Testing in 30+ Open Source Tools

Second Edition

Rahul Shende
MS, MCM, MBA

Testing in 30+ Open Source Tools

Second Edition

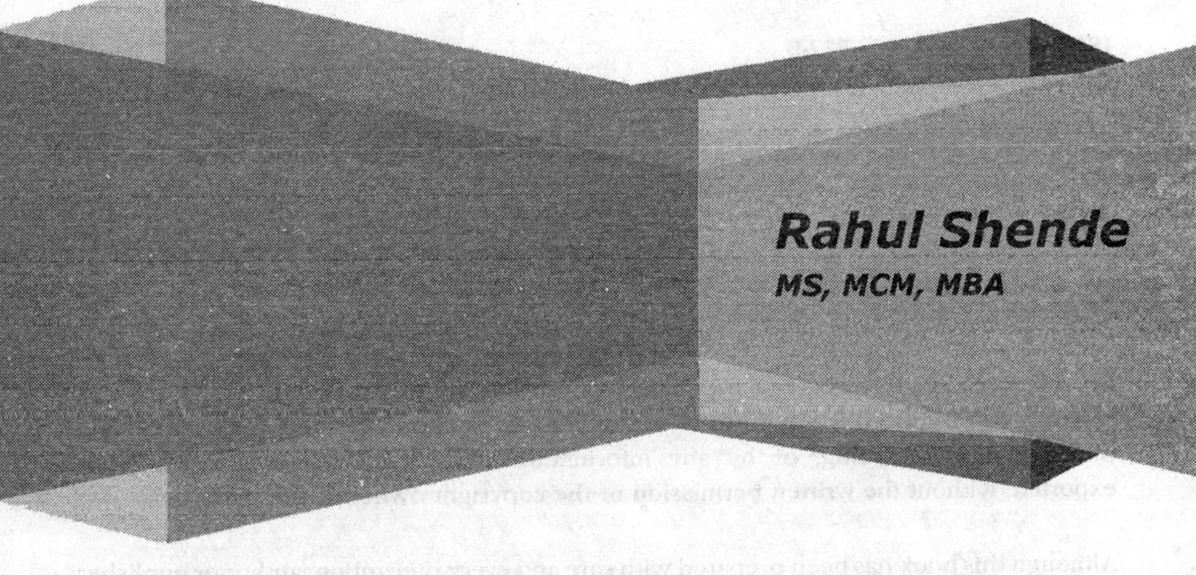

Rahul Shende

MS, MCM, MBA

SHROFF PUBLISHERS & DISTRIBUTORS PVT. LTD.

Mumbai *Bangalore* *Kolkata* *New Delhi*

Testing in 30^+ Open Source Tools,
Second Edition

by Mr. Rahul Shende

First Edition: September 2010

Second Edition: November 2012

ISBN 13: 978-93-5023-712-0

Published by **Shroff Publishers & Distributors Pvt. Ltd.** C-103, T.T.C. Industrial Area, M.I.D.C., Pawane, Navi Mumbai - 400 705. Tel.: (91-22) 4158 4158 Fax: (91-22) 4158 4141 E-mail: spdorders@shroffpublishers.com. Printed at Decora Book Prints Pvt. Ltd., Mumbai.

Acknowledgement:

I want to dedicate this book to my mother Mrs. Rohini Shende & father Mr. Ramesh Shende who always supported me in ups and downs in my life, to my lovely caring wife Mrs. Raksha Shende and my charming baby boy, Family members Mr. Rajesh, Mrs. Archana and Shreyas Shende, friends and well wishers. I am very thankful to all those who have been with me including my support team.

For any queries or suggestions please do write:

Rahul_Shende11@yahoo.com

opensourcetestingtools@gmail.com

opensourcetestingtools@yahoo.com

opensourcetestingtools@hotmail.com

Contents

Introduction

Open Source Definition

The Open Source Definition

Introduction

Open source doesn't just mean access to the source code. The distribution terms of open-source software must comply with the following criteria:

1. Free Redistribution

The license shall not restrict any party from selling or giving away the software as a component of an aggregate software distribution containing programs from several different sources. The license shall not require a royalty or other fee for such sale.

2. Source Code

The program must include source code, and must allow distribution in source code as well as compiled form. Where some form of a product is not distributed with source code, there must be a well-publicized means of obtaining the source code for no more than a reasonable reproduction cost preferably, downloading via the Internet without charge. The source code must be the preferred form in which a programmer would modify the program. Deliberately obfuscated source code is not allowed. Intermediate forms such as the output of a preprocessor or translator are not allowed.

3. Derived Works

The license must allow modifications and derived works, and must allow them to be distributed under the same terms as the license of the original software.

4. Integrity of The Author's Source Code

The license may restrict the source-code from being distributed in modified form only if the license allows the distribution of "patch files" with the source code for the purpose of modifying the program at build time. The license must explicitly permit distribution of software built from modified source code. The license may require derived works to carry a different name or version number from the original software.

5. No Discrimination Against Persons or Groups

The license must not discriminate against any person or group of persons.

6. No Discrimination Against Fields of Endeavor

The license must not restrict anyone from making use of the program in a specific field of endeavor. For example, it may not restrict the program from being used in a business, or from being used for genetic research.

7. Distribution of License

The rights attached to the program must apply to all to whom the program is redistributed without the need for execution of an additional license by those parties.

8. License Must Not Be Specific to a Product

The rights attached to the program must not depend on the program's being part of a particular software distribution. If the program is extracted from that distribution and used or distributed within the terms of the program's license, all parties to whom the program is redistributed should have the same rights as those that are granted in conjunction with the original software distribution.

9. License Must Not Restrict Other Software

The license must not place restrictions on other software that is distributed along with the licensed software. For example, the license must not insist that all other programs distributed on the same medium must be open-source software.

10. License Must Be Technology-Neutral

No provision of the license may be predicated on any individual technology or style of interface.

Open Source Licenses

Open Source Licenses which have successfully gone through the approval process and comply with the Open Source Definition are listed here:

- Licenses by name
- Licenses by category

Open Source Licenses by Category

- Open Group Test Suite License
- Reciprocal Public License

.:: License Index ::.

- License Approval Process
- License Information
- Origins and definitions of categories from the License Proliferation Committee report

.:: Licenses that are popular and widely used or with strong communities ::.

- Apache License, 2.0
- New and Simplified BSD licenses
- GNU General Public License (GPL)
- GNU Library or "Lesser" General Public License (LGPL)
- MIT license
- Mozilla Public License 1.1 (MPL)
- Common Development and Distribution License
- Eclipse Public License

.:: Special purpose licenses ::.

- Educational Community License
- IPA Font License
- NASA Open Source Agreement 1.3
- Open Font License 1.1 (OFL 1.1)

.:: Other/Miscellaneous licenses ::.

- Adaptive Public License
- Artistic license 2.0
- Open Software License
- Qt Public License (QPL)
- zlib/libpng license

.:: Licenses that are redundant with more popular licenses ::.

- Academic Free License
- Attribution Assurance Licenses
- Eiffel Forum License V2.0
- Fair License
- Historical Permission Notice and Disclaimer
- Lucent Public License Version 1.02
- University of Illinois/NCSA Open Source License
- X.Net License

.:: Non-reusable licenses ::.

- Apple Public Source License
- Computer Associates Trusted Open Source License 1.1
- CUA Office Public License Version 1.0
- EU DataGrid Software License
- Entessa Public License
- Frameworx License
- IBM Public License
- Motosoto License
- Multics License
- Naumen Public License
- Nethack General Public License
- Nokia Open Source License
- OCLC Research Public License 2.0
- PHP License
- Python license (CNRI Python License)
- Python Software Foundation License
- RealNetworks Public Source License V1.0
- Ricoh Source Code Public License
- Sleepycat License
- Sun Public License
- Sybase Open Watcom Public License 1.0
- Software License v. 1.0
- W3C License
- wxWindows Library License
- Zope Public License

.:: Superseded licenses ::.

- Apache Software License 1.1
- Common Public License 1.0
- Artistic license 1.0
- Eiffel Forum License V1.0
- Lucent Public License (Plan9)
- Mozilla Public License 1.0 (MPL)

.:: Licenses that have been voluntarily retired ::.

- Intel Open Source License
- Open Source License
- MITRE Collaborative Virtual Workspace License (CVW License)
- Sun Industry Standards Source License (SISSL)

.:: Uncategorized Licenses ::.

- Affero GNU Public License
- Boost Software License (BSL1.0)
- Common Public Attribution License 1.0 (CPAL)
- European Union Public License (link to every language's version on their site)
- GNU General Public License version 3.0 (GPLv3)
- GNU Library or "Lesser" General Public License version 3.0 (LGPLv3)
- ISC License
- Microsoft Public License (Ms-PL)
- Microsoft Reciprocal License (Ms-RL)
- MirOS Licence
- Non-Profit Open Software License 3.0
- NTP License
- The PostgreSQL License
- Reciprocal Public License 1.5 (RPL1.5)
- Public License 2.0

Licenses by Name

The following licenses have been approved by the OSI via the License Review Process.

- Academic Free License 3.0 (AFL 3.0)
- Affero GNU Public License
- Adaptive Public License
- Apache License, 2.0
- Apple Public Source License
- Artistic license 2.0
- Attribution Assurance Licenses

- New and Simplified BSD licenses
- Boost Software License (BSL1.0)
- Computer Associates Trusted Open Source License 1.1
- Common Development and Distribution License
- Common Public Attribution License 1.0 (CPAL)
- CUA Office Public License Version 1.0
- EU DataGrid Software License
- Eclipse Public License
- Educational Community License, Version 2.0
- Eiffel Forum License V2.0
- Entessa Public License
- European Union Public License (link to every language's version on their site)
- Fair License
- Frameworx License
- GNU General Public License (GPL)
- GNU General Public License version 3.0 (GPLv3)
- GNU Library or "Lesser" General Public License (LGPL)
- GNU Library or "Lesser" General Public License version 3.0 (LGPLv3)
- Historical Permission Notice and Disclaimer
- IBM Public License
- IPA Font License
- ISC License
- Lucent Public License Version 1.02
- MirOS Licence
- Microsoft Public License (Ms-PL)
- Microsoft Reciprocal License (Ms-RL)
- MIT license
- Motosoto License
- Mozilla Public License 1.1 (MPL)
- Multics License
- NASA Open Source Agreement 1.3
- NTP License
- Naumen Public License
- Nethack General Public License

- Nokia Open Source License
- Non-Profit Open Software License 3.0 (Non-Profit OSL 3.0)
- OCLC Research Public License 2.0
- Font License 1.1 (OFL 1.1)
- Open Group Test Suite License
- Open Software License 3.0 (OSL 3.0)
- PHP License
- The PostgreSQL License
- Python license (CNRI Python License)
- Python Software Foundation License
- Qt Public License (QPL)
- RealNetworks Public Source License V1.0
- Public License 1.5 (RPL1.5)
- Ricoh Source Code Public License
- Public License 2.0
- License
- Sun Public License
- Open Watcom Public License 1.0
- University of Illinois/NCSA Open Source License
- Vovida Software License v. 1.0
- W3C License
- wxWindows Library License
- .Net License
- Public License
- zlib/libpng license

You can also view a list of open source licenses grouped by category, and licenses which have been superceded or retired.

References:

http://www.opensource.org/licenses/category

Purpose & Objective:

Purpose of this book is to prove that how open source tool can be used in Real life scenario with cost effective solution. Open source tools are the new market trends and this is beneficial for companies to set Test Lab with Open Source tools in no license cost.

Today open source software has become critical for almost every organization. Almost everything requires open source software, be it telecommunication systems, inventory, accounting, personal productivity applications, contact management and operating systems amongst others.

Advantages of Open Source software

Why is "Open Source code "and" Open Source software" good for the customer/user?

Financial savings

In the majority of cases of Open Source software, the software will be available for free. In other words, the acquisition costs are considerably lower than those of the traditional, proprietary software that may be purchased.

In many cases people also want the services connected with the software acquisition that will cost; installation, operation, training support, however compared with proprietary software the same case often applies here.

Software code that sustains a critical eye!

The people who originally write the software always know that anyone can see in full detail how it works or what solutions have been chosen. They will therefore naturally do as good a job as possible in order that they can be as proud as possible of the product and avoid criticism as much as possible.

It is perhaps simplest to conceal the source code and thereby obtain a little more freedom as long as the end product is ok. However by producing in accordance with the "Open Source code" concept, one makes a clear statement that "my method withstands the light of day and a critical eye!"

Easy integration and interaction

Open Source code means that it is relatively simple to adapt programs so that they can work with each other because you can see from the source codes how a program "thinks" and how you should approach it to share or exchange data, for example.

Rapid debugging, rapid further development

Because the source code is open, the developer/producer does not just receive feedback on any errors or problems, or proposals for new functions, but feedback reports that can specify down to the code level what should be done – it is therefore far simpler for the producer to implement changes on the basis of feedback reports since these often say precisely what program changes must be made and also any errors in the original source code may be corrected by the person who detects the error without having to wait for the original programmer.

Avoiding lock-in to one supplier

It is obviously great to have one software supplier to turn to – perhaps to provide services connected with the software, such as installation assistance, courses, operation, support and more, and you have someone to ring if you need help or information concerning the software.

But you decide to whom you turn! Don't end up in the situation where by acquiring a product from a supplier, you have simultaneously locked yourself into only being able to obtain related assistance from the same supplier. For example, if you have other software must interact with the initial software, you are forced to be grateful for what this single supplier has to offer and if the supplier goes bankrupt or your collaboration ends in another way, you are left high and dry when it comes to future debugging or new versions.

The very basis of Open Source software is an openness that ensures interaction between products and makes it impossible for one player to lock customers to their products by concealing the source code.

With Open Source you can:

- Use it as you want
- Study the program's working method
- Changing the work method of the program
- Share the program with others

Advantages with Open Source

- Better products
- Better services
- Lower costs
- Greater flexibility
- Greater freedom of choice

References:

http://www.redpill-linpro.com/About-Open-Source/Advantages-of-Open-Source-software

http://assets1.csc.com/fr/downloads/4819_1.pdf

Section 1

Automation Testing Approach

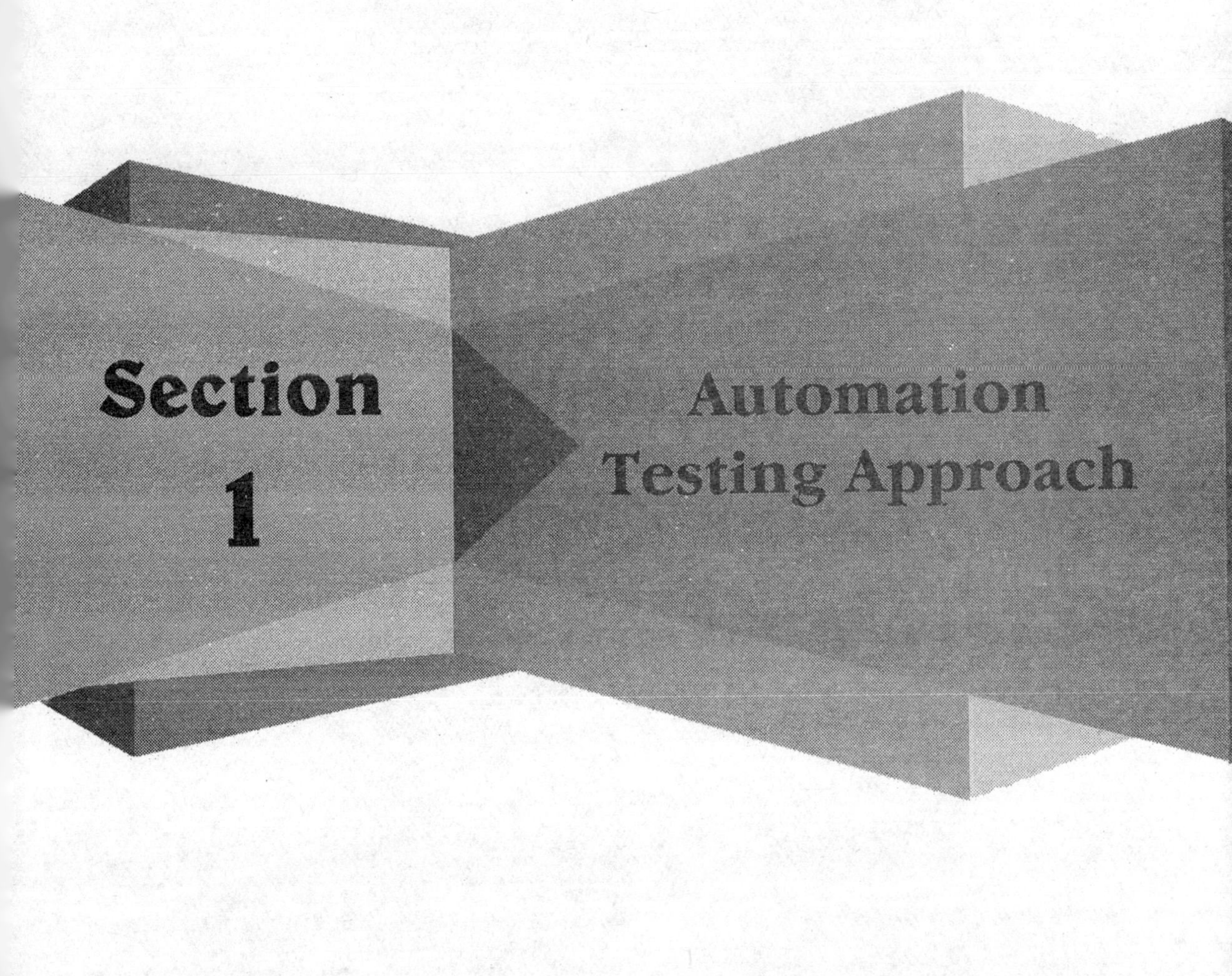

Introduction:

What is Automation?

— Automation is making a process *Automatic* eliminating the need for human intervention.

— Is a self-controlling or self-moving processes.

— Automation Software offers automation wizards and commands of its own in addition to providing task recording and re-play capabilities.

— Using these programs you can record an IT or business task.

— Then if needed use the editor to edit the task, add new actions to the task, use variables or prompt user for values or even write an automation script from scratch using GUI automation commands or using GUI automation wizards.

Benefits of Automation

Fast	**Test Automation tool runs faster than human users**
Reliable	**Test automation tool performs precisely the same operations at each time eliminating the human errors**
Repeatable	**Test Automation tool performs same operations with different combination of data in a less time**
Programmable	**We can program sophisticated tests that brings out hidden information (defects)**
Reusable	**We can develop reusable components which can run on different versions of application under test**
Regression Testing	**Test Automation tool makes it easy to conduct regression test**
Enabling 24x7 testing	**Test can be schedule and supports unattended recovery**
Robust verification	**Support Robust verification mechanism than other testing tools**

Automation Test Workflow

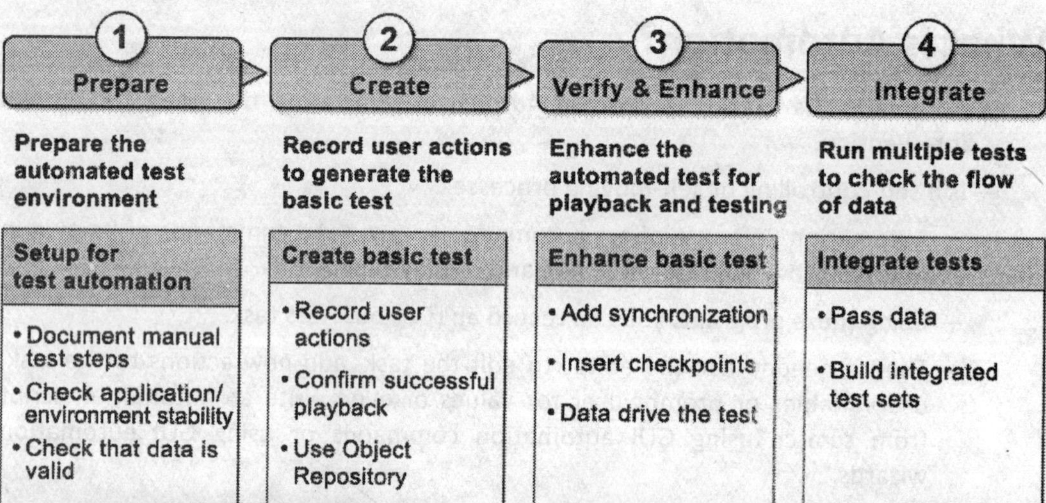

What Tests should we Automate?

Good Candidate

- Tests executed for each software build
- Business critical tests
- "Easy to automate" tests
  - Many similar test cases, different data
  - Repetitive operations
  - No customization required
- Tests that are difficult or tedious to perform manually

Bad Candidate

- Tests without predictable results
- Tests that are executed infrequently
- Emergency tests
- Tests that are difficult to automate

Test Automation Approach

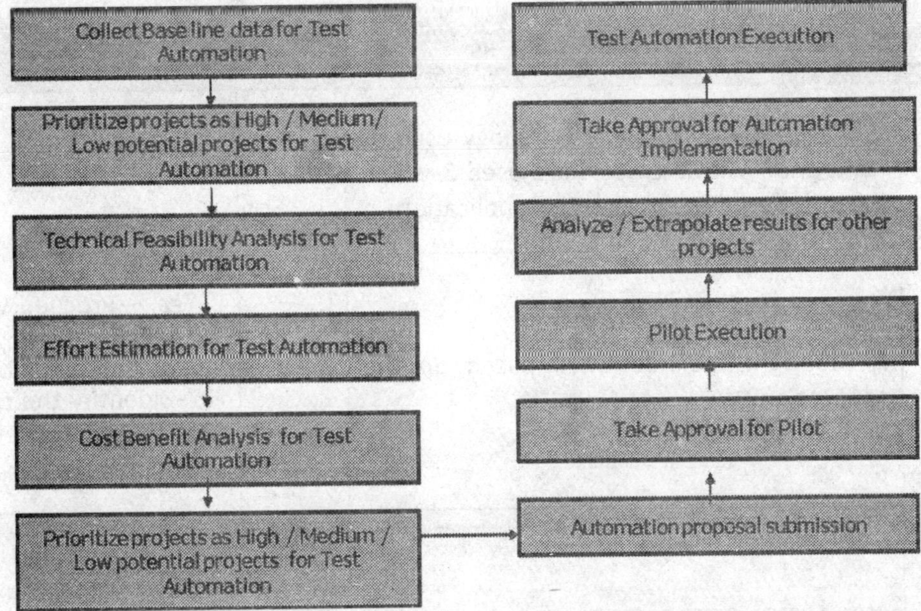

Regression Test Automation Methodology

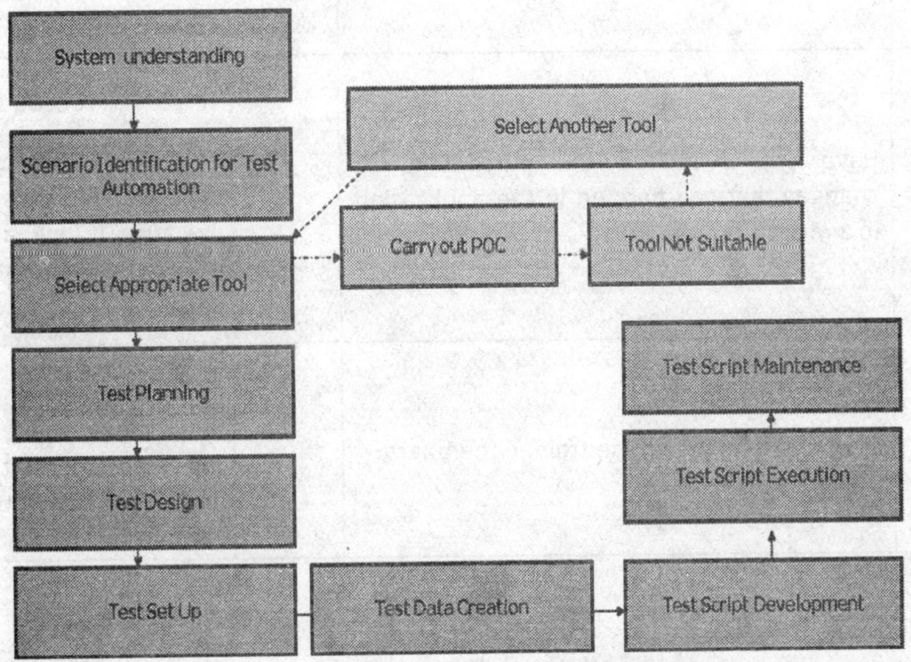

CheckList of Automation Feasibility Study

Sl. No	Items	Y/N	Comments
1	What is the application technology used as front end, What browsers are used & which database used to develop this application?		
2.	Is the right tool identified based on the application?		If Yes - Proceed with Automation Testing No – Identify the right tool based on tool selection guidelines
3.	Are there any custom objects in the application?		If Yes – Need to Analyze the extra effort required No - Proceed with Automation Testing
4.	Have you evaluated the percentage of changes that can happen in the application in a month/quarter/year?		If Yes - Proceed with Automation Testing No – Need to consider, because it will affect the maintenance effort.
5.	Does the team comprise trained members?		if Yes - Proceed with Automation Testing No – provide suitable training for team members.

6.	Is the Application stable?		If Yes – Proceed with Automation Testing No – Not recommend for Automation
7.	Are the test cases and test scenarios frozen?		If Yes – Proceed with Automation Testing No – request to freeze/ finalize
8.	Are the steps (in the test) repeatable and short?		If Yes – Easy to identified the reusable components. No – recommended to go for individual test scripts
9.	Do these automated tests usually execute very rapidly?		If Yes – Scheduling of those test cases become easy to automate No – Need to execute individual scripts
10.	Is Requirements Tractability Matrix prepared for mapping a test case to a script?		If Yes – Easy to go for Automation approach No – Need to map Test cases
11	Is test Data and Test Bed ready?		If Yes – Proceed with Automation Testing No – Need to prepare test data and setup Test-Bed

Automation Frameworks:

There are mainly three types of Automation Frameworks:

Choosing test Automation Framework :

- Automation is the key to reducing 'test cycle time'.
- One of the key factors for successful test automation is to choose a suitable framework.
- What is a Test Automation Framework?
- A test Automation framework is a set of concepts, techniques and guidelines, which are to be followed when developing test automation scripts.
- The test Automation framework helps by isolating the application under test from the test scripts by providing functions and test data separately.

A good place to start any discussion on test automation frameworks is to understand how automation is done today, the fundamental problems in approach and how these can be addressed through the frameworks presented in this document. We will start with listing some common problems:

- The structure of most of automated test scripts are rarely designed, rather it is created in an ad hoc manner on the fly during capture/playback.
- Most automated test scripts cannot easily adapt to changing application requirements and environments.
- Majority of the time is then spent modifying these automated test scripts, often to the point of abandoning their use because of this.
- Software testing once an area receiving the least focus is now critical, but the time to do testing has reduced in the hurry to get releases out the door on schedule.
- Despite the plethora of automation tools in the market today, test automation has rarely gone beyond the capture/ playback paradigm.
- Testers like others within the software community do not stand on the shoulders of others, meaning that there is very little reuse, we rarely see automated test scripts as a part of a sharable library.
- Test automation design for a project is done very informally.

Any good framework must successfully address some or all of the problems listed above. This document describes five such frameworks- they are discussed in increasing order of complexity to implement.

As a starting point in solving some of the problems listed above we should consider the attributes that any well structured automation framework have, they are:

- Partitioning (modularity) into parts having well-identified and understandable boundaries.
- Functional decomposition that helps achieves identification and isolation of common functions.
- Representing the mass of automated test scripts as a hierarchy and,
- Maximizing the independence among the parts of the system – both data and instruction independence.

A test automation framework is a set of assumptions, concepts and practices that provide support for automated software testing.

Basing an automated testing effort on using only a capture tool to record and play back test cases has its drawbacks. Running complex and powerful tests is time consuming and expensive when using only a capture tool. Because these tests are created ad hoc, their functionality can be difficult to track and reproduce, and they can be costly to maintain.

A better choice for an automated testing team is to use a test automation framework, defined as a set of assumptions, concepts, and practices that constitute a work platform or support for automated testing.

1. ***Data-Driven Framework.***
2. ***Keyword-Driven Framework.***
3. ***Hybrid Framework.***

Data-Driven Framework:

- A data-driven framework is where test input and output values are read from data files (ODBC sources, CSV files, Excel files, DAO objects, ADO objects, and such) and are loaded into variables in captured or manually coded scripts.
- In this framework, variables are used for both input values and output verification values.
- Navigation through the program, reading of the data files, and logging of test status and information are all coded in the test script.

Keyword-Driven Framework

- This requires the development of data tables and keywords, independent of the test automation tool used to execute them and the test script code that "drives" the application-under-test and the data.

- Keyword-driven tests look very similar to manual test cases.
- In a keyword-driven test, the functionality of the application-under test is documented in a table as well as in step-by-step instructions for each test.
- In this method, the entire process is data-driven, including Functionality.

Hybrid Framework

- It is combination of Data-Driven & Keyword-Driven Frameworks.
- This hybrid test automation framework is what most frameworks evolve into over time and multiple projects.
- This allows data driven scripts to take advantage of the powerful libraries and utilities that usually accompany a keyword driven architecture.
- On the other hand, the framework can use scripts to perform some tasks that might be too difficult to re-implement in a pure keyword driven approach, or where the keyword driven capabilities are not yet in place.

Benefits of Framework based architecture :

- ***Maintainability***- of the test suite increases.
- ***Increased productivity***– Due to the structured approach test scripts can be re-used and hence new scripts can be developed quickly. This greatly improves the productivity.
- ***Early test case development*** – test cases can be written early in the development cycle, before the code under test has been written.
- ***Overall reduction in test cycle time***- Once test scripts are developed they can be re-executed unmanned for each build with low maintenance and thus reduce the test cycle time.
- ***Tool independent scripts*** – Most of the test script code is in the functions used to implement keywords. Porting the test cases to another functional test tool will only require the keyword functions to be written.
- ***Analysis:*** Results logged after execution can be used for analysis of test execution.
- ***Traceability:*** The requirements can be mapped to appropriate test cases and scripts.
- ***Version Control:*** The test scripts can be checked into a version control tool and a new version can be created for new changes in the script.

How to choose the Framework for your application?

- Analyze your application.
- Analysis of test scenarios.
  - Analyze the steps of the test scenarios
  - Identify the input data required for scenario.
  - Identify common re-usable functions.
- Categorize the type of your application.
  - Non-GUI based application
  - GUI based application
    - Application requiring high volumes of data
    - Applications interfacing with multiple subsystems
    - Type of application web/client server/mainframe

Steps followed for Framework Selection :

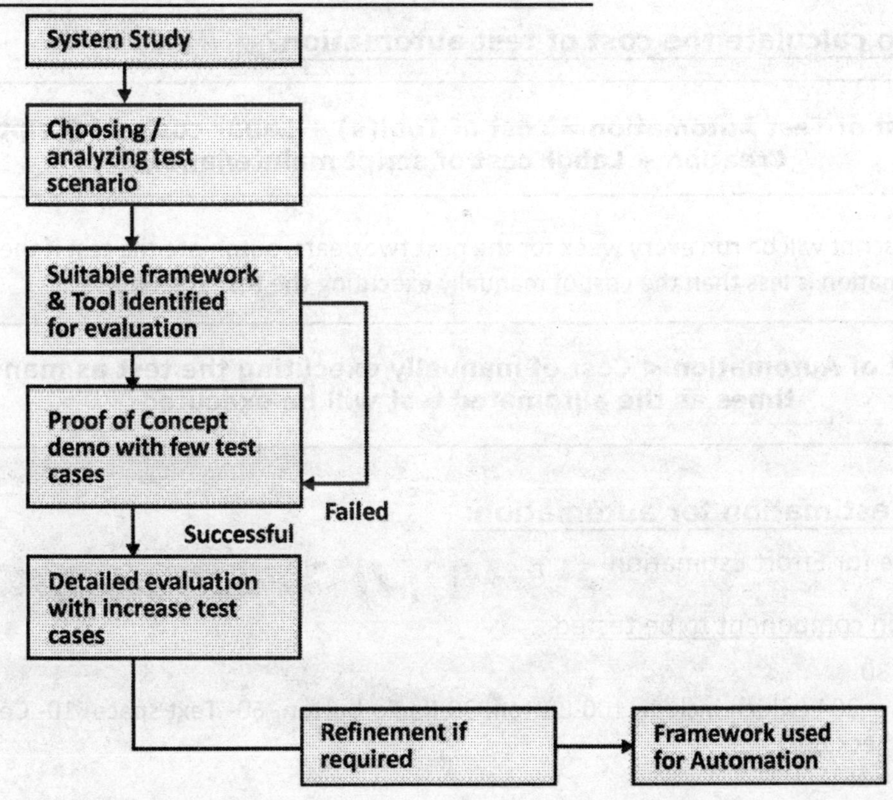

How is it done practically?

1. *Phase1* – Information gathering, assessment, estimation and planning. Information gaps are identified and agreement reached with component teams to supply the information.
2. *Phase2* – Setup, knowledge transfer and framework building, update the estimate/ plan
3. *Phase3* – Build and verify tests, sampling level of SME reviews, iterative releases of automated tests to test execution library

The plan must follow test methodology. The key points to incorporate are:

- Short time-bound steps in the project (i.e. fortnightly sprints),
- Continuous improvement: reflection and improvement process,
- Delivery of real value to customers (the most critical/useful tests should be automated early)
- Continuous review using techniques such as pair programming

How to calculate the cost of test automation?

Cost of Test Automation = cost of Tool(s) + Labor costs of Script Creation + Labor cost of script maintenance

If a test script will be run every week for the next two years, automate the test if the cost of automation is less than the cost of manually executing the test 104 times.

Cost of Automation < Cost of manually executing the test as many times as the automated test will be executed

Effort estimation for automation:

Example for Effort Estimation

The main component to be tested

Forms = 30
Controls = 204 (which include 100-Button, 30 Radio button, 60- Text space, 10- Combo box, 4- check Box)
Reports = 15

Time Calculation :

Type of Testing, on the scale of 10

Functionality testing = 6 hrs
Usability Testing = 3 hrs
Look and Feel Testing = 0.7 hrs
Security testing = 0.3 hrs
Manpower Available Testers = 4

Total Time taken on:

Item	Test Cases	Time Time Req.
Text Box –60	4	5 Mins
Button –100	3	5 Mins
Radio Button-30	3	3 Mins
Combo Box-10	4	2 Mins
Check Box-4	4	2 Mins

Time Calculation at large

Item	Calc	Time Req. (Each)
Text Box –60	60X20	20 hrs
Button –100	100X15	25 hrs
Radio Button-30	30X9	3 hrs
Combo Box-10	10X8	1.3 hrs
Check Box-4	4X8	0.6 hrs
	Total	**50 hrs**

Total days available = 6

Work hrs per day = 50 / 6 = **8.3 Hrs/per day**

Per Day hrs for Each Tester

8.3/4 = 2.1 Hrs

So daily each Tester will give 2.1 hrs for 6 days.

Out of Total 50 hrs, the following testing techniques will get:

Functionality testing = 30 hrs
Usability Testing = 15 hrs
Look and Feel Testing = 3.5 hrs
Security Testing = 1.5 hrs

Test artifacts:

- **Requirements:** The requirements that are being tested are stored into the repository. This feature enables us to map the requirements to test cases and test scripts.
- **Test Plan:** Design the tests and build the test plan on it using the Test Management Tool. The test plan will be maintained in a central repository. This will help to produce reusable test plans or individual test cases in future. The information is shareable and preserved.
- **Test Case:** Contains description of test case and test steps.
- **Test Script:** Automated test Script associated with each test case will be stored in the quality center repository.
- **Test Sets:** This will be a set of selected test cases and associated test scripts. The test sets are executed from Quality Center onto remote machines. The status of each execution is stored in the respective test case execution status. The status can be either pass/fail, it doesn't mention exact details of execution.
- **Test Logs:** The test script execution logs are stored in a global repository. The log repository contains status of each test execution and logs in the steps that are performed, data and status of execution of the data. The log enables the tester to analyze the test execution results.
- **Reusable Components:** The repetitive functions that are invoked in most of the functions are stored. These reusable components enable us to reduce the coding redundancy.
- **Object Repository:** The object repository contains the declaration of the application objects. The objects are global to all the scripts. The script reads the object classes and properties from the object repository location.
- **Data Sheets:** The data sheet contains the test data used for execution. The data sheets can be populated from a database or manually store the data so that the same set of data can be used for all iterations. These data sheets may contain few hundreds of combinations of data for same feature or separate data sheet for each feature.

Automation activities:

- ✓ **Record the application GUI.**
- ✓ **Write script.**
- ✓ **Execute script.**
- ✓ **Review the script.**
- ✓ **Modify script if any changes.**
- ✓ **Execute script on at least two machines.**
- ✓ **Store the script in Central Repository.**
- ✓ **Execute the script from central repository.**
- ✓ **Verify the execution status in Central Repository.**
- ✓ **Verify the test logs on common server.**
- ✓ **Prepare Test Reports.**

Test automation implementation:

The following diagram represents pictorial representation of the phases for Test Automation Implementation.

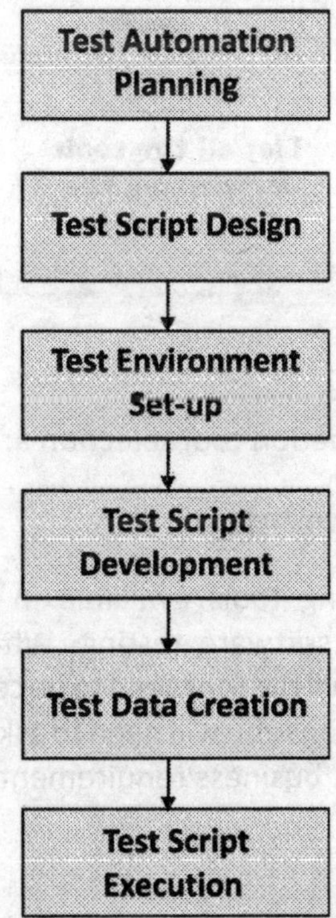

Tool Selection Criteria

With the emerging trends and technologies, a huge number of automation tools are available in the market. Therefore, it is difficult to identify an appropriate tool for the project needs. Hence tool evaluation is inevitable for selecting the automation tool that meets the project expectations. It requires prior experience and process to reduce the complexity of the tool selection process and the general concerns include:

- How to be abreast of the automation tools available for project use
- Decide when to start using the automation tool
- Evaluate the tool based on different criteria
- Select the tool based on different technology.

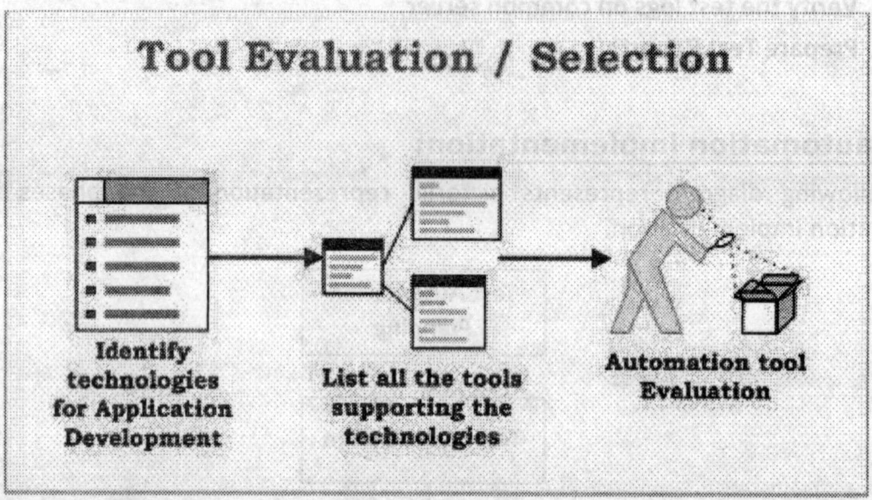

Evaluation Process

The steps to software test automation tool selection are as follows:

a. Determine your requirements

Before looking at any testing tools available in the market, make a list of the requirements you have for software testing. What problems will the tool solve? What technical capabilities, will the tool need to be compatible with your environment? Some of the important questions you will need to ask should be related to compatibility requirements, tool audience, business requirements, and testing requirements.

b. Identify your constraints

The factors that will restrict your choice of tool need to be evaluated early in this process. Some factors will allow you to exclude certain tools from your selection process at an early stage, such as environmental constraints, supplier constraints, quality constraints, quality characteristics.

c. Identify a possible list of tools for evaluation

Some basic research needs to be done to determine tools available in the market. Evaluation process should focus on feature categorization, such as:

- **Mandatory features:** These are the features that are essential to accomplish your goal in meeting your requirements within the constraints.
- **Desirable features:** These are features that will distinguish the best tools from the others.
- **Irrelevant features:** Features that are not important and will not provide any real benefit to your situation.

d. Evaluation Process

All tests should be run on the same test application. This will give a very good idea of how each tool compares against the others.

Features to be evaluated and compared are described below:

Record and Playback

This category details how easy it is to record & playback a test. Does the tool support low-level recording (mouse drags, exact screen location)? Is there object recognition when recording and playing back or does it appear to record ok but then on playback (without environment change or unique ID etc. changes) fails? How easy is it to read the recorded script?

When automating, this is the first thing that most test professionals try to evaluate and rightly so. They will record a simple script; look at the code and then playback. This is very similar to recording a macro in say, Microsoft Excel. Eventually record and playback becomes less and less part of the automation process as it is usually more robust to use the built-in functions to directly test objects, databases, etc. However this should be done as a minimum in the evaluation process because if the tool of choice cannot recognize the applications' objects then the automation process will be a very tedious experience.

Web Testing

Web based functionality on most applications is now a part of everyday life. As such the test tool should provide good web based test functionality in addition to its client/server functions.

Tool of choice should provide native support for HTML tables, frames, DOM, various platforms for browsers, Web site maps and links. Web testing can be riddled with problems if various considerations are not taken into account. Here are a few examples:

- Are there functions to tell me when the page has finished loading?
- Can I tell the test tool to wait until an image appears?
- Can I test whether links are valid or not?
- Can I test web based objects functions like is it enabled, does it contain data, etc.?
- Are there facilities that will allow me to programmatically look for objects of a certain type on a ..web page or locate a specific object?
- Can I extract data from the web page itself? e.g.: the title? A hidden form element?

Database Tests

Checking what is in the backend database usually verifies the proper validation of tests carried out on the front end of an application. Because of the many databases available e.g. Oracle, DB2, SQL Server, Sybase, Informix, Ingres, etc. all of them support a universal query language known as SQL and a protocol for communicating with these databases called ODBC (JDBC can be used on Java environments). Tools should be evaluated for the support for SQL, ODBC and how they hold returned data e.g. is this in an array, a cursor, a variable, etc. How does the tool manipulate this returned data? Can it call stored procedures and supply required input variables? What is the range of functions supplied for this testing?

Data Functions

Applications usually provide a facility for storing data off line. So to test this, we will need to create data to input into the application. Tools should provide facilities for creating and manipulating data. Does the tool allow you to specify the type of data you want? Can you automatically generate data? Can you interface with files, spreadsheets, etc to create, extract data? Can you randomize the access to that data? Is the data access truly random? This functionality is normally more important than database tests as the databases will usually have their own interface for running queries.

These functions are also very important as you move from the record/playback phase, to data-driven to framework testing. Data-driven tests are tests that replace hard coded names, address, numbers; etc with variables supplied from an external source usually a CSV (Comma Separated variable) file, spreadsheet or database.

Object Mapping

If you are in a role that can help influence the design of a product, try to get the development/design team to use standard and not custom objects. Then hopefully you will not need this functionality. However you may find that most (hopefully) of the application has been implemented using standard objects supported by your test tool vendor but there may be a few objects that are custom ones.

Most custom objects will behave like a similar standard control. Here are a few standard objects that are seen in everyday applications:

- Push buttons
- Check boxes
- Radio buttons
- List views
- Edit boxes
- Combo boxes

If you have a custom object that behaves like one of these, you should be able to map the custom object to tell the test tool that the custom control behaves like the standard control

Test/Error Recovery

This can bc one of the most difficult areas to automate but if it is automated, it provides the foundation to produce a truly robust test suite. Suppose the application crashes while test execution is in progress, if a function does not receive the correct information; how can this be handled? If there is an error message, how to do deal with that? If I access a web site and get a warning what do I do? I cannot get a database connection, how do I skip those tests?

The test tool should provide facilities to handle the above scenarios. Some tools have built in wizards for standard test recovery (when you finish tests or when a script fails). Error recovery caused by the application and environment. How easy is it to build this into your code?

Object Identity Tool

Once you become more proficient with automation testing, one of the primary means of identifying objects will be via an ID Tool; a sort of spy that looks at the internals of the object giving you details like the object name, ID and similar. This will allow you to reference that object within a function call.

The tool should give you details of some of the object's properties, especially those associated with uniquely identifying the object or window. The tool will usually provide the tester with a point and ID service where you can use the mouse to point at the object and in some window you will see all of that objects IDs and properties.

A lot of the tools will allow you to search all the open applications in one swoop and show you the result in a tree that you can look at when required.

Extensible Language

If the standard test language does not support a feature or function for the problem in question, the same should be possible through a DLL or extend the language in some way to do it? This is usually an advanced topic and is not encountered until the trained tester has been using the tool for some time. However, when this is encountered the tool should support language extension. If via DLLs, then the tester must have knowledge of a traditional development language e.g. C, C++ or VB.

Some tools provide extension by providing features to create user defined functions, methods, classes, etc. but these are normally a mixture of the already supported data types, functions, etc. rather than extending the tool beyond its released functionality.

The tool should ideally support any of the standard languages, than its own proprietary language. A standard language support has the following benefits:

- It would be cheaper to maintain as you do not require as many people developing your own niche ..language
- There will be a lot more books available to explain the intr cacies of the language
- There will be a lot more skilled resources who have knowledge of the language
- It would be a more desirable profession as you will obtain more transferable and sought after skills
- The language will be richer
- The test tool vendor can concentrate on supplying test functionality rather than providing functions like opening a file, string manipulation, etc. which are already provided in existing languages

Environment Support & Compatibility

Ultimately this is the most important part of automation: environment support.

How many environments does the tool support out of the box? Does it support the latest Java release, Oracle, Power Builder, WAP, etc? Most tools can interface to unsupported environments if the developers in that environment provide classes, DLLs etc. that expose some of the applications details.

Any testing tool you choose will need to be compatible with:

- The operating systems your application supports
- The development environments used to create your application
- Third party software with which your application integrates

Integration

How well does the tool integrate with other tools. This is becoming more and more important. Does the tool allow you to run it from various test management suites? Can you raise a bug directly from the tool and feed the information gathered from your test logs into it? Does it integrate with products like Word, Excel or requirements management tools?

When managing large test projects with an automation team, the management aspect and the tools integration moves further up the importance ladder.

You may also have the requirement for configuration management, so you may evaluate the following:

- Does the tool come with integrated version control capability?
- Can the tool be integrated with other version control tools

Supports

Points to look for are:

- Maturity of product
- Market share of product
- Vendor qualifications, such as financial stability and length of existence. What is the vendor's track record?
- Are software patches provided, if deemed necessary?

- Are upgrades provided on a regular basis?
- Customer support - validity of responses from the help desk, speed of responses and similar.
- Training availability
- Is a tool Help feature available? Is the tool well documented?
- Availability and access to tool user groups
- Online resources like documentation, knowledge base contributed by the vendor and users
- Availability of skilled resources

Web Testing using Selenium IDE 1.0.6 tool

Introduction of Selenium Components

Selenium is composed of three major tools. Each one has a specific role in aiding the development of web application test automation.

Selenium-IDE

Selenium-IDE is the Integrated Development Environment for building Selenium test cases. It operates as a Firefox add-on and provides an easy-to-use interface for developing and running individual test cases or entire test suites. Selenium-IDE has a recording feature, which will keep account of user actions as they are performed and store them as a reusable script to play back. It also has a context menu (right-click) integrated with the Firefox browser, which allows the user to pick from a list of assertions and verifications for the selected location. Selenium-IDE also offers full editing of test cases for more precision and control. Although Selenium-IDE is a Firefox only add-on, tests created in it can also be run against other browsers by using Selenium-RC and specifying the name of the test suite on the command line.

Selenium-RC (Remote Control)

Selenium-RC allows the test automation developer to use a programming language for maximum flexibility and extensibility in developing test logic. For instance, if the application under test returns a result set, and if the automated test program needs to run tests on each element in the result set, the programming language's iteration support can be used to iterate through the result set, calling Selenium commands to run tests on each item.

Selenium-RC provides an API (Application Programming Interface) and library for each of its supported languages: HTML, Java, C#, Perl, PHP, Python, and Ruby. This ability to use Selenium-RC with a high-level programming language to develop test cases also allows the automated testing to be integrated with a project's automated build environment.

Selenium Remote Control (RC) is a test tool that allows you to write automated web application UI tests in any programming language against any HTTP website using any mainstream JavaScript-enabled browser.

Selenium RC comes in two parts.

1. A server which automatically launches and kills browsers, and acts as a HTTP proxy for web requests from them.
2. Client libraries for your favourite computer language.

The RC server also bundles Selenium Core, and automatically loads it into the browser.

Architectural representation....

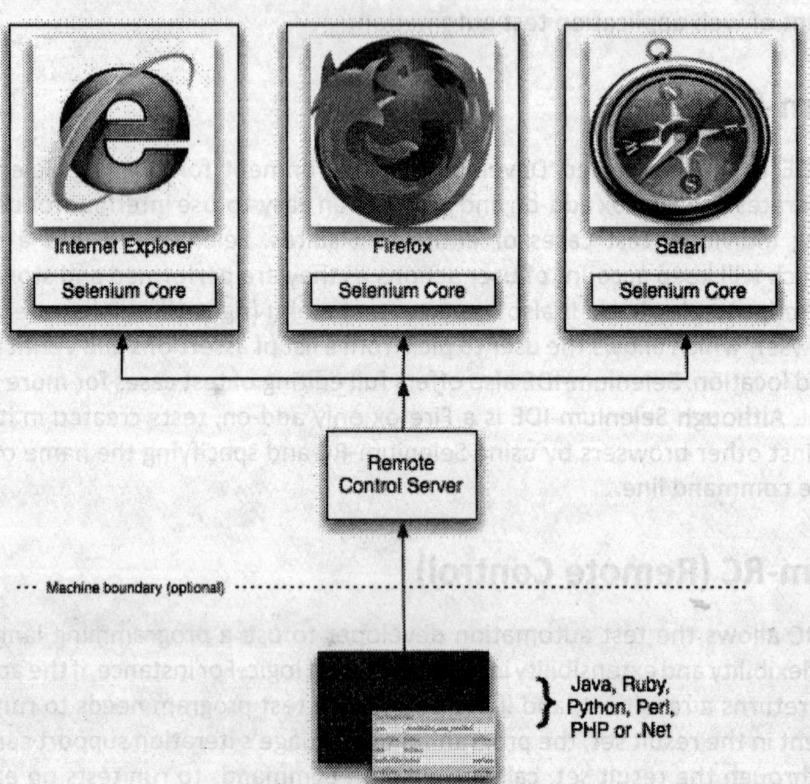

Selenium Remote Control is great for testing complex AJAX-based web user interfaces under a Continuous Integration system. It is also an ideal solution for users of Selenium Core or Selenium IDE who want to write tests in a more expressive programming language than the Selenese HTML table format customarily used with Selenium Core.

Download Selenium RC from http://seleniumhq.org/download/

Selenium-Grid

Selenium-Grid allows the Selenium-RC solution to scale for large test suites or test suites that must be run in multiple environments. With Selenium-Grid, multiple instances of Selenium-RC are running on various operating system and browser configurations; Each of these when launching register with a hub. When tests are sent to the hub they are then redirected to an available Selenium-RC, which will launch the browser and run the test. This allows for running tests in parallel, with the entire test suite theoretically taking only as long to run as the longest individual test.

How Selenium Works

Selenium IDE

Firefox Plugin

Records and plays back tests in Firefox; a great way to get started writing tests.

Selenium IDE allows you export your tests to many programming languages, (including Ruby, PHP, Java, perl, C#, and Python) so you can tweak your tests and even put them into your existing testing framework.

Your tests

Your tests are made of a series of Selenium commands, which are sent to the Selenium Remote Control server or the Selenium Grid server.

OR

Selenium Remote Control

Java-based command line server

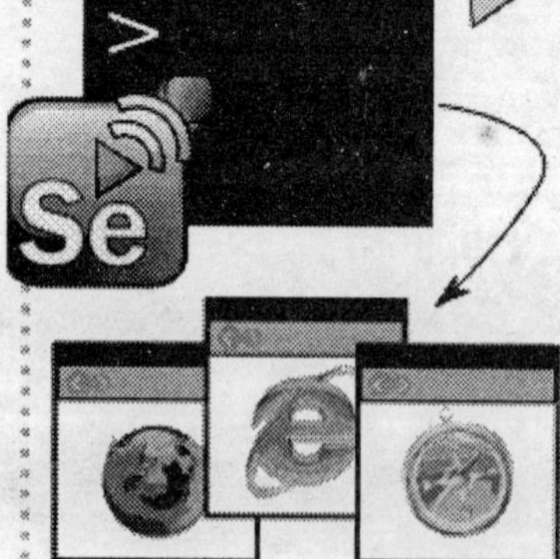

Selenium Remote Control starts up browsers (one at a time) and then runs commands you pass along from your tests

Selenium Grid

Java-based command line server

Selenium Grid coordinates multiple Selenium Remote Control servers so you can run tests on lots of platforms at the same time, which saves lots of time and allows wider testing.

Selenium Introduction:

Selenium is a high quality **open source test automation tool for web application testing.** The Selenium-IDE (**Integrated Development Environment**) is the tool you use to develop your Selenium test cases. It's an easy-to-use Firefox plug-in and is generally the most efficient way to develop test cases. It also contains a context menu that allows you to first select a UI element from the browser's currently displayed page and then select from a list of Selenium commands with parameters pre-defined according to the context of the selected UI element. This is not only a time-saver, but also an excellent way of learning Selenium script syntax. **Selenium IDE** is an integrated development environment for Selenium tests. It is implemented as a Firefox extension, and allows you to record, edit, and debug tests. Selenium IDE includes the entire Selenium Core, allowing you to easily and quickly record and play back tests in the actual environment that they will run.

Selenium IDE is not a only recording tool: **it is a complete IDE**. You can choose to use its recording capability, or you may edit your scripts by hand. With auto complete support and the ability to move commands around quickly, Selenium IDE is the ideal environment for creating Selenium tests no matter what style of tests you prefer.

Supported Environments:-

Selenium runs in Internet Explorer, Mozilla and Firefox on Windows, Linux, and Macintosh, Safari on the Mac.

Installation

Download Pre-requisite software

Download the Selenium IDE from http://seleniumhq.org/download/

Steps:

1. Using Firefox, first, download the Selenium IDE from http://seleniumhq.org/download/

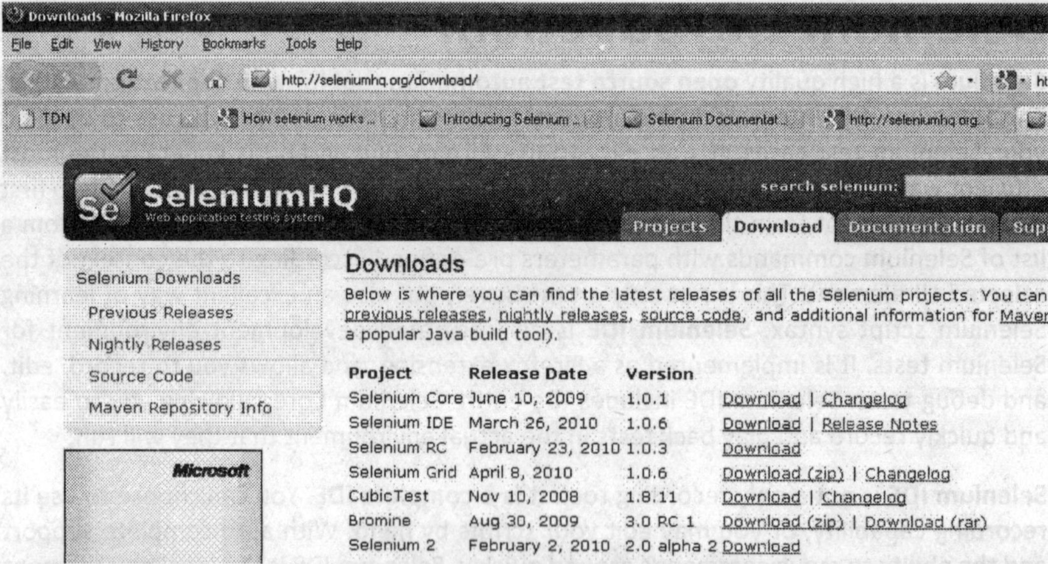

When clicking on Download link, you'll be presented with the following popup message window. "Firefox prevented this site (seleniumhq.org) from asking you to install software on your computer".

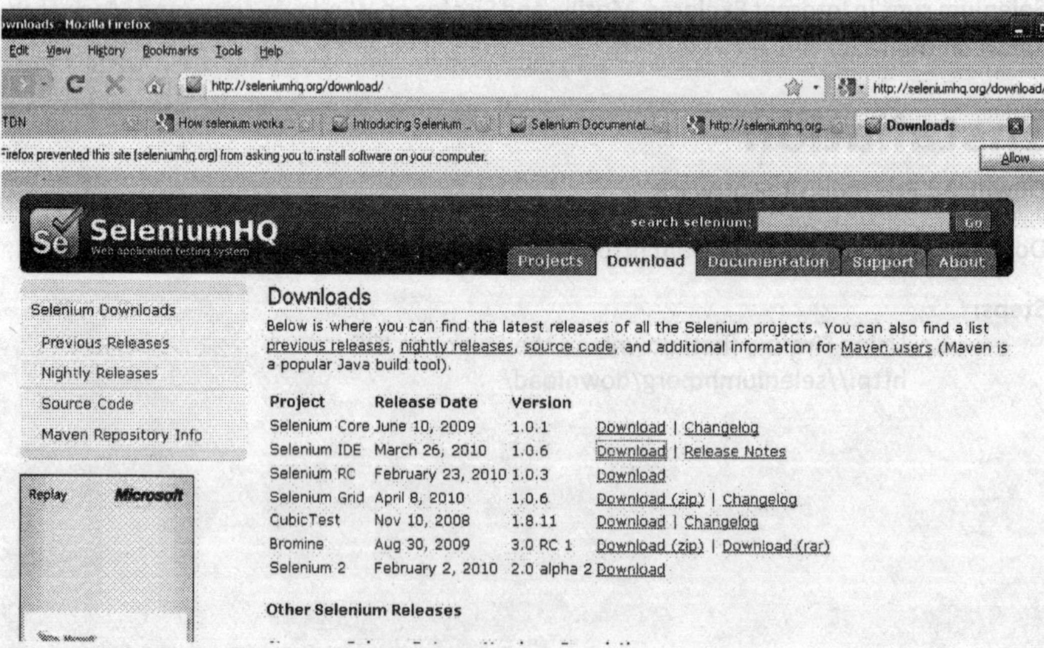

Click on Allow button to install Selenium IDE

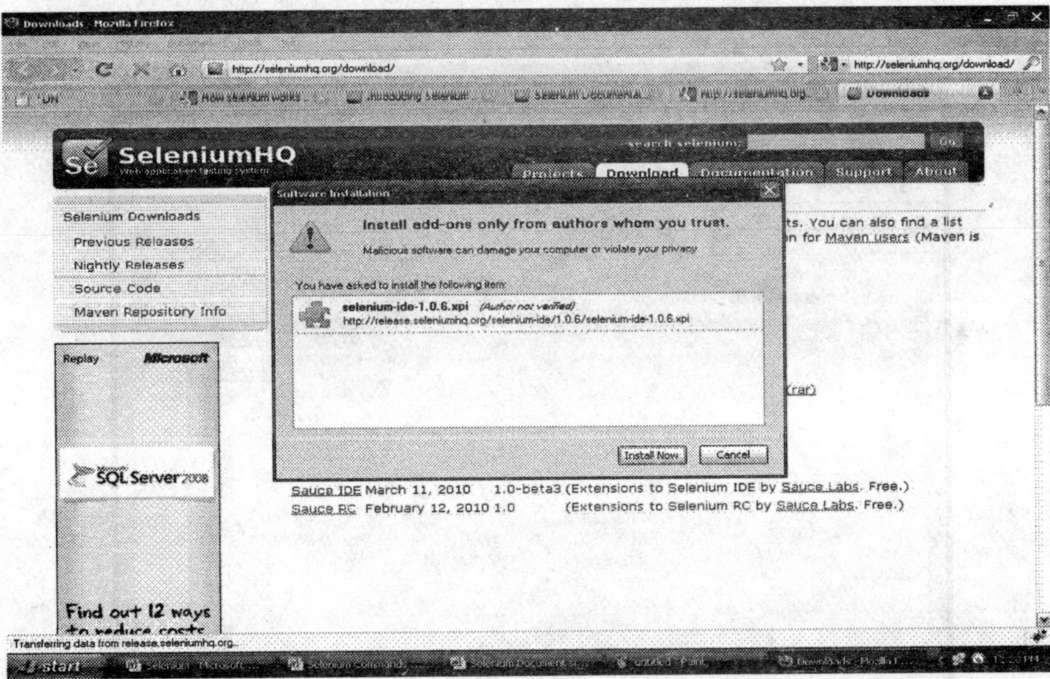

Select Install Now. The Firefox Add-ons window pops up, first showing a progress bar.

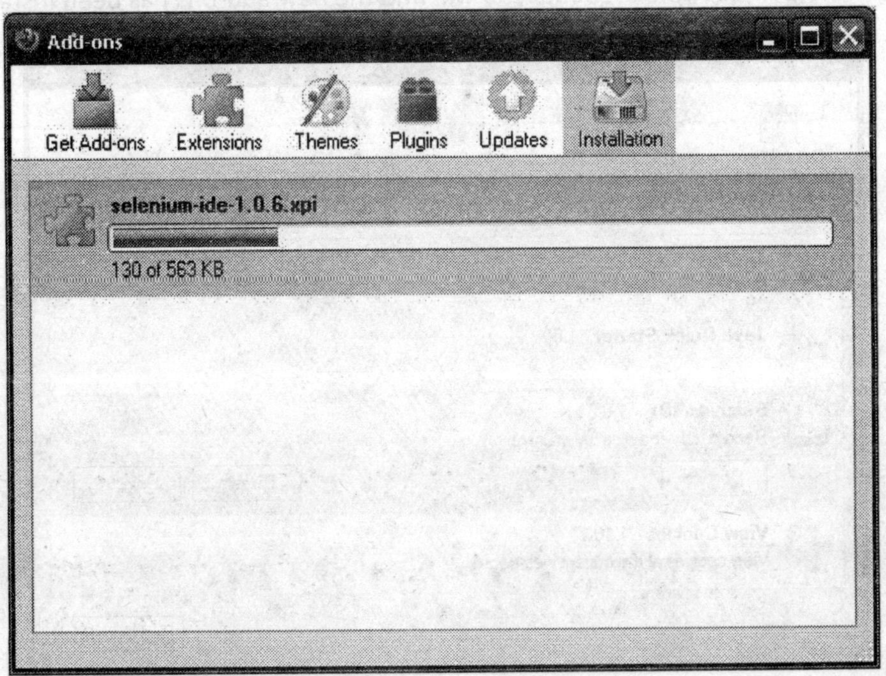

when the download is complete, displays the following.

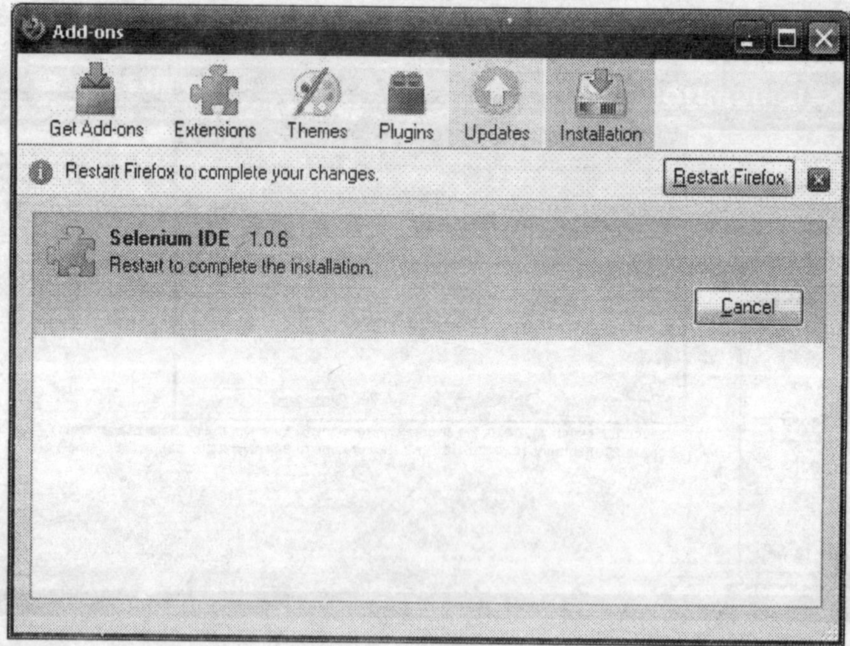

Restart Firefox. After Firefox reboots you will find the new add-ons has been installed.

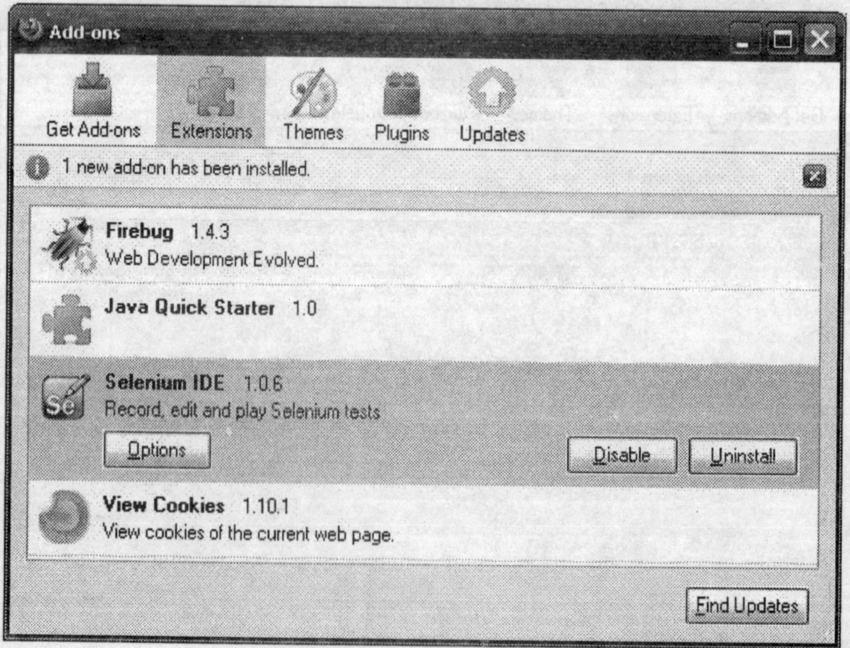

After Firefox reboots you will find the Selenium-IDE listed under the Firefox Tools menu.

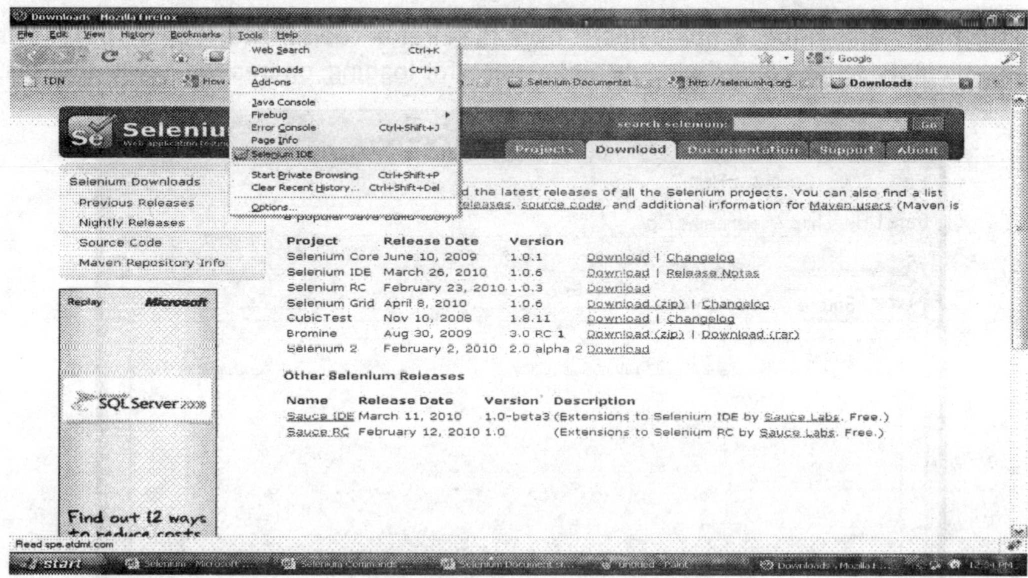

Click on Selenium IDE. It opens as follows with an empty script-editing window and a menu for loading, or creating new test cases.

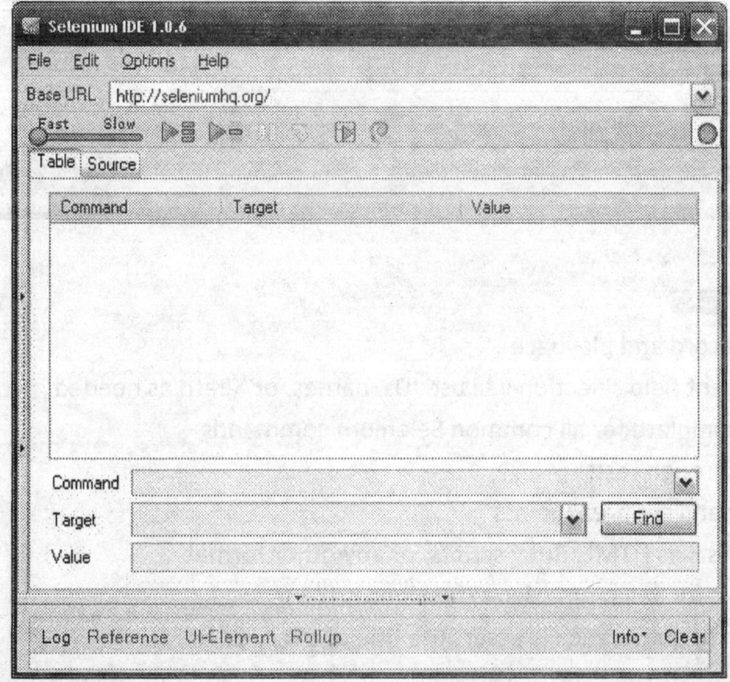

How to Open Selenium IDE

To run the Selenium-IDE, simply select it from the Firefox Tools menu. It opens as follows with an empty script-editing window and a menu for loading, or creating new test cases.

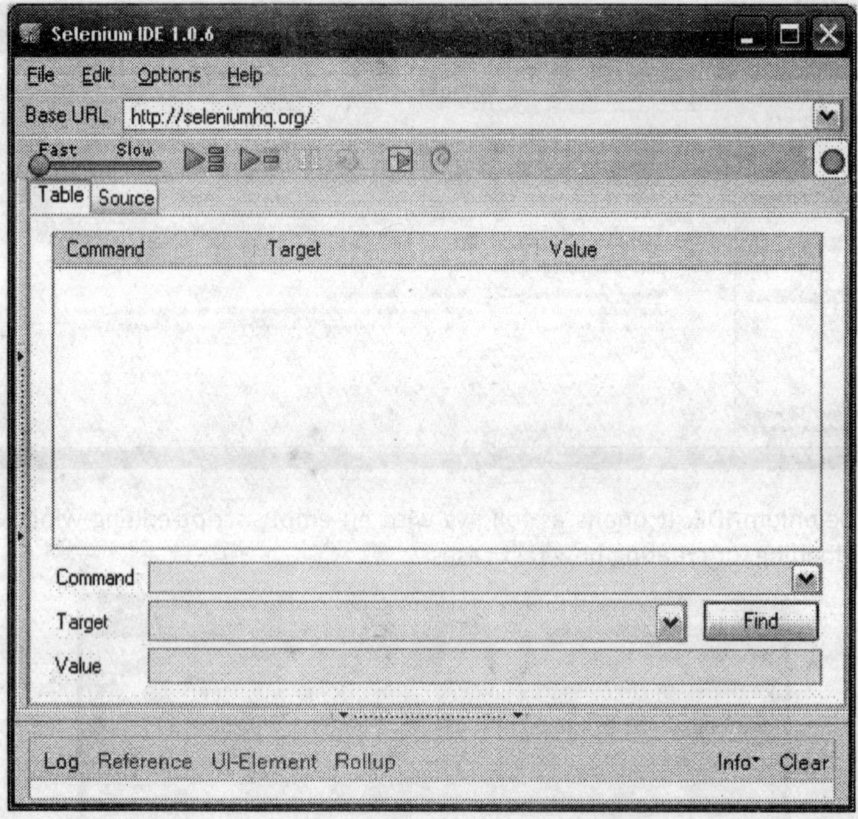

Features

- Easy record and playback
- Intelligent field selection will use IDs, names, or XPath as needed
- Auto complete for all common Selenium commands
- Walk through tests
- Debug and set breakpoints
- Save tests as HTML, Ruby scripts, or any other format
- Support for Selenium user-extensions.js file
- Option to automatically assert the title of every page

Menu Bar

The File menu allows you to create, open, and save test case and test suite files. The Edit menu allows copy, paste, delete, undo, and select all operations for editing the commands in your test case. The Options menu allows the changing of settings. You can set the timeout value for certain commands, add user-defined user extensions to the base set of Selenium commands, and specify the format (language) used when saving your test cases. The Help menu is the standard Firefox Help menu; only one item on this menu–UI-Element Documentation–pertains to Selenium-IDE.

Toolbar

The toolbar contains buttons for controlling the execution of your test cases, including a step feature for debugging your test cases. The right-most button, the one with the red-dot, is the record button.

Speed Control: controls how fast your test case runs.

 Run All: Runs the entire test suite when a test suite with multiple test cases is loaded.

 Run: Runs the currently selected test. When only a single test is loaded this button and the Run All button have the same effect.

 Pause/Resume: Allows stopping and re-starting of a running test case.

 Step: Allows you to "step" through a test case by running it one command at a time. Use for debugging test cases.

 TestRunner Mode: Allows you to run the test case In a browser loaded with the Selenium-Core TestRunner. The TestRunner is not commonly used now and is likely to be deprecated. This \ button is for evaluating test cases for backwards compatibility with the TestRunner. Most users will probably not need this button.

 Apply Rollup Rules: This advanced feature allows repetitive sequences of Selenium commands to be grouped into a single action. Detailed documentation on rollup rules can be found in the UI-Element Documentation on the Help menu.

 Record: Records the user's browser actions.

TestRunner:-

To install TestRunner first download Selenium Core 1.0.1 from

http://seleniumhq.org/download/

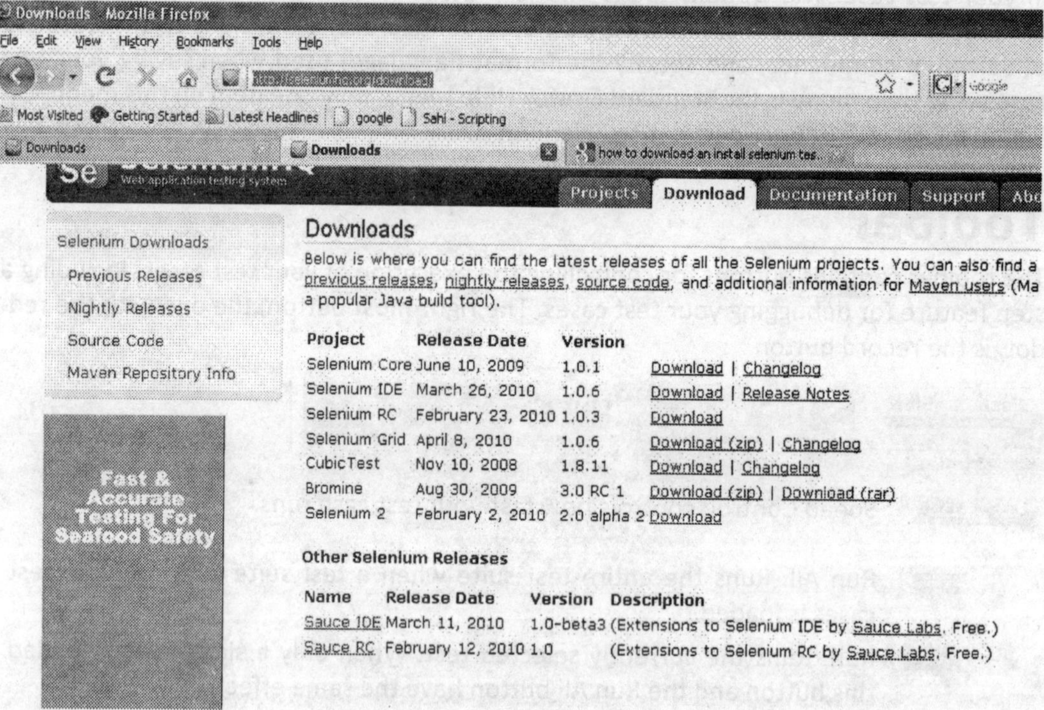

Save Selenium Core-1.0.1.zip file

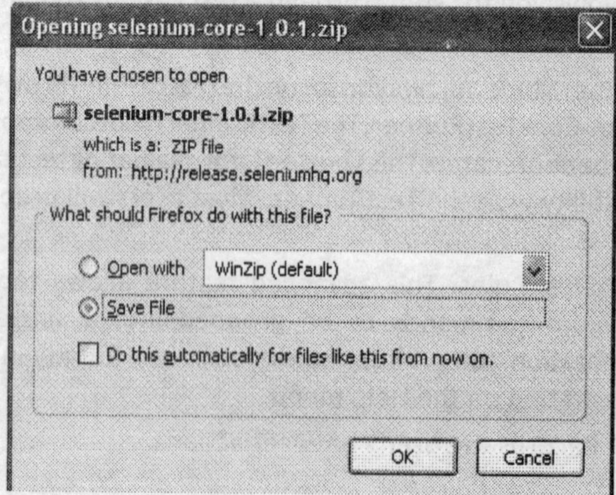

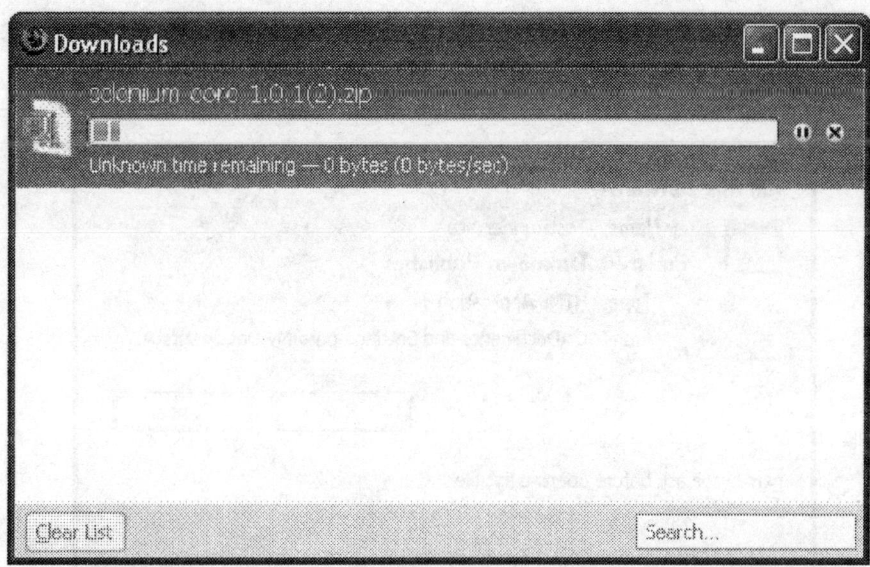

Unzip Selenium Core-1.0.1 file to desired location.
Open Selenium Core-1.0.1 folder. Select Core folder.
C:\Documents and Settings\pqrs\My Documents\Ashwini\selenium-core-1.0.1\core

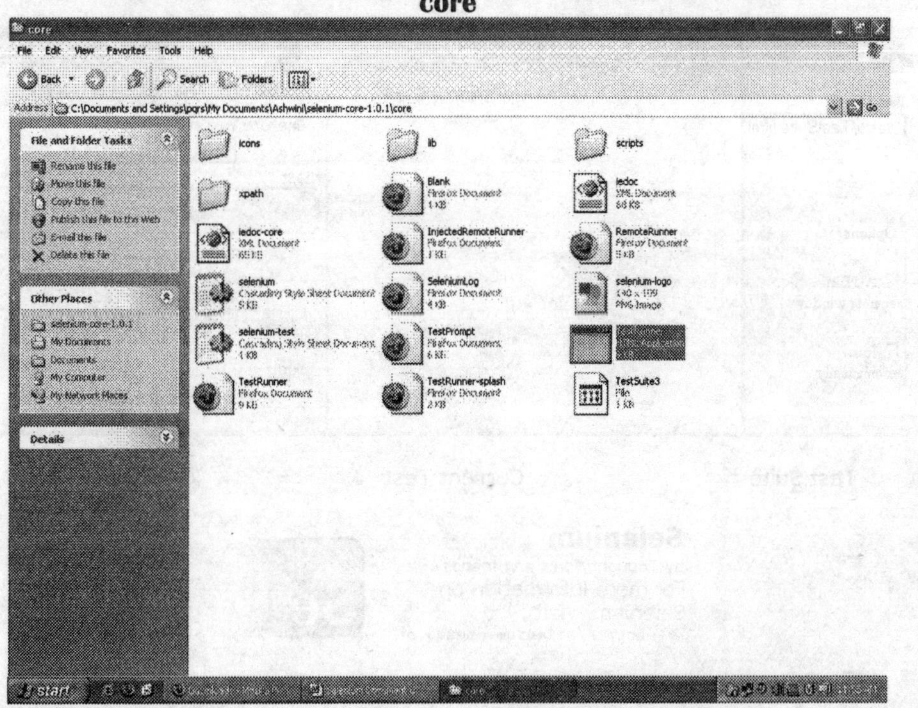

Double Click on TestRunner HTML file,

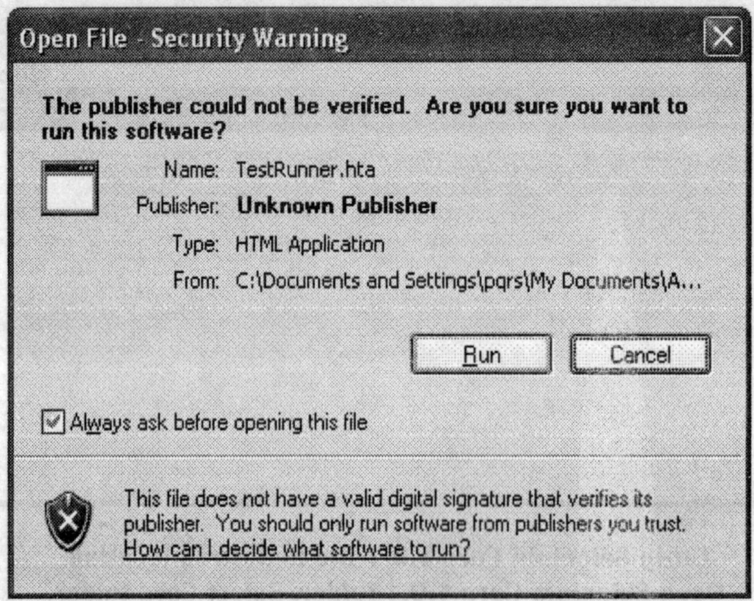

Click on Run button, your TestRunner Looks like

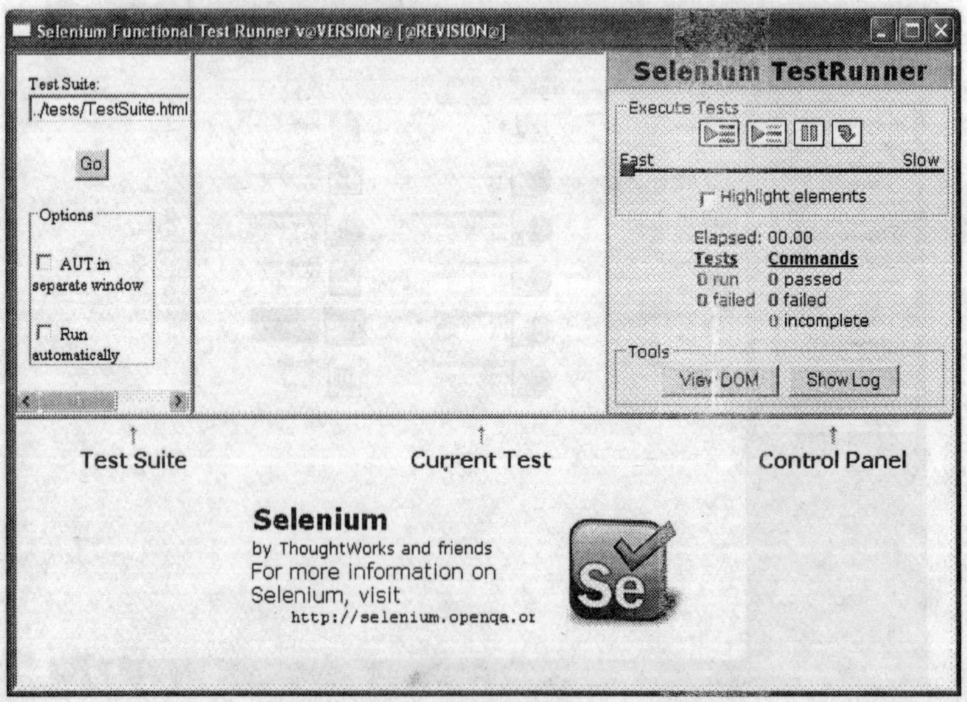

Test Case Pane

Your script is displayed in the test case pane. It has two tabs, one for displaying the command and their parameters in a readable "table" format.

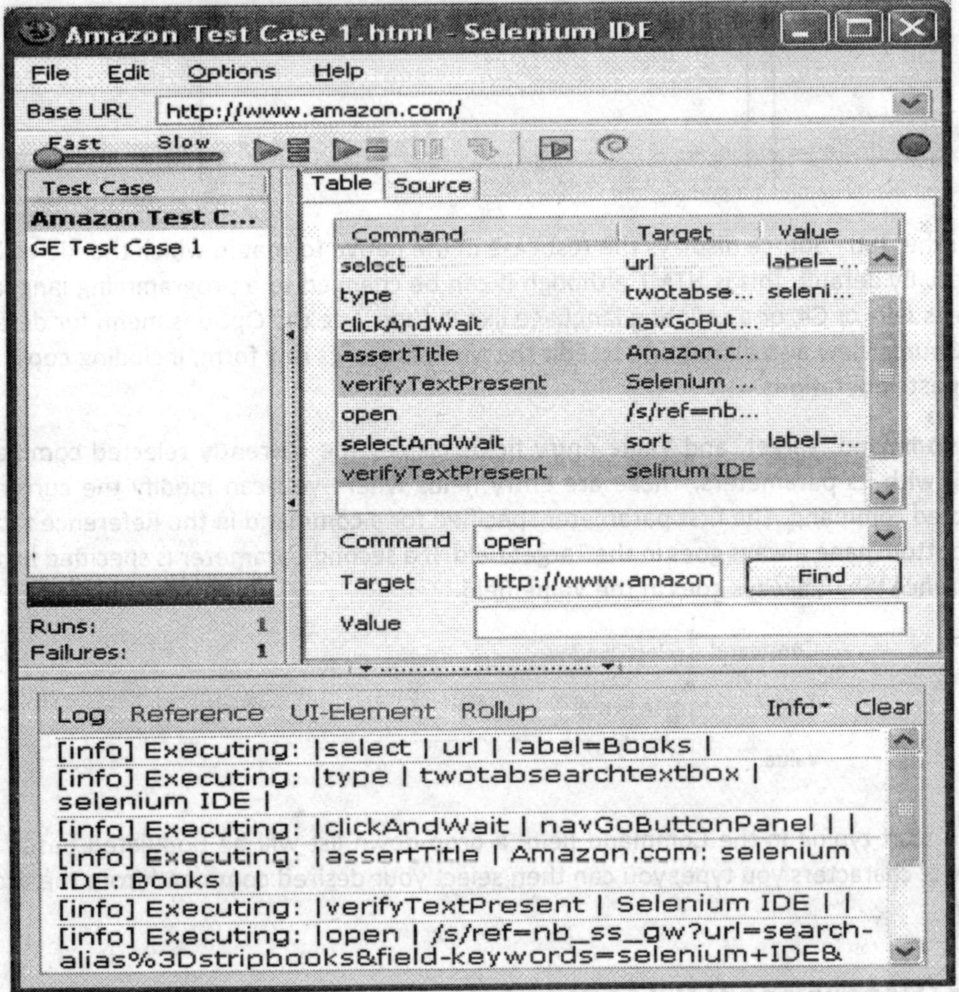

Light Green indicates the step is executed successfully

Dark Green indicates the step command is verified successfully

Red indicates the step is failed during execution

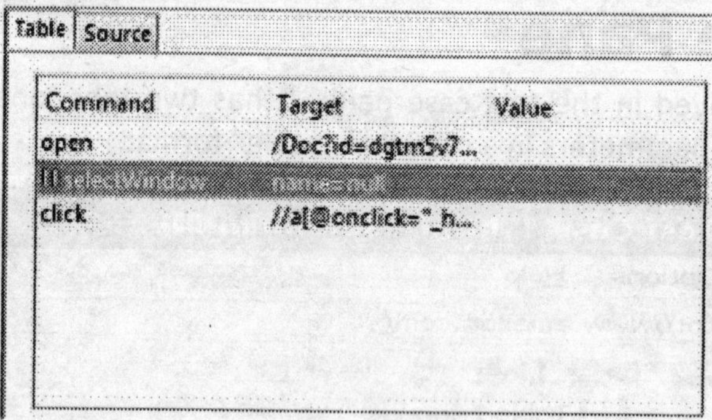

The other tab - Source displays the test case in the native format in which the file will be stored. By default, this is HTML although it can be changed to a programming language such as Java or C#, or a scripting language like Python. See the Options menu for details. The Source view also allows one to edit the test case in its raw form, including copy, cut and paste operations.

The Command, Target, and Value entry fields display the currently selected command along with its parameters. These are entry fields where you can modify the currently selected command. The first parameter specified for a command in the Reference tab of the bottom pane always goes in the Target field. If a second parameter is specified by the Reference tab, it always goes in the Value field.

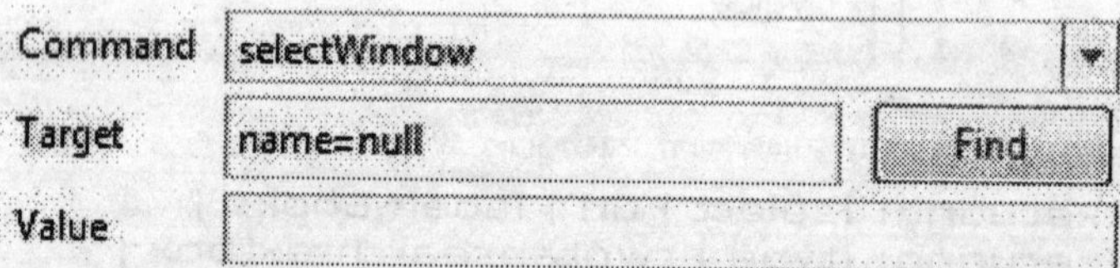

If you start typing in the Command field, a drop-down list will be populated based on the first characters you type; you can then select your desired command from the drop-down.

Log/Reference/UI-Element/Rollup Pane

The bottom pane is used for four different functions–Log, Reference, UI-Element, and Rollup–depending on which tab is selected.

Log

When you run your test case, error messages and information messages showing the progress are displayed in this pane automatically, even if you do not first select the Log tab. These messages are often useful for test case debugging. Notice the Clear button for clearing the Log. Also notice the Info button is a drop-down allowing selection of different levels of information to log.

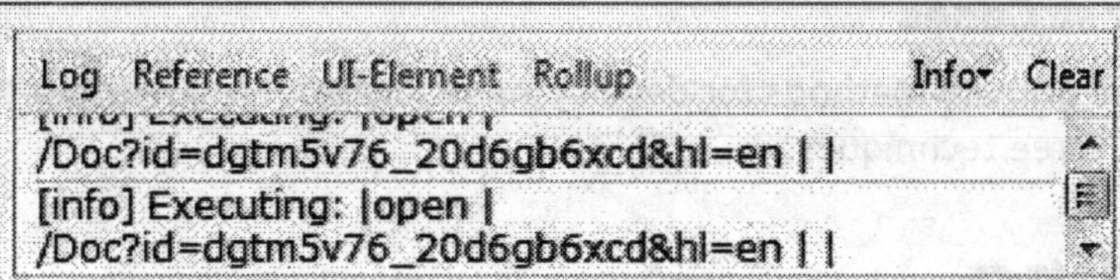

Reference

The Reference tab is the default selection whenever you are entering or modifying Selenese commands and parameters in Table mode. In Table mode, the Reference pane will display documentation on the current command. When entering or modifying commands, whether from Table or Source mode, it is critically important to ensure that the parameters specified in the Target and Value fields match those specified in the parameter list in the Reference pane. The number of parameters provided must match the number specified, the order of parameters provided must match the order specified, and the type of parameters provided must match the type specified. If there is a mismatch in any of these three areas, the command will not run correctly.

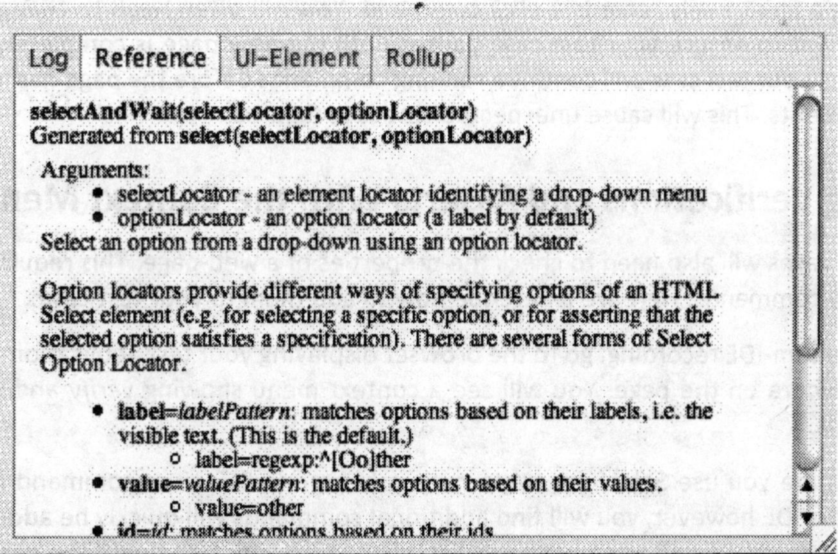

While the Reference tab is invaluable as a quick reference, it is still often necessary to consult the Selenium **Reference** document.

UI-Element and Rollup

The UI Element name refers to the type of HTML element.

Building Test Cases

There are three primary methods for developing test cases. Frequently, a test developer will require all three techniques.

Recording

When Selenium-IDE is first opened, the record button is ON by default.

During recording, Selenium-IDE will automatically insert commands into your test case based on your actions. Typically, this will include:

- clicking a link - *click* or *clickAndWait* commands
- entering values - *type* command
- selecting options from a drop-down listbox - *select* command
- clicking checkboxes or radio buttons - *click* command
- The *type* command may require clicking on some other area of the web page for it to record.

Following a link usually records a *click* command. You will often need to change this to *clickAndWait* to ensure your test case pauses until the new page is completely loaded. Otherwise, your test case will continue running commands before the page has loaded all its UI elements. This will cause unexpected test case failures.

Adding Verifications and Asserts With the Context Menu

Your test cases will also need to check the properties of a web-page. This requires *assert* and *verify* commands. Here we'll describe how to add them to your test case.

With Selenium-IDE recording, go to the browser displaying your test application and right click anywhere on the page. You will see a context menu showing *verify* and/or *assert* commands.

The first time you use Selenium, there may only be one Selenium command listed. As you use the IDE however, you will find additional commands will quickly be added to this menu. Selenium-IDE will attempt to predict what command, along with the parameters, you will need for a selected UI element on the current web-page.

Open a web-page of your choosing and select a block of text on the page. A paragraph or a heading will work fine. Now, right-click the selected text. The context menu should give you a *verifyTextPresent* command and the suggested parameter should be the text itself.

Also, the Show All Available Commands menu option. This shows many, many more commands, again, along with suggested parameters, for testing your currently selected UI element.

Try a few more UI elements. Try right-clicking an image, or a user control like a button or a checkbox. You may need to use Show All Available Commands to see options other than *verifyTextPresent.* Once you select these other options, the more commonly used ones will show up on the primary context menu. For example, selecting *verifyElementPresent* for an image should later cause that command to be available on the primary context menu the next time you select an image and right-click.

Editing

Insert Command

Table View

Select the point in your test case where you want to insert the command. To do this, in the Test Case Pane, left-click on the line where you want to insert a new command. Right-click and select Insert Command; the IDE will add a blank line just ahead of the line you selected. Now use the command editing text fields to enter your new command and its parameters.

Source View

Select the point in your test case where you want to insert the command. To do this, in the Test Case Pane, left-click between the commands where you want to insert a new command, and enter the HTML tags needed to create a 3-column row containing the Command, first parameter (if one is required by the Command), and second parameter (again, if one is required). Be sure to save your test before switching back to Table view.

Insert Comment

Comments may be added to make your test case more readable. These comments are ignored when the test case is run.

Comments may also be used to add vertical white space (one or more blank lines) in your tests; just create empty comments. An empty command will cause an error during execution; an empty comment won't.

Table View

Select the line in your test case where you want to insert the comment. Right-click and select Insert Comment. Now use the Command field to enter the comment. Your comment will appear in purple font.

Source View

Select the point in your test case where you want to insert the comment. Add an HTML-style comment, i.e., *<!– your comment here –>*.

Edit a Command or Comment

Table View

Simply select the line to be changed and edit it using the Command, Target, and Value fields.

Source View

Since Source view provides the equivalent of a WYSIWYG editor, simply modify which line you wish–command, parameter, or comment.

Opening and Saving a Test Case

The File=>Open, Save and Save As menu commands behave similarly to opening and saving files in most other programs. When you open an existing test case, Selenium-IDE displays its Selenium commands in the Test Case Pane.

Test suite files can also be opened and saved via the File menu. However, such operations have their own menu entries near the bottom; the Open, Save, and Save As items are only for files.

Running Test Cases

The IDE allows many options for running your test case. You can run a test case all at once, stop and start it, run it one line at a time, run a single command you are currently developing, and you can do a batch run of an entire test suite. Execution of test cases is very flexible in the IDE.

Run a Test Case

Click the Run button to run the currently displayed test case.

Run a Test Suite

Click the Run All button to run all the test cases in the currently loaded test suite.

Stop and Start

The Pause button can be used to stop the test case while it is running. The icon of this button then changes to indicate the Resume button. To continue click Resume.

Stop in the Middle

You can set a breakpoint in the test case to cause it to stop on a particular command. This is useful for debugging your test case. To set a breakpoint, select a command, right-click, and from the context menu select Toggle Breakpoint.

Start from the Middle

You can tell the IDE to begin running from a specific command in the middle of the test case. This also is used for debugging. To set a startpoint, select a command, right-click, and from the context menu select Set/Clear Start Point.

Run Any Single Command

Double-click any single command to run it by itself. This is useful when writing a single command. It lets you immediately test a command you are constructing, when you are not sure if it is correct. You can double-click it to see if it runs correctly. This is also available from the context menu.

Using Base URL to Run Test Cases in Different Domains

The *Base URL* field at the top of the Selenium-IDE window is very useful for allowing test cases to be run across different domains. Suppose that a site named http://news.portal.com had an in-house beta site named http://beta.news.portal.com. Any test cases for these sites that begin with an *open* statement should specify a *relative URL* as the argument to *open* rather than an *absolute URL* (one starting with a protocol such as http: or https :). Selenium-IDE will then create an absolute URL by appending the *open* command's argument onto the end of the value of Base URL. For example, the test case below would be run against http://news.portal.com/about.html:

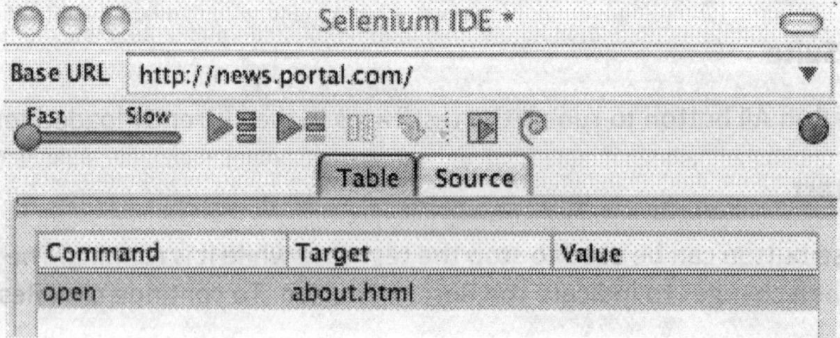

This same test case with a modified Base URL setting would be run against http://beta.news.portal.com/about.html:

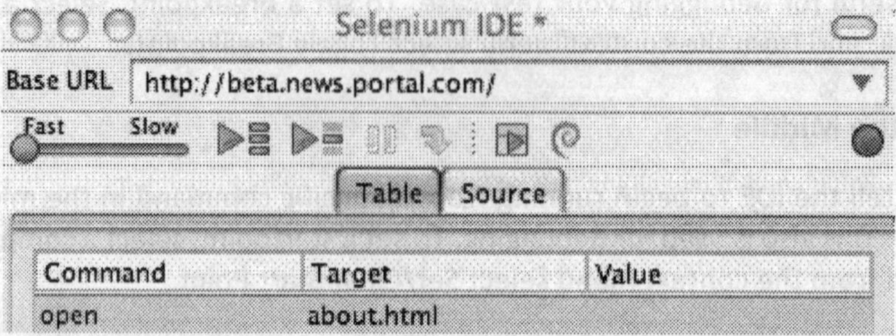

Debugging

Debugging means finding and fixing errors in your test case. This is a normal part of test case development.

Breakpoints and Startpoints

The Sel-IDE supports the setting of breakpoints and the ability to start and stop the running of a test case, from any point within the test case. That is, one can run up to a specific command in the middle of the test case and inspect how the test case behaves at that point. To do this, set a breakpoint on the command just before the one to be examined.

To set a breakpoint, select a command, right-click, and from the context menu select *Toggle Breakpoint*. Then click the Run button to run your test case from the beginning up to the breakpoint.

It is also sometimes useful to run a test case from somewhere in the middle to the end of the test case or up to a breakpoint that follows the starting point. For example, suppose your test case first logs into the website and then performs a series of tests and you are trying to debug one of those tests. However, you only need to login once, but you need to keep rerunning your tests as you are developing them. You can login once, then run your test case from a startpoint placed after the login portion of your test case. That will prevent you from having to manually logout each time you rerun your test case.

To set a startpoint, select a command, right-click, and from the context menu select *Set/ Clear Start Point*. Then click the Run button to execute the test case beginning at that startpoint.

Stepping Through a Testcase

To execute a test case one command at a time ("step through" it), follow these steps:

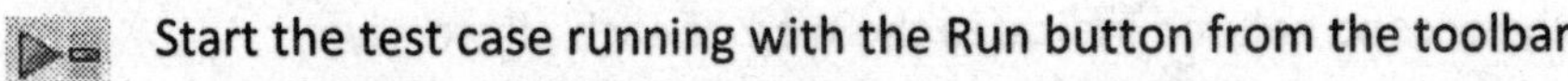

Start the test case running with the Run button from the toolbar.

Immediately pause the executing test case with the Pause button.

Repeatedly select the Step button.

Find Button

The Find button is used to see which UI element on the currently displayed webpage (in the browser) is used in the currently selected Selenium command. This is useful when building a locator for a command's first parameter. It can be used with any command that identifies a UI element on a webpage, i.e. *click*, *clickAndWait*, *type*, and certain *assert* and *verify* commands, among others.

From Table view, select any command that has a locator parameter. Click the Find button. Now look on the webpage: There should be a bright green rectangle enclosing the element specified by the locator parameter.

Page Source for Debugging

Often, when debugging a test case, you simply must look at the page source (the HTML for the webpage you're trying to test) to determine a problem. Firefox makes this easy. Simply right-click the webpage and select 'View->Page Source. The HTML opens in a separate window. Use its Search feature (Edit=>Find) to search for a keyword to find the HTML for the UI element you're trying to test.

Alternatively, select just that portion of the webpage for which you want to see the source. Then right-click the webpage and select View Selection Source. In this case, the separate HTML window will contain just a small amount of source, with highlighting on the portion representing your selection.

Locator Assistance

Whenever Selenium-IDE records a locator-type argument, it stores additional information which allows the user to view other possible locator-type arguments that could be used instead. This feature can be very useful for learning more about locators, and is often needed to help one build a different type of locator than the type that was recorded.

This locator assistance is presented on the Selenium-IDE window as a drop-down list accessible at the right end of the Target field (only when the Target field contains a recorded locator-type argument). Below is a snapshot showing the contents of this drop-down for one command. Note that the first column of the drop-down provides alternative locators, whereas the second column indicates the type of each alternative.

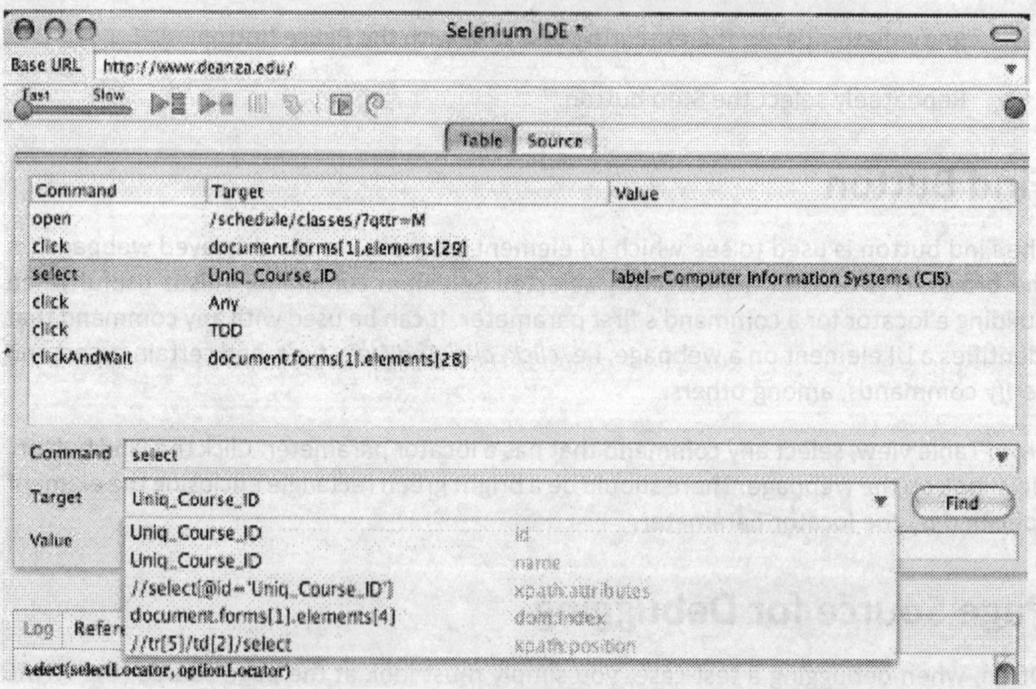

Writing a Test Suite

A test suite is a collection of test cases which is displayed in the leftmost pane in the IDE. The test suite pane can be manually opened or closed via selecting a small dot halfway down the right edge of the pane (which is the left edge of the entire Selenium-IDE window if the pane is closed).

The test suite pane will be automatically opened when an existing test suite is opened *or* when the user selects the New Test Case item from the File menu. In the latter case, the new test case will appear immediately below the previous test case.

Selenium-IDE does not yet support loading pre-existing test cases into a test suite. Users who want to create or modify a test suite by adding pre-existing test cases must manually edit a test suite file.

A test suite file is an HTML file containing a one-column table. Each cell of each row in the <tbody> section contains a link to a test case. The example below is of a test suite containing four test cases:

```
<html>
<head>
  <meta http-equiv="Content-Type" content="text/html; charset=UTF-8">
  <title>Sample Selenium Test Suite</title>
</head>
<body>
  <table cellpadding="1" cellspacing="1" border="1">
    <thead>
      <tr><td>Test Cases for De Anza A-Z Directory Links</td></tr>
    </thead>
  <tbody>
    <tr><td><a href="./a.html">A Links</a></td></tr>
    <tr><td><a href="./b.html">B Links</a></td></tr>
    <tr><td><a href="./c.html">C Links</a></td></tr>
    <tr><td><a href="./d.html">D Links</a></td></tr>
  </tbody>
  </table>
</body>
</html>
```

Note

Test case files should not have to be co-located with the test suite file that invokes them. And on Mac OS and Linux systems, that is indeed the case. However, at the time of this writing, a bug prevents Windows users from being able to place the test cases elsewhere than with the test suite that invokes them.

User Extensions

User extensions are JavaScript files that allow one to create his or her own customizations and features to add additional functionality. Often this is in the form of customized commands although this extensibility is not limited to additional commands.

There are a number of useful extensions created by users.

Perhaps the most popular of all Selenium-IDE extensions is one which provides flow control in the form of while loops and primitive conditionals. This extension is the goto_sel_ide.js. For an example of how to use the functionality provided by this extension, look at the page created by its author.

To install this extension, put the pathname to its location on your computer in the **Selenium Core extensions** field of Selenium-IDE's Options=>Options=>General tab.

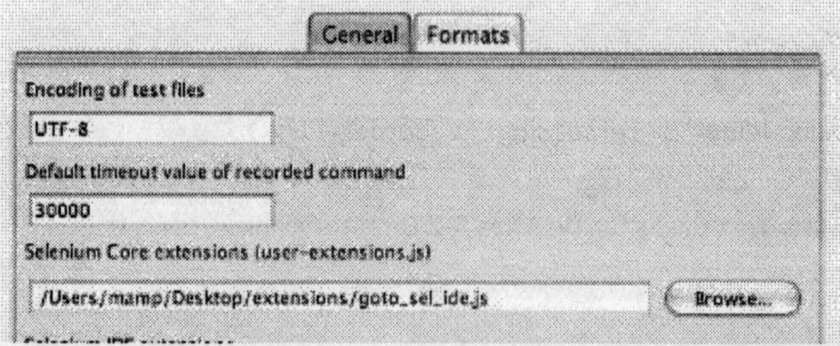

After selecting the **OK** button, you must close and reopen Selenium-IDE in order for the extensions file to be read. Any change you make to an extension will also require you to close and reopen Selenium-IDE.

Information on writing your own extensions can be found near the bottom of the Selenium Reference document.

Format

Format, under the Options menu, allows you to select a language for saving and displaying the test case. The default is HTML.

If you will be using Selenium-RC to run your test cases, this feature is used to translate your test case into a programming language. Select the language, i.e. Java, PHP, you will be using with Selenium-RC for developing your test programs. Then simply save the test case using File=>Save. Your test case will be translated into a series of functions in the language you choose. Essentially, program code supporting your test is generated for you by Selenium-IDE.

Also, note that if the generated code does not suit your needs, you can alter it by editing a configuration file which defines the generation process. Each supported language has configuration settings which are editable. This is under the Options=>Options=>Format tab.

Executing Selenium-IDE Tests on Different Browsers

While Selenium-IDE can only run tests against Firefox, tests developed with Selenium-IDE can be run against other browsers, using a simple command-line interface that invokes the Selenium-RC server. This topic is covered in the *Run Selenese tests* section on Selenium-RC chapter. The *-htmlSuite* command-line option is the particular feature of interest.

Troubleshooting

Below is a list of image/explanation pairs which describe frequent sources of problems with Selenium-IDE:

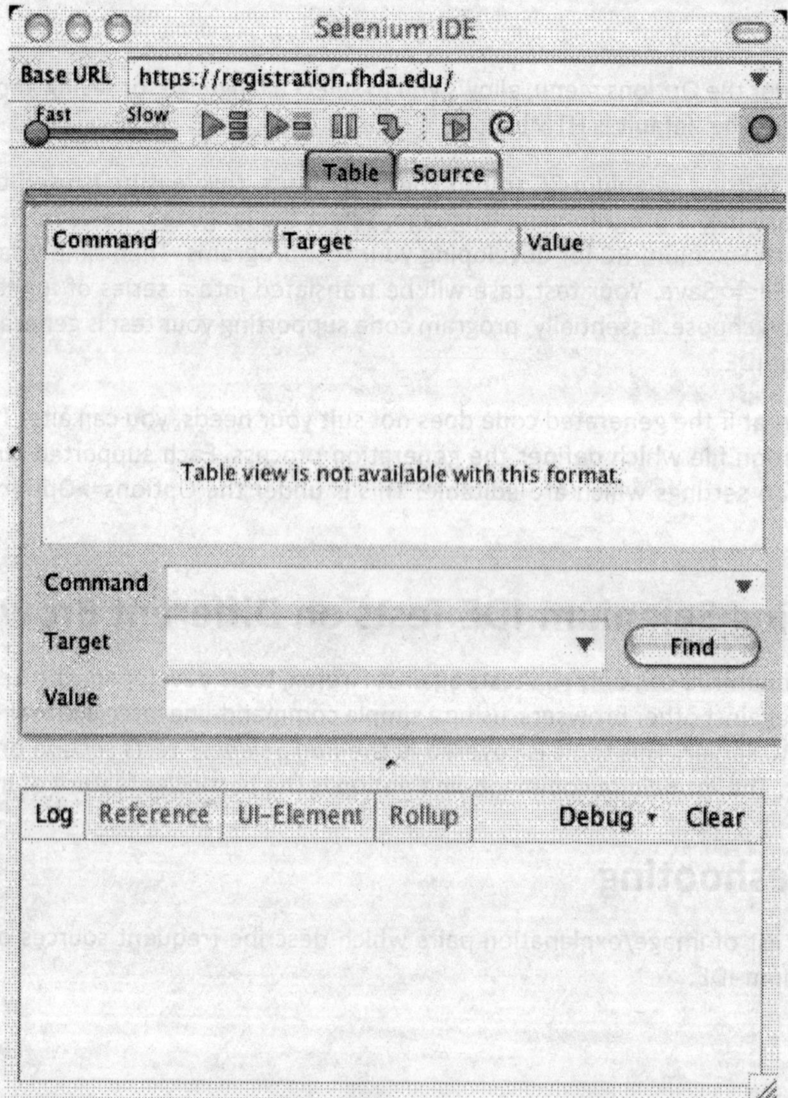

This problem occurs occasionally when Selenium IDE is first brought up. The solution is to close and reopen Selenium IDE. The bug has been filed as SIDE-230.

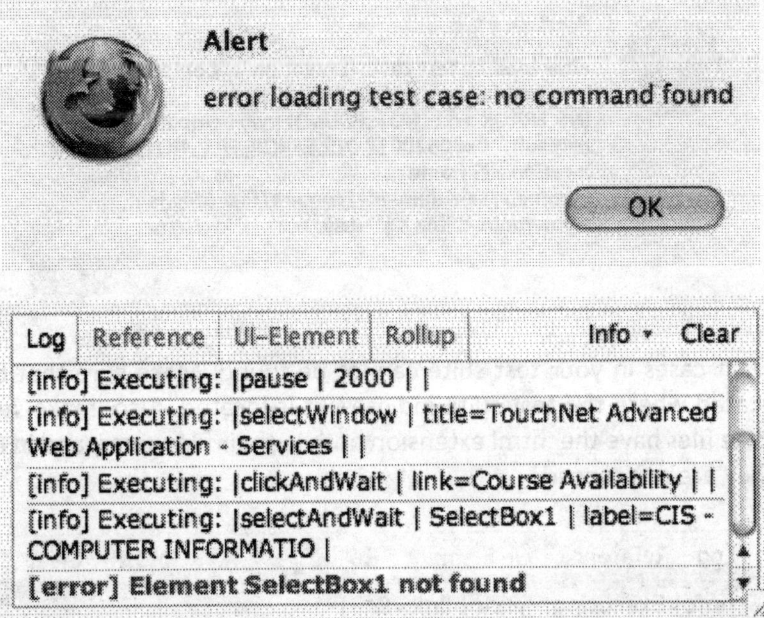

This type of **error** may indicate a timing problem, i.e., the element specified by a locator in your command wasn't fully loaded when the command was executed. Try putting a **pause 5000** before the command to determine whether the problem is indeed related to timing. If so, investigate using an appropriate **waitFor*** or ***AndWait** command immediately before the failing command.

Log	Reference	UI-Element	Rollup	Info ▾ Clear

[info] Executing: |store | URL | http://www.deanza.edu |
[info] Executing: |open | ${URL} | |

Whenever your attempt to use variable substitution fails as is the case for the **open** command above, it indicates that you haven't actually created the variable whose value you're trying to access. This is sometimes due to putting the variable in the **Value** field when it should be in the **Target** field or vice versa. In the example above, the two parameters for the **store** command have been erroneously placed in the reverse order of what is required. For any Selenese command, the first required parameter must go in the **Target** field, and the second required parameter (if one exists) must go in the **Value** field.

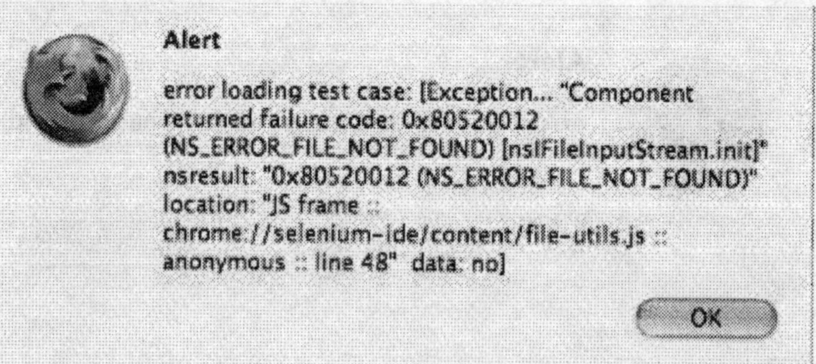

One of the test cases in your test suite cannot be found. Make sure that the test case is indeed located where the test suite indicates it is located. Also, make sure that your actual test case files have the .html extension both in their filenames, and in the test suite file where they are referenced.

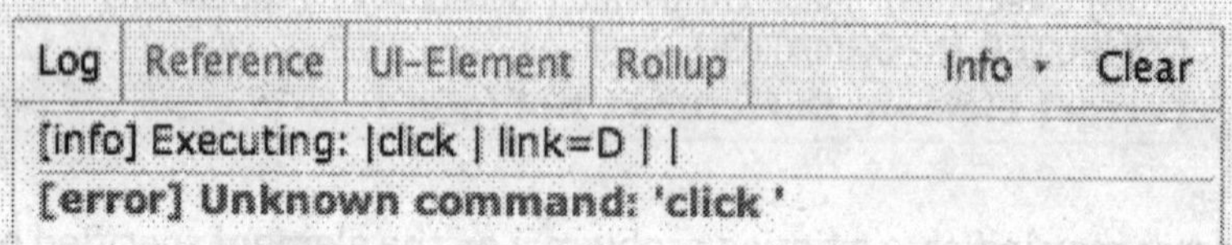

Selenium-IDE is very *space-sensitive*! An extra space before or after a command will cause it to be unrecognizable.

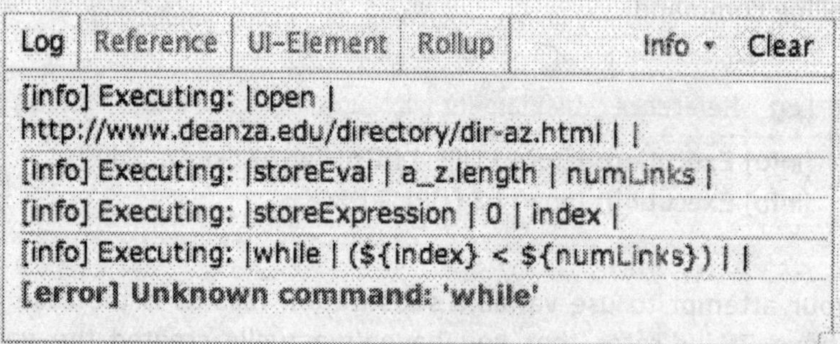

Your extension file's contents have not been read by Selenium-IDE. Be sure you have specified the proper pathname to the extensions file via **Options=>Options=>General** in the **Selenium Core extensions** field. Also, Selenium-IDE must be restarted after any change to either an extensions file *or* to the contents of the **Selenium Core extensions** field.

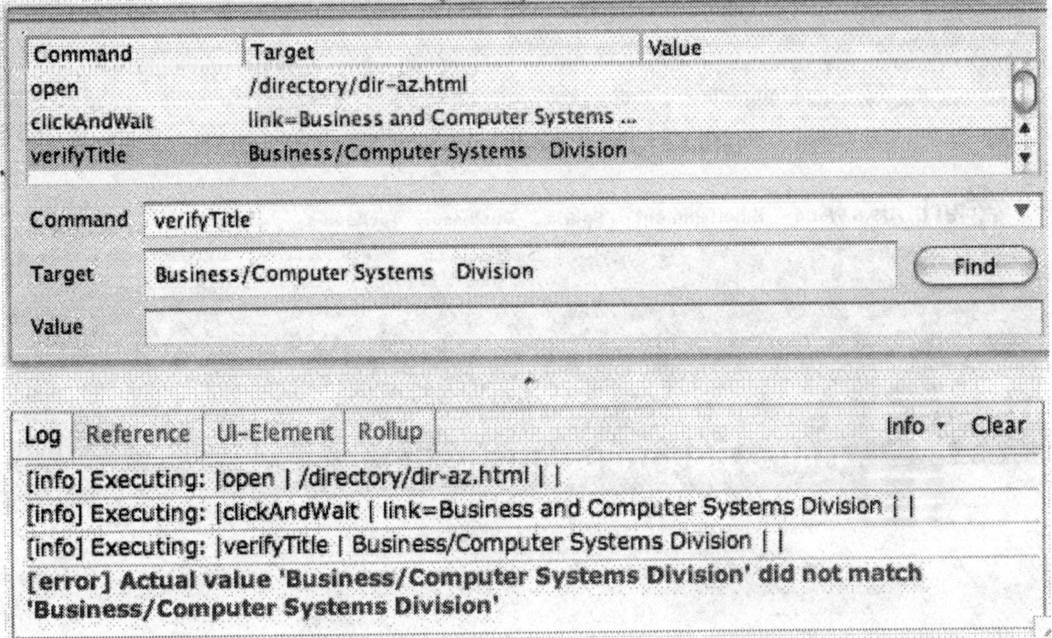

This type of error message makes it appear that Selenium-IDE has generated a failure where there is none. However, Selenium-IDE is correct that the actual value does not match the value specified in such test cases. The problem is that the log file error messages collapse a series of two or more spaces into a single space, which is confusing. In the example above, note that the parameter for **verifyTitle** has two spaces between the words "System" and "Division." The page's actual title has only one space between these words. Thus, Selenium-IDE is correct to generate an error, but is misleading in the nature of the error.

Selenium Example

1. Open Selenium IDE. Type www.evri.com in base url of Selenium IDE. When Selenium-IDE is first opened, the record button is ON by default

2. Open Firefox. Type www.evri.com address bar and press enter key.

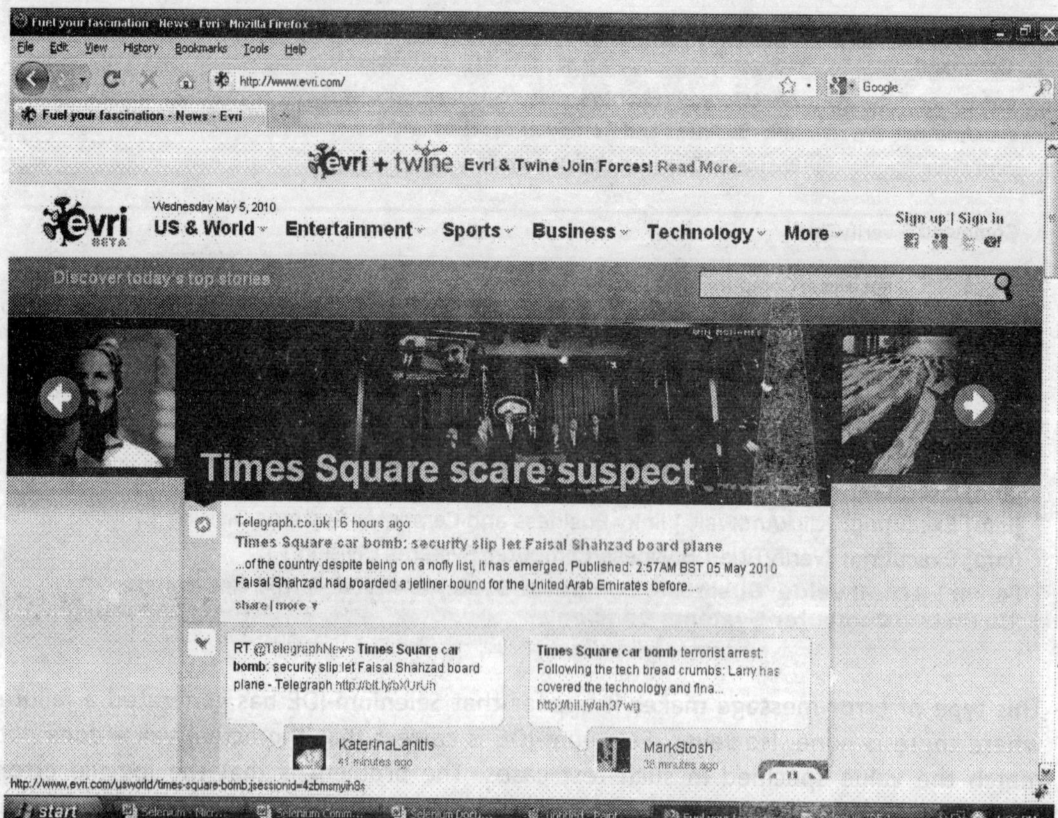

3. Select a block of text on the page or a heading. Now, right-click the selected text. The context menu should give you a *verifyTextPresent* command and the suggested parameter should be the text itself.

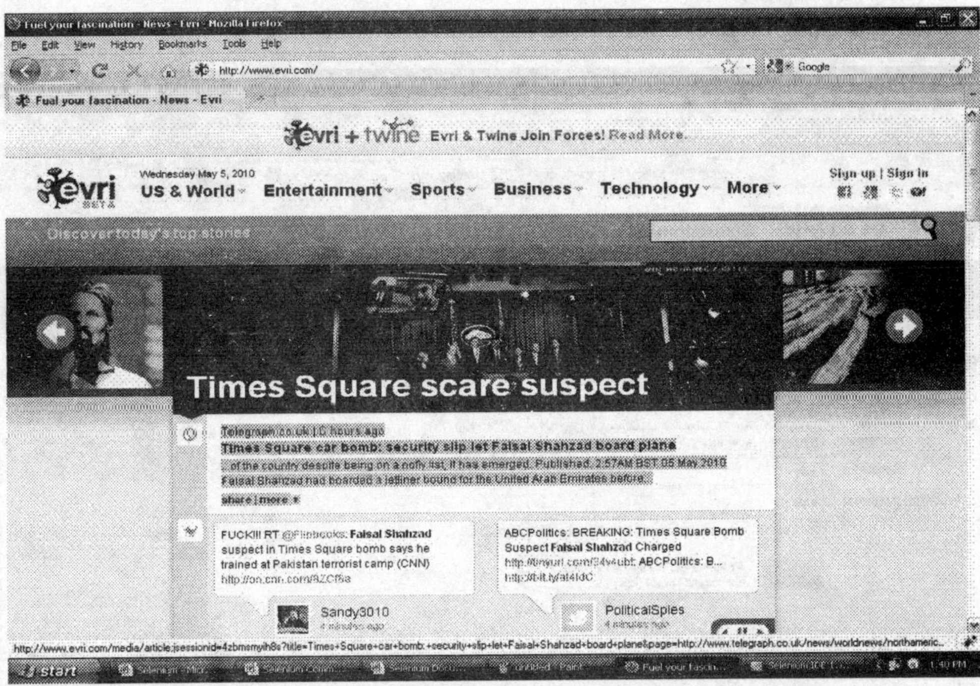

4. Right-clicking an image. Selecting *verifyElementPresent* for an image.

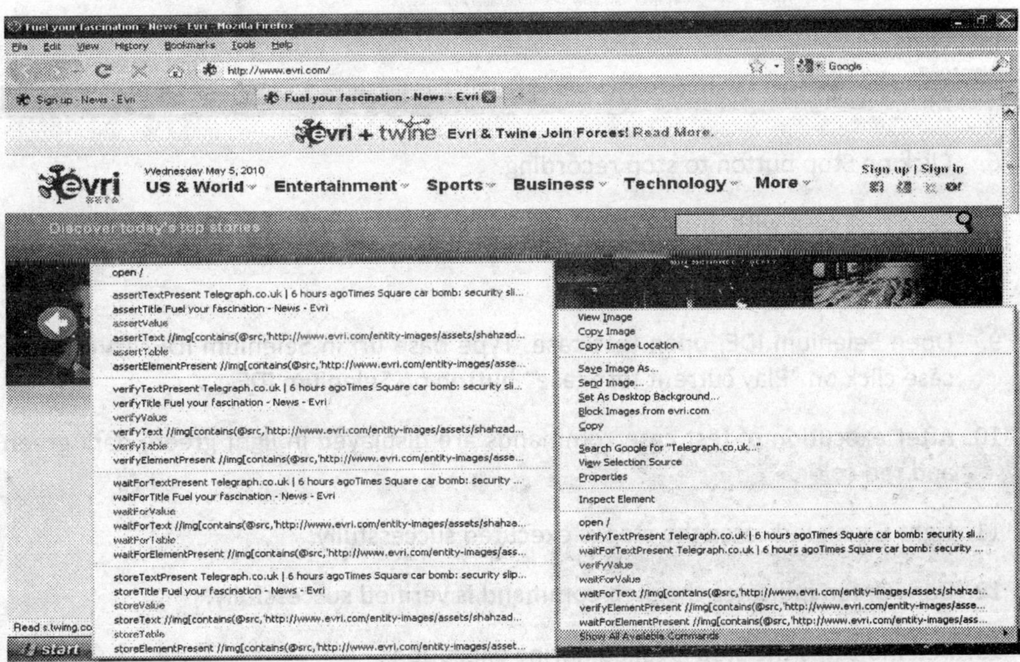

5. Right clicking on user control like a button or a checkbox

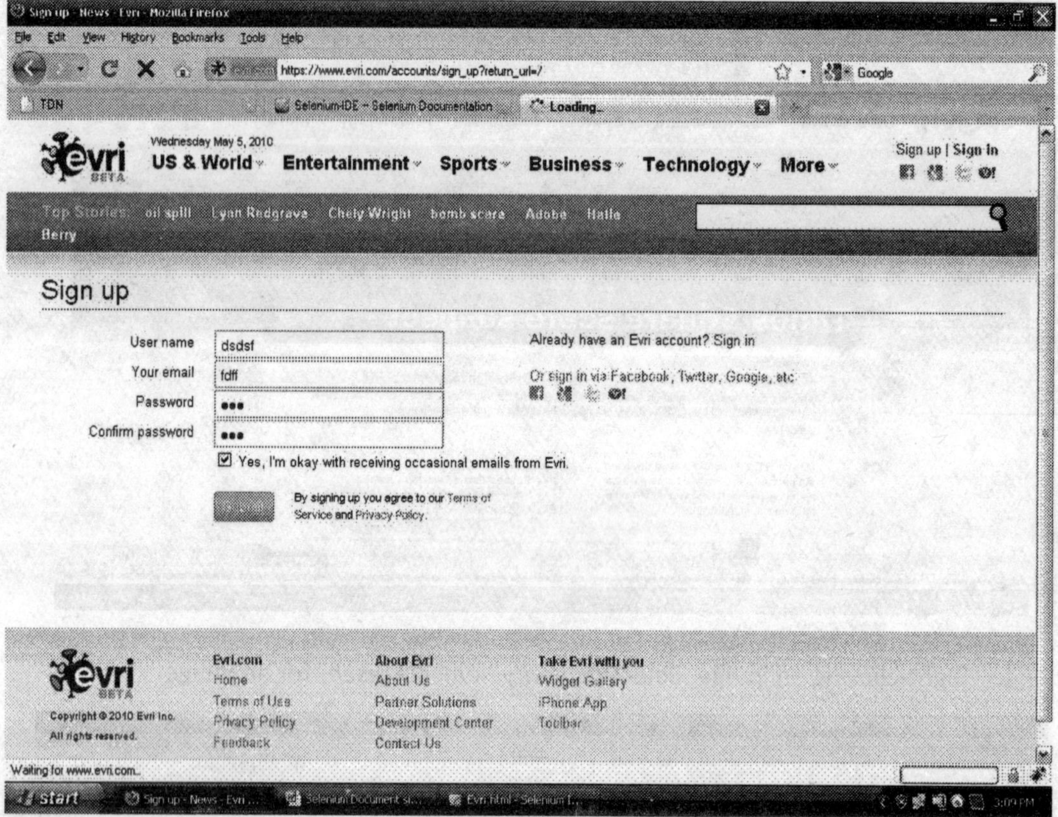

6. Click on Stop button to stop recording.

7. Save test case with .html extension.

8. Open Firefox.

9. Open Selenium IDE, open test case. Type base url in Selenium IDE. To run test case click on "Play current test case" button on Selenium IDE.

10. After execution of test case commands are displayed in light green, dark green and red color.

11. Light Green indicates the step is executed successfully.

12. Dark Green indicates the step command is verified successfully.

13. Red indicates the step is failed during execution

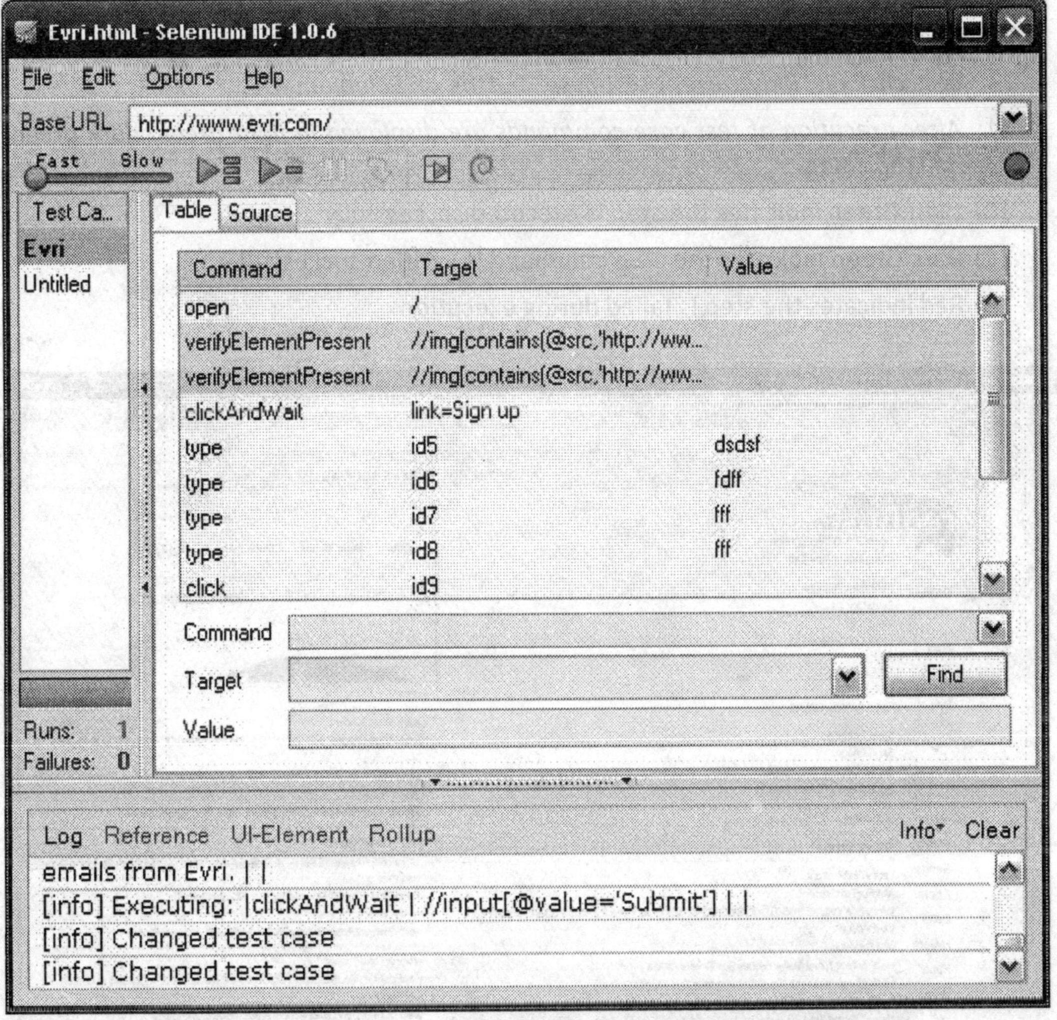

www.redbus.in

1) Open Selenium IDE. Type www.reredbus.in in base url of Selenium IDE. When Selenium-IDE is first opened, the record button is ON by default.
2) Open Firefox. Type www.redbus.in address bar and press enter key.
3) *Click on drop down list to select bus.*
4) Store value of drop down list.
5) Select Type of bus from drop down list.
6) *Save test case with .html extension.*

7) *Open Firefox.*

8) *Open Selenium IDE, open test case. Type base url in Selenium IDE. To run test case click on "Play current test case" button on Selenium IDE.*

9) *After execution of test case commands are displayed in light green, dark green and red color.*

10) Light Green indicates the step is executed successfully.

11) Dark Green indicates the step command is verified successfully.

12) Red indicates the step is failed during execution

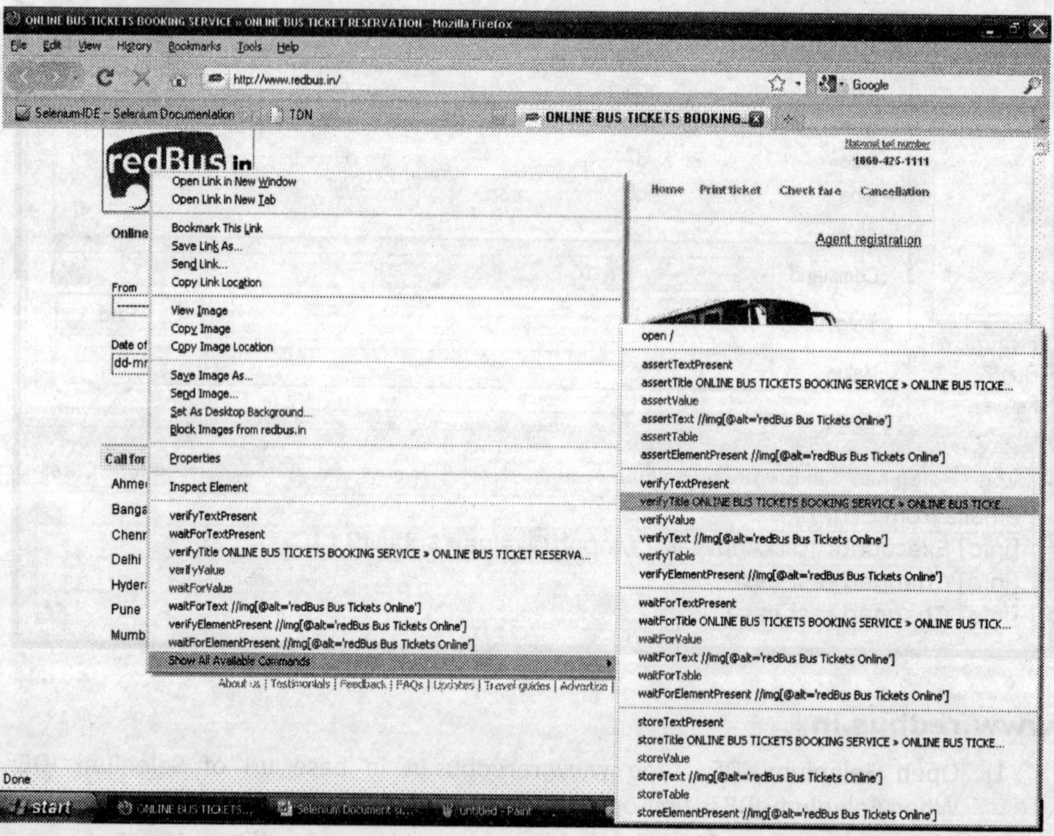

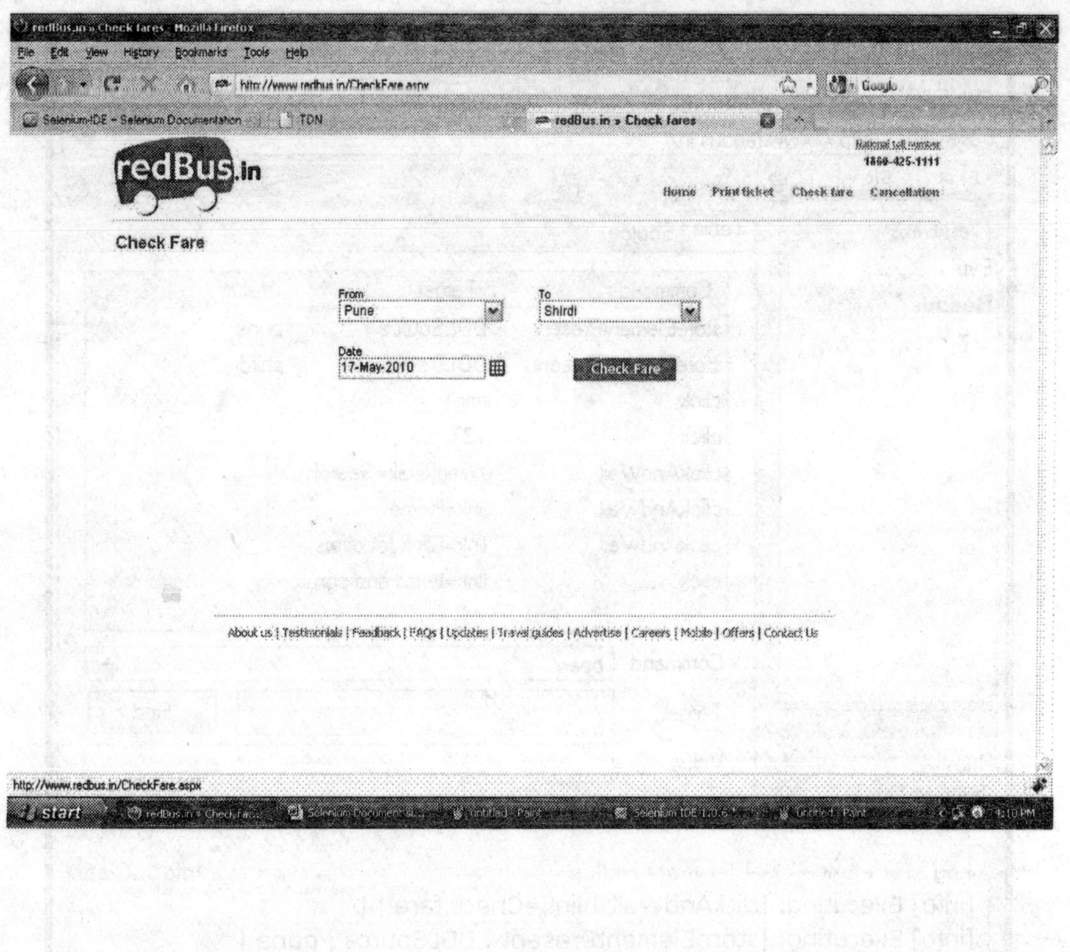
redBus.in » Check fares - Mozilla Firefox
File Edit View History Bookmarks Tools Help
http://www.redbus.in/CheckFare.aspx
Selenium-IDE - Selenium Documentation
TDN
redBus.in » Check fares
National toll number
1860-425-1111
redBus.in
Home Print ticket Check fare Cancellation
Check Fare
From
Pune
To
Shirdi
Date
17-May-2010
Check Fare
About us | Testimonials | Feedback | FAQs | Updates | Travel guides | Advertise | Careers | Mobile | Offers | Contact Us
http://www.redbus.in/CheckFare.aspx
start

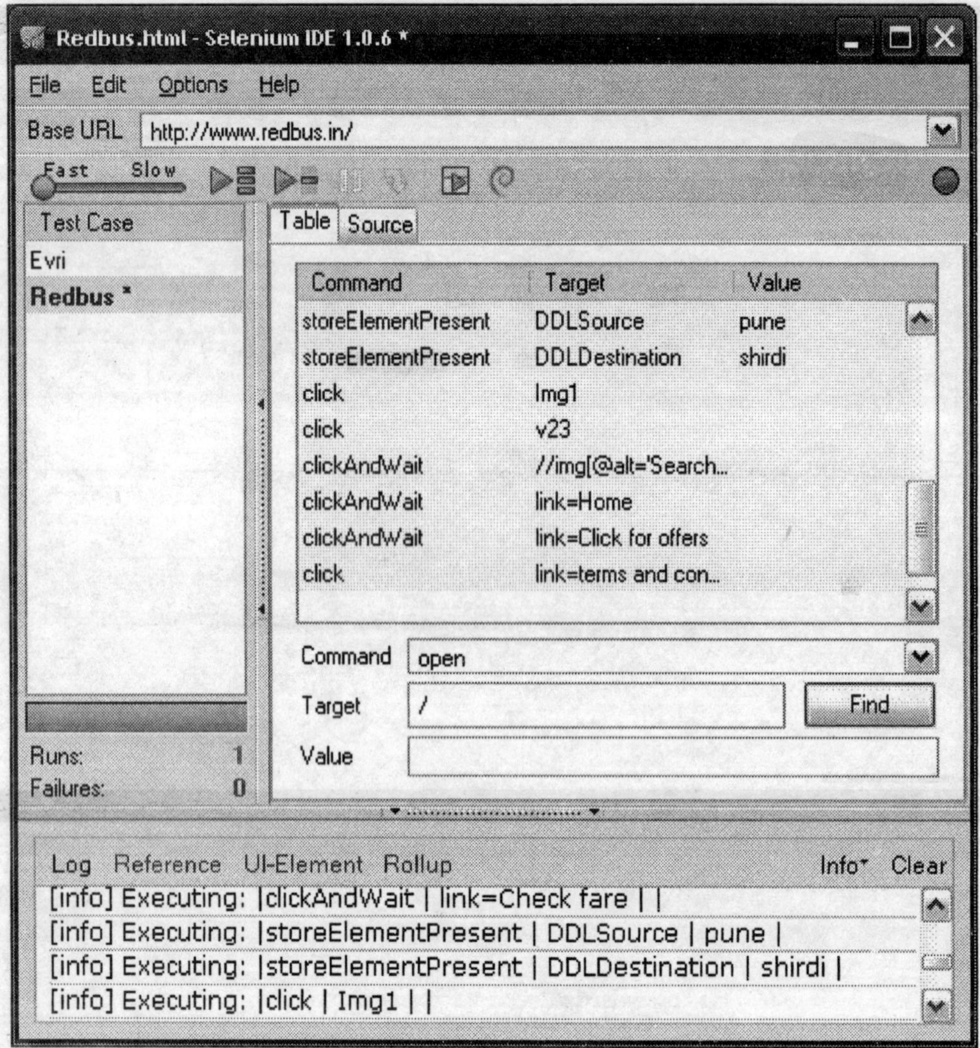
Redbus.html - Selenium IDE 1.0.6 *
File Edit Options Help
Base URL http://www.redbus.in/
Fast Slow
Test Case
Evri
Redbus *
Table Source
Command Target Value
storeElementPresent DDLSource pune
storeElementPresent DDLDestination shirdi
click Img1
click v23
clickAndWait //img[@alt='Search...
clickAndWait link=Home
clickAndWait link=Click for offers
click link=terms and con...
Command open
Target /
Find
Value
Runs: 1
Failures: 0
Log Reference UI-Element Rollup Info Clear
[info] Executing: |clickAndWait | link=Check fare | |
[info] Executing: |storeElementPresent | DDLSource | pune |
[info] Executing: |storeElementPresent | DDLDestination | shirdi |
[info] Executing: |click | Img1 | |

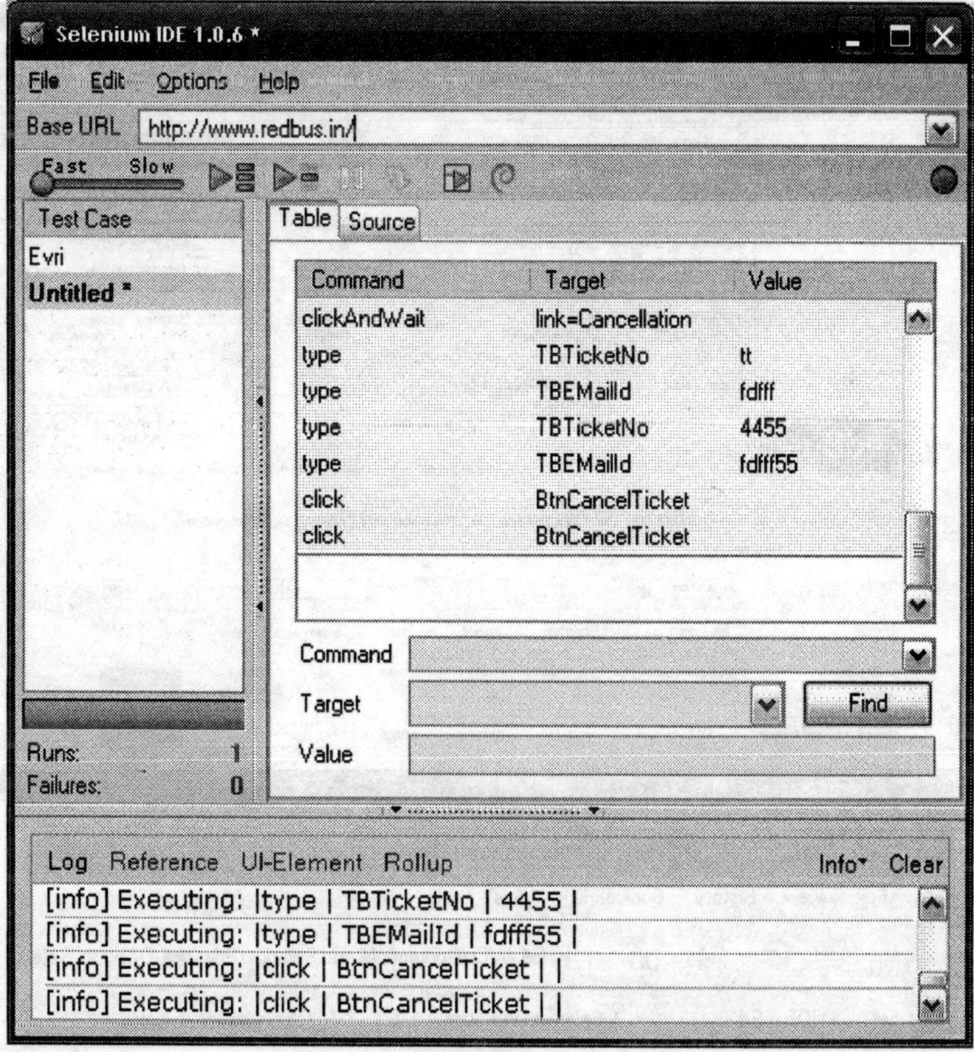

Test Suite

Testsuite.html contains Evri.html and Redbus.html test cases.

To run test suite click on "Play with Selenium Testrunner" button on Selenium IDE.

Opens the testrunner.

Click on testsuite.html to run test cases.

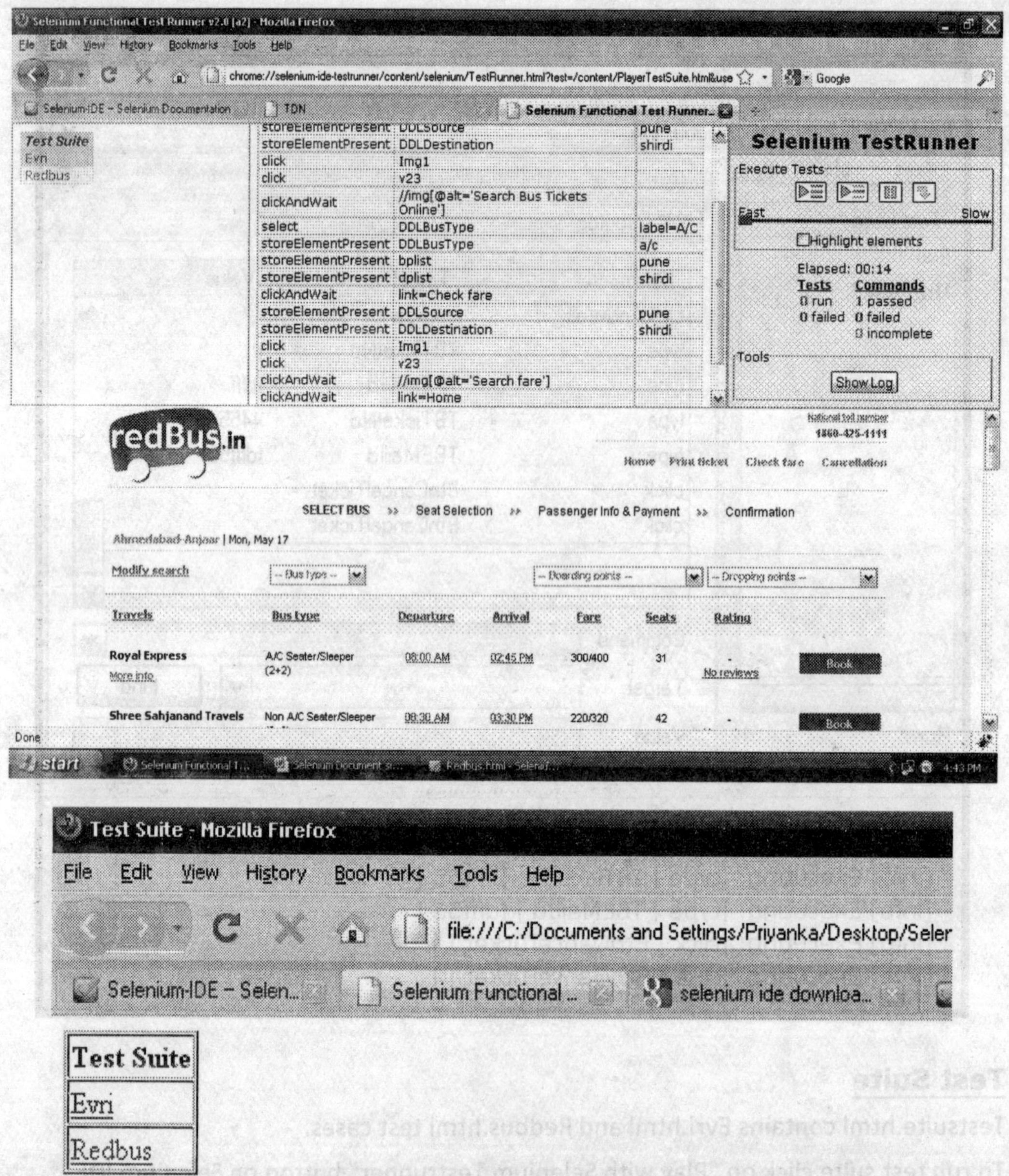
Selenium Functional Test Runner v2.0 [a2] - Mozilla Firefox
File Edit View History Bookmarks Tools Help
chrome://selenium-ide-testrunner/content/selenium/TestRunner.html?test=/content/PlayerTestSuite.html&use
Selenium-IDE - Selenium Documentation
TDN
Selenium Functional Test Runner...
Test Suite
Evri
Redbus
storeElementPresent DDLSource pune
storeElementPresent DDLDestination shirdi
click Img1
click v23
clickAndWait //img[@alt='Search Bus Tickets Online']
select DDLBusType label=A/C
storeElementPresent DDLBusType a/c
storeElementPresent bplist pune
storeElementPresent dplist shirdi
clickAndWait link=Check fare
storeElementPresent DDLSource pune
storeElementPresent DDLDestination shirdi
click Img1
click v23
clickAndWait //img[@alt='Search fare']
clickAndWait link=Home
Selenium TestRunner
Execute Tests
Fast
Slow
Highlight elements
Elapsed: 00:14
Tests
0 run
0 failed
Commands
1 passed
0 failed
0 incomplete
Tools
Show Log
redBus.in
Home Print ticket Check fare Cancellation
SELECT BUS » Seat Selection » Passenger Info & Payment » Confirmation
Ahmedabad-Anjaar | Mon, May 17
Modify search
-- Bus type --
-- Boarding points --
-- Dropping points --
Travels Bus type Departure Arrival Fare Seats Rating
Royal Express A/C Seater/Sleeper (2+2) 08:00 AM 02:45 PM 300/400 31
More info
No reviews
Book
Shree Sahjanand Travels Non A/C Seater/Sleeper 08:30 AM 03:30 PM 220/320 42
Book
Done
start
Test Suite - Mozilla Firefox
File Edit View History Bookmarks Tools Help
file:///C:/Documents and Settings/Priyanka/Desktop/Seler
Selenium-IDE - Selen...
Selenium Functional ...
selenium ide downloa...
Test Suite
Evri
Redbus

References

1. http://seleniumhq.org/download/
2. http://seleniumhq.org/docs/03_selenium_ide.html
3. For advance coding in Selenium:
4. http://www.open2test.org/QAT_Tech_Docs/Selenium_framework_quick_start.pdf
5. http://www.open2test.org
6. http://www.open2test.org/techdocs.html

Selenium RC tool

Introduction

Selenium-RC is the solution for tests that need more than simple browser actions and linear execution. Selenium-RC uses the full power of programming languages to create more complex tests like reading and writing files, querying a database, and emailing test results.

You'll want to use Selenium-RC whenever your test requires logic not supported by Selenium-IDE. What logic could this be? For example, Selenium-IDE does not directly support:

- condition statements
- iteration
- logging and reporting of test results
- error handling, particularly unexpected errors
- database testing
- test case grouping
- re-execution of failed tests
- test case dependency
- screenshot capture of test failures

Although these tasks are not supported by Selenium directly, all of them can be achieved by using programming techniques with a language-specific Selenium-RC client library.

How Selenium-RC Works

First, we will describe how the components of Selenium-RC operate and the role each plays in running your test scripts.

RC Component

Selenium-RC components are:

- The Selenium Server which launches and kills browsers, interprets and runs the Selenese commands passed from the test program, and acts as an *HTTP proxy*, intercepting and verifying HTTP messages passed between the browser and the AUT.
- Client libraries which provide the interface between each programming language and the Selenium-RC Server.

Here is a simplified architecture diagram....

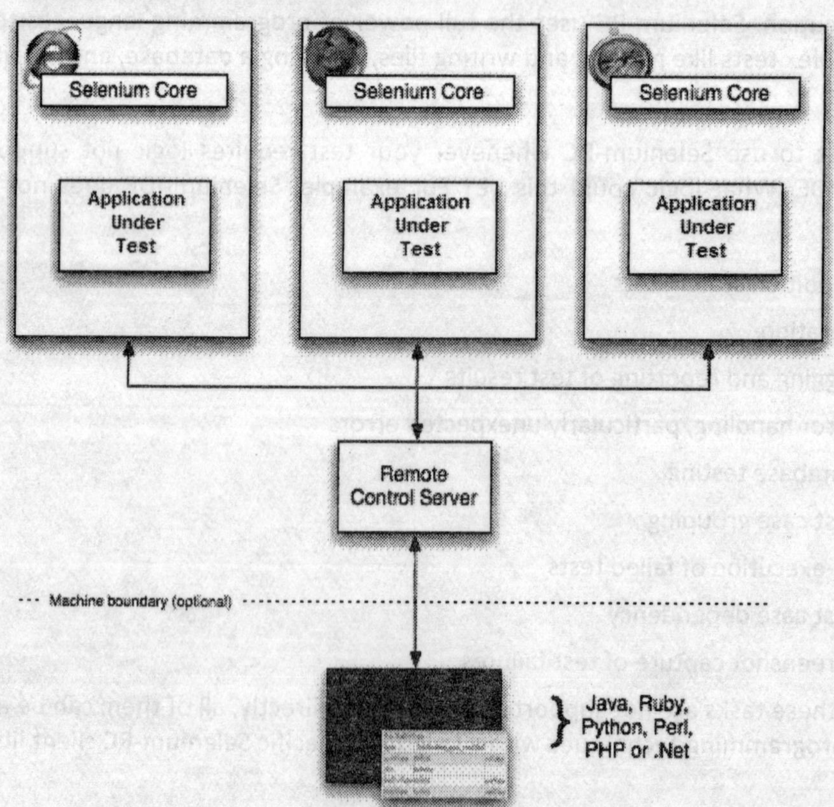

The diagram shows the client libraries communicate with the Server passing each Selenium command for execution. Then the server passes the Selenium command to the browser using Selenium-Core JavaScript commands. The browser, using its JavaScript interpreter, executes the Selenium command. This runs the Selenese action or verification you specified in your test script.

Selenium Server

Selenium Server receives Selenium commands from your test program, interprets them, and reports back to your program the results of running those tests.

The RC server bundles Selenium Core and automatically injects it into the browser. This occurs when your test program opens the browser (using a client library API function). Selenium-Core is a JavaScript program, actually a set of JavaScript functions which interprets and executes Selenese commands using the browser's built-in JavaScript interpreter.

The Server receives the Selenese commands from your test program using simple HTTP GET/POST requests. This means you can use any programming language that can send HTTP requests to automate Selenium tests on the browser.

Client Libraries

The client libraries provide the programming support that allows you to run Selenium commands from a program of your own design. There is a different client library for each supported language. A Selenium client library provides a programming interface (API), i.e., a set of functions, which run Selenium commands from your own program. Within each interface, there is a programming function that supports each Selenese command.

The client library takes a Selenese command and passes it to the Selenium Server for processing a specific action or test against the application under test (AUT). The client library also receives the result of that command and passes it back to your program. Your program can receive the result and store it into a program variable and report it as a success or failure, or possibly take corrective action if it was an unexpected error.

So to create a test program, you simply write a program that runs a set of Selenium commands using a client library API. And, optionally, if you already have a Selenese test script created in the Selenium-IDE, you can *generate the Selenium-RC code*. The Selenium-IDE can translate (using its Export menu item) its Selenium commands into a client-driver's API function calls. See the Selenium-IDE chapter for specifics on exporting RC code from Selenium-IDE.

Installation

After downloading the Selenium-RC zip file from the downloads page, you'll notice it has several sub-folders. These folders have all the components you need for using Selenium-RC with the programming language of your choice.

Once you've chosen a language to work with, you simply need to:

- Install the Selenium-RC Server.
- Set up a programming project using a language specific client driver.

Installing Selenium Server

The Selenium-RC server is simply a Java *jar* file (*selenium-server.jar*), which doesn't require any special installation. Just downloading the zip file and extracting the server in the desired directory is sufficient.

Running Selenium Server

Before starting any tests you must start the server. Go to the directory where Selenium-RC's server is located and run the following from a command-line console.

java -jar selenium-server.jar

This can be simplified by creating a batch or shell executable file (.bat on Windows and .sh on Linux) containing the command above. Then make a shortcut to that executable on your desktop and simply double-click the icon to start the server.

For the server to run you'll need Java installed and the PATH environment variable correctly configured to run it from the console. You can check that you have Java correctly installed by running the following on a console:

java -version

If you get a version number (which needs to be 1.5 or later), you're ready to start using Selenium-RC.

Using the Java Client Driver

- Download Selenium-RC from the SeleniumHQ downloads page.
- Extract the file *selenium-java-client-driver.jar*.

- Open your desired Java IDE (Eclipse, NetBeans, IntelliJ, Netweaver, etc.)
- Create a new project.
- Add the selenium-java-client-driver.jar files to your project as references.
- Add to your project classpath the file *selenium-java-client-driver.jar*.
- From Selenium-IDE, export a script to a Java file and include it in your Java project, or write your Selenium test in Java using the selenium-java-client API. The API is presented later in this chapter. You can either use JUnit, or TestNg to run your test, or you can write your own simple main() program. These concepts are explained later in this section.
- Run Selenium server from the console.
- Execute your test from the Java IDE or from the command-line.

For details on Java test project configuration, see the Appendix sections *Configuring Selenium-RC With Eclipse* and *Configuring Selenium-RC With Intellij.*

Using the Python Client Driver

- Download Selenium-RC from the SeleniumHQ downloads page
- Extract the file *selenium.py*
- Either write your Selenium test in Python or export a script from Selenium-IDE to a python file.
- Add to your test's path the file *selenium.py*
- Run Selenium server from the console
- Execute your test from a console or your Python IDE

For details on Python client driver configuration, see the appendix *Python Client Driver Configuration.*

Using the .NET Client Driver

- Download Selenium-RC from the SeleniumHQ downloads page
- Extract the folder
- Download and install NUnit (Note: You can use NUnit as your test engine. If you're not familiar yet with NUnit, you can also write a simple main() function to run your tests; however NUnit is very useful as a test engine.)
- Open your desired .Net IDE (Visual Studio, SharpDevelop, MonoDevelop)

- Create a class library (.dll)
- Add references to the following DLLs: nmock.dll, nunit.core.dll, nunit. framework. dll, ThoughtWorks.Selenium.Core.dll, ThoughtWorks.Selenium. IntegrationTests. dll and ThoughtWorks.Selenium.UnitTests.dll
- Write your Selenium test in a .Net language (C#, VB.Net), or export a script from Selenium-IDE to a C# file and copy this code into the class file you just created.
- Write your own simple main() program or you can include NUnit in your project for running your test. These concepts are explained later in this chapter.
- Run Selenium server from console
- Run your test either from the IDE, from the NUnit GUI or from the command line

For specific details on .NET client driver configuration with Visual Studio, see the appendix *.NET client driver configuration.*

Using the Ruby Client Driver

- If you do not already have RubyGems, install it from RubyForge
- Run `gem install selenium-client`
- At the top of your test script, add `require "selenium/client"`
- Write your test script using any Ruby test harness (eg Test::Unit, Mini::Test or RSpec).
- Run Selenium-RC server from the console.
- Execute your test in the same way you would run any other Ruby script.

For details on Ruby client driver configuration, see the Selenium-Client documentation

From Selenese to a Program

The primary task for using Selenium-RC is to convert your Selenese into a programming language. In this section, we provide several different language-specific examples.

Sample Test Script

Let's start with an example Selenese test script. Imagine recording the following test with Selenium-IDE.

Open	/	
type	q	selenium rs
clickAndWait	btnG	
assertTextPresent	Results * for selenium rc	

Note: This example would work with the Google search page http://www.google.com

Selenese as Programming Code

Here is the test script exported (via Selenium-IDE) to each of the supported programming languages. If you have at least basic knowledge of an object- oriented programming language, you will understand how Selenium runs Selenese commands by reading one of these examples. To see an example in a specific language, select one of these buttons.

In the next section we'll explain how to build a test program using the generated code.

Programming Your Test

Now we'll illustrate how to program your own tests using examples in each of the supported programming languages. There are essentially two tasks:

- Generate your script into a programming language from Selenium-IDE, optionally modifying the result.
- Write a very simple main program that executes the generated code.

Optionally, you can adopt a test engine platform like JUnit or TestNG for Java, or NUnit for .NET if you are using one of those languages.

Here, we show language-specific examples. The language-specific APIs tend to differ from one to another, so you'll find a separate explanation for each.

- Java
- C#
- Python
- Ruby
- Perl, PHP

Java

For Java, people use either JUnit or TestNG as the test engine. Some development environments like Eclipse have direct support for these via plug-ins. This makes it even easier. Teaching JUnit or TestNG is beyond the scope of this document however materials may be found online and there are publications available. If you are already a "java-shop" chances are your developers will already have some experience with one of these test frameworks.

You will probably want to rename the test class from "NewTest" to something of your own choosing. Also, you will need to change the browser-open parameters in the statement:

```
selenium = new DefaultSelenium("localhost", 4444, "*iehta",
"http://www.google.com/");
```

The Selenium-IDE generated code will look like this. This example has comments added manually for additional clarity.

```
package com.example.tests;
// We specify the package of our tests

import com.thoughtworks.selenium.*;
// This is the driver's import. You'll use this for
instantiating a
// browser and making it do what you need.

import java.util.regex.Pattern;
// Selenium-IDE add the Pattern module because it's sometimes
used for
// regex validations. You can remove the module if it's not
used in your
// script.

public class NewTest extends SeleneseTestCase {
// We create our Selenium test case

      public void setUp() throws Exception {
        setUp("http://www.google.com/", "*firefox");
             // We instantiate and start the browser
      }

      public void testNew() throws Exception {
```

```
            selenium.open("/");
            selenium.type("q", "selenium rc");
            selenium.click("btnG");
            selenium.waitForPageToLoad("30000");
            assertTrue(selenium.isTextPresent("Results * for
selenium rc"));
            // These are the real test steps
    }
}
```

C#

The .NET Client Driver works with Microsoft.NET. It can be used with any .NET testing framework like NUnit or the Visual Studio 2005 Team System.

Selenium-IDE assumes you will use NUnit as your testing framework. You can see this in the generated code below. It includes the *using* statement for NUnit along with corresponding NUnit attributes identifying the role for each member function of the test class.

You will probably have to rename the test class from "NewTest" to something of your own choosing. Also, you will need to change the browser-open parameters in the statement:

```
selenium = new DefaultSelenium("localhost", 4444, "*iehta",
"http://www.google.com/");
```

The generated code will look similar to this.

```
using System;
using System.Text;
using System.Text.RegularExpressions;
using System.Threading;
using NUnit.Framework;
using Selenium;

namespace SeleniumTests

{
    [TestFixture]
```

```
public class NewTest

{
private ISelenium selenium;

private StringBuilder verificationErrors;

[SetUp]

public void SetupTest()

{
    selenium = new DefaultSelenium("localhost", 4444,
"*iehta",
   "http://www.google.com/");

   selenium.Start();

   verificationErrors = new StringBuilder();
}

[TearDown]

public void TeardownTest()
{
   try
   {
   selenium.Stop();
   }

   catch (Exception)
   {
   // Ignore errors if unable to close the browser
   }
   Assert.AreEqual("", verificationErrors.ToString());
```

```
    }
    [Test]

    public void TheNewTest()
    {
        // Open Google search engine.
        selenium.Open("http://www.google.com/");

        // Assert Title of page.
        Assert.AreEqual("Google", selenium.GetTitle());

        // Provide search term as "Selenium OpenQA"
        selenium.Type("q", "Selenium OpenQA");

        // Read the keyed search term and assert it.
                Assert.AreEqual("Selenium OpenQA", selenium.
GetValue("q"));

        // Click on Search button.
        selenium.Click("btnG");

        // Wait for page to load.
        selenium.WaitForPageToLoad("5000");

      // Assert that "www.openqa.org" is available in search
results.
           Assert.IsTrue(selenium.IsTextPresent("www.openqa.
org"));

          // Assert that page title is - "Selenium OpenQA -
Google Search"
        Assert.AreEqual("Selenium OpenQA - Google Search",
                     selenium.GetTitle());
    }
    }
}
```

You can allow NUnit to manage the execution of your tests. Or alternatively, you can write a simple main() program that instantiates the test object and runs each of the three methods, SetupTest(), TheNewTest(), and TeardownTest() in turn.

Python

Pyunit is the test framework to use for Python. To learn Pyunit refer to its *official documentation* <http://docs.python.org/library.org/library/unittest.html>_.

The basic test structure is:

```
from selenium import selenium
# This is the driver's import.  You'll use this class for
instantiating a
# browser and making it do what you need.

import unittest, time, re
# This are the basic imports added by Selenium-IDE by
default.
# You can remove the modules if they are not used in your
script.

class NewTest(unittest.TestCase):
# We create our unittest test case

    def setUp(self):
        self.verificationErrors = []
          # This is an empty array where we will store any
verification errors
        # we find in our tests

                self.selenium = selenium("localhost", 4444,
"*firefox",
                "http://www.google.com/")
        self.selenium.start()
        # We instantiate and start the browser
```

```
    def test_new(self):
        # This is the test code.  Here you should put the
actions you need
        # the browser to do during your test.

        sel = self.selenium
        # We assign the browser to the variable "sel" (just
to save us from
        # typing "self.selenium" each time we want to call
the browser).

        sel.open("/")
        sel.type("q", "selenium rc")
        sel.click("btnG")
        sel.wait_for_page_to_load("30000")
        self.failUnless(sel.is_text_present("Results  *  for
selenium rc"))
        # These are the real test steps

    def tearDown(self):
        self.selenium.stop()
        # we close the browser (I'd recommend you to comment
this line while
        # you are creating and debugging your tests)

        self.assertEqual([], self.verificationErrors)
        # And make the test fail if we found that any verif-
ication errors
        # were found
```

Ruby

Selenium-IDE generates reasonable Ruby, but requires the old Selenium gem. This is a problem because the official Ruby driver for Selenium is the Selenium-Client gem, not the old Selenium gem. In fact, the Selenium gem is no longer even under active development.

Therefore, it is advisable to update any Ruby scripts generated by the IDE as follows:

1. On line 1, change `require "selenium"` to `require "selenium/client"`
2. On line 11, change `Selenium::SeleniumDriver.new` to `Selenium::Client::Driver.new`

You probably also want to change the class name to something more informative than "Untitled," and change the test method's name to something other than "test_untitled."

Here is a simple example created by modifying the Ruby code generated by Selenium IDE, as described above.

```
# load the Selenium-Client gem
require "selenium/client"

# Load Test::Unit, Ruby 1.8's default test framework.
# If you prefer RSpec, see the examples in the Selenium-
Client
# documentation.
require "test/unit"

class Untitled < Test::Unit::TestCase

  # The setup method is called before each test.
  def setup

    # This array is used to capture errors and display them
at the
    # end of the test run.
    @verification_errors = []

    # Create a new instance of the Selenium-Client driver.
    @selenium = Selenium::Client::Driver.new \
      :host => "localhost",
      :port => 4444,
      :browser => "*chrome",
```

```
      :url => "http://www.google.com/",
      :timeout_in_second => 60

    # Start the browser session
    @selenium.start

     # Print a message in the browser-side log and status
bar
    # (optional).
    @selenium.set_context("test_untitled")

  end

  # The teardown method is called after each test.
  def teardown

    # Stop the browser session.
    @selenium.stop

    # Print the array of error messages, if any.
    assert_equal [], @verification_errors
  end

  # This is the main body of your test.
  def test_untitled

    # Open the root of the site we specified when we created
the
    # new driver instance, above.
    @selenium.open "/"

    # Type 'selenium rc' into the field named 'q'
    @selenium.type "q", "selenium rc"

    # Click the button named "btnG"
    @selenium.click "btnG"
```

```
    # Wait for the search results page to load.
    # Note that we don't need to set a timeout here, because
that
    # was specified when we created the new driver instance,
above.
    @selenium.wait_for_page_to_load

    begin

      # Test whether the search results contain the expected
text.
       # Notice that the star (*) is a wildcard that matches
any
        # number of characters.
           assert @selenium.is_text_present("Results * for
selenium rc")

    rescue Test::Unit::AssertionFailedError

        # If the assertion fails, push it onto the array of
errors.
        @verification_errors << $!

    end
  end
end
```

Perl, PHP

The members of the documentation team have not used Selenium-RC with Perl or PHP. If you are using Selenium-RC with either of these two languages please contact the Documentation Team (see the chapter on contributing). We would love to include some examples from you and your experiences, to support Perl and PHP users.

Learning the API

The Selenium-RC API uses naming conventions that, assuming you understand Selenese, much of the interface will be self-explanatory. Here, however, we explain the most critical and possibly less obvious aspects.

Starting the Browser

Each of these examples opens the browser and represents that browser by assigning a "browser instance" to a program variable. This program variable is then used to call methods from the browser. These methods execute the Selenium commands, i.e. like *open* or *type* or the *verify* commands.

The parameters required when creating the browser instance are:

host

Specifies the IP address of the computer where the server is located. Usually, this is the same machine as where the client is running, so in this case *localhost* is passed. In some clients this is an optional parameter.

port

Specifies the TCP/IP socket where the server is listening waiting for the client to establish a connection. This also is optional in some client drivers.

browser

The browser in which you want to run the tests. This is a required parameter.

url

The base url of the application under test. This is required by all the client libs and is integral information for starting up the browser-proxy-AUT communication.

Note that some of the client libraries require the browser to be started explicitly by calling its *start()* method.

Running Commands

Once you have the browser initialized and assigned to a variable (generally named "selenium") you can make it run Selenese commands by calling the respective methods from the browser variable. For example, to call the *type* method of the selenium object:

```
selenium.type("field-id","string to type")
```

In the background the browser will actually perform a *type* operation, essentially identical to a user typing input into the browser, by using the locator and the string you specified during the method call.

Reporting Results

Selenium-RC does not have its own mechanism for reporting results. Rather, it allows you to build your reporting customized to your needs using features of your chosen programming language. That's great, but what if you simply want something quick that's already done for you? Often an existing library or test framework can meet your needs faster than developing your own test reporting code.

Test Framework Reporting Tools

Test frameworks are available for many programming languages. These, along with their primary function of providing a flexible test engine for executing your tests, include library code for reporting results. For example, Java has two commonly used test frameworks, JUnit and TestNG. .NET also has its own, NUnit.

We won't teach the frameworks themselves here; that's beyond the scope of this user guide. We will simply introduce the framework features that relate to Selenium along with some techniques you can apply. There are good books available on these test frameworks however along with information on the internet.

Test Report Libraries

Also available are third-party libraries specifically created for reporting test results in your chosen programming language. These often support a variety of formats such as HTML or PDF.

What's The Best Approach?

Most people new to the testing frameworks will being with the framework's built-in reporting features. From there most will examine any available libraries as that's less time consuming than developing your own. As you begin to use Selenium no doubt you will start putting in your own "print statements" for reporting progress. That may gradually lead to you developing your own reporting, possibly in parallel to using a library or test framework. Regardless, after the initial, but short, learning curve you will naturally develop what works best for your own situation.

Test Reporting Examples

To illustrate, we'll direct you to some specific tools in some of the other languages supported by Selenium. The ones listed here are commonly used and have been used extensively (and therefore recommended) by the authors of this guide.

Test Reports in Java

- If Selenium Test cases are developed using JUnit then JUnit Report can be used to generate test reports. Refer to JUnit Report for specifics.
- If Selenium Test cases are developed using TestNG then no external task is required to generate test reports. The TestNG framework generates an HTML report which list details of tests. See TestNG Report for more.
- ReportNG is a HTML reporting plug-in for the TestNG framework. It is intended as a replacement for the default TestNG HTML report. ReportNG provides a simple, colour-coded view of the test results. See ReportNG for more.
- Also, for a very nice summary report try using TestNG-xslt. A TestNG-xslt Report looks like this

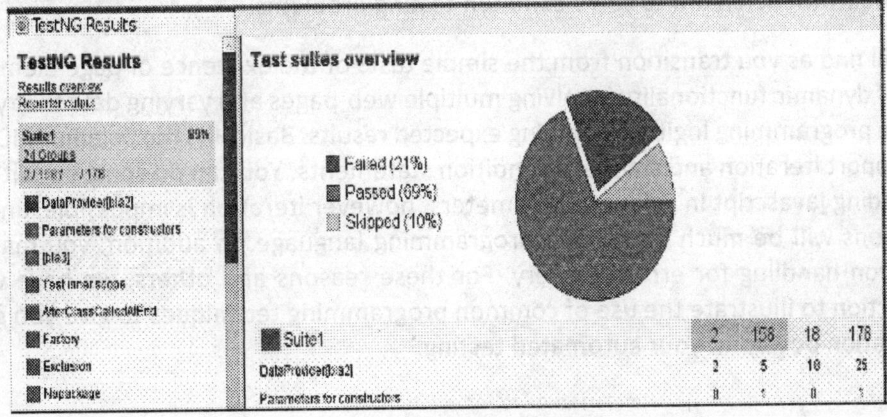

- See TestNG-xsit for more.

Logging the Selenese Commands

- Logging Selenium can be used to generate a report of all the Selenese commands in your test along with the success or failure of each. Logging Selenium extends the Java client driver to add this Selenese logging ability. Please refer to Logging Selenium.

Test Reports for Python

- When using Python Client Driver then HTMLTestRunner can be used to generate a Test Report. See HTML TestRunner.

Test Reports for Ruby

- If RSpec framework is used for writing Selenium Test Cases in Ruby then its HTML report can be used to generate a test report. Refer to RSpec Report for more.

Note

If you are interested in a language independent log of what's going on, take a look at Selenium Derver Logging

Adding Some Spice to Your Tests

Now we'll get to the whole reason for using Selenium-RC, adding programming logic to your tests. It's the same as for any program. Program flow is controlled using condition statements and iteration. In addition you can report progress information using I/O. In this section we'll show some examples of how programming language constructs can be combined with Selenium to solve common testing problems.

You will find as you transition from the simple tests of the existence of page elements to tests of dynamic functionality involving multiple web-pages and varying data that you will require programming logic for verifying expected results. Basically, the Selenium-IDE does not support iteration and standard condition statements. You can do some conditions by embedding javascript in Selenese parameters, however iteration is impossible, and most conditions will be much easier in a programming language. In addition, you may need exception handling for error recovery. For these reasons and others, we have written this section to illustrate the use of common programming techniques to give you greater 'verification power' in your automated testing.

The examples in this section are written in C# and Java, although the code is simple and can be easily adapted to the other supported languages. If you have some basic knowledge of an object-oriented programming language you shouldn't have difficulty understanding this section.

Iteration

Iteration is one of the most common things people need to do in their tests. For example, you may want to to execute a search multiple times. Or, perhaps for verifying your test results you need to process a "result set" returned from a database.

Using the same Google search example we used earlier, let's check the Selenium search results. This test could use the Selenese:

open	/	
type	q	selenium rc
clickAndWait	btnG	
assertTextPresent	Results * for selenium rc	
type	q	selenium ide
clickAndWait	btnG	
assertTextPresent	Results * for selenium ide	
type	q	selenium grid
clickAndWait	btnG	
assertTextPresent	Results * for selenium grid	

The code has been repeated to run the same steps 3 times. But multiple copies of the same code is not good program practice because it's more work to maintain. By using a programming language, we can iterate over the search results for a more flexible and maintainable solution.

In C#:

```
// Collection of String values.
String[] arr = {"ide", "rc", "grid"};

// Execute loop for each String in array 'arr'.
```

```
foreach (String s in arr) {
    sel.open("/");
    sel.type("q", "selenium " +s);
    sel.click("btnG");
    sel.waitForPageToLoad("30000");
    assertTrue("Expected text: " +s+ " is missing on page."
    , sel.isTextPresent("Results * for selenium " + s));
}
```

Condition Statements

To illustrate using conditions in tests we'll start with an example. A common problem encountered while running Selenium tests occurs when an expected element is not available on page. For example, when running the following line:

```
selenium.type("q", "selenium " +s);
```

If element 'q' is not on the page then an exception is thrown:

```
com.thoughtworks.selenium.SeleniumException: ERROR: Element
q not found
```

This can cause your test to abort. For some tests that's what you want. But often that is not desirable as your test script has many other subsequent tests to perform.

A better approach is to first validate if the element is really present and then take alternatives when it it is not. Let's look at this using Java.

```
// If element is available on page then perform type
operation.
if(selenium.isElementPresent("q")) {
    selenium.type("q", "Selenium rc");
} else {
    System.out.printf("Element: " +q+ " is not available on
page.")
}
```

The advantage of this approach is to continue with test execution even if some UI elements are not available on page.

Executing JavaScript from Your Test

JavaScript comes very handy in exercising an application which is not directly supported by selenium. The **getEval** method of selenium API can be used to execute java script from selenium RC.

Consider an application having check boxes with no static identifiers. In this case one could evaluate JavaScript from selenium RC to get ids of all check boxes and then exercise them.

```
public static String[] getAllCheckboxIds () {
            String script = "var inputId  = new Array();";//
Create array in java script.
             script += "var cnt = 0;"; // Counter for check
box ids.
            script += "var inputFields  = new Array();"; //
Create array in java script.
             script += "inputFields = window.document.getEl
ementsByTagName('input');"; // Collect input elements.
              script += "for(var i=0; i<inputFields.length;
i++) {"; // Loop through the collected elements.
             script += "if(inputFields[i].id !=null " +
             "&& inputFields[i].id !='undefined' " +
                 "&& inputFields[i].getAttribute('type') ==
'checkbox') {"; // If input field is of type check box and
input id is not null.
             script += "inputId[cnt]=inputFields[i].id ;" +
// Save check box id to inputId array.
             "cnt++;" + // increment the counter.
             "}" + // end of if.
             "}"; // end of for.
                script += "inputId.toString();" ;// Convert
array in to string.
            String[] checkboxIds = selenium.getEval(script).
split(","); // Split the string.
             return checkboxIds;
  }
```

To count number of images on a page:

```
selenium.getEval("window.document.images.length;");
```

Remember to use window object in case of DOM expressions as by default selenium window is referred to, not the test window.

Server Options

When the server is launched, command line options can be used to change the default server behaviour.

Recall, the server is started by running the following.

```
$ java -jar selenium-server.jar
```

To see the list of options, run the server with the `-h` option.

```
$ java -jar selenium-server.jar -h
```

You'll see a list of all the options you can use with the server and a brief description of each. The provided descriptions will not always be enough, so we've provided explanations for some of the more important options.

Proxy Configuration

If your AUT is behind an HTTP proxy which requires authentication then you should configure http.proxyHost, http.proxyPort, http.proxyUser and http.proxyPassword using the following command.

```
$ java -jar selenium-server.jar -Dhttp.proxyHost=proxy.
com -Dhttp.proxyPort=8080 -Dhttp.proxyUser=username -Dhttp.
proxyPassword=password
```

Multi-Window Mode

If you are using Selenium 1.0 you can probably skip this section, since multiwindow mode is the default behavior. However, prior to version 1.0, Selenium by default ran the application under test in a sub frame as shown here.

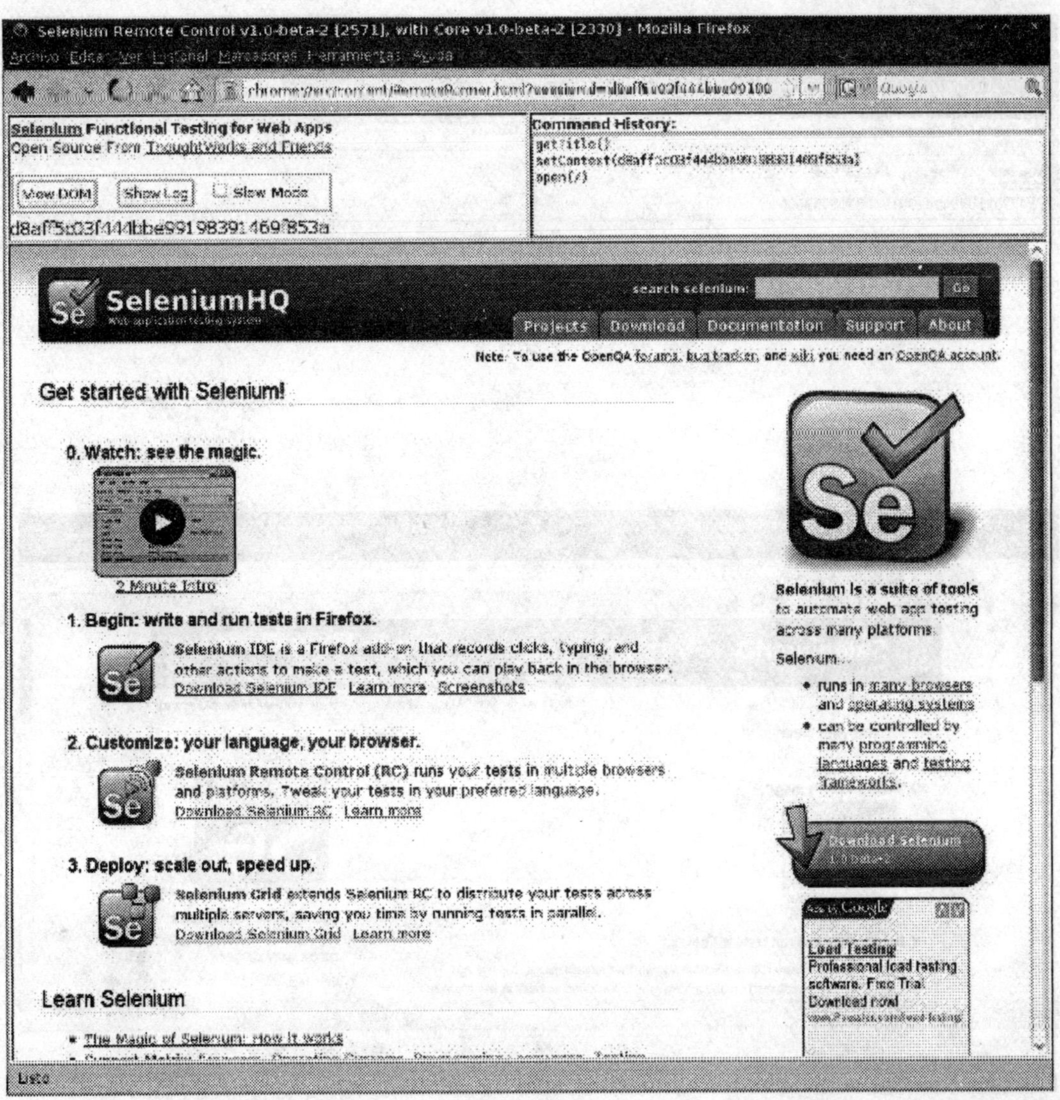

Some applications didn't run correctly in a sub frame, and needed to be loaded into the top frame of the window. The multi-window mode option allowed the AUT to run in a separate window rather than in the default frame where it could then have the top frame it required.

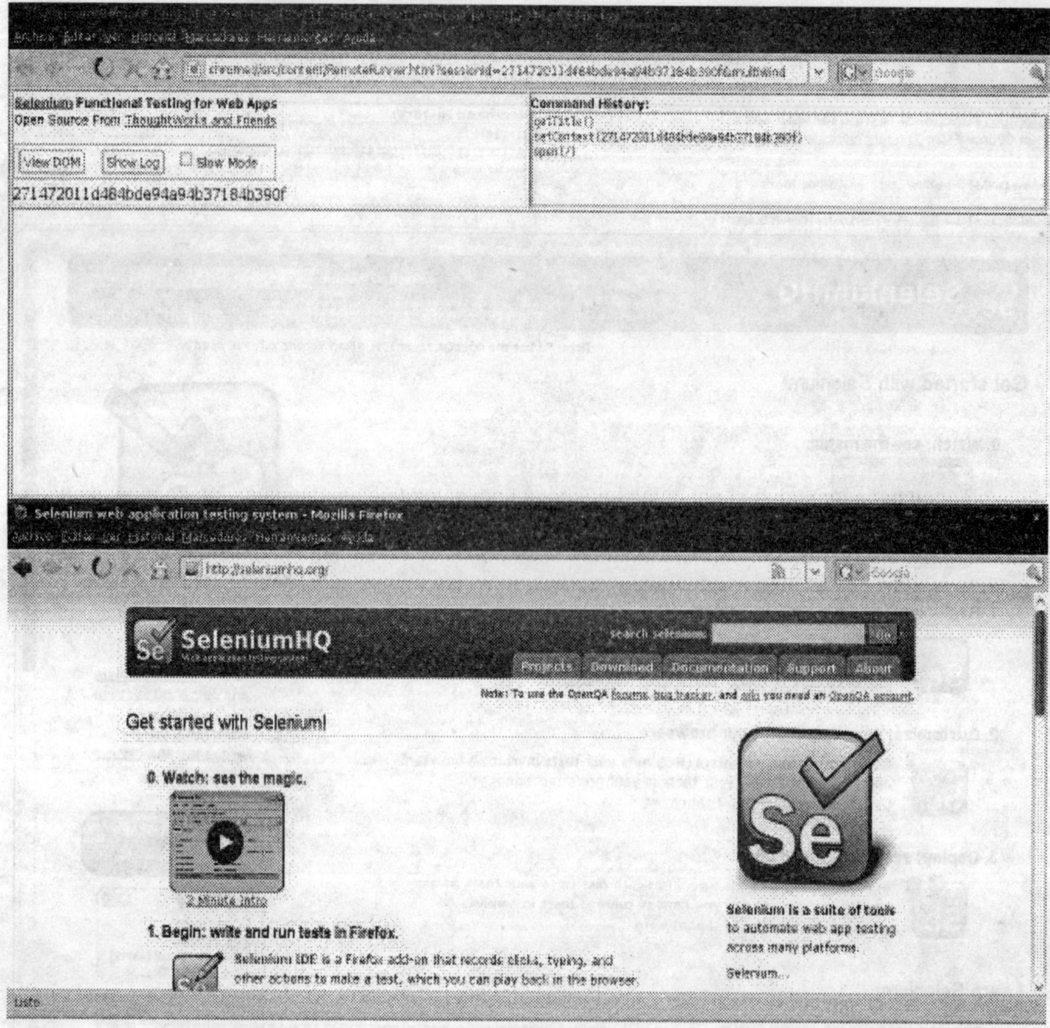

For older versions of Selenium you must specify multiwindow mode explicitly with the following option:

```
-multiwindow
```

In Selenium-RC 1.0, if you want to run your test within a single frame (i.e. using the standard for earlier Selenium versions) you can state this to the Selenium Server using the option

```
-singlewindow
```

Specifying the Firefox Profile

Firefox will not run two instances simultaneously unless you specify a separate profile for each instance. Selenium-RC 1.0 and later runs in a separate profile automatically, so if you are using Selenium 1.0, you can probably skip this section. However, if you're using an older version of Selenium or if you need to use a specific profile for your tests (such as adding an https certificate or having some addons installed), you will need to explicitly specify the profile.

First, to create a separate Firefox profile, follow this procedure. Open the Windows Start menu, select "Run", then type and enter one of the following:

```
firefox.exe -profilemanager
firefox.exe -P
```

Create the new profile using the dialog. Then when you run Selenium Server, tell it to use this new Firefox profile with the server command-line option *-firefoxProfileTemplate* and specify the path to the profile using it's filename and directory path.

```
-firefoxProfileTemplate "path to the profile"
```

Warning

Be sure to put your profile in a new folder separate from the default!!! The Firefox profile manager tool will delete all files in a folder if you delete a profile, regardless of whether they are profile files or not.

More information about Firefox profiles can be found in Mozilla's Knowledge Base

Run Selenese Directly Within the Server Using -htmlSuite

You can run Selenese html files directly within the Selenium Server by passing the html file to the server's command line. For instance:

```
java -jar selenium-server.jar -htmlSuite "*firefox"
"http://www.google.com"
"c:\absolute\path\to\my\HTMLSuite.html"
"c:\absolute\path\to\my\results.html"
```

This will automatically launch your HTML suite, run all the tests and save a nice HTML report with the results.

Note

When using this option, the server will start the tests and wait for a specified number of seconds for the test to complete; if the test doesn't complete within that amount of time, the command will exit with a non-zero exit code and no results file will be generated.

This command line is very long so be careful when you type it. Note this requires you to pass in an HTML Selenese suite, not a single test. Also be aware the -htmlSuite option is incompatible with `-interactive` You cannot run both at the same time.

Selenium Server Logging

Server-Side Logs

When launching selenium server the **-log** option can be used to record valuable debugging information reported by the Selenium Server to a text file.

```
java -jar selenium-server.jar -log selenium.log
```

This log file is more verbose than the standard console logs (it includes DEBUG level logging messages). The log file also includes the logger name, and the ID number of the thread that logged the message. For example:

```
20:44:25 DEBUG [12]
org.openqa.selenium.server.SeleniumDriverResourceHandler
 -
Browser 465828/:top frame1 posted START NEW
```

The message format is

```
TIMESTAMP(HH:mm:ss) LEVEL [THREAD] LOGGER - MESSAGE
```

This message may be multiline.

Browser-Side Logs

JavaScript on the browser side (Selenium Core) also logs important messages; in many cases, these can be more useful to the end-user than the regular Selenium Server logs. To access browser-side logs, pass the **-browserSideLog** argument to the Selenium Server.

```
java -jar selenium-server.jar -browserSideLog
```

-browserSideLog must be combined with the **-log** argument, to log browserSideLogs (as well as all other DEBUG level logging messages) to a file.

Specifying the Path to a Specific Browser

You can specify to Selenium-RC a path to a specific browser. This is useful if you have different versions of the same browser and you wish to use a specific one. Also, this is used to allow your tests to run against a browser not directly supported by Selenium-RC. When specifying the run mode, use the *custom specifier followed by the full path to the browser's executable:

```
*custom <path to browser>
```

Selenium-RC Architecture

This topic tries to explain the technical implementation behind Selenium-RC. It's not fundamental for a Selenium user to know this, but could be useful for understanding some of the problems you might find in the future.

The Same Origin Policy

The main restriction that Selenium faces is the Same Origin Policy. This security restriction is applied by every browser in the market and its objective is to ensure that a site's content will never be accessible by a script from another site. The Same Origin Policy dictates that any code loaded within the browser can only operate within that website's domain. It cannot perform functions on another website. So for example, if the browser loads JavaScript code when it loads www.mysite.com, it cannot run that loaded code against www.mysite2.com–even if that's another of your sites. If this were possible, a script placed on any website you open would be able to read information on your bank account if you had the account page opened on other tab. This is called XSS (Cross-site Scripting).

To work within this policy, Selenium-Core (and its JavaScript commands that make all the magic happen) must be placed in the same origin as the Application Under Test (same URL).

Historically, Selenium-Core was limited by this problem since it was implemented in JavaScript. Selenium-RC is not, however, restricted by the Same Origin Policy. Its use of the Selenium Server as a proxy avoids this problem. It, essentially, tells the browser that the browser is working on a single "spoofed" website that the Server provides.

Note

You can find additional information about this topic on Wikipedia pages about Same Origin Policy and XSS.

Proxy Injection

The first method Selenium used to avoid the The Same Origin Policy was Proxy Injection. In Proxy Injection Mode, the Selenium Server acts as a client-configured [1] **HTTP proxy** [2], that sits between the browser and the Application Under Test. It then masks the AUT under a fictional URL (embedding Selenium-Core and the set of tests and delivering them as if they were coming from the same origin).

[1] The proxy is a third person in the middle that passes the ball between the two parts. It acts as a "web server" that delivers the AUT to the browser. Being a proxy gives Selenium Server the capability of "lying" about the AUT's real URL.

[2] The browser is launched with a configuration profile that has set localhost:4444 as the HTTP proxy, this is why any HTTP request that the browser does will pass through Selenium server and the response will pass through it and not from the real server.

Here is an architectural diagram.

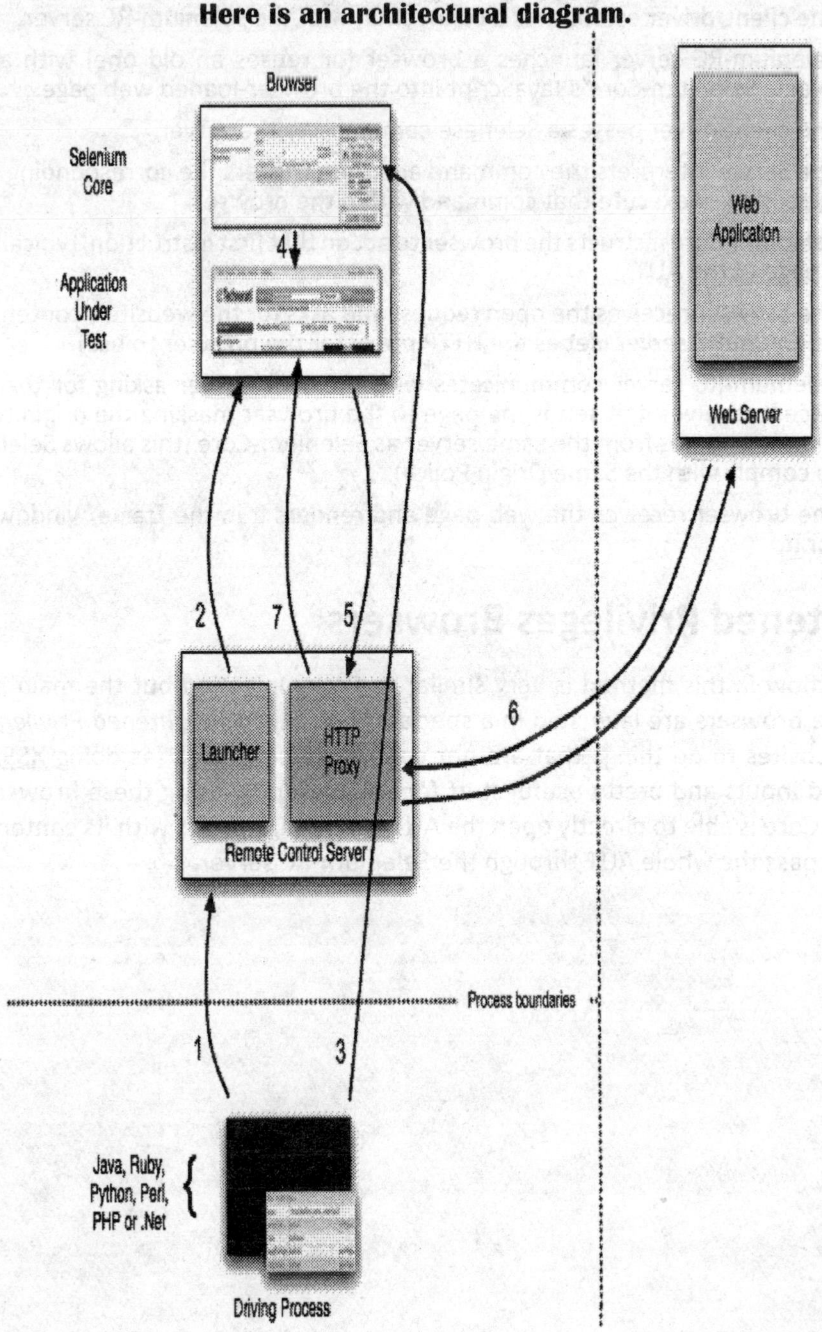

As a test suite starts in your favorite language, the following happens:

1. The client/driver establishes a connection with the selenium-RC server.
2. Selenium-RC server launches a browser (or reuses an old one) with a URL that injects Selenium-Core's JavaScript into the browser-loaded web page.
3. The client-driver passes a Selenese command to the server.
4. The Server interprets the command and then triggers the corresponding JavaScript execution to execute that command within the browser.
5. Selenium-Core instructs the browser to act on that first instruction, typically opening a page of the AUT.
6. The browser receives the open request and asks for the website's content from the Selenium-RC server (set as the HTTP proxy for the browser to use).
7. Selenium-RC server communicates with the Web server asking for the page and once it receives it, it sends the page to the browser masking the origin to look like the page comes from the same server as Selenium-Core (this allows Selenium-Core to comply with the Same Origin Policy).
8. The browser receives the web page and renders it in the frame/window reserved for it.

Heightened Privileges Browsers

This workflow in this method is very similar to Proxy Injection but the main difference is that the browsers are launched in a special mode called *Heightened Privileges*, which allows websites to do things that are not commonly permitted (as doing **XSS**, or filling file upload inputs and pretty useful stuff for Selenium). By using these browser modes, Selenium Core is able to directly open the AUT and read/interact with its content without having to pass the whole AUT through the Selenium-RC server.

Here is the architectural diagram.

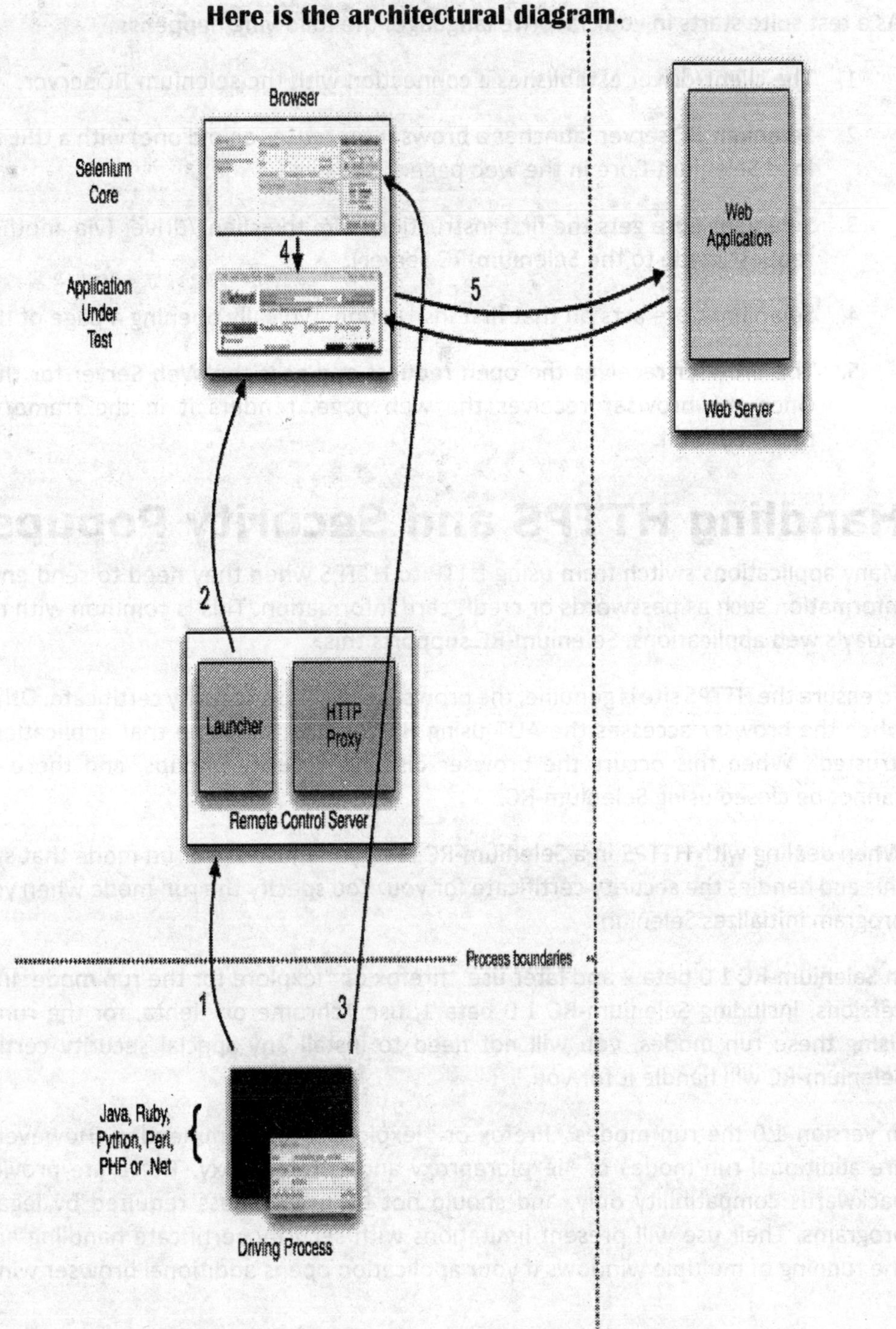

As a test suite starts in your favorite language, the following happens:

1. The client/driver establishes a connection with the selenium-RC server.

2. Selenium-RC server launches a browser (or reuses an old one) with a URL that will load Selenium-Core in the web page.

3. Selenium-Core gets the first instruction from the client/driver (via another HTTP request made to the Selenium-RC Server).

4. Selenium-Core acts on that first instruction, typically opening a page of the AUT.

5. The browser receives the open request and asks the Web Server for the page. Once the browser receives the web page, renders it in the frame/window reserved for it.

Handling HTTPS and Security Popups

Many applications switch from using HTTP to HTTPS when they need to send encrypted information such as passwords or credit card information. This is common with many of today's web applications. Selenium-RC supports this.

To ensure the HTTPS site is genuine, the browser will need a security certificate. Otherwise, when the browser accesses the AUT using HTTPS, it will assume that application is not 'trusted'. When this occurs the browser displays security popups, and these popups cannot be closed using Selenium-RC.

When dealing with HTTPS in a Selenium-RC test, you must use a run mode that supports this and handles the security certificate for you. You specify the run mode when your test program initializes Selenium.

In Selenium-RC 1.0 beta 2 and later use *firefox or *iexplore for the run mode. In earlier versions, including Selenium-RC 1.0 beta 1, use *chrome or *iehta, for the run mode. Using these run modes, you will not need to install any special security certificates; Selenium-RC will handle it for you.

In version 1.0 the run modes *firefox or *iexplore are recommended. However, there are additional run modes of *iexploreproxy and *firefoxproxy. These are provided for backwards compatibility only, and should not be used unless required by legacy test programs. Their use will present limitations with security certificate handling and with the running of multiple windows if your application opens additional browser windows.

In earlier versions of Selenium-RC, *chrome or *iehta were the run modes that supported HTTPS and the handling of security popups. These were considered experimental modes although they became quite stable and many people used them. If you are using Selenium 1.0 you do not need, and should not use, these older run modes.

Security Certificates Explained

Normally, your browser will trust the application you are testing by installing a security certificate which you already own. You can check this in your browser's options or Internet properties (if you don't know your AUT's security certificate ask your system administrator). When Selenium loads your browser it injects code to intercept messages between the browser and the server. The browser now thinks untrusted software is trying to look like your application. It responds by alerting you with popup messages.

To get around this, Selenium-RC, (again when using a run mode that support this) will install its own security certificate, temporarily, to your client machine in a place where the browser can access it. This tricks the browser into thinking it's accessing a site different from your AUT and effectively suppresses the popups.

Another method used with earlier versions of Selenium was to install the Cybervillians security certificate provided with your Selenium installation. Most users should no longer need to do this however; if you are running Selenium-RC in proxy injection mode, you may need to explicitly install this security certificate.

Supporting Additional Browsers and Browser Configurations

The Selenium API supports running against multiple browsers in addition to Internet Explorer and Mozilla Firefox. See the SeleniumHQ.org website for supported browsers. In addition, when a browser is not directly supported, you may still run your Selenium tests against a browser of your choosing by using the "*custom" run-mode (i.e. in place of *firefox or *iexplore) when your test application starts the browser. With this, you pass in the path to the browsers executable within the API call. This can also be done from the Server in interactive mode.

```
cmd=getNewBrowserSession&1=*custom c:\Program
Files\Mozilla
Firefox\MyBrowser.exe&2=http://www.google.com
```

Running Tests with Different Browser Configurations

Normally Selenium-RC automatically configures the browser, but if you launch the browser using the "*custom" run mode, you can force Selenium RC to launch the browser as-is, without using an automatic configuration.For example, you can launch Firefox with a custom configuration like this:

```
cmd=getNewBrowserSession&1=*custom c:\Program
Files\Mozilla
Firefox\firefox.exe&2=http://www.google.com
```

Note that when launching the browser this way, you must manually configure the browser to use the Selenium Server as a proxy. Normally this just means opening your browser preferences and specifying "localhost:4444" as an HTTP proxy, but instructions for this can differ radically from browser to browser. Consult your browser's documentation for details.

Be aware that Mozilla browsers can vary in how they start and stop. One may need to set the MOZ_NO_REMOTE environment variable to make Mozilla browsers behave a little more predictably. Unix users should avoid launching the browser using a shell script; it's generally better to use the binary executable (e.g. firefox-bin) directly.

Troubleshooting Common Problems

When getting started with Selenium-RC there's a few potential problems that are commonly encountered. We present them along with their solutions here.

Unable to Connect to Server

When your test program cannot connect to the Selenium Server, an exception will be thrown in your test program. It should display this message or a similar one:

```
"Unable to connect to remote server???.Inner Exception
Message:
    No connection could be made because the target machine
actively
    refused it???."


    (using .NET and XP Service Pack 2)
```

If you see a message like this, be sure you started the Selenium Server. If so, then there is a problem with the connectivity between the Selenium Client Library and the Selenium Server.

When starting with Selenium-RC, most people begin by running thier test program (with a Selenium Client Library) and the Selenium Server on the same machine. To do this use "localhost" as your connection parameter. We recommend beginning this way since it reduces the influence of potential networking problems which you're getting started. Assuming your operating system has typical networking and TCP/IP settings you should have little difficulty. In truth, many people choose to run the tests this way.

If, however, you do want to run Selenium Server on a remote machine, the connectivity should be fine assuming you have valid TCP/IP connectivity between the two machines.

If you have difficulty connecting, you can use common networking tools like *ping*, *telnet*, *ipconfig(Unix)/ifconfig* (Windows), etc to ensure you have a valid network connection. If unfamilar with these, your system administrator can assist you.

Unable to Load the Browser

Ok, not a friendly error message, sorry, but if the Selenium Server cannot load the browser you will likley see this error.

```
(500) Internal Server Error
```

This could be caused by

- Firefox (prior to Selenium 1.0) cannot start because the browser is already open and you did not specify a separate profile. See the section on Firefox profiles under Server Options.
- The run mode you're using doesn't match any browser on your machine. Check the parameters you passed to Selenium when you program opens the browser.
- You specified the path to the browser explicitly (using "*custom"–see above) but the path is incorrect. Check to be sure the path is correct. Also check the user group to be sure there are no known issues with your browser and the "*custom" parameters.

Selenium Cannot Find the AUT

If your test program starts the browser successfully, but the browser doesn't display the website you're testing, the most likely cause is your test program is not using the correct URL.

This can easily happen. When you use Selenium-IDE to export your script, it inserts a dummy URL. You must manually change the URL to the correct one for your application to be tested.

Firefox Refused Shutdown While Preparing a Profile

This most often occurs when your run your Selenium-RC test program against Firefox, but you already have a Firefox browser session running and, you didn't specify a separate profile when you started the Selenium Server. The error from the test program looks like this:

```
Error:  java.lang.RuntimeException: Firefox refused shutdown
while
preparing a profile
```

Here's the complete error message from the server:

```
16:20:03.919 INFO - Preparing Firefox profile...
16:20:27.822 WARN - GET /selenium-server/driver/?cmd=getNew
BrowserSession&1=*fir
efox&2=http%3a%2f%2fsage-webapp1.qa.idc.com HTTP/1.1
java.lang.RuntimeException: Firefox refused shutdown while
preparing a profile
        at
org.openqa.selenium.server.browserlaunchers.FirefoxCusto
mProfileLaunc
her.waitForFullProfileToBeCreated(FirefoxCustomProfileLaunc
her.java:277)
????????????????????????.
Caused by:
org.openqa.selenium.server.browserlaunchers.FirefoxCustom
ProfileLaunc
her$FileLockRemainedException: Lock file still present! C:\
DOCUME~1\jsvec\LOCALS
~1\Temp\customProfileDir203138\parent.lock
```

To resolve this, see the section on Specifying a Separate Firefox Profile

Versioning Problems

Make sure your version of Selenium supports the version of your browser. For example, Selenium-RC 0.92 does not support Firefox 3. At times you may be lucky (I was). But don't forget to check which browser versions are supported by the version of Selenium you are using. When in doubt, use the latest release version of Selenium with the most widely used version of your browser.

Error message: "(Unsupported major.minor version 49.0)" while starting server

This error says you're not using a correct version of Java. The Selenium Server requires Java 1.5 or higher.

To check double-check your java version, run this from the command line.

```
java -version
```

You should see a message showing the Java version.

```
java version "1.5.0_07"
Java(TM) 2 Runtime Environment, Standard Edition (build 1.5.0_07-b03)
Java HotSpot(TM) Client VM (build 1.5.0_07-b03, mixed mode)
```

If you see a lower version number, you may need to update the JRE, or you may simply need to add it to your PATH environment variable.

404 error when running the getNewBrowserSession command

If you're getting a 404 error while attempting to open a page on "http://www.google.com/selenium-server/", then it must be because the Selenium Server was not correctly configured as a proxy. The "selenium-server" directory doesn't exist on google.com; it only appears to exist when the proxy is properly configured. Proxy Configuration highly depends on how the browser is launched with *firefox, *iexplore, *opera, or *custom.

- *iexplore: If the browser is launched using *iexplore, you could be having a problem with Internet Explorer's proxy settings. Selenium Server attempts To configure the global proxy settings in the Internet Options Control Panel. You must make sure that those are correctly configured when Selenium Server launches the browser. Try looking at your Internet Options control panel. Click on the "Connections" tab and click on "LAN Settings".

- If you need to use a proxy to access the application you want to test, you'll need to start Selenium Server with "-Dhttp.proxyHost"; see the Proxy Configuration for more details.
    - You may also try configuring your proxy manually and then launching the browser with *custom, or with *iehta browser launcher.
        - ***custom: When using *custom you must configure the proxy correctly(manually),**

otherwise you'll get a 404 error. Double-check that you've configured your proxy settings correctly. To check whether you've configured the proxy correctly is to attempt to intentionally configure the browser incorrectly. Try configuring the browser to use the wrong proxy server hostname, or the wrong port. If you had successfully configured the browser's proxy settings incorrectly, then the browser will be unable to connect to the Internet, which is one way to make sure that one is adjusting the relevant settings.

- For other browsers (*firefox, *opera) we automatically hard-code the proxy for you, and so ther are no known issues with this functionality. If you're encountering 404 errors and have followed this user guide carefully post your results to user group for some help from the user community.

Permission Denied Error

The most common reason for this error is that your session is attempting to violate the same-origin policy by crossing domain boundaries (e.g., accesses a page from http://domain1 and then accesses a page from http://domain2) or switching protocols (moving from http://domainX to https://domainX).

This error can also occur when JavaScript attempts to find UI objects which are not yet available (before the page has completely loaded), or are no longer available (after the page has started to be unloaded). This is most typically encountered with AJAX pages which are working with sections of a page or subframes that load and/or reload independently of the larger page.

This error can be intermittent. Often it is impossible to reproduce the problem with a debugger because the trouble stems from race conditions which are not reproducible when the debugger's overhead is added to the system. Permission issues are covered in some detail in the tutorial. Read the section about the The same Origin Policy, Proxy Injection carefully.

References:

http://seleniumhg.org/docs/

http://seleniumhq.org/docs/appendix installing java driver client.html#configuring-selenium-rc-with-eclipse

Selenium RC tool

The Eclipse IDE

First Install Eclipse:

Visit **http://www.eclipse.org/** for more information

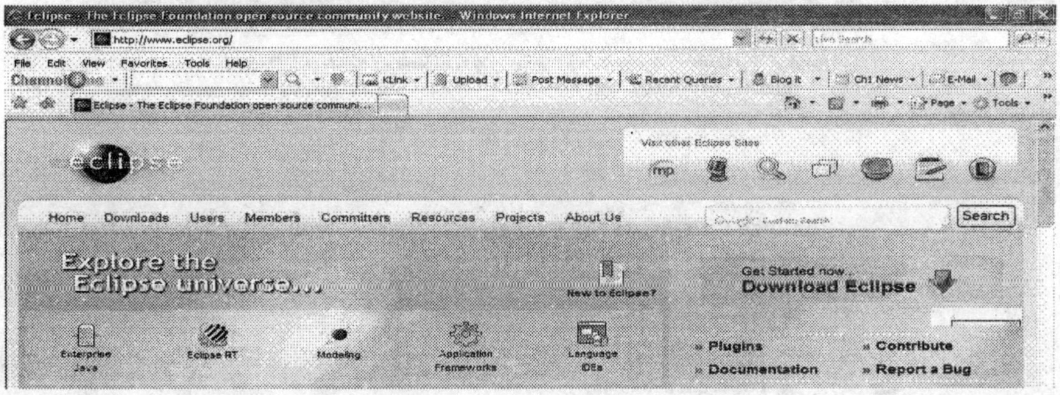

Go to below site and click on **download Ganymede** button. http://www.eclipse.org/ganymede/

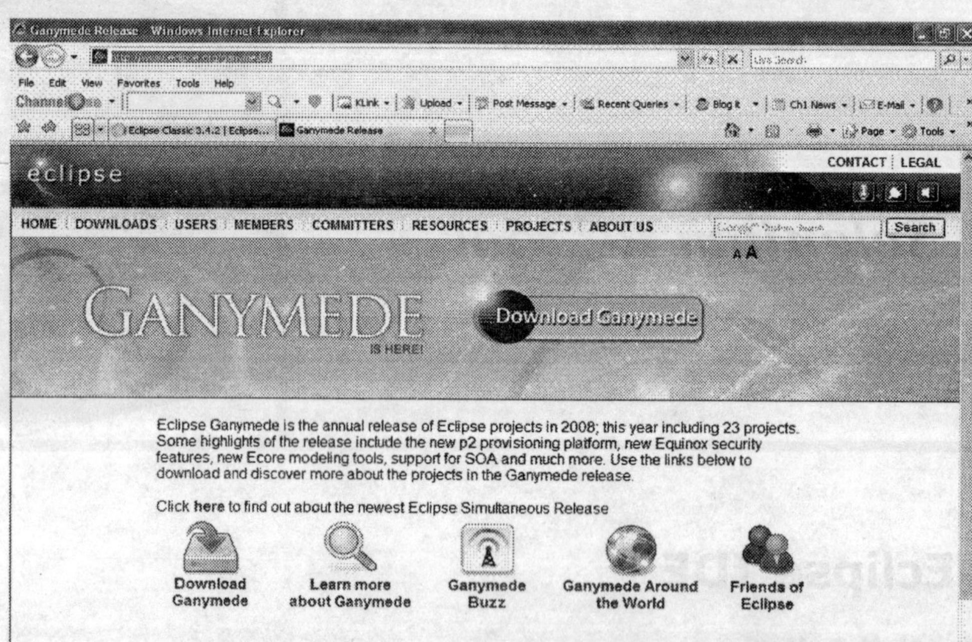

Click on Eclipse Classic 3.4.2 link

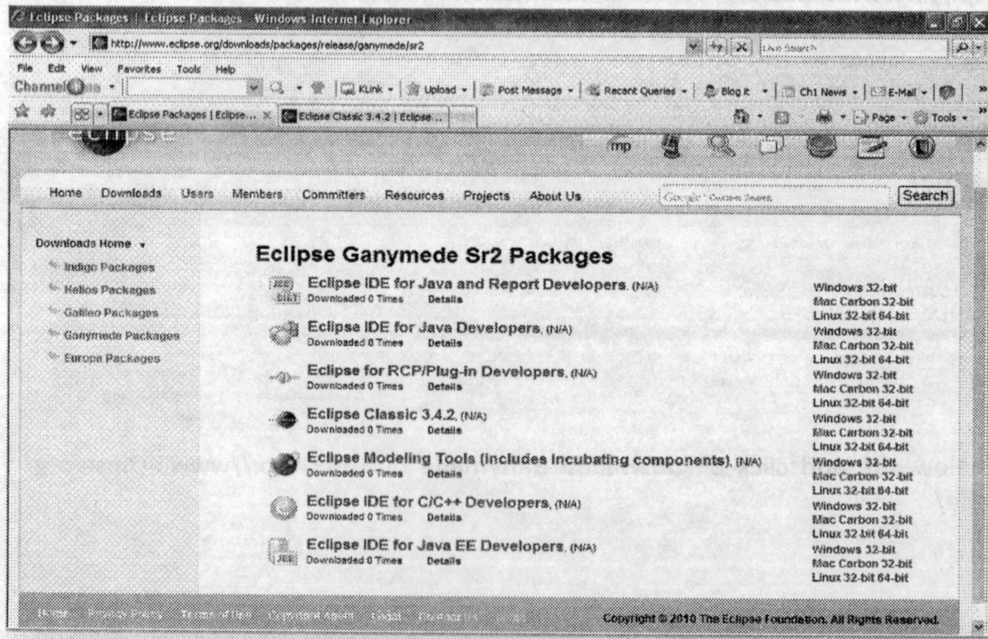

Click on **Windows 32-bit link to download the setup**

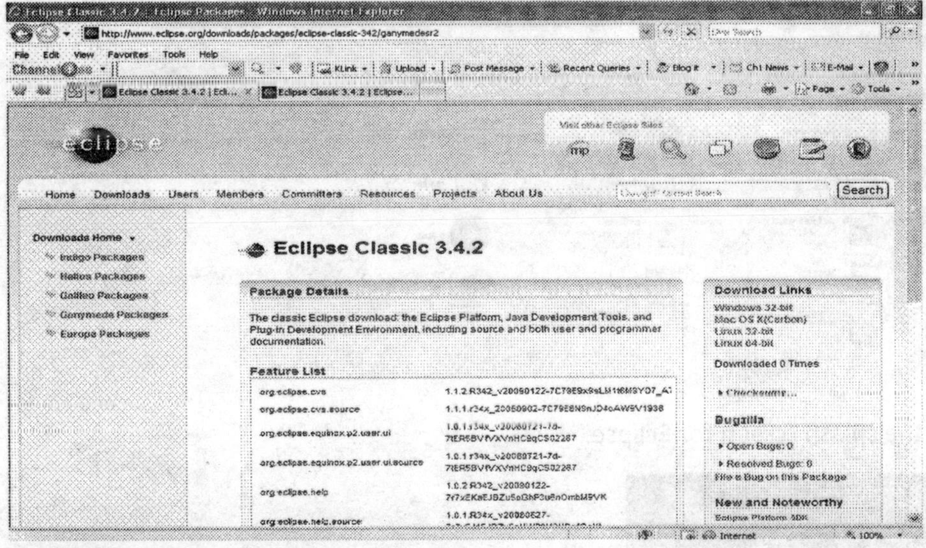

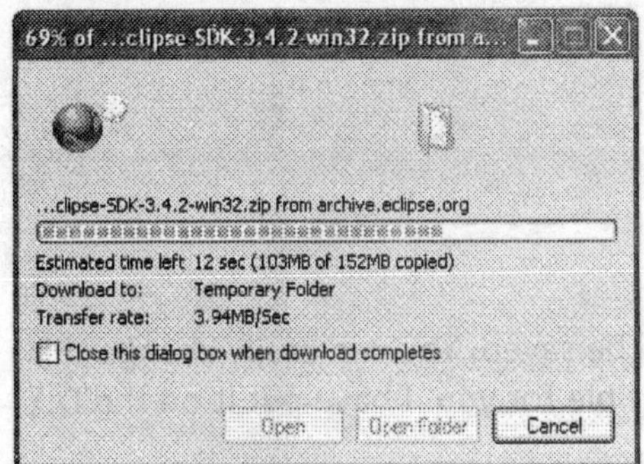

Save the folder on local drive

Second- Run Eclipse:

Run Eclipse by double clicking on “eclipse.exe” from the local drive where you have saved the eclipse setup.

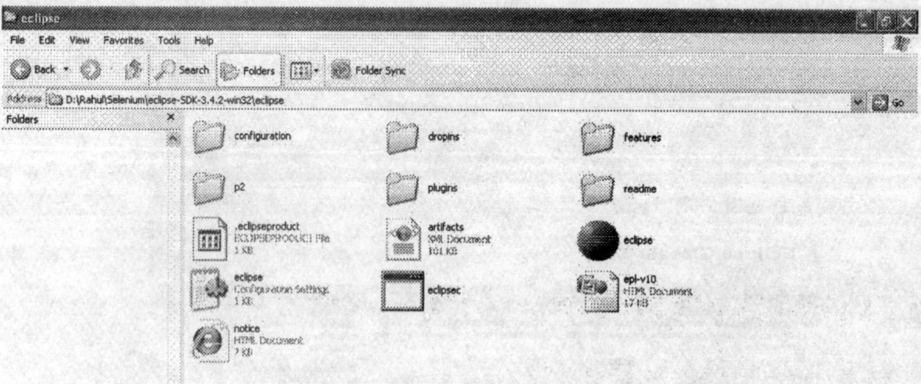

You will see the splash screen for Eclipse.

Choose a 'workspace' - where your project files will be saved. You can easily change this at a later date so choose a location that seems sensible for you. I have put it on the **D:\Rahul\Selenium\Selenium-JUnit-Example**

Click on **'OK'**

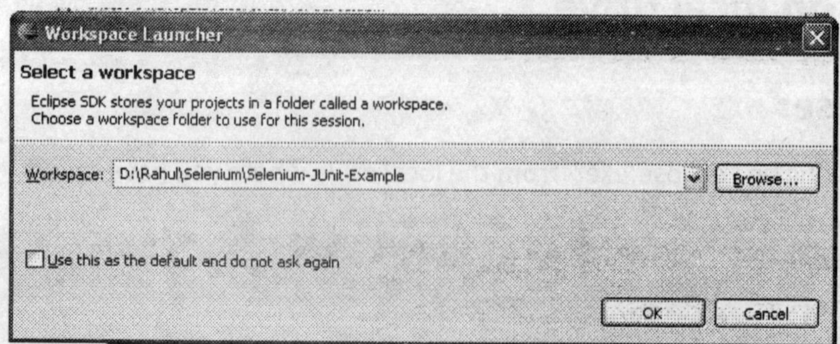

And then you will see the Eclipse "Welcome" screen, You want to click on the curved arrow to the right which displays the text "Workbench" "Goto the Workbench" when you hover the mouse over it.

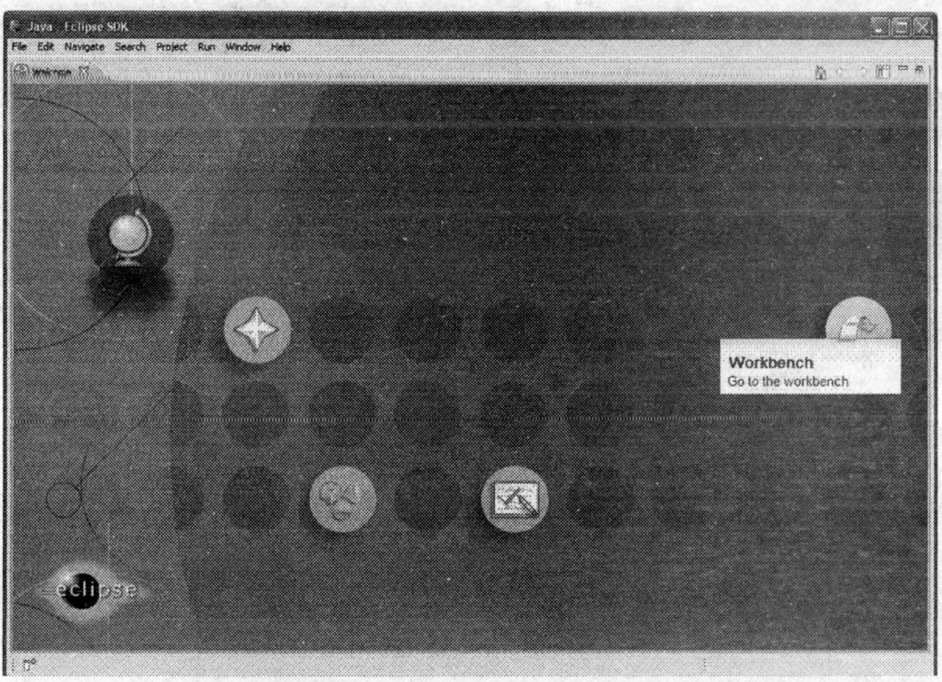

And then you will see the Eclipse workbench screen that will become very familiar

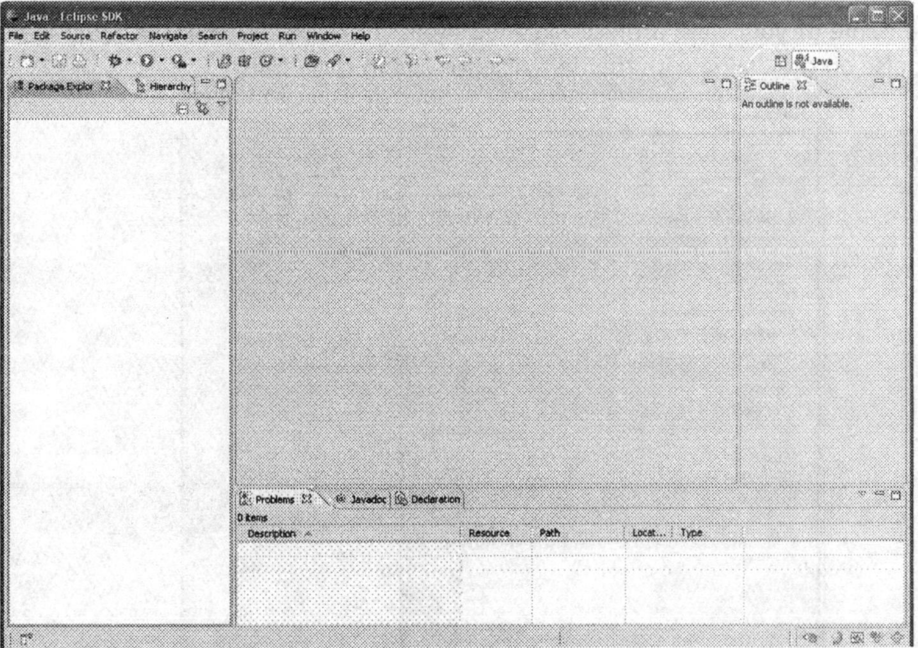

Third - create a new Java project

We are going to create tests in Java so to do that we need a Java project to store them in. Start by using the file menu in Eclipse to create a new Java project.

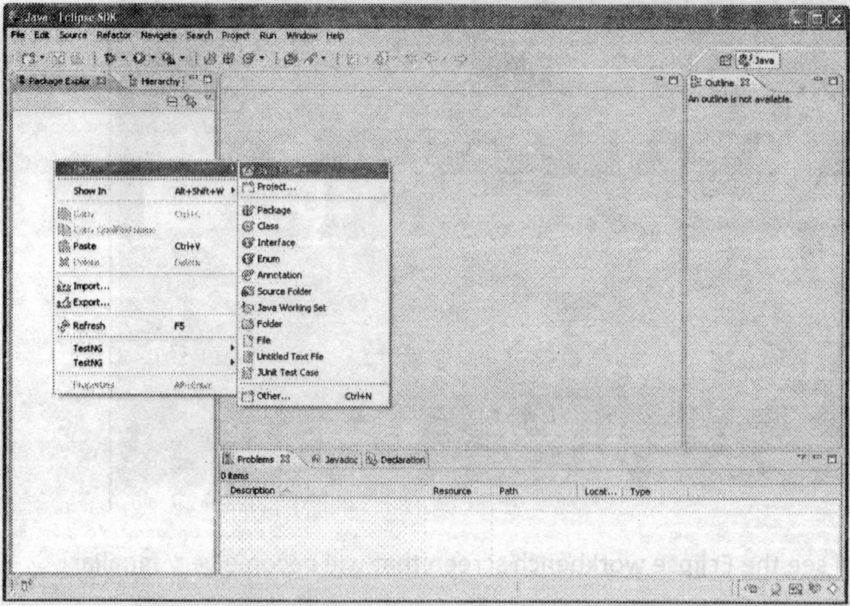

Type in the name of your new project - I called mine "**InitialSeleniumTests**", just leave everything else on the dialog with the default entries and click 'finish'.

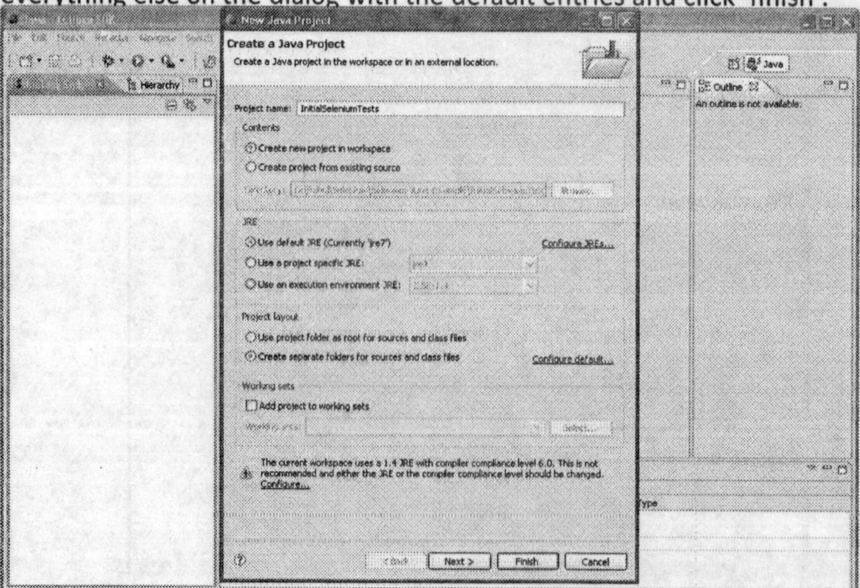

This will create a folder in your workspace directory called "InitialSeleniumTests" which has the basic folders that you need when working with Java in Eclipse.

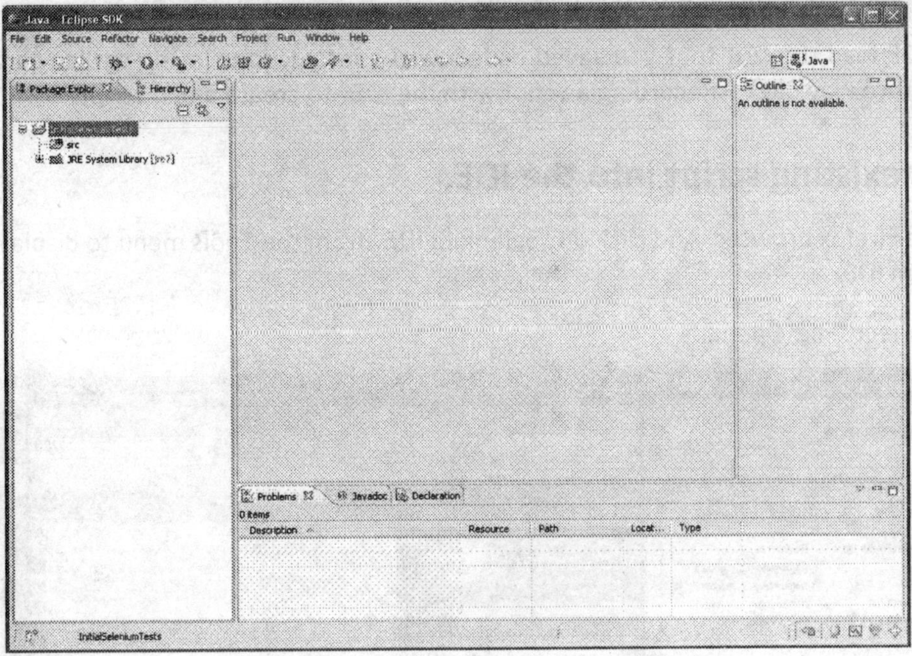

In Eclipse, in the Package Explorer tab on the left, you will see a tree with a root node named "InitialSeleniumTests", this is your project.

Now you are ready to start creating Selenium tests in Eclipse. We still have a few changes to make in the Eclipse configuration, but we will make those changes in the context of writing tests so that you will see and understand why we make them.

Create a JUnit test Using the JUnit export from Selenium-IDE

Introduction

- export an IDE script as a Java JUnit test
- get the exported test running in Eclipse

Export an IDE script as a JUnit test

We have already done this in the preceding part.

So in the IDE load the test that you saved or follow the instructions in the earlier part about "Capture Play Back – Recording a Script with the IDE" to create a test script.

Load an existing script into the IDE

Start up the Firefox browser. And click on "Selenium IDE" from the Tools menu to display the Selenium IDE.

In the IDE select "File\Open..."

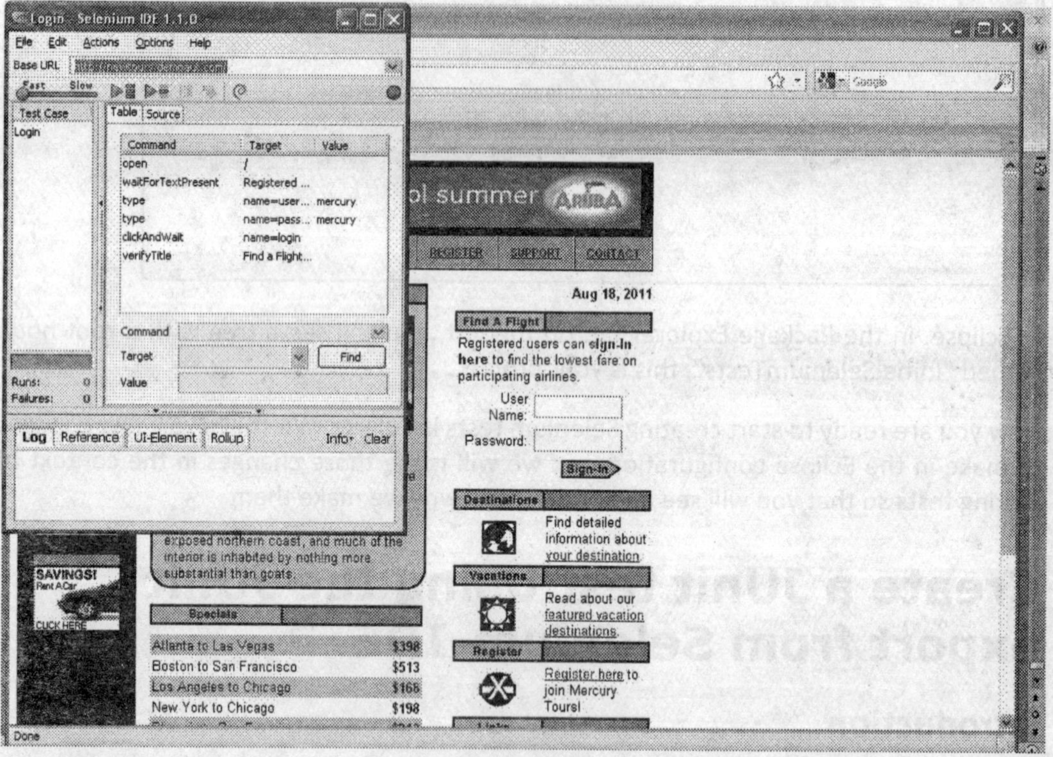

Then navigate to the test case and Open it in the IDE. You should see the test loaded into the IDE in the table view.

Change the format of the script to Java

We need to convert this test into a Java test and we do this by changing the format of the test from the options menu.

If you open the options menu from the IDE then you will see that the current format of the recorded test script is "HTML". This is the default recording and playback option for the IDE using an Action Word scripting language called "Selenese".

So select "Junit 4 (Remote Control)" from the "Format" menu.

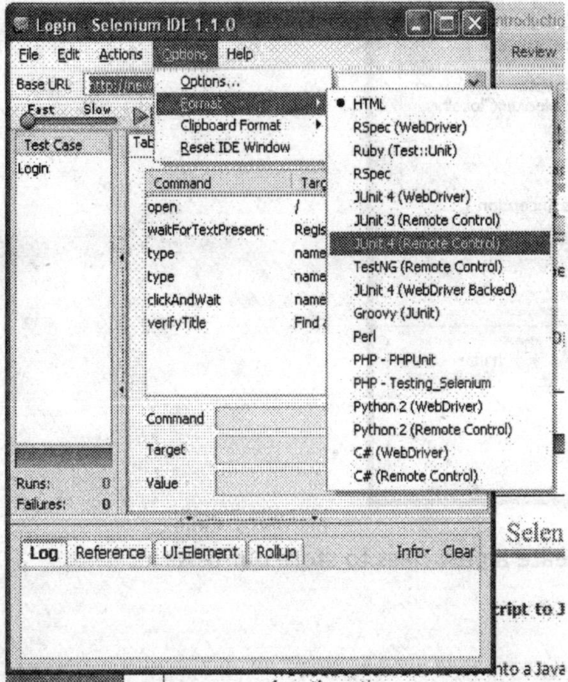

Click on 'OK'

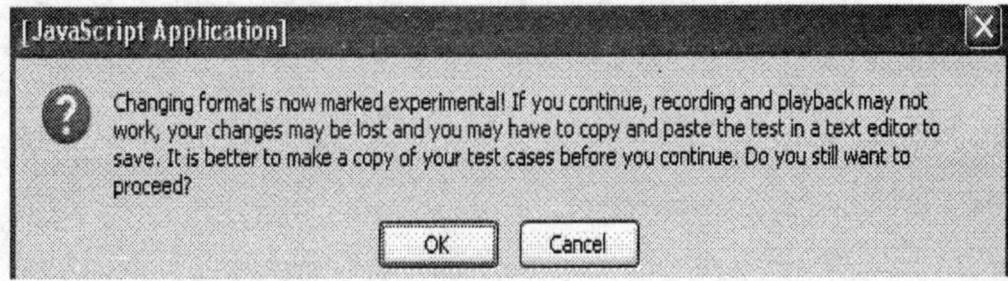

You should now see the "Source" tab selected and some Java source code displayed.

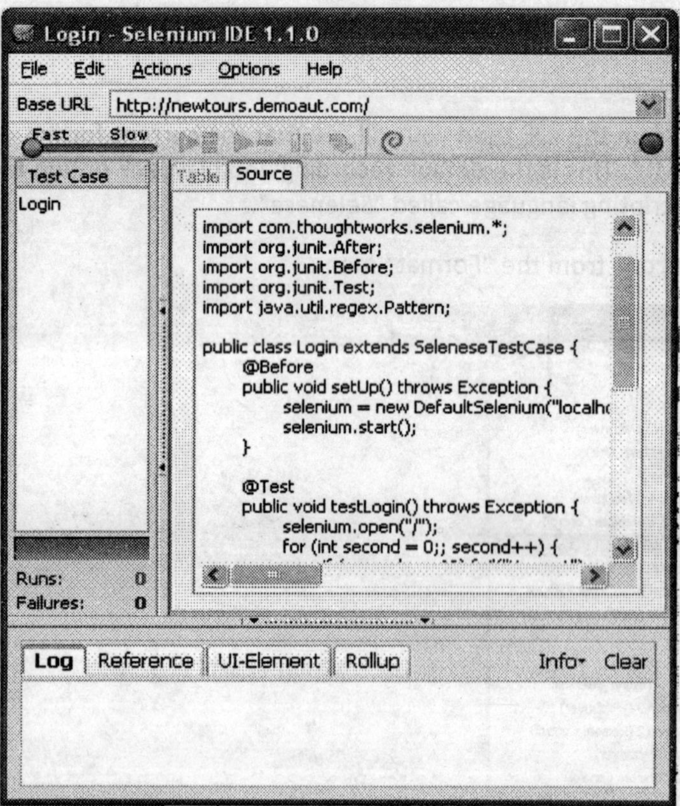

So the first thing we are going to do is create a new class to store our tests in.

Create a New Class in Eclipse

In Java all of our 'tests' are going to be 'methods' of a Java Class.

Java is an Object Oriented programming language so all of the code is built from classes. And the only way to have the program do something is to execute a method of one of the classes.

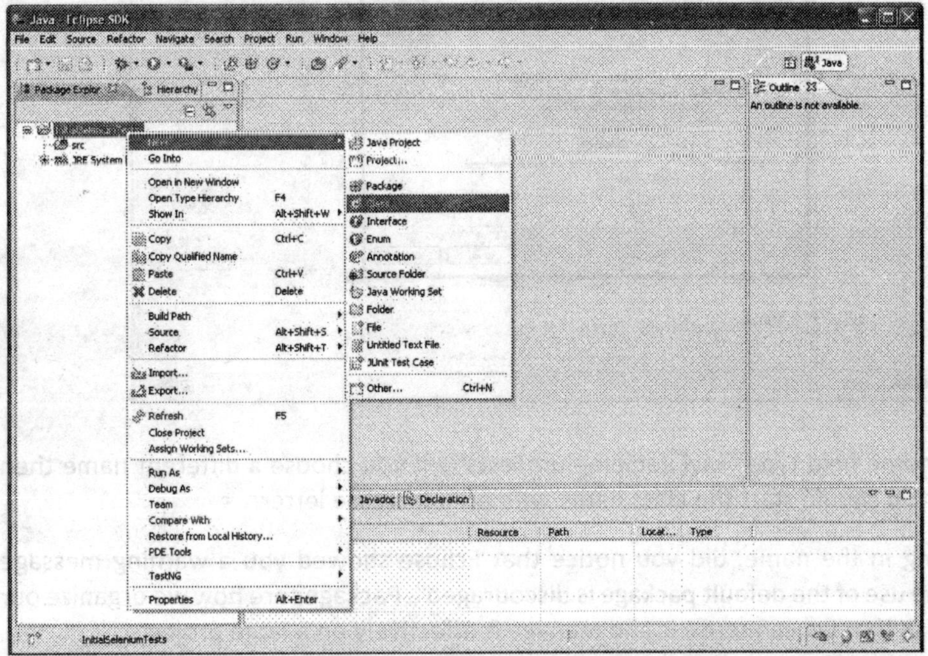

The Eclipse "New Java Class" wizard will appear and we can use this to create our basic class - Right now, we just want to create a simple class called "MyFirstSeleniumTests".

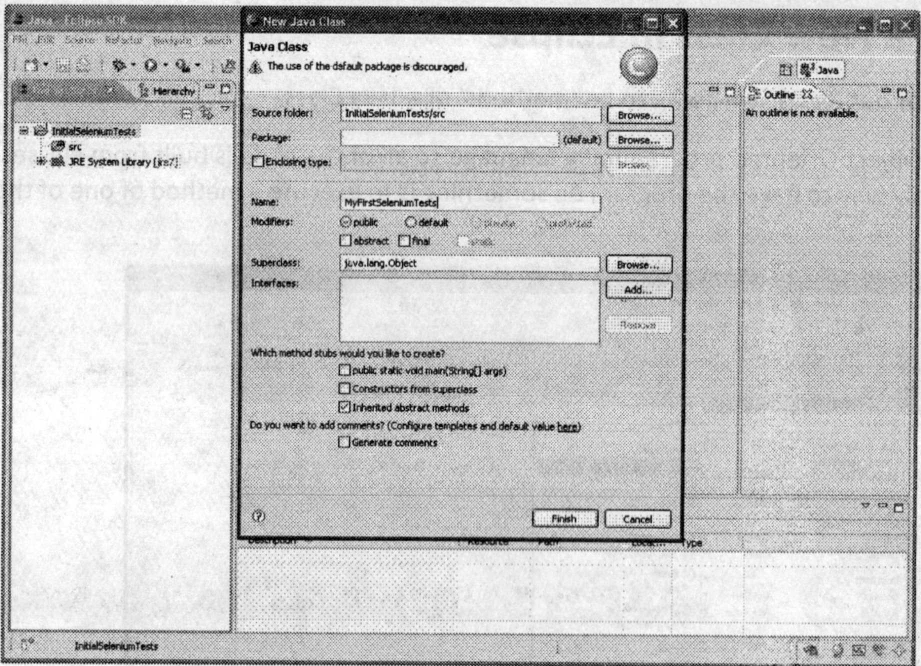

So in the name field type "MyFirstSeleniumTests" - if you choose a different name then note that you should start the class name with an uppercase letter.

After typing in the name, did you notice that Eclipse showed you a warning message saying "The use of the default package is discouraged". Packages are how we organize our Java code so that we can reuse it and manage it effectively on a large project.

Eclipse provides plenty of warnings to help you code. This warning means that we should really type in a package name - and we will.

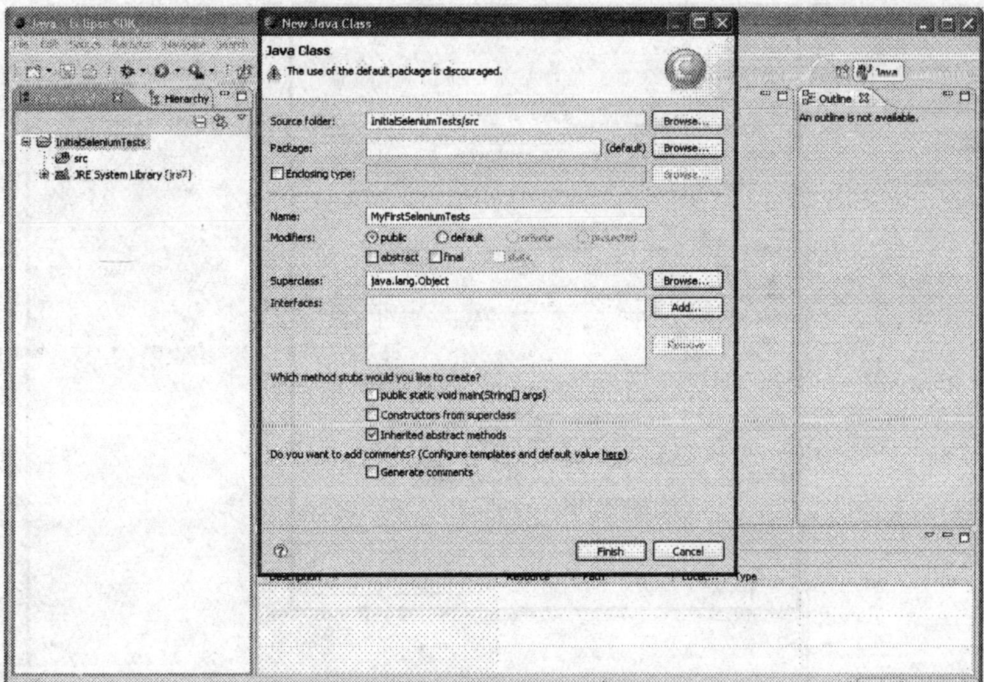

Sun provide some guidance on package names (see links below), I will use "**com. RahulFirstSeleniumJUnit.seleniumtutorials**" and type that into the "Package" field.

- http://java.sun.com/docs/codeconv/html/CodeConventions.doc8.html
- http://java.sun.com/docs/books/jls/third_edition/html/packages.html#7.7

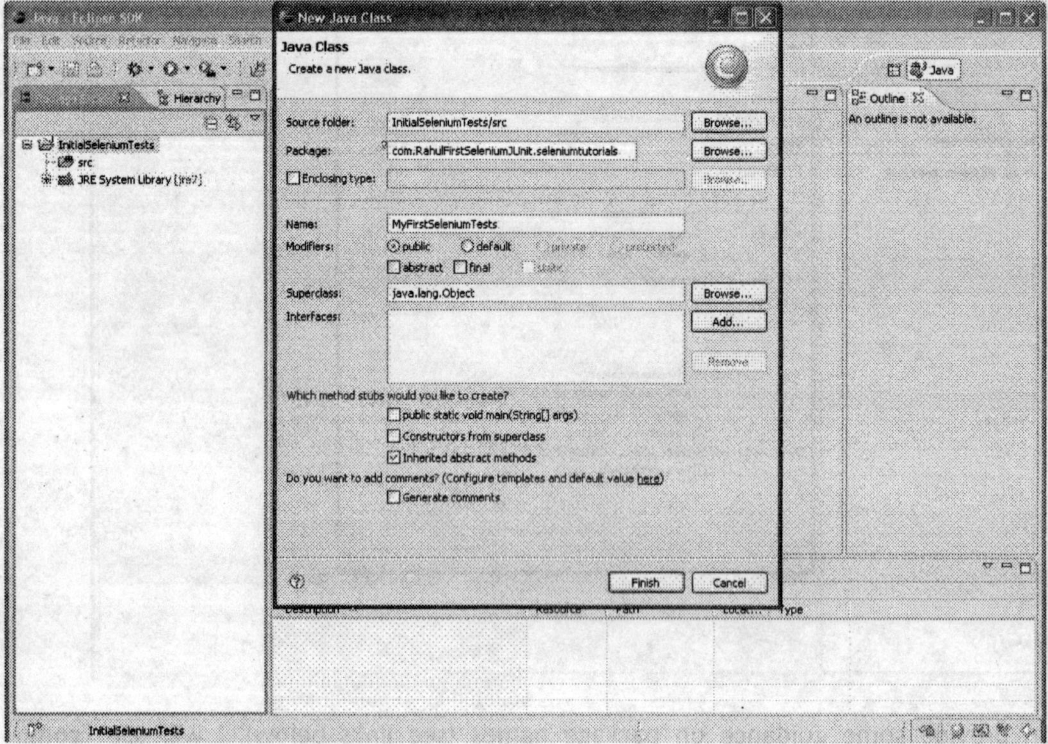

The rest of the dialog can be left with the default values provided by the wizard

And then press finish.

Eclipse will have created an empty class and a package for you.

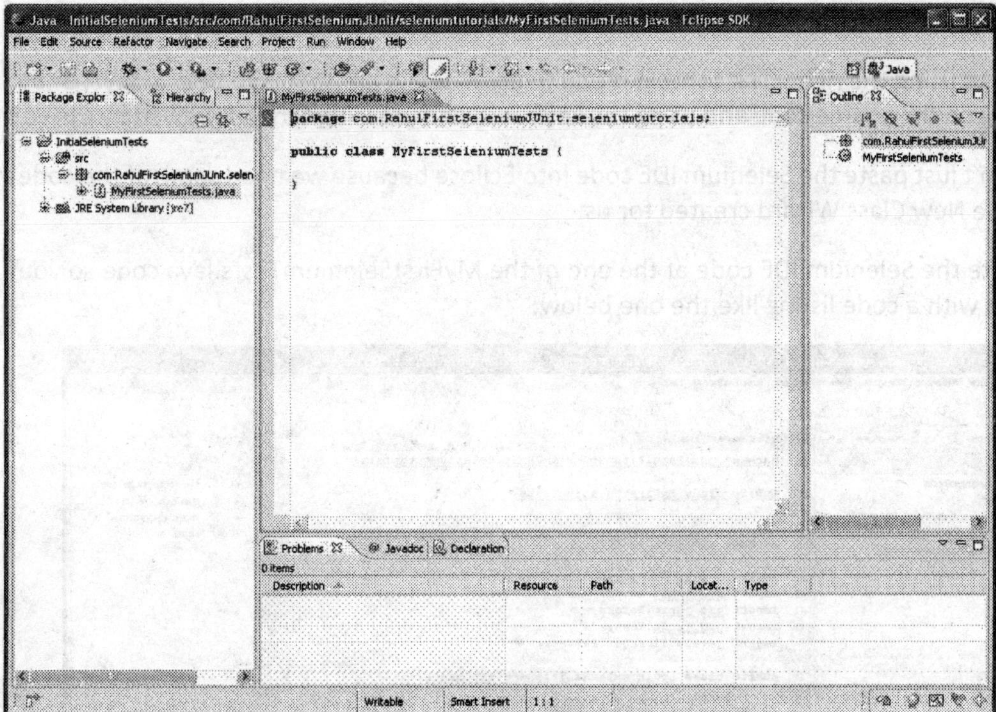

Now we just have to add the code from the IDE.

Copy & Paste the code from Selenium IDE into Eclipse.

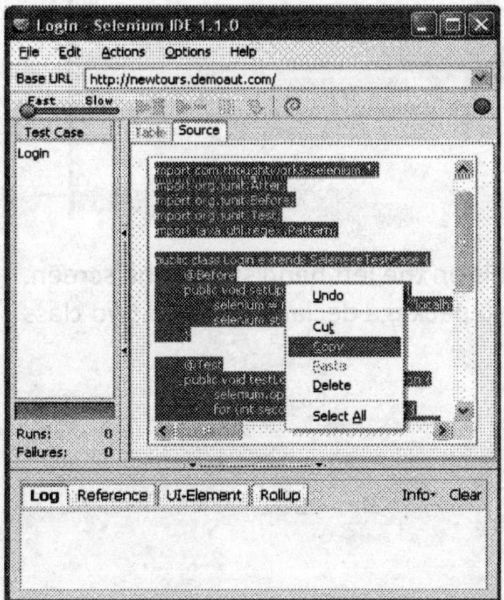

Copy the code from the IDE into the clipboard.

Either by using the right click context menu to do a "select all" followed by a "copy", or by clicking on the source code and using the keyboard and pressing Ctrl+a followed by Ctrl+c.

We can't just paste the Selenium IDE code into Eclipse because we need some of the code that the New Class Wizard created for us.

So paste the Selenium IDE code at the end of the MyFirstSeleniumTests.java code so you end up with a code listing like the one below.

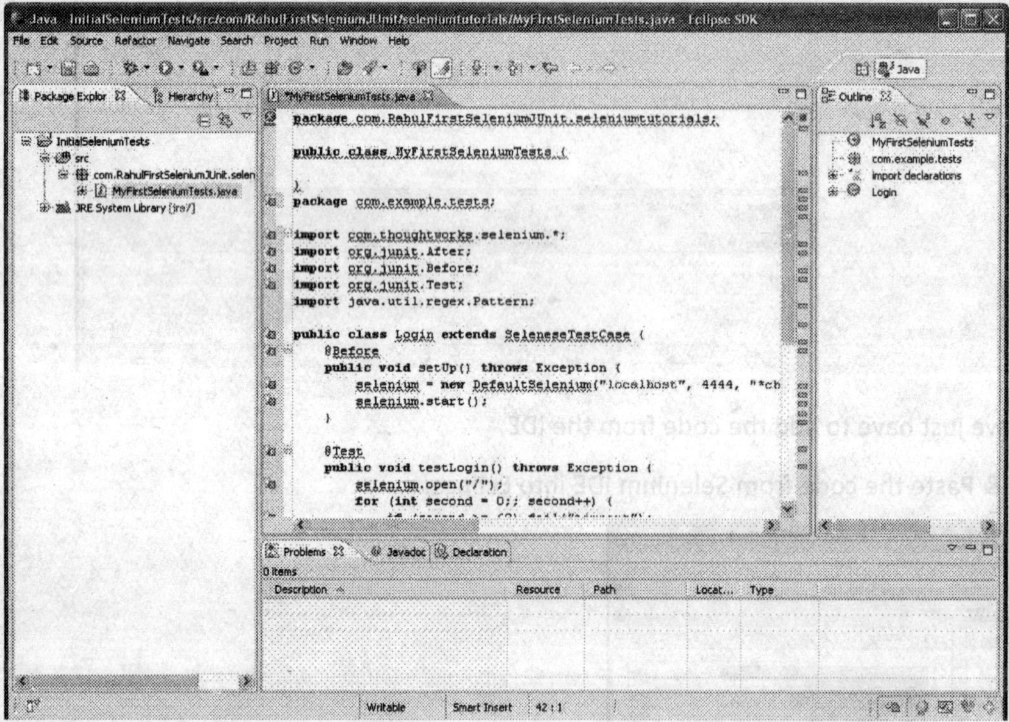

As you can see there are a lot of Eclipse error symbols on the left hand side of the screen. This is because we have written invalid Java with two package declarations and two class declarations. So we will tidy that up:

Important notes:

- rcmovc thc linc "package com.example.tests,"
    - We can only have one package declaration in each class, and it is at the top of the file.
- copy MyFirstSeleniumTests and overwrite Login
- then remove the declaration of MyFirstSeleniumTests that the wizard generated ie. "public class MyFirstSEleniumTests { }"
    - We only want one class declaration per file.

This should give you a listing like the following, which although valid Java is not yet correct because we need to make a few more changes to make it work in Eclipse:

```
package com.RahulFirstSeleniumJUnit.seleniumtutorials;

import com.thoughtworks.selenium.*;
import org.junit.After;
import org.junit.Before;
import org.junit.Test;
import java.util.regex.Pattern;

public class MyFirstSeleniumTests extends SeleneseTestCase {
   @Before
   public void setUp() throws Exception {
      selenium = new DefaultSelenium("localhost", 4444,
"*chrome", "http://newtours.demoaut.com/");
      selenium.start();
   }

   @Test
   public void testLogin() throws Exception {
      selenium.open("/");
      for (int second = 0;; second++) {
         if (second >= 60) fail("timeout");
         try { if (selenium.isTextPresent("Registered users
can sign-in here to find the lowest fare on participating
airlines.")) break; } catch (Exception e) {}
         Thread.sleep(1000);
      }
```

```
    selenium.type("name=userName", "mercury");
    selenium.type("name=password", "mercury");
    selenium.click("name=login");
    selenium.waitForPageToLoad("30000");
    verifyEquals("Find a Flight: Mercury Tours:", selenium.
getTitle());
  }

  @After
  public void tearDown() throws Exception {
    selenium.stop();
  }
}
```

Resolve Import Errors

Select 'InitialSeleniumTests' folder then Right Click and then select 'Properties'

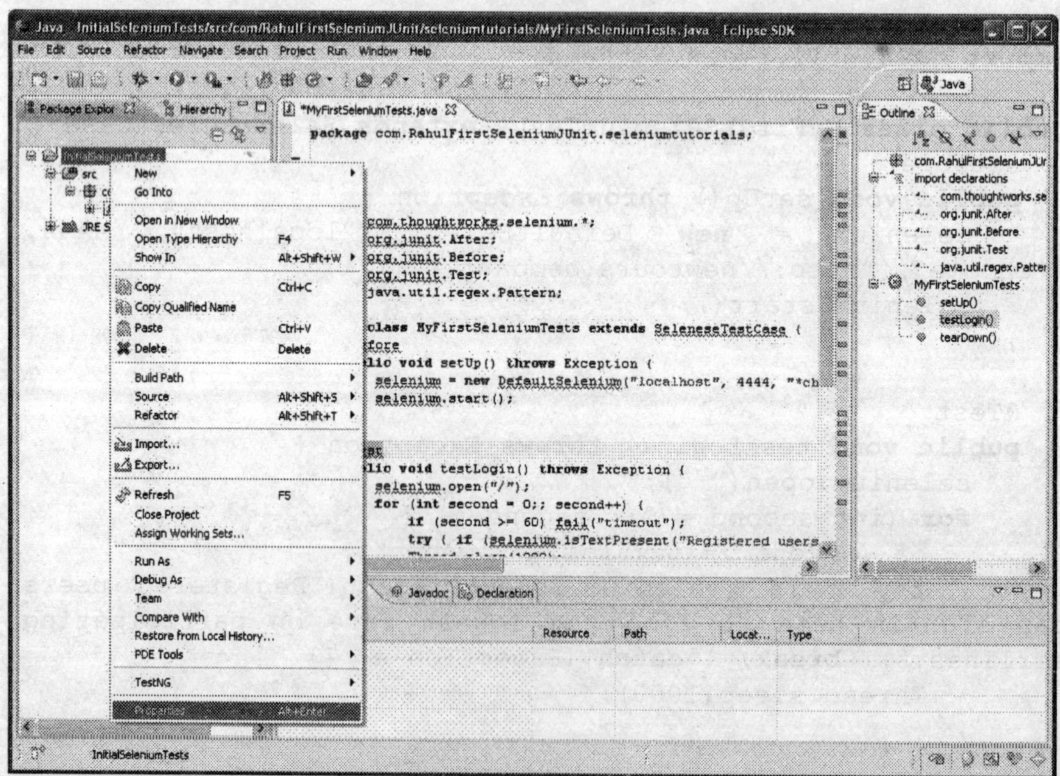

Then go to 'Java Build Path'

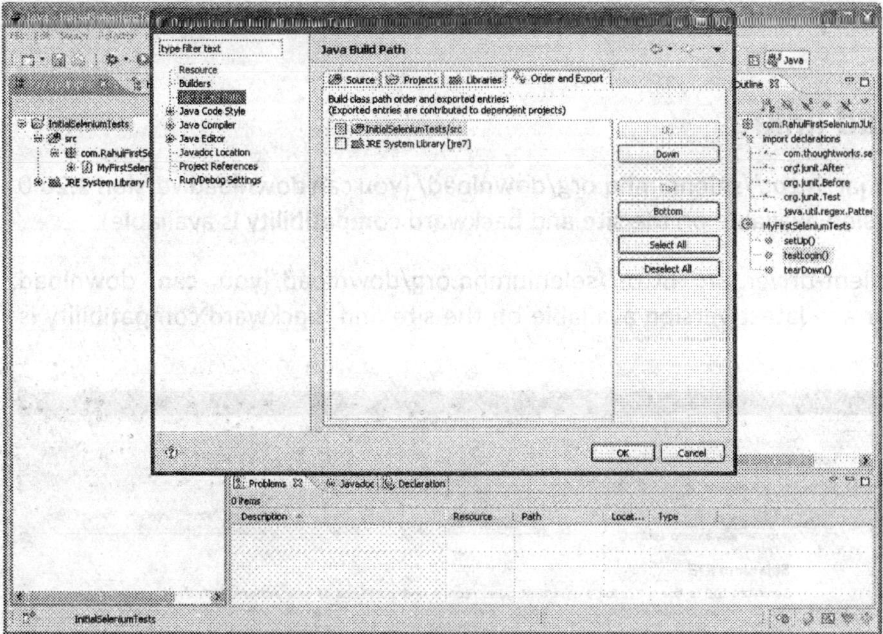

Then go to 'Java Build Path' - > Select 'Libraries' tab

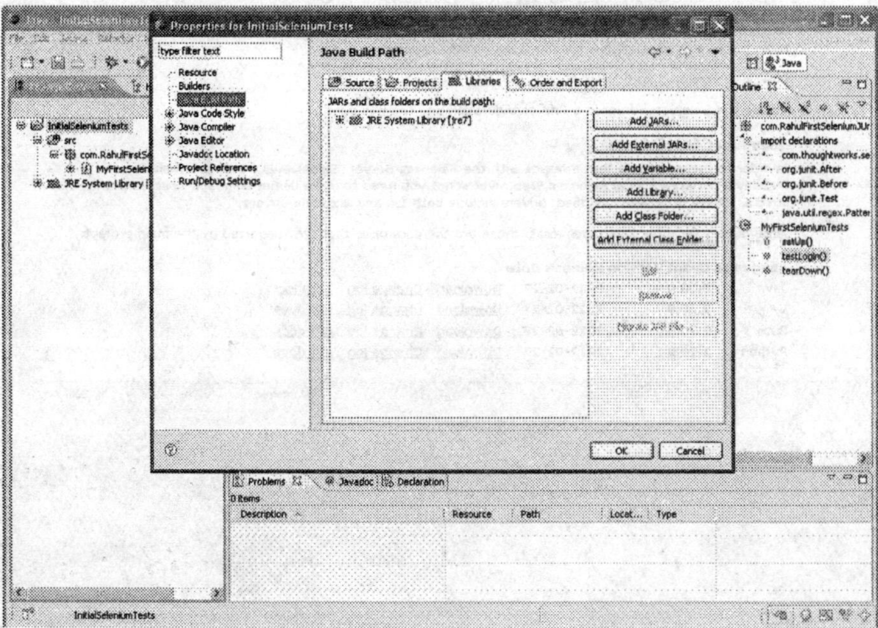

Then click on 'Add External JARs' and all the library files .

Jar download link:

Selenium-server.jar: http://seleniumhq.org/download/ (you can download version 2.20.0 or any latest version available on the site and backward compatibility is available)

Selenium-Java-client-driver.jar: http://seleniumhq.org/download/(you can download version 2.20.0 or any latest version available on the site and backward compatibility is available)

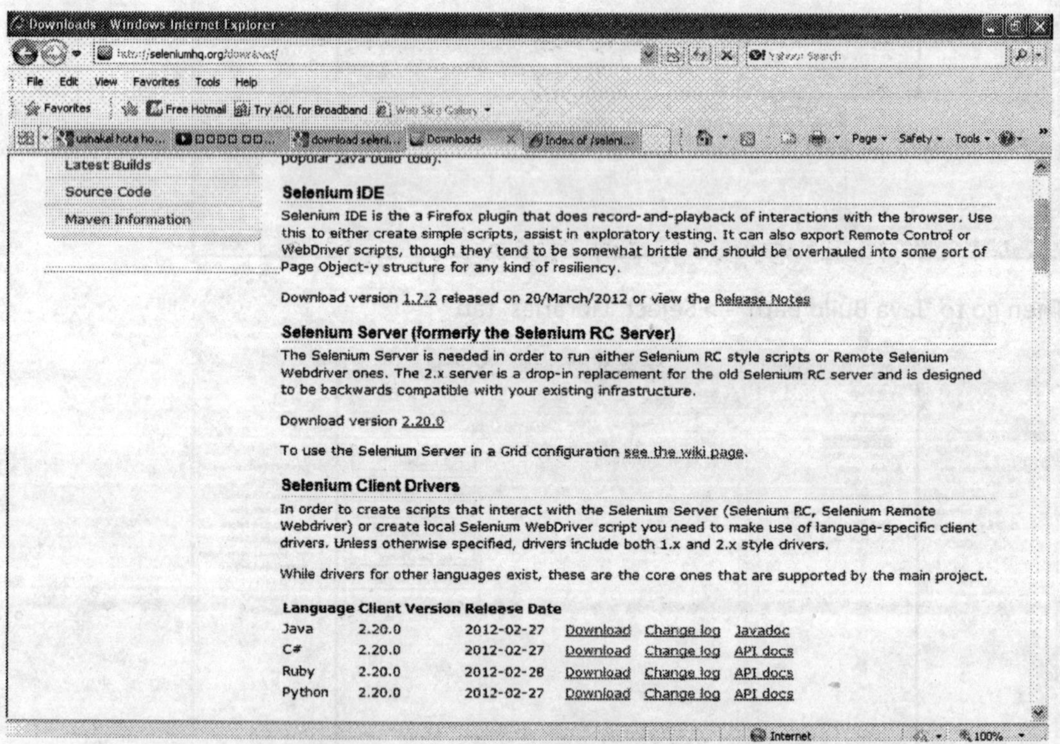

Jxl.jar: http://sourceforge.net/projects/jxl/

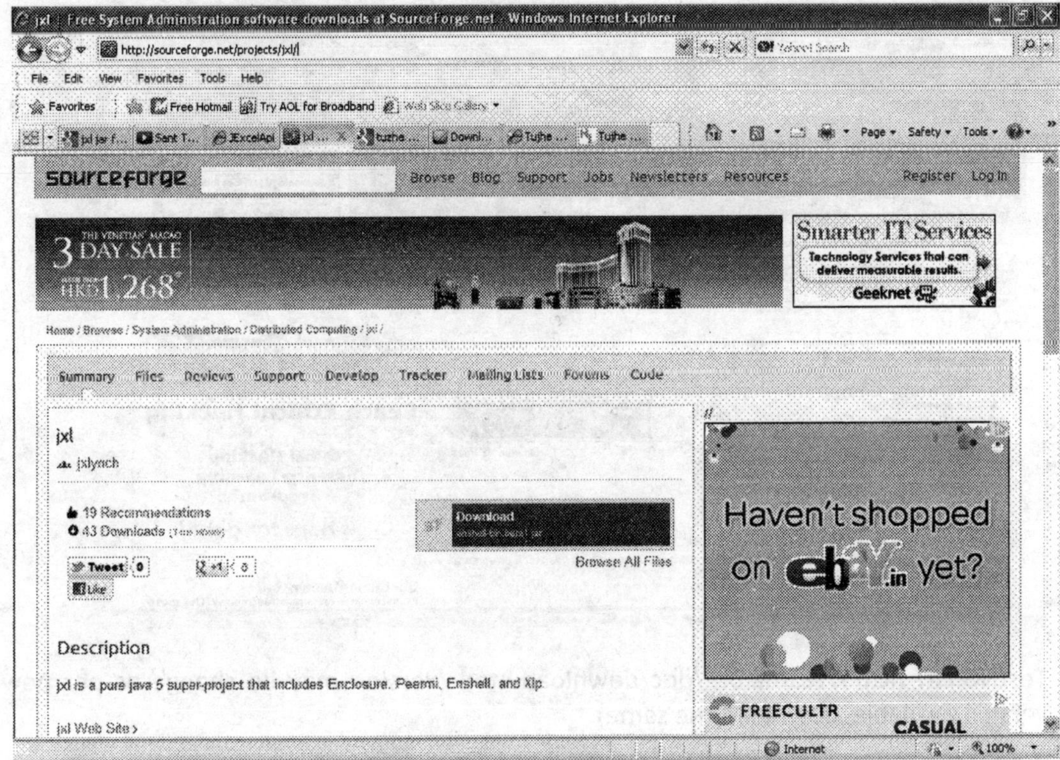

Junit.jar: http://sourceforge.net/projects/junit/

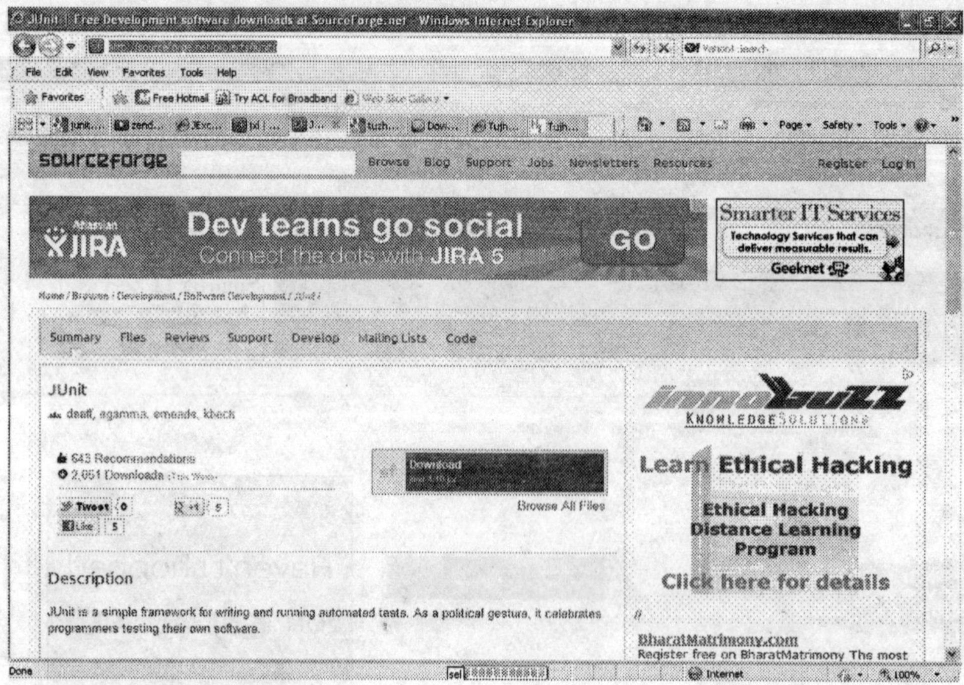

TestNG.jar: http://testng.org/doc/download.html (version may be change as per new version available, download the same)

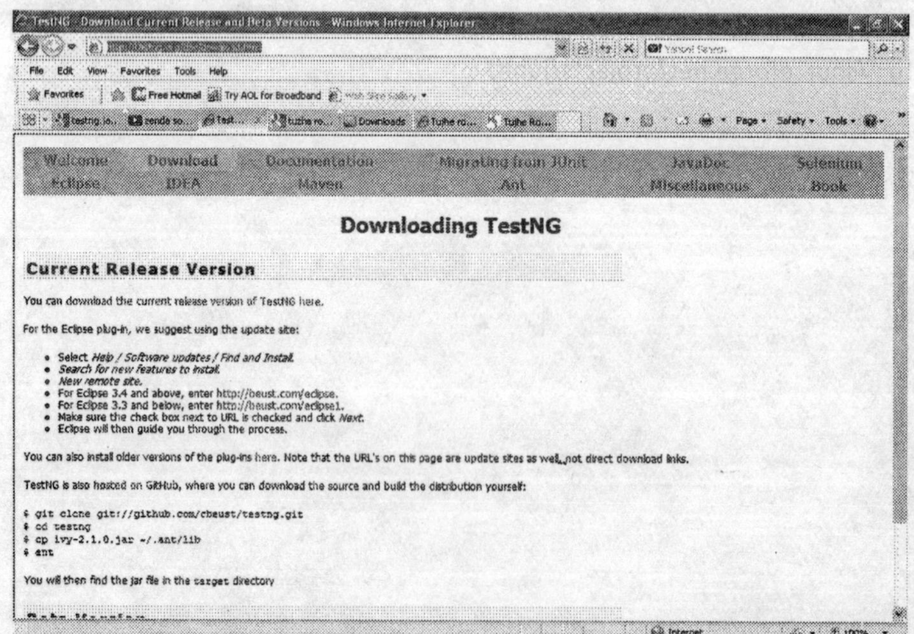

Note : Jar files are included in CD

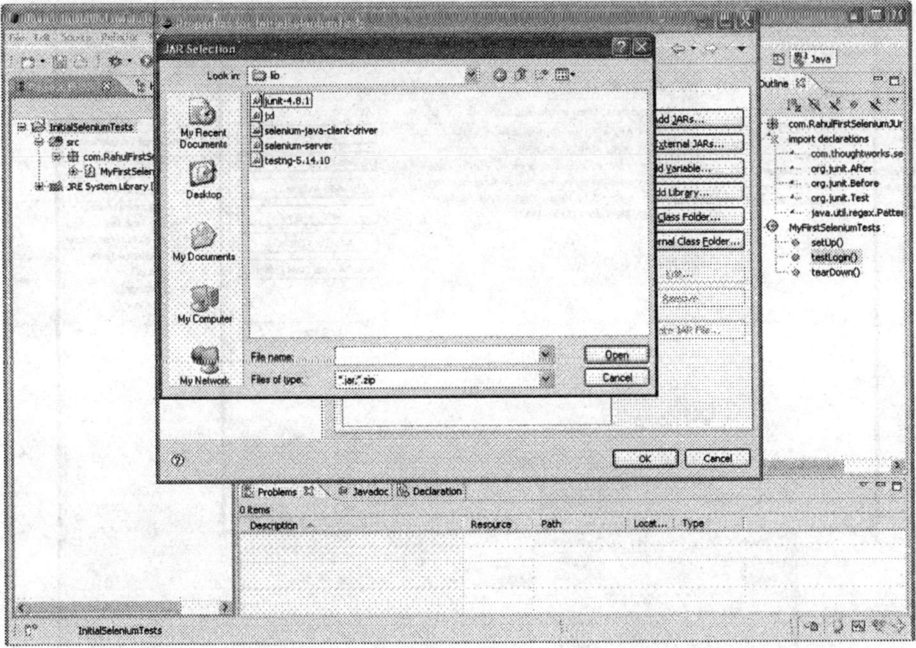

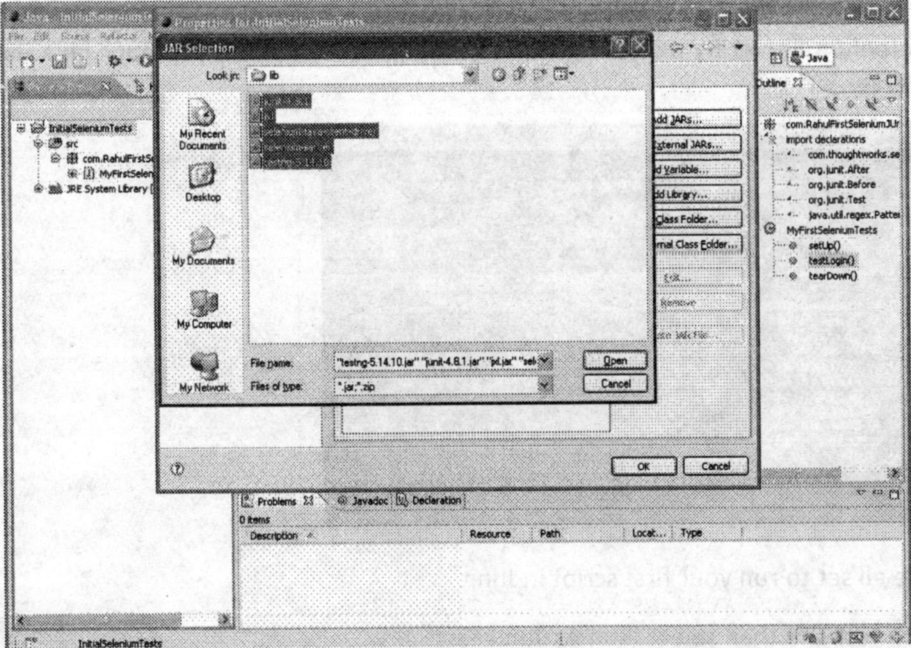

You can See the jar files in 'Libraries' tab .

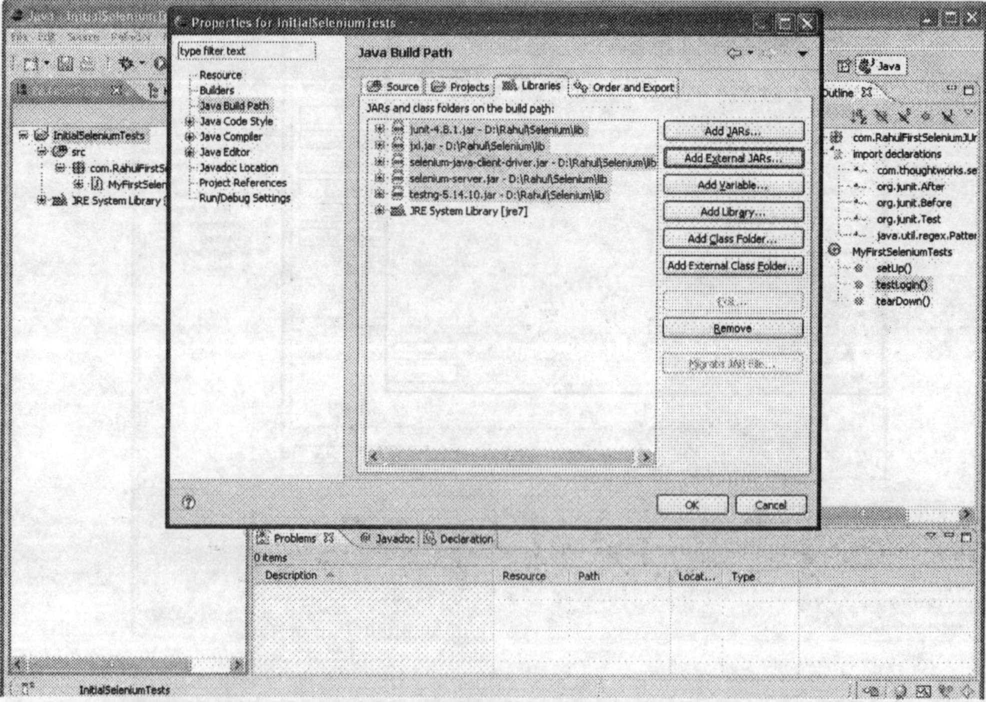

Start the selenium Server by executing this command on command prompt ' java -jar selenium-server.jar'

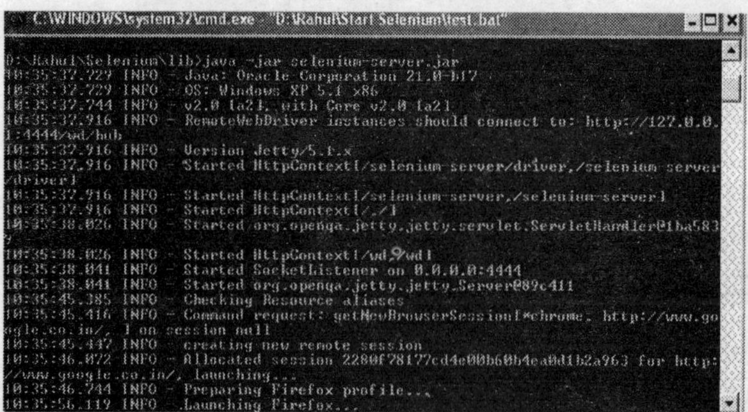

Now you are all set to run your first script in Junit

Right click on test and then select 'Run As-Junit test'

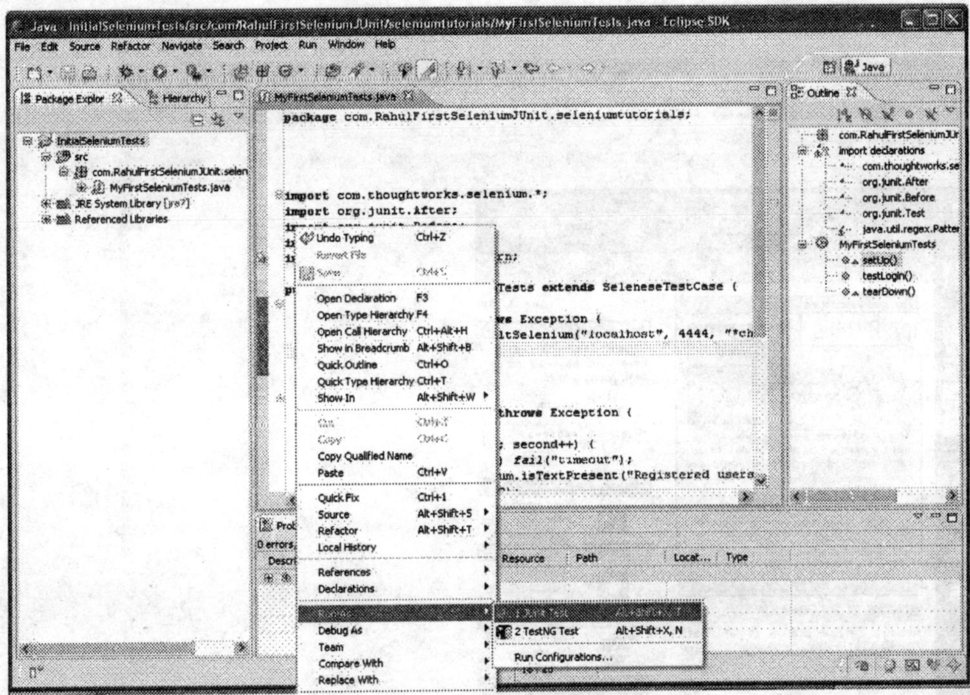

Executing is started on Selenium RC server.

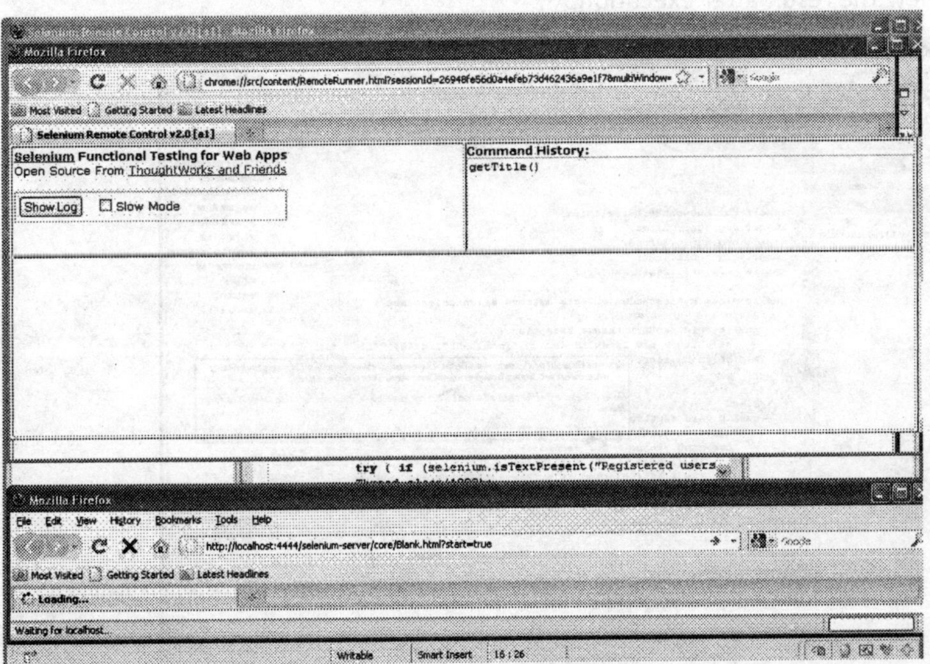

Executing is started on Selenium RC server.

You can view the result after execution.

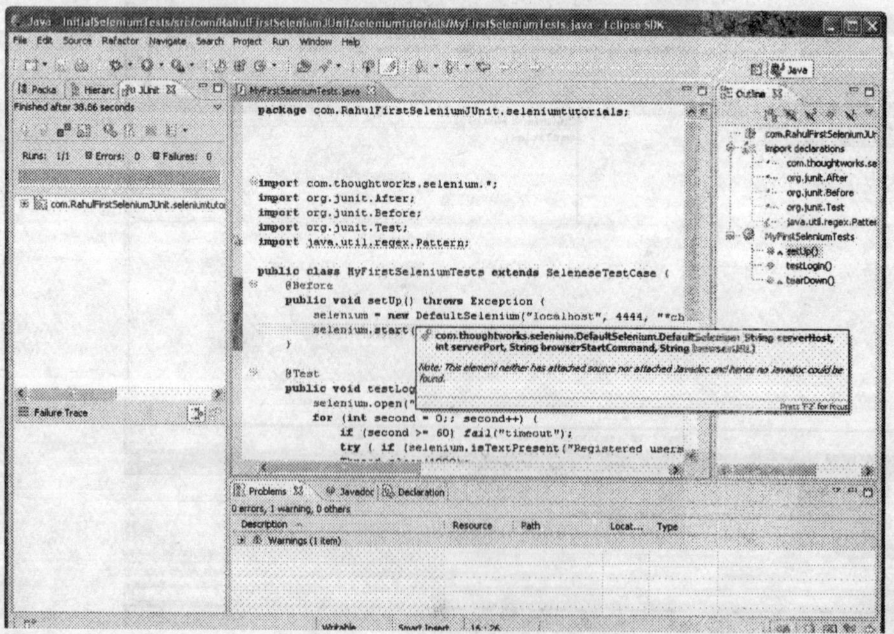

Web Testing using Sahi tool

Introduction:

Sahi is an open source automation and testing tool for web applications, with the facility to record and playback scripts. Sahi runs on any modern browser which supports javascript.

Sahi is written in Java and Javascript and hosted on SourceForge since October 2005. It is released under an Apache License 2.0 Open Source License. Sahi claims to be independent of the browser or operating system. Sahi runs as a proxy server and users configure their browser's proxy settings to point to Sahi's proxy. Sahi then injects its javascript code into web pages, which allows it to record and playback events on the browser. Scripts are recorded or written in Sahi Script which is similar to javascript.

How does Sahi work?

- Sahi is a proxy server written in java
- The proxy injects javascript code
- Javascript code handles all record and playback
- Configure browser to point to the Sahi proxy

Why a proxy?

Easiest way to control any browser by injecting javascript.

Allows manipulation of web content if needed.

–Eg. Remove ad links while testing

Installation

Prerequisites

Java 1.5 or above
Sahi
Browser:- Internet Explorer, Firefox

Download Pre-requisite software

You require Java 1.5 or above is needed for running Sahi.

You can download Java from here: http://www.java.com/download.

Download Sahi from: - http://sourceforge.net/projects/sahi/files/

Download Sahi V3 (2010-03-21) from SourceForge

Download Firefox or Internet Explorer.

Steps:

1) Download Sahi

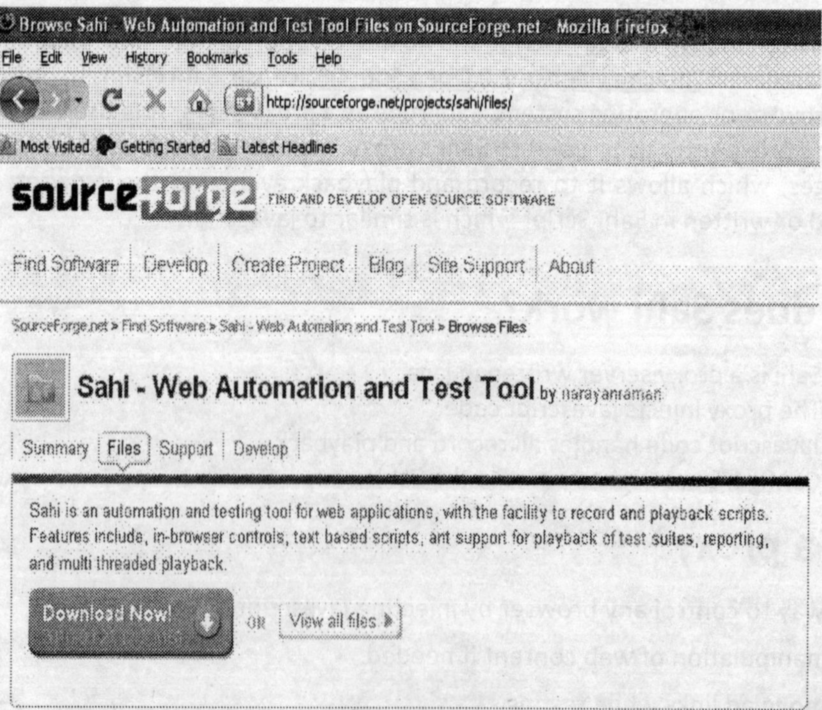

2) Save Sahi_20100321.zip file

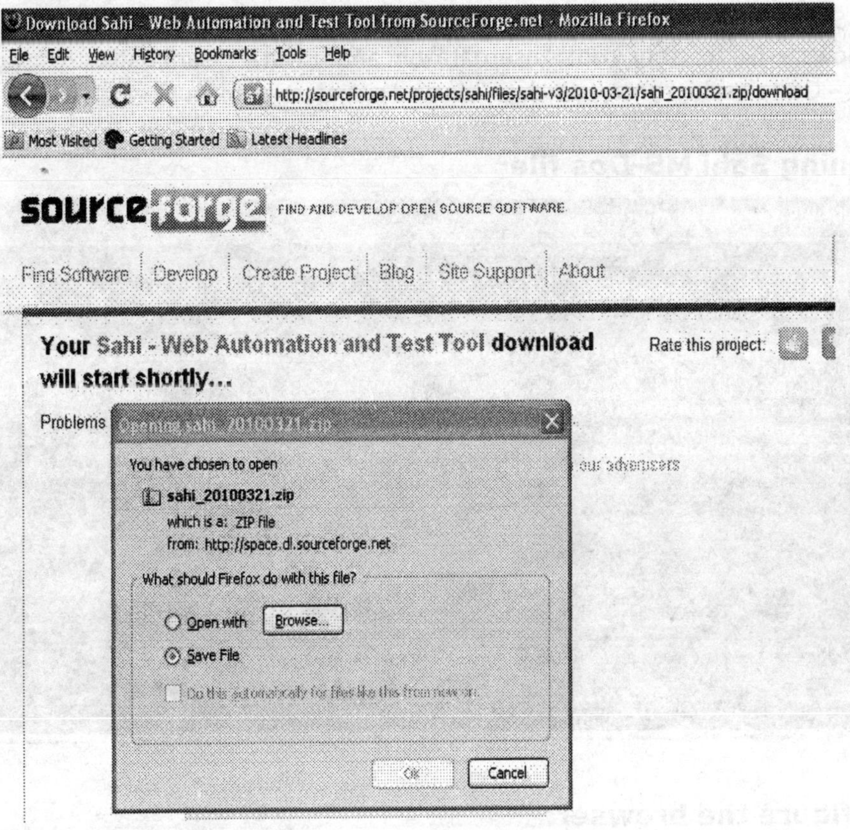

3) Downloading processes

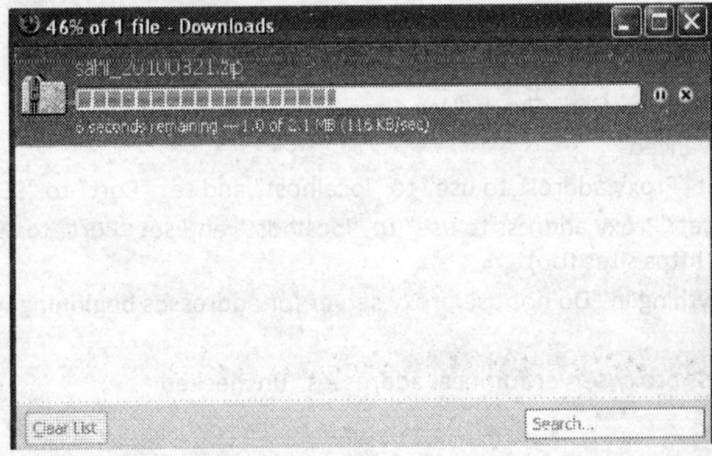

4) Unzip sahi.zip to a desired location

Start Sahi's proxy:

Windows: – Go to <sahi_root>\userdata\bin and run start_sahi.bat

Linux – Go to <sahi_root>/userdata/bin and run start_sahi.sh

5) Running Sahi MS-Dos file

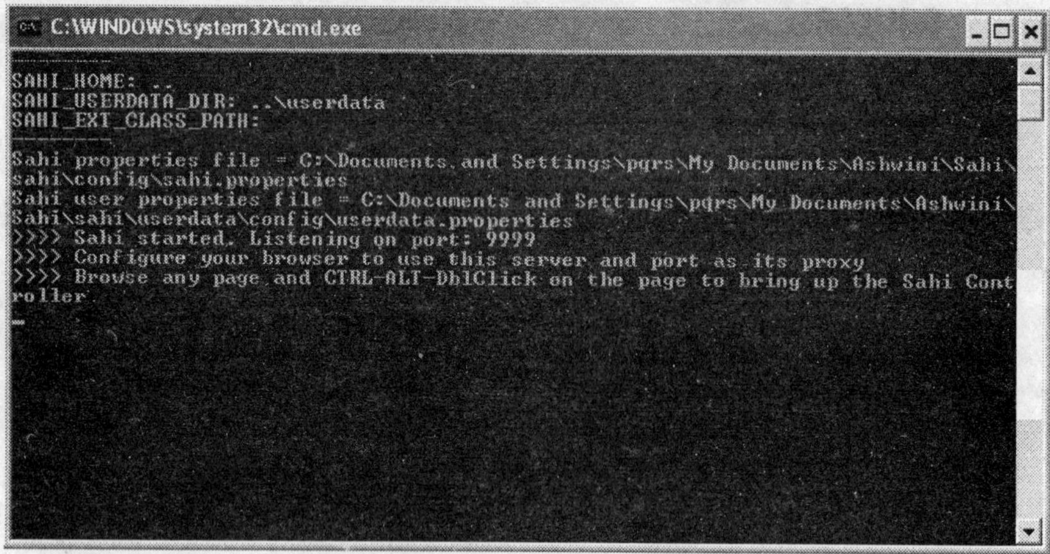

6) Configure the browser:

You need to change your browser's proxy setting to use Sahi's proxy.

a) Internet Explorer:

Go to Tools > Internet Options > Connections > LAN Settings >

In "Proxy server" section, Check "Use a proxy server for your LAN"

Click on "Advanced"

For HTTP: set "Proxy address to use" to "localhost" and set "Port" to "9999"

For Secure: set "Proxy address to use" to "localhost" and set "Port" to "9999" (if you want to test https sites too)

Clear out anything in "Do not use proxy server for addresses beginning with:"

OK

Leave "Bypass proxy server for local addresses" unchecked

OK > OK

LAN Settings

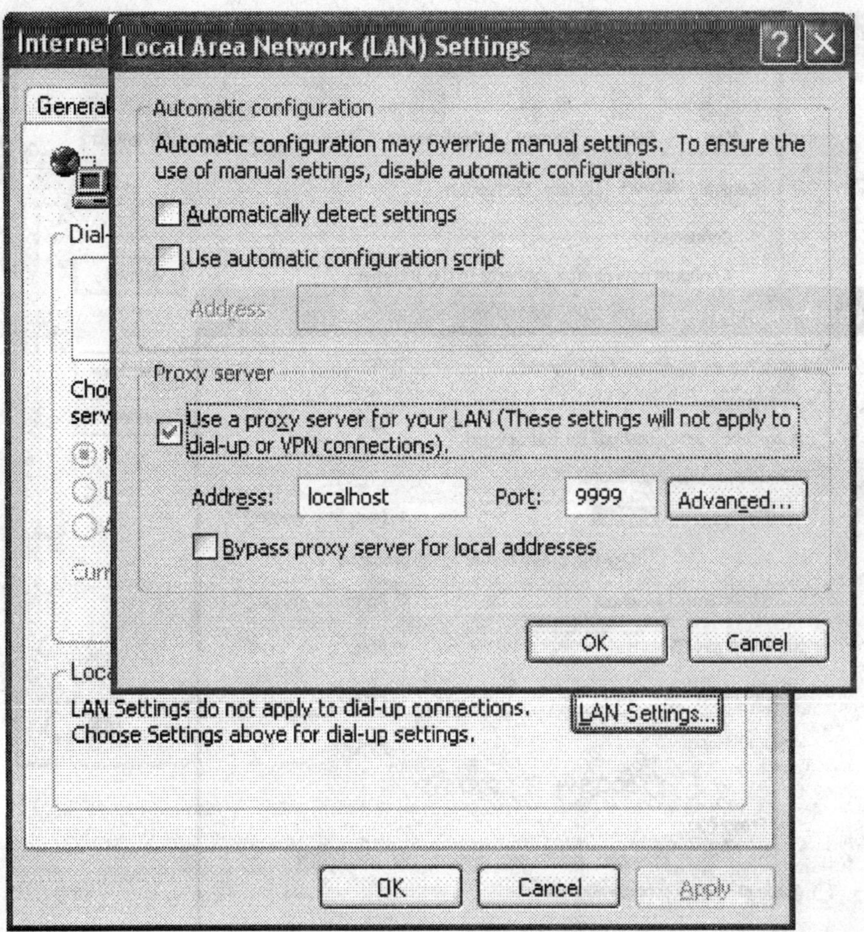

b) Firefox:

Go to Tools > Options > General > Connection Settings >

Set to "Manual Proxy Configuration"

Set "HTTP Proxy" to "localhost"

Set "Port" to "9999". (This setting can be modified through /config/sahi.properties)

Do the same for "SSL Proxy" too, if you wish to record and playback https sites

Keep "Use the same proxy for all protocol" unchecked as Sahi does not understand protocols other than HTTP

NOTE: "No Proxy for" should NOT have localhost in it.

Connection Settings

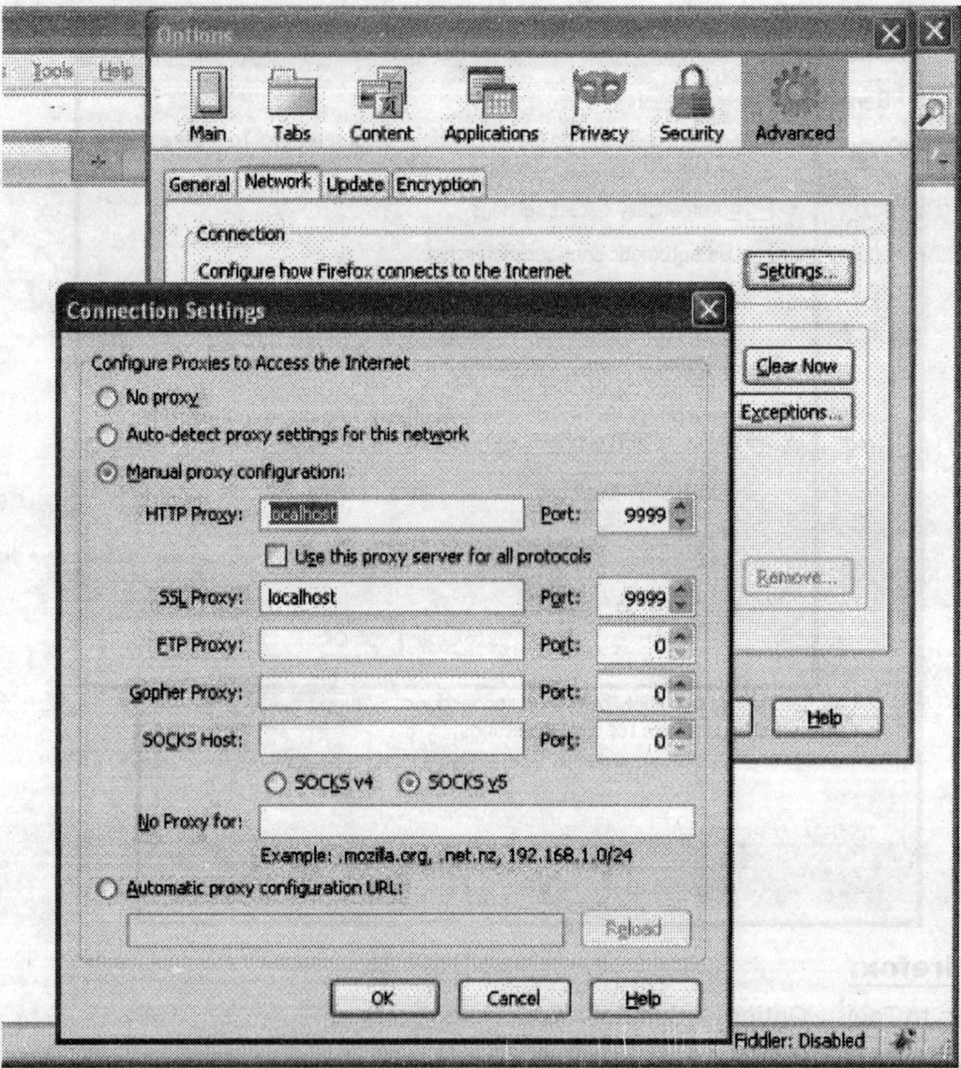

7) Open Sahi Controller

Press ALT and double click on the window which you want to record. Sahi's Controller window will pop up. (If that does not work, press CTRL and ALT keys together and then double click. Make sure popup blockers are turned off.

After Installation your Sahi Controller looks like

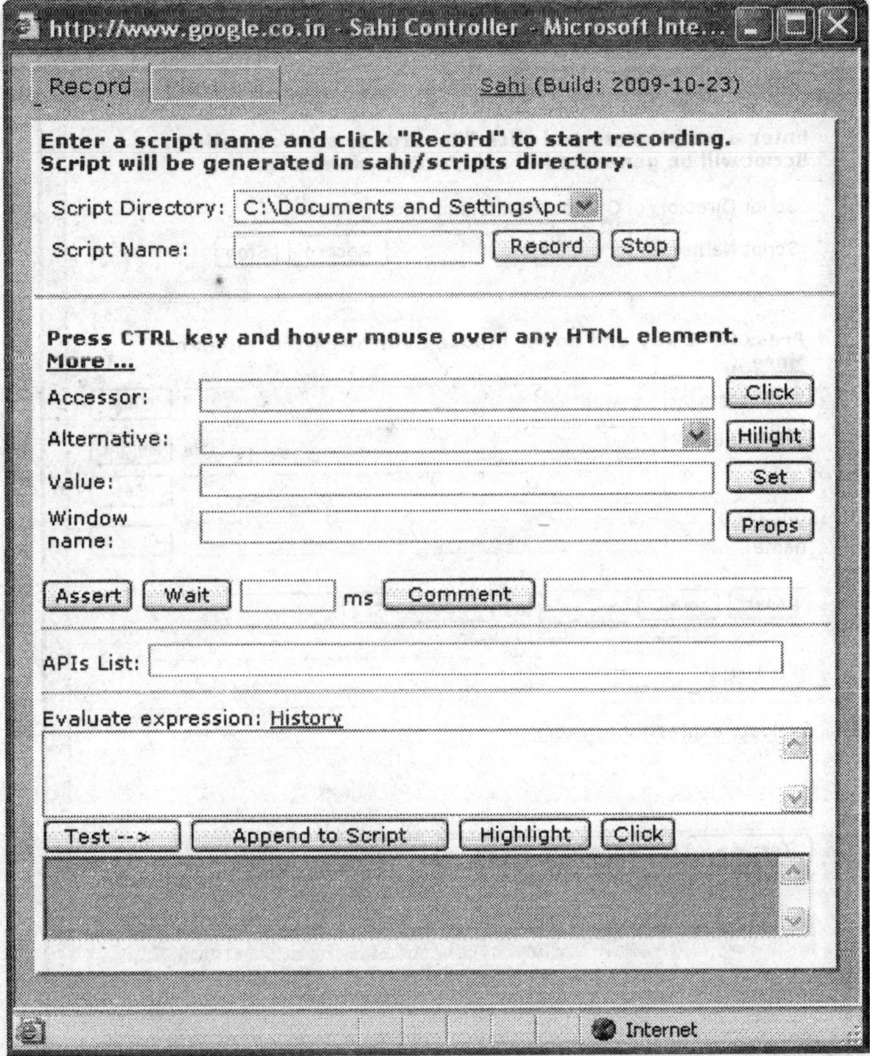

How to Open Sahi Contorller

1) Run Sahi MS-Dos file.
2) Open http://www.Google.com/ in your web browser
3) After Google loads, hold down the Ctrl and Alt keys and thendouble-click the web page. Sahi's Controller window will pop up. (If that does not work, press CTRL and ALT keys together and then double click. Make sure popup blockers are turned off.

The Sahi Controller should now appear

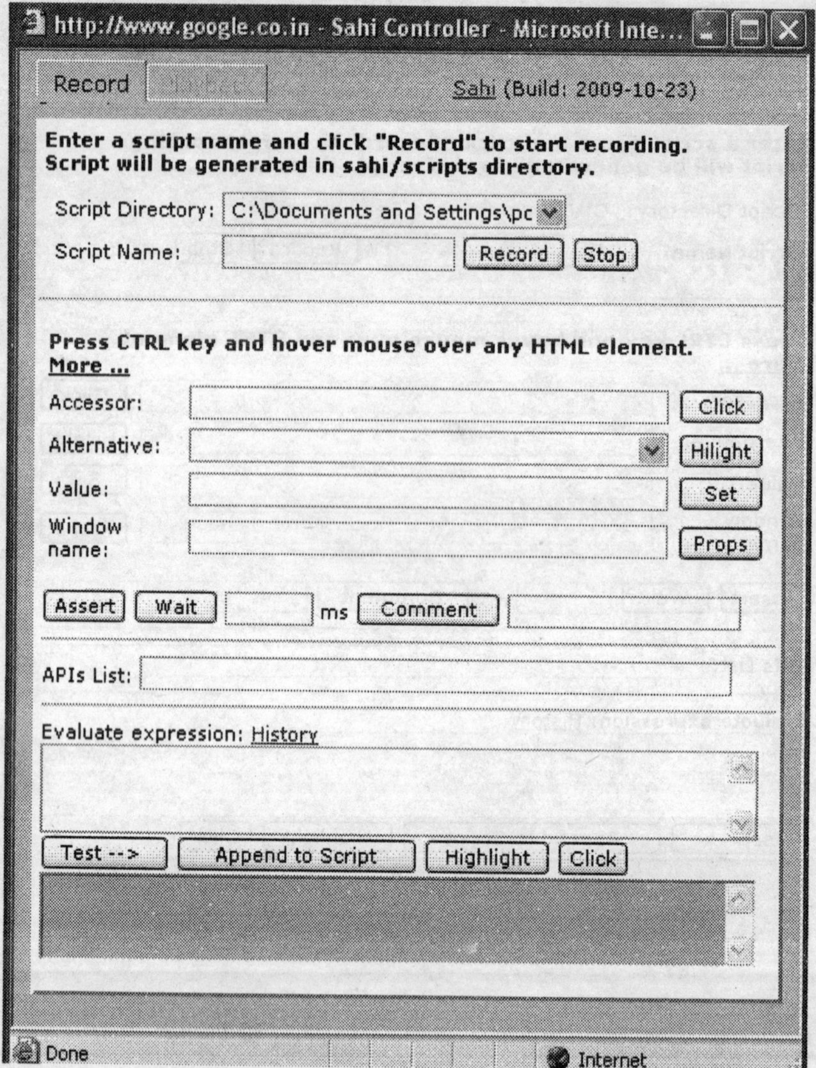

How to Record

The Sahi Controller has two tabs: Record and Playback. We will start by recording the navigation steps.

The "Script Directory" field shows you where the script will be saved. By default Sahi saves to the "scripts" directory.

NOTE: This directory can be changed via sahi.properties in the "config" directory.

Enter "Test" in the "Script Name" text field and press the "Record" button
In the web browser, enter "Sahi" in the Google search box
Now click the "Google Search" button
Click the "Stop" button in the Sahi Controller

View the recorded script

The recoded script can be viewed and edited by opening the .sah file in the <sahi_root>\userdata\scripts directory. Sahi scripts are simple text files which use Javascript syntax.

The script can be edited even while recording, so that logical segregation into functions etc. can be done as recording happens.

View Logs

On the Controller, go to Playback tab and click on "View Logs" link at the bottom right. It will open a window with the results neatly formatted in HTML.

Clicking on a line in the logs will drill down to exact line in script.

You can also view the logs at http://localhost:9999/logs

How to Playback

Now to play back what we just recorded:

Click the "Playback" tab in the Sahi Controller
Select "Test.sah" in the "File" selection list
Enter "http://www.Google.com/" in the "Start URL" text field
Click the "Set" button
Wait for the web page in the browser to reload
Click the "Play" button

Features

- Browser and Operating System independent
- Powerful recorder which works across browsers
- Powerful Object Spy
- Intuitive and simple APIs
- Javascript based scripts for good programming control
- Version Controllable text-based scripts

- In-built reports
- In-built multithreaded or parallel playback of tests
- Tests do not need the browser window to be in focus
- Command line and ant support for integration into build processes
- Supports external proxy, HTTPS, 401 & NTLM authentications
- Supports browser popups and modal dialogs
- Supports AJAX and highly dynamic web applications
- Scripts very robust
    - No wait statements required even for AJAX and page loads
    - Intuitive APIs like _near and _in eliminates need for XPaths
- Works on applications with random auto-generated ids
- Very lightweight and scalable
- Supports data-driven testing. Can connect to database, Excel or CSV file.
- Ability to invoke any Java library from scripts

Reporting

Two-level reports will be generated. First level is consolidated report as shown in the below screenshot, where report just says the script name and its result. Sahi follows the color code (green for pass and red for fail) for reporting which helps to locate the failed script easily.

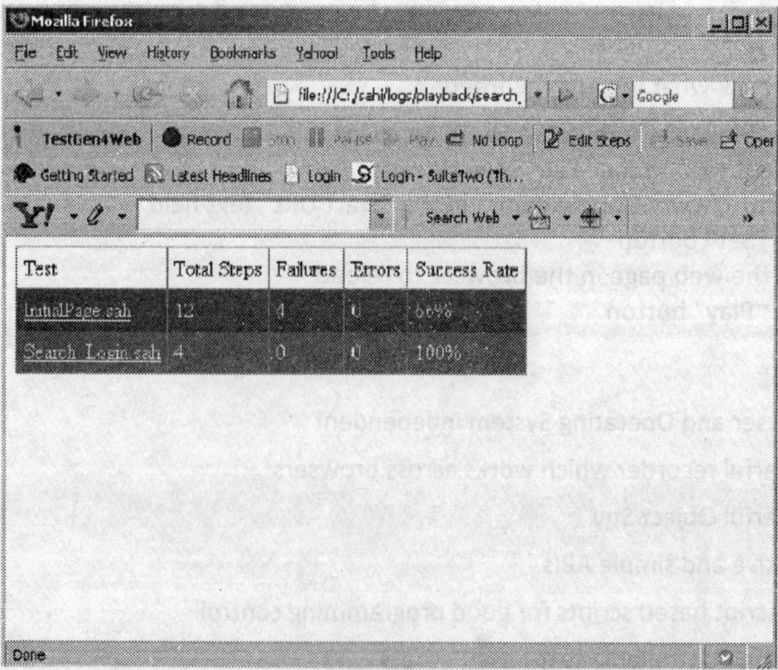

Test	Total Steps	Failures	Errors	Success Rate
InitialPage.sah	12	4	0	66%
Search_Login.sah	4	0	0	100%

Sample Examples

1) Open Sahi controller.
2) Using the "Record" tab on Sahi controller, enter your script name in the "Script Name" field.
3) Select "Record" button to start recording

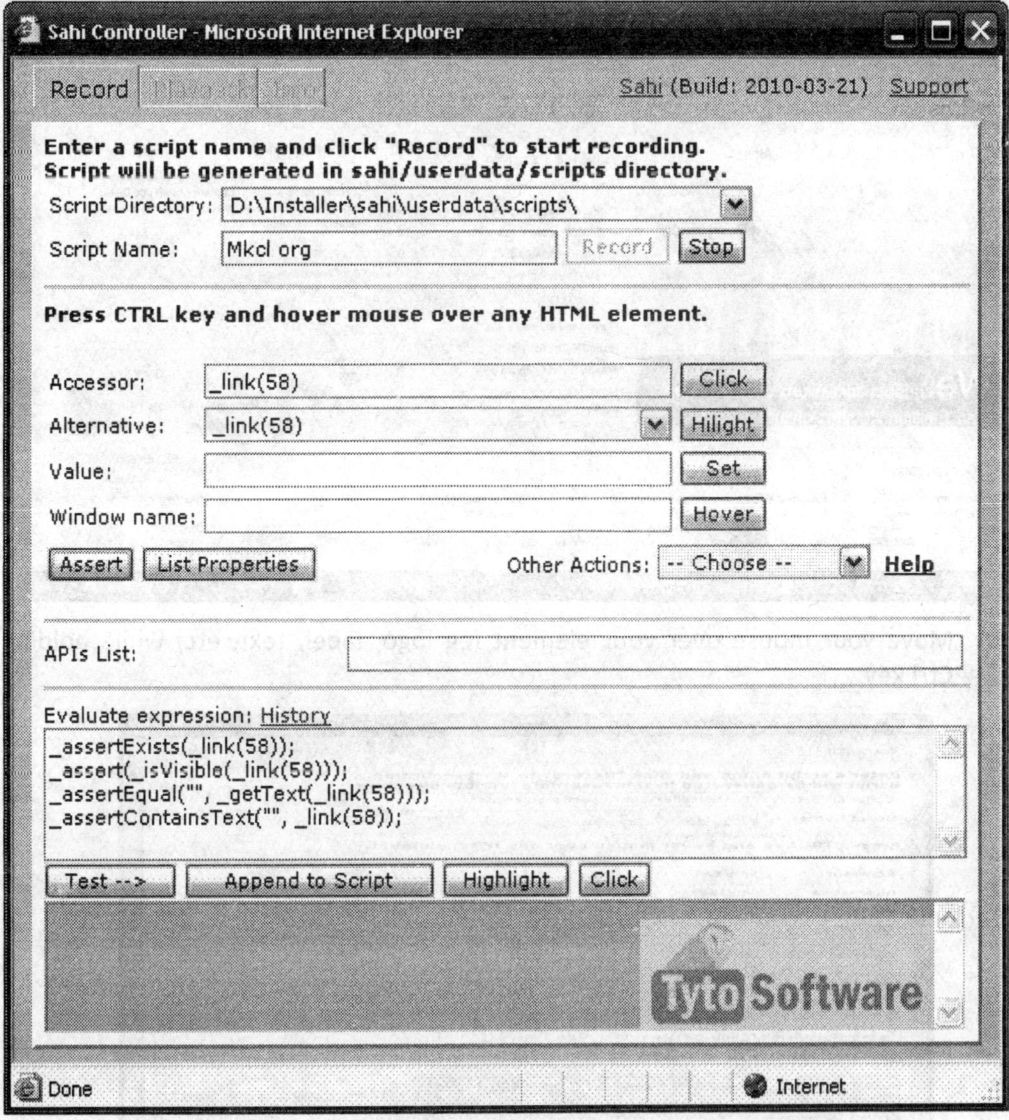

4) Navigate your website. Type www.mkcl.org

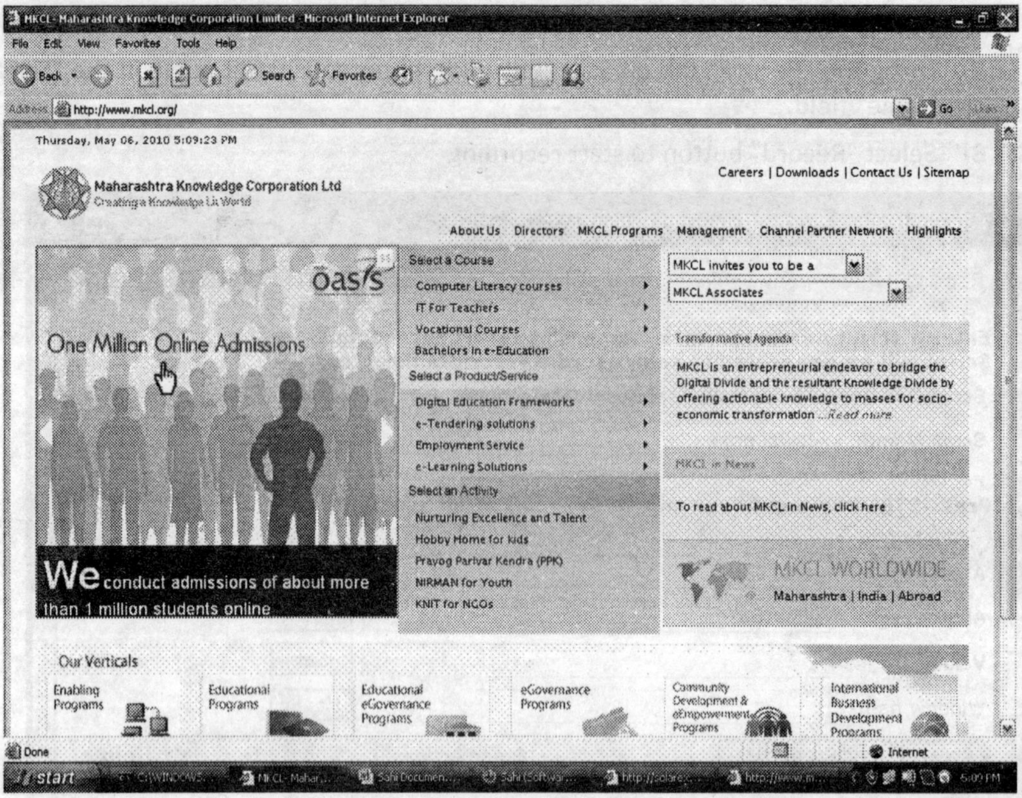

5) Move your mouse over your element (eg logo, label, text, etc) while holding Ctrl key.

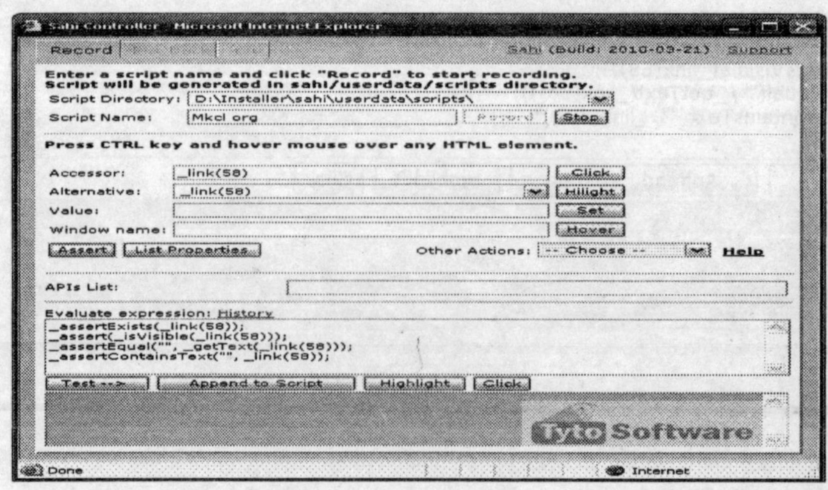

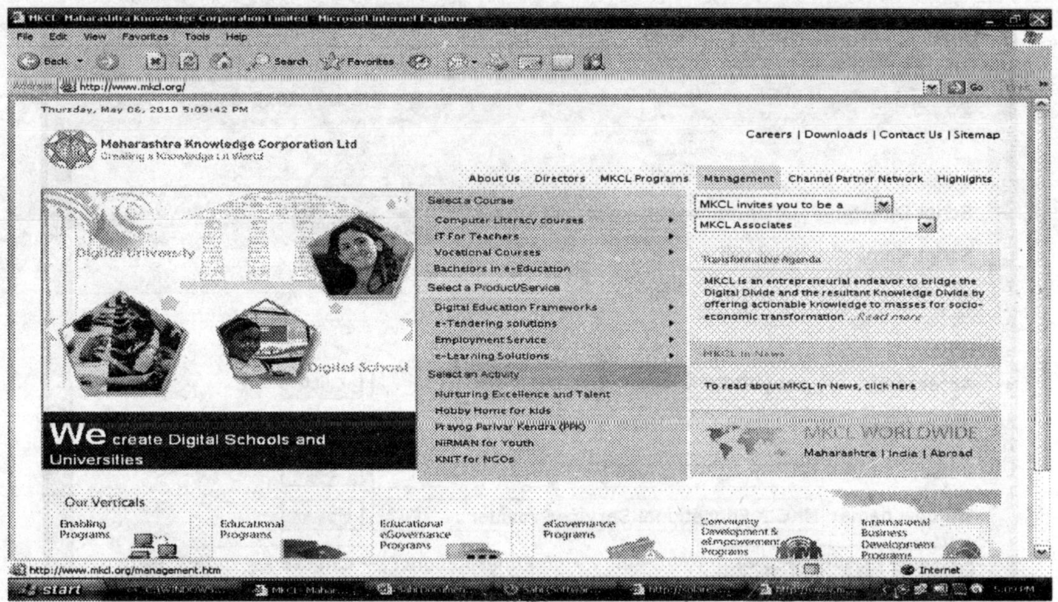

6) Verify a right value/element is shown on the Accessor and/or Value fields on Sahi controller.

7) Select "Assert" control.

8) Verify a right value/element is shown on "Evaluate expression:" text box.

9) Select "Append to Script" control to add the element/value to your recorded script

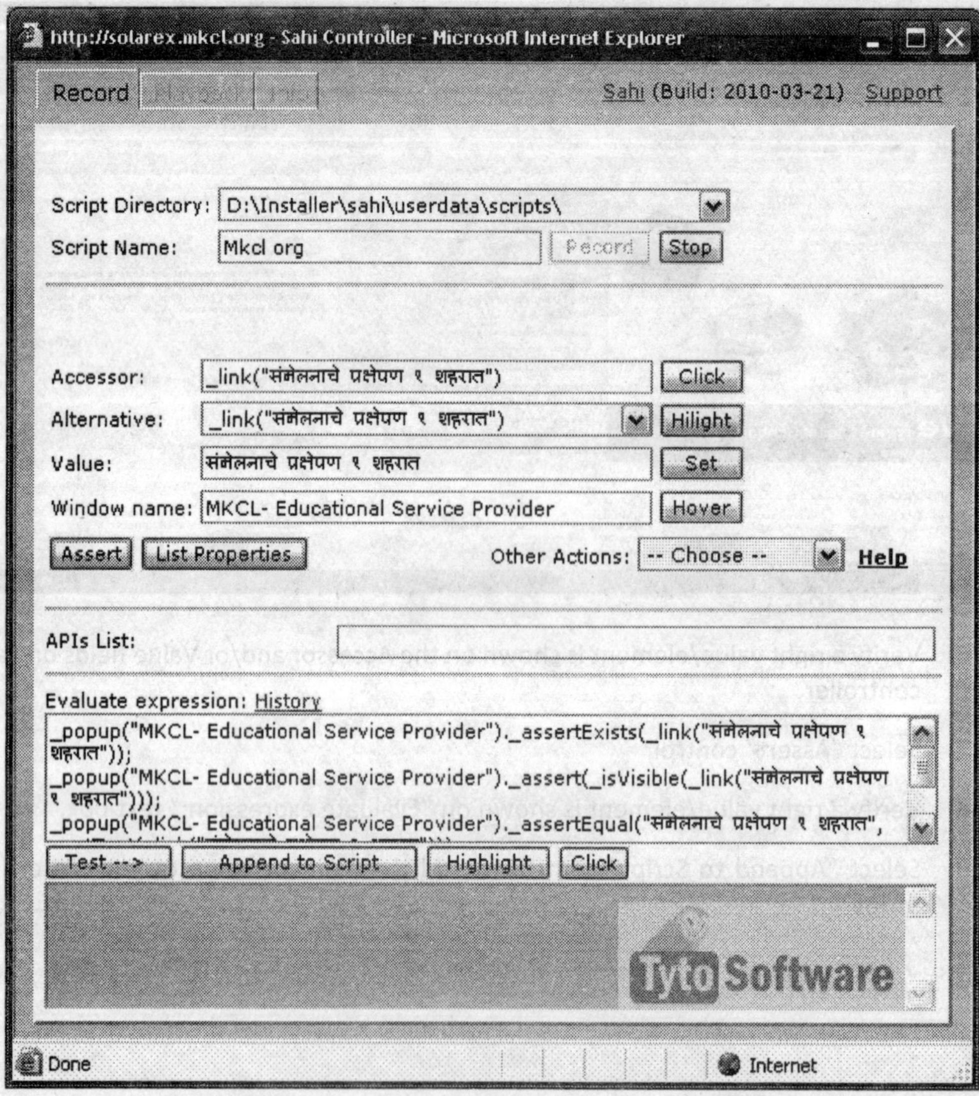

10) Once you are done recording, select "Stop" control to stop recording.

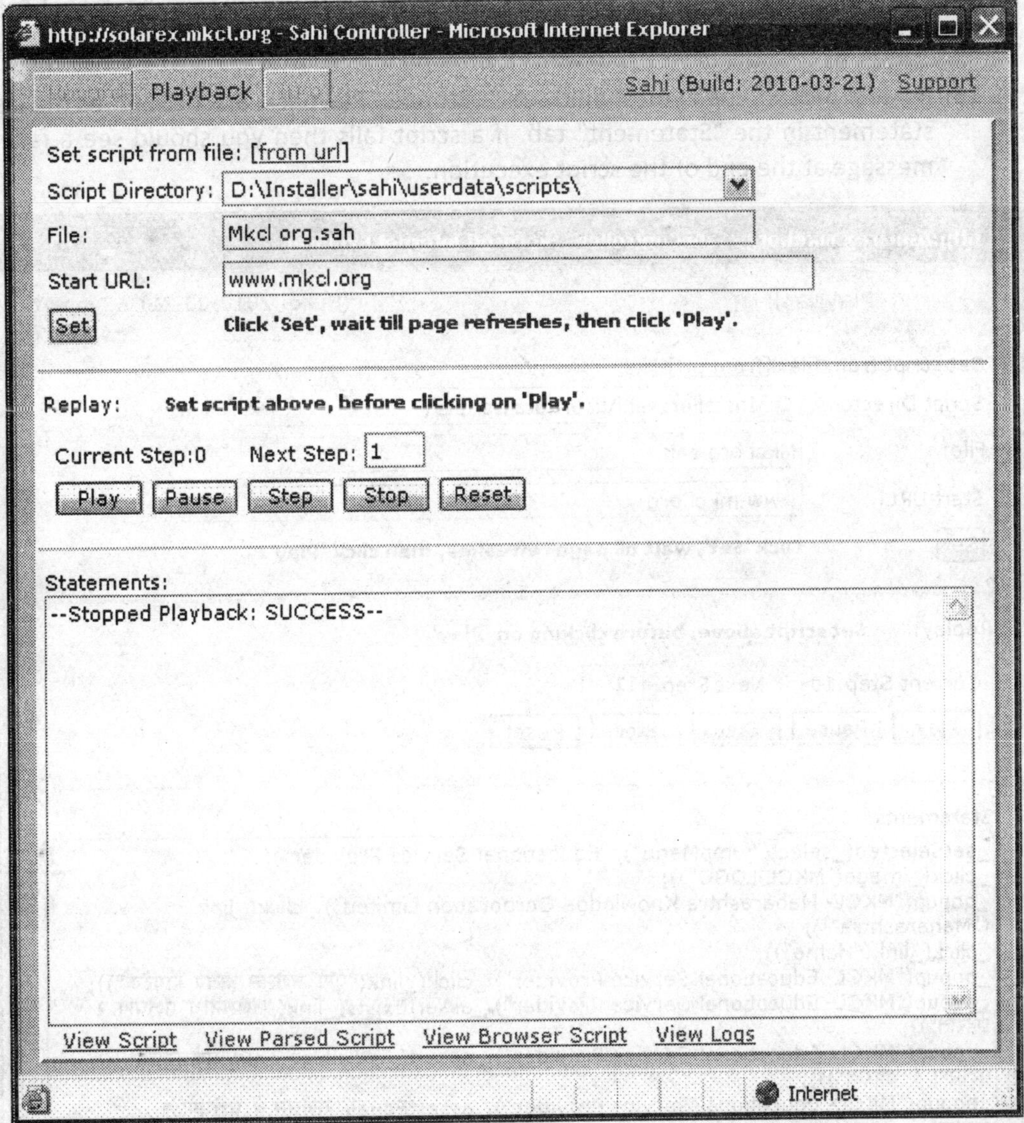

11) If Sahi controller is already opened then select the "Playback" tab.

12) Select your recorded Sahi script file from the "File" drop down.

13) Enter the required starting URL on your browser URL and on the "Start URL" textbox on Sahi controller.

14) From Sahi controller, click 'Set' control and ensure your browser is refreshed/ reloaded.

15) Click 'Play' control and watch script execution on the "Statements" tab of Sahi controller against your browser.

16) If a test passed, then you should see "--Stopped Playback: SUCCESS-- " as the last statement in the "Statement" tab. If a script fails then you should see a failed message at the end of the script execution.

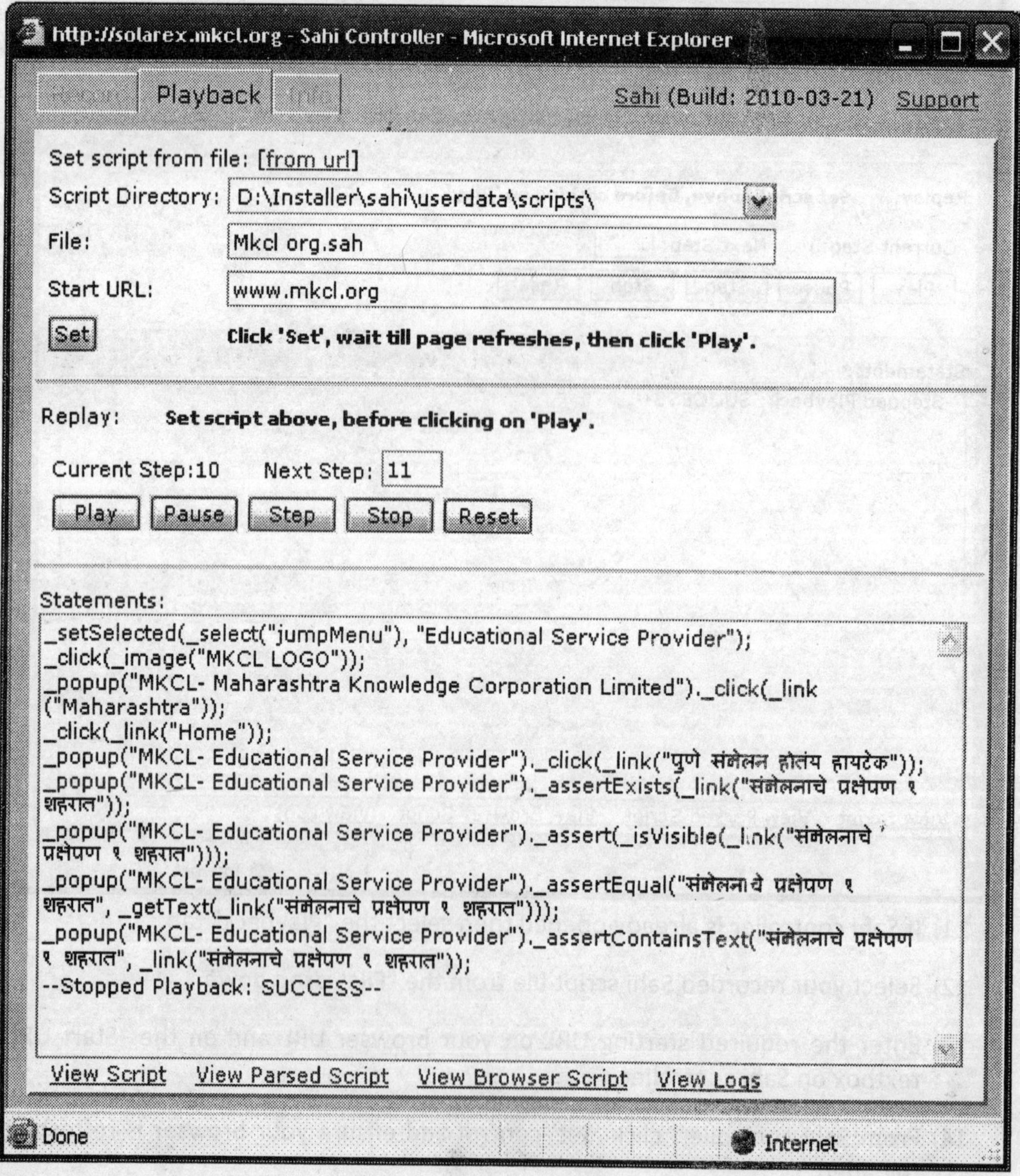

To view script

On the Controller, go to Playback tab and click on "View Script" link at the bottom right. It will open a window with the recorded script.

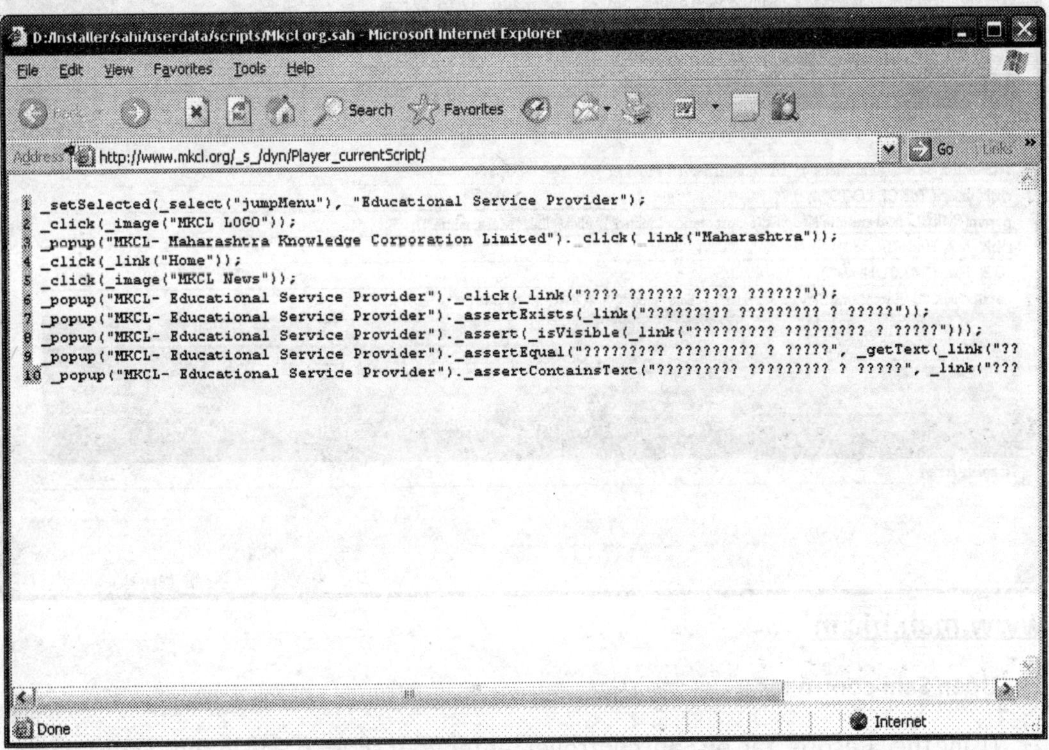

View Logs

On the Controller, go to Playback tab and click on "View Logs" link at the bottom right. It will open a window with the results neatly formatted in HTML.

Clicking on a line in the logs will drill down to exact line in script.

You can also view the logs at http://localhost:9999/logs

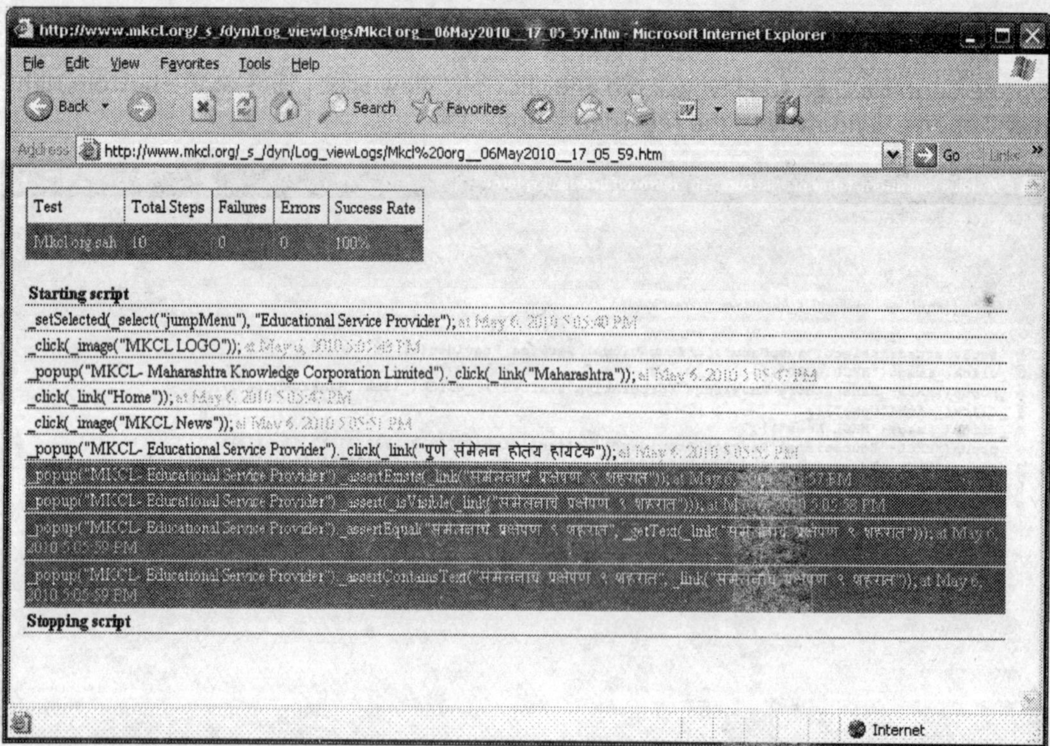

www.mah.nic.in

1) Open Sahi controller.

2) Using the "Record" tab on Sahi controller, enter your script name in the "Script Name" field.

3) Select "Record" button to start recording

4) Navigate your website. Type www.mkcl.org

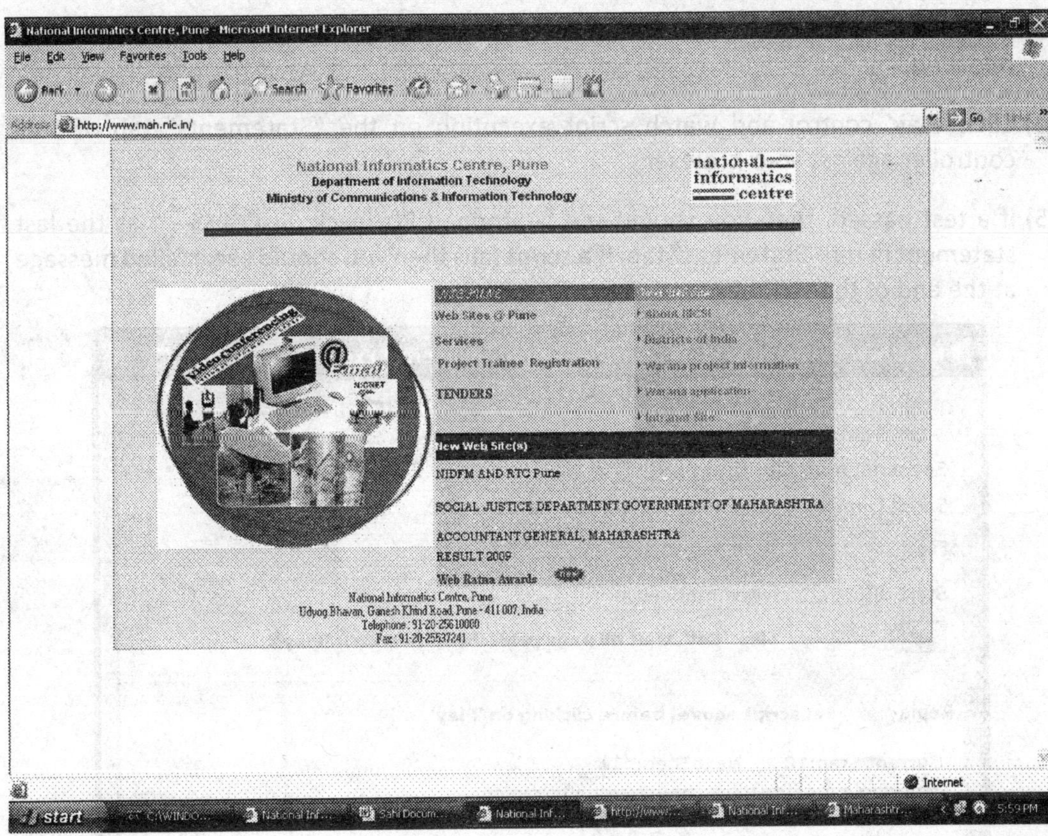

5) Move your mouse over your element (eg logo, label, text, etc) while holding Ctrl key.

6) Verify a right value/element is shown on the Accessor and/or Value fields on Sahi controller.

7) Select "Assert" control.

8) Verify a right value/element is shown on "Evaluate expression:" text box.

9) Select "Append to Script" control to add the element/value to your recorded script

10) If Sahi controller is already opened then select the "Playback" tab.

11) Select your recorded Sahi script file from the "File" drop down.

12) Enter the required starting URL on your browser URL and on the "Start URL" textbox on Sahi controller.

13) From Sahi controller, click 'Set' control and ensure your browser is refreshed/ reloaded.

14) Click 'Play' control and watch script execution on the "Statements" tab of Sahi controller against your browser.

15) If a test passed, then you should see "--Stopped Playback: SUCCESS-- " as the last statement in the "Statement" tab. If a script fails then you should see a failed message at the end of the script execution.

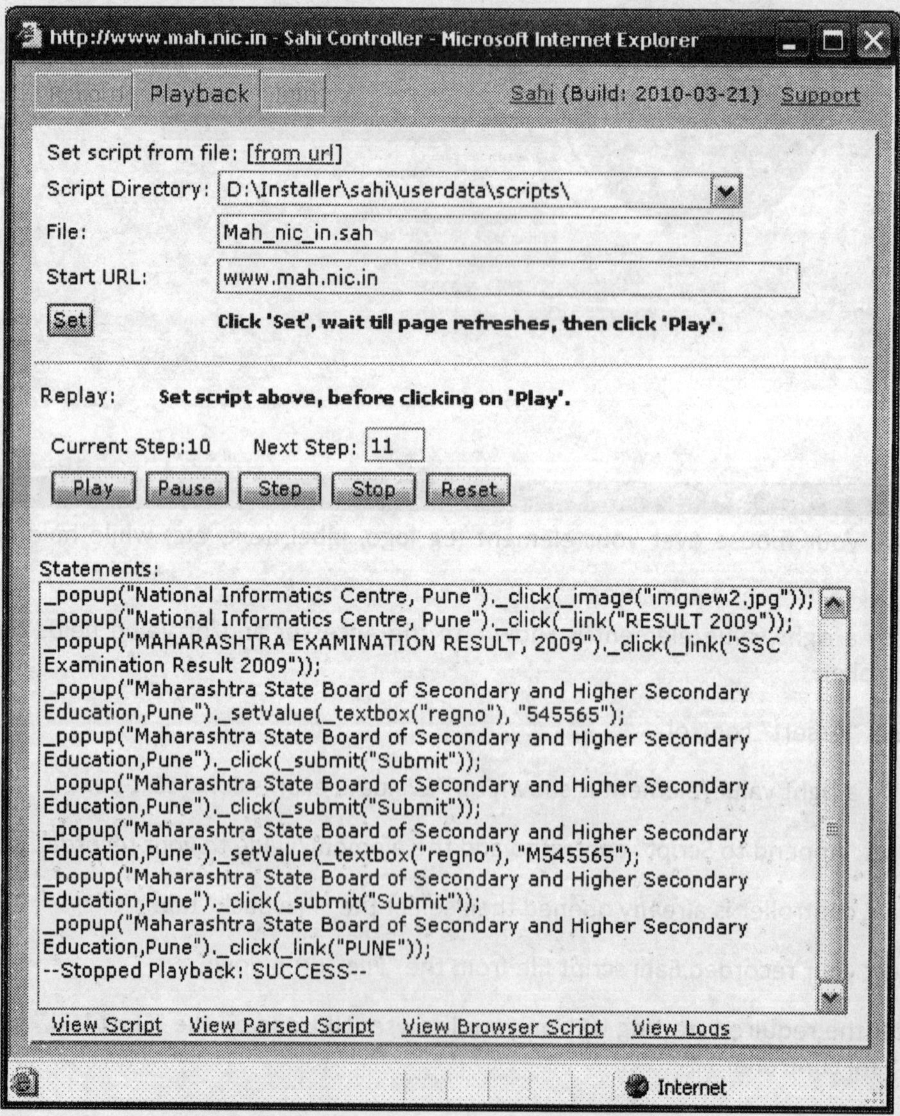

To view script

On the Controller, go to Playback tab and click on "View Script" link at the bottom right. It will open a window with the recorded script.

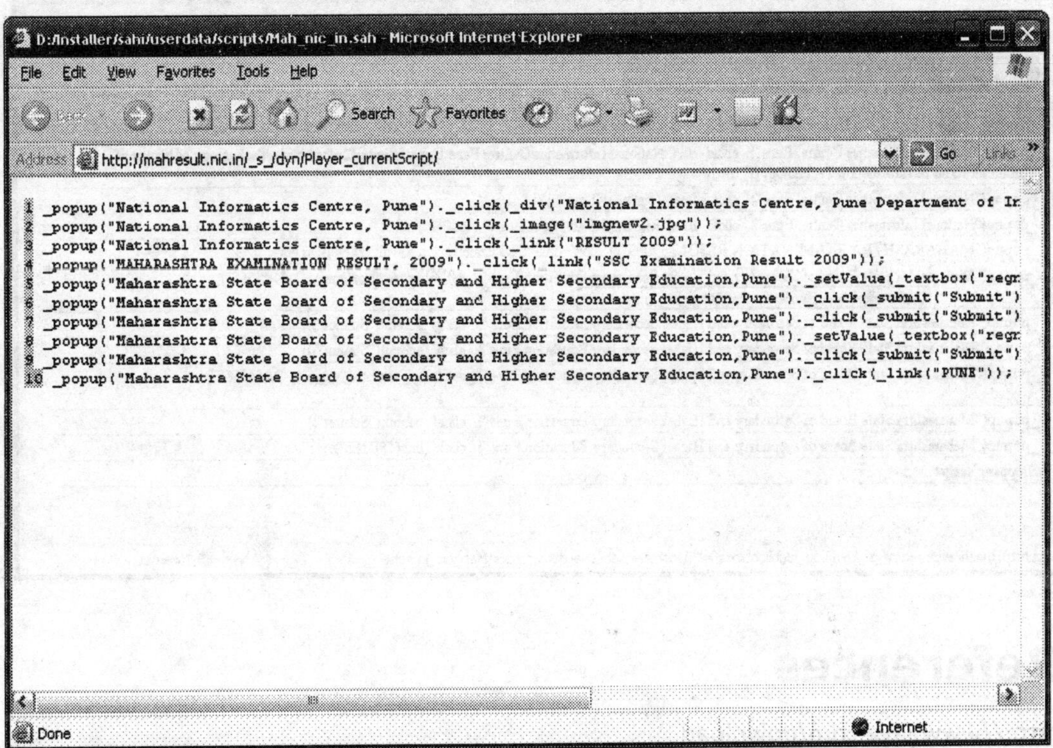

View Logs

On the Controller, go to Playback tab and click on "View Logs" link at the bottom right. It will open a window with the results neatly formatted in HTML.

Clicking on a line in the logs will drill down to exact line in script.

You can also view the logs at http://localhost:9999/logs

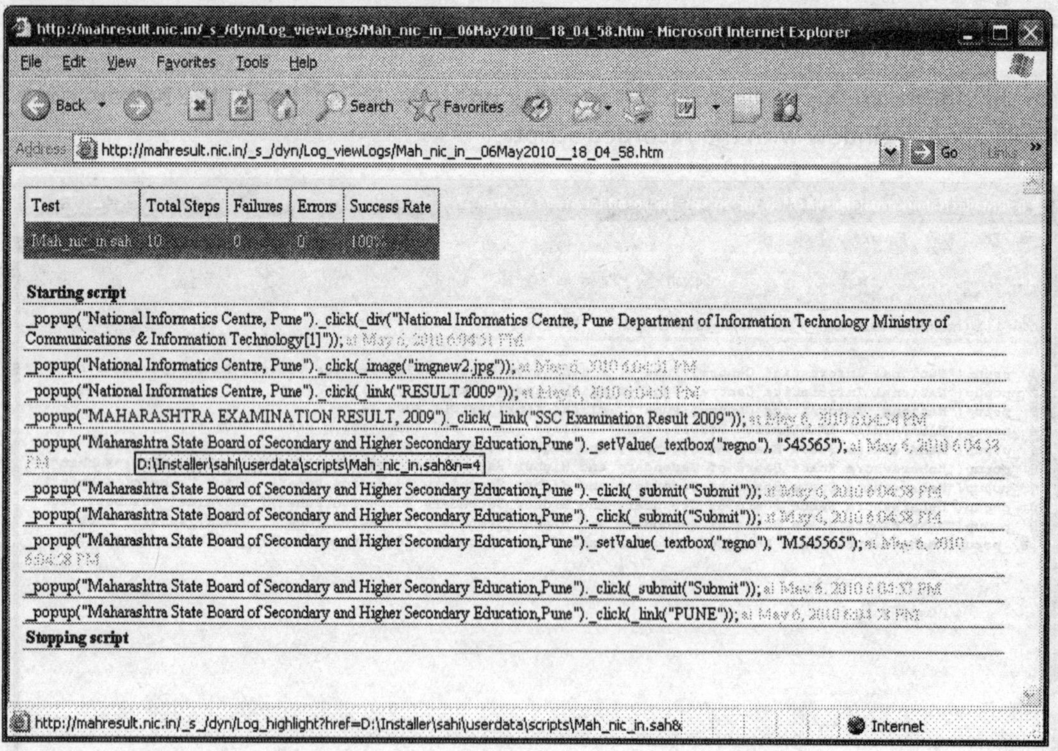

References

http://www.java.com/download

http://sourceforge.net/projects/sahi/files/

Download Sahi V3 (2010-03-21)

http://en.wikipedia.org/wiki/Sahi (Software)#Executing Sahi Scripts .\28Recor

Web Testing using WatiR tool

1. Introduction

"Watir" stands for **"Web Application Testing in Ruby".** Watir is an automated test tool which uses the Ruby scripting language to drive the Internet Explorer web browser using Microsoft's OLE (Object Linking and Embedding) interface. Watir provides a toolkit for automated tests to be developed and run against a web browser.

- A free, open-source functional testing tool for web applications.
- It is a Ruby library which drives Internet Explorer the same way people do, clicks links, fills in forms, and presses buttons.
- Watir also checks results, such as whether expected text appears on the page.
- Because it's build on Ruby, you have the power to connect to databases, read data files, export XML and structure your code into reusable libraries.

- WatirMarker recently was renamed WatirRecorder. It's easier to use, remaining useful for creating the framework of a testing script. WatirRecorder can't record all of what you do on your site, so many recorded scripts will require editing or further coding.
- WET Web Tester
- WET is a powertool for Watir. WET stands for Watir Extension Toolkit. Because the WET classes inherit from the Watir classes, WET provides all of the Watir
- Functionality plus additional features, including powerful pop-up handling mechanisms.

WatiN

- WatiN (pronounced What-in) is a similar tool as Watir for .NET. Tests can be written in C# (or any other .NET language like VB.NET, F# or IronPython) and are executed using Internet Explorer and Mozilla Firefox.

Watij

- Watij (pronounced "wattage") stands for Web Application Testing in Java. Watij is a pure Java API created to allow for the automation of web applications. Based on the simplicity of Watir and enhanced by the power of Java, Watij automates functional testing of web applications through a real browser. Currently Watij supports automating Internet Explorer on Windows only.

Why Use WATIR?

- Free
- Powerful
- Simple (easy to use and learn)
- Excellent Support
- It uses Ruby, a full-featured object-oriented scripting language, rather than a proprietary vendorscript.
- Don't just take our word for it, read what our users are saying.
- As a testing tool: It's as robust & sophisticated as 'professional' tools such as Rational, Mercury & Segue.
- As a library of a programming language [Ruby] : It's powerful.
- (You have the power to connect to databases, read data files, export XML, structure your code into reusable libraries, and pretty much anything else you can think of...)
- It has a supportive online community for when you get 'stuck'.

What Does Watir Work With?

Watir will drive web applications that are served up as HTML pages in a web browser. Watir will not work with ActiveX plugin components, Java Applets, Macromedia Flash, or other plugin applications. To determine whether Watir can be used to automate a part of a web application, right click on the object and see if the *View Source* menu option is available. If you can view the HTML source, that object can be automated using Watir.

How WATIR Drives Internet Explorer

How does Watir work?

- Uses the COM interface of Internet Explorer (IE)
    - a.k.a ActiveX or OLE
- Allows an external program to control IE
    - Similar interfaces exist for Word, Excel, PowerPoint and Outlook.
- Full access to the contents of an HTML page
- Provides different ways to access objects

Installation

Prerequisites

To use the tool, users should have a basic understanding of:

- HTML: this is a basic HTML tutorial.
- Programming: users should understand programming basics (ie. what a "for" loop is, etc.)
- Ruby: users do not need to know how to program in Ruby to use the tool, but it is recommended to learn some Ruby basics if they would like to write more powerful scripts.
- check out the Ruby Cheat Sheet document for more information

Download Pre-requisite software

Ruby-186-26

(http://rubyforge.org/projects/rubyinstaller/)

On Windows, the simplest way to install Ruby is to download the One Click Windows Installer. If you prefer, you can download and install a Windows version of Ruby from here.

OR

How to download RUBY

Go to browser and type this link http://rubyforge.org/projects/rubyinstaller/

Once Ruby is installed on your machine, you can run files with the ".rb" extension by clicking them or running them from the command line.

How to download WATIR

Watir - (http://rubyforge.org/frs/download.php/5677/watir-1.4.1.exe)

To download the latest fully tested release, go to the Project Home Page Under the **Latest File Releases** section, find the *Watir* Package, and click the **Download** link for that package.

On the files list page, scroll down to the **watir** section. Click on the latest release ex. watir-v "n">.zip, (where "n" is the version number). The file will be downloaded on to your machine. Unzip it into a temprorary directory, and then run the installer.

Step 1 - Install Ruby

Save The File

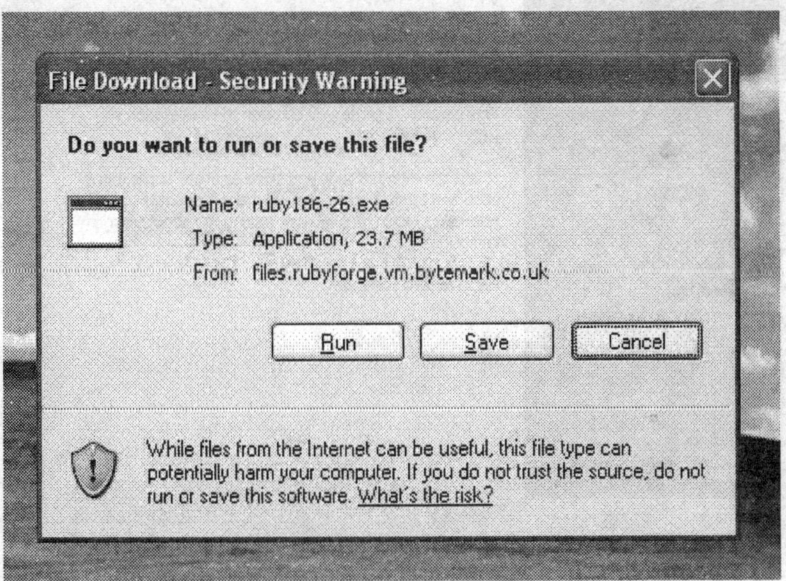

Click on Run for Ruby Installer

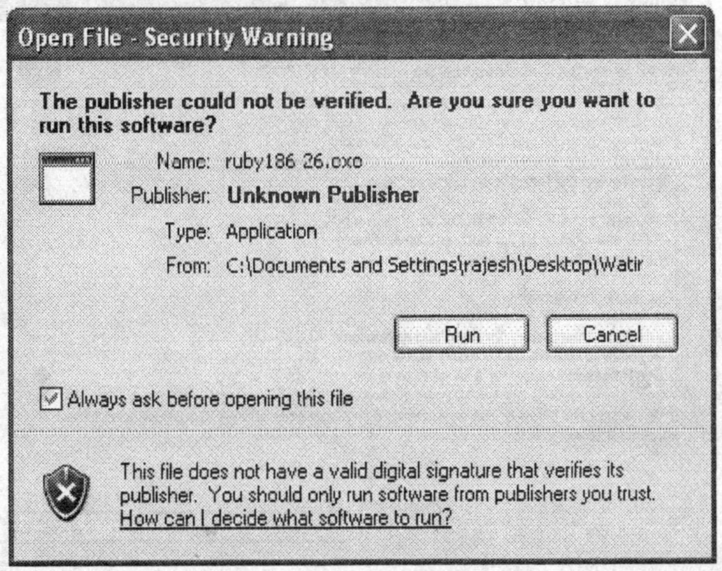

Click next

Accept the term

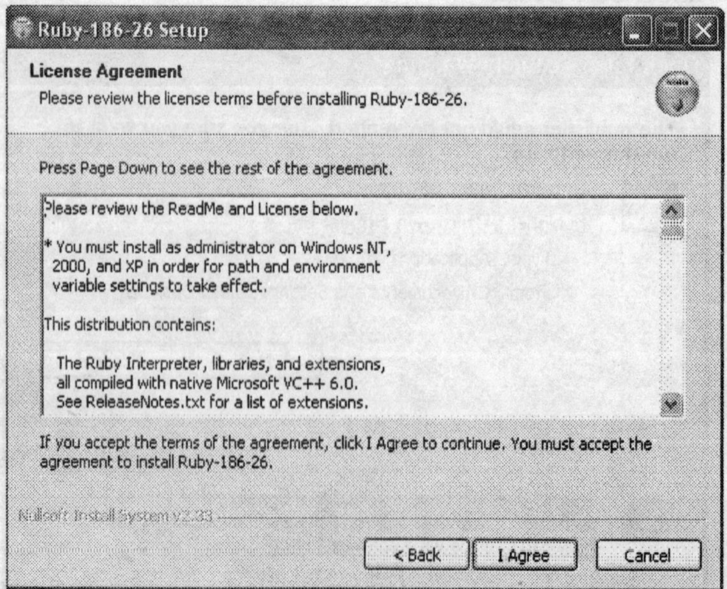

Click to next

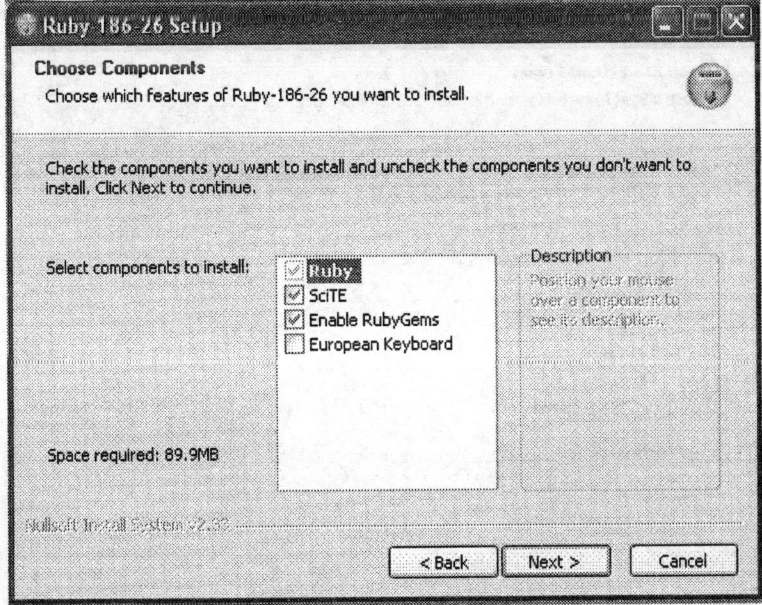

Choose Install Location & Click on Next

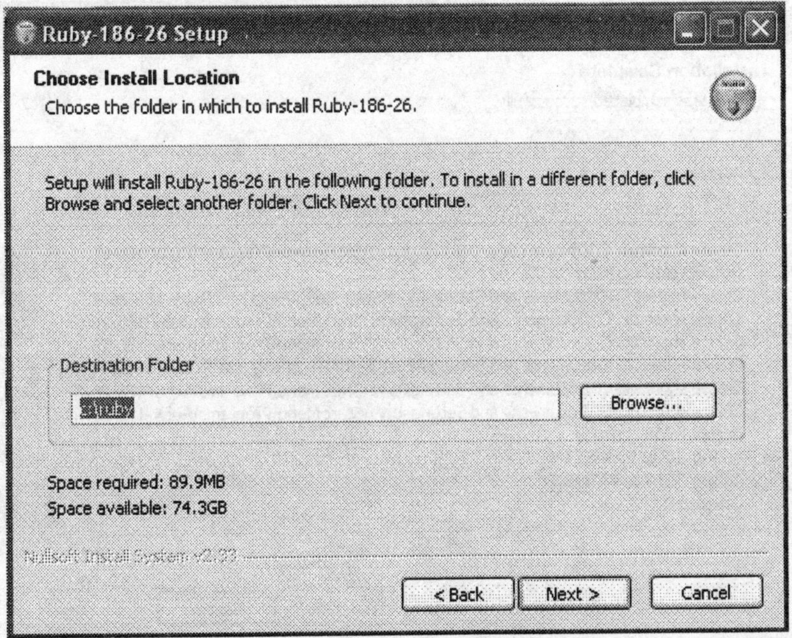

Choose Start Menu Folder & Click on Install

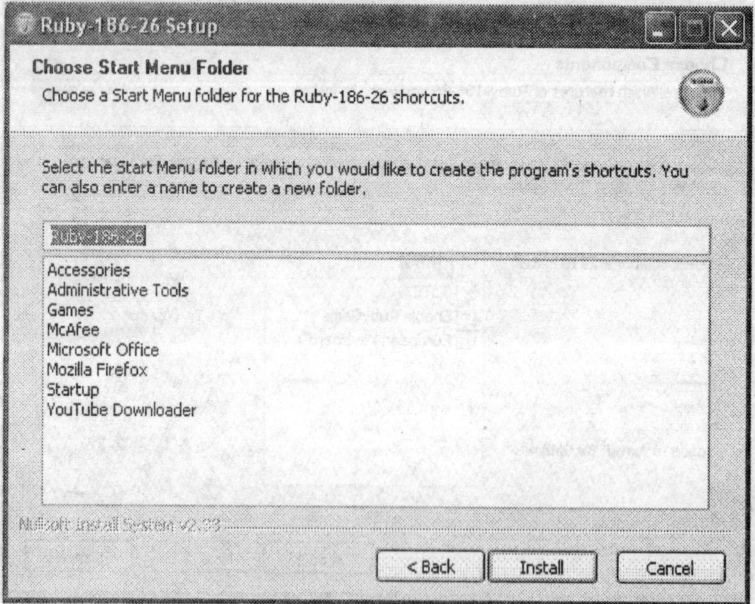

Installation Complete & Click on Next

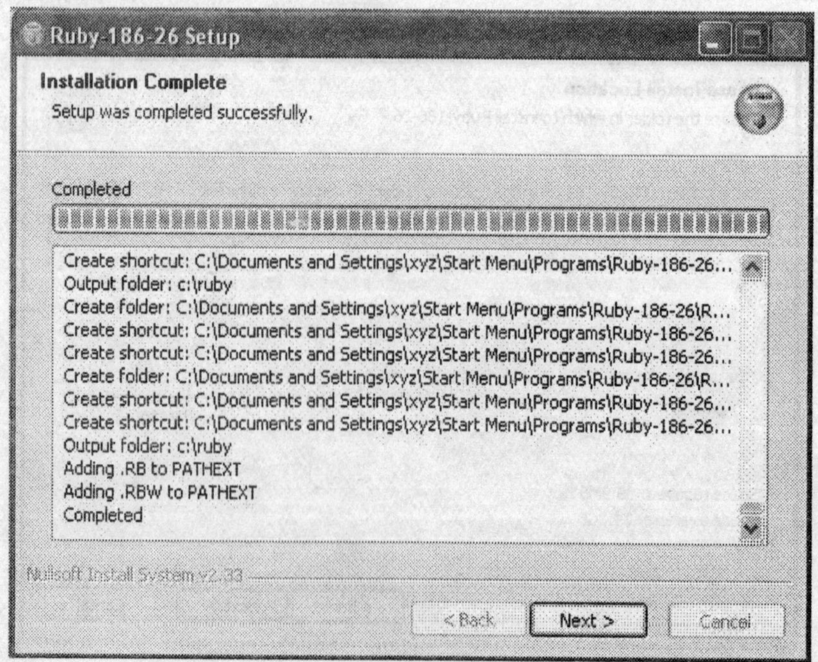

Ruby Installation on Computer & Click on Finish

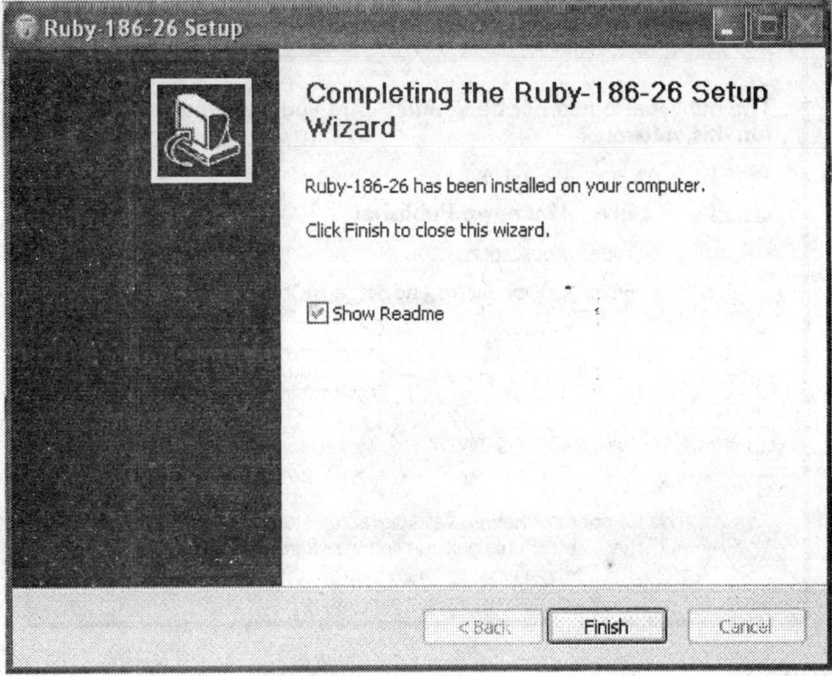

Step 2 - Install Water

1) Save the File

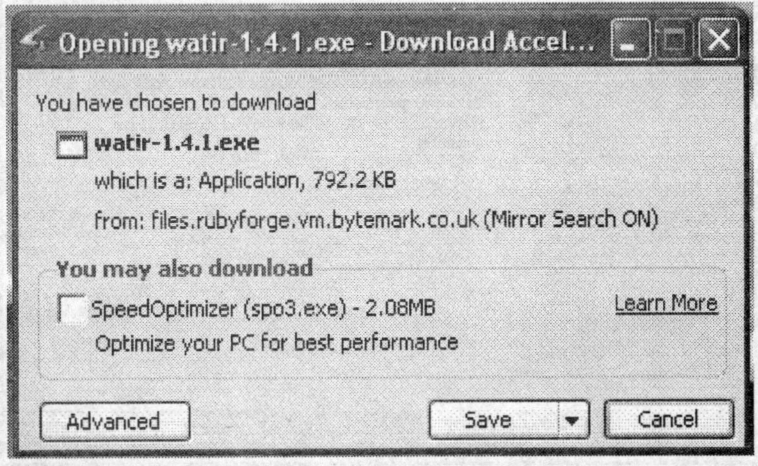

2) Click on Run for Ruby Installer

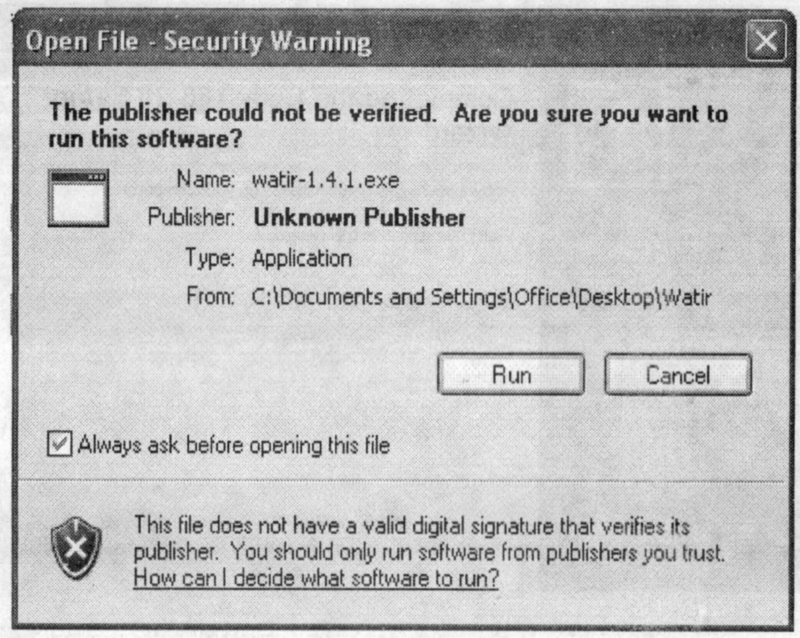

3) Click next

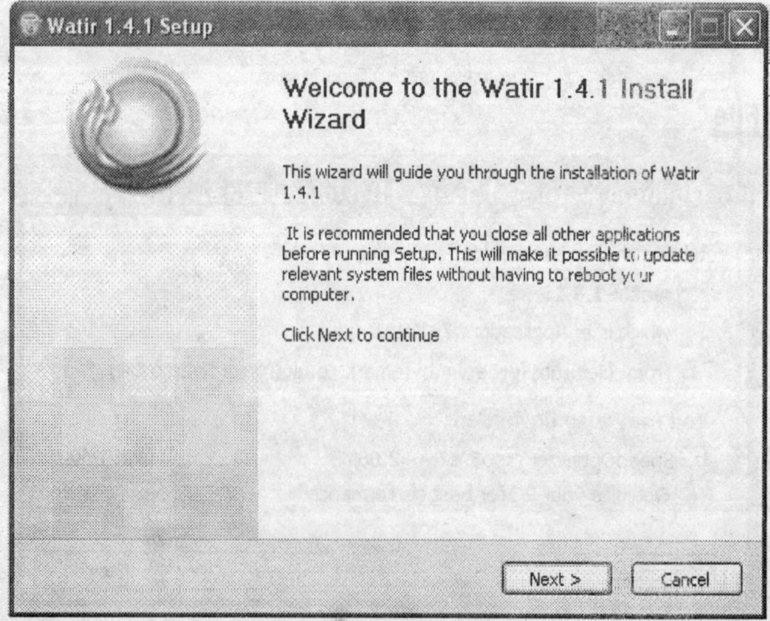

4) Accept the terms

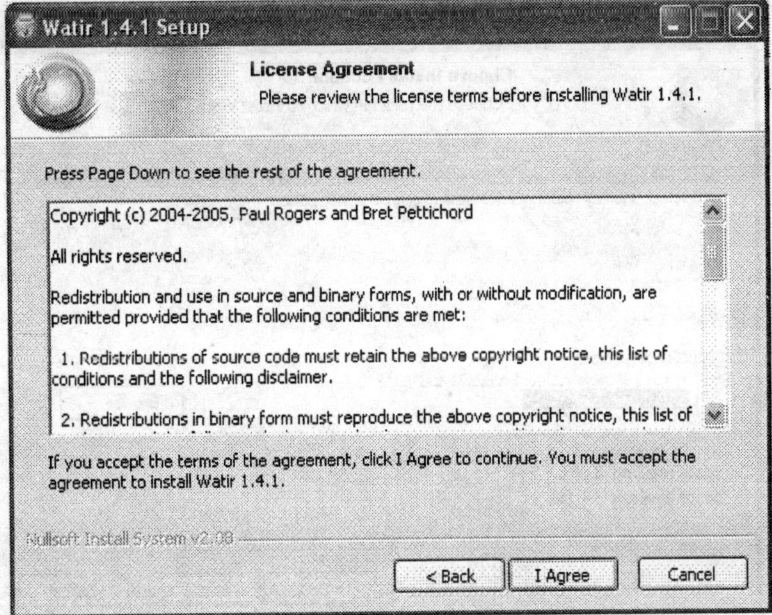

5) Click to next

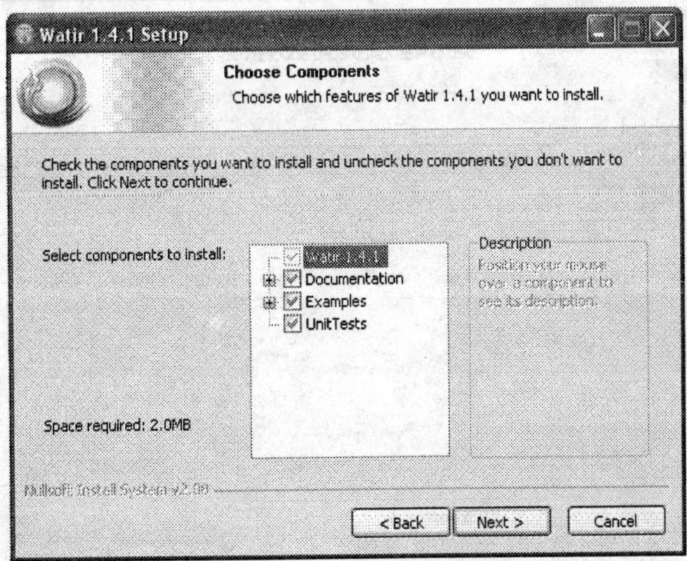

6) Choose Install Location & Click on Next

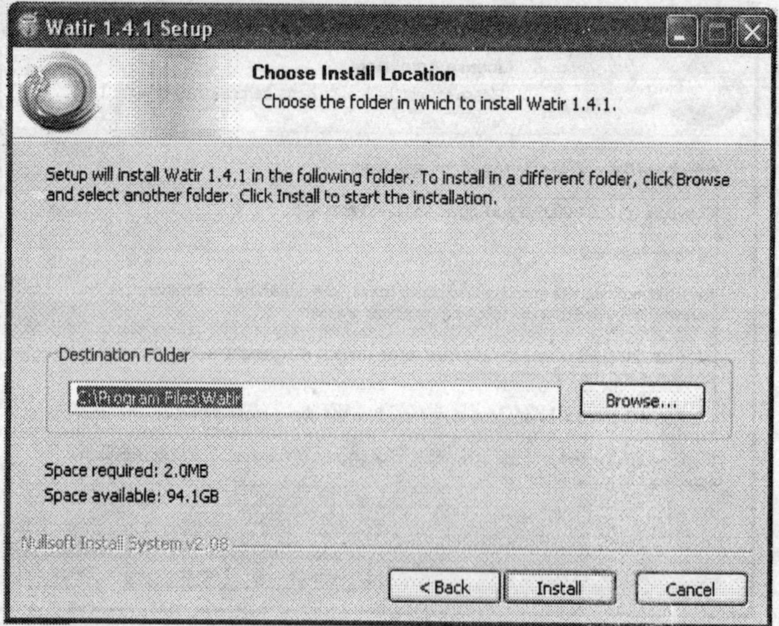

7) Click on Close

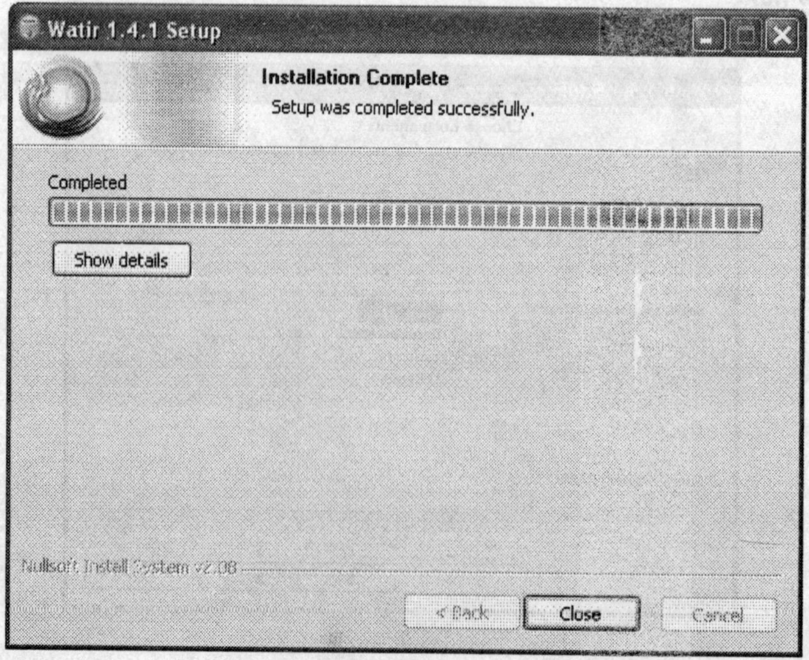

Using Ruby's Interactive Command Interpreter (IRB)

What is it?

- Irb = Interactive Ruby
- It evaluates Ruby expressions from the terminal

Use it to:

- Attach to IE windows and quickly identify browser objects
- -Run quick experiments to see if things will work in your tests

How to Use Watir

Watir Syntax

The Watir syntax is shown below with three views. One is the view that we see objects on a web page while viewing them in a web browser. The next view is an example of the Watir code that would be needed to automate an action using that web page object. The third view is the object on the web page shown in its HTML form. This is the way it looks when we view the source of a web page, or open the file in a text editor.

Include the Watir Tool

To use the Watir tool, first enter the following in your test script:

require 'watir'

This allows our test script to use the Watir tool.

Create a Test Instance of Internet Explorer

To create a test instance of Internet Explorer, enter the following in your test script:

$ie = IE.new

Watir sends a message to Internet Explorer, telling to create a new instance of itself, and assigns that instance to "$ie".

Site Navigation

To direct your test script to the web application you are testing, enter the URL in this command:

$ie.goto("http://mytestsite")

In the example above, enter in your application's URL in place of *mytestsite*.

Watir sends the goto message to Internet Explorer, telling it to enter the address you entered as a method argument in the Address bar, and to direct the browser to that site.

Manipulating Web Page Objects

These examples will demonstrate how to use Watir to interact with objects on the page.

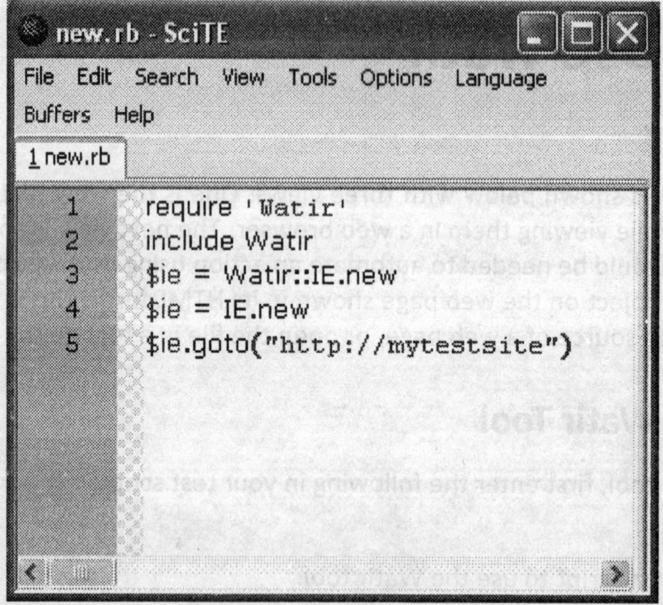

Examples

Eg.1.: www.google.com

Now open the windows shell (`cmd.exe`), and type '`irb`' to launch the interactive ruby shell.

```
C:\>irb <-- start the interactive ruby shell, 'irb'
irb(main):001:0> require 'watir' <-- tell irb you'll be using the 'watir'
library
=> true
irb(main):002:0> ie = Watir::IE.new <-- open an IE browser, in a var called
'ie'
=> #<Watir::IE:0x2bad438 @url_list=[], @typingspeed=0.08, @form=nil,
@ie=#<WIN32
OLE:0x2bad3d8>, @logger=#<Watir::DefaultLogger:0x2bad378 @progname=nil,
@logdev=
#<Logger::LogDevice:0x2bad318 @filename=nil, @dev=#<IO:0x27ce7d0>,
@shift_size=n
il, @shift_age=nil>, @level=2, @datetime_format="%d-%b-%Y %H:%M:%S">,
@error_che
ckers=[#<Proc:0x029198e8@./watir.rb:1135>], @defaultSleepTime=0.1,
@activeObject
HighLightColor="yellow", @enable_spinner=false>
irb(main):003:0> ie.goto("http://google.com") <-- tell 'ie' to browse to
google
=> 2.797
irb(main):004:0> ie.text_field(:name, "q").set("Yukihiro Matsumoto")

                 ^^^^-- put the text 'Yukihiro Matsumoto' in the textbox named
'q'
=> true
irb(main):005:0> ie.button(:name, "btnG").click <-- click the button called
'btnG'
=> nil
irb(main):006:0>
```

Alternatively, you can type below commands into notepad and then save the file with a '`.rb`' extension.

require 'watir'

include Watir

ie = Watir::IE.new

ie.goto("http://google.com")

ie.text_field(:name, "q").set("Yukihiro Matsumoto")

ie.button(:name, "btnG").click

Look at the source code of the examples and compare it to the web application that it tests

Right click on the Ruby test file and select *Edit* to view its source code in the SciTE editor.

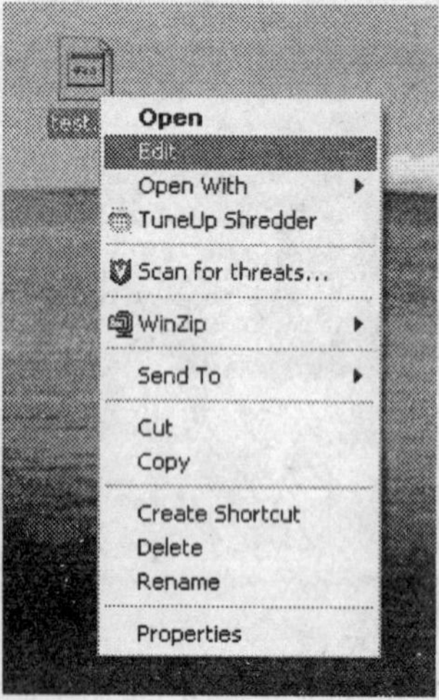

Now Select Tool Button & Click on Go or Press F5

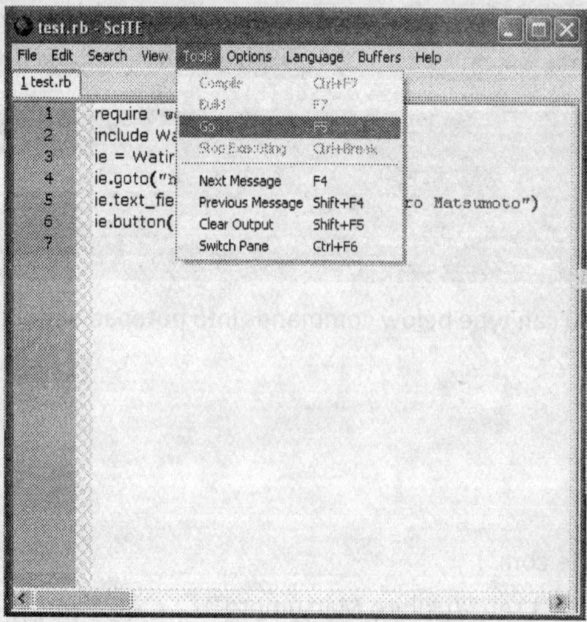

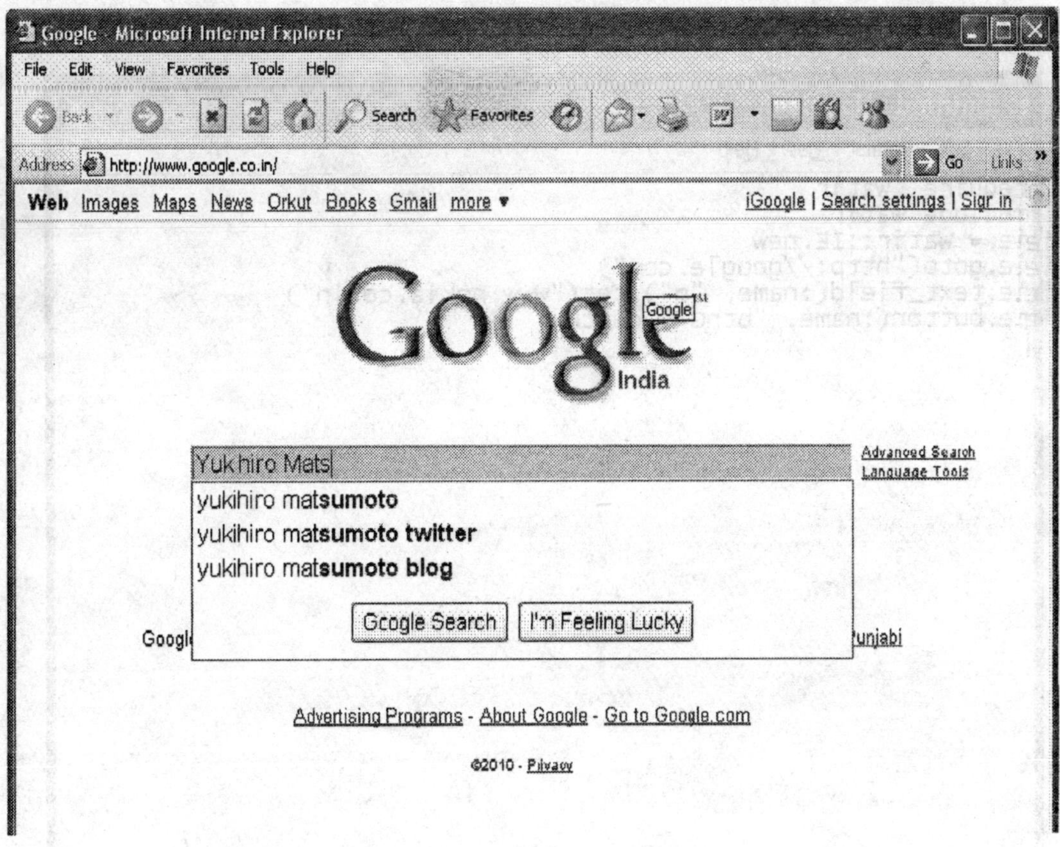
Google - Microsoft Internet Explorer
File Edit View Favorites Tools Help
Back Search Favorites
Address http://www.google.co.in/ Go Links
Web Images Maps News Orkut Books Gmail more
iGoogle | Search settings | Sign in
Google
India
Yukhiro Mats
Advanced Search
Language Tools
yukihiro matsumoto
yukihiro matsumoto twitter
yukihiro matsumoto blog
Google Search I'm Feeling Lucky
Punjabi
Advertising Programs - About Google - Go to Google.com
©2010 - Privacy

Eg.2 www.nokia.co.in

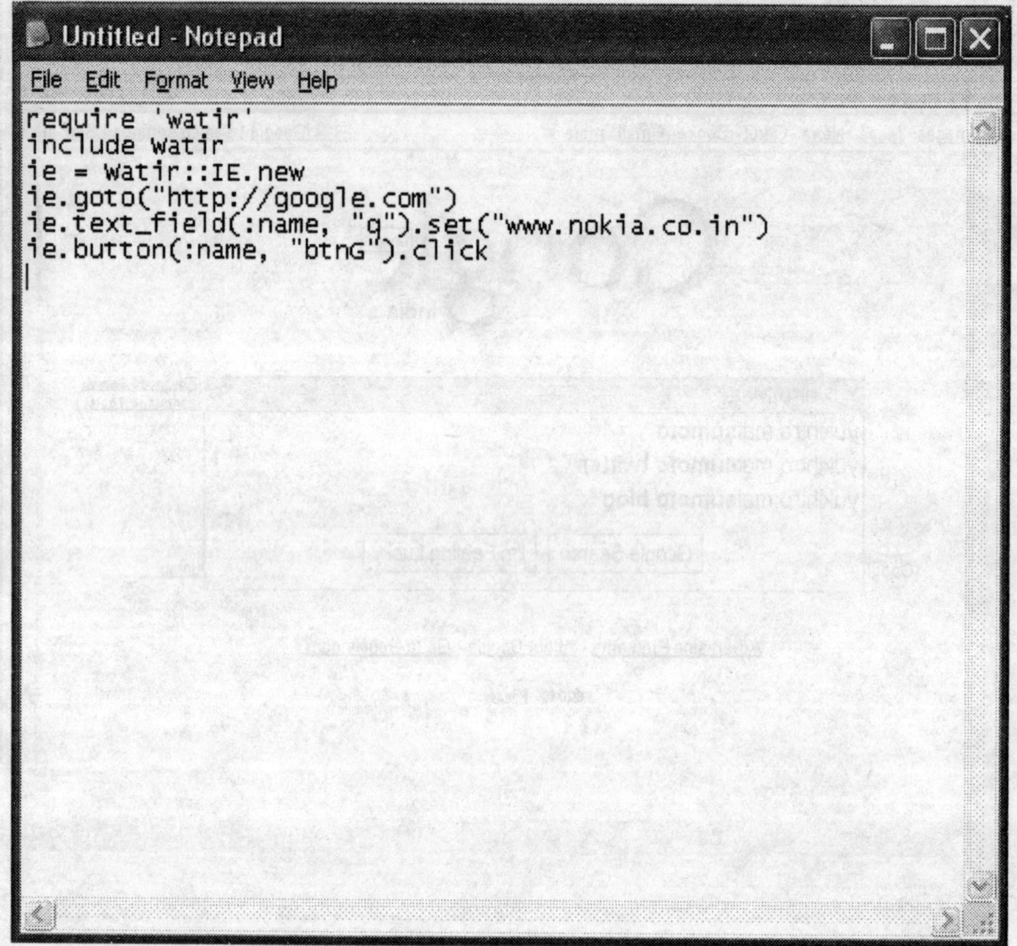

Save the file with a '.rb' extension

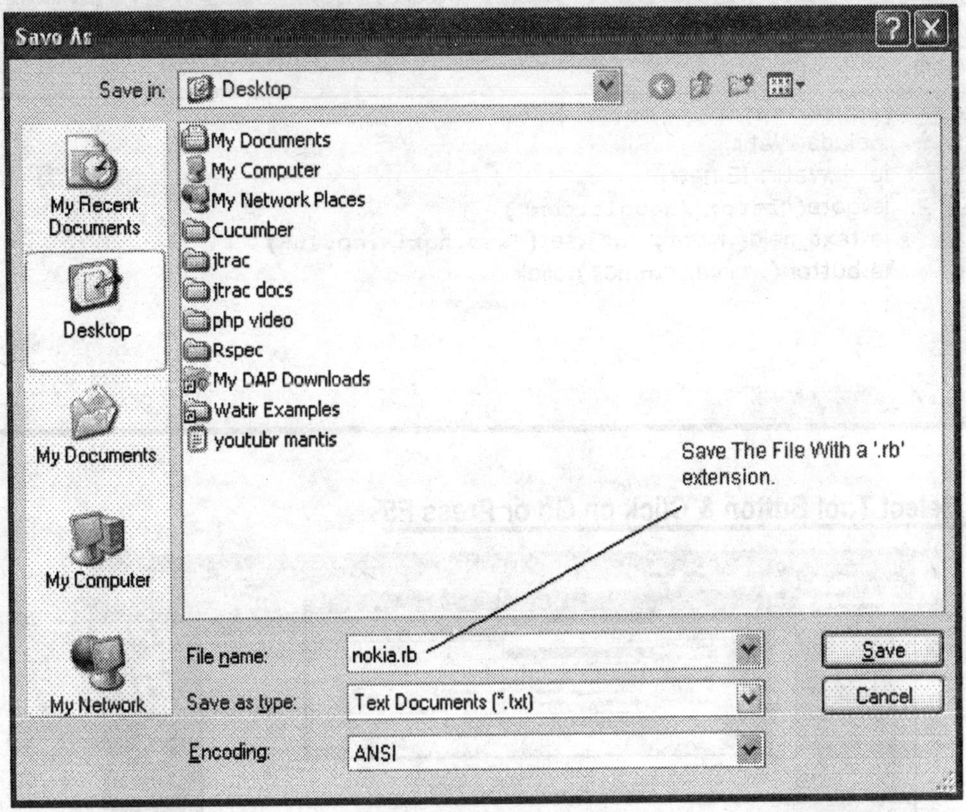

Right click on the Ruby test file and select Edit to view its source code in the SciTE editor.

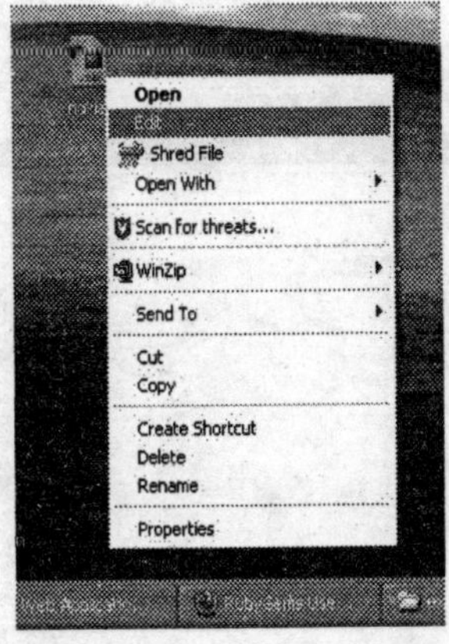

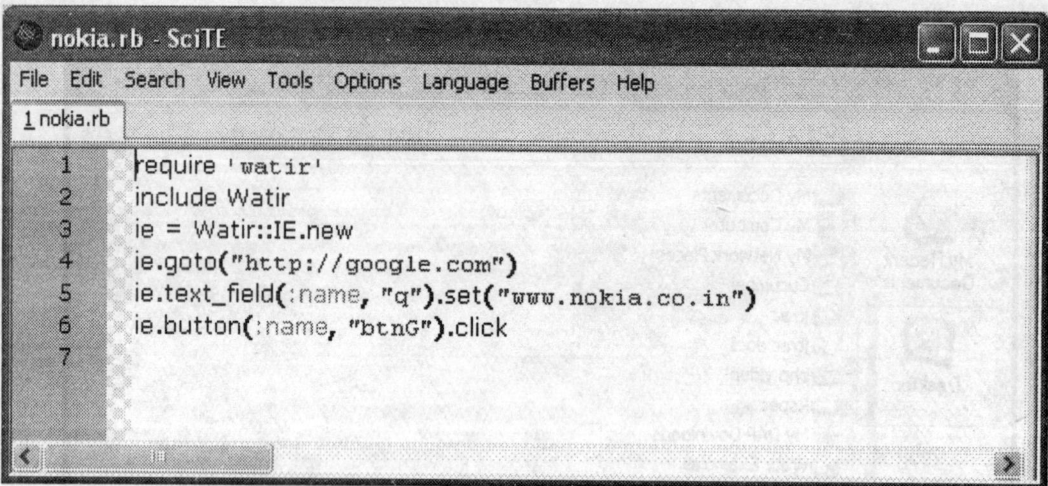

Now Select Tool Button & Click on Go or Press F5

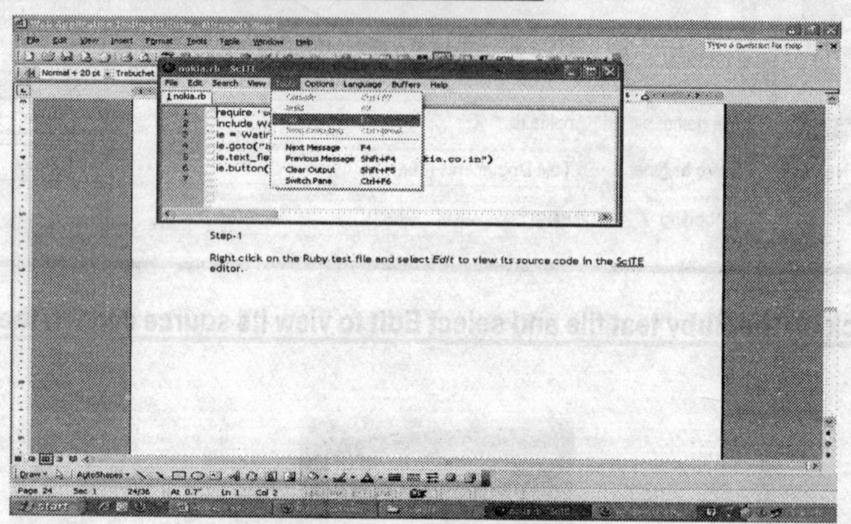

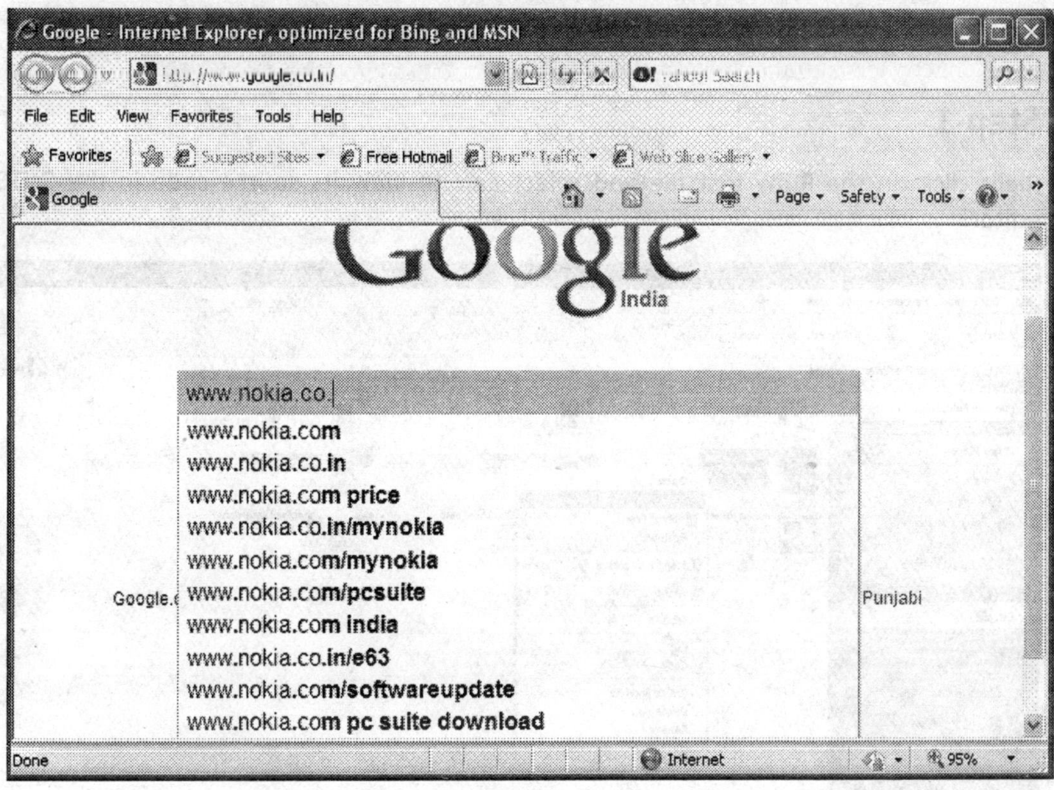
Google - Internet Explorer, optimized for Bing and MSN
File Edit View Favorites Tools Help
Favorites
Free Hotmail
Google
Page Safety Tools
Google
India
www.nokia.co.
www.nokia.com
www.nokia.co.in
www.nokia.com price
www.nokia.co.in/mynokia
www.nokia.com/mynokia
www.nokia.com/pcsuite
www.nokia.com india
www.nokia.co.in/e63
www.nokia.com/softwareupdate
www.nokia.com pc suite download
Punjabi
Done
Internet
95%

Eg.3.: Google map from Watir Example folder

Step-1

Right click on the Ruby test file and select *Edit* to view its source code in the SciTE editor.

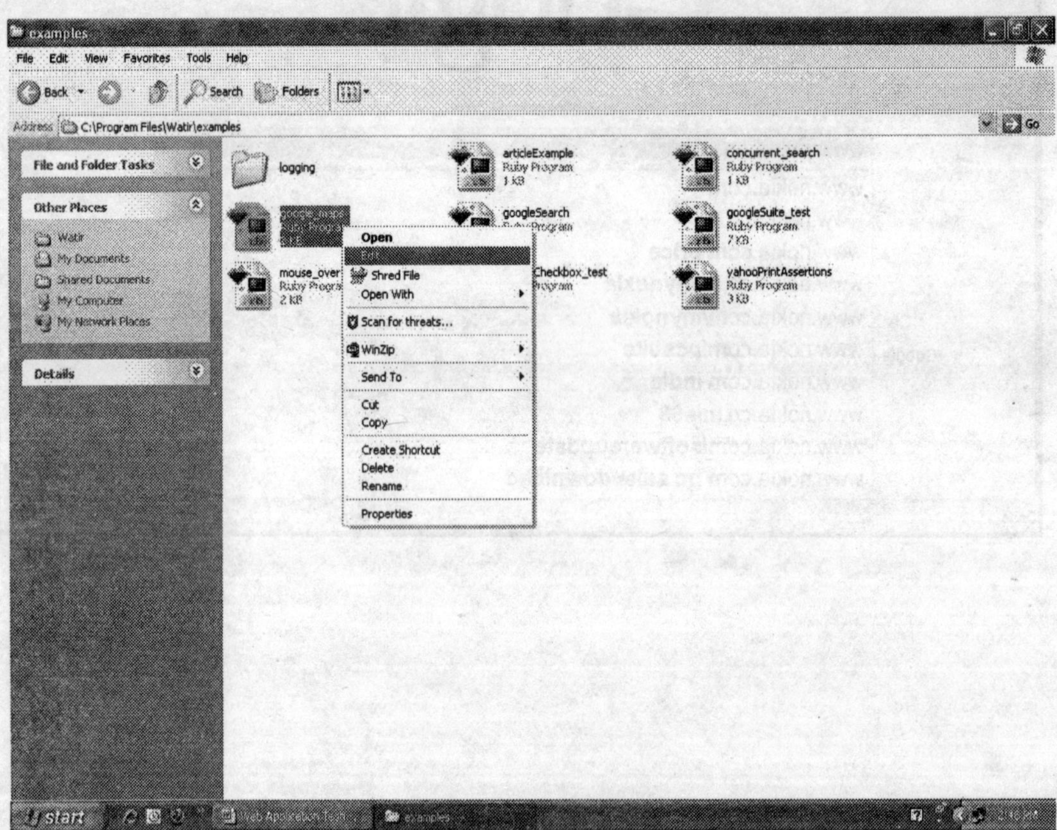

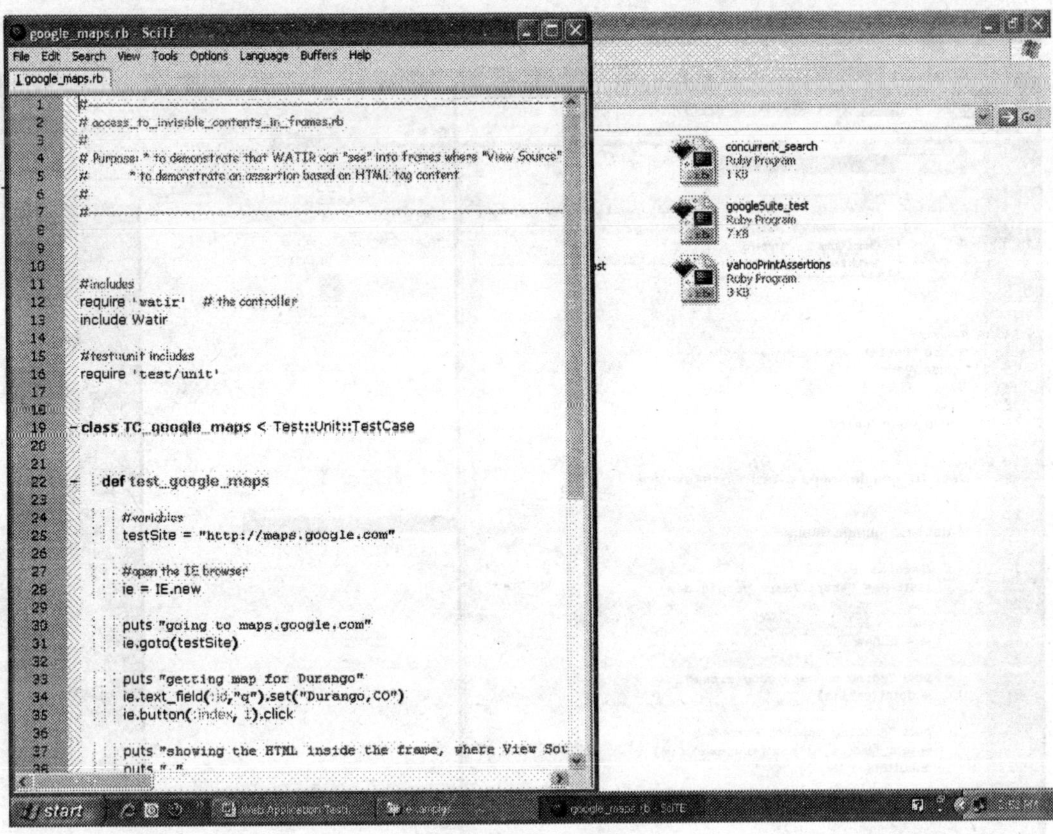

google_maps.rb - SciTE
File Edit Search View Tools Options Language Buffers Help
#
access_to_invisible_contents_in_frames.rb
#
Purpose: * to demonstrate that WATIR can "see" into frames where "View Source"
* to demonstrate an assertion based on HTML tag content
#includes
require 'watir' # the controller
include Watir
#testunit includes
require 'test/unit'
class TC_google_maps < Test::Unit::TestCase
def test_google_maps
#variables
testSite = "http://maps.google.com"
#open the IE browser
ie = IE.new
puts "going to maps.google.com"
ie.goto(testSite)
puts "getting map for Durango"
ie.text_field(:id,"q").set("Durango,CO")
ie.button(:index, 1).click
puts "showing the HTML inside the frame, where View Sou
concurrent_search
Ruby Program
googleSuite_test
Ruby Program
yahooPrintAssertions
Ruby Program
start

Now Select Tool Button & Click on Go or Press F5

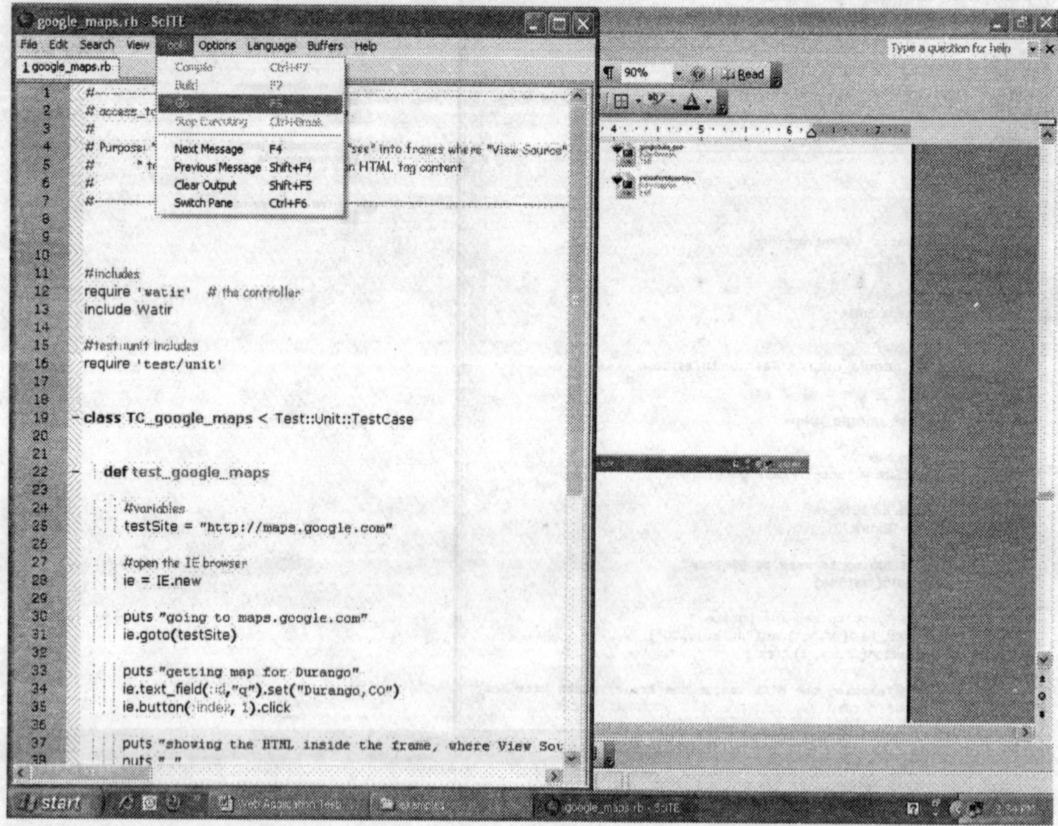

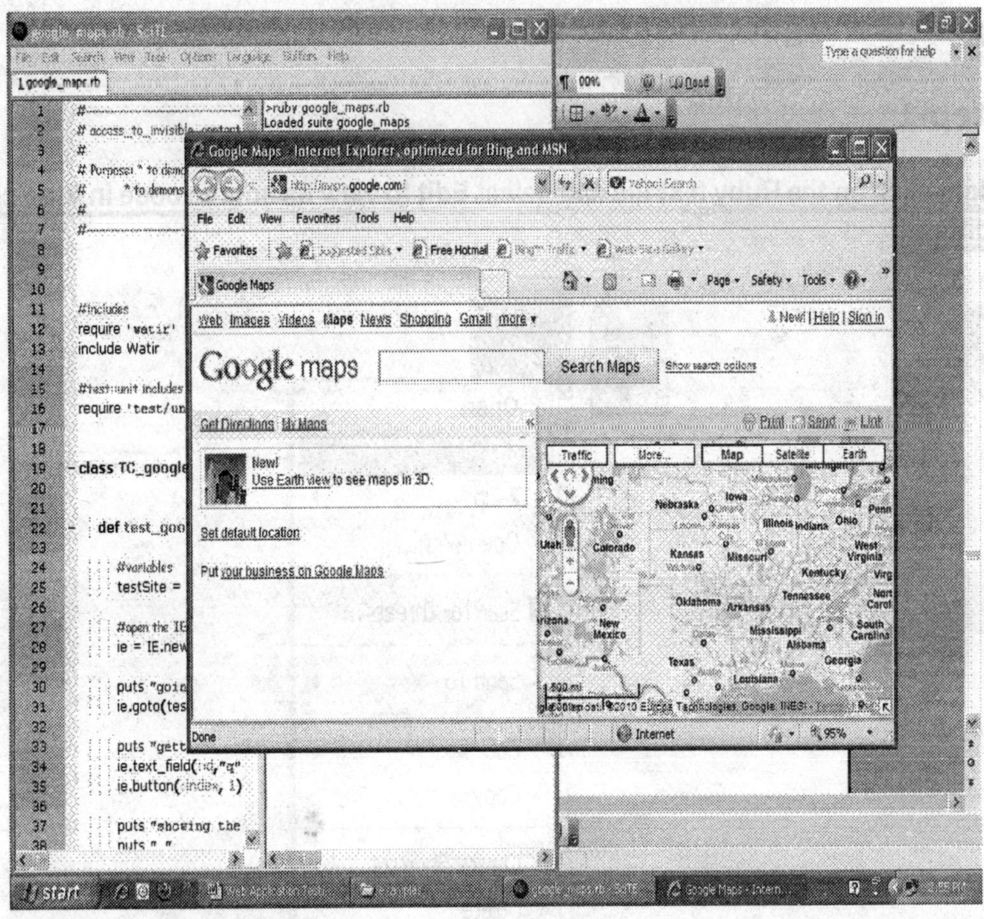

>ruby google_maps.rb
Loaded suite google_maps
Google Maps - Internet Explorer, optimized for Bing and MSN
File Edit View Favorites Tools Help
Favorites
Free Hotmail
Google Maps
Page Safety Tools
Web Images Videos Maps News Shopping Gmail more
New! | Help | Sign in
Google maps
Search Maps
Show search options
Get Directions My Maps
Print Send Link
Traffic More... Map Satellite Earth
New!
Use Earth view to see maps in 3D.
Set default location
Put your business on Google Maps
Done
Internet
95%
#includes
require 'watir'
include Watir
require 'test/un
class TC_google
def test_goo
#variables
testSite =
ie = IE.new
puts "goin
ie.goto(tes
puts "gett
ie.text_field(:id,"q"
ie.button(:index, 1)
puts "showing the
start

Eg.4.: www.guccishoes.com

Step-1

Right click on the Ruby test file and select Edit to view its source code in the SciTE editor

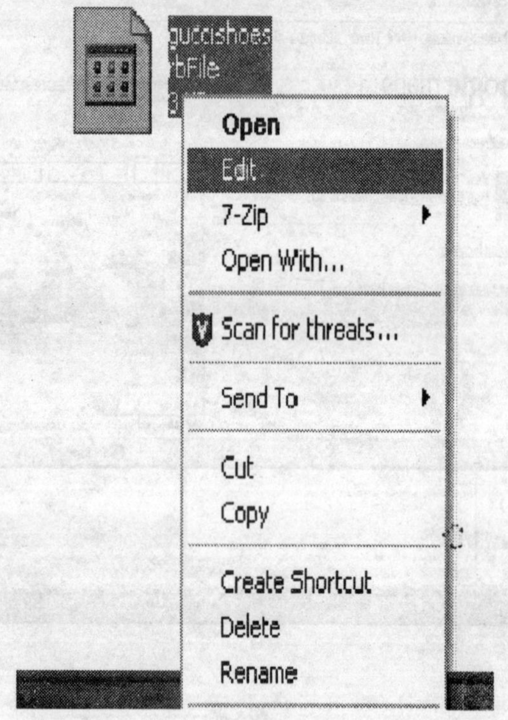

Now Select Tool Button & Click on Go or Press F5

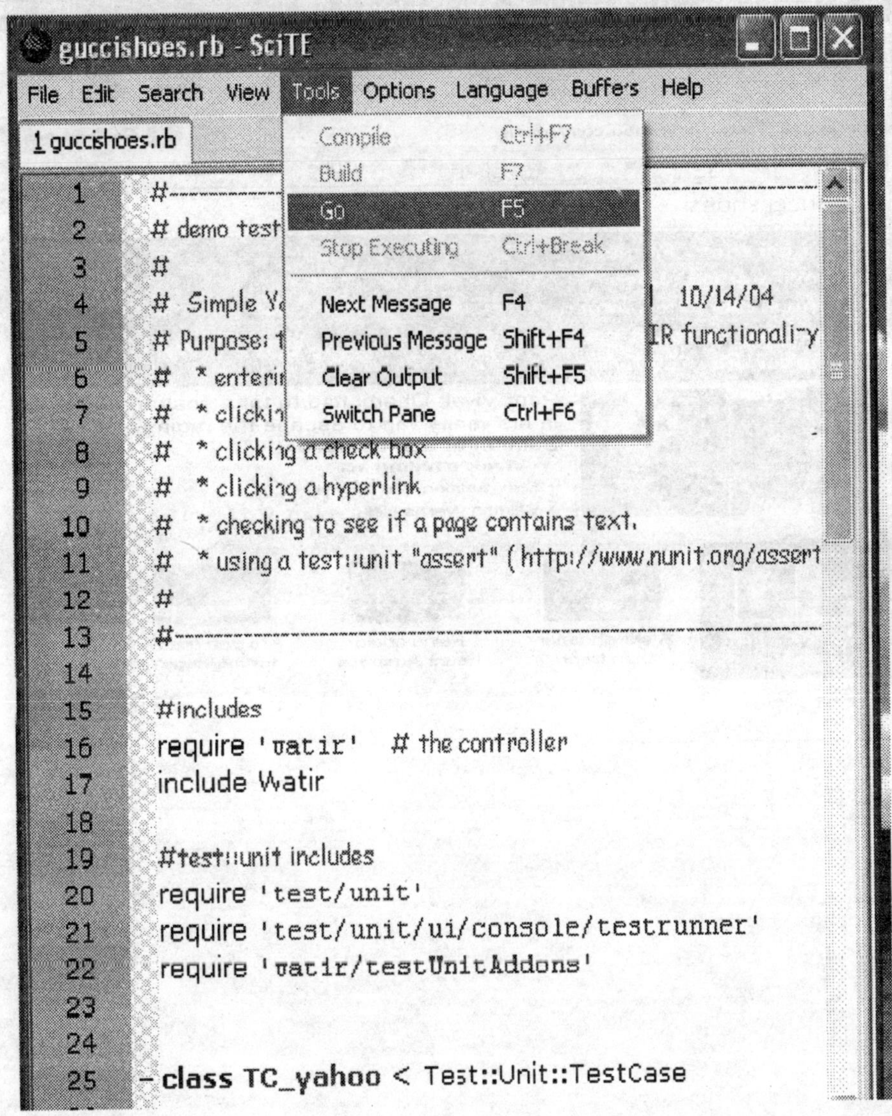

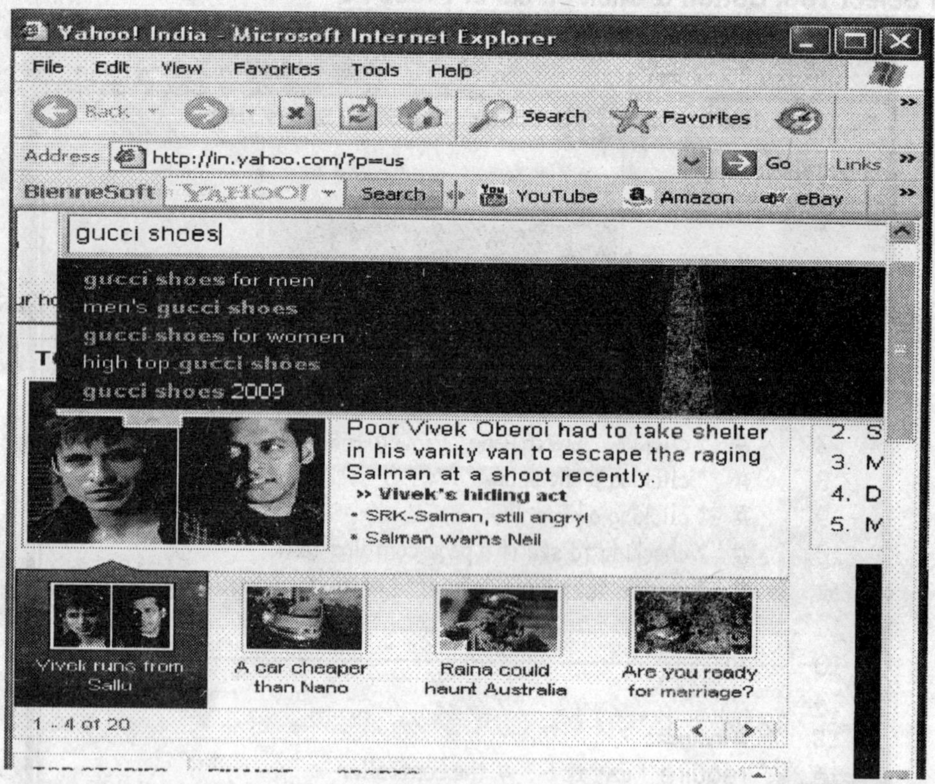
Yahoo! India - Microsoft Internet Explorer
File Edit View Favorites Tools Help
Back
Search
Favorites
Address http://in.yahoo.com/?p=us
Go
Links
BienneSoft
Search
YouTube
Amazon
eBay
gucci shoes
gucci shoes for men
men's gucci shoes
gucci shoes for women
high top gucci shoes
gucci shoes 2009
Poor Vivek Oberoi had to take shelter in his vanity van to escape the raging Salman at a shoot recently.
» Vivek's hiding act
• SRK-Salman, still angry!
• Salman warns Neil
Vivek runs from Sallu
A car cheaper than Nano
Raina could haunt Australia
Are you ready for marriage?
1 - 4 of 20

Eg.4. : www.gojiyo.com

Step-1

Right click on the Ruby test file and select Edit to view its source code in the SciTE editor

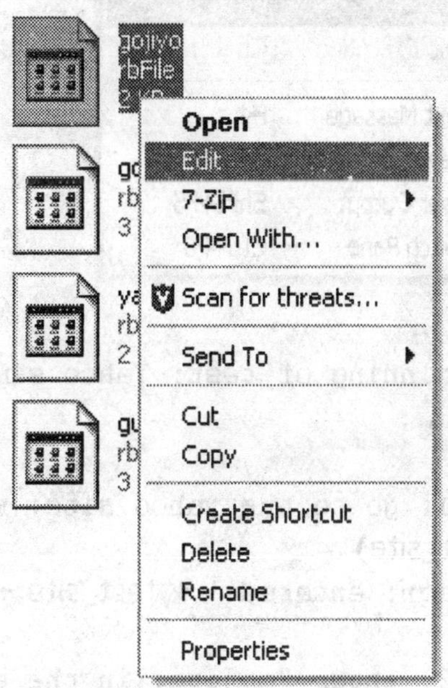

Now Select Tool Button & Click on Go or Press F5

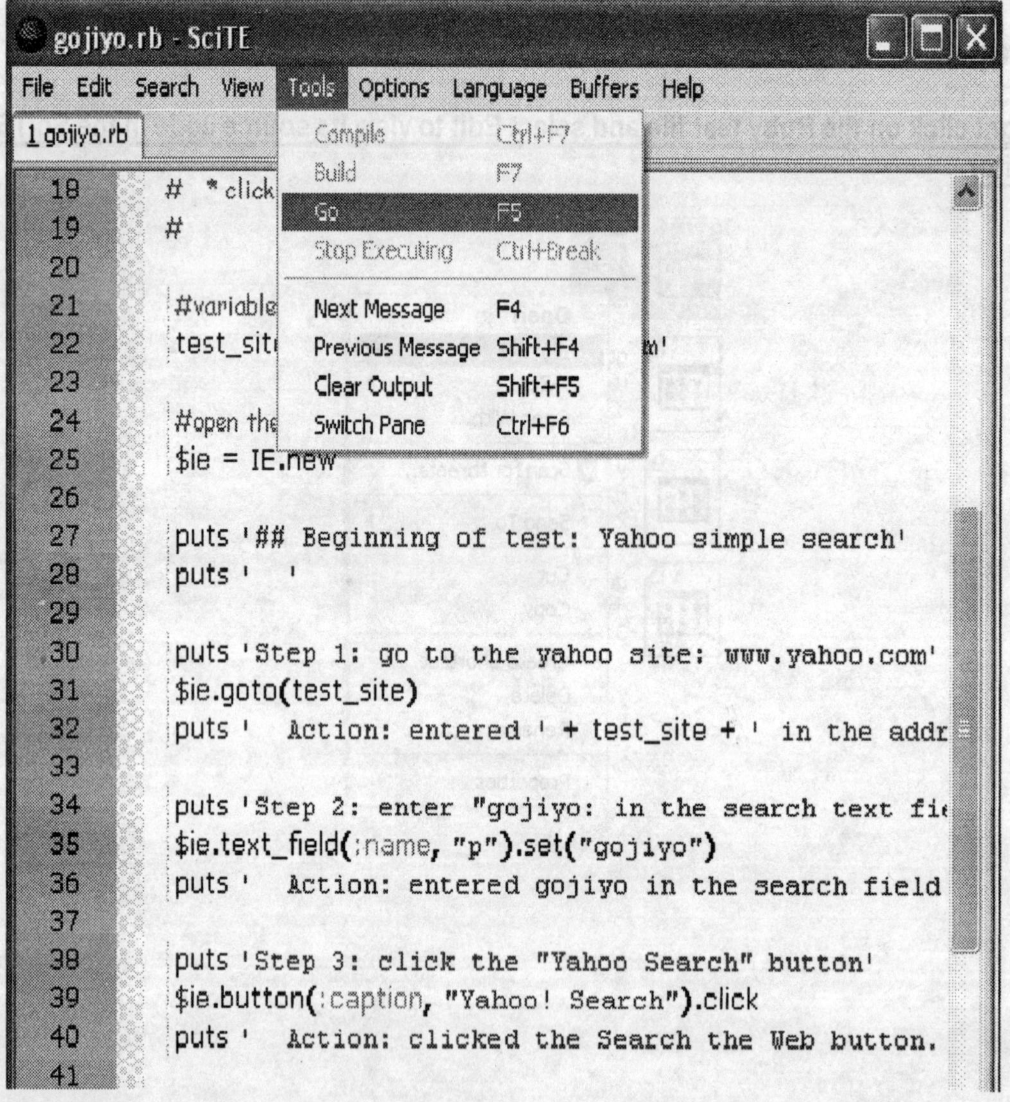

Navigating the Browser

 # Always Load the Watir library at the top of your script require 'watir'

#Start IE and navigate to a given URL

ie = Watir::IE.start('http://news.google.com')

#or..Attach to an existing IE window by title or url

ie = Watir::IE.attach(:title,'title')

ie = Watir::IE.attach(:url,/regex matching url/)

#Navigate to a different URL

ie.goto("http://mentorweb/")

#Close IE.

ie.close

Finding <HTML> Elements

TextBox	IE.text_field(***how, what***)
Button	IE.button(***how, what***)
DropDownList	IE.select_list(***how, what***)
CheckBox	IE.checkbox(***how, what***)
RadioButton	IE.radio(***how, what***)
HyperLink	IE.link(***how, what***)
Form	IE.form(***how, what***)
Frame	IE.frame(***how, what***)
And many, many more (div, label, image, etc...)...	

How's tell your method how to find the element you're looking for. What's tell your method the value for "how".

<u>**How's:**</u>

- :name
- :id
- :index
- :value
- :text
- :title

What's:

- String value of "how"
- /Regular expression/

Interacting with Elements

#Set the text field (or text area) specified name specified value.

ie.text_field(:name,'name').set('value')

#Sets the select with to the specified value

ie.select_list(:name,'name').select('value')

#Click the button with the specified value (label)

ie.button(:value,'value').click

#Clicks the link matching 'text'

ie.link(:text,'text').click

#Accessing elements in a "frame" or "iframe"

ie.frame(:name,"someFrame").text_field(:name,'name').set('value')

Checking Output

```
#Get the title of the page
ie.title
#Get all the text displayed on the page
ie.text
#Get all the HTML in the body of the page ie.html
#Return true if 'text' is displayed on the page
ie.contains_text('text')
```

Creating and using Methods

#Here is an example method for logging into a web application. Its two parameters are a user and password (both of which have defaults). It returns an instance of IE

```
def login(user="test_admin",password = "Password123")
    ie=Watir::IE.start('http://someURL.com/login')
    ie.text_field(:name,/user/i).set(user)
    ie.text_field(:name,/password/i).set(password)
    ie.button(:value,/login/i).click
    return ie
End
```

```
#Now we can easily login with the default user..
ie = login
#or with a unique user
ie = login("Fred","flinstone")
```

Creating Formal Test Cases

```
require 'test/unit'   #includes Ruby's test case functionality
Require 'util'        #Assuming our login method is saved in util.rb
#Test cases are contained within classes which extend Ruby's base test case class
class MyTest  < Test::Unit::TestCase
    def setup #Optional, will be run before each test method.
        @ie = login()  #call our login function.
    end

    def test_some_link #Test methods must begin with "test_"
        @ie.link(:text,"some_link").click    #click on some link

        #verify that the proper page loaded
        assert(@ie.contains_text("My Some Link Page"))
    end

    def teardown #Optional, will be run after each test method.
        @ie.close
    end
end
```

Debugging with IRB

- IRB = Interactive Ruby Shell
- Command line-like interface that allows immediate running of Ruby script
- Great for debugging one line at a time, rather then having to run through an entire script
- Great for testing single lines

Try ruby out using an online IRB. This is a great way to learn ruby basics!

Features

- Watir supports frames and also nested frames.
- Watir supports visible and invisible running of test cases.

- Watir supports links, options, radio buttons, tables, forms, button, select list, checkboxes, labels, pre, p, div and a lot more. When it does not support an element you can reach them via getObject method. Also most of these supports iterators.
- Watir supports send_keys method using (autoit com dll)
- Watir automatically waits for page to be loaded.
- Watir have helper methods to find interested object in page. Like show_forms,show_images,show_links
- Watir supports file uploads
- Watir supports saving images in a page.
- Watir supports hidden fields
- Watir supports pop-up dialogs, though this support is limited to very simple cases and does not support modal dialogs.
- Watir supports capturing of screens.

Some Helpful Tools:

Editors:

- Scite (A good light-weight editor installed with Ruby - ruby\scite\scite.exe)
- RDT (Eclipse plug-in for Ruby, great if you need a graphical debugger)

Tips for finding/accessing HTML elements:

- IE Developer Tool bar (Lets you explore the HTML elements behind the visible elements on a web page by clicking on the elements
- FireBlue (Excellent FireFox extension for identifying HTML elements while writing scripts.)
- WATIR: SuportsSubElements (Watir API for accessing html elements)

Reference

Ruby Link- (http://rubyforge.org/projects/rubyinstaller/)

Watir Link- (http://rubyforge.org/frs/download.php/5677/watir-1.4.1.exe)

Watir homepage: http://wtr.rubyforge.org

Watir User Guide: http://wiki.openqa.org/display/WTR/User+Guide

Scripting 101 Tutorial: http://wtr.rubyforge.org/s101/doc/

Watir

Watir main site: http://wiki.openga.org/display/WTR/

Watir user guide: wtr.rubyforge.org/watir_user_guide.html

Watir API: wtr.rubyforge.org/rdoc/index.html

Mailing List: rubyforge.org/mailman/listinfo/wtr-general

Project site: http://wiki.openqa.org/display/WTR/

User Contributions/examples: http:// wiki.openqa.org/display/WTR/Contributions

Watir FAQ: http://wiki.openqa.org/display/WTR/FAQ

Ruby

Ruby site: http://ruby-lang.org

Ruby docs: http://ruby-doc.org/

Ruby Quickstart: ruby-lang.org/en/documentation/quickstart/

Web Testing using WatiN tool

Introduction

WatiN Overview

Welcome at the WatiN *(pronounced as What-in)* **website**. Inspired by Watir development of WatiN started in December 2005 to make a similar kind of Web Application Testing possible for the .Net languages. Since then WatiN has grown into an easy to use, feature rich and stable framework. WatiN is developed in C# and aims to bring you an easy way to automate your tests with Internet Explorer and FireFox using .Net.

Installation Getting started with WatiN

This article explains some of the basics to get you up and running to automate your web applications with WatiN. A German version is also available here.

Index

Download and install WatiN.

1. Using WatiN from a console application.
2. Using IE Developer Toolbar with WatiN.

Download and install WatiN

http://sourceforge.net/projects/watin/files/

If you haven't already done this, you should download the latest release of WatiN. Alternatively you could get the latest source from the Subversion repository (using TortoiseSVN) and build it yourself. After you downloaded the version run the installer or Unzip the download in a directory. Lets assume you used the msi installer, then WatiN will be installed in c:\Program Files\WatiN\<version>-<.net version>

Using WatiN from a console application

Start your favourite .Net ide. In this example I will use Visual Studio 2003. Create a new console application named WatiNGettingStarted. Next, add a reference to WatiN.Core.dll by opening the Add Reference dialog and selecting the assembly from the WatiN installation directory.

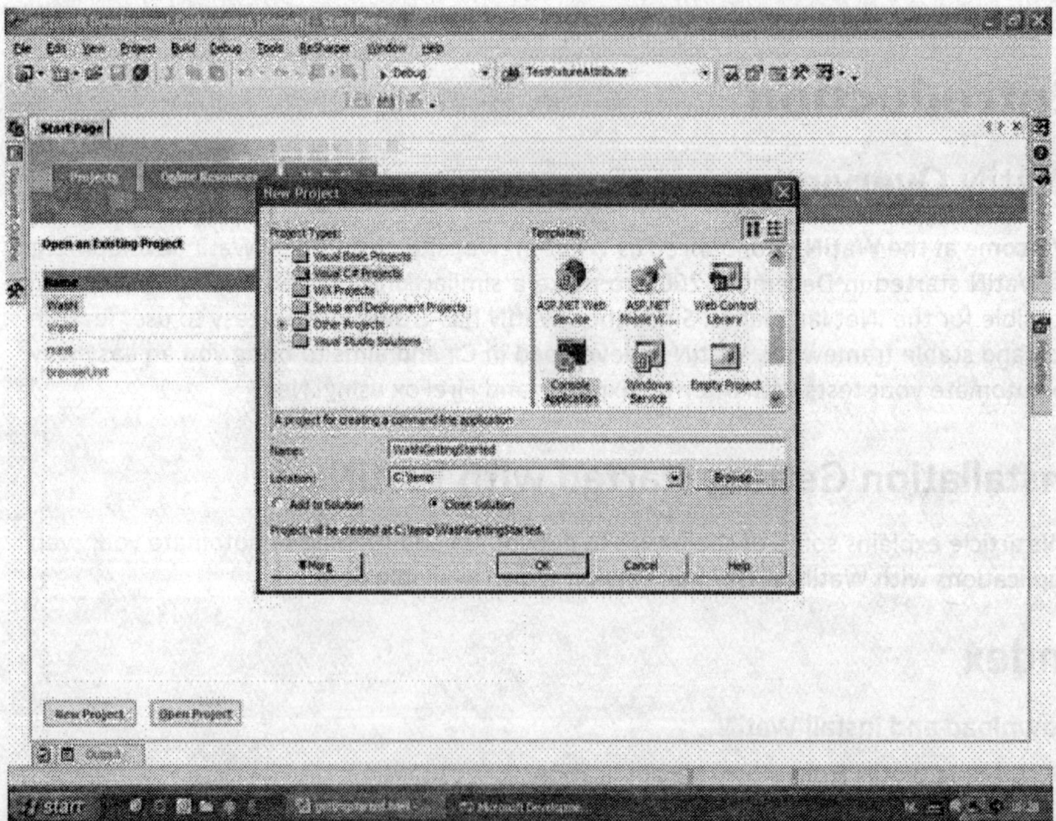

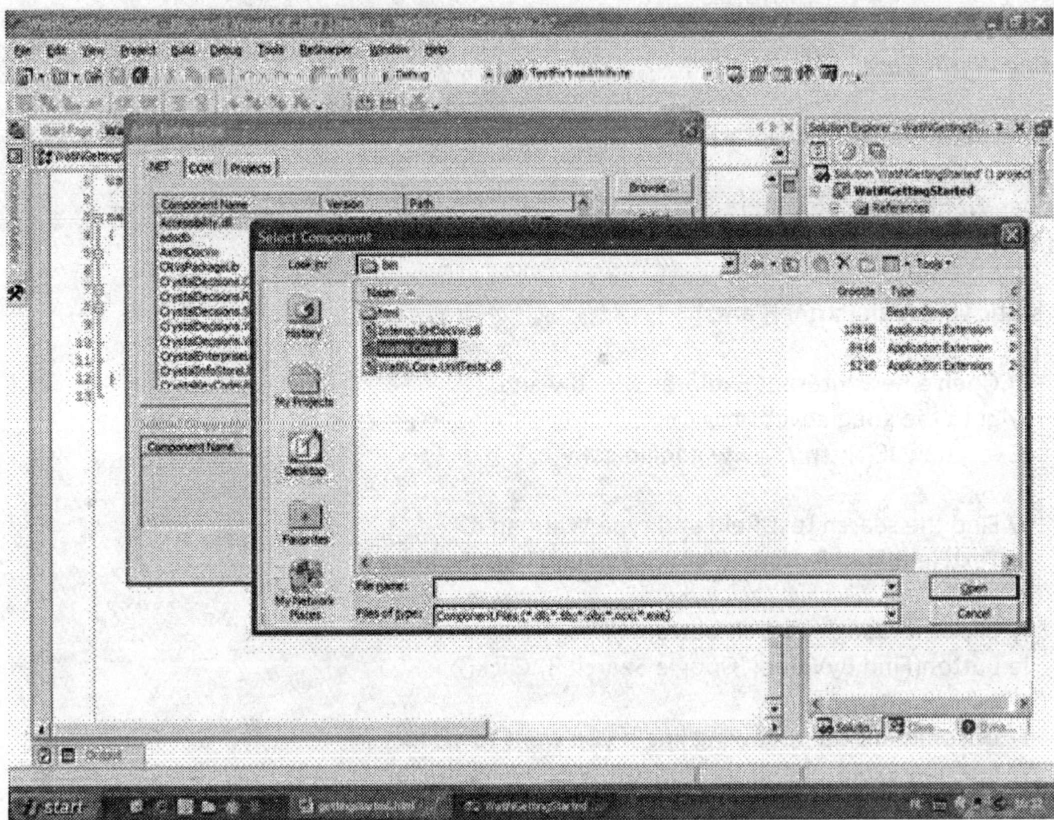

Rename the file Class1.cs to WatinConsoleExample.cs and replace the existing code with the following code. This code will:

1. Open a new Internet Explorer window and go to the Google.com website (it might be redirected to a localised version).

2. Type the text WatiN in the search text field which can be uniquely identified in the html code by the name q.

3. Click the search button which can be uniquely identified by the text Google Search (this is the value attribute of the html input element).

```
using System;
using WatiN.Core;

namespace WatiNGettingStarted
{
 class WatiNConsoleExample
 {
  [STAThread]
  static void Main(string[] args)
  {
   // Open a new Internet Explorer window and
   // goto the google website.
   IE ie = new IE("http://www.google.com");

   // Find the search text field and type Watin in it.
   ie.TextField(Find.ByName("q")).TypeText("WatiN");

   // Click the Google search button.
   ie.Button(Find.ByValue("Google Search")).Click();

   // Uncomment the following line if you want to close
   // Internet Explorer and the console window immediately.
   //ie.Close();
  }
 }
}
```

Build and start the project and see Internet Explorer go to the Google website, search for WatiN and finally show the results webpage.

Internet Explorer Developer Toolbar Installation

Step – 1 Click on "Next" Button

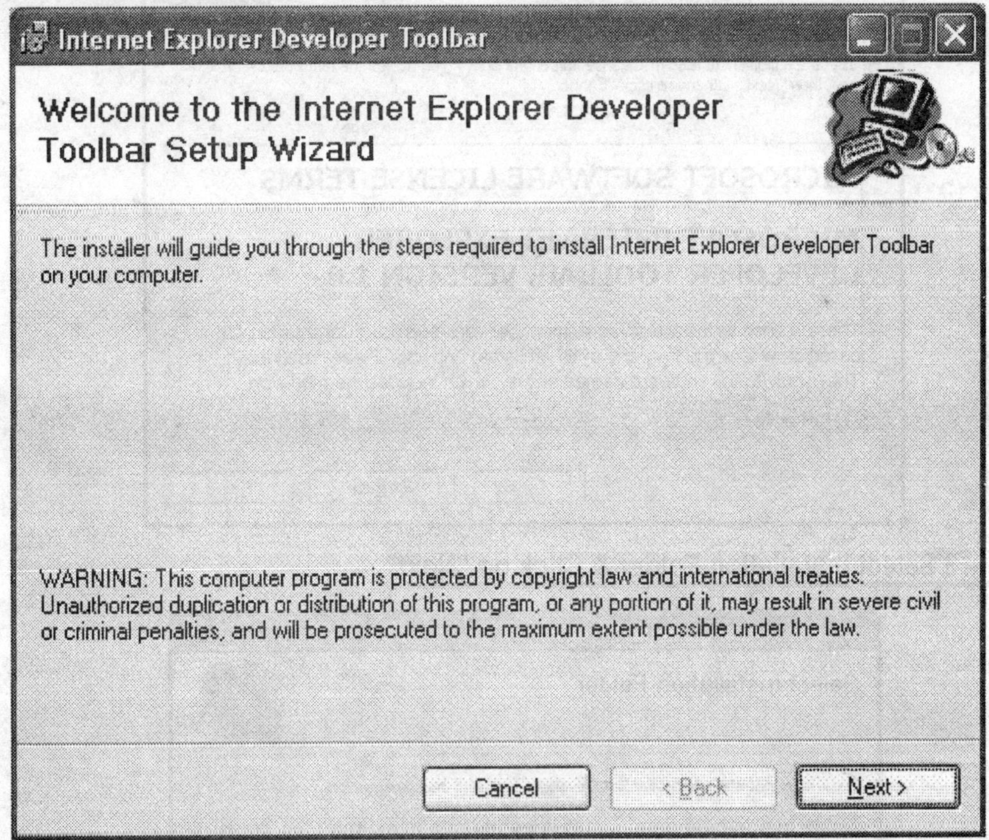

Step – 2 Click "I Agree",then "Next" Otherwise Click "Cancel"

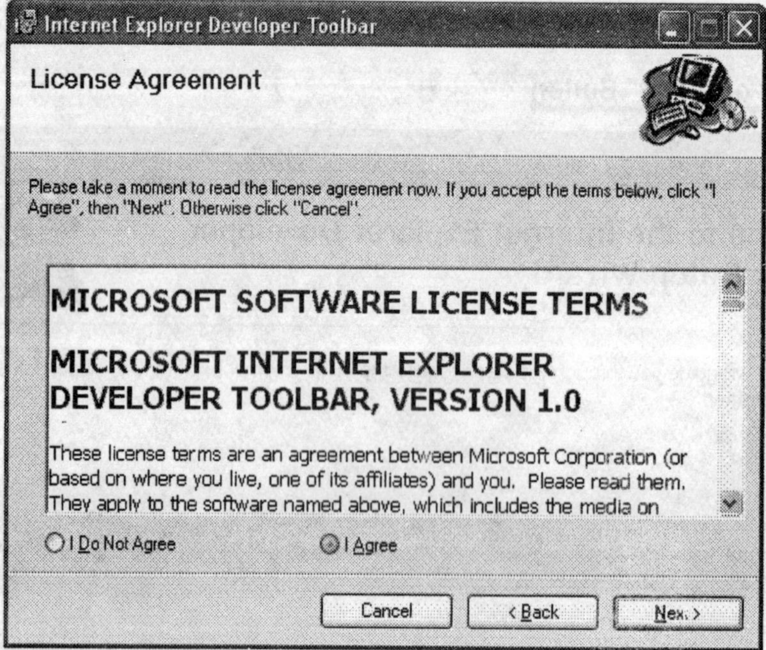

Step – 3 Select Installation Folder & Click on "Next"

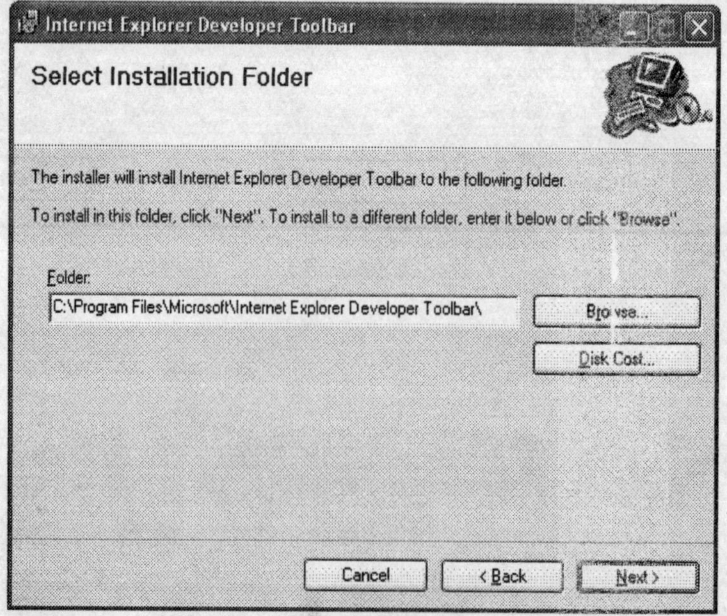

Step – 4 Select Installation Folder & Click on "Next"

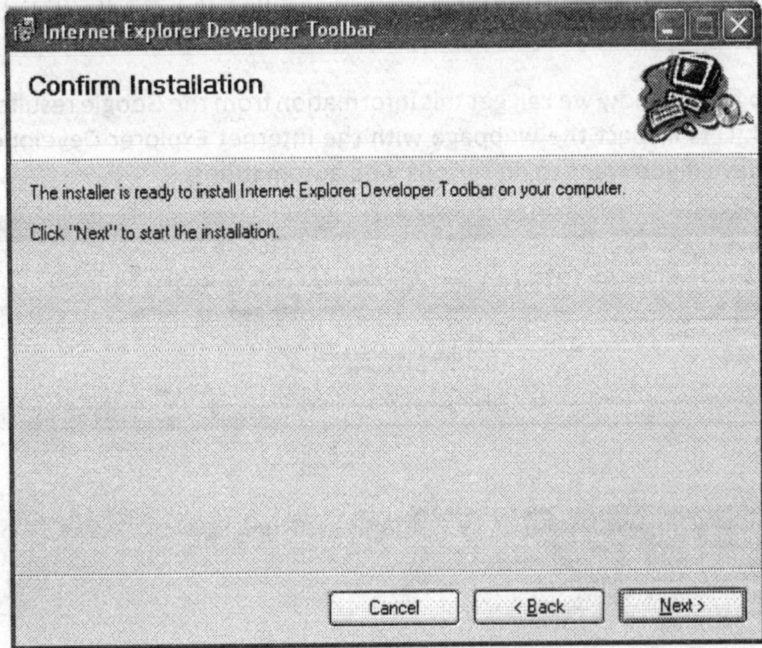

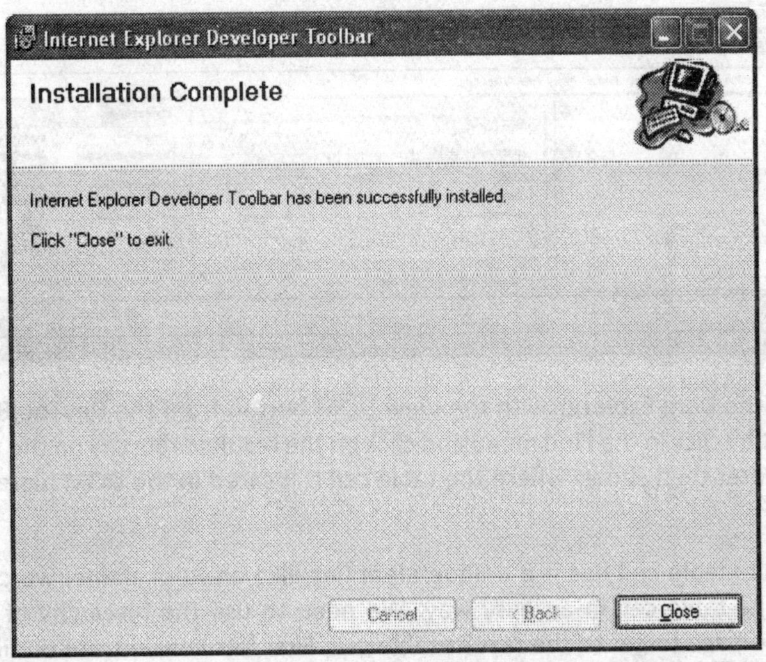

Using IE Developer Toolbar with WatiN

Lets make this example a bit more interesting by writing the results statistics to the console window.

First we need to find out how we can get this information from the Google results webpage by using WatiN. Lets inspect the webpage with the Internet Explorer Developer toolbar (this is a must have if you want to do serious web automation!).

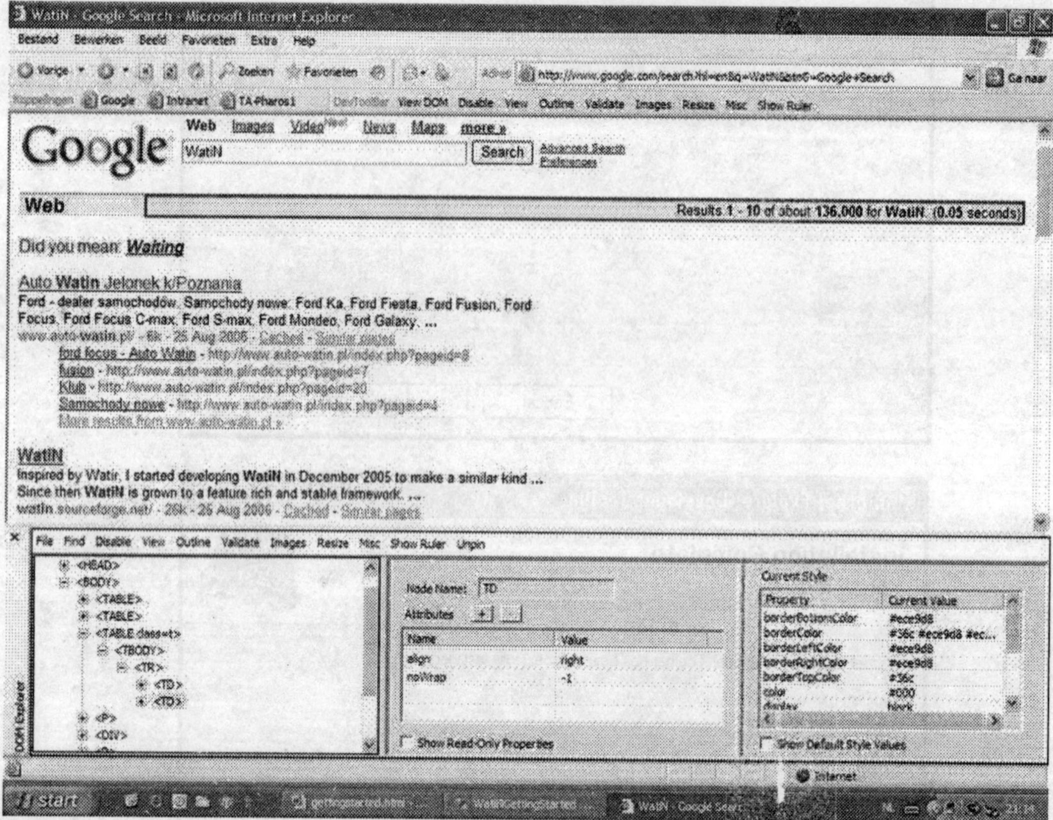

After opening the Dom Explorer with the View DOM button from the DevToolBar, select Select element by click in the Find menu and click on the results table cell on the webpage. The DOM Explorer then shows where the table cell is located in the DOM hierarchy (see screenshot).

Since the results table cell hasnt a unique identifier, like an Id or name, we cant get a reference to the table cell in an easy way. We need to use the hierarchy of the html elements in the page to get to the results table cell. First lets concentrate on finding the table the results table cell is located in. The table is the third table so we could use the

Table collection to get a reference to this table. The code would look like this:

```
Table table = ie.Tables[2];
```

There is another way to get this same table, using the classname of this Table. Since no other table has the classname t assigned to it, this makes it unique to the table we are looking for. To find this table by its classname we will use the Find.By factory method like this:

```
Table table = ie.Table(Find.By("classname","t"));
```

At this point we have a reference to the table the results statistics are in. Next, find the table row and table cell the actual info is located in.

Finding the right table row is simple, there is only one row (<TR>) in this table. To get the results table cell we will use the TableCells collection. The text in the second table cell (<TD>) contains the info we are looking for. This results in the following code:

```
string resultStats = table.TableRows[0].TableCells[1].Text;
```

The last thing we have to do is write this info to the Console window. And here is the final code for this example.

```
using System;
using WatiN.Core;

namespace WatiNGettingStarted
{
 class WatiNConsoleExample
 {


  [STAThread]
  static void Main(string[] args)
  {
   // Open an new Internet Explorer Window and
   // goto the google website.
   IE ie = new IE("http://www.google.com");

   // Find the search text field and type Watin in it.
   ie.TextField(Find.ByName("q")).TypeText("WatiN");

   // Click the Google search button.
   ie.Button(Find.ByValue("Google Search")).Click();

   // Find the table cell which shows the search result statistics.
   Table table = ie.Table(Find.By("classname","t"));
   string resultStats = table.TableRows[0].TableCells[1].Text;

   // Write these statistics to the console window.
   Console.WriteLine(resultStats);

   // Uncomment the following line if you want to close
   // Internet Explorer and the console window immediately.
   //ie.Close();
  }
 }
}
```

Build and start the project and you will see something like this:

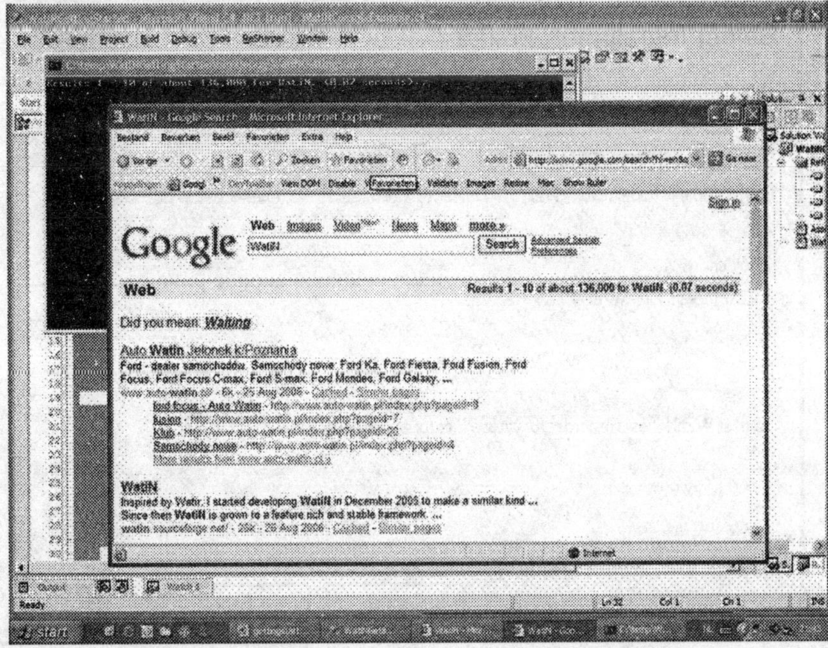

Watin Test Recorder Installation

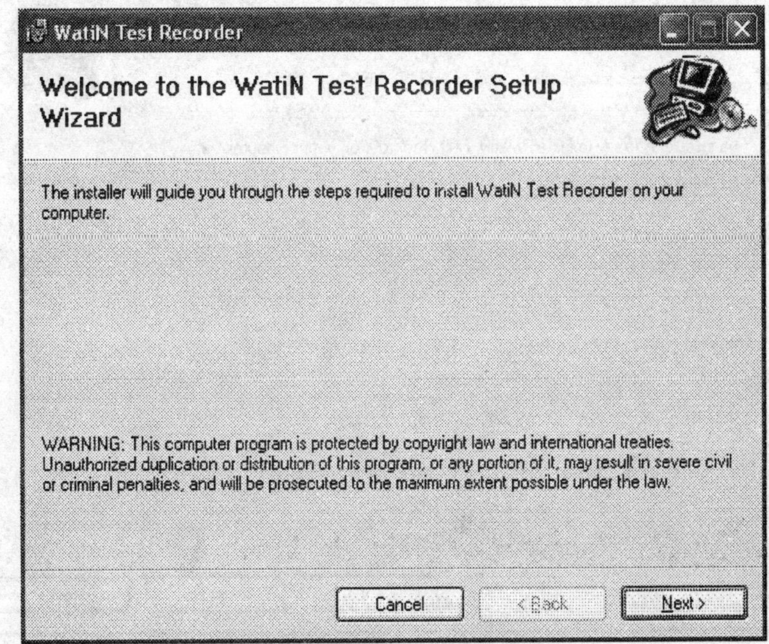

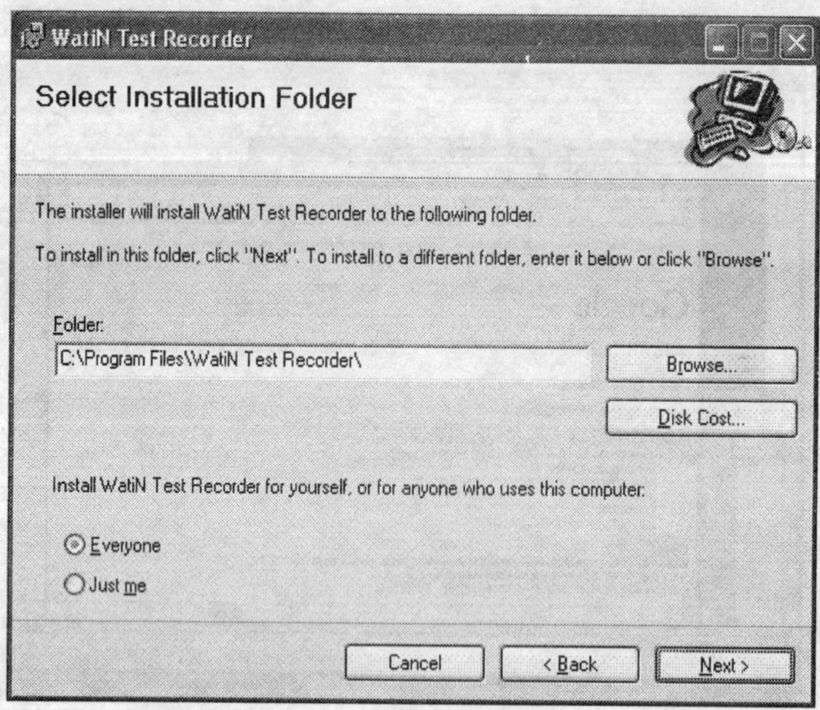
WatiN Test Recorder
Select Installation Folder
The installer will install WatiN Test Recorder to the following folder.
To install in this folder, click "Next". To install to a different folder, enter it below or click "Browse".
Folder:
C:\Program Files\WatiN Test Recorder\
Browse...
Disk Cost...
Install WatiN Test Recorder for yourself, or for anyone who uses this computer:
Everyone
Just me
Cancel
< Back
Next >

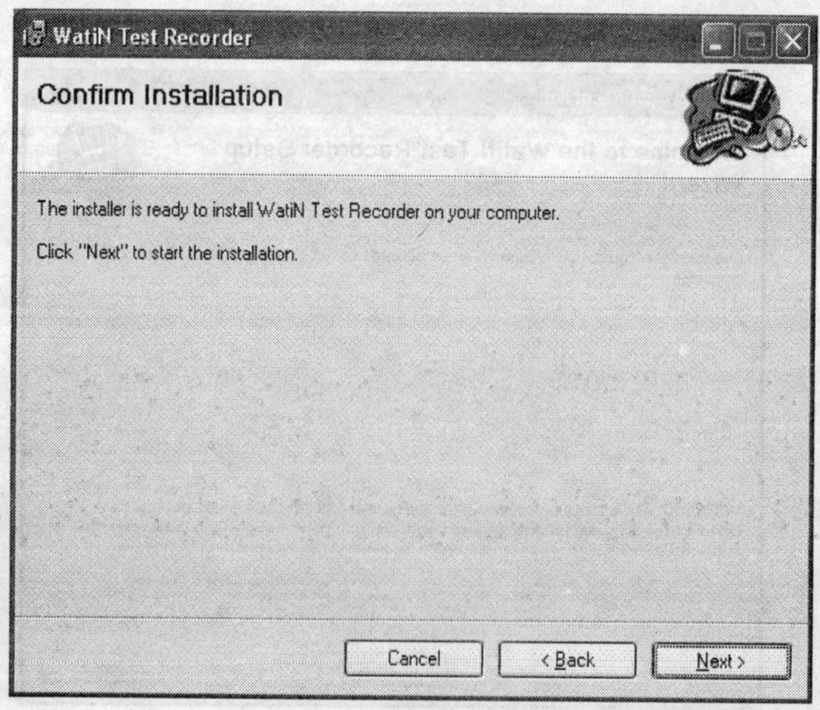
WatiN Test Recorder
Confirm Installation
The installer is ready to install WatiN Test Recorder on your computer.
Click "Next" to start the installation.
Cancel
< Back
Next >

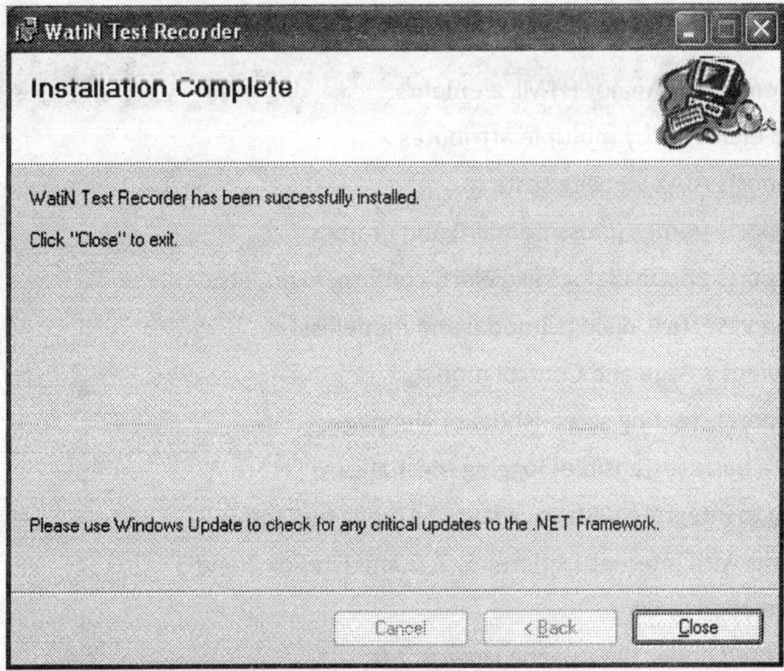
WatiN Test Recorder
Installation Complete
WatiN Test Recorder has been successfully installed.
Click "Close" to exit.
Please use Windows Update to check for any critical updates to the .NET Framework.
Cancel
< Back
Close

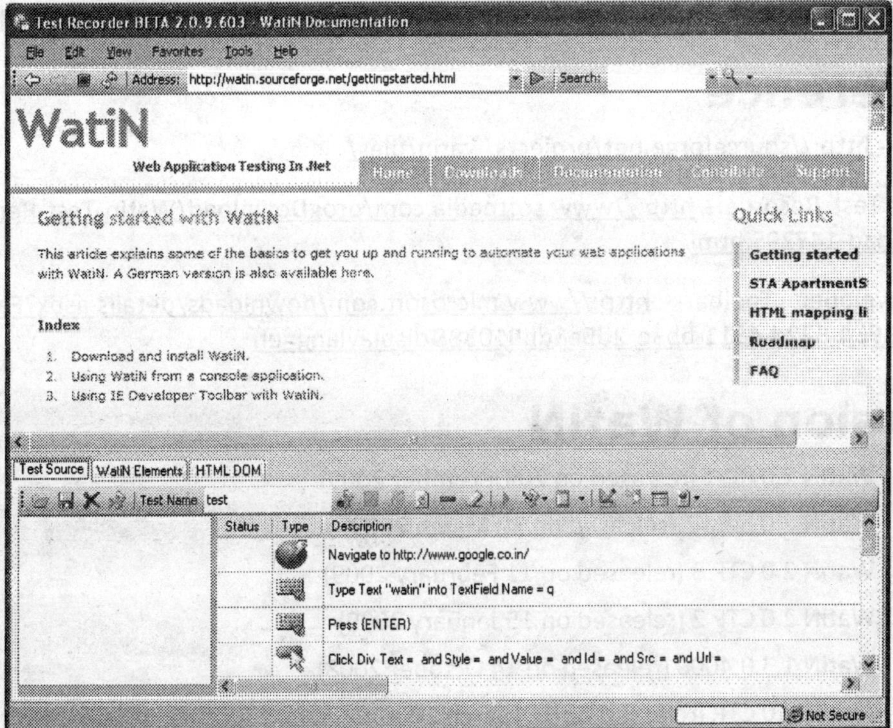
Test Recorder BETA 2.0.9.603 - WatiN Documentation
Address: http://watin.sourceforge.net/gettingstarted.html
WatiN
Web Application Testing In .Net
Getting started with WatiN
This article explains some of the basics to get you up and running to automate your web applications with WatiN. A German version is also available here.
Index
1. Download and install WatiN.
2. Using WatiN from a console application.
3. Using IE Developer Toolbar with WatiN.
Quick Links
Getting started
STA ApartmentS
HTML mapping li
Roadmap
FAQ
Test Source
WatiN Elements
HTML DOM
Test Name test
Status
Type
Description
Navigate to http://www.google.co.in/
Type Text "watin" into TextField Name = q
Press {ENTER}
Click Div Text = and Style = and Value = and Id = and Src = and Url =
Not Secure

WatiN Feature List

- Automates all major HTML elements
- Find elements by multiple attributes
- Supports AJAX website testing
- Supports frames (cross domain) and iframes
- Supports popup dialogs like alert, confirm, login, etc..
- Supports HTML dialogs (modal and modeless)
- Provides a Page and Control model.
- Supports creating screenshots of webpages
- Has a basic (extensible) logging mechanism
- Easy to integrate with your favorite (unit) test tool
- Works with Internet Explorer 6, 7, 8 and FireFox 2 and 3
- Developed in C#
- Licensed under the Apache License 2.0
- And since its open source you can add and contribute new features yourself!

Reference

WatiN - http://sourceforge.net/projects/watin/files/

WatiN Test Recorder- http://www.softpedia.com/progDownload/Watin-Test-Recorder-Download-147295.html

IE Developer Toolbar- http://www.microsoft.com/downloads/details.aspx?FamilyID=e59c3964-672d-4511-bb3e-2d5e1db91038&displaylang=en

Version of WatiN

- WatiN 2.0 RC 1 (released on 20 December 2009)
- WatiN 2.0 beta 1 (released on 30 March 2009)
- WatiN 2.0 CTP 3 (released on 11 February 2009)
- WatiN 2.0 CTP 2 (released on 15 January 2009)
- WatiN 1.3.0.4000 (released on 14 October 2008)
- WatiN 2.0 CTP (released on 12 March 2008)

- WatiN 1.2.1.4000 (released on 23 October 2007)
- WatiN 1.2.0.4000 (released on 4 October 2007)
- WatiN 1.1.2.4000 (released on 16 May 2007)
- WatiN 1.1.1.4000 (released on 15 May 2007)
- WatiN 1.1.0.4000 (released on 2 May 2007)
- WatiN 1.0.0.4000 (released on 1 March 2007)
- WatiN 0.9.5.4000 (released on 31 December 2006)
- WatiN 0.9.0.4000 (released on 31 October 2006)
- WatiN 0.8.0.4000 (released on 31 August 2006)
- WatiN 0.7.0.4000 (released on 8 July 2006)
- WatiN 0.6.0.3000 (released on 31 May 2006)

Reference

WatiN - http://sourceforge.net/projects/watin/files/

WatiN Test Recorder- http://www.softpedia.com/progDownload/Watin-Test-Recorder-Download-147295.html

IE Developer Toolbar- http://www.microsoft.com/downloads/details.aspx?FamilyID=e59c3964-672d-4511-bb3e-2d5e1db91038&displaylang=en

Web Testing using Watij tool

Introduction

Watij – Web Application Testing in Java

Watij (*pronounced wattage*) stands for Web Application Testing in Java. **Watij** is a pure Java API created to allow for the automation of web applications. Based on the simplicity of Watir and enhanced by the power of Java, **Watij** automates functional testing of web applications through a real browser. Currently **Watij** supports automating Internet Explorer on Windows only. Future plans are in place to support others like Mozilla.

Watij is a Java API that provides control and automation of Internet Explorer in order to test web applications. It was created out of the need to have a reliable, easy to use, and robust web application testing tool using Java as the scripting language. But why Java?

With Java at your fingertips you have access to a tremendous amount of existing libraries and tools. This means in your test scripts you are not restricted to testing only web applications. For example with Java you can write a test that calls a web service to do some processing and in the same test bring up your web application using Watij and validate that everything is correct. And if your web application is developed in Java, Watij integrates nicely into your already existing environment.

With Watij you can imitate real user interaction with your web application. Simple user actions like navigating, clicking links, filling out forms, and validating content are a breeze with Watij. Watij also makes it easy to handle more complex actions like file downloading and uploading, popup windows and dialogs, and screen captures.

Finding HTML elements on a page can be a cumbersome task using the traditional DOM. To make this easier Watij includes a powerful element finding capability that allows your scripts to find, access, and control any HTML element on the page. It even supports XPath expressions that are lightning fast.

Watij is a standalone Java API that purposely doesn't force you into using a proprietary testing framework or IDE. Two of the most popular Java testing frameworks are JUnit and TestNG, and Watij integrates seamlessly with either one. Watij is just like any other Java library, so it's very is easy to import into your favorite Java IDE like Eclipse or IntelliJ. And even though its main use is in testing web applications, because it is a standalone Java API Watij is not limited to the testing paradigm.

Installation

Download Watij

- Click here to get the current release of Watij

http://sourceforge.net/projects/watij/files/

- Unzip the watij_X_x.x.zip

Note: You can also [Get the Latest Source] and build it yourself

Setting up

Step – 1

Place the jniwrap.dll into your system32 folder(Typically C: /WINDOWS/system32/ or anywhere on your PATH)

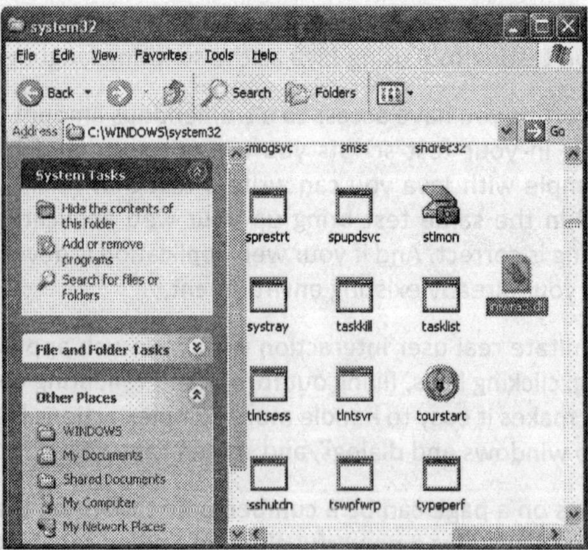

Step – 2

Include watij.jar and all the jars in the lib folder in your classpath

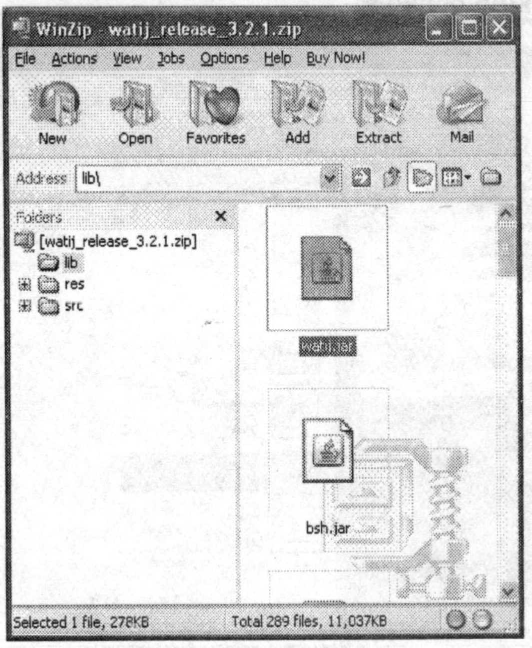

Step – 3

Extract the File

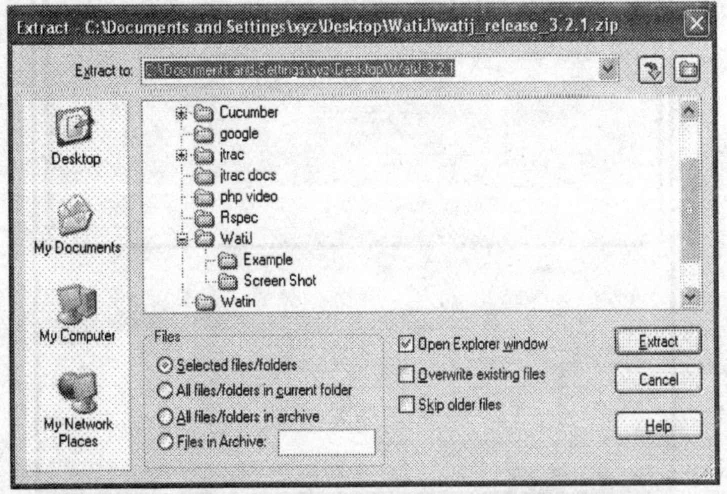

Step – 4

Double-click on the launchWatijBeanShell.bat and you are ready to start scripting in the BeanShell Desktop console.

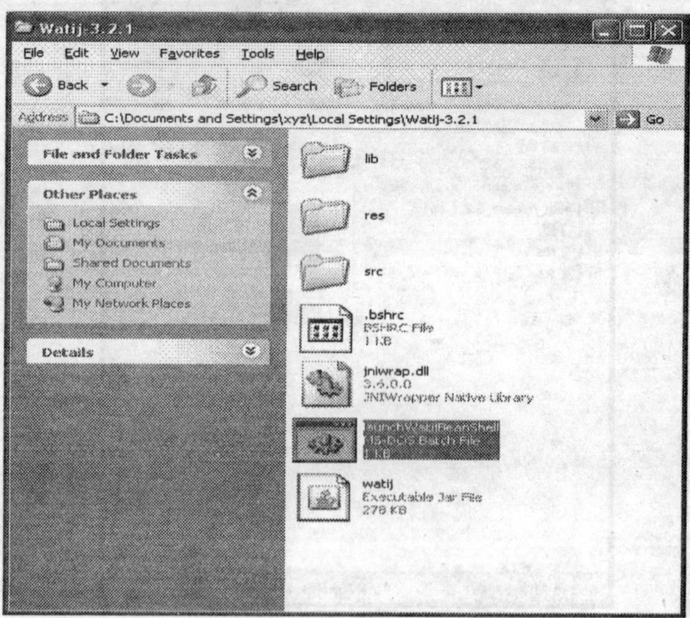

BeanShell Window Will Display

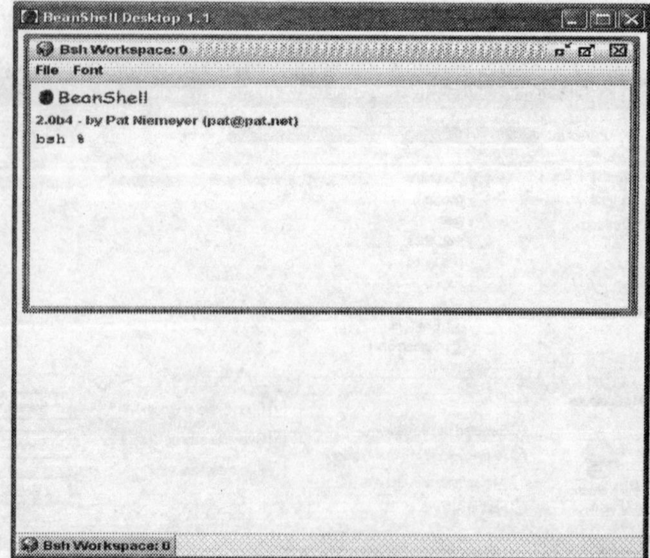

Example Google Search Test

```
import junit.framework.TestCase;
import static watij.finders.SymbolFactory.*;

public class GoogleTest extends TestCase {
   public void testGoogleSearch() throws Exception{
      IE ie = new IE();
      ie.start("http://www.google.com");
      ie.textField(name,"q").set("Watij");
      ie.button("Google Search").click();
      assertTrue(ie.containsText("/Web Application Testing in Java/"));
   }
}
```

Usage Guide

Automating Internet Explorer

Eg.Starting Up Internet Explorer

To begin you must create an instance of the IE object, but at this point the actual Internet Explorer browser has not been created.

```
IE ie = new IE();
```

It's not until you call start that the instance of Internet Explorer browser appears

```
IE ie = new IE()
ie.start(); //starts up Internet Explorer
```

As a convenience you can also provide the url to navigate to

```
IE ie = new IE
//starts up Internet Explorer and navigates to www.google.
comie.start("http://www.google.com");
```

Attaching To An Existing Internet Explorer Browser

Watij allows you connect to and control an instance of Internet Explorer that is already open. You can find an IE browser by url or by title.

Attaching by url:

```
IE ie = new IE()
//connects to the first open browser with the provided url
ie.attach(url,"http://www.google.com");
```

Attaching by title:

```
IE ie = new IE()
//connects to the first open browser with the provided title
ie.attach(title,"Google");
```

Once you are attacted to the target browser, you can now use your IE object as if you started it up yourself.

Site Navigation

Several means of navigating Internet Explorer are available to you at any time:

```
//navigates IE to www.mysite.com
ie.goTo("http://www.mysite.com");
//also navigates IE to www.mysite.com
ie.navigate("http://www.mysite.com");
//navigates forward one item in the history list
ie.forward();
//navigates back one item in the history list
ie.back();
```

Window Focus, Positioning, Sizing, and Modes

Watij allows you to position your Internet Explorer instance virtually anywhere on the desktop, toggle visual modes, as well as size the window to your needs.

```
//brings the Iternet Explorer window to the foreground, in front of every
other window
```

```
ie.bringToFront();
//gives the window focus
ie.focus();

//maximizes the window to take up the entire desktop screen
ie.maximize();
//minimizes the window to the desktop taskbar
ie.minimize();
//restores the window to its previous positioned state
ie.restore();

//turns the window's full screen mode on
ie.fullScreen(true);
//turns the window's screen mode back to normal
ie.fullScreen(false);

//turns the window's theatre mode on
ie.theatreMode(true);
//turns the window's screen mode back to normal
ie.theatreMode(false);
 //hides the window from being seen on the desktop
ie.visible(false);
//make the window visible on the desktop
ie.visible(true);
 //sets the screen coordinate of the left edge of the window to 100
ie.left(100);
//sets the screen coordinate of the top edge of the window to 200
ie.top(200);
```

Finding HTML Elements

Finding HTML elements on the page is handled through **Watij Symbols, Finders,** and **XPath Expressions**.

Symbols

Watij brought over from Watir (Web Application Testing in Ruby) the concept of using Symbols to specify what to search by. The following code uses the Symbol name to search for a button with the attribute name="button1".

```
ie.button(name,"button1");
```

Every HTML element modeled in Watij provides the singular form and the plural form of the object. So the object **Button represents a single button**, and the object **Buttons represents a collection of Buttons**.

Using Symbols we can find a collection of all the HTML elements on the page with specific properties.

```
//returns all the HTML buttons on the page with the name="deleteButton"
ie.buttons(name,"deleteButton");
```

You can also access an HTML element in a returned collection by index. **Indexes in Watij are zero-based**, so the first element is at index 0.

```
//returns the 2nd Button in the collection
ie.buttons(name,"deleteButton").get(1);
// OR
//returns the 2nd Button in the collection
ie.buttons(name,"deleteButton").button(1);
```

You are not limited to the amount of filtering using Symbols, so anything is possible:

```
//finds the 3 Button with value="Delete" and name="deleteButton"
button = ie.buttons(name,"deleteButton").
buttons(value,"Delete").button(2);
```

Watij also provides a **generic object named HtmlElement** that will allow you to access any other Html element not modeled in the API. For example if you have the following html:

```
<MYTAG>My Text1</MYTAG>
```

One way of accessing MYTAG is with the following code:

```
ie.htmlElement(tag,"MYTAG");
```

Finders

To better equip you with the ability to access any element on the page in a simple easy to manner, Watij introduced a new concept called **Finders**. Finders are like Symbols except they are not limited by a single parameter. In fact later on you will see that the sky is the limit when it comes to Finders, especially when creating your own custom ones. For now let's say you have the following html:

```
<MYTAG myattr1="attribute1">My Text</MYTAG>
<MYTAG myattr2="attribute2">My Text2</MYTAG>
```

By using the Finder named attribute which takes in a name and value you can do the following:

```
//returns the HtmlElement with myattr1="attribute1"
ie.htmlElement(attribute("myattr1","attribute1"));
```

The following Finder objects are accessible via:

```
import static watij.finders.FinderFactory.*;
```

tag(String tagName)
attribute(String name, String value)
index(int index)
text(String text)
name(String value)
value(String value)
caption(String value)
id(String value)
title(String value)
alt(String value)
src(String value)
action(String value)
method(String value)
url(String value)
href(String value)
xpath(String expression)

Custom Finders

Automating HTML Elements

Hyperlinks

Your browser would disply a link to Google as Google. The actual HTML would look something like:

```
<a href="http://google.com>Google</a>
```

There are many ways to have Watij click the above link to Google. You can find and click the link using the **text** or **url** attribute, which both also accept regular expressions. You can also use **xpath** to find the link.

```
ie.link(text,"Google").click();

ie.link(text,"/oogl/").click();

ie.link(url,"http://google.com").click();

ie.link(url,"/google.com/").click();

ie.link(xpath, "//A[@url='http://google.com']").click();
```

See the Watij API for a complete list of methods available for links

Checkboxes

Watij *sets* or *clears* checkboxes based on the name and value attributes provided in the checkbox HTML tag. The HTML of a check box looks like:

```
Check Me: <input name="checkme" value="1" type="checkbox">
```

We can search for this checkbox using our **Symbols**

```
ie.checkbox(name,"checkme").set();

ie.checkbox(value,"1").set();

ie.checkbox(xpath, "//INPUT[@name='checkme' and @value='1']")
.set();
```

We can also use the clear method on a checkbox. **See the Watij API for a complete list of methods available for checkboxes**

Radios

Watij *sets* or *clears* radios based on the name and value attributes provided in the radio HTML tag. The HTML code of a radio looks like:

```
Click Me: <input name="clickme" id="1" type="radio">
```

We can search for this radio using our **Symbols**

```
ie.radio(name,"clickme").set();
ie.radio(id,"1").set();
ie.radio(xpath, "//INPUT[@name='clickme' and @id='1']").
set();
```

We can also use the clear method on a radio. **See the Watij API for a complete list of methods available for radios**

Buttons

Watij can submit HTML buttons on a web page based on the *name, value (caption)* and *id* attributes. The HTML code of a button looks like:

```
<input type="submit" value="ClickTheButton" name="b1>
```

We can search for this select box using our **Symbols**

```
ie.button(name, "b1").click();
ie.button(value,"ClickTheButton").click();
```

The default way to find a button is through its value. Because of this, there is a simple way to find a button:

```
ie.button("ClickTheButton").click();
```

See the Watij API for a complete list of methods available for buttons

Select Lists

Watij selects an item in a select list (or dropdown box) based on the *name* and option *value* attributes provided in the select HTML tag. Or we can identify it based on the *name* and attribute, and the value we want to set. The HTML code of a SelectList looks like:

```
<select name="selectme">
  <option name="1">O1</option>
  <option name="2">O2</option>
</select>
```

We can search for this select list using our *Symbols*

```
//(finds the option in the select list with name 1)
ie.selectList(name, "selectme").option(name,"1").select();

//(finds the second option in the list)
ie.selectList(name, "selectme").option(index,1).select();

//(returns whether the select list is disabled)
ie.selectList(name, "selectme").disabled();
```

You can also clear a select list using the clearSelection() method. **See the Watij API for a complete list of methods available for select boxes**

Images

Watij *clicks* images based on the *name, id, src, alt* and other attributes provided in the image HTML tag. The HTML code of a image looks like:

```
<img src=images/square.jpg id=square title="square_image">
```

We can search for this select box using our **Symbols**

```
ie.image(src, "/square/").click();

ie.image(title, "square_image").hasLoaded();

ie.image(id,"square").width();

ie.image(xpath, "//IMAGE[@id='square']").click();
```

See the Watij API for a complete list of methods available for images

TextFields and TextAreas

Watij *sets* textfields and textareas based on the *name* and *id* and other attributes provided in the HTML tag. The HTML code of a textfield looks like:

```
<input name="username" type="text">
```

We can search for this textfield using our **Symbols**

```
ie.textField(name, "username").set("myusername");

ie.textField(name, "username").value();
```

See the Watij API for a complete list of methods available for textfields and textareas

Handling Child Browsers

Watij supports attaching to child browsers that are created from a parent window. For example, you might have a link that creates a new popup window. This is easily handled in watij:

```
IE ie = new IE().start("www.mysite.com");
//lets click a link that causes a new window to popup
ie.link(name, "mylink").click();
//now lets get a handle on the child browser;
IE new_ie = ie.childBrowser();
```

Wasn't that easy! You can also get the child browser at a specific index away from the parent window. The third child browser would be ie.childBrowser(2). **See the Watij API for a complete list of methods available for browsers**

Handling Popup Dialogs

TODO: Document This Validation

Watij supports many methods for validation. You may check to see if an object is *disabled*, *enabled*, *isSet*, *readOnly*, or any other available element attribute. When writing Watij tests, you extend Junit, so you have the full capability for validation that JUnit and java have to offer. I would highly suggest looking at the Watij unit tests to get a deeper understanding of the validation capabilities of Watij, JUnit, and Java. The Unit Tests are a great resource – and they all work, too!!

Interactive Runtime Via BeanShell

Watij is packaged with a preconfigured version of BeanShell. You can always run Beanshell and just start using Watij to explore an automation idea.

Release Note

Release 3.1.0

IMPORTANT!

- Please recopy the jniwrap.dll to your system32 dir.
- Most of the jars in the lib directory have been upgraded, so you will need to update your environment to use the new jars.

Design Changes:

- Upgraded to JExplorer 1.7.4x
- Changed the way Watij waits until the browser is ready so that the next call will process the wait. This fixes many browser closing and javascript timing issues. However if you are currently timing actions for performance monitoring you will need to call ie.waitUntilReady to get the full duration of the action. You could also stop the timer after the next call to ie or it's elements.

IE Support:

- Added support for handling dialogs (alert, confirm, prompt, file download). Please take a look at the PopupsTest for examples on how to use the new api.
- Added IEUtil.closeAllDialogs which will close all open dialogs on all browsers

Bug Fixes:

- Running your tests from Eclipse is no longer an issue.

Release 3.0.2 (BETA)

IMPORTANT!

- With latest version, Eclipse compiler/runtime has a bug and Watij will not run in it. Any other compiler/runtime will work. TeamDev has been notified of the issue.
- Please recopy the jniwrap.dll to your system32 dir.

Design Changes:

- Upgraded to JExplorer 1.6
- IE class delegates to IESupport which extends BrowserSupport (JExplorer)
- It's possible to use separate message loops for each browser instance...this is to enable modal dialog support.

IE Support:

- Added support for Modal Dialogs (see ModalDialogTest)
- Added IEUtil.closeAllBrowsers which will close all IE instances
- Added IEUtil.browserCount which will return the number of open browsers

Element Support:

- You can now chain finders together in one call. For example: ie.button(name("butt on1"),value("Button 1"),index(1)).click(); this will click the 2nd button on the page with the name "button1" and the value "Button 1"
- There is a generic attribute and tag finder that will allow one to access any element on the page. For example: ie.htmlElement(tag("MyTag"), attribute("myattr","myvalue")).click(); this will click the first element on the page that matches <MyTag myattr="myvalue"/>

Bug fixes

- Fixed child browser threading issues
- Fixed browser initialization issues
- Fixed issue where you have to call close() on child browsers that are closed via javascript

Release 3.0.1 (beta)

Design Changes:

- New system property BROWSER_TIMEOUT can be configured. This property is the amount of time in seconds that watij should wait for a browser to be initialized.
- Added ability to run single unit test. Example: launchAnt.bat run.single.test -DtestName=watij.NavigateTest
- Added static import to beanshell.
- Refactored IEController and IE to single class.
- Refactored to bind all calls to OLEMessageLoop to increase stability.

Element Support:

- Added ability to use "/i" construct as in perl for regular expressions inorder to do case insensitive searches.
- Added ability to get/set screen mode to full screen or theatre mode.
- Added ability to get/set top and left position of IE.
- Added ability to get/set visible state of ie.
- Added ability to capture only IE window.
- Added additional waitWhileBusy lines in IE when iWebBrowser2 is being affected for stability.
- Added additional waitUntilDocComplete lines in various element classes when actions are performed (click, set, dblclick, etc..) for stability.
- Changed method of minimizing, maximizing, and restoring IE from using sendKeys to using Wnd object.
- Changed method of closing IE browser to ensure RPC Server Unavilable error is not received.

Bug Fixes:

- Fixed bug that prevented use of "/" in regex expression for finders.
- Fixed typo for firing ONKEYDOWN and ONKEYUP.

Release 3.0 (beta)

IMPORTANT!

We are releasing a beta of Watij that utilizes our new Java-to-Com bridge ComfyJ. We are no longer using Jacob and Jiffie. During this beta phase we will be updating Watij with api changes, and performance improvements.

- Please copy jniwrap.dll to your system32 dir.
- Include the following jars from the lib dir in your classpath: comfyj-2.1.jar, jniwrap-3.1.jar, watijcom.jar, and winpack-3.0.jar.

Design Changes:

- Symbol and the symbols package has moved and been renamed to SymbolFactory and the finders package (import static watij.symbols.Symbol.* is now import static watij.finders.SymbolFactory.*)
- There is a new FinderFactory that contains finders that you can use to find elements. This is an alternative to using symbols and will allow for custom finders. So instead of using ie.button(name,"button1"); you can now do the same with ie.button(name("button1"));
- You can create your own custom finders by implementing the Finder interface or extending the BaseFinder class. For example: ie.button(new MyButtonFinder()).click();
- Symbol index is no longer supported, you can use ie.htmlElement(int index) instead

Element Support:

- Initial table support (table, tablerow, tablecell, tablebody)
- Initial support for bahavior tags (e.g. <x:y>)

Bug Fixes:

- Fixed flash bug on collections

Release 2.2.3

IMPORTANT! We are releasing with the latest Jacob 1.10.1

- **This includes a new jacob.dll that you must (re)copy to your system32 folder or place in your java.library.path**
- There is also a new jacob.jar and jiffie.jar in the lib dir

Bug Fixes

- Fixed issue with http headers prepending null

Release 2.2.2

IE Support:

- Additional Http Headers support (somewhat experimental method setAdditional HttpHeaders(String) will cause every navigation to include the set http headers. Doesn't work with frames – will cause frame navigation issues)

Element Support:

- File Field support (input type=file)

Release 2.2.1

IE Support:

- Access to native Document through method getOLEDocument()
- Frame.title now returns the title for the frame

Element Support:

- Html Form support

Unit Tests:

- WatijTestCase now uses a global setup and teardown (unit tests run twice as fast)
- WatijTestCase now uses a System property for finding the HTML_ROOT (you will need to add this to your IDE as a vm parameter)

Release 2.2

All indexes in Watij are now zero-based. Please update your existing one-based tests.
IE Support:

- Execute Javascript (you can now call ie.executeScript(String) to run your own custom javascript in IE)
- Enhanced screenCapture (will automatically bring IE to front, maximize, do screenshot, and then restore)
- Show (calling ie.show() will print out all html elements on IE in JSON format)
- Calling sendKeys on IE will automatically wait until IE is finished processing
- Fixed IE.close bug where failures caused IE to hang
- Improved childBrowser logic to wait on new child window (this ensures you don't access a child window before the parent window has a handle to it)
- Indexes to child browsers are now zero-based

Element Support:

- Button tag (button finder supports \<button\> html syntax)
- Get style on html element (e.g. ie.buttons(2).style())
- Show (calling show() will print out the html element in JSON format)

Element Collection Support:

- Show (calling show() will print out all the html elements in the collection in JSON format)
- Indexes to html elements are now zero-based

Release 2.1

IE Support:

- Dynamic sizing of IE (you can set the width and height)
- Fixed sendKeys issue (added title, if no title supplied will use active IE's title)
- Screen capture (default image is png, supports other formats as well: bmp, jpg, etc)
- Restore (after calling maximize you can call restore to bring back to original size)

Element Support:

- Flash for element (calling flash() will cause element to flicker on the page)
- Flash for element collections (calling flash() on a collection will cause all elements to flicker on page at the same time)
- Focus (calling focus() will put cursor on element)

Release 2.0

This landmark release of watij introduces **frame support, iframes, and embedded elements**. We also have spruced up http://watij.xwiki.com with a Basic User Guide. The Javadocs also now show unimplemented items by throwing a NotImplementedYetException. Check out the Release Notes for 2.0 for more info.

WatiJ version List

Watij Release 3.2.1

Watij Release 3.2.0

Watij Release 3.1.0

Watij 3.0.2 BETA

Watij 3.0.1 BETA

Watij 3.0 BETA

Watij Release 2.2.3

Watij Release 2.2.2

Watij Release 2.2.1

Watij Release 2.2

Watij Release 2.1

Watij Release 2.0.1

Watij Release 2.0

Watij beta 1.1

Reference:

http://souceforge.net/projects/watij/files/watij/Watij%20Release%203.2.1/watij_release_3.2.1.zip/download

Web Testing using WebDriver tool

WEBDRIVER

Overview

Webdriver™ is a simple to use web testing tool based on open source Perl script modules. Perl is a scripting language that requires a Perl interpreter to be present on the host machine. The tool requires the installation of some web-related Perl modules to operate properly.

The tool makes extensive use of the WWW:Mechanize (known as Mech to most people) module written by Andy Lester. In effect, Webdriver™ is simply an easy-to-use front end to the Mech facility. Webdriver™ used comma-separated-value files as an input.

Architecture

Webdriver™ implements a very simple scripting model. Scripts are CSV files having just four columns. The four columns format is described in section 0 CSV Four-Column Scripts.

CSV files can be edited using any text editor such as notepad. However, it is most useful to use a program like MS Excel to edita the tabular data. Note that the files must be saved as CSV files, so any formatting will be lost on exit from the program.

Webdriver™ uses a single configuration file referenced on the command line to drive it. The tools accesses one or more web sites, generates dump files with screen content and a log to the console.

Webdriver™ generates a log file on output which can be read using a standard browser. This file has links to copies of downloaded forms, test case results and reporting files.[1]

Software Requirements

Webdriver™ will work on Windows and Unix/Linux platforms. As a single user script driver, it does not have large resource demands, so should be usable on any computer capable of running standard office applications.

- Webdriver™ has been tested on:
- Windows XP Professional SP2.
- Windows 2000 Server SP4
- Windows 2003 Server SP1
- Windows Vista.

Since test scripts are stored in CSV files, these files can be edited any basic text editor such as Windows notepad, wordpad or programmers editors such as UltaEdit™. On the Unix/Linux platform, any text editor such a vi or emacs are suitable.

However, CSV files are most easily edited using a spreadsheet program capable of opening and tabulating the CSV data. It is important that the tool used saves files in CSV format, rather than it's own format of course. Formatting, calculated fields, macros and formatting information cannot be stored in CSV files, so should not be used.

However, for documentation purposes, a traditional spreadsheet could be used to hold complete scripts, with formatting, macros etc. When saving the file for use in Webdriver™ however, use the "Save as..." facility to create the CSV file. The exported CSV file must comply with the four-column format specified in section 0 Webdriver™ Script Format.

Installation and set up

Installing Required Software

Installing the ActiveState Perl Interpreter

Perl is an interpreted script language and there are several interpreters that could be used. The most popular interpreter is that supplied by ActiveState and we'll use that in out example installation process below.

---

1 Need to generate log file data in HTML format. Also, keep dump files in separate files, linked to the main log output file.

1 Go to the ActiveState website and download the free Perl interpreter from www.activestate.com

If you are a windows user, you have the choice of downloading a Zip file or standard Microsoft installer (.msi) file. Choose either.

2 To install Perl, double click on the downloaded file and use the default settings to complete the installation.

3. You need to check that Perl installation directory is in the directory path by opening a command prompt window. At the command prompt, enter

C:\>perl –h

You should see the standard perl header message and a list of perl command line options.

Installing the Required Perl Modules

4 Webdriver™ uses XXX open source modules that must be installed from the internet. Perl package manager, or PPM, is used to perform the module download and installation. PPM is installed as part of the ActiveState standard install.

PPM uses libraries of freely available Perl modules called repositories. The default repositories that are automatically referenced by PPM may not always have the latest versions of the required module. PPM can be run from the Start->Programs->ActivePerl. Note that PPM needs an internet connection to connect to the repositories and download the required modules.

We recommend you add the following repository in addition to the standard ActiveState repository:

University of Winnipeg

http://theoryx5.uwinnipeg.ca/ppms/package.xml

5 Next, you need to then install the five modules as below.

Note that between the two repositories you now have, the same module might be available multiple times. Make sure you install the latest version of each module.

Webdriver™ 1.0.6 required the following Modules and versions:

WWW-Mechanize (1.20)
Test-WWW-Mechanize (1.06)

Crypt-SSLeay (0.53)
Test-Longstring (0.11)
Webservice-Validator-HTML-W3C (0.18)

```
Note that the new GUI version of PPM will download and install all of the additional modules these depend on.
```

6 Perl and the modules it requires to run Webdriver™ are now ready for use.

Command Line Options

Running webdriver

The Webdriver programme is run from the command line as follows:
In windows:

```
C:\> perl webdir\webdriver.pl -c configfile
```

In unix/linux:

```
# perl webdir/webdriver.pl -c configfile
```

Where:

Webdir	is the location of the webdriver script
Configfile	Is the name of the configuration file (usually a .csv (comma separated value) file

```
is the location of the webdriver script\webdriver.pl -c configfile
```

Command-line options

-c configfile	Specifies the configuration file
-v	Verbose mode produces more output to the console

-d seconds	Specifies the delay between HTTP messages sent to the server under test. Default is 1. A zero delay means the messages are sent instantaneously use –d zero to do this – but only on your own sites, please.

Webdriver™ Scripting

Webdriver™ Script Format

A CSV file is a plain text file containing textual data in fields separated by commas. The basic rules are:

All text is human readable character data

The field separator is a comma

Fields that contain test values with embedded commas should be surrounded in quotation marks ("......")

Where quotation marks are used in the fields themselves, the field should be surrounded in quotes, and the quotes in the field should be 'doubled'

Webdriver™ configuration files use CSV files with only four fields.

Examples of valid Webdriver™ script lines are:

```
Link,text,Update my profile,Edit the users profile
Link,text,"This is a link in quotes",My comment here
Link,text,"A link, with ""commas"", and quotes"
And so on…
```

CSV Four-Column Scripts

Webdriver™ scripts are simple to use because the require a maximum of only four columns. The four columns are described below:

Command (or verb) – the command to be interpreted by Webdriver™. There is a limited, but constantly growing set of commands possible. A simple example would be link command that tells Webdriver™ to follow a link on the currently open webpage. The verb is highlighted in the example below:

```
link, text, http://www.msn.com, my comment here
```

Object – typically, this is the object or object type upon which the command will operate. Many objects act as a qualification for the Command. For example, links may be found using plain text (link, text,...) or as a regular expression (regex) that is a search pattern, rather than a simple link name (link, regex,...) The object is highlighted in the example below:

```
link, text, http://www.msn.com, my comment here
validate, regex, /\d\d:\d\d/
```

Data – this column contains the value an object might be assigned, the name of an object type, the URL to be fetched and so on. The data is highlighted in the example below:

```
link, text, http://www.msn.com, my comment here
```

Comment – this is an entirely optional column to be used to document the script. The comment is highlighted in the example below:

```
link, text, http://www.msn.com, my comment here
```

Script Command Summary

Verb	*Object*	*Data*	*Comment*
Test	Name	n/a	Is a name for the test – printed on the console when the test is run
Case		name	A name for the current test case. Just used as a label for the current group of commands
Comment	n/a	Your comment to be printed at the console	Just documentation relevant to your test. Any number of comments may be added throughout the script
*****	n/a	Your comment to be printed at the console	An asterisk in the first column is entirely equivalent to the comment verb
authdomain	domain plus port number 80	Realm	Domain is the web URL domain to be accessed. Realm is the area on the web site to be accessed. When you try and access the site through a browser, you should see a message like "realm on domain – enter username and password". Be sure to append the port number to the domain. E.g. www.mytestportal.com:80

Authcred	Username	Password	Username and password associated with the domain and realm assigned using the authdomain command.
Txn	transactionname	n/a	Enter a name for the current transaction. The console will label the next log message relating to a link or form submission. The transaction name will then reset. When the next transaction is executed, the transaction label will be set to: • the text of the url for a "get url" command • the text of a "link text" command • the name of the button for a "button name" command
Get	url	urltext	Uses an HTTP GET command to retrieve the page. Normally used to retrieve a home page.
Form	number	formnumber	Used to select the form on the currently loaded page. Pages with multiple forms are numbered from 1. If there is only one form on the page, this command isn't required.
field	fieldname	fieldvalue	This command sets the value of a text or radio button field to the value provided.
fieldselect	Fieldname	Fieldvalue(s)	This command sets the values of a SELECT MULTIPLE field that may have multiple values selected. Values should be comma separated.
checkon	fieldname	fieldvalue	This identifies a checkbox with name and value provided and checks its value to ON
checkoff	fieldname	fieldvalue	This identifies a checkbox with name and value provided and checks its value to OFF

link	**text**	Link name	Finds the link on the current page labelled with the text provided and simulated a button click. Note that this field is case sensitive
button	**Name**	Name of the button to be clicked	The named button is clicked
button	**Value**	Value for the button to be clicked	The button with the value provided is clicked
Submit			Submits the form without clicking a button
loop	**labelname**	count	Initiates a loop of the script between this script line and the line with label labelname
label	**labelname**		This statement is the end of the loop defined by the loop earlier in the script.
visiblefields	Field values		The visible fields on the form are set to the values provided in a comma separated list. Quotes should be used to longer text phrases with commas in. Fields are set in the order in which they appear in the HTML. NB this will change button values too, so use dumpforms first, then reassign the same value to the button before clicking it. NB 2: note that select field allowing multiple selections CANNOT be set this way, and the script will fail if you attempt this.
validate	**string**	searchstring	Searches the HTML returned by the last GET, LINK or form submission for the string searchstring. If a match is found, it reports a MATCH, otherwise it reports NO MATCH. Note that the search string may contain HTML tags etc.

validate	**regex**	regexstring	Searches the HTML returned by the last GET, LINK or form submission for the regular expression regexstring. If a match is found, it reports a MATCH, otherwise it reports NO MATCH. More information can be found at http://www.regular-expressions.info/ e.g. validate,regex,/found/ would find the string 'found'
checkhtml			Validates the HTML returned by the last GET, LINK or form submission. It uses the W3C HTML Validation service at http://validator.w3.org/ Note that you should not abuse this service.
dump			The currently loaded page is stored in the dump file dump.html. This file is over written the first tie dump is called, and appended to on each subsequent call during the test run. Note that the page content should present a good representation of the actual web pages downloaded, but this may not always be the case.
dumpforms			Prints out the Forms and fields for each form in the HTML returned by the last GET, LINK or form submission. This is useful for identifying the field names in a form to create script commands to assign values and submit the form by button click or
dumplinks			Prints out the details of all the links in the current web page.

dumplinks	code		Prints out the details of all the links in the current web page in the form of webdriver™ script code. This is a convenient way to generate a script to visit all links on a page. Note that javascript links cannot be automated.
dumpheaders			Prints out the details of all the header entries in the current web page.
dumptree			Prints out the complete HTML tree structure for the current web page on the console. (Can be large).
back			Simulates the back or previous command in the browser. If there is no previous page, this command is ignored.
Exit			Ends the script immediately.
Blank field			Blank commands are ignored by the tool. Entering a comment in the data column is a convenient way to document the script.

Webdriver output

Console messages

DUMP Output files

DUMPFORMS Output

An example output from a DUMPFORMS command in a test script has been extracted from a test and shown below.

```
23,========== FORM DEFINITION ==========
Form name: form1  Action: form1Handler.asp  Method: post
  INPUT Field (1) name=TextField1 Type=text
  INPUT Field (2) name=CheckBox1 Type=checkbox
  INPUT Field (3) name=Radio1 Type=radio Value=1
  INPUT Field (4) name=Radio1 Type=radio Value=2
  INPUT Field (5) name=Radio1 Type=radio Value=3
```

```
SELECT Field (6) name=_ctl27:_ctl17 MULTIPLE SELECTION ALLOWED
                   1 Safety
                   2 Fire Safety
     SELECTED-> 3 Fire Safety Equipment
                   4 Fire Safety Risk Assessment
                   5 Fire Safety Regulation
                   6 Water Safety
                   7 Water Safety Equipment
                   8 Water Safety Risk Assessment
                   9 Water Safety Regulation
                   10 Road Safety
                   11 Road Safety Equipment
                   12 Road Safety Risk Assessment
                   13 Road Safety Regulation
  INPUT Field (7) name=response Type=submit Value=submit
  INPUT Field (8) name=fields Type=submit Value=fields
   *** WARNING *** Radio buttons found, field numbers may need
adjusting[2]
  *** WARNING *** Select field with multiple selections
      allowed on this form
      YOU CANNOT USE VISIBLEFIELDS COMMAND IN YOUR SCRIPT[3]
2,======= END OF FORM DEFINITION ======
```

Error Messages

xx, Warning! Unknown verb: in line badverb.....	Denoted an unrecognized keyword in the verb column.

Test Development

Test Structure

There is a fairly standard approach to script development. Because the scripts themselves cannot be modularized easily and are straightforward sequential series of instructions, the structuring of tests can only be done in two ways:

- using batch files or shell scripts
- by sequencing series of test cases in a single script files.

---

2 Radio buttons intended to be treated as a group are usually given the same name, so this usually increases the field number (in brackets)

3 Note that the VISIBLEFIELDS command cannot be used with select fields that allow multiple options to be selected.

Scripts can be executed by a batch file or shell script. Multiple scripts files can be executed by the same batch file. Scripts themselves can be split into a sequential series of test cases.

Batch file or shell scripts might look like:

```
perl \webdriver\webdriver.pl -v -c test1.csv
copy *.log ..\test1
perl \webdriver\webdriver.pl -v -c test1.csv
copy *.log ..\test2
perl \webdriver\webdriver.pl -v -c test1.csv
copy *.log ..\test3

and so on…
```

A script might be structured as follows:

```
Test,name,Test 4A

Case,name,Test Case 4.1
…
    Scripts commands for test case 4.1
…

Case,name,Test Case 4.2
…
    Scripts commands for test case 4.2
…

Case,name,Test Case 4.3
…
    Scripts commands for test case 4.3
…
And so on…
```

Looping

Webdriver™ scripts can have loops embedded in the code so you can repeat sequences of script commands. Loops can be nested, one inside the other.

Here's an example:

```
loop, myloop, 31
...
More script commands
...
Label, myloop
```

In this case, the script commands between the loop and label verbs will be executed 31 times, with the variable myloop as the counter.

Here is another example:

```
loop, years, 5
...
More script commands (executed 5 times)
...
loop, months, 12
...
More script commands (executed 60 times (12 per 'year'))
...
label, months
...
More script commands (executed 5 times)
...
label, years
```

In this case, there are two loops, one nested inside the other. The first loop is executed five times. The second loop is executed twelve times within the first loop – i.e. sixty times.

Notes:

1. Loops can be nested one inside the other, but no checking of the consistency of loops is done. One loop could overlap, rather than include the other. This might lead to some interesting situations.

2. There is no maximum limit to the size of loops. Please be considerate of websites that belong to other organizations. Large numbers of iterations of resource-intensive transactions could be regarded as a denial of service attack. Use the 'delay' command line parameter to increase the time between transactions.

Script Development

Because the scripts comprise a fixed series of commands always executed in the same order, the best way to develop the scripts is to work sequentially through the script, writing come lines (perhaps only one or two), then testing the script, debugging the script, then extending the script by another few lines. This incremental approach to script development is probably the easiest.

Sequential, Independent Tests in Reverse Order

If your script will comprise a number of distinct test cases that are independent, it is probably best to write and debug them in the reverse order you expect to execute them. That is, script test 5 say. Then, when it is working, insert a number of rows BEFORE that working code to make room for the previous script – the script you will not work on. Insert an exit command just before the working script. Now, when you run test 4, it will run and end before test 5 is reached in the script.

When script 4 is working, move the exit command to the point just before test 4, and create test 3 before the exit command.

When all your tests are coded and debugged, remove the exit command before test 2 and run the script in its entirety.

NB this approach will only work if your tests can all be run completely independently. **Typically, every test will start with a get, url to start that test at a common position.**

Script development?

Very broadly, an automated test will start at a particular web site home page or other page on the site. The first command in the script will typically be:

```
get,url,http://www.mysite.com/,start at the home page
```

For the first

Getting started with Script development: Your First Test Script Now as we've got an overview of the tool, its technical aspects and the scripting format it uses, its time to really get to work. In this section you are going to have a detailed explanation of getting to write your 1St test script.

The way this section has been organized is to begin with simple COMMANDS. Once you've had a basic idea of how the scripts look, the way they work, and how the generated output looks like, we would then be looking at how to integrate these commands to generate test scripts to illustrate simple functionality.

For the purpose of this illustration we would be using a simple web based application called rowsquad.mytestportal.com. To enhance your understanding screen shots have been provided. This would give you a good feel and some hands-on experience to start with.

Before getting started to write a test script, you need to get to know to create and name a test script. Doing so helps you organize your content.

The steps involved are:

- Create a separate folder for your test scripts. Let the folder name be for example "Scripts". You can however give a different name of your choice. Make sure this folder is present in the same path of the Perl directory.
- The next step is to create a test script. To do this open a new MS- Excel book (choose FILE->NEW->BLANK WORKBOOK)

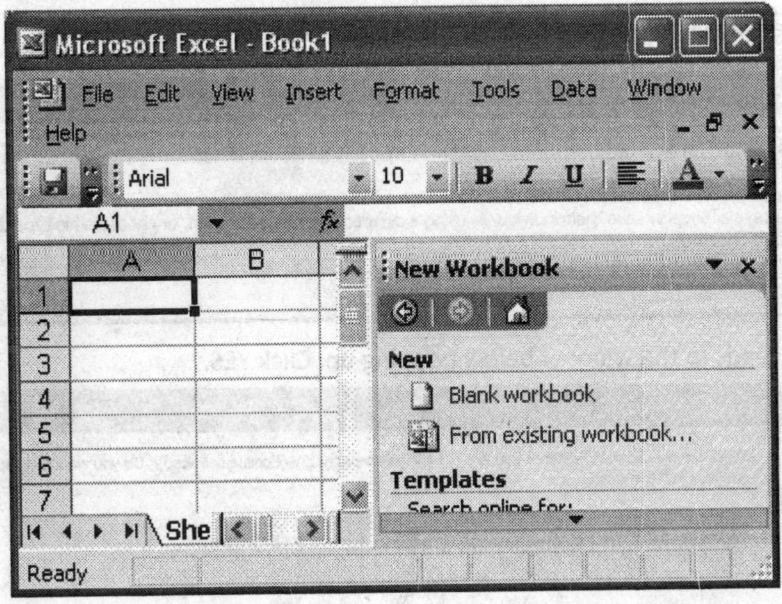

- The next step is to name and save the test script. To save the file (choose FILE -> SAVE AS). The window below pops up. Save the file with the name script1 as file type comma delimited (*.csv) in the folder we have just created called "Scripts".

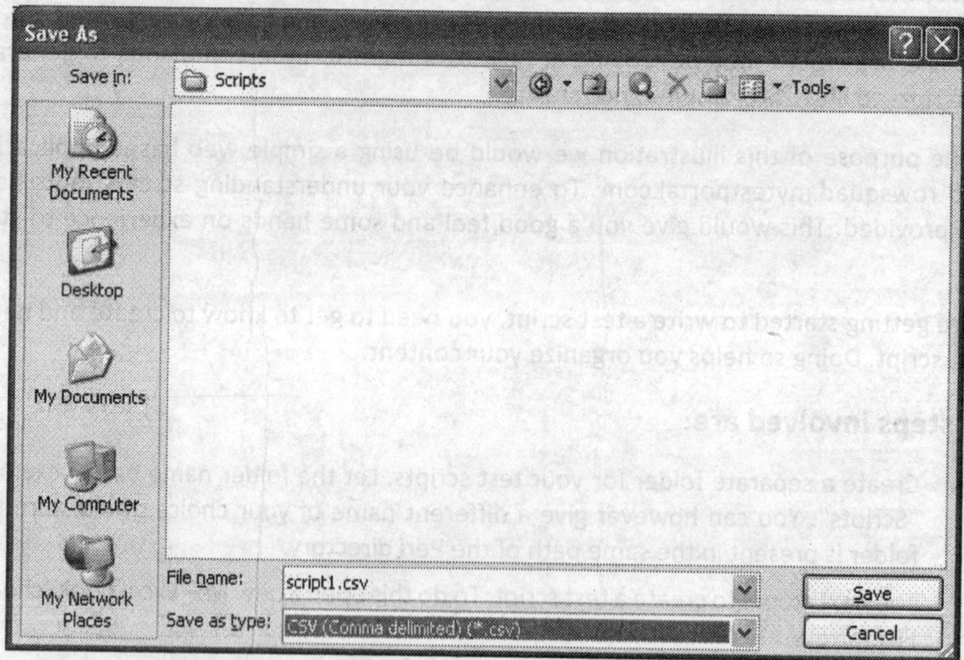

- When we click the save button, the window below pops up. Click OK

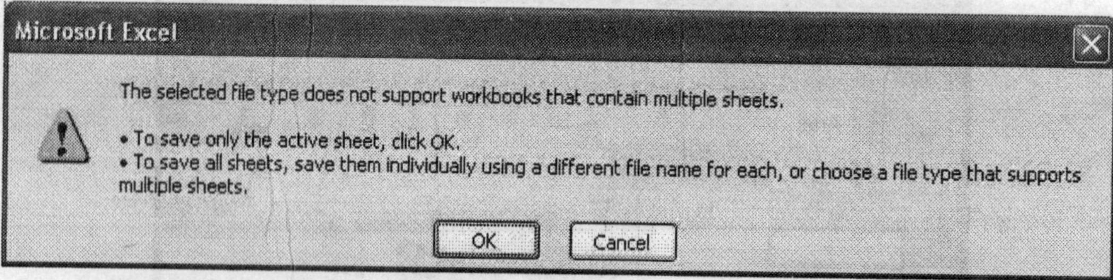

- This leads to the window below popping up. Click YES.

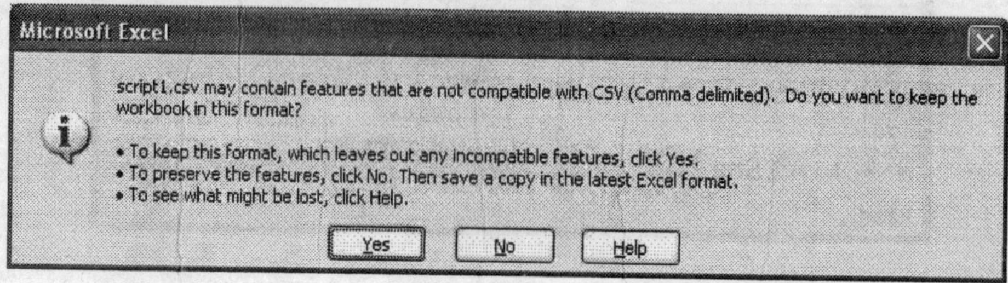

The above 3 actions of naming and saving a test script, results in the creation of the new test script "script1". This is seen in the window below

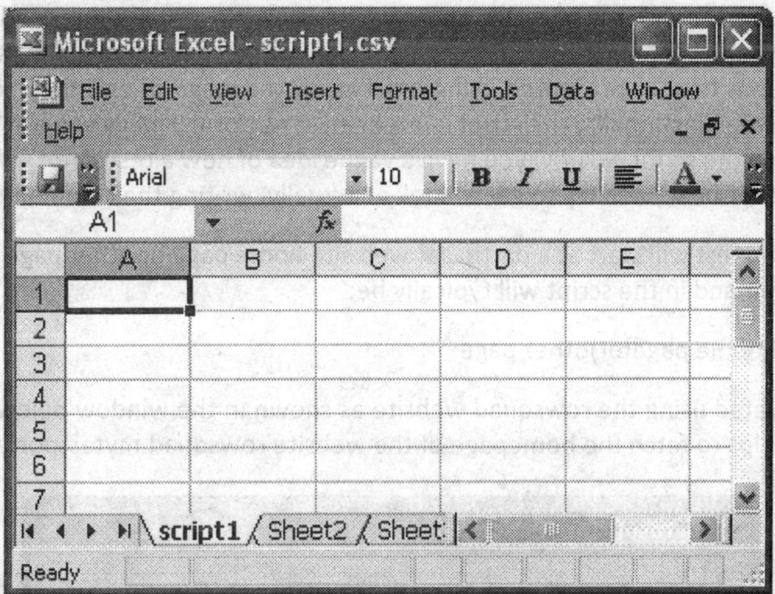

Having created and named the 1st test script (script1.csv), we can now proceed to the next level of writing the steps in the body of the script. Broadly speaking the body of the script would be typically something like:

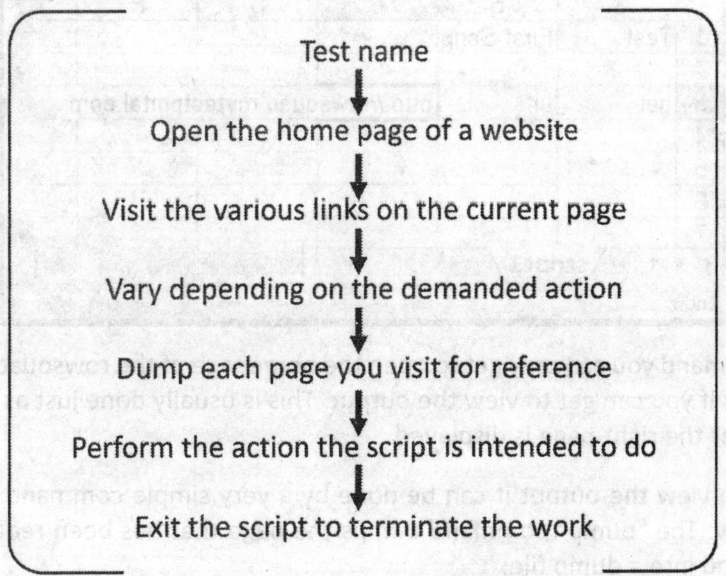

The above diagram gives a clear explanation of how the body of the test script would look like. This is not a strictly rigid procedure to be followed as it various from one script to another depending on the action to be performed. However every script starts with a name for the script, which is normally about what action the script, is intended to achieve. This is followed by fetching for a homepage or any other page. We then have a set of steps which has been represented using brackets in the diagram and they keep varying according to the functionality the script is intended to perform. Finally you exit the process and terminate the script. So now you have a vague idea of how a test script will look. Let's proceed a step ahead, and try to get to look at actually, writing the commands.

An automated test will start at a particular web site home page or other page on the site. The first command in the script will typically be:

get,url,home page(or)other page

This is illustrated using the rowsquad website as shown in the window below. The "get" command helps to fetch the homepage of the website rowsquad.mytestportal.com

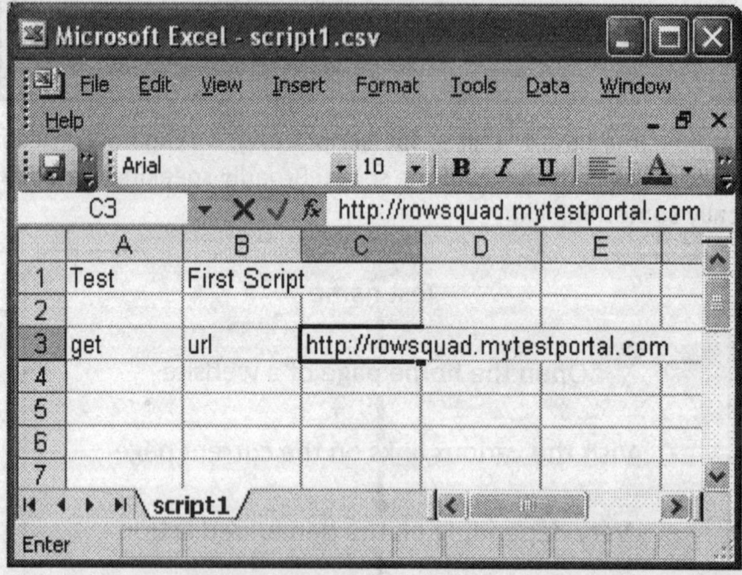

With this command you can only get to open the homepage of the rowsquad website. But it will be nicer if you can get to view the output. This is usually done just as a cross check to see whether the right page is displayed.

If you need to view the output it can be done by a very simple command shown in the window below. The "dump" command dumps the page that has been requested by the "get "command into a dump file.

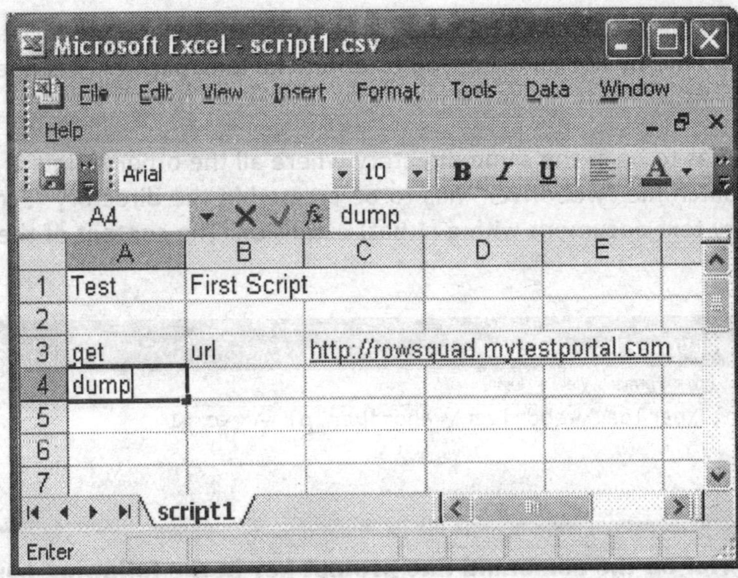

The next step is to end the process to terminate the script, so that the script can be executed to view the results. To end the process the command used is "exit".

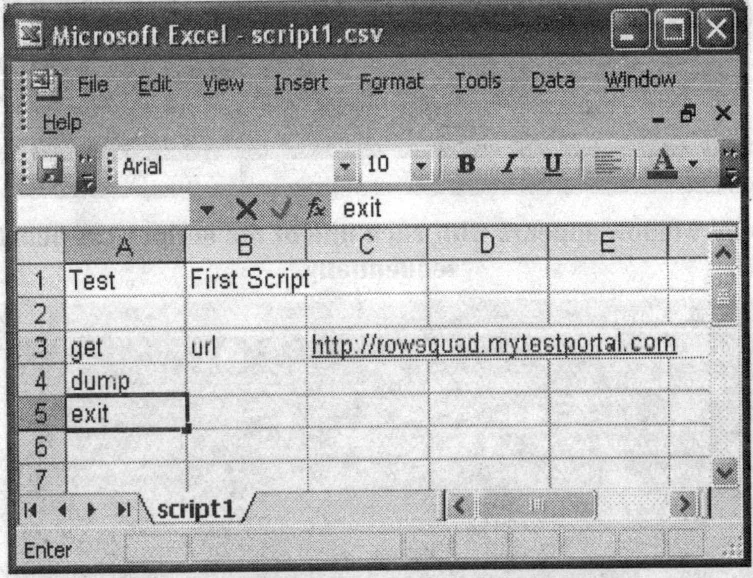

Save the script and open the command line prompt to run the script.

Before you run the script, you need to make sure that you are in the directory where the test scripts exist. To run the script on the command line prompt you need to use a batch file called "webdriver" along with the name of the script (script1.csv) you have just created. A batch file is one single file that has a bunch of several other files within it. A batch file saves time by not allowing you to enter the long path of files need to run the current script.

This batch file has to be in the same directory where all the other scripts are created. In this case the batch file "webdriver" has to be created in the directory "Scripts". This is just an ordinary text document with a (*.bat) extension. The content of the batch file is as follows

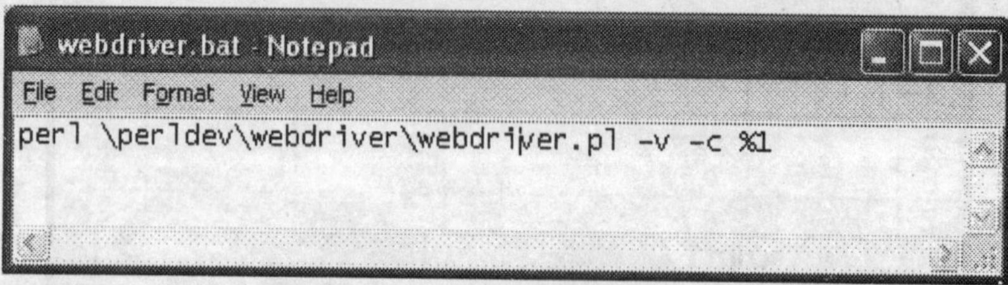

To run the script on the command line prompt key in the following command and hit return

The following window appears with each line of the script1.csv being executed sequentially.

```
Command Prompt
C:\Scripts>webdriver script1.csv

C:\Scripts>perl \perldev\webdriver\webdriver.pl -v -c script1.csv
==========================================
webdriver v 1.0.5 (c) 2006 Paul Gerrard
==========================================
Using script file: script1.csv
==========================================
1, test first script  //  //
==========================================

3, http://rowsquad.mytestportal.com, 2006-8-4 11:52:16, 1154688736, 200, text/ht
ml, 6814, 0.417222023010254
Using dumpfile: dump.html
4, DUMP 1 - HTML form written to dump.html
5, Ending test... bye.

C:\Scripts>
```

Thus the above window clearly shows that, Line 1 displays the name of the script. Line 2 doesn't appear because it's a blank line, so the Perl interpreter ignores that line.

Line 3 retrieves the homepage of the rowsquad website. It also displays other relevant information like the URL, date-time, epoch-time, HTTP response code, the type of content downloaded, number of characters (bytes) contained in the downloaded page, and the time taken to download the page in seconds.

Line 4 dumps the page to a file called "dump.html"and it also says that there is only one dump file. Line 5 terminates the process.

So now you know that the homepage has been retrieved from the server and it is being dumped in a file. But how do you get to view the output in order to make sure the right page has been retrieved. This can be done by entering the dump file (dump.html) on the command line as shown in the window below.

```
Command Prompt

C:\Scripts>webdriver script1.csv

C:\Scripts>perl \perldev\webdriver\webdriver.pl -v -c script1.csv
==============================================
webdriver v 1.0.5 (c) 2006 Paul Gerrard
==============================================
Using script file: script1.csv
========================================
1, test first script  //  //
========================================

3, http://rowsquad.mytestportal.com, 2006-8-4 11:52:16, 1154688736, 200, text/ht
ml, 6814, 0.417222023010254
Using dumpfile: dump.html
4, DUMP 1 - HTML form written to dump.html
5, Ending test... bye.

C:\Scripts>dump.html

C:\Scripts>_
```

By doing so this in turn opens the content of the dump.html file which is nothing other than the homepage of the rowsquad website on to a browser window as shown below.

This example would have given you an idea of how to write the script, run a script and check for the output. You can now proceed to explore other commands.

A page could contain loads of information like, list of links to other pages in the website, links to other external sites and other relevant information. As you've already retrieved the homepage of a website, you might also like to browse through the various links on the page to get to know more information about the website. This can be done by using a simple command as shown in the script below.

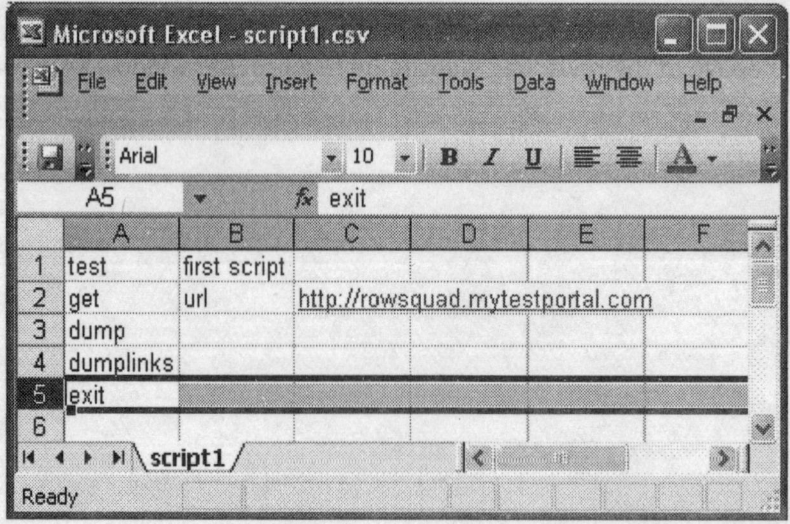

The command "dumplinks" prints a complete list of links of the current page on the console.

When this script is executed on the command line prompt, it displays information about all the links on the homepage of the rowsquad website and also information about the java script.

```
Command Prompt
=========================================
1, test first script  //  //
=========================================

2, http://rowsquad.mytestportal.com, 2006-8-4 12:43:0, 1154691780, 200, text/htm
1, 6814, 0.262022018432617
Using dumpfile: dump.html
3, DUMP 1 - HTML form written to dump.html
---> LINK --->
URL: squadmain.asp?mode=home
Text: Squad Home
Name:
Tag: a
URL ABS: http://rowsquad.mytestportal.com/squadmain.asp?mode=home
---> LINK --->
URL: squadlogin.asp?mode=login
Text: Login
Name:
Tag: a
URL ABS: http://rowsquad.mytestportal.com/squadlogin.asp?mode=login
```

```
Command Prompt
---> LINK --->
URL: #top
Text: Top of Page
Name:
Tag: a
URL ABS: http://rowsquad.mytestportal.com#top
---> LINK --->
URL: javascript:GoBack()
Text: Go Back
Name:
Tag: a
URL ABS: javascript:GoBack()
---> LINK --->
URL: squadmain.asp
Text: Home
Name:
Tag: a
URL ABS: http://rowsquad.mytestportal.com/squadmain.asp
---> LINK --->
URL: javascript:Privacy('/privacy.htm')
```

The "dumplinks" command just displays the links of the website. Using this command you cannot actually view the content of the links. To do this you need to use the command shown below link, text, link name(case sensitive)

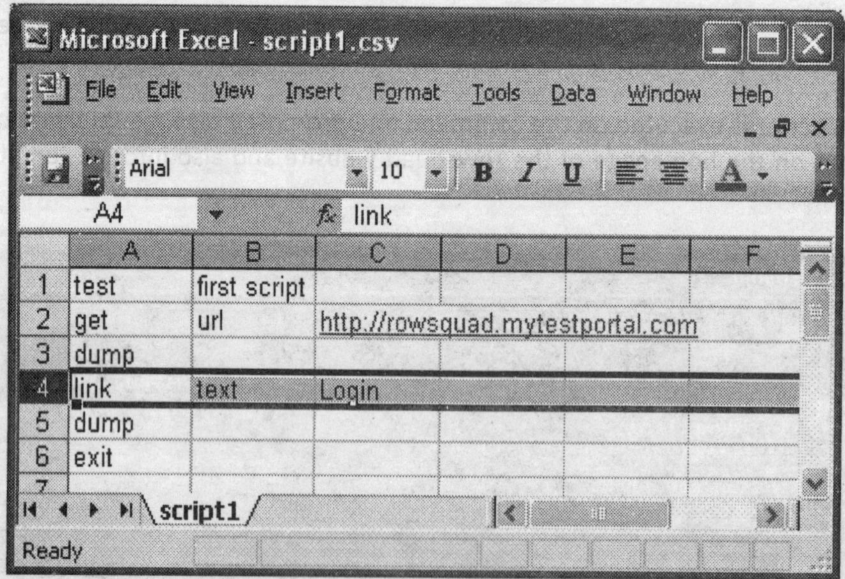

	A	B	C
1	test	first script	
2	get	url	http://rowsquad.mytestportal.com
3	dump		
4	link	text	Login
5	dump		
6	exit		

The "link" command opens the link on the current page with the text "Login". The content of the "Login" page is then dumped.

When you run the script on the command line the following screen appears.

```
Command Prompt
Using script file: script1.csv
=====================================
1, test first script  //  //
=====================================

2, http://rowsquad.mytestportal.com, 2006-8-4 13:13:25, 1154693605, 200, text/ht
ml, 6813, 0.294770956039429
Using dumpfile: dump.html
3, DUMP 1 - HTML form written to dump.html
DEBUG: Link.Text absolute URL=http://rowsquad.mytestportal.com/squadlogin.asp?mo
de=login
4, Login, 2006-8-4 13:13:25, 1154693605, 200, text/html, 4481, 0.078560113906860
4
5, DUMP 2 - HTML form written to dump.html
6, Ending test... bye.

C:\Scripts>dump.html

C:\Scripts>
```

From the screen shot above we clearly understand that, firstly, the homepage is retrieved and dumped. Secondly the link "Login" is retrieved and dumped. So the output dump. html file should now have 2 dump files (dump1 and dump2)

A "link" command helps you to retrieve only the specified page. Let's consider a scenario where in which a page has 25 links. Using the "link" command you can retrieve the 25 links on the page, but it is time consuming and tedious as you need to enter the command for each of the link on the page. There should be an efficient way in which you could generate the command for each link. This can be done using the command shown below.

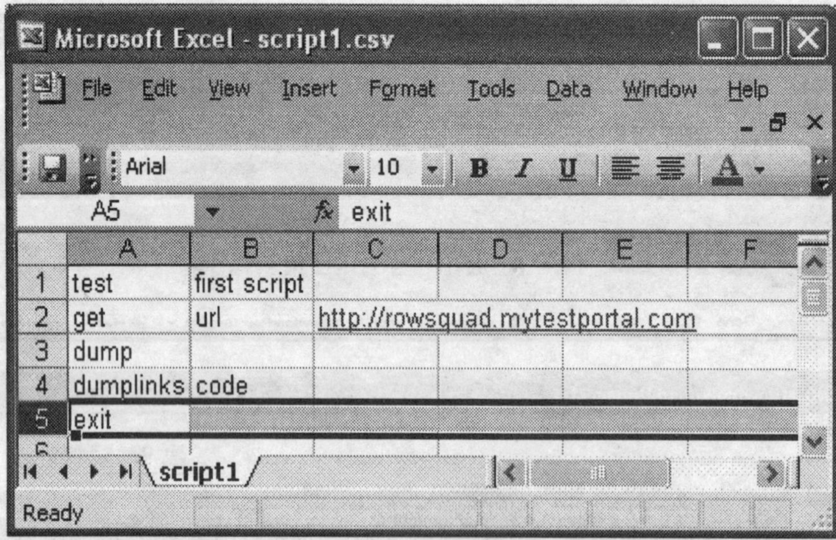

When you run this script, the following window appears

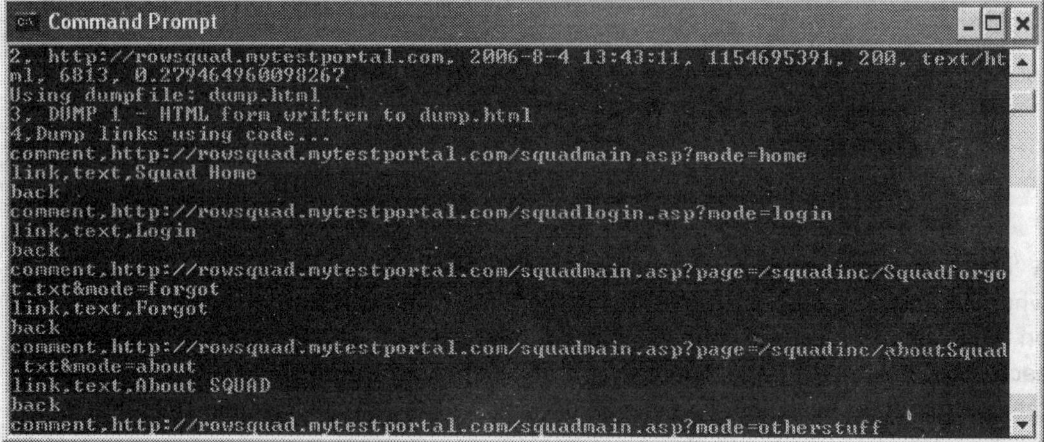

From the window displayed above you can read that the "link" command for each link on the page has been retrieved. These commands are comma separated because it can be easily reused in the test scripts which are (*.csv) file.

To access certain features of the website it is necessary that you log in as authorized user and to prevent unauthorized access you need to logout as well. Let's try to work on a small functionality of login and logout. The diagrammatic representation below gives you a typical idea of how the login/logout functionality is going to work.

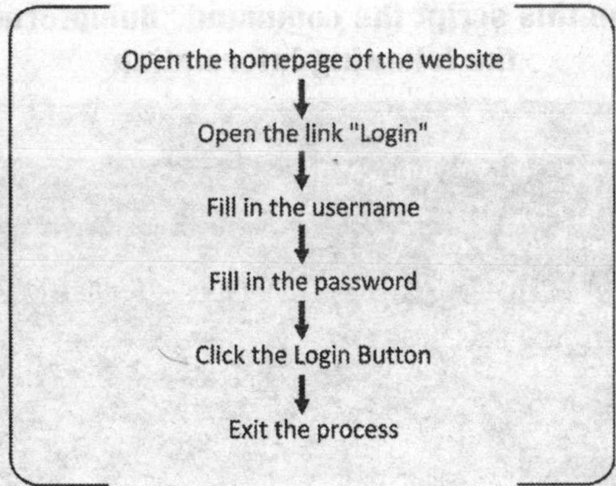

This representation can be implemented in a test script as follows. In this script you could also find another command “comment”, which is being used to document the script better. Before we proceed further we need to understand that the login page has a login form on it.

To obtain details of this form like filed name, type of field etc you need to use a command called “dumpforms”. The purpose of this command is to display details of the form which could aid the user to create the script.

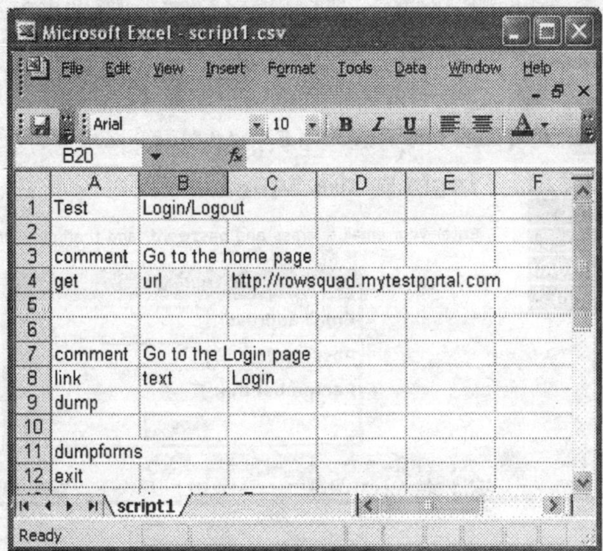

	A	B	C	D	E	F
1	Test	Login/Logout				
2						
3	comment	Go to the home page				
4	get	url	http://rowsquad.mytestportal.com			
5						
6						
7	comment	Go to the Login page				
8	link	text	Login			
9	dump					
10						
11	dumpforms					
12	exit					

When you run this script the command "dumpforms" displays the following information

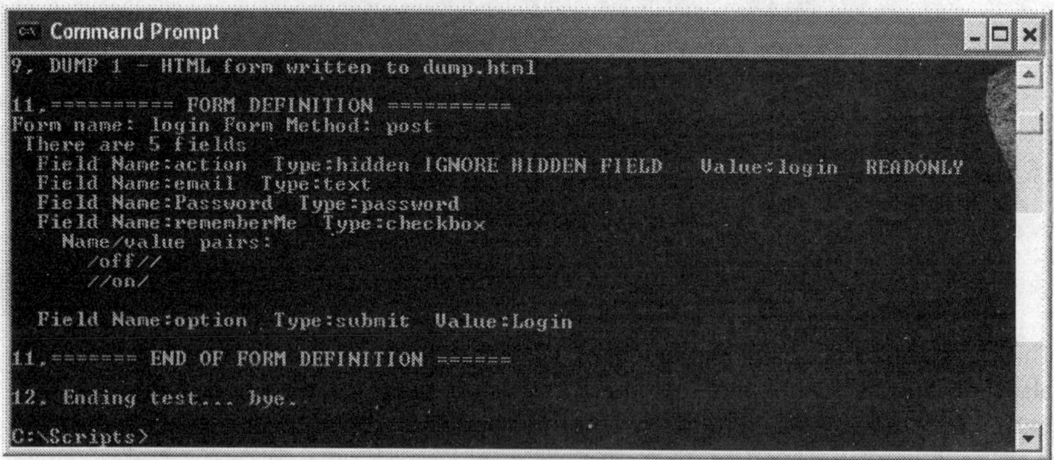

The dump.html file has the dumped the Login page as shown below

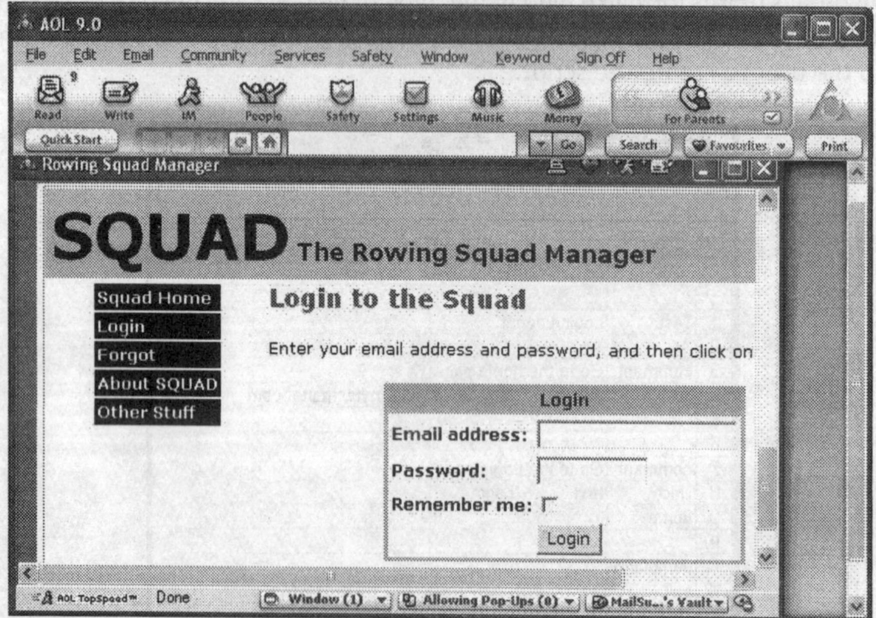

Once you obtain details of the form you can create your test script with the form details in it as shown below.

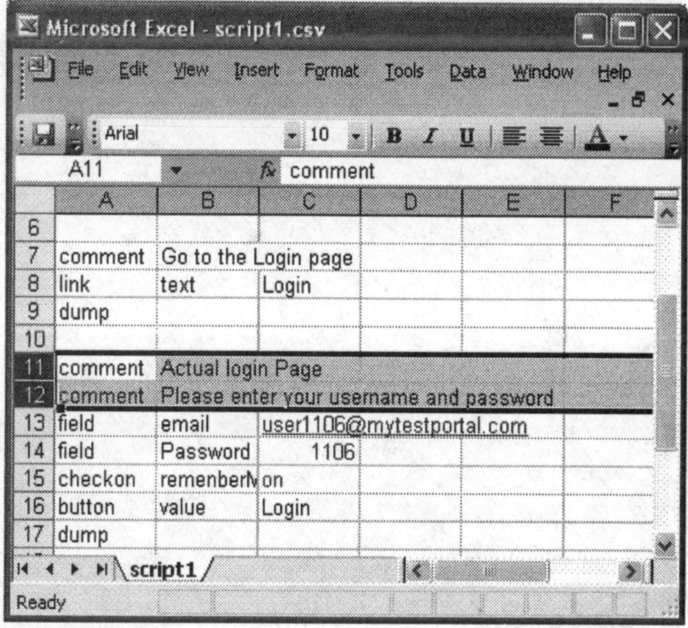

References:

www.gerrardconsulting.com

Automation using Auto IT Tool

Introduction:

AutoIt v3 is a freeware BASIC-like scripting language designed for automating the Windows GUI and general scripting. It uses a combination of simulated keystrokes, mouse movement and window/control manipulation in order to automate tasks in a way not possible or reliable with other languages (e.g. VBScript and Send Keys). AutoIt is also very small, self-contained and will run on all versions of Windows out-of-the-box with no annoying “runtimes” required!

AutoIt was initially designed for PC “roll out” situations to reliably automate and configure thousands of PCs. Over time it has become a powerful language that supports complex expressions, user functions, loops and everything else that veteran scripter’s would expect.

Download Pre-requisite software

http://www.autoitscript.com/autoit3/scite/

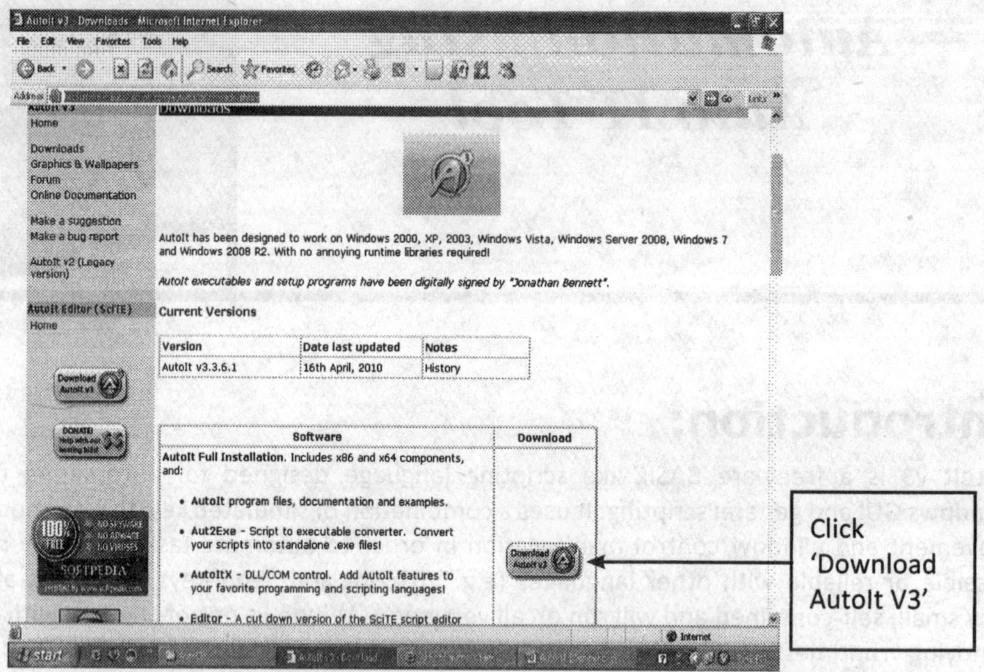

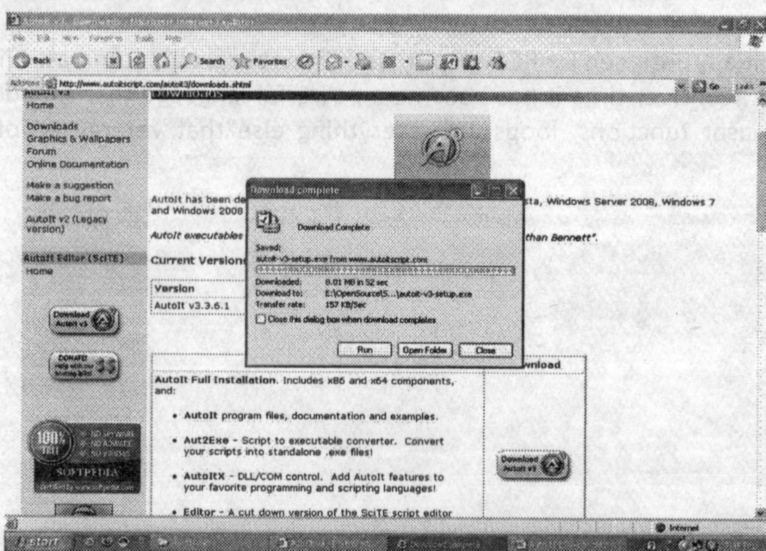

Click on 'Run'

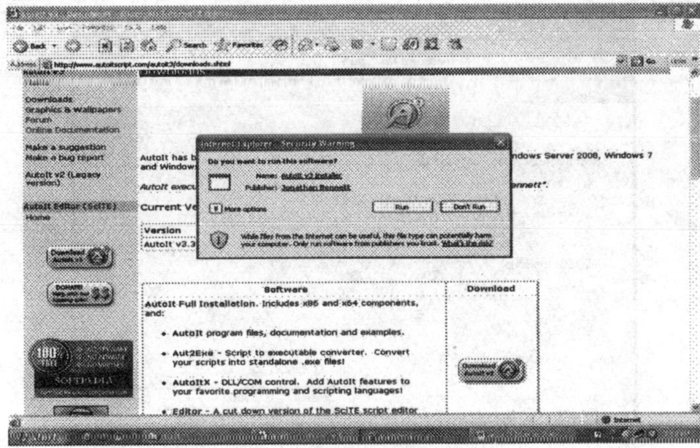

Click 'Next'

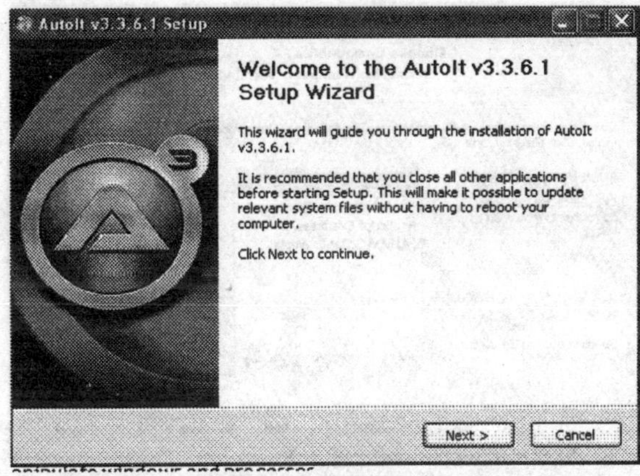

Click 'I Agree'

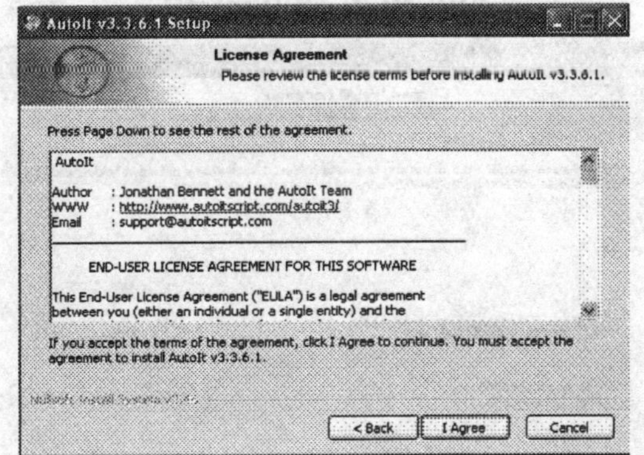

Click 'Run the script' radio button & click 'Next'

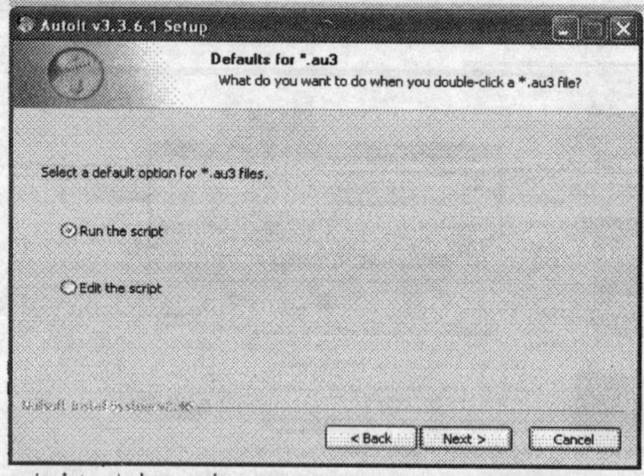

Select all the check box and click 'Next'

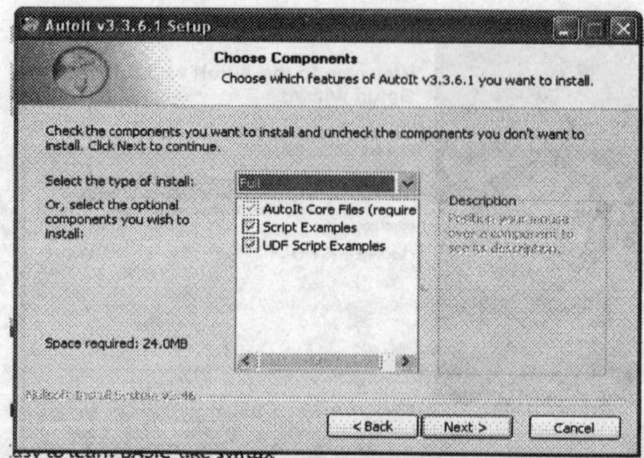

Select 'Destination Folder' as 'C:\Program Files\AutoIt3' path and click on 'Install'

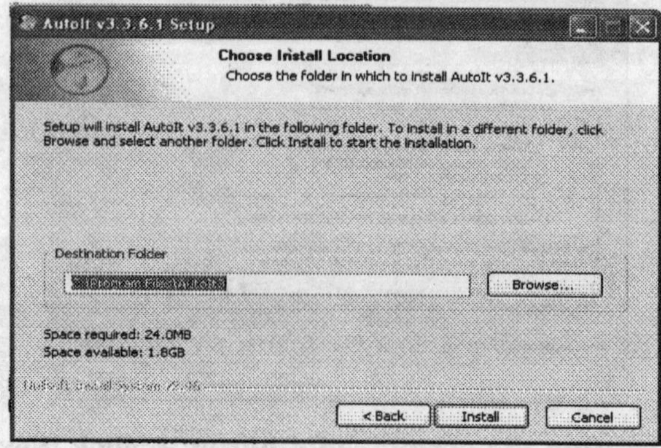

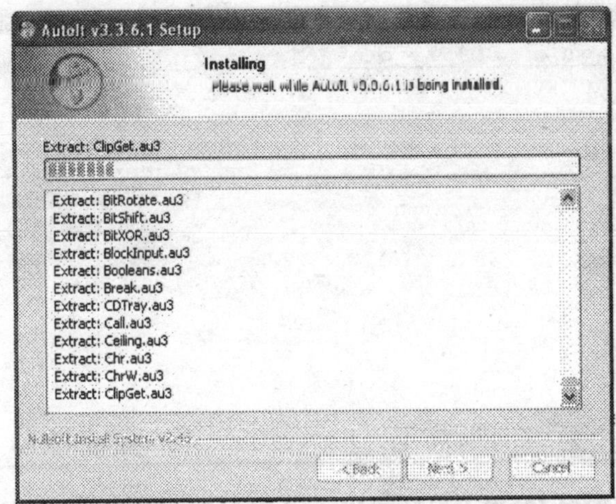

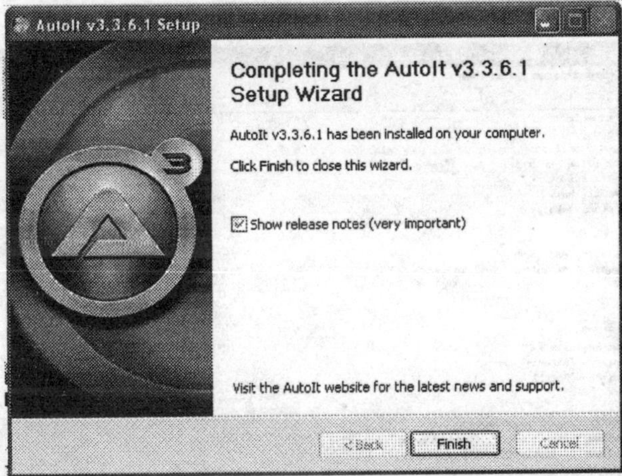

Click Start-> Program-> AutoIt v3->SciTE Script Editor'

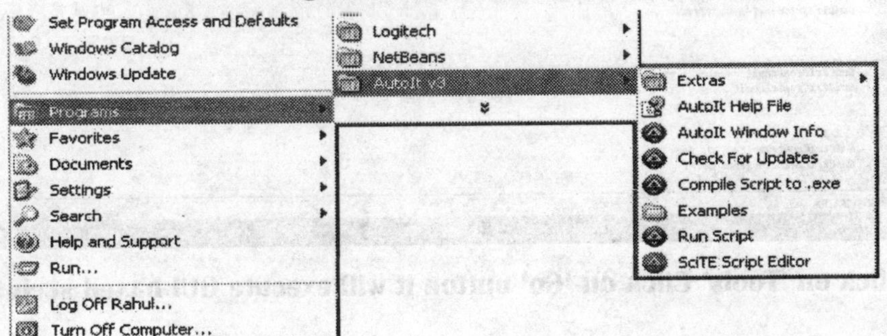

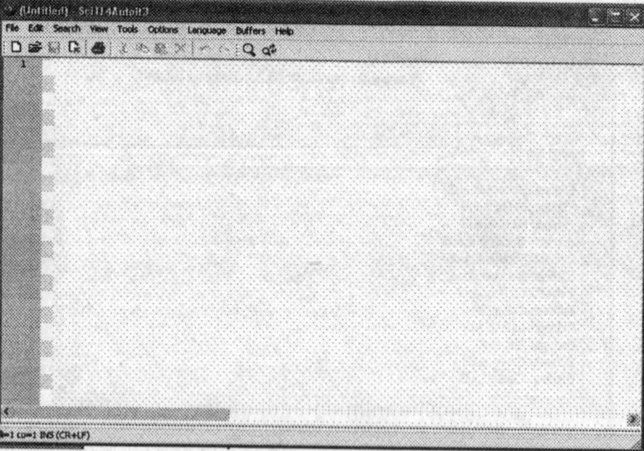

Open Sample program from 'C:\Program Files\AutoIt3\Examples\GUI' and click on 'SampleControls.au3' scirpt

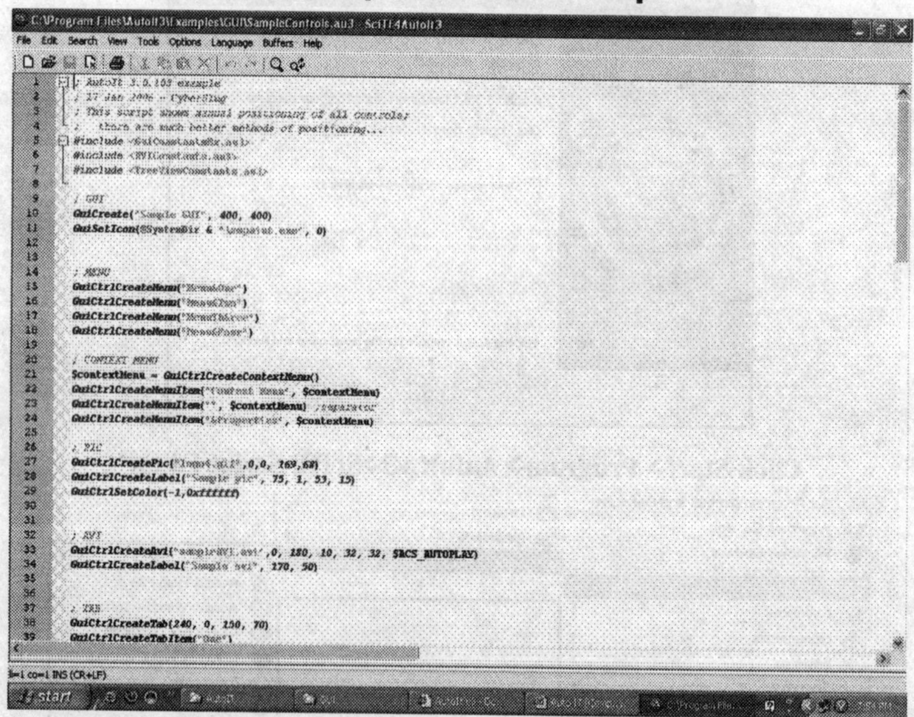

Click on 'Tools' Click on 'Go' button it will execute GUI based script.

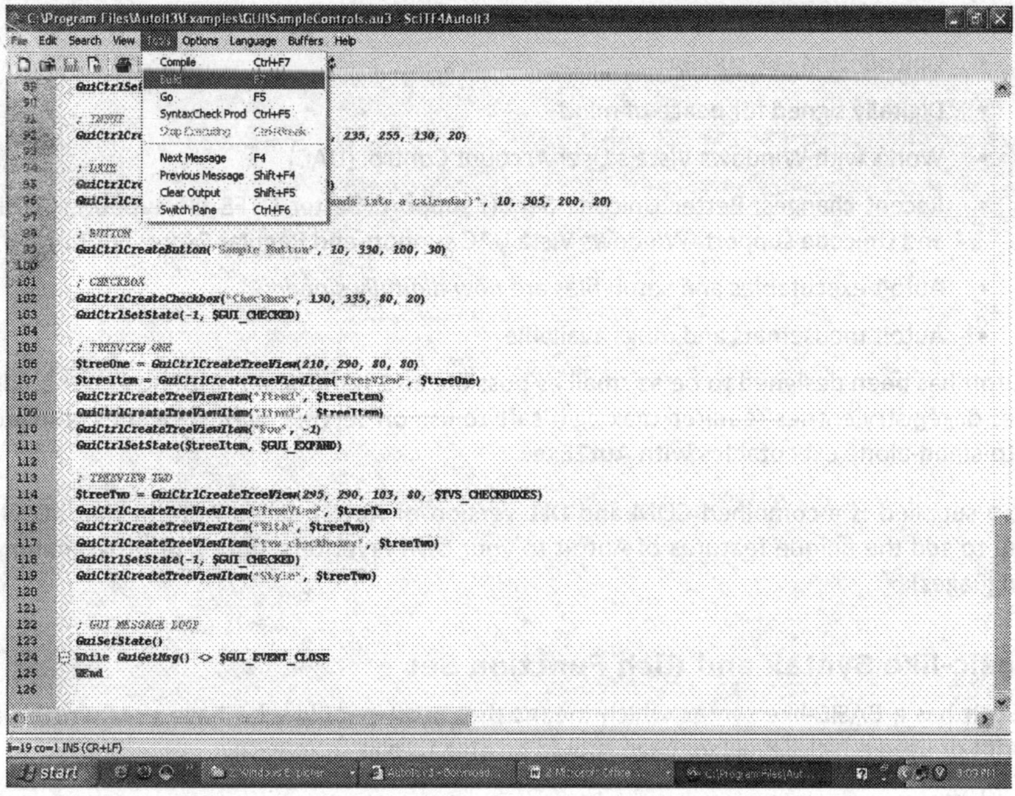

Features:

- Easy to learn BASIC-like syntax
- Simulate keystrokes and mouse movements
- Manipulate windows and processes
- Interact with all standard windows controls
- Scripts can be compiled into standalone executables
- Create Graphical User Interfaces (GUIs)
- COM support
- Regular expressions
- Directly call external DLL and Windows API functions
- Scriptable RunAs functions
- Detailed help file and large community-based support forums

- Compatible with Windows 95 / 98 / ME / NT4 / 2000 / XP / 2003 / Vista / 2008
- Unicode and x64 support
- Digitally signed for peace of mind
- Works with Windows Vista's User Account Control (UAC)
- Recent changes: Better Unicode Send() support. Better UTF8 file support, 64-bit and Unicode support. Windows Vista UAC support and Regular Expressions.
- AutoIt executables and setup files are now *digitally signed*
- AutoIt mousemats and mugs available

AutoIt has been designed to be as small as possible and stand-alone with no external .dll files or registry entries required making it safe to use on Servers. Scripts can be compiled into stand-alone executables with **Aut2Exe**.

Also supplied is a combined COM and DLL version of AutoIt called AutoItX that allows you to add the unique features of AutoIt to your own favorite scripting or programming languages!

Basic-like Syntax and Rich Function Set

AutoIt has a BASIC-like syntax which means that most people who have ever written a script or used a high-level language should be able to pick it up easily.

Although it started life as a simple automation tool, AutoIt now has functions and features that allow it to be used as a general purpose scripting language (with awesome automation as well of course!). Language features include:

- The usual high-level elements for functions, loops and expression parsing
- A staggering amount of string handling functions **and** a Perl compatible regular expression engine (using the PCRE library).
- COM support
- Call Win32 and third-party DLL APIs

Built-in Editor with Syntax Highlighting

AutoIt comes with a customised "lite" version of SciTe that makes editing scripts easy. Users can also download a complete version of SciTe that includes additional tools to make things even easier.

Standalone and Small

AutoIt is a very small and standalone application with no reliance on massive runtimes like .NET or VB. All you need to run AutoIt scripts are the main AutoIt executable (AutoIt3.exe) and the script. Scripts can also be encoded into standalone executables with the built-in script compiler **Aut2Exe.**

International and 64-bit Support

AutoIt is fully Unicode aware and also includes x64 versions of all the main components! How many other free scripting languages can you say that about?

Key and Mouse Simulation

Much time has been spent optimizing the keystroke and mouse simulation functions to be as accurate as possible on all versions of Windows. All the mouse and keyboard routines are highly configurable both in terms of simulation "speed" and functionality.

Window Management

You can expect to move, hide, show, resize, activate, close and pretty much do what you want with windows. Windows can be referenced by title, text on the window, size, position, class and even internal Win32 API handles.

Controls

Directly get information on and interact with edit boxes, check boxes, list boxes, combos, buttons, status bars without the risk of keystrokes getting lost. Even work with controls in windows that aren't active!

Graphical User Interfaces (GUIs)

AutoIt v3 will also allow you to create some complex GUIs - just like those below!

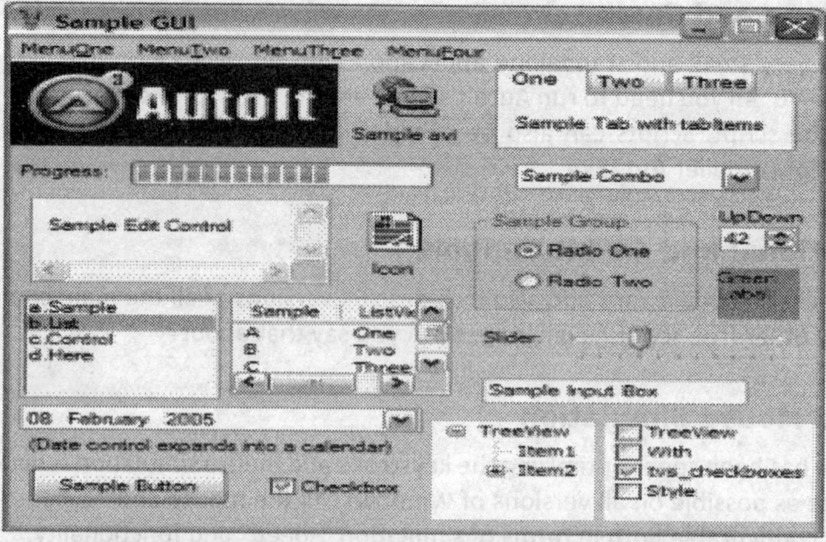

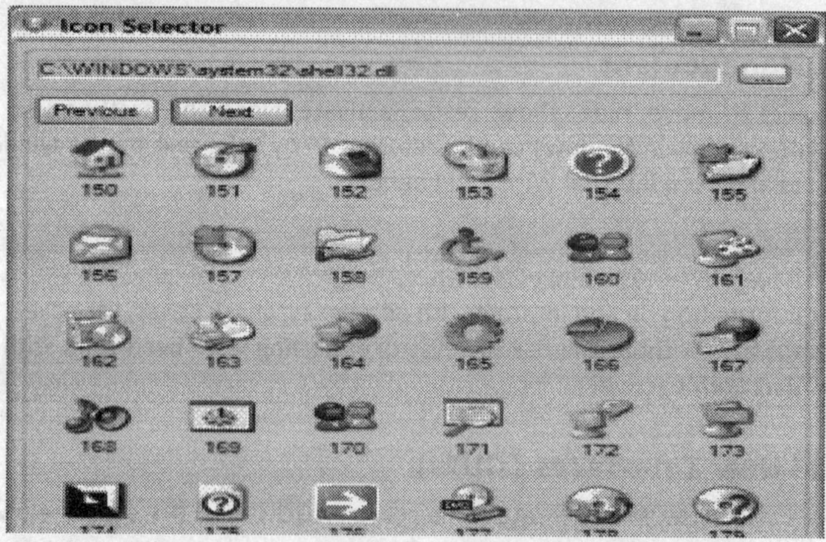

➢ Usage

AutoIt can be used to produce utility software for Microsoft Windows and automate common tasks, such as website monitoring, network monitoring, disk defragging and backup. It is also used to simulate application users, whereby an application is *driven* by an AutoIt script in place of manual application control during software testing.

➢ Test Cases

While creating a POC for this tool on a Web Base Application, we have considered the following test cases for the verification of its functionality the test cases are:

Web Application use (www.webftp.co.uk)

- Body text read
- Checkboxes
- Display Source
- Navigation of Web Site
- Navigation of Image link
- Navigation of Text link
- Radio Button
- Drop Down menu
- Title of Window
- Status Bar
- Refresh Action
- Error Notification
- Submit of Form
- Login Form
- Using Excel file as Data Base for Login Form
- Search Form (If there is a search form in Web Application)

Testing Approach With Auto IT Tool:

➢ Scripts in Auto It

A scripting language, script language or extension language is a programming language that allows control of one or more software applications. "Scripts" are distinct from the core code of the application, which is usually written in a different language, and are often created or at least modified by the end-user. Scripts are often interpreted from source code or bytecode, whereas the applications they control are traditionally compiled to native machine code. Scripting languages are nearly always embedded in the applications they control.

Notes:

Below is code for different controls, Open SciTE Script Editor from Program File-> AutoIt3 and save script as 'Scriptname1.au3' or any specified named.

1) Script for Body text read

```
#include <IE.au3>
$oIE = _IECreate ("http://www.webftp.co.uk")
Sleep(5000)
$sText = _IEBodyReadText ($oIE)
Sleep(5000)
MsgBox(0, "Body Text", $sText)
_IEQuit ($oIE)
```

2) Script for Checkboxes

```
#include <IE.au3>
$oIE = _IECreate ("http://www.webftp.co.uk")
Sleep(5000)
$oForm = _IEFormGetObjByName($oIE,"LoginForm")
_IEFormElementCheckboxSelect ($oForm, "1", "anonymous", 1, "byValue")
Sleep(5000)
_IEFormElementCheckboxSelect ($oForm, "yes", "passivemode", 1, "byValue")
Sleep(5000)
_IEFormElementCheckboxSelect ($oForm, "yes", "sslconnect", 1, "byValue")
_IEQuit ($oIE)
```

3) Script for Display Source

```
#include <IE.au3>
$oIE = _IECreate("http://www.webftp.co.uk")
Sleep(5000)
$sHTML = _IEDocReadHTML ($oIE)
MsgBox(0, "Document Source", $sHTML)
_IEQuit ($oIE)
```

4) Script for Navigation of Web Site

```
#include <IE.au3>

$oIE = _IECreate ("www.webftp.co.uk")
Sleep(5000)
_IENavigate ($oIE, "Insert Link of the Page Within that Web Application , Where you want to Navigate")
Sleep(5000)
_IENavigate ($oIE, "Insert Link of the Page Within that Web Application , Where you want to Navigate")
_IEQuit ($oIE)
```

5) Script for Login Form

```
#include <IE.au3>
$oIE = _IECreate ("http://www.webftp.co.uk")
Sleep(5000)

$oForm = _IEFormGetObjByName ($oIE, "LoginForm")
$oText = _IEFormElementGetObjByName ($oForm, "ftpserver")
_IEFormElementSetValue ($oText,"ABC")
Sleep(5000)
$oText = _IEFormElementGetObjByName ($oForm, "username")
_IEFormElementSetValue ($oText,"Vikas Wadhwa")
Sleep(5000)
$oText = _IEFormElementGetObjByName ($oForm, "password")
_IEFormElementSetValue ($oText,"11223344")
Sleep(5000)
$oText = _IEFormElementGetObjByName ($oForm, "directory")
_IEFormElementSetValue ($oText,"Vikas Wadhwa")
Sleep(5000)
$oSelect = _IEFormElementGetObjByName ($oForm, "skin")
_IEFormElementOptionSelect ($oSelect, "india", 1, "byText")
_IEQuit ($oIE)
```

6) Script for Drop Down menu

```
#include <IE.au3>

$oIE = _IECreate ("http://10.2.0.178/powerapps_NLB/loginscreen.
asp")

$oForm = _IEFormGetObjByName ($oIE, "LOGIN")

Sleep(5000)

$oSelect = _IEFormElementGetObjByName ($oForm, "intranet")

_IEFormElementOptionSelect ($oSelect, "ENC", 1, "byText")

_IEQuit ($oIE)
```

7) Script for Radio Button

```
#include <IE.au3>

$oIE = _IECreate ("http://www.webftp.co.uk")

$oForm = _IEFormGetObjByName ($oIE, "LoginForm")

_IEFormElementRadioSelect  ($oForm,  "binary",  "ftpmode",  1,
"byValue")

Sleep(5000)

_IEFormElementRadioSelect  ($oForm,  "automatic",  "ftpmode",  1,
"byValue")

Sleep(5000)

_IEQuit ($oIE)
```

8) Script for Submit the Form

```
#include <IE.au3>

$oIE = _IECreate ("http://www.webftp.co.uk")

Sleep(5000)

$oForm = _IEFormGetObjByName ($oIE, "LoginForm")

$oText = _IEFormElementGetObjByName ($oForm, "ftpserver")

_IEFormElementSetValue ($oText,"ABC")
```

```
Sleep(5000)
$oText = _IEFormElementGetObjByName ($oForm, “username”)
_IEFormElementSetValue ($oText,”Vikas Wadhwa”)
Sleep(5000)
$oText = _IEFormElementGetObjByName ($oForm, “password”)
_IEFormElementSetValue ($oText,”11223344”)
Sleep(5000)
$oText = _IEFormElementGetObjByName ($oForm, “directory”)
_IEFormElementSetValue ($oText,”Vikas Wadhwa”)
Sleep(5000)
$oSelect = _IEFormElementGetObjByName ($oForm, “skin”)
_IEFormElementOptionSelect ($oSelect, “india”, 1, “byText”)
Sleep(5000)
_IEFormSubmit ($oForm)
_IEQuit ($oIE)
```

9) Script for Link click by text

```
#include <IE.au3>
$oIE = _IECreate (“http://www.webftp.co.uk”)
Sleep(5000)
_IELinkClickByText ($oIE, “Clear cookies”)
Sleep(5000)
_IELinkClickByText ($oIE, “privacy policy”)
Sleep(5000)
_IELinkClickByText ($oIE, “Further Ftp and Web Ftp information”)
_IEQuit ($oIE)
```

10) Script for image click

```
#include <IE.au3>

$oIE = _IECreate ("http://www.webftp.co.uk")

_IEImgClick ($oIE, "WebFTP Logo", "alt")

_IEQuit ($oIE)
```

11) Script for Search Form

```
#include <IE.au3>

$oIE = _IECreate ("http://www.yahoo.com")

$oForm = _IEFormGetObjByName ($oIE, "sf1")

$oQuery = _IEFormElementGetObjByName ($oForm, "p")

_IEFormElementSetValue ($oQuery, "sap")

_IEFormSubmit ($oForm, 0)

_IELoadWait($oIE)
```

12) Script for Excel Connectivity with login form

```
#include <IE.au3>

#include <Excel.au3>

$sFilePath1 = "D:\Vikas Wadhwa\WebSite Testing\Webftp Testing\
vikas.xls" ;This file should already exist

$oExcel = _ExcelBookOpen($sFilePath1,0)

If @error = 1 Then

MsgBox(0, "Error!", "Unable to Create the Excel Object")

    Exit

ElseIf @error = 2 Then

MsgBox(0, "Error!", "File does not exist - Shame on you!")

    Exit

EndIf
```

```
$sCellValue = _ExcelReadCell ($oExcel, 2 ,1)
$sCellValue1 = _ExcelReadCell($oExcel, 2 ,2)
$sCellValue2 = _ExcelReadCell($oExcel, 2 ,3)
$sCellValue3 = _ExcelReadCell($oExcel, 2 ,4)
$sCellValue4= _ExcelReadCell ($oExcel, 2 ,5)
$sCellValue5 = _ExcelReadCell($oExcel, 2 ,6)
$sCellValue6 = _ExcelReadCell($oExcel, 2 ,7)
$sCellValue7 = _ExcelReadCell($oExcel, 2 ,8)
$sCellValue8 = _ExcelReadCell($oExcel, 2 ,9)
$oIE = _IECreate ("http://www.webftp.co.uk")
Sleep(2000)
$oForm = _IEFormGetObjByName ($oIE, "LoginForm")
$oText = _IEFormElementGetObjByName ($oForm,"ftpserver" )
_IEFormElementSetValue ($oText,$sCellValue)
Sleep(2000)
$oText = _IEFormElementGetObjByName ($oForm,"Username" )
_IEFormElementSetValue ($oText,$sCellValue1)
Sleep(2000)
$oText = _IEFormElementGetObjByName ($oForm, "password")
_IEFormElementSetValue ($oText,$sCellValue2)
Sleep(2000)
$oText = _IEFormElementGetObjByName ($oForm, "directory")
_IEFormElementSetValue ($oText,$sCellValue3)
Sleep(2000)

$oSelect = _IEFormElementGetObjByName ($oForm, "skin")
```

```
_IEFormElementOptionSelect ($oSelect, $sCellValue4, 1, "byText")

_IEFormElementRadioSelect ($oForm, "binary", "ftpmode", $sCellValue5, "byValue")

Sleep(2000)

_IEFormElementRadioSelect ($oForm, "automatic", "ftpmode", $sCellValue6, "byValue")

Sleep(2000)

_IEFormElementRadioSelect ($oForm, "binary", "ftpmode", $sCellValue6, "byValue")

Sleep(2000)

_IEFormElementRadioSelect ($oForm, "automatic", "ftpmode", $sCellValue5, "byValue")

Sleep(2000)

_IEFormElementCheckboxSelect ($oForm, "1", "anonymous", $sCellValue7, "byValue")

Sleep(2000)

_IEFormElementCheckboxSelect ($oForm, "1", "anonymous", 0, "byValue")

Sleep(2000)

_IEFormElementCheckboxSelect ($oForm, "yes", "passivemode" ,$sCellValue7, "byValue")
Sleep(2000)

_IEFormElementCheckboxSelect ($oForm, "yes", "passivemode",0, "byValue")

Sleep(2000)

_IEFormElementCheckboxSelect ($oForm, "yes", "sslconnect", $sCellValue7, "byValue")

Sleep(2000)

_IEFormElementCheckboxSelect ($oForm, "yes", "sslconnect", 0,
```

```
"byValue")
Sleep(2000)
_IEFormSubmit ($oForm)
Sleep(2000)
_IEQuit ($oIE)
```

13) Script for Refresh Action

```
#include <IE.au3>
$oIE = _IECreate ("http://www.webftp.co.uk")
$oSubmit = _IEGetObjByName ($oIE, "LoginForm")
Sleep(2000)
_IEAction ($oSubmit, "refresh")
_IELoadWait ($oIE)
_IEQuit ($oIE)
```

14) Script for Error Notification

```
#include <IE.au3>
$oIE = _IECreate ("www.webftp.co.uk")
If _IEErrorNotify () Then
    MsgBox(0, "_IEErrorNotify Status", "Notification is ON, turning it
    OFF")
    _IEErrorNotify (False)
Else
    MsgBox(0, "_IEErrorNotify Status", "Notification is OFF, turning it
    ON")
    _IEErrorNotify (True)
EndIf
_IEQuit ($oIE)
```

15) Script for Status Bar text

```
#include <IE.au3>

$oIE = _IECreate ("http://www.webftp.co.uk")

;Sleep(5000)

;$oForm = _IEFormGetObjByName($oIE,"LoginForm")


If Not _IEPropertyGet ($oIE, "statusbar") Then _IEPropertySet ($oIE,
"statusbar", True)

_IEPropertySet ($oIE, "statustext", "Look What I can Do")

Sleep(1000)

_IEPropertySet ($oIE, "statustext", "I can change the status text"

_IEQuit ($oIE)
```

16) Script for title of window

```
#include <IE.au3>

$oIE = _IECreate ("http://www.webftp.co.uk")

;Sleep(5000)

;$oForm = _IEFormGetObjByName($oIE,"LoginForm")


 _IEPropertyGet ($oIE, "title" )

MsgBox(0, "title", "Mozila")

_IEQuit ($oIE)
```

➢ Scripts to .exe

We can easily convert our generated scripts into .exe that will run on any machine that is, will be independent of the Auto It software. Auto It provides a Special Feature known as **Compile Script to .exe** as shown below:

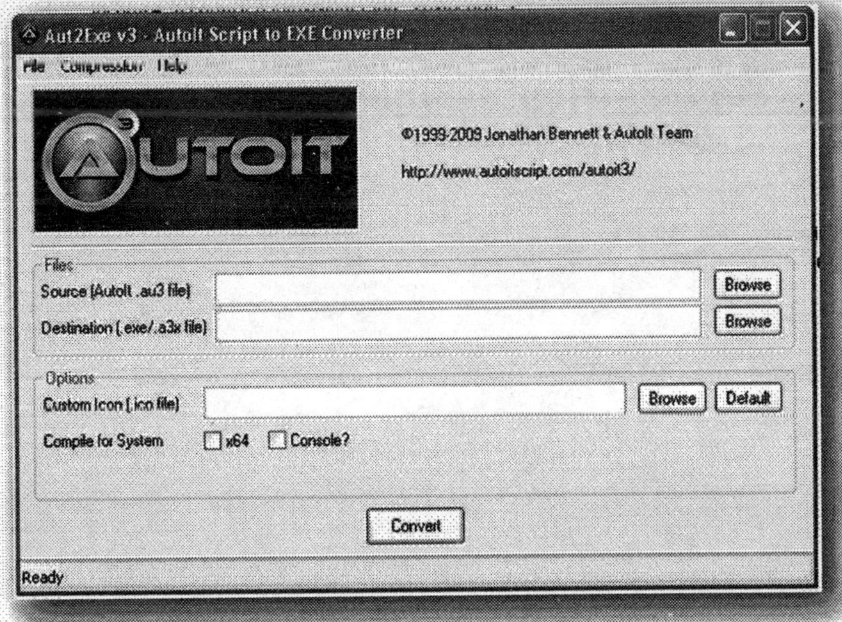

Compile Scripts to .exe

Steps for converting Script into .exe

- Open AutoIt
- Click on Compile Script to .exe
- Specify the Source file
- Specify the Destination path , where you want your .exe file
- Select the Options by Check & Uncheck it , depending upon your application
- Click on Convert

After performing all these steps, User will be available with the .exe file that can be run on any machine that is it will independent of the AutoIt Software.

➢ Execution of Scripts

AutoIt provides a feature by which we can generate & edit our scripts. We can perform this with the help of AutoIt SciTE Script Editor. The AutoIt SciTE Script Editor window is shown as below:

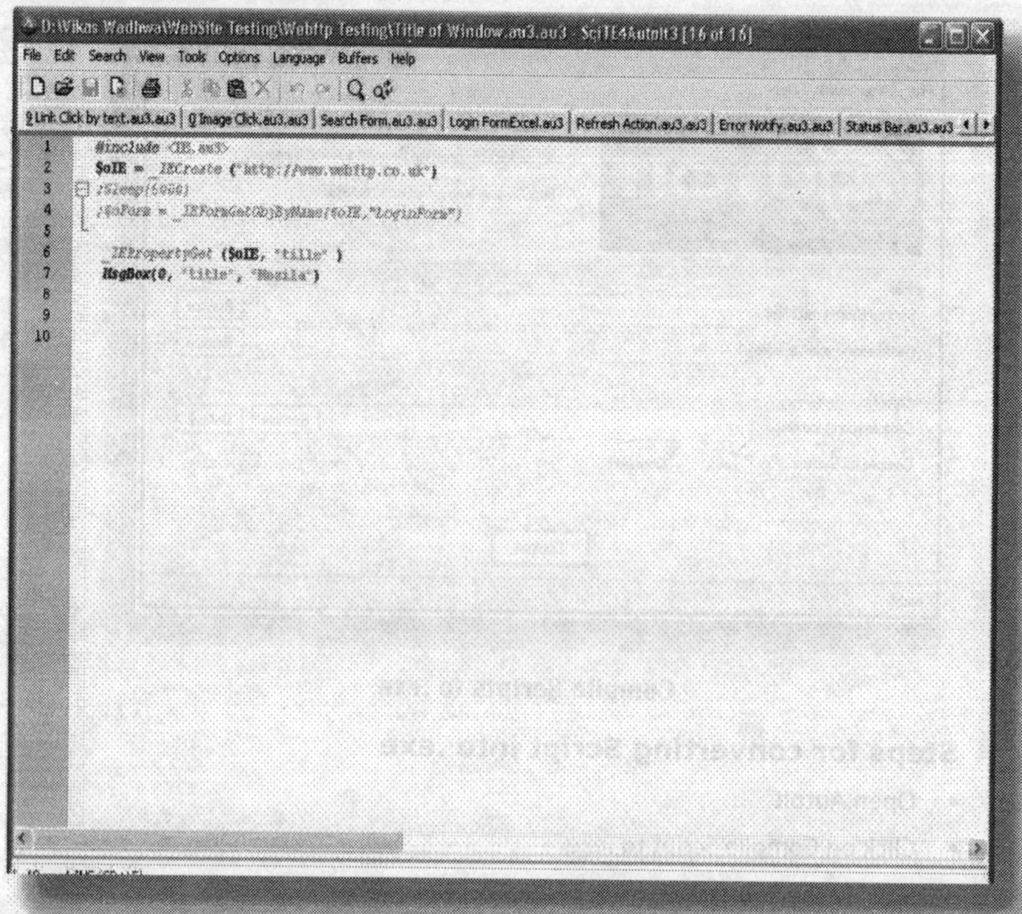

AutoIt SciTE Script Editor Window

Steps for creating Scripts in AutoIt SciTE Script Editor

- Open AutoIt
- Click on SciTE Script Editor
- AutoIt SciTE Script Editor Window will open
- There you can create your scripts
- Save it with .au3
- Run the Script with F5 or by double clicking on it

These all are the steps by which you can create and run a Script.

➢ AutoIt v3 Window Info

AutoIt v3 Window Info is used to find the properties of a window applicaton like:

- Window
- Control
- Visible Text
- Hidden Text
- Status Bar
- Tool Bar
- Mouse (Position)
- Summary

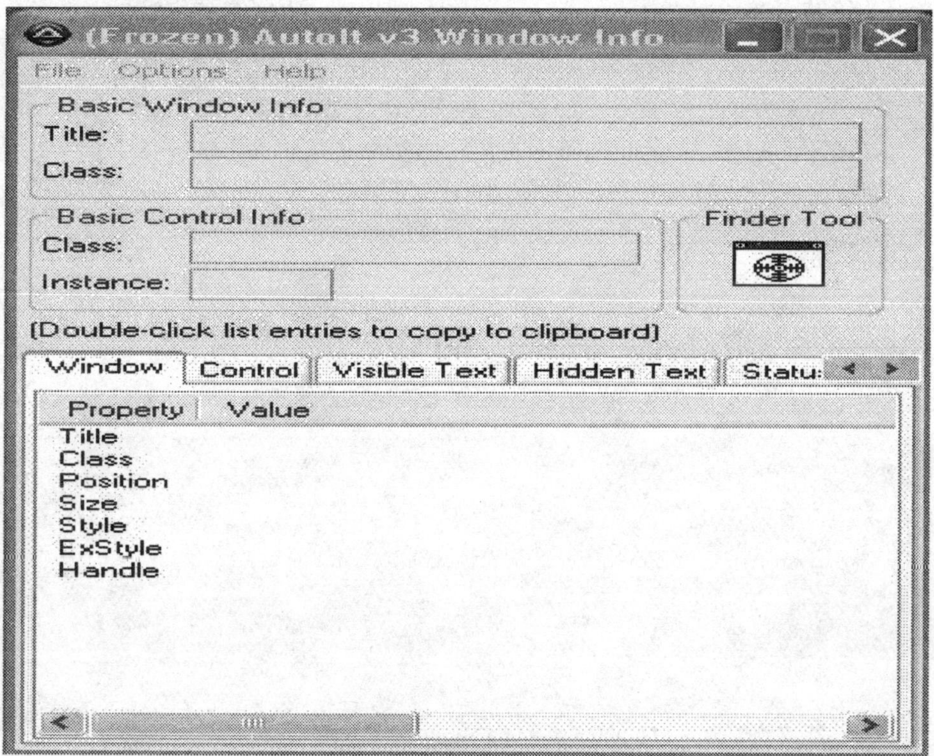

AutoIt v3 Window Info

Flex Automation using FlexMonkey tool

1) Selenium Handling windows Popup using Auto-it

Step 1: Go to AutoIT-> click on 'AutoIT Window Info' menu

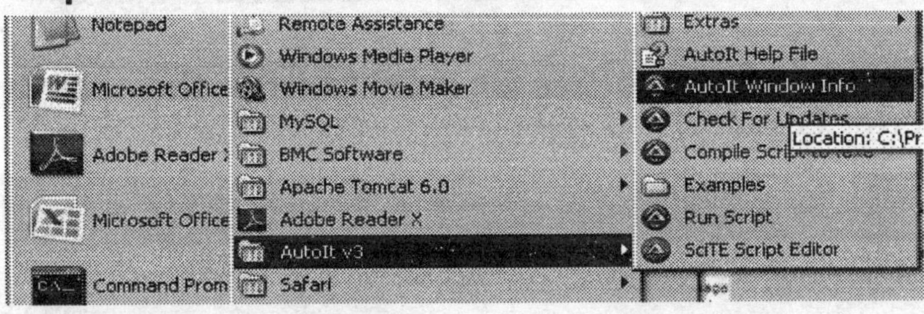

Step 2: got to the window pop-up and highlight the window objects using 'Finder Tool'

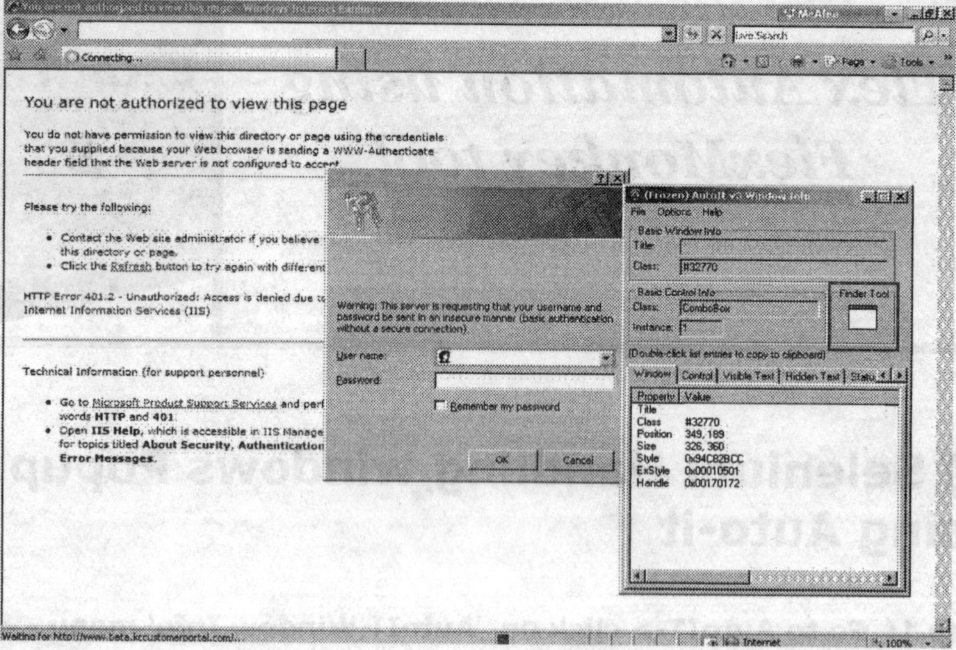

Step 3: after checking the properties we need to write the code in AutoIT 'SciTE Script Editor'

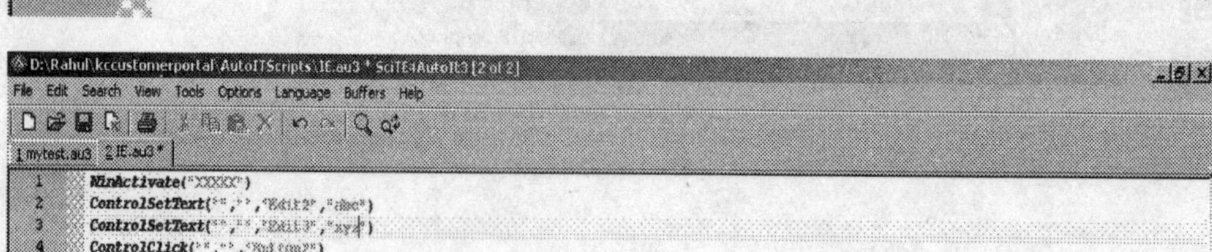

Example code:

```
WinActivate("XXXXX")
ControlSetText("","","Edit2","abc")
ControlSetText("","","Edit3","xyz")
ControlClick("","","Button2")
```

Step 4: Save the file on the local drive and then we need to create exe of this file: So open 'Compile Script to EXE converter'

Give the below details
Source file: as saved by you
Destination file: the file name with .exe extension

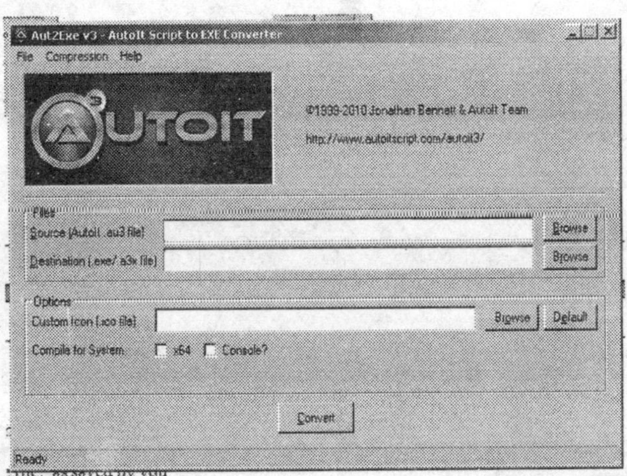

Then click on 'Convert'

So it will save the exe file on the drive specified by you.

Step 5: Calling the .exe file in java

How to call the exe file from JAVA?

Java Code sample 1:

```
Runtime.getRuntime().exec("C:\\NEW.EXE " + date1);
 //call Autoit script with one parameter date1
```

Java Code sample 2:

```
Runtime r=Runtime.getRuntime();
String athToExe="D:/Rahul/AutoITScripts/
Firefox1.exe";
r.exec(pathToExe);
```

2) Selenium - File Upload/Download using Autoit:

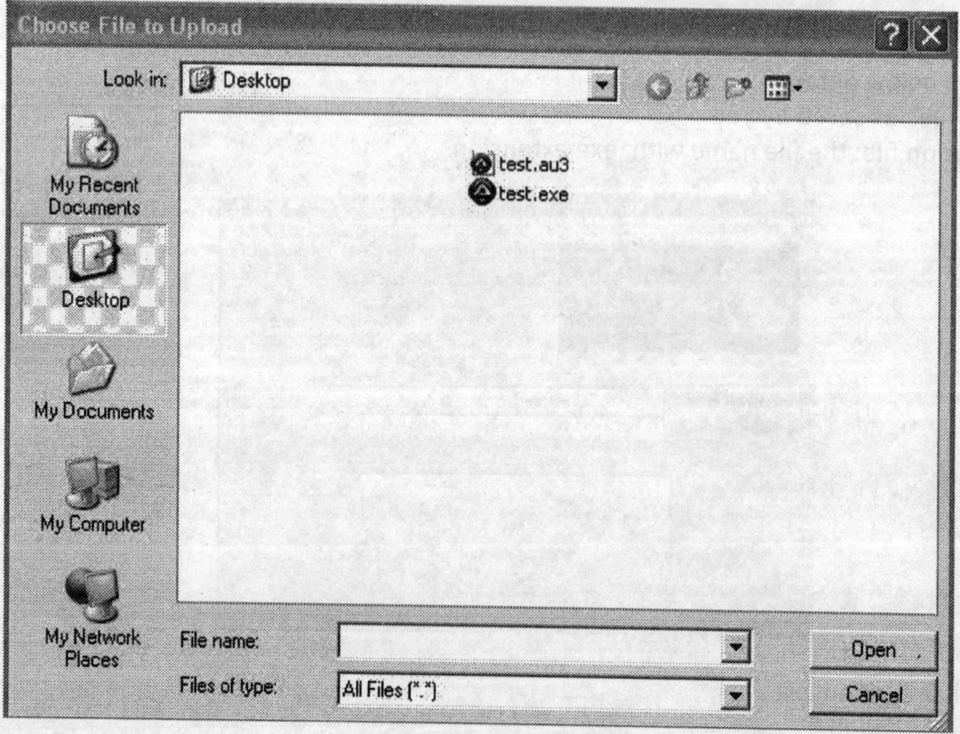

What are the different steps that need to be performed by the Autoit to select the file from the above window.

1. Select the window and get the focus on it.

2. Type the file name with path in the text box.

3. Select open button, so that all the selection details are transferred into web page control and selenium can take control of the next activity.

Following is the Autoit script for the above steps, compile and convert into exe file and call from selenium.

How to call the exe file from JAVA?

Java Code

```
Runtime.getRuntime().exec("C:\\NEW.EXE " + date1); //call Autoit script with one parameter date1
```

AutoIt Script sample code:

```
;MsgBox(0,"Parameters",$CmdLine[1])    ;Sending   parameters through command line
FileCopy("C:\W3C.png",   "C:\"&$CmdLine[1]&".png")  ;Make  a duplicate copy of the file, as same file name is not accepted
sleep(3000);delay for 3 seconds for the file to create
WinWaitActive("#32770", "Choose File to Upload",10)
WinFlash("Choose File to Upload","", 4, 500) ; Just to Flash the window
ControlSetText("Choose  File  to  Upload",  "",  "[CLASS:Edit; INSTANCE:1]", "C:\"&$CmdLine[1]&".png")
ControlClick("Choose  File  to  Upload",  "","[CLASS:Button; INSTANCE:2]");
```

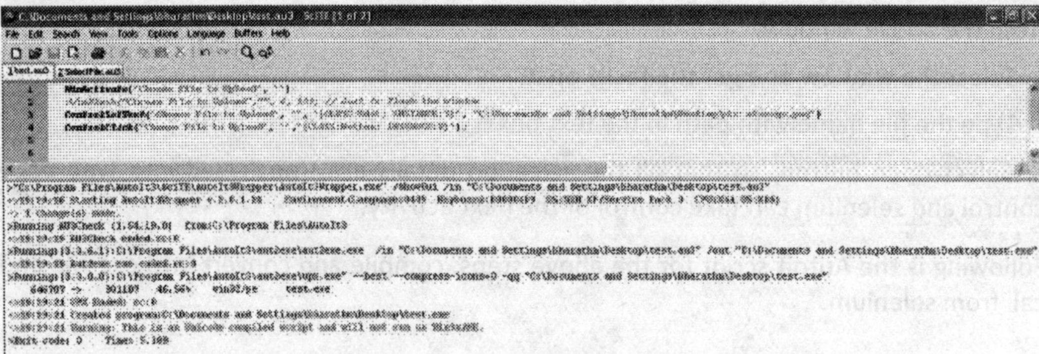

How to capture the Windows object properties, by using Auto it Windows Info tool, following screen shot demonstrates how to open and capture the windows controls.

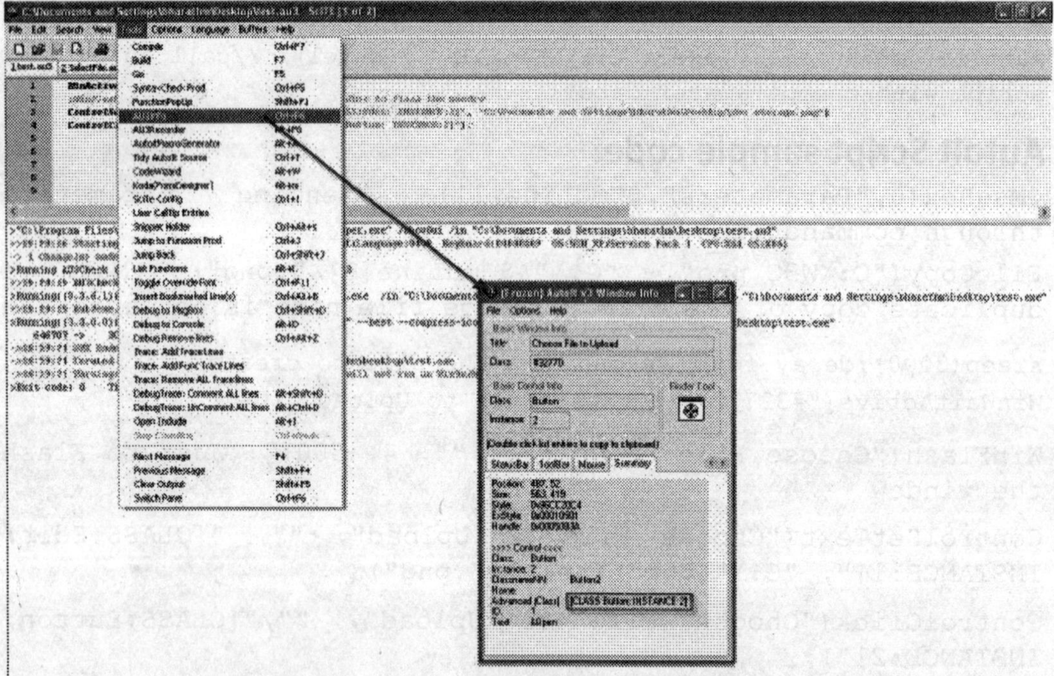

Drag and drop the finder tool icon on the windows objects to get its corresponding properties. Verify help to understand the syntax of Autoit commands.

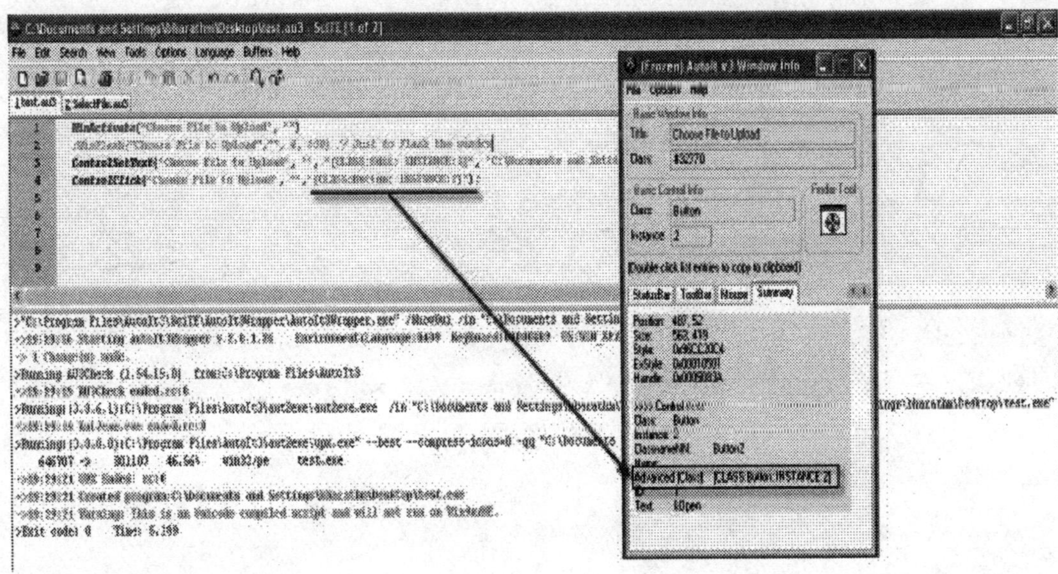
(Frozen) AutoIt v3 Window Info
Choose File to Upload
Button
Finder Tool
(Double click list entries to copy to clipboard)
StatusBar
ToolsBar
Mouse
Summary
Advanced (Class) [CLASS:Button; INSTANCE:2]
&Open

Flex Automation using FlexMonkey tool

Introduction:

Flex Monkey is an Adobe AIR application used for testing Flex- and AIR-based applications. Providing the functionality to record, playback and verify Flex UI interactions, Flex Monkey also generates Action Script-based testing scripts that you can easily include within a continuous integration environment.

Download

http://www.gorillalogic.com/flexmonkey

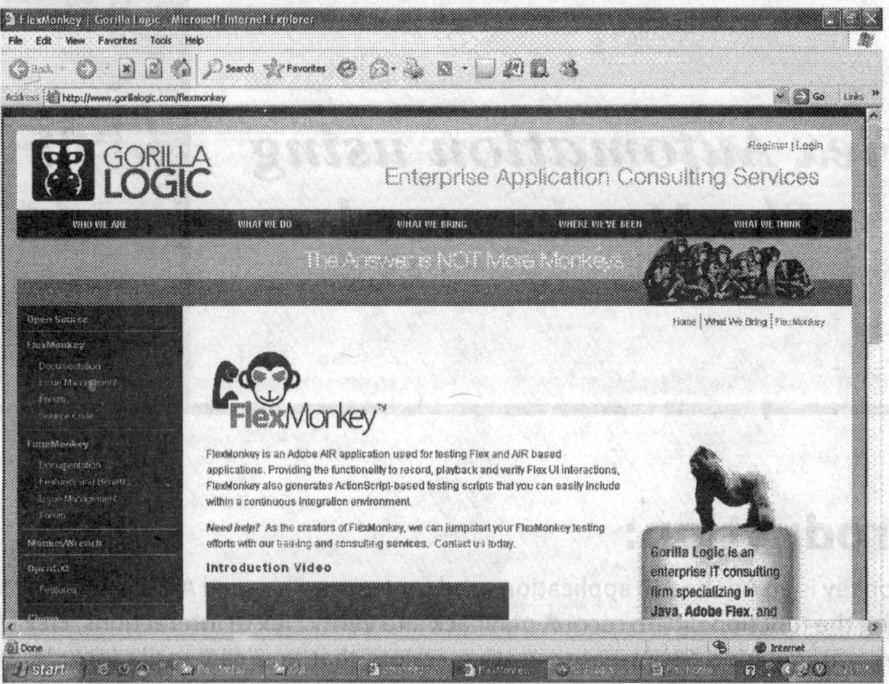

Note: You have to Register to download 'FlexMonkey'

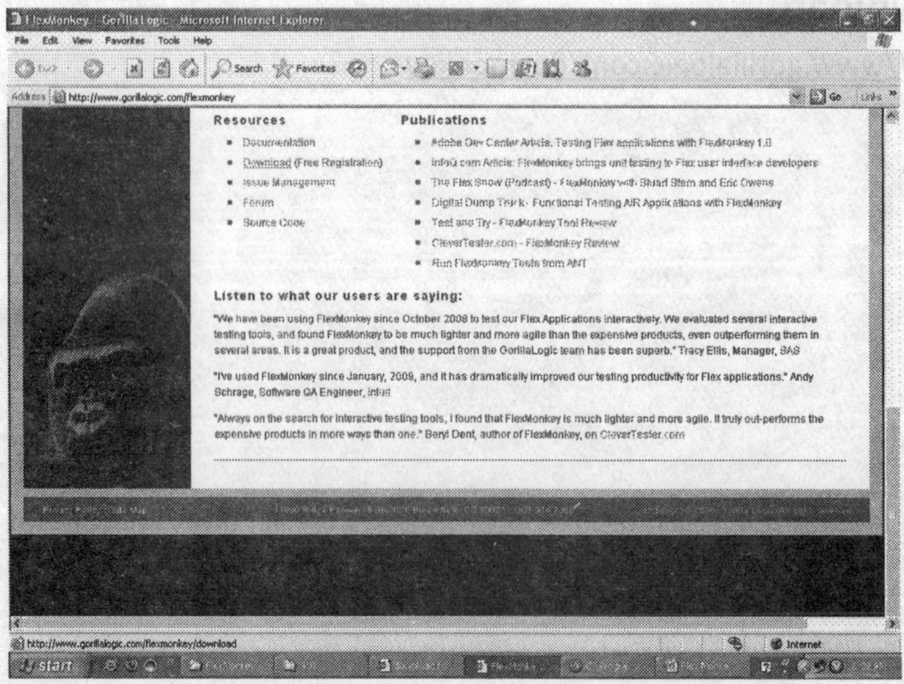

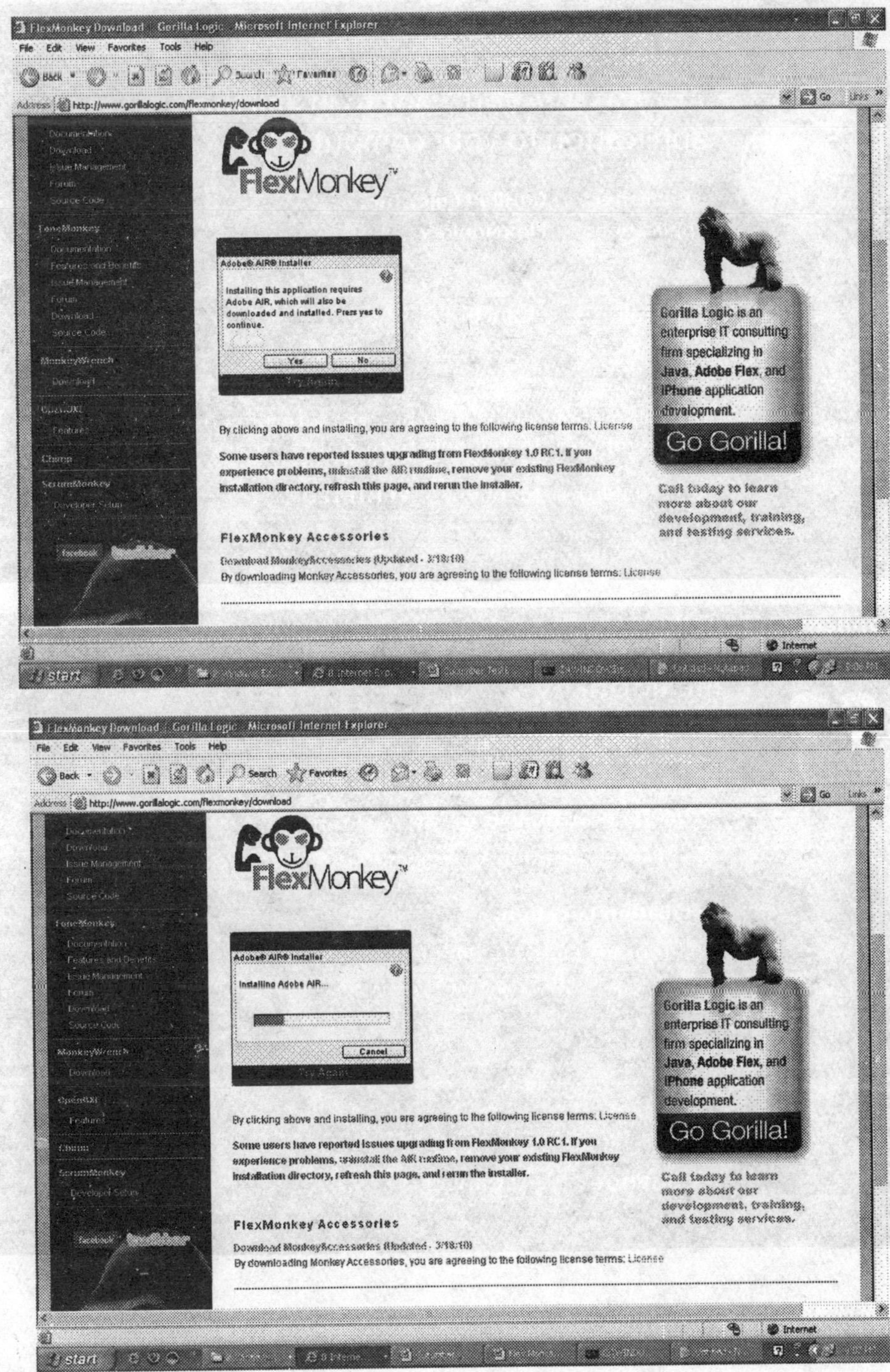
FlexMonkey Download - Gorilla Logic - Microsoft Internet Explorer
File Edit View Favorites Tools Help
Address http://www.gorillalogic.com/flexmonkey/download
FlexMonkey
Adobe® AIR® Installer
Installing this application requires Adobe AIR, which will also be downloaded and installed. Press yes to continue.
Yes
No
Gorilla Logic is an enterprise IT consulting firm specializing in Java, Adobe Flex, and iPhone application development.
Go Gorilla!
Call today to learn more about our development, training, and testing services.
By clicking above and installing, you are agreeing to the following license terms: License
Some users have reported issues upgrading from FlexMonkey 1.0 RC1. If you experience problems, uninstall the AIR runtime, remove your existing FlexMonkey installation directory, refresh this page, and rerun the installer.
FlexMonkey Accessories
Download MonkeyAccessories (Updated - 3/18/10)
By downloading Monkey Accessories, you are agreeing to the following license terms: License
Internet
start
FlexMonkey Download - Gorilla Logic - Microsoft Internet Explorer
File Edit View Favorites Tools Help
Address http://www.gorillalogic.com/flexmonkey/download
FlexMonkey
Adobe® AIR® Installer
Installing Adobe AIR...
Cancel
Gorilla Logic is an enterprise IT consulting firm specializing in Java, Adobe Flex, and iPhone application development.
Go Gorilla!
Call today to learn more about our development, training, and testing services.
By clicking above and installing, you are agreeing to the following license terms: License
Some users have reported issues upgrading from FlexMonkey 1.0 RC1. If you experience problems, uninstall the AIR runtime, remove your existing FlexMonkey installation directory, refresh this page, and rerun the installer.
FlexMonkey Accessories
Download MonkeyAccessories (Updated - 3/18/10)
By downloading Monkey Accessories, you are agreeing to the following license terms: License
Internet
start

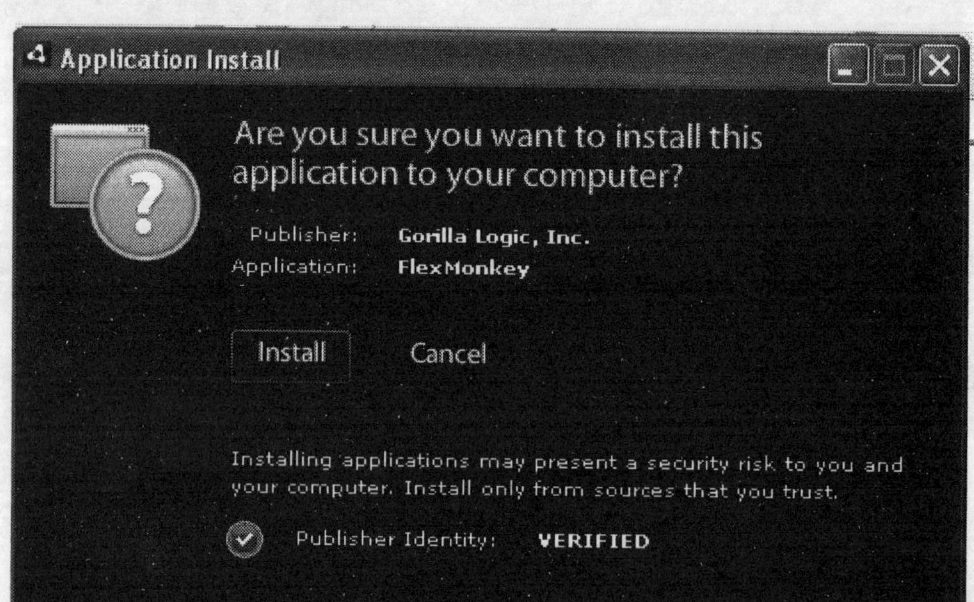
Application Install
Are you sure you want to install this application to your computer?
Publisher: Gorilla Logic, Inc.
Application: FlexMonkey
Install
Cancel
Installing applications may present a security risk to you and your computer. Install only from sources that you trust.
Publisher Identity: VERIFIED

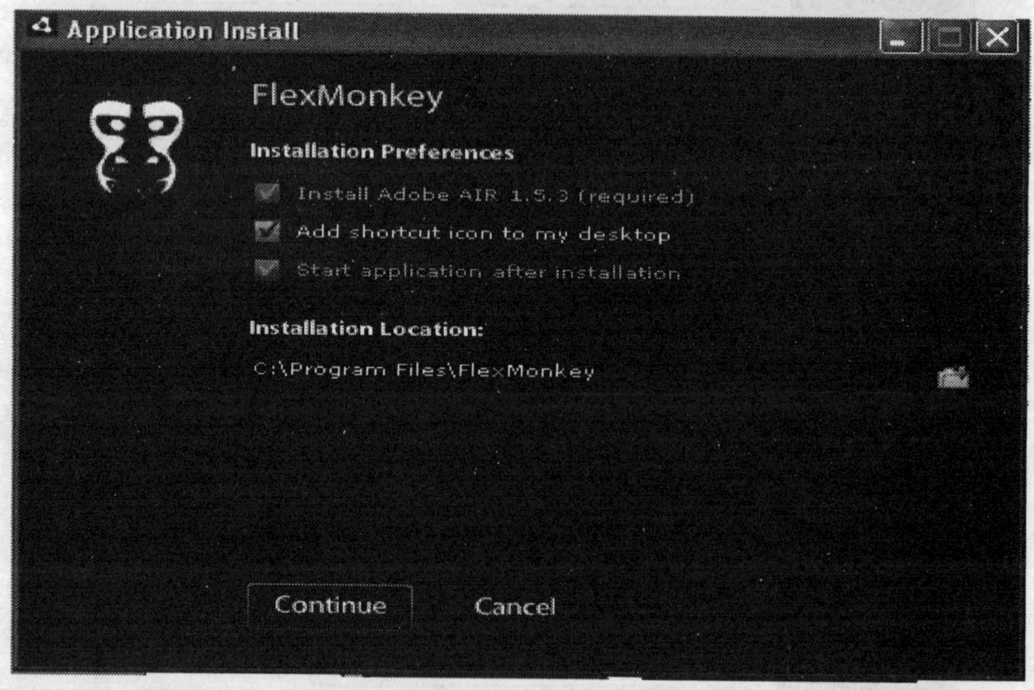
Application Install
FlexMonkey
Installation Preferences
Install Adobe AIR 1.5.3 (required)
Add shortcut icon to my desktop
Start application after installation
Installation Location:
C:\Program Files\FlexMonkey
Continue
Cancel

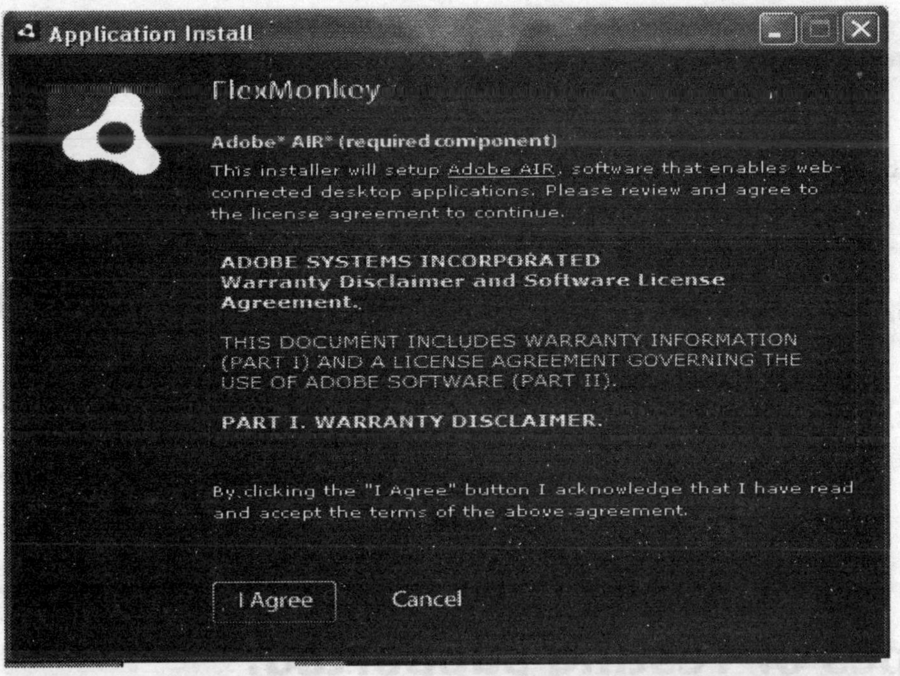
Application Install
FlexMonkey
Adobe® AIR® (required component)
This installer will setup Adobe AIR, software that enables web-connected desktop applications. Please review and agree to the license agreement to continue.
ADOBE SYSTEMS INCORPORATED
Warranty Disclaimer and Software License Agreement.
THIS DOCUMENT INCLUDES WARRANTY INFORMATION (PART I) AND A LICENSE AGREEMENT GOVERNING THE USE OF ADOBE SOFTWARE (PART II).
PART I. WARRANTY DISCLAIMER.
By clicking the "I Agree" button I acknowledge that I have read and accept the terms of the above agreement.
I Agree
Cancel

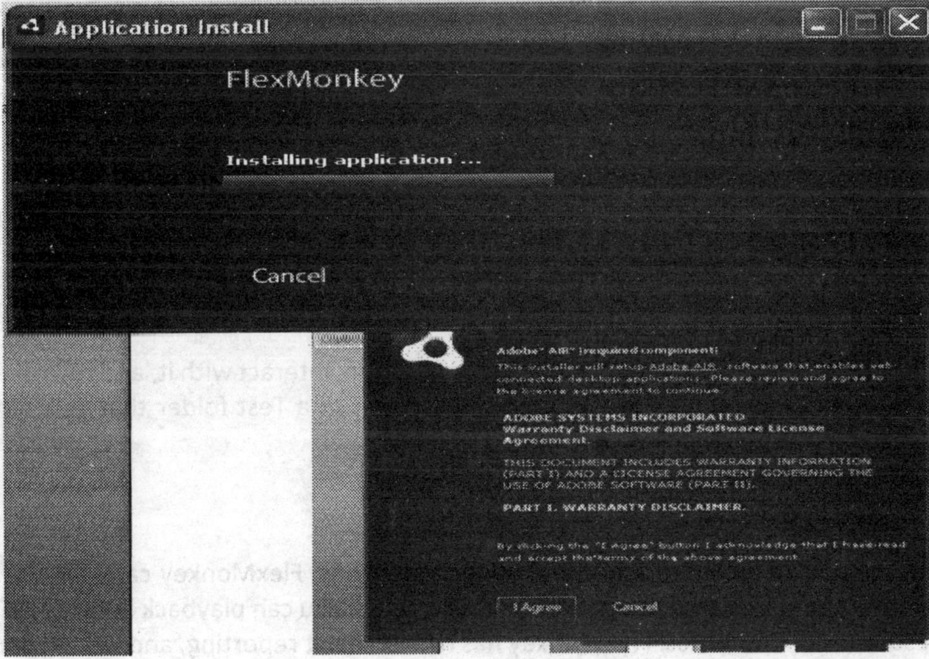
Application Install
FlexMonkey
Installing application ...
Cancel
ADOBE SYSTEMS INCORPORATED
Warranty Disclaimer and Software License Agreement.
PART I. WARRANTY DISCLAIMER.

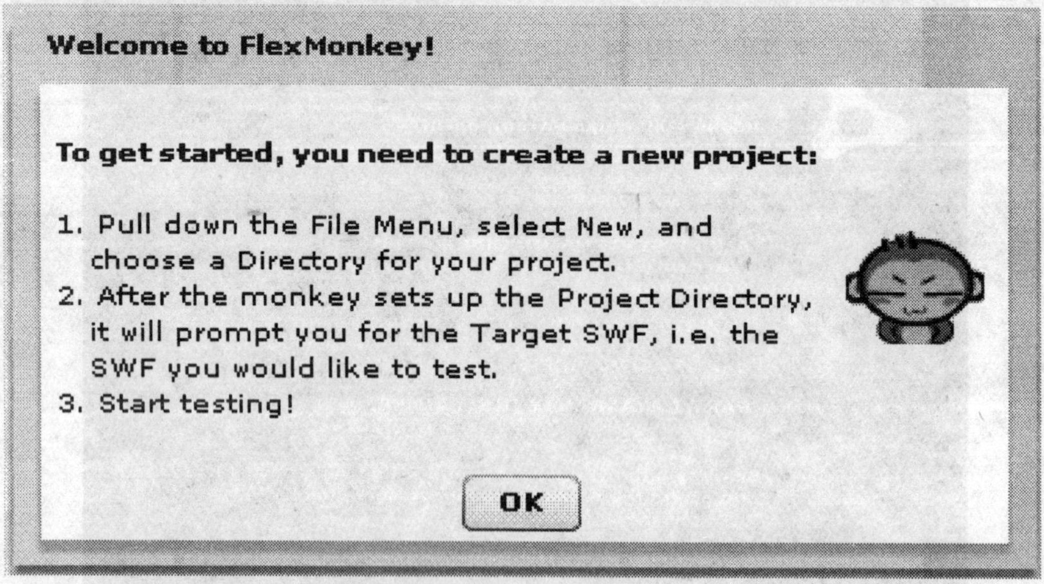

Welcome to FlexMonkey!

To get started, you need to create a new project:

1. Pull down the File Menu, select New, and choose a Directory for your project.
2. After the monkey sets up the Project Directory, it will prompt you for the Target SWF, i.e. the SWF you would like to test.
3. Start testing!

OK

Types of Testing supported:

- **Regression Testing**
- **Functional Testing**
- **Unit Testing.**

Features:

a) Recording:

With FlexMonkey, you can run your Flex application, interact with it, and record those interactions. FlexMonkey stores your interactions in a Test folder that you can see and edit in the FlexMonkey Console

b) PlayBack :

Once you have recorded a test and added assertions, FlexMonkey can play the test, and you can watch as your application is exercised. You can playback individual Tests, TestCases, or TestSuites. FlexMonkey has robust result reporting, and when your test run is completed, FlexMonkey allows you to browse the results.

c) Organizing the tests :

FlexMonkey allows you to organize your Test folders into TestCase folders, and your TestCase folders into TestSuite folders, in accordance with XUnit test organization.

d) Assertions :

You can add assertions to your FlexMonkey test that check your application's response when the test runs. Assertions can check the values of a component's properties or styles, or you can capture the bitmap of a visible component and compare it to actual bitmap when your test runs.

e) Generating Action scripts :

FlexMonkey can generate a Fluint/FlexUnit-compatible Actionscript version of your TestSuite that you can run from ANT. When you run from ANT, FlexMonkey will create jUnitReport-compatible output that you can integrate with other jUnitReports.

f) Testing AIR Applications :

You can test AIR applications with FlexMonkey, but the Flex 3 Adobe Automation platform imposes some limitations. Recording and playback will only work for the main application window and pop-ups from there. Sub-windows and their pop-ups are ignored. Also, File dialogs are ignored.Adobe is improving the automation system in Flex 4 to cover subwindows, and FlexMonkey will support Flex 4 in a future release.

Advanced Features :

- Automation of Flex 4 AIR applications.
- Supports 'mx.core.Application, Halo'.
- Supports Automation of Marshalled Flex and AIR applications

Flex Automation tools :

- Flex Monkey
- Selenium with Flex

Testing Approach With Flex Monkey Tool:

When you install Flex Monkey and start it for the first time, you'll see a Welcome dialog box with instructions on getting started (see Figure 1). Click OK.

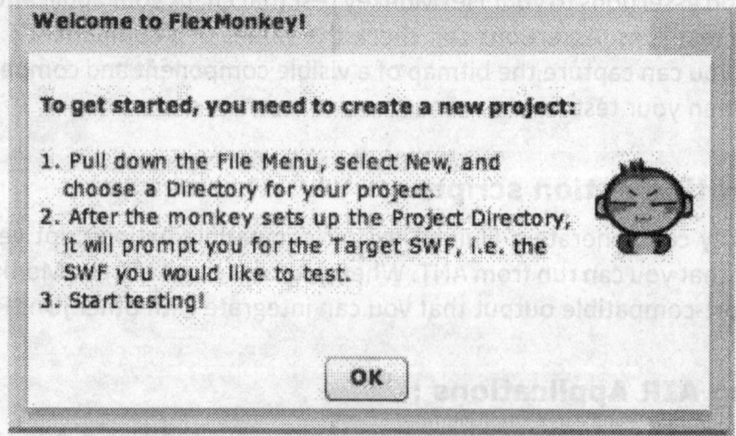

Figure 1. The FlexMonkey welcome screen

To create your first FlexMonkey project, download and extract this article's sample files and then follow these steps:

1. Choose File > New Project (see Figure 2).

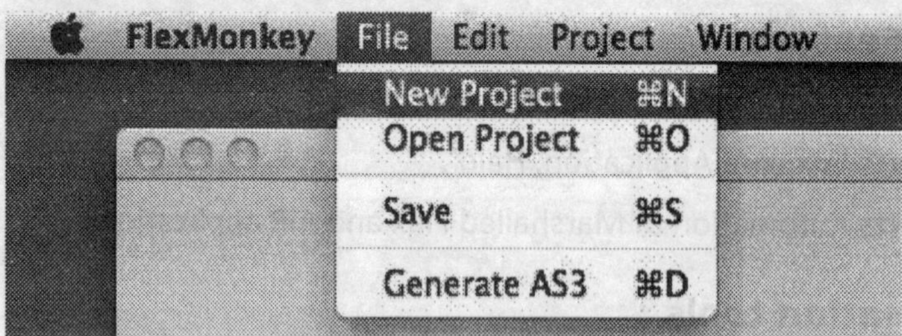

Figure 2. Creating a new project in FlexMonkey

2. In the New Project dialog box, select a directory to hold your FlexMonkey project files (see Figure 3). For this example, select the Flex Builder project directory for the sample MonkeyContactsIntroExample project.

3. Click Select, and FlexMonkey will create files to hold your tests and your project preferences.

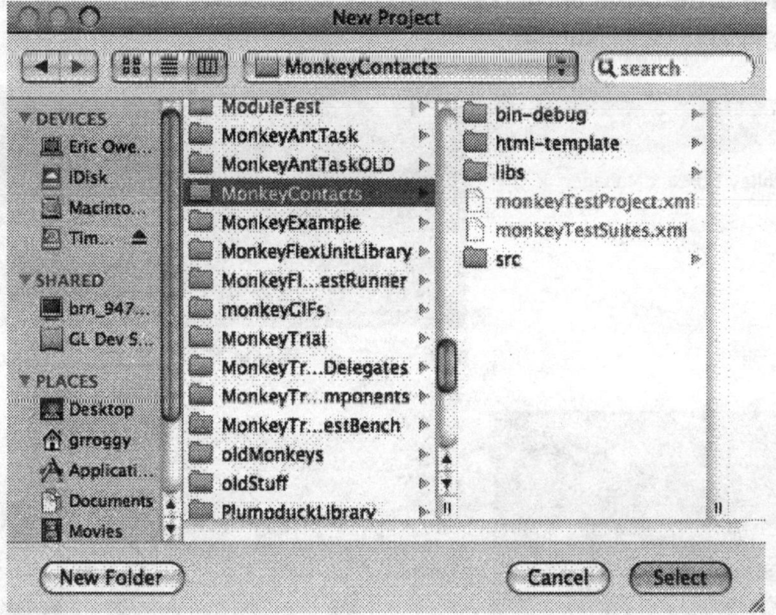

Figure 3. The New Project dialog box

4. In the Project Properties window, specify the target SWF (that is, the SWF file that you want to test). In this case, click Browse and select MonkeyContacts.swf in the bin-debug directory of the project (see Figure 4).

   Note: If the SWF you want to test is remote, you can just type in the URL.

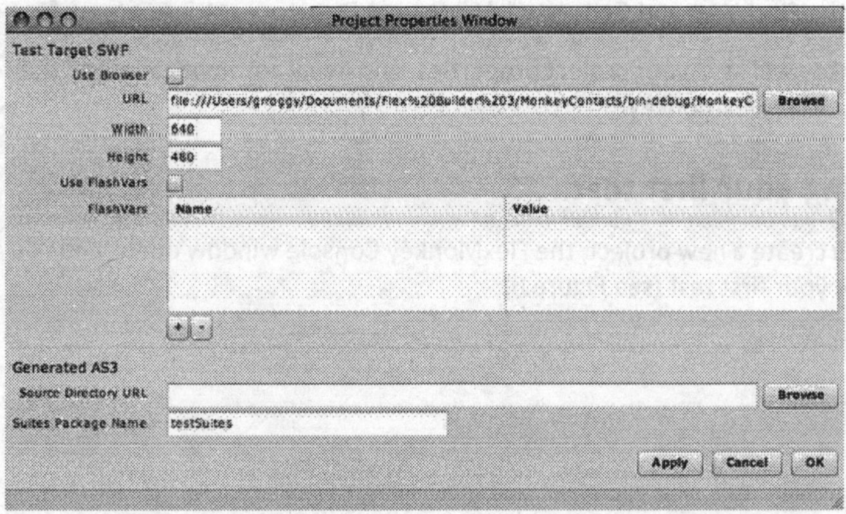

Figure 4. The FlexMonkey Project Properties window

5. Leave Use Browser unchecked, and click Apply. A window will open displaying the target SWF (see Figure 5).

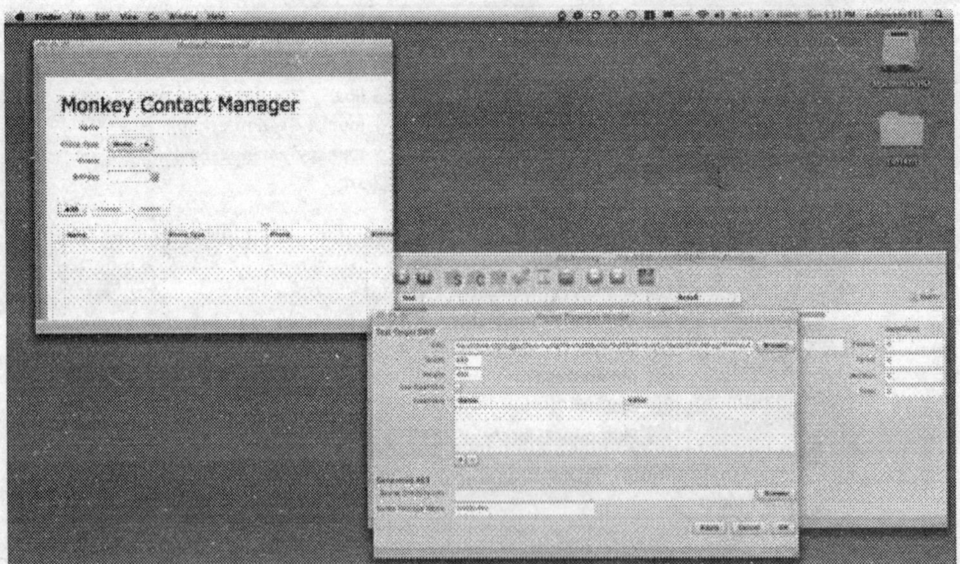

Figure 5. The target SWF window opens on your desktop

6. Adjust the size of the target SWF window using the Project Properties Width and Height settings and click Apply to see the effect.

7. When you are satisfied with the size of the target SWF window, click OK. (Leave the FlashVars and Generated AS3 Source Directory settings empty for now.)

FlexMonkey will save your project properties, and it will automatically load them the next time you start FlexMonkey.

Creating your first test

After you create a new project, the FlexMonkey Console window opens and you are ready to create your first test (see Figure 6).

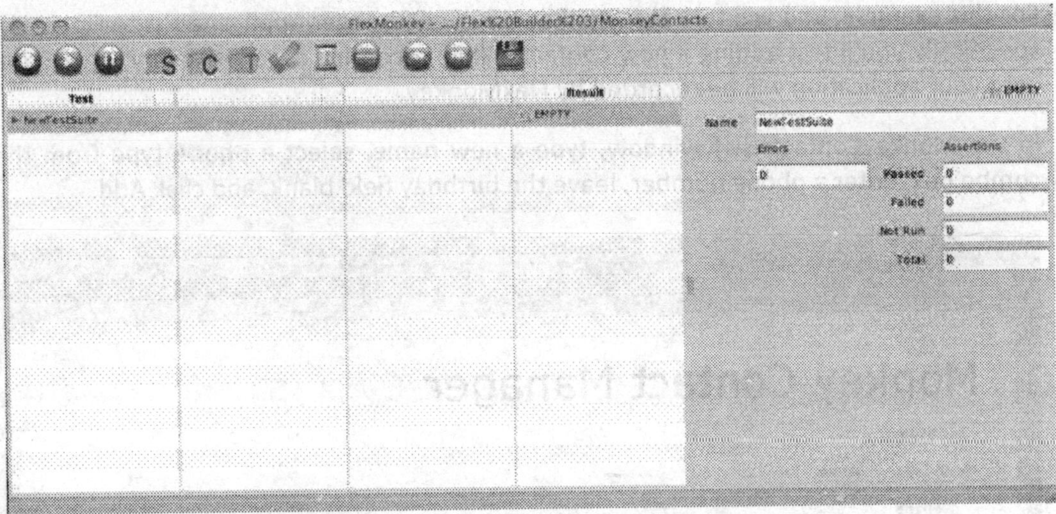

Figure 6. The FlexMonkey Console window

Expand NewTestSuite (by clicking the triangle next to it) and then expand NewTestCase to show NewTest (see Figure 7). If you are familiar with xUnit, you will recognize the standard hierarchical test organization in FlexMonkey. Select NewTest by clicking its row. NewTest is *Empty* because you haven't added any UI commands to it yet. When you select NewTest, the Record button will be enabled. Click the Record button and it glows red to indicate that you are now in Record mode.

Figure 7. The FlexMonkey Console window in Record mode

For this example, you will test the Monkey Contact Manager application (see Figure 8); specifically you'll test adding a new contact. While recording is active, every interaction with your application will be recorded by FlexMonkey.

In the MonkeyContacts.swf window, type a new name, select a phone type from the combo box, enter a phone number, leave the birthday field blank, and click Add.

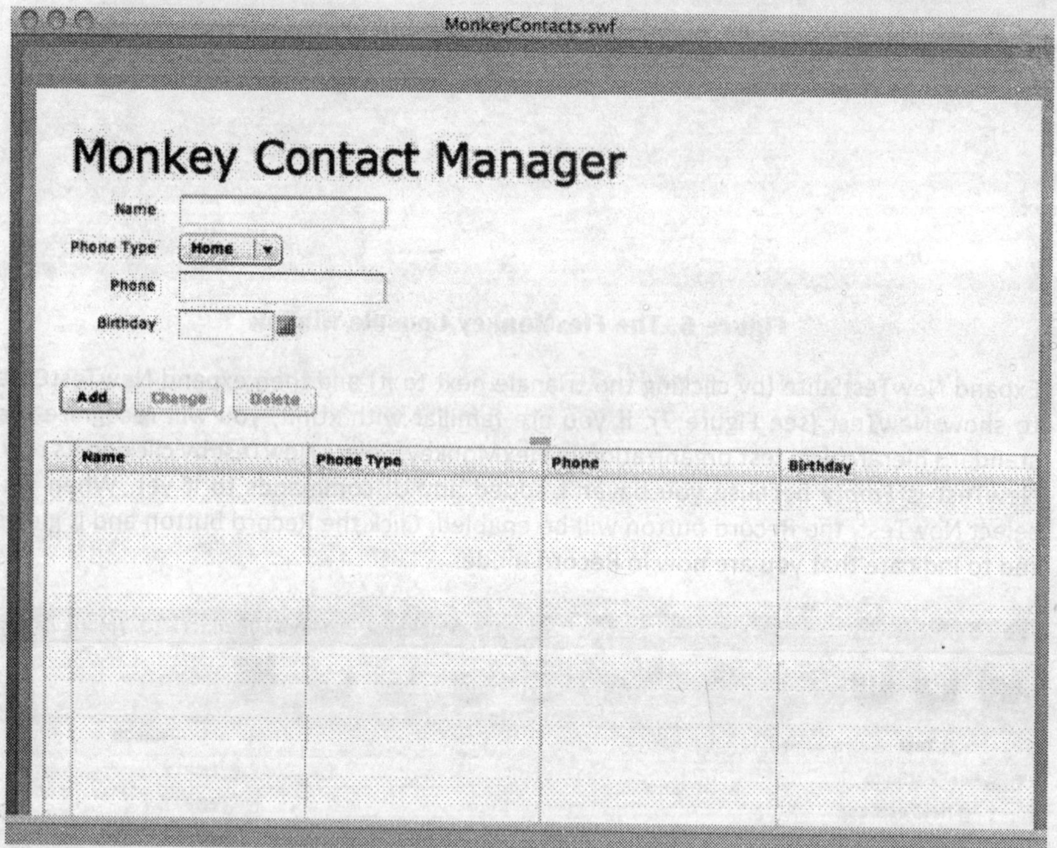

Figure 8. The Contact Manager application to be tested

When you have finished adding the contact in the MonkeyContacts.swf window, click the Record button again to toggle Record mode off. Figure 9 shows the FlexMonkey console window after recording the new test.

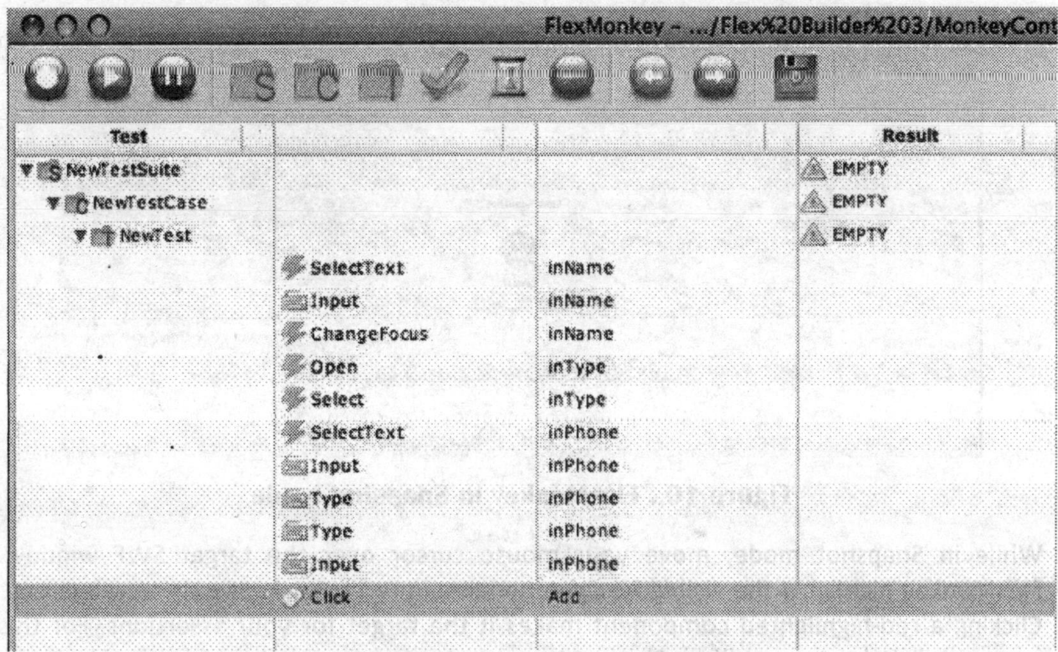

Figure 9. The Console window shows the UI commands that were recorded

As you can see, FlexMonkey inserted a sequence of UI commands into *NewTest*. In the second column, there are entries for *Open* and *Select* events, keyboard input, and mouse clicks. In the third column, the id of the target component for the UI command is listed.

In the contact manager application, the id property of the Name field is inName, the id property of the Phone Type field is inType, and the id property of the Phone field is inPhone.

Adding assertions

Now you're ready to add an assertion to your test. With the last command in the test (Click Add) still selected, click the Add Verify button, which is the green check mark in the tool bar. The Take Snapshot dialog box will appear over the FlexMonkey Console window indicating that FlexMonkey is in Snapshot mode (see Figure 10).

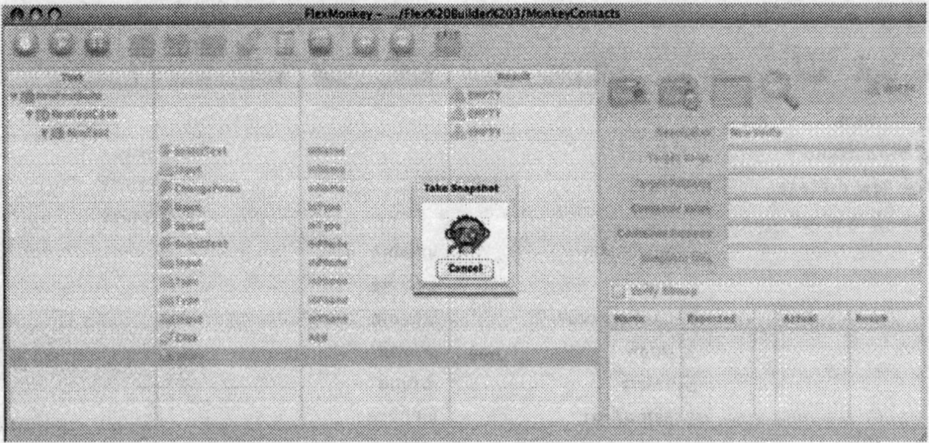

Figure 10 . FlexMonkey in Snapshot mode

While in Snapshot mode, move your mouse cursor over the target SWF window. FlexMonkey highlights the visible Flex components in red to make it easy to select one. Clicking a red-highlighted component makes it the target for your assertions. For this example click the data grid (see Figure 11).

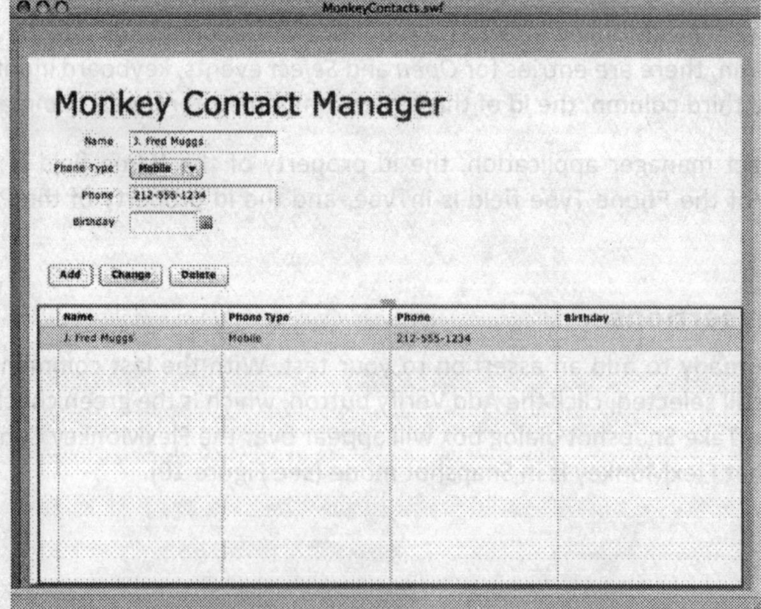

Figure 11. The data grid of the Contact Manager application highlighted in Snapshot mode

After you select a target component for your assertions, FlexMonkey displays the Spy window, which shows the current properties and styles for the target component. Click the selectedIndex property, which is currently set to 0 (see Figure 12). Click OK, and FlexMonkey will add an assertion that the selectedIndex property of the data grid will be 0 when the Verify command executes.

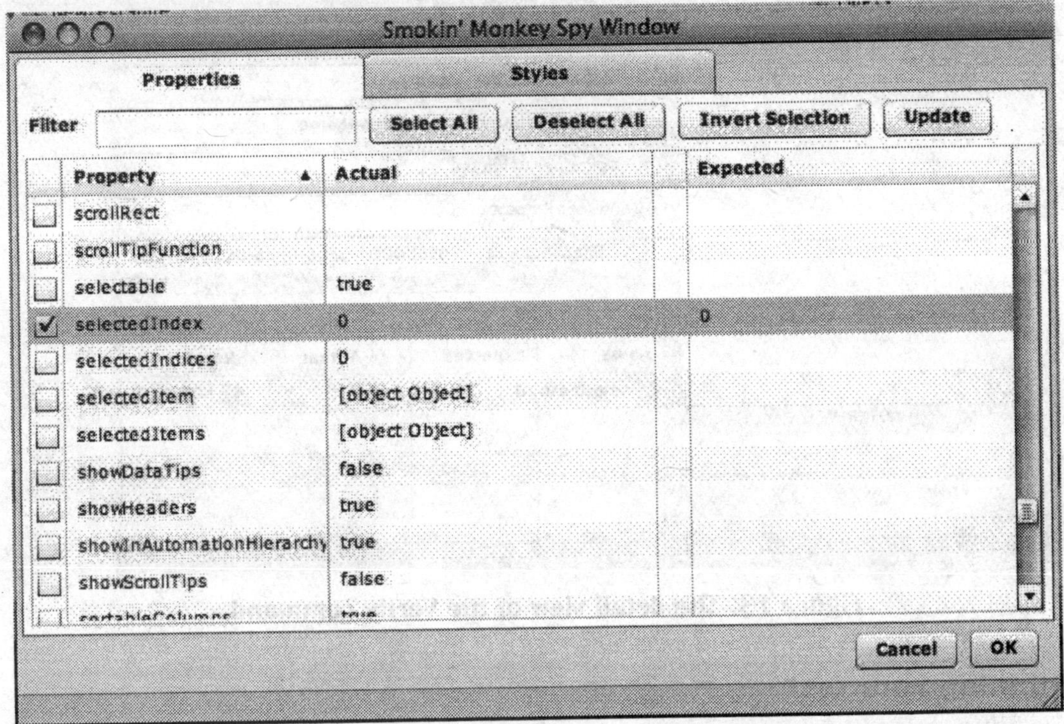

Figure 12. The FlexMonkey Spy window

Back in the FlexMonkey Console window, you can see the added assertion on the right. The detail view for the Verify command shows that the selectedIndex property is expected to be equal to 0 when the command executes (see Figure 13).

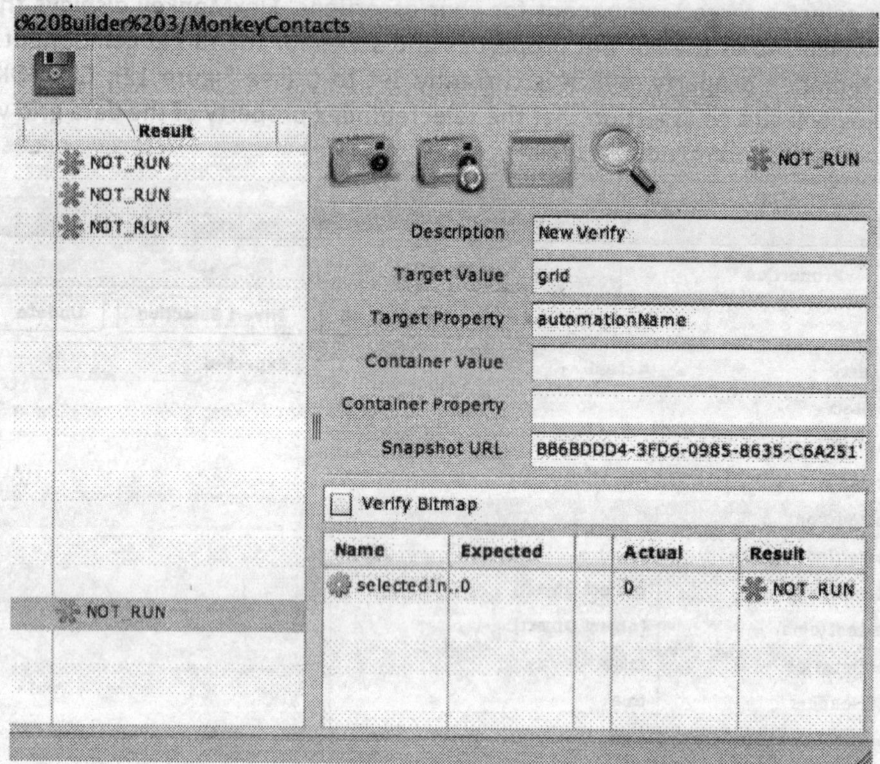

Figure 13. The detail view of the Verify command

Running your test

Now it's time to have FlexMonkey play back the test. First, select *NewTest* as shown in Figure 14. Click Play (the button just to the right of the Record button), and FlexMonkey will execute all of the UI commands in NewTest.

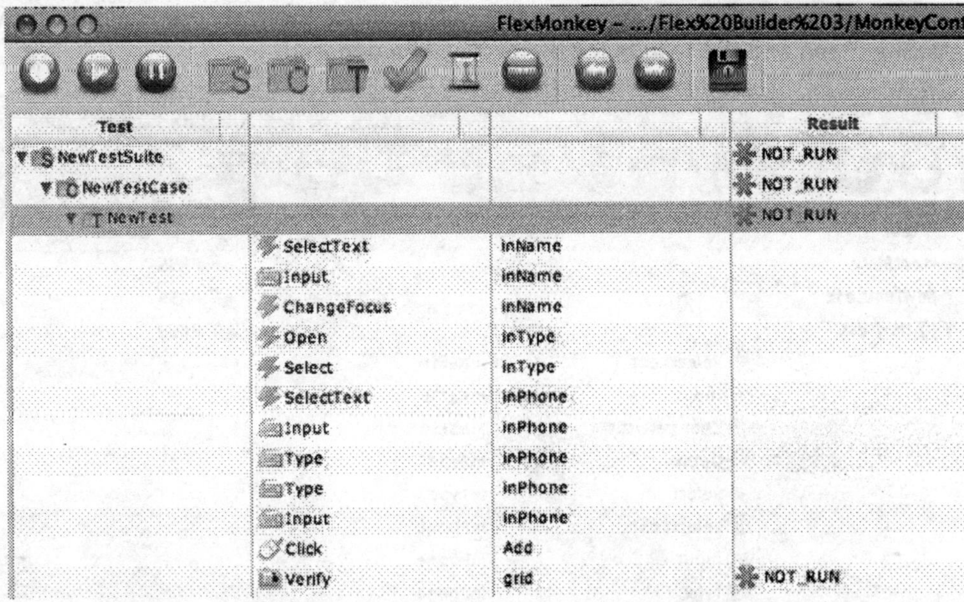

Figure 14. Select NewTest and then click Play to run the test

When FlexMonkey is playing, the Play button will glow green as shown in Figure 15. As FlexMonkey plays, it highlights each UI command in the console window as it is executing. Of course, you can also watch as the commands are executed in the target SWF window.

Figure 15. UI commands are highlighted as they are executed

When FlexMonkey is finished playing the last command of the test, the Play button will stop glowing green and the results for the test will be updated.

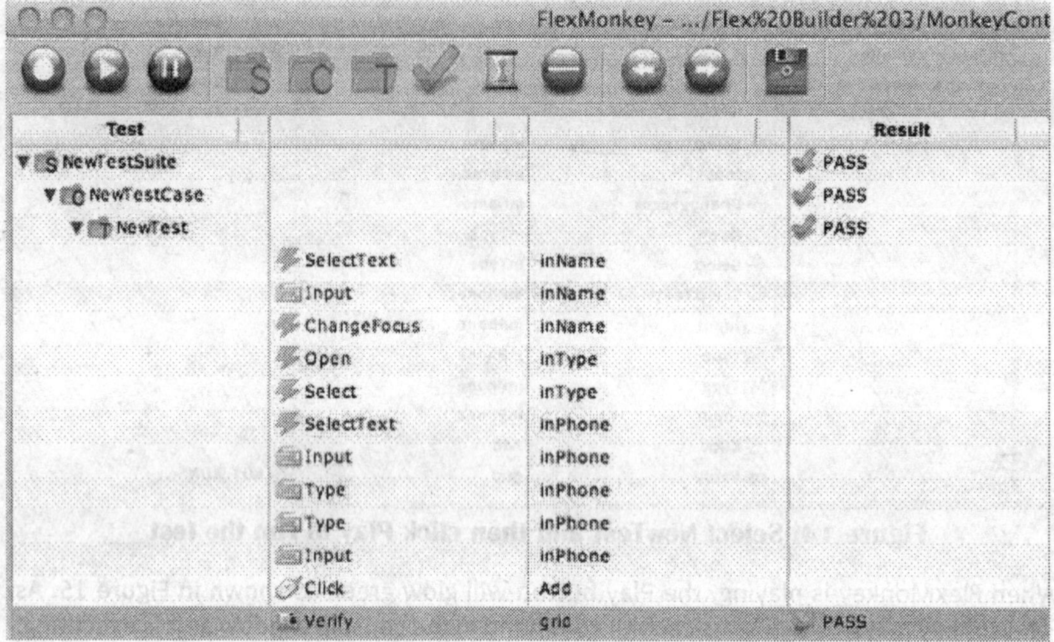

Figure 16. FlexMonkey displaying the results of NewTest

Save your work and shut down

You can save your work at any time by clicking the Save button (the blue diskette at the far right of the tool bar). If you don't, and you quit FlexMonkey, you'll be prompted to save your work (see Figure 17).

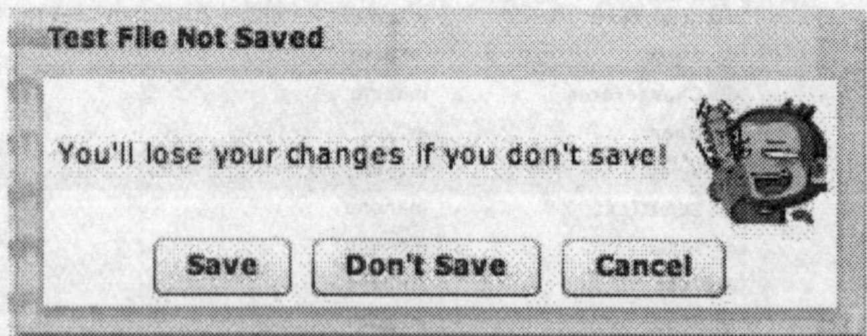

Figure 17. FlexMonkey prompts you to save changes

The next time you open FlexMonkey, it will reopen this project, and load the test file and target SWF.

Silverlight / Ajax Testing using Telerik Webaii tool

Telerik Introduces Free Web Testing Framework for ASP.NET AJAX and Silverlight

***WebAii Testing** Framework enables developers to automate AJAX or Silverlight applications in all major browsers and simplifies testing of RadControls*

NEWTON, Mass.– (BUSINESS WIRE)–Telerik, the leading vendor of development tools and user interface components for .NET, today announced a new addition to its portfolio – **WebAii Testing Framework** (Beta), a product by ArtOfTest. WebAii Testing Framework is a free web automation framework that helps developers and Quality Assurance professionals easily write functional tests for AJAX and Silverlight applications. The framework offers one consistent application programming interface (API) that allows users to automate the user interface (UI) of web applications as part of regression testing. Besides Silverlight support, a key benefit of WebAii Testing Framework is the browser abstraction, which allows developers to create a test once and execute it against all major browsers.

"WebAii Testing Framework has been designed in partnership with ArtOfTest to address developers' challenges in testing modern web applications.

The WebAii Testing Framework has been specifically built to cater to users' advanced testing needs. AJAX-based applications can be easily automated including complex UI actions like Drag'n'drop, Hover, Right-click, and more. Waiting on document object model changes is also supported as well as the option to invoke JavaScript functions from test code.

In addition to testing AJAX-based applications, Telerik's new WebAii Testing Framework also incorporates Silverlight Extension which makes automating Silverlight applications finally possible. It has a UI object model that mimics the complete list of UI XAML elements in Silverlight allowing developers to access everything as if inside the Silverlight application. Beside the ability to perform basic automation actions like clicking, moving and setting text, it also gives access to all properties such as brushes, borders and even transform matrices.

"The addition of the WebAii Testing Framework to the Telerik portfolio of .NET tools and components is another step in our strategy of serving the developer community in more aspects of the application development lifecycle," continued Georgiev.

Availability

WebAii Testing Framework is available for free download at Telerik Testing Tools section of its website or as a part of RadControls for ASP.NET AJAX and RadControls for Silverlight licenses. General availability of the free WebAii Testing Framework will be available later in the second quarter 2009.

About Telerik

Telerik is a leading vendor of development tools and components for the Microsoft .NET platform. Developers from most of the Fortune 2000 companies, many of the world's leading educational and non-profit organizations and thousands of consultants rely on Telerik products to build applications with unparalleled richness, responsiveness and interactivity. Read more at http://www.telerik.com/

Getting Started with WebAii

Thanks for using WebAii Automation infrastructure. To get started using WebAii, please follow the instructions below.

IMPORTANT

- WebAii 1.1 and 2.0 were designed coexist on the same machine.
- Please uninstall any previous WebAii 1.x installations on your machine before installing the current version. of WebAii 1.x.
- Please uninstall any previous WebAii 2.0 installations on your machine before installing the current version. of WebAii 2.0.
- If you are upgrading from 1.0 to 1.1, please make sure to also uninstall the WebAii 1.0 Firefox extension before installing 1.1. WebAii 1.1 and 2.0 beta versions automatically install their respective Firefox extensions. No manual steps are required.

Installing and Setting Up the Infrastructure

Once the installation is complete, you will have all of the following placed in the WebAii %InstallDir% folder:

- The WebAii Automation Infrastructure library. **ArtOfTest.WebAii.dll & ArtOfTest.Common.dll.**
- WebAii's Internet Explorer client. **ArtOfTest.InternetExplorer.dll.**
- WebAii's Firefox client: **Automatically installed in your install directory.**
- Safari client: **Automatically installed in your install directory.**
- Silverlight plug-in: **ArtOfTest.WebAii.Mime.dll.**
- Our HTTP Proxy: **ArtOfTest.WebAii.HttpProxy.exe.**
- ASP.NET TestRegion Custom Control. **ArtOfTest.WebAii.AspNet.dll.**
- Visual Studio item templates for VS Team Test, NUnit, MbUnit and xUnit (Both VB.NET and C#).**These are automatically registered with Visual Studio.**
- 90+ Unit Test Code Samples to help illustrate the different features of WebAii. You will find 4 zipped solutions: (QuickStarts_NUnit_CS.zip, QuickStarts_VSTS_CS.zip, QuickStarts_NUnit_VB.zip, QuickStarts_VSTS_VB.zip). You can use the sample solution that fits your language and testing framework of preference.
- Release notes. **ReleaseNotes.txt**
- API Reference help file. **Documentation.chm**
- Link to the online Documentation including the Getting Started Guide.
- Link to the online community forums.
- Link to WebAii Premier Support description.

<u>Only needed when using WebAii 1.0</u>

Both the WebAii library and the Internet Explorer client are installed and ready to use once the installation is complete. The templates are also installed into your local templates for the current user. You also have a copy of these templates under %InstallDir%\Visual Studio Templates\. Firefox client is not automatically installed in WebAii 1.0. If you wish to also support Firefox in WebAii 1.0, you can simply install the Firefox client using the following simple <u>steps</u>. In WebAii 1.1 and above the Firefox client is automatically installed by the WebAii installer.

How to Download & Install:

http://www.telerik.com/login.aspx?ReturnUrl=%2fcommunity%2flicense-agreement.aspx%3fpld%3d691

Download webaii

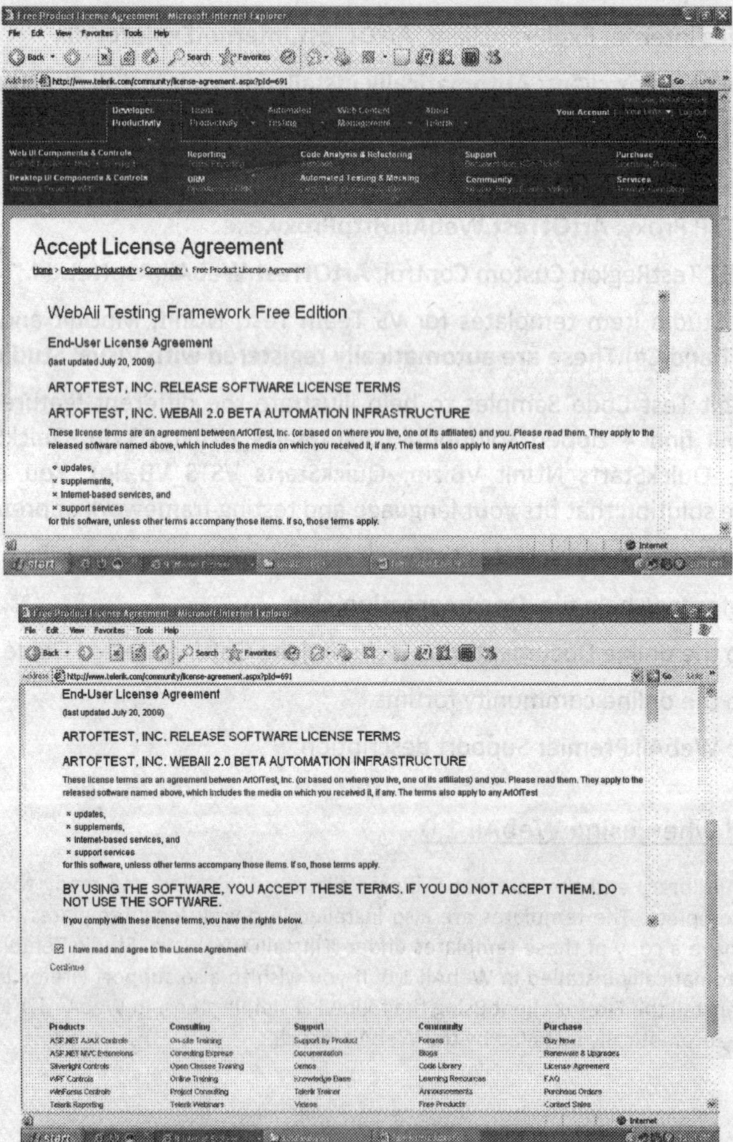

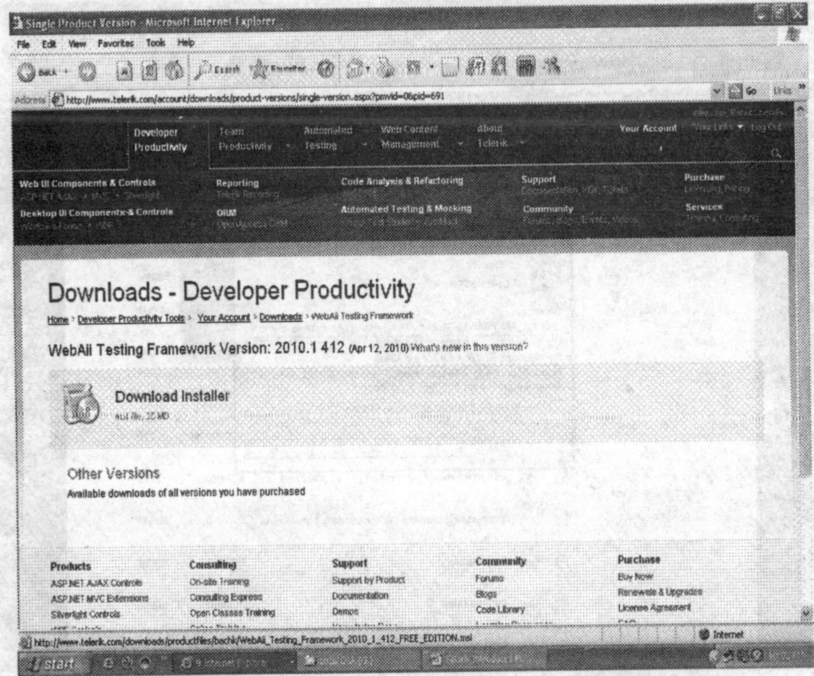

Click on 'Download Installaer' to download Webaii

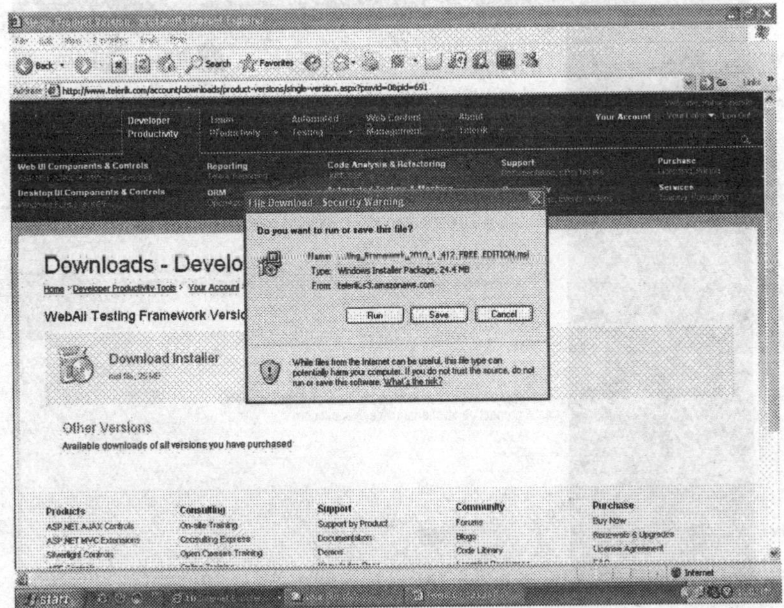

Click on 'Run'

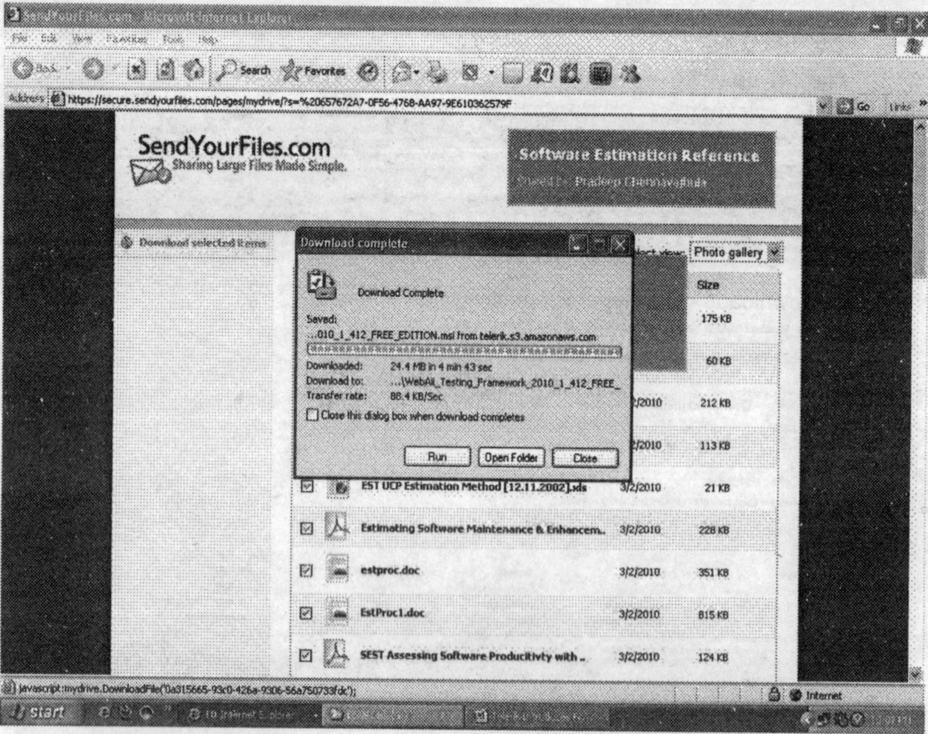
https://secure.sendyourfiles.com/pages/mydrive/?s=%20657672A7-0F56-4768-AA97-9E610362579F
SendYourFiles.com
Sharing Large Files Made Simple.
Software Estimation Reference
Download selected items
Download complete
Download Complete
Saved:
...010_1_412_FREE_EDITION.msi from telerik.s3.amazonaws.com
Downloaded: 24.4 MB in 4 min 43 sec
Download to: ...\WebAii_Testing_Framework_2010_1_412_FREE_
Transfer rate: 88.4 KB/Sec
Close this dialog box when download completes
Run
Open Folder
Close
Photo gallery
Size
175 KB
60 KB
212 KB
113 KB
EST UCP Estimation Method [12.11.2002].xls 3/2/2010 21 KB
Estimating Software Maintenance & Enhancem.. 3/2/2010 228 KB
estproc.doc 3/2/2010 351 KB
EstProc1.doc 3/2/2010 815 KB
SEST Assessing Software Producitivty with .. 3/2/2010 124 KB
javascript:mydrive.DownloadFile('0a315665-93c0-426a-9306-56a750733fdc');
Internet
start

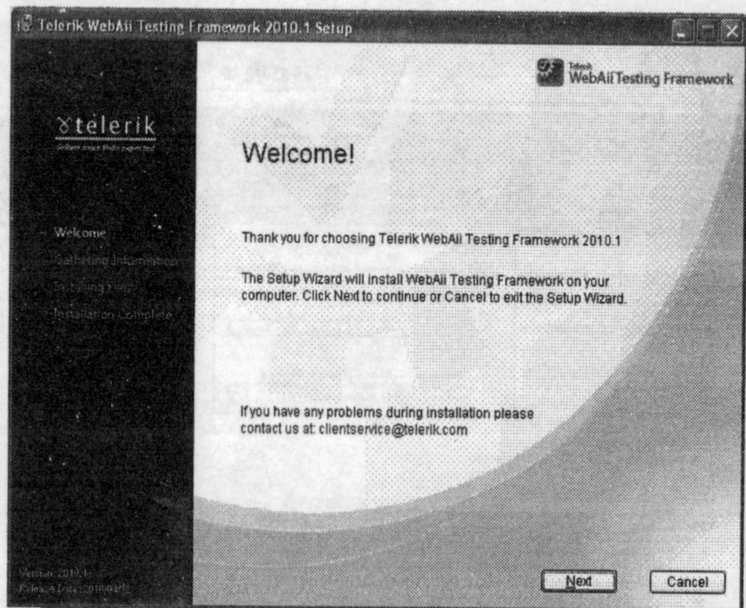
Telerik WebAii Testing Framework 2010.1 Setup
WebAii Testing Framework
telerik
Welcome
Welcome!
Thank you for choosing Telerik WebAii Testing Framework 2010.1
The Setup Wizard will install WebAii Testing Framework on your computer. Click Next to continue or Cancel to exit the Setup Wizard.
If you have any problems during installation please contact us at: clientservice@telerik.com
Next
Cancel

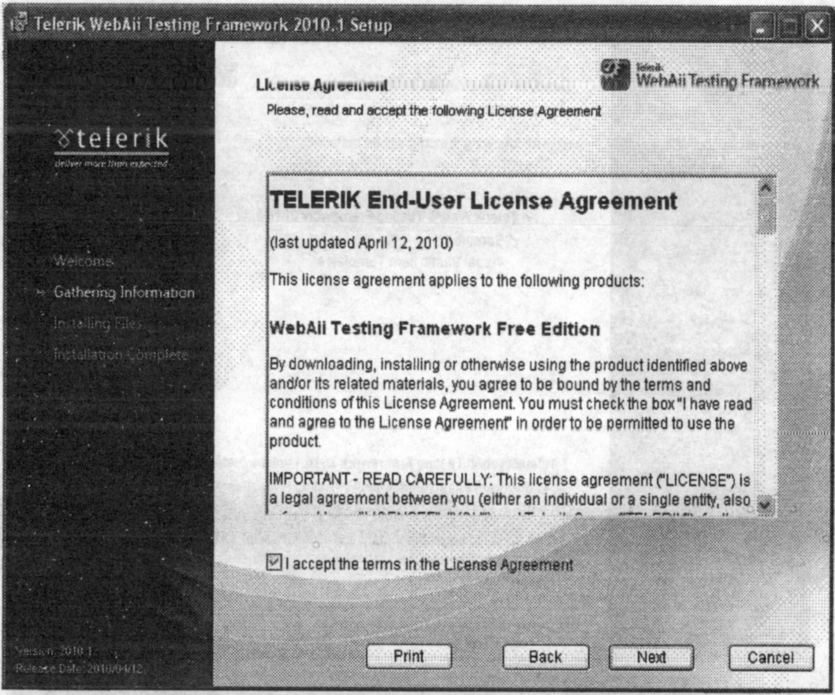
Telerik WebAii Testing Framework 2010.1 Setup
License Agreement
Please, read and accept the following License Agreement
WebAii Testing Framework
telerik
Welcome
Gathering Information
Installing Files
Installation Complete
TELERIK End-User License Agreement
(last updated April 12, 2010)
This license agreement applies to the following products:
WebAii Testing Framework Free Edition
By downloading, installing or otherwise using the product identified above and/or its related materials, you agree to be bound by the terms and conditions of this License Agreement. You must check the box "I have read and agree to the License Agreement" in order to be permitted to use the product.
IMPORTANT - READ CAREFULLY: This license agreement ("LICENSE") is a legal agreement between you (either an individual or a single entity, also
I accept the terms in the License Agreement
Print
Back
Next
Cancel

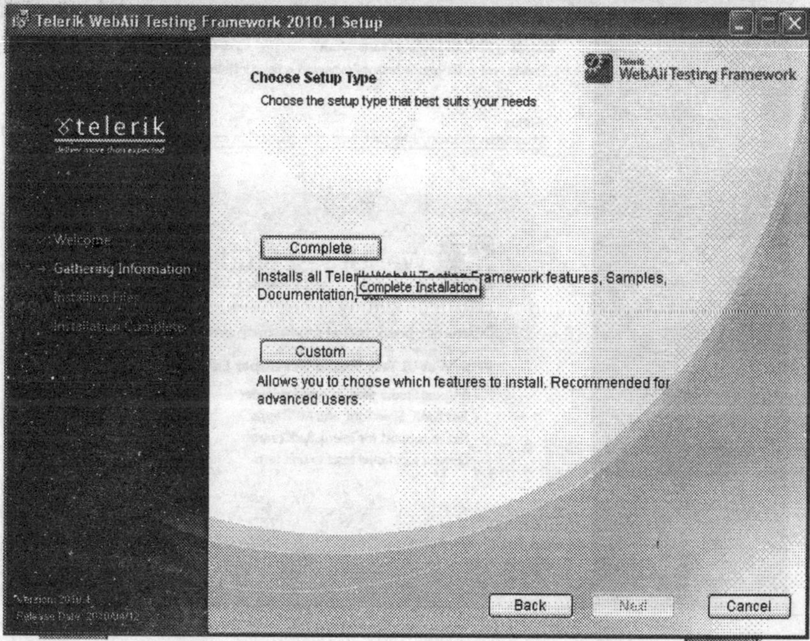
Telerik WebAii Testing Framework 2010.1 Setup
Choose Setup Type
Choose the setup type that best suits your needs
WebAii Testing Framework
telerik
Welcome
Gathering Information
Complete
Installs all Telerik WebAii Testing Framework features, Samples, Documentation, etc.
Complete Installation
Custom
Allows you to choose which features to install. Recommended for advanced users.
Back
Next
Cancel

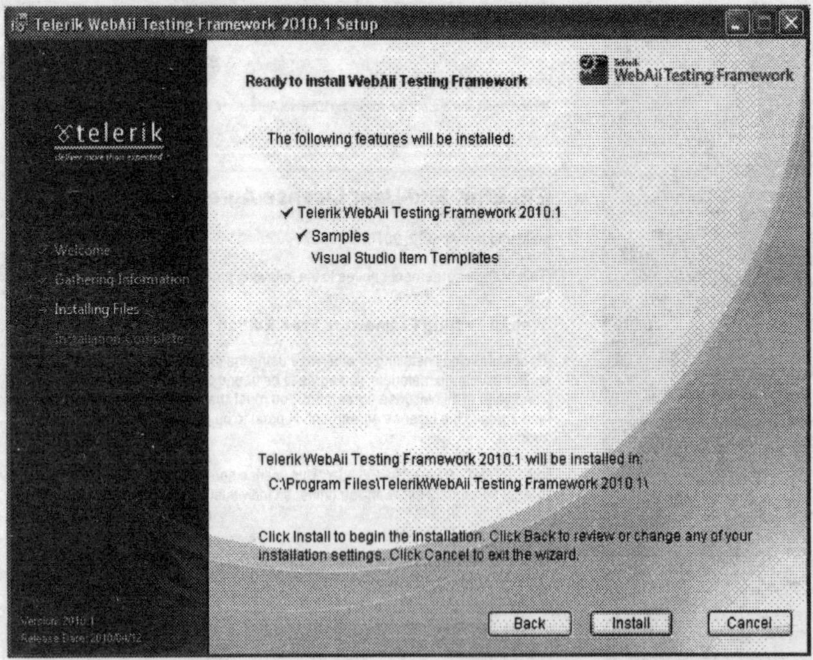
Telerik WebAii Testing Framework 2010.1 Setup
Ready to install WebAii Testing Framework
WebAii Testing Framework
telerik
The following features will be installed:
Telerik WebAii Testing Framework 2010.1
Samples
Visual Studio Item Templates
Welcome
Gathering Information
Installing Files
Telerik WebAii Testing Framework 2010.1 will be installed in:
C:\Program Files\Telerik\WebAii Testing Framework 2010.1\
Click Install to begin the installation. Click Back to review or change any of your installation settings. Click Cancel to exit the wizard.
Back
Install
Cancel

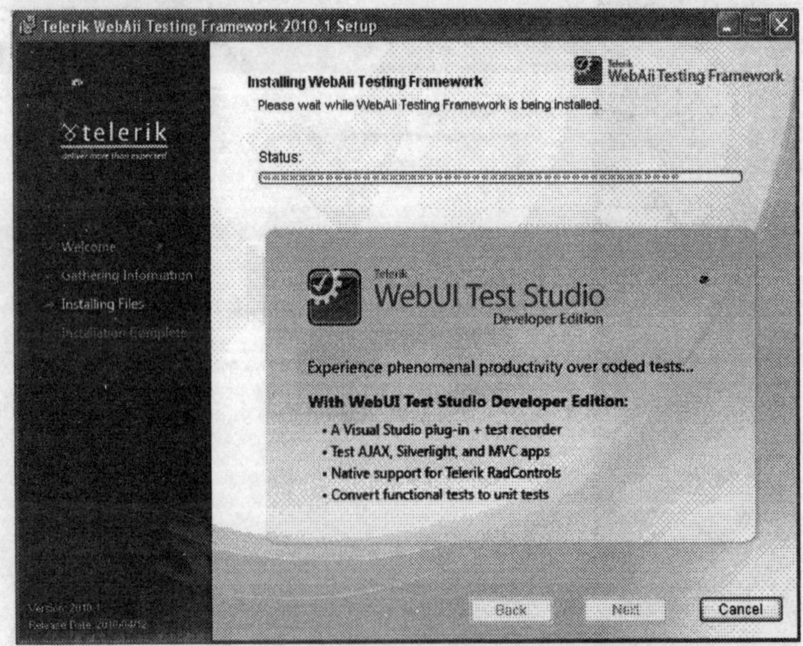
Telerik WebAii Testing Framework 2010.1 Setup
Installing WebAii Testing Framework
WebAii Testing Framework
Please wait while WebAii Testing Framework is being installed.
telerik
Status:
Welcome
Gathering Information
Installing Files
WebUI Test Studio
Developer Edition
Experience phenomenal productivity over coded tests...
With WebUI Test Studio Developer Edition:
• A Visual Studio plug-in + test recorder
• Test AJAX, Silverlight, and MVC apps
• Native support for Telerik RadControls
• Convert functional tests to unit tests
Back
Next
Cancel

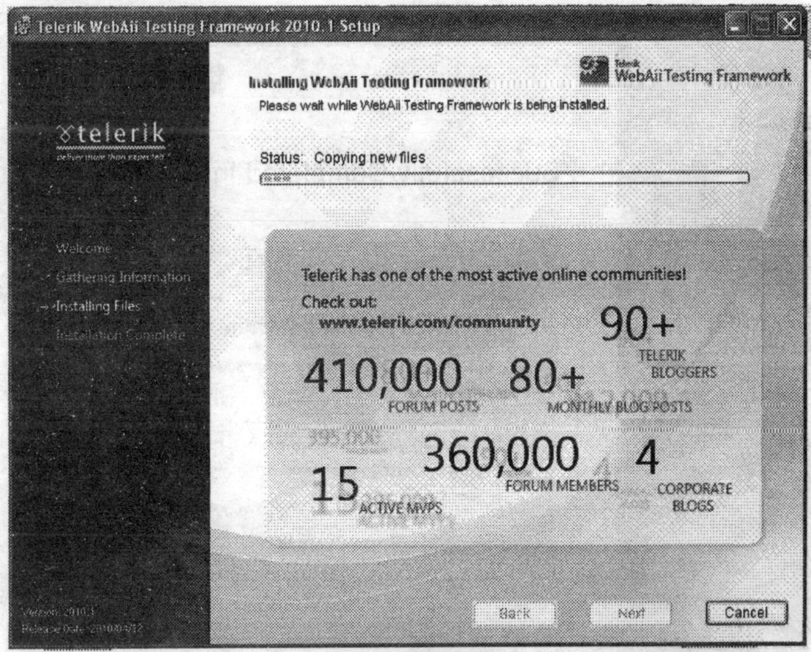
Telerik WebAii Testing Framework 2010.1 Setup
Installing WebAii Testing Framework
Please wait while WebAii Testing Framework is being installed.
WebAii Testing Framework
telerik
Status: Copying new files
Welcome
Gathering Information
Installing Files
Installation Complete
Telerik has one of the most active online communities!
Check out:
www.telerik.com/community
90+
TELERIK BLOGGERS
410,000
FORUM POSTS
80+
MONTHLY BLOG POSTS
360,000
FORUM MEMBERS
4
CORPORATE BLOGS
15
ACTIVE MVPS
Back
Next
Cancel

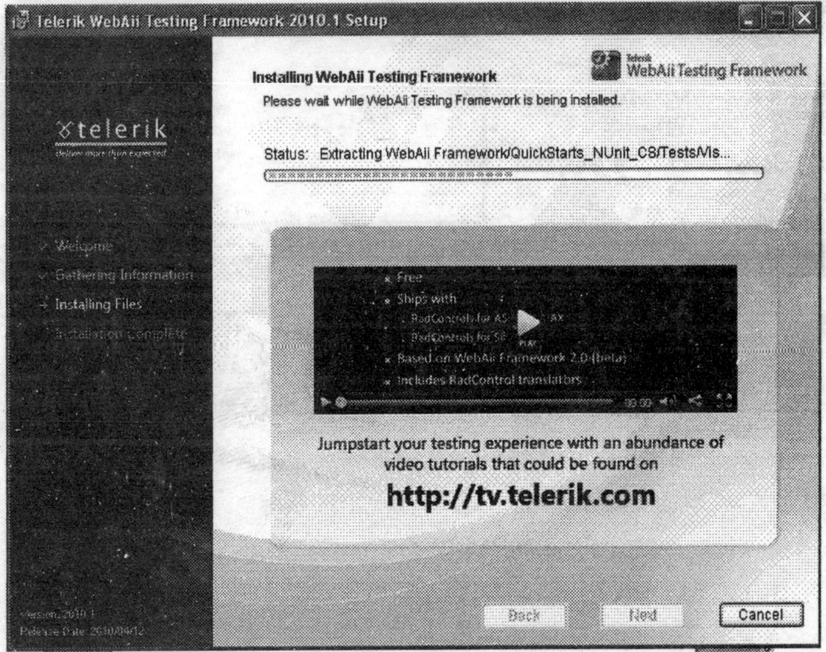
Telerik WebAii Testing Framework 2010.1 Setup
Installing WebAii Testing Framework
Please wait while WebAii Testing Framework is being installed.
WebAii Testing Framework
telerik
Status: Extracting WebAii Framework/QuickStarts_NUnit_C8/Tests/Ms...
Welcome
Gathering Information
Installing Files
Installation Complete
Free
Ships with
Based on WebAii Framework 2.0 (beta)
Includes RadControl translators
Jumpstart your testing experience with an abundance of video tutorials that could be found on
http://tv.telerik.com
Back
Next
Cancel

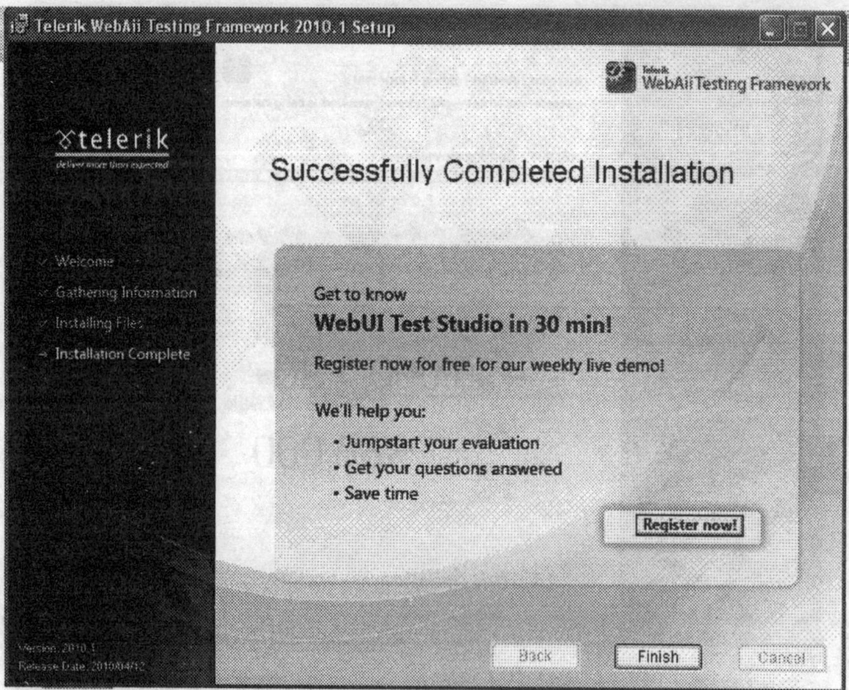
Telerik WebAii Testing Framework 2010.1 Setup
WebAii Testing Framework
telerik
Successfully Completed Installation
Welcome
Gathering Information
Installing Files
Installation Complete
Get to know
WebUI Test Studio in 30 min!
Register now for free for our weekly live demo!
We'll help you:
• Jumpstart your evaluation
• Get your questions answered
• Save time
Register now!
Back
Finish
Cancel

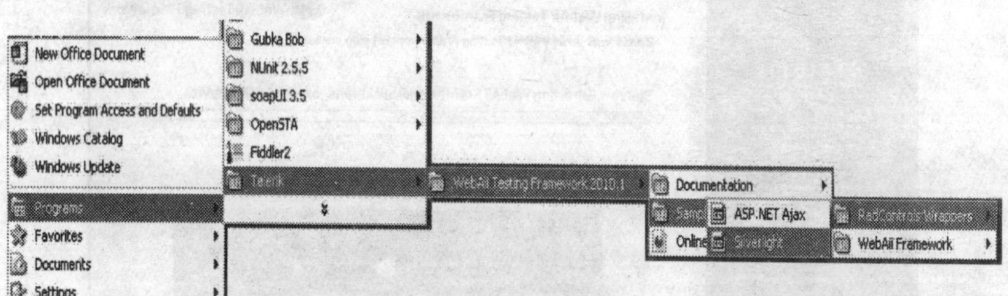
New Office Document
Open Office Document
Set Program Access and Defaults
Windows Catalog
Windows Update
Programs
Favorites
Documents
Settings
Gubka Bob
NUnit 2.5.5
soapUI 3.5
OpenSTA
Fiddler2
Telerik
WebAii Testing Framework 2010.1
Documentation
ASP.NET Ajax
Silverlight
RadControls Wrappers
WebAii Framework

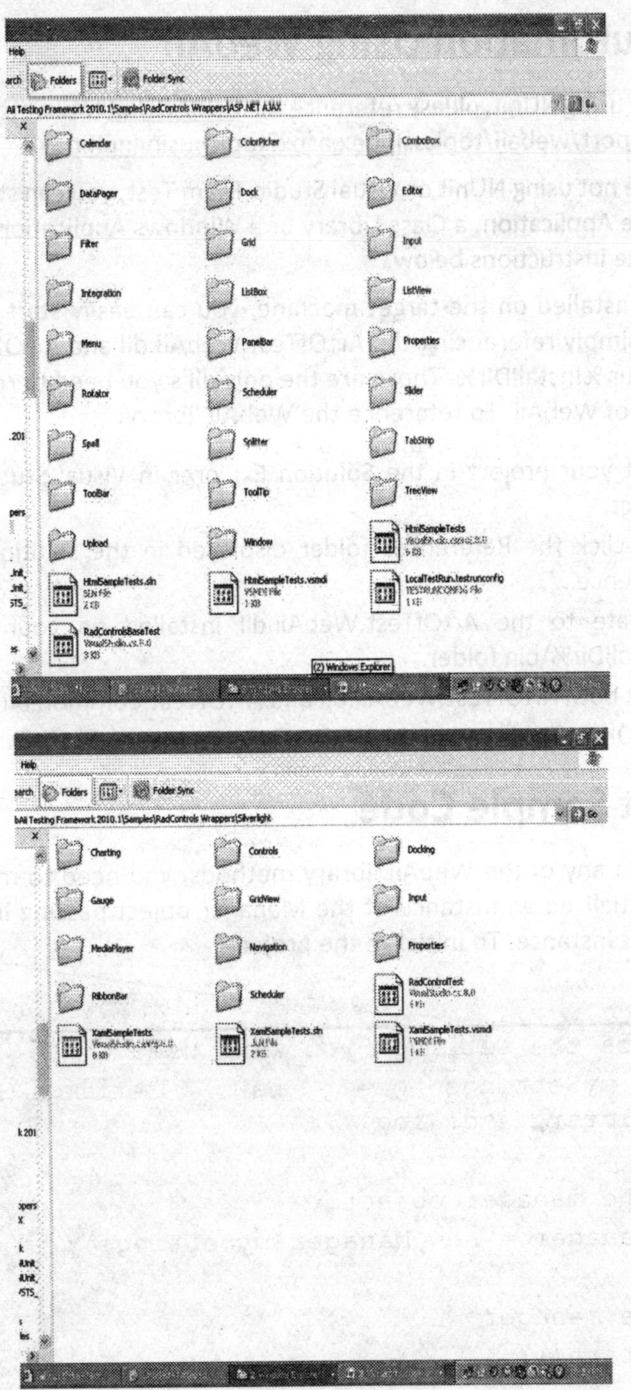
Help
Folders
Folder Sync
All Testing Framework 2010.1\Samples\RadControls Wrappers\ASP.NET AJAX
Calendar
ColorPicker
ComboBox
DataPager
Dock
Editor
Filter
Grid
Input
Integration
ListBox
ListView
Menu
PanelBar
Properties
Rotator
Scheduler
Slider
Spell
Splitter
TabStrip
ToolBar
ToolTip
TreeView
Upload
Window
HtmlSampleTests
HtmlSampleTests.sln
HtmlSampleTests.vsmdi
LocalTestRun.testrunconfig
RadControlsBaseTest
(2) Windows Explorer
Help
Folders
Folder Sync
bAll Testing Framework 2010.1\Samples\RadControls Wrappers\Silverlight
Charting
Controls
Docking
Gauge
GridView
Input
MediaPlayer
Navigation
Properties
RibbonBar
Scheduler
RadControlTest
XamlSampleTests
XamlSampleTests.sln
XamlSampleTests.vsmdi

Starting Automation Using WebAii

- If you are using NUnit, please reference the Using NUnit topic. http://www.artoftest.com/support/webaii/topicssindex.aspx?topic=usingnunit
- If you are not using NUnit or Visual Studio Team Test, you can still use WebAii from a Console Application, a Class Library or a Windows Application. Simply follow the rest of the instructions below.

Once WebAii is installed on the target machine, you can easily start using it from your .NET project by simply referencing the ArtOfTest.WebAii.dll and ArtOfTest.Command.dll files placed in your %InstallDir%. Those are the only dll's you need to reference to get the full functionality of WebAii. To reference the WebAii library:

- Select your project in the Solution Explorer in Visual Studio, or start a new project.
- Right-click the References folder displayed in the solution and select 'Add Reference...'.
- Navigate to the ArtOfTest.WebAii.dll installed on your machine in your %InstallDir%\bin folder.
- Select both ArtOfTest.WebAii.dll and ArtOfTest.Common.dll files.
- Click OK to finish added the WebAii references needed.

Quick Start Sample Code

Before calling into any of the WebAii library methods, you need to make sure that you have properly initialized an instance of the Manager object passing in the settings you want used for this instance. To initialize the project:

```
C#
// Initialize the settings you want used.
Settings    mySettings    =    new    Settings(BrowserType.
InternetExplorer, @"c:\log\");

// Create the manager object
Manager myManager = new Manager(mySettings);

// Start the manager
myManager.Start();
```

```
// Launch a new browser instance. [This will launch an IE
instance qiven the setting above]
myManager.LaunchNewBrowser();

// Navigate to a certain web page
myManager.ActiveBrowser.NavigateTo("http://www.google.
com");

// Perform your automation actions.
Element mybtn = myManager.ActiveBrowser.Find.
ByTagIndex("input", 3);
myManager.ActiveBrowser.Actions.Click(mybtn);

// Shut-down the manager and do all clean-up
myManager.Dispose();
Visual Basic
' Initialize the settings you want used.
Dim mySettings As Settings = New Settings(BrowserType.
InternetExplorer, "c:\log\")

' Create the manager object
Dim myManager As Manager = New Manager(mySettings)

' Start the manager
myManager.Start()

' Launch a new browser instance. [This will launch an IE
instance given the setting above]
myManager.LaunchNewBrowser()

' Navigate to a certain web page
myManager.ActiveBrowser.NavigateTo("http://www.google.com")

' Perform your automation actions.
Dim mybtn As Element = myManager.ActiveBrowser.Find.
ByTagIndex("input", 3)
```

```
myManager.ActiveBrowser.Actions.Click(mybtn)

' Shut-down the manager and do all clean-up
myManager.Dispose()
```

The Manager object exposes all methods/properties needed to perform browser automation, element identification, logging and DOM traversal including TestRegion identification. Below is a brief description of the key objects exposed off the Manager and their corresponding key object properties/methods:

Object	Type Name	Brief Description	Key Objects/ Methods Exposed	Quick Start Tutorials
Manager. ActiveBrowser	**ArtOfTest.WebAii. Core.Browser**	The most recent launched browser instance. You can use it to invoke actions, access the loaded document DOM and perform element identification and extraction using the Browser.Find object.	Browser.Actions, Browser.Find, Brower.DomTree, Browser.Window	**Automating Browser Actions, Finding Page Elements, Multi-Browser Instance Support, JavaScript Support**
Manager. ActiveBrowser. Actions	**ArtOfTest.WebAii. Core.Actions**	Used to invoked direct DOM actions against the loaded document.	Actions. Click, Actions. SetText, Actions. Check, Actions. WaitForElement	**Automating Browser Actions, Ajax support, JavaScript Support**
Manager. ActiveBrowser. Find	ArtOfTest.WebAii. Core.Find	Used to search the DOM elements of the associated browser.	Find.SearchRegion	**Finding Page Elements, Introduction to TestRegion's, FindParam's as External Xml DataSource**
Manager. ActiveBrowser. DomTree	**ArtOfTest.WebAii. Core.TreeBuilder**	The full DOM Tree of the currently loaded document.	TreeBuilder. TestRegion's, TreeBuilder.Root	**Finding Page Elements**
Manager. ActiveBrowser. Window	**ArtOfTest.WebAii. Win32.Window**	The window representation of this browser window. Use this object to manipulate the browser window and capture bitmaps.	Window.Handler, Window.GetBitmap()	**Native Win32 Windows Handling, Visual Capturing**

Manager. ActiveBrowser. Frames	ArtOfTest. WebAii.Core. FramesCollection	Retrieves a list of the child frames contained in the browser window.	ById, BySrc, RefreshAllDomTrees, WaitUntilReady()	Frames Support
Manager. ActiveBrowser. Regions	ArtOfTest.WebAii. ObjectModel. TestRegionCollection	Retrieves a list of the test regions identified in the DOM.	Count, Item, Items	Intro to TestRegion's. Using Asp.Net TestRegion Control
Manager. Desktop	ArtOfTest.WebAii. Core.Desktop	Used to invoke pure UI automation events from the Mouse & Keyboard.	Desktop.Mouse, Desktop.Keyboard	Automating Browser Actions
Manager.Log	ArtOfTest.WebAii. Core.Log	Provides logging support for the current manager session.	Log.WriteLine, Log. CaptureBrowser()	none

How to do Silverlight Test Automation with WebAii

One of the latest hot web development technologies on the market is Microsoft's Silverlight framework. When Microsoft introduced WPF/e (now known as Silverlight Beta), the focus was on building rich media applications - similar to what you can do today with Flash - using a subset of their latest client development technology known as the Windows Presentation Foundation (aka WPF). Later Microsoft introduced Silverlight Alpha which expanded the scope of Silverlight by introducing a light-weight CLR that allows developers to write managed code applications and host these applications inside the browser. To allow Silverlight applications to integrate well with current HTML/Ajax applications, Silverlight also enabled easy access to the HTML document DOM hosting these applications. Pretty cool!

As many in the development community ponder the feature set of this technology and how it can be leveraged in future development projects, we at ArtOfTest and others in the software testing community began investigating how automated testing would work in Silverlight world! There are quite a few challenges to overcome!

When thinking about Silverlight applications and automated testing, there are a couple of different approaches that come to mind:

To get started, let's use a simple application and demo some basic automation scenarios like button click and set text. Then we will expand into more advanced topics and scenarios. Let's take the following simple Silverlight application that contains a button and a text box. When you click the button, it simply displays hello in a text block on the canvas. The application looks like this:

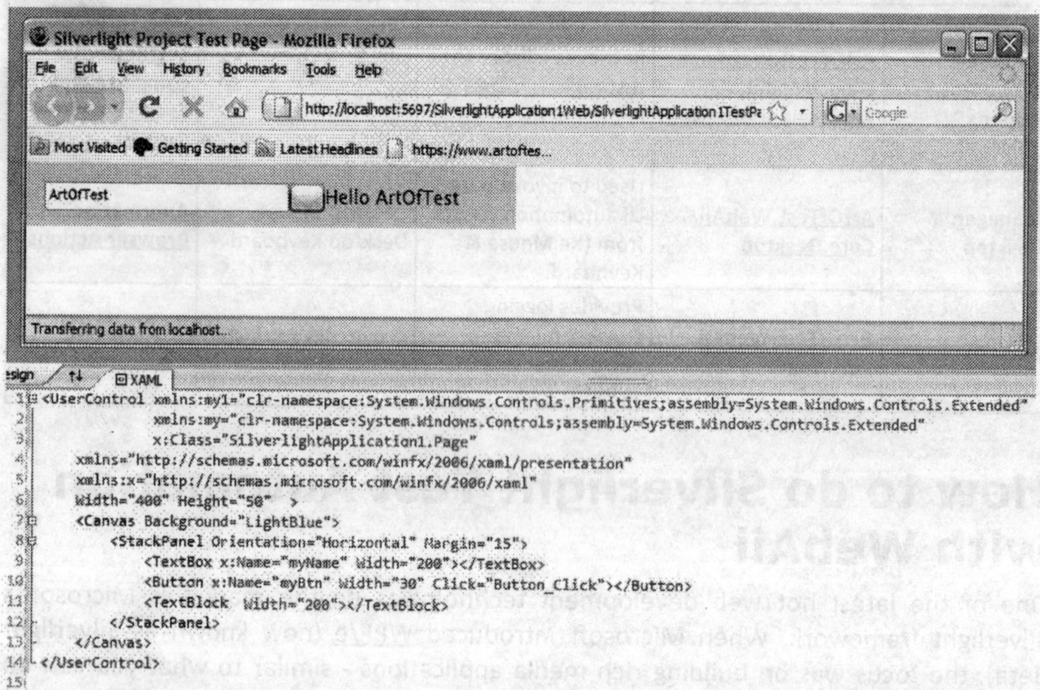

To automate the application above to set the text, click the button and then verify the hello text in WebAii, we can simply write the following code using WebAii's Silverlight Extension (which resides under **ArtOfTest.WebAii.Silverlight**).

```
C#
    [TestMethod]
    public void SLDemo()
    {
        // Launch a browser instance
        Manager.LaunchNewBrowser();

        // Navigate to the page
        ActiveBrowser.NavigateTo("http://localhost:5697/
SilverlightApplication1Web/SilverlightApplication1TestPage.
html");
```

```
        // Get an instance of our Silverlight app.
    SilverlightApp app = ActiveBrowser.SilverlightApps()[0];

        // Set the text of the text box
              app.FindName<TextBox>("myName").Text = "ArtOfTest";

        // Click the button
        app.FindName<Button>("myBtn").User.Click();

        // Verify the text
         Assert.IsTrue(app.Find.ByText("p:Hello").Text.Equals("Hello ArtOfTest"));
    }
```

Visual Basic

```
    <TestMethod()> _
   Public Sub SLDemo()

       ' Launch a browser instance
      Manager.LaunchNewBrowser()

        ' Navigate to the page
       ActiveBrowser.NavigateTo("http://localhost:5697/SilverlightApplication1Web/SilverlightApplication1TestPage.html")

        ' Get an instance of our Silverlight app.
          Dim app As SilverlightApp = ActiveBrowser.SilverlightApps()(0)

        ' Set the text of the text box
             app.FindName(Of TextBox)("myName").Text = "ArtOfTest"

```

```
331         ' Click the button
332        app.FindName(Of Button)("myBtn").User.Click()
333
334         ' Verify the text
335             Assert.IsTrue(app.Find.ByText("p:Hello").Text.
Equals("Hello ArtOfTest"))
336    End Sub
```

Let's take a closer look at the code above line by line:

Line 319-323

This is basic WebAii code that launches the browser and navigates to a specific page.

Line 326

As soon as you include the Silverlight extension namespace in your test, (**ArtOfTest.WebAii.Silverlight**), the 'SilverlightApps()' extension method is added to the ActiveBrowser. The extension method offers you a list of all Silverlight applications found on that page. The extension method returns a list that has two accessors. An **index** accessor that takes an int (as shown above) and a string accessor that takes a **hostid** [The ID of the HTML element that contains the <object> tag for the plug-in]. You can pick and choose what works for you. In this sample, given that we only have one Silverlight plug-in on the page, we simply accessed the first and only one.

Line 329

As soon as you have an instance of a **SilverlightApp,** you now have full access to the application including the entire **VisualTree**. The app offers a short-cut method '**FindName**', that can be used to search the application using an element name. In the above sample, given that the **TextBox** has a name associated with it, we can use **FindName** to locate it. The **SilverlightApp** object offers two versions of '**FindName**': The first is a generic method that can return a strongly-typed object of the element (As shown above, i.e. a Button, a TextBox, a Grid�etc). The second is simpler and returns the base **FrameworkElement** object. We will discuss the strongly-typed object model offered in WebAii Silverlight Extension later.

To go back to the line above, we are simply accessing the **TextBox** that has a name '**myName**' and then setting its **Text** property to "**ArtOfTest**". Note that given we are accessing a property on the element, this is analogous to **SetText** on a DOM element in WebAii automation. You are not really typing the text in the textbox but rather setting the **Text** property inside the application to that text. Our extension enables you to access and set properties directly against any **FrameworkElement**. If we wanted to simulate real typing of the text we would have written code like thls:

```
app.FindName<TextBox>("myName").User.TypeText("ArtOfTest", 50);
```

Line 332

Same as above in terms of accessing the button. The difference here is that we are using the '**User**' object to click the button. The **User** object is present on all elements that inherit from **FrameworkElement** and offers real user interactions with Silverlight elements. So a click using the 'User' object will actually move the mouse over that button and click it. That is exactly what this line does.

Line 335

Now that the button is clicked, we need to verify that the message is correct. The difference here is that we can't really use **FindName** to locate the **TextBlock** because the **TextBlock** doesn't really have a name. The **SilverlightApp** object offers extensive search support within the **VisualTree** beyond **FindName()** by utilizing similar approach to the Find object off the ActiveBrowser (that is used for HTML DOM searches) but adapted to specific **XAML** search scenarios.

In our code above, we are searching for a TextBlock (All Find.xxText() routines return TextBlocks) that partially contains **'Hello'**, hence **'p:Hello'** (Similar to Find.ByContent in HTML search). Once we find the **TextBlock,** we then verify that the **Text** of that label is actually **'Hello ArtOfTest'** using the **Assert.IsTrue**.

Now that we understand this sample, let's dig into some of the key objects available in WebAii's Silverlight Extension.

>> NOTE: In WebAii 2.0 Beta there is a new Setting.EnableSilverlight flag that needs to be set to enable WebAii to connect to Silverlight applications. By default this setting is <u>not</u> on. Setting this flag will activate the built-in proxy that we use to detect Silverlight applications.

Current limitations with this release:

1. On Vista, if you are automating an external website, then make sure to add the URL to your Trusted Websites list in IE.
2. Our automation supports Silverlight 2.0 (and above). We do not support any previous versions.

3. The automation only supports the XAP deployment method.
4. EnableHtmlAccess needs to be set to 'True' on your application.
5. There are known issues with Silverlight applications that attempt to perform web service calls within the application.
6. The application needs to be running off http:// not C:\...
7. Running the application under HTTPS is not supported.
8. When using localhost as your server name, it must end with a trailing '.' character e.g. http://localhost./.

Ajax Support

Ajax is one of the latest and fastest growing web development technologies that is fuelling today's Web 2.0 era. The technology enables developers to build great and rich web content. However at the same time it adds great complexity to the testing methods required to validate the web applications that use it. To a certain extent, websites that rely heavily on Ajax can no longer rely on using the legacy HTTP record/replay methods to test the entire functionality given that major portions of the website logic are executed within the browser JavaScript engine and in some cases no HTTP requests are being made to the server at all!

WebAii has been built from the ground up with features like Ajax in mind. WebAii supports the following features that help ease the testing and automation authoring for Ajax applications. These features also lay the ground work for a rich, consistent and comprehensive infrastructure that developers and quality assurance professionals can rely on to test rich web content. WebAii offers:

- **Direct DOM interaction** with web pages allowing you to perform automation actions from within the browser to automate and exercise your Ajax scripts. This topic is covered in detail under Automating Browser Actions.
- **Perform complex UI actions** like DragAndDrop and pure UI actions on web pages (i.e. Hover, Right-click, etc). You have both worlds of automation (DOM + UI) accessible to you using WebAii. This topic is covered in detail under Automating Browser Actions.
- **Waiting on DOM changes**. With Ajax, you can no longer rely on the load complete of pages or the browsers ready flag to know when a specific page or scenario has finished. WebAii supports a WaitForElement(s) method exposed off of the Actions object. The WaitForElement(s) allows you to wait for 1-N elements using the

rich identification support available in WebAii. For example you can wait for an element to show up at a specific DOM location or wait for some of its attributes to be set to certain values ...etc. This is covered in more detail below.

- **Retrieve dynamic property values directly from the DOM** of any element hosted by the browser. This is also covered in more detail below.
- **Visual capturing of browser states and elements** to more easily diagnose test failures and application behaviors and do visual comparison of specific elements. This topic is covered in detail under Visual Capturing.
- **Invoke JavaScript functions** from your test code and **perform logging** directly from JavaScript. This topic is covered in detail under JavaScript Invocation and JavaScript Logging.
- **Invoke JavaScript events** directly from your test code. For example, invoke the OnBlur() event on an element or the OnMouseOut(), etc. This topic is covered in detail under JavaScript Events.
- **Attach event handlers** directly to JavaScript events. This topic is covered in detail under JavaScript Events.

Waiting on DOM Changes: WaitForElement(s)

WaitForElement(s) is a great method to use when trying to suspend test execution until a certain element is present or has changed or a specific value of a certain attribute for an element has been set (or even a combination of values). This is a common scenario when automating Ajax applications. WaitForElement(s) requires a basic understanding of FindParam's and how to define them. Once you know how to craft FindParam's, you will be able to write custom and rich wait routines using a consistent pattern.

Let's examine a couple of examples to illustrate how WaitForElement(s) is used. Assume that you are waiting for a table to be inserted in your DOM tree at a certain location and you want to wait until the whole table is built including the sixth row. The following is the DOM segment before the Ajax call is made:

```
<!--testregion id="ajaxupdate"-->
<div>
</div>
<!--/testregion-->
```

Here is the DOM after the call has been made:

```
<!--testregion id="ajaxupdate"-->
<div>
  <table>
     <tr><td>Data</td></tr>
     <tr><td>Data</td></tr>
     <tr><td>Data</td></tr>
     <tr><td>Data</td></tr>
     <tr><td>Data</td></tr>
     <tr><td>Data</td></tr>
  </table>
</div>
<!--/testregion-->
```

The following code will perform this wait.

```
C#
// Get the ajaxupdate region.
// Notice how using a testregion simplifies our identification
and makes it
// more isolated to the current DOM region being targeted and
less prone
// to be affected by other DOM sections.
TestRegion ajaxupdate = ActiveBrowser.Regions["ajaxupdate"];

// First wait for the table to show up inside the region. (the
first table tag, index=0)
FindParam table = new FindParam("table", 0);

// Next wait for the sixth row to be there.
FindParam sixth_row = new FindParam("tr", 6);

// perform the wait for both elements. WaitForElements() takes
1-N FindParam objects to
// to wait for.
```

```
ActiveBrowser.Actions.WaitForElements(500, ajaxupdate, false,
table, sixth_row);
```

```
Visual Basic
' Get the ajaxupdate region.
' Notice how using a testregion simplifies our identification and
makes it
' more isolated to the current DOM region being targeted and less
prone
' to be affected by other DOM sections.
Dim ajaxupdate As TestRegion = ActiveBrowser.Regions.
Item("ajaxupdate")

' First wait for the table to show up inside the region. (the first
table tag, index=0)
Dim table As FindParam = New FindParam("table", 0)

' Next wait for the sixth row to be there.
Dim sixth_row As FindParam = New FindParam("tr", 6)

' perform the wait for both elements. WaitForElements() takes 1-N
FindParam objects to
' to wait for.
ActiveBrowser.Actions.WaitForElements(500, ajaxupdate, False,
table, sixth_row)
```

In the above code sample, we used TestRegion's to make our automation simpler and targeted at the DOM region we are interested in. If you choose to not use TestRegion's, you can simply use the WaitForElement(s) overload that takes in only the FindParam and the Timeout. In that case, all identification will be performed with reference to the root element of the DomTree.

You can also use "Chained Identification" to wait for an element. For example if we have a DOM segment that looks like the sample below:

```
<spanid="myspan">
   <div>
```

```
    <table>
      <tr><td>Data</td></tr>
      <tr><td>Data</td></tr>
      <tr><td>Data</td></tr>
      <tr><td>Data</td></tr>
      <tr><td>Data</td></tr>
      <tr><td>Data</td></tr>
    </table>
  </div>
</span>
```

... and we want to wait until we have six rows available, then we can use chained identification as follows:

```
C#
// First find the span by id
FindParam myspan = new FindParam("id=myspan");

// Next wait for the sixth row to be there.
FindParam sixth_row = new FindParam("tr", 5);

// perform the wait for the row element.
ActiveBrowser.Actions.WaitForElement(new   FindParam[]   {
myspan, sixth_row }, 500);
```

```
Visual Basic
' First find the span by id
Dim myspan As FindParam = New FindParam("id=myspan")

' Next wait for the sixth row to be there.
Dim sixth_row As FindParam = New FindParam("tr", 5)

' perform the wait for the row element.
ActiveBrowser.Actions.WaitForElement(New  FindParam()  {myspan,
sixth_row}, 500)
```

The above scenario is one of the most common when testing Ajax apps. Therefore, the WaitForElement provides an easy to use overload for these common scenarios where you need to first identify an element by id/name then validate a certain attribute list. This helps reduce the lines of code each time you need to identify an element. If you need a more complex identification, you can use chained identification as described above.

Retrieving Dynamic Property Values Directly From the DOM

When using Ajax the application, in most scenarios, updates the document's DOM using JavaScript. The DOM tree provided to your test code by WebAii is automatically updated after each command gets executed against the browser if Browser.AutoDomRefresh property is set to 'true', which is the default value. In most scenarios the DOM tree is the latest up-to-date DOM tree from the browser. In cases where the DOM tree is updated without using WebAii browser commands (for example, the page auto-refreshes based on an internal timer, or you are using Pure UI automation), you can always refresh the DOM by calling Browser.RefreshDomTree().

In some scenarios that might not even be enough. For example, you want to retrieve a property value that doesn't usually get emitted into the DOM when serialized like the default or inherited values of an unset property or in Firefox the 'value' property of input tags.

To help address this issue and potentially other issues, the WebAii infrastructure supports a generic and simple method of retrieving any property of any element directly from the live DOM hosted in the browser. Each Element object in WebAii has a GetValue<T>() method that you can use to evaluate any custom or standard attribute of your Dom element at any point in your test code or application.

For example, if you want to retrieve the text set by a user in an input textbox in Firefox, you can simply do the following:

```
C#
// Get the element.
Element input = ActiveBrowser.Find.ById("myinput");

// Get its 'value' property from the DOM
string value = input.GetValue<string>("value");
```

```
// Get its 'display' property from the DOM
string display = input.GetValue<string>("display");

// Get its 'visibility' property from the DOM
string visibility = input.GetValue<string>("visibility");
Visual Basic
' Get the element.
Dim input As Element = ActiveBrowser.Find.ById("myinput")

' Get its 'value' property from the DOM
Dim value As String = input.GetValue(Of String)("value")

' Get its 'display' property from the DOM
Dim display As String = input.GetValue(Of String)
("display")

' Get its 'visibility' property from the DOM
Dim visibility As String = input.GetValue(Of String)
("visibility")
```

References:

http://www.telerik.com/community/code-library/web-testing-tools/webaii-testing-framework/continuous-integration-with-webaii-tests-for-silverlight-nunit-and-cruisecontrol-net.aspx

http://www.artoftest.com/support/webaii/topicsindex.aspx

http://www.telerik.com/products/web-testing-tools/webaii-framework-features.aspx

http://www.artoftest.com/support/webaii/topicsindex.aspx?topic=usingnunit

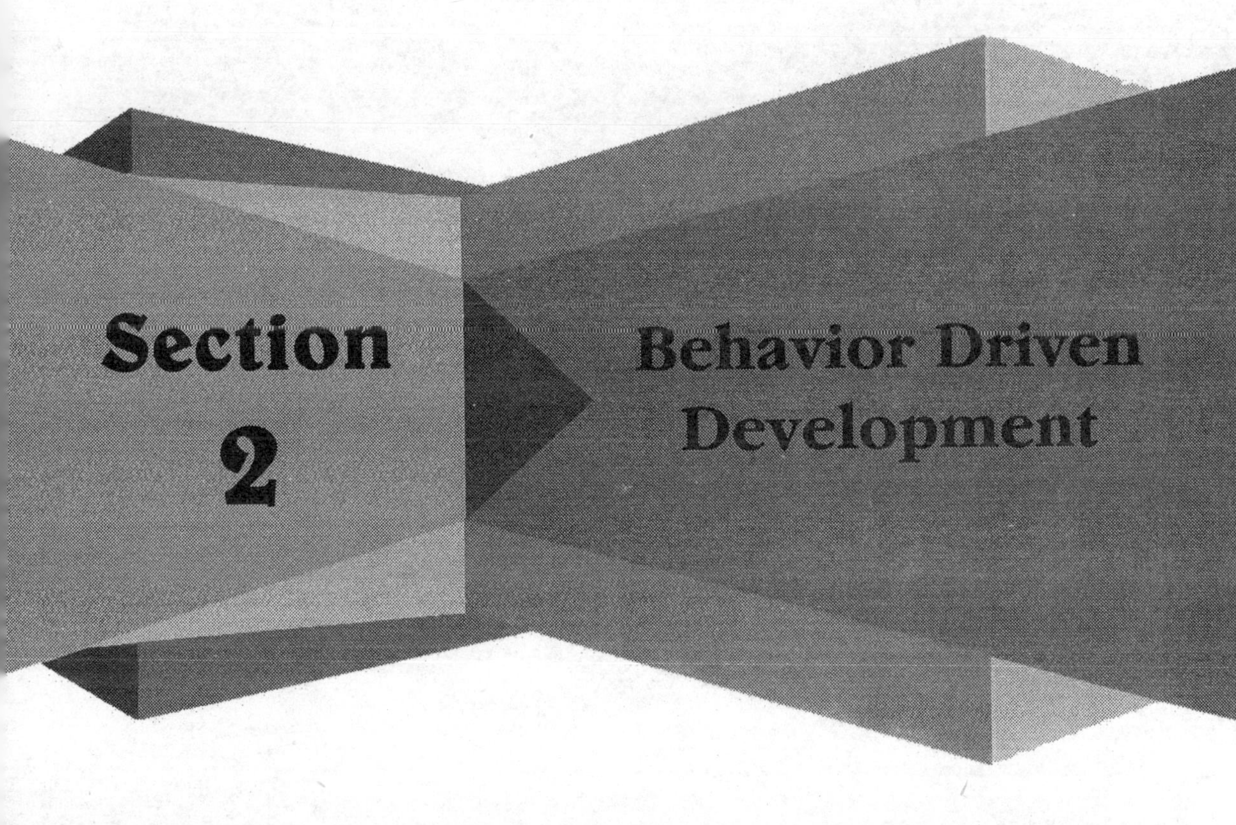
Section
2
Behavior Driven
Development

Behavior Driven Development (or **BDD**) is an Agile software development technique that encourages collaboration between developers, QA and non-technical or business participants in a software project. It was originally named in 2003 by Dan North[1] as a response to Test Driven Development, and to Framework for Integrated Tests concepts, from the Customer Test practice in Extreme Programming. It has evolved over the last few years[2].

On the "Agile Specifications, BDD and Testing eXchange" in November 2009 in London, Dan North[3] gave the following definition of BDD:

BDD is a second-generation, outside-in, pull- based, multiple-stakeholder, multiple-scale, high-automation, agile methodology. It describes a cycle of interactions with well- defined outputs, resulting in the delivery of working, tested software that matters.

BDD focuses on exposing internal logic (typically business rules) to review by stakeholders. It extends TDD by writing test cases in a natural language that non-programmers can read. Behavior-driven developers use their native language in combination with the *ubiquitous language* of Domain Driven Design to describe the purpose and benefit of their code. This allows the developers to focus on why the code should be created, rather than the technical details, and minimizes translation between the technical language in which the code is written and the domain language spoken by the business, users, stakeholders, project management etc.

Dan North created the first ever BDD framework, JBehave[1], followed by a story-level BDD framework for Ruby called RBehave[4] which was later integrated into the RSpec project[5]. He also worked with David Chelimsky, Aslak Hellesøy and others to develop RSpec and also to write "The RSpec Book: Behaviour Driven Development with RSpec, Cucumber, and Friends". The first story-based framework in RSpec was later replaced by Cucumber mainly developed by Aslak Hellesøy.

In 2008, Chris Matts, who was involved in the first discussions around BDD, came up with the idea of Feature Injection[6], allowing BDD to cover the analysis space and provide a full treatment of the software lifecycle from vision through to code and release.

Some of those are not really benefits of BDD, however - rather, they are benefits of Designing. Many programmers (particularly in the less sophisticated parts of the agile movement) tend to focus on code and ignore the rest. BDD provides them with a neat, coder-friendly way of doing design and specification. Of course that helps! There's a reason why the industry standard development processes include a *design* phase, after all - it's not just to delay the project!

I think there's another important reason why BDD is better, *as a test suite*. It helps make your test suite less brittle *in the face of specification changes*. Here's the reasoning.

Update: *Please have a look at this article from Pat Maddox. BDD is a fairly new field that's still evolving, and Pat's article is right on the money. The approach I outline in this article is what Pat would call "pure interaction testing" and, as he points out, it should not be a goal - only an available technique. Currently, I use pure interaction testing for Rails controller testing, and state-based testing for ActiveRecord models. There's certainly a place for the ideas exposed in this article, but they shouldn't be used blindly everywhere.*

BDD focuses on specifying what will happen next. The basic sentence structure of a BDD spec is:

> This should happen; then this should happen; then this. Tell me if that doesn't happen when I say "foo". Foo.

TDD, on the other hand, focuses on setting up a set of conditions and then looking at the output:

> Foo. Is Bar set to the right value? What about Baz?

Put in other words, BDD specifies behaviours while TDD specifies outcomes. The difference is more than just language, though. It's a paradigm shift that has some severe consequences.

The main one, in my view, is that behaviours can be layered, while outcomes cannot. This might sound a bit cryptic, so let me explain. Let's use the analogy of a big machine. At one end, you put a variety of raw materials, and at the other, you get a widget. Outcome testing will examine the widget from all angles. It will ask "Does this widget perform the functions that I expect a widget to perform?". This is basically black box testing - and that's what most integration tests do (and, sadly, many unit tests, as it's often hard to separate the two without extensive mocking, which requires deep knowledge of the internals of the module you're testing).

Behaviour specification turns this upside down. Instead of trying to specify the outcome, and using mocking only where you absolutely need to in order to get the thing working, you start with the goal to specify precisely those internals that you tried to avoid in TDD. "The machine should be able to turn sand and gold flakes into gold flaked glass; to do this, it should heat up the sand into molten glass. Then it should insert the gold flakes." This requires internal knowledge of the machine.

Hopefully this is clear so far. Now here's the clincher, the real advantage of behaviour specification over outcome testing. In order to test an outcome, you need all the parts up to that outcome to have done their job. If I want to test that my widget has a gold-flaked glass pane in it, I need the rest of the widget-building to have succeeded and not produced a molten lump of goo. In other words, outcome testing is quite brittle. If one of the parts malfunctions, there will be many knock-on effects onto other tests. You might point out that this is why we have unit tests, but my point is, BDD enables you to design your unit tests properly. Let's take a fairly simple method as an example.

```
class Mogrifier < Polator
def transmogrify(foo, bar)
   foo.extrapolate!
   bar.extrapolate!

   baz = intrapolate(foo, bar)

   return ultrapolate(baz)
  end
end
```

With a Test-First approach, we might have written something like this as a test, before writing this code:

```
def test_mogrifier
 foo = test_foo
 bar = test_bar

 test_result = Mogrifier.new.transmogrify(foo, bar)

 assert test_result.ultrapolated?
 assert test_result.intrapolated?
 assert test_result.contains(foo.relevant_bit)
 assert test_result.contains(bar.relevant_bit)
end
How would you write this as a specification?
describe Mogrifier, "transmogrify" do

  before(:each) do
   @mogrifier = Mogrifier.new
```

```
  end

  it "should extrapolate foo" do
    foo = "foo"
    foo.should_receive(:extrapolate!).and_return("extrapolated foo")

    @mogrifier.my_method(foo, "bar")
  end

  it "should extrapolate bar" do
    bar = "bar"
    bar.should_receive(:extrapolate!).and_return("extrapolated bar")

    @mogrifier.my_method("foo", bar)
  end

  it "should intrapolate" do
    @mogrifier.should_receive(:intrapolate)
    @mogrifier.my_method("foo", "bar")
  end

  it "should ultrapolate" do
    @mogrifier.should_receive(:ultrapolate)
  end

end
```

Why is the test more brittle? It's brittle because if the specification changes and states that actuallly, the transmogrifier should also encrypt its results, your test will break, whereas **not one** of your specs will break. In a BDD world, you'd write:

```
  it "should encrypt" do
    mock_baz = mock("baz")
```

```
  mock_baz.should_receive(:encrypt)
  @mogrifier.should_receive(:ultrapolate).and_return(mock_baz)
end
```

And then you'd add the encrypt call to the transmogrify method. With TDD, on the other hand, any of your tests that depend on the outcome of the transmogrifier will have to change. You might even be quite stuck at this point, in this specific example, if the encryption happens to be one-way - if that were the case, you won't be able to test the outcome at all, since it will be opaque! Then you'd have to redesign your code so that transmogrify doesn't actually encrypt stuff, but some other method does. What a pain!

Behaviour specifications enable you to ensure that your transmogrifier code keeps extrapolating and intrapolating as required - no matter what it does with its input later. If it needs to do other stuff too, that's fine, you can specify it as well - but each specification will (or should) focus on a single behaviour and that way, as long as your spec passes, you know that the specification is being met, and that foo and bar are still being extrapolated (in this example).

As the behaviours multiply, and the layering increases, this becomes even more useful. Because of the focus of each specification, there is rarely any need to change more than a handful of specifications when the code changes (if the specs are well-written and cleanly split out into small and specific behaviours). For instance, if the Polator changes its processes (but retains its interface), the Transmogrifier test code will remain the same. BDD encourages low coupling of tests, which, to be fair, TDD doesn't encourage. In TDD, it's easier to write a test that uses real objects (at least at first). In BDD, you simply cannot specify behaviours without using mocks.

Different Flavours in Driven Development

- Behavior-Driven Development
- Domain-Driven Design
- Acceptance-Test Driven Development
- Feature-Driven Development
- Example-Driven Development
- Hope-Driven Development

Introduction of TDD/BDD/DDD

Test Driven Development (TDD) has established itself as a useful--and at its best, profound--improvement in the software development process. It delivers a variety of benefits to its practitioners; some of them are related to testing, but the most important benefits are not.

1. The developer starts writing unit tests around their code using a test framework like JUnit or NUnit.
2. As the body of tests increases the developer begins to enjoy a strongly increased sense of confidence in their work.
3. At some point the developer has the insight (or is shown) that writing the tests before writing the code, helps them to focus on writing only the code that they need.
4. The developer also notices that when they return to some code that they haven't seen for a while, the tests serve to document how the code works.
5. A point of revelation occurs when the developer realises that writing tests in this way helps them to "discover" the API to their code. TDD has now become a design process.
6. Expertise in TDD begins to dawn at the point where the developer realizes that TDD is about defining behaviour rather than testing.
7. Behaviour is about the interactions between components of the system and so the use of mocking is fundamental to advanced TDD.

We have observed this progression in many developers, but unfortunately while most, with a little help, find their way to step 4, many miss the big wins found at steps 5, 6 and 7.

We started wondering why this was, and wondering what we could do to help people get to the good stuff more quickly. Looking closely at this evolution in understanding, while step 1 may be considered to be related to testing, the rest really are not. For the remainder of the steps in this process, the test aspect is very much a secondary concern. The issue at the heart of this learning process is the behaviour of the system. Developers gain confidence in the systems they build when the behaviour of that system is confirmed.

By writing tests in advance of code, the developer defines the behavioural intent of the system that they are developing. Tests that document the behavioural intent of the system are most valuable as documentation of that system. By specifying the behaviour of the code in tests, developers are able to best consider the interface from the perspective of the consumer of the service rather than as the producer – thinking more abstractly about the nature of the solution and so hiding technical detail.

This focus on behaviour ahead of testing is a focus on the real value in TDD, and in our experience is the mark of the genuinely experienced TDD practitioner.

It is not too surprising that it takes apprentice TDD practitioners a while to realize that TDD is not about testing when all of the nomenclature surrounding it is described in terms of testing.

The aim of Behaviour Driven Development (BDD) is to address this shortcoming. By using terminology focused on the behavioural aspects of the system rather than testing, BDD attempts to help direct developers towards a focus on the real value to be found in TDD at its most successful.

BDD aims to bridge the gap between the differing views of computer systems held by Business users and Technologists. It is deeply rooted in the success of TDD and is influenced by ideas like Domain Driven Design. Its focus is on minimizing the hurdles between specification, design, implementation and confirmation of the behaviour of a system. Thus enabling the incremental delivery of business systems, and in particular in allowing teams new to agile development to quickly get up to speed using these extremely productive techniques.

BDD relies on the use of a very specific (and small) [:BddVocabulary:Vocabulary] to minimize miscommunication and to ensure that everyone – the business, developers, testers, analysts and managers – are not only on the same page but using the same words. It must be stressed that BDD is a rephrasing of existing good practice, it is not a radically new departure. Its aim is to bring together existing, well-established techniques under a common banner and with a consistent and unambiguous terminology. In fact, "Getting the Words Right" was the starting point for the development of BDD, and is still very much at its core. "Getting the Words Right" is intended to produce a [:BddVocabulary:vocabulary] that is accurate, accessible, descriptive and consistent.

Agile Development

Agile Development is an approach to software development that attempts to reduce the cost of change, and so deliver software that meets business needs in a more predictable, timely manner.

It encompasses a variety of approaches and methods, but all share common features and are grounded in principles of the AgileManifesto.

Agile development practitioners believe that planning too far ahead is doomed to failure, because, however good we are, we are not prescient and we will make mistakes. They further believe that many TraditionalDevelopment processes are based on such predictions and that this is a fundamental reason why so many software projects fail.

Agile processes accept that mistakes will happen, that people will change their minds, misunderstand things and generally behave like human beings.

Instead of mitigating risk by trying to anticipate problems, agile projects are designed to avoid the increase in the CostOfChange completely. By accepting that change will happen and relying on several techniques to reduce the impact of late changes, agile processes alter the CostOfChange curve.

There are several techniques used on agile projects to effect this reduction in the cost of change. Instead of taking a qualitative approach to development, agile projects try as much as possible to take a quantitative approach.

- Estimates for this week are based on what was accomplished last week.
- Progress is measured by how much software is actually working.
- The usefulness of the software produced is measured by users using it and reporting back if it meets, or fails to meet, their needs.

These are pragmatic, measurable things. Of course, there remain times when guesses must be made based on experience. Agile projects attempt to reduce the impact of getting those guesses wrong by not extrapolating too far ahead, typically only one or two weeks ahead.

Agile projects are characterized by the following:

- IterativeDevelopment
- SmallTeams
- ContinuousIntegration
- MinimalDocumentation
- No BigDesignUpFront
- IterativePlanning

BddWiki: AgileDevelopment (last edited 2009-10-04 14:13:25 by JacobAndresen)

Here are some tools to help implementing BDD:

- BOO - Specter: A tool written for the Boo language, a .Net and Mono programming language.
- C - CSpec
- C++ - CppSpec Spec-CPP
- C# .Net - NSpec
- .Net - NBehave
- .Net - NSpecify (incomplete site)
- Delphi - dSpec
- Groovy - GSpec, http://easyb.org easyb, tspec a non-English BDD framework with Thai syntax.
- Java - JBehave, JDave, beanSpec, Instinct, GivWenZen (Java and FitNesse)
- Javascript - JSSpec, jspec
- PHP - PHPSpec
- Python - Specipy, spec plugin for nose
- Ruby - RSpec, Shoulda, test-spec & bacon, Cucumber
- Scala - Specs
- Smalltalk - SSpec

BddWiki: Implementations (last edited 2009-10-05 02:28:38 by WesWilliams)

References:

http://behaviour-driven.org/Implementations

http://inter-sections.net/2007/10/03/the-difference-between-tdd-and-bdd

http://behaviour driven.org/

http://behaviour-driven.org/BDDProcess

http://behaviour-driven.org/Implementations

http://behaviour-driven.org/DescriptionsOfBDD

http://behaviour-driven.org/AgileDevelopment

www.cornetdesign.com/files/TDDMVP-AgileTampa1208.ppt

BDD using Cucumber tool

Introduction

What is Cucumber?

Cucumber is a tool that can execute plain-text documents as automated functional tests. Cucumber works with Ruby, .NET, Flex, Java or web applications written in any language. Cucumber has been translated to over 30 spoken languages. Cucumber also supports more succinct tests in tables - similar to what fit does. Dig around in the examples and documentation to learn more about Cucumber tables.

Cucumber understands Gherkin language. Here is an example:

Feature: Search courses
  In order to ensure better utilization of courses
  Potential students should be able to search for courses

  Scenario: Search by topic
    Given there are 240 courses which do not have the topic "biology"
    And there are 2 courses A001, B205 that each have "biology" as one of the topics
    When I search for "biology"
    Then I should see the following courses:
    | Course code |
    | A001 |
    | B205 |

The Cucumber tool is to support BDD (Behavior Driven Development). This means that the "tests" (plain text feature descriptions with scenarios) are typically written before anything else and verified by business analysts, domain experts, etc. non technical stakeholders. The production code is then written outside-in, to make the stories pass.

Cucumber itself is written in Ruby, but it can be used to "test" code written in Ruby or other languages including but not limited to Java, C# and Python. Cucumber only requires minimal use of Ruby programming and Ruby is easy.

Supported Environments

Windows, Linux.

Requirements:

Ruby, JRuby and Java

Download Ruby from

http://www.ruby-lang.org/en/downloads/

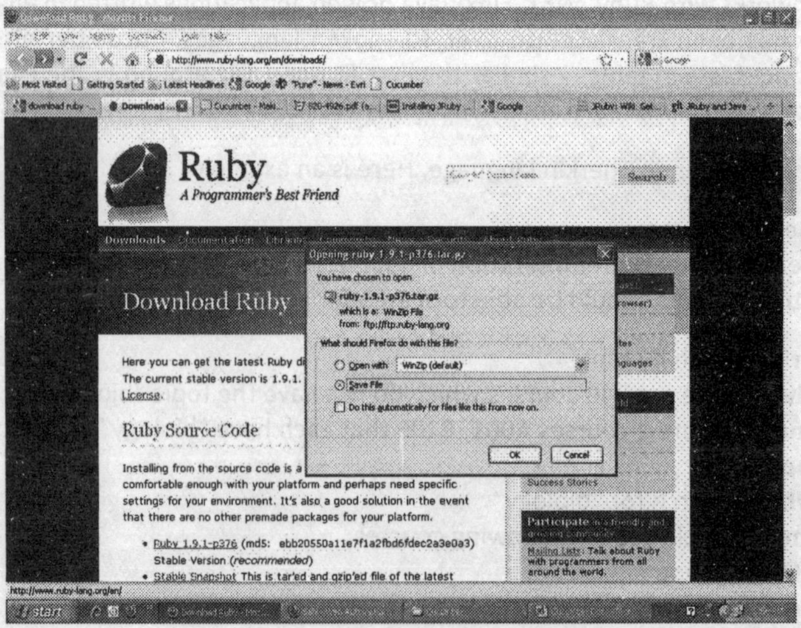

Save ruby 1.9.1 p376.tar.gz file.

Extract ruby 1.9.1 p376.tar.gz to desired location.

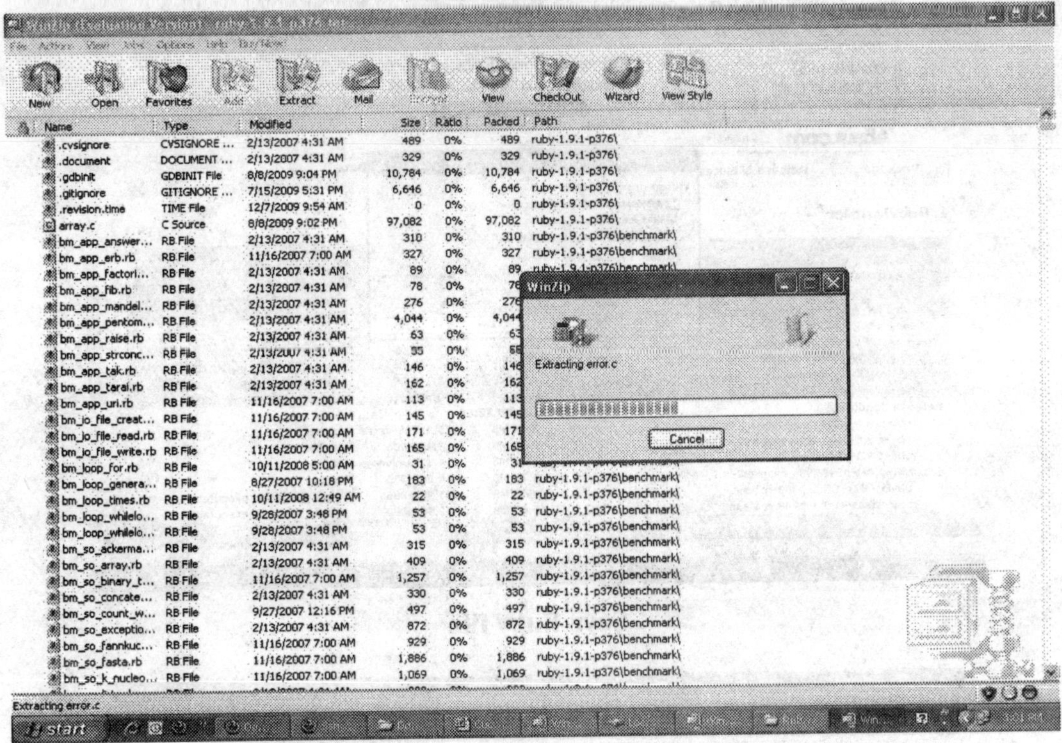

Click to Download Ruby

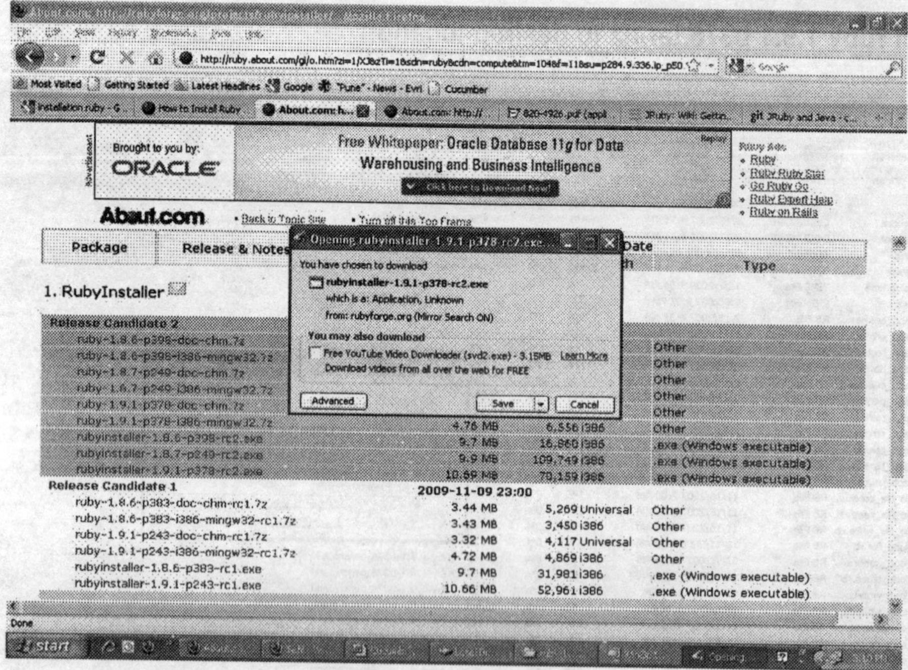

Save Ruby file

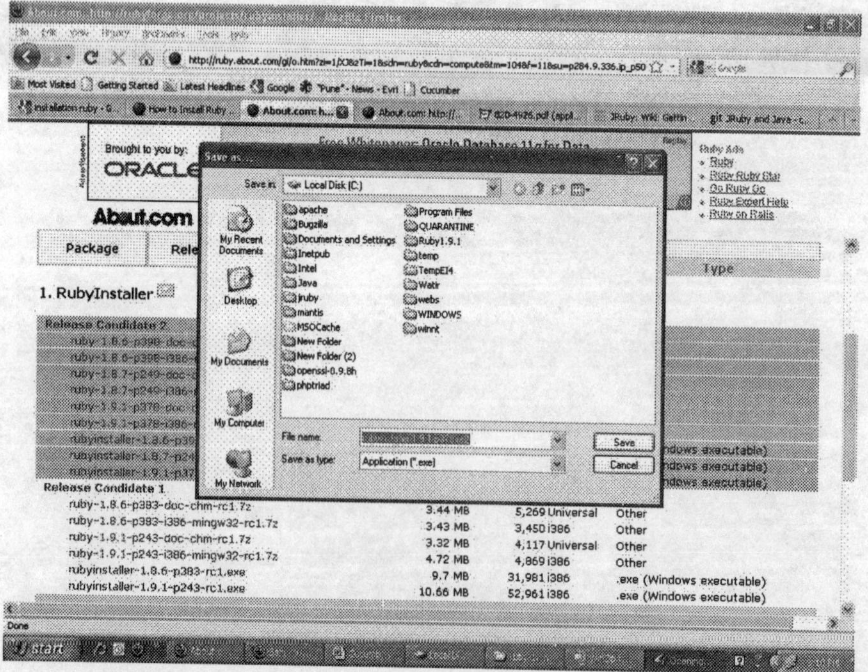

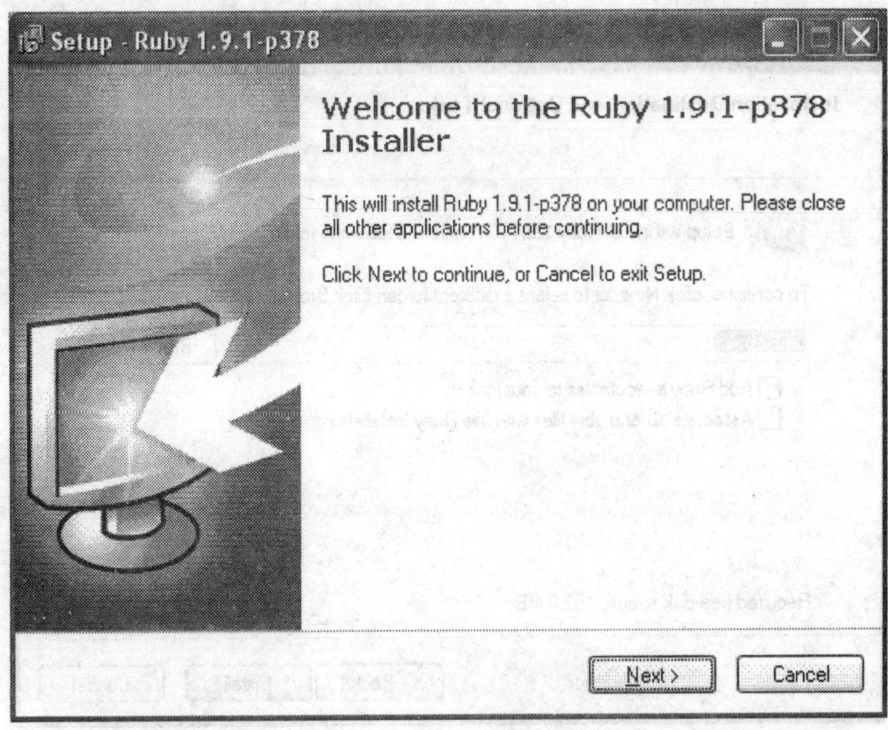
Setup - Ruby 1.9.1-p378
Welcome to the Ruby 1.9.1-p378 Installer
This will install Ruby 1.9.1-p378 on your computer. Please close all other applications before continuing.
Click Next to continue, or Cancel to exit Setup.
Next >
Cancel

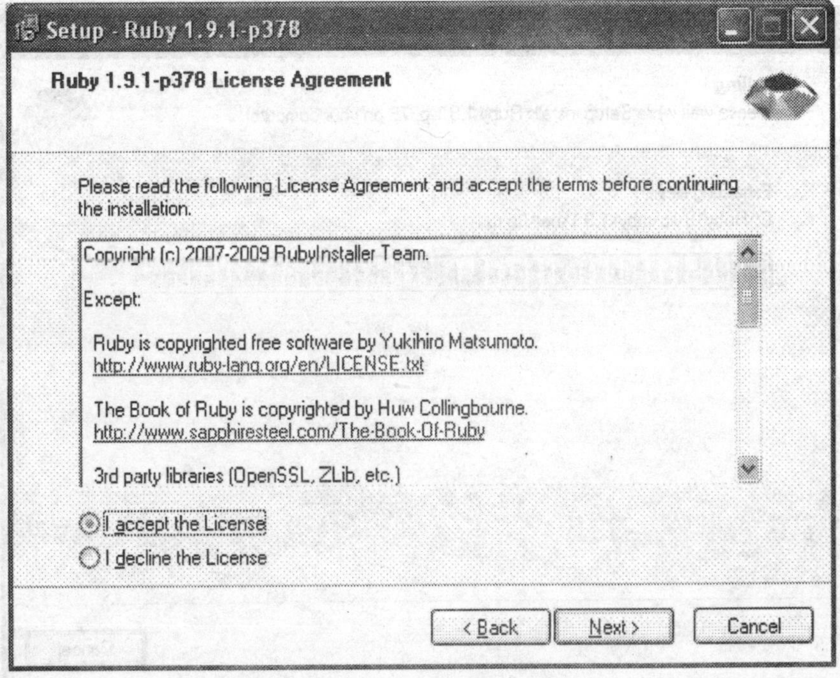
Setup - Ruby 1.9.1-p378
Ruby 1.9.1-p378 License Agreement
Please read the following License Agreement and accept the terms before continuing the installation.
Copyright (c) 2007-2009 RubyInstaller Team.
Except:
Ruby is copyrighted free software by Yukihiro Matsumoto.
http://www.ruby-lang.org/en/LICENSE.txt
The Book of Ruby is copyrighted by Huw Collingbourne.
http://www.sapphiresteel.com/The-Book-Of-Ruby
3rd party libraries (OpenSSL, ZLib, etc.)
I accept the License
I decline the License
< Back
Next >
Cancel

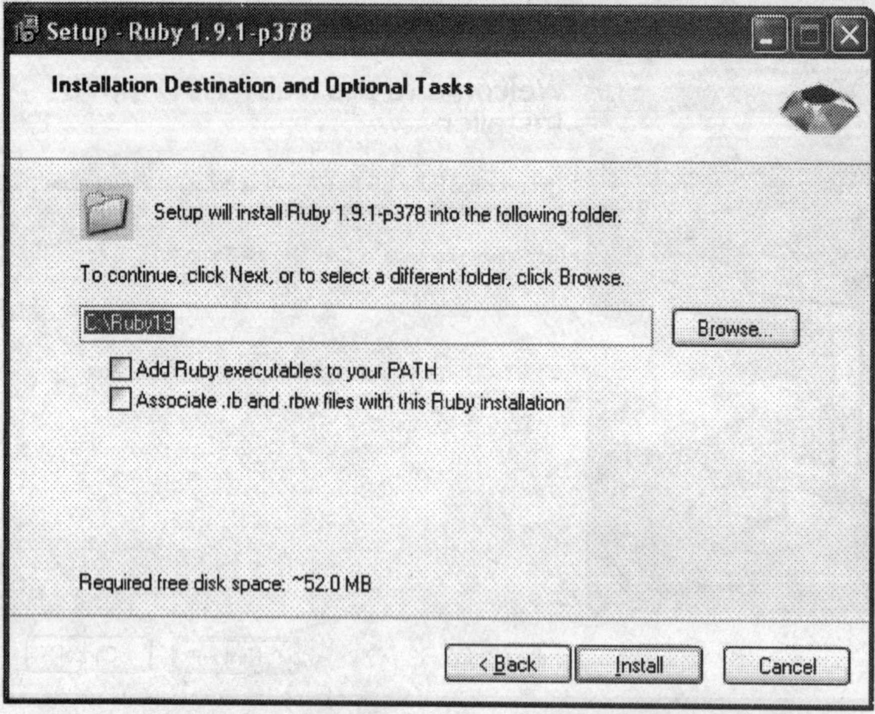
Setup - Ruby 1.9.1-p378
Installation Destination and Optional Tasks
Setup will install Ruby 1.9.1-p378 into the following folder.
To continue, click Next, or to select a different folder, click Browse.
C:\Ruby19
Browse...
Add Ruby executables to your PATH
Associate .rb and .rbw files with this Ruby installation
Required free disk space: ~52.0 MB
< Back
Install
Cancel

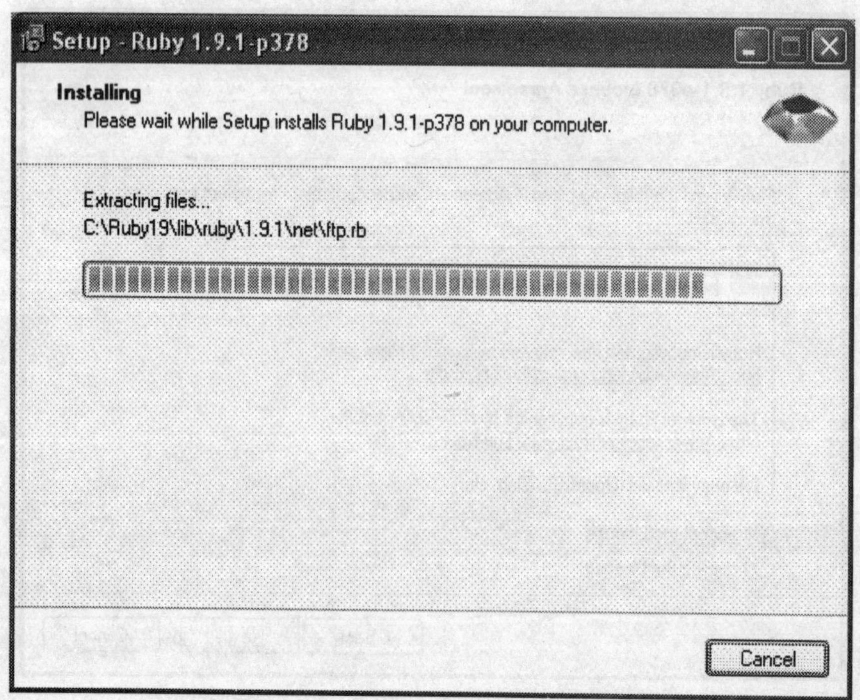
Setup - Ruby 1.9.1-p378
Installing
Please wait while Setup installs Ruby 1.9.1-p378 on your computer.
Extracting files...
C:\Ruby19\lib\ruby\1.9.1\net\ftp.rb
Cancel

Click on Start -> All Programs ->Start Command Prompt with Ruby

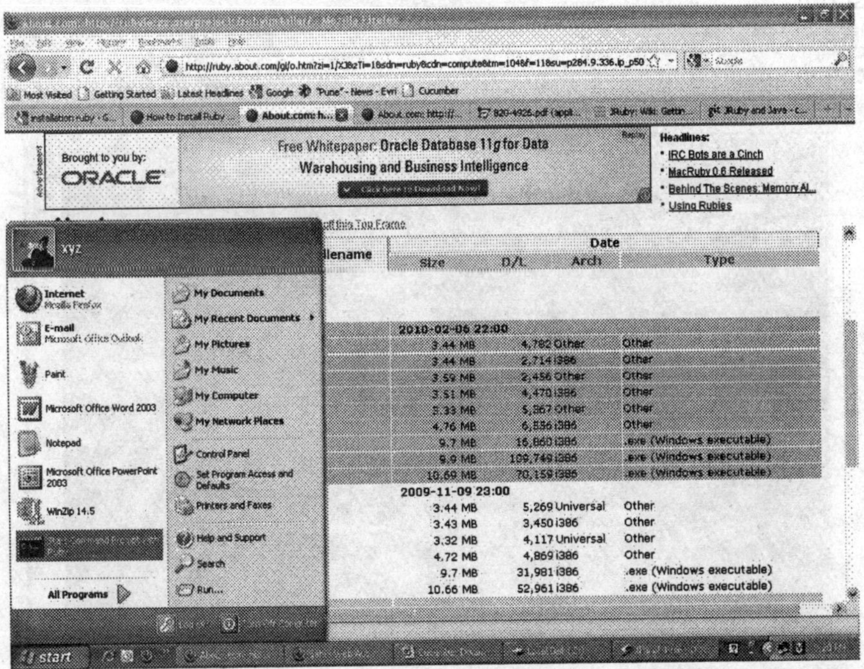

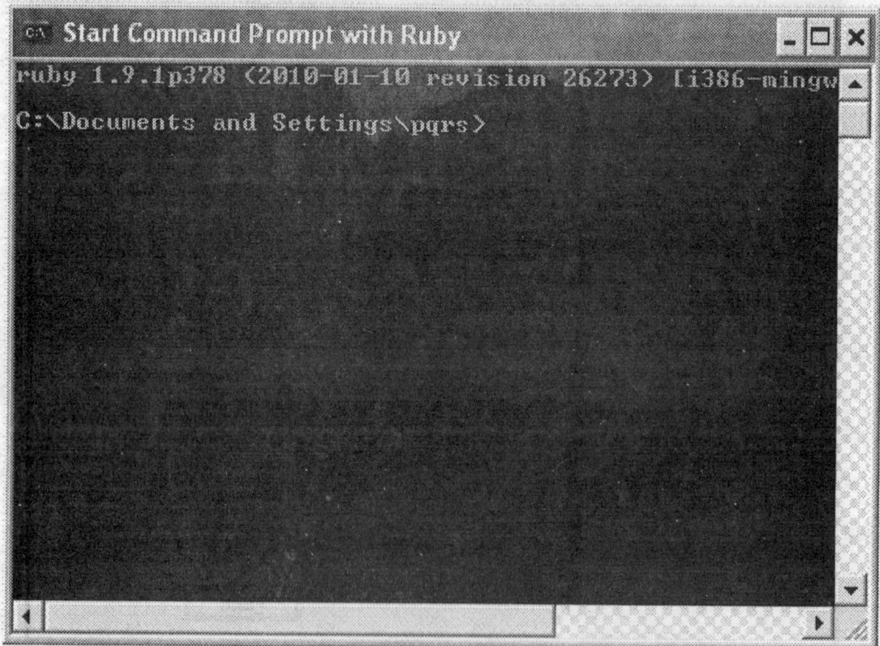

Start Command Prompt with Ruby

Then just run

```
gem install cucumber
```

from a command prompt.

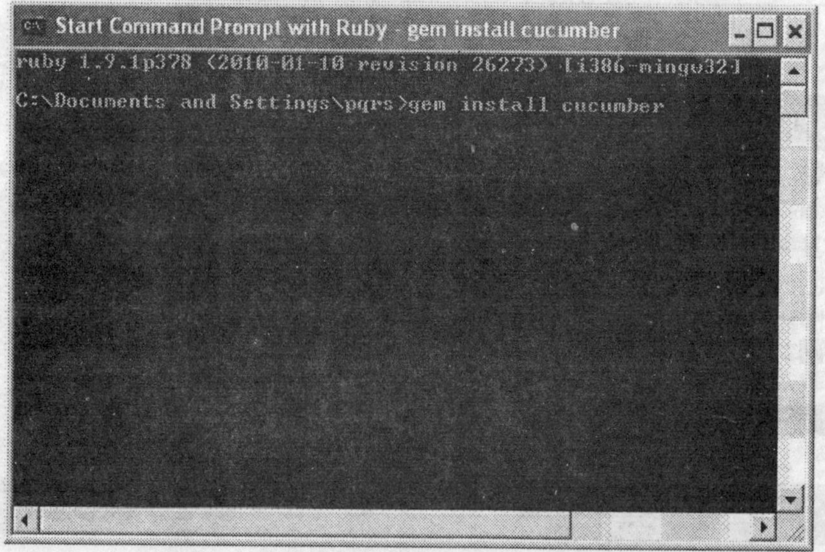

Now, run

```
cucumber --help
```

You need Ruby installed. Then just run

```
gem install cucumber
```

from a command prompt. Now, run

```
cucumber --help
```

You can install development snapshots too:

```
gem sources --add http://gems.github.com
gem install aslakhellesoy-cucumber
```

Download

Cucumber from this website

http://mac.softpedia.com/progDownload/Cucumber-Download-57041.html

1: Describe behaviour in plain text

```
Feature: Addition
  In order to avoid silly mistakes
  As a math idiot
  I want to be told the sum of two numbers

  Scenario: Add two numbers
    Given I have entered 50 into the calculator
    And I have entered 70 into the calculator
    When I press add
    Then the result should be 120 on the screen
```

2: Write a step definition in Ruby

```
Given /I have entered (.*) into the calculator/ do |n|
  calculator = Calculator.new
  calculator.push(n.to_i)
end
```

3: Run and watch it fail

```
$ cucumber features/addition.feature
Feature: Addition
  In order to avoid silly mistakes
  As a math idiot
  I want to be told the sum of two numbers
  Scenario: Add two numbers

    And I have entered 70 into the calculator
    When I press add
    Then the result should be 120 on the screen
```

4. Write code to make the step pass

```
class Calculator
  def push(n)
    @args ||= []
    @args << n
  end
end
```

5. Run again and see the step pass

```
$ cucumber features/addition.feature
Feature: Addition
  In order to avoid silly mistakes
  As a math idiot
  I want to be told the sum of two numbers
  Scenario: Add two numbers
    Given I have entered 50 into the calculator
    And I have entered 70 into the calculator
    When I press add
    Then the result should be 120 on the screen
```

6. Repeat 2-5 until green like a cuke

```
$ cucumber features/addition.feature
Feature: Addition
  In order to avoid silly mistakes
  As a math idiot
  I want to be told the sum of two numbers
  Scenario: Add two numbers
    Given I have entered 50 into the calculator
    And I have entered 70 into the calculator
    When I press add
    Then the result should be 120 on the screen
```

Outcomes and bottom-up scenarios

The value provided by a system is what you can get out of it – not what you put into it. Just like the value is expressed at the top of a feature (In order to...), the value should be in the steps of a scenarios too, more precisely in the **Then** steps.

Cucumber scenarios consist of steps, also known as Givens, Whens and Thens.

Cucumber doesn't technically distinguish between these three kind of steps. However, we strongly recommend that you do! These words have been carefully selected for their purpose, and you should know what the purpose is to get into the BDD mindset.

Robert C. Martin has written a great post about BDD's Given-When-Then concept where he thinks of them as a finite state machine.

Given

The purpose of givens is to **put the system in a known state** before the user (or external system) starts interacting with the system (in the When steps). Avoid talking about user interaction in givens. If you had worked with usecases, you would call this preconditions.

Examples:

- Create records (model instances) / set up the database state.
- It's ok to call into the layer "inside" the UI layer here (in Rails: talk to the models).
- Log in a user (An exception to the no-interaction recommendation. Things that "happened earlier" are ok).

And for all the Rails users out there – we recommend using a Given with a multiline table argument to set up records instead of fixtures. This way you can read the scenario and make sense out of it without having to look elsewhere (at the fixtures).

When

The purpose of When steps is to **describe the key action** the user performs (or, using Robert C. Martin's metaphor, the state transition).

Examples:

- Interact with a web page (Webrat/Watir/Selenium *interaction* etc should mostly go into When steps).
- Interact with some other user interface element.
- Developing a library? Kicking off some kind of action that has an observable effect somewhere else.

Then

The purpose of Then steps is to **observe outcomes**. The observations should be related to the business value/benefit in your feature description. The observations should also be on some kind of *output* – that is something that comes *out* of the system (report, user interface, message) and not something that is deeply buried inside it (that has no business value).

Examples:

- Verify that something related to the Given+When is (or is not) in the output
- Check that some external system has received the expected message (was an email with specific content sent?)

While it might be tempting to implement Then steps to just look in the database – resist the temptation. You should only verify outcome that is observable for the user (or external system) and databases usually are not.

And, But

If you have several givens, whens or thens you can write

```
Scenario: Multiple Givens
Given one thing
Given an other thing
Given yet an other thing
When I open my eyes
Then I see something
Then I don't see something else
```

Or you can make it read more fluently by writing

```
Scenario: Multiple Givens
  Given one thing
    And an other thing
    And yet an other thing
  When I open my eyes
  Then I see something
    But I don't see something else
```

To Cucumber steps beginning with And or But are exactly the same kind of steps as all the others.

that need to be in place in order for the When/Then to make sense.

Example:

- Feature: Login
    - As an admin
    - I want be able to login with my credentials
    - So that I get to the home page

- Scenario: Able to successfully login
    - Given that I am on page "http://www.blahblah.com"
    - When I provide my username "admin"
    - And I provide my password "admin"
    - Then I should be at "HomePage"

Develop the application driven by the behavior described earlier in the feature file Run the application

- $ cucumber login.feature

Run and watch it fails:

```
C:\WINDOWS\system32\cmd.exe
C:\dev\projects\callcenter\QA\vcc-tests/lib/firewatir-1.6.2/lib/firewatir/htmlel
ements.rb:1897: warning: already initialized constant TAG
C:\dev\projects\callcenter\QA\vcc-tests/lib/firewatir-1.6.2/lib/firewatir/htmlel
ements.rb:1902: warning: already initialized constant TAG
C:\dev\projects\callcenter\QA\vcc-tests/lib/firewatir-1.6.2/lib/firewatir/htmlel
ements.rb:1907: warning: already initialized constant TAG
C:\dev\projects\callcenter\QA\vcc-tests/lib/firewatir-1.6.2/lib/firewatir/firefo
x.rb:93: warning: already initialized constant FIRST_ORDERED_NODE_TYPE
C:\dev\projects\callcenter\QA\vcc-tests/lib/firewatir-1.6.2/lib/firewatir/versio
n.rb:3: warning: already initialized constant VERSION
Feature: Login
        As an admin
        I want to be able to login with my credentials
        So that I get to the home page

  Scenario: Able to successfully Login                           # login.feature:6
    Given that I am on page "http://www.blahblah.com"  # login.feature:7
    When I provide my username "admin"                  # login.feature:8
    And I provide my password "admin"                   # login.feature:9
    Then I should be at "HomePage"                      # login.feature:10

1 scenario (1 undefined)
4 steps (4 undefined)
0m2.375s
```

A template provided in order to write the automation script

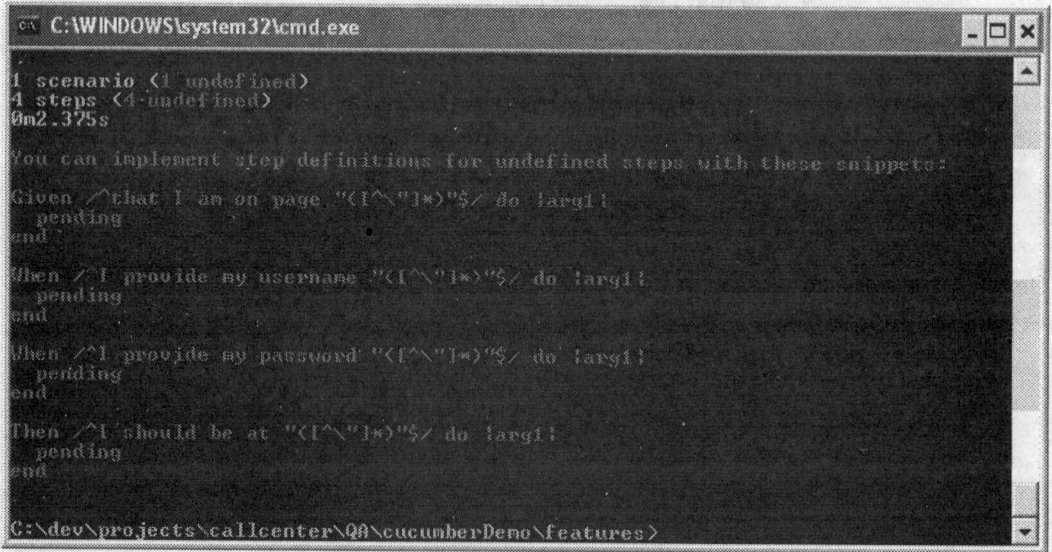

Given /^I am on "([^\"]*)"$/ do |url|

- **pending**
- **end**

- **When /^I enter username "([^\"]*)"$/ do |userName|**
- **pending**
- **end**
- **When /^I enter password "([^\"]*)"$/ do |password|**
- **pending**
- **end**
- **When /^I click the button with name "([^\"]*)"$/ do |buttonValue|**
- **pending**
- **end**
- **Then /^I should be at "([^\"]*)"$/ do |url|**
- **pending**
- **end**

They are called ***step definitions***
Essentially bunch of ruby code
A library called Watir is used for the API

Run it again and watch it fails:

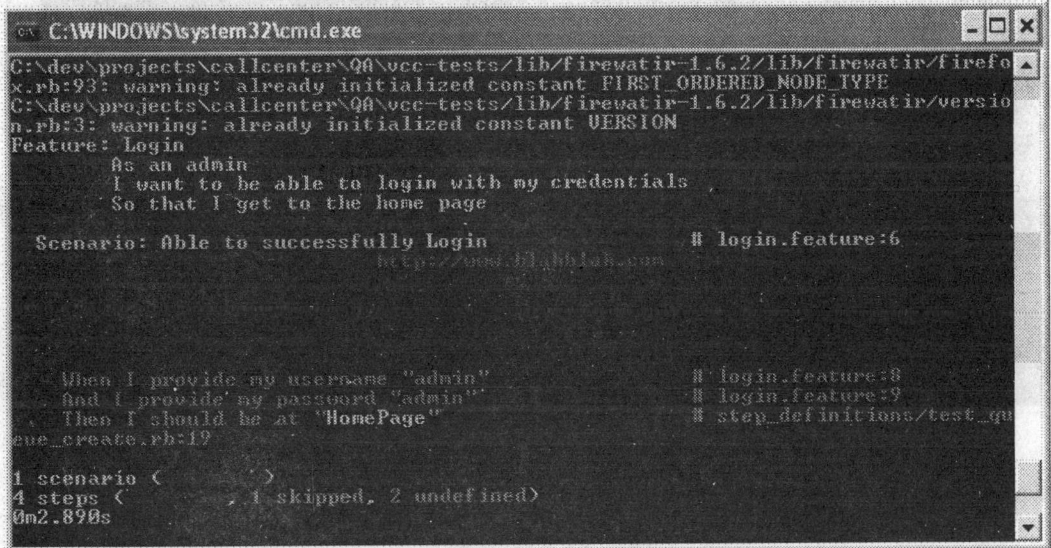

Make the necessary changes

Given /^I am on "([^\"]*)"$/ do |url|

- **@browser.goto(url)**

- end
- When /^I enter username "([^\"]*)"$/ do |userName|
- pending
- end
- When /^I enter password "([^\"]*)"$/ do |password|
- pending
- end
- When /^I click the button with name "([^\"]*)"$/ do |buttonValue|
- pending
- end
- Then /^I should be at "([^\"]*)"$/ do |url|
- pending
- end

Go back to step definitions and write the script in order to satisfy the behavior

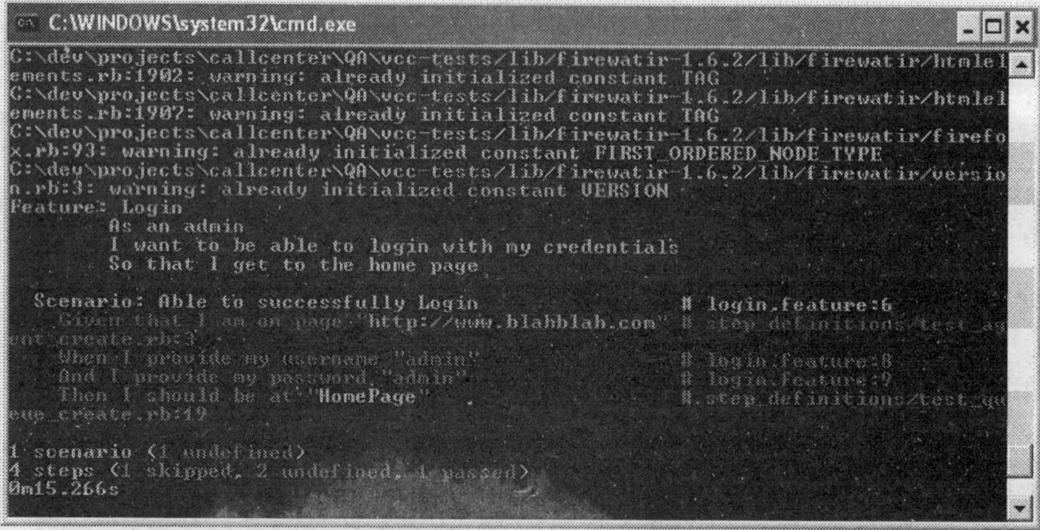

- Keep on running the feature file until all of them turns *green* like a *Cucumber*

```
C:\WINDOWS\system32\cmd.exe
Feature: Contact Center
        If I am an       admin
        I want to create a callcenter
        I am expected to login without failure
        I am also expected to create the call center without failure

  Scenario: Contact Center Creation
                                                         # CC_create_test.feature:7
    Given I am on "http://10.0.0.36:8080/callcenter-web"
                                                         # step_definitions/test_queue_cre
ate.rb:3
    When I login as Admin
                                                         # step_definitions/test_CC_create
.rb:1
    Then I should be at "home"
                                                         # step_definitions/test_queue_cre
ate.rb:19
    Then I enter the Individual Contact Center Management
                                                         # step_definitions/test_CC_create
.rb:5
    Then I create the call center with "AutoCC" and "CallCenter for Automation T
est" and "autogroup" and "autoccadmin" and "a" # step_definitions/test_CC_create
.rb:12
    Then the call center with id "AutoCC" should be present
                                                         # step_definitions/test_CC_create
.rb:16
    Then I delete the callcenter with id "AutoCC"
                                                         # step_definitions/test_CC_create
.rb:23

1 scenario (1 passed)
7 steps (7 passed)
1m4.765s

C:\dev\projects\callcenter\QA\cucumberDemo\features>
```

References:

http://mac.softpedia.com/progDownload/Cucumber-Download-57041.html

http://www.ruby-lang.org/en/downloads/

http://austinonrails.org/files/austin-on-rails_cukes.pdf

http://docs.rubygems.org/read/chapter/3 - RubyGems installation

http://wiki.github.com/dchelimsky/rspec/ - RSpec Installation

Keep on running the feature file until all of them turns green like as shown

References:

BDD using JBehave tool

What is JBehave?

JBehave is a framework for Behaviour-Driven Development (BDD). BDD is an evolution of test-driven development (TDD) and acceptance-test driven design, and is intended to make these practices more accessible and intuitive to newcomers and experts alike. It shifts the vocabulary from being test-based to behaviour-based, and positions itself as a design philosophy.

Features of JBehave include:

- Pure Java implementation, which plays well with Java-based enterprises
- Allows users to specify and run text-based scenarios, which allows "out-in" development.
- Annotation-based binding of textual steps to Java methods
- Auto-conversion of string arguments to any parameter type (including generic types) via custom parameter converters.
- Scenario reporter - outputs scenarios executed in human-readable form
- Auto-generation of pending steps so the build is not broken by a missing step, but has option to configure breaking build for pending steps.
- Scenario can be run as JUnit tests, providing easy integration with your favourite IDE. Using alternative annotation-based unit test frameworks is equally easy.
- Ant integration: allows scenarios to be run via Ant task
- Maven integration: allows scenarios to be run via Maven plugin at given build phase

JBehave Web provides a web-integration layer for the JBehave framework for Behaviour-Driven Development (BDD).

Features of JBehave Web include:

- A Web Runner to allow generic scenarios to be run via a simple web interface.
- A Selenium integration module to allow automation of scenarios for web applications

Running Scenarios with Selenium

Selenium is a powerful open-source tool for automated web testing. To demonstrate the use of JBehave with Selenium, we'll draw upon the fully-functional **Ajax Email example webapp** from **Pico Web** project.

Let's see how we can easily use Selenium to run web-based scenarios. As usual, we'll have a Scenario class that maps to a textual scenario, e.g.

Scenario: User logs in successfully

Given nobody is logged in
When user Gill Bates with password 1234 attempts to log in
Then the Inbox is selected
And there are some messages listed

Scenario: User fails to login with invalid password

Given nobody is logged in
When user Gill Bates with password 99999 attempts to log in
And there are no messages listed
And the text "Invalid Login" should be visible

Scenario: User fails to login with invalid username

Given nobody is logged in
When user Fred with password 1234 attempts to log in
Then the Inbox should not be visible
And the text "Invalid Login" should be visible

The objective in creating a DSL is to represent the business-domain functionality whilst abstracting away the details of the implementation, in this case the access to the web layer via a specific testing tool, such as Selenium. The same DSL should be re-usable with different testing tools.

The Scenario class will specify the Steps class is where all the Selenium magic happens:

```
public class AjaxEmailSteps extends SeleniumSteps {

   private Main main;
   private String[] lastFormValues;
   private String prefix;

   @Given("nobody is logged in")
   public void nobodyLoggedIn() {
      Main.logout(selenium);
   }

   @Given("user is viewing their Inbox")
   public void theyreInTheirInbox() {
      nobodyLoggedIn();
      logIn("Gill Bates", "1234");
      boxIsSelected("Inbox");
   }

   @When("user $userName with password $password attempts to log in")
   public void logIn(String userName, String password) {
      main = new LoginForm(selenium, runner).login(userName, password);
   }

   @Then("the Inbox should not be visible")
   public void inBoxIsNotVisible() {
   main.textIsNotVisible("Instant Millionaire");
   }

   @Then("the text \"$text\" should be visible")
   public void textIsVisible(String text) {
   main.waitFor(new Text(text));
   }

   @Then("the text \"$text\" should not be visible")
  public void textIsNotVisible(String text) {
```

```
waitFor(new Not(new Text(text)));
  }

  private void waitFor(Condition condition) {
  runner.waitFor(condition);
  waitFor(1);
  }
}
```

The **@BeforeScenario** and **@AfterScenario** annotations in the SeleniumSteps methods allow to start and stop the selenium server before and after scenario. Users can of course override the default behaviour, but generally don't need to bother for most use cases.

NOTE: To get the Selenium based tests running in an automated way, you need to run both a webapp server (e.g. Jetty) and the Selenium server. See the **Ajax Email example webapp** for a way to do this using **Maven**

More accurate is a JBehave

Behaviour Driven Development, BDD, Framework for Java.
Ie Java package that you can use as guides to work with BDD.

Features

- Pure Java implementation, which plays well with Java-based enterprises
- Allows users to specify and run text-based scenarios, which allows "out-in" development.
- Annotation-based binding of textual steps to Java methods
- Auto-conversion of string arguments to any parameter type (including generic types) via custom parameter converters.
- Scenario reporter - outputs scenarios executed in human-readable form
- Auto-generation of pending steps so the build is not broken by a missing step, but has option to configure breaking build for pending steps.
- Scenario can be run as JUnit tests, providing easy integration with your favourite IDE. Using alternative annotation-based unit test frameworks is equally easy.
- Ant integration: allows scenarios to be run via Ant task
- Maven integration: allows scenarios to be run via Maven plugin at given build phase

Write a text scenario

Create a scenario using the words `Given`, `When`, `Then` and `And`.

Given I am not logged in
When I log in as Liz with a password JBehaver
Then I should see a message, "Welcome, Liz!"

Save the scenario in file. The file should have a meaningful name, but use lowercase letters and underscores, eg: `user_logs_in_successfully`

Create matching Java Scenario class

Create a Java class, that matches the text scenario name. It should have the same name as your scenario, but use CamelCase, e.g. UserLogsInSuccessfully.java.

This class should extend Scenario and be in the same package.

```
public class UserLogsInSuccessfully extends Scenario {
  public UserLogsInSuccessfully() {
      super(new LoginSteps());
  }
}
```

where LoginSteps extends Steps

```
public class LoginSteps extends Steps {
}
```

Try running your scenario

The Scenario class is a JUnit test. You can right-click and run it in most new IDEs, or use a build script that runs JUnit tests. You can also run scenarios as Ant tasks or Maven goals. Learn more about scenarios

You will notice an output of the kind:

Given I am not logged in (PENDING)
When I log in as Liz with a password JBehaver (PENDING)
Then I should see a message, "Welcome, Liz!" (PENDING)

What's happening is that JBehave cannot find matching methods in the Steps class corresponding the to steps in the text scenario.

NOTE: from JUnit's perspective the behaviour has been successfully run (you'll see it marked as green). This silent pending error strategy is meant to allow textual scenarios to be written before any Java matching them is written – but to avoid breaking the build.

One can configure different ways of handling scenarios misbehaving, e.g. it is possible to define a pending error strategy that throws an exception, and thus breaking the build.

Define the steps for your scenario

In the LoginSteps, write a method for each step, then annotate that method using @ Given, @When or @Then JBehave annotations, depending on whether the step sets up a context (Given), performs some events that you're interested in (When) or describes the desired outcome (Then).

The value of the annotations should match the steps you described in your scenario. You can capture arguments to pass through to your steps using a prefix, "$", before the argument.

```
package my.domain.app;

// Ensure extends JUnit's Assert
// It works just like JUnit with Hamcrest's matchers
// or you can create your own

import static org.jbehave.Ensure.ensureThat;

import org.jbehave.scenario.steps.Steps;
import org.jbehave.scenario.annotations.Given;
import org.jbehave.scenario.annotations.When;
import org.jbehave.scenario.annotations.Then;

public class LoginSteps extends Steps {

   // Some code to set up our browser and pages
   //...

   @Given("I am not logged in")
   public void logOut() {
      currentPage.click("logout");
   }

   @When("I log in as $username with a password $password")
   public void logIn(String username, String password) {
      currentPage.click("login");
   }
```

```
    @Then("I should see a message, \"$message\"")
    public void checkMessage(String message) {
        ensureThat(currentPage, containsMessage(message));
    }
}
```

Run your successful scenario!

If you now re-run your scenario as a JUnit test, you'll find that the PENDING messages are gone and your scenario has run successfully.

What is the difference between Test-Driven

Development TDD and BDD?

They are addressed to different targets and therefore complementary, ie BDD TDD does not replace but complements TDD.

TDD

is more to test the devices / components regardless of other units and where you can use Mocha to test each of unit itself.

BDD

• Are more focused on design direction and deleted at the outside. Best suited for Regression and Acceptance Test

• Do focus on the development of priority and verified business benefits. Want to be independent of the chosen language technology eg java, but would rather rely on the domain's language, ie plain language

Competitors to JBehave

RSpec is a similar tool for Ruby - the creator
Fitness - http://fitnesse.org/

On Wikipedia there is this list
• RSpec - Ruby

• Cucumber - Plain text + Ruby. Works Against Java,. NET, Ruby, Flex or Any web application via

Watir or Selenium.

• JBehave
- Java
• NUnit
- Another implementation of BDD framework in. Net with focus on specification testing

• StoryQ
-. Net 3.5, Can Be Integrated with NUnit to Provide Both specification Readability and Testing

• NSpec
-. Net

• NSpecify
-. Net
• NBehave
-. Net

• Specter
- Another implementation of BDD framework in. Net with focus on specification Readability

• GSpec
- Groovy

• easyb
- Groovy

• tspec
- Groovy (Thai syntax)

• Specs
- Scala

• dSpec
- Delphi

• JSSpec
- JavaScript

• JSpec
- JavaScript (Focus on Readability)

- PHPSpec

- PHP

- Instinct

- Java

- JDave

- Java

- bean Spec

- Java

- BDD into Python

ice core module doctest

- CSpec

- C

- cfSpec

- Cold Fusion

Mockning

Mockning recommended to be performed with Mockito Also JMock, EasyMock JUnit 4.4

- JUnit 4.4 includes hamcrest assertions.
- Hamcrest is a library on matches which allows one to declare matching rules for validation.
- Hamcrest assertions from JMock

Where can I find good example ...?
Ryan Green Hall is one of those who wrote a good example of this ...
http://www.ryangreenhall.com/articles/bdd-by-example.html

- When you implement the methods required you think in a top-down perspective
- Scenarios themselves are excellent sources for find classes and class name - which allows ubigitous a language!

Parameter converter

There is a built ParameterConverters class that can be used to convert parameter values to Java object. There are built-in converter that JBehave supports:
Number Converter
List Number Converter
String List Converter

BDD more concrete on grade level .....

- The BDD test classes should be called instead of Behaviour Test
- Behaviour These classes will include techniques such as that has the word "Should"
- Note - the jbehaves website does not use the otherwise Should that typical concepts and Behaviour!
- By contrast with the example of the subversion repository ...
- The focus should be on the specification of behavior
- Behavior class should therefore have oxå Dealer, When, Then

"BDD is a collaborative design process, associate wing Rich Communication Between the stakeholders of the software and Those Responsible for ITS development. This That ensures the Software Being Developed is of high value, Meeting the Needs of real users. If Those Do Not Conversations happen, then 'no-tool, or JBehave Other wise Will Be variable to save a Project That Developing unwanted ice or low priority features."

Feel again about 5 minutes!
Then we'll see what we do ...
Planning is that we intend to jointly and coding jointly by me from my computer.

References:

http://jbehave.org

http://jbehave.org/reference/web/latest/download.html

http://jbehave.org/reference/web/latest/selenium-steps.html

http://jbehave.org/reference/web/latest/customising-web-runner.html

http://jbehave.org/reference/web/latest/using-web-runner.html

http://repository.codehaus.org/org/jbehave/web/

BDD using RSpec tool

Introduction:

RSpec is the original Behaviour Driven Development framework for Ruby.

RSpec was created by Steven Baker in 2005, inspired by Dave's aforementioned article. One of Dave's suggestions was that with languages like Smalltalk and Ruby, we could more freely explore new frameworks that could encourage focus on behaviour.

While the syntactic details have evolved since Steven's original version of RSpec, the basic premise remains. We use RSpec to write executable examples of the expected behaviour of a small bit of code in a controlled context.

Download RSpec from http://rspec.rubyforge.org/rspec/1.3.0/

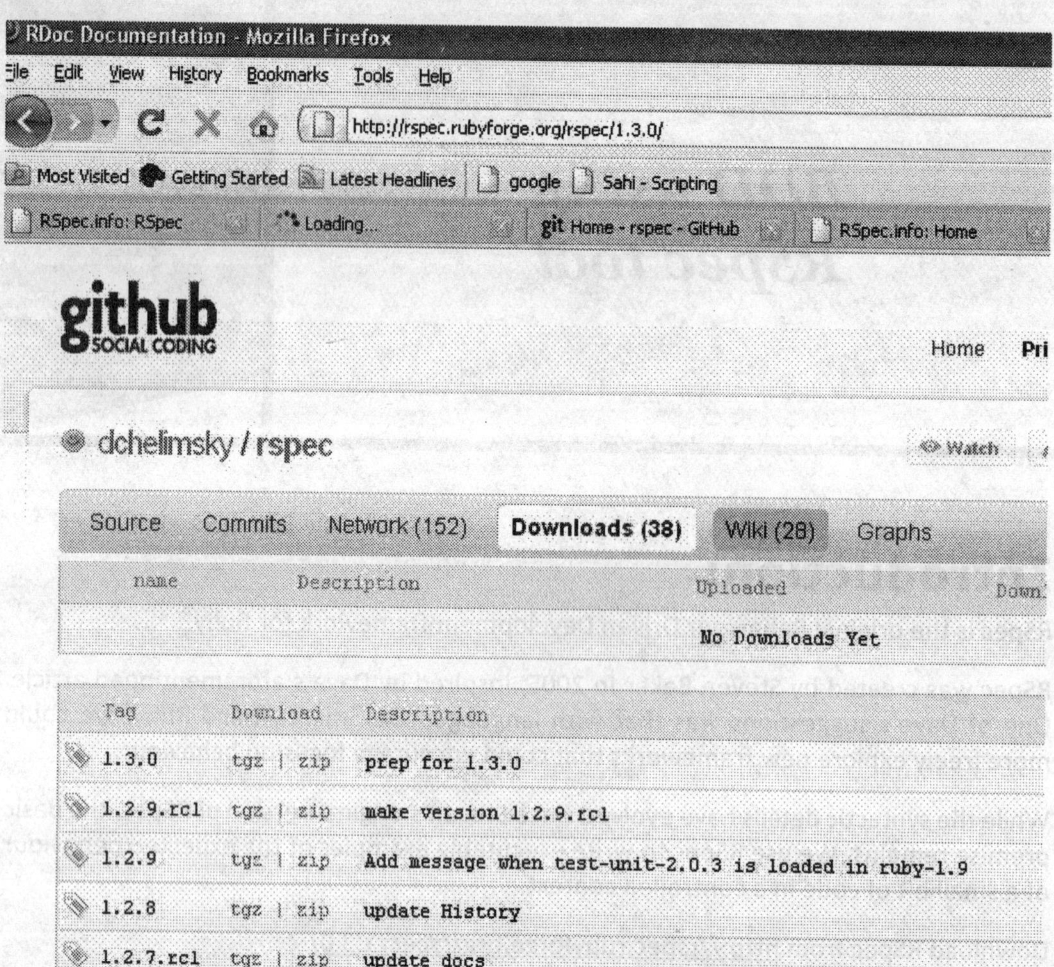
RDoc Documentation - Mozilla Firefox
File Edit View History Bookmarks Tools Help
http://rspec.rubyforge.org/rspec/1.3.0/
Most Visited
Getting Started
Latest Headlines
google
Sahi - Scripting
RSpec.info: RSpec
Loading...
Home - rspec - GitHub
RSpec.info: Home
github SOCIAL CODING
Home
dchelimsky / rspec
Watch
Source
Commits
Network (152)
Downloads (38)
Wiki (28)
Graphs
name
Description
Uploaded
No Downloads Yet
Tag
Download
Description
1.3.0 tgz | zip prep for 1.3.0
1.2.9.rc1 tgz | zip make version 1.2.9.rc1
1.2.9 tgz | zip Add message when test-unit-2.0.3 is loaded in ruby-1.9
1.2.8 tgz | zip update History
1.2.7.rc1 tgz | zip update docs

Save dchelimsky-rspec-1.3.0-0-g87ab554 file

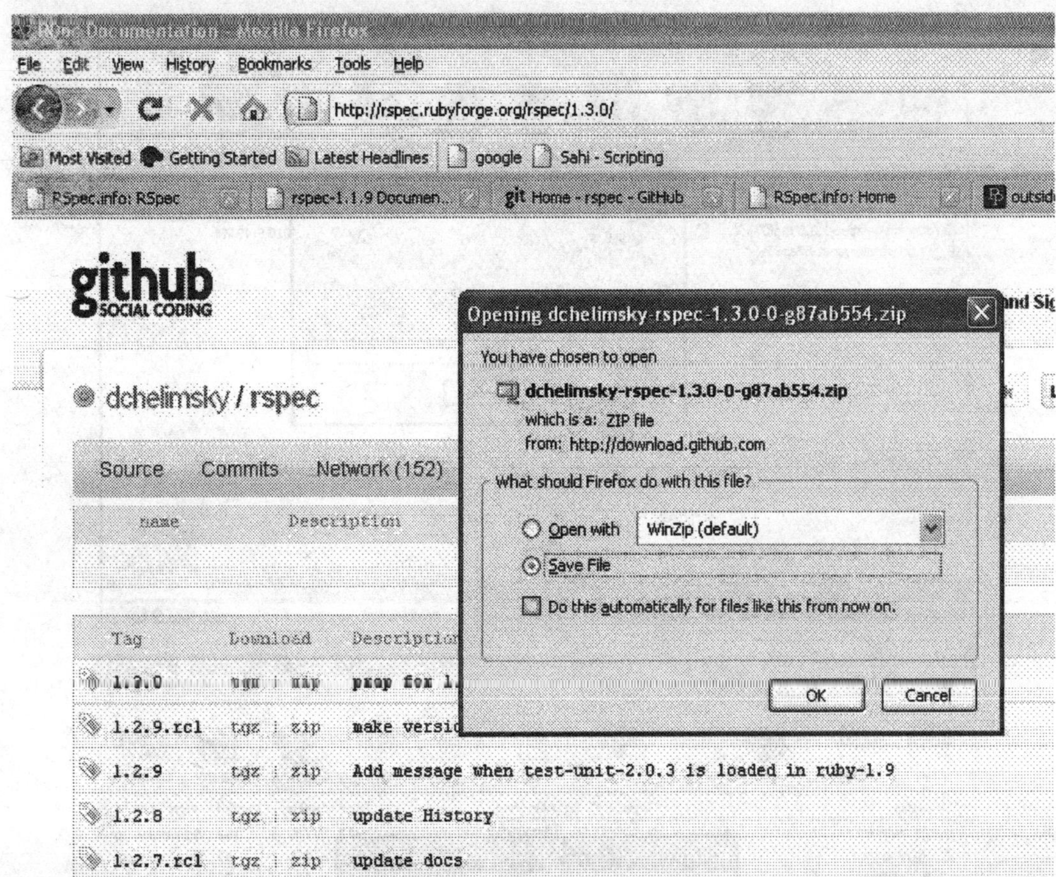

Extract zip file

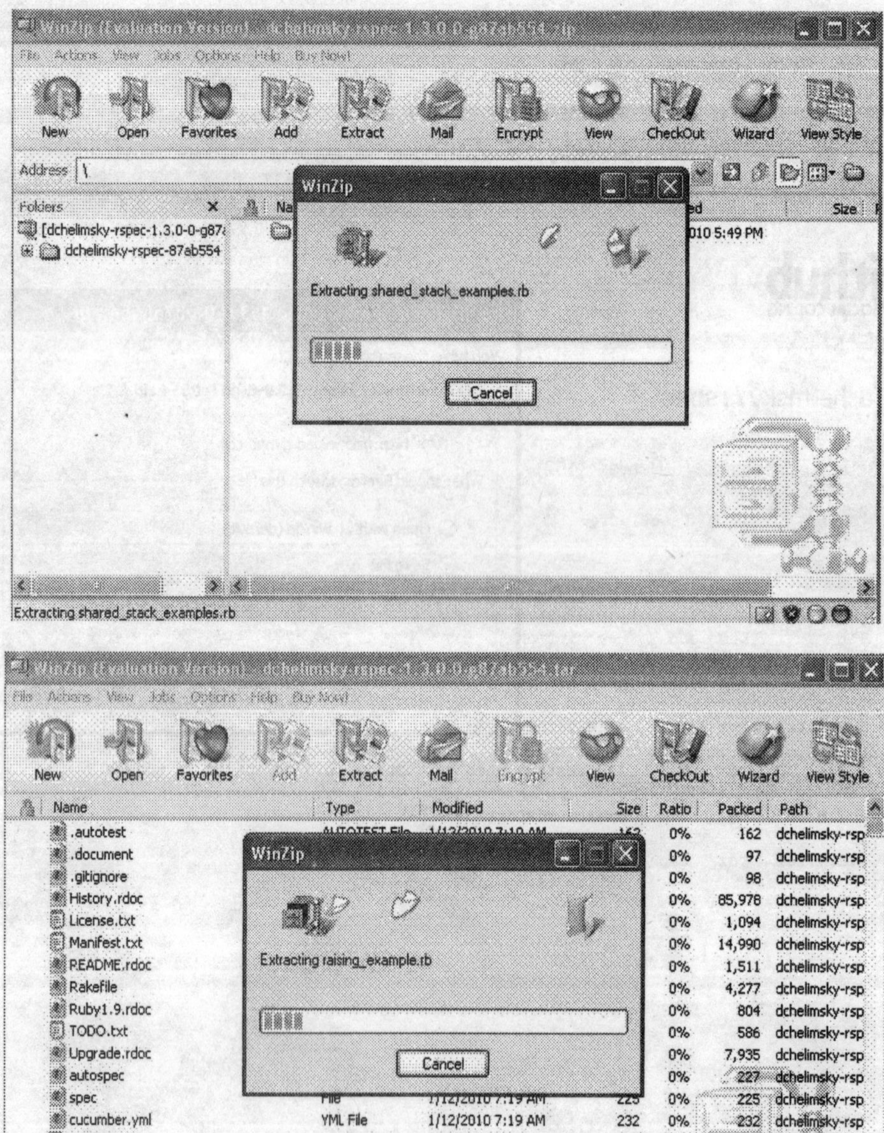

First upgrade to the latest version of Ruby gems:

> gem update --system

Before installing Buildr, please set the JAVA_HOME environment variable to point to your JDK distribution. Next, use Ruby Gem to install Buildr:

> gem install buildr

To upgrade to a new version or install a specific version:

> gem update buildr

> gem install buildr -v 1.3.6

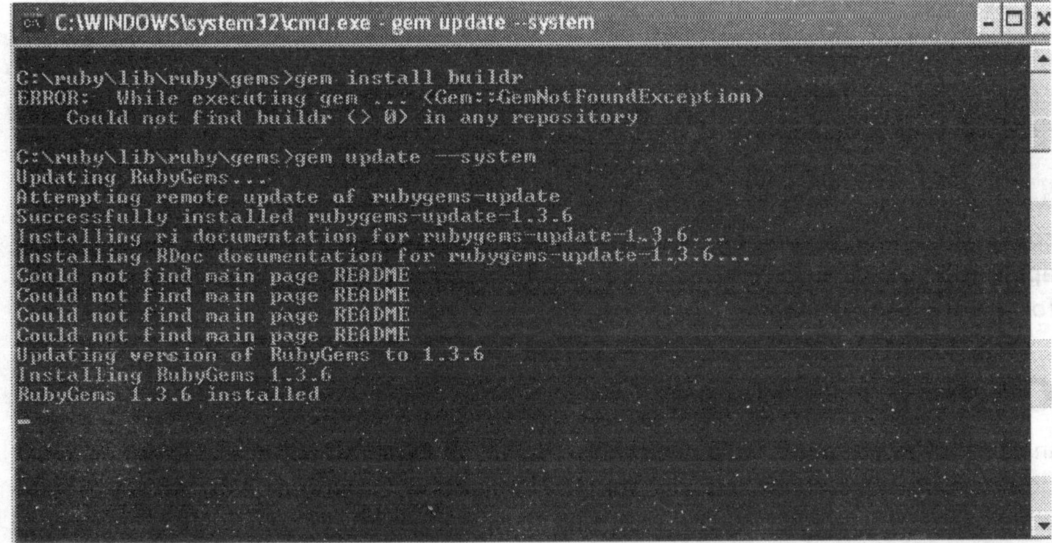

RSpec example

```
describe MovieList do
context "when first created" do
it "should be empty" do
movie_list = MovieList.new
movie_list.should be_empty
end
end
end
```

The it( ) method creates an *example* of the behaviour of a MovieList, with the *context* being that the MovieList was just created. The expression movie_list.should be_empty should be self-explanatory. Just read it out loud. You'll see how be_empty( ) interacts with the movie_list in Section

Running this code in a shell with the spec command yields the following specification:

MovieList when first created
- should be empty

Add some more contexts and examples, and the resulting output looks even more like a specification for a MovieList object:

MovieList when first created
- should be empty

MovieList with 1 item
- should not be empty
- should include that item

we're talking about the specification of an object, not necessarily a whole system. You *could* specify application behaviour with RSpec. Many do. Ideally, however, for specifying application behaviour, we want something that communicates in broader strokes. And for that, we use Cucumber.

Code Examples

In this part of the book, we'll explore the details of RSpec's built-in expectations, mock objects framework, command line tools, IDE integration, extension points, and even show you how to integrate RSpec with Test::Unit so that you can take advantage of the myriad extensions that are written for both frameworks.

Our goal is to make Test Driven Development a more joyful and productive experience with tools that elevate the design and documentation aspects of TDD to first class citizenship. Here are some words you'll need to know as we reach for that goal:

subject code The code whose behaviour we are specifying with RSpec.

expectation An expression of how the subject code is expected to behave.

code example An executable example of how the subject code can be used, and its expected behaviour (expressed with expectations) in a given context. In BDD, we write the code examples before the subject code they document.

The *example* terminology started with Brian Marick, whose website is even named http://exampler.com. Using "example" instead of "test" reminds us that the writing them is a design and documentation practice, even though once they are written and the code is developed against them they become regression tests. **example group** A group of code examples.

RSpec provides a Domain Specific Language for specifying the behaviour of objects. It embraces the metaphor of describing behaviour the way we might express it if we were talking to a customer, or another developer. A snippet of such a conversation might look like this:

You: *Describe a new account*

Somebody else: *It should have a balance of zero*
Here's that same conversation expressed in RSpec:

```
describe "A new Account" do
it "should have a balance of 0" do
account = Account.new
account.balance.should == Money.new(0, :USD)
end
end
```

We use the describe( ) method to define an example group. The string we pass to it represents the facet of the system that we want to describe (a new account). The block holds the code examples that make up that group.

The it( ) method defines a code example. The string passed to it describes the specific behaviour we're interested in specifying about that facet (should have a balance of zero). The block holds the example code that exercises the subject code and sets expectations about its behaviour. Using strings like this instead of legal Ruby class names and method names provides a lot of flexibility. Here's an example from RSpec's own code examples:

```
it "should match when value < (target + delta)" do be_close(5.0, 0.5).matches?(5.49).
should be_true end
```

This is an example of the behaviour of code, so the intended audience is someone who can read code. In Test::Unit, we might name the method test_should_match_when_value_is_less_than_target_plus_delta, which is pretty readable, but the ability to use non-alpha-numeric characters makes the name of this example more expressive.1 To get a better sense of how you can unleash this expressiveness, let's take a closer look at the describe( ) and it( ) methods.

The describe( ) method:

The describe( ) method can take an arbitrary number of arguments and a block, and returns a subclass of Spec::Example::ExampleGroup.2 We generally only use one or two arguments, which represent the facet of behaviour that we wish to describe. They might describe an object, perhaps in a pre-defined state, or perhaps a subset of the behaviour we can expect from that object. Let's look at a few examples, with the output they produce so we can get an idea of how the arguments relate to each other.

describe "A User" { ... }
=> A User
describe User { ... }
=> User
describe User, "with no roles assigned" { ... }
=> User with no roles assigned
describe User, "should require password length between 5 and 40" { ... }
=> User should require password length between 5 and 40

The first argument can be either a reference to a Class or Module, or a String. The second argument is optional, and should be a String. Using the class/module for the first argument provides an interesting benefit:

when we wrap the ExampleGroup in a module, we'll see that module's name in the output. For example, if User is in the Authentication module, we could do something like this:

module Authentication
describe User, "with no roles assigned" do

The resulting report would look like this:
Authentication::User with no roles assigned

So by wrapping the ExampleGroup in a Module, we see the fully qualified name Authentication::User, followed by the contents of the second argument. Together, they form a descriptive string, and we get the fully qualified name for free. This is a nice way to help RSpec help *us* to understand where things live as we're looking at the output. You can also nest example groups, which can be a very nice way of expressing things in both input and output. For example, we can nest the input like this:

describe User do
describe "with no roles assigned" do
it "should not be allowed to view protected content" do

This produces output like this:

User with no roles assigned
- should not be allowed to view protected content
Or, with the --nested flag on the command line, the output looks like this:
User
with no roles assigned
should not be allowed to view protected content
To understand this example better, let's explore describe( )'s yang, the it( ) method.

Here's how we express that conversation in RSpec:

```
describe Account, "when first created" do
  it "should have a balance of $0" do
    ...
  end
end
```

The `describe()` method returns an `ExampleGroup` class, which contains a group of examples of a particular behaviour of the system that you wish to describe.

The `it()` method returns an instance of the `ExampleGroup` in which that example is run.

When you run this example, RSpec can provide a report like this:

```
Account when first created
- should have a balance of $0
```

before() and after()

You can use `before()` and/or `after()` to define code that executes before and after each example or only once per `ExampleGroup`:

```
describe Thing do
  before(:all) do
     # This is run once and only once, before all of the
examples
    # and before any before(:each) blocks.
  end

  before(:each) do
```

```
    # This is run before each example.
  end

  before do
      # :each is the default, so this is the same as
before(:each)
  end

  it "should do stuff" do
    ...
  end

  it "should do more stuff" do
    ...
  end

  after(:each) do
    # this is after each example
  end

  after do
      # :each is the default, so this is the same as
after(:each)
  end

  after(:all) do
     # this is run once and only once after all of the
examples
    # and after any after(:each) blocks
  end

end
```

Warning: The use of `before(:all)` and `after(:all)` is generally discouraged because it introduces dependencies between the Examples. Still, it might prove useful for very expensive operations if you know what you are doing.

Helper Methods

You can write helper methods directly within an Example Group:

```
describe "..." do

  it "..." do
    helper_method
  end

  def helper_method
    ...
  end

end
```

Reusable Helper Methods

You can include helper methods in multiple ExampleGroups by expressing them within a module, and then including that module in your ExampleGroup:

```
module AccountExampleHelperMethods
  def helper_method
    ...
  end
end

describe "A new account" do
  include AccountExampleHelperMethods
  before do
    @account = Account.new
  end

  it "should have a balance of $0" do
    helper_method
    @account.balance.should eql(Money.new(0, :dollars))
  end
end
```

Shared Example Groups

You can create shared example groups and include those groups into other groups.

Suppose you have some behavior that applies to all editions of your product, both large and small.

First, factor out the "shared" behavior:

```
shared_examples_for "all editions" do
  it "should behave like all editions" do
  end
end
```

then when you need define the behavior for the Large and Small editions, reference the shared behavior using the `it_should_behave_like()` method.

```
describe "SmallEdition" do
  it_should_behave_like "all editions"

  it "should also behave like a small edition" do
  end
end

describe "LargeEdition" do
  it_should_behave_like "all editions"

  it "should also behave like a large edition" do
  end
end
```

`it_should_behave_like` will search for an Example Group by its description string, in this case, "all editions"

All of the following are included from a shared group:

- before(:all)
- before(:each)
- after(:each)
- after(:all)

- all included modules
- all methods

Shared example groups may not extend classes.
Multiple shared example groups may be referenced in one (non-shared) group.
Shared example groups may be included in other shared groups:

```
shared_examples_for "All Employees" do
  it "should be payable" do
    @employee.should respond_to(:calculate_pay)
  end
end

shared_examples_for "All Managers" do
  it_should_behave_like "All Employees"
  it "should be bonusable" do
    @employee.should respond_to(:apply_bonus)
  end
end

describe Officer do
  before(:each) do
    @employee = Officer.new
  end

  it_should_behave_like "All Managers"

  it "should be optionable" do
    @employee.should respond_to(:grant_options)
  end
end

$ spec officer_spec.rb

Officer
- should be payable
- should be bonusable
- should be optionable
```

Pending Examples

There are three ways to mark an example as "pending."

Leave out the block:

```
it "should say foo"
```

The output will say PENDING (Not Yet Implemented).

Use the pending method with no block:

```
it "should say foo" do
  pending("get the vocal chords working")
  subject.should say("foo")
end
```

The output will say PENDING (get the vocal chords working).

Use the pending method with a block:

```
it "should say foo" do
  pending("get the vocal chords working") do
    subject.should say("foo")
  end
end
```

Reference:

http://wiki.github.com/dchelimsky/rspec

http://rspec.lighthouseapp.com

http://blog.davidchelimsky.net

http://rspec.info/documentation/

http://wiki.github.com/dchelimsky/rspec-rails/

BDD using GoSpecify

Introduction

Gospecify

Gospecify is a behavior-driven development (BDD) framework for Go. It helps a programmer produce an executable specification of that code's behavior. Go's syntax allowed gospecify to be almost as expressive as Ruby's rpsec; however, a few tricks had to be used to achieve the best readability.

Download Gospecify from http://github.com/stesla/gospecify/downloads

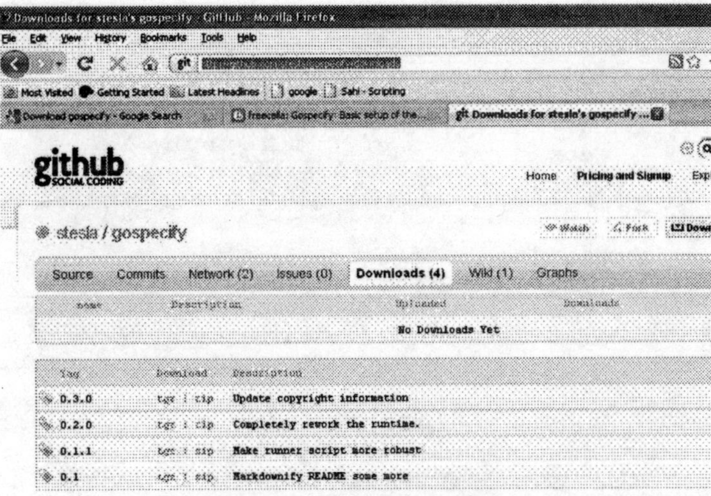

Click to download zip file

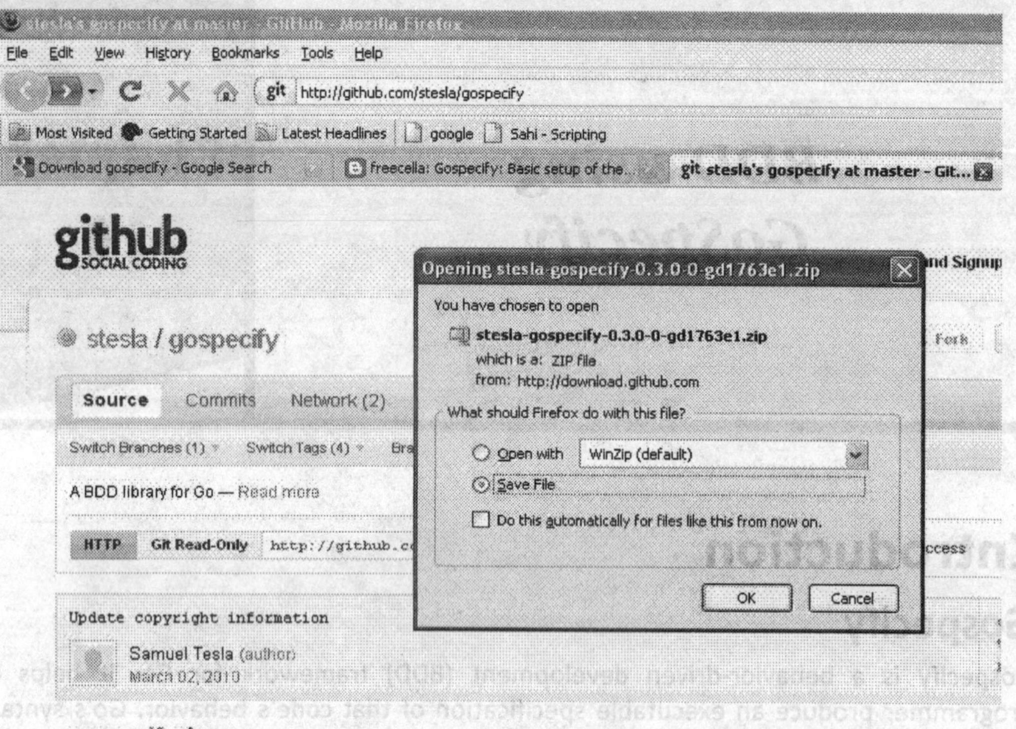

Save fie stesla-gospecify-0.3.0-0-gd1763e1.tar file

Extract zip file to desired location.

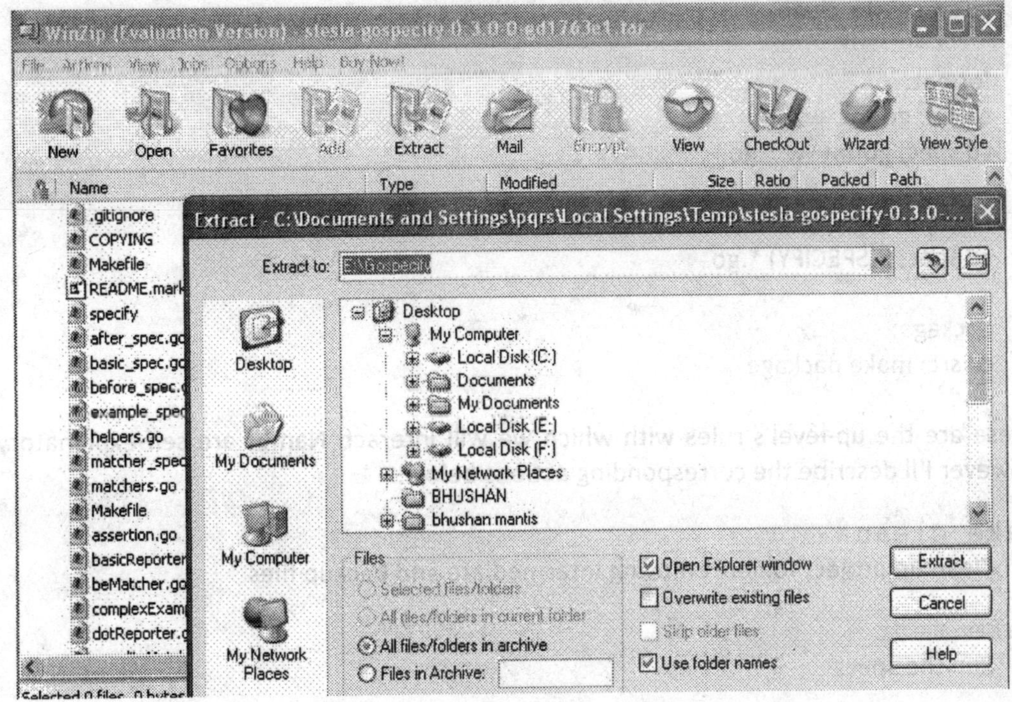

First, create the project folder

mkdir fib

eg. Fibonacci sequence implementation

Move in `fib` folder and create a basic project structure
cd fib
mkdir src
mkdir spec

A `src` will contain source files and `spec` will contain the specs. Now let's go creating a `Makefile` in the project base path. Create an empty `Makefile` using your favourite text editor and copy/paste the code below:

```
GOBIN=$(HOME)/bin
SPECIFY=specify

all: test

clean:
```

```
cd src; make clean

format:
cd src; gofmt -w *.go
cd spec; gofmt -w *.go

test: package
cd spec; $(SPECIFY) *.go

package:
cd src; make package
```

These are the up-level's rules with which we will interact. Names are self-explanatory however I'll describe the corresponding actions below:

`make clean`
: Clean up project folder removing intermediate and backup files

`make test`
: Run the specs

`make format`
: Format the source files using `gofmt`

`make package`
: Build the package

As you can see, some of the rules above assume there is another `Makefile` inside `src/` folder. Thus, move on `src/` and create the following `Makefile`:

```
PACKAGE=fib
TESTPROG=test_$(PACKAGE)

include $(GOROOT)/src/Make.$(GOARCH)
export GC
export LD
export O

SRC=$(wildcard *.go)

all: test
clean:
```

```
rm -rf *.[a68] $(TESTPROG) _test *~

test: testpackage

package: $(PACKAGE).a

$(PACKAGE).a: $(PACKAGE).$O
gopack grc $@ $(PACKAGE).$O

$(PACKAGE).$O: $(SRC)
$(GC) -o $@ $(SRC)
```

Note that we have to set the `PACKAGE` variable with the name of the package (`fib` in this case). Also, note that the `testpackage` rule in the `Makefile` above will create a package named `test$(PACKAGE).a`. So, in our case, we will get `src/testfib.a`. We will import this package in our test code to actually run the specs.

At this point, the basic project structure and makefiles are done. Now, we can populate `src/` folder with an empty source file (with just the basic `package` clause within):

```
cd src
echo "package fib" > fib.go
```

Now, following BDD convention (test-first approach), let's write our test. Enter in `spec/` folder and create `spec/fib_spec.go` with the code below:

```
package main
import . "specify"
import t "../src/fib"
func init() {
	Describe("Fib", func() {
		It("should return Fibonacci's next number", func(e Example) {
			fib := new(t.Fib)
			fib.N0, fib.N1 = 0, 1
			e.Value(fib.Next()).Should(Be(1))
			e.Value(fib.Next()).Should(Be(1))
			e.Value(fib.Next()).Should(Be(2))
			e.Value(fib.Next()).Should(Be(3))
			e.Value(fib.Next()).Should(Be(5))
		})
	})
}
```

The spec above tell us **how we expect the system behaves before actually implement it**. In particular, we setup two seed values `N0` and `N1` and then we query `fib` about the next value in the sequence using `fib.Next()` method. For the first five calls we expect the sequence: 1, 1, 2, 3, 5.

If we try to run the specs at this point we get an error of course (we haven't an implementation yet):

```
$ make
...
fib_spec.go:9: undefined: testfib.Fib
...
```

Open the text editor and paste in `src/fib.go` the code below:

```
package fib
type Fib struct {
    N0, N1 int
}
func (state *Fib) Next() int {
    state.N0, state.N1 = state.N0 + state.N1, state.N0
    return state.N0
}
```

If you're new to Go, take your time reading the code. Also consider that I'm still learning this language from the ground up so this could not be the best **idiomatic** implementation (waiting for suggestions in this case). BTW, for the purpose of this post, our code behave as we expect. In fact, running the specs

```
$ make test
.
Passing: 1  Failing: 0  Pending: 0  Errors: 0
```

they all pass.

References:

http://github.com/stesla/gospecify

http://freecella.blogspot.com/2010/01/gospecify-basic-setup-of-projects.html

http://www.testingtv.com/2010/03/15/go-behave-a-bdd-framework-for-the-go-programming-language/

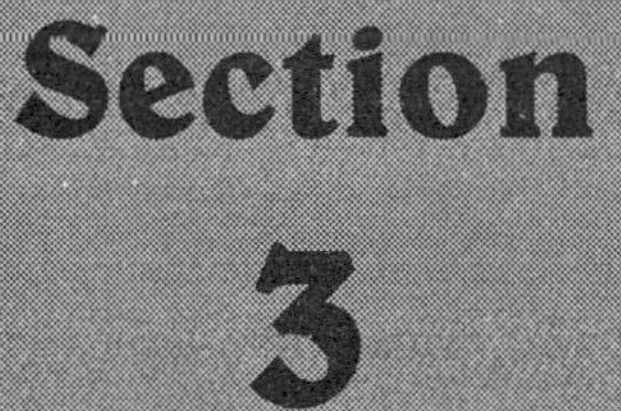

Section 3

Open Source Automation Framework

STAF and STAX Automation Framework

Practical Approaches to End-to-End Automation with STAF and STAX

- Introduction
- STAF Services
- STAX Service
- Automation Tasks
- Extending the Infrastructure

Introduction

- STAF (Software Testing Automation Framework) is a multi-platform, multi-language framework designed around the idea of reusable components, called services (which provide functionality such as process invocation, resource management, logging, and monitoring)
- STAF helps you increase the efficiency, productivity, and quality of your testing by improving your level of automation and reuse in your individual testcases as well as your overall test environment
- STAF removes the tedium of building an automation infrastructure, thus enabling you to focus on building your automation solution

STAF Services

- A STAF service is a reusable component which provides a focused set of functionality (such as logging)
- STAF's services can be leveraged to provide end-to-end automation of your test environment. Here are some examples.

Event	Provides a publish/subscribe notification system
EventManager	Allows you to call STAF services when a specified Event occurs
Cron	Calls into STAF services at a specified time interval
Process	Allows you to start, stop ,and query processes
Queue	Provides a network-enabled IPC mechanism for STAF programs
Monitor	Allows a testcase to publish its current running execution status for others to read
Log	Provides a full-featured logging facility
Semaphore	Provides network-enabled named event and mutex semaphores
FileSystem	Allows you to get and copy files across the network, list directories, and delete files
HTTP	Allows you to quickly and easily make HTTP requests
ResourcePool	Allows you to manage exclusive access to pools of elements, e.g. UserIDs or Software Licenses
Email	Allows you to send email messages

Introduction

- STAX is an execution engine which helps you thoroughly automate your entire test environment
  - » System Setup
  - » Product Installation
  - » Testcase Distribution
  - » Testcase Execution/Monitoring
  - » Results Analysis
  - » Notification
- STAX builds on top of three existing technologies, STAF, XML, and Python, to place great automation power in the hands of testers
- STAX provides a powerful GUI monitoring application which allows you to interact with and monitor the progress of your jobs

STAX Service

- The STAX Service is what drives all of your testcase automation, from beginning to end. Your end-to-end testcase automation may be comprised of a single STAX job, or multiple STAX jobs.
- Features provided by the STAX Service
  - » Support for sequential and parallel execution
  - » User-defined granularity of execution control
  - » Support for nested testcases
  - » Ability to control amount of execution time
  - » Ability to import modules at run time
  - » Support for existing Python and Java modules/packages
  - » XML-based
  - » Includes common utility modules
  - » Ability to extend the STAX XML language
- Features provided by the STAX Monitor GUI
  - » Ability to view and interact with your entire test environment from any number of remote machines
  - » Dynamic updating of the GUI to reflect the current state of the job
  - » Ability to extend the STAX Monitor GUI

Automation Tasks

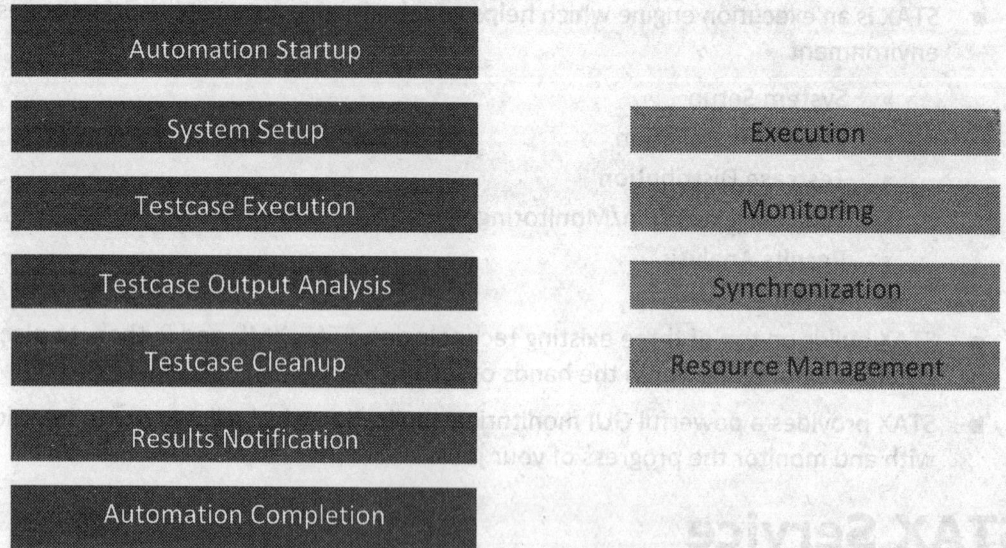

Automation Tasks - Automation Startup

- Automation startup refers to the stage where your end-to-end automation begins and is usually the result of a prior piece of work, such as a product build successfully completing or by the passage of a designated time interval
  - » In the first case, the Event and EventManager services can be used to initiate STAF/STAX automation
    - STAF-enabled testcases can register for a certain Event, and take appropriate action when the Event (such as a product build completion) occurs
    - Instead of using STAF-enabled testcases to listen for these events, you can use the EventManager service to execute an arbitrary STAF command when the Event occurs
    - In most scenarios, the STAF command is the submission of a STAX Job which will kick off the target automation
  - » In the second case, the Cron service can be used to execute an arbitrary STAF command at a designated time interval (for example, every hour, every day at 12 midnight, every 15th day of month, etc.)
    - In most cases, the STAF command is the submission of a STAX Job which will kick off the target automation

Automation Tasks - System Setup

- During the setup phase, a baseline OS can be established by using Ghost/Drive images and/or VMWare images. STAF's Process Service allows you to boot these images.
- Prior to testcase execution, STAF's FileSystem and Process services can be used to install the product under test and any pre-requisite software
- In most cases, testcase files will need to be extracted from a server or a code repository. STAF's Process service allows testcases to be extracted from code repositories, and STAF's FileSystem service allows testcase files to be transferred from a server machine to test machines.

Automation Tasks - Testcase Execution

- Testcases are typically files (such as binary executables, Java class files, shell scripts, Perl/Python/Tcl/Rexx scripts etc.) or system commands that will be executed on a test machine
- STAF and STAX allow you to start any executable file/script/command, just as if you were executing that file or command while logged into a terminal on the machine
- Testcases are executed in the STAF environment by the Process service
  - » The Process service can execute testcases that are completely unaware that they are being executed by STAF/STAX, or they can leverage STAF services in order to take advantage of additional automation capabilities
  - » In your STAX job, the <process> element is used to submit a START command to the Process service
- To automate GUI testing, you would need to use tools such as SilkTest, Rational Robot, WinRunner, etc.
  - » Once you have the GUI testing automated, you would then use STAF/STAX to kick off the GUI automation tools to run the tests
  - » After the tests complete, STAF/STAX can analyze the output to determine if the tests were successful, and take appropriate action

Automation Tasks - Testcase Execution - Monitoring

- It is desirable to have the means to easily determine the status of testcases as they are executing
- Testcases can leverage the Monitor service in order to publish their current

execution status

  » As an example, a testcase that loops through a set of tests 1000 times could publish the current loop number as its latest status
  » By using the Monitor service, you could then, from a central machine in the STAF environment, query the current status of all of your testcases
  » Furthermore, when using the STAX Monitor, all of your testcases' current status will be dynamically updated in the STAX Monitor
  » The STAX Monitor allows you to remotely view all of your executing testcases in a single view

- Throughout your STAX job, you can define blocks, which represent a portion of your job over which you would like to have runtime control
  » The STAX Monitor allows you to hold, release, and terminate any blocks that are defined in your job

Automation Tasks - Testcase Execution – Synchronization

- Testcases may need to synchronize at certain points before proceeding with additional execution. STAF and STAX allow testcases, even when on remote machines, to synchronize via the Semaphore service.
- The STAX service allows you to synchronize the completion of multiple activities via the <parallel> and <paralleliterate> elements
- The STAX service also allows you to place time constraints on portions of your automation jobs via the <timer> element
  » Allows cleanup of "infinite" tasks after the time limit is reached
  » Allows detection and cleanup of "hung" tasks
  » The STAX engine handles all cleanup activities and gives you direct control over the outcome of an expired timer

Automation Tasks - Testcase Execution - Resources

- Testcases can have pools of resources that can be shared among a number of other testcases. Resources are typically a set of machines, printers, or other hardware devices to which you want to manage access. Resources can also be "logical" resources, such as software licenses or userids.
  » One example would be if part of your test effort includes a certain

software package for which you only have 5 software licenses, but you have 20 testcases that may, at some point during their execution, need to obtain one of these software licenses. The ResourcePool service could be used to set up a resource pool with 5 software licenses, from which the 20 testcases would request acquisition of one of the resources before continuing with their execution.

» Another example would be if you had 3 userids that your testcases could use to log into a system. You could again use the ResourcePool service to control access to the 3 userids.

» A third example would be if you had a machine pool of 10 machines on which your testcases can execute. You could leverage the ResourcePool service to control access to the machines.

Automation Tasks - Testcase Output Analysis

- Testcases often write output to log files or to the standard output stream
- When using STAF and STAX, you can have any number of files and/or the entire standard error/output stream returned when the testcase completes
- Every STAF command and process returns a return code which can be used to determine the automation flow
- The files and/or standard error/output stream can then be parsed through, or otherwise analyzed in STAX, and appropriate action can then be taken depending on the content of the files and/or standard error/output
- Throughout your STAX job, you can define <testcase> elements and corresponding <tcstatus> elements to record testcase passes and failures
- The FileSystem service can be used to check for the presence/absence of files as part of the output analysis
- The FSExt service can be used to search files for particular strings as part of the output analysis
- Within your STAX job, you can use Python's Regular Expression search capabilities to analyze testcase output

Automation Tasks - Testcase Cleanup, Results Notification

- Testcase Cleanup
  - » After your testcases have completed execution, STAF's FileSystem and Process services allow you to cleanup any temporary output and/or the testcases themselves
  - » The FileSystem service can also transfer any output or log files that have been created by the testcases to a central server

- Results Notification
  - » After your automation has completed, you can use STAF's Email service to distribute the automation results
  - » STAF's HTTP Service allows you to post forms with the automation results on the web

End-to-End Automation with STAF and STAX

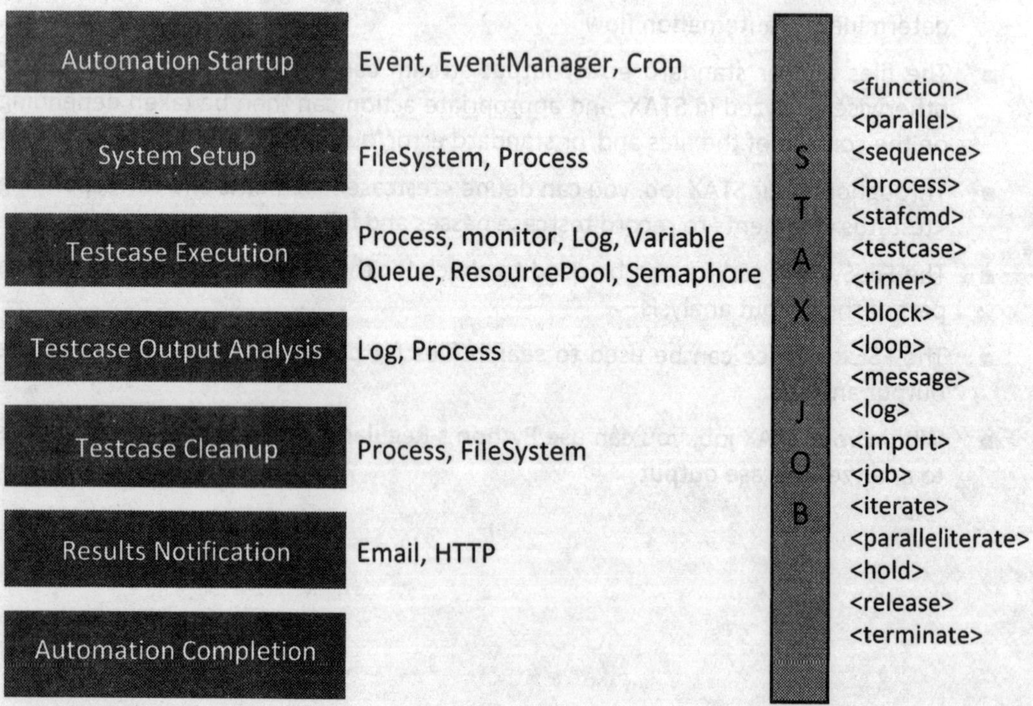

End-to-End Automation with STAF and STAX

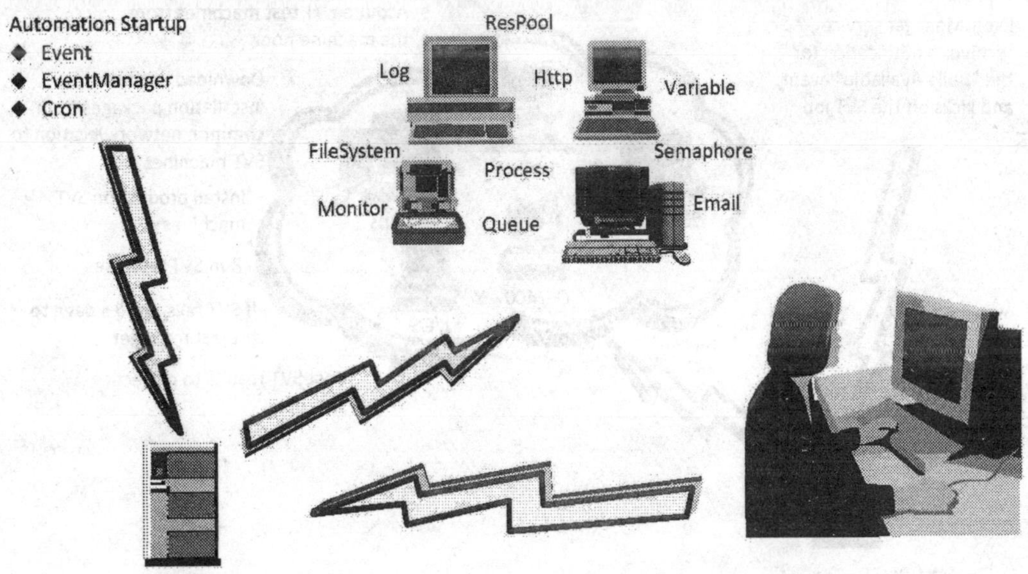

End-to-End Automation with STAF and STAX

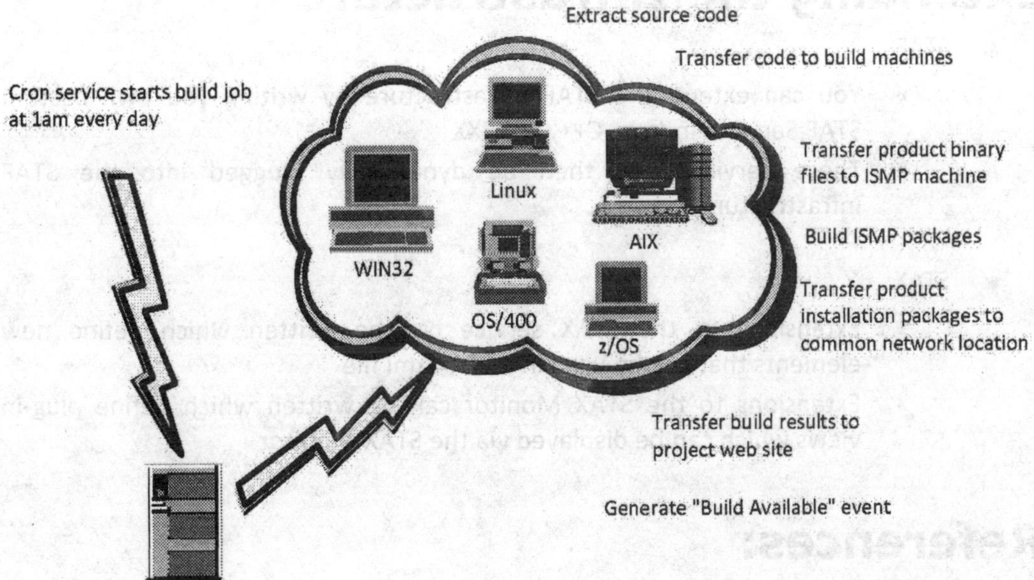

End-to-End Automation with STAF and STAX

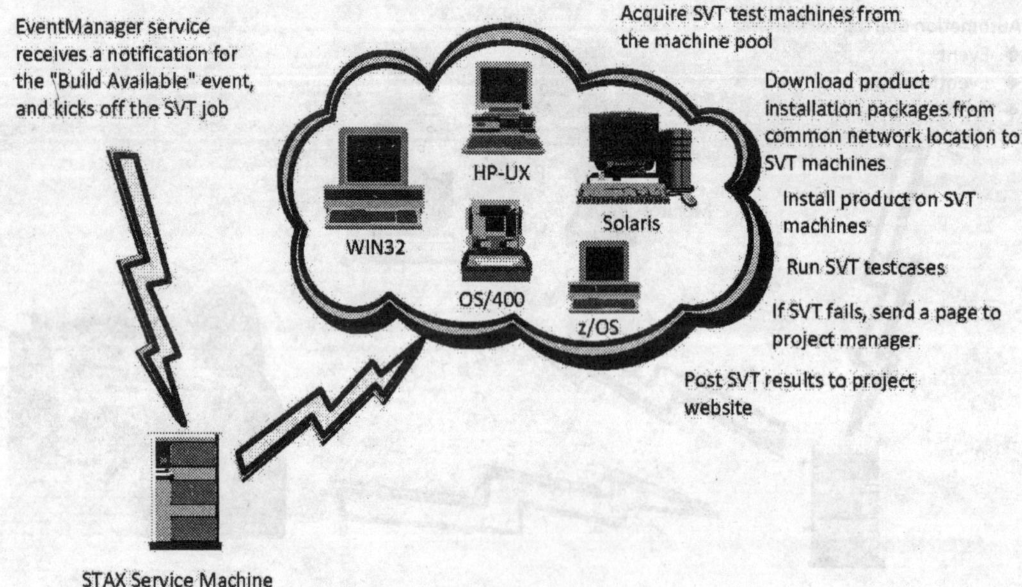

Extending the Infrastructure

- STAF
  - » You can extend the STAF infrastructure by writing you own custom STAF Services in Java, C++, or REXX
  - » These services can then be dynamically plugged into the STAF infrastructure
- STAX
  - » Extensions to the STAX service can be written which define new elements that can be used in a STAX xml file
  - » Extensions to the STAX Monitor can be written which define plug-in views which can be displayed via the STAX Monitor

References:

http://staf.sourceforge.net/

Canoo Web Test Automation Framework

Introduction

Canoo Webtest Automation Framework and apply it to automate testing Web Applications.

Test Automation? Yes please.

- Enables a more frequent feedback
- Provides a built-in safety net
- Facilitates change
- Tests as executable specifications

Critical **for agile software development**

Canoo Webtest Automation Framework

- A keyword driven framework that facilitates automated testing of Web applications with Canoo Webtest.
- Simplify test creation and maintenance, allowing more automated testing with fewer technical resources.
- Focus on automated smoke and regression testing.

Canoo Webtest

- A popular free open-source testing tool for webapplications
- Simple but expressive XML scripting language
- ANT integration
- HTMLUnit browser
- Easy to extend using Groovy, Java
- Comprehensive test reports

Framework Features

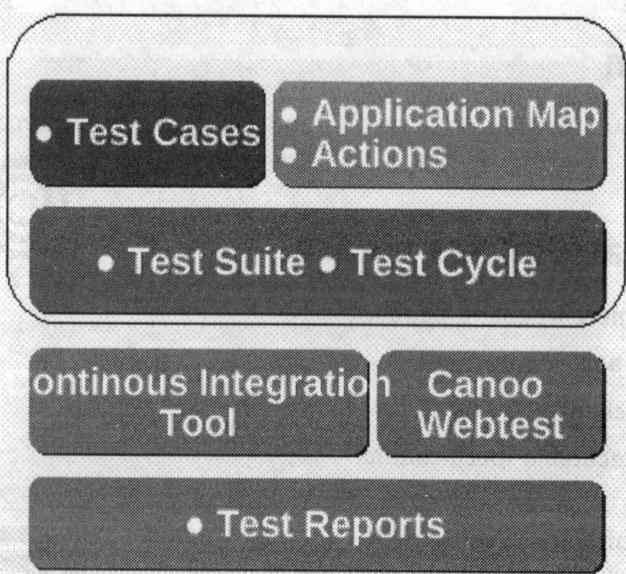

1. Test Cases simulate user actions and business processes using a simple spread sheet format
   - Easy to understand by non-technical users
   - Independent of the test tool
   - Independent of the GUI of the application being tested
2. Application Map maps GUI objects from names that humans can recognize to a data format that is useful for the automation tool
   - Single point of maintenance for GUI objects

3. Action Words mimic user actions like navigation and form filling and Submission
    - Developed by the toolsmith
4. Test suites and test cycles are modular ANT scripts that enable Canoo Webtest to read and execute the test cases based on the information in the Application Map.
5. Comprehensive test reports.
6. Interoperability with Continuous Integration Tools like Cruise Control or Hudson.

Getting Started

Install the framework	environment.properties
Test Design	Test Cases
Test Build	Application Maps Action words
Test Execution	Test Suites Test Cycle
Analyze Test Result	Test Reports

Install the framework

Download and install Canoo Webtest 2.6

http://webtest.canoo.com

- Requires JDK version 5 or higher

Extract the framework archive to a directory of your choice

Update the following properties in the environment.properties file to point to your local settings:

- webtest.home: Canoo Webtest installation folder
- webtest.testdir: Canoo Webtest Automation Framework installation folder

Test Design

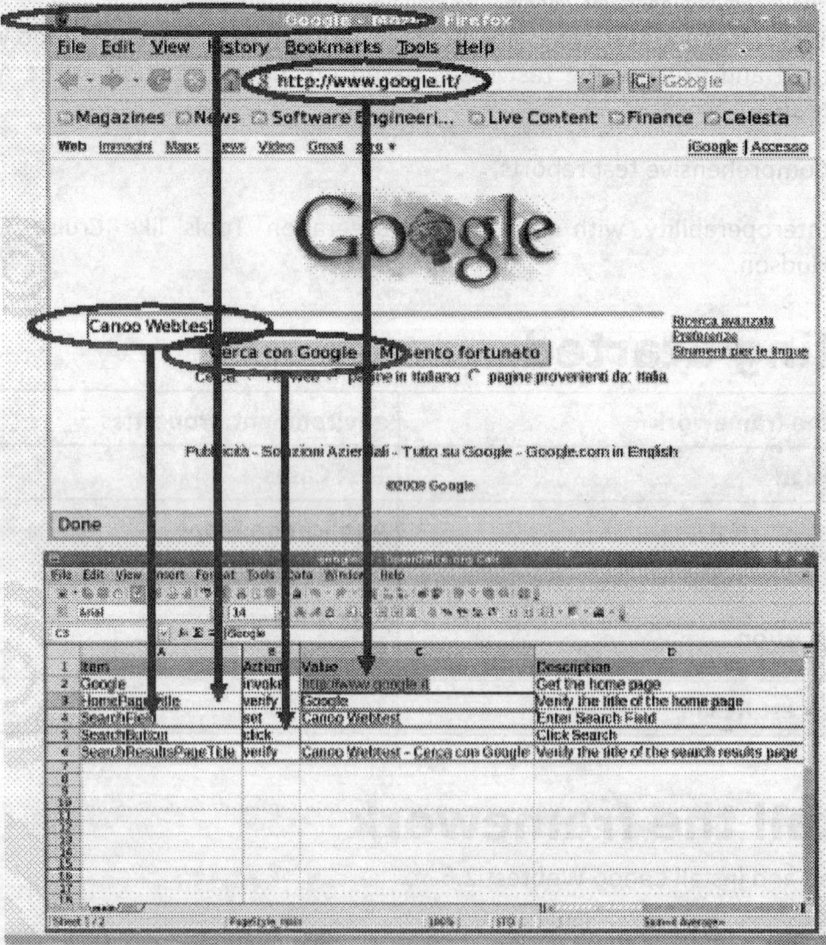

Test cases simulate typical user actions like page invocation, navigation via links and form entry and submission using a simple spreadsheet format:

- Item: A unique logical name for an application field or object
- Action: The action to be performed on the item
- Value: The argument value associated with the action being performed
- Description: A textual description of what the step does

Test Build

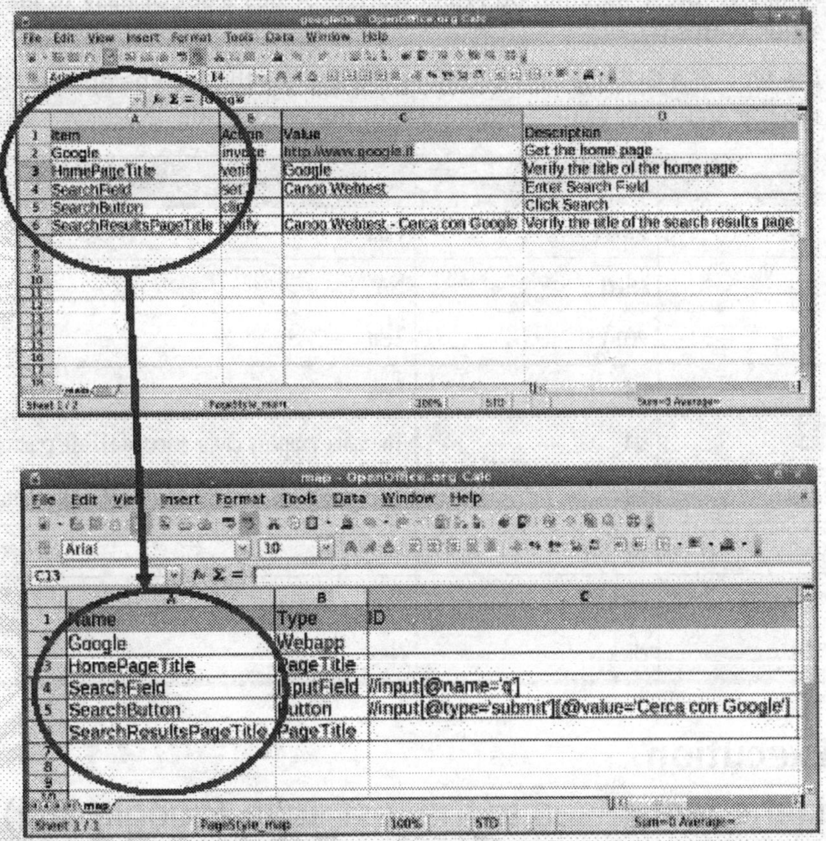

The application map associates each item name to the identification scheme needed by the automation tool to recognize and manipulate the correct GUI object

- Name: The logical name associated with the GUI object used in the test cases
- Type: The type of the GUI object
- ID: A XPath identification scheme that uniquely identifies the object in the HTML page

Test Build

- Canoo Webtest Automation Framework provides a set of easy to learn, intuitive action words.
- The type of a GUI object determines the actions that can be applied to the object and the argument value associated with the used action.

Type	Action	Value
Webapp	invoke	Path
Window	select	NA
PageTitle	verify	Text
InputField	set	Text
RadioButton	set	The value property of the selected HTML control
SelectField	set	The value property of the selected HTML control
Checkbox	set	true or false
Button	click	NA
Link	click	NA

Test Execution

- Add the test cases to the test suite (google.xml)

```
<project name="google" default="suite">
    <target name="suite">
        <antcall target="testcase">
            <param name="description" value="Google Search Canoo Webt
            <param name="container" value="googleOk.xls"/>
        </antcall>
    </target>
</project>
```

Test case

- Add the test suites to the test cycle (demo.xml)

```
<project name="demo" default="wt.full">
    ...
    <property name="wt.testInWork" value="usecases/google/google.xml
    ...
</project>
```

Test suite

- Run the test cycle

Test Reports

Comprehensive test reports that show the exit of each test case and the details of each test step

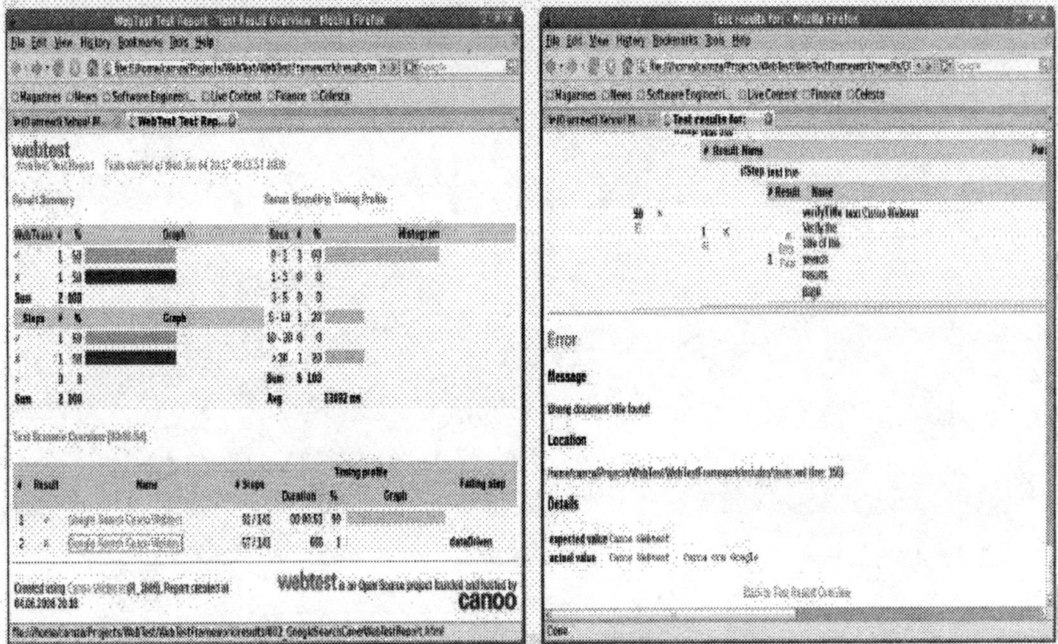

References:

http://webtest.canoo.com/webtest/manual/Downloads.html

TestNG Automation Framework

Software Versions

- This presentation refers to the following versions of software:
  - » TestNG 5.5 & 5.1 for maven-surefire-plugin
  - » TestNG Eclipse plugin 5.5
  - » Maven 2.0.6
  - » Ant 1.7
  - » Eclipse 3.2 (3.2.1 or 3.2.2)

What is TestNG?

TestNG is a testing framework designed to simply a broad range of testing needs, from unit testing (testing a class in isolation of the others) to Integration testing (testing entire systems made of several classes, several packages and even several external frameworks, such as application servers).

Writing a test is typically a three-step process:

- Write the business logic of your test and insert TestNG annotations in your code.
- Add the information about your test (e.g. the class name, the groups you wish to run, etc...) in a `testng.xml` file or in build.xml.
- Run TestNG.

You can find a quick example on the Welcome page.

The concepts used in this documentation are as follows:

- A suite is represented by one XML file. It can contain one or more tests and is defined by the `<suite>` tag.
- A test is represented by `<test>` and can contain one or more TestNG classes.
- A TestNG class is a Java class that contains at least one TestNG annotation. It is represented by the `<class>` tag and can contain one or more test methods.
- A test method is a Java method annotated by `@Test` in your source.

A TestNG test can be configured by `@BeforeXXX and @AfterXXX` annotations which allows to perform some Java logic before and after a certain point, these points being either of the items listed above.

The rest of this manual will explain the following:

- A list of all the annotations with a brief explanation. This will give you an idea of the various functionalities offered by TestNG but you will probably want to consult the section dedicated to each of these annotations to learn the details.
- A description of the testng.xml file, its syntax and what you can specify in it.
- A detailed list of the various features and how to use them with a combination of annotations and testng.xml.

- It is an annotation-driven Java testing framework inspired by JUnit and NUnit "Testing, the Next Generation"

Why TestNG?

- Not built just for Unit testing
- Build upon your JUnit know-how
- Superset of JUnit 3 and JUnit 4 features
- Can run JUnit tests
- IDE Integration – Eclipse, Intellij, NetBeans
- Plethora of features not offered by JUnit

TestNG Features

- Annotations; no mandatory naming patterns for test methods or extending classes
- Also Supports Javadoc annotations for Java 1.4
- Powerful test-fixture set-up and tear-down options

TestNG Features (2)

- Group tests – test classes or test methods
- Specify dependencies on test method(s) and/or group(s) of tests with annotations
- Create a suite of tests or groups of tests
- Suite metadata, and execution control via xml file (eclipse-testng.xml)

TestNG Features (3)

- If dependent test fails - TestNG skips subsequent tests in the dependency chain
- TestNG can rerun failed tests only

Features – Overview

- JDK5 Annotations
- Flexible Testconfiguration
- Support for Data Driven testing
- Introduction of Tests Granularities
- Parallel Testing
- Full JDK 1.4 Support (through JavaDoc Tags)
- Full JUnit Support
- Automatic TestSuite of failed Tests
- TestScenarios and dependent Testing
- Expected Exceptions (more than 1 per Method)
- Easy to write Extension (own loggers, reporters etc..)
- ....

TestNG Testmodel

TestNG Test Model

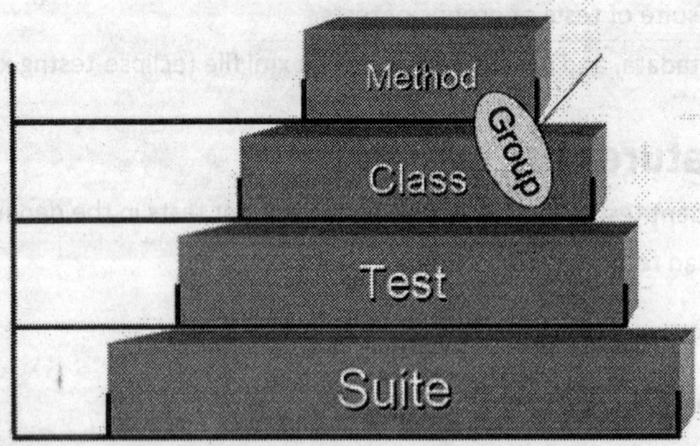

Features – TestConfiguration

testng.xml

```
<!DOCTYPE suite SYSTEM «http://testng.org/testng-1.0.dtd»>
<suite name="testsuite">
    <test verbose="1" name= "testname">
        <packages>
            <package name= „test.*" />
        </packages>
        <groups>
            <include name="groupsToRun">
        </groups>
    </test>
</suite>
```

Testng.xml DTD

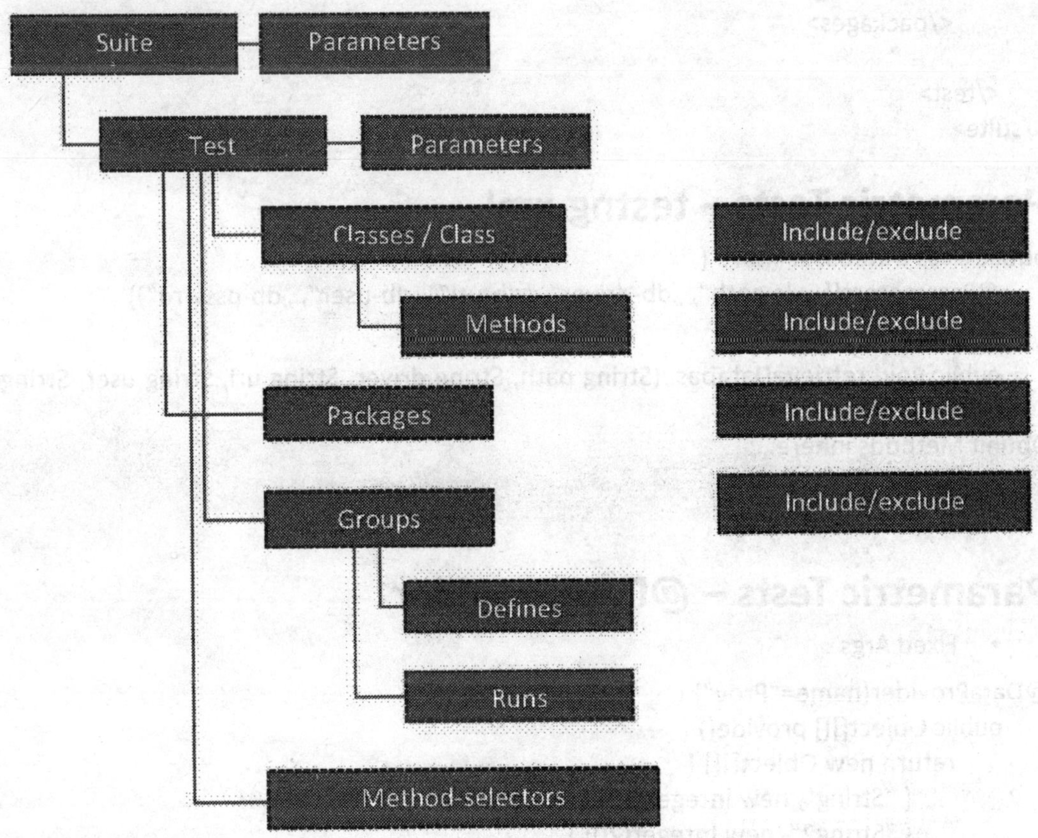

Parametrisierte Tests – testng.xml

In testng.xml:

```
<!DOCTYPE suite SYSTEM «http://testng.org/testng-1.0.dtd»>

<suite name=„db suite“>

    <parameter name="xls-path" value="conf/projects.xls" />
    <parameter name="db-driver" value="org.postgresql.Driver" />
    <parameter name="db-url" value="jdbc:postgresql://localhost:5432/postgres" />
    <parameter name="db-user" value="postgres" />
    <parameter name="db-psswrd" value="postgres" />
    <test verbose="10" name="database test">
```

```
        <packages>
            <package name="db.*" />
        </packages>

    </test>
</suite>
```

Parametric Tests – testng.xml

```
public class DatabaseFixture {
    @Parameters({ „xls-path", „db-driver", „db-url", „db-user", „db-psswrd"})
    @BeforeTest
    public void retrieveDatabase(String path, String driver, String url, String user, String
    pssword) {
Dbunit Methods inhere...;
}
```

Parametric Tests – @DataProvider

- Fixed Args

```
@DataProvider(name="Prov") {
    public Object[][] provide() {
        return new Object[][] {
            { "String", new Integer(10) },
            { "String2", new Integer(20) },
            };
        }

@Test (dataProvider = "Prov")
Public void testSomethng(String string, Integer intgr) {
    ......
}
```

Parametric Tests – @DataProvider

- Parametric DataProvider

```
@DataProvider (name="pDP") {
Public Object[][] createData(Method m) {
    if(m.getName().equals("atest")) {
```

```
        return new Object[][] {}}
    if(m.getName().equals("btest")) {
        return new Object[][] {}}
}

@Test (dataProvider="pDP")
Public void atest() {
}
```

Getting started

- Create POJO
- Declare a Test with TestNG Annotation

```
Import org.testng.annotation.Test;
Import static org.testng.Assert.assertEquals;

Public class First {
    @Test
    public void firstTest() {
        assertEquals("1","1");
    }
```

Getting started – JDK4

```
import org.testng.Assert;

Public class First {
    /**
     * @testng.test
     */
    public void firstTest() {
        Assert.assertEquals("1","1");
    }
```

Testng - @Test Annotation

- @Test (name="example",
    description="example test",
    expectedExceptions=IOException.class,
    dataProvider="dataProv",

```
groups={"functional","stress"},
dependsOnGroups="database",
dependsOnMethods={"init","setup"},
enabled=true,
successPercentage=80,
timeout=10000,
invocationCount=10,
threadPoolSize=10,
sequential=true)
```

Testng – Scope Annotations

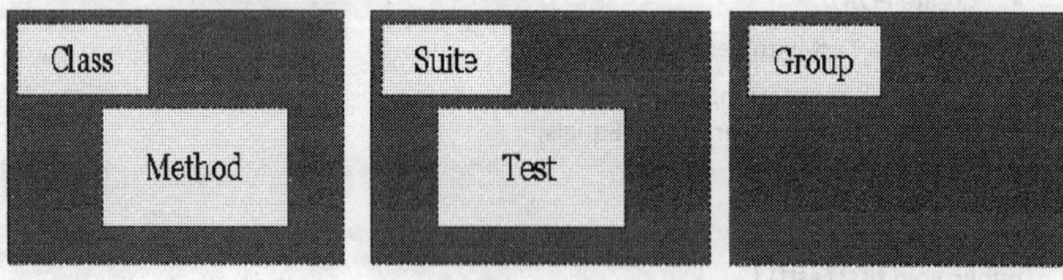

@BeforeClass	@BeforeSuite	@BeforeGroups
@AfterClass	@AfterSuite	@AfterGroups
@BeforeMethod	@BeforeTest	
@AfterMethod	@AfterTest	

IDE Integration / Plugins

- Eclipse Plugin – just like JUnit
- Maven 1 – Plugin doesnt work Λ
- Maven 2 – works ok – with problems

Literatur

- Next Generation Testing
  - Stefan Edlich, Mark Rambow
  - Entwickler Press (Oktober 2006)

- www.testng.org
- Forums.opensymphony.com/forum.jspa?forumID=14

TestNG Demo 1

- Eclipse project – TestNG 5.5
- Use annotations
- Run test and test suite
- Specify dependency between tests
- Run failed test
- Check test reports in test-output directory

TestNG Features (4)

- Specify the number of times a test is run
- Specify timeout for test execution
- Parameterized test methods – specify parameter values in
  - Method returning Object[][] with @DataProvider annotation
  - eclipse-testng.xml (inconvenient)
- Factories to create tests dynamically

TestNG Features (5)

- Run tests in parallel in separate threads
  - Specify number of threads
    - Runs dependent tests in a single thread
  - Specify set of tests to be run in a single thread in eclipse-testng.xml
- Supports BeanShell for specifying test inclusion in eclipse-testng.xml

TestNG Demo 2

- Specify the number of times a test is run
- Specify timeout for a test execution

- Run tests in parallel in separate threads
- Parameterized test methods

TestNG vs. Junit 4

- Except annotations, JUnit 4 does not support other features available in TestNG
- JUnit 4 enforces annotated @BeforeClass methods to be static, TestNG does not

TestNG-Spring Integration

- **Retrofitting existing class for TestNG**

```
public abstract class MyAbstractSpringTests extends
AbstractTransactionalDataSourceSpringContextTests {
// The following two methods are for converting this into a TestNG class
@BeforeMethod
protected final void nGSetup() throws Exception {
    super.setUp();
}

@AfterMethod
protected final void nGTearDown() throws Exception {
    super.tearDown();
}
}
```

TestNG-Spring Integration

- Retrofit any of the existing classes for TestNG based on your needs
    - AbstractDependencyInjectionSpringContextTests
    - AbstractTransactionalSpringContextTests
    - AbstractTransactionalDataSourceSpringContextTests
- OR, use TestNG provided drop in replacements of spring root classes
  http://testng.googlecode.com/svn/trunk/spring/src/common

TestNG – Build Tools

- Maven integration
    - maven-surefire-plugin

- Ant integration
  - TestNG Ant tasks

TestNG Demo 3

- Run tests using Maven 2
  - On the command line in the TestNGDemo folder type "mvn test" - pom.xml must be in this folder
- Run tests using Ant
  - In Eclipse right click on build.xml and run the provided ant file

TestNG Hiccups

- IDE plugin
  - cannot create a new test class from the class to be tested
  - Eclipse TestNG plugin recognizes "groups" annotation attributes only at the class level and not at the method level
- Suite xml file does not support regular expression to select tests
- maven-surefire-plugin does not work with TestNG version 5.5 but works with 5.1. For details check:

http://www.goi18n.com/testngdemo/testng-usage.html

TestNG Adoption

- Project with existing JUnit test
  - Write new tests with TestNG
  - Plan converting existing JUnit tests to TestNG
    - Use the convert option in the IDE plugin. However, this does not work for a class that doesn't directly extend junit.framework.TestCase class.
- Project using maven-surefire-plugin 2.3 and TestNG 5.1 (because of the issues)
  - End your test classes' name with "Test"
  - If you integration tests take longer consider separating them into a integration package instead of using TestNG groups, and use Maven profiles to run them in the integration-test phase.

Resources

- http://www.testng.org
- The discussion forum
    - http://forums.opensymphony.com/category.jspa?categoryID=9
- Spring Source
    - http://testng.googlecode.com/svn/trunk/spring/src/common/
- http://testng.org/doc/download.html
- http://testng.org/doc/documentation-main.html#introduction

Functional testing tools list

Chapter 20

1. AUTOIT
2. Watir
3. MacQ
4. Selenium
5. Junit
6. XMl Unit
7. Test NG
8. DBUnit
9. SQL Unit
10. Nuint
11. WET
12. csUnit
13. Sahi
14. Fit
15. JTR(java Test Runner)
16. Regression Tester

Automation Framework tool:

Maveryx is an open and extensible automated testing framework powered by an innovative engine that eliminates dependency on GUI Maps providing a dynamic test objects handling

- Maveryx at runtime during test execution:
- takes "snapshots" of the current user interface
- turn them into a XML documents
- searches within snapshots for the GUI objects to test
- executes the test actions on the test objects
- Gets the GUI objects hierarchy by the Java Virtual Machine where the application-under-test is running
- Based on Java Accessibility technology
- Builds a snapshot using an XML syntax and semantics

http://sourceforge.net/projects/maveryx

Section 4

Manual Testing, Test Management & Bug Tracking

Manual Testing Concepts

Test Plan

A test plan is a document detailing a systematic approach to testing a system such as a machine or software. The plan typically contains a detailed understanding of what the eventual workflow will be.

Test Plan Template:

Name of the Product

Prepared by:

Names of Preparers
Date

Contents

1. Introduction
2. Objectives & Tasks
    - Objectives
    - Tasks
3. Testing Strategy
    - Alpha Testing
    - System & Integration Testing
    - Performance & Stress testing
    - User acceptance Testing
    - Batch Testing
    - Automated Regression Testing
    - Beta Testing
4. Hardware Requirements
5. Environment Requirements
    - Mainframe
    - Work Station

6. Test Schedule
7. Control Procedures
8. Features to Be Tested
9. Features Not to Be Tested
10. Resources/Roles & Responsibilities
11. Schedules
12. Significantly Impacted Departments (SIDs)
13. Dependencies
14. Risks/Assumptions
15. Tools
16. Approvals

1. Introduction:

A brief summary of the product being tested. Outline all the functions at a high level.

2. Objectives & tasks:

- **Objectives**

Describe the objectives supported by the Master Test Plan, eg., defining tasks and responsibilities, vehicle for communication, document to be used as a service level agreement, etc.

- **Tasks**

List all tasks identified by this Test Plan, i.e., testing, post-testing, problem reporting, etc.

3. Testing Strategy:

Describe the overall approach to testing. For each major group of features or feature combinations, specify the approach which will ensure that these feature groups are adequately tested. Specify the major activities, techniques, and tools which are used to test the designated groups of features.

The approach should be described in sufficient detail to permit identification of the major testing tasks and estimation of the time required to do each one.

Unit Testing

Definition:
Specify the minimum degree of comprehensiveness desired. Identify the techniques which will be used to judge the comprehensiveness of the testing effort (for example, determining which statements have been executed at least once). Specify any additional completion criteria (for example, error frequency). The techniques to be used to trace requirements should be specified.

Participants:

List the names of individuals/departments that would be responsible for Unit Testing.

Methodology:

Describe how unit testing will be conducted. Who will write the test scripts for the unit testing, what would be the sequence of events of Unit Testing and how will the testing activity take place?

System and Integration Testing

Definition:
List what is your understanding of System and Integration Testing for your project.

Participants:

Who will be conducting System and Integration Testing on your project? List the individuals that will be responsible for this activity.

Methodology:

Describe how System & Integration testing will be conducted. Who will write the test scripts for the unit testing, what would be sequence of events of System & Integration Testing, and how will the testing activity take place?

Performance and Stress Testing

Definition:
List what is your understanding of Stress Testing for your project.

Participants:

Who will be conducting Stress Testing on your project? List the individuals that will be responsible for this activity.

Methodology:

Describe how Performance & Stress testing will be conducted. Who will write the test scripts for the testing, what would be sequence of events of Performance & Stress Testing, and how will the testing activity take place?

User Acceptance Testing

Definition:

The purpose of acceptance test is to confirm that the system is ready for operational use. During acceptance test, end-users (customers) of the system compare the system to its initial requirements.

Participants:

Who will be responsible for User Acceptance Testing? List the individuals' names and responsibility.

Methodology:

Describe how the User Acceptance testing will be conducted. Who will write the test scripts for the testing, what would be sequence of events of User Acceptance Testing, and how will the testing activity take place?

Batch Testing

4.6 Automated Regression Testing

Definition:

Regression testing is the selective retesting of a system or component to verify that modifications have not caused unintended effects and that the system or component still works as specified in the requirements.

Participants:

Methodology:

- **Beta Testing**

4. Hardware Requirement:

Computers
Modems

5. Environment Requirement:

Main Frame

Specify both the necessary and desired properties of the test environment. The specification should contain the physical characteristics of the facilities, including the hardware, the communications and system software, the mode of usage (for example, stand-alone), and any other software or supplies needed to support the test. Also specify the level of security which must be provided for the test facility, system software, and proprietary components such as software, data, and hardware.

Identify special test tools needed. Identify any other testing needs (for example, publications or office space). Identify the source of all needs which are not currently available to your group.

Workstation

6. Test Schedule:

Include test milestones identified in the Software Project Schedule as well as all item transmittal events.

Define any additional test milestones needed. Estimate the time required to do each testing task. Specify the schedule for each testing task and test milestone. For each testing resource (that is, facilities, tools, and staff), specify its periods of use.

7. Control Procedure:

Problem Reporting

Document the procedures to follow when an incident is encountered during the testing process. If a standard form is going to be used, attach a blank copy as an "Appendlx" to the Test Plan. In the event you are using an automated incident logging system, write those procedures in this section.

Change Requests

Document the process of modifications to the software. Identify who will sign off on the changes and what would be the criteria for including the changes to the current product. If the changes will affect existing programs, these modules need to be identified.

8. Features to be tested:

Identify all software features and combinations of software features that will be tested.

9. Features not to be tested:

Identify all features and significant combinations of features which will not be tested and the reasons

10. Resources/Role & Responsibility:

Specify the staff members who are involved in the test project and what their roles are going to be (for example, Mary Brown (User) compiles Test Cases for Acceptance Testing). Identify groups responsible for managing, designing, preparing, executing, and resolving the test activities as well as related issues. Also identify groups responsible for providing the test environment. These groups may include developers, testers, operations staff, testing services, etc.

11. Schedules:

Major Deliverables

Identify the deliverable documents. You can list the following documents:

- Test Plan
- Test Cases
- Test Incident Reports
- Test Summary Reports

12. Significantly Impacted Departments (SIDs):

Department/Business Area Bus. Manager Tester(s)

13. Dependencies:

Identify significant constraints on testing, such as test-item availability, testing-resource availability, and deadlines.

14. Risks/Assumptions:

Identify the high-risk assumptions of the test plan. Specify contingency plans for each (for example, delay in delivery of test items might require increased night shift scheduling to meet the delivery date).

15. Tools:

List the Automation tools you are going to use. List also the Bug tracking tool here.

16. Approvals:

Specify the names and titles of all persons who must approve this plan. Provide space for the signatures and dates.

Test case

Definition

A test case is also defined as a sequence of steps to test the correct behavior of a functionality/feature of an application.

OR

A test case is a list of the conditions or issues of what the tester want to test in software. Test case helps to come up with test data. A test case has an input description, Test sequence and an expected behavior.

Why we write test cases?

The basic objectives of writing test cases are to validate the testing coverage of the application. If you are working in any CMMi company then you will strictly follow test cases standards. So writing test cases brings some sort of standardization and minimizes the adhoc approach in testing.

Test Case Template:

Test Case ID	Test Case Name	Test Case description	Test steps	Expected result	Actual result	Pass/Fail

Bug Life Cycle

Introduction:

Bug can be defined as the abnormal behavior of the software. No software exists without a bug. The elimination of bugs from the software depends upon the efficiency of testing done on the software. A bug is a specific concern about the quality of the Application under Test (AUT).

In software development process, the bug has a life cycle. The bug should go through the life cycle to be closed. A specific life cycle ensures that the process is standardized. The bug attains different states in the life cycle. The life cycle of the bug can be shown diagrammatically as follows:

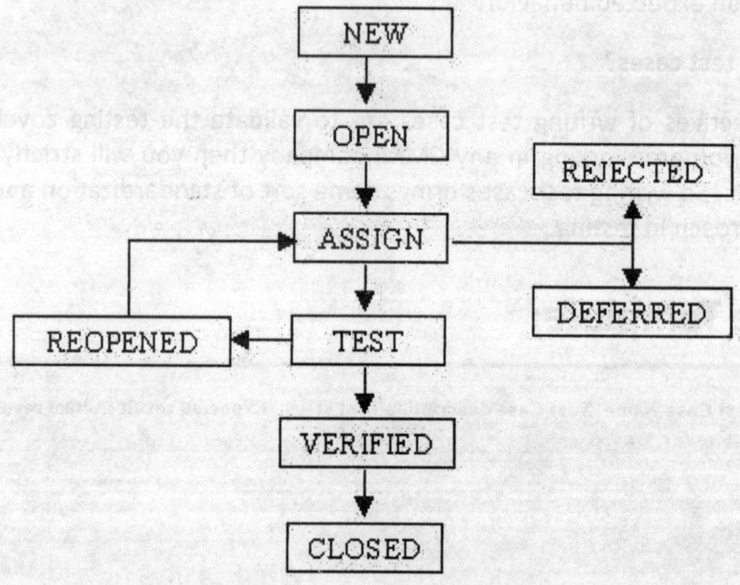

The different states of a bug can be summarized as follows:

1. New
2. Open
3. Assign
4. Test
5. Verified
6. Deferred
7. Reopened

8. Duplicate
9. Rejected and
10. Closed

Description of Various Stages:

1. New: When the bug is posted for the first time, its state will be "NEW". This means that the bug is not yet approved.

2. Open: After a tester has posted a bug, the lead of the tester approves that the bug is genuine and he changes the state as "OPEN".

3. Assign: Once the lead changes the state as "OPEN", he assigns the bug to corresponding developer or developer team. The state of the bug now is changed to "ASSIGN".

4. Test: Once the developer fixes the bug, he has to assign the bug to the testing team for next round of testing. Before he releases the software with bug fixed, he changes the state of bug to "TEST". It specifies that the bug has been fixed and is released to testing team.

5. Deferred: The bug, changed to deferred state means the bug is expected to be fixed in next releases. The reasons for changing the bug to this state have many factors. Some of them are priority of the bug may be low, lack of time for the release or the bug may not have major effect on the software.

6. Rejected: If the developer feels that the bug is not genuine, he rejects the bug. Then the state of the bug is changed to "REJECTED".

7. Duplicate: If the bug is repeated twice or the two bugs mention the same concept of the bug, then one bug status is changed to "DUPLICATE".

8. Verified: Once the bug is fixed and the status is changed to "TEST", the tester tests the bug. If the bug is not present in the software, he approves that the bug is fixed and changes the status to "VERIFIED".

9. Reopened: If the bug still exists even after the bug is fixed by the developer, the tester changes the status to "REOPENED". The bug traverses the life cycle once again.

10. Closed: Once the bug is fixed, it is tested by the tester. If the tester feels that the bug no longer exists in the software, he changes the status of the bug to "CLOSED". This state means that the bug is fixed, tested and approved.

While defect prevention is much more effective and efficient in reducing the number of defects, most organization conducts defect discovery and removal. Discovering and removing defects is an expensive and inefficient process. It is much more efficient for an organization to conduct activities that prevent defects.

Guidelines on deciding the Severity of Bug:

Indicate the **impact** each defect has on **testing efforts** or users and administrators of the application under test. This information is used by developers and management as the **basis** for assigning **priority** of work on defects.

A sample guideline for assignment of Priority Levels during the product test phase includes:

1. **Critical / Show Stopper** — An item that prevents further testing of the product or function under test can be classified as Critical Bug. No workaround is possible for such bugs. Examples of this include a missing menu option or security permission required to access a function under test.

2. **Major / High** — A defect that does not function as expected/designed or cause other functionality to fail to meet requirements can be classified as Major Bug. The workaround can be provided for such bugs. Examples of this include inaccurate calculations; the wrong field being updated, etc.

3. **Average / Medium** — The defects which do not conform to standards and conventions can be classified as Medium Bugs. Easy workarounds exists to achieve functionality objectives. Examples include matching visual and text links which lead to different end points.

4. **Minor / Low** — Cosmetic defects which does not affect the functionality of the system can be classified as Minor Bugs.

Guidelines on writing Bug Description:

Bug can be expressed as "Result followed by the action". That means, the unexpected behavior occurring when a particular action takes place can be given as bug description.

1. Be **specific**. State the expected behavior which did not occur - such as after pop-up did not appear and the behavior which occurred instead.
2. Use **present tense.**
3. Don't use unnecessary words.

4. Don't add exclamation points. End sentences with a period.
5. DON'T USE ALL CAPS. Format words in upper and lower case (mixed case).

Advantages of CTE_XL

- Configurable dependency rules
- Automated test case generation
- Methodical linking with test automation tool
- Open interfaces to industry standards
- Linking with test platform for model-based ECU function development MESINA
- The implementation of usual design features like color and font of classification-tree
- An auto-layout function for classification trees
- Unlimited canvas for generating the tree
- Systematic and common classification tree method

A The defect tracking system is a program that testers use to record and track defects. It routes each defect between testers, developers, the project manager and others, following a workflow designed to ensure that the defect is verified and repaired.

- Every defect encountered in the test run is recorded and entered into a defect tracking system so that it can be prioritized.

- The defect workflow should track the interaction between the testers who find the defect and the programmers who fix it. It should ensure that every defect can be properly prioritized and reviewed by all of the stakeholders to determine whether or not it should be repaired. This process of review and prioritization referred to as triage.

Test Management using Test Link

TestLink (Version 1.7)

TestLink Introduction:

TestLink is web based **Test Management system**. This manual should serve as source for users to understand processes, terms and organization of work with TestLink.

Overall structure

There are three cornerstones: **Test Project, Test Plan** and **User**. All other data are relations or attributes of this base. First, we will define terms that are used throughout the documentation and testing world.

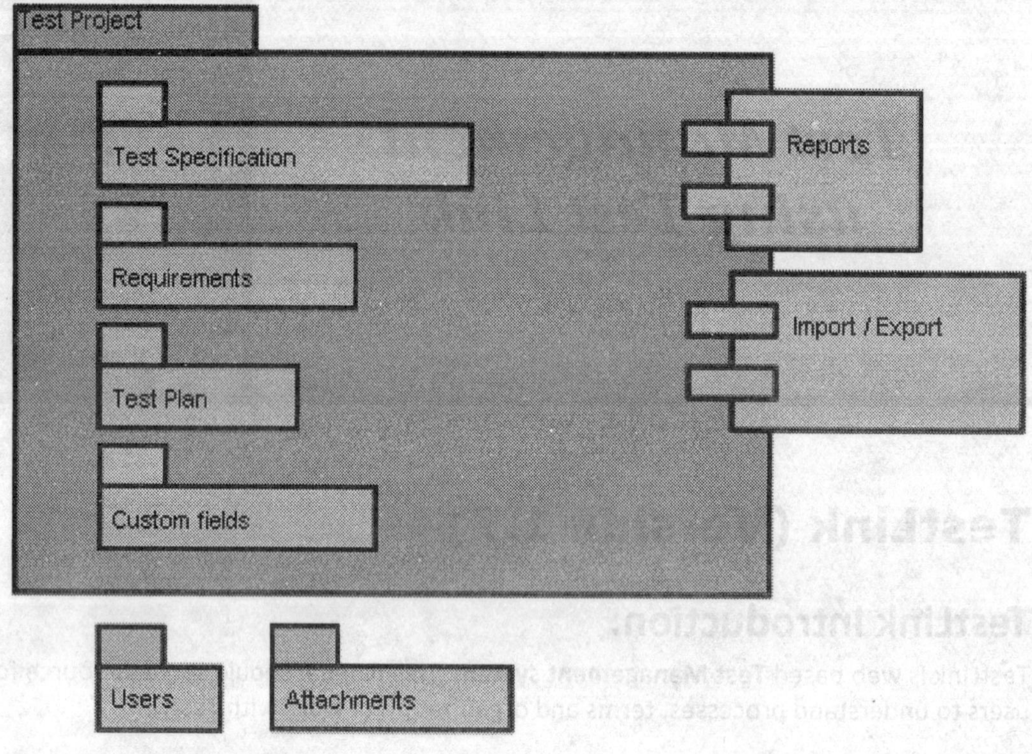

Basic Terminology

Test Case describes a testing task via steps (actions, scenario) and expected results. Test Cases are the fundamental piece of TestLink.

Test Suite (Test Case Suite) organizes Test Cases to units. It structures Test Specification into logical parts.

**Test Suite replaces the components and categories in TL 1.6 and earlier.*

Test Plan is created when you'd like to execute Test Cases. Test Plans can be made up of the Test Cases from one or many Test Projects. Test Plan includes Builds, Milestones, user assignment and Test Results.

Test Project is something that will exist forever in TestLink. Test Project will undergo many different versions throughout its lifetime. Test Project includes Test Specification with Test Cases, Requirements and Keywords. Users within the project have defined roles.

**Test Project was called Product in TL 1.6 and earlier.*

User: each TestLink user has a Role that defines available TestLink features. See more in chapter "User Administration". Illustration 2 shows common activities according to user roles.

Example of TestLink simple work-flow

1. Administrator creates a **Test Project** "Fast Food" and two users, Adam with rights "Leader" and Beta with rights "Senior Tester".

2. Leader Adam imports **Software Requirements** and for part of these requirements generates empty Test Cases. He reorganizes them into two Test Suites: "Fish" and "Chips".

3. Tester Beta describes a test scenario (create a content of empty Test Cases) using these **Test Specification** that is organized into Test Suites.

4. Adam creates keyword "Regression testing" and assigns this keyword to ten of these Test Cases.

5. Adam creates a **Test Plan** "Fish & Chips 1", **Build** "Fish 0.1" and links all Test Cases in Test Suite "Fish" to this Test Plan. He assigns himself and Beta as resources to this Test Plan too.

6. Now developers produce a first build. Adam and Beta execute and record the testing with the result: 5 passed, 1 failed and 4 is blocked.

7. Developers make a new Build "Fish 0.2" and Beta tests the failed and blocked Test Cases only. This time these all blocked and failed Test Cases passed. They retest also all Test Cases with keywords "Regression testing" in addition.

8. A **manager** of this team would like to see the results. Administrator explains to him that he can create an account himself on the login page. Manager does it. He has default "Guest" rights and can see **Test Results** and Test Cases. He can see that everything passed in the overall report ;-) and problems in Build "Fish 0.1" in a report for that particular Build.1

9. Later, developers finally add also "Chips" functionality. Adam creates a **Test Plan** "Fish & Chips 2". He can reuse the first Test Plan as template. All "Fish" Test Cases and roles will be automatically added. He creates a new Build "Fish 1.1" and links all "Chips" Test Cases to this Test Plan too.

10. Now, a testing starts as usually.

11. Later, Admin creates a new **Test Project** for another product "Hot Dog". But this is another test team and different story.

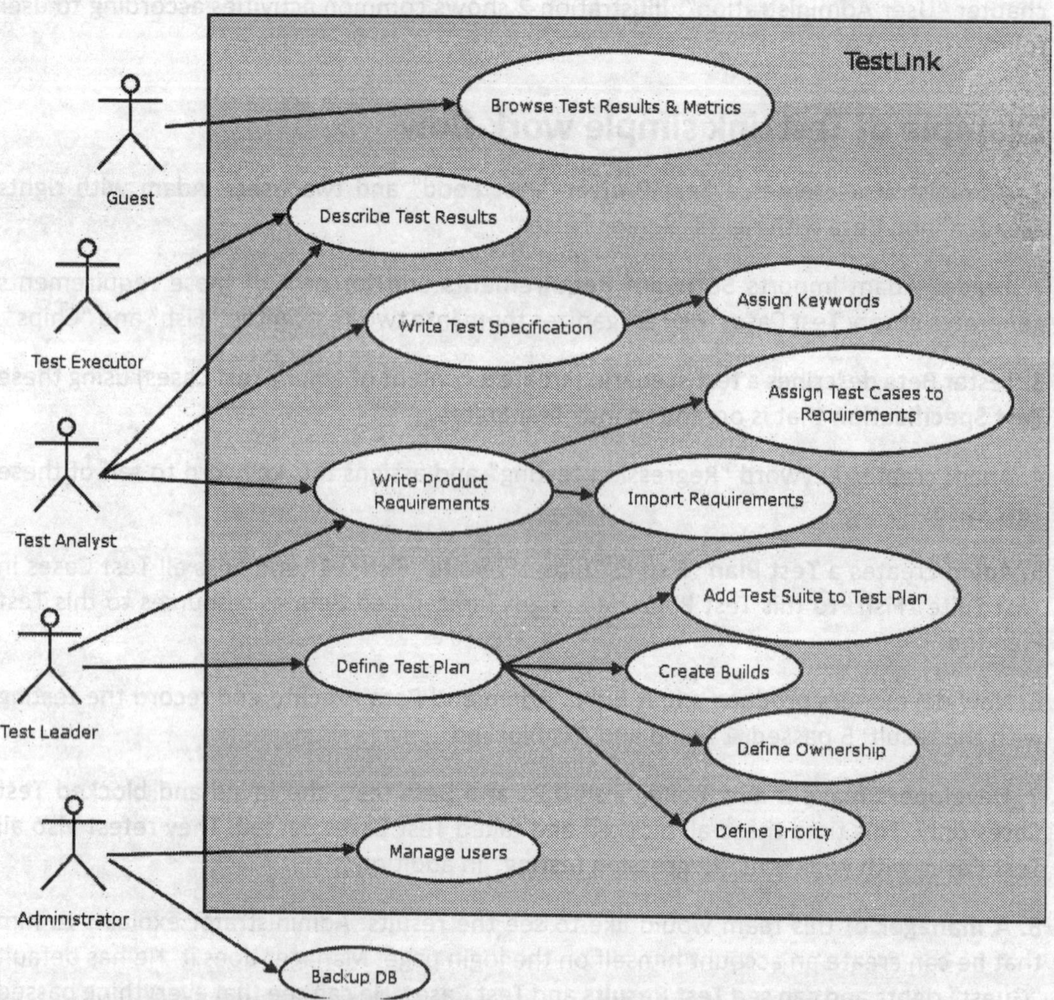

Installation Steps:

Apache HTTP Server 2.2.4

The Apache HTTP Server Project is a collaborative software development effort aimed at creating a robust, commercial-grade, feature and freely-available source code implementation of an HTTP (Web) server. The project is jointly managed by a group of volunteers located around the world, using the Internet and the Web to communicate, plan, and develop the server and its related documentation. This project is part of the Apache Software Foundation.

1. Download Apache HTTP Server

- Go to browser & type link
  http://archive.apache.org/dist/httpd/binaries/win32/
- Download
- Save the file

2. Install Apache HTTP Server

Step 1: Double Click on your setup file

Step 2 : Click on 'Run' button

Step 3 : Click the "next" button in the Installation Wizard

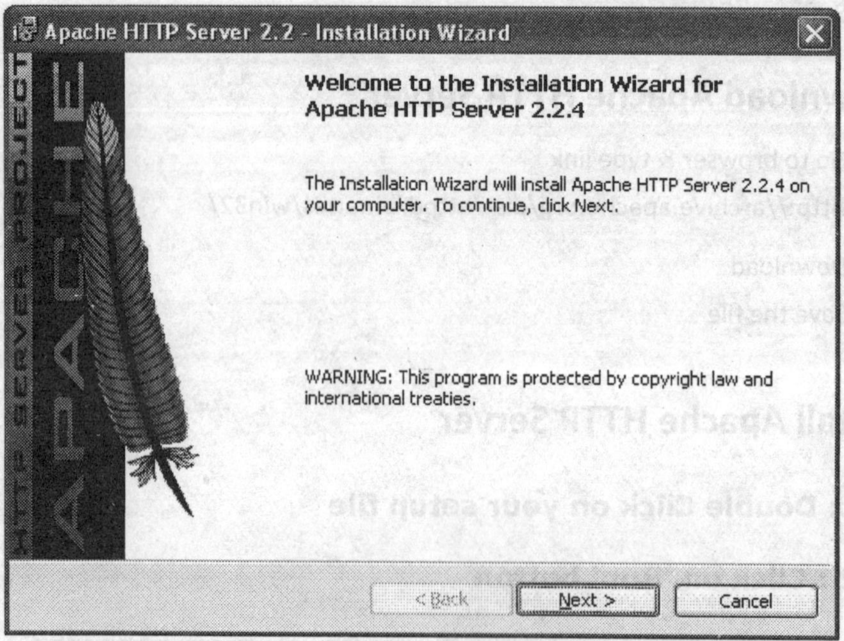

Step 4 : Accept the License agreement and click the "next" button

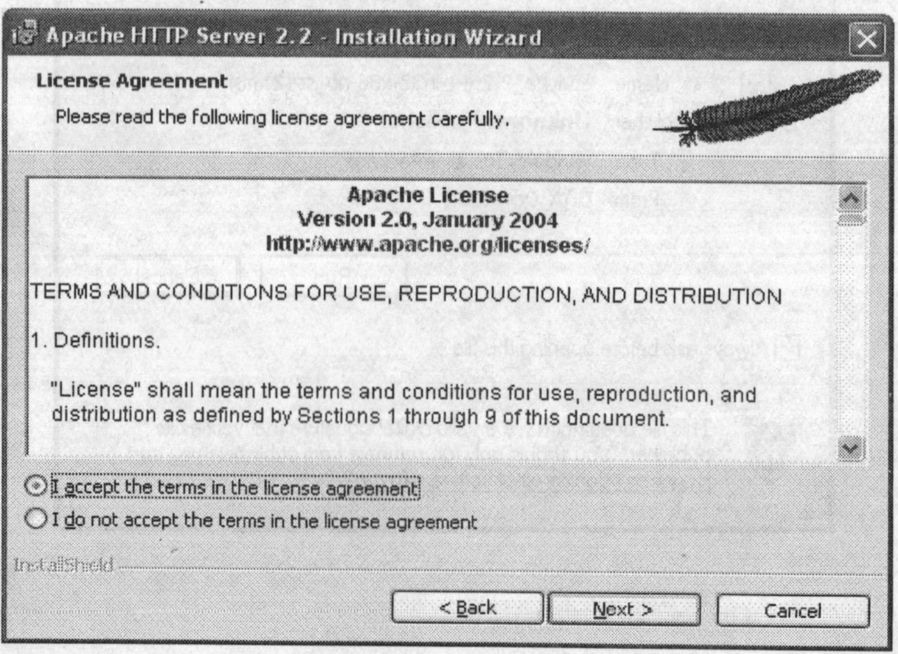

Step 5 : Read Apache HTTP Server & Click on Next button

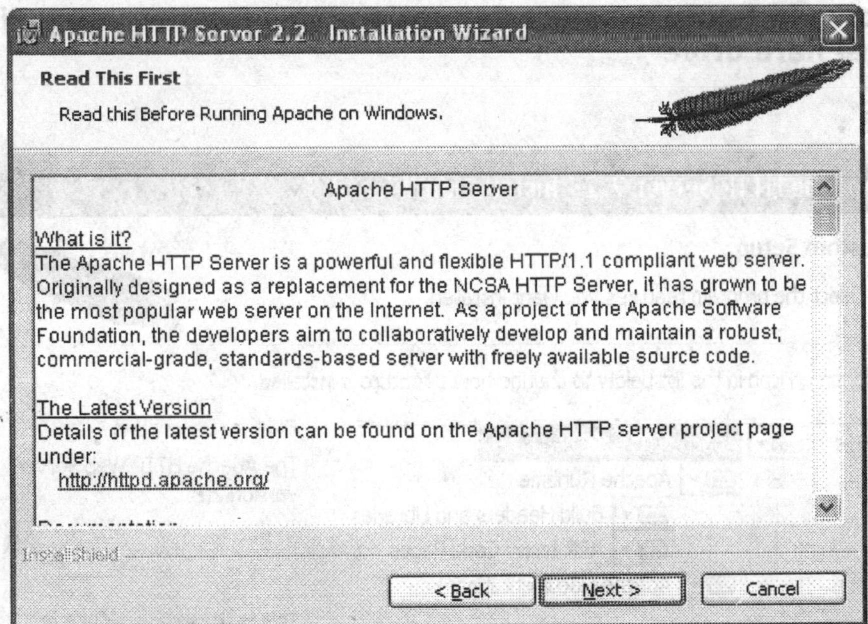

Step 6 : Provide the Server information details in the window. Network Domain & Server Name as "localhost", Admin email address as "admin@localhost"

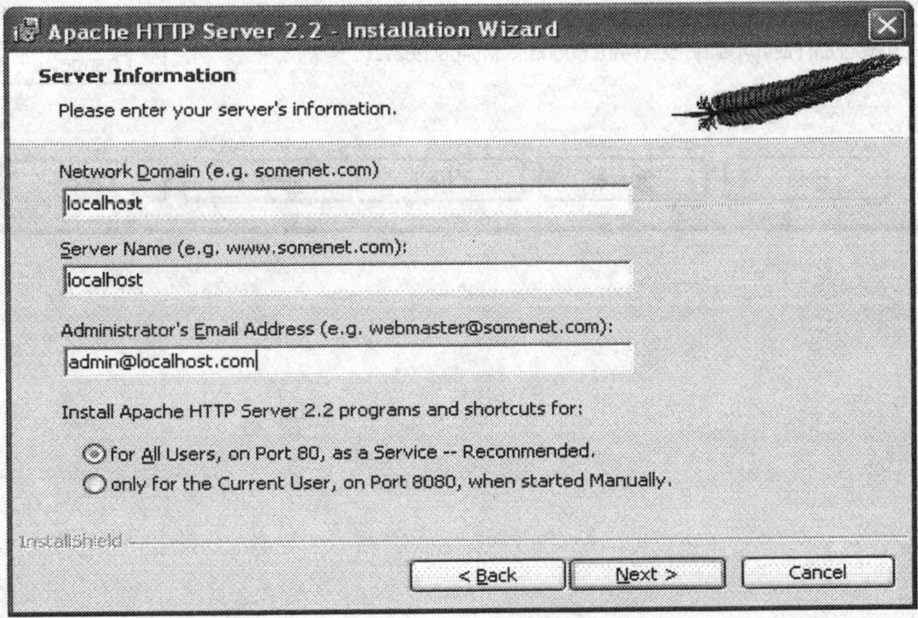

Step 7: Click on Build Headers and Libraries which is in Red cross as shown in figure & select the option 'This feature will be install on local hard drive'

Step 8 :

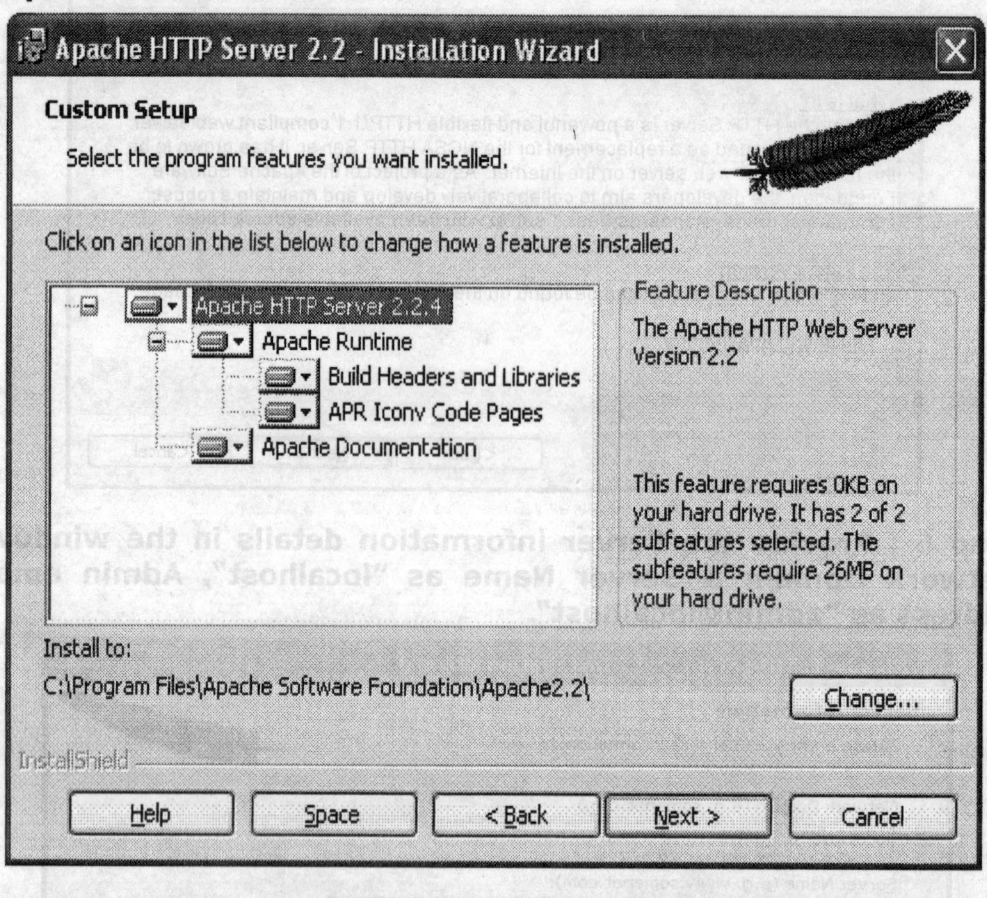

Step 9 : On the following screen you will see the default path of Apache to installs. Click the \"Change...\" , and choose whatever other name you choose your created directory structure. Click \"Next\".

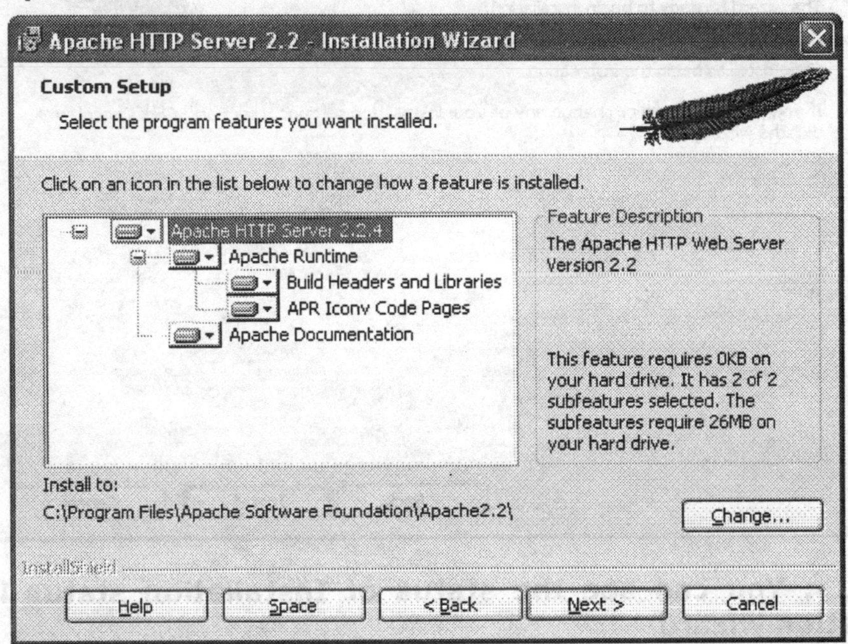

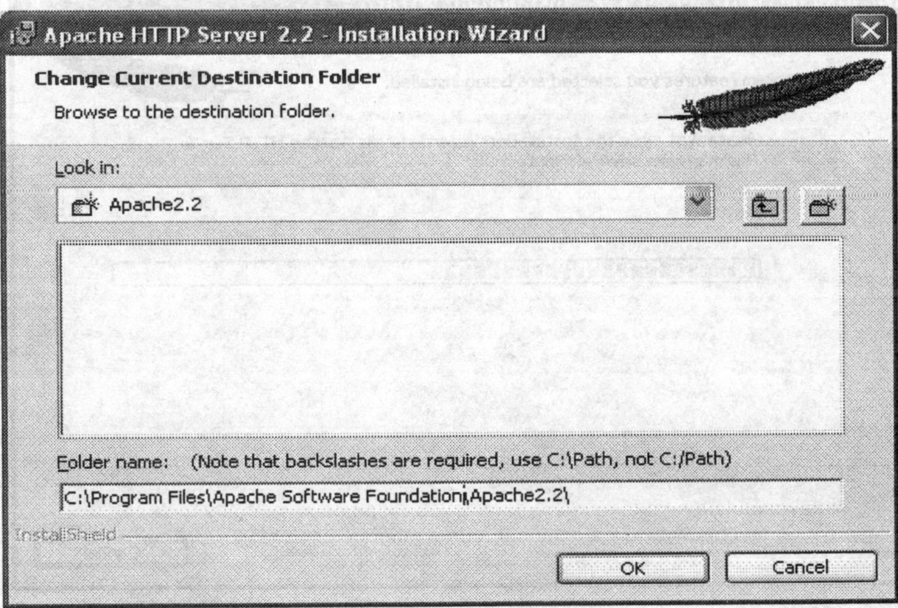

Step 10 : Click on 'Install' button to install Apache HTTP Server

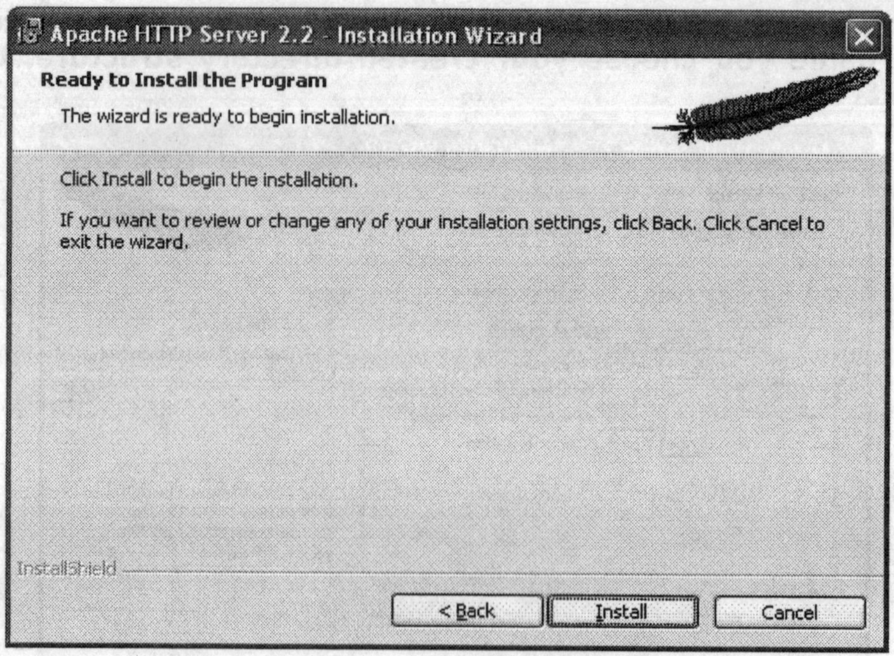

Step 11 : You can see the status of Installation status in the Installation wizard

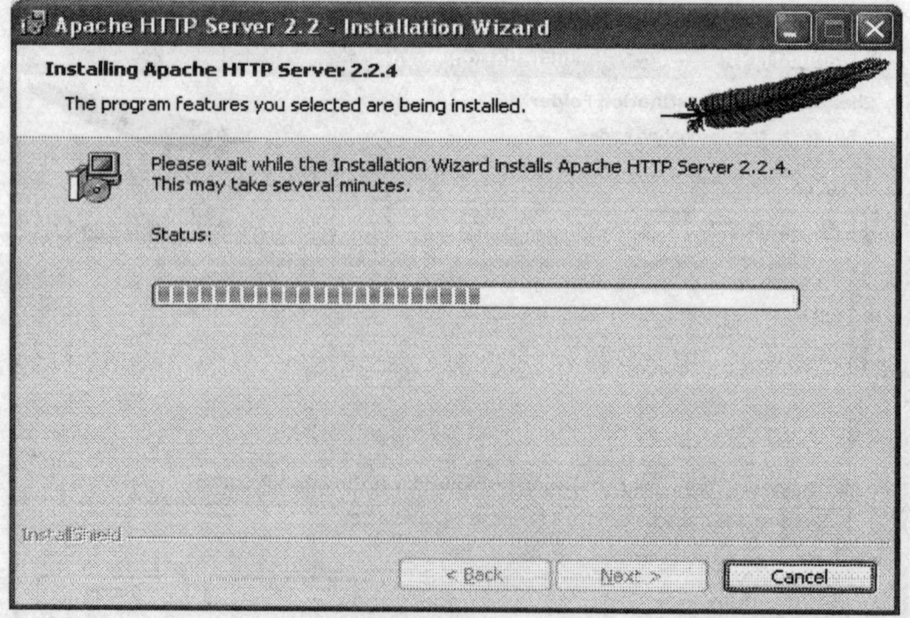

Step 12 : Once the installation has been completed, following window will get displayed. Click finish.

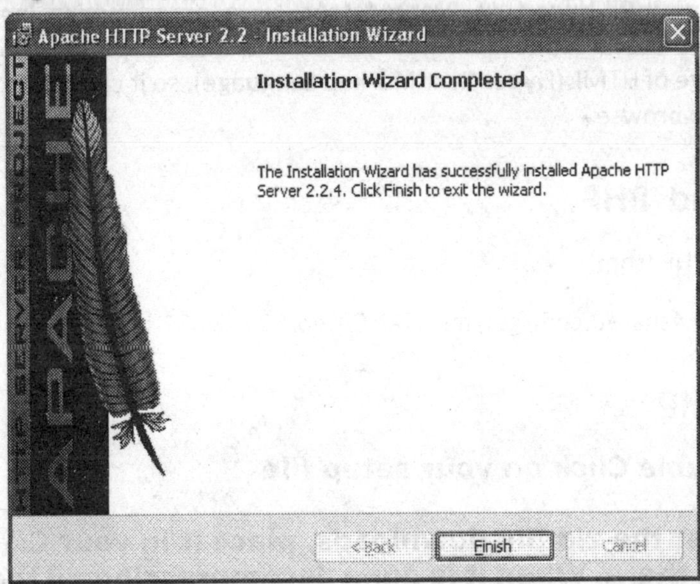

To Test Apache installation, type in the browser http://localhost/ The following window should appear.

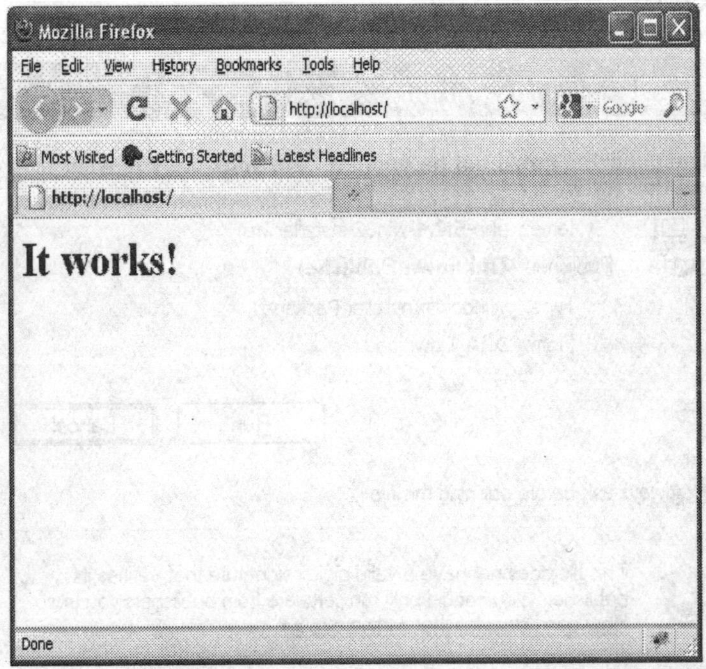

PHP

PHP (stands for **PHP: Hypertext Preprocessor**), is a programming language that is intended for web-based applications. PHP job is to "**translate**" programming commands into the language of HTML (**Hyper Text Markup Language**), so it can be displayed on your computer's web browse

1. Download PHP

Download PHP from

http://www.4shared.com/get/mlJp4XNC/php-524-win32-installer.html

2. Install PHP

Step 1 : Double Click on your setup file

Step 2 : After the zip file downloads, place it in your C:\ directory, and unzip it there. When it is done decompressing all the files, you can delete the zip file. Now your PHP is in C:\Program Files\php

Step 3 : Click on 'Run' button

Step 4 : Accept the License agreement and click the "next" button

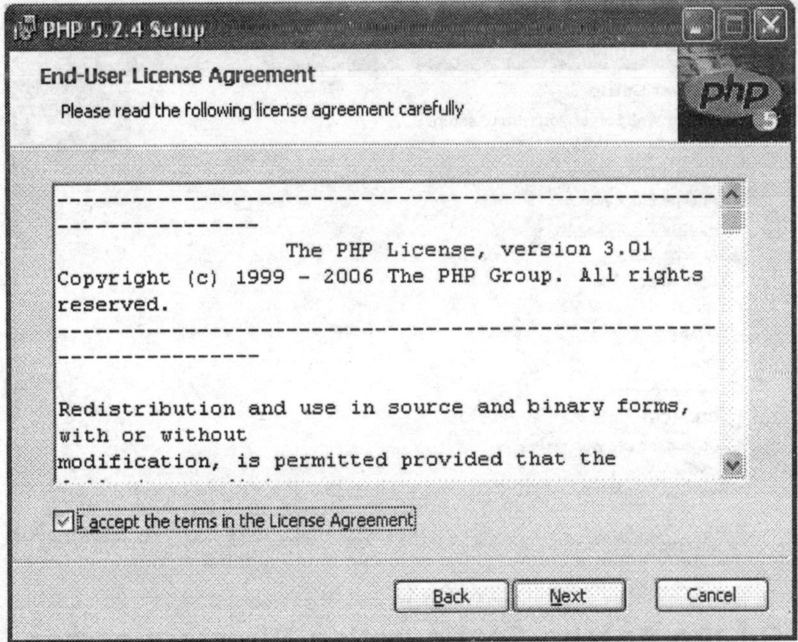

Step 5 : Change your PHP installation path OR just accept the default path – C:\Program Files\PHP\ and click "*Next*

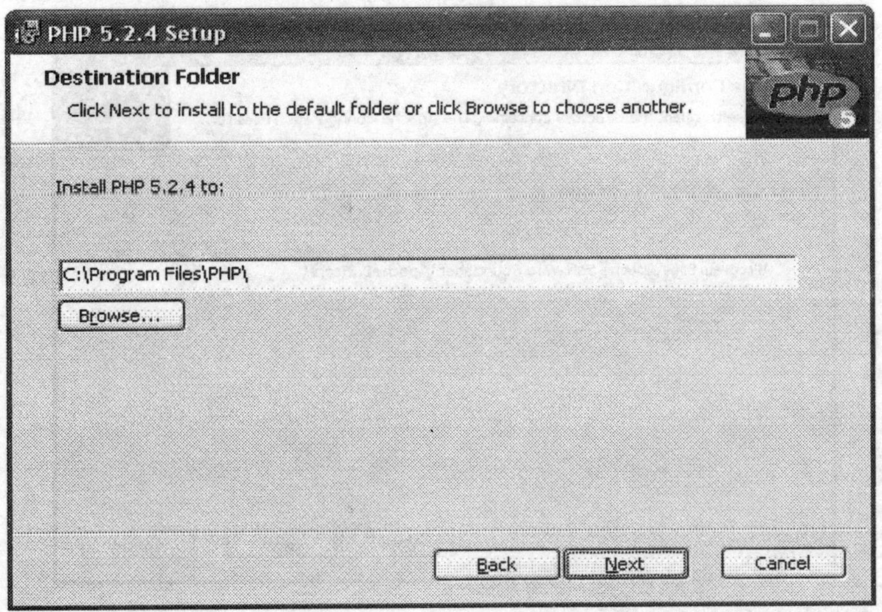

Step 6: On the Web Server Setup screen, select the Apache 2.2.x Module and click "*Next*

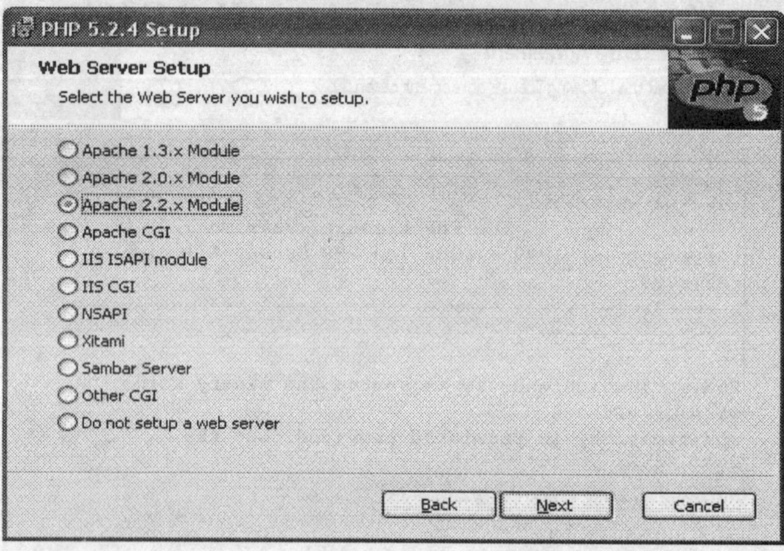

Step 7 :-On the Apache Configuration Directory screen, browse for the Apache configuration directory (conf) OR just enter C:\Program Files\Apache Software Foundation\Apache2.2\conf\ and click "*Next*" to proceed with the installation.

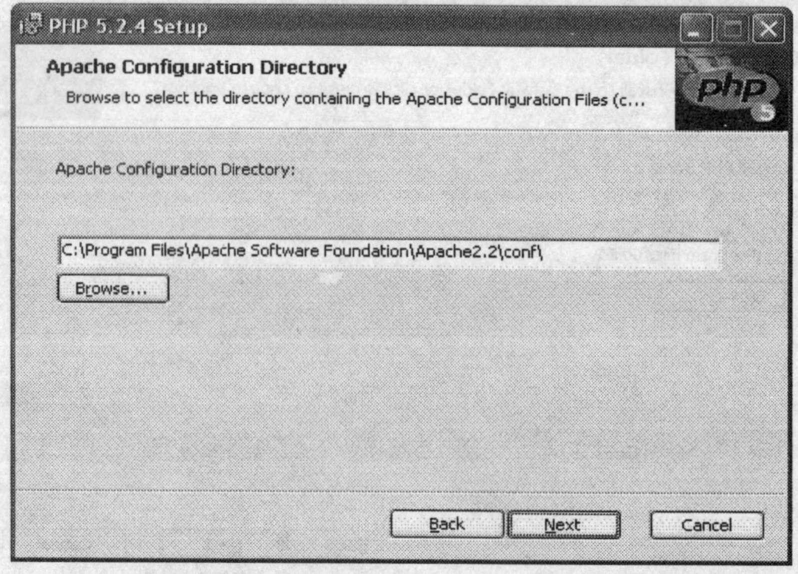

Step 8: For now, accept the default selection and click "*Next*".

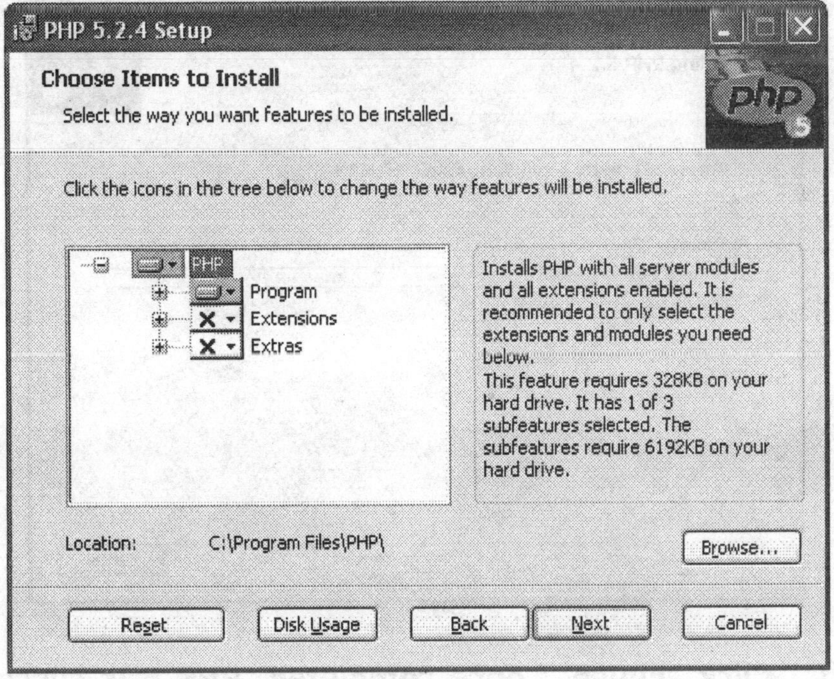

Step 9 : Click "*Install* " to install PHP 5 on Windows.

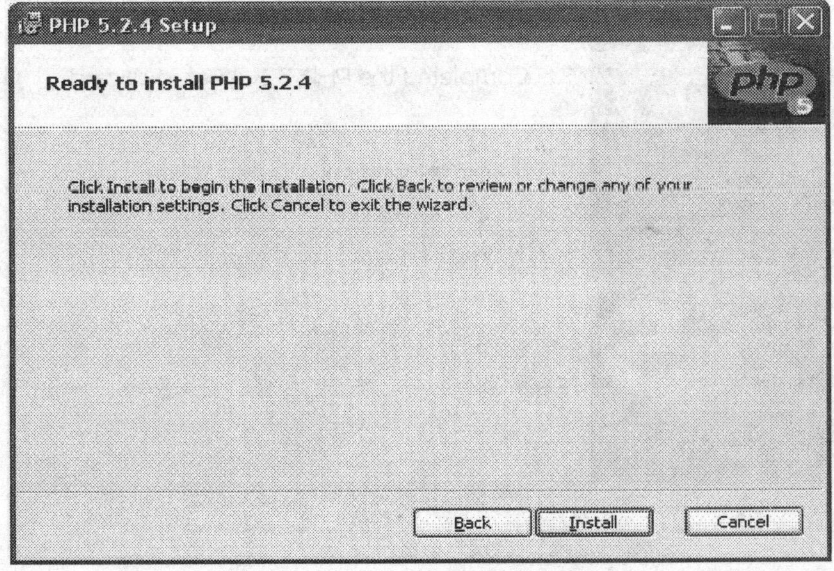

Step 10 : Installation Status

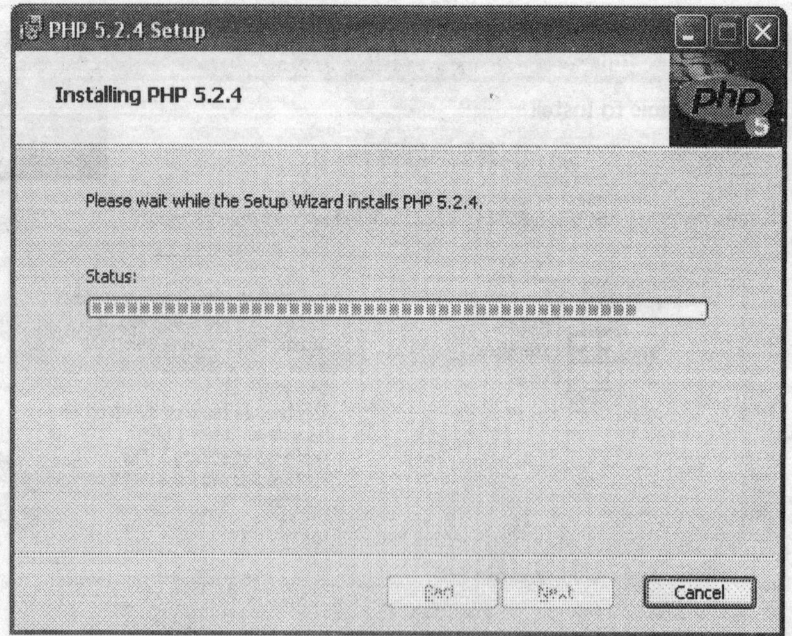

Step 11 : Click "Finish " once completed. PHP 5 is successfully installed.

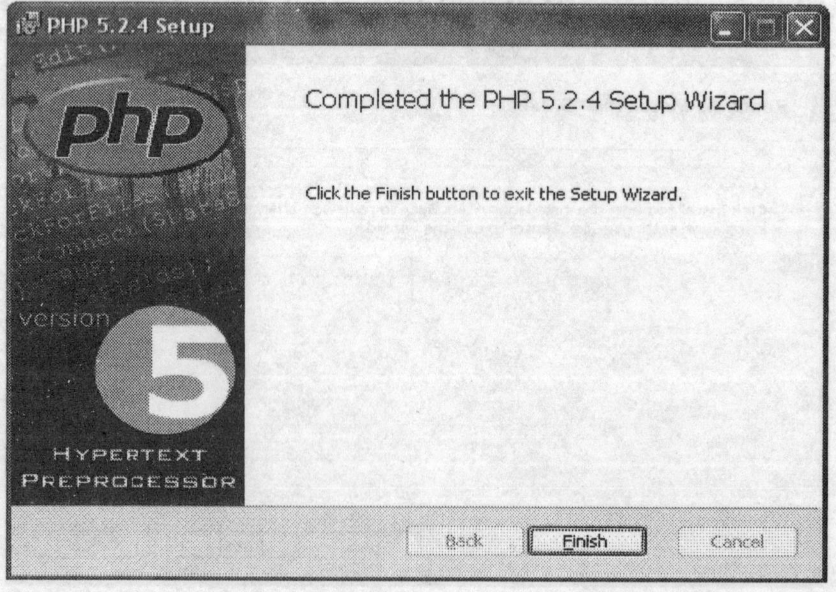

Start your Apache 2.2 server using the "Monitor Apache Servers" console (*Start -> Apache HTTP Servers 2.2.4 -> Monitor Apache Servers*). You can see that PHP was successfully Installed by checking the Apache status at the bottom of the console.

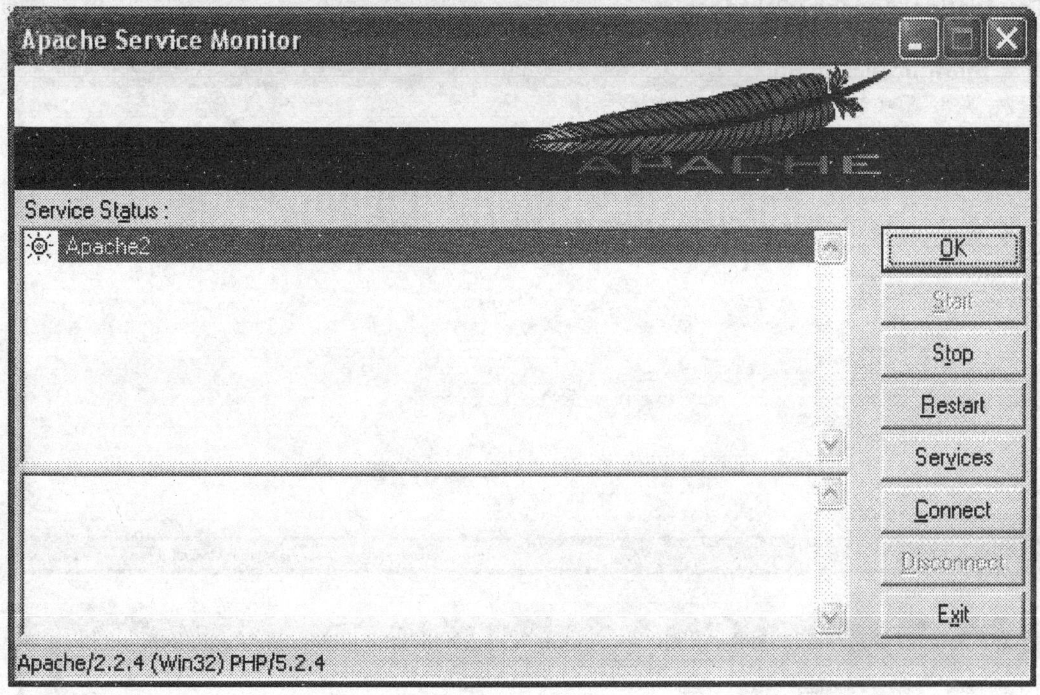

Test your PHP 5 Installation

1- Open up your Windows Notepad. Type in "<?php phpinfo(); ?>" inside the file. Save this file as "info.php" inside your Apache root directory, C:\Program Files\Apache Software Foundation\Apache2.2\htdocs.

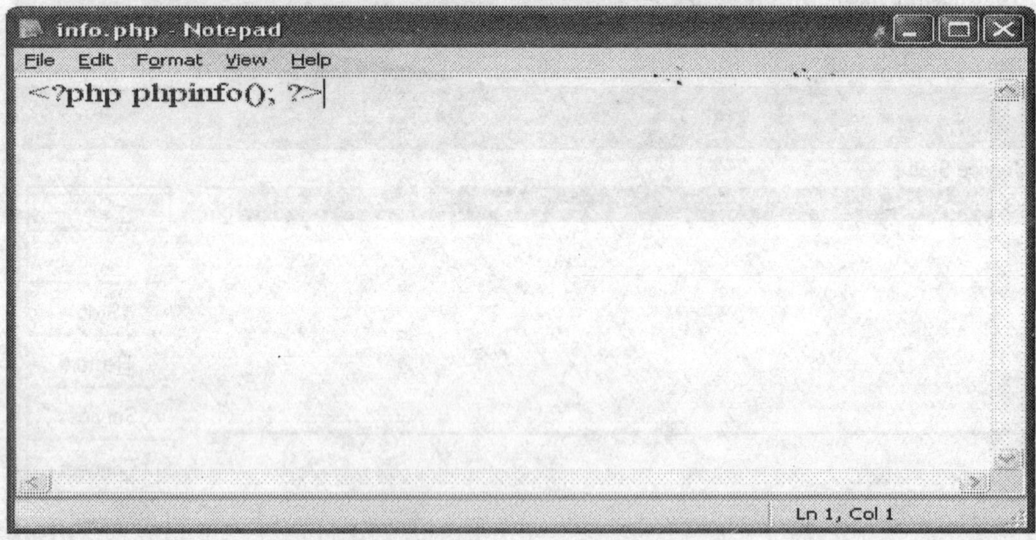

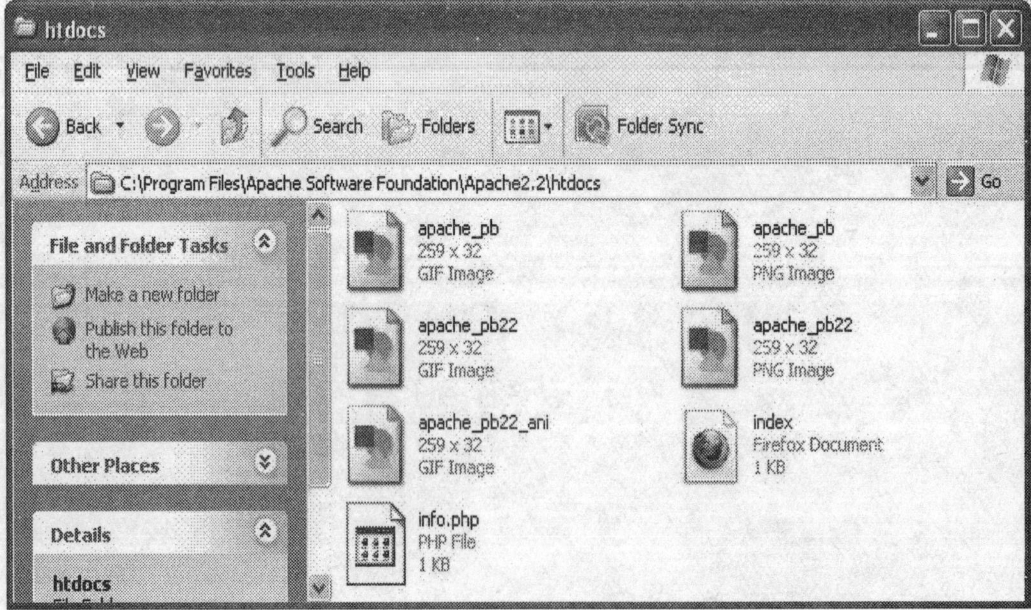

2- Open up your web browser. In the address bar, type in your web server domain name plus info.php **as the file name. Example:** *http://www.syahid.com/info.php* **. You should get a PHP configuration page just like the one below.**

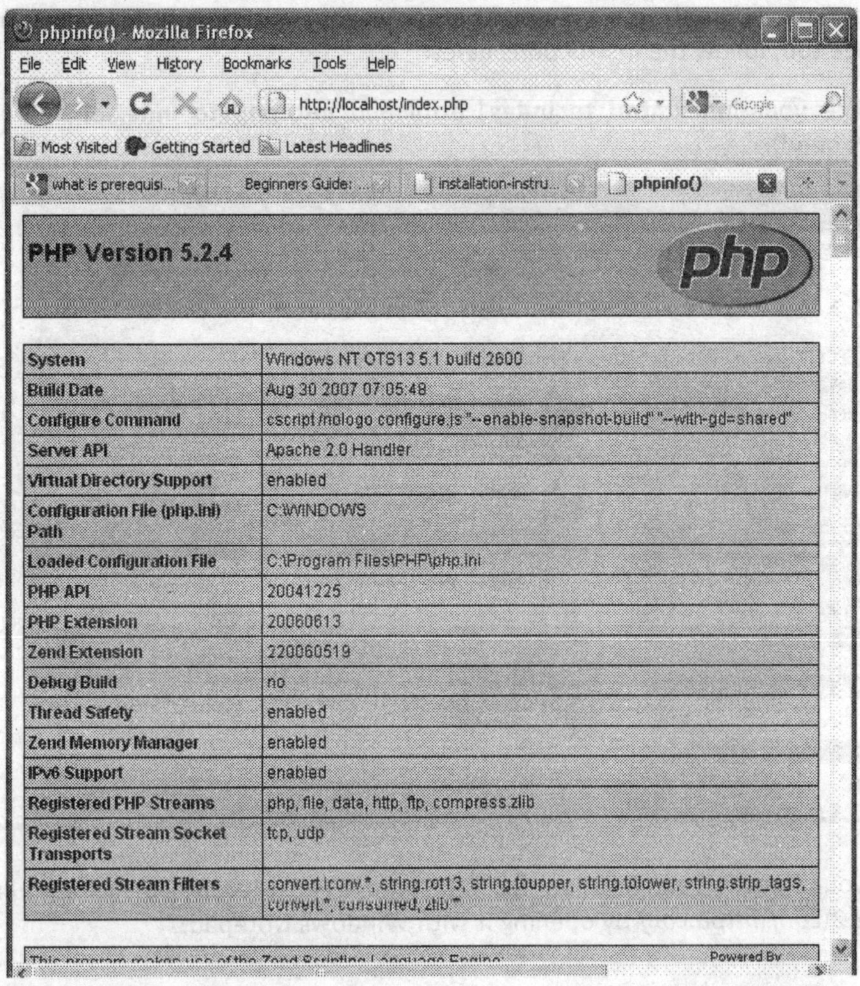

Configuration of Apache 2.2.4 & php 5.2.4

What happens if you change your index.html (default web server homepage) to index.php and try to access your homepage? Apache will not recognize it and you won't see anything displayed on the page. To **make sure Apache recognizes index.php as a default homepage** too, follow the instructions below.

1- Rename your **index.html to index1.html** and **info.php to index.php** (for testing purposes only!).

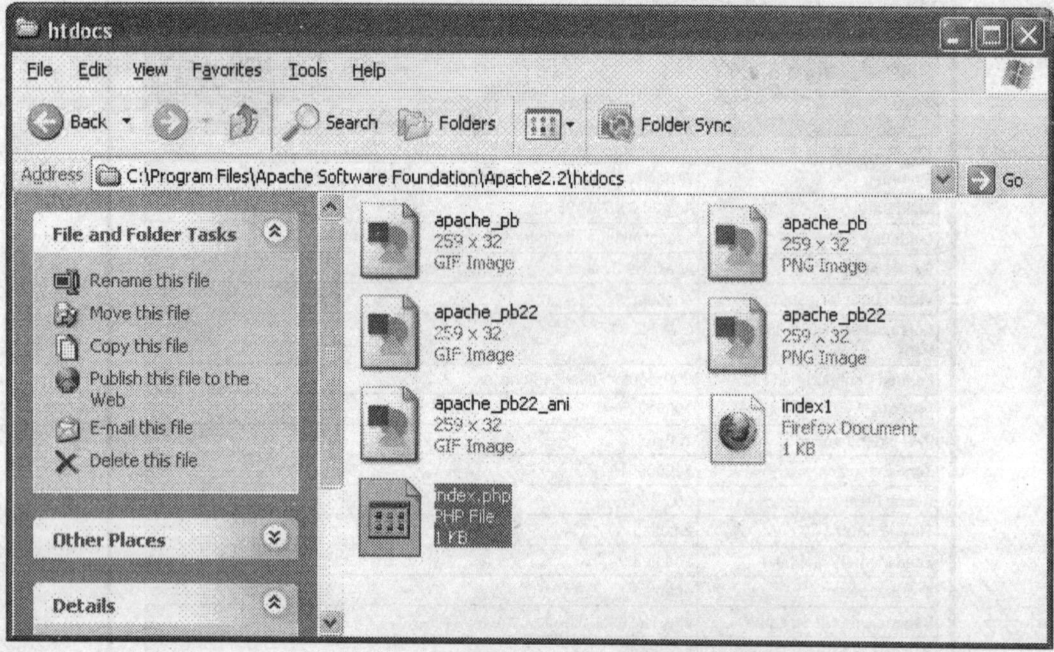

2- Edit your Apache configuration file, *C:\Program Files\Apache Software Foundation\Apache2.2\conf\httpd.conf* by opening it with Windows Notepad.

3- Find a line that starts with "**DirectoryIndex index.html…**". Add index.php at the end of the line . Save the file and restart your Apache Server from the "Monitor Apache Servers" console.

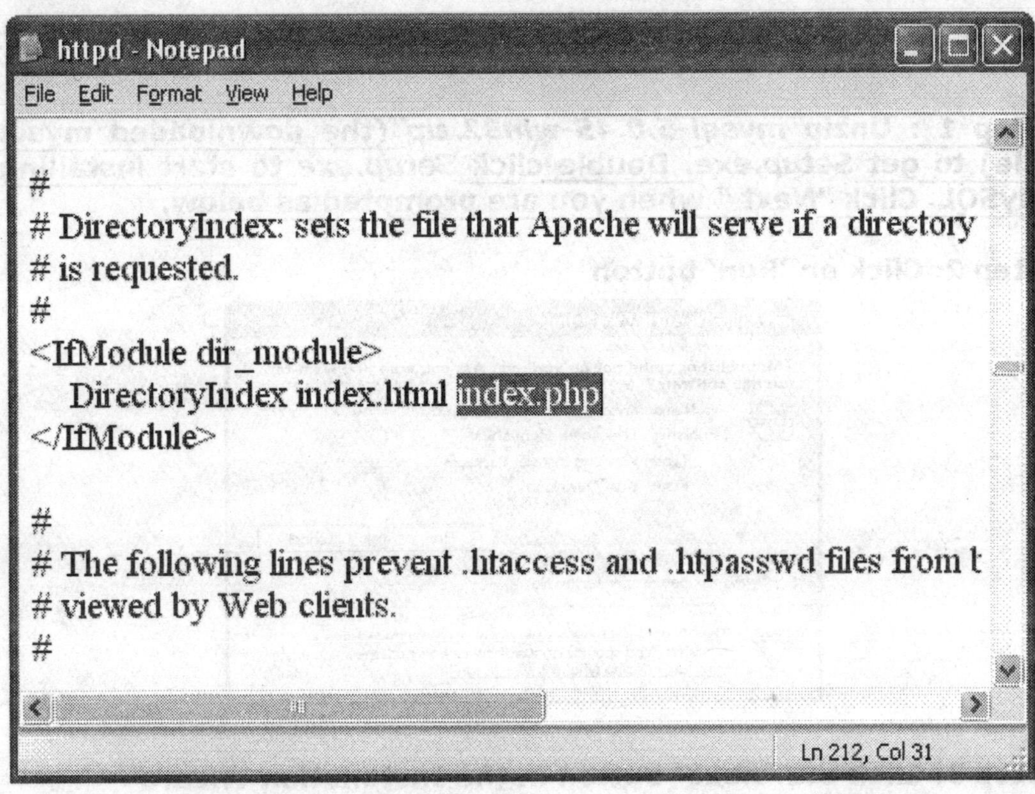

Install MySQL 5.0 Community Edition on Windows

Download from

http://mysql.mirror.iweb.ca/Downloads/MySQL-5.0/

Step 1 : Unzip *mysql-5.0.45-win32.zip* (the downloaded mysql file) to get *Setup.exe*. Double click *Setup.exe* to start installing MySQL. Click "*Next* " when you are prompted as below.

Step 2: Click on 'Run' button

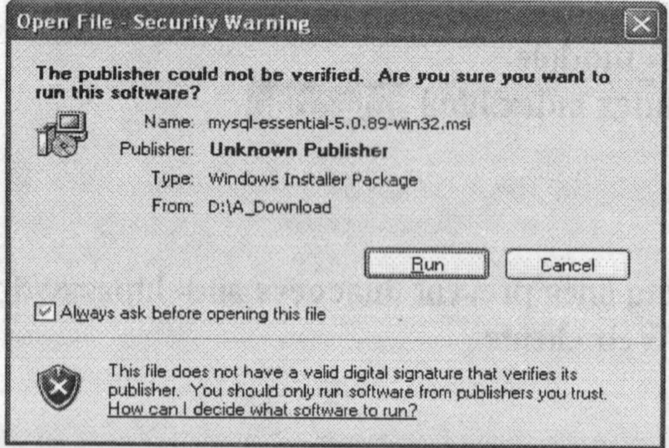

Step 3: Click the "next" button in the Installation Wizard

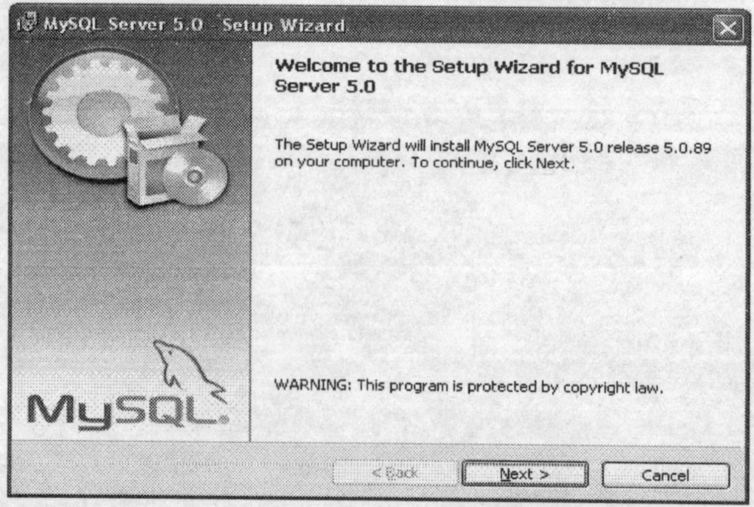

Step 4 : Choose Custom and press \"Next

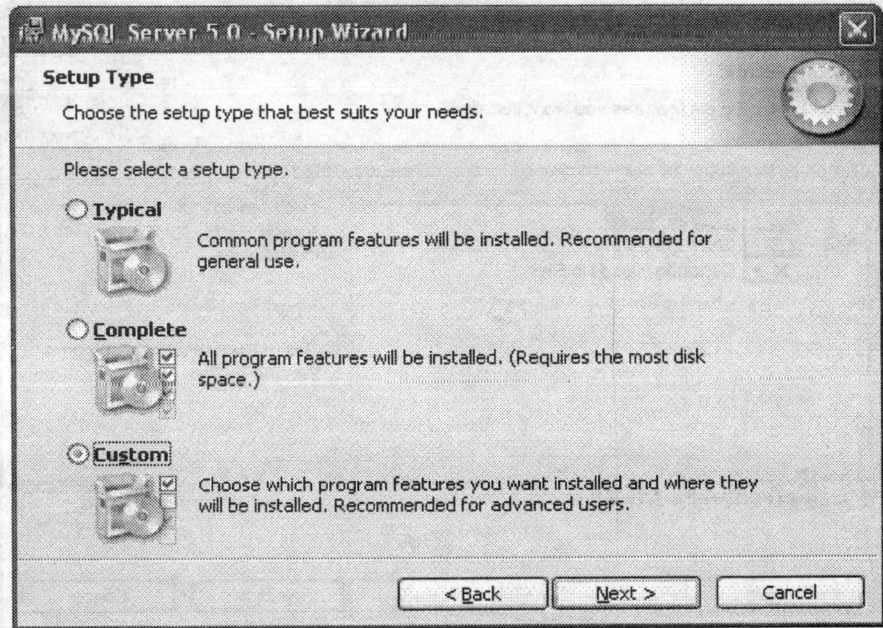

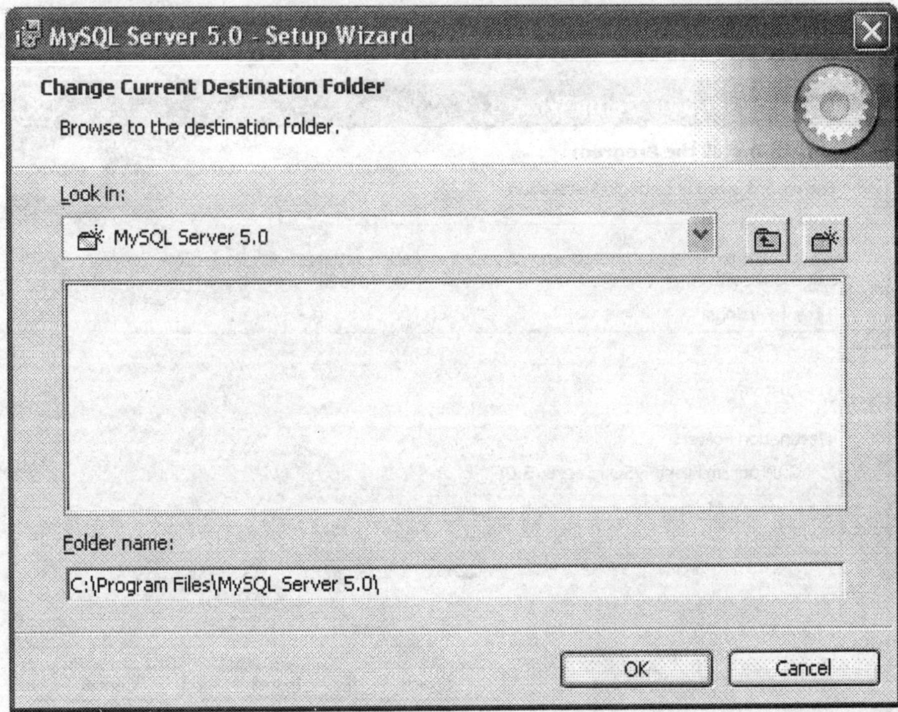

Step 5 : Specify the path to install

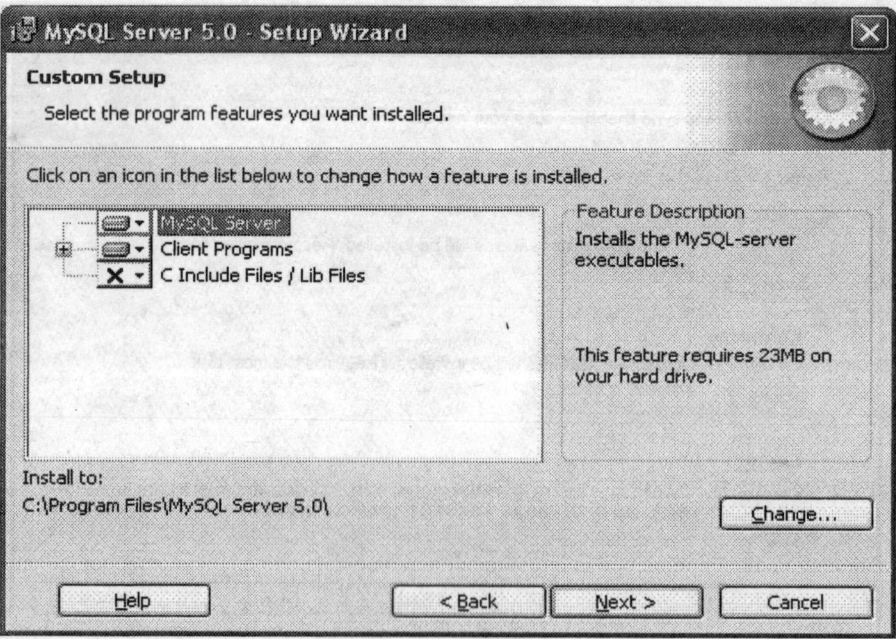

Step 7 : Click on install button to install MySql

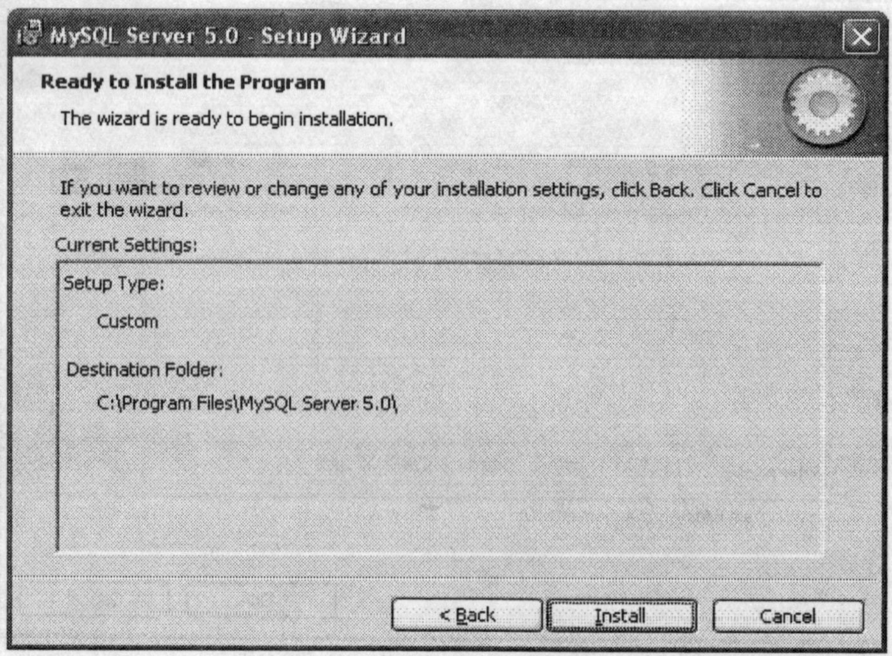

Step 8 : You can see the status of Installation status in the Installation wizard

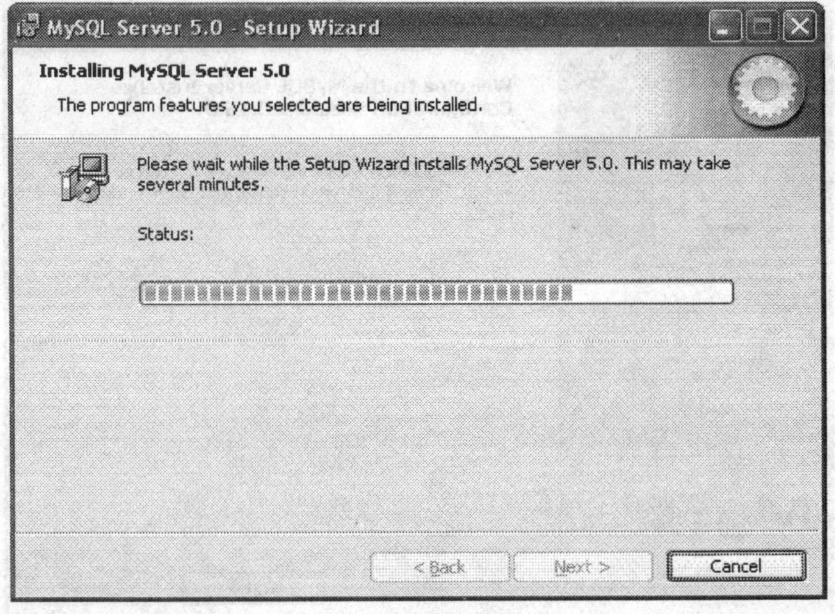

Step 10 : Click finish" Now you finished installation but you need to configure mysql.

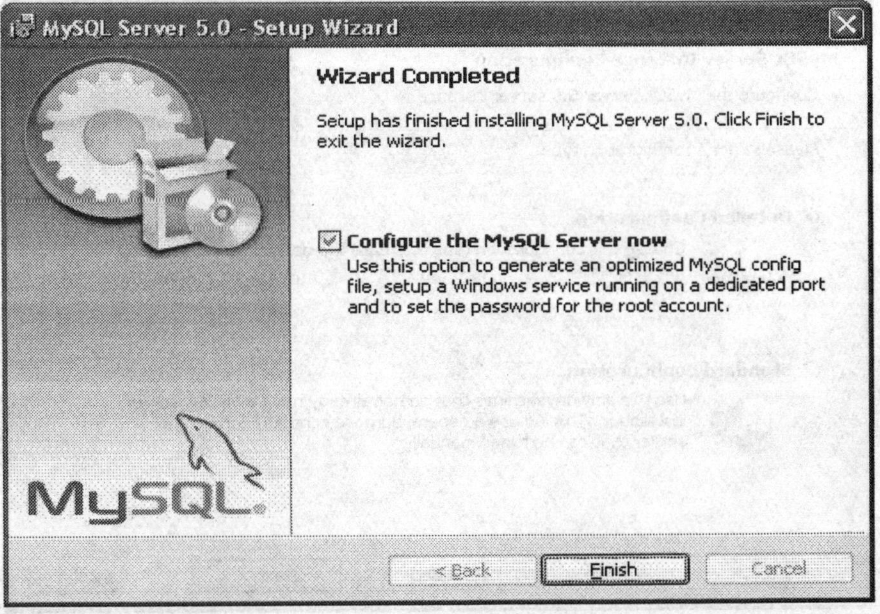

Step 11 : MySQL Configuration file wizard will open after your setup wizard. Click "Next" to proceed

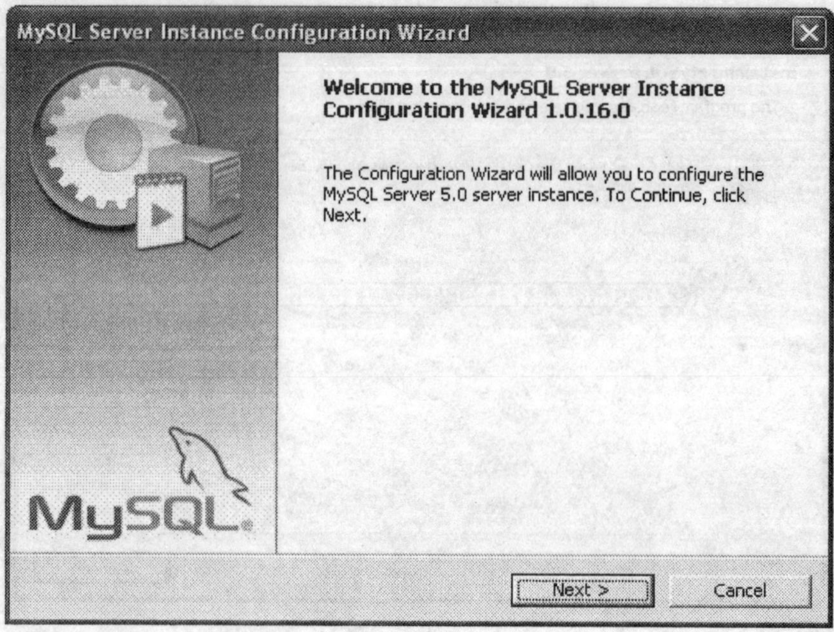

Step 12 : Select "Detailed configuration" & Click on "Next" button

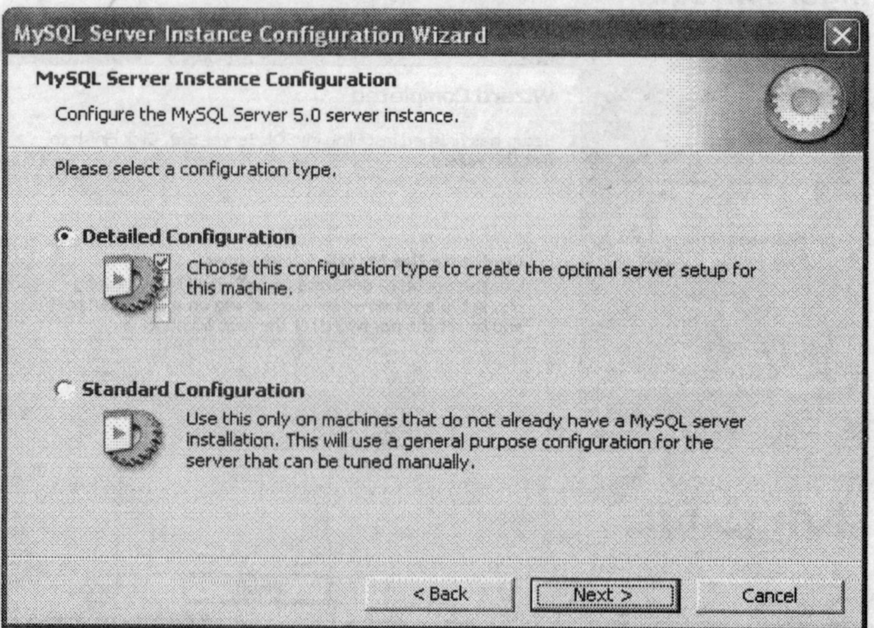

Step 13 : Next you will be getting a server type wizard. Choose "Developer machine" then click "Next" button

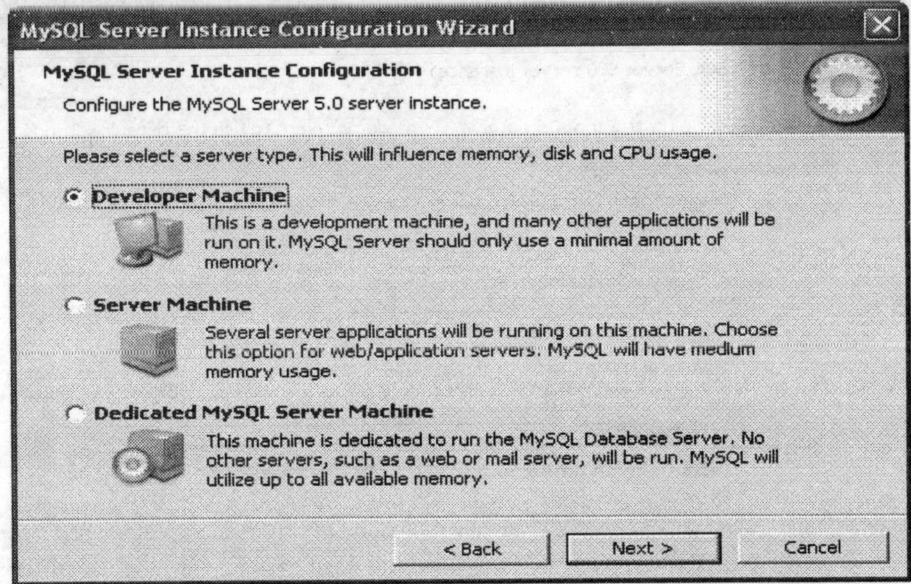

Step 14 : Choose "Multifunctional Database" and click "Next"

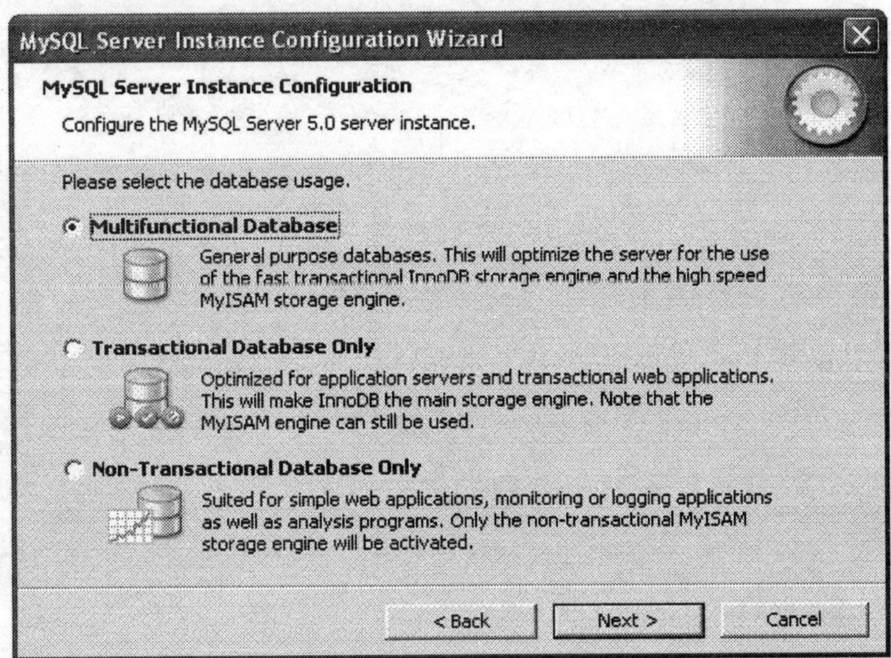

Step 15 : Click on Next

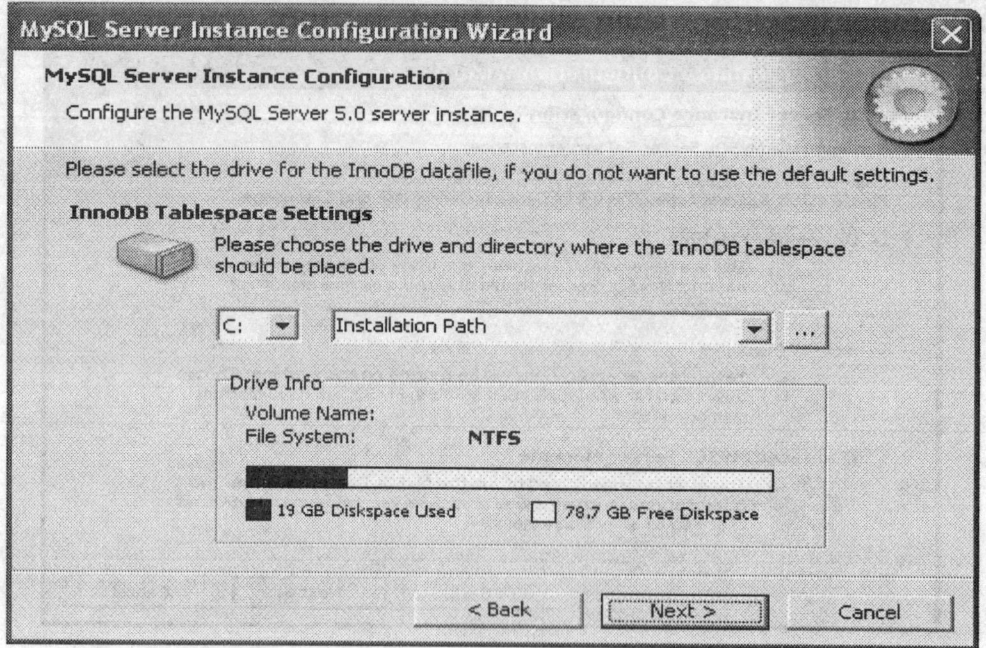

Step 16 : Click if the no. of concurrent connection is less than 20 then go for "Decision support (DSS)/OLAP. If the no. of concurrent connection is 500 at a time (load is heavy) then go for Online Transaction Processing (OLTP) If the no. of concurrent connection is neither 20 or else not heavy like 500 then go for manual testing. In this documentation, I had chosen "Decision support (DSS)/OLAP".

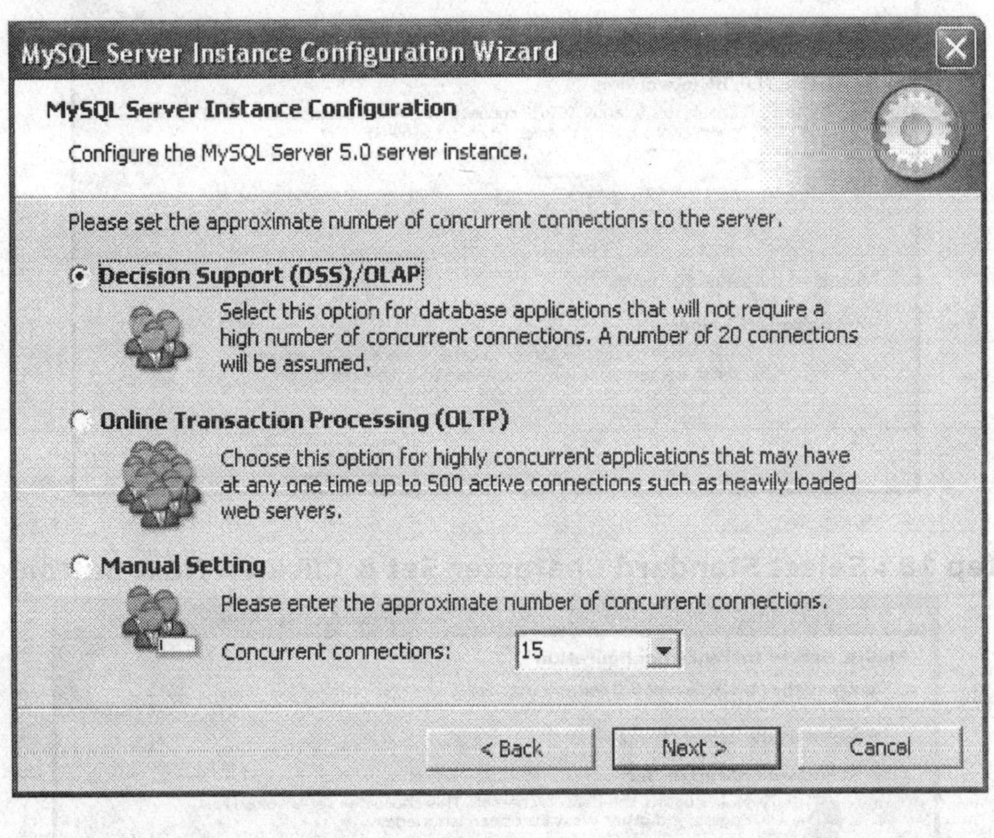

Step 17 : Now you have to set the network port. By default MySQL you will be having 3306 port, if in your machine some other Database server is using 3306 port then go for different PORT(3307, 3308,3309).

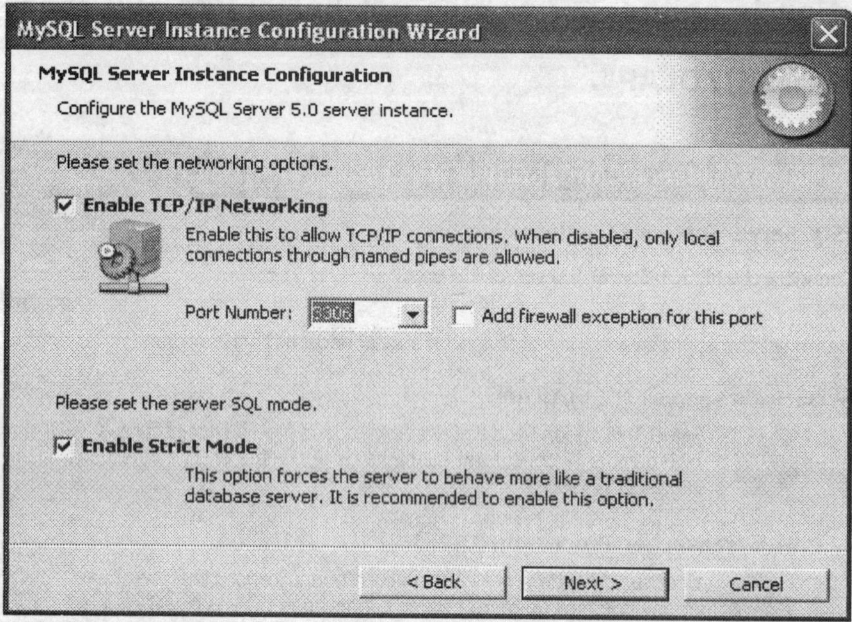

Step 18 : Select Standard Character Set & Click on Next button

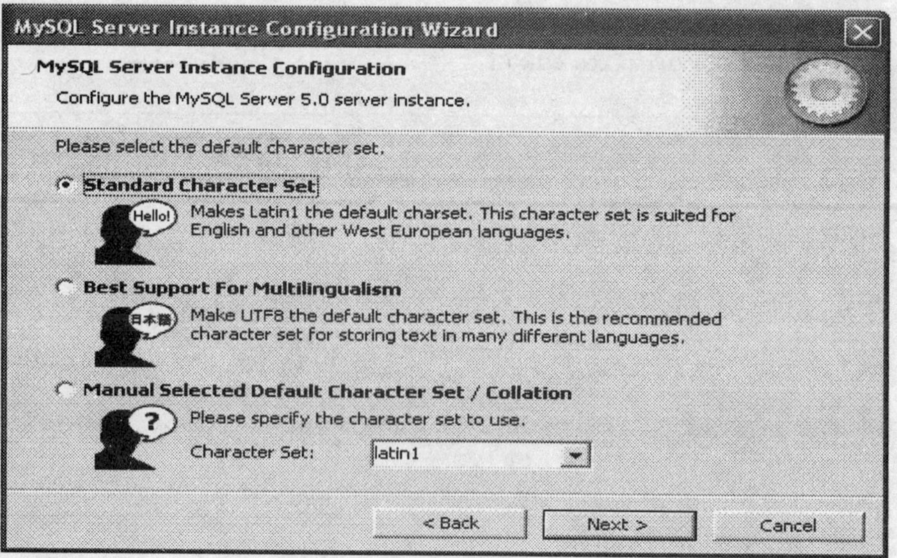

Step 19 : Now you will be getting Windows option window, where you can set the name for mysql service (By default MySQL). Choose Service Name as MySql & Click on "Next" button

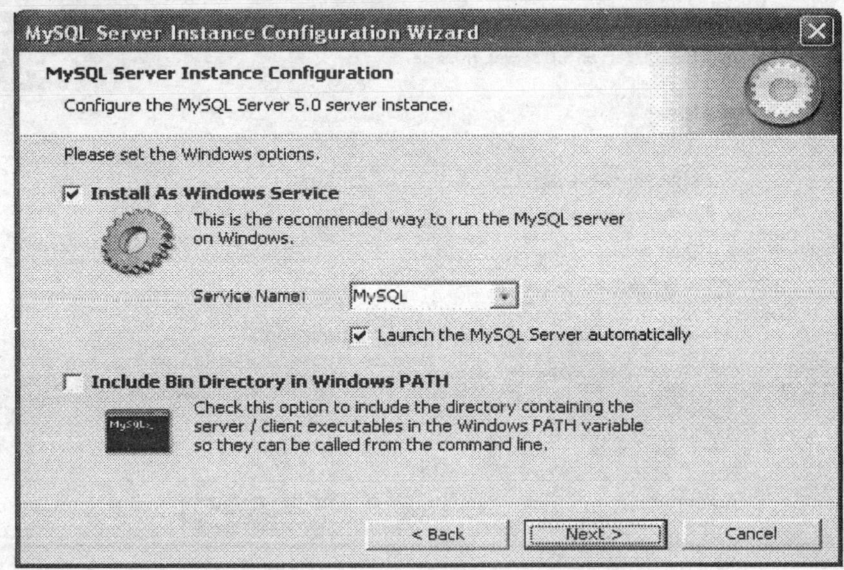

Step 20 : Give root password for mysql (for e.g. I gave root as password) & click on Next button

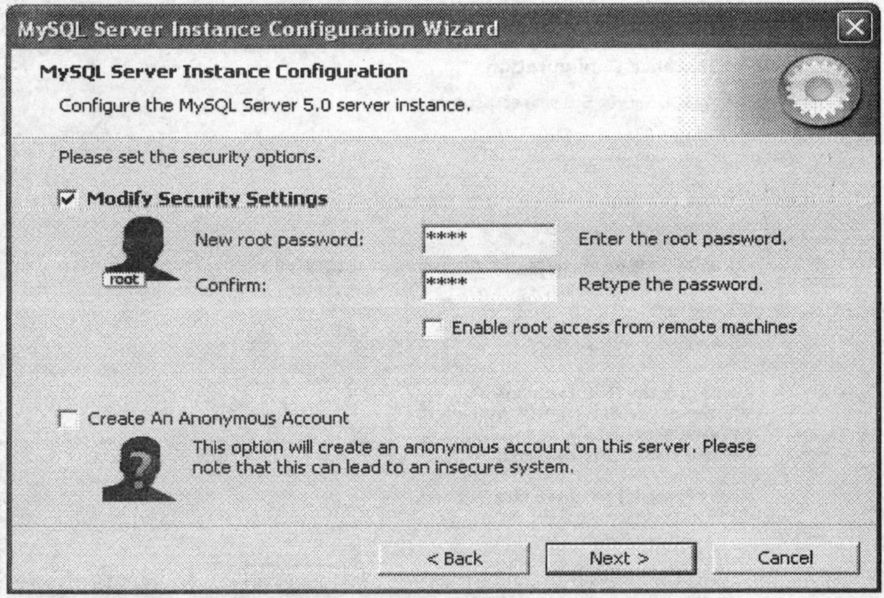

Step 21 : The Wizard will check whether mysql is configured properly & services are running or not.

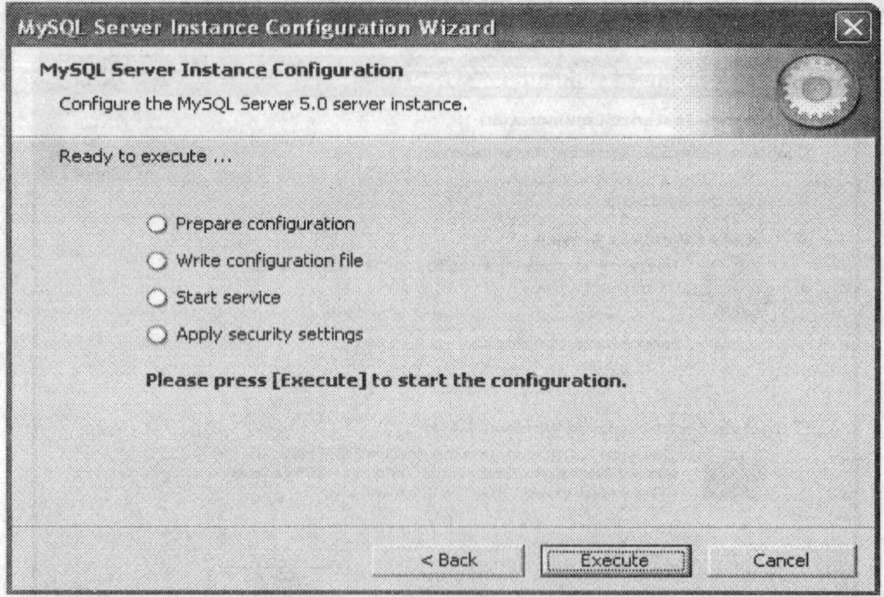

Step 22 : Following window appears, click on finish to complete the configuration.

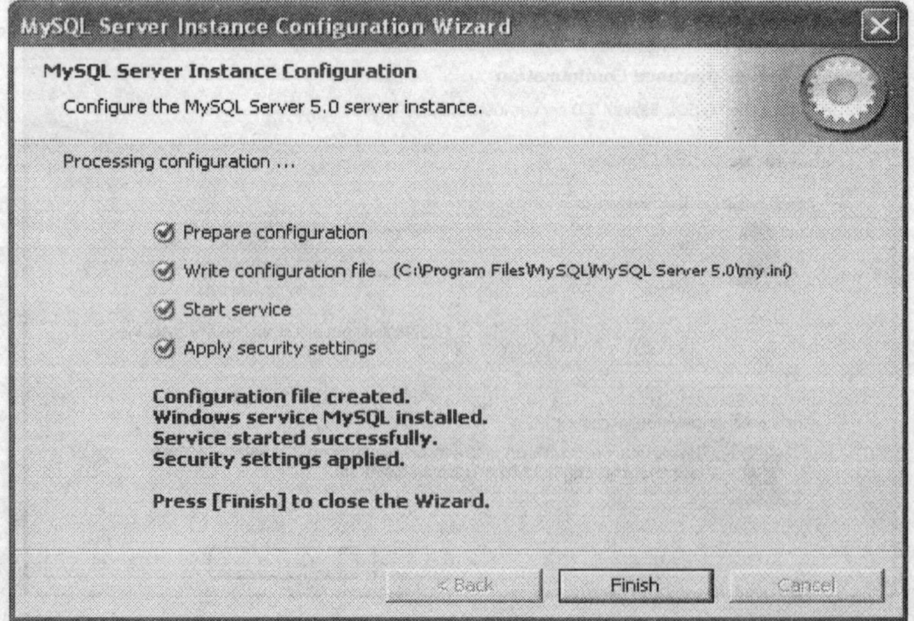

Step 23 : Make sure MySQL runs automatically after installation. You can check the status from Administrative Tools Services snap in (*Start -> Programs -> Administrative Tools -> Services*), also available via Control Panel.

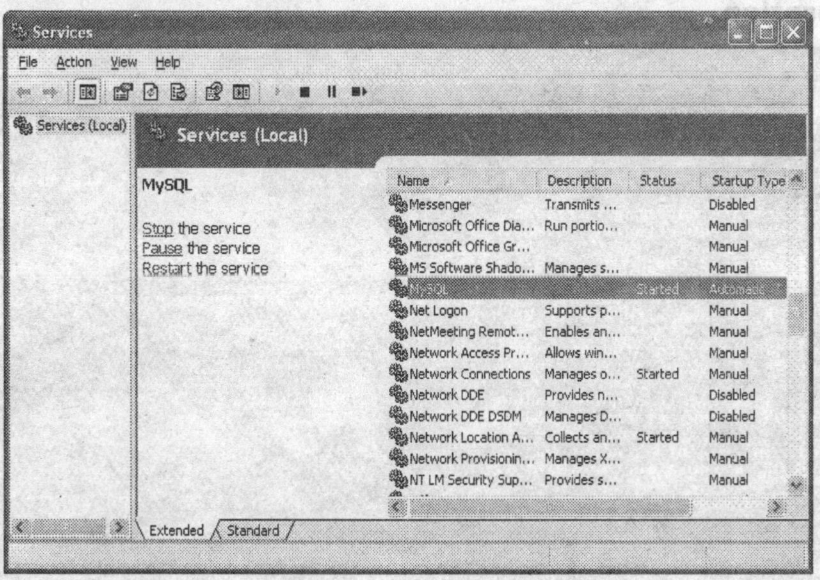

Step 24 : (OPTIONAL) Open your DOS command prompt (*Run -> cmd*). Type in "*net stat -na*". Check out ports opened by MySQL (3306) and Apache (80). That means the services are up and running

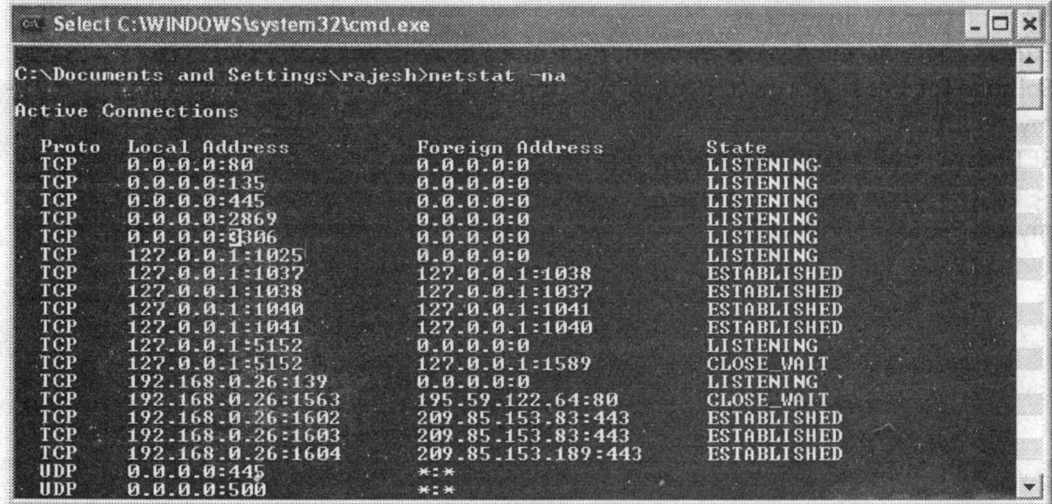

Step 25 : (OPTIONAL) Run some of MySQL commands to further ensure that the installation is a success. Check out and follow the commands as pictured below. User account is root and password depends on what you have entered previously during your MySQL configuration.

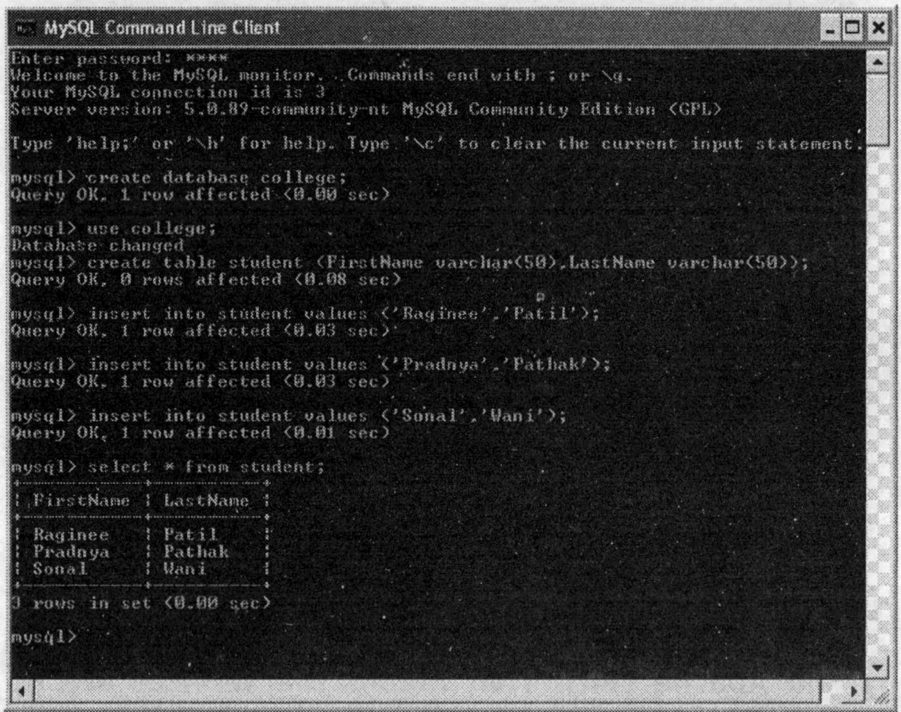

Note : If there is an error as
ERROR 1045: Access denied for user: 'root@localhost' (Using password: NO)
Solution for this is that go to your mysql prompt & type
mysql> UPDATE mysql.user
SET Password=PASSWORD('newpwd')
-> WHERE User='root';
mysql> FLUSH PRIVILEGES;

Configure PHP 5.2.4 with MySQL 5.0.89

Previously, we have installed PHP with minimal modules / extension. To add MySQL support to PHP, you need to change your PHP installation – by adding the MySQL extension on top of your PHP installation. Please make sure that your original PHP 5 MSI installer still remains at its original place .

Step 1: Open the *Add / Remove Programs* console via Windows Control Panel. Find the PHP 5.x.x entry and click "*Change* ".

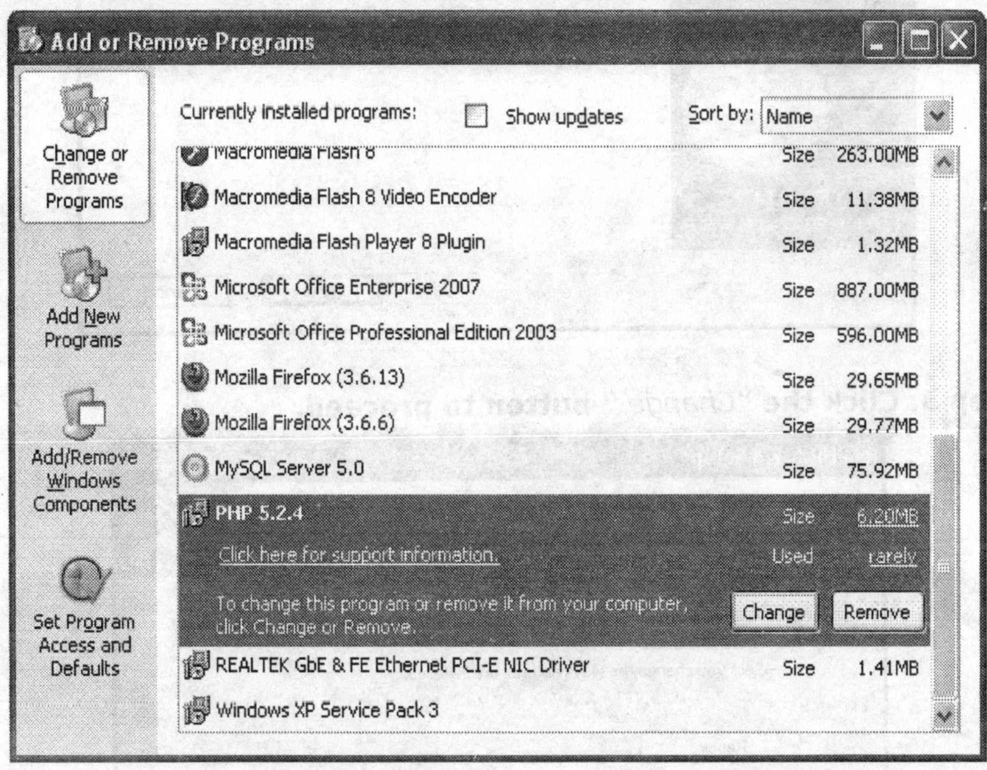

Step 2 : Click "*Next* " once you are prompted the Welcome page.

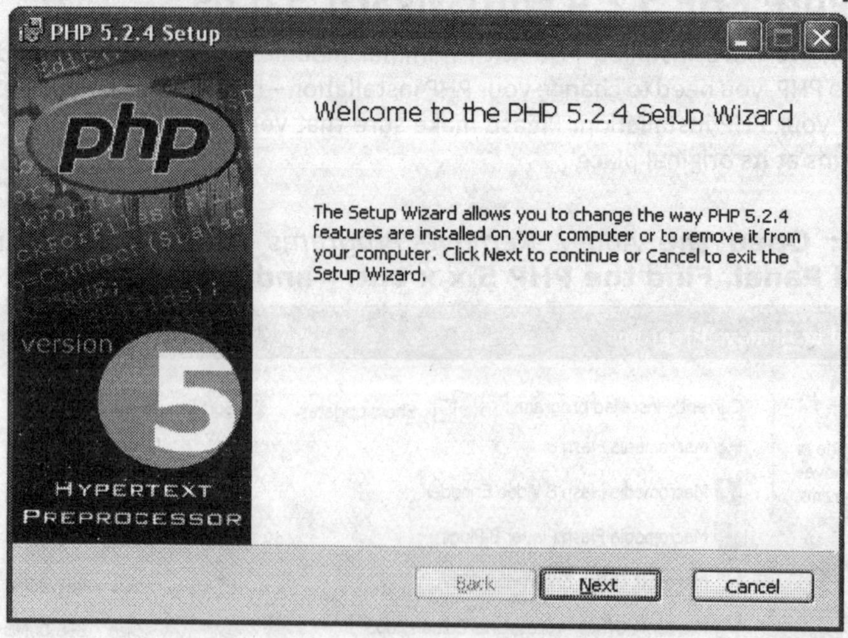

Step 3: Click the "*Change* " button to proceed.

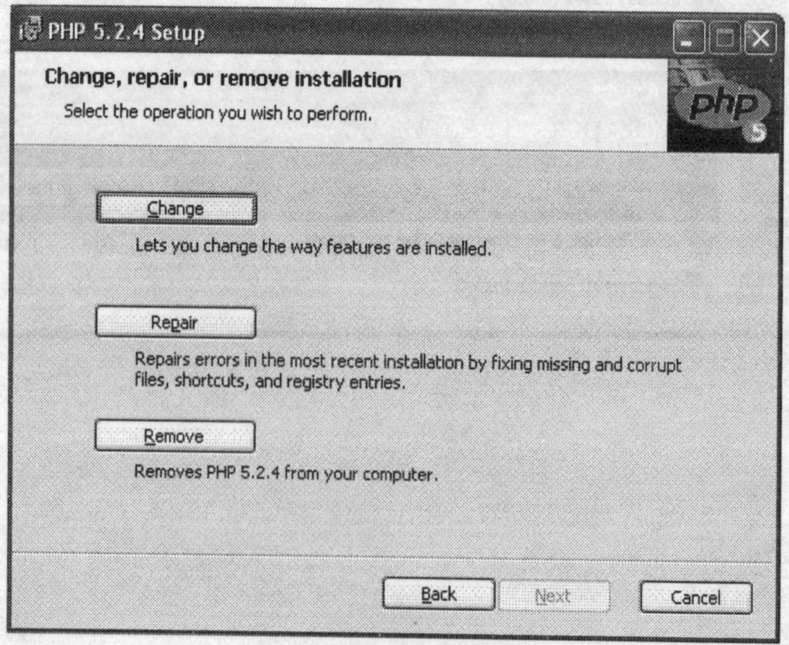

Step 4: Select Apache 2.2.x as shown in the picture below. Click "*Next*" once again

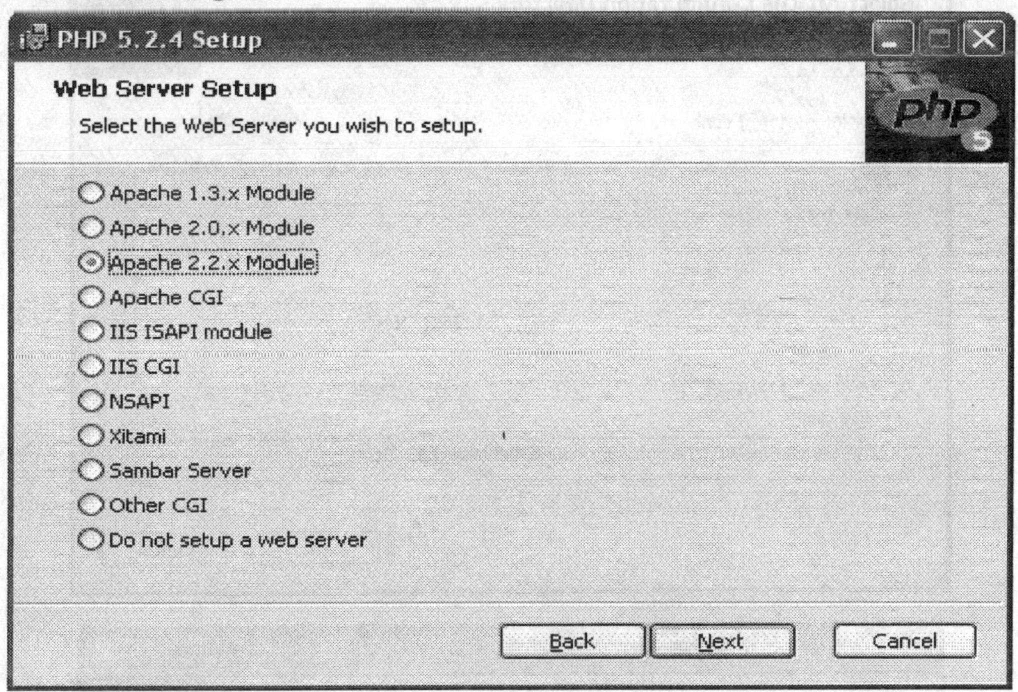

Step 5: Select your Apache configuration directory (conf) – the directory where your httpd.conf resides. Click "*Next*" once done.

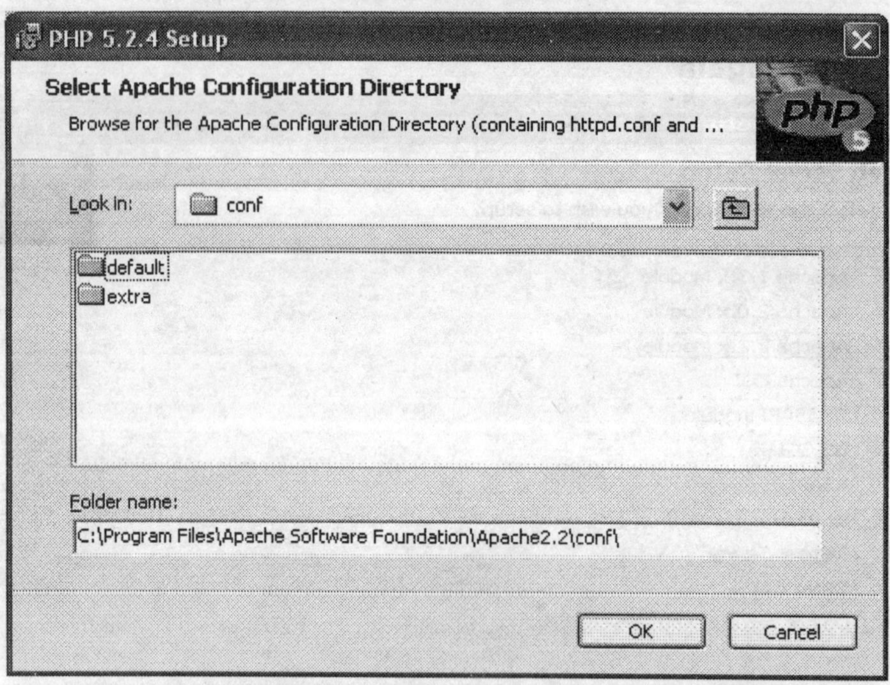
PHP 5.2.4 Setup
Select Apache Configuration Directory
Browse for the Apache Configuration Directory (containing httpd.conf and ...
Look in:
conf
default
extra
Folder name:
C:\Program Files\Apache Software Foundation\Apache2.2\conf\
OK
Cancel

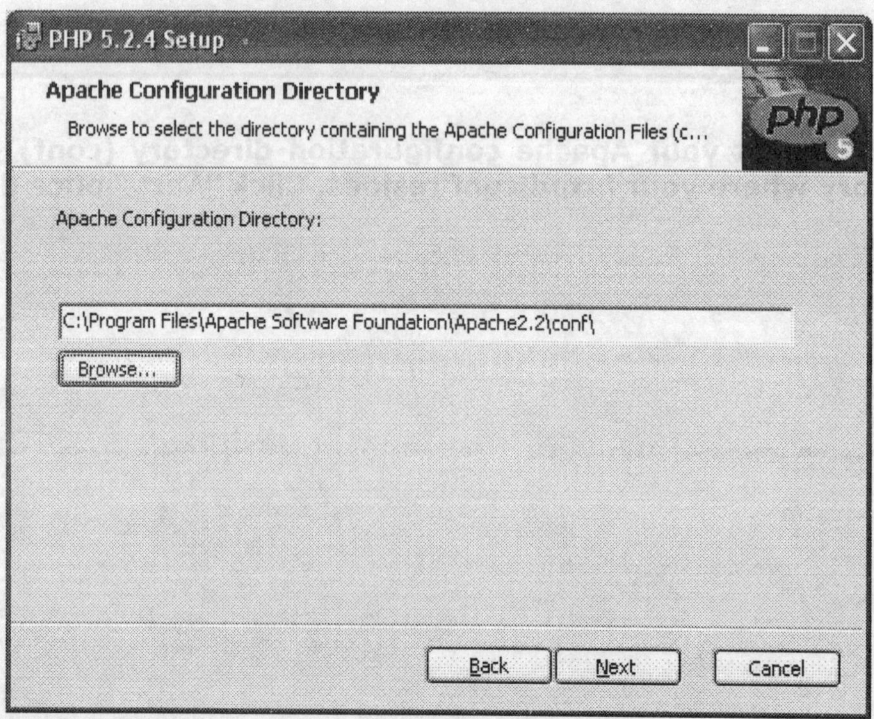
PHP 5.2.4 Setup
Apache Configuration Directory
Browse to select the directory containing the Apache Configuration Files (c...
Apache Configuration Directory:
C:\Program Files\Apache Software Foundation\Apache2.2\conf\
Browse...
Back
Next
Cancel

Step 6 : On the "Choose items to install" screen, click on the plus (+) icon next to Extensions to expand the list.

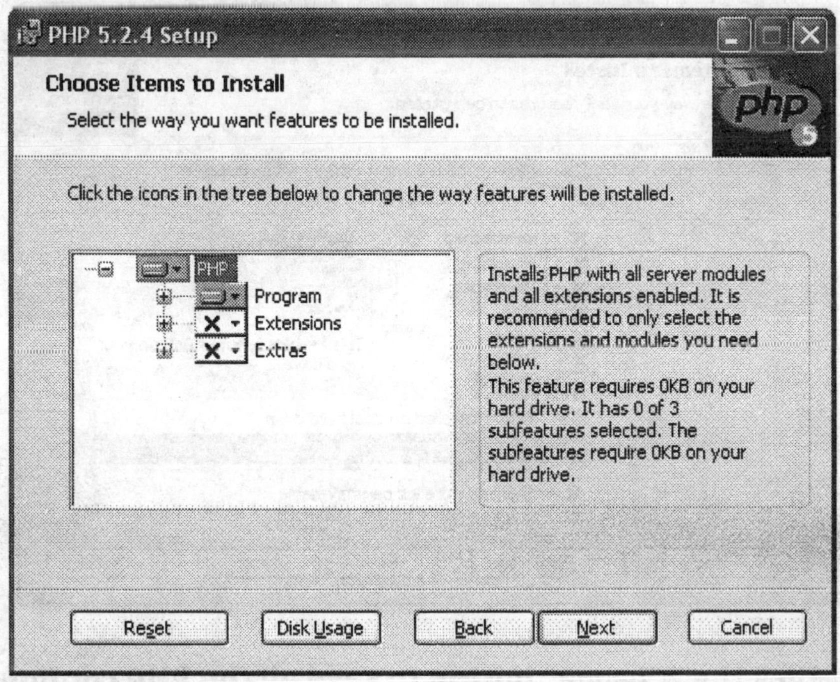

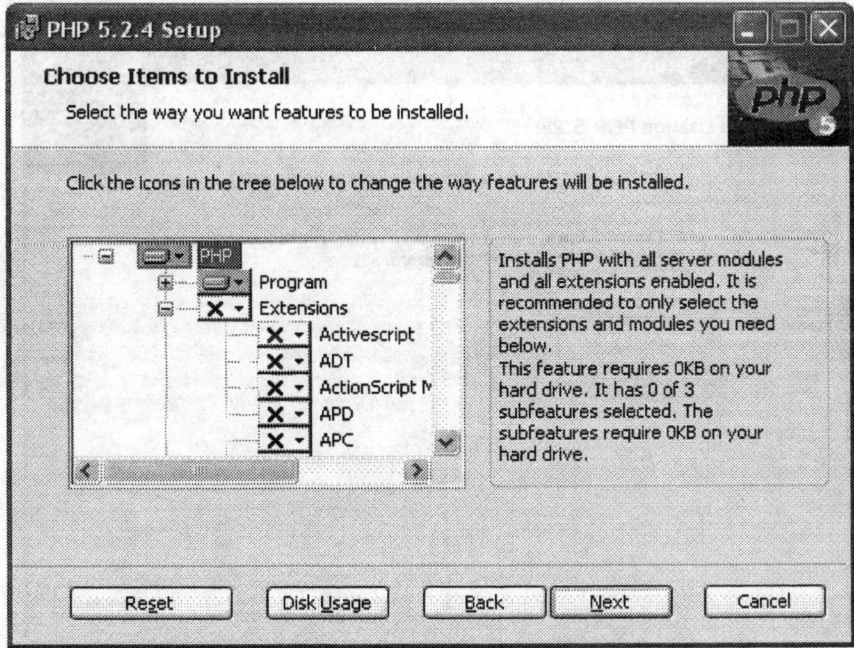

Step 7: Select on the "*X*" next to "MySQL" and select "Entire feature will be installed on local hard drive". Click "*Next*" again.

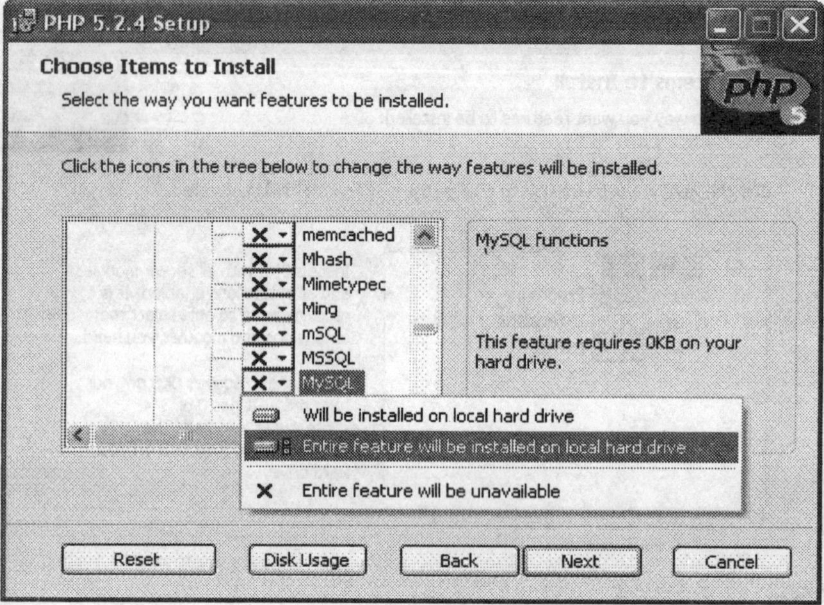

Step 8 : Click the "*Change*" button to save all the PHP configuration changes

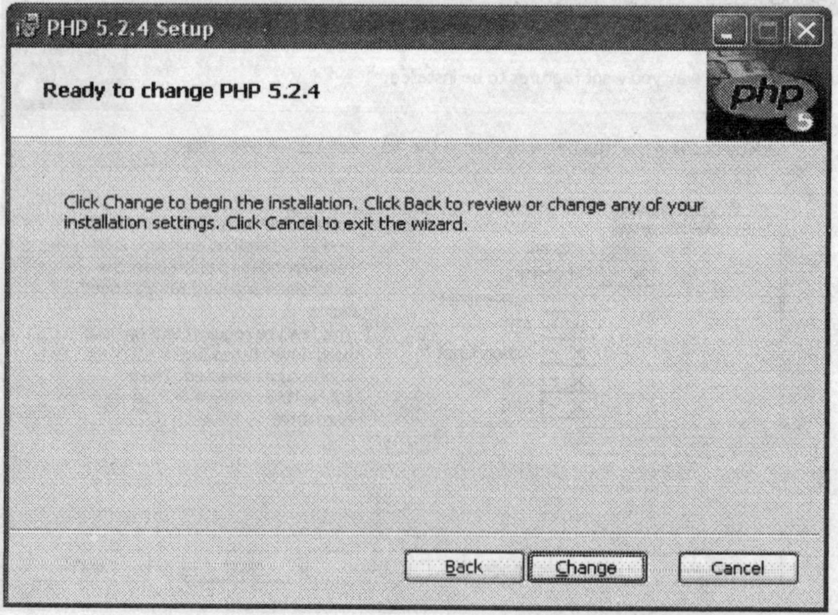

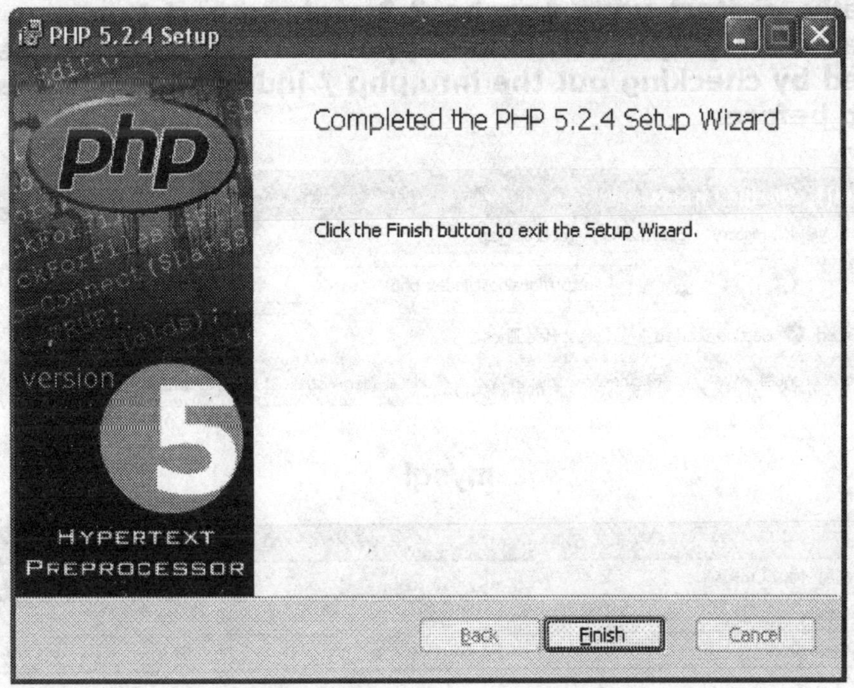
PHP 5.2.4 Setup
php
version
5
HYPERTEXT
PREPROCESSOR
Completed the PHP 5.2.4 Setup Wizard
Click the Finish button to exit the Setup Wizard.
Back
Finish
Cancel

9- Finally, restart your Apache 2.2 web server! You can check out that the MySQL extension support for PHP was successfully installed by checking out the info.php / index.php page that was created before.

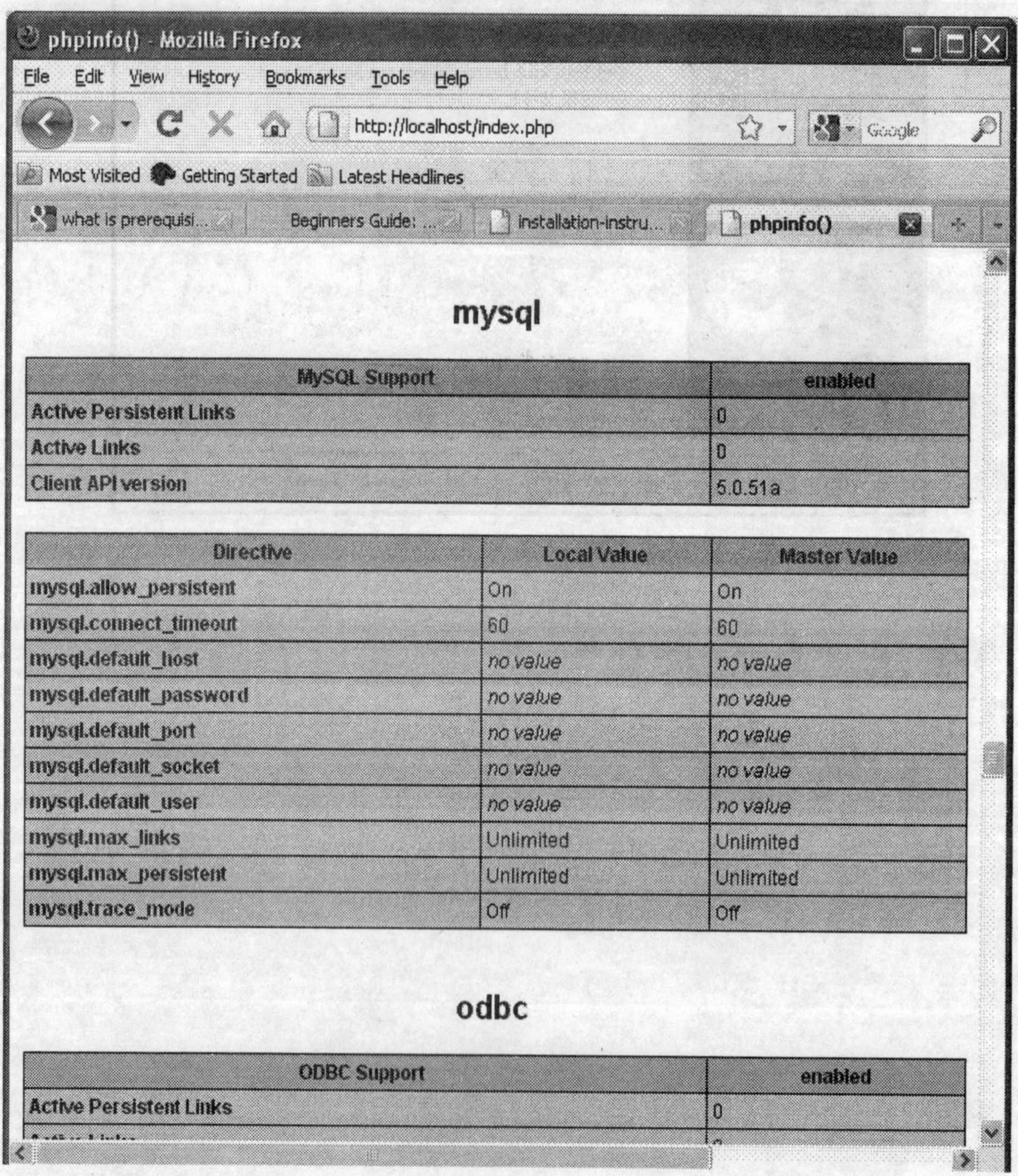

TestLink 1.7.5

Step 1: Download the testlink

http://sourceforge.net/project/showfiles.php?group_id=90976

Step 2 : Unzip and paste the testlink in root directory(ie. Paste the Testliink in C:\ProgramFiles\Apache Software Foundation\ Apache2.2\htdocs\"Testlink")

Step 3 : Now open any browser (ex: Internet explorer , mozilla firefox) and type the following to access Testlink

http://localhost/Testlink/ or
http://ipaddress/Testlink/

Step 4 : Click on New Installation link

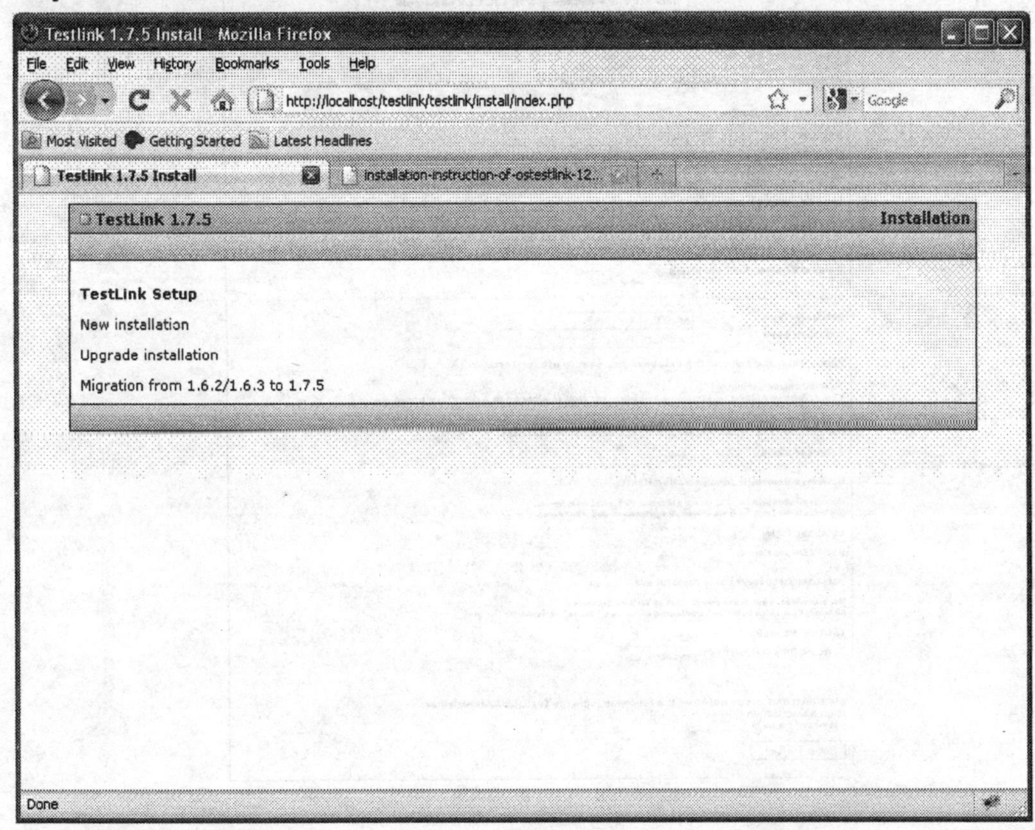

Step 5 : Enter all the required information in the field. Especially Database username and password(root, admin) .Enter the Database name & TestLink DB Login & Password (admin, admin). The testlink will create a database in mysql for the testlink and give connection to the testlilnk.

Click on Setup TestLink

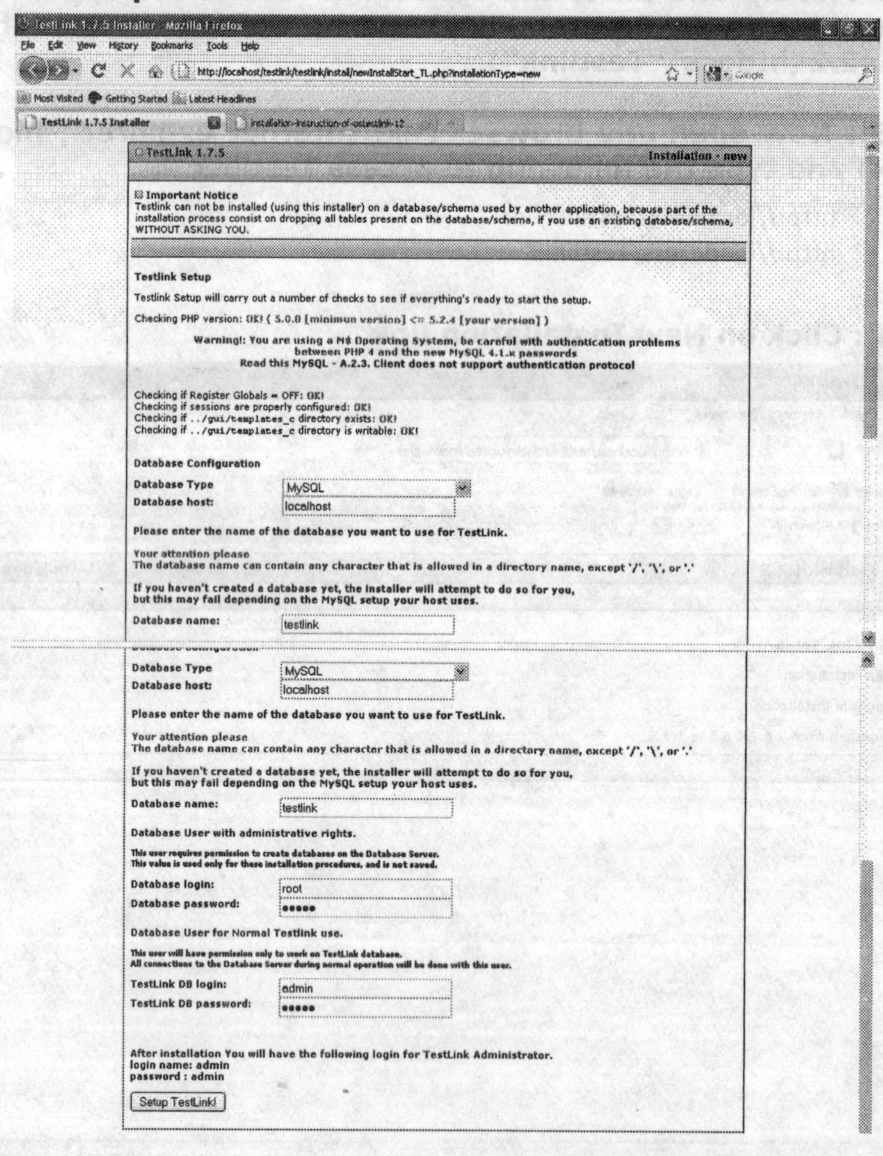

Step 6 : Select the checkbox & click on Proceed

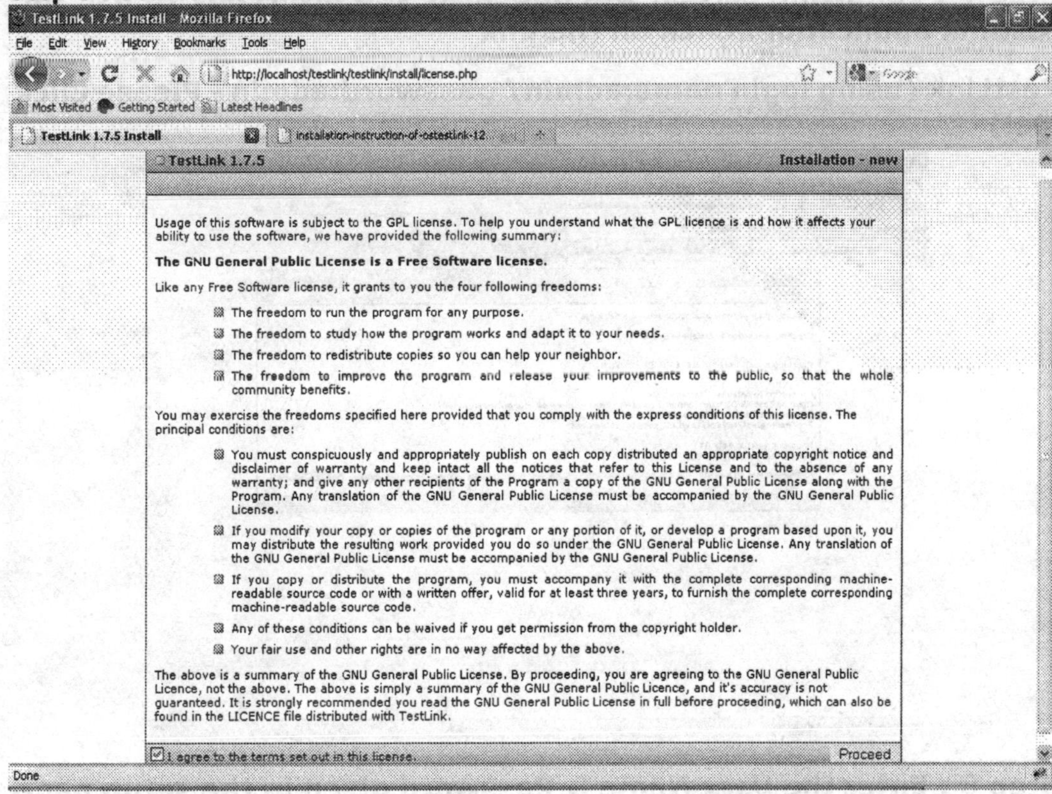

Note : If there is an error as
ERROR 1045: Access denied for user: 'root@localhost' (Using password: NO)
Solution for this is that go to your mysql prompt & type

```
mysql> UPDATE mysql.user
SET Password=PASSWORD('newpwd')
-> WHERE User='root';
mysql> FLUSH PRIVILEGES;
```

Step 7 : Following screen will appear & you are ready to use the testlink application. Click on the link

TestLink (using login name:admin/ password:admin - Please Click Me!)

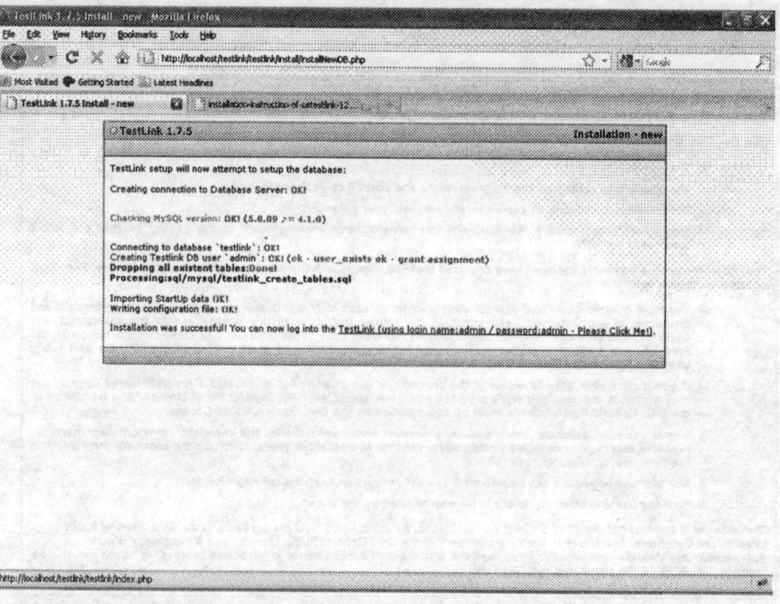

Step 8 : Enter the User Name & Password given in the setup page to login

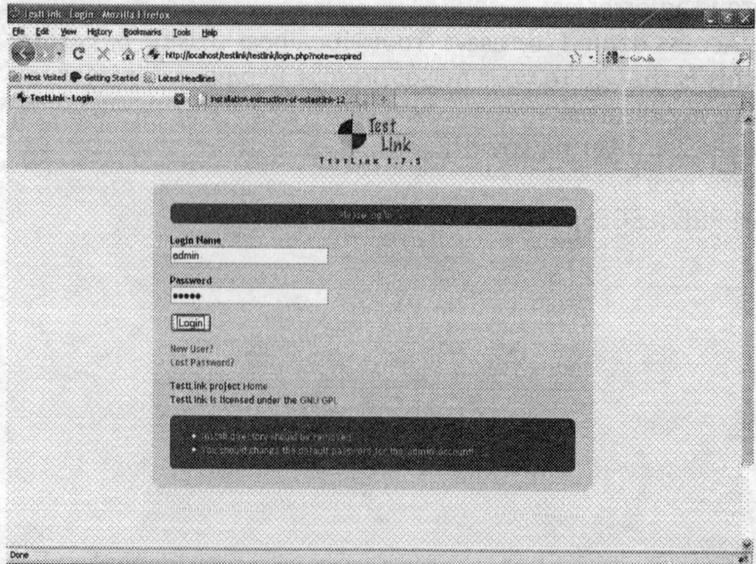

Step 9 : Following TestLink 1.7.5 screen will display

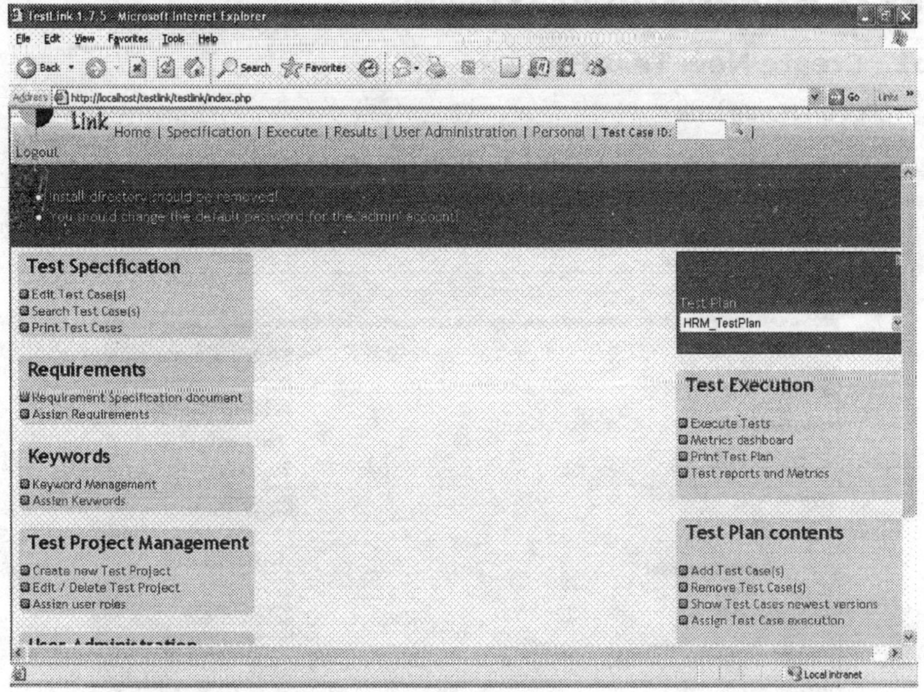

Steps to be perform in TestLink

Step1 : Create New Test Project

- Click on Home Link
- Click on Create new Test Project as shown in figure (red color)

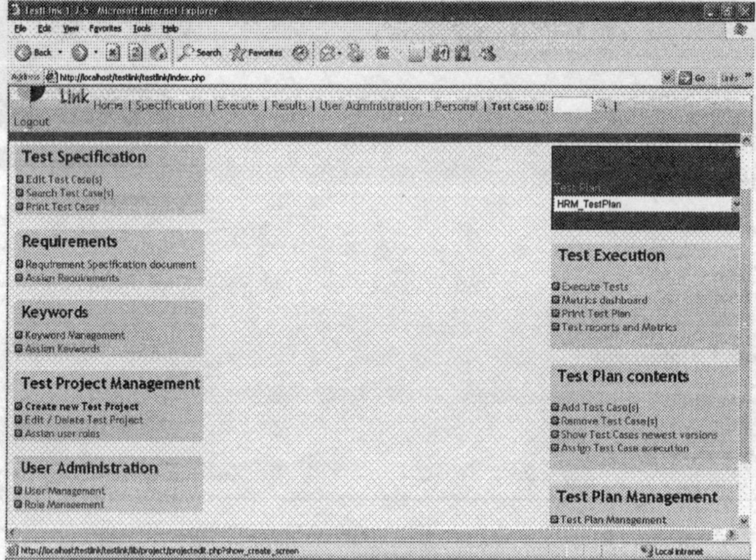

- Type Project Name, Notes & Click on Create button

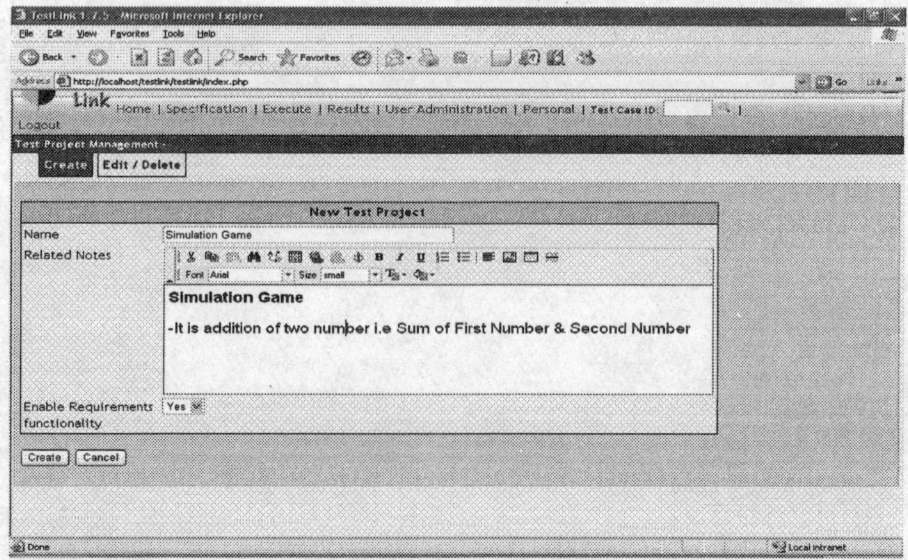

- Click on Home link, then select Test Project (right-upper corner) Simulation Game. The following screen will display

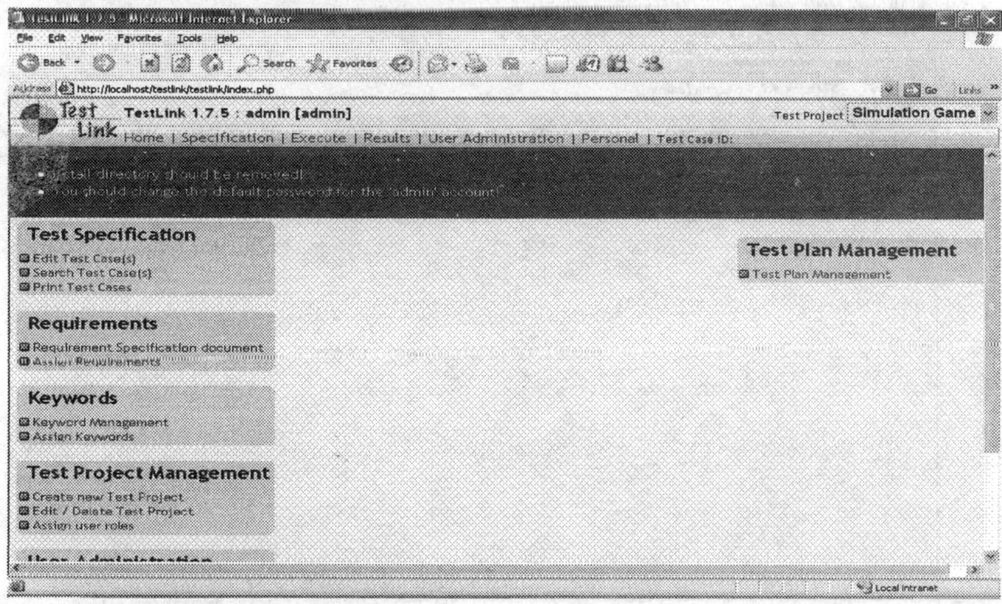

Step 2: Create Test Plan.

- Click on Test Plan Management & then click on create .Following screen will appear. Enter Test Plan Name, Description, & click on create button.

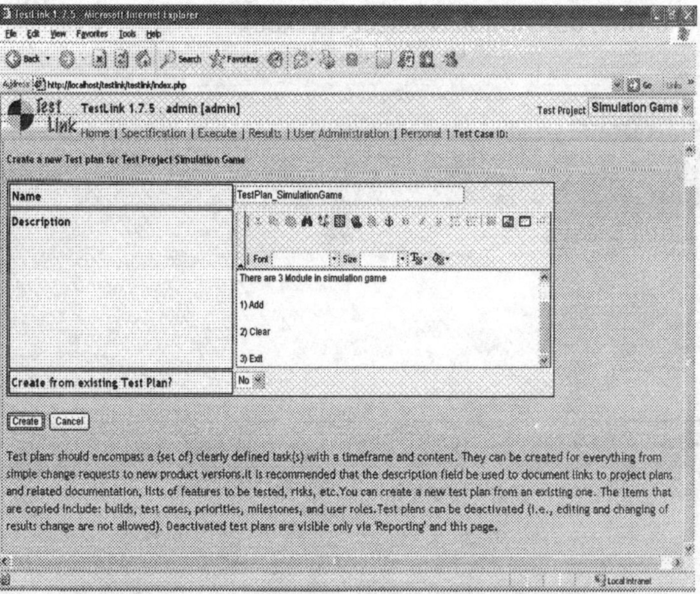

- After clicking on create button, test plan will create & following screen will appear.

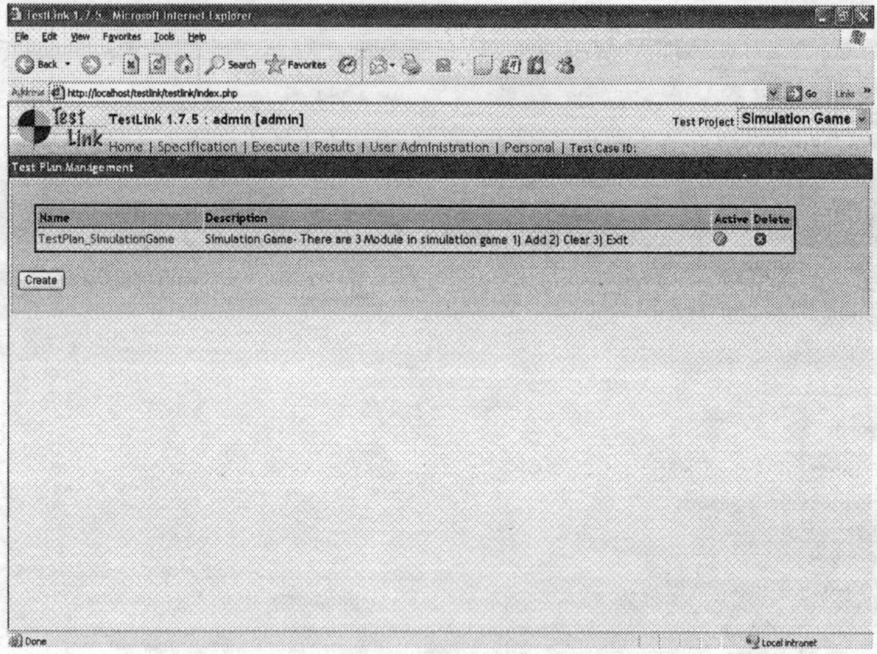

Step 3 : Create Builds

- Click on Home link.
- In Test Plan Management, click on Build Management & then click on Create button
- Enter Build Title, description & select checkbox

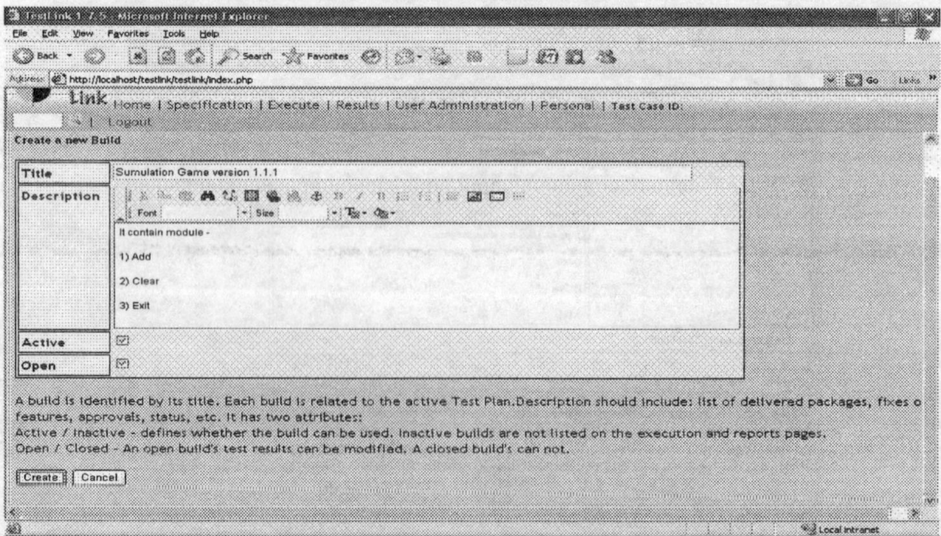

- After creating New Build following screen will appear.

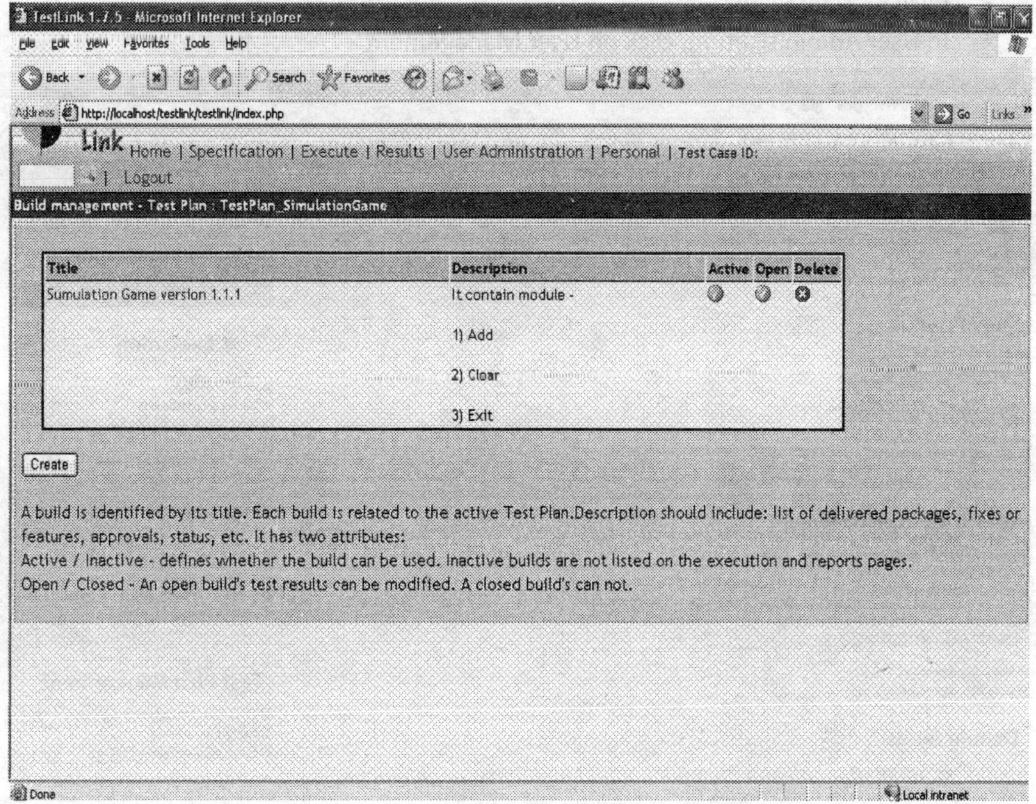

Step 4 : Create Users

- Click on Home link
- In User Administration, click on User Management

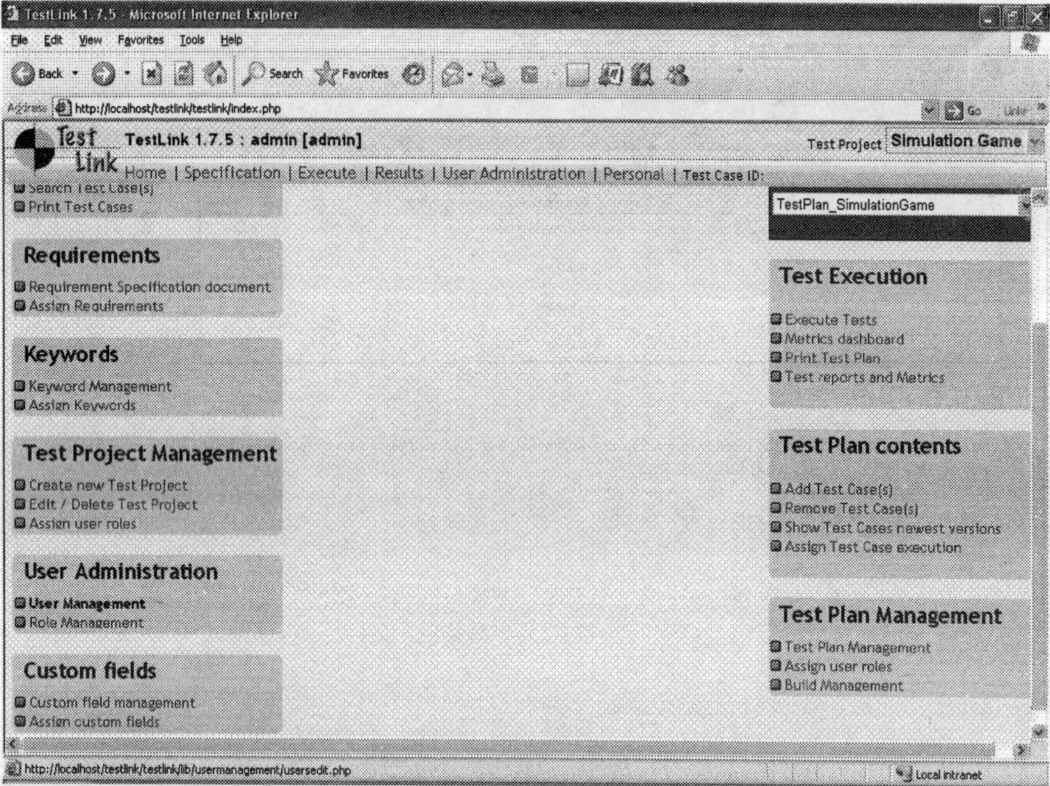

- In User Management, you can create number of users like

1. Tester
2. Guest
3. leader
4. Senior Tester

- For Example Tester (Create user)

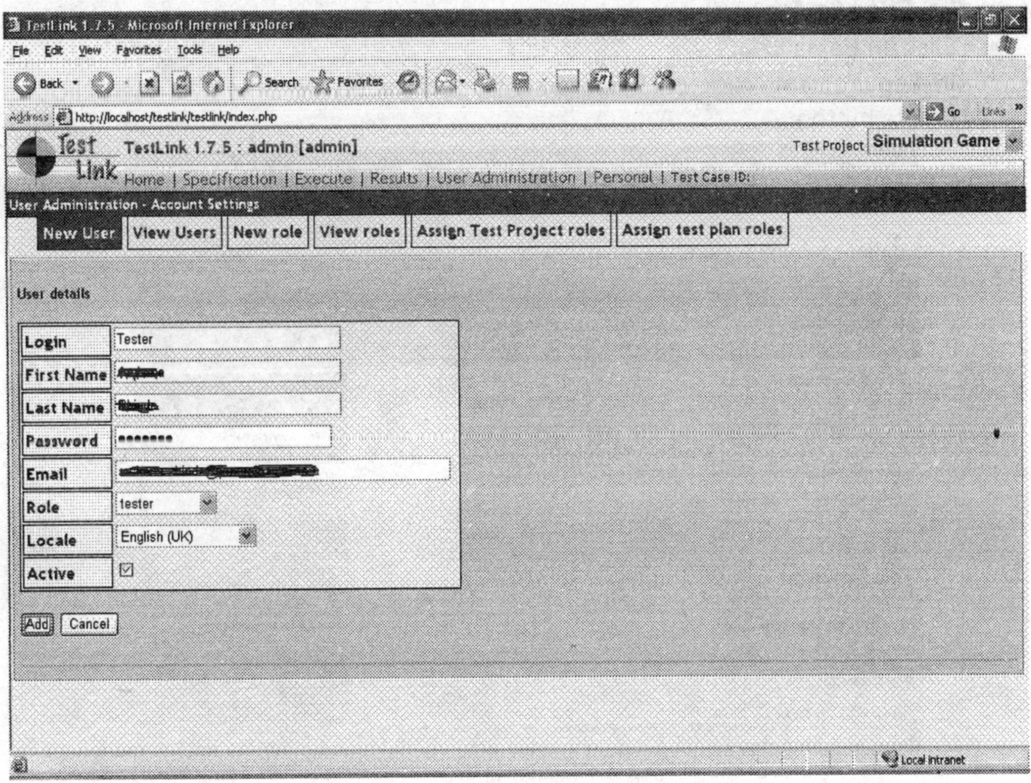
TestLink 1.7.5 - Microsoft Internet Explorer
File Edit View Favorites Tools Help
Back Search Favorites
Address http://localhost/testlink/testlink/index.php
Go Links
TestLink 1.7.5 : admin [admin]
Test Project Simulation Game
Home | Specification | Execute | Results | User Administration | Personal | Test Case ID:
User Administration - Account Settings
New User
View Users
New role
View roles
Assign Test Project roles
Assign test plan roles
User details
Login
Tester
First Name
Last Name
Password
Email
Role
tester
Locale
English (UK)
Active
Add
Cancel
Local intranet

Step 5 : Create Requirements

- Click on Home link
- In Requirement, click on Requirement Specification Document & then click on Create button

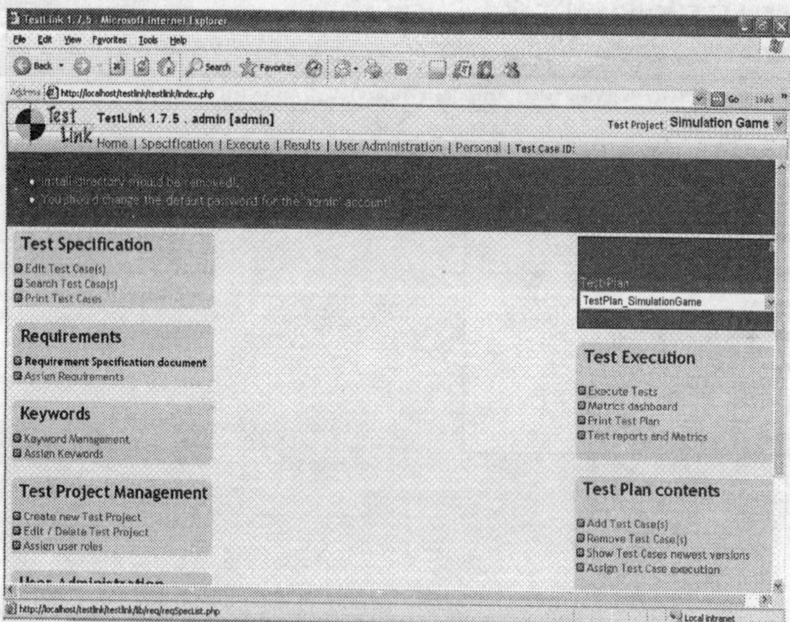

- Enter Requirement Specification Document Title, Scope, & click on create button

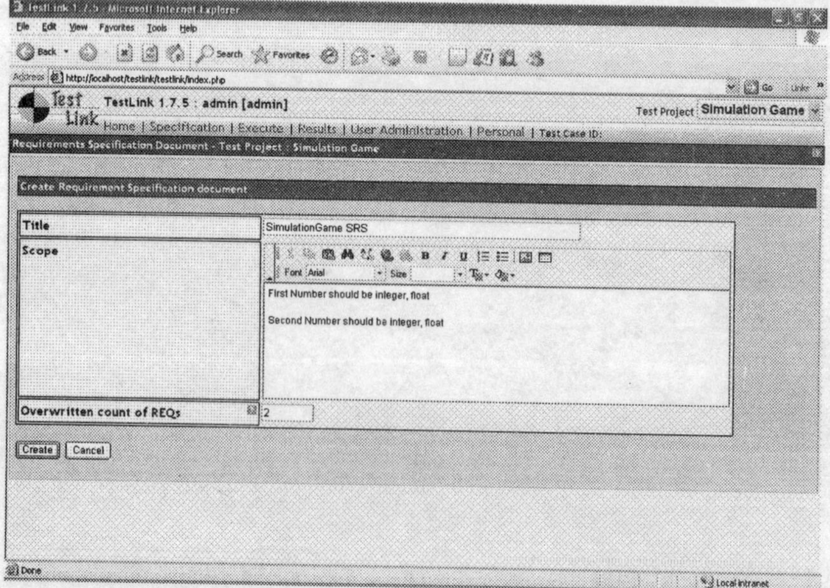

- After creating requirement specification document , following screen will display

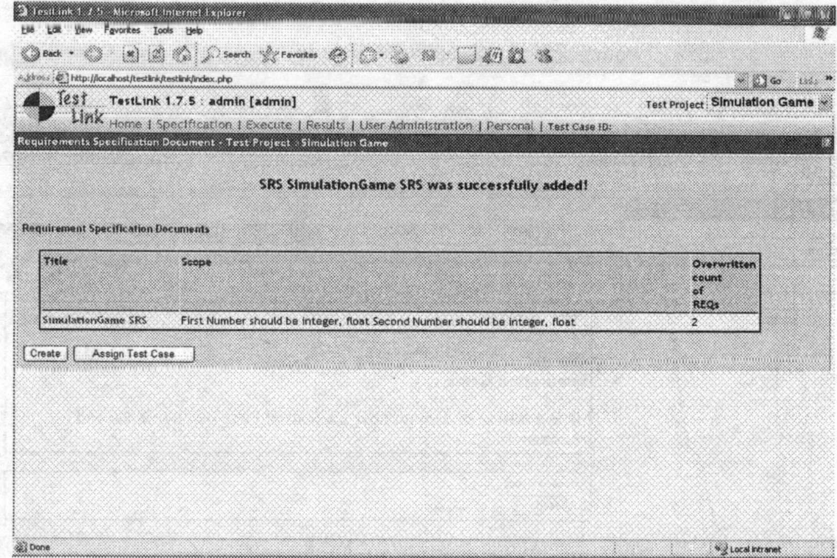

Step 6 : Create Test Suite

- Click on Home link
- In Test Specification, click on Edit Test Case(s)

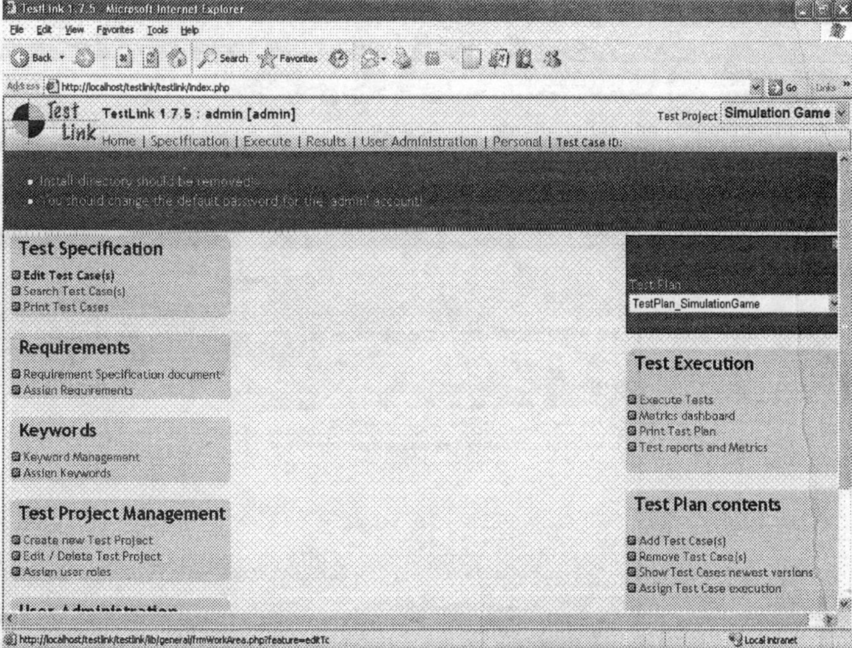

- Click on Simulation Game, following screen will appear
- Click on New Test Suite

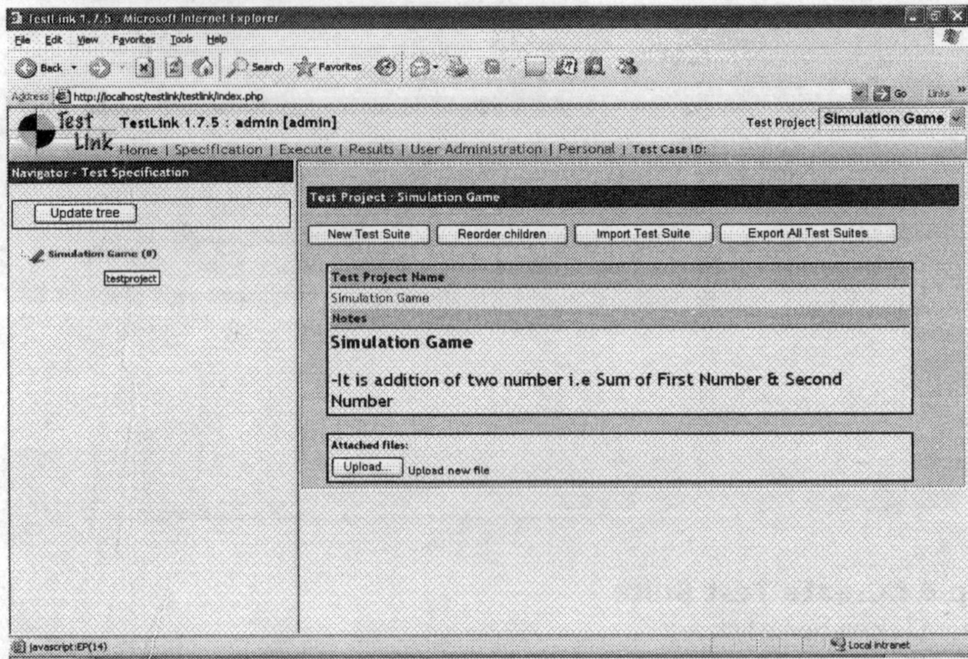

- Enter Test Suite Name, Details & click on save button.

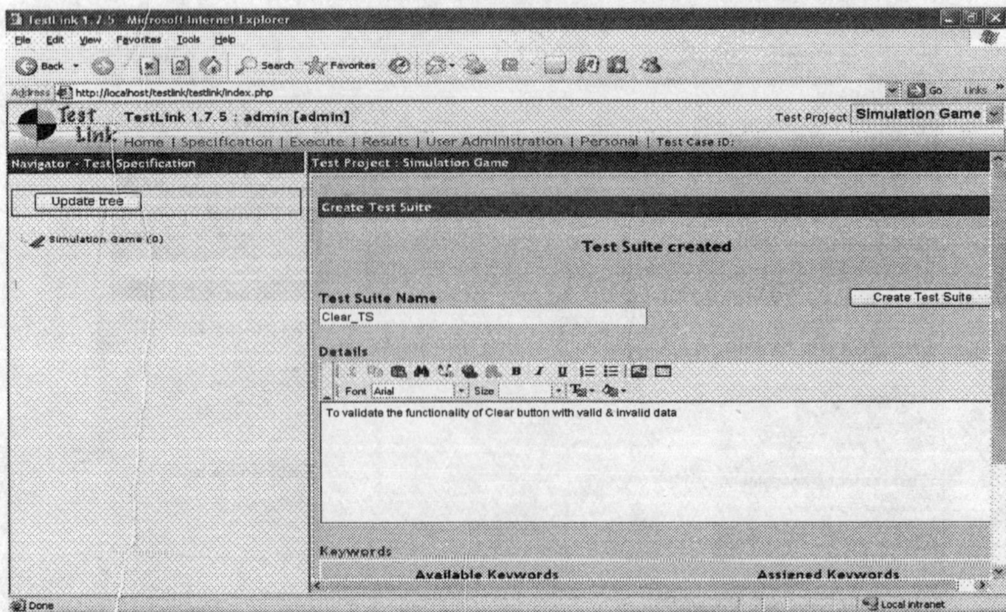

- Similarly you can create number of Test Suits as shown in the following figure (Add, Clear, Exit in the left side).

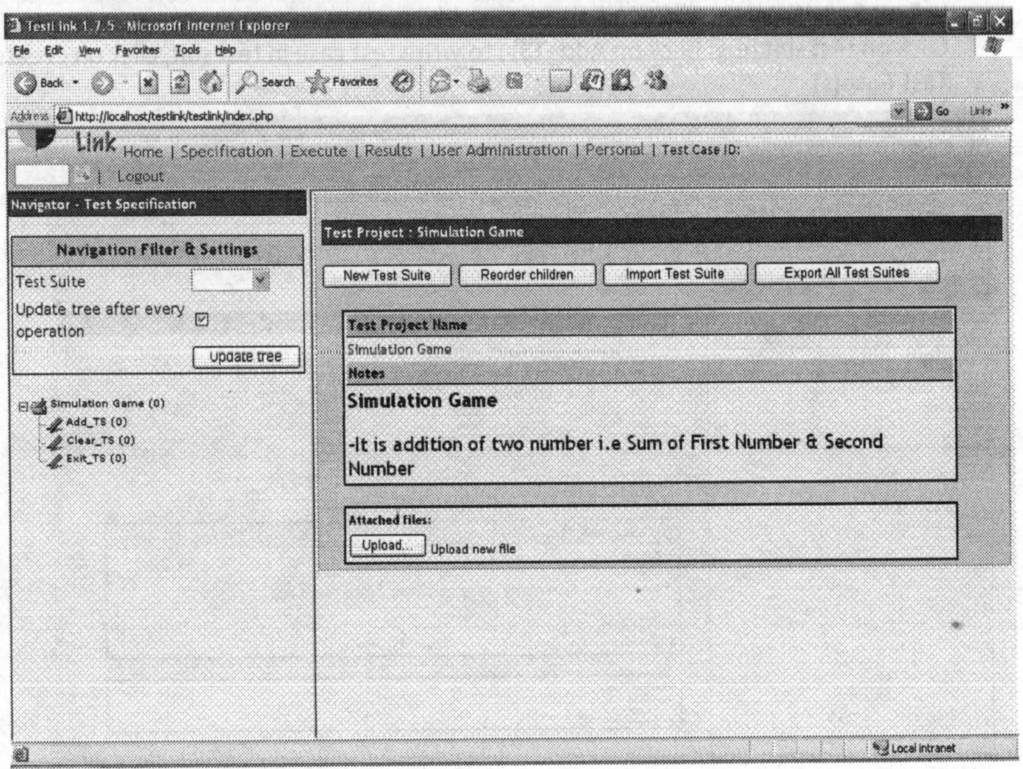

Step 7 : Create Test Cases

- Click on Home Link
- In Test Specification, Click on Edit Test Case(s).
- Click on test suit (e.g. Click on Add_TS) , to write test case in test suit, click on Create Test Case(s).

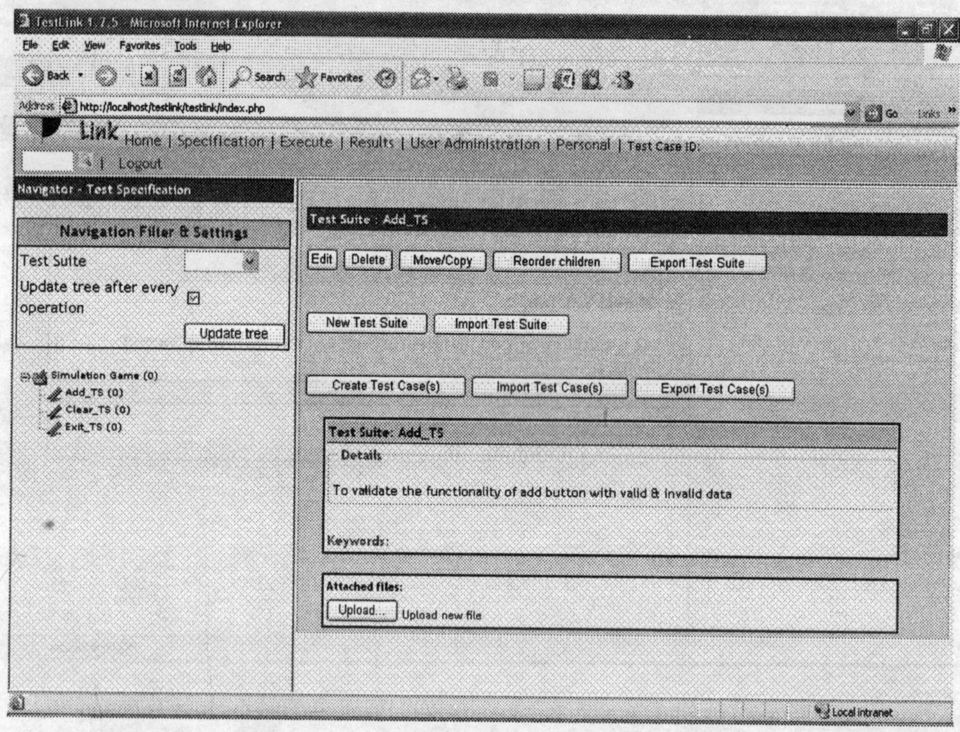

- Enter Test Case Title, Summary, Steps, & Expected Result & Click on save button.

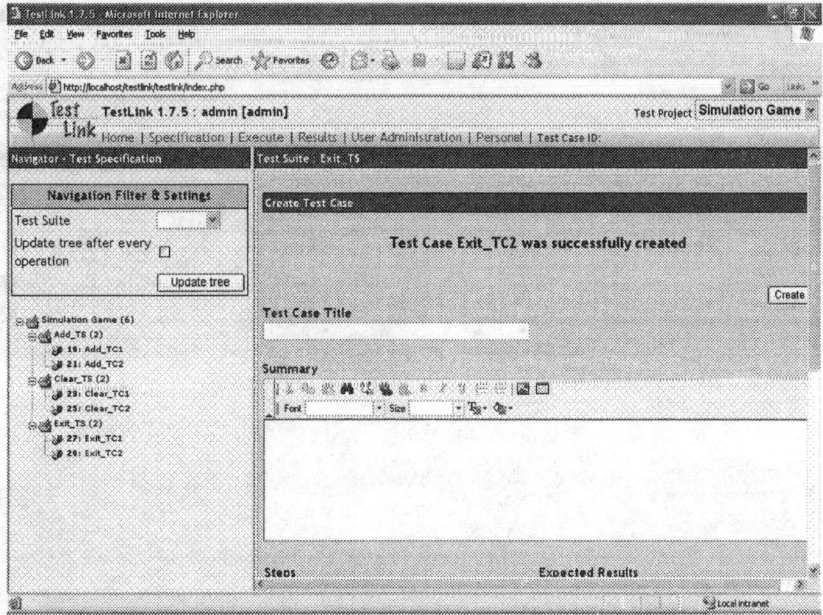

Step 8 : Create Document

- Click on Home link
- In Requirements, click on Requirement Specification Document

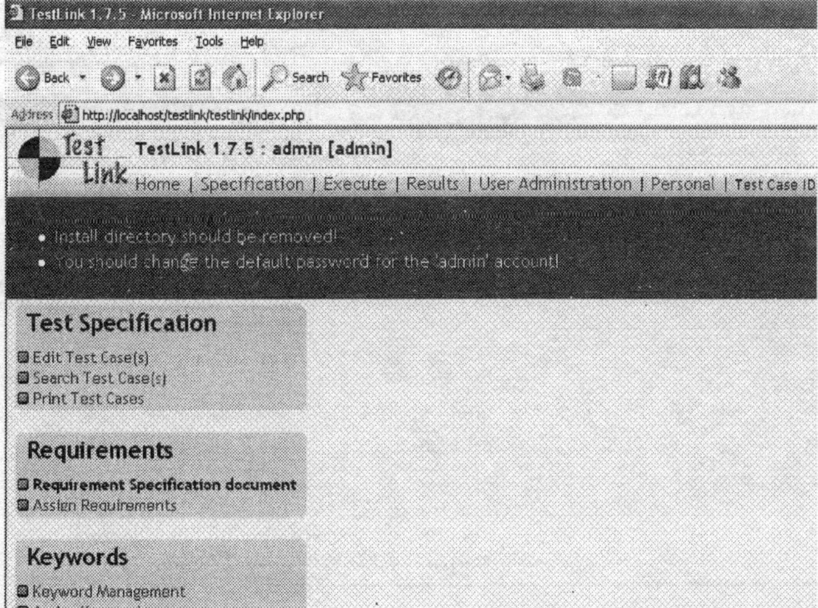

- Click on SimulationGameSRS

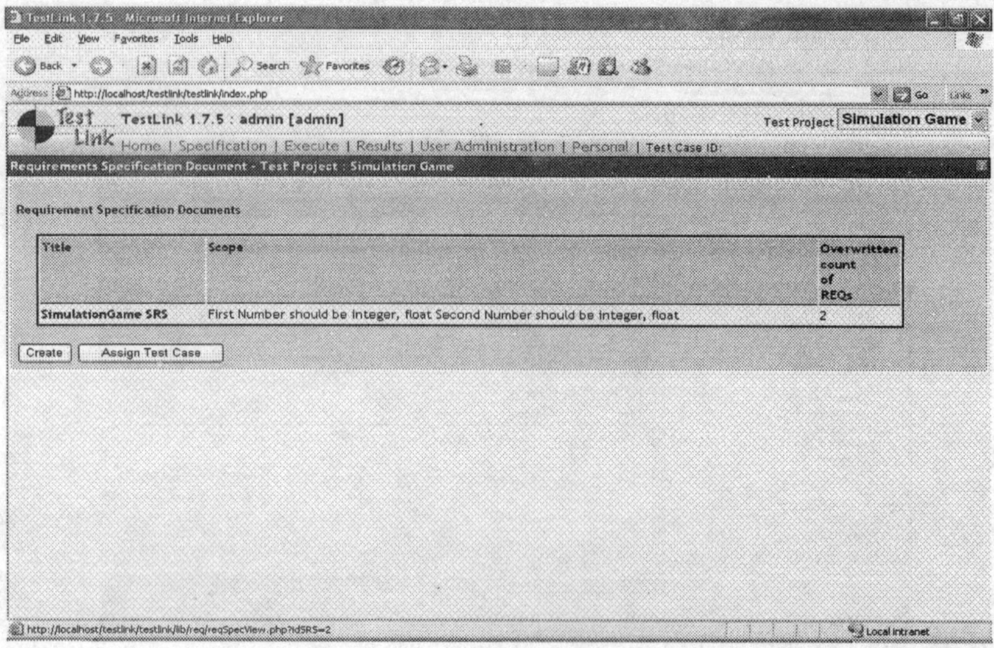

- Click on Create New REQ

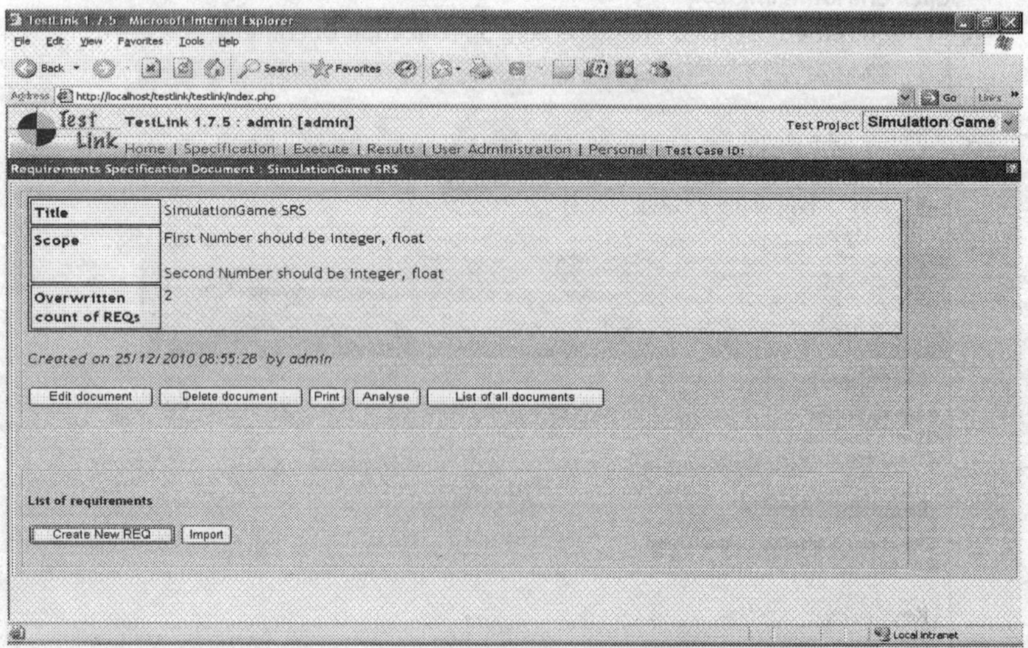

- Enter Requirement DOC-ID, Title ,Scope, Status & then click on Create button

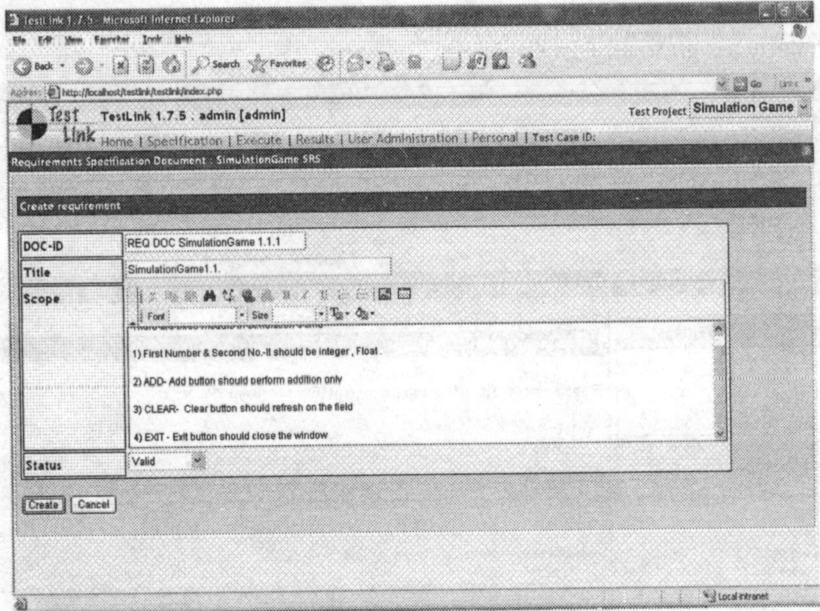

Step 9 : Assign Requirement to Test Case

- Click on Home link.
- In Requirements, click on Assign Requirements

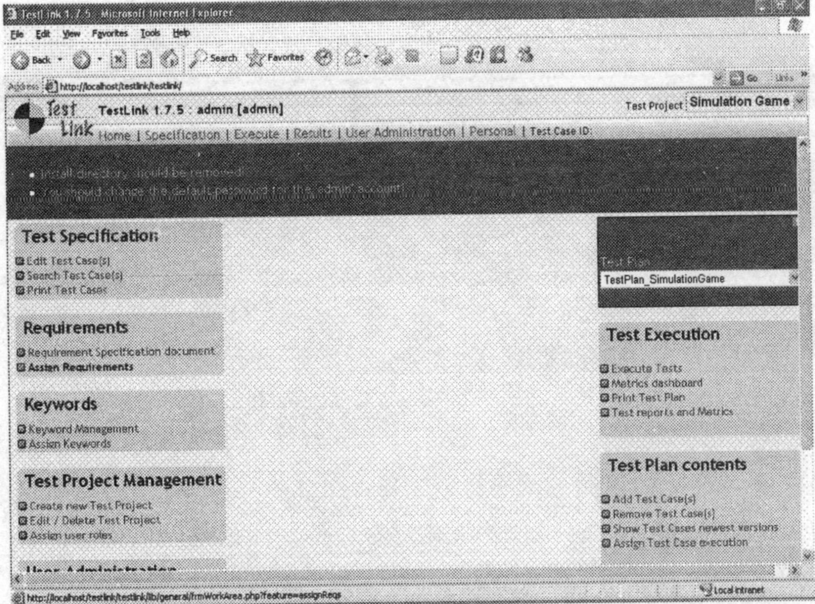

- Click on the Test Case (i.e. Add_TC1)
- Select the checkbox & Click on Assign button.
- Similarly assign to all Test Cases.

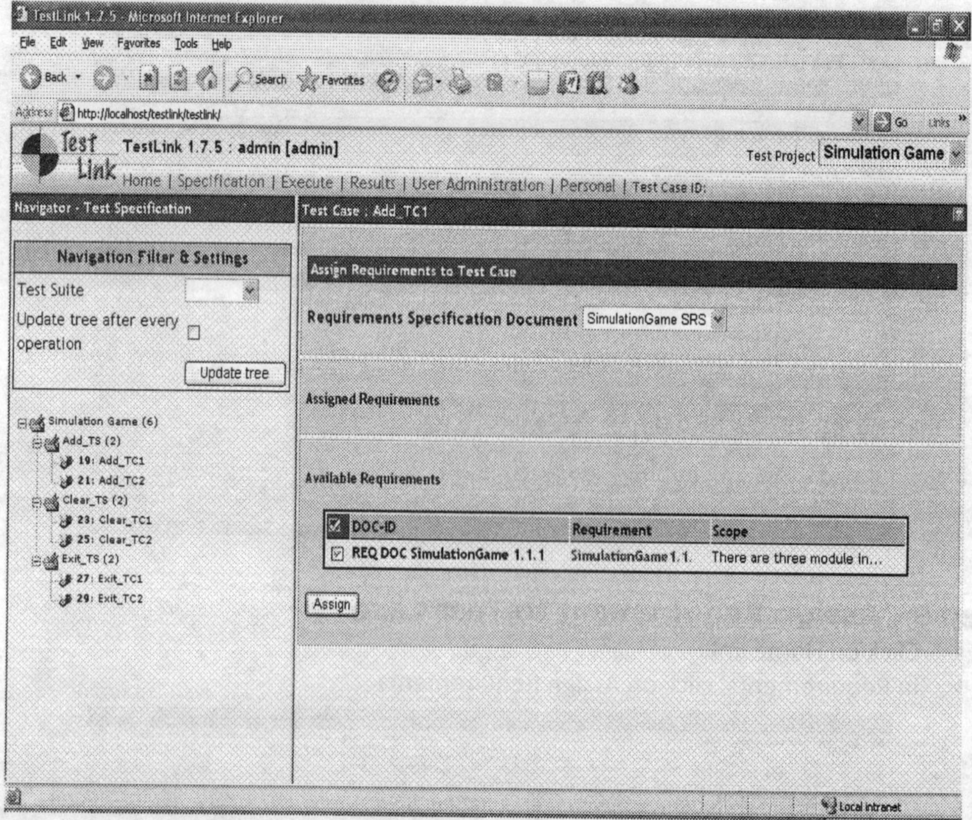

Step 10 : Add Test Cases to Test Plan

- Click on Home link.
- In Test Plan Contents, Click on Add Test Case(s)

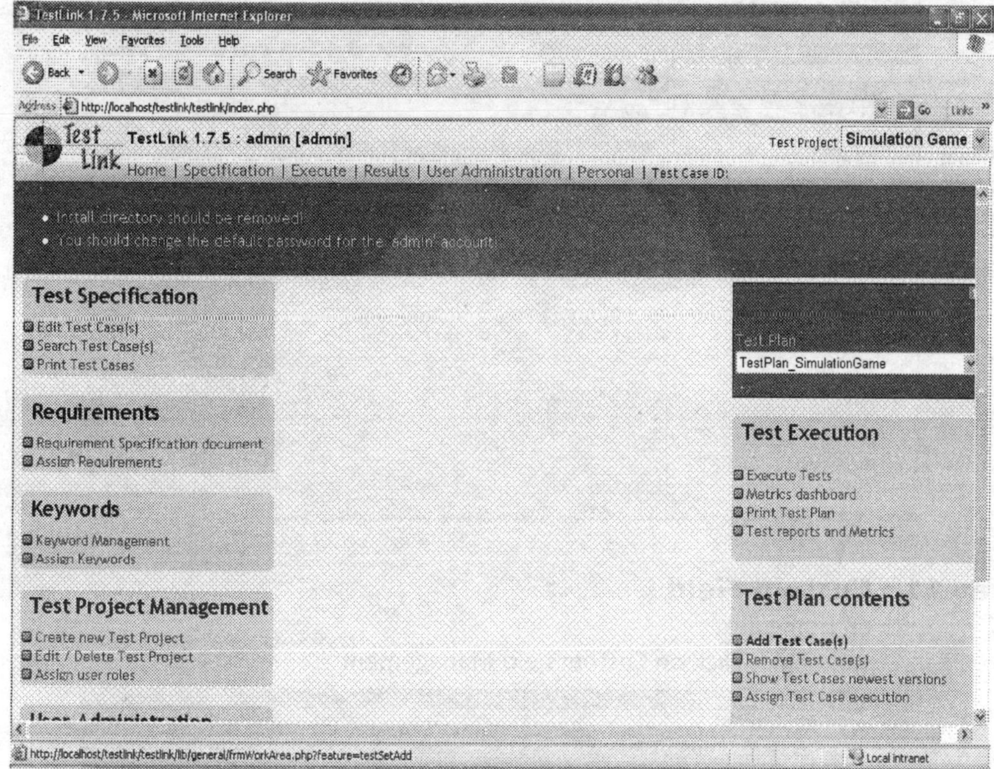

- Click on Test Suit i.e Add_TC1, Select Checkbox & then Click on Add Selected button. Similarly add all test case to test plan.

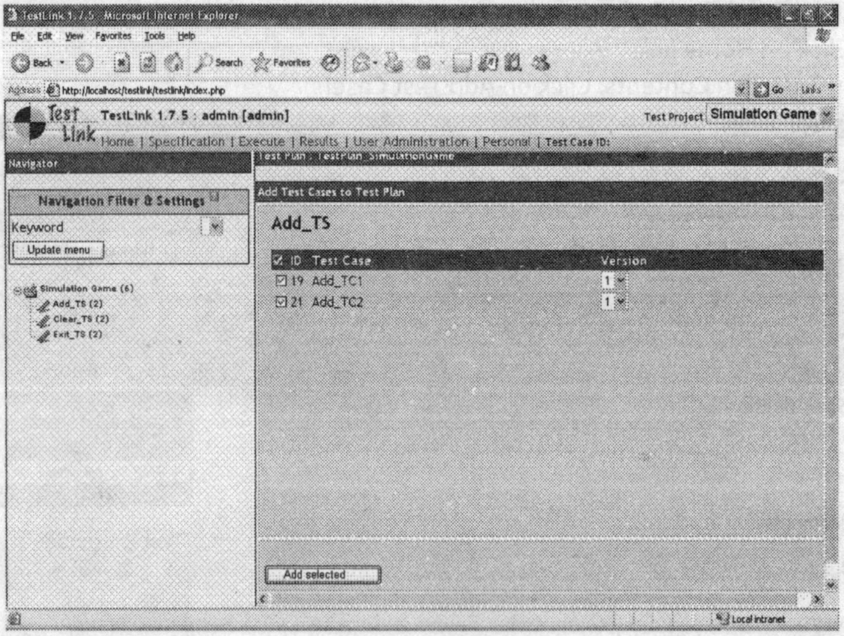

Step 11 : Custom Field

- Click on Home link.
- In Custom field, Click on Custom field Management

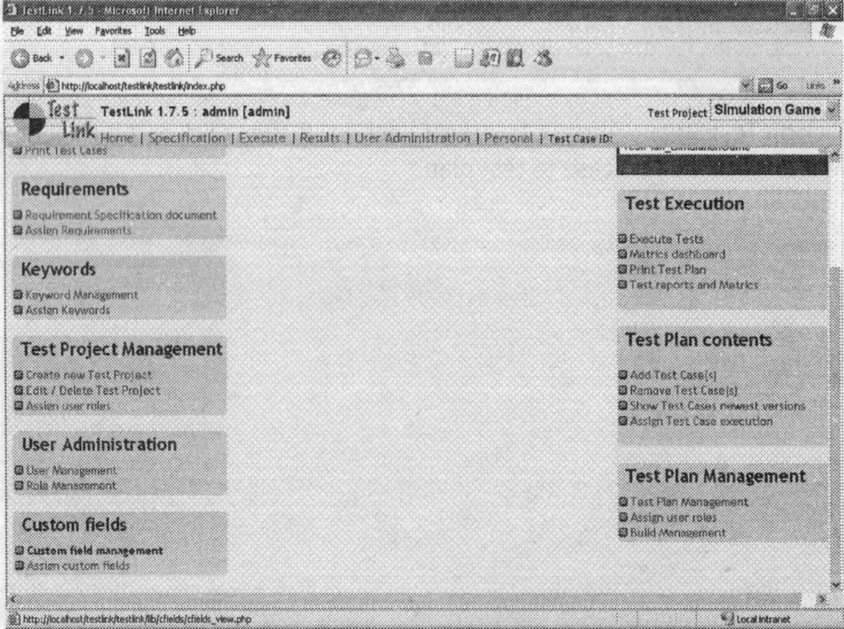

- Enter all the fields & click on Add button.

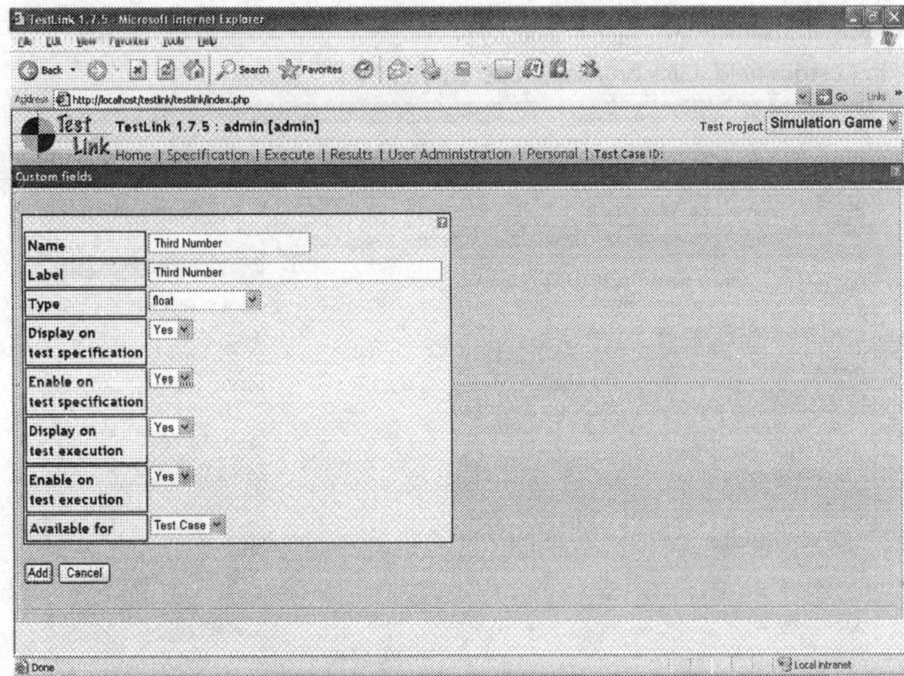

- Following window will display

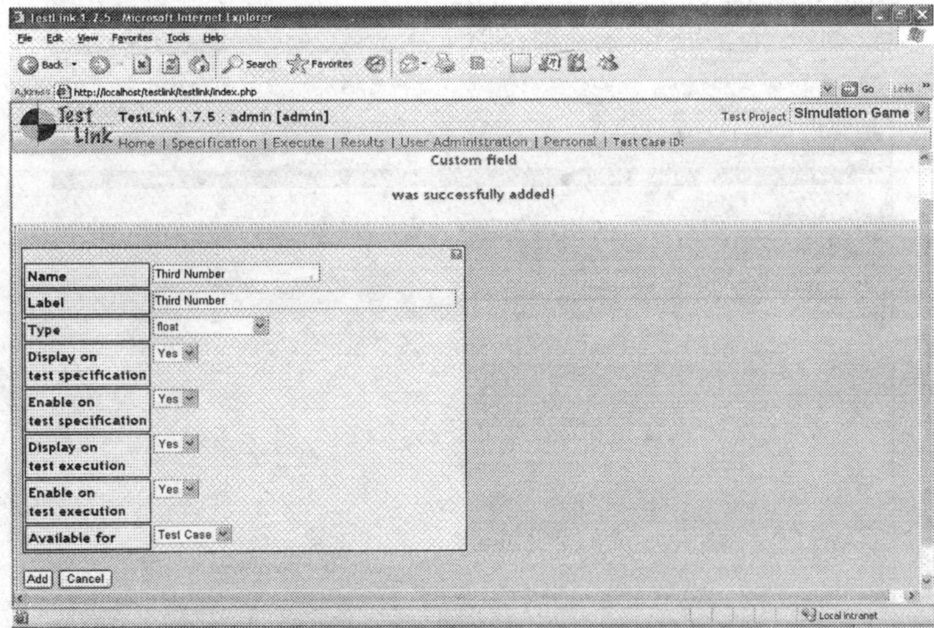

Step 12 : Assign Custom Field

- Click on Home link.
- In Custom field, Click on Assign Custom field.

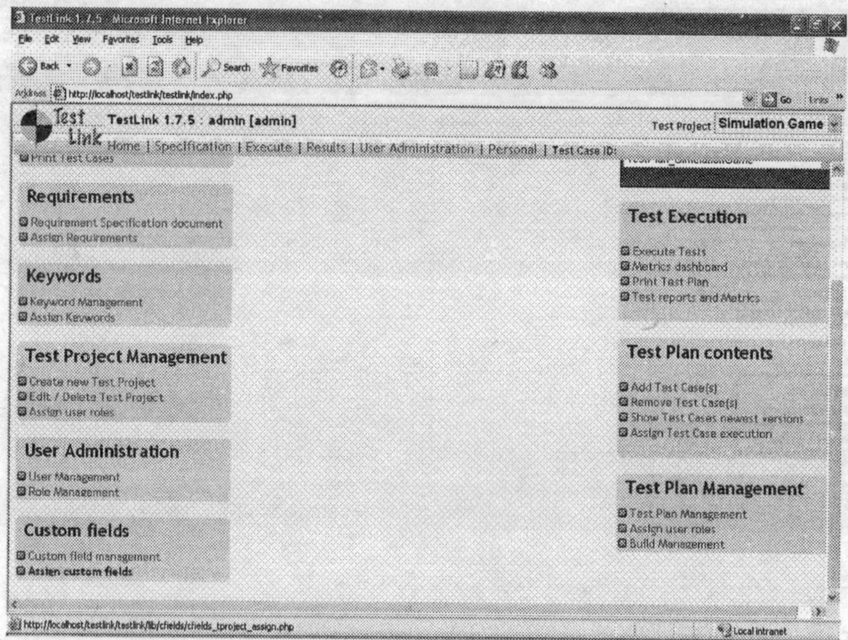

- Select checkbox & click on Assign button.

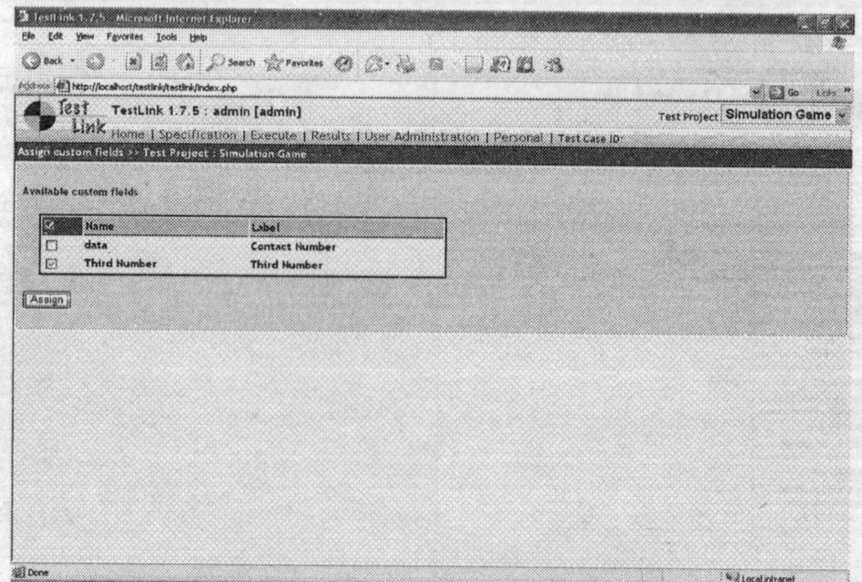

- Following screen will display.

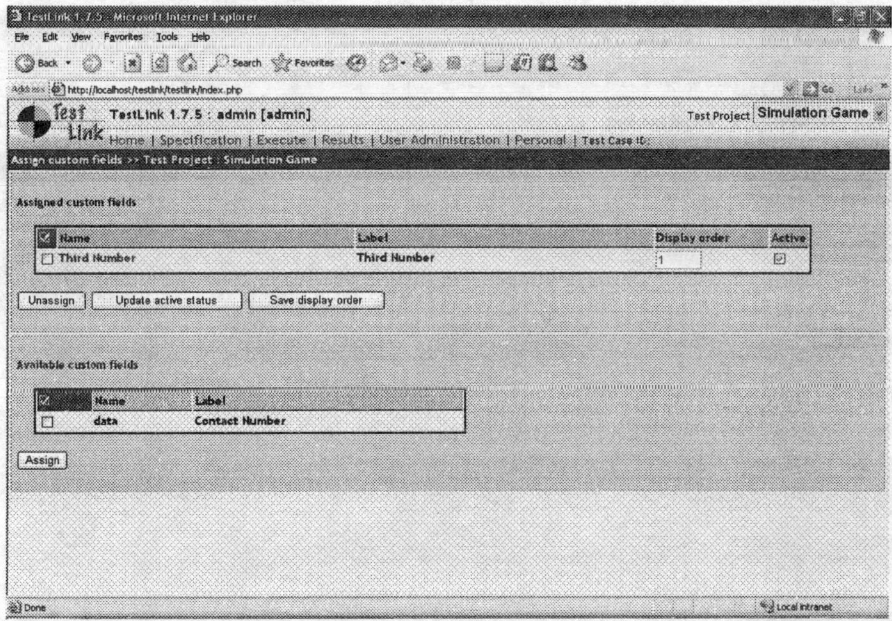

Step 13 : Create Keyword

- Click on Home link.
- In Keywords, Click on Keyword Management.

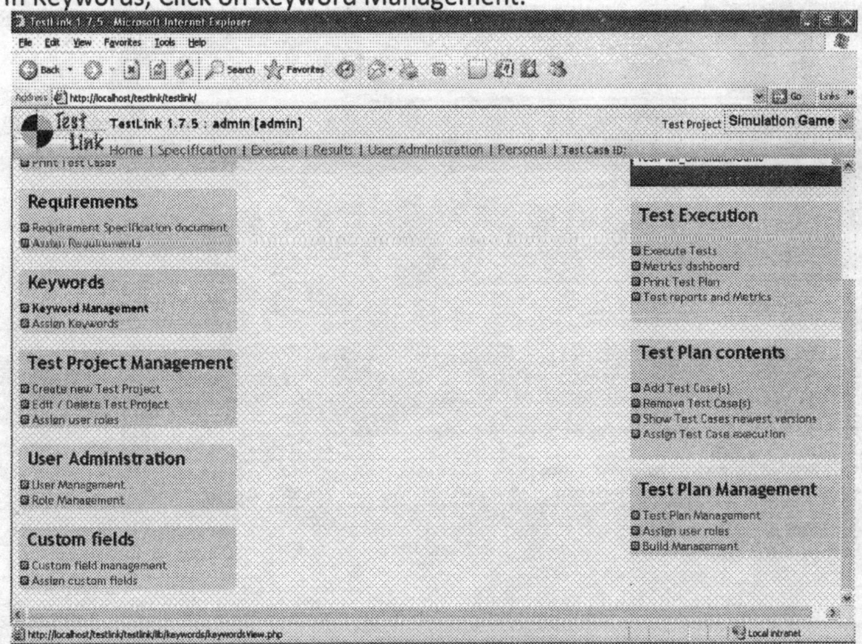

- Enter Keyword, notes, & Click on Create Keyword button.

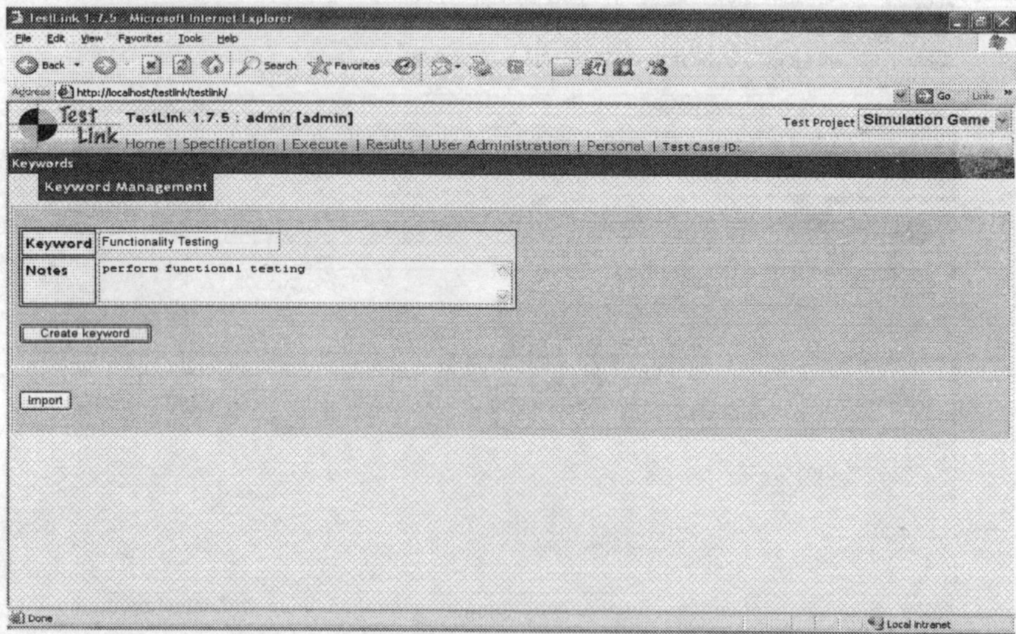

- Similarly you can create number of keywords as shown in the screen (i.e. Functionality testing & Usability Testing)

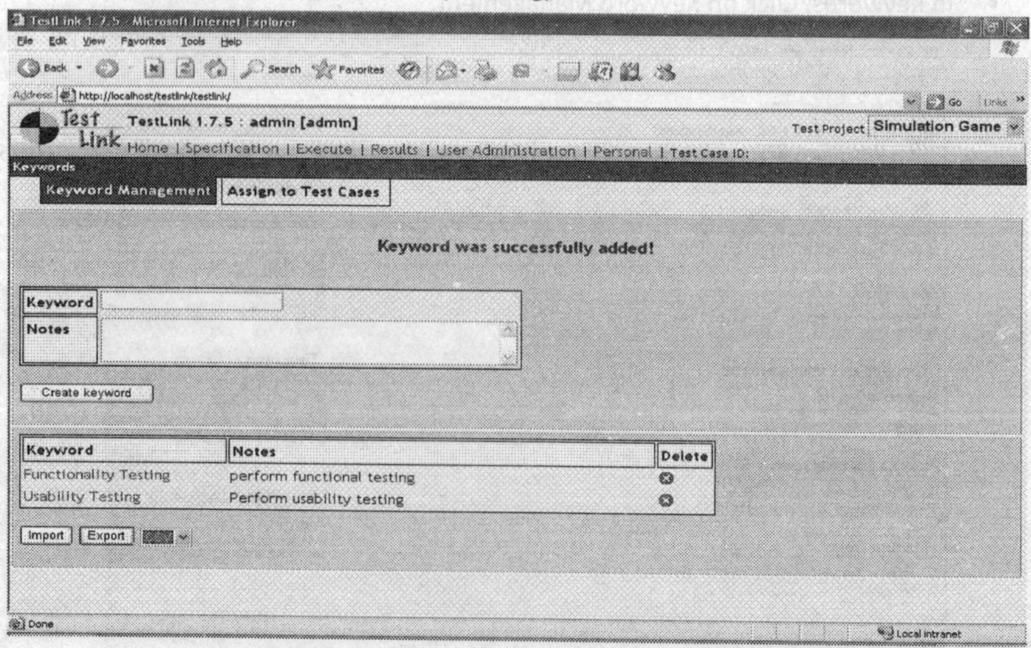

Step 14 : Assign Keyword

- Click on home link.
- In Custom fields, click on Assign Custom Fields.

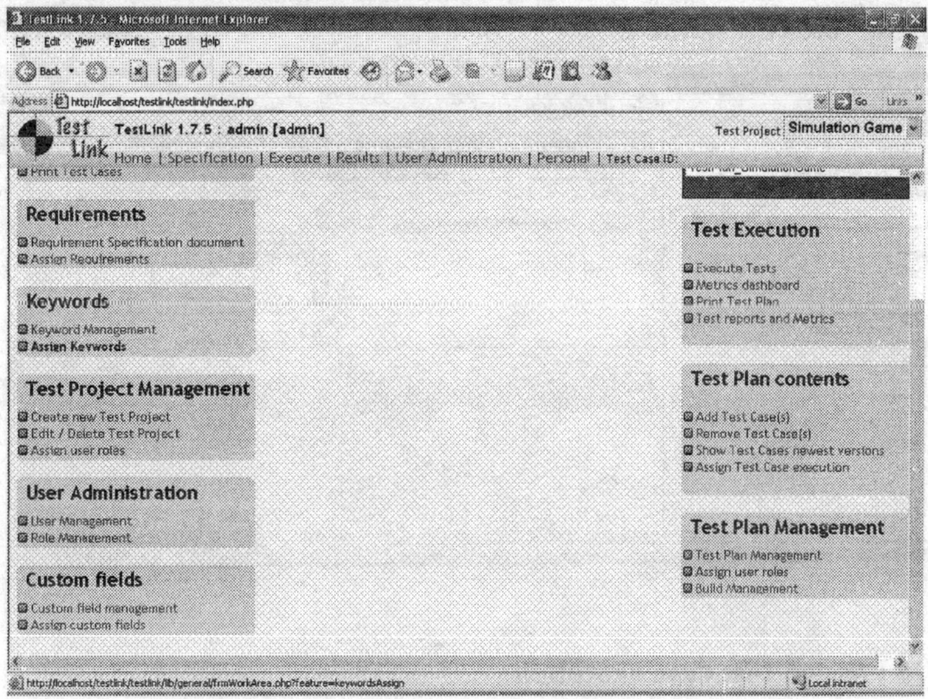

- Select Available Keyword, then click on arrow button & then on Save button

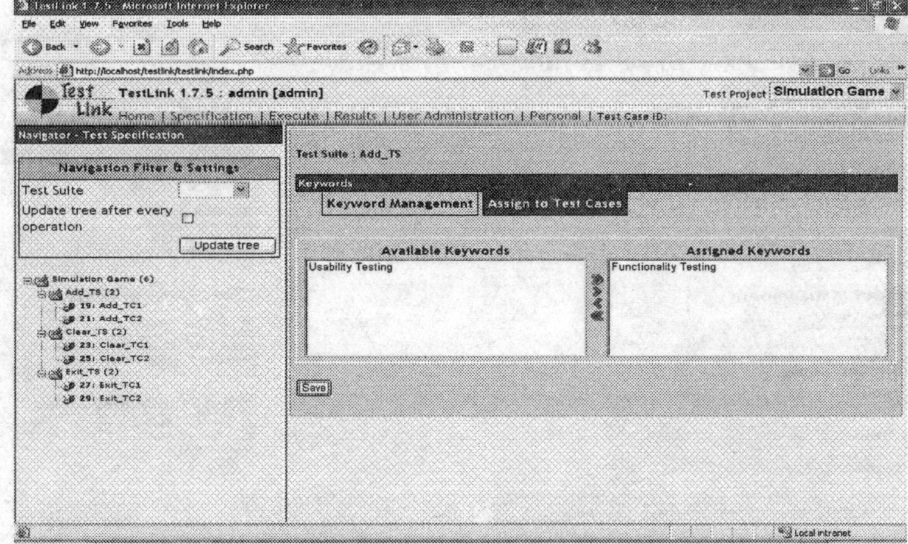

- Assign Keyword to each test case.

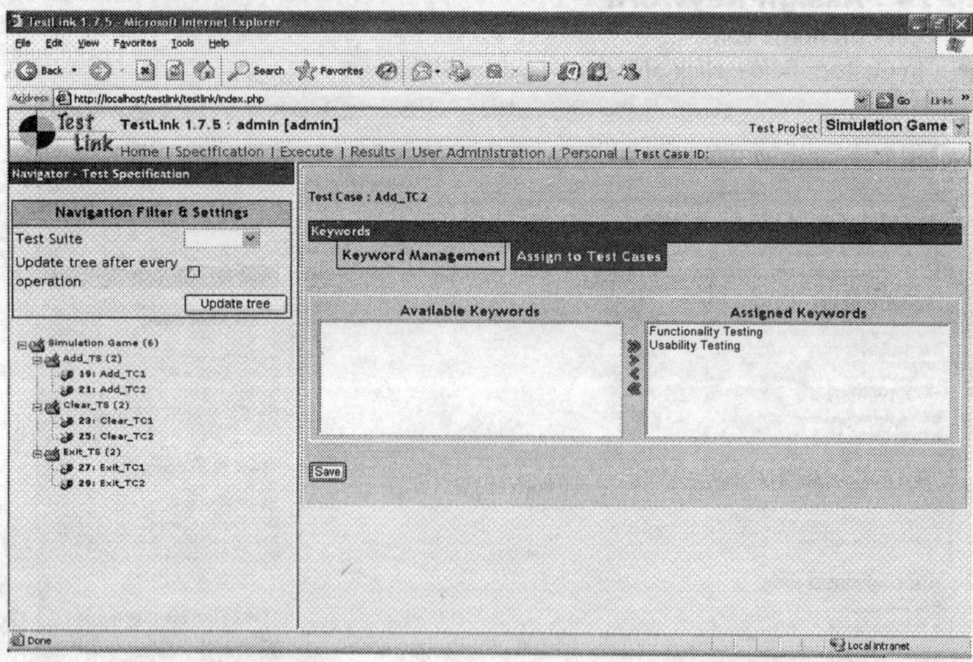

Step 15 : Assign Test Case execution

- Click on Home link.
- In Test Plan Contents, Click on Assign test Case Execution.

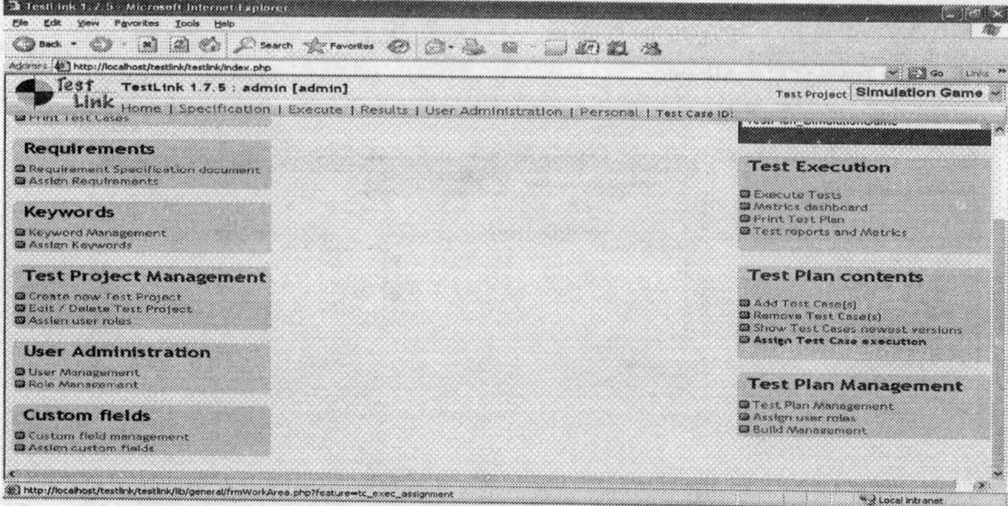

- To assign test case execution, select Checkbox & User to whom the test case to be assign. Do the same for the remaining test case.

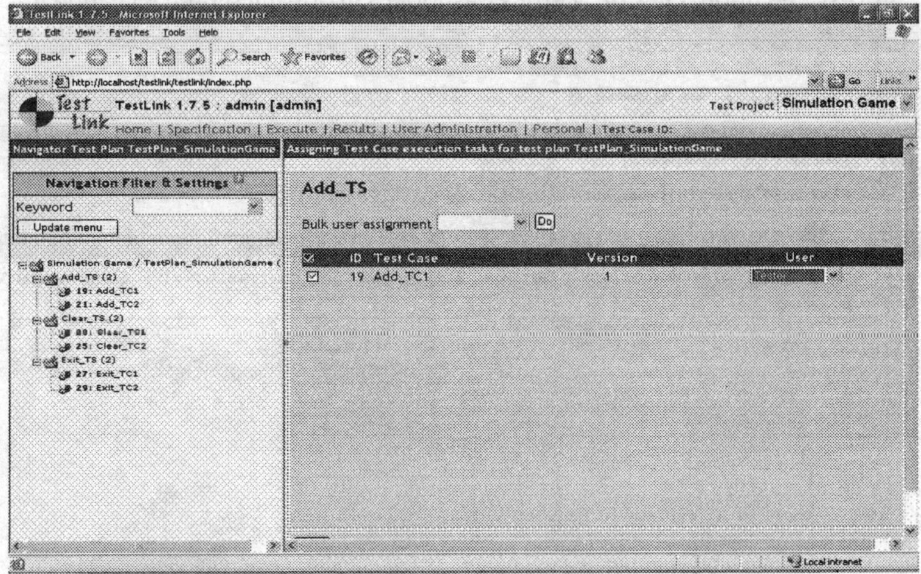

Step 16 : Execute Test Case

- To execute test case login from user e.g. login from "Archana" Tester
- So, Tester Archana will execute only two test case because only two test cases there assigned to it.

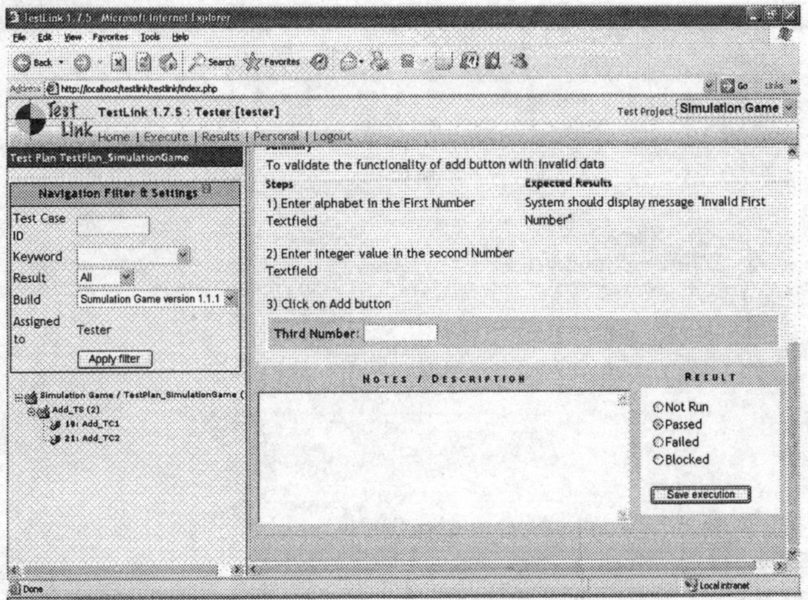

Step 17 : Metrics Dashboard

- Click on Home link.
- In Test Execution, Click on Metrics Dashboard, following screen will appear.

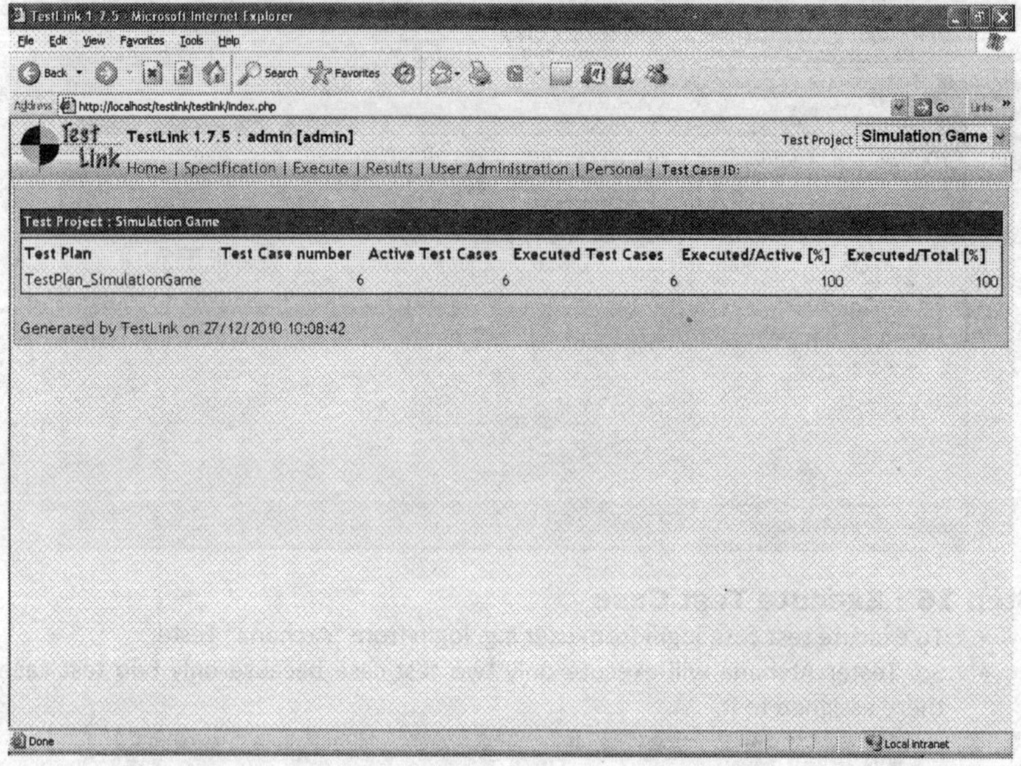

Step 18 : Test Reports & Metrics

- Click on Home link.
- In Test Execution, Click on Test Reports & Metrics.

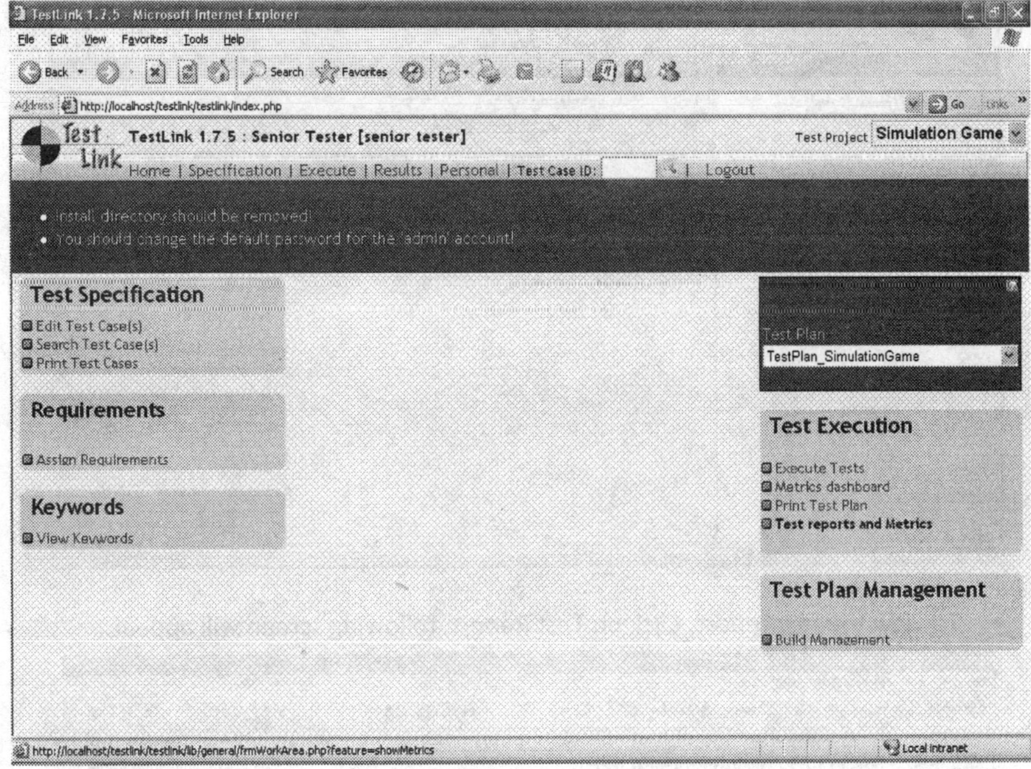

- Click on Overall Build Status

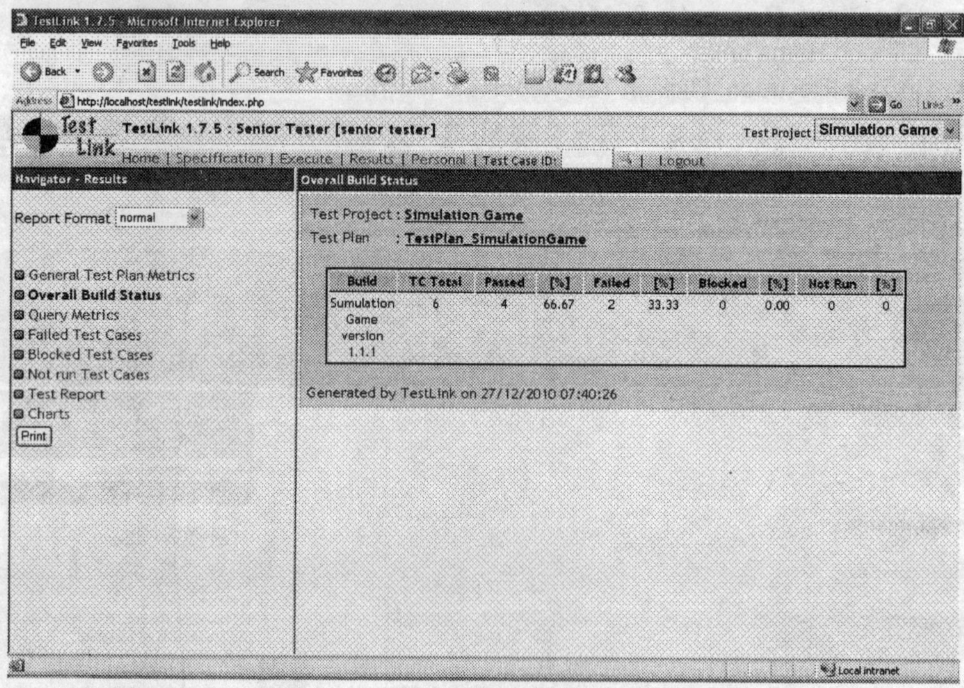

Build	TC Total	Passed	[%]	Failed	[%]	Blocked	[%]	Not Run	[%]
Sumulation Game version 1.1.1	6	4	66.67	2	33.33	0	0.00	0	0

- To view the test report, Click on Test Report, following screen will appear.

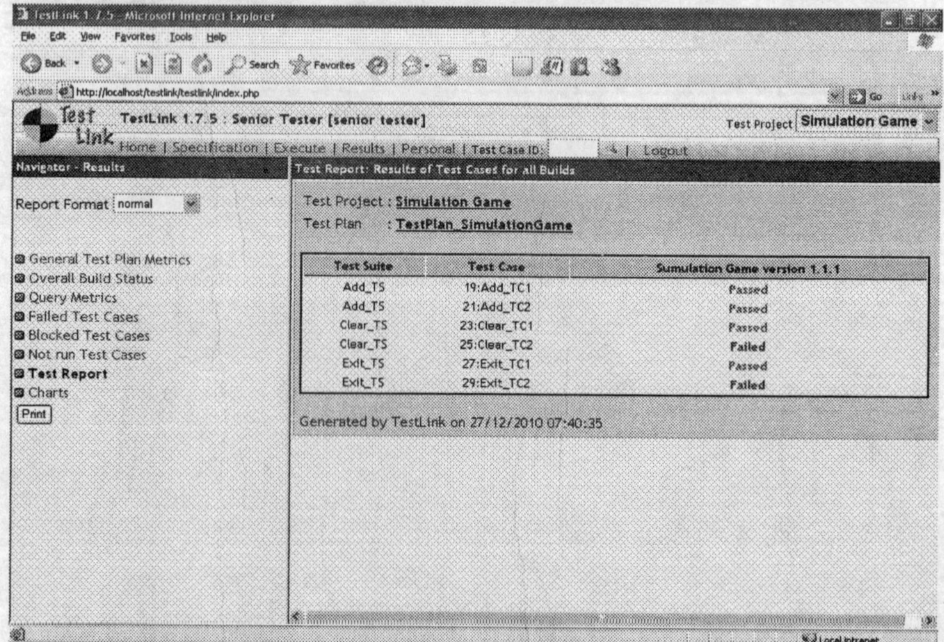

Test Suite	Test Case	Sumulation Game version 1.1.1
Add_TS	19:Add_TC1	Passed
Add_TS	21:Add_TC2	Passed
Clear_TS	23:Clear_TC1	Passed
Clear_TS	25:Clear_TC2	Failed
Exit_TS	27:Exit_TC1	Passed
Exit_TS	29:Exit_TC2	Failed

References:

Documentation available on: http://www.teamst.org/ or http://www.teamst.org/index.php/doc

Manual Test case writing using CTE-XL

Classification Tree Editor eXtended Logics

Introduction :

- The CTE XL is a completely new and revised version of the CTE, written entirely in Java.
- The tool CTE is based on the classification-tree method, a special approach to (black-box) partition testing.
- The classification-tree method is a self-development partly using and improving ideas from the category-partition method defined by Ostrand and Balcer (OSTR).
- The CTE is a graphical editor supporting the application of the classification-tree method.
- The classification-tree method (CTM) is a testing method for the systematic design of test cases on basis of the specification. CTM and CTE are widely used in industrial practice.
- The classification-tree method is a self-development partly using and improving ideas from the category-partition method defined by Ostrand and Balcer (OSTR).

Using CTE XL Tool :

Classification Tree Method is very well supported by CTE XL tool. We used CTE XL tool to:

- Draw the classification tree
- Select the test cases
- Working with CTE XL was made easier because of:
- Simple classification tree
- Moderate number of test cases

Open interfaces of CTE-XL

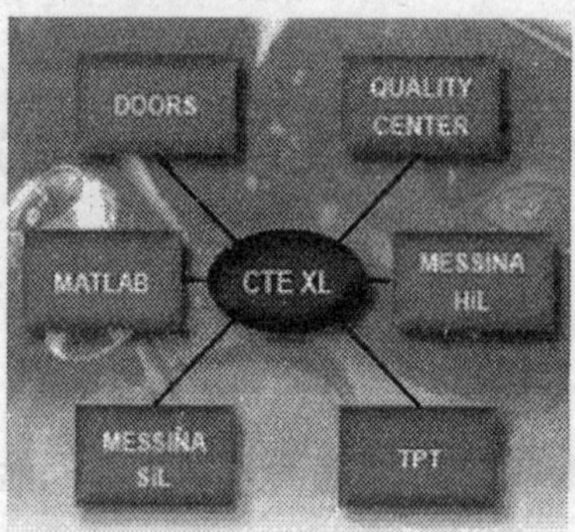

Top features of CTE XL

- Systematic and common classification tree method
- Universally applicable
- Configurable dependency rules
- Automated test case generation
- Methodical linking with test automation tool
- Open interfaces to industry standards
- Linking with test platform for model-based ECU function development MESINA

Installation Steps of CTE-XL

Download CTE XL 1.9.3

- Go to browser & type link http://www.berner-mattner.com/en/berner-mattner-home/products/cte/download.html
- Download & Save the file

1. Double Click on your setup file

2. Click on 'Run' button

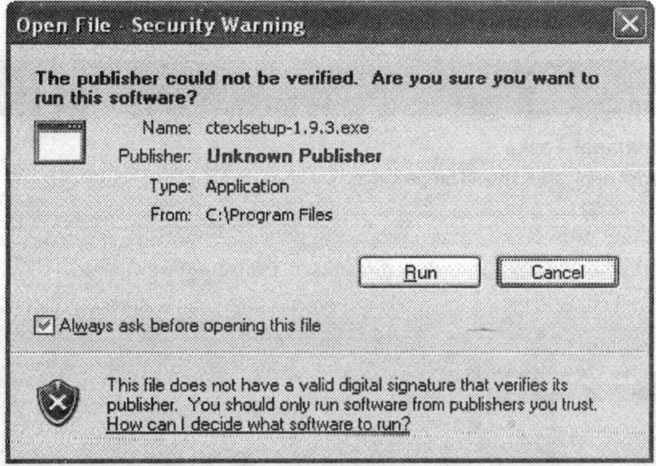

3. Choose Language

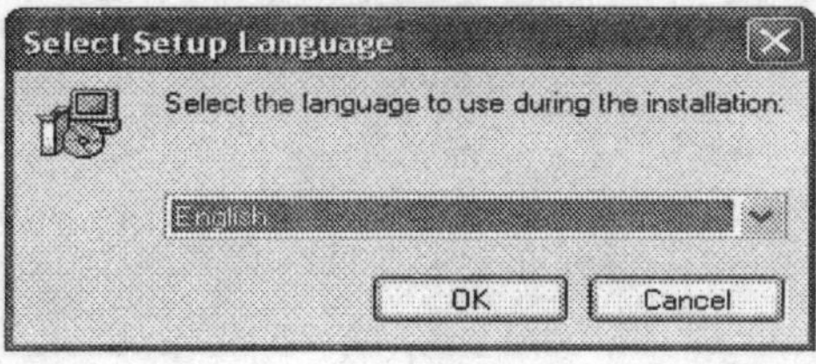

4. Choose installation directory & Click the “next” button to proceed further

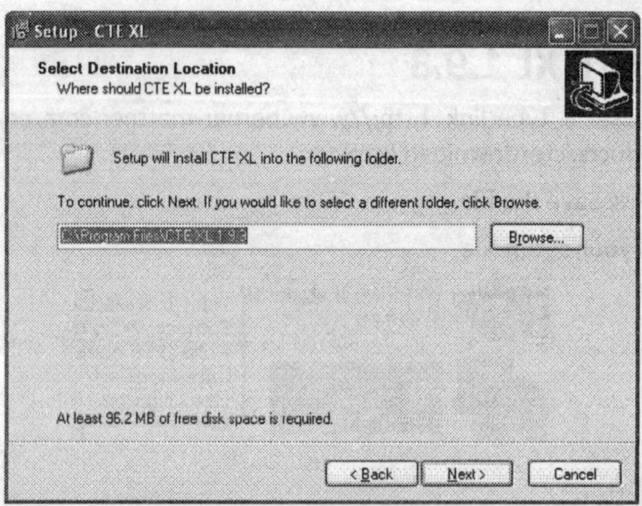

5. Select ‘Create a desktop icon’ & click on Next

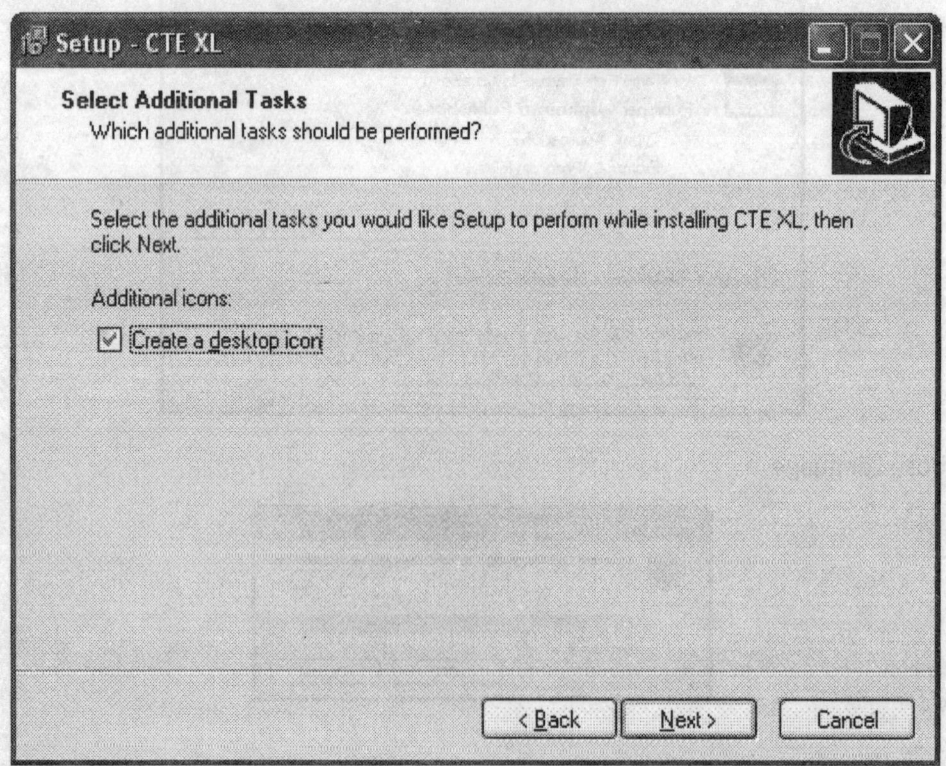

6. Click on 'Install' button

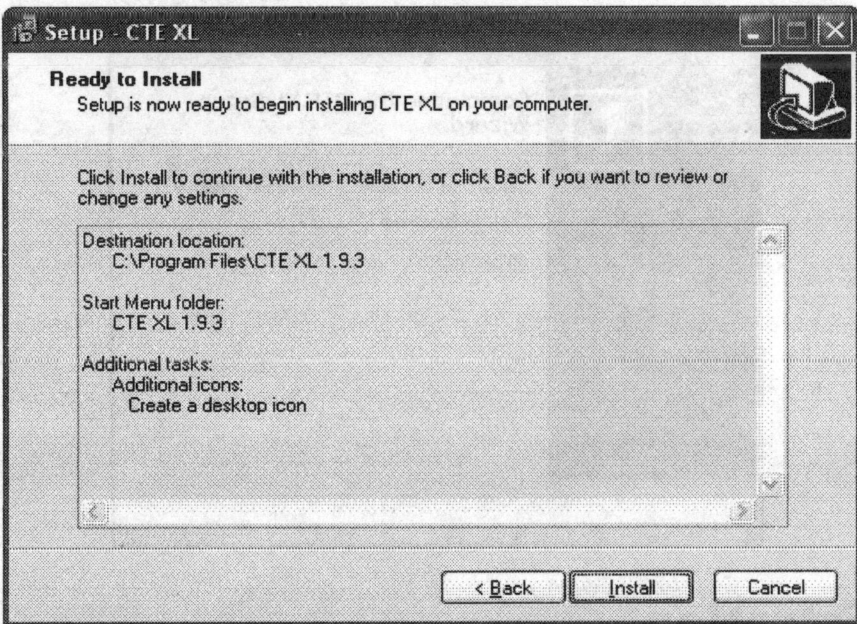

7. You can see the status of Installation status in the Installation wizard

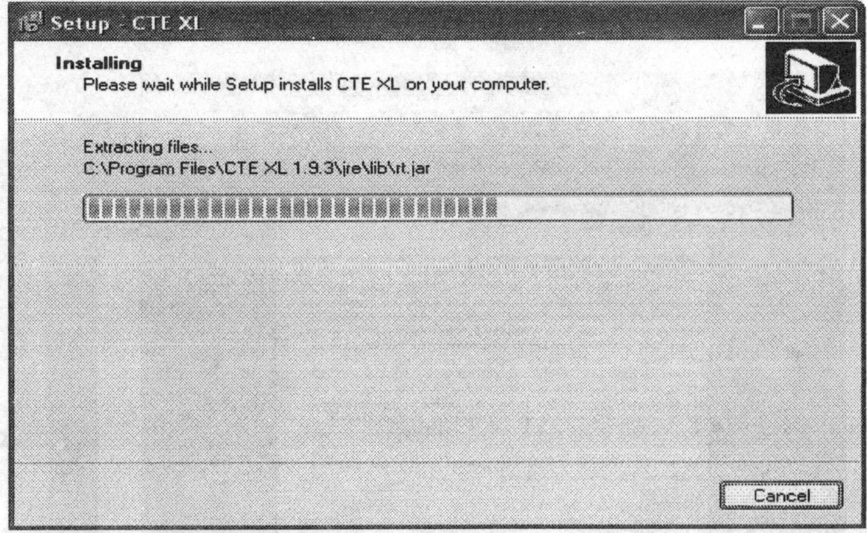

8. Once the installation has been completed, you will get the following window. Click finish.

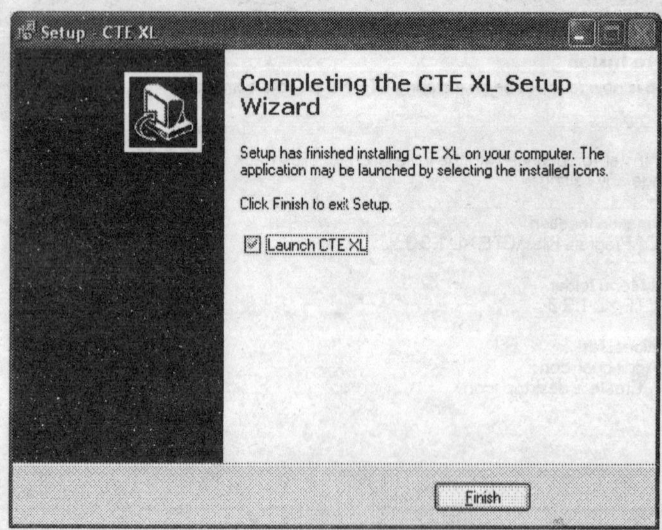

Registration

When you start the CTE-XL for the first time, it asks for the license agreement & following window will appear. Click on **I agree** button.

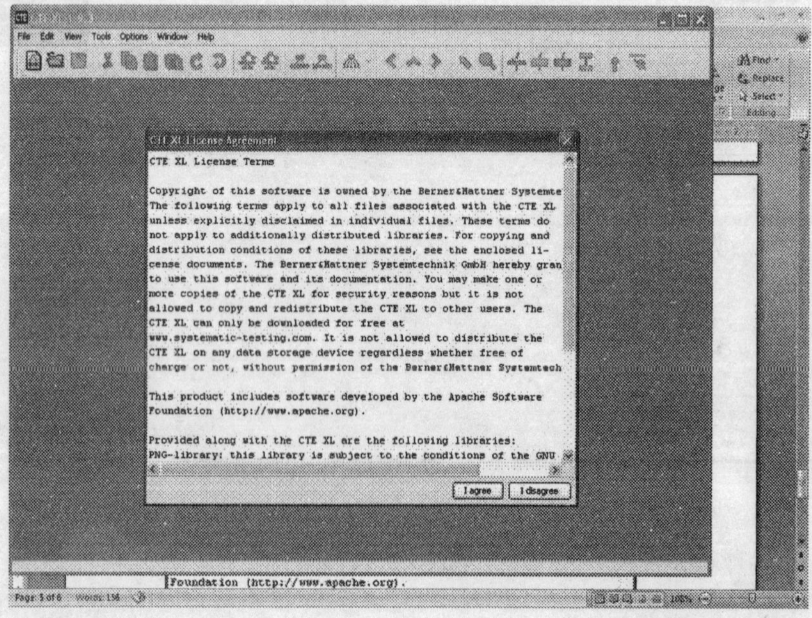

Enter all details in the field & click on **Get License** button.

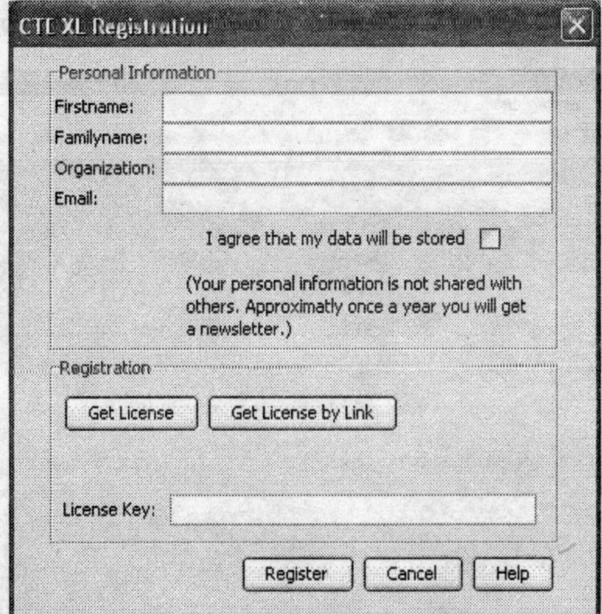

Status Window appear

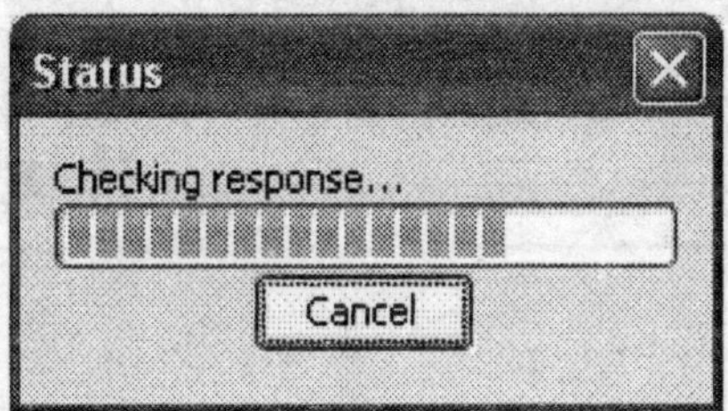

After a successful registration the following dialog box will appear:

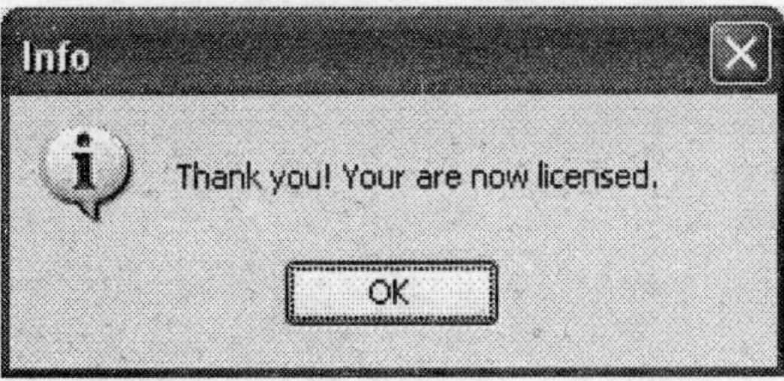

How to open CTE-XL

To open CTE-XL double Click on CTE-XL icon, following window will appear.

CTE-XL Window Areas

The CTE window is divided into three areas, the **Draw Pad, the Table Pad and the Test Item List**. Each area has certain functionality:

- The **Draw Pad** is used for the step-by-step creation of the classification tree. The classification tree elements will be displayed using different symbols.
- The **Table Pad** (combination table) is used to specify the contents of the test items by marking elements of the classification tree. These mark combinations form the specification that is one of the results of the classification tree method.
- The **Test Item List** is used to define test cases, test sequences and test steps. Every test item creates a new line in the Table Pad.

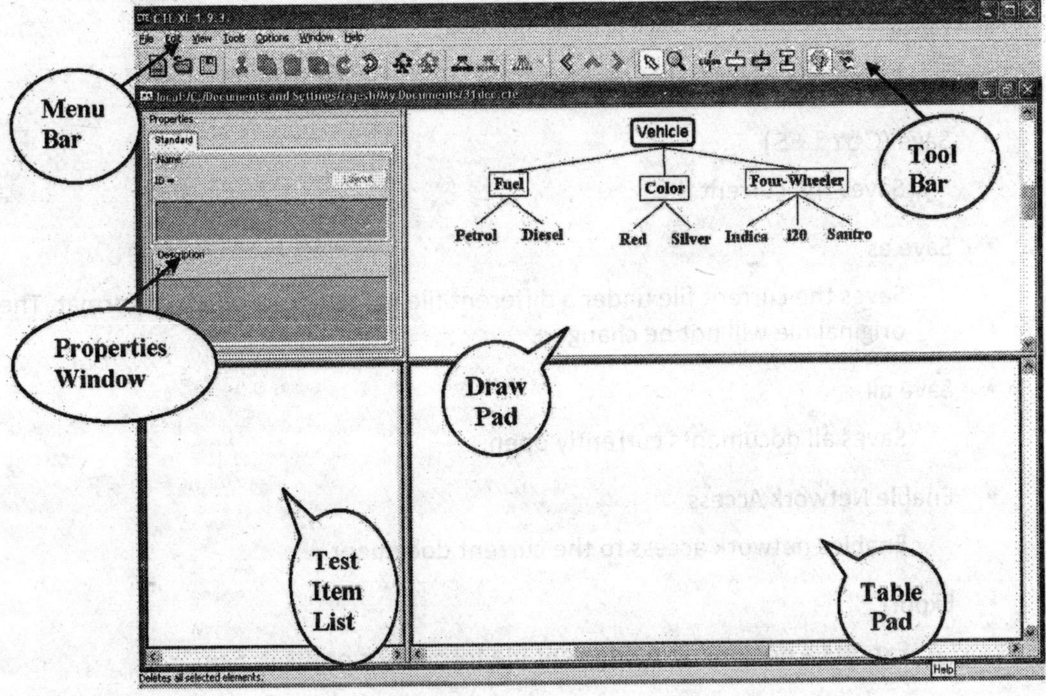

Menu Bar Contain-

1) File-

- New (`Ctrl+N`)

  Opens a new window with a new document.

- Open(`Ctrl+O`)

  Opens a dialog box in which you can select a file which is to be opened.

- Remot Project

  Opens a dialog box in which you can open a file provided by a network.

- Close

  Closes the current document.

- Save (`Ctrl+S`)

  Saves the current file.

- Save as

  Saves the current file under a different file name or in a different format. The original file will not be changed.

- Save all

  Saves all documents currently open.

- Enable Network Access

  Enables network access to the current document.

- Export

  Exports a document in different file formats or prints it. See

- Page setup

  Here you can make settings, such as paper size or margins, for printing.

- Print (`Ctrl+P`)

  Prints the current document with recently made print settings.

- Quit (`Ctrl+Q`), (`Alt+F4`)

  Closes the program.

2) Edit

- Copy (`Ctrl+C`)

  Copies the currently marked tree element or the current test case onto the Windows clipboard.

- Cut (`Ctrl1+X`)

  Copies the currently marked tree element or the current test case onto the Windows clipboard and deletes it from the classification tree.

- Paste (`Ctrk+V`)

  Inserts an element from the clipboard into the document.

- Delete (`Del`)

  Deletes the marked element.

- Select all (`Ctrl+A`)

  Marks all elements in the classification tree window.

3) View

- Zoom in (Ctrl+ numeric +)

  Maximizes the view on the classification tree.

- Zoom out (Ctrl+ numeric -)

  Minimizes the view on the classification tree.

- TagTable

  Shows the values of test steps in a table nest to the test case list.

- Properties

  Switches the properties field in the upper left-hand corner on and off.

- Statistics

  Displays statistics for the current document.

4) Tools

- Tags

Opens the tags dialog box in which you can make adjustments to the tags in the properties field.

- Auto Layout (Ctrl+L)

  Puts the whole classification tree into a new order.

- Auto Layout subtree

  Puts all elements of the classification under the current element into a new order.

- Generate Test cases

  Automatically generates test cases according to set rules.

- Dependency rules

  Opens the dependency editor with which you can define dependency rules.

- Requirements

  In the requirements dialog you can import requirements from Requirements Management tools.

- Tree Templates

  Opens the Classification Tree Library, used to insert tree elements from existing CTE XL files.

5) Options

- General

  Here you can make adjustments for general settings in the appearance of the CTE XL.

- Tag icons

  Here you can enter new icons, which can serve as marking for tree elements.

- Dialogs

  Here you can make adjustments for the behavior of the properties field.

- Default layout

  Determines the default layout for tree elements and test cases.

6) Window

- Cascade

  Puts all windows opened into cascade order.

- Tile

  Puts all windows opened into tile order.

- Window List

  Displays a list of all windows opened, the window selected will come to the fore.

7) Help

- Help

  Displays the help available.

- Register

  Opens the registration dialog for activating the CTE XL license.

- About

  Displays information about the CTE XL version used and the license.

Creating, Opening, Saving a document

Creating a new document:-

1. Create CTE XL new document by clicking new in file menu or

2. Click create new project on toolbar. You will get following window.

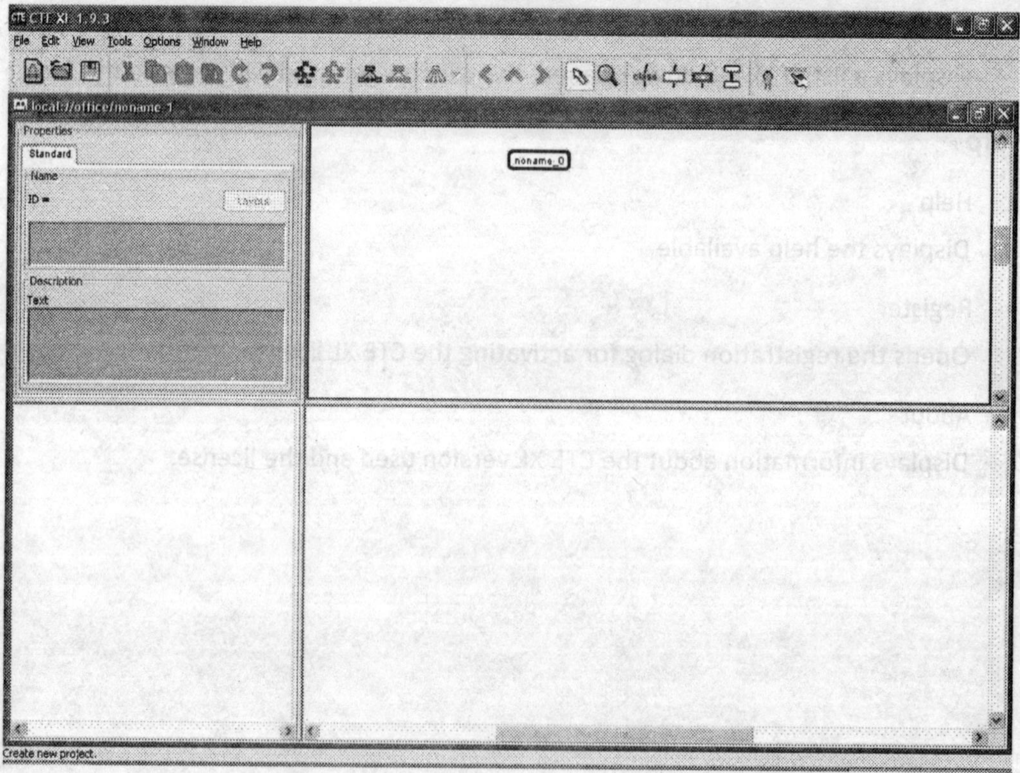

Opening a document:-

For opening existing CTE XL document:

1. Click on open in the File menu

2. In the toolbar click on open existing project

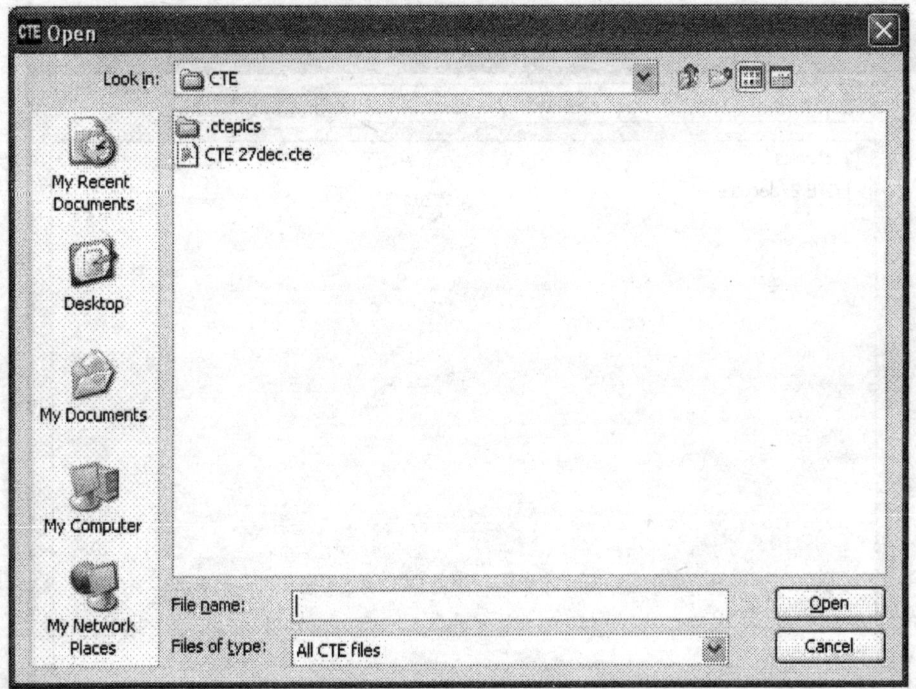

Select a file or enter a file name and then click on **Open**.

Saving a document:

For saving a document:

1. Click on Save in the File menu or

2. On toolbar, click on save project

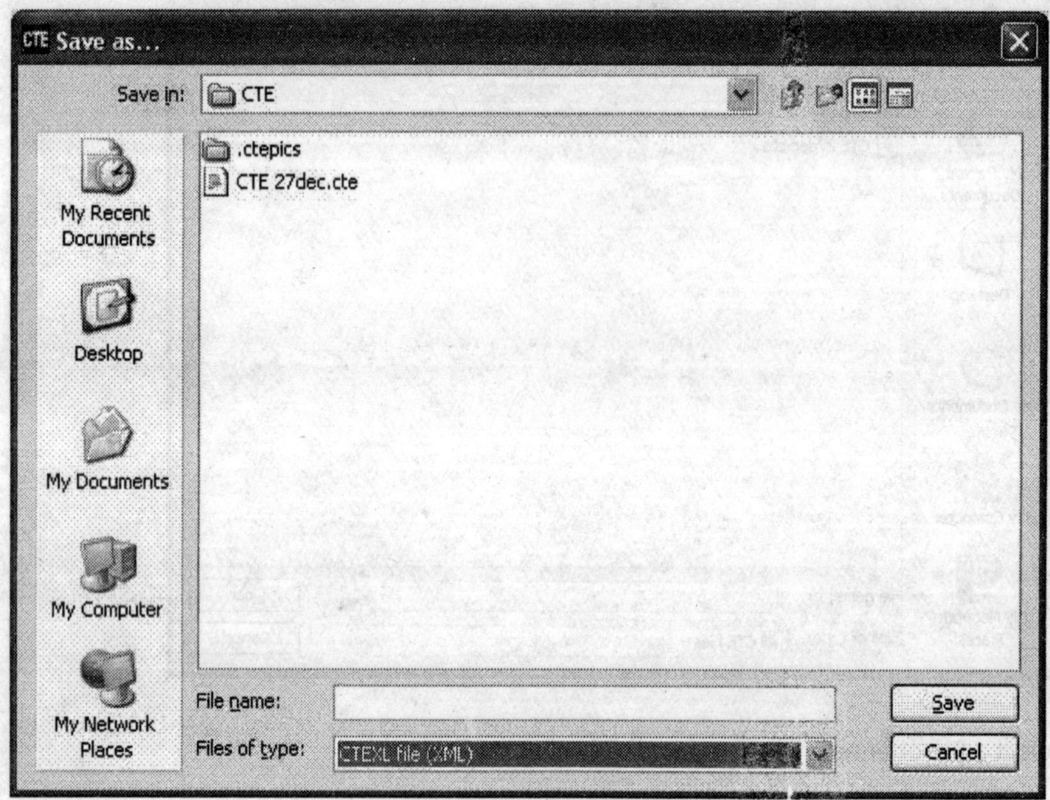

If you want to save a document under different format, select Save as in the file menu

CTE XL provides following formats –

1. CTE XL file (XML) (standard)

2. CTE32 file version 2.0

3. CTE file version 1.0

4. All Files

The Classification Tree

Creating elements in the tree :

1. Root element - This element is the root of the classification tree and represents the object which is to be tested. The root element cannot be deleted.

E. g. Root – Vehicle

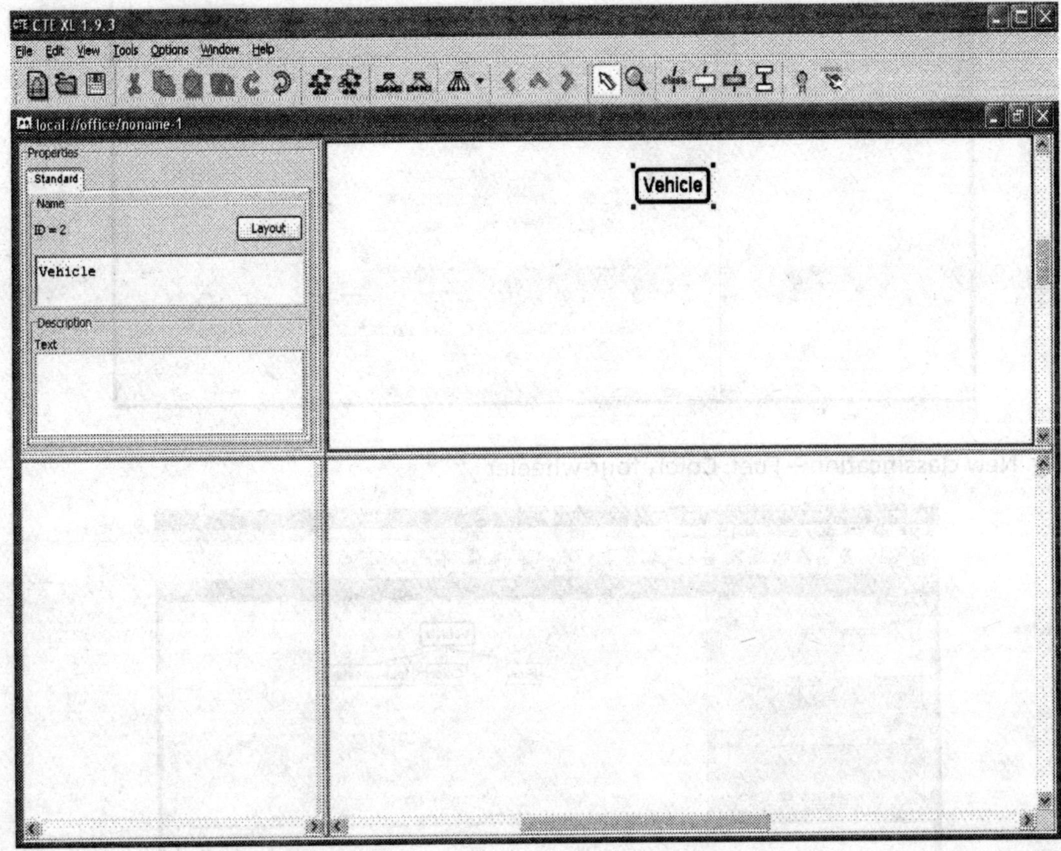

2. Classification – To create classification, right click on vehicle (Root) & select create classification.

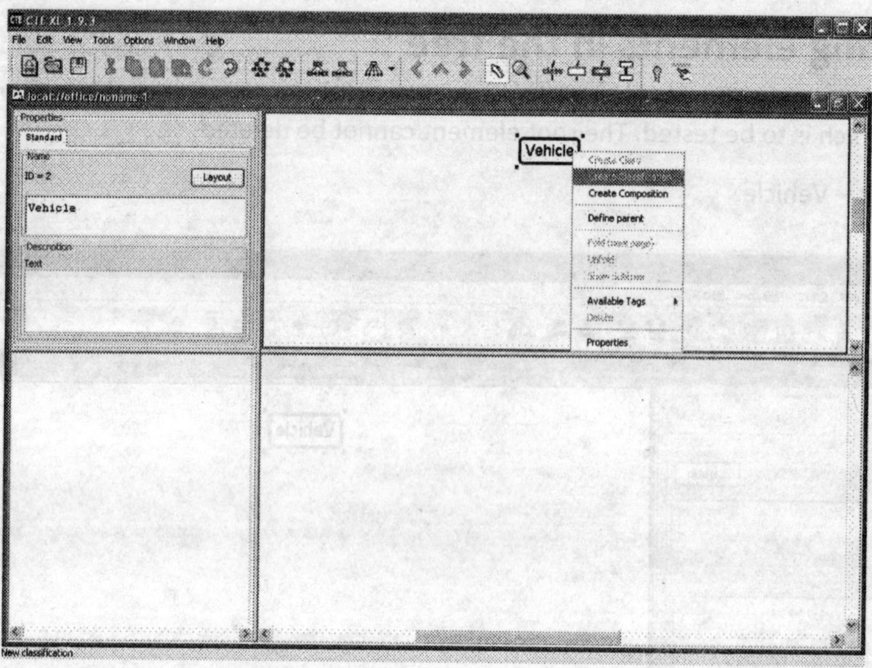

E.g. New classification – Fuel, Color, four-wheeler

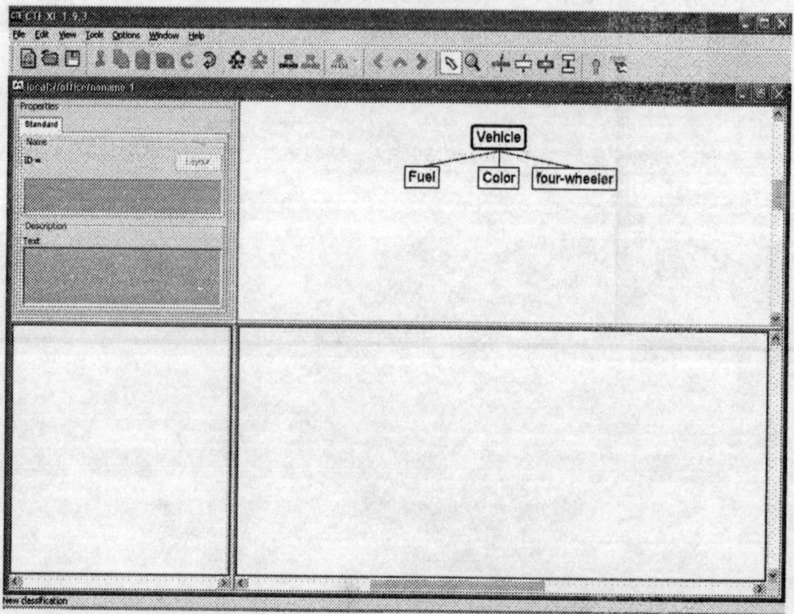

3. Class - Classes may be connected to test cases in the combination table. Classifications and compositions can be created under a class.

To create class, right click on classification & select create class.

E.g. Fuel: Petrol, Diesel

Color: Red, Silver

Four-wheeler: Indica, i20, Santro

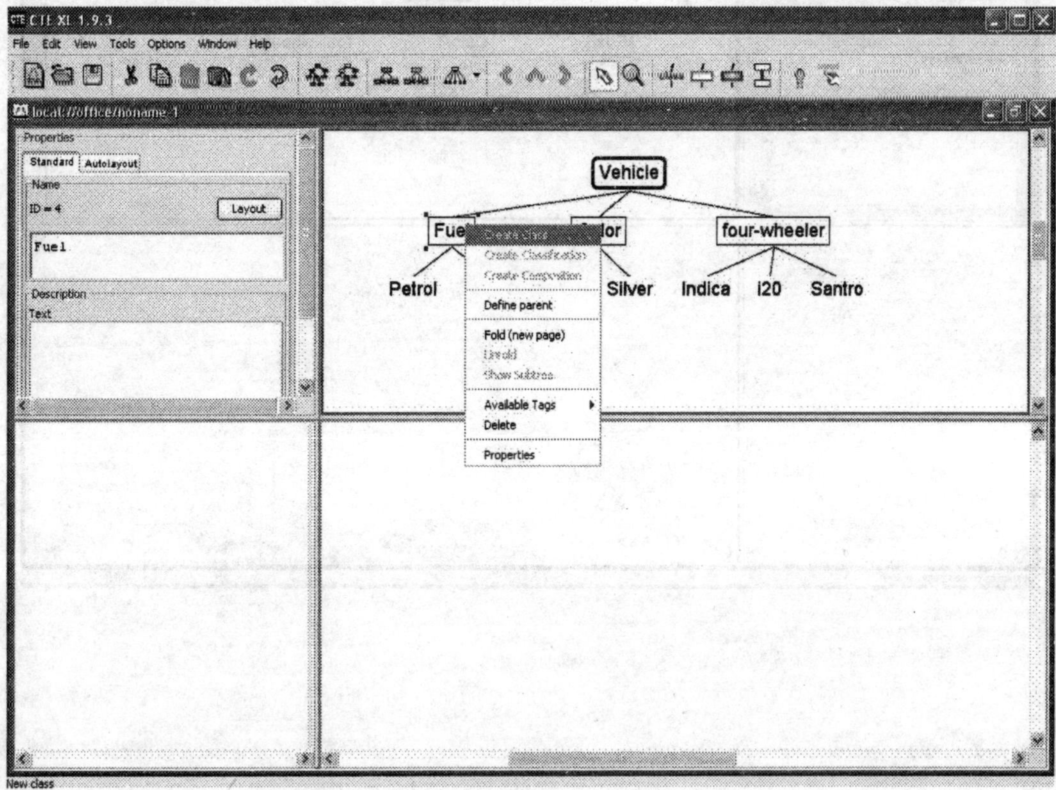

Folding a subtree:

If you want to fold a subtree, right click on the element & select fold (new page), folded tree should look like following window.

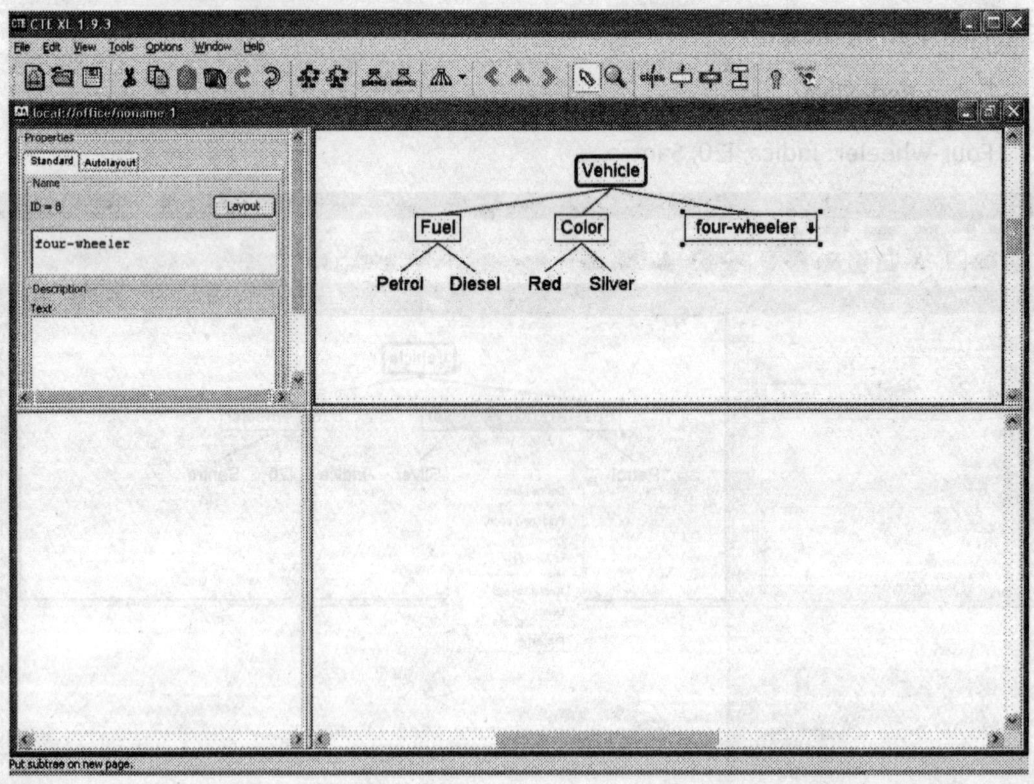

Unfolding a subtree:

Right click on the parent symbol (arrow pointing downwards).Select Unfold from the context menu. Here we will get our previous window.

Working on folded subtree

Right click on element (arrow pointing downward) & select show subtree, following window will be displayed.

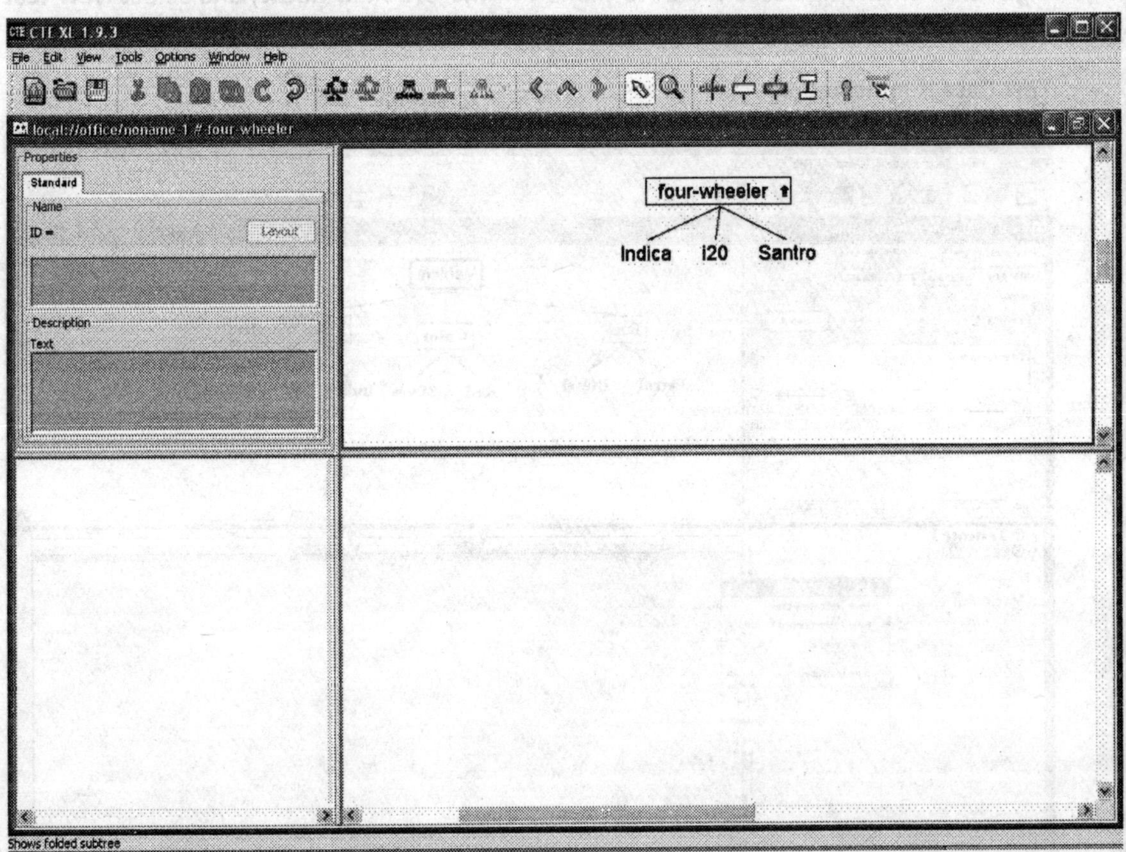

If you want to return to the main tree from the subtree window, right click on arrow pointing upward & select **show Anchor**.

Generating test cases

Generating simple test cases

There are two methods to generate test cases:

1. Generating test cases manually.

Right click on the test case table (to the left in the CTE XL window) and select **New test case** from the context menu. A new test case will be inserted.

Test Case is indicated by ◯

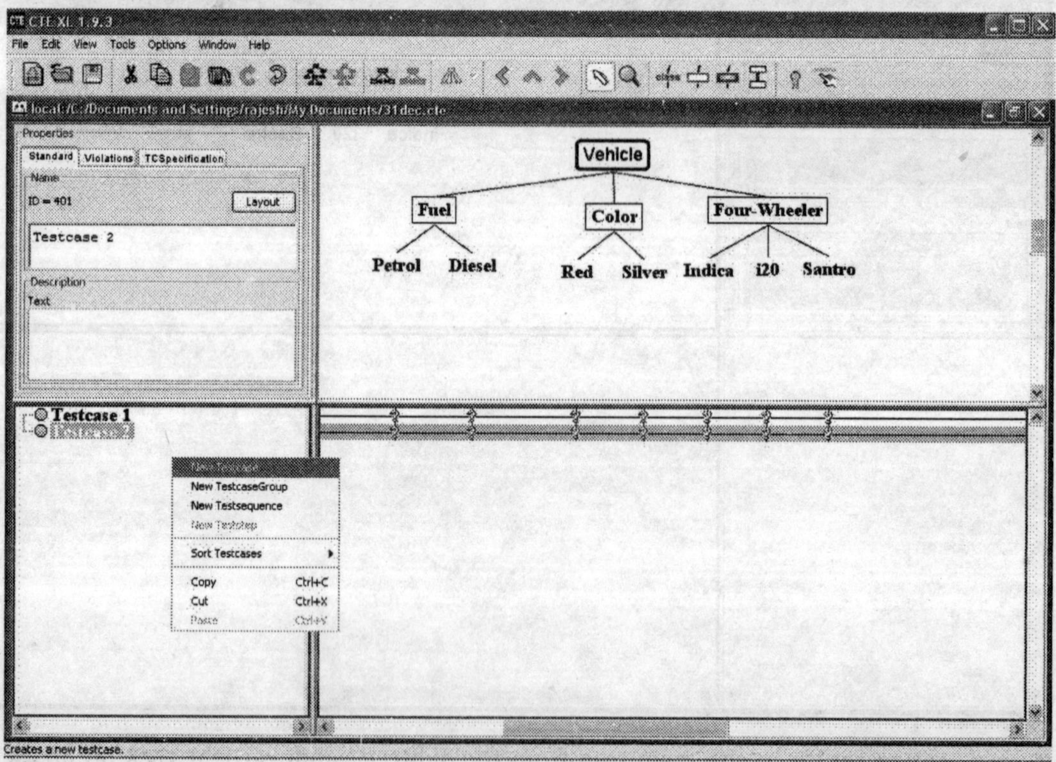

Generating test case groups

Click with the right-hand mouse button on the test case list field and select **NewTestcaseGroup** in the context menu.

TestCaseGroup is indicated by

To generate new test cases in this test case group, mark the test case group and insert new test cases.

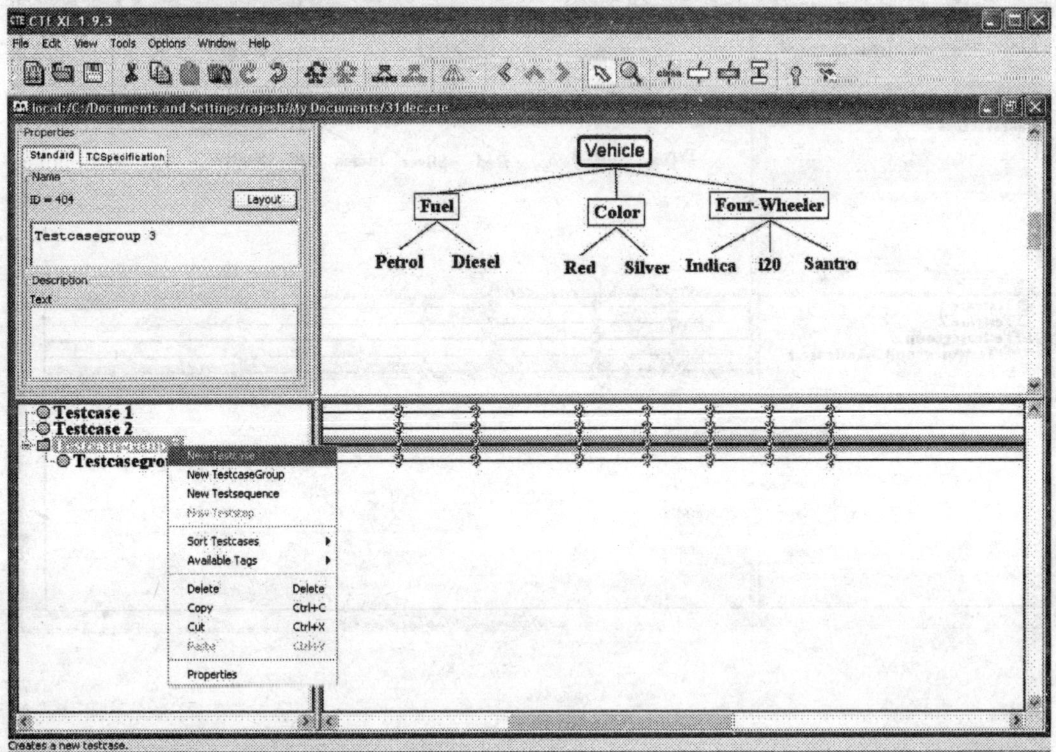

Note : *It is possible to create further test case groups within a test case group. Thereby, a testcase hierarchy emerges*

Generating test sequences

Test sequences are a collection of test steps. To generate a test sequence, click with the right-hand mouse button on the test case field and select **New test sequence** from the context menu.

Test Sequences is indicated by

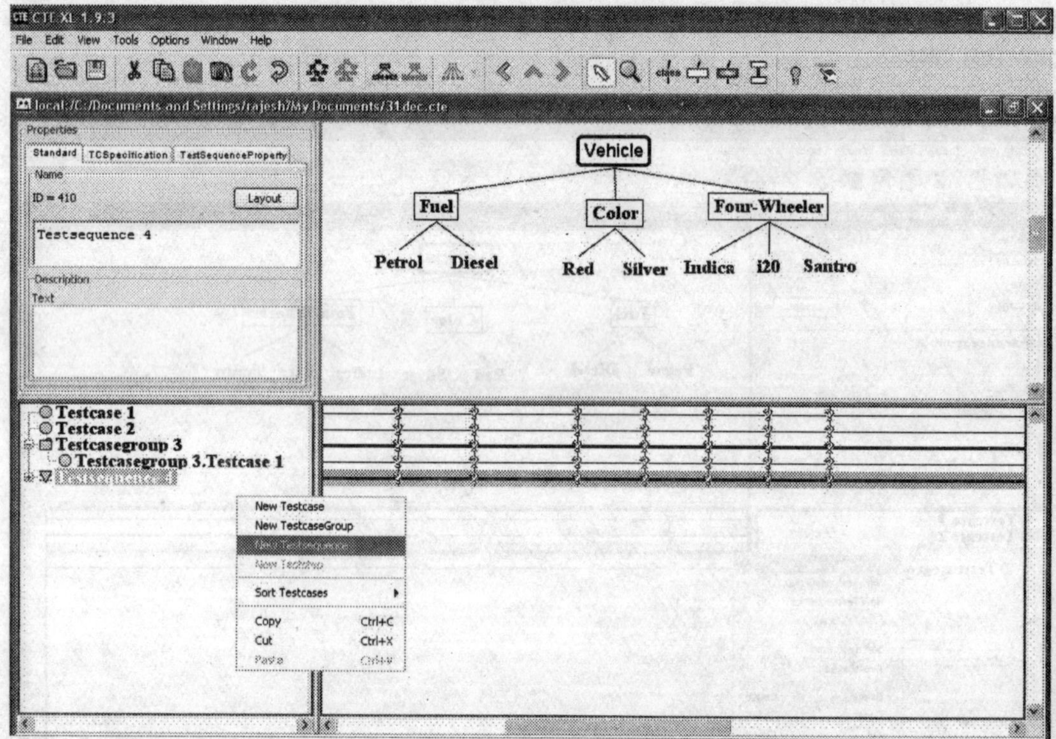

Creating test steps

Each test sequence contains a certain amount of test steps. To create test steps, click with the right-hand mouse button on the test sequence and then on **New test step**. A new test step will appear within the test sequence. Test Steps are indicated by

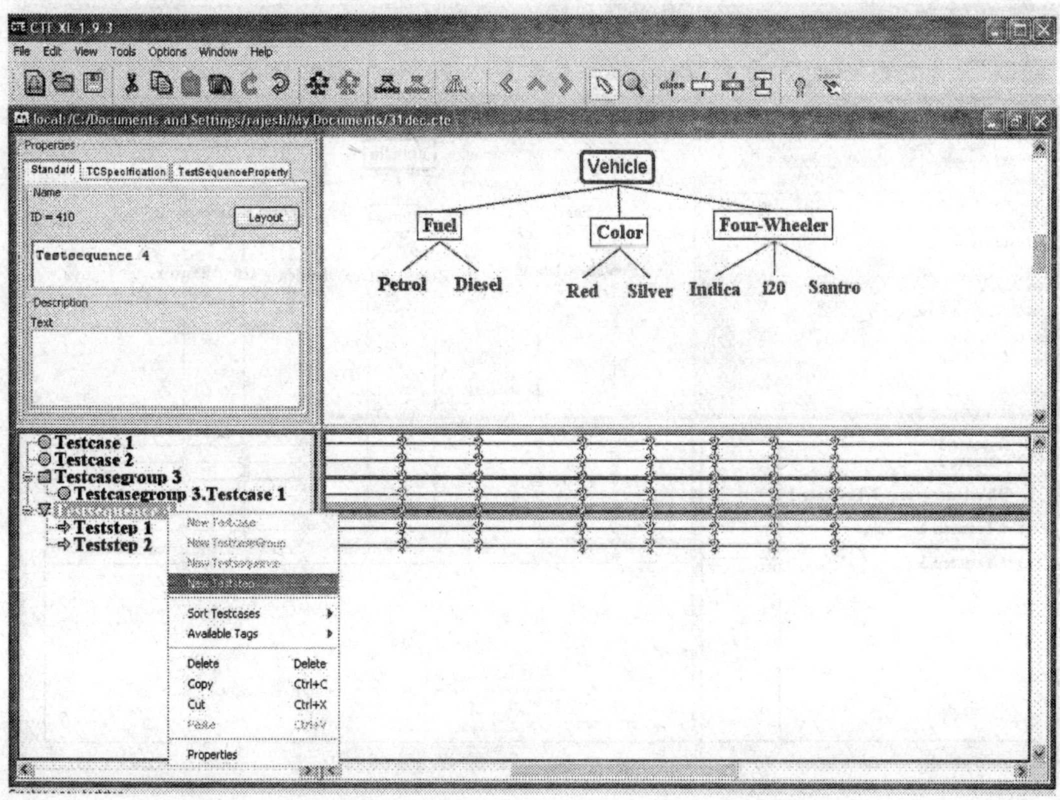

Displaying a tag table

It is possible to have test step values displayed in a table in the test case list by selecting **Tag table** in the **View** selection menu.

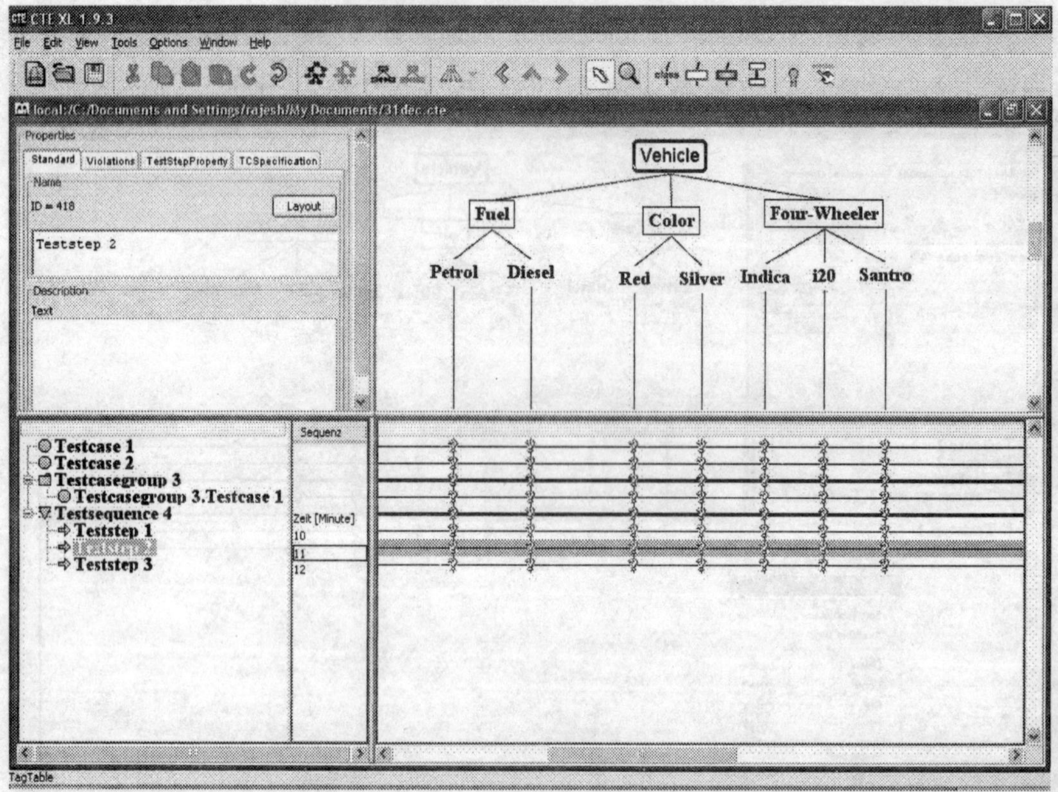

2. Generating test cases automatically.

In order to open the test case generator, select the Generate test cases option in the Tools menu. The window of the test case generator will appear.

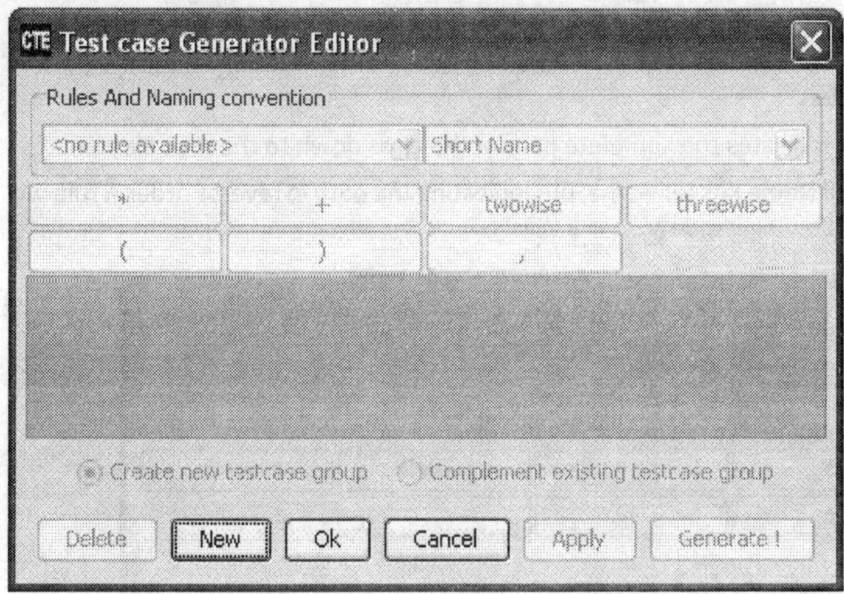

1. Click on the New button to create a new rule for the test cases to be generated. Here we can set up rule.

Setting up a rule :

2. Enter a name for the rule in the dialog box and click on OK.. E.g. rule 1

3. You can drag & drop classification tree elements directly.

4. There are different types of inserting links(*, +, (,), twowise & etc.) on Test Case Generator Editor window. You can select anyone of them.

5. Choose one of the following options:

- **Create new testcase group:** Creates the test cases within a new test case group on top of the test case hierarchy.
- **Complement existing testcase group:** Select a test case group in the test case list. When generating test cases, this test case group will be complemented by test cases whose markings are not yet covered by existing test cases.

6. Naming conventions :

- **Shortname** : Indicates the name of class only.
- **Unambiguous Name:** Indicates the path if there are two classes with the same name.
- **Reverse Unambiguous Name:** As unambiguous name, but indicating the path in reverse order.
- **Full Name:** Indicates the complete path of the class down to the root element.
- **Reverse Full Name** : As full name, but indicating the path in reverse order A rule will look like following window.

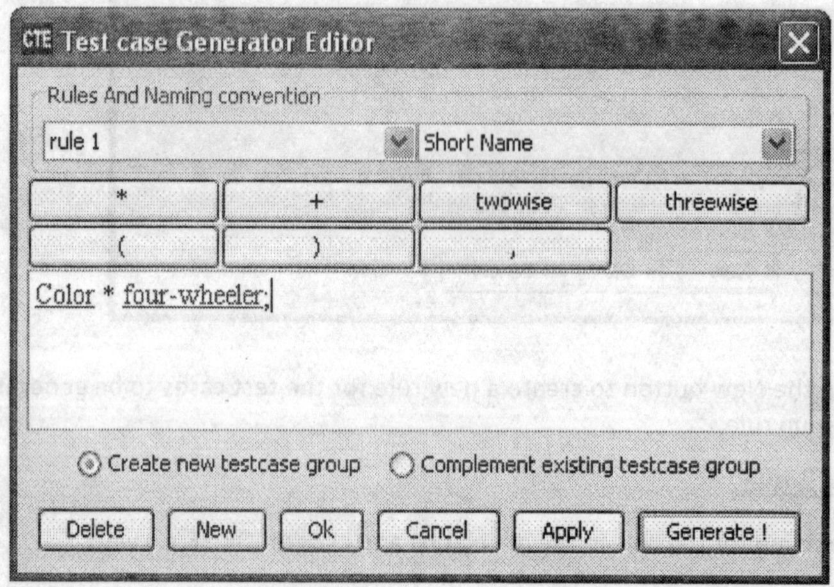

7. Click on Generate & then apply button.

The editor will now create the test cases and insert them, with the name of the rule, into a test case group in the test case table. The rule editor checks the rule for syntax errors and, if necessary, gives warning.

Meaning of Each Marking

A question mark means that no class has yet been marked in the classification indicated.

A solid circle means that the class is assigned to the test case.

If there is no symbol above a marking, another class of the same classification has already been marked. You may still mark it, but in this case the marking in the other class will be deleted.

A grey circle indicates for test case groups that in the test cases of this group the class has been marked at least once. If it has been marked in all the test cases a solid circle will appear

The triangle denotes a **Don't care marking**. This symbol will appear in all classes of the same classification.

The class is assigned to the test case and a circle has been chosen as mark type.

The class is assigned to the test case and a solid square has been chosen as mark type

The class is assigned to the test case and a square has been chosen as mark type

Setting markings

To set markings do the following:

1. Choose a test case or test step from the test item list and a suitable element from the classification tree.
2. Move the mouse pointer to their intersection in the combination table.
3. Press the left mouse button. The desired intersection will be marked

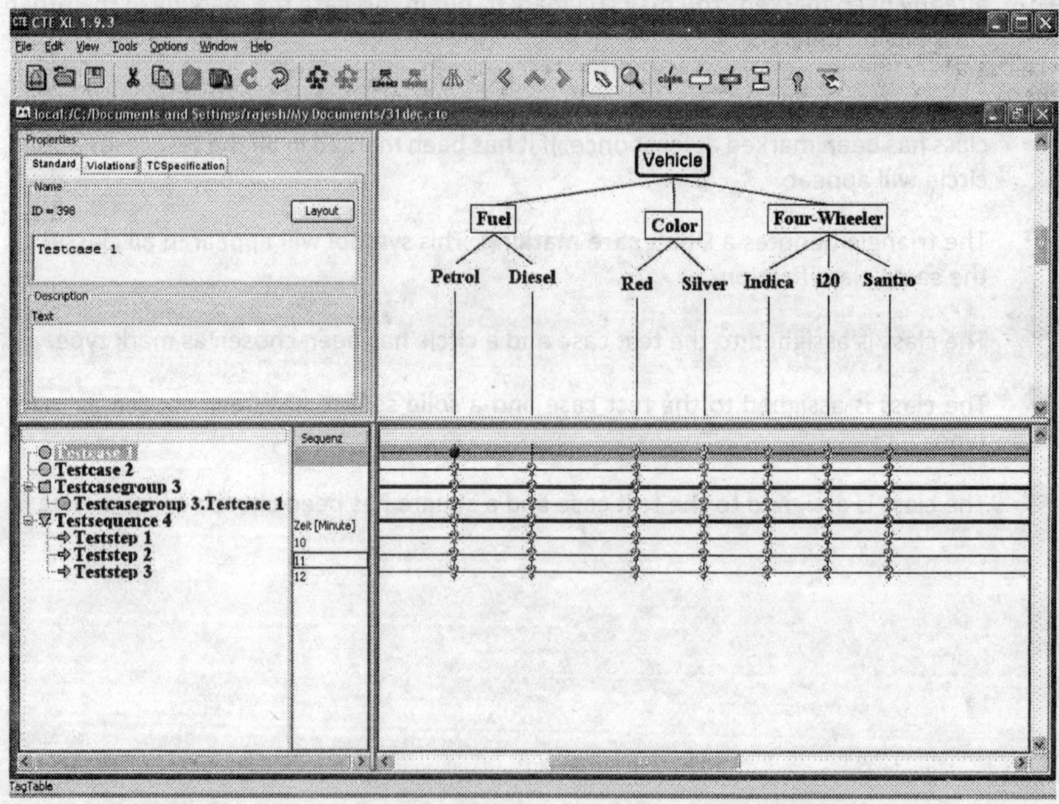

A single marking can be changed as follows:

Open the context menu with the right mouse button

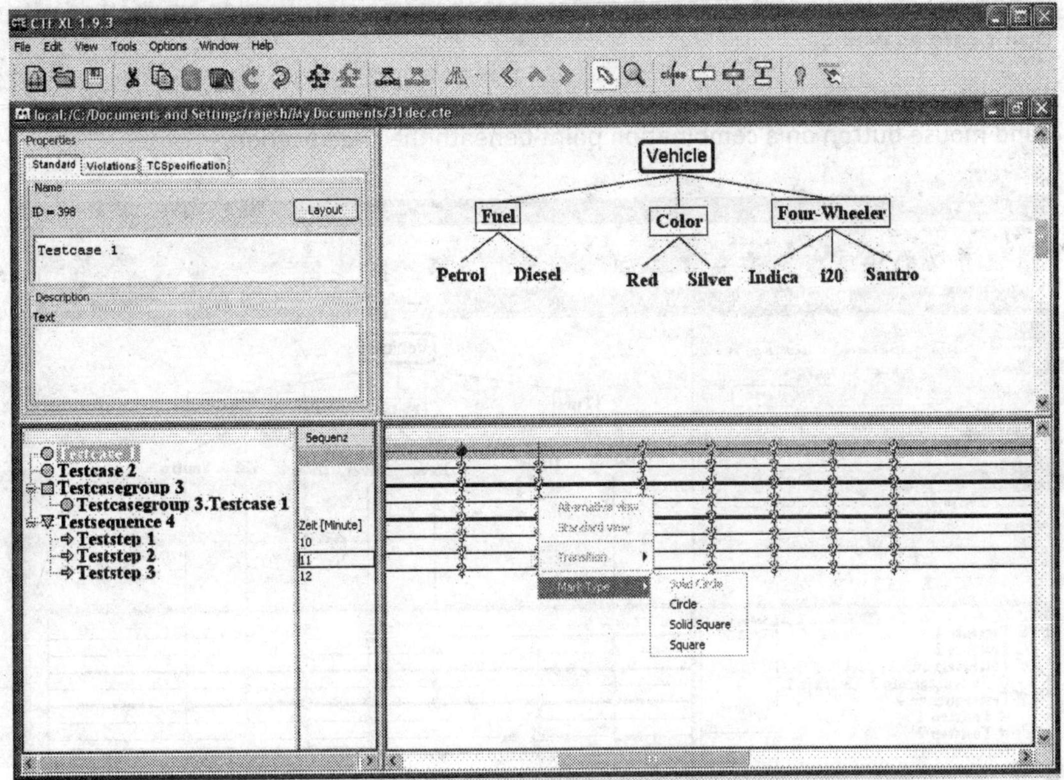

Don't Care Marking

The **don't care** symbol can be used to mark combinations. If one class in a classification is marked with **Don't care** all the other classes in the same classification are marked with **Don't care** as well.

To mark a test case with **Don't care**, keep the shift key pressed and click with the left-hand mouse button on a combination point beneath the classification.

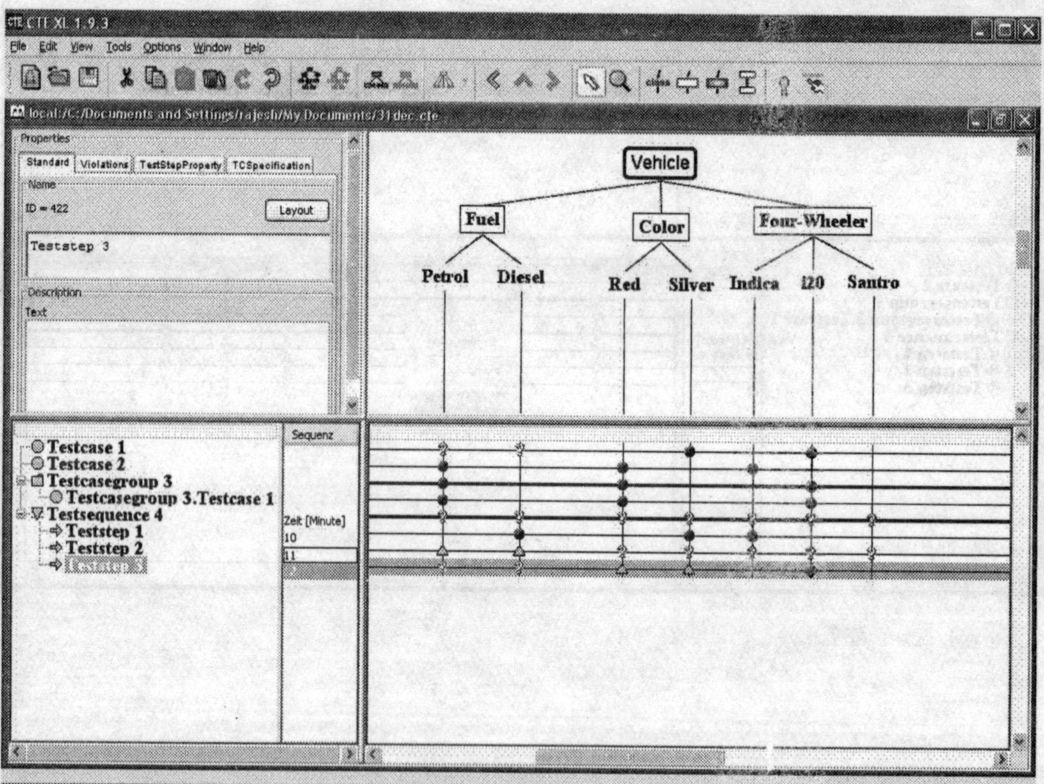

Transition

Transitions represent connections between the test steps of a test sequence. Transitions may be used to further specify changes of values from one test step of a test sequence to another test step.

Insert transitions

To insert transitions in a test sequence do the following:

1. Move the mouse pointer over the marking of a test step in the combination table. *The mouse pointer changes to a circle.*

2. Open the context menu with the right mouse button.

3. Choose **Transition** and **Create Transition** from the sub menu.

According to the selected type of *Transitions* in the **TablePad**, the following test step will be automatically connected with a predefined *transition type.*

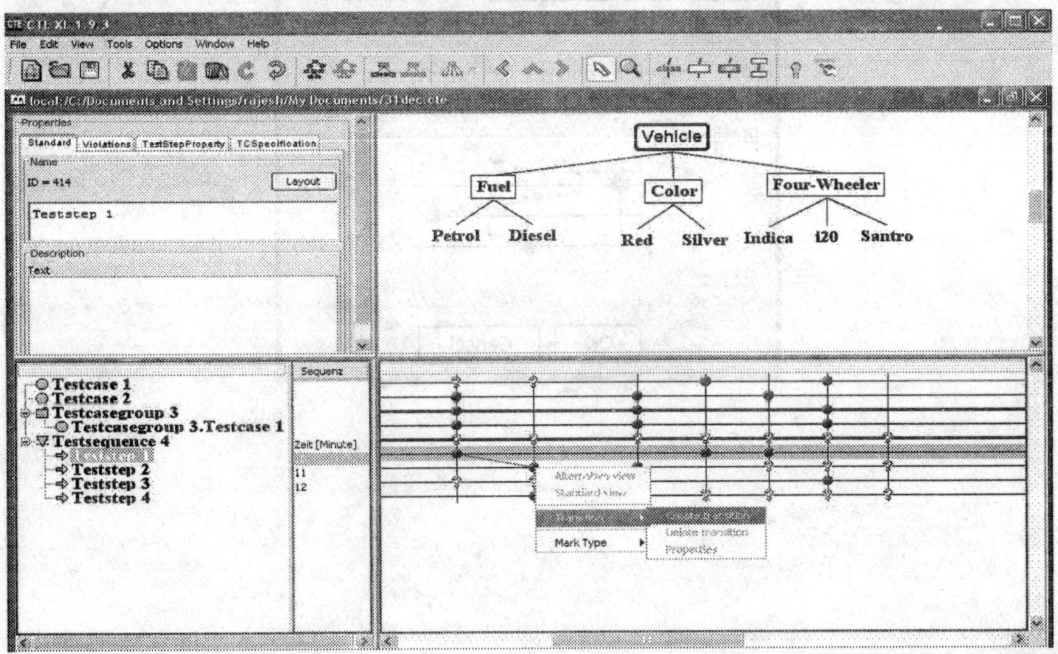

Transition properties

You can change the line type of the transition.

1. Click with the right-hand mouse button on the starting point of a transition. Select the **Properties** option in the context menu under **Transition**. The following dialogue box will appear:
2. Here you can adjust the following settings like Transition type in name, line type in Linetype, transition color.
3. Click on **OK** button.

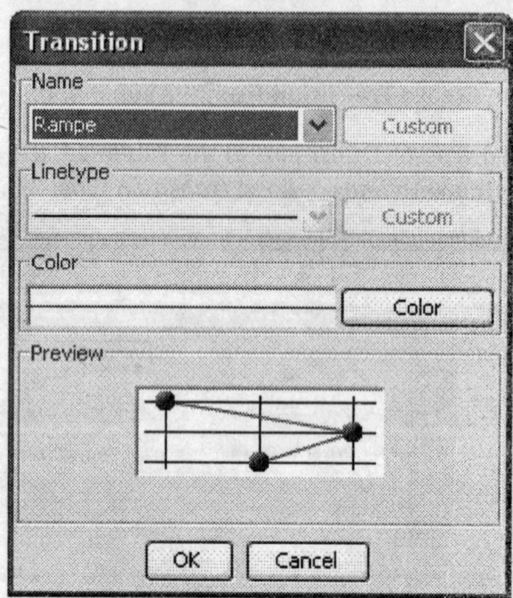

Deleting Transitions

1. Move the mouse pointer over a marking with a transition. *The mouse pointer changes to a circle.*

2. Open the context menu with the right mouse button.

3. Choose **Delete Transition.**

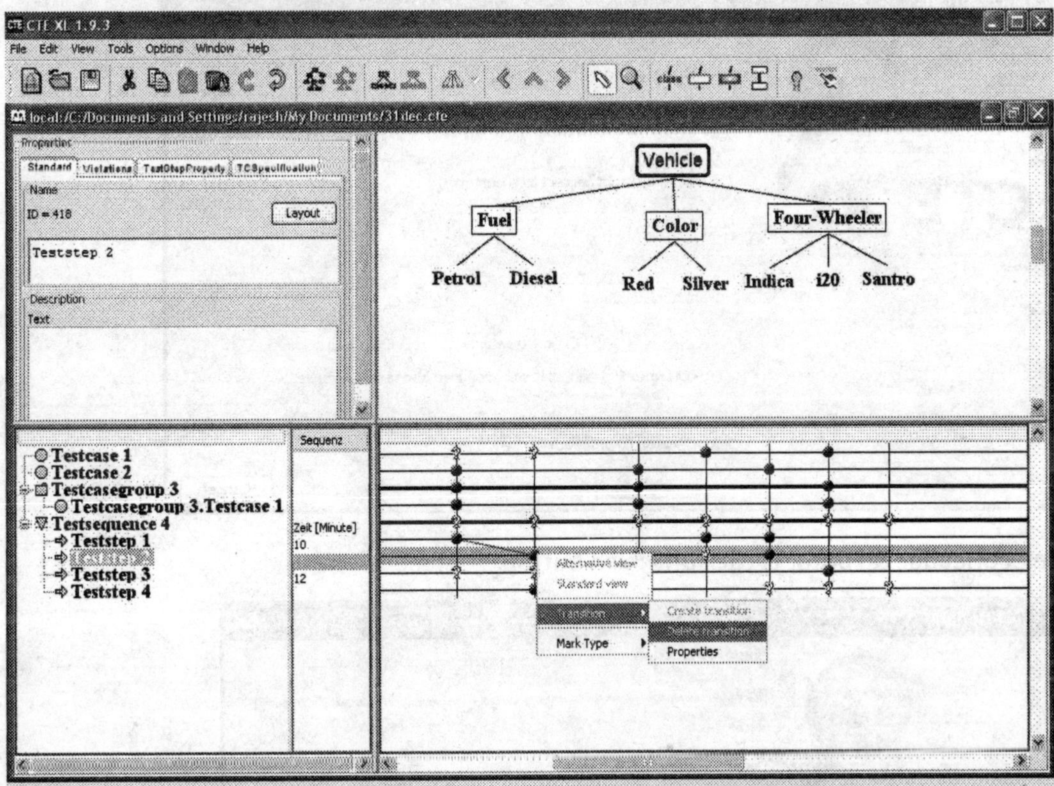

Printing & Exporting a Document

Printing a Document

In file, click on Export, select PRINT formats from drop-down list. Following window will appear. Click on Next button

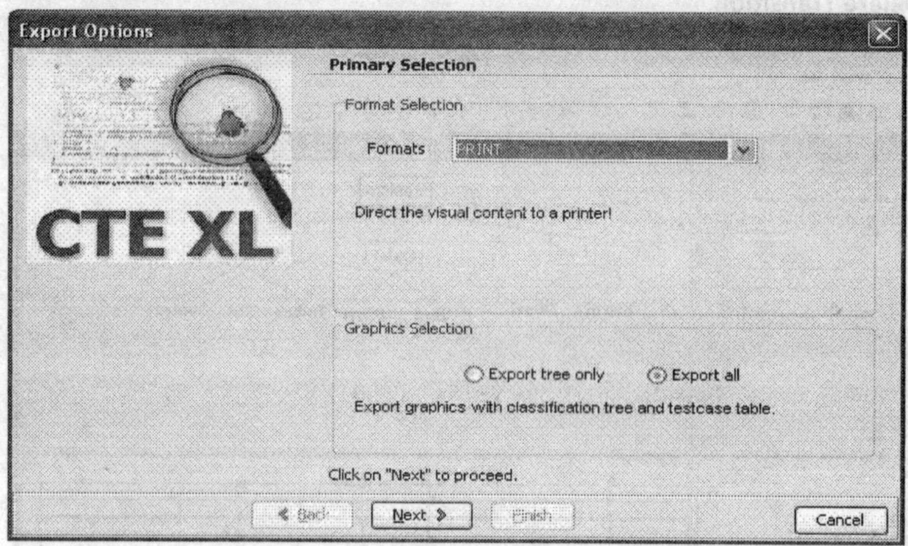

Select Header & Footer & click on Finish button

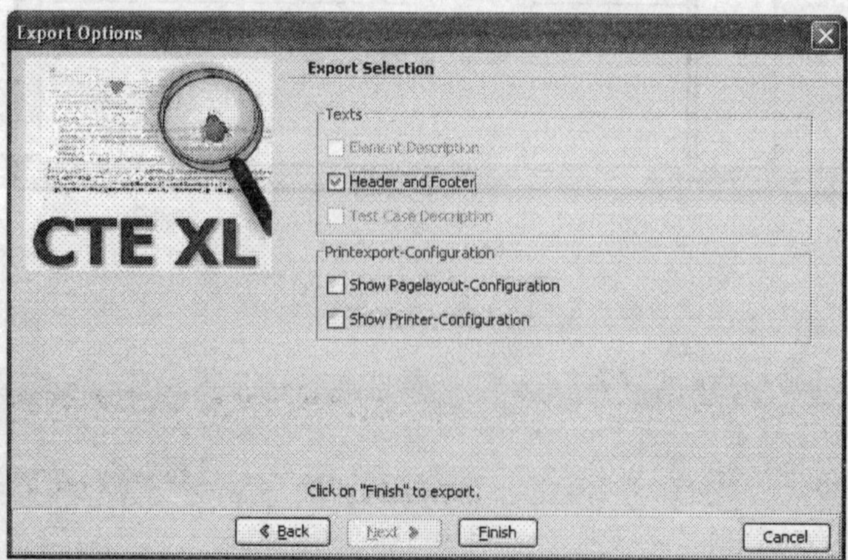

Exporting a document

You can export the document into different file format.

Select **Export** from the **File** menu. The **Export Options** dialog box will open.

Select the format from drop down list. Select graphical section & click on **Next** button

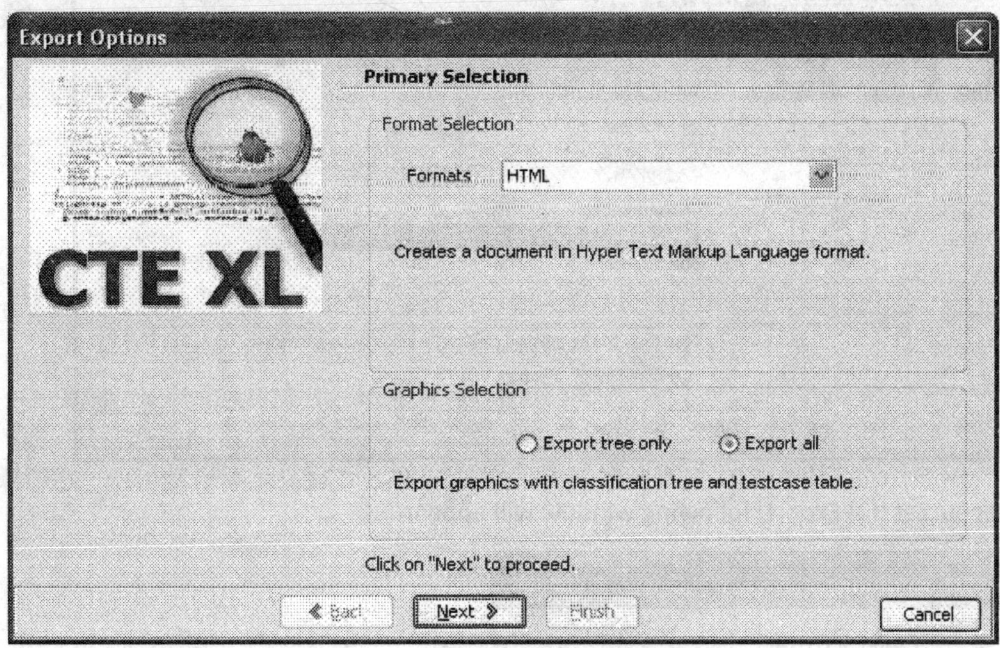

Select file name & path for the output file & Click on **Finish** button.

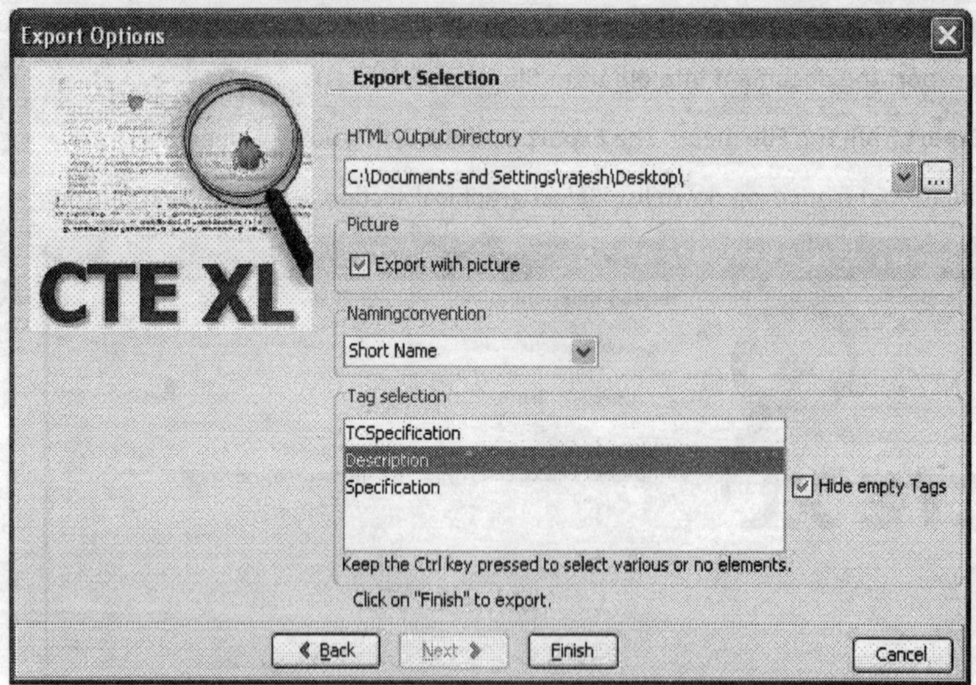

After successful Export, following window will appear.

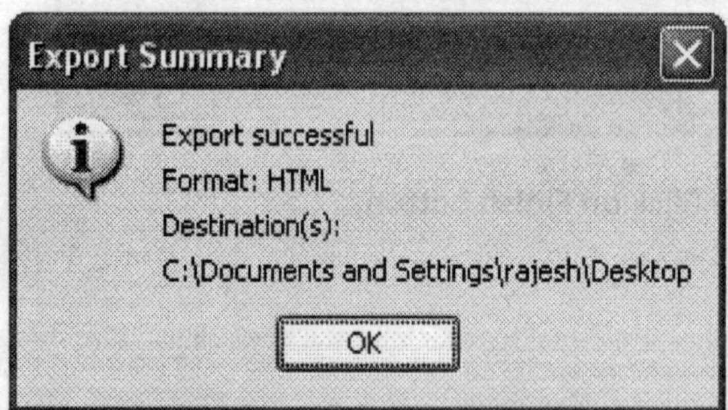

Dependencies

In order to preclude logical errors when generating test cases, there is a dependency manager in the CTE XL, warning the user if an inadmissible or impossible combination of classes has been selected.

For this, logical rules must first be set up in the **dependencies editor**. The **dependencies manager** will follow these rules when marking the test cases. If an inadmissible combination is marked, the dependency manager marks the test case symbol red.

Generating a dependency rule

Dependency rules are generated in **dependency editor.** Open the dependency editor by clicking on **Dependency rules** in the **Tools** menu.

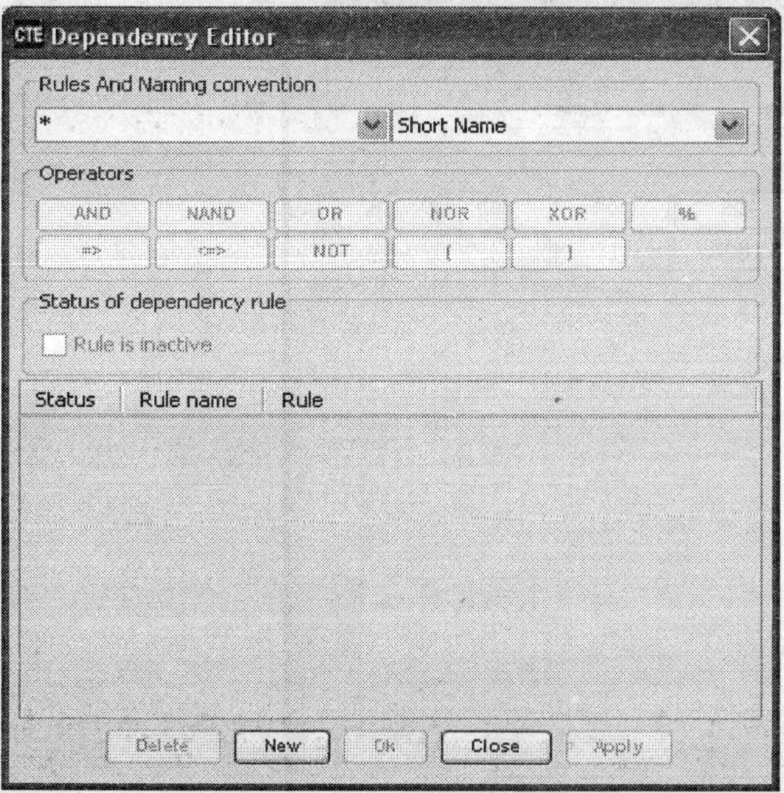

Setting up a rule

To set up a new rule:

1. Click on **New**.

2. Enter a name for the rule and click on **OK**.

3. You will return to the dependency editor. Now you can create a rule. A rule consists of classes linked by logical operators. Enter the rule in the text field, using the logical links of classes. An example: If it needs to be ensured that all Vehicles of the **i20** have the color **silver** a rule needs to be created which only allows such class combinations in a test case.

4. Click on apply button & then on OK button.

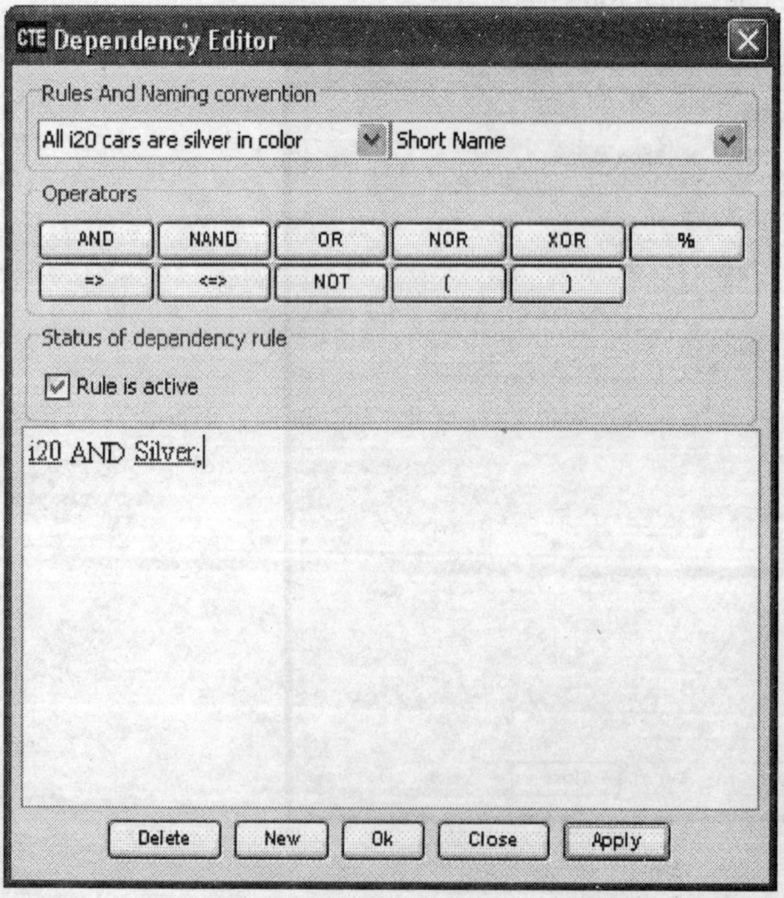

Meaning of operators-

AND	Logical AND (A and B)
NAND	Negated AND (not A and B)
OR	Logical OR (A or B, or A and B)
NOR	Negated OR (neither A nor B)
XOR	Exclusive OR (A or B)
= >	from A follows B
<=>	A is equivalent to B
NOT	NOT-operator: reverses the statement
(and)	Brackets in order to combine statement

Note : 1) You do not need to enter the class names directly. Instead, you can extract item from the classification tree via drag & drop.

2) In order to enter names you can also use the automatic name completion function. To do so, enter the first letter of the class name and press the tab key.

The dependency manager

To have the dependency rules monitored, turn on the dependency manager.

Click on the **Activate dependency manager** symbol on the toolbar. 

If the light bulb is switched on the dependency manager is activated.

It is indicated by

The dependency manager checks the existing test cases for inconsistencies. Test cases in which there are no inconsistencies are marked **green**; if inconsistencies occur they are marked **red**. All test cases which have not been tested are marked yellow.Test case groups are marked red if they contain a test case with errors.If you make changes in the document the dependency manager will check these and react if necessary.You can switch off the dependency manager by clicking on the symbol again.

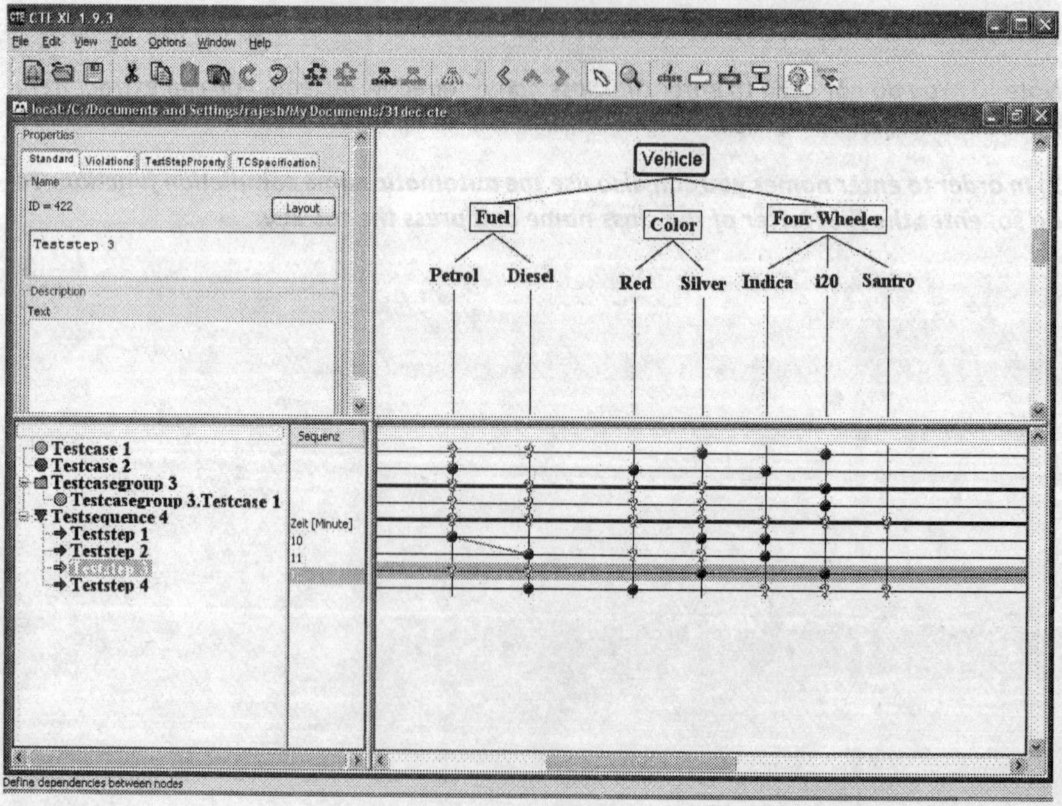

Tools

There are some tools within the CTE XL.There are some topics comes under tool

Tags

Creating tree links

Generating test cases automatically

Dependencies

Requirements

Tree templates

Tags

- The project-specific attributes can be linked to tree elements or testcase elements as so called tags.
- Therefore it is first necessary to define, which attributes shall be linked to which elements.
- You can edit the tag list. Select Tags option from the Tools menu. The tag dialog box will be displayed.

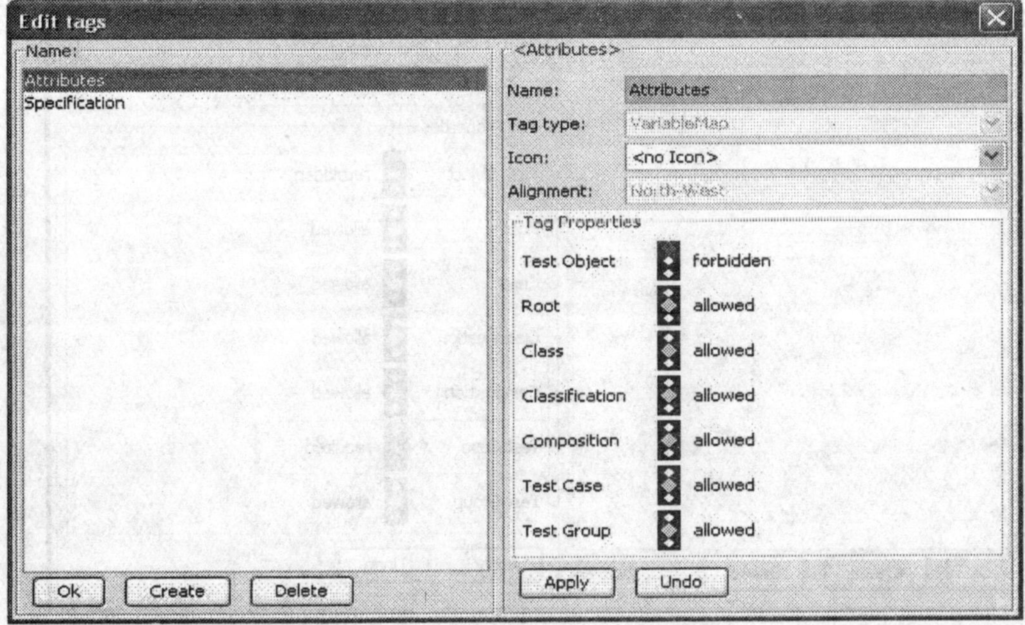

Tags provide different facilities like :

1. Configuring the appearance of tag.
2. Creating new tabs.
3. Use tags.
4. Creating tree links.

1. Configuring the appearance of tags

1. Click on the name of the desired tag on the left-hand side of the dialog box.

On the right-hand side, there is a list of those objects that may contain tags. They are classification tree elements, test cases and test case groups.

2. In order to change the status of an object group, click one of the light symbols until you will get the desired status.

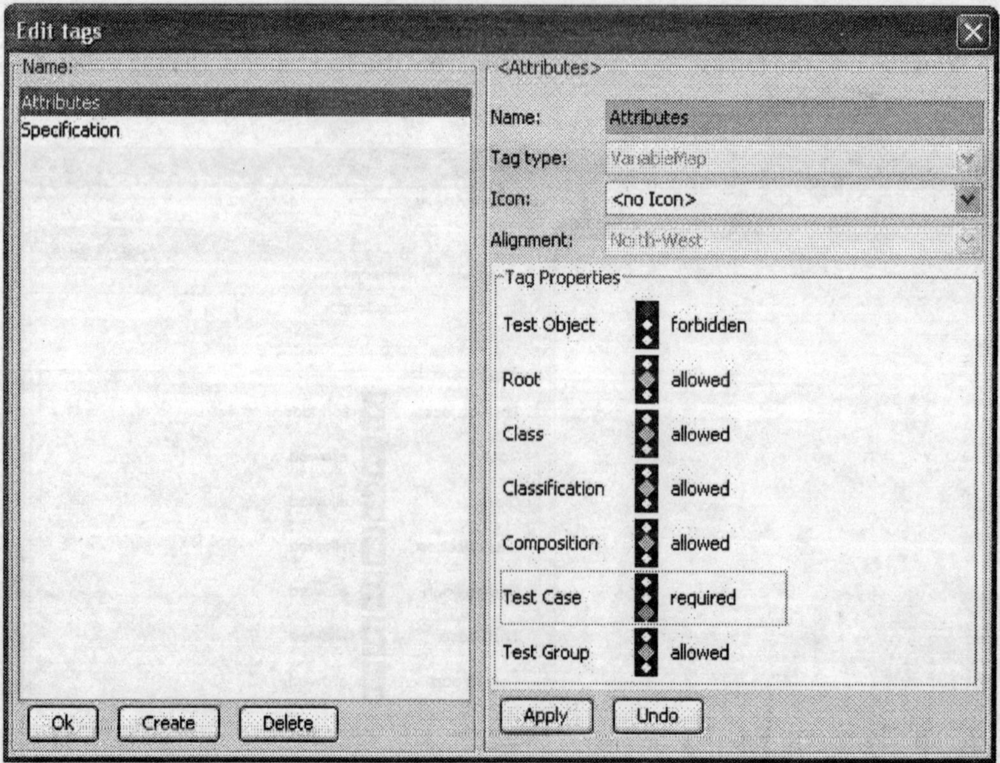

The following possibilities are available:

Forbidden - Tag is never displayed

Allowed - The tag can be added manually to an element through its context menu.

Required - Tag is always on display.

2. Creating new tags

1. Click on **create** in the tags dialog box.
2. Enter a name for the tag in the **Name** column in the upper right-hand corner.

   E.g. Info33
3. Choose under **Tag type** what kind of content tag should have.

   E.g. Texual tag
4. Under **Icon**, select a picture which should be displayed with the elements containing this tag.

   E. g. tag_picture.gif

We can create our own icon:

Go to option on menubar - tag icons – click icons

To create new icon with which you can mark tags.

I. Click on **New**, enter, in the appearing dialog, a name for the icon and click on **OK**.

II. Now mark this file name in the icon list. Then, enter the file name in the field at the bottom or click on the three dots next to the field in order to select the file.

III. Click on **Set**.

IV. In the preview field, a preview of the icon appears (possibly enlarged). Click on **OK** to accept the icon.

Now the newly created icon will come in the icon list of edit tag window.

1. Under **Alignment** you can choose the corner of the tree element in which the icon will be displayed.

2. Choose for which kind of elements the tag should be automatically displayed, manually displayed (Here you can change the possibilities of root, class, classification & etc.)

3. Click on **Apply.** Following window will be displayed.

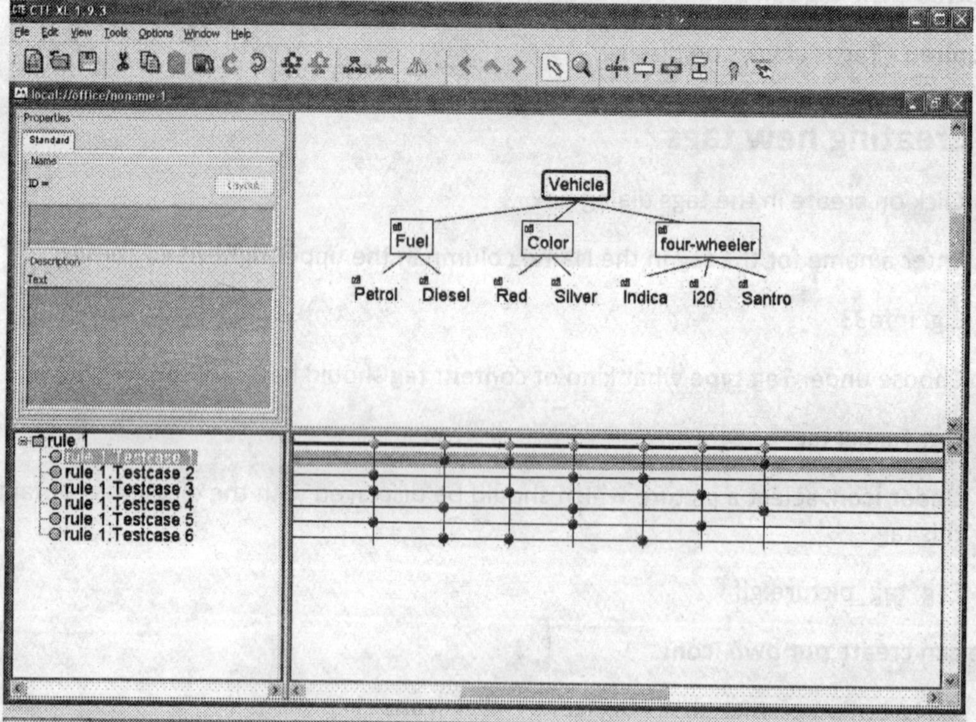

Use tags

For linking a tag with status **allowed** to a tree element or a testcase element follow these steps:

- Click with the right-hand mouse button on the element that you wish to link to the tag.
- Select **Available Tags** from the context menu and then select the tag.

A new tab with the name of the tag appears in the properties field. Click on the tab. Depending on the tag type there are different possibilities of using the tag:

TextualTag -

Here you can enter a free text as an attribute for the element.

VariableMap -

Here you can define attribute-value pairs for the element. Right click in the empty attributes field and select Insert Attribute. Click in the row Name or Value respectively and enter the name and value of the attribute.

Creating Tree Links

Using a tree link it is possible to import the test cases of a different test object into the current classification tree. In this way, you can link test cases of a test object with different properties and classification trees or test it according to further aspects.

In order to create a tree link:

1. Click on tools, select tag then click on create.
2. Name: TreeLink
3. Tag type: TreeLinkTag.
4. Set tag properties like following window.
5. Click on Apply & ok button.

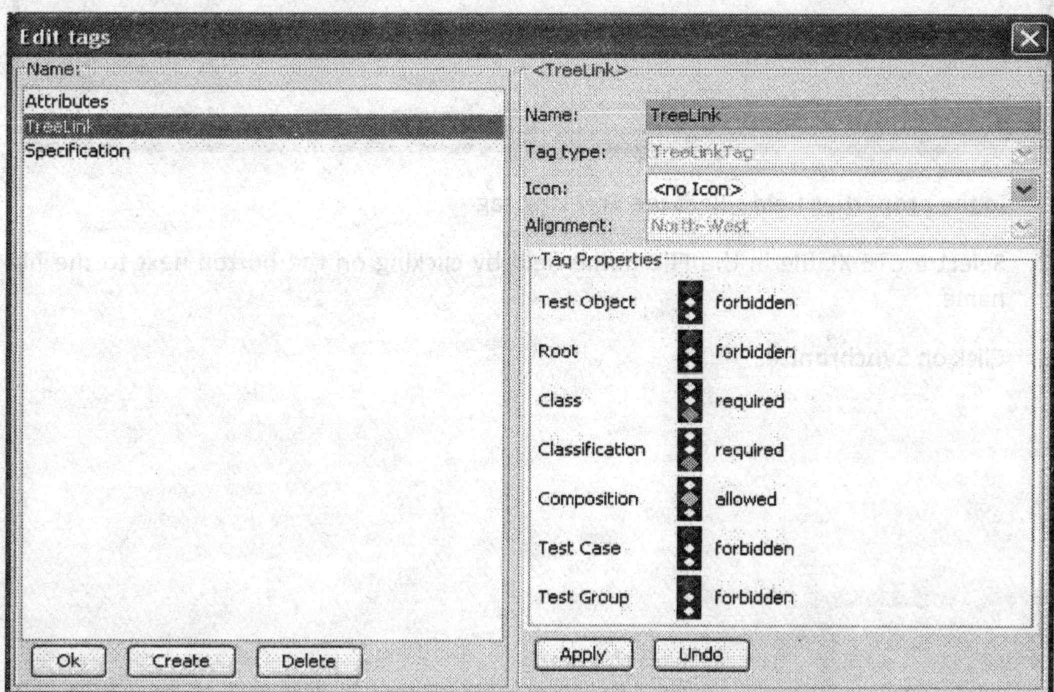

The CTE XL window should look like following window

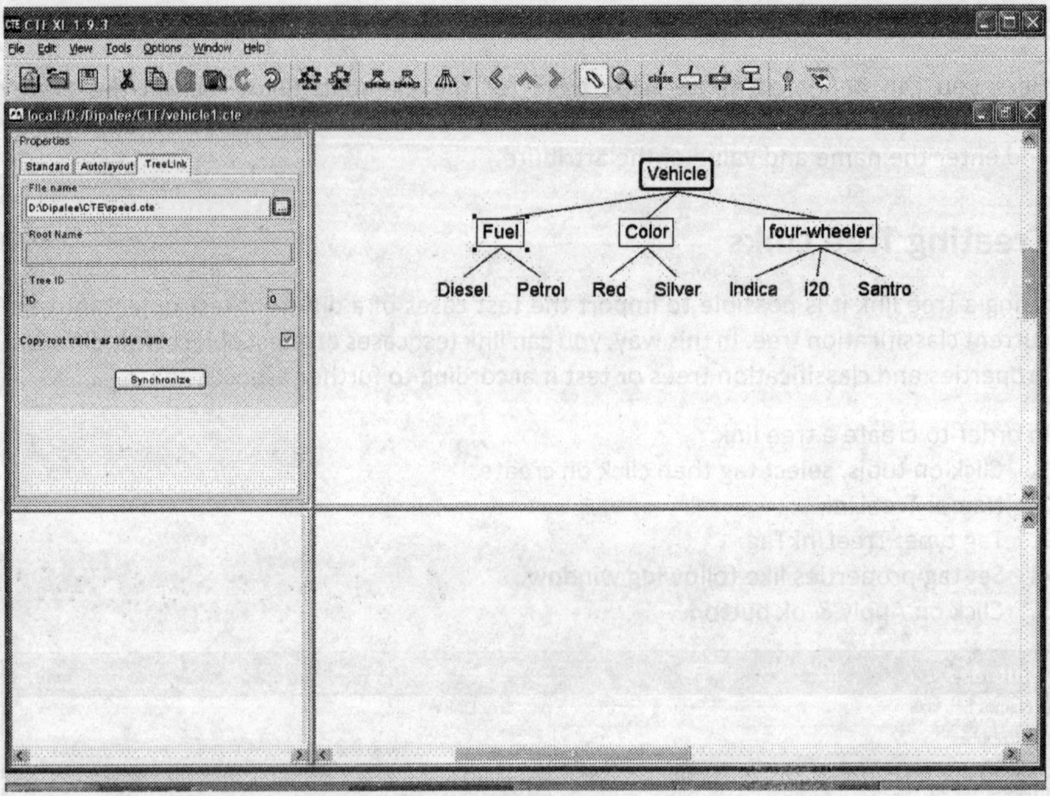

1. In the properties field select the **TreeLink** tag
2. Select a CTE XL file in the **File name** field by clicking on the button next to the file name.
3. Click on **Synchronize.**

Following window will be displayed.

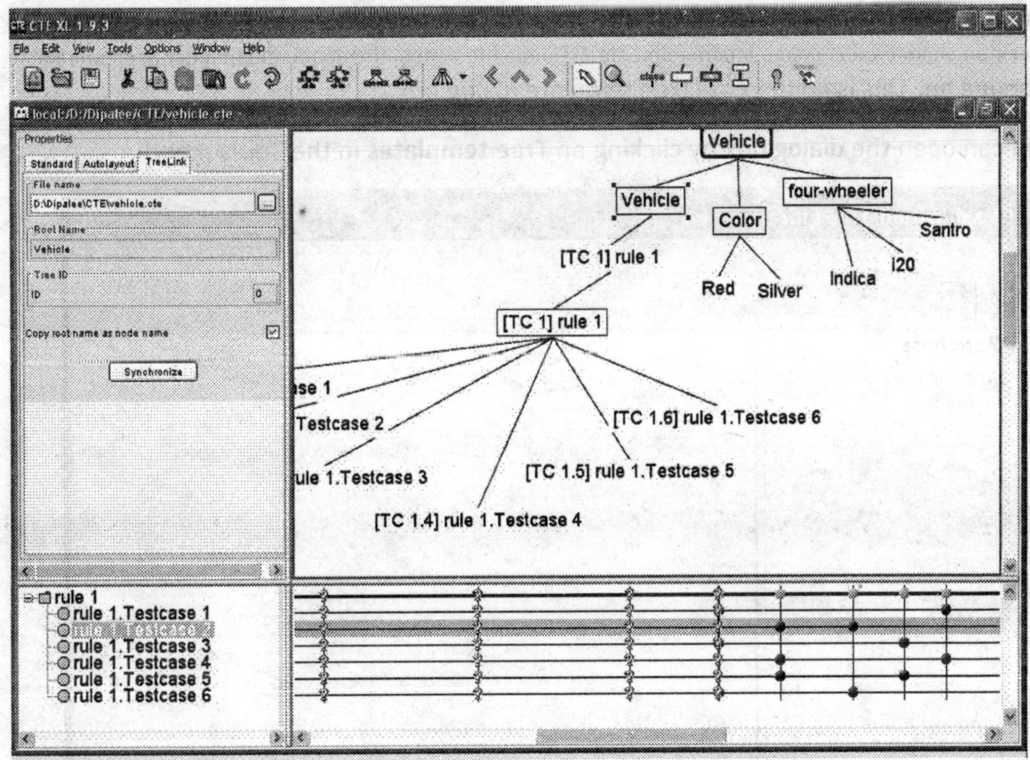

Tree templates

To avoid having to continually recreate classification tree structures which are often used, you can insert tree parts from existing CTE XL files into the document you are currently working on. This is done in the tree template dialog box.

You can open the dialog box by clicking on **Tree templates** in the **Tools** menu

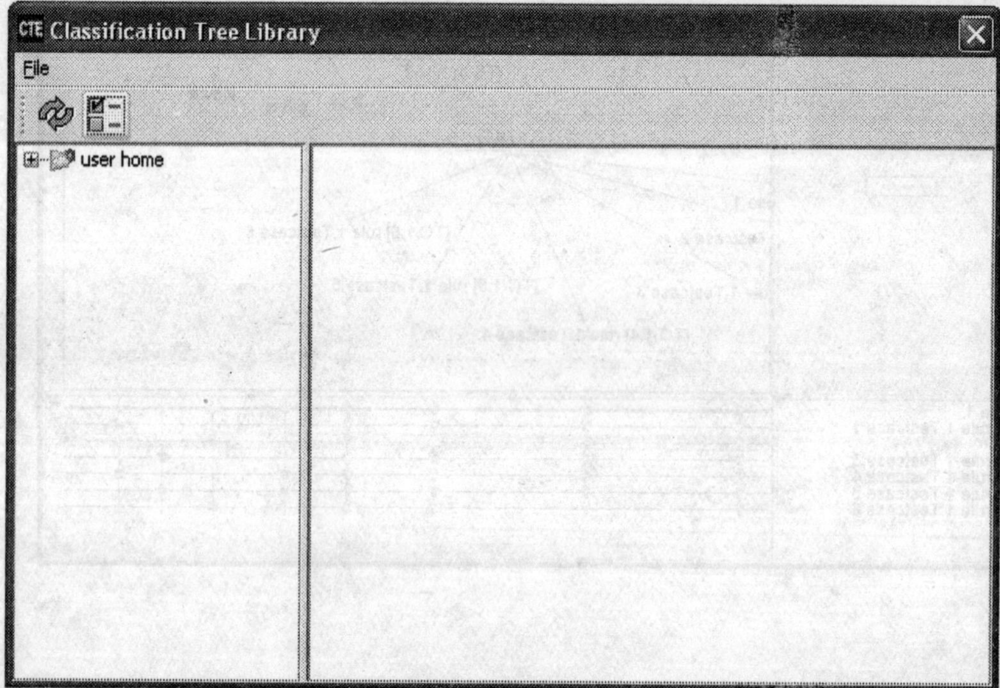

Tree template covers following topics:

1. Adding paths
2. The tree library dialog
3. Inserting elements into a document

1. Adding paths –

Click on **Configure** in the **File** menu.

Following window will be displayed.

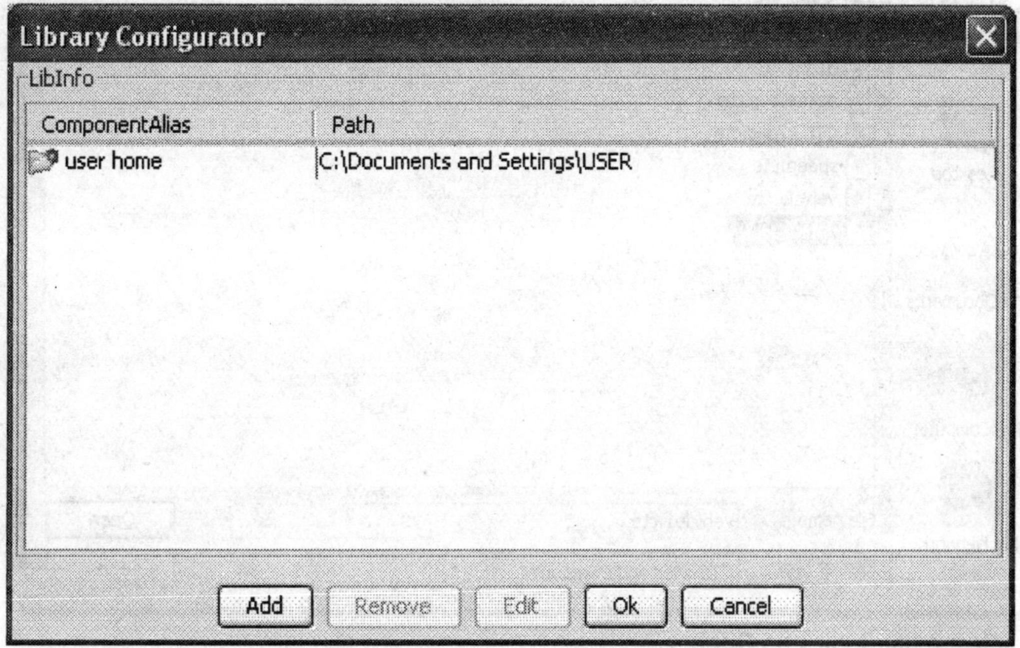

In the window which appears, click on **Add**, a dialog box will appear, in which you can choose the folder which contains the files.

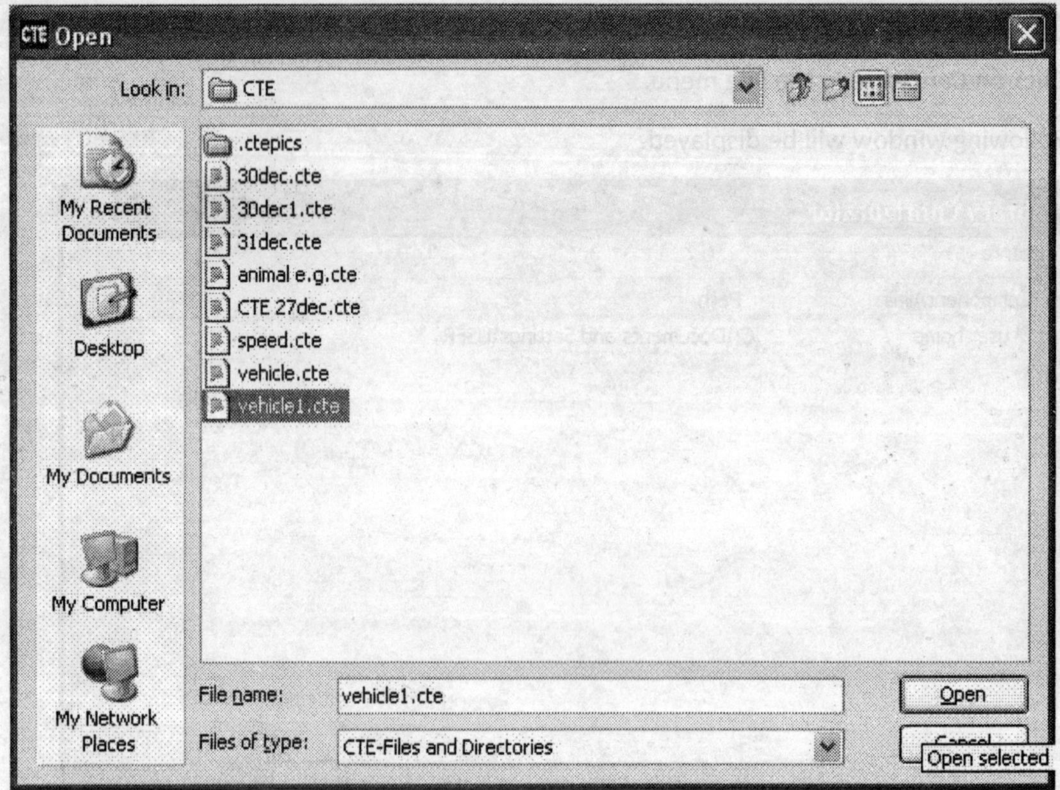

3. Select a file & click on **Open**.
4. The file has now been included in the list.

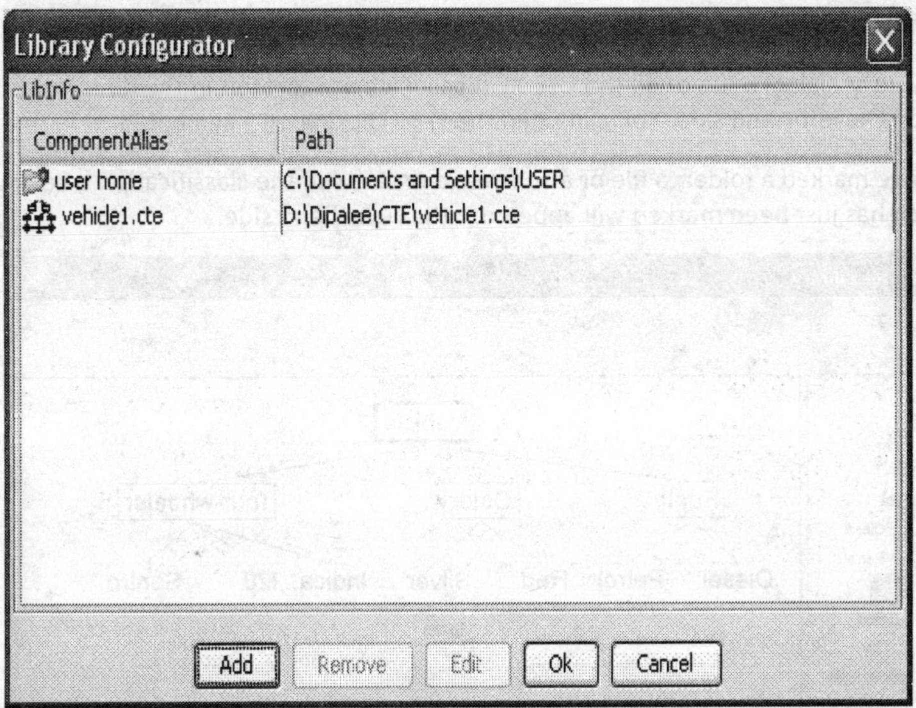

Select vehicle 1.cte & click on ok.

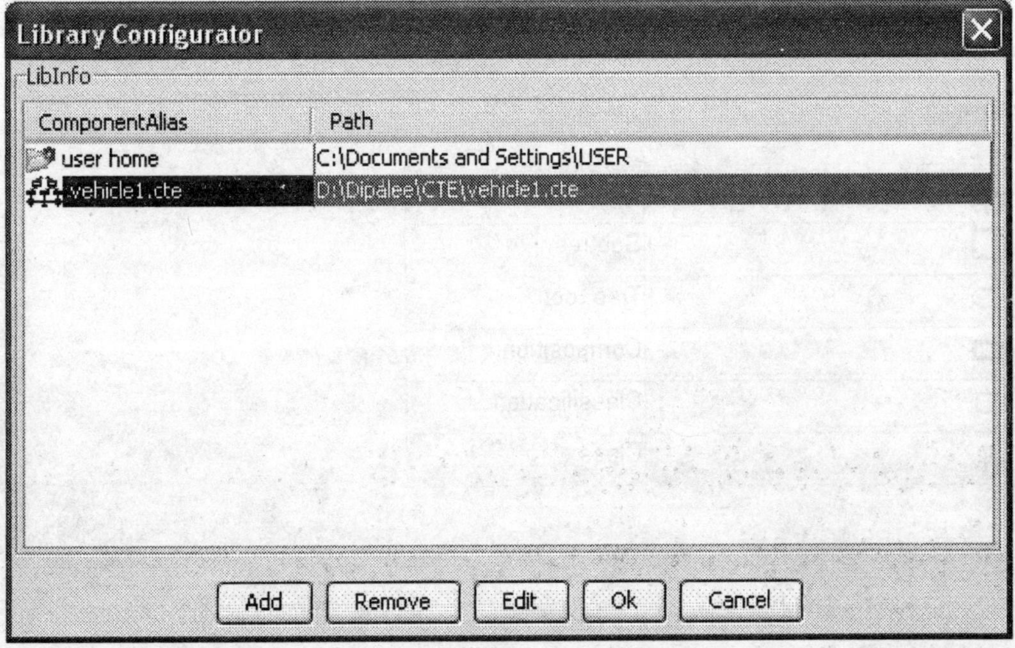

2. The tree Library Dialog -

In the tree library dialog, a list of all the CTE XL files which are located in the directories will appear on the left-hand side. You can open these by clicking on + symbol

When you have marked a folder, a file or a subtree, a preview of the classification tree or subtree which has just been marked will appear on the right-hand side.

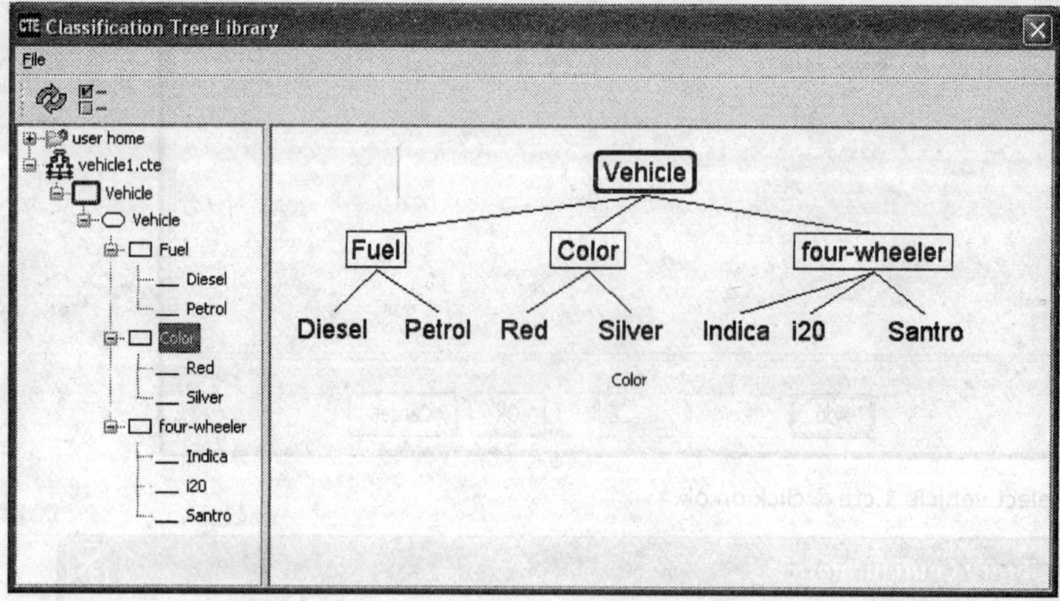

Symbols:

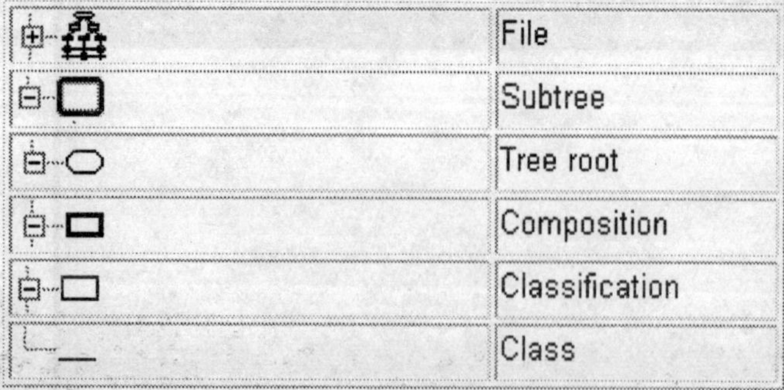

Symbol	Meaning
⊞ (file icon)	File
⊟ (thick box)	Subtree
⊟ (oval)	Tree root
⊟ (bold box)	Composition
⊟ (box)	Classification
└──	Class

3. Inserting elements into a document -

For inserting an element in the classification tree, select required element from classification tree library which is on the left part of the window drag& drop it onto the place you have selected.

E. g. Vehicle (Selected element)

The window will look like:

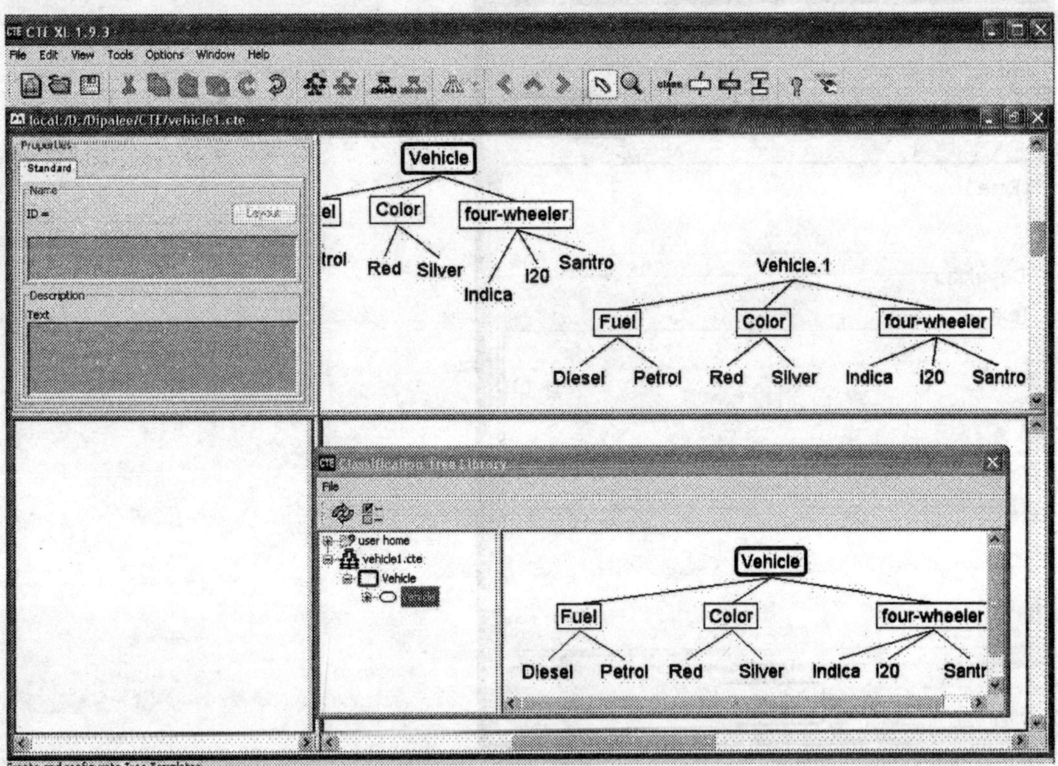

The selected element will now be inserted into the document you are currently working on. Here, we can choose any element for insertion.

Properties Field

Standard

In this tab you can look up or change the name, layout and description of the marked element.

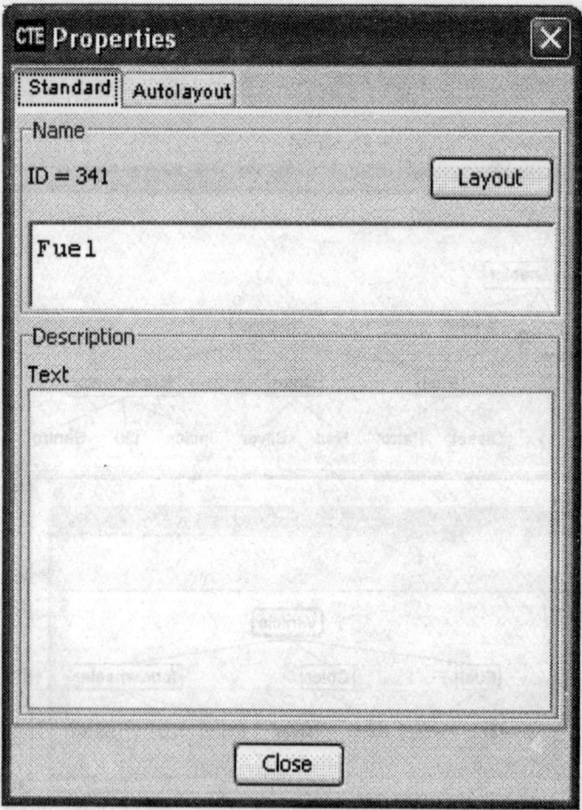

Name

Under ID you can find the unique number of the marked element. This cannot be changed. In the upper text field you can enter a name for the tree element. The name may contain more than one line.

Layout

Clicking on **Layout** will open the layout window. Here you can adjust the font, its style and size of the marked element.

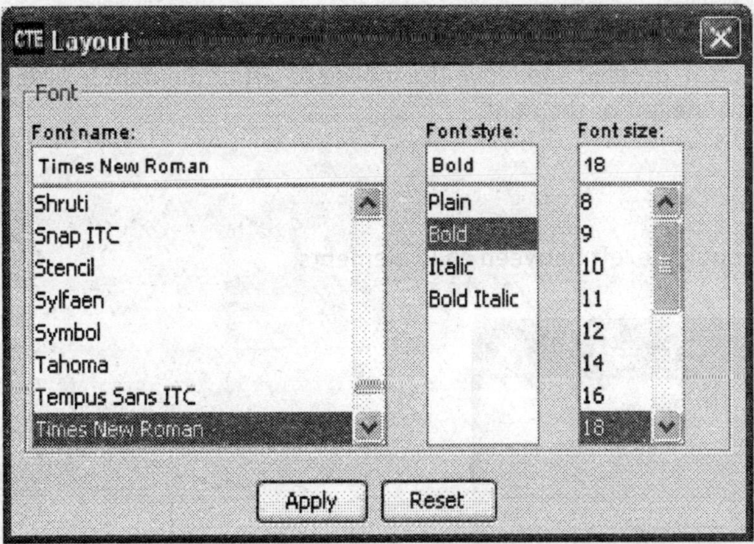

Description

In the lower text field it is possible to enter a description for the marked element.

Adjusting the autolayout function

The **Autolayout** tab is only available for elements of the classification tree if Autolayout has been executed at least once. Here, you can adjust the placement of tree elements by the autolayout function.

Fixed

This option fixes the position of the marked tree element in the window. This means that the position of the element will not be changed by the autolayout function

Layout type

Here you can select one of 4 modes of aligning the child elements of the currently selected node

Position

This regulator determines the relative position of the child elements. Click on the slide control, keep the mouse button pressed and move the mouse to left or the right in order to move the subelements to the left or the right.

Space:

Defines how much space should be left between child elements

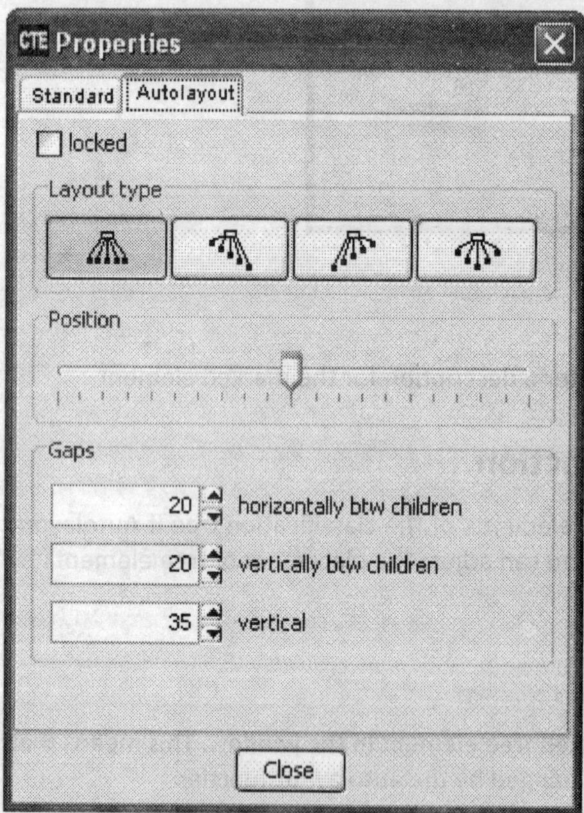

Rule Violation

This tag is available only for test cases and test steps. Those dependency rules are displayed which were violated by the marked test case.

Right click on inconsistent test case or test step & click on properties & then select violation. Double-clicking on a rule will open the dependencies editor, which offers the possibility of looking at the rule.

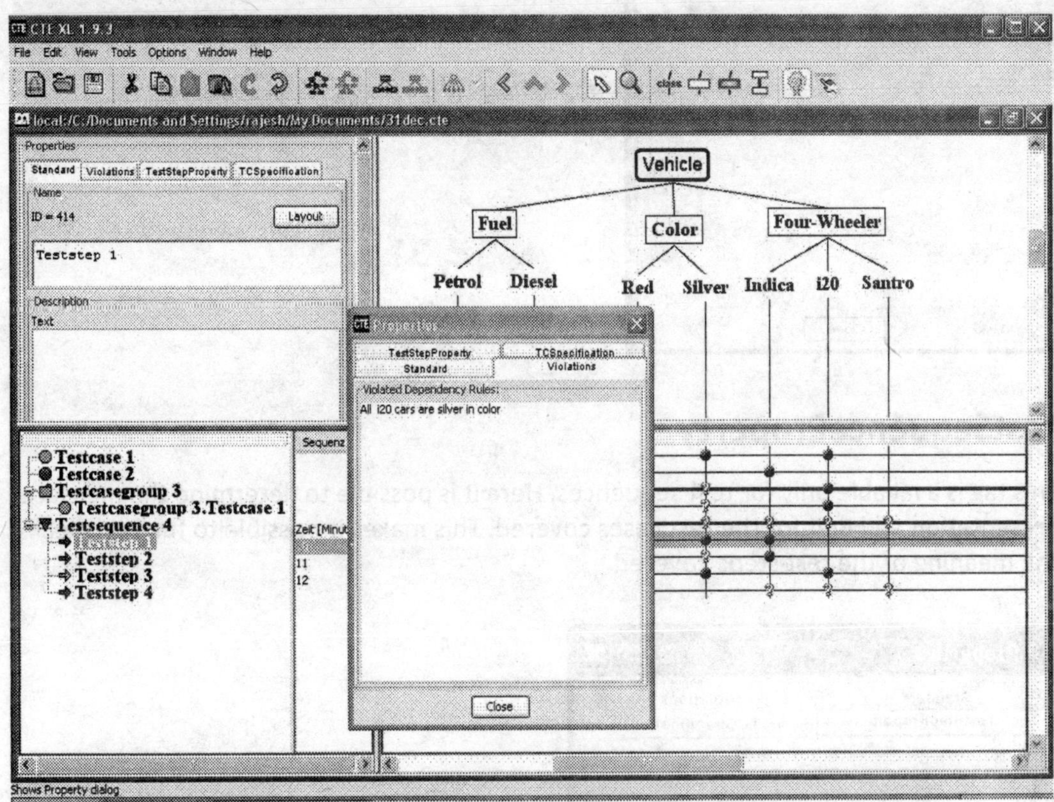

TCSpecification

This tag is available only for the elements of the test case table. The test case specification is being displayed. It results from the classes, with which the test case, the test sequence or the test case group are combined, as well as from the superordinate classification.

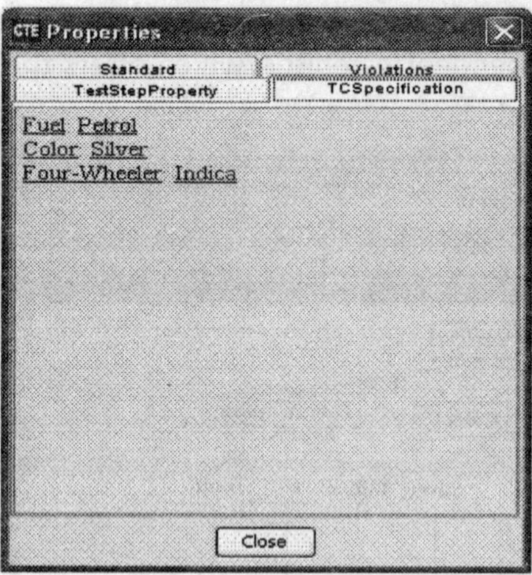

TestSequenceProperty

This tag is available only for test sequences. Here it is possible to determine the measure, presentation and unit for the test cases covered. This makes it possible to further specify the meaning of the test steps covered.

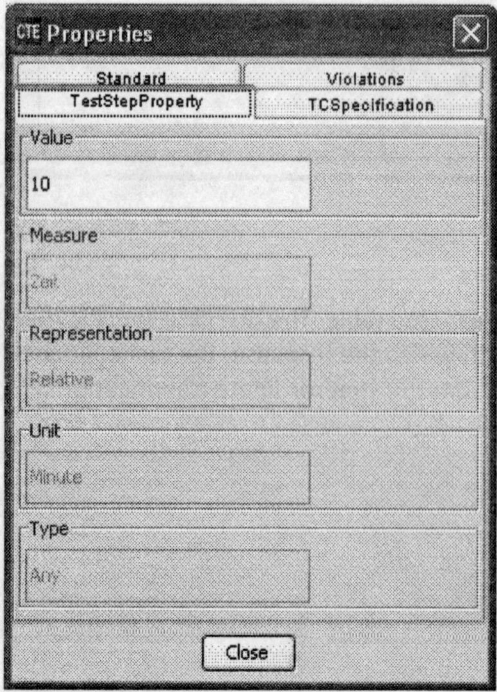

Under **Measure** you can select which value should be represented by the test sequence. The following values are selectable: **Distance, Angle** and **Time.**

Under **Representation** you can select whether you would like to specify the value of a test step as being **absolute** or **relative** to the preceding test step.

The **Unit** depends on the measure selected. The following options are possible:

- For distance: **meter, centimeter** or **millimeter**
- For angle: **degree** or **radian**
- For time: **hour, minute, second** or **millisecond**

Bug Tracking using JTRAC tool

Introduction:

JTrac is a generic issue-tracking web-application that can be easily customized by adding custom fields and drop-downs. Features include customizable workflow, field level permissions, e-mail integration, file attachments and a detailed history view.

JTrac was created after the author felt that he could write a much better alternative to a commercial defect tracking tool that he was having to use. Development started in 2004. JTrac is ideal for issue tracking or bug-tracking, but it has been designed to be generic and you can define custom fields to track almost anything you need.

JTrac is extremely easy to install and the only pre-requisite is a Java 5 (or higher) Runtime Environment. You can be up and running in seconds because JTrac comes bundled with a small-footprint web-application server called Jetty and an embedded database called HSQLDB. Please refer to the installation section of this documentation for details. You can also choose to drop the WAR file into an application server of your choice and start using JTrac right away.

Installation

Prerequisites

All you require in order to start using JTrac is Java 5 (or higher). Only a JRE (Java Runtime Environment) is required and not the full-blown JDK (Java Development Kit).

There is a good chance that Java is already installed on your system and you can verify whether it is ready to run JTrac by opening a command prompt and typing the following command:

```
java -version
```

If the system responds with a java version that is 1.5 or greater, you are ready to download and run JTrac.

You can download Java from here: http://www.java.com/download.

Download Pre-requisite software

- Jtrac(http://sourceforge.net/projects/j-trac/)
- Apache tomcat
- Java runtime environment 1.6 (http://java.com/en/download/index.jsp)

Installing the Apache HTTP Server

- The Apache HTTP Server Project is a collaborative software development effort aimed at creating a robust, commercial-grade, featureful, and freely-available source code implementation of an HTTP (Web) server

How to download AHHTPS

- Go to browser and type this link http://httpd.apache.org/
- Download from a mirror
- Choose: Win32 Binary including OpenSSL 0.9.8m (MSI Installer): httpd-2.2.15-win32-x86-openssl-0.9.8m-r2.msi [PGP] [MD5] [SHA1]

Steps:

1) Save The File

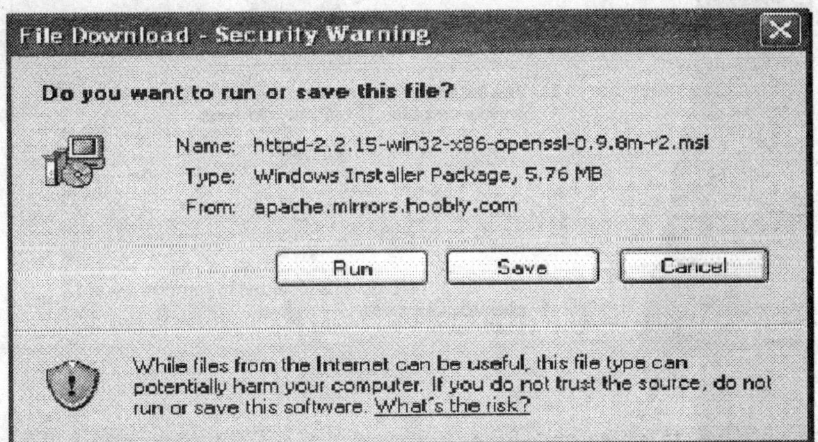

2) Run apache http server

3) Click next

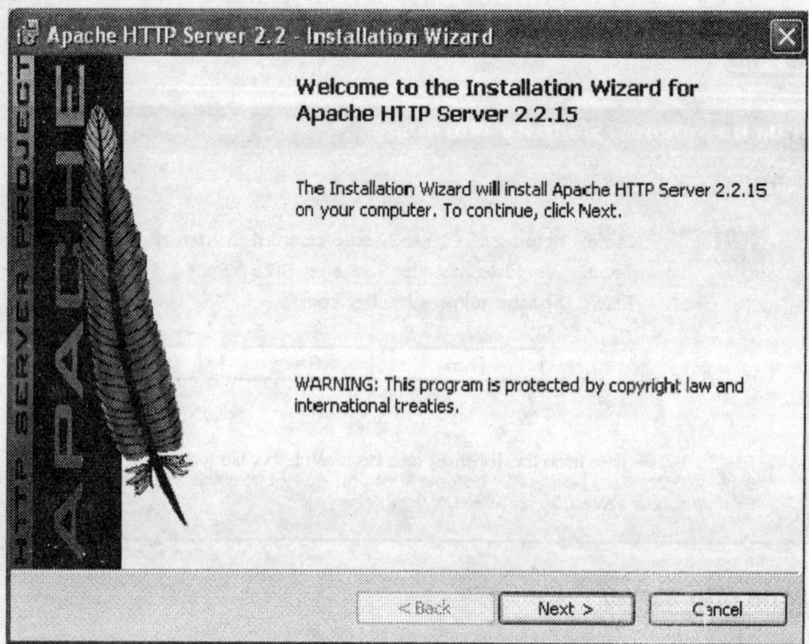

4) Accept the terms

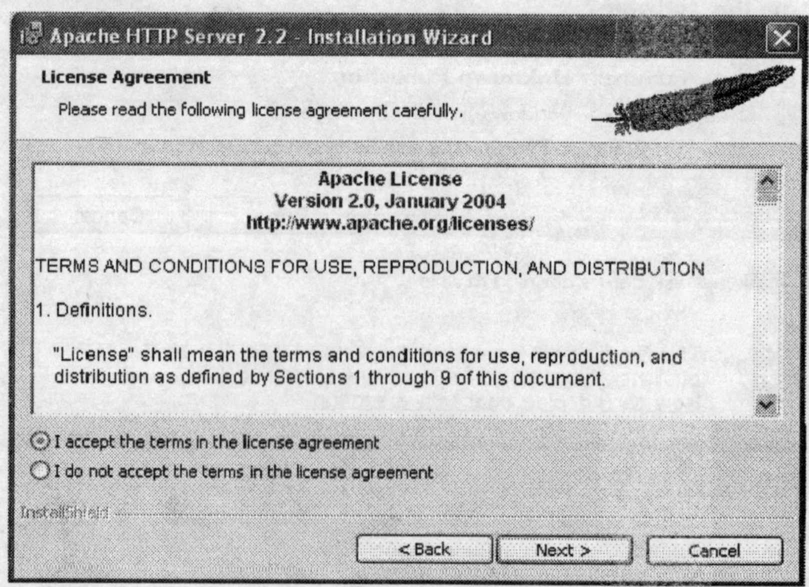

5) Read AHTTP server and click to next

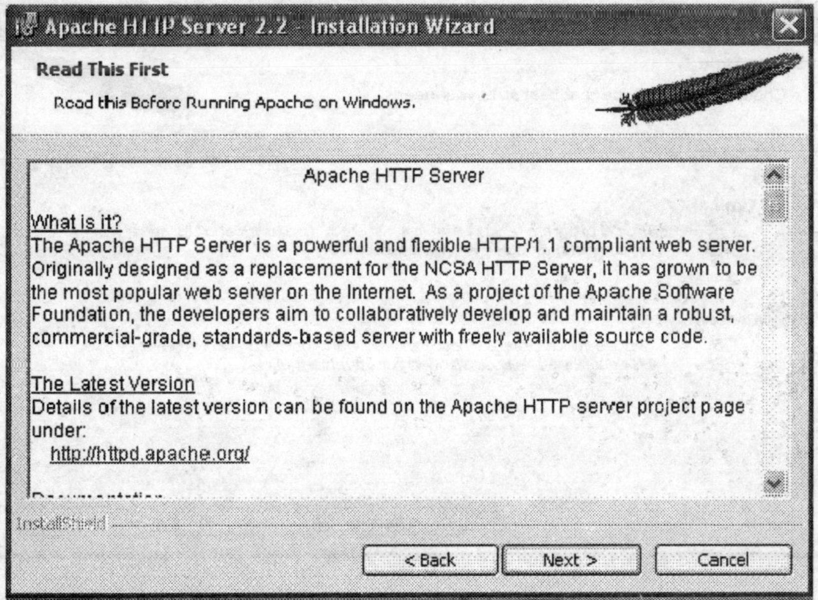

6) type "local host" in network domain and server name field and type 'admin@ localhost' in admin email address

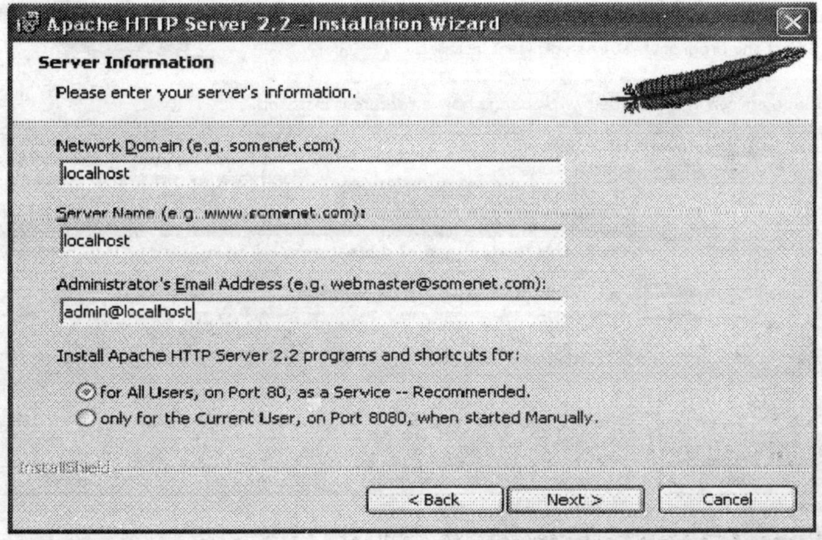

7) Choose 'Custom'

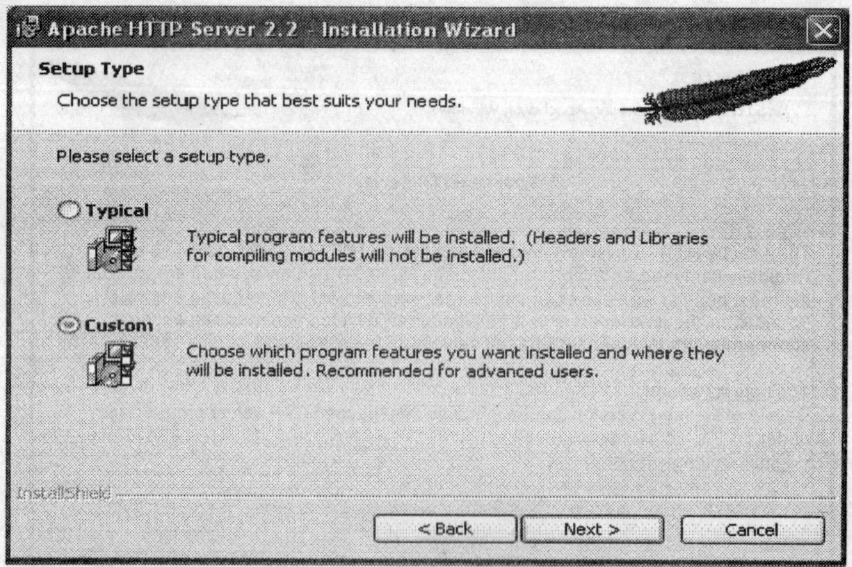

8) Click on "This feature will be installed on local hard drive"

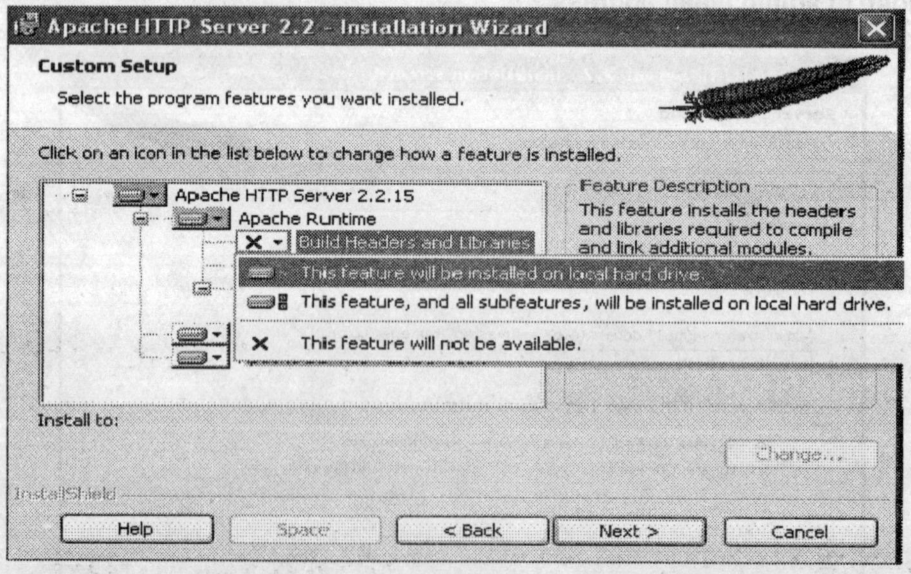

9) Click 'Next'

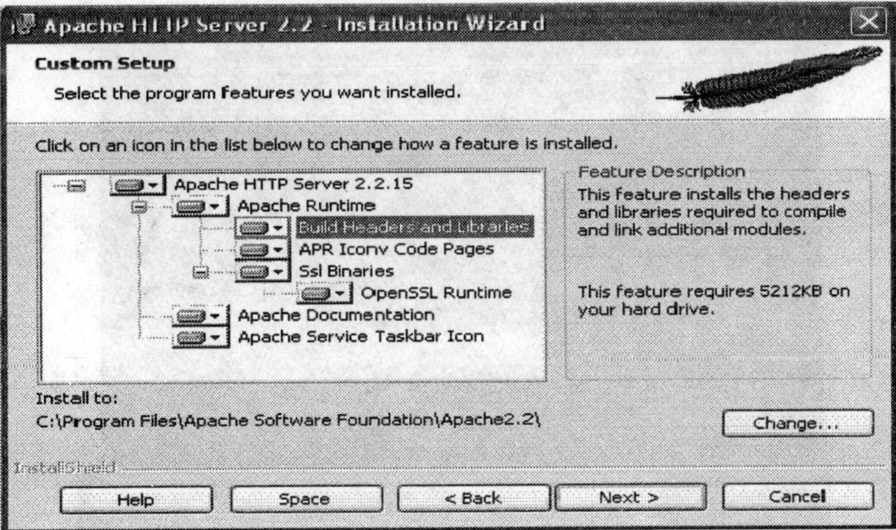

10) Click to 'Install'

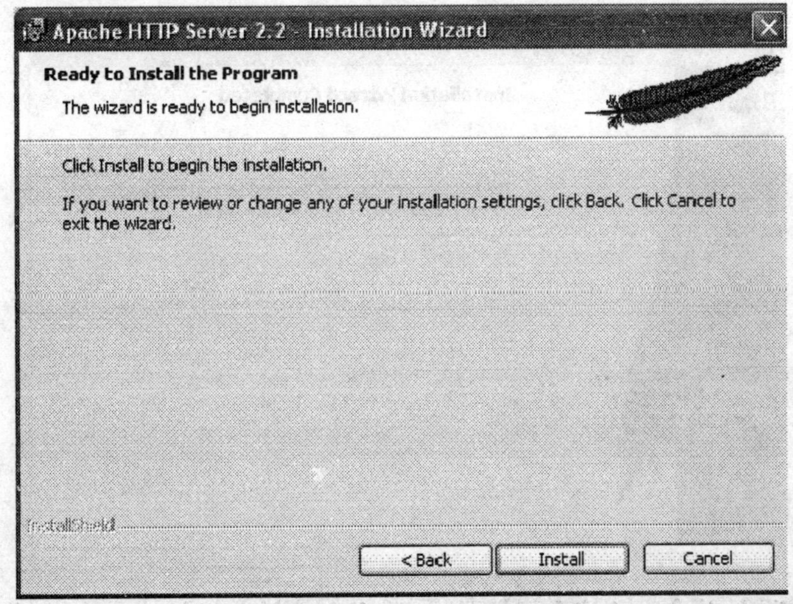

11) Testing http server

12) Click to Finish

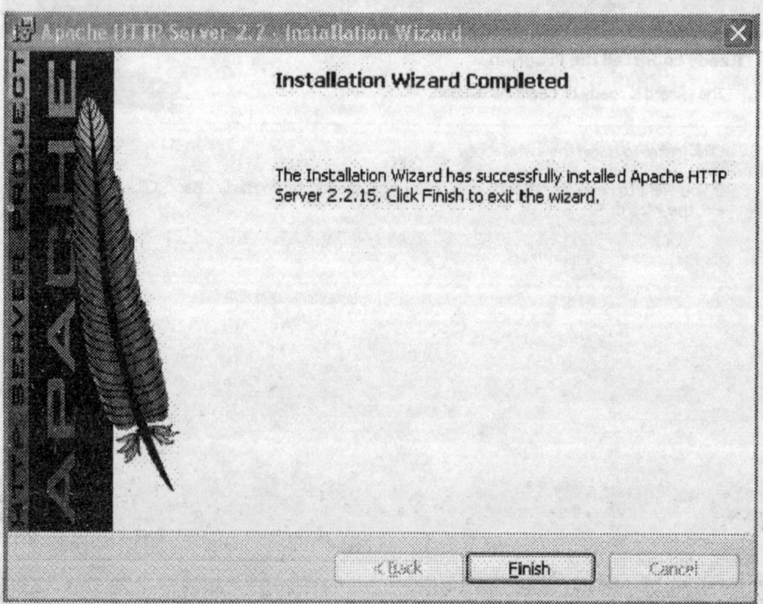

13) To Check it whether running or not type http://localhost/It gives a message " It works" if it runs

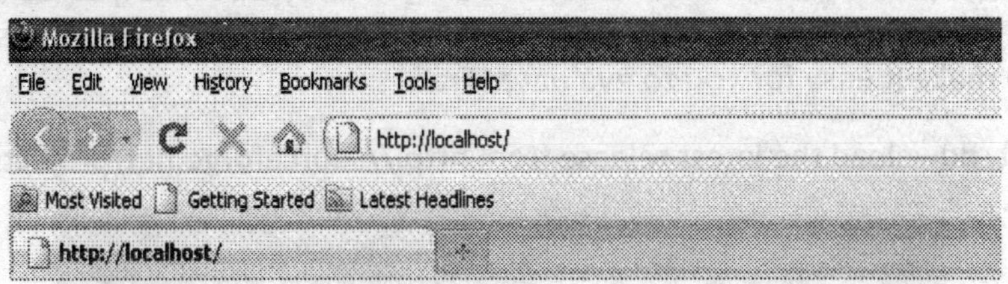

It works!

Apache Installation Successful

JTRAC Quick Installation

Once you have Java you can start using JTrac right away because you do not need to configure a web-application server or a database. JTrac embeds both of these (Jetty and HSQLDB) to make it easy for you to evaluate JTrac.

- First, download the latest release from http://sourceforge.net/projects/j-trac/)

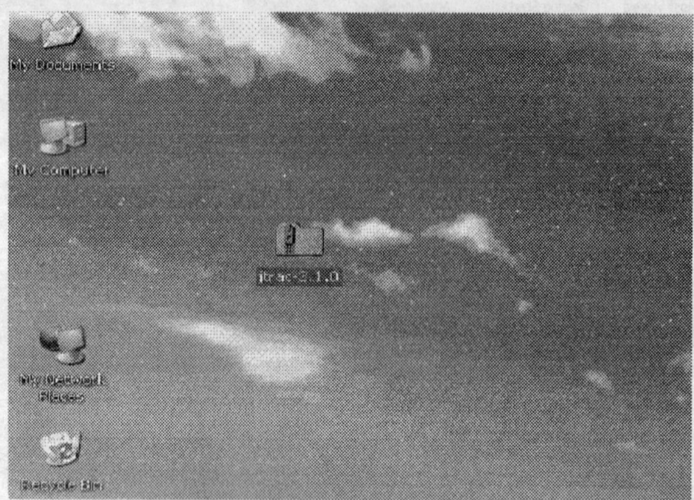

- Extract the zip file into a directory of your choiceYour jtrac folder looks like this

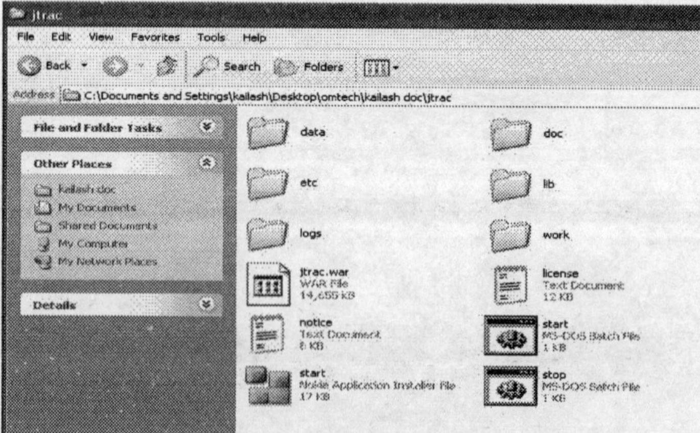

- Create a folder name as "apache software foundation" into program files

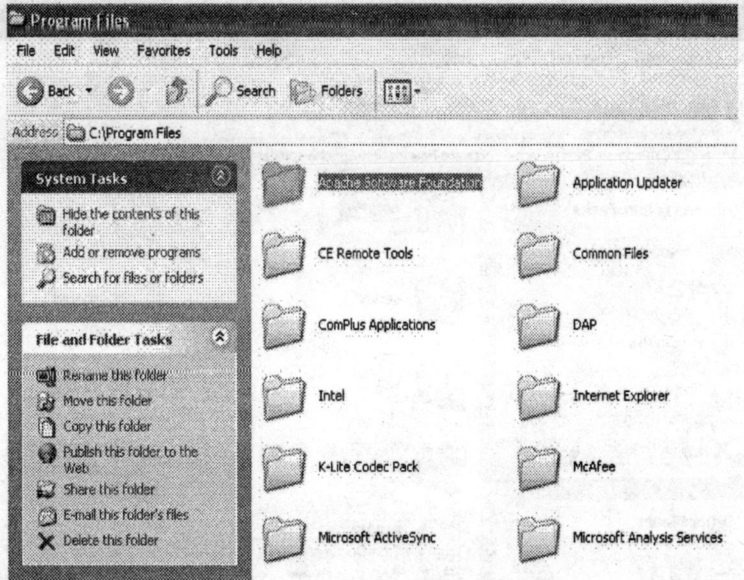

- Copy your "apache-tomcat-5.5.28" into "Apache Software Foundation" folder

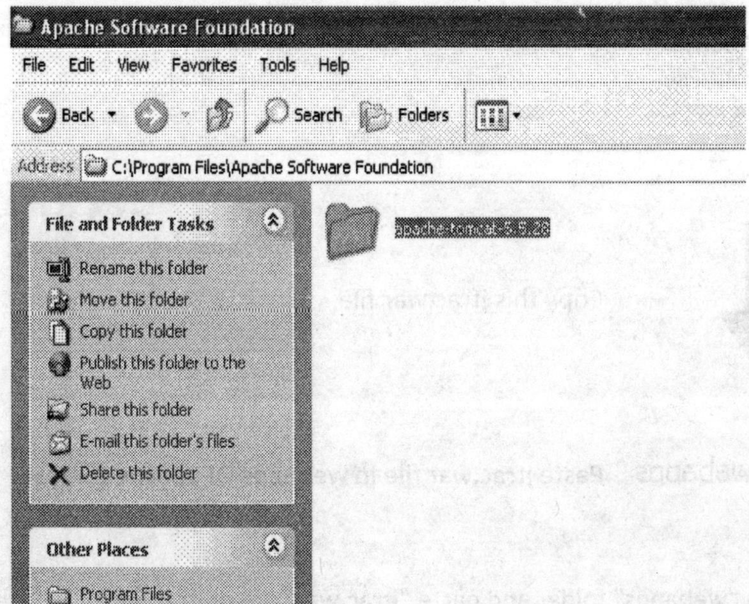

- Open "apache-tomcat-5.5.28" folder you'll see "webapps" folder

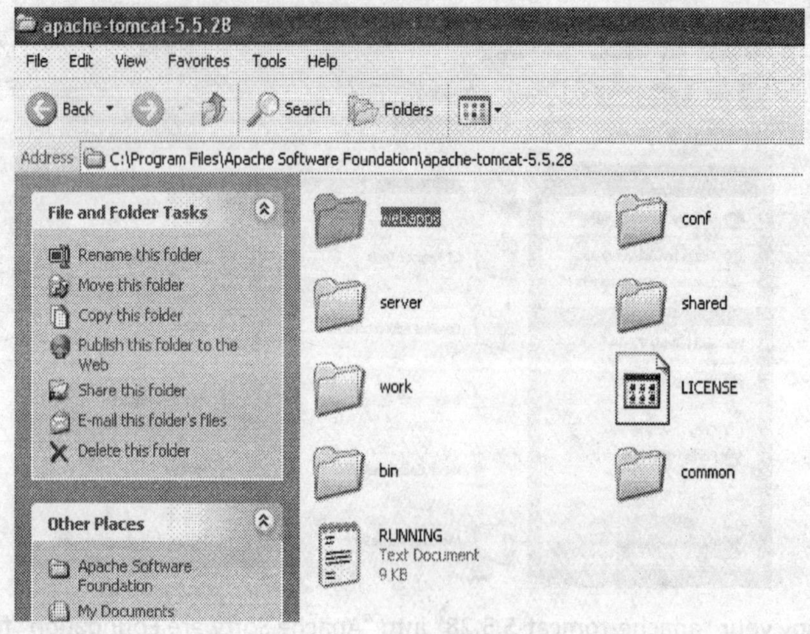

Copy this jtrac.war file

webapps Paste jtrac.war file in webapps Of apache tomcat

- Open "webapps" folder and paste "jtrac.war" file of jtrac

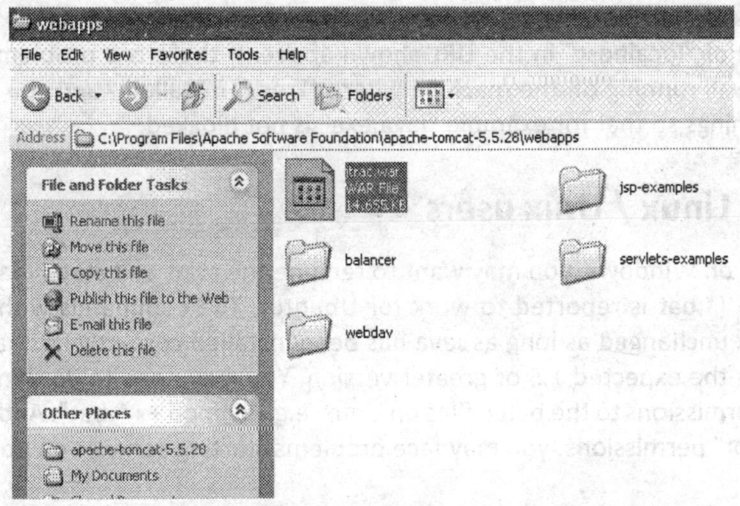

- Double-click or run “start.bat” to start JTrac

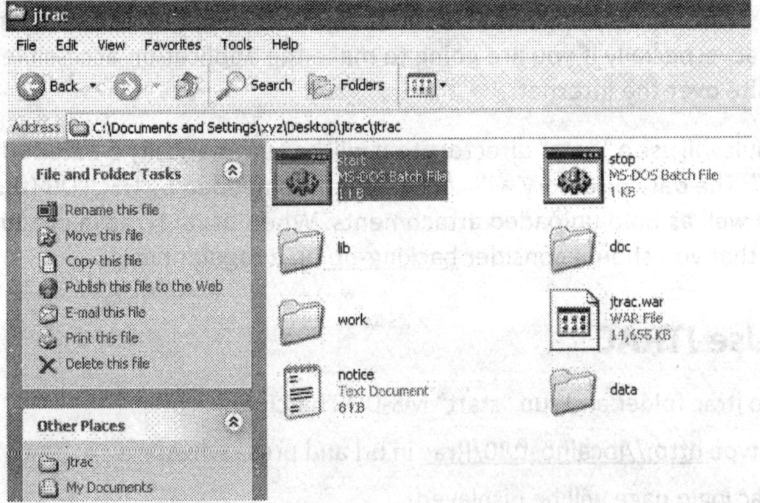

- Point your web-browser to
- http://localhost:80/jtrac
- Sign on with the user name “admin” and password “admin”
- Start using Jtrac

You can use the “stop.bat” script to stop the application. The “start.bat” file configures the Jetty server to use port 80 which you can easily change by editing “start.bat”. You may need to do this if for example JTrac does not start because a web-server (like Apache or IIS) is already running on port 80.

Remote users should be able to access JTrac over the network by using the machine name instead of "localhost" in the URL shown above. If there is a problem, it could be due to a firewall running on the machine where JTrac is installed - and you may have to reconfigure things so that for example "java.exe" is not blocked.

Notes for Linux / Unix users

If you are not on Windows, you may want to rename the start and stop *.bat files to e.g. *.sh for Linux (*.bat is reported to work for Ubuntu). The commands within the batch files will work unchanged as long as Java has been installed correctly i.e. "java" is in the PATH and it is the expected 1.5 or greater version. You may need to do things like apply executable permissions to the batch files on Linux, e.g. "chmod +x *.bat". And also - unless you have "root" permissions, you may face problems starting services on port 80 etc.

Security and Backup

For security reasons, it is best that you change the default "admin" password after installing JTrac, especially if you are going to make the application accessible on a public-facing web-site over the internet.

JTrac by default will use a "data" directory that will be automatically created within the root folder "jtrac". The data directory will contain the files needed by HSQLDB (the embedded database) as well as hold uploaded attachments. When using JTrac in production, this is the location that you should consider backing-up on a regular basis.

How to Use JTRAC

- Go to jtrac folder and run "start" MS-DOS batch file
- And type http://localhost:80/jtrac in url and press enter.
- A jtrac login page will be displayed

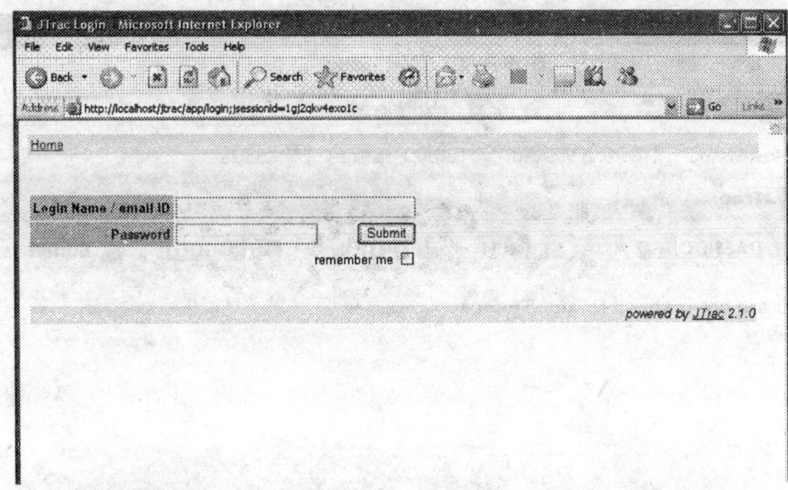

Type "admin" in login name/email ID and password

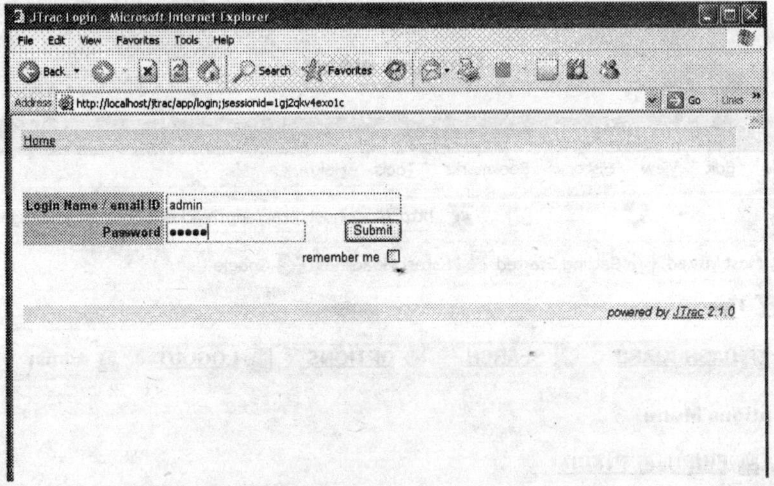

Logged in as admin

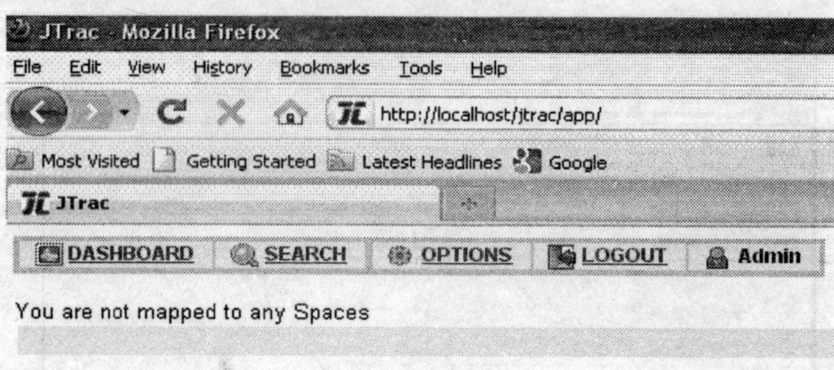

Options menu

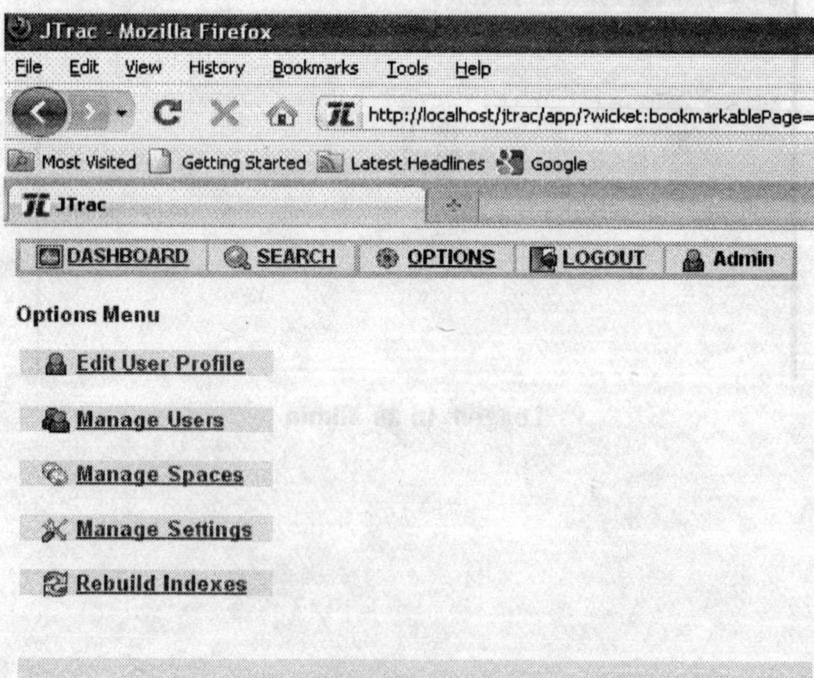

Select Edit user profile

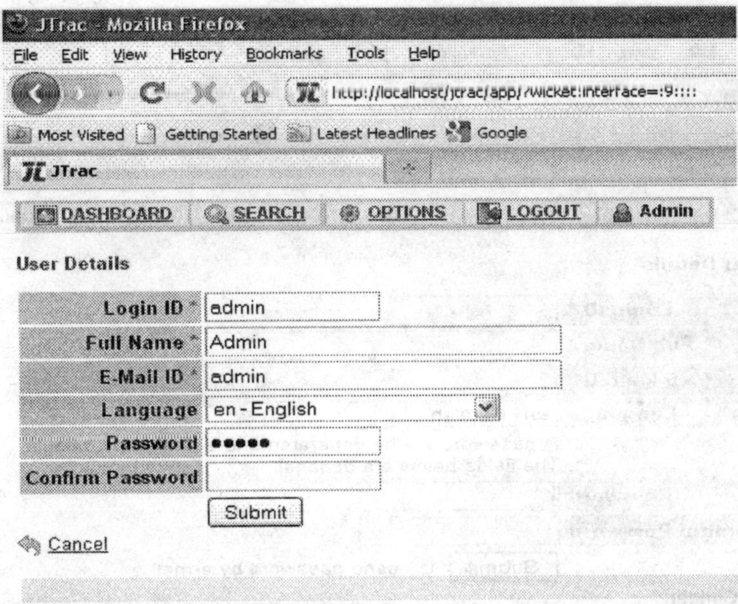

How to create user

→ Go to manage user to create new user

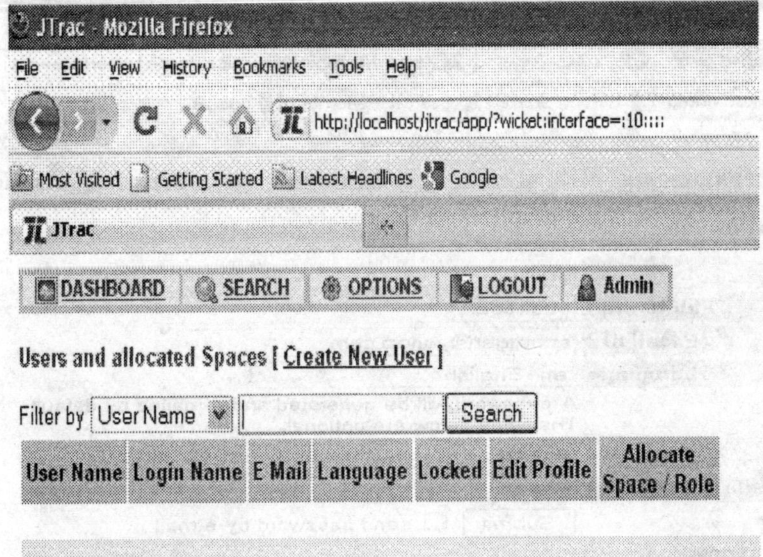

Create user here

- Fill all the user details

JTrac - Mozilla Firefox
File Edit View History Bookmarks Tools Help
http://localhost/jtrac/app/?wicket:interface=:11::::
Most Visited Getting Started Latest Headlines Google
JTrac
DASHBOARD SEARCH OPTIONS LOGOUT Admin
User Details
Login ID *
Full Name *
E-Mail ID *
Language en - English
A password will be generated and e-mailed by default.
The fields below are optional.
Password
Confirm Password
Submit send password by e-mail
Cancel

New User details are filled

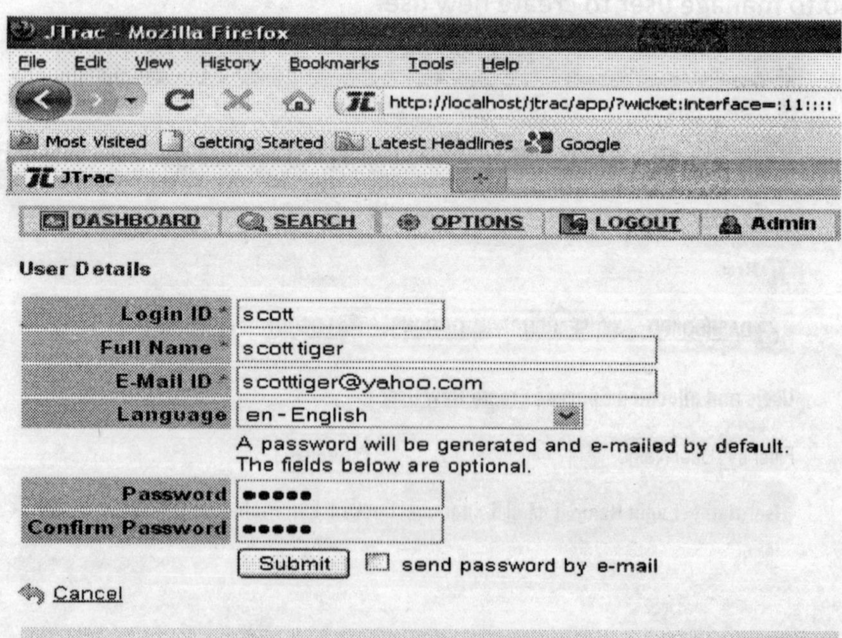

New user created

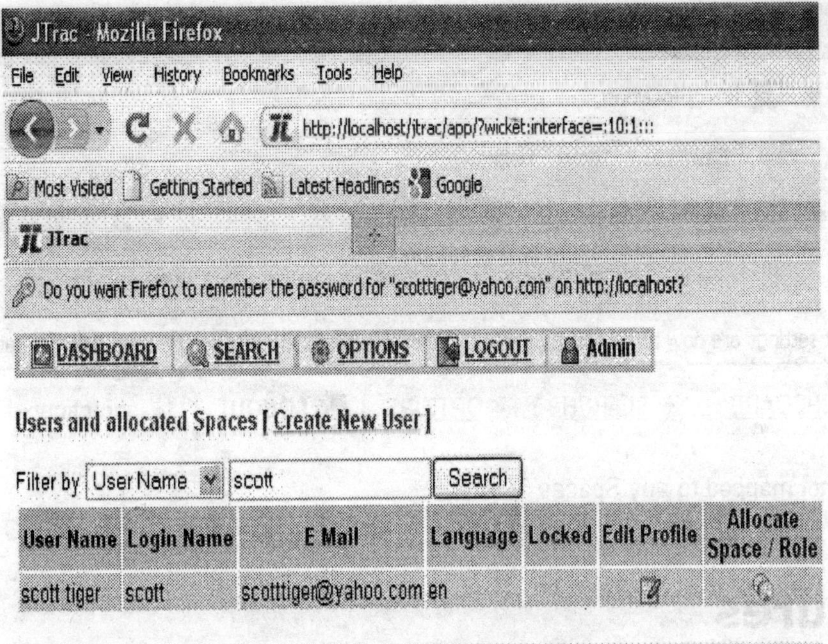

Login as new created user

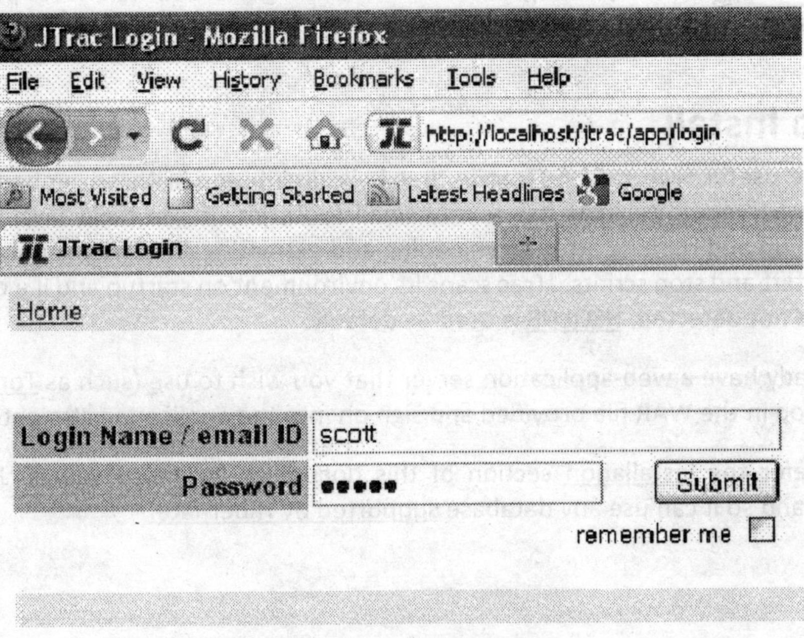

Logged in as "scott" ,"tiger"

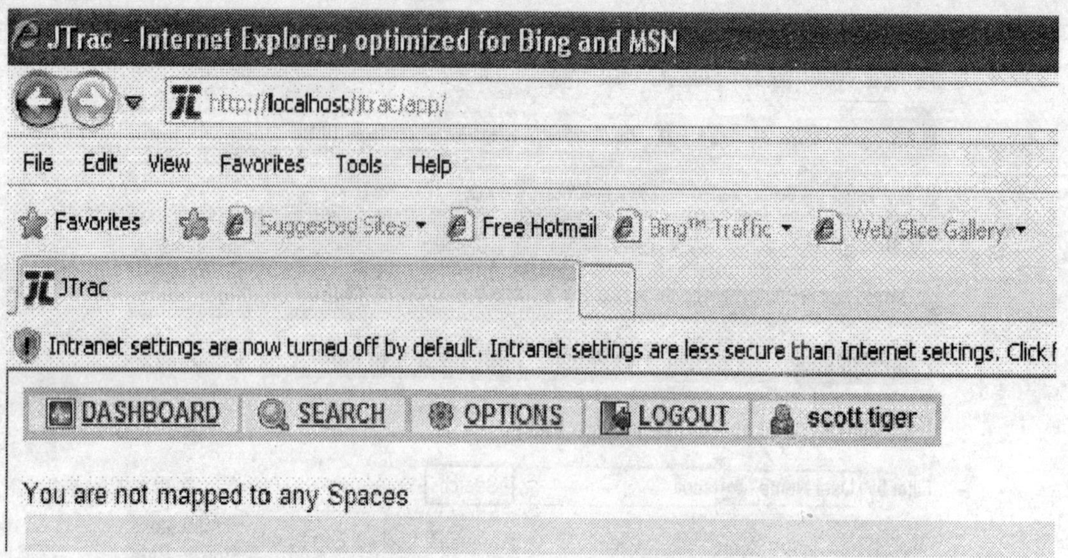

Features

JTrac has all the features that you would expect from a standard issue-tracking application such as support for file-attachments and e-mail integration. JTrac offers powerful customization options, especially in the areas of workflow and field-level permissions and compares well to even commercial tools.

Easy to Install

One of the useful features of JTrac is that it is distributed with an embedded web-application server (Jetty) that has a very small footprint. If you have Java 5 installed you can be up and running after downloading and extracting JTrac - by simply using the provided start and stop scripts. JTrac scans its environment on startup and if a configured database is not detected, HSQLDB is used by default.

If you already have a web-application server that you wish to use (such as Tomcat), you can just drop in the WAR file provided and sign on into the application straight-away.

You can refer the installation section of this document for more details. JTrac uses Hibernate and so it can use any database supported by Hibernate.

Custom Fields

JTrac can be used to effectively track various kinds of things such as Bugs, Action Items and Tasks. You can easily add the following types of custom fields to a tracker Project (Space):

- Drop Down List
- Free Text Field
- Date Picker
- (Decimal) Number

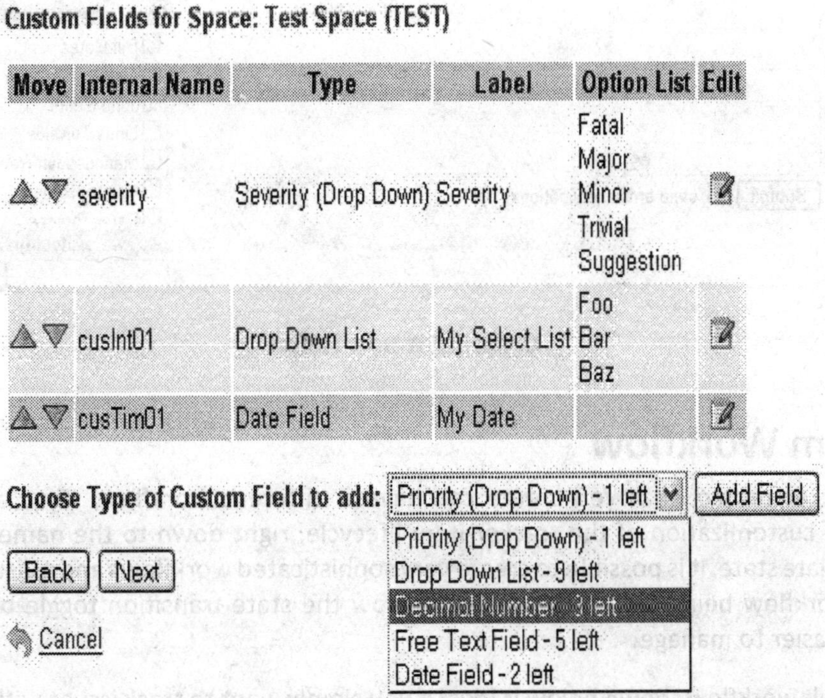

Custom Fields for Space: Test Space (TEST)

Move	Internal Name	Type	Label	Option List	Edit
▲▼	severity	Severity (Drop Down)	Severity	Fatal Major Minor Trivial Suggestion	
▲▼	cusInt01	Drop Down List	My Select List	Foo Bar Baz	
▲▼	cusTim01	Date Field	My Date		

Choose Type of Custom Field to add: Priority (Drop Down) - 1 left [Add Field]

- Priority (Drop Down) - 1 left
- Drop Down List - 9 left
- Decimal Number - 3 left
- Free Text Field - 5 left
- Date Field - 2 left

[Back] [Next]

Cancel

Setting up custom fields for a project

There is a limit to how many custom fields of each type that you can configure for a Space. These limits have been set after careful consideration and would very rarely fail to suffice. They are as follows: Drop Down - 10, Free Text - 5, Numeric - 3, Date/Time - 3.

The screenshot below shows how creating a new item would look like for the typical project (space) where 'Severity', 'Module', 'Type' and 'Priority' have been defined as custom fields.

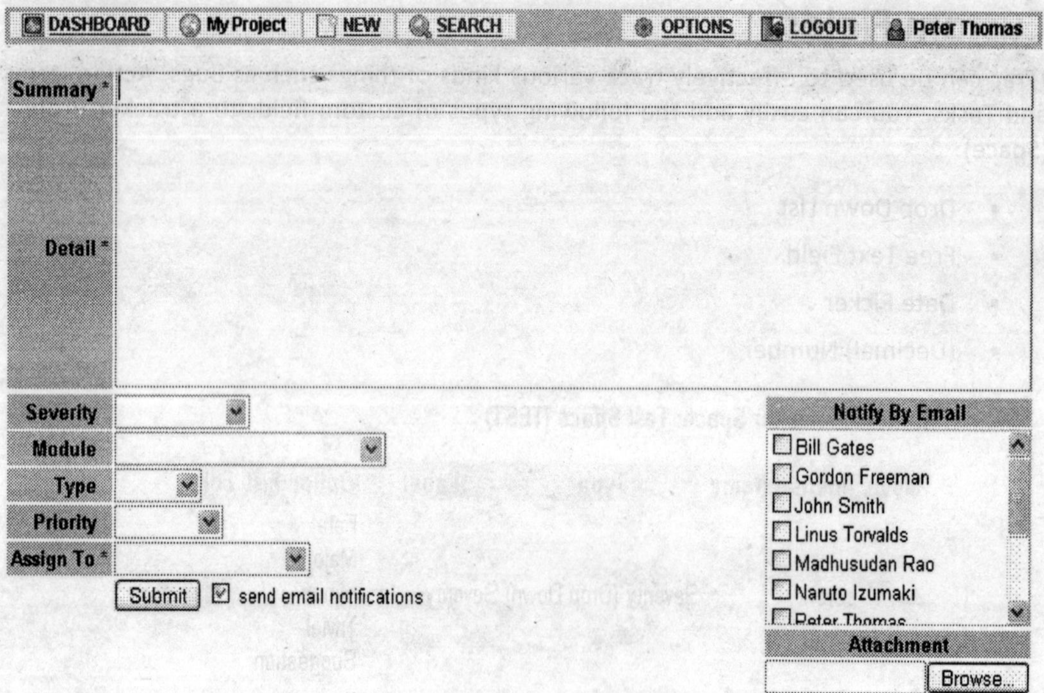

Creating a new item

Custom Workflow

Each tracker project that you create can have a different workflow. JTrac allows for complete customization of the tracker-item lifecycle, right down to the names of each intermediate state. It is possible to create very sophisticated workflows and a visual "map" of the workflow being edited is displayed below the state-transition toggle-buttons to make it easier to manage.

The default workflow shown below is ideal if you simply want to track issues with just two states - Open and Closed. However, with just a few mouse clicks, you can turn this into a complex workflow involving multiple states.

Space Roles and State-Transitions (Workflow) for Space: Test Space (TEST)

				Next Allowed State		Field Level Permissions M Mandatory O Optional R Read-Only		
State	✚	**Role**	✚	Open	Closed	Severity	My Select List	My Date
New		DEFAULT	✎	●		M	M	M
Open	✎	DEFAULT		●	●	R	R	R
Closed	✎	DEFAULT		●	●	R	R	R

Back Save

Cancel

New DEFAULT Open
DEFAULT Closed DEFAULT Open
DEFAULT Open

Default workflow - before customization

Space Roles and State-Transitions (Workflow) for Space: Test Space (TEST)

				Next Allowed State				Field Level Permissions M Mandatory O Optional R Read-Only		
State	✚	**Role**	✚	Assigned	Fixed	Rejected	Closed	Severity	My Select List	My Date
New		DEFAULT	✎	●				M	M	M
Assigned	✎	DEFAULT		●	●	●	●	R	R	R
Fixed	✎	DEFAULT		●	●	●	●	R	R	R
Rejected	✎	DEFAULT		●	●	●	●	R	R	R
Closed	✎	DEFAULT		●	●	●	●	R	R	R

Back Save

Cancel

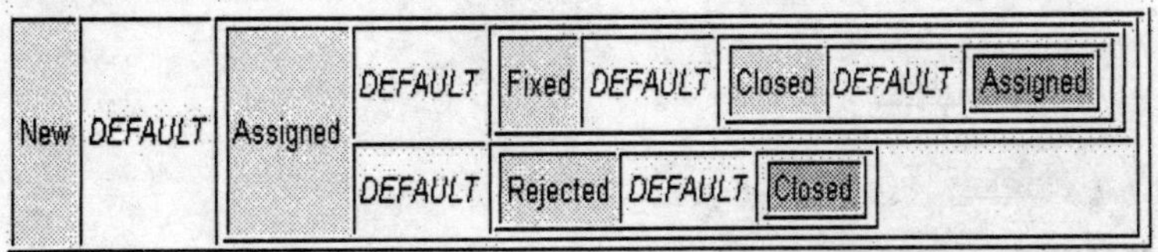

Example of a workflow - after customization

You can even configure whether or not changing of values is permitted given the current state within the workflow - and that too at a field-level. This flexibility allows for some interesting possibilities. For example, assume that you want to maintain a "percentage complete" field that can be updated at any time during the life-cycle of an item. The screenshot below demonstrates how you can set up a drop down field called "% Complete":

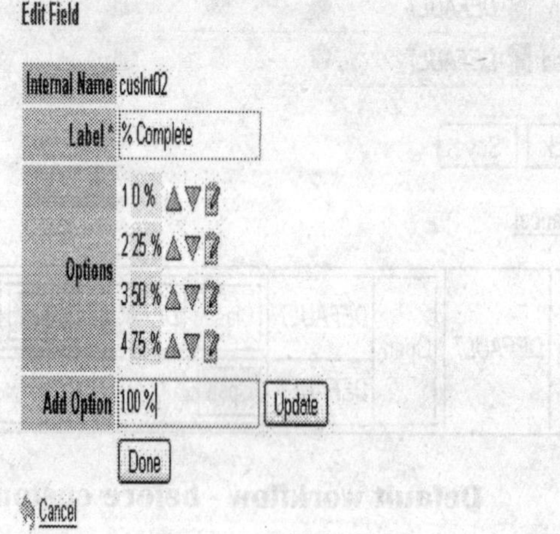

Setting up of a drop down custom field called "% Complete"

Then when customizing the roles and field-level permissions, all you need to do is specify that the "% Complete" field is editable even when the status is "Open".

Space Roles and State-Transitions (Workflow) for Space: Another Space (ABC)

		Next Allowed State		Field Level Permissions M Mandatory O Optional R Read-Only
State	Role	Open	Closed	% Complete
New	DEFAULT	●		M
Open	DEFAULT	●	●	M
Closed	DEFAULT	●	●	R

Back Save

Cancel

Making a custom field editable when updating an item (after new item has been created)

This results in the "% Complete" field being available for updating whenever anyone views an item with a status of "Open". Notice also how the "% Complete" field is added as a column to the "History" section so that the complete history of changes to this custom field can be viewed.

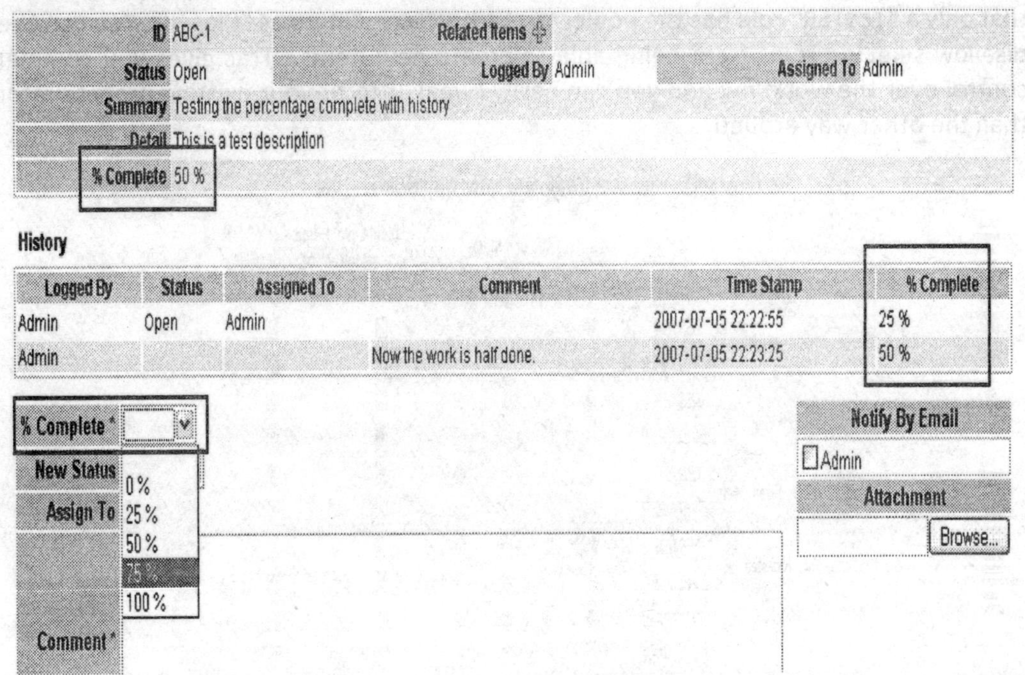

Example of a custom field that can be updated even when status is "Open"

Detailed History View

JTrac provides a very detailed history view that completely captures all comments or status changes for an item. The history can be seen when viewing an item as shown above.

Attachments Support

You can upload file attachments at the time of creating of an item or as many times as required after an item has been created.

Custom Roles

JTrac customization does not stop at workflow - you can also define different roles for each tracker project that you set up. This allows for power and flexibility. For example you could enforce that a "DEVELOPER" role can only mark "Assigned" items as "Fixed" and that only a "TESTER" role has the power to mark a "Fixed" item as "Closed". You can even disallow selected roles from being able to create new items. JTrac gives you complete control over the workflow and you can easily tweak it to fit your existing process rather than the other way around.

Space Roles and State-Transitions (Workflow) for Space: Workflow Demo (FLOW)

		Next Allowed State				Field Level Permissions (M Mandatory, O Optional, R Read-Only)	
State	Role	Assigned	Fixed	Rejected	Closed	Severity	Priority
New	TESTER					M	M
	DEVELOPER					M	M
Assigned	TESTER					R	R
	DEVELOPER					R	R
Fixed	TESTER					R	R
	DEVELOPER					R	R
Rejected	TESTER					R	R
	DEVELOPER					R	R
Closed	TESTER					R	R
	DEVELOPER					R	R

Back Save

Cancel

New	TESTER	Assigned	DEVELOPER	Fixed	TESTER	Closed	TESTER DEVELOPER	Assigned
			DEVELOPER	Rejected	TESTER	Closed		

Example of workflow where each role has clearly defined responsibilities.

In the example above, the roles highlighted in red on the visual "map" of the workflow being edited mean that at these points in the workflow - a user with the given role can assign only to other roles. So in this case, the TESTER can assign a New item only to a DEVELOPER role and not another TESTER. And when an item is in the "Assigned" state, a DEVELOPER can only assign to a TESTER when changing the status to "Fixed" or "Rejected".

Field-level permissions can be mapped to roles which allows for even more flexibility. For example, you can set a project up so that only a "MANAGER" can change the "Severity" level after a bug is submitted. JTrac makes it possible for you to define very complex workflows, complete with both Status and Role dependent field-level permissions, and you can do all this within a single admin screen.

Search Custom Fields

The intuitive search screen (shown below) allows for easy execution of common queries such as find all items "logged by" or "assigned to" a user (or users). JTrac allows for filtering even on custom fields.

You can navigate back to the search setup screen from the search results screen and have the search parameters still active. This is useful when trying to tweak complex queries by trial and error.

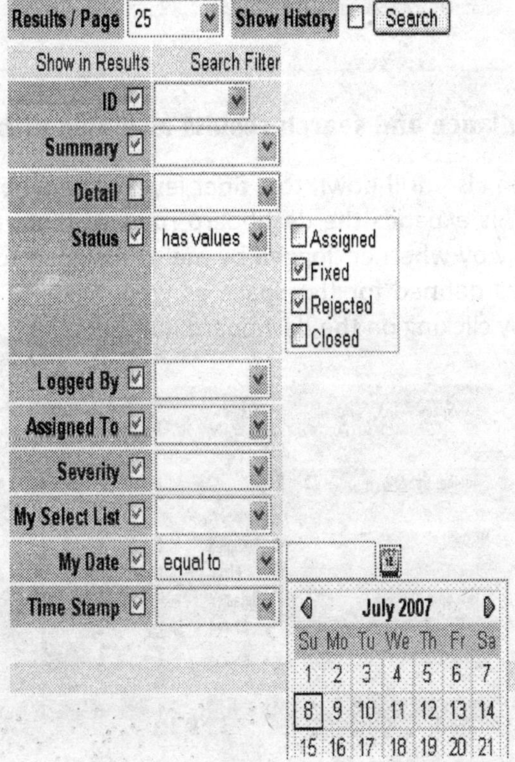

The search screen - which allows filtering on custom fields

Dashboard

The default view when you log into JTrac is a very handy dashboard view that provides the most frequently used statistics at a glance. You can click on any of the numbers to immediately bring up the search results view listing the items matched. For example, clicking on the count of items "Logged By Me" would immediately display the list of items initiated by the currently logged in user.

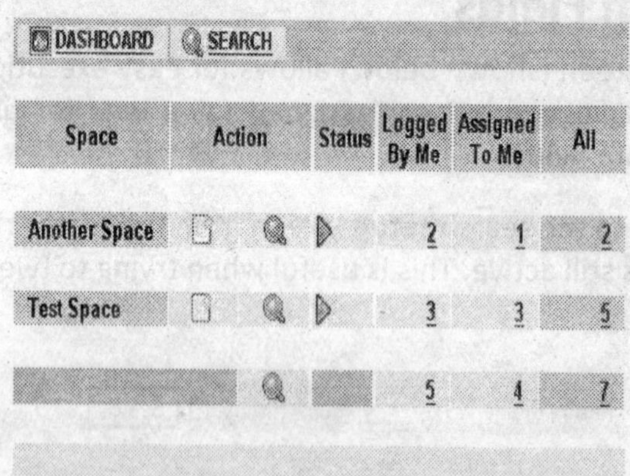

Statistics at a glance and search results available with just one click

For each Space, you can also drill-down to a finer level of detail by clicking on the right-arrow 'expand' icon. This expands the dashboard rows so that you can see a break-up of item counts, not only by whether 'logged by me' / 'assigned to me' - but against the custom workflow states defined for the Space as well. Again, it is possible to directly navigate to the items by clicking on the dashboard numbers.

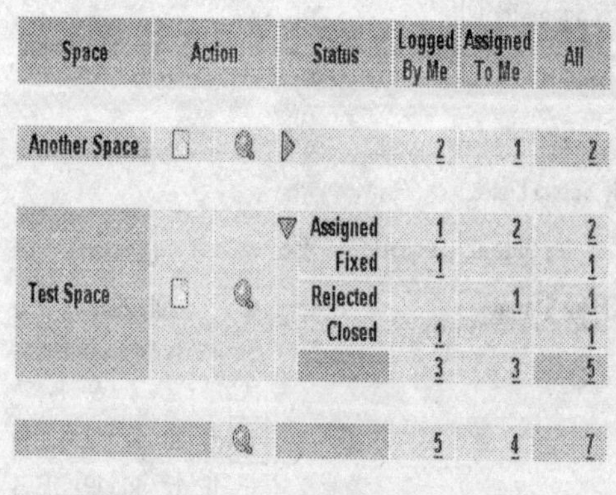

Expanded statistics for a Space showing counts by workflow status

Search Across All Projects

In addition to be able to search within a single space (project) JTrac allows for searching across all (or a sub set of) projects that a user is mapped to. For example, in the screenshot of the dashboard above, there are two projects. The "SEARCH" link at the top of the page (as well as the "search" link on the "totals" row) would bring up the search wizard that can search across all (or a subset of) the spaces assigned to the currently logged in user.

Full Text Search

The summary and even the detailed descriptions of items are indexed and can be searched. Note that if you are upgrading or migrating databases, you may need to "re-index" which is an option available to admin users.

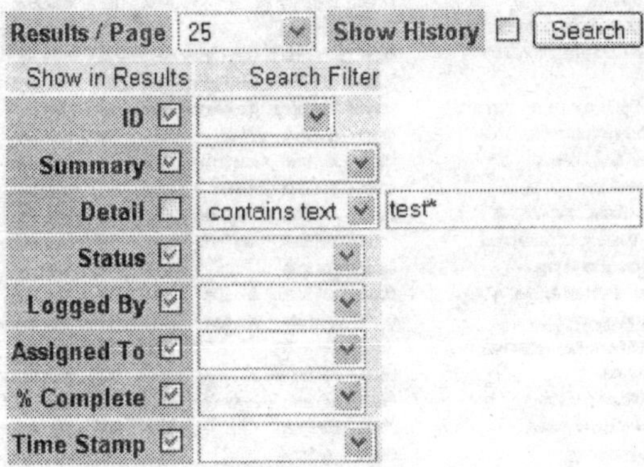

Lucene powered full text search with wildcard support

Export to Excel

JTrac Is able to export the results of any search (or all items in a Space) as an Excel Sheet. The link for this appears at the top right of the search results screen.

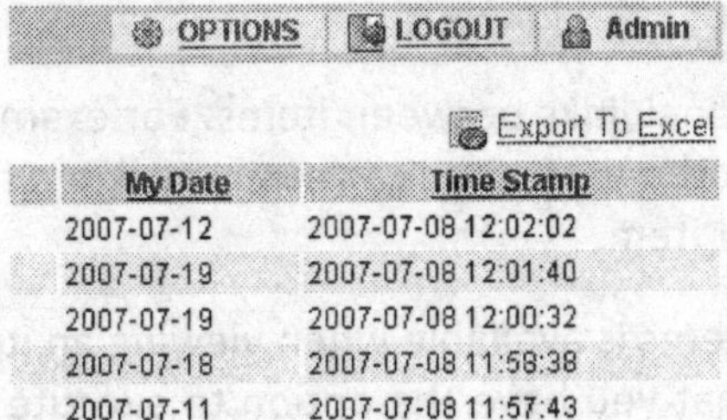

Download search results as an excel sheet

Once the data is in a spreadsheet, it is very easy to analyze data and do things like creating pivot-tables and charts. Many users use the 'export to Excel' feature to fulfil custom reporting requirements.

Simple Navigation

Most users will use only five screens in JTrac: Dashboard, Create, View, Search and Results. Navigation has been designed with usability and simplicity in mind. A screenshot of the search results screen is shown below.

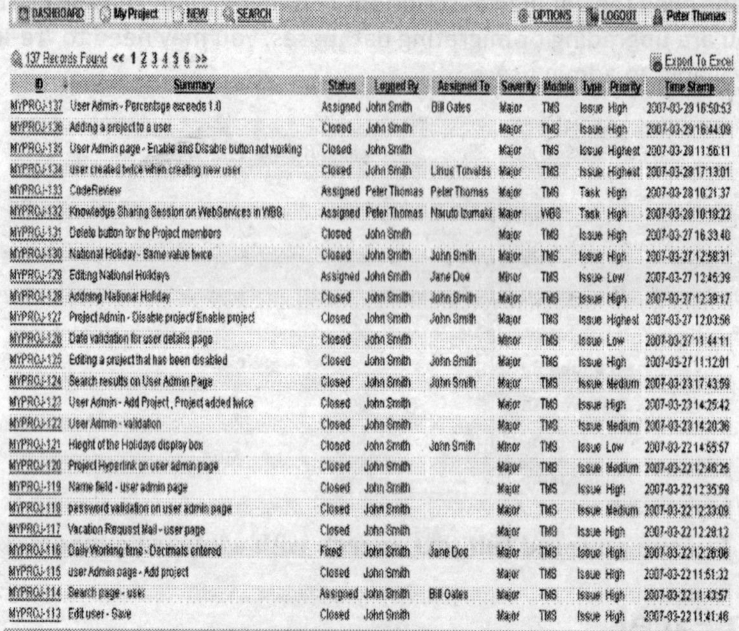

ID	Summary	Status	Logged By	Assigned To	Severity	Module	Type	Priority	Time Stamp
MYPROJ-137	User Admin - Percentage exceeds 1.0	Assigned	John Smith	Bill Gates	Major	TMS	Issue	High	2007-03-29 16:50:53
MYPROJ-136	Adding a project to a user	Closed	John Smith		Major	TMS	Issue	High	2007-03-29 16:44:09
MYPROJ-135	User Admin page - Enable and Disable button not working	Closed	John Smith		Major	TMS	Issue	Highest	2007-03-28 11:56:11
MYPROJ-134	user created twice when creating new user	Closed	John Smith	Linus Torvalds	Major	TMS	Issue	Highest	2007-03-28 17:13:01
MYPROJ-133	CodeReview	Assigned	Peter Thomas	Peter Thomas	Major	TMS	Task	High	2007-03-28 10:21:37
MYPROJ-132	Knowledge Sharing Session on WebServices in WBS	Assigned	Peter Thomas	Naruto Izumaki	Major	WBS	Task	High	2007-03-28 10:18:22
MYPROJ-131	Delete button for the Project members	Closed	John Smith		Major	TMS	Issue	High	2007-03-27 16:33:48
MYPROJ-130	National Holiday - Same value twice	Closed	John Smith	John Smith	Major	TMS	Issue	High	2007-03-27 12:58:31
MYPROJ-129	Editing National Holidays	Assigned	John Smith	Jane Doe	Minor	TMS	Issue	Low	2007-03-27 12:45:39
MYPROJ-128	Addning National Holiday	Closed	John Smith	John Smith	Major	TMS	Issue	High	2007-03-27 12:39:17
MYPROJ-127	Project Admin - Disable project/ Enable project	Closed	John Smith	John Smith	Major	TMS	Issue	Highest	2007-03-27 12:03:56
MYPROJ-126	Date validation for user details page	Closed	John Smith		Minor	TMS	Issue	Low	2007-03-27 11:44:11
MYPROJ-125	Editing a project that has been disabled	Closed	John Smith	John Smith	Major	TMS	Issue	High	2007-03-27 11:12:01
MYPROJ-124	Search results on User Admin Page	Closed	John Smith	John Smith	Major	TMS	Issue	Medium	2007-03-23 17:43:59
MYPROJ-123	User Admin - Add Project , Project added twice	Closed	John Smith		Major	TMS	Issue	High	2007-03-23 14:25:42
MYPROJ-122	User Admin - validation	Closed	John Smith		Major	TMS	Issue	Medium	2007-03-23 14:20:36
MYPROJ-121	Hieght of the Holidays display box	Closed	John Smith	John Smith	Minor	TMS	Issue	Low	2007-03-22 14:55:57
MYPROJ-120	Project Hyperlink on user admin page	Closed	John Smith		Major	TMS	Issue	Medium	2007-03-22 12:46:25
MYPROJ-119	Name field - user admin page	Closed	John Smith		Major	TMS	Issue	High	2007-03-22 12:35:59
MYPROJ-118	password validation on user admin page	Closed	John Smith		Major	TMS	Issue	Medium	2007-03-22 12:33:09
MYPROJ-117	Vacation Request Mail - user page	Closed	John Smith		Major	TMS	Issue	High	2007-03-22 12:28:12
MYPROJ-116	Daily Working time - Decimals entered	Fixed	John Smith	Jane Doe	Major	TMS	Issue	High	2007-03-22 12:26:06
MYPROJ-115	user Admin page - Add project	Closed	John Smith		Major	TMS	Issue	High	2007-03-22 11:51:32
MYPROJ-114	Search page - user	Assigned	John Smith	Bill Gates	Major	TMS	Issue	High	2007-03-22 11:43:57
MYPROJ-113	Edit user - Save	Closed	John Smith		Major	TMS	Issue	High	2007-03-22 11:41:46

The search results screen

Cross Referencing of Items

You can establish bi-directional links between items. For example you can mark an item as being a "duplicate of" another item. You can easily navigate to related items (and back) when viewing any particular item.

The option to add related items is available when viewing an item after it is created. The navigation is designed so that you have the option to execute a search before selecting an item to cross-reference.

Read-Only Access

When setting up a Space you can define whether this space can be viewed by users without having to log-in.

Specify if read-only anonymous access is allowed per-space

E-mail Integration

All status changes for an item will trigger e-mail notifications by default. You can choose to add multiple users into a "notify list" at the time of raising a new item or updating the history for an item.

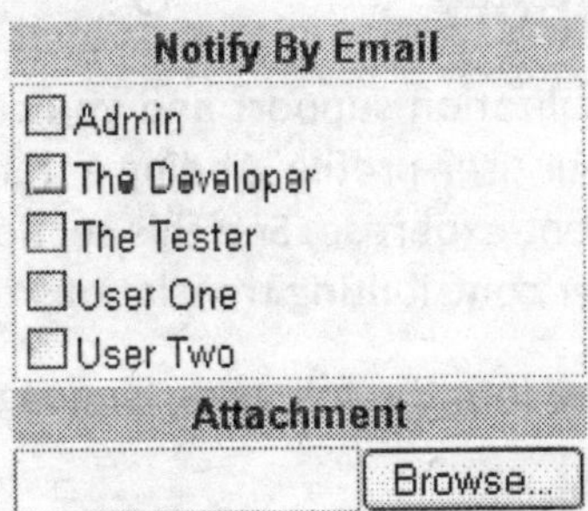

Add multiple users to a "notify list" while creating or updating an item

The e-mail content is very nicely formatted HTML and is laid out in the same way as how the screen looks within JTrac when viewing an item. Users do not need to get used to a different or possibly less pleasing format such as plain-text.

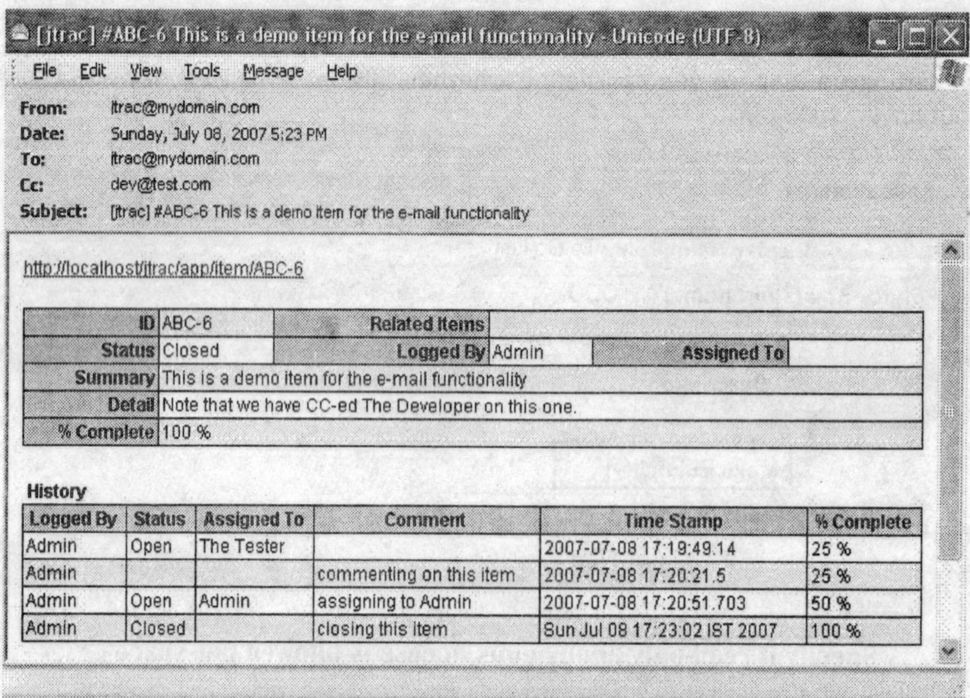

[jtrac] #ABC-6 This is a demo item for the e-mail functionality - Unicode (UTF-8)

File Edit View Tools Message Help

From: jtrac@mydomain.com
Date: Sunday, July 08, 2007 5:23 PM
To: jtrac@mydomain.com
Cc: dev@test.com
Subject: [jtrac] #ABC-6 This is a demo item for the e-mail functionality

http://localhost/jtrac/app/item/ABC-6

ID	ABC-6	Related Items			
Status	Closed	Logged By	Admin	Assigned To	
Summary	This is a demo item for the e-mail functionality				
Detail	Note that we have CC-ed The Developer on this one.				
% Complete	100 %				

History

Logged By	Status	Assigned To	Comment	Time Stamp	% Complete
Admin	Open	The Tester		2007-07-08 17:19:49.14	25 %
Admin			commenting on this item	2007-07-08 17:20:21.5	25 %
Admin	Open	Admin	assigning to Admin	2007-07-08 17:20:51.703	50 %
Admin	Closed		closing this item	Sun Jul 08 17:23:02 IST 2007	100 %

Example of an e-mail sent by JTrac

Admin users can configure the SMTP / e-mail server that JTrac should use in the "Manage Setting" page. This page can be accessed from the "OPTIONS" menu. JTrac also can handle an e-mail server that requires authentication or even a secure connection over HTTPS.

Multi-Language Support

JTrac has complete internationalization support and you can change the user interface language instantly by editing your user-profile. Adding a translation is very easy and does not require any Java development expertise. See this section of the developer guide for more details and please consider contributing translations to the JTrac project.

JTrac has already been translated into the following languages:

- German - de
- Greek - el
- Spanish - es
- Spanish (Argentina) - es_AR
- Spanish (Mexico) - es_MX
- French - fr
- Hungarian - hu

- Italian - it
- Japanese - ja
- Dutch nl
- Polish - pl
- Portugese (Brazil) - pt_BR
- Russian - ru
- Chinese (China) - zh_CN
- Chinese (Taiwan) - zh_TW

LDAP / CAS authentication support

JTrac has built-in support for authenticating user credentials against an LDAP or Active Directory server. Please refer the LDAP section of the installation guide for more details.

JTrac also has support for integrating with a Central Authentication Service (CAS) installation. The install guide has more details on how to configure single sign-on using CAS.

Settings

For e-mail notifications to work, an SMTP server needs to be configured in JTrac. Users who have the ADMIN role will be able to access the JTrac configuration settings screen from a link on the "OPTIONS" screen. Note that you will need to provide values for the "mail.from" and the "jtrac.url.base" properties also, for things like the hyperlinks within e-mail to work properly. JTrac also supports mail servers that require authentication or secure connections using SSL. You can refer the descriptions of the available configuration property settings available from the settings screen as shown below.

If you have trouble getting e-mail to work, one of the things to watch out for is whether there is any firewall blocking the communication between JTrac and the mail server - for example you may have a firewall runnning on the machine where JTrac is installed. It is very common for mail servers to be configured to prevent mail-relay requests from unknown applications or IP addresses so you may need to check with your mail server administrator.

Configuration Settings

Parameter Key	Value	Edit	Description
mail.server.host	123.45.67.89		Hostname or IP address of the SMTP server to be used for sending e-mail
mail.server.port			Port used by the SMTP server (default 25)
mail.server.username			Username for the SMTP server if it requires authentication
mail.server.password			Password for the SMTP server if it requires authentication
mail.server.starttls.enable			Use "true" for secure (SSL) connection if required by the SMTP server
mail.subject.prefix			Text that will be prefixed to the e-mail subject-line (default [jtrac])
mail.from	admin@mydomain.com		When generating e-mail, this will be used as the 'from' address
mail.session.jndiname			javax.mail.Session JNDI name - if present, this will be used instead of the SMTP server details above
jtrac.url.base	http://myserver/jtrac		Base URL of your JTrac installation (e.g. http://myserver/jtrac) required for links in the e-mails to work
locale.default			Default language used for this JTrac installation e.g. "de" for German
session.timeout			Time in minutes after which user session expires (default 30 minutes)
attachment.maxsize			Maximum size in MB of file-attachments. (default 5 MB) Use -1 for no-limit

The JTrac settings screen where you can configure an e-mail / SMTP server

JTrac also can lookup and use a JNDI mail session (javax.mail.Session) if required. If you provide a JNDI name, JTrac will ignore the SMTP server details provided.

Using only the WAR file

JTrac is designed so that you can be up and running by just deploying the WAR file into your existing web-application server. Note that you need a servlet 2.4 compliant container. For example, if you have Apache Tomcat 5.5.X, you can either copy the WAR file into the [tomcat.home]/webapps folder or choose to upload the WAR file through the Tomcat console.

JTrac saves database information and uploaded attachments into a directory on the server. This directory is logically called the "jtrac.home". When you do a "quick-install" of JTrac by just deploying the WAR file, JTrac creates a ".jtrac" folder in the user home folder and uses that location as the home directory. This is great for quickly evaluating JTrac but when you actually use JTrac in production you should configure the JTrac home directory as a location that can easily be backed-up for example.

Custom Installation

To customize the location of "jtrac.home" you have the following three options. On startup, JTrac tries to detect the value of "jtrac.home", and checks the following configuration options in the order listed below.

Edit the "jtrac-init.properties" file

If you explode (unzip) the WAR file, you can edit the /WEB-INF/classes/jtrac-init.properties file and customize the location of "jtrac.home". Note that you can choose to deploy JTrac as an exploded-war and it is not mandatory that you re-package (zip) the WAR file after editing "jtrac-init.properties".

Set a Servlet context parameter

For example you can specify the jtrac.home using the Tomcat administration console or as follows using a <Context> parameter.

```
<Context docBase="${catalina.home}/jtrac/jtrac.war">
    <Parameter name="jtrac.home" value="C:/data/jtrac_
home"/>
</Context>
```

Set a System / JVM parameter

If you can easily set a system property called "jtrac.home" within the environment of your application server then you don't need to edit the WAR file. Please look at the contents of "start.bat" to see an example of how the appropriate JVM (Java Virtual Machine) parameters can be set when deploying JTrac. For example, if you are using Apache Tomcat 5.5.X, you can set an environment variable called JAVA_OPTS before invoking the startup script (startup.bat / startup.sh). Here is an example for Tomcat 5.5.X on Windows:

```
set JAVA_OPTS=-Djtrac.home=C:/data/jtrac_home -Dfile.
encoding=UTF-8
```

If "jtrac.home" has not been configured in any of the above ways, JTrac will create a folder called ".jtrac" in the user home directory and proceed to use that as "jtrac.home".

Using a different database such as MySQL

You can configure the database that JTrac uses by editing the "jtrac.properties" file that JTrac expects within the "jtrac.home" folder. Note that if JTrac does not find a "jtrac.properties" file in the expected location, JTrac creates a fresh one which is pre-configured for HSQLDB. The contents of this file are as follows:

```
database.driver=org.hsqldb.jdbcDriver
database.url=jdbc:hsqldb:file:${jtrac.home}/db/jtrac
database.username=sa
database.password=
hibernate.dialect=org.hibernate.dialect.HSQLDialect
hibernate.show_sql=false
```

You can change the database values and the hibernate dialect to match the settings of a database that you have already. When JTrac starts, it will connect to the database and create the schema if one does not already exist.

If you edit the "jtrac.properties" file, ensure that there are no trailing spaces in the entries shown above (especially when cutting and pasting from somewhere). This can save you a lot of frustration!

Don't forget to make the database driver available for the web-application. If you are using the bundled Jetty web-app server, this is as simple as copying the jar file into the "lib" folder along with the jetty jar files. If you are using Tomcat, you can either place the jar file under "shared/lib" or within the "/WEB-INF/lib" folder of the "jtrac" (exploded) WAR itself.

Given below is a sample jtrac.properties file for MySQL. Using the default "root" user is obviously not advisable from a security point of view and you should try and have a separate user for the database used by JTrac.

```
database.driver=com.mysql.jdbc.Driver
database.url=jdbc:mysql://localhost/jtrac
database.username=root
database.password=
hibernate.dialect=org.hibernate.dialect.MySQLDialect
hibernate.show_sql=false
```

For MySQL, do not use the "autoReconnect=true" parameter in the MySQL URL, this is not recommended by the MySQL team. The Apache DBCP connection pool used internally by JTrac is configured to refresh stale database connections.

The default query to test idle database connections is "SELECT 1". This has been reported to not work for databases such as Derby and Progress because they consider this invalid SQL. You can customize the validation query by adding a "database.validationQuery" property in "jtrac.properties. If you set the validation query to an empty string, this effectively disables the periodic testing of idle database connections that Apache DBCP performs.

Using a JNDI Datasource

You can provide a JNDI datasource name as an additional property called "database. datasource.jndiname" in the "jtrac.properties" file. JTrac will ignore the other database properties in this case.

LDAP Authentication

A couple of extra entries in "jtrac.properties" are required in order to configure LDAP authentication. JTrac will attempt LDAP authentication if an "ldap.url" config entry is present.

```
ldap.url=ldap://myldaphost
ldap.searchBase=DC=foo,DC=bar,DC=org
```

The following additional entry is recommended if you are using Active Directory. This switches on an LDAP optimization that is specific to Active Directory.

```
ldap.activeDirectoryDomain=MYDOMAIN
```

The benefit of LDAP authentication is that users can sign-on to JTrac by using their existing LDAP credentials (username and password). At the moment, LDAP support is limited to authentication and not authorization. Users still have to be created by an administrator and mapped to the relevant Spaces using the JTrac administration screens before they can start using JTrac.

Integrating with CAS for Single Sign On

In order to integrate JTrac with CAS you have to edit a couple of XML files within the "WEB-INF" folder ('web.xml' and 'applicationContext-acegi-cas.xml'). The changes that you need to make are described below.

Changes to web.xml

- Change "applicationContext-acegi.xml" to "applicationContext-acegi-cas.xml". This appears towards the start of the file in the 'contextConfigLocation' context-param.
- Uncomment the filter and filter-mapping XML for the 'acegi' FilterToBeanProxy
- Uncomment the servlet and servlet-mapping XML for the 'casProxy' ProxyTicketReceptor. You should also uncomment the associated context-param called 'edu.yale.its.tp.cas.proxyUrl' and customize the value for your environment.

Changes to applicationContext-acegi-cas.xml

In the XML corresponding to bean id "casProxyTicketValidator" - edit the following property values to suit your environment:

- casValidate
- proxyCallbackUrl
- trustStore
- loginUrl
- logoutUrl

For more details and troubleshooting, you can refer to the Acegi documentation on CAS integration.

Installing as a Windows Service

Note that this approach can reportedly apply to other operating systems. If you have been able to do this successfully on Linux or Mac environments, please consider contributing some documentation on this.

If you choose to use the bundled Jetty web-application server, you can easily install JTrac as a Windows service so that it can start automatically when the host machine is switched on. One of the big advantages of this is that the console window will be invisible and will run in the background. You can therefore avoid the possibility of the Jetty server getting terminated because somebody decided to close "that pesky DOS Window that gets in the way". Having JTrac start automatically without requiring someone to log-in is ideal when you have a server that may be restarted occasionally due to power outages or maintenance.

JTrac can be configured as a Windows service by using the Java Service Wrapper project. For convenience, the JTrac distribution contains a "wrapper.conf" file in the "etc" folder that is pre-configured for the Java Service Wrapper. But first you have to download the Java Service Wrapper distribution separately. Note that the Java Service Wrapper project supports other operating systems such as Linux or Mac also.

Place some of the files from the Java Service Wrapper distribution into the JTrac folder structure as follows:

- From the "bin" folder, copy "wrapper.exe" to the "jtrac" root folder
- From the "lib" folder, copy "wrapper.jar" and "wrapper.dll" into the "jtrac/etc" folder

To install JTrac as a windows service, open a command prompt, change to the "jtrac" directory (where you extracted the JTrac distribution) and run the following command:

```
wrapper.exe -i etc/wrapper.conf
```

This will install a windows service called "JTrac-Jetty". You can now go to the Windows - Control Panel :: Administrative Tools :: Services dialog to start the "JTrac-Jetty" service. Note that this service is configured to automatically start when Windows starts, by default. To remove the service, you can use the following command:

```
wrapper.exe -r etc/wrapper.conf
```

The "wrapper.conf" file in the "etc" folder can be modified in case you need JTrac to run on a different port from the default (80). Look for the "-Djetty.port=80" entry. When running as a service under the Java Service Wrapper, you can look at the "wrapper.log" file in the "jtrac/logs" folder for troubleshooting.

What to Backup

Although in practice JTrac has been found to be extremely stable in production - to safeguard against hardware failures, you should regularly backup the database and stored attachments. If you are using JTrac with the embedded HSQLDB database, backing up the contents of "jtrac.home" will be sufficient. The HSQLDB data will be stored as files in a directory called "db" under the JTrac home.

If you are using the JTrac distribution as-is, i.e. if you are using the bundled Jetty application server - the JTrac home directory will be called "data" and this is created automatically under the folder where you un-zipped JTrac.

Of course, if you are using a different database you will have to backup the database separately. The "jtrac.home" would still need to be backed up because this is where uploaded attachments are stored.

References

http://java.com/en/download/index.jsp

http://sourceforge.net/projects/j-trac/

Bug Tracking using Mantis tool

Mantis

Mantis introduction

Mantis is a web based bugtracking system. It is currently in development and is considered a beta.

It is written in the PHP scripting language and requires a MySQL database and a webserver. Mantis has been installed on Windows, MacOS, OS/2, and a variety of Unix operating systems. Any web browser should be able to function as a client. It is released under the terms of the GNU General Public License (GPL).

Mantis is free to use and modify. It is free to redistribute as long as you abide by the distribution terms of the GPL.

PRE-REQUISITE :

Operating System	**Windows 2003 Server, MacOS, OS/2, Linux, Solaris**
Database	MySQL database 3.23.2 and higher
Software	PHP 4.0.6 and higher
Application Server	Apache 1.3, Apache 2.0.54, IIS 6.0 with Web Services Extension
Browser	IE6 and above, Mozilla Firefox

Apache HTTP Server 2.2.4

The Apache HTIP *Server* Project is a collaborative software development effort aimed at creating a robust, commercial-grade, featureful and freely-available source code implementation of an HTTP (Web) server.The project is jointly managedby a groupof volunteers located around the world,using the Internet and the Web to communicate, plan, and develop the server and its related documentation.This project is part of the Apache SoftwareFoundation.

1. Download Apache HTIP Server

- Go to browser & type link http://archive.apache.org/dist/httpd/binaries/win32/
- Download
- Save the file

Install Apache HTIP Server

Step 1:Oouble Click on your setup file

Step 2 :Click on 'Run'button

Step 3 : Click the "next" button in the Installation Wizard

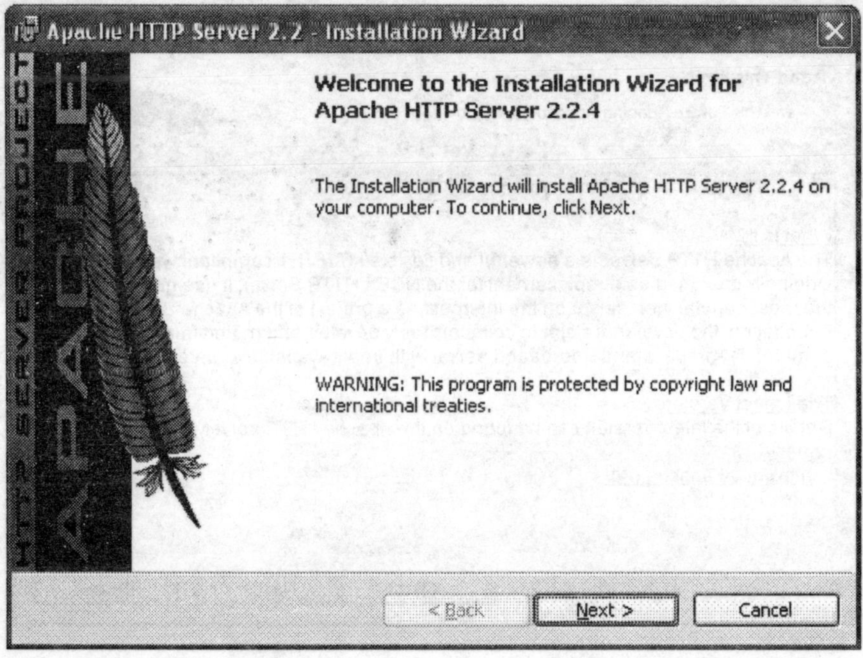

Step 4 : Accept the License agreement and click the "next" button

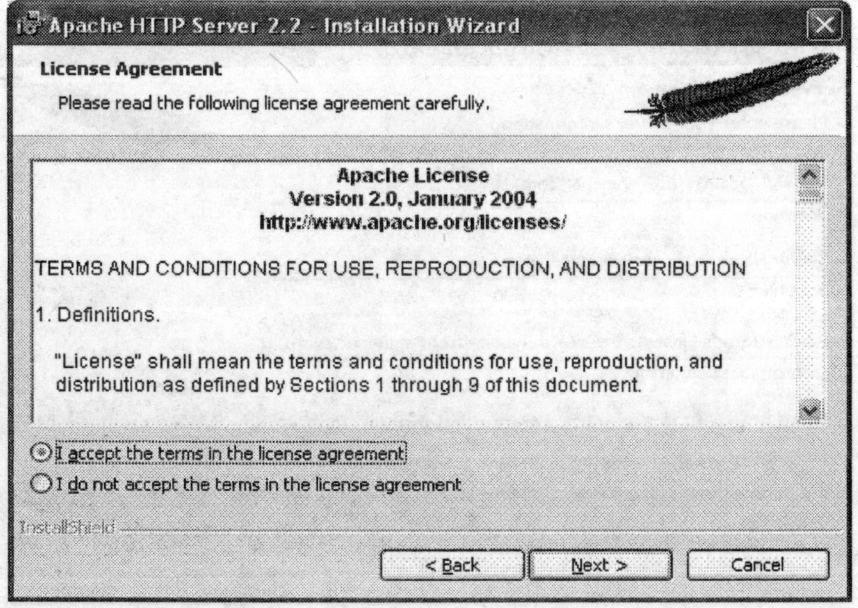

Step 5 : Read Apache HTTP Server & Click on Next button

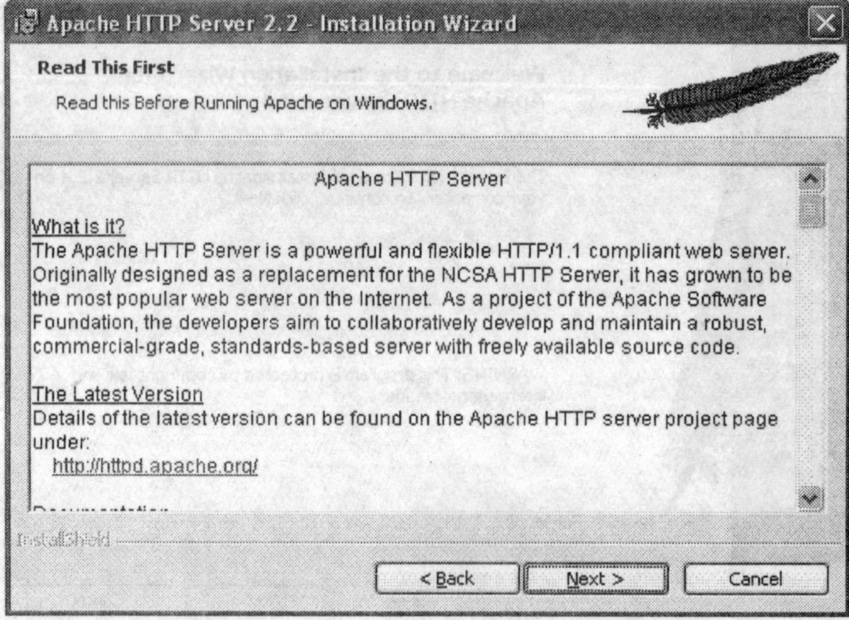

Step 6 : Provide the Server information details in the window. Network Domain & Server Name as "localhost", Admin email address as "admin@localhost"

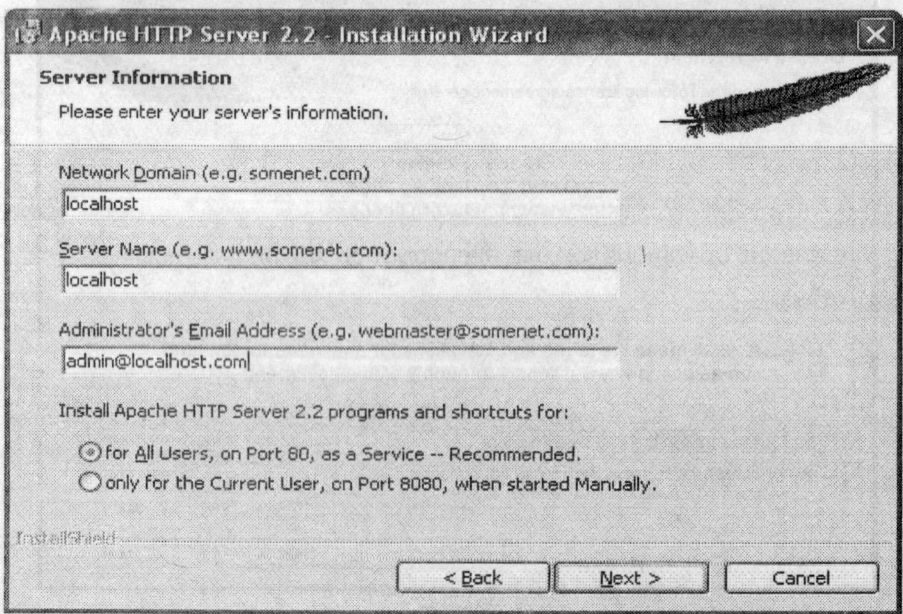

Step 8 : Click on Build Headers and Libraries which is in Red cross as shown in figure & select the option 'This feature will be install on local hard drive'

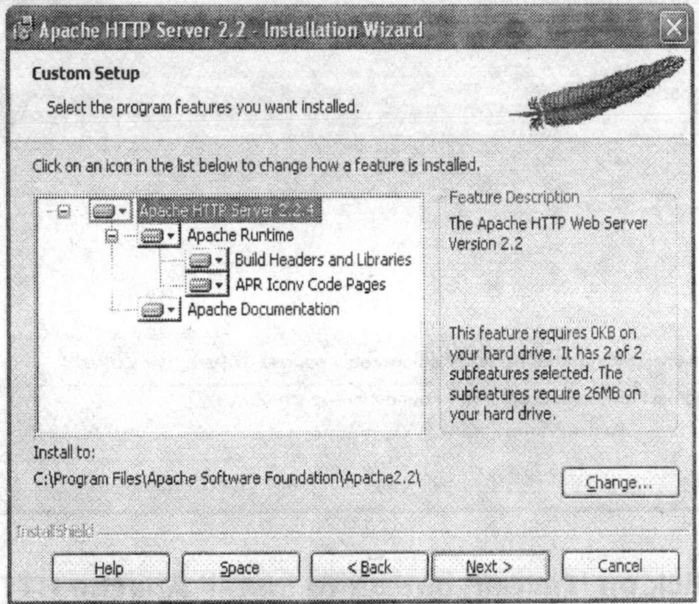

Step 9 : On the following screen you will see the default path of Apache to installs. Click the \"Change...\", and choose whatever other name you choose your created directory structure. Click \"Next\".

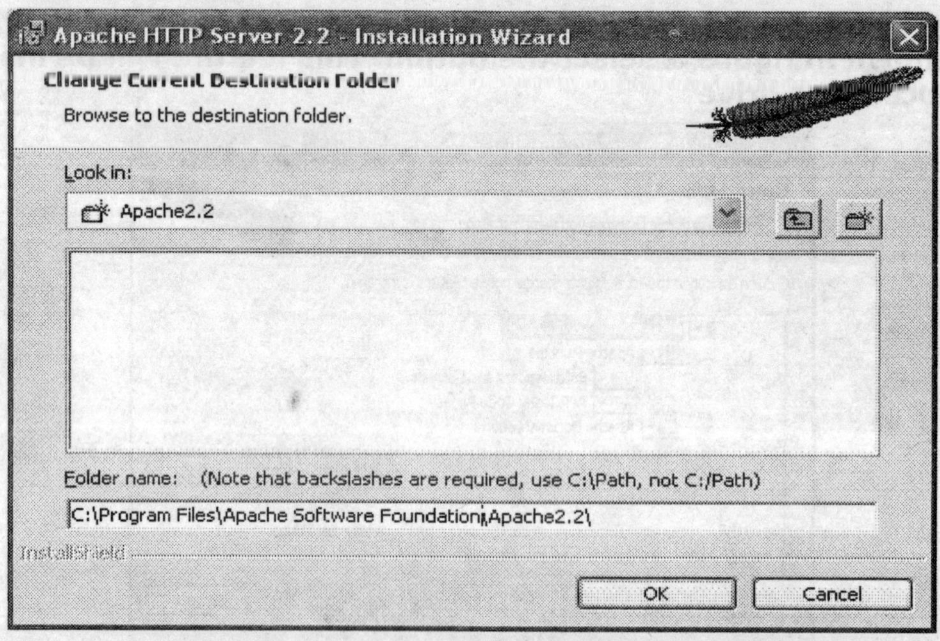

Step 10 : Click on 'Install' button to install Apache HTTP Server

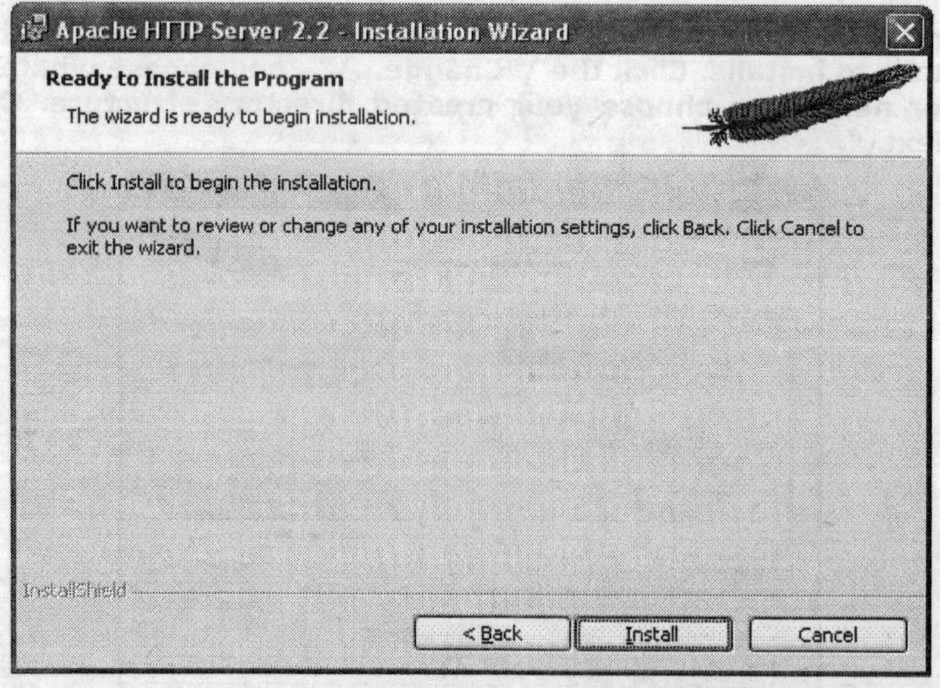

Step 11 : You can see the status of Installation status in the Installation wizard

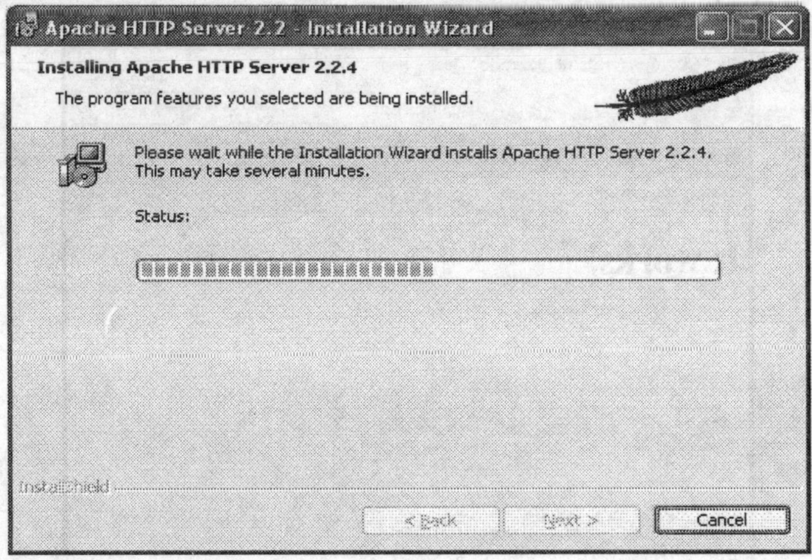

Step 12 : Once the installation has been completed, following window will get displayed. Click finish.

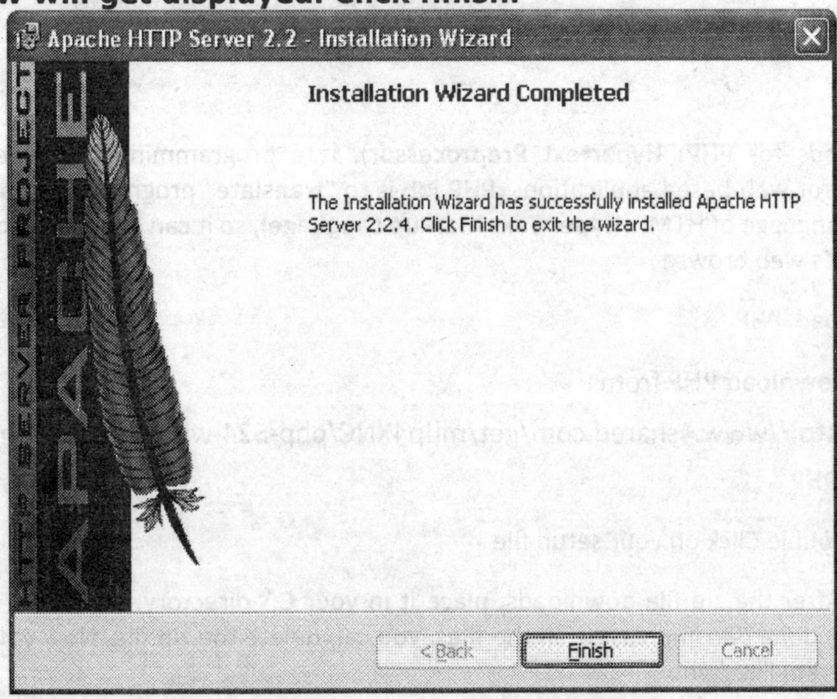

To Test Apache installation, type in the browser http://localhost/ The following window should appear.

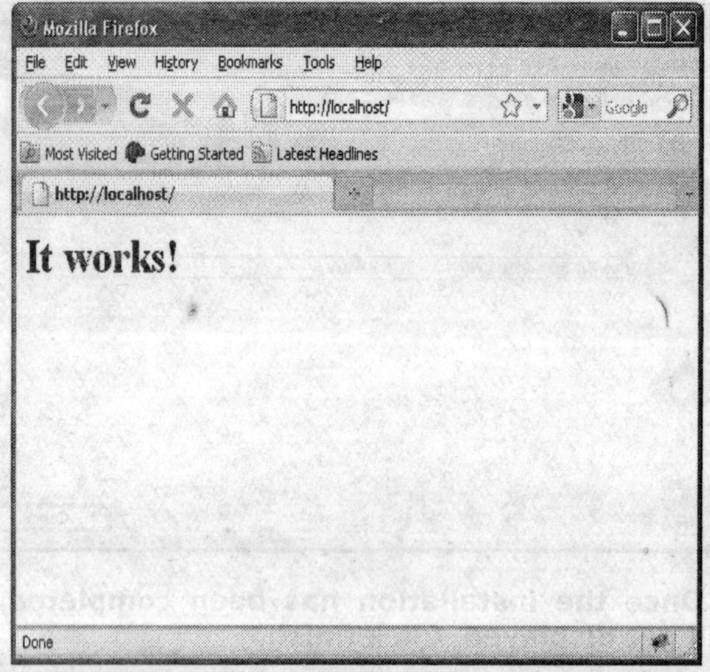

PHP

PHP (stands for **PHP: Hypertext Preprocessor**), is a programming language that is intended for web-based applications. PHP job is to "**translate**" programming commands into the language of HTML (**Hyper Text Markup Language**), so it can be displayed on your computer's web browse

1) Download PHP

- Download PHP from
- http://www.4shared.com/get/mlJp4XNC/php-524-win32-installer.html

2) Install PHP

Step 1 : Double Click on your setup file

Step 2 : After the zip file downloads, place it in your C:\ directory, and unzip it there. When it is done decompressing all the files, you can delete the zip file. Now your PHP is in C:\Program Files\php

Step 3 : Click on 'Run' button

Step 4 : Accept the License agreement and click the "next" button

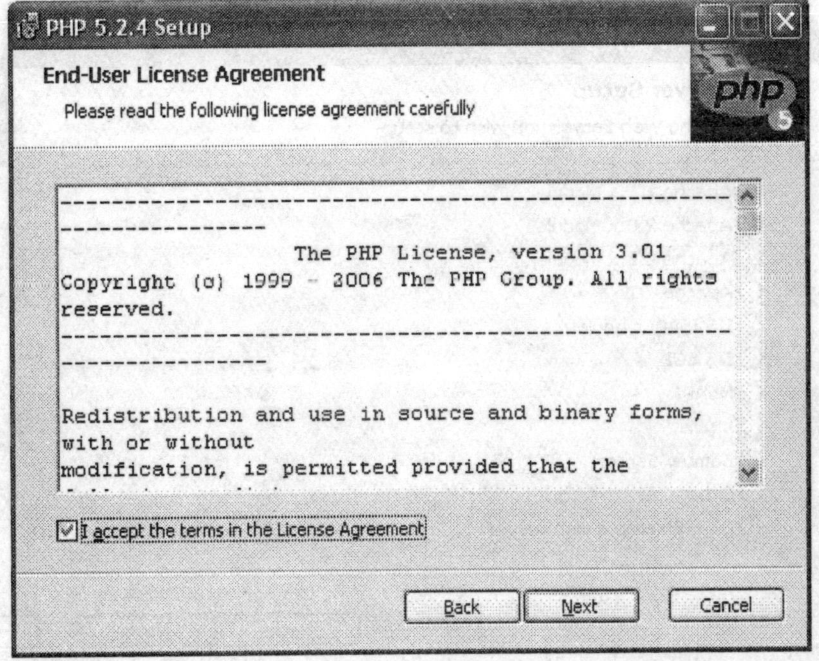

Step 5 : Change your PHP installation path OR just accept the default path – **C:\Program Files\PHP** and click *"Next*

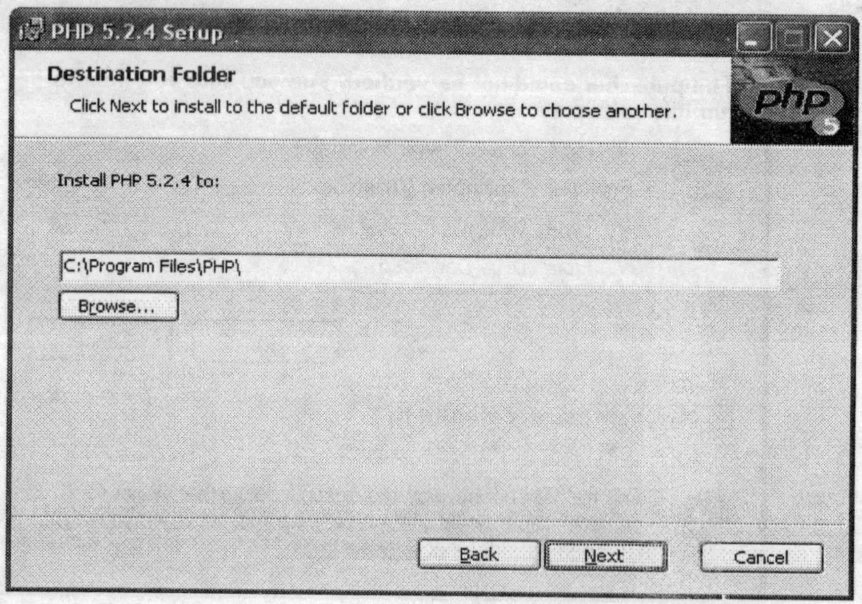

Step 6: On the Web Server Setup screen, select the **Apache 2.2.x Module** and click *"Next*

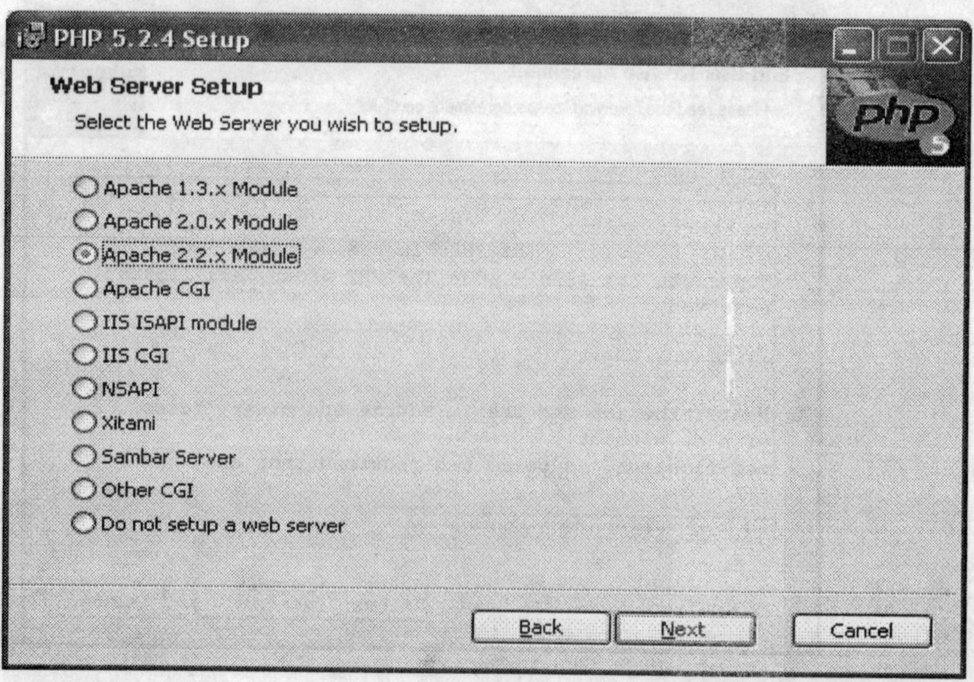

Step 7 :-On the **Apache Configuration Directory** screen, browse for the Apache configuration directory (conf) OR just enter **C:\Program Files\Apache Software Foundation\Apache2.2\conf** and click *"Next"* to proceed with the installation.

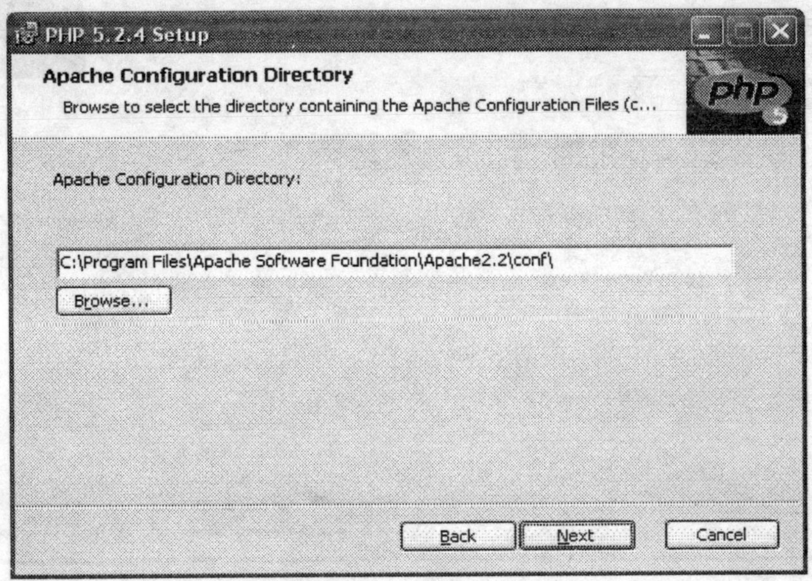

Step 8: For now, accept the default selection and click *"Next"*.

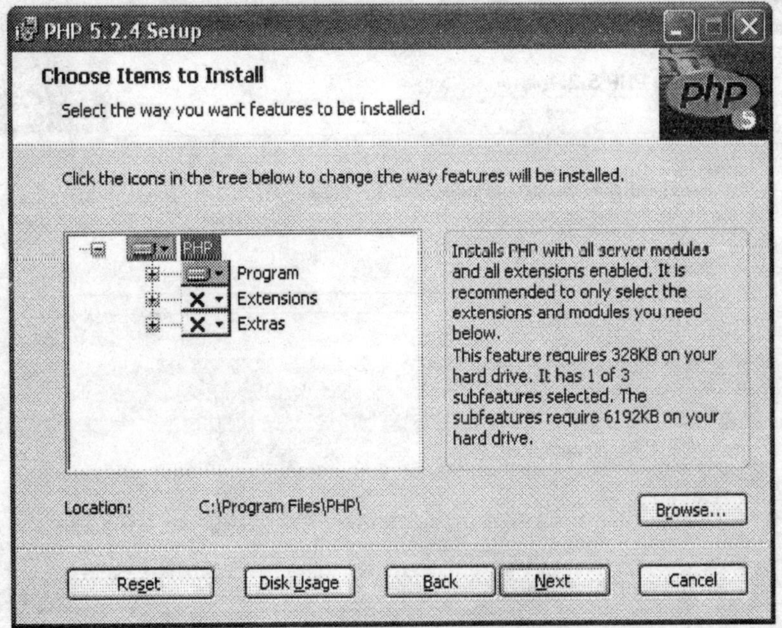

Step 9 : Click "*Install*" to install PHP 5 on Windows.

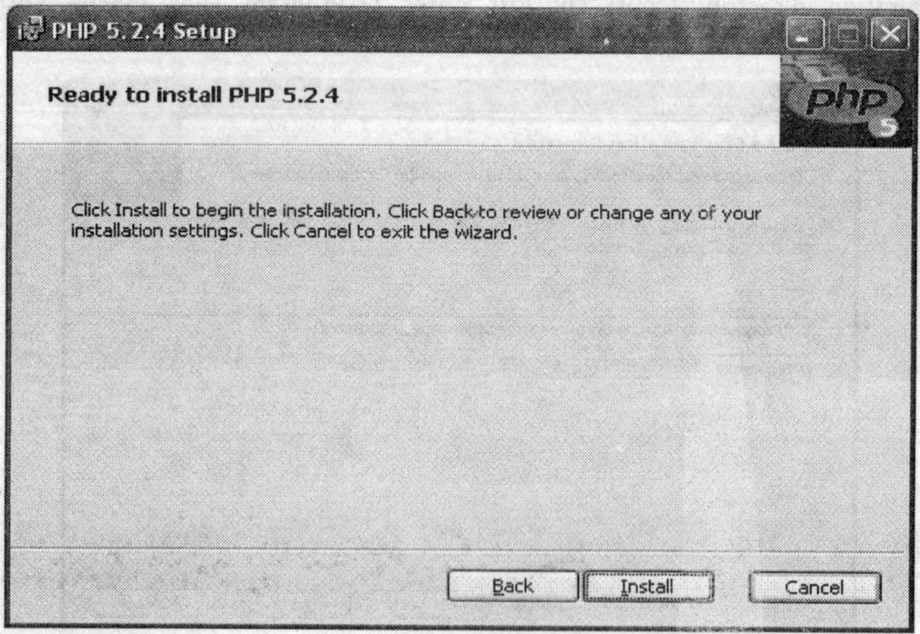

Step 10 : Installation Status

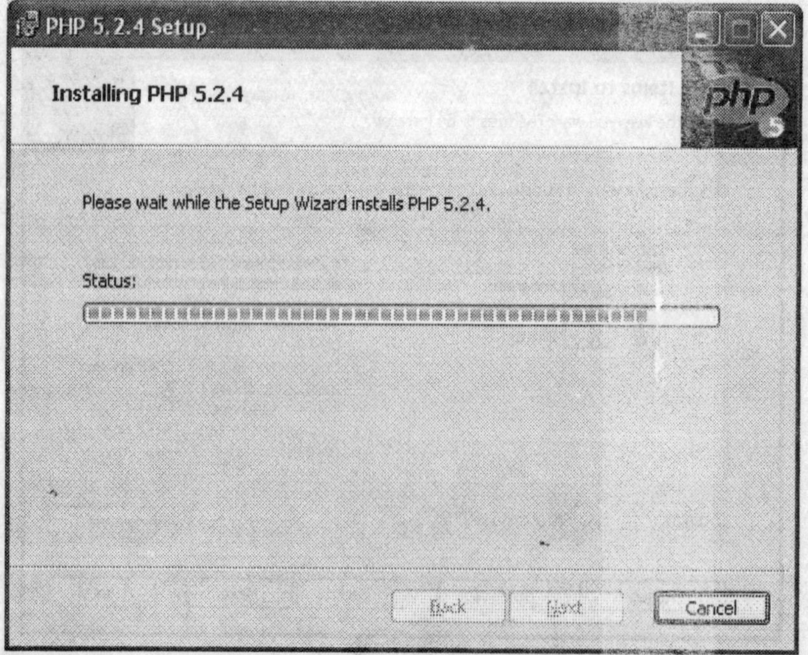

Step 11 : Click *"Finish"* once completed. PHP 5 is successfully installed.

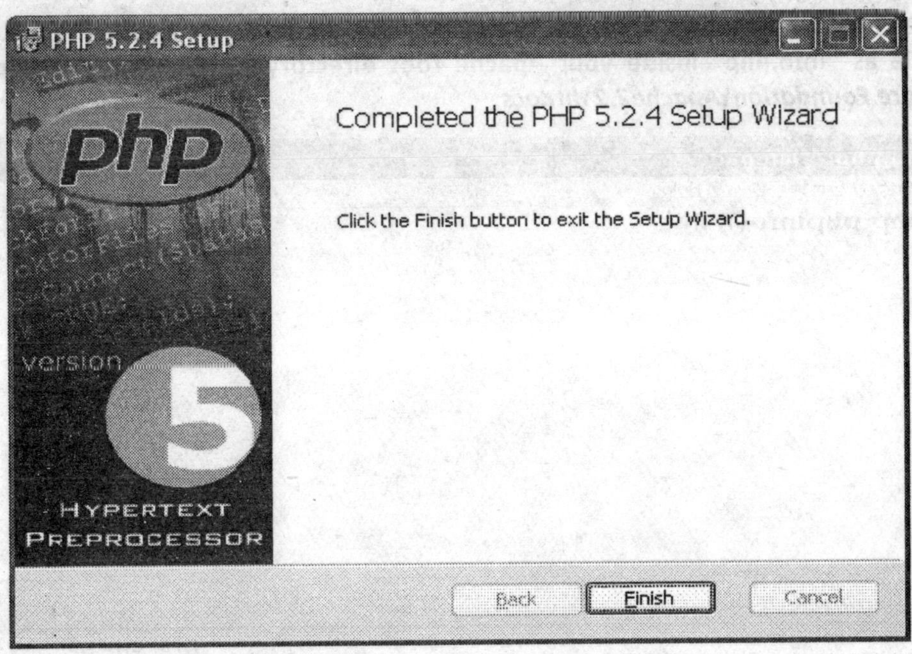

Start your Apache 2.2 server using the "**Monitor Apache Servers**" console (*Start -> Apache HTTP Servers 2.2.4 -> Monitor Apache Servers*). You can see that PHP was successfully installed by checking the Apache status at the bottom of the console.

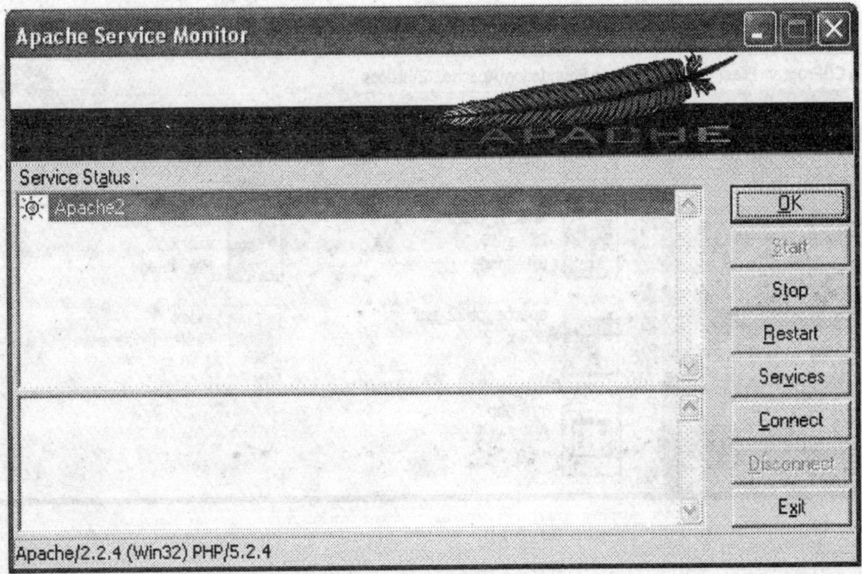

Test your PHP 5 Installation

1- Open up your Windows Notepad. Type in *"<?php phpinfo(); ?>"* inside the file. Save this file as "info.php" inside your Apache root directory, *C:\Program Files\Apache Software Foundation\Apache2.2\htdocs*.

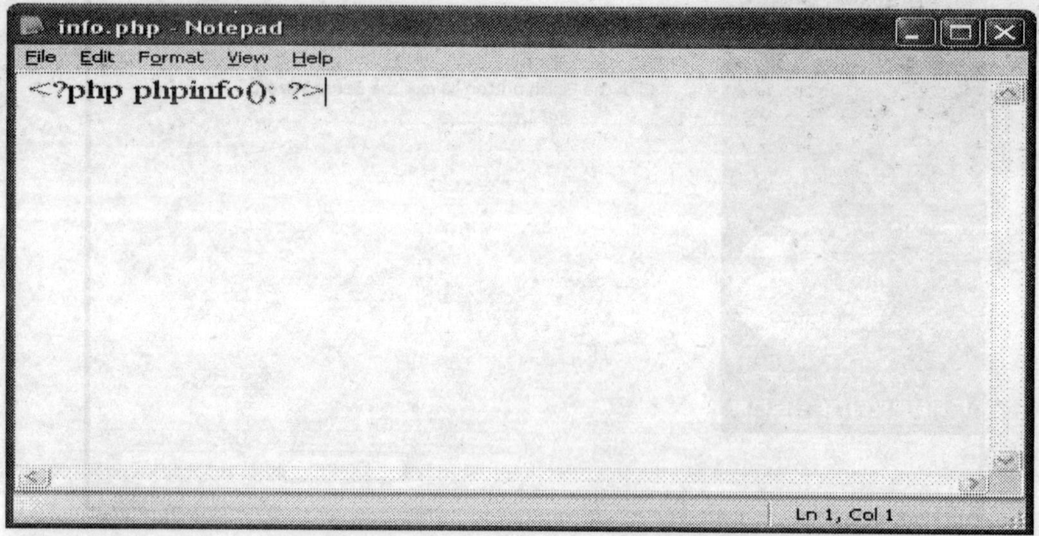

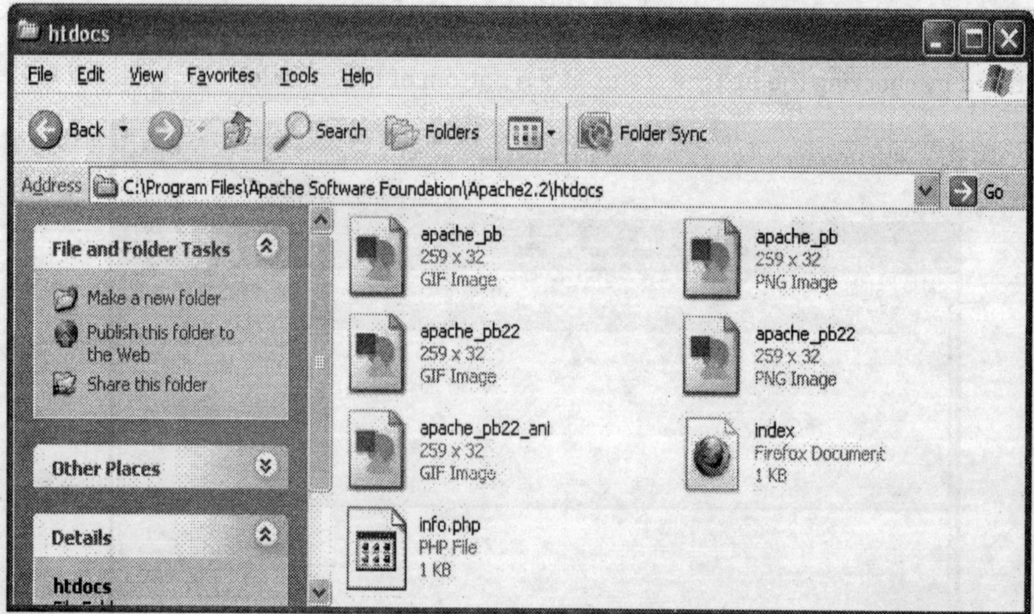

2- Open up your web browser. In the address bar, **type in your web server domain name plus info.php** as the file name. Example: *http://www.syahid.com/info.php* . You should get a PHP configuration page just like the one below.

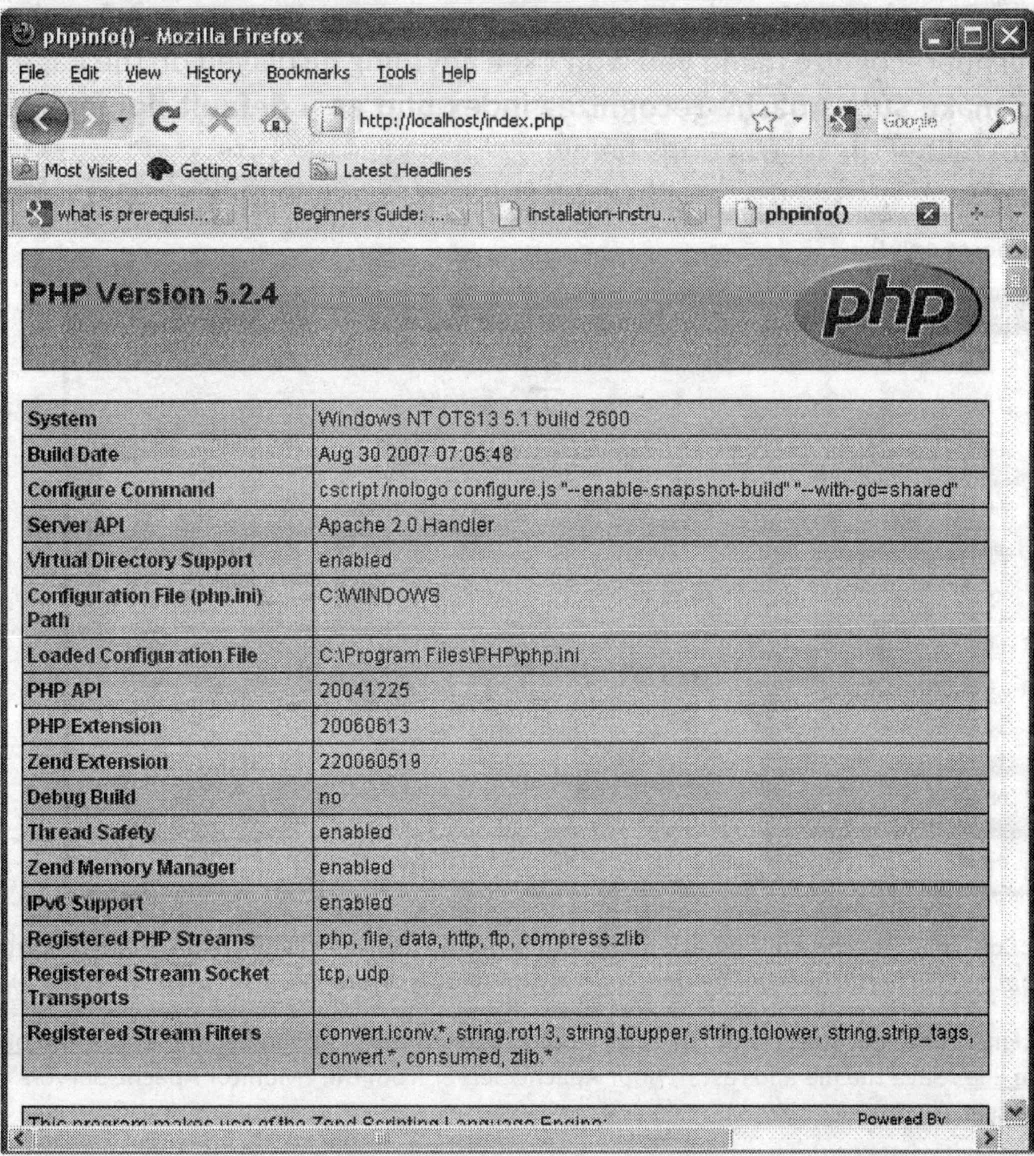

Configuration of Apache 2.2.4 & php 5.2.4

What happens if you change your index.html (default web server homepage) to index.php and try to access your homepage? Apache will not recognize it and you won't see anything displayed on the page. To **make sure Apache recognizes index.php as a default homepage** too, follow the instructions below.

1- Rename your **index.html to index1.html** and **info.php to index.php** (for testing purposes only!).

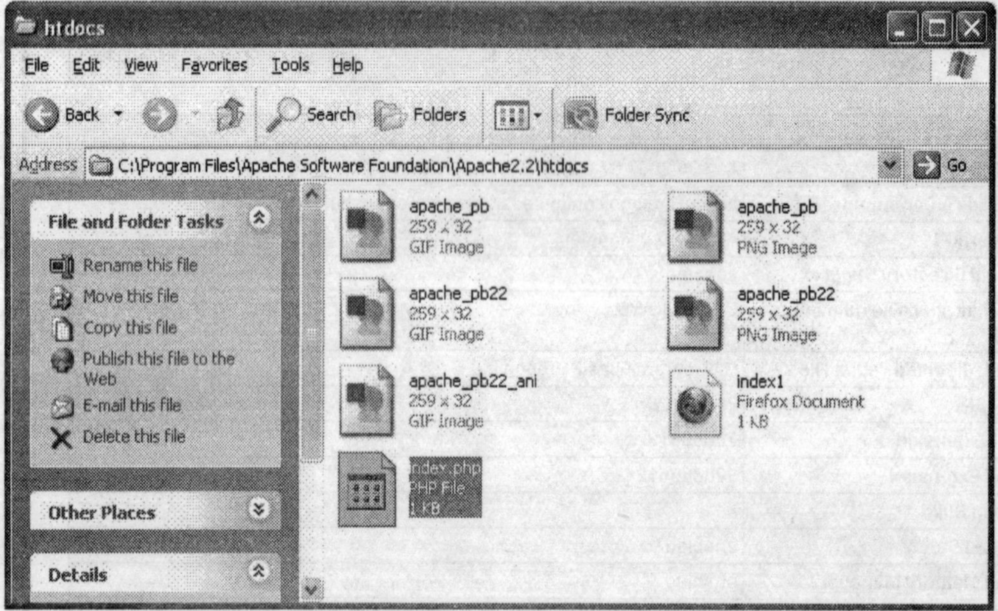

2- Edit your Apache configuration file, *C:\Program Files\Apache Software Foundation\Apache2.2\conf\httpd.conf* by opening it with Windows Notepad.

3- Find a line that starts with "***DirectoryIndex index.html...***". <u>Add index.php at the end of the line</u> . Save the file and restart your Apache Server from the "Monitor Apache Servers" console.

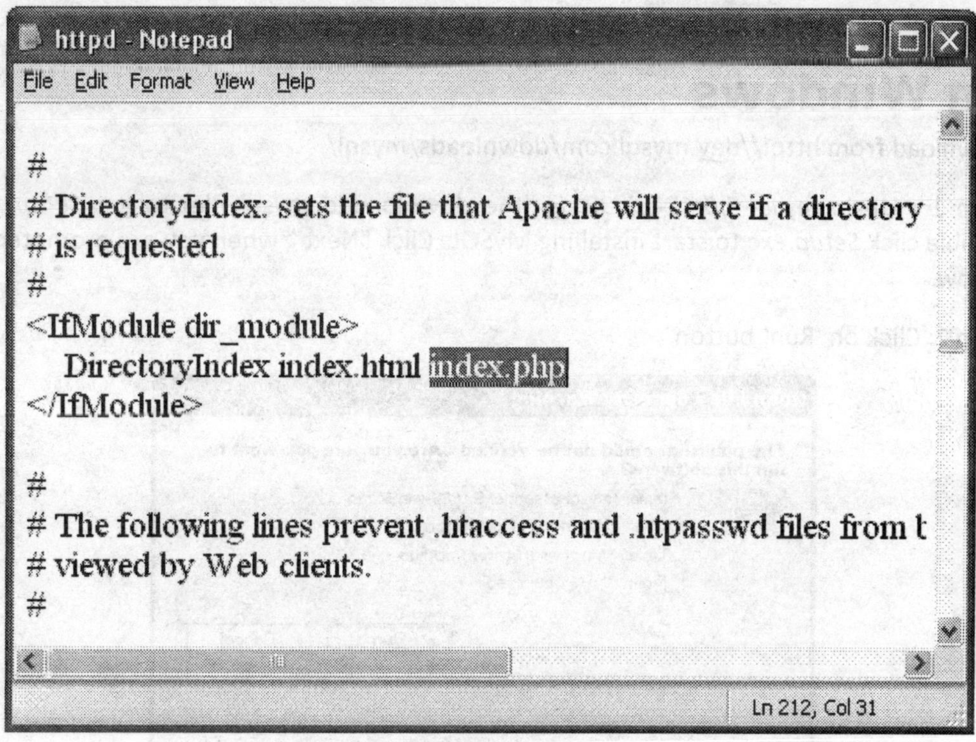
httpd - Notepad
File Edit Format View Help
#
DirectoryIndex: sets the file that Apache will serve if a directory
is requested.
#
<IfModule dir_module>
DirectoryIndex index.html index.php
</IfModule>
#
The following lines prevent .htaccess and .htpasswd files from t
viewed by Web clients.
#
Ln 212, Col 31

Install MySQL 5.0 Community Edition on Windows

Download from http://dev.mysql.com/downloads/mysql/

Step 1 : Unzip *mysql-5.0.45-win32.zip* (the downloaded mysql file) to get *Setup.exe*. Double click *Setup.exe* to start installing MySQL. Click "Next " when you are prompted as below.

Step 2: Click on 'Run' button

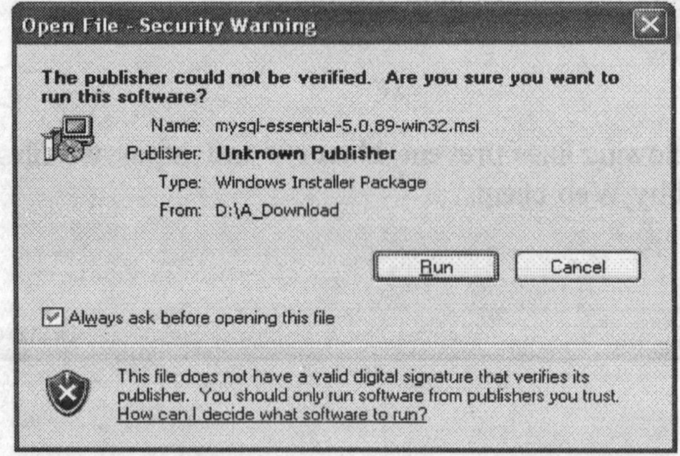

Step 3: Click the "next" button in the Installation Wizard

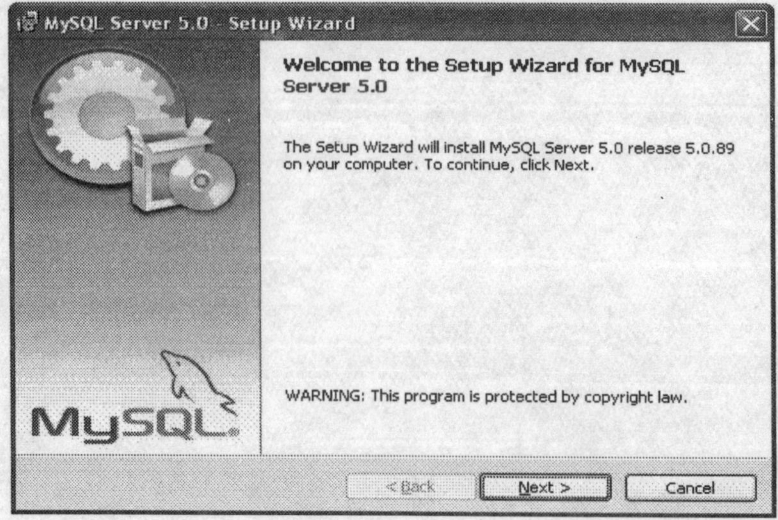

Step 4 : Choose Custom and press \"Next

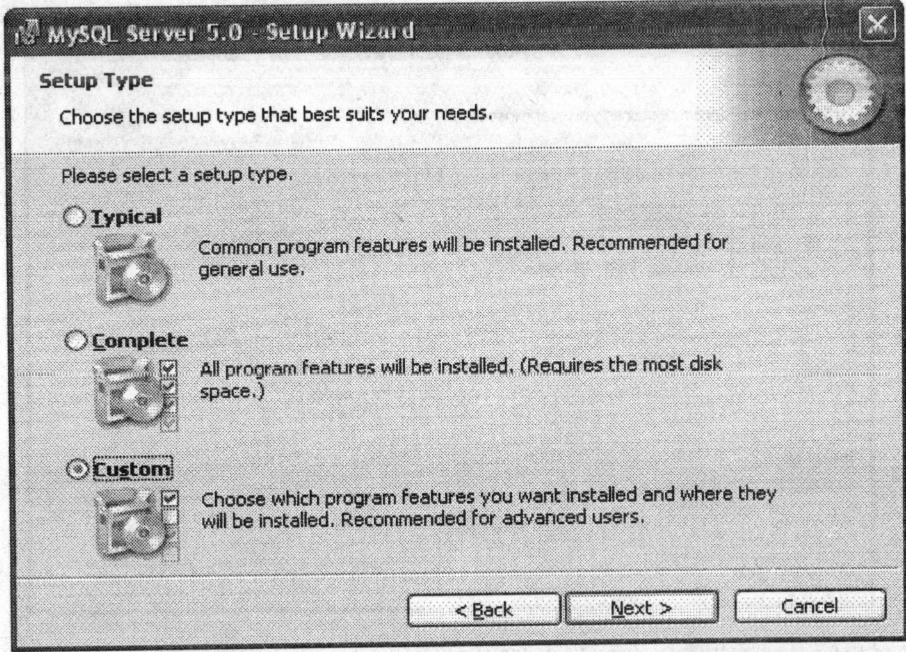

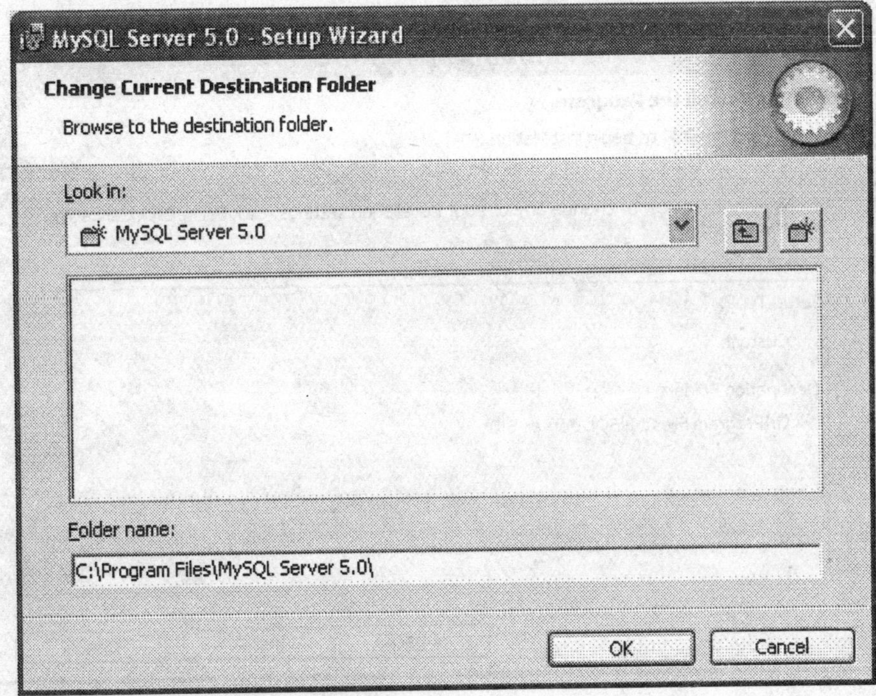

Step 5 : Specify the path to install

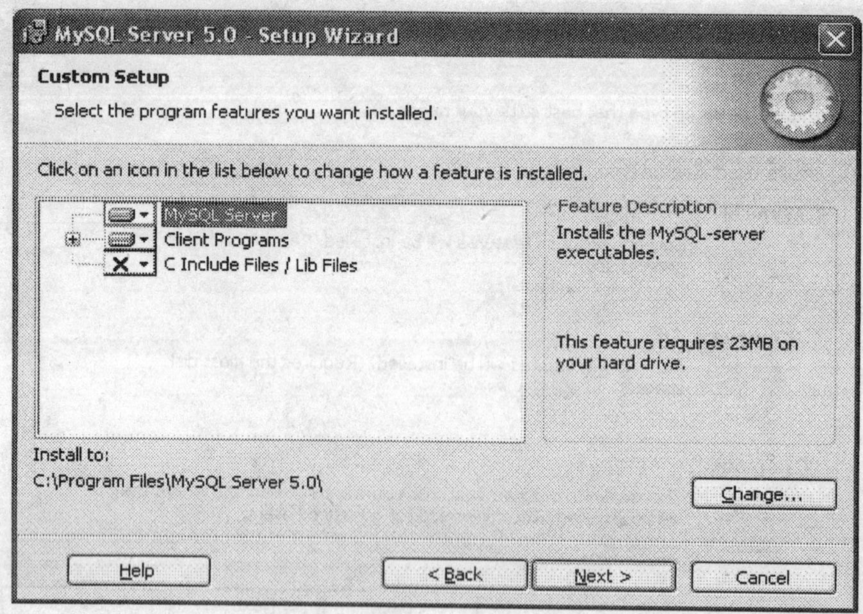

Step 7 : Click on install button to install MySql

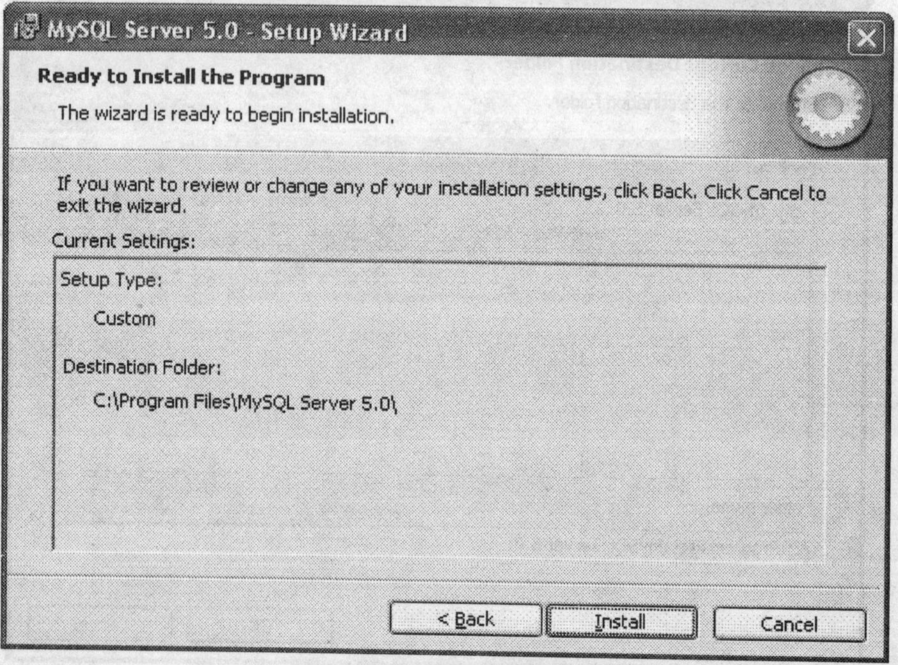

Step 8 : You can see the status of Installation status in the Installation wizard

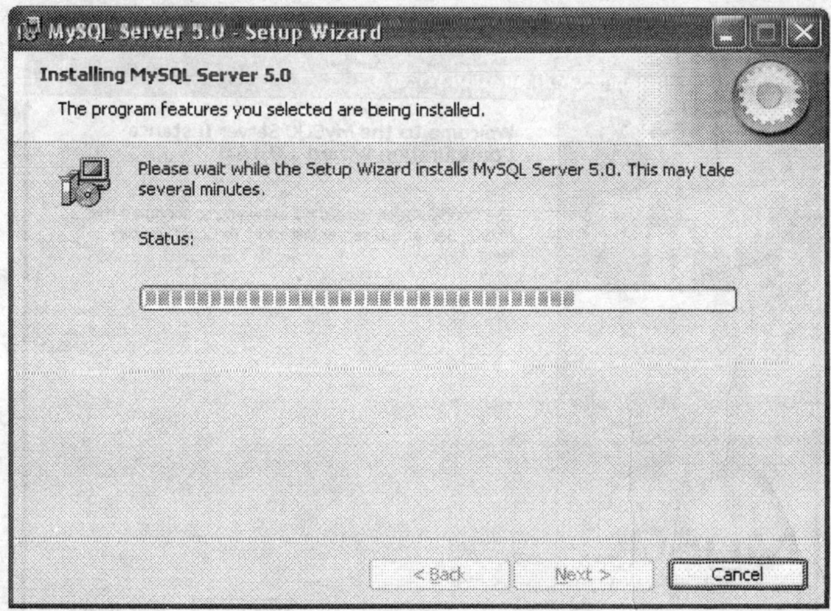

Step 10 : Click finish" Now you finished installation but you need to configure mysql.

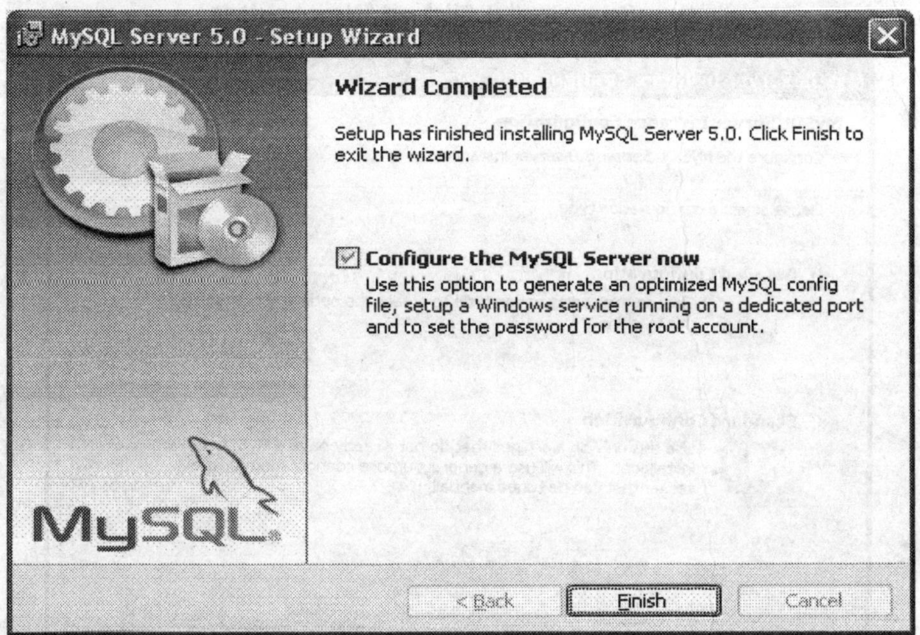

Step 11 : MySQL Configuration file wizard will open after your setup wizard. Click "Next" to proceed

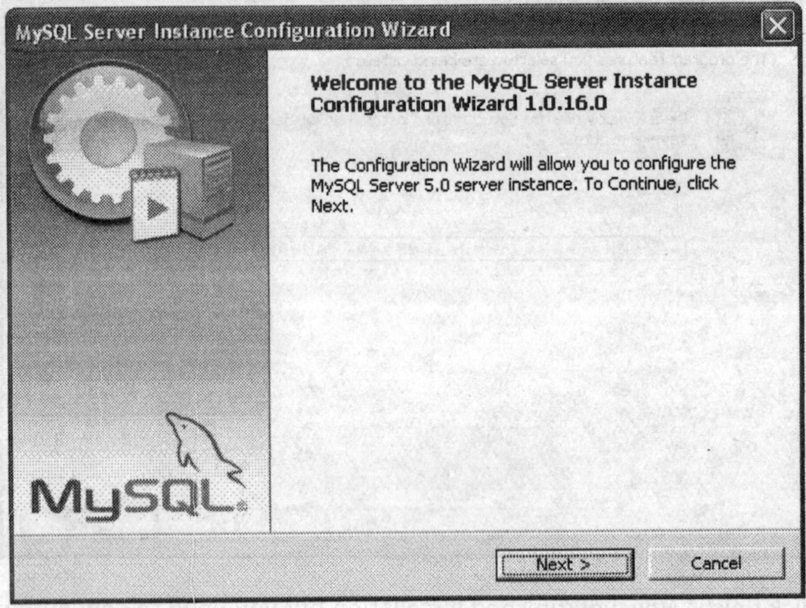

Step 12 : Select "Detailed configuration" & Click on "Next" button

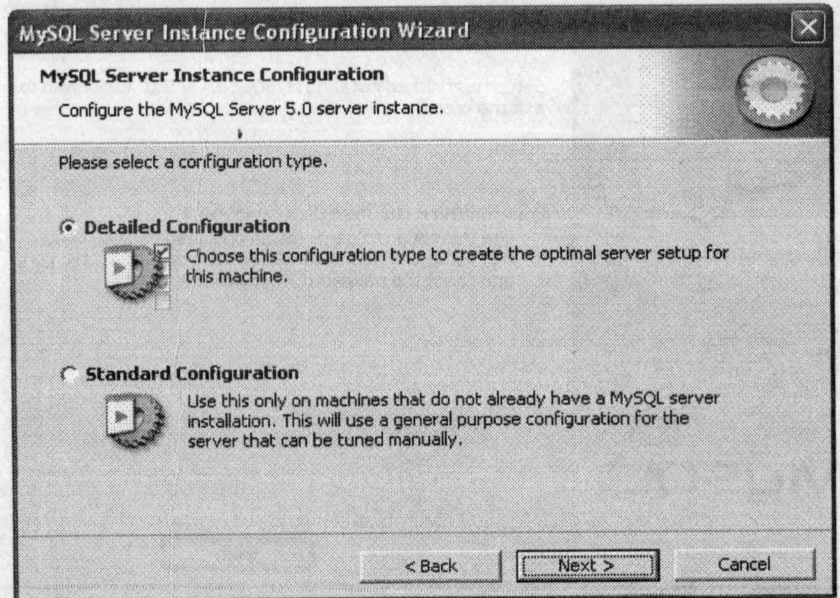

Step 13 : Next you will be getting a server type wizard. Choose "Developer machine" then click "Next" button

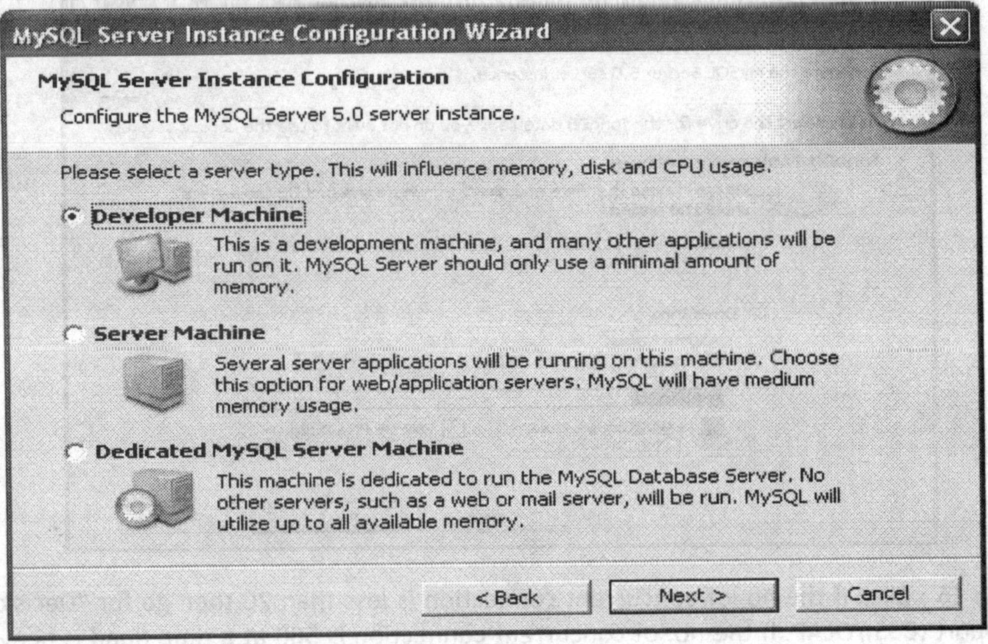

Step 14 : Choose "Multifunctional Database" and click "Next"

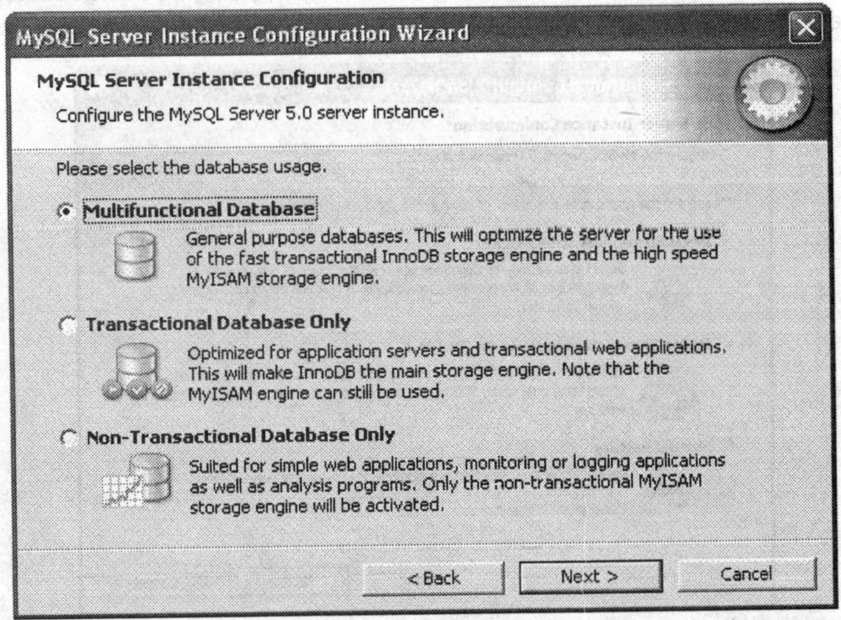

Step 15 : Click on Next

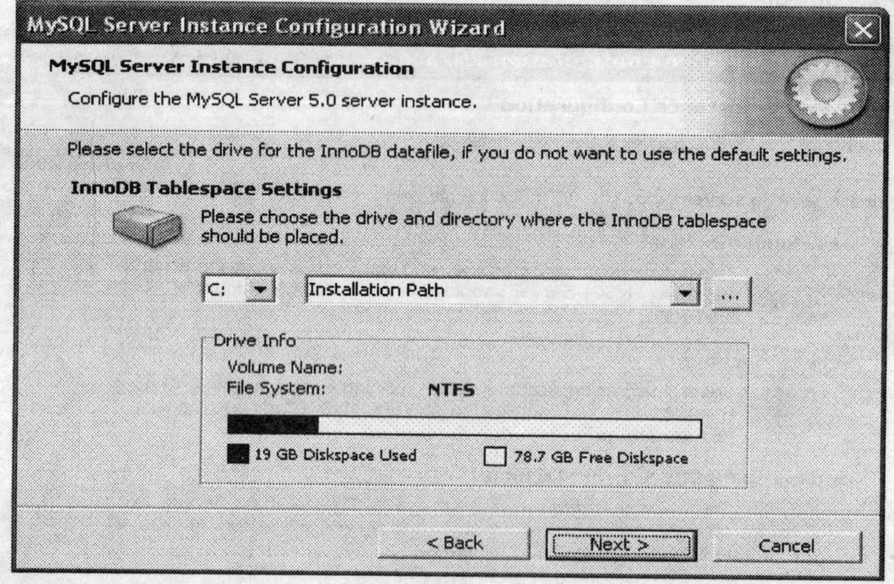

Step 16 : Click if the no. of concurrent connection is less than 20 then go for "Decision support (DSS)/OLAP. If the no. of concurrent connection is 500 at a time (load is heavy) then go for Online Transaction Processing (OLTP) If the no. of concurrent connection is neither 20 or else not heavy like 500 then go for manual testing. In this documentation, I had chosen "Decision support (DSS)/OLAP".

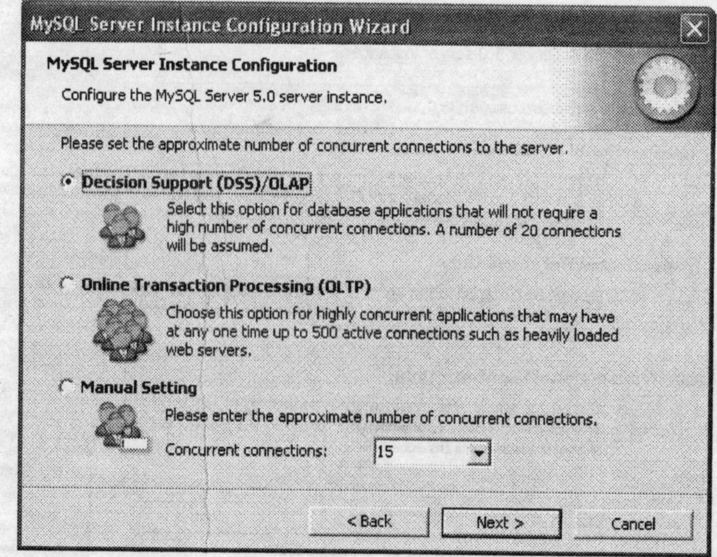

Step 17 : Now you have to set the network port. By default MySQL you will be having 3306 port, if in your machine some other Database server is using 3306 port then go for different PORT(3307, 3308,3309).

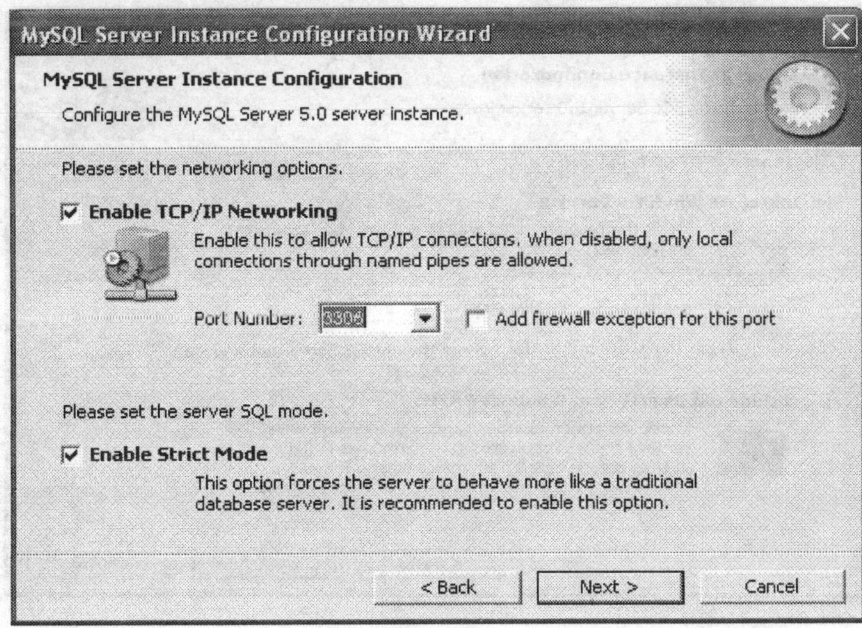

Step 18 : Select Standard Character Set & Click on Next buttom

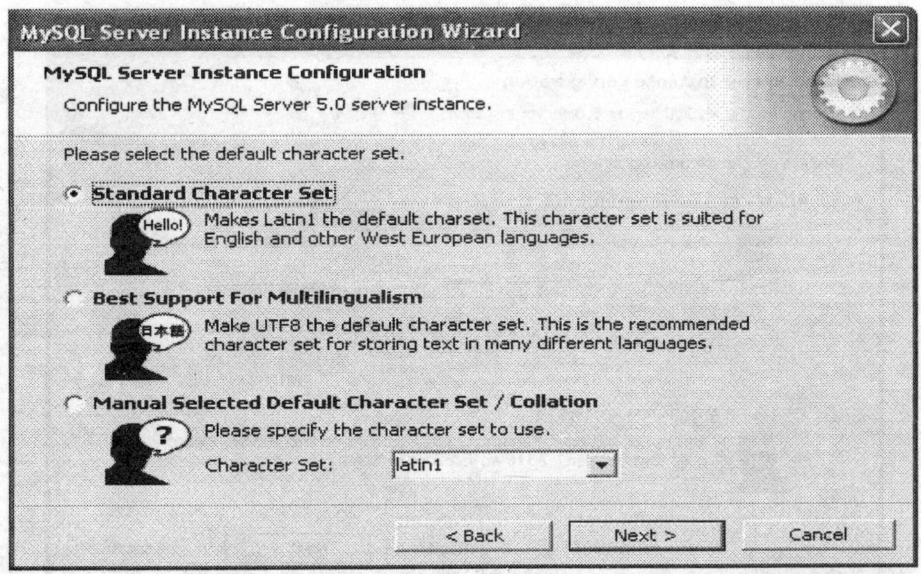

Step 19 : Now you will be getting Windows option window, where you can set the name for mysql service (By default MySQL). Choose Service Name as MySql & Click on "Next" button

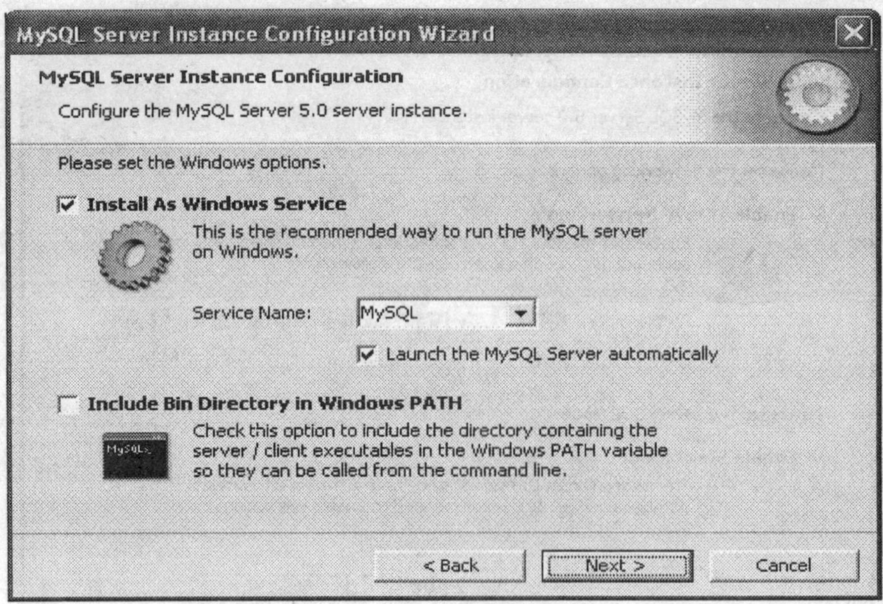

Step 20 : Give root password for mysql (for e.g. I gave root as password) & click on Next button

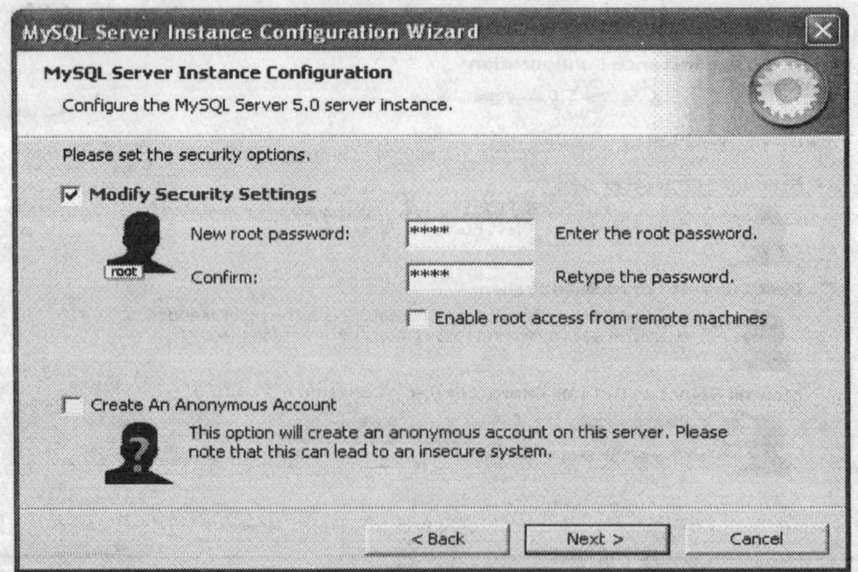

Step 21 : The Wizard will check whether mysql is configured properly & services are running or not.

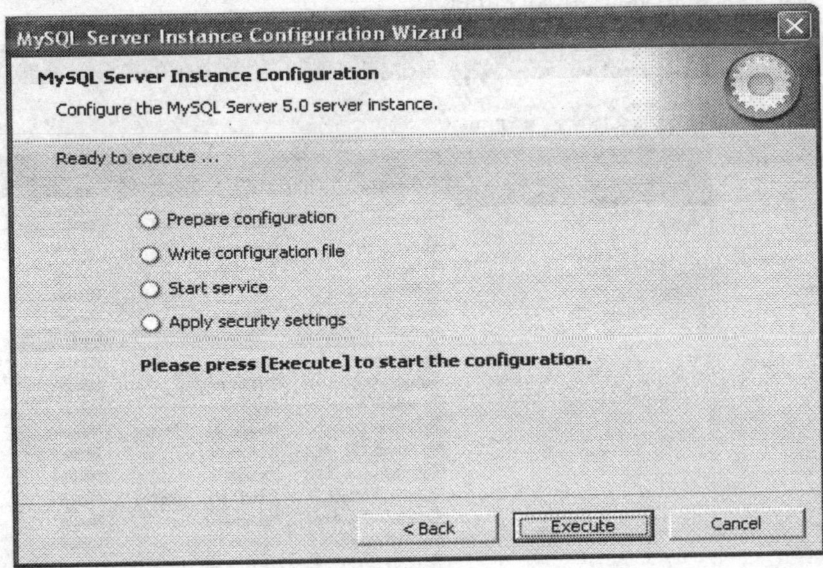

Step 22 : Following window appears, click on finish to complete the configuration.

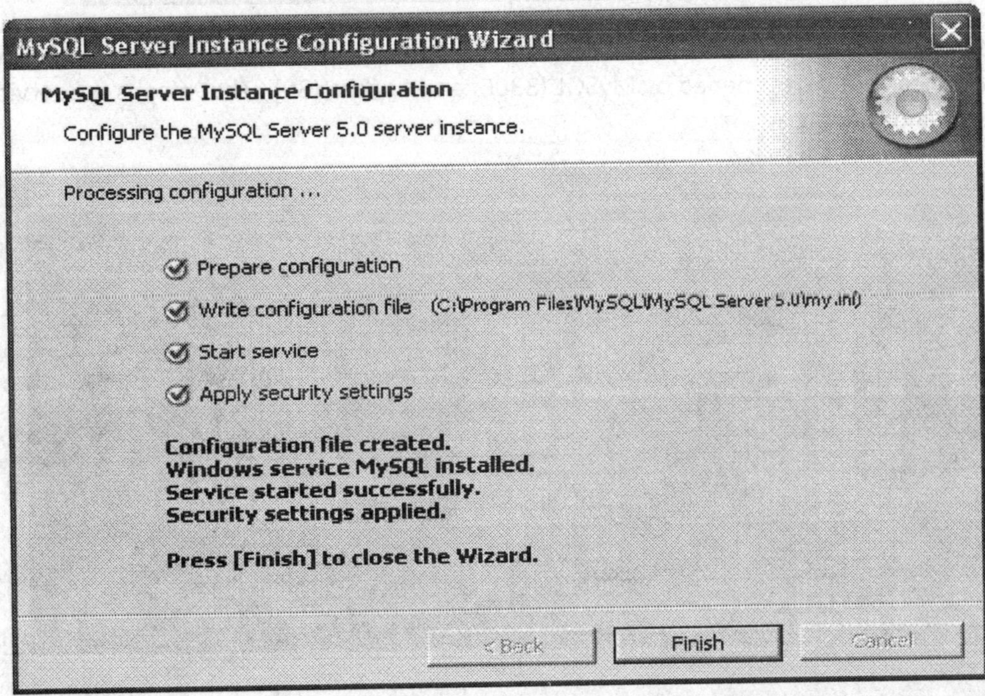

Step 23 : Make sure MySQL runs automatically after installation. You can check the status from Administrative Tools Services snap in (Start -> Programs -> Administrative Tools -> Services), also available via Control Panel.

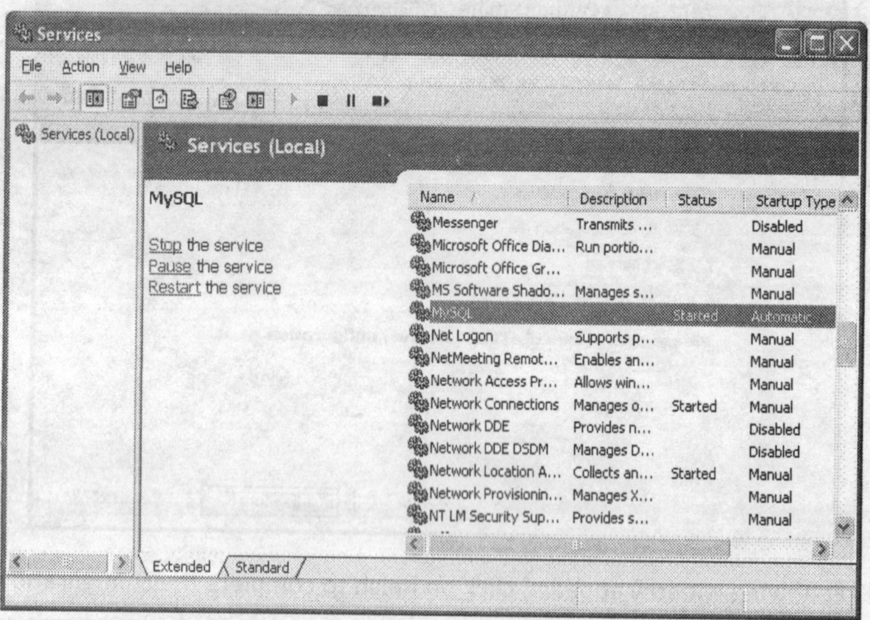

Step 24 : (OPTIONAL) Open your DOS command prompt (Run -> cmd). Type in "net stat -na". Check out ports opened by MySQL (3306) and Apache (80) . That means the services are up and running

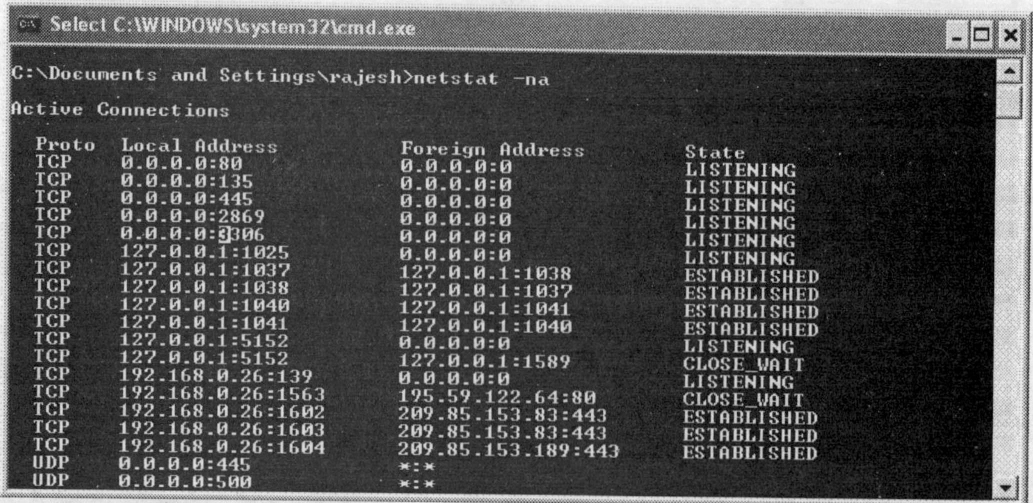

```
Select C:\WINDOWS\system32\cmd.exe

C:\Documents and Settings\rajesh>netstat -na

Active Connections

  Proto  Local Address          Foreign Address        State
  TCP    0.0.0.0:80             0.0.0.0:0              LISTENING
  TCP    0.0.0.0:135            0.0.0.0:0              LISTENING
  TCP    0.0.0.0:445            0.0.0.0:0              LISTENING
  TCP    0.0.0.0:2869           0.0.0.0:0              LISTENING
  TCP    0.0.0.0:3306           0.0.0.0:0              LISTENING
  TCP    127.0.0.1:1025         0.0.0.0:0              LISTENING
  TCP    127.0.0.1:1037         127.0.0.1:1038         ESTABLISHED
  TCP    127.0.0.1:1038         127.0.0.1:1037         ESTABLISHED
  TCP    127.0.0.1:1040         127.0.0.1:1041         ESTABLISHED
  TCP    127.0.0.1:1041         127.0.0.1:1040         ESTABLISHED
  TCP    127.0.0.1:5152         0.0.0.0:0              LISTENING
  TCP    127.0.0.1:5152         127.0.0.1:1589         CLOSE_WAIT
  TCP    192.168.0.26:139       0.0.0.0:0              LISTENING
  TCP    192.168.0.26:1563      195.59.122.64:80       CLOSE_WAIT
  TCP    192.168.0.26:1602      209.85.153.83:443      ESTABLISHED
  TCP    192.168.0.26:1603      209.85.153.83:443      ESTABLISHED
  TCP    192.168.0.26:1604      209.85.153.189:443     ESTABLISHED
  UDP    0.0.0.0:445            *:*
  UDP    0.0.0.0:500            *:*
```

Step 25 : (OPTIONAL) Run some of MySQL commands to further ensure that the installation is a success. Check out and follow the commands as pictured below. User account is root and password depends on what you have entered previously during your MySQL configuration.

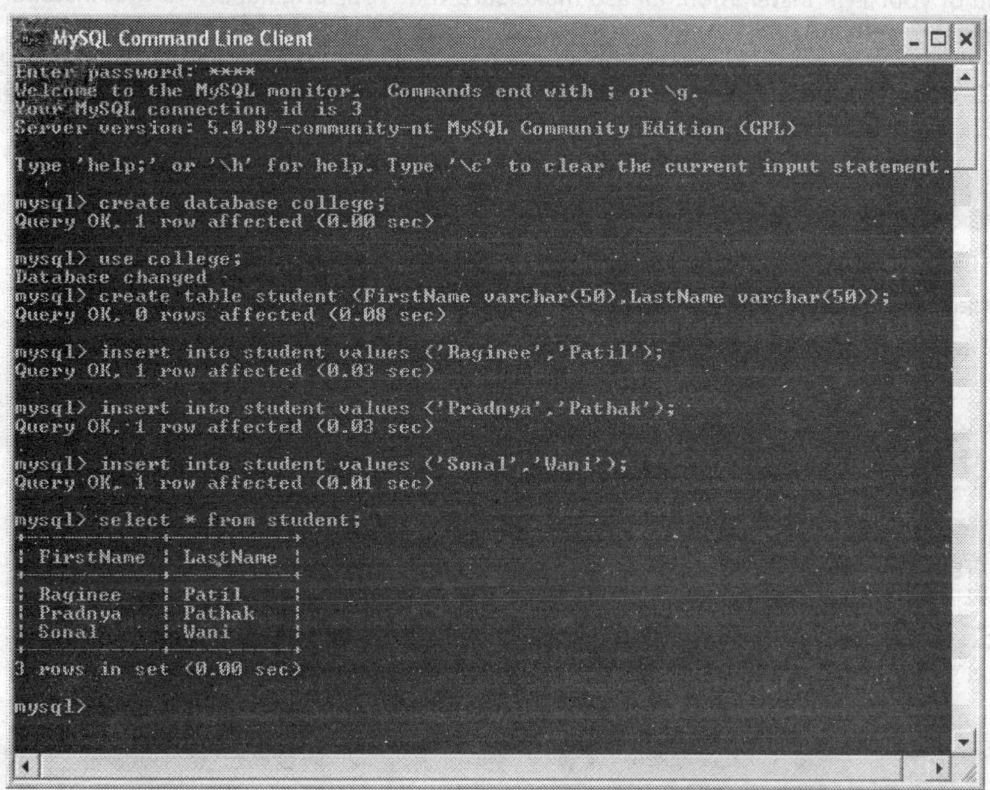

Note : If there is an error as
ERROR 1045: Access denied for user: 'root@localhost' (Using password: NO)
Solution for this is that go to your mysql prompt & type
mysql> UPDATE mysql.user
SET Password=PASSWORD('newpwd')
-> WHERE User='root';
mysql> FLUSH PRIVILEGES;

Configure PHP 5.2.4 with MySQL 5.0.89

Previously, we have installed PHP with minimal modules / extension. To add MySQL support to PHP, you need to change your PHP installation – by adding the MySQL extension on top of your PHP installation. Please make sure that your original PHP 5 MSI installer still remains at its original place .

Step 1: Open the Add / Remove Programs console via Windows Control Panel. Find the **PHP 5.x.x entry** and click "Change " .

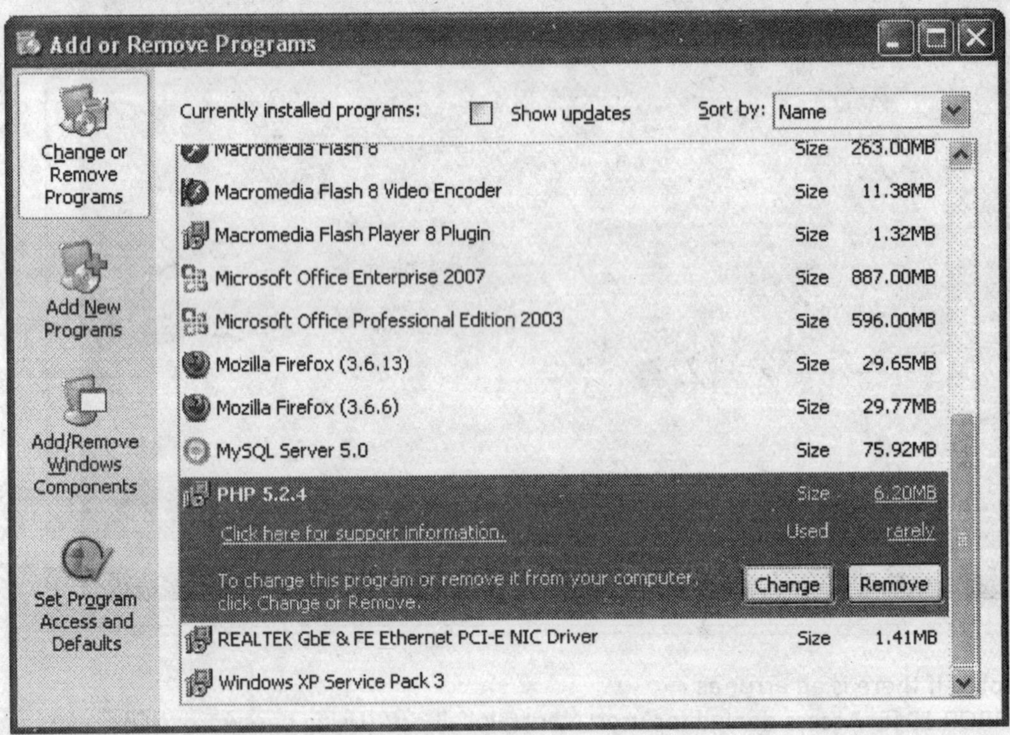

Step 2 : Click *"Next"* once you are prompted the Welcome page.

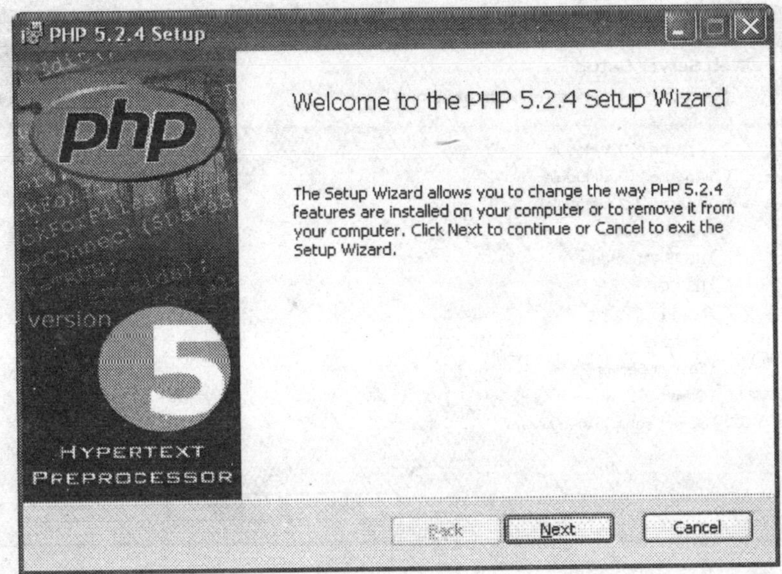

Step 3: Click the *"Change"* button to proceed.

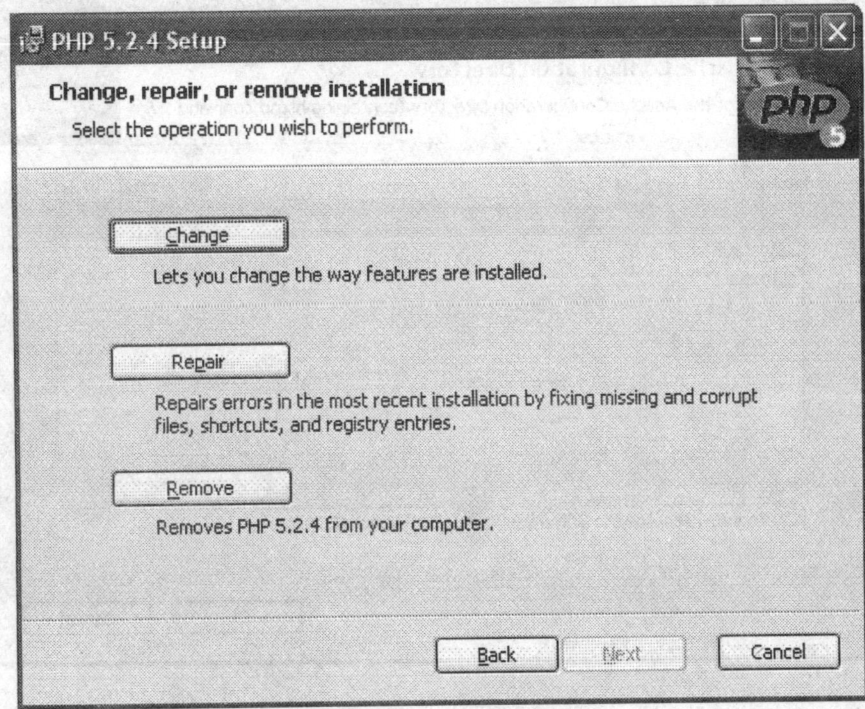

Step 4: Select **Apache 2.2.x** as shown in the picture below. Click *"Next"* once again

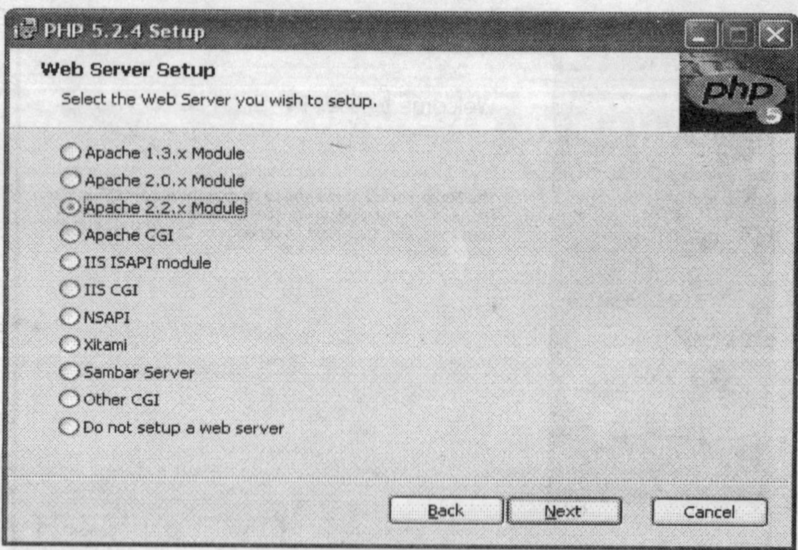

Step 5: Select your Apache configuration directory (conf) – the directory where your httpd.conf resides. Click *"Next"* once done.

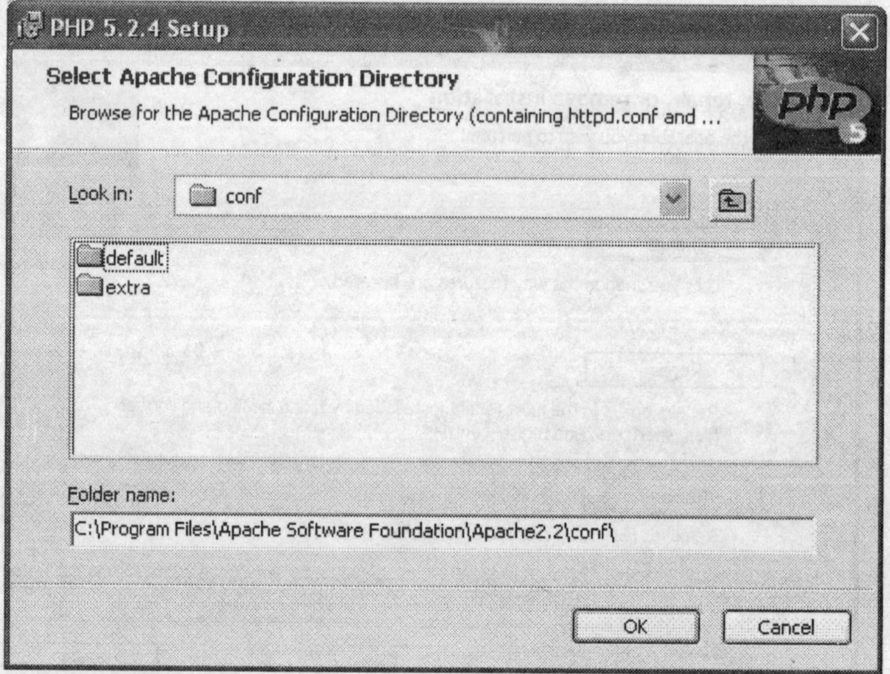

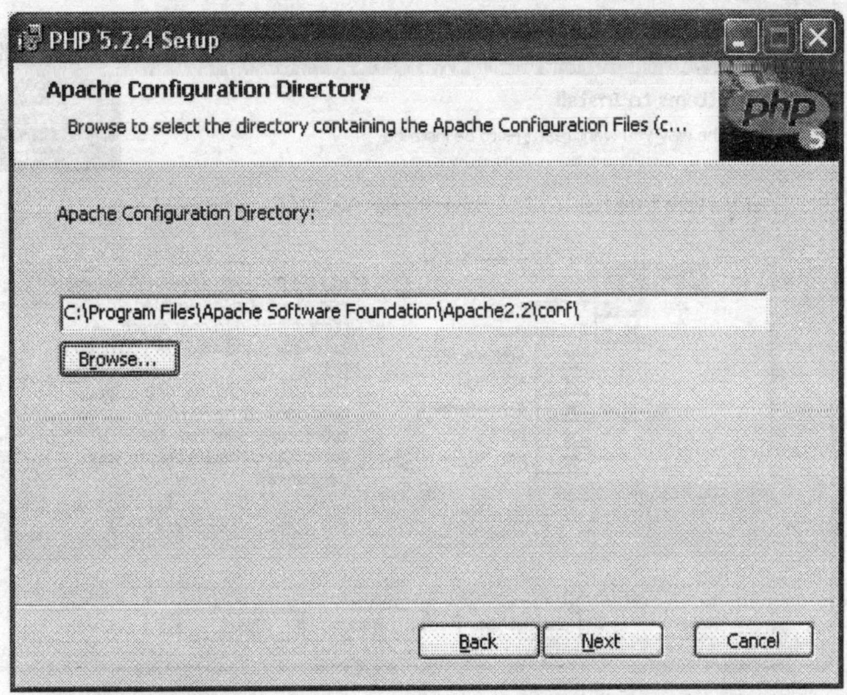

Step 6 : On the "**Choose items to install**" screen, click on the plus (+) icon next to Extensions to expand the list.

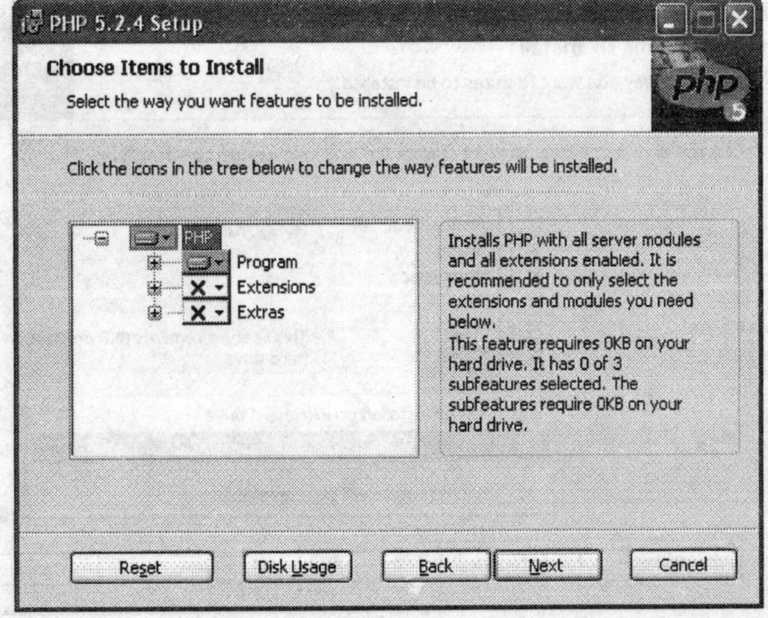

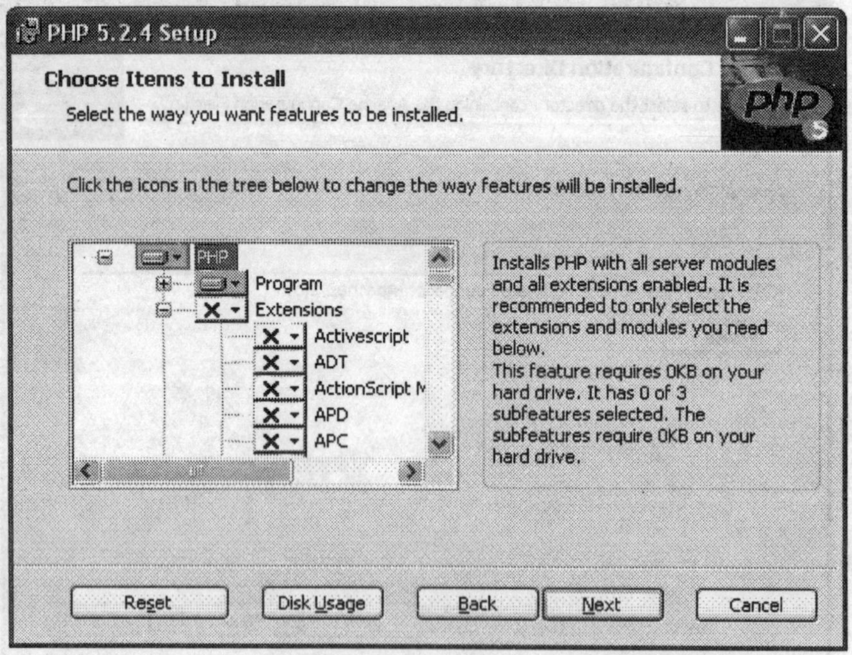

Step 7: Select on the "X" next to "**MySQL**" and **select "Entire feature will be installed on local hard drive"**. Click "Next" again.

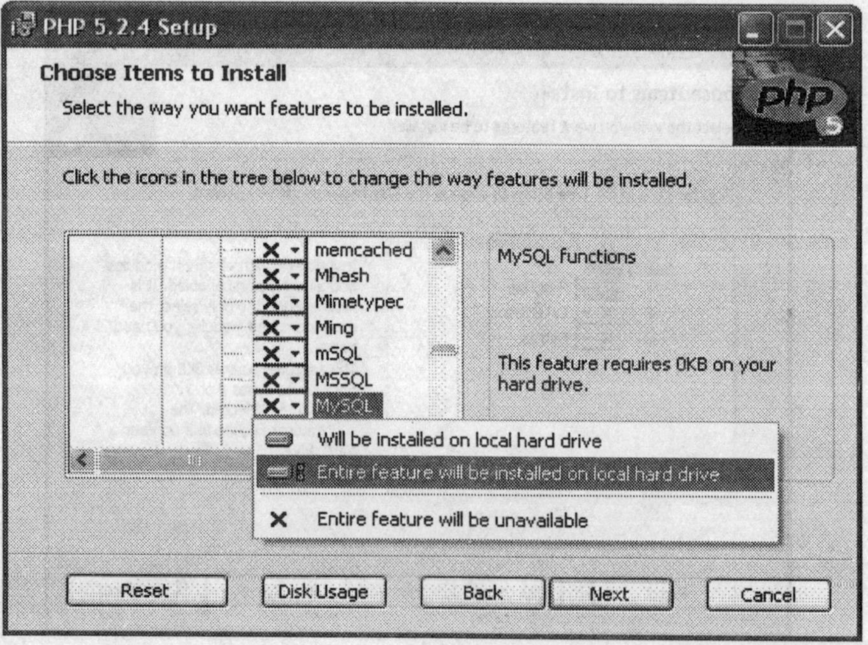

Step 8 : Click the "*Change*" button to save all the PHP configuration changes

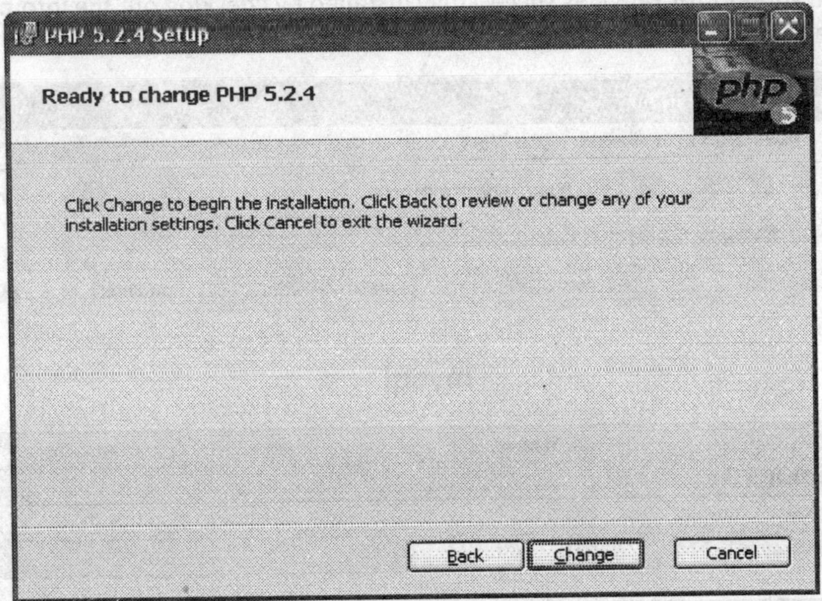

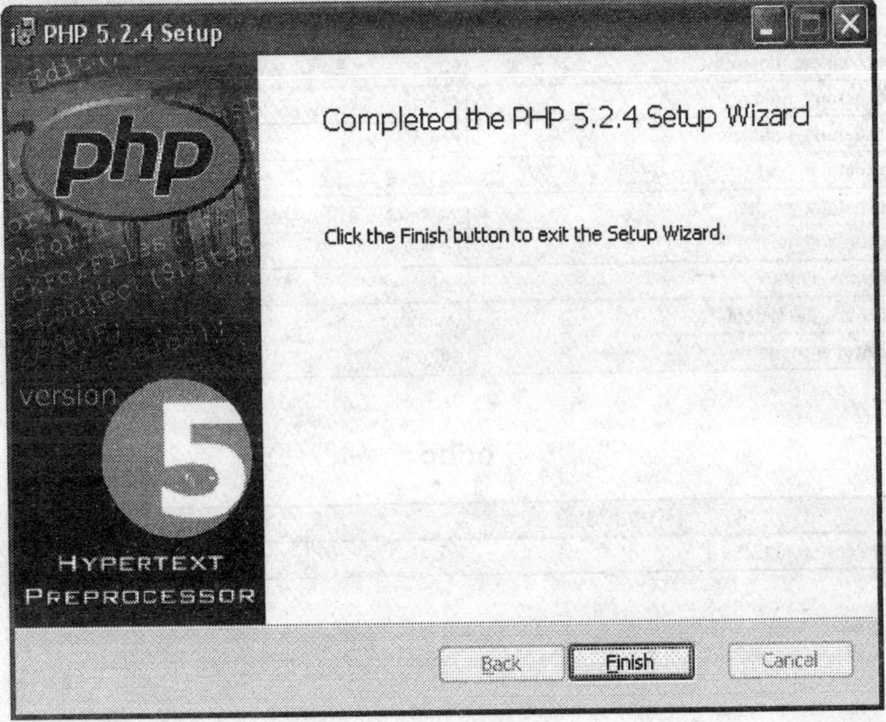

9- Finally, **restart your Apache 2.2 web server!** You can check out that the MySQL extension support for PHP was successfully installed by checking out the info.php / index.php page that was created before.

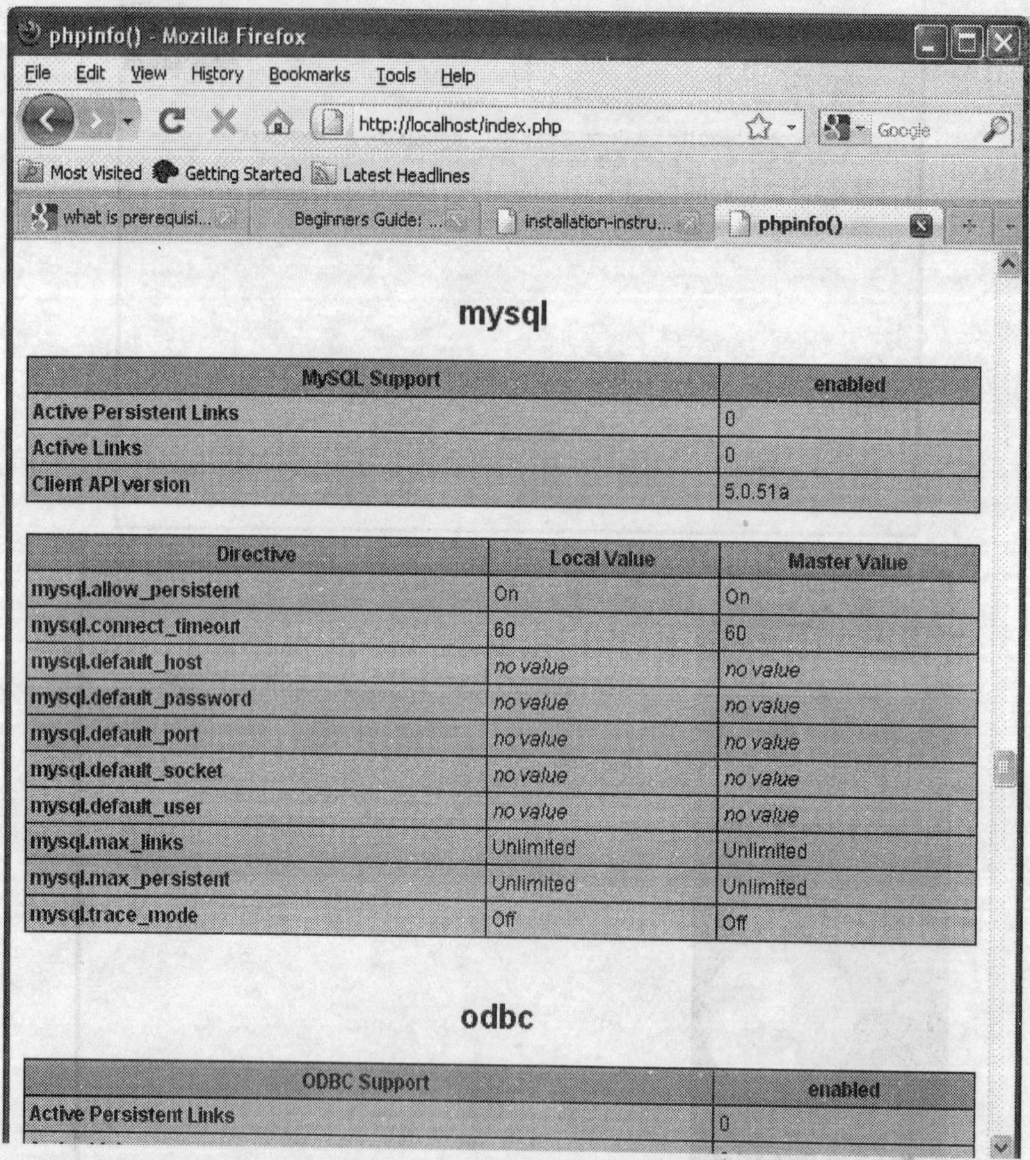

mysql

MySQL Support	enabled
Active Persistent Links	0
Active Links	0
Client API version	5.0.51a

Directive	Local Value	Master Value
mysql.allow_persistent	On	On
mysql.connect_timeout	60	60
mysql.default_host	*no value*	*no value*
mysql.default_password	*no value*	*no value*
mysql.default_port	*no value*	*no value*
mysql.default_socket	*no value*	*no value*
mysql.default_user	*no value*	*no value*
mysql.max_links	Unlimited	Unlimited
mysql.max_persistent	Unlimited	Unlimited
mysql.trace_mode	Off	Off

odbc

ODBC Support	enabled
Active Persistent Links	0

Mantis

Step 1. Download the Mantis

http://www.mantisbt.org/download.php

Step 2 : Unzip and paste the mantis in root directory(ie. Paste the Mantis in C:\ ProgramFiles\Apache Software Foundation\Apache2.2\htdocs\"Mantis")

Step 3 : Now open any browser (ex: Internet explorer , mozilla firefox) and type the following to access Mantis

http://localhost/Mantis/ or

http://ipaddress/Mantis/

Step 4- After clicking on above link you will get following screen. In that screen click on admin link.

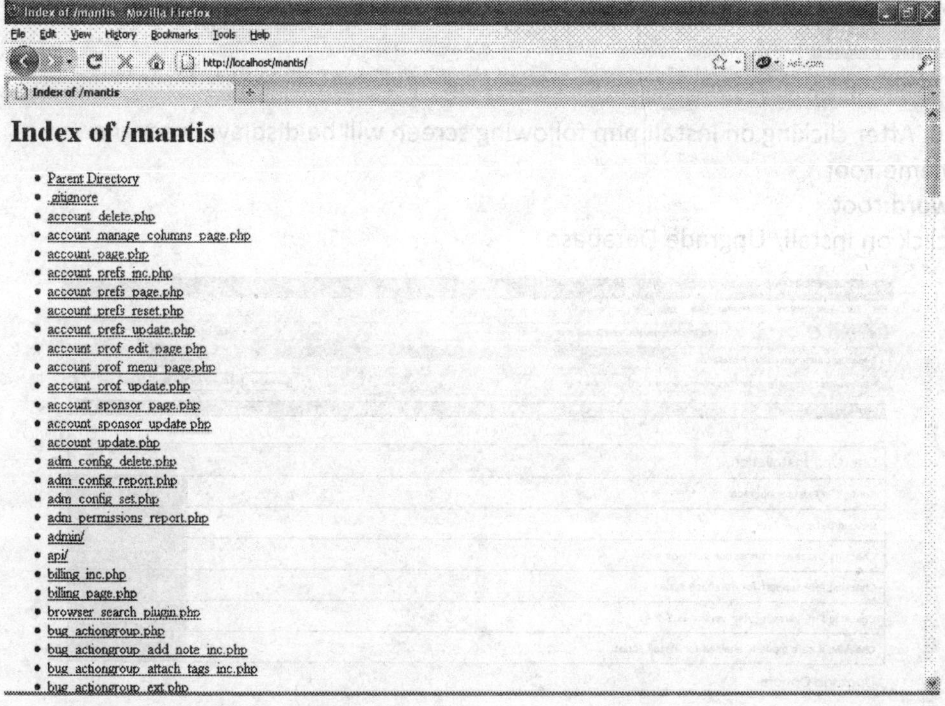

Step 5: After clicking on admin link following screen will display In that screen click on install.php link.

Step 6: After clicking on install.php following screen will be display. Enter the
Username:root
Password:root
And click on Install/ Upgrade Database

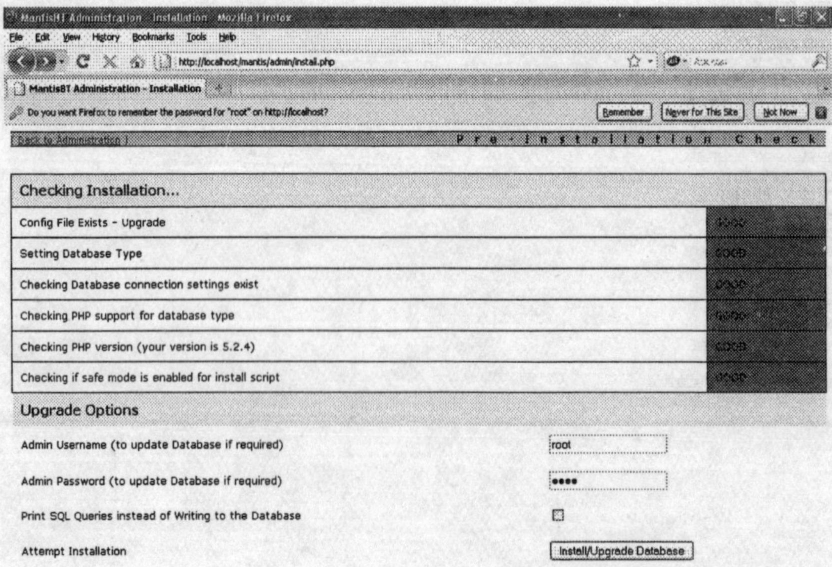

Note : If there is an error as
ERROR 1045: Access denied for user: 'root@localhost' (Using password: NO)
Solution for this is that go to your mysql prompt & type
mysql> UPDATE mysql.user
SET Password=PASSWORD('newpwd')
-> WHERE User='root';
mysql> FLUSH PRIVILEGES;

Step 7: Click on Continue.

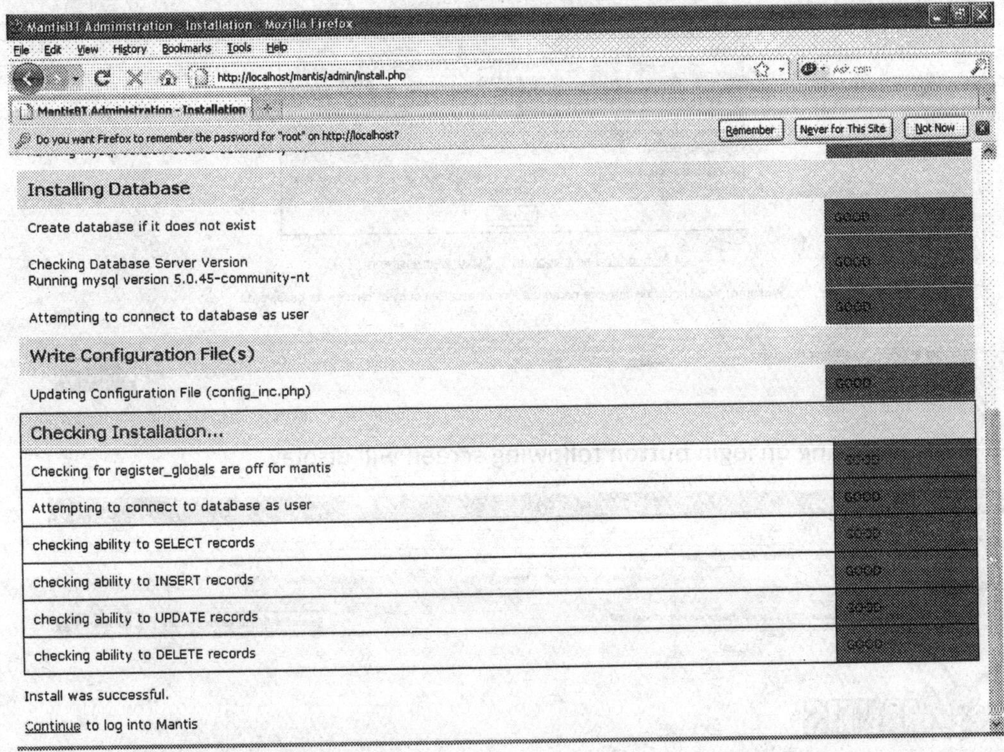

Step 8: Enter Username as 'Administrator' & Password as 'root' and click on login button.

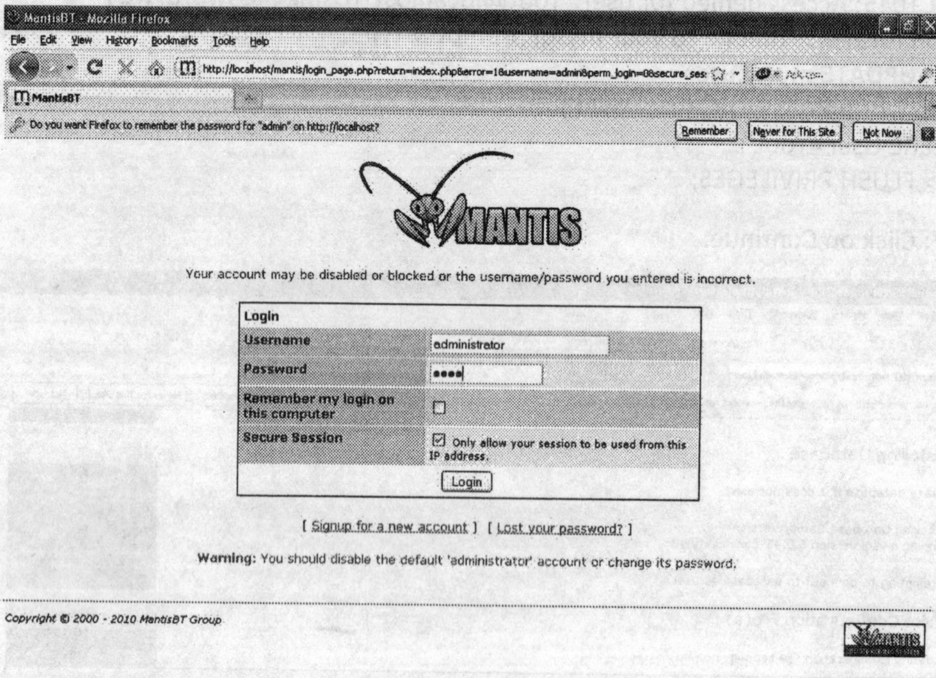

Step 9: After clicking on login button following screen will display.

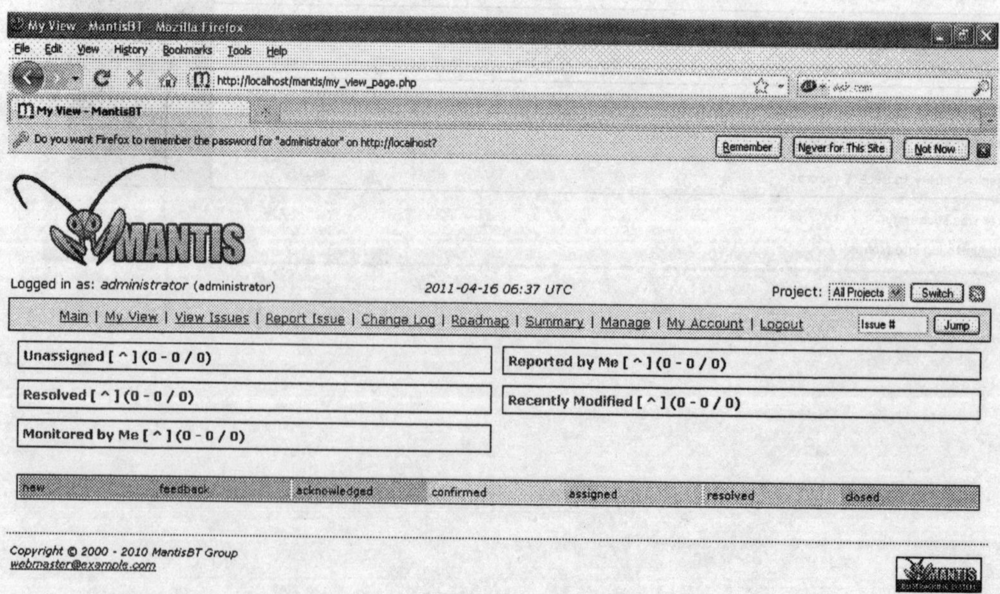

How To Add User

Step 1: Login into Mantis as an administrator and click the Manage Tab->Manage Users and click <Create New Account> button.

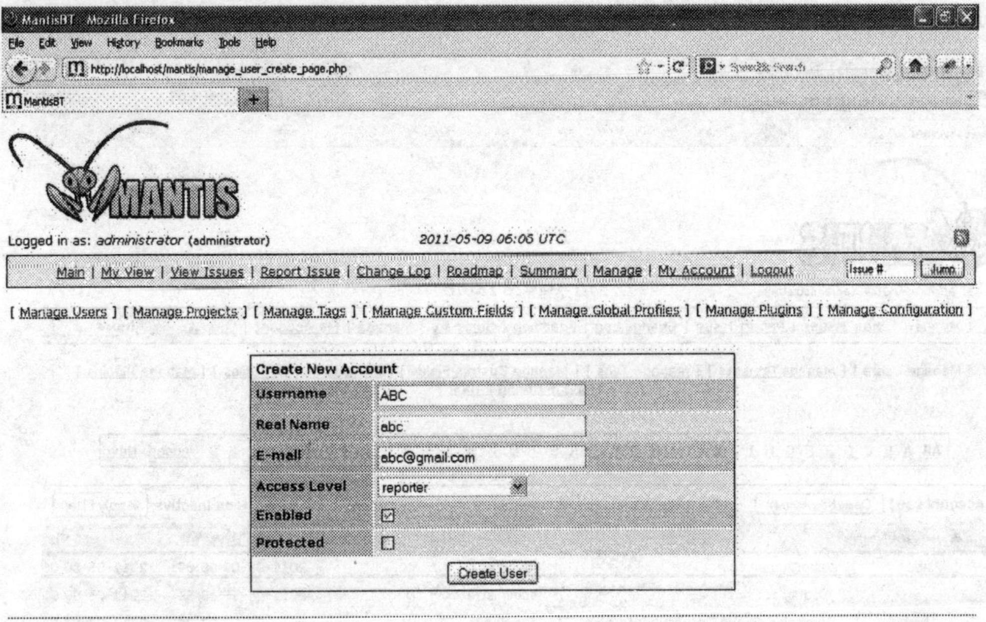

Step 2 : The above screen gets displayed. Provide the desired user name and the appropriate access level. The available access levels are:

Viewer, Reporter, Updater, Developer, Manager, Administrator

User will be created.

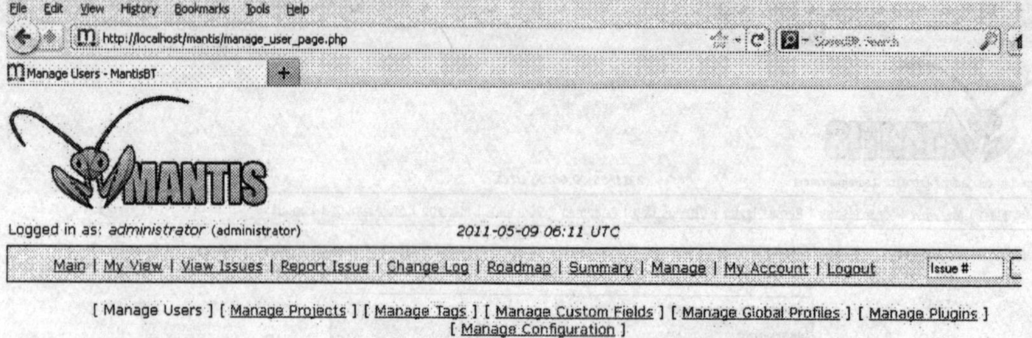

All A B C D E F G H I J K L M N O P Q R S T U V W X Y Z 0 1 2 3 4 5 6 7 8 9 Unused New

Manage Accounts [6] Create New Account   Hide Inactive Apply Filter

Username▲	Real Name	E-mail	Access Level	Enabled		Date Created	Last Visi
ABC	abc	abc@gmail.com	reporter	X		2011-05-09 06:09	2011-05-09 06
administrator		root@localhost	administrator	X		2011-04-15 08:54	2011-05-09 06
Archana	archu	archana.shinde@preeminents.com	developer	X		2011-04-27 07:24	2011-04-27 07
Dipali	dips	dipali.bhave@preeminents.com	reporter	X		2011-04-27 07:25	2011-04-27 07
madhavi	mady	madhavi.sutar@preeminents.com	reporter	X		2011-04-27 07:23	2011-04-27 07

Project Creation

Step 1: Login into Mantis as an administrator and click the Manage Tab->Manage Projects. Click on <Create New Project> button.

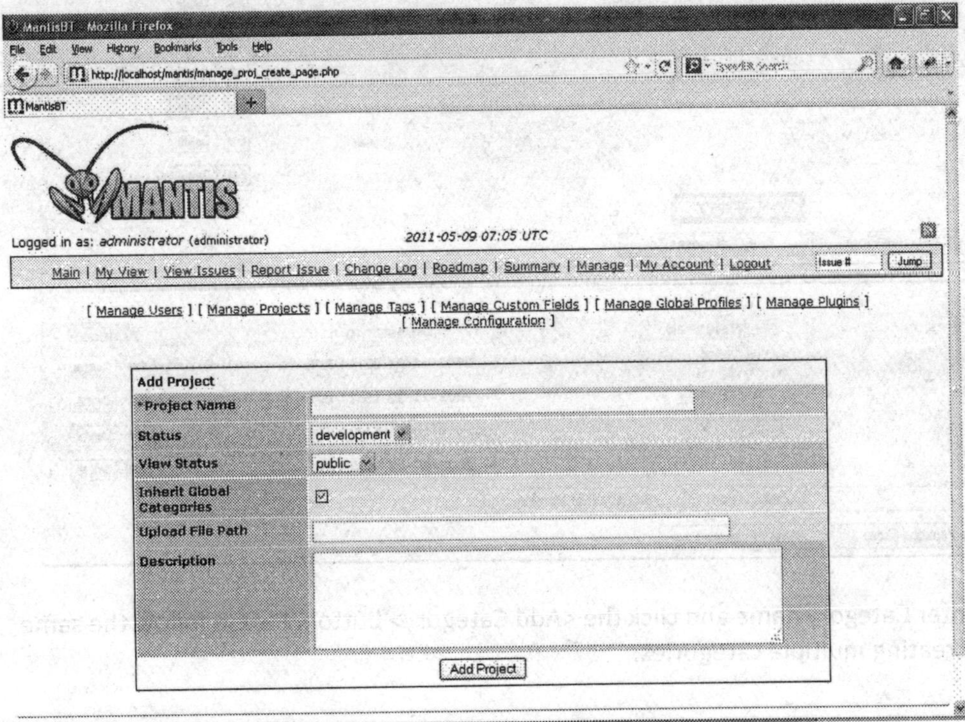

Step 2: The above screen gets displayed. Provide the desired Project name and the required details and then click the <Add project> button.

How to add Defect Category

Step 1: After the Project has been created, then create the various categories for defects which are going to be selected at the time of defect reporting. To create Defect Category, login as an

Administrator and Click Manage Tab->Manage Projects->Select the Project. On the edit project page scroll down and locate the Add Category button.

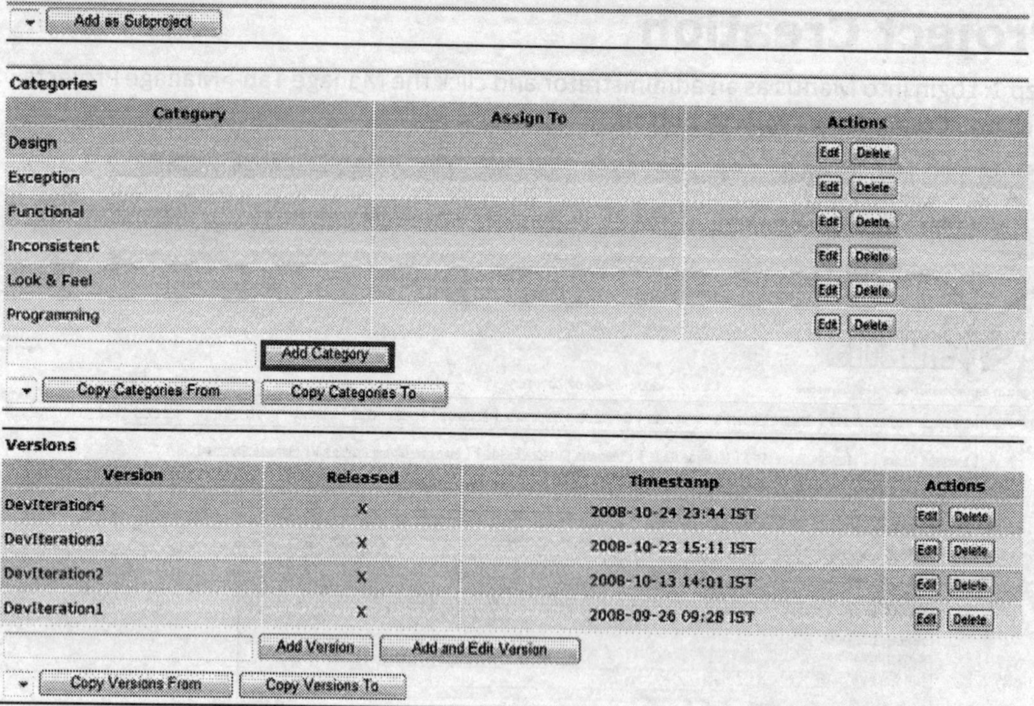

Category	Assign To	Actions
Design		Edit Delete
Exception		Edit Delete
Functional		Edit Delete
Inconsistent		Edit Delete
Look & Feel		Edit Delete
Programming		Edit Delete

Version	Released	Timestamp	Actions
DevIteration4	X	2008-10-24 23:44 IST	Edit Delete
DevIteration3	X	2008-10-23 15:11 IST	Edit Delete
DevIteration2	X	2008-10-13 14:01 IST	Edit Delete
DevIteration1	X	2008-09-26 09:28 IST	Edit Delete

Step 3: Enter Category name and click the <Add Category> button. Please follow the same step for creating multiple categories.

Version Creation

Step 1: After the Project has been created, then create the versions to be selected while reporting the defects. To create Version, login as an Administrator and Click Manage Tab-> Manage Projects

-> Select the Project. On the edit project page scroll down and locate the <Add Version> button.

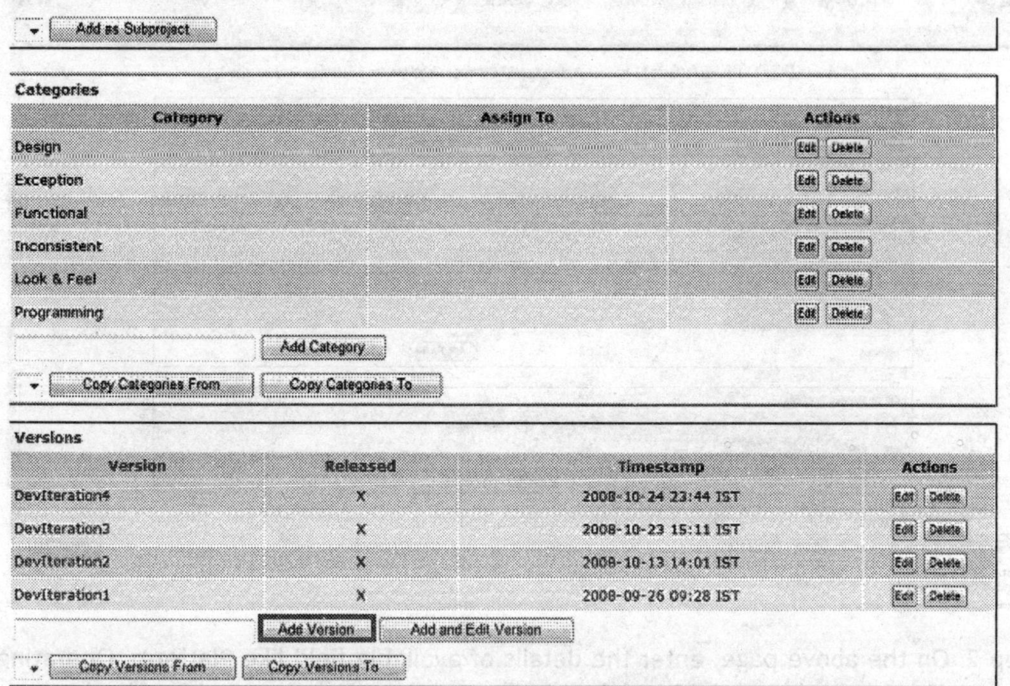

Step 2: Enter Version name and click the Add Version button. Please follow the same step for creating multiple Versions.

Global Profile Creation

Step 1: You can create a global profile to indicate the environment on which you are doing the testing of the application. To create a global profile, login as an administrator and click Manage Tab->Manage Global Profile.

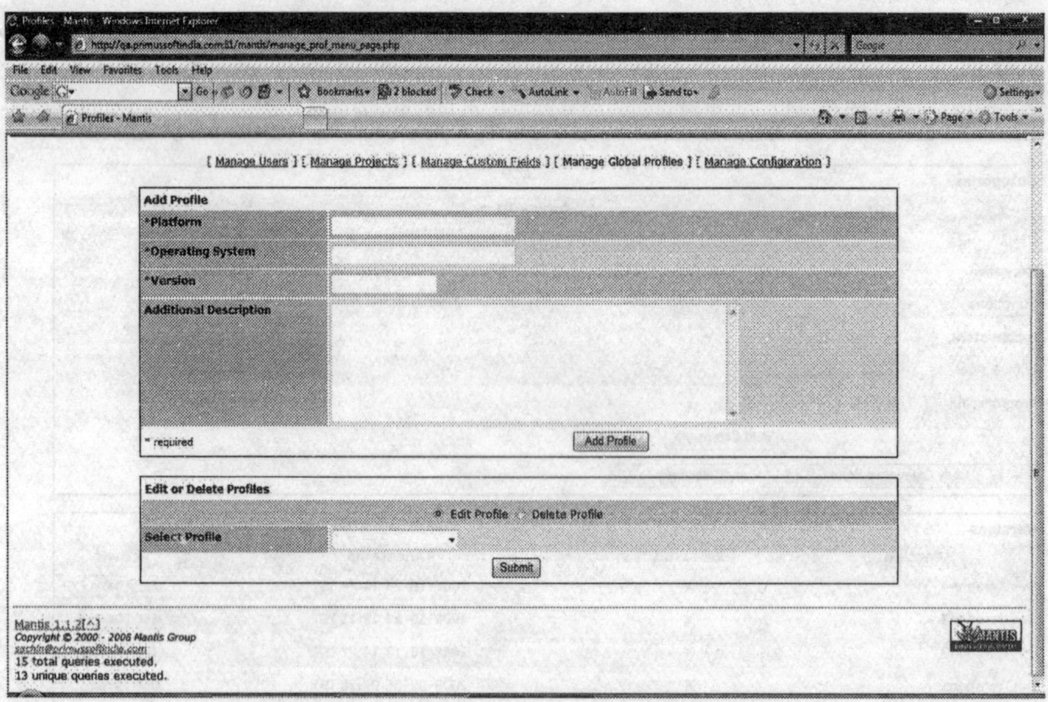

Step 2: On the above page, enter the details of available field like Platform, Operating System, Version, and any additional description and then click the <Add Profile> button.

Defect Management

Defect Life Cycle in Mantis:

Users	Defect Status	Resolution
Reporter	New	Open
Manager	Assigned	Open
Developer	Resolved Acknowledged – in case defect is planned to be fixed in future releases	Open or Fixed or Duplicate or No Change Required or Unable to Reproduce. The Resolution Open can be selected only when Status is set to Acknowledged.
Reporter	Closed	Reopen If defect is reopened, then Status remains Resolved until the defect has been again fixed. In other cases the i.e. where a reported is closing the defect, then do not make any changes in the Resolution set by developer

Defect Reporting

The users (Reporter) who have the rights to report the defect can use Mantis to report the defects while doing testing of the application. The steps for reporting defects are as follows:

Step 1: Click on Report issue tab.

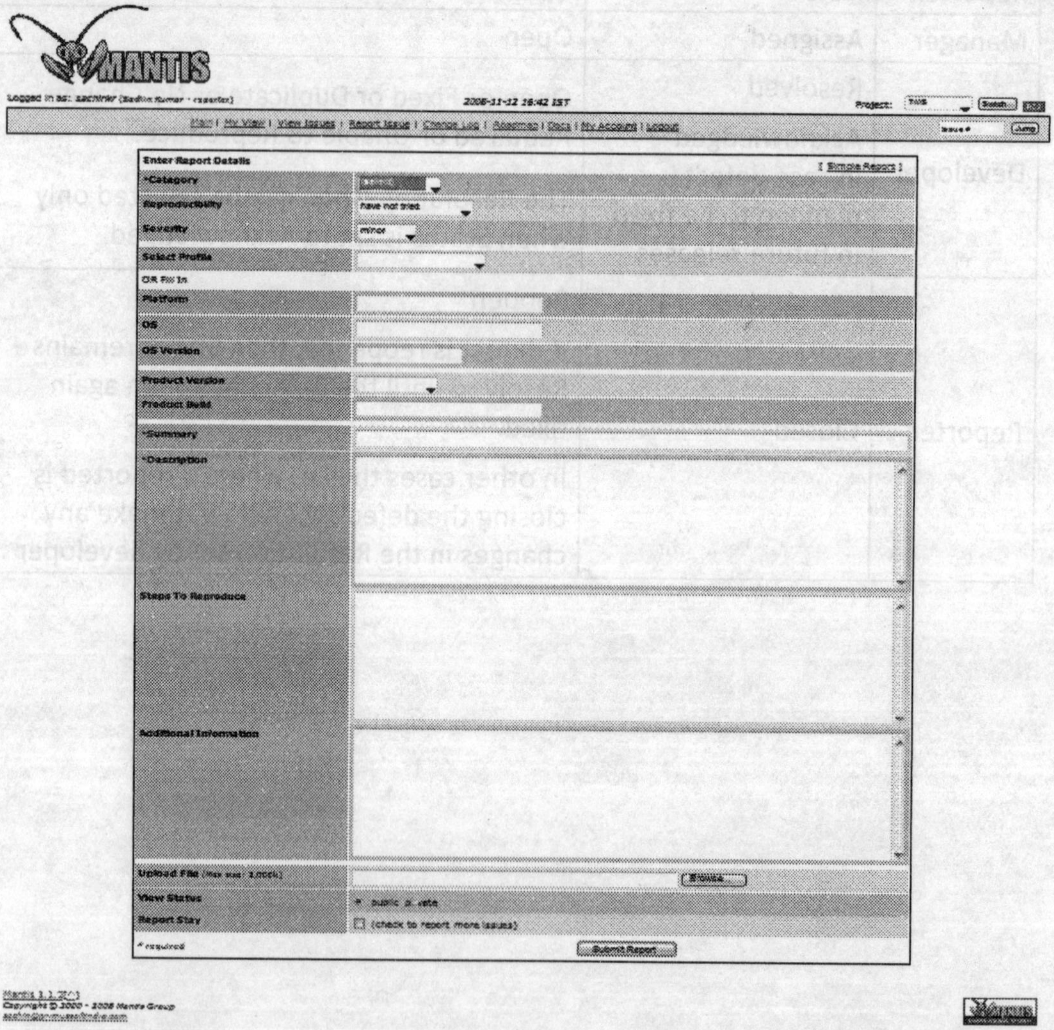

MANTIS

Project: TWS Switch

Main | My View | View Issues | Report Issue | Change Log | Roadmap | Docs | My Account | Logout

Issue # Jump

Enter Report Details [Simple Report]

*Category

Reproducibility: have not tried

Severity: minor

Select Profile

OR Fill In

Platform

OS

OS Version

Product Version

Product Build

*Summary

*Description

Steps To Reproduce

Additional Information

Upload File

View Status

Report Stay: (check to report more issues)

* required

Submit Report

- Login using your valid user id and password.
- Click Report Issue link.
- The above page gets displayed. In case you are not able to view all the above field

shown in the screen shot, then click the Advance Report link available in upper right section of the page.

- Select the Defect Category, Reproducibility, Severity, Select Profile, Product Version. (You may select mandatory field only but as a good practice please input as much information as one can).
- Enter a Summary for the defect – would be one liner.
- Enter Defect Description
- Enter the Steps to Reproduce the Defects.
- You can also enter any other additional information.
- In case you want to upload supporting document for the defects like screen shot, video etc., then upload the desired file.
- Set the View Status to either Public or Private. Recommended is Private so that only authorized user can view the detail of defect.
- Submit the Report

Once the Defect has been submitted, its Status is Set to New and Resolution is Open.

Defect Assignment

The authorized user (Manager) can assign the reported defect to the respective developer. The Steps for assigning defect(s) to developer are as follows:

Step 1: Click on View Issue tab and then click on <User Filter> button.

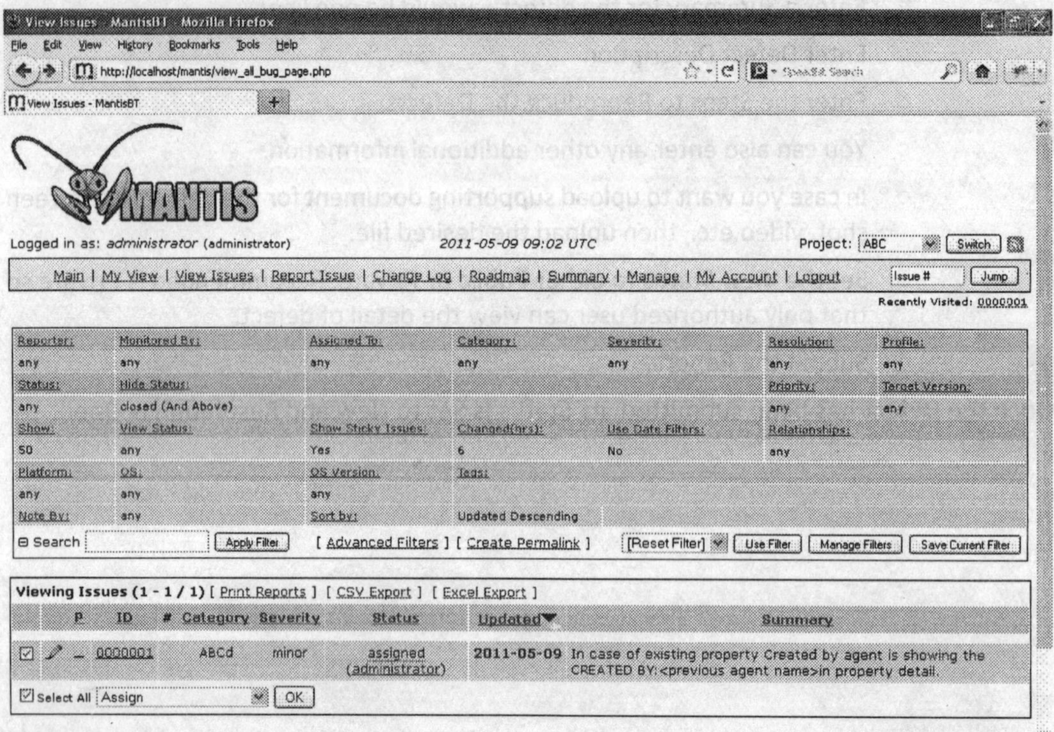

Step 2: The defect will be added as shown in above screen. Check the Select All and select Assign.

Step 3: Click on <OK> button.

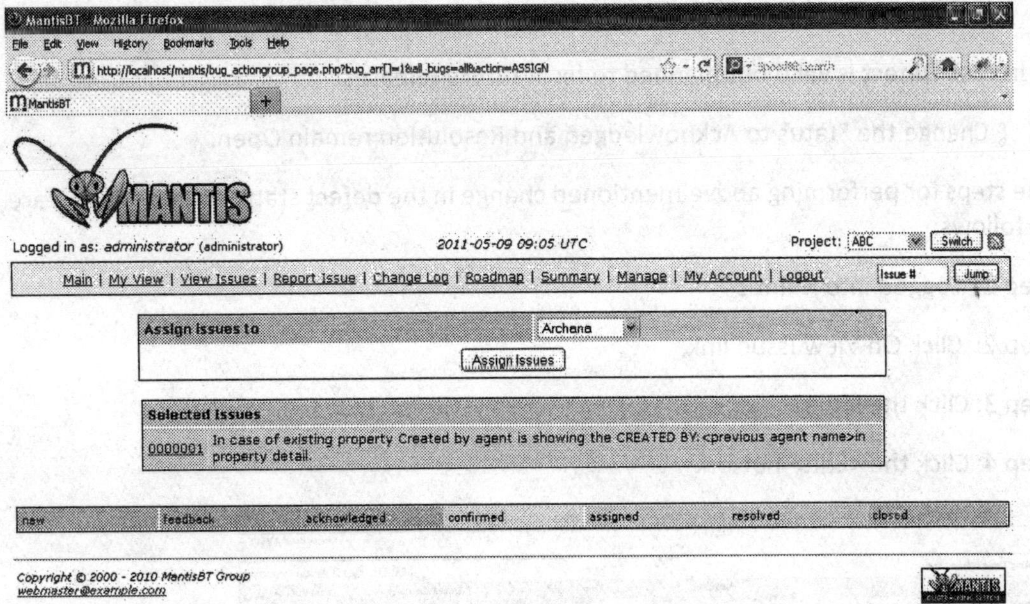

- Logged into Mantis
- Click View Issues link
- Select the Issue which should be assigned. (as shown above)
- Select Assign from the drop down
- Click OK (see above screen shot)
- Select the developer name from the drop-down and click the Assign Issues button.

Once the defect has been assigned, the status is set to Assigned and Resolution remains open.

Defect Resolution

After the defect has been assigned, the developer got email notification of all the issue(s) assigned to him/her. The developer can change the Status and provide the correct Resolution based on his/her defect analysis. The below mentioned scenarios can happen at the developer end:

1. In case Defect is valid:

    § Change the Status to Resolved and Resolution to Fixed

2. In case Defect is not valid:

   § Change the Status to Resolved and Resolution to either Duplicate or No Change

3. In case Defect is valid but planned to fix in future releases:

   § Change the Status to Acknowledged and Resolution remain Open.

The steps for performing above mentioned change in the defect status and resolution are as follows:

Step 1: Logged into Mantis

Step 2: Click On View Issue link.

Step 3: Click the Issue.

Step 4: Click the <Edit> button.

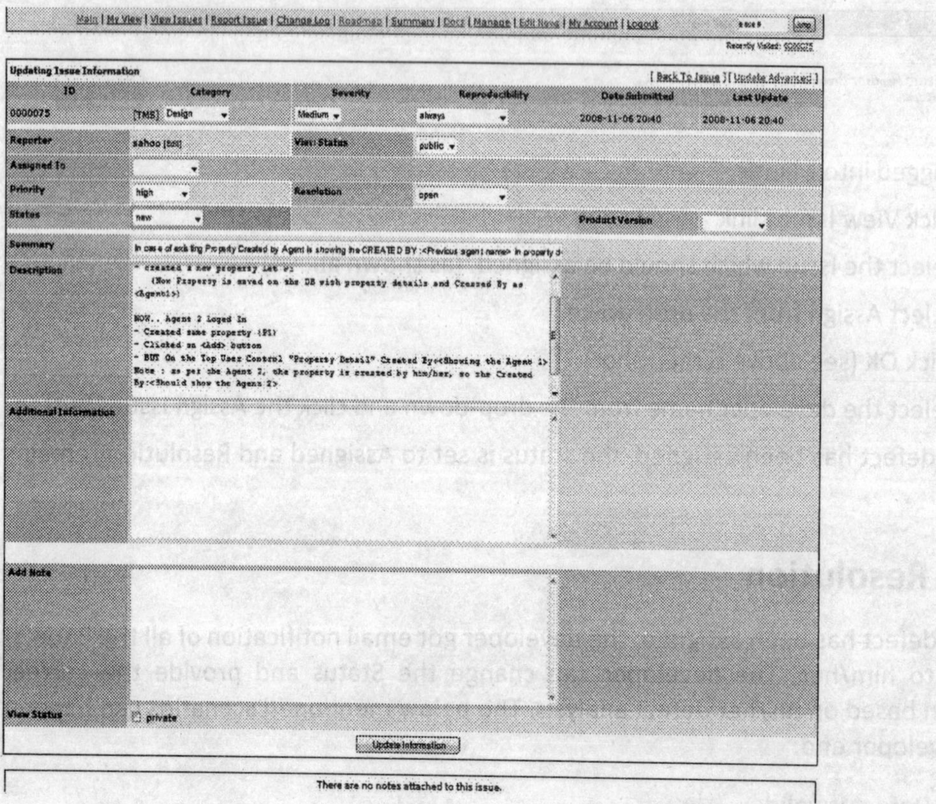

Step 5: Change the Status and Resolution and Save the changes.

Defect Closure

After the defect status has been marked as Resolved, then the reporter verifies the defect for its closure. The below mentioned scenarios can happen at Reporter end:

1. In case defect is found to be fixed during verification:

    - Change the Defect Status from Resolved to Closed. Do not make any changes in Resolution.

2. In case defect is found not fixed during verification:

    - Do not change the Status but change the Resolution from Fixed to Reopen In such cases the defect again moves to Assigned and so on.

3. In case defect is dropped by developer and reporter found that the defect still exists:

    - Do not change the Status but change the Resolution to Reopen.

The Reporter follows the same steps as developer to change the Defect Status.

Bug Tracking using BugZilla tool

Bugzilla

Introduction

Bugzilla is a web-based tool that lets you: * report bugs * assign bugs to the appropriate developers * prioritize bugs * set bug dependencies * arrange bugs by product and component With these features, you can also use Bugzilla as a to-do list manager. Bugzilla is a web application that lets users report and look up existing bugs. Changes made to a bug's status are automatically sent to users concerned with it.

The installation proceeds as follows:

1. Install Perl (5.8.1 or above)
2. Install a Database Engine
3. Install a Web server
4. Install Bugzilla
5. Install Perl modules
6. Configure all of the above.

1. Perl

Installed Version Test:

perl -v Any machine that doesn't have Perl on it is a sad machine indeed. If you Don't have it and your OS doesn't provide official packages, visit http://www.perl.org. Although Bugzilla runs with Perl 5.8.1, it's a good Idea to be using the latest stable version.

2. Database Engine

Bugzilla supports MySQL, PostgreSQL and Oracle as database servers. You only Require one of these systems to make use of Bugzilla.

i). MySQL

Installed Version Test:
mysql -V

If you don't have it and your OS doesn't provide official packages, visit http://www.mysql.com. You need MySQL version 4.1.2 or higher.

ii). PostgreSQL

Installed Version Test:
psql -V

If you don't have it and your OS doesn't provide official packages, visit http://www.postgresql.org/. You need PostgreSQL version 8.00.0000 or higher.

If you install from something other than a packaging/installation system, such as .rpm (Redhat Package), .deb (Debian Package), .exe (Windows Executable), or .msi (Microsoft Installer), make sure the PostgreSQL server is started when the machine boots.

iii). Oracle

Installed Version Test:
select * from v$version

(you first have to log in into your DB)

If you don't have it and your OS doesn't provide official packages, visit http://www.oracle.com/. You need Oracle version 10.02.0 or higher.

If you install from something other than a packaging/installation system, such as .rpm (Redhat Package), .deb (Debian Package), .exe (Windows Executable), or .msi (Microsoft Installer), make sure the Oracle server is started when the achine boots.

3. Web Server

Installed Version Test: view the default welcome page at
http://<your-machine>/

You have freedom of choice here, pretty much any web server that is capable of running

CGI scripts will work. However, we strongly recommend using the Apache web server (either 1.3.x or 2.x), and the installation instructions usually assume you are using it. If you have got Bugzilla working using another web server, please share your experiences with us by filing a bug in Bugzilla Documentation.

If you don't have Apache and your OS doesn't provide official packages, visit http://httpd.apache.org/.

4. Bugzilla

Download a Bugzilla tarball (or check it out from CVS) and place it in a suitable directory, accessible by the default web server user (probably "apache" or "www"). Good locations are either directly in the web server's document directories or in /usr/local with a symbolic link to the web server's document directories or an alias in the web server's configuration.

5. Perl Modules

Bugzilla's installation process is based on a script called checksetup.pl. The first thing it checks is whether you have appropriate versions of all the required Perl modules.

At this point, you need to su to root. You should remain as root until the end of the install. To check you have the required modules, run: bash# ./checksetup.pl --check-modules

checksetup.pl will print out a list of the required and optional Perl modules, together with the versions (if any) installed on your machine. The list of required modules is reasonably long; however, you may already have several of them installed.

The preferred way of installing Perl modules is to use the install-module.pl script on Unix, or PPM on Windows (see Section 2.5.1.2). If for some reason you need to install the Perl modules manually, see Appendix C. For instance, on Unix: bash# perl install-module.pl <modulename>

Tip

Here is a complete list of modules and their minimum versions. Some modules have special installation notes, which follow.

Required Perl modules:

1. CGI (3.21)
2. Date::Format (2.21)

3. DateTime (0.28)
4. DateTime::TimeZone (0.71)
5. DBI (1.41)
6. DBD::mysql (4.00) if using MySQL
7. DBD::Pg (1.45) if using PostgreSQL
8. DBD::Oracle (1.19) if using Oracle
9. Digest::SHA (any)
10. Email::Send (2.00)
11. Email::MIME (1.861)
12. Email::MIME::Encodings (1.313)
13. Email::MIME::Modifier (1.442)
14. Template (2.22)
15. URI (any)

Optional Perl modules:

1. GD (1.20) for bug charting
2. Template::Plugin::GD::Image (any) for Graphical Reports
3. Chart::Lines (2.1) for bug charting
4. GD::Graph (any) for bug charting
5. GD::Text (any) for bug charting
6. XML::Twig (any) for bug import/export
7. MIME::Parser (5.406) for bug import/export
8. LWP::UserAgent (any) for Automatic Update Notifications
9. PatchReader (0.9.4) for pretty HTML view of patches
10. Net::LDAP (any) for LDAP Authentication
11. Authen::SASL (any) for SASL Authentication
12. Authen::Radius (any) for RADIUS Authentication
13. SOAP::Lite (0.710.06) for the web service interface
14. JSON::RPC (any) for the JSON-RPC interface
15. Test::Taint (any) for the web service interface
16. HTML::Parser (3.40) for More HTML in Product/Group Descriptions
17. HTML::Scrubber (any) for More HTML in Product/Group Descriptions
18. Email::MIME::Attachment::Stripper (any) for Inbound Email
19. Email::Reply (any) for Inbound Email
20. TheSchwartz (any) for Mail Queueing
21. Daemon::Generic (any) for Mail Queueing
22. mod_perl2 (1.999022) for mod_perl

Download the Bugzilla from

http://www.bugzilla.org/download/

Download bugzilla

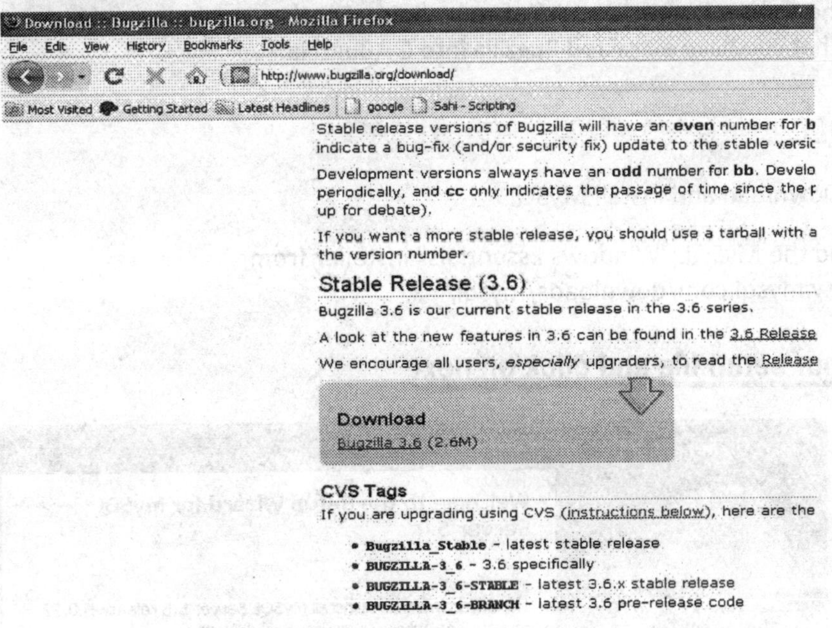

Click to save

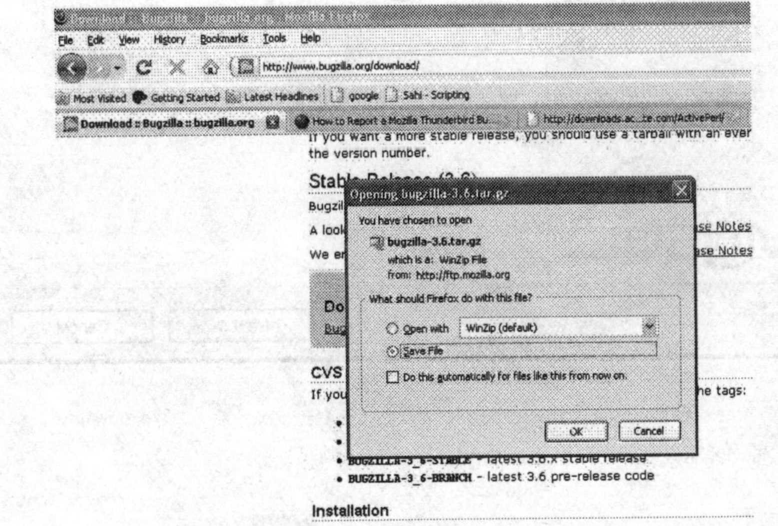

For extracting tar file download 7-zip software and extract the file.

Link is given below:
http://www.7-zip.org/ (Extract tar file)

Extract the archive to the directory of your choice. For the remainder of this document I will assume that you have extracted Bugzilla into C :\Bugzilla.

MySQL

How to Download and install MySQL

Download the MySQL "Windows Essentials" installer from:
http://dev.mysql.com/downloads/mysql/

Click your setup file and click on next

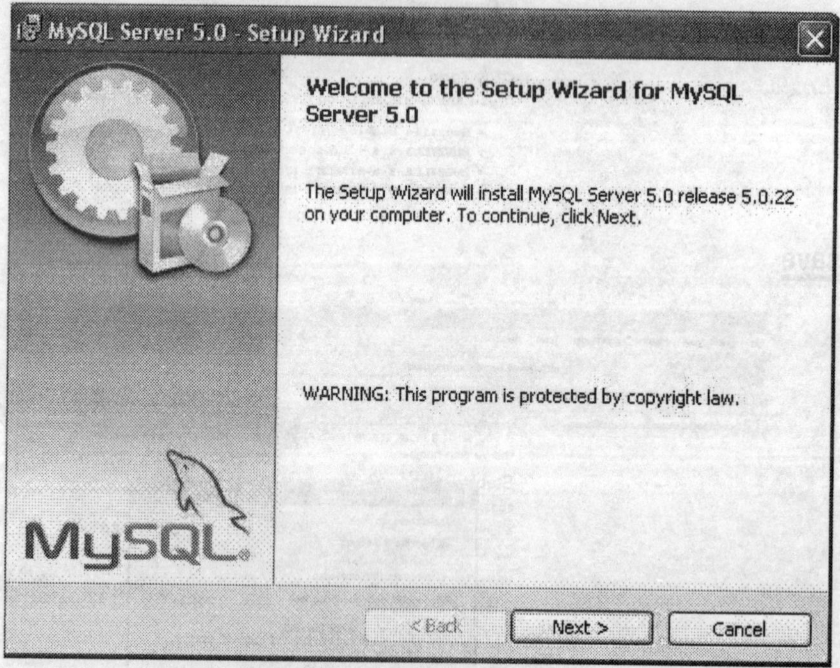

Choose typical/custom

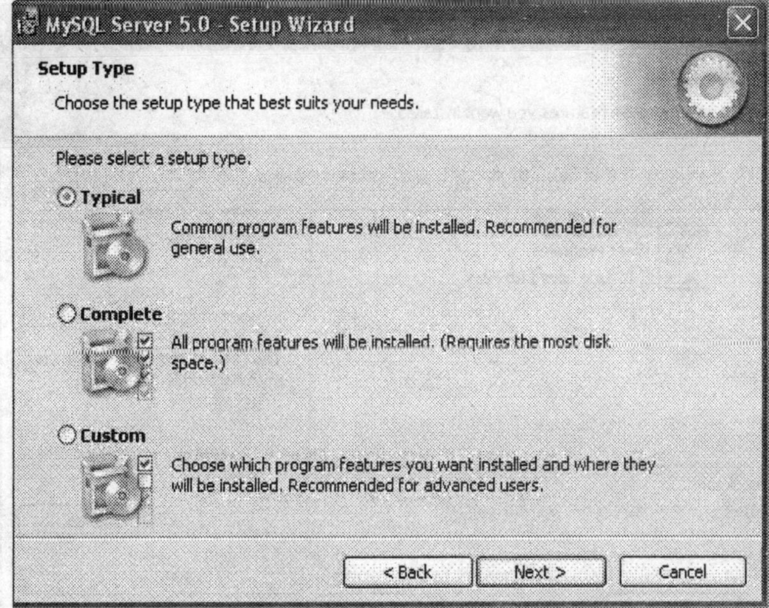

choose custom

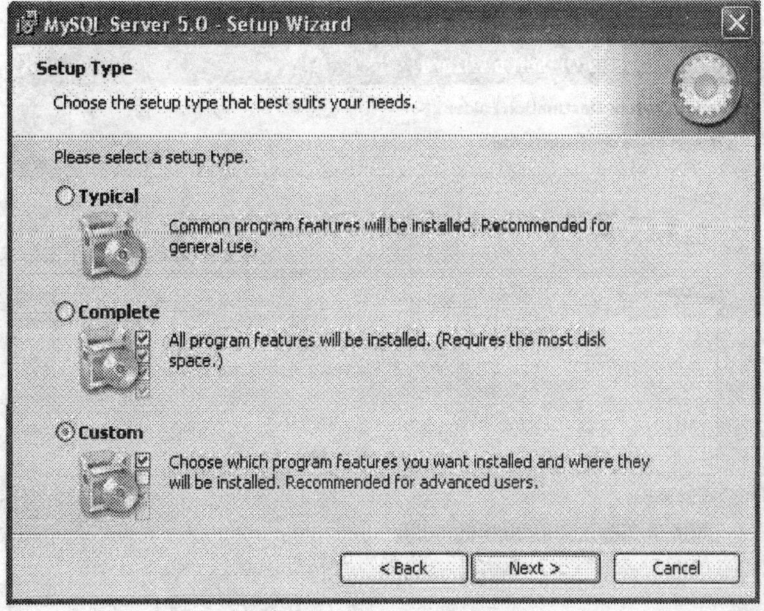

Specify the path to install

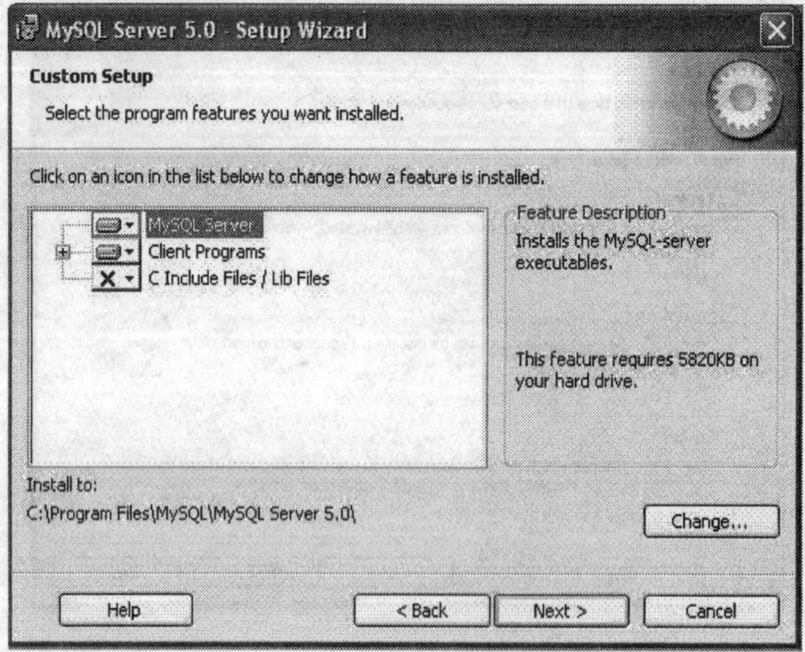

continue

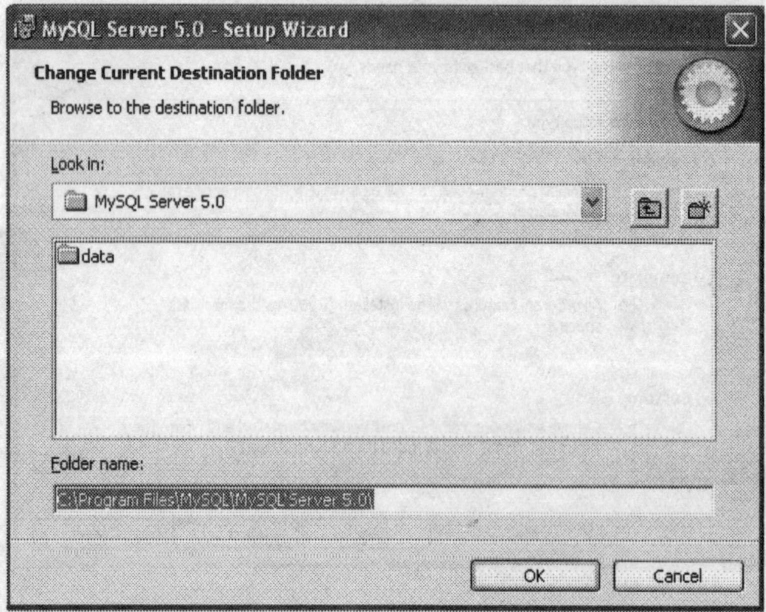

Click on install

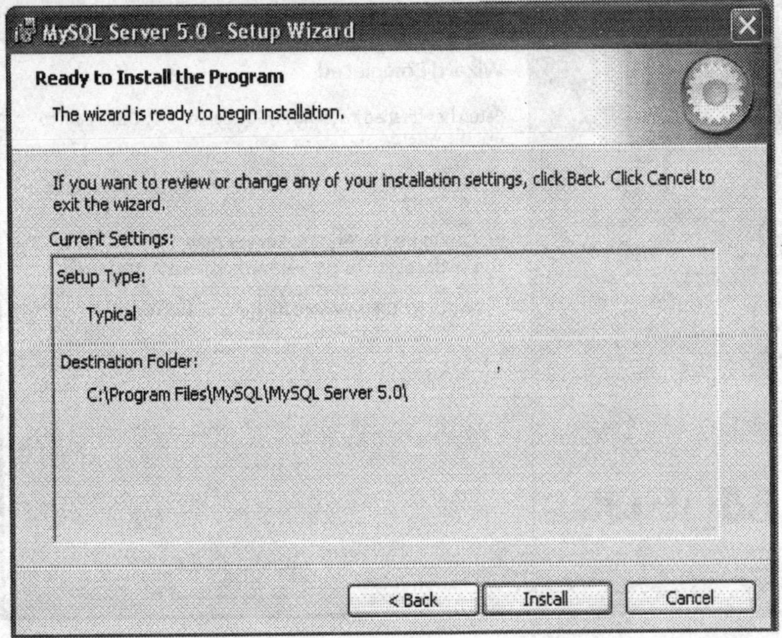

Installation status

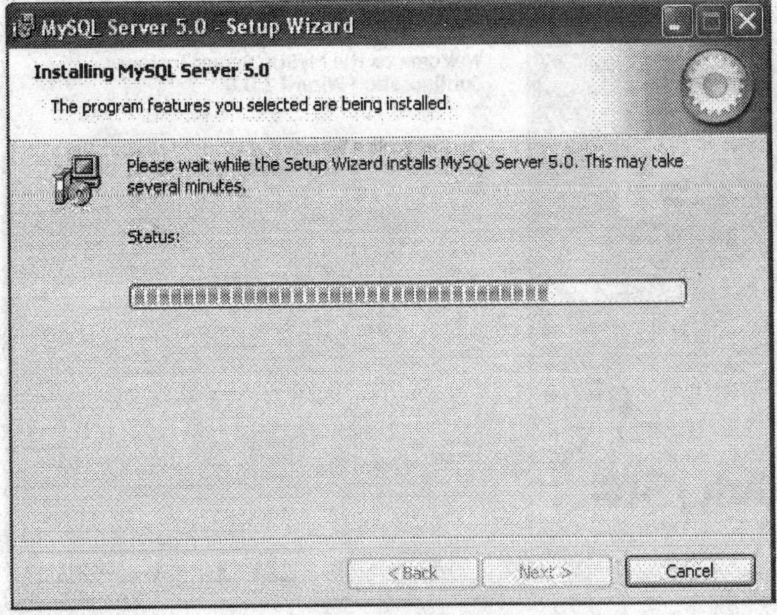

Installation is finished, conf the mysql server now

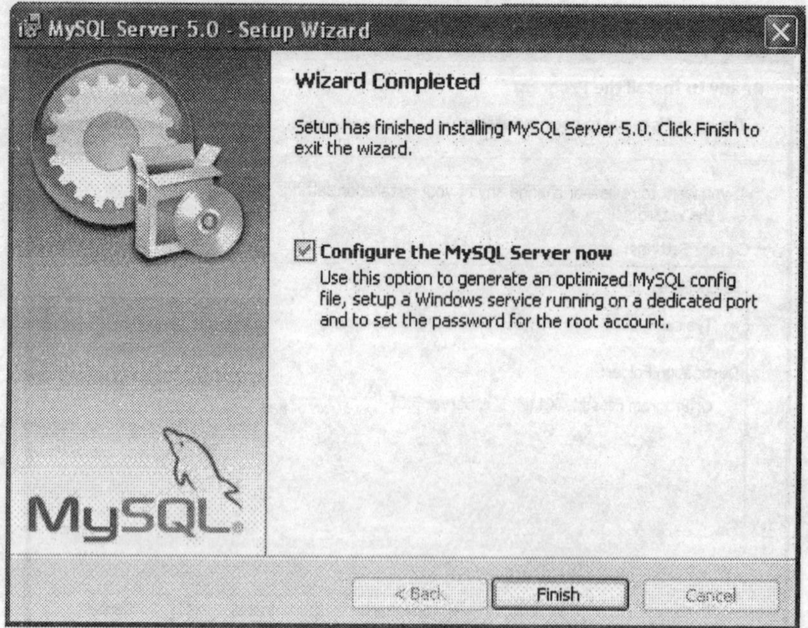

Click to next button

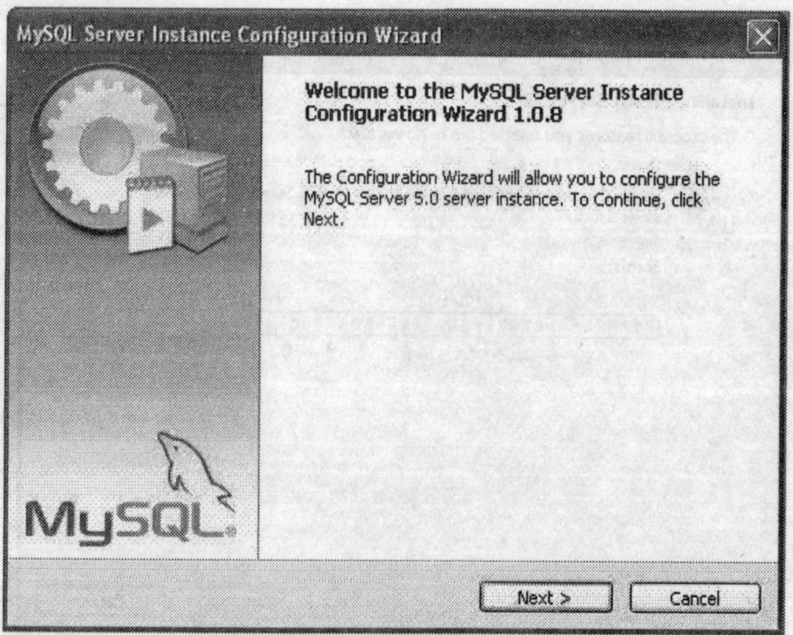

Click on detailed configuration

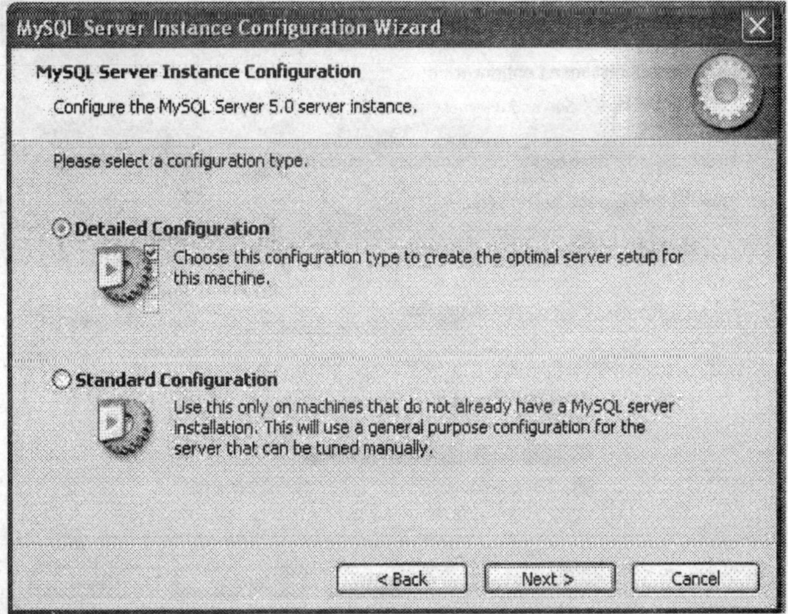

Click the developer machine

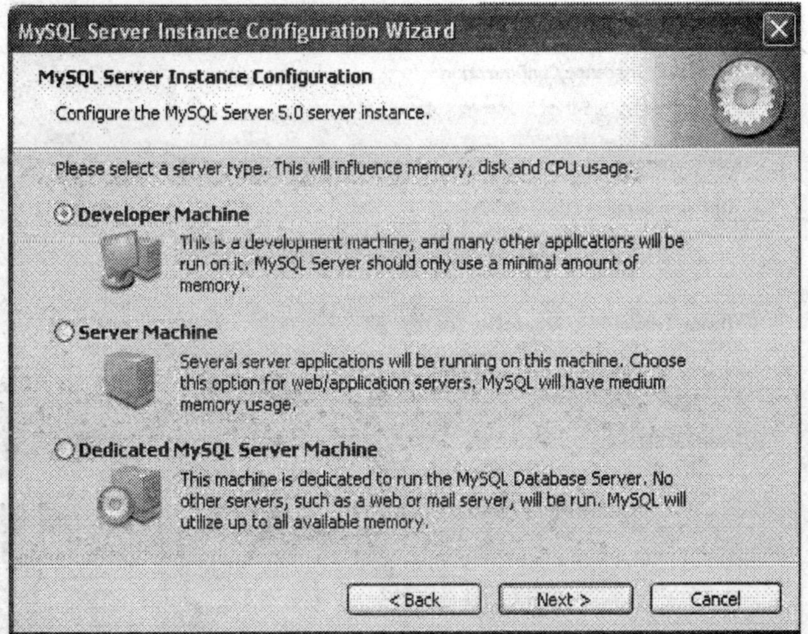

Click next to proceed

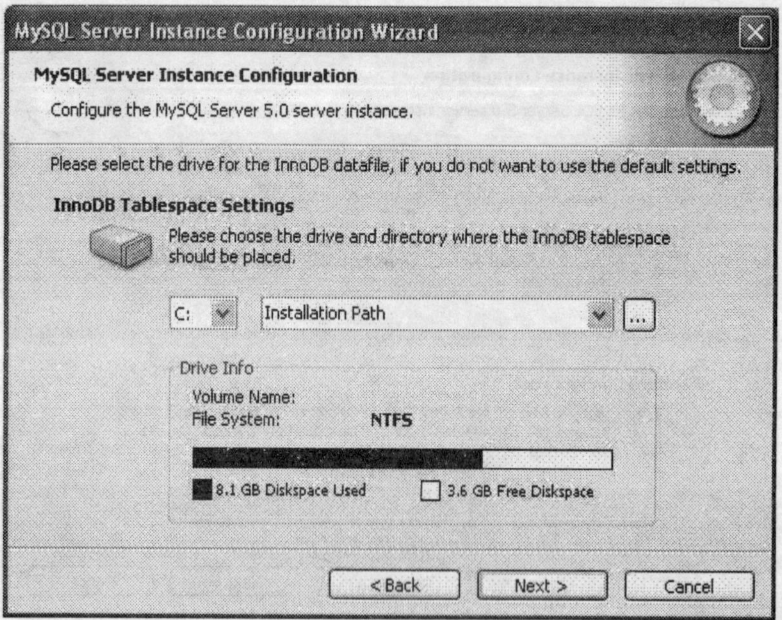

Click the decision support (DSS)/OALP

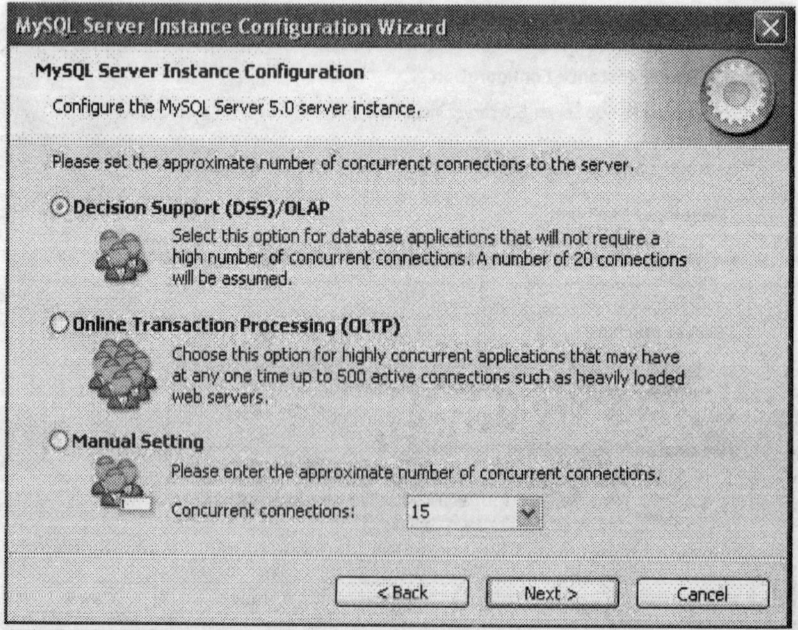

Choose the port for mysql and click the next button

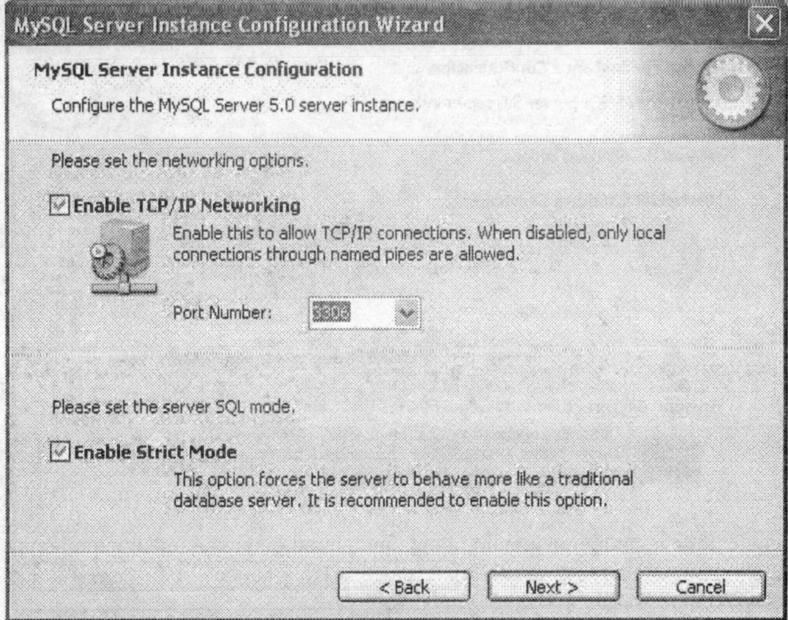

Click standard character set and click next button

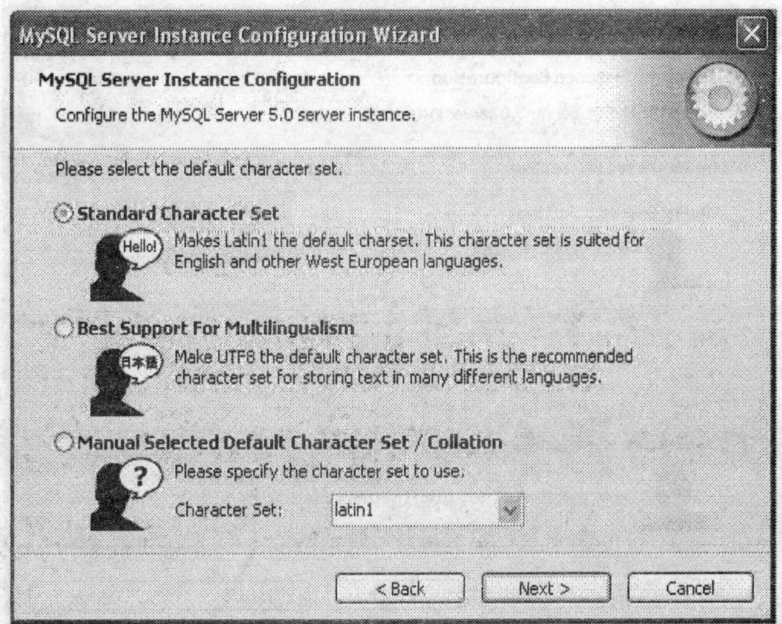

Choose the service name and click next button

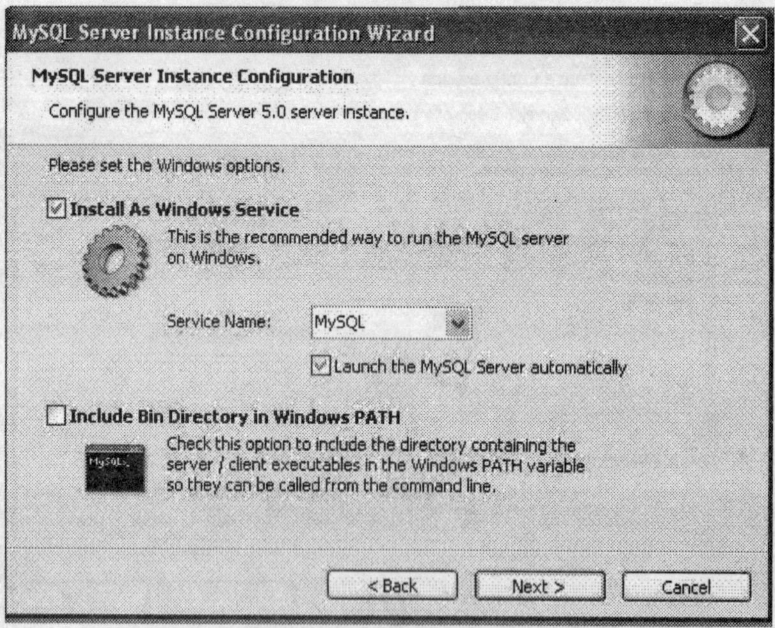

Give root password for mysql (for ex: I gave root as the password)

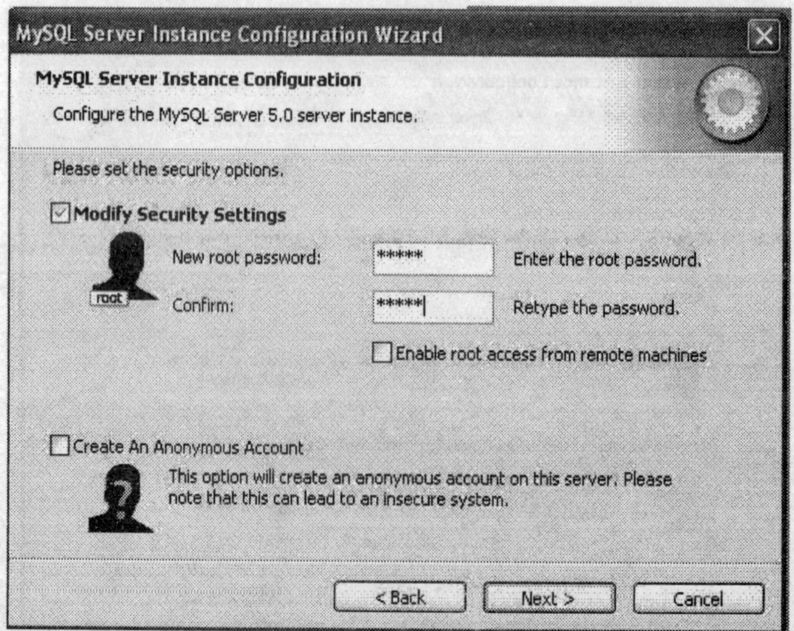

The wizard will check whether mysql configured properly and servicesis running or not.

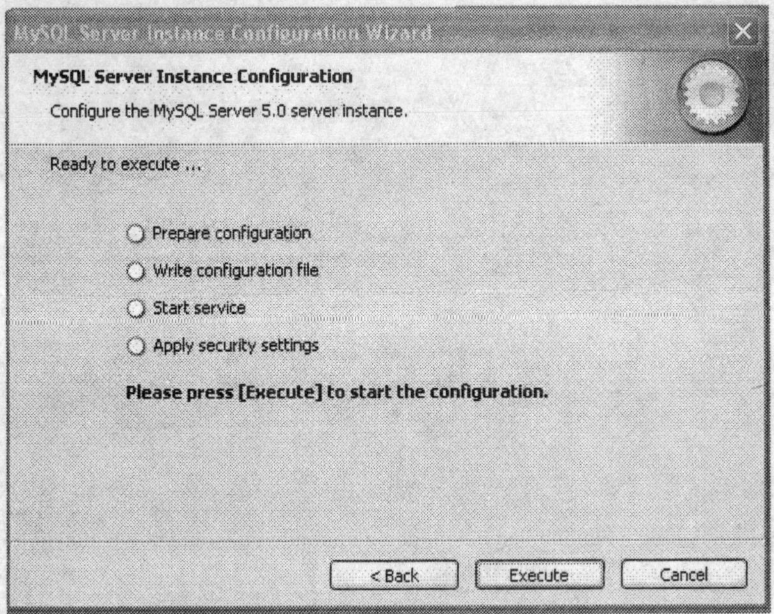

Click finish and mysql is installed successfully

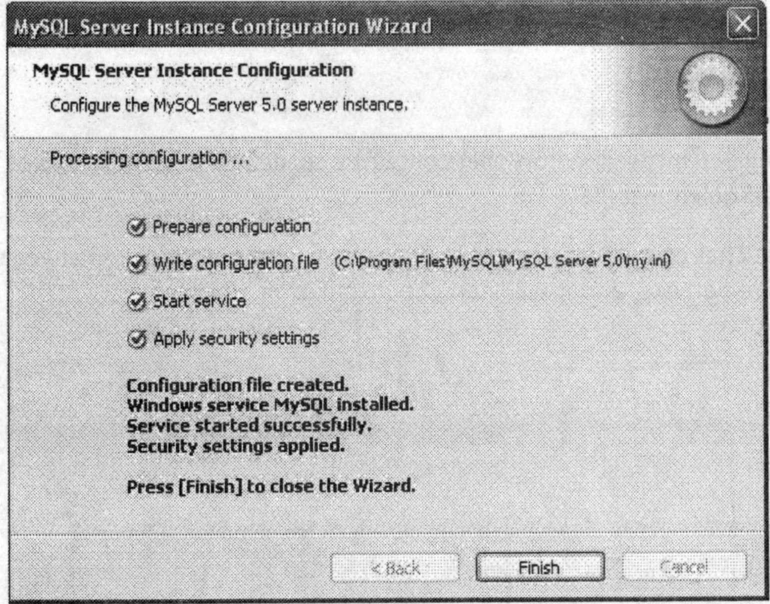

Create Bugs Database and User

```
C:\mysql\bin>mysql --user=root -p mysql
Enter password: ********
Welcome to the MySQL monitor.  Commands end with ; or \g.
Your MySQL connection id is 15 to server version: 4.0.20a-debug

Type 'help;' or '\h' for help. Type '\c' to clear the buffer.

mysql> create database bugs;

Query OK, 1 row affected (0.11 sec)

mysql> grant all privileges on bugs.* to 'bugs'@'localhost' identified by 'sockmonkey';
Query OK, 0 rows affected (0.03 sec)

mysql> flush privileges;
Query OK, 0 rows affected (0.00 sec)

mysql> quit

Bye

C:\mysql\bin>
```

Install

ActiveState Perl uses a standard Windows Installer. Install, sticking with the defaults, which will install Perl into

C:\Perl

Note: Installing Perl into a directory that contains a space (eg "C:\Program Files") will break the Template-Toolkit installer

Once the intsall has completed, log out and log in again to pick up the changes to the PATH Click the Active perl exe, and it will start the installation.

Click next

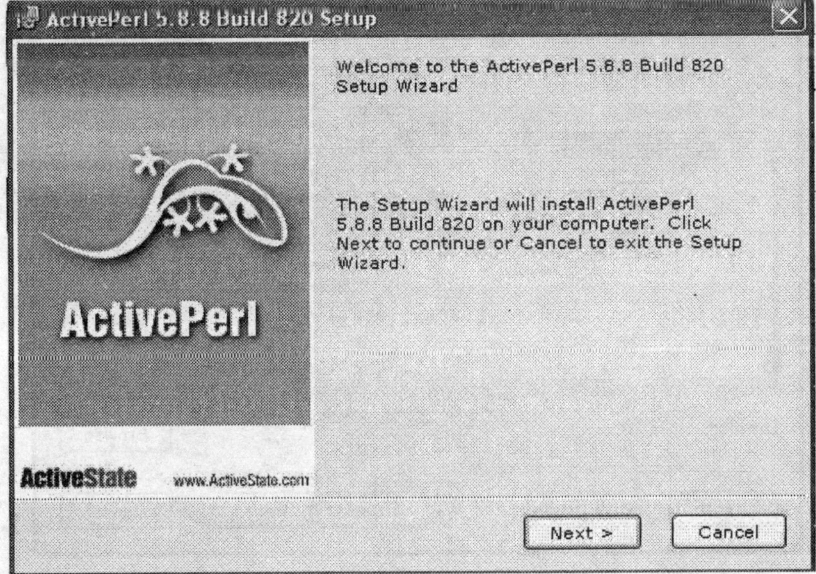

Accept the license agreement

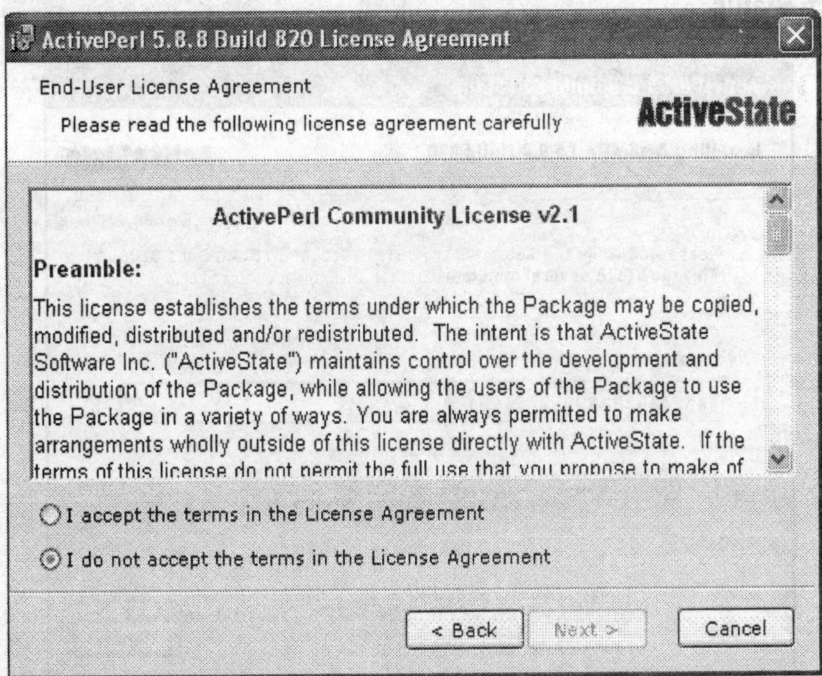

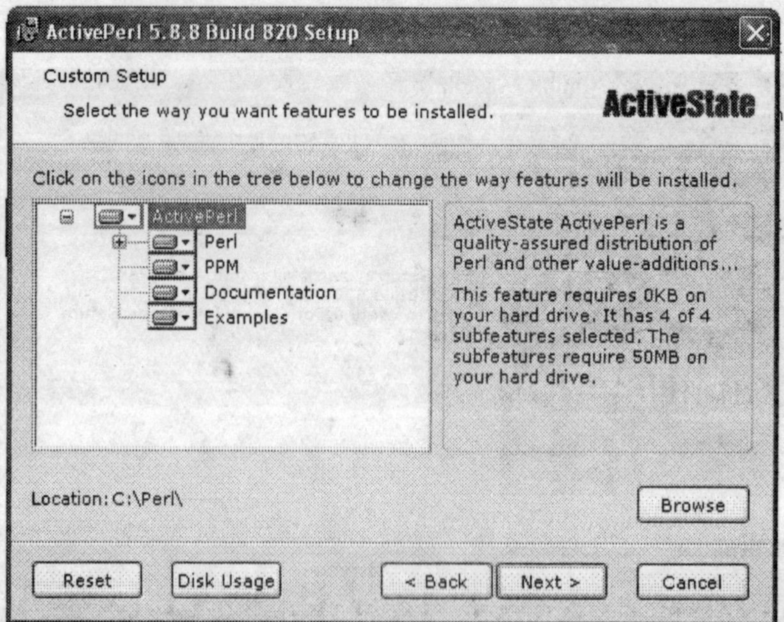

Choose a directory for Active Perl

Click the Install button to proceed for installation

Installation Status

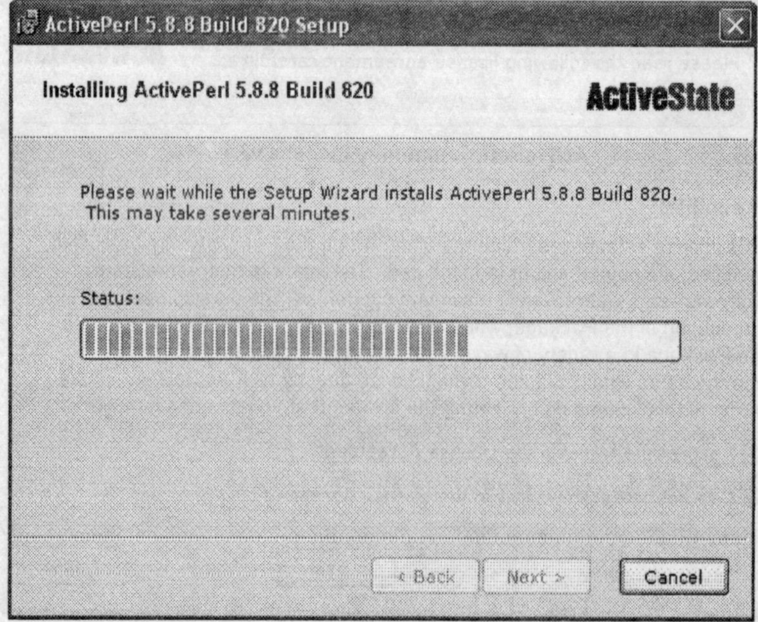

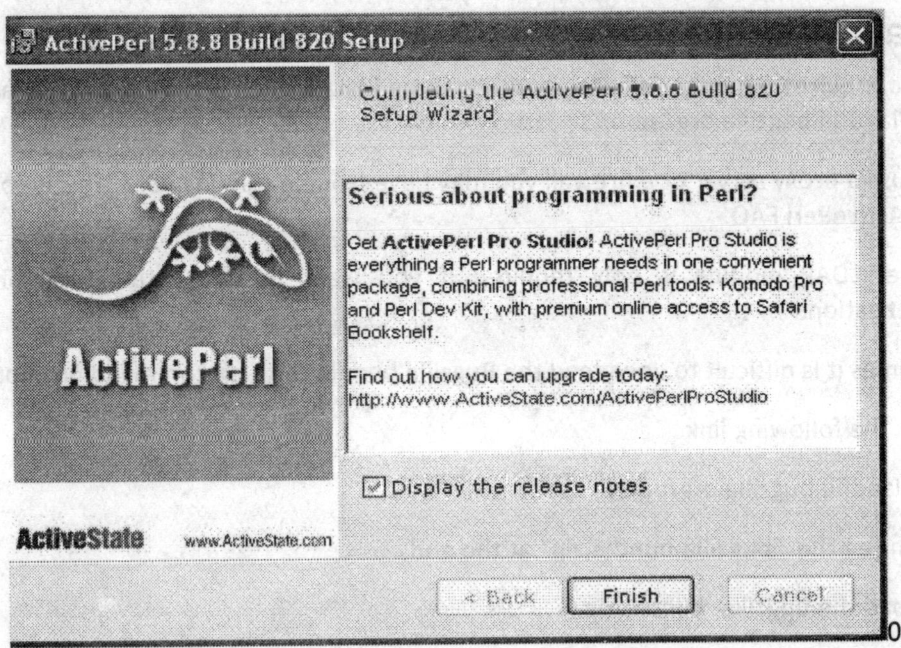

Click finish, the active perl is installed successfully

Upgrading Existing Installs

If you already have ActiveState Perl installed, now's a good time to ensure you're running the latest version of ActiveState Perl, along with the latest versions of the modules.

To upgrade ActiveState Perl, follow the directions at:
http://aspn.activestate.com/ASPN/docs/ActivePerl/install.html
To upgrade your modules, simply run
ppm upgrade
Create Temp Directory
On Windows, Perl has a hard time of locating the correct directory to write its temporary files (CGI.pm, File::Spec). Basically it has a list of paths hard coded to use, instead of querying Windows for the correct path.
To avoid problems, create the
C:\Temp
directory (it has to be on drive C) and ensure SYSTEM has write and modify access

Install Modules

Bugzilla requires a number of perl modules to be installed, all of which are available at http://landfill.bugzilla.org/ppm/.

If you use a proxy server or a firewall you may have trouble running PPM. This is covered in the ActivePerl FAQ.

The Net::LDAP module is only required if you want to use Active Directory for authentication.

Sometimes it is difficult to download the Bugzilla bundle through command prompt.

So click the following link

http://landfill.bugzilla.org/ppm/

You can see the "bugzilla-bundle.zip" at the end.

Download the bugzilla- bundle.zip.

Unzip the bundle and put it in some folder. Then unzip the bundle in "c:\bugzilla-bundle".

In commond Prompt:

Type "ppm path of the Perl Modules perlmodule.ppd (For Ex: ppm c:\bugzilla- bundle\AppConfig.ppd)

```
C:\WINDOWS\system32\cmd.exe
threads 1.77 (have 1.75)
threads-shared 1.33 (have 1.32)
version 0.82 (have 0.78)

C:\>ppm install appconfig
No missing packages to install

C:\>ppm install AppConfig
No missing packages to install

C:\>ppm install TimeDate
No missing packages to install

C:\>ppm install DBI
No missing packages to install

C:\>ppm install DBD-mysql
Downloading DBD-mysql-4.011...redirect
Downloading DBD-mysql-4.011...done
Unpacking DBD-mysql-4.011...ppm install failed: Can't extract files from
ME~1\pqrs\LOCALS~1\Temp\ppm-USa5tI/DBD-mysql-4.011.tgz

C:\>ppm install Template-Toolkit
Downloading Template-Toolkit-2.22...done
Unpacking Template-Toolkit-2.22...done
Generating HTML for Template-Toolkit-2.22...done
Updating files in site area...done
 140 files installed

C:\>ppm install MailTools
No missing packages to install

C:\>ppm install GD
No missing packages to install

C:\>ppm install GDGraph
Downloading GDGraph-1.44...done
Unpacking GDGraph-1.44...done
Generating HTML for GDGraph-1.44...done
Updating files in site area...done
  21 files installed

C:\>ppm install PatchReader
Downloading PatchReader-0.9.5...done
Unpacking PatchReader-0.9.5...done
Generating HTML for PatchReader-0.9.5...done
Updating files in site area...done
```

Note: Install DateTime and DateTime-TimeZone

(removed the ActiveState Package Repository, used the ppm install commands, then reinstalled the ActiveState Package Repository)

1. Use ppm repo list to view the list of repositories that are enabled.
2. Then use ppm repo off *num*, where *num* is the id number of the ActiveState Package Repository. At the command prompt you can do a C:\bugzilla>ppm repo list That will tell you what order your repo's are listed then you can do C:\bugzilla>ppm repo off [number of repo you want turned off]

3. Then attempt to install DateTime and DateTime-TimeZone again using the ppm install commands.
4. Then run checksetup.pl again to verify everything is installed.
5. Use ppm repo on *num* to re-enable the repository.

The Apache HTTP Server

The Apache HTTP Server Project is a collaborative software development effort aimed at creating a robust, commercial-grade, featureful, and freely-available source code implementation of an HTTP (Web) server

How to download AHHTPS

Go to browser and type this link http://httpd.apache.org/

Download from a mirror

Choose: Win32 Binary including OpenSSL 0.9.8m (MSI Installer): httpd-2.2.15-win32-x86-openssl-0.9.8m-r2.msi [PGP] [MDS] [SHA1]

Save the file

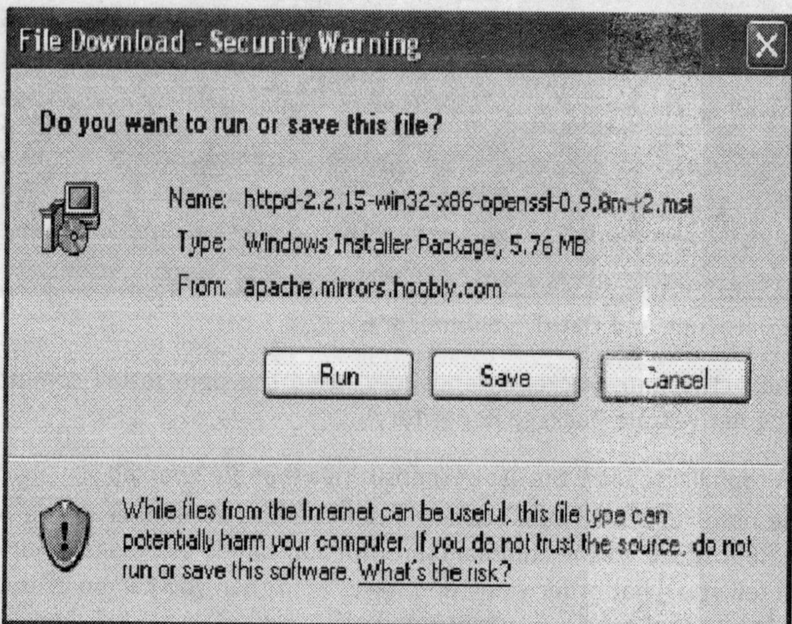

How to install Apache HTTP Server

Run apache http server

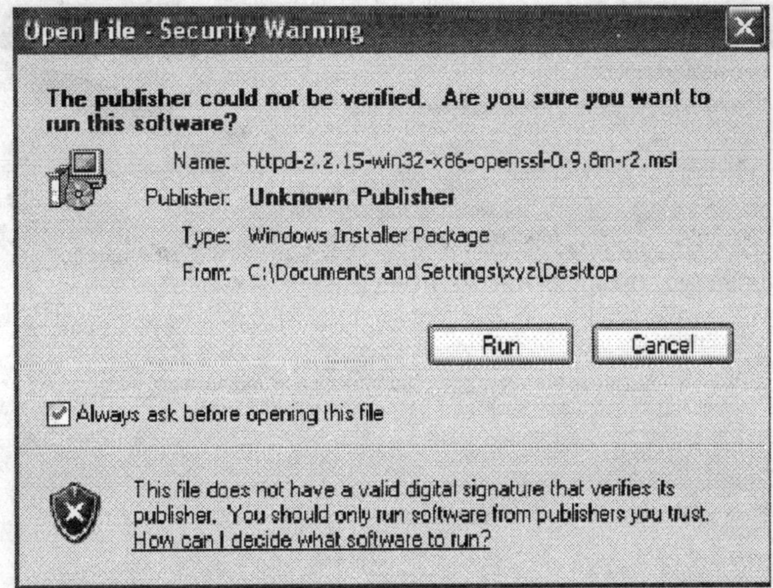

Click next

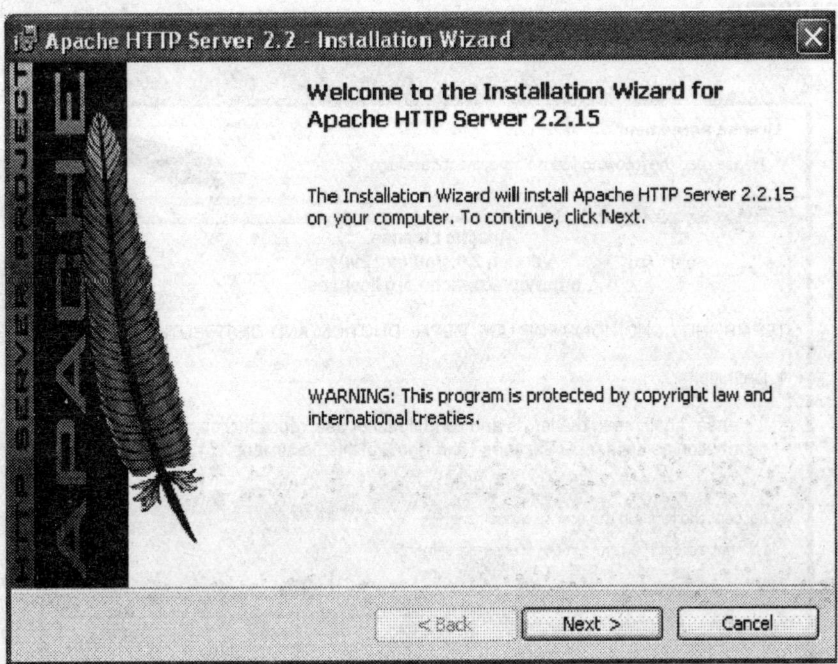

License agreement

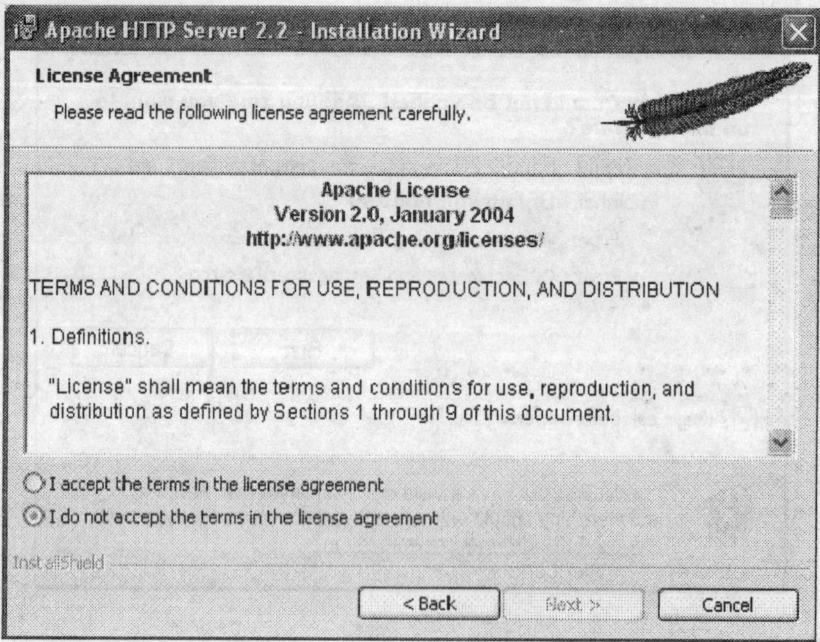

Accept the terms

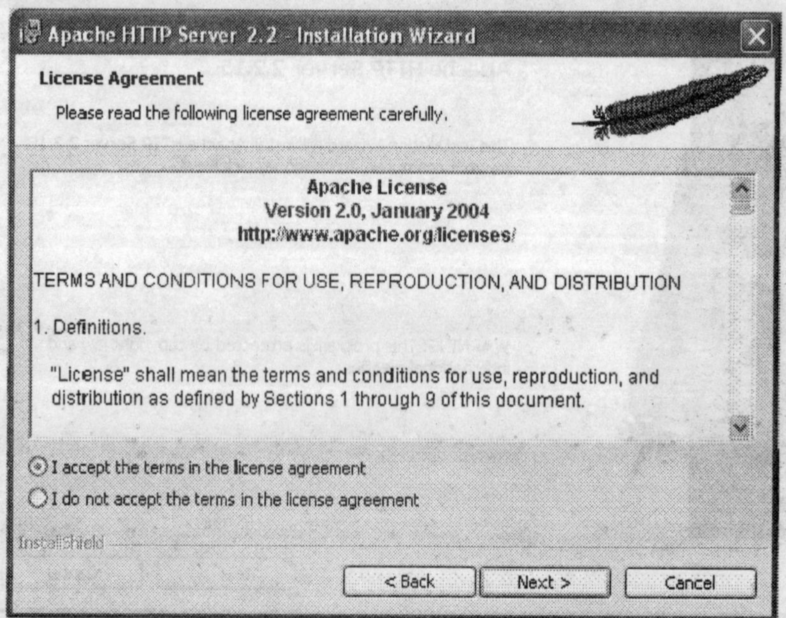

Read AHTTP server and click to next

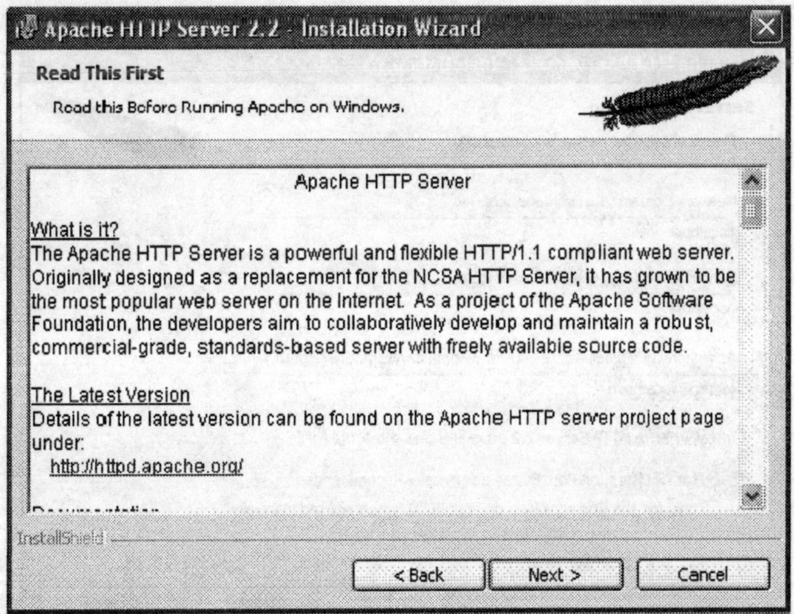

You'll asked to fill network domain, server name,adm's email adds

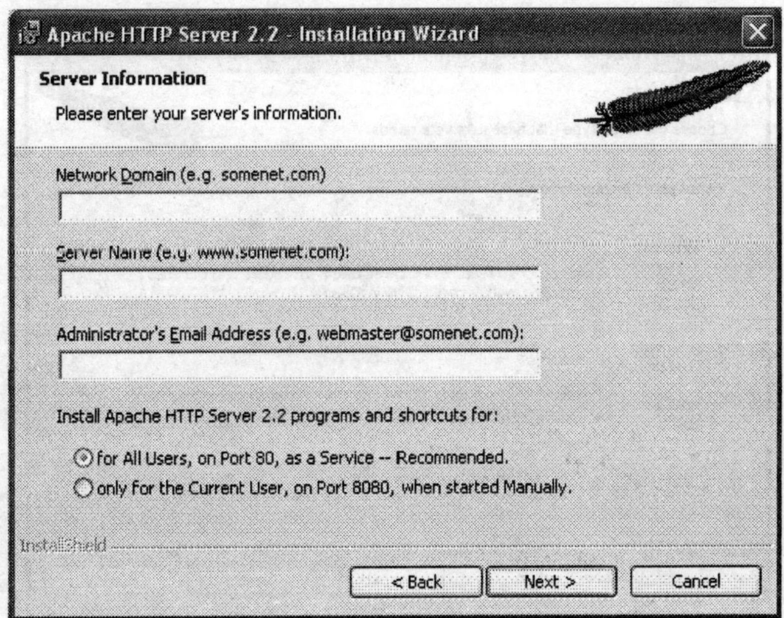

type "local host" in network domain and server name field. and type admin@localhost in adm's email adds.

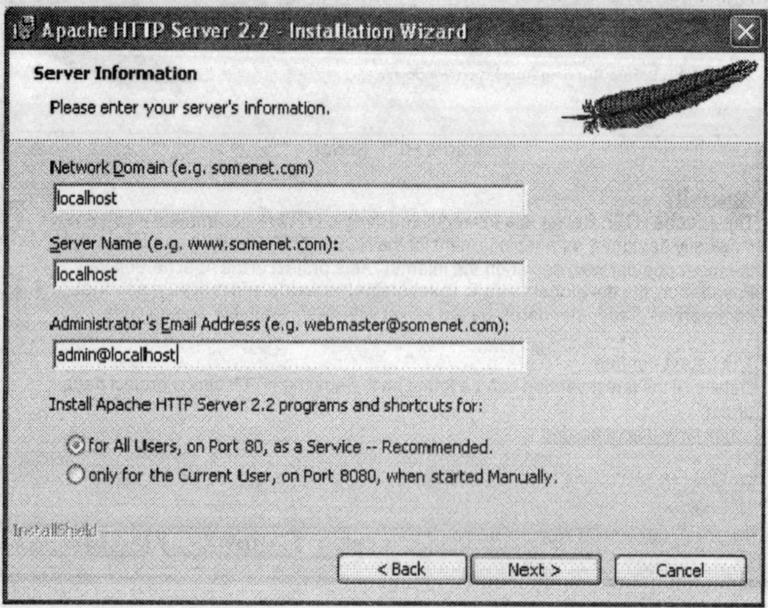

Choose custom

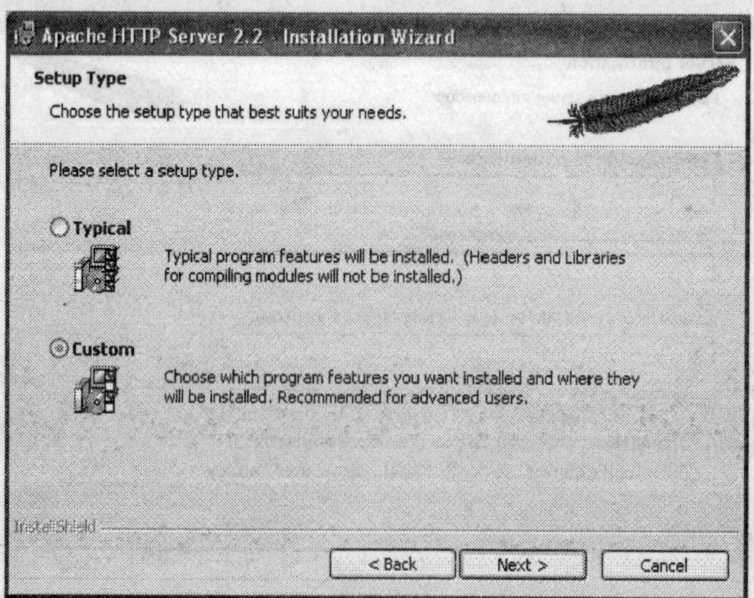

click on build headers and........As shown red cross in fig

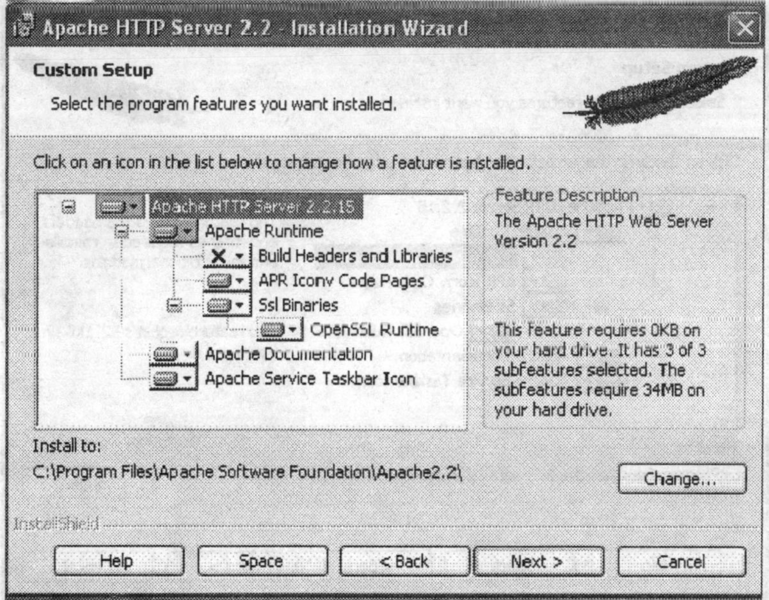

Click on "This feature will be installed on local hard drive"

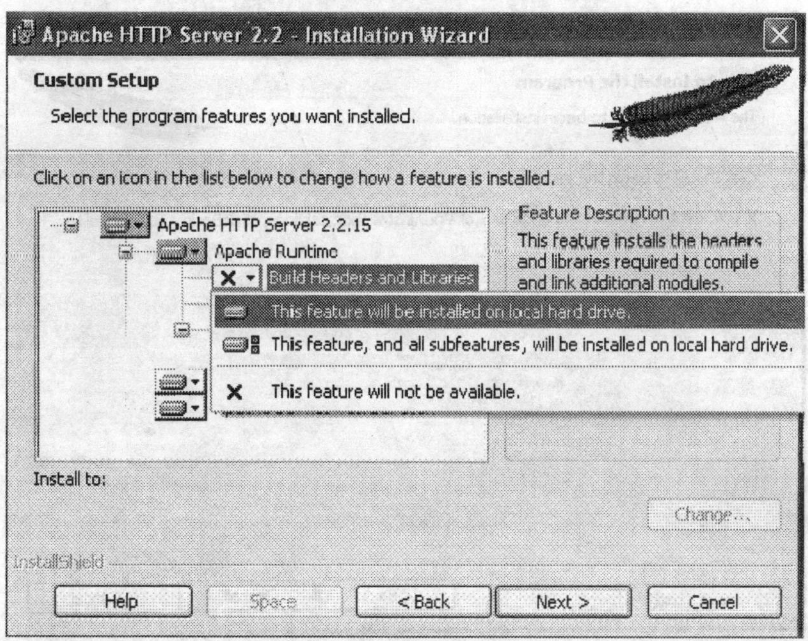

Click to next

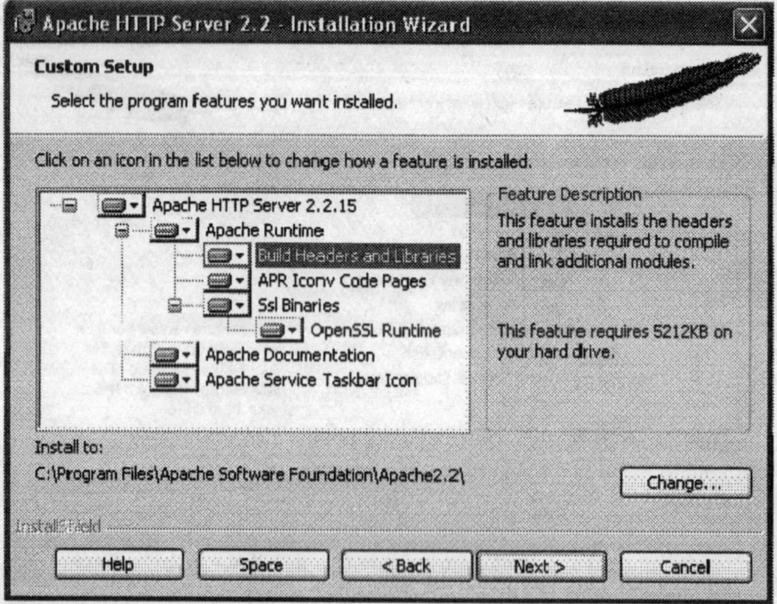

Click to install apache http server

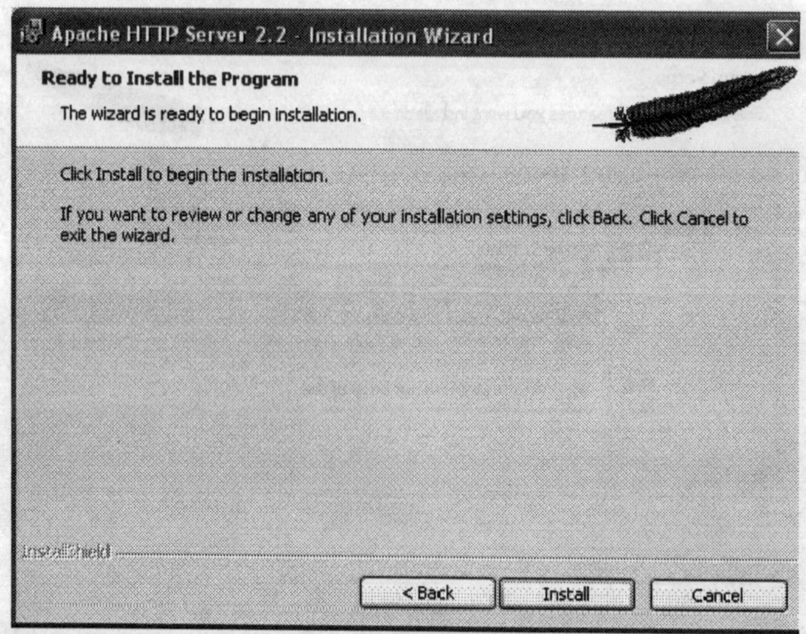

Installing status

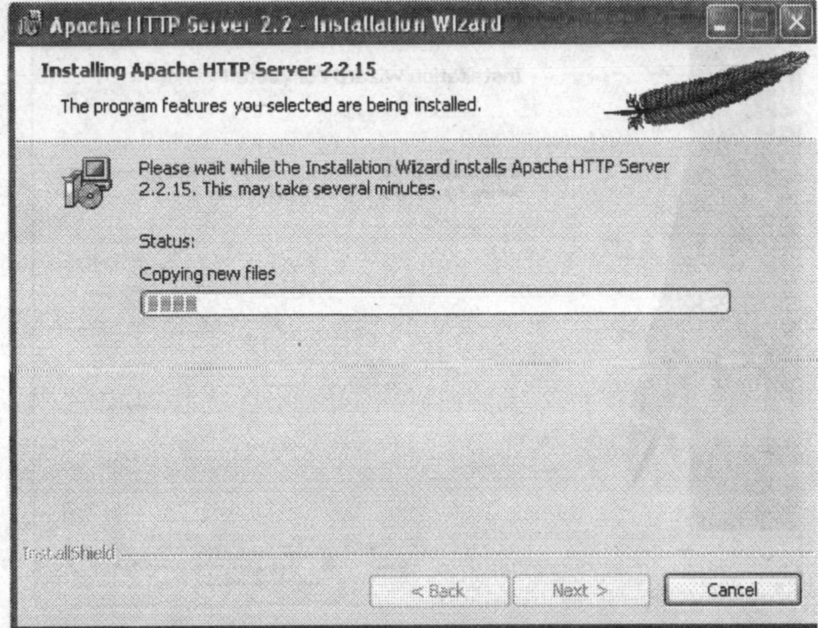

Testing http server

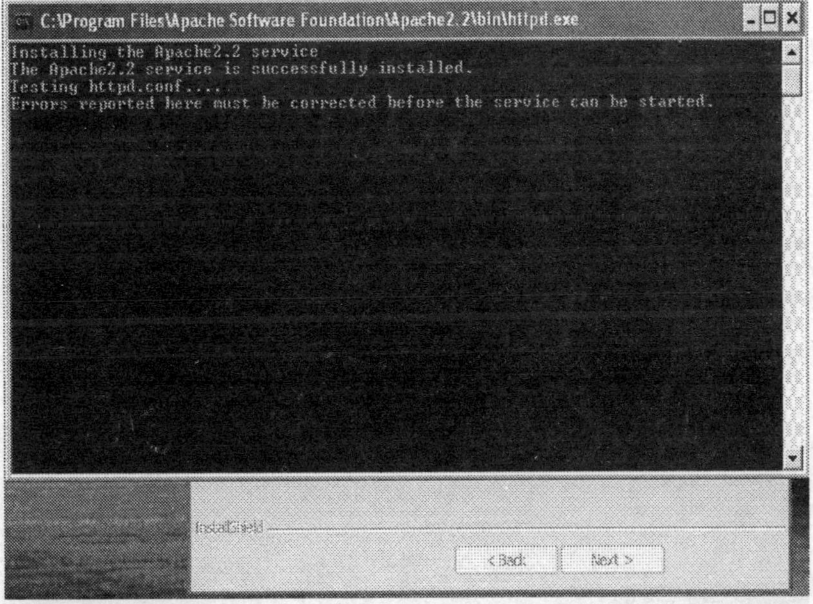

Click to finish

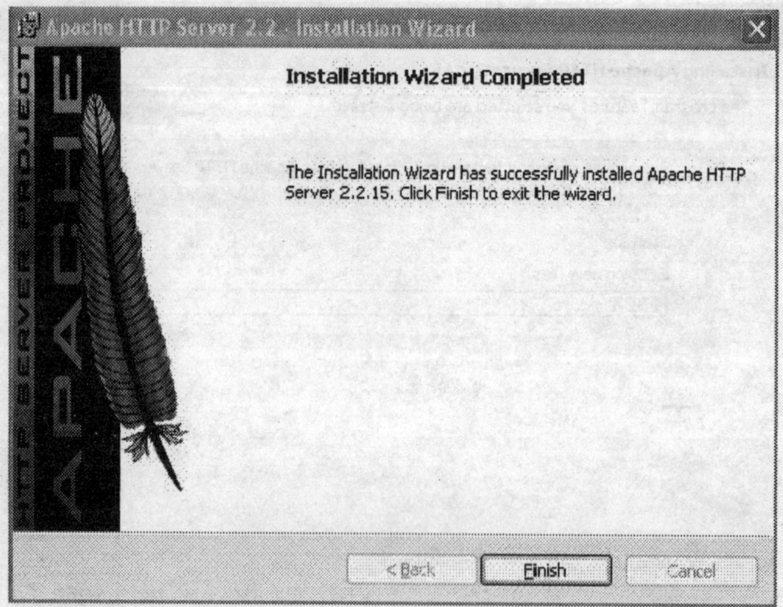

To Check it whether running or not type http://localhost/

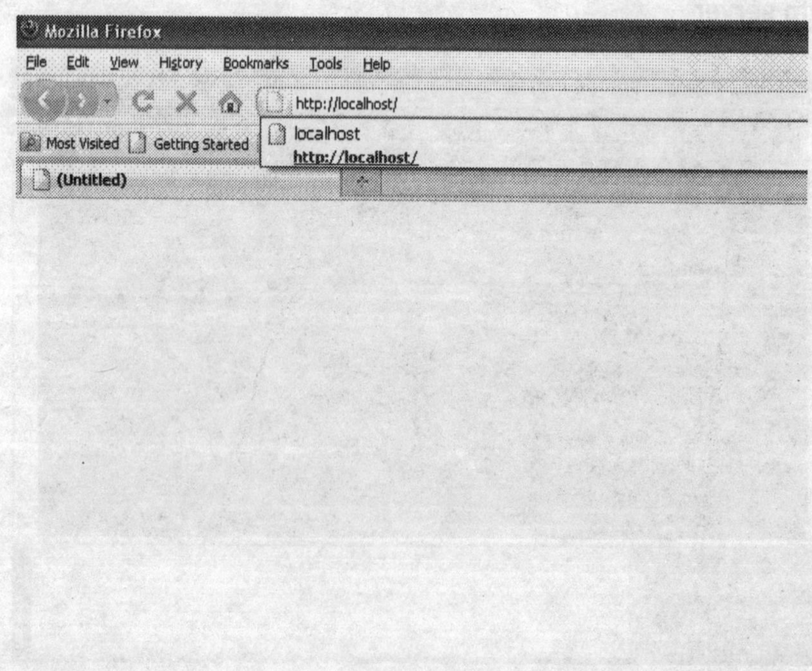

It gives a message " It works" if it runs

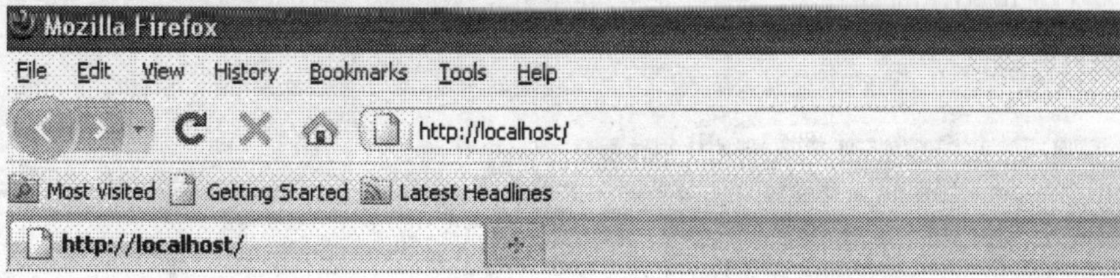

It works!

Note that C:\Bugzilla\data is created the first time you run checksetup.pl. Configure Port and DocumentRoot Edit C:\Program Files\Apache Group\Apache2\conf\httpd.conf with your favourite text editor.

To change the port that Apache runs on (listens on, or binds to), edit the below Listen option.

```
# Listen: Allows you to bind Apache to specific IP addresses and/or
# ports, instead of the default. See also the <VirtualHost>
# directive.
#
# Change this to Listen on specific IP addresses as shown below to
# prevent Apache from glomming onto all bound IP addresses.
#
#Listen 12.34.56.78:80
Listen 80
```

Change the DocumentRoot setting to point to C:\Bugzilla. Note there are two locations in httpd.conf that need to be updated. Note you need to use / instead of \ as a path separator

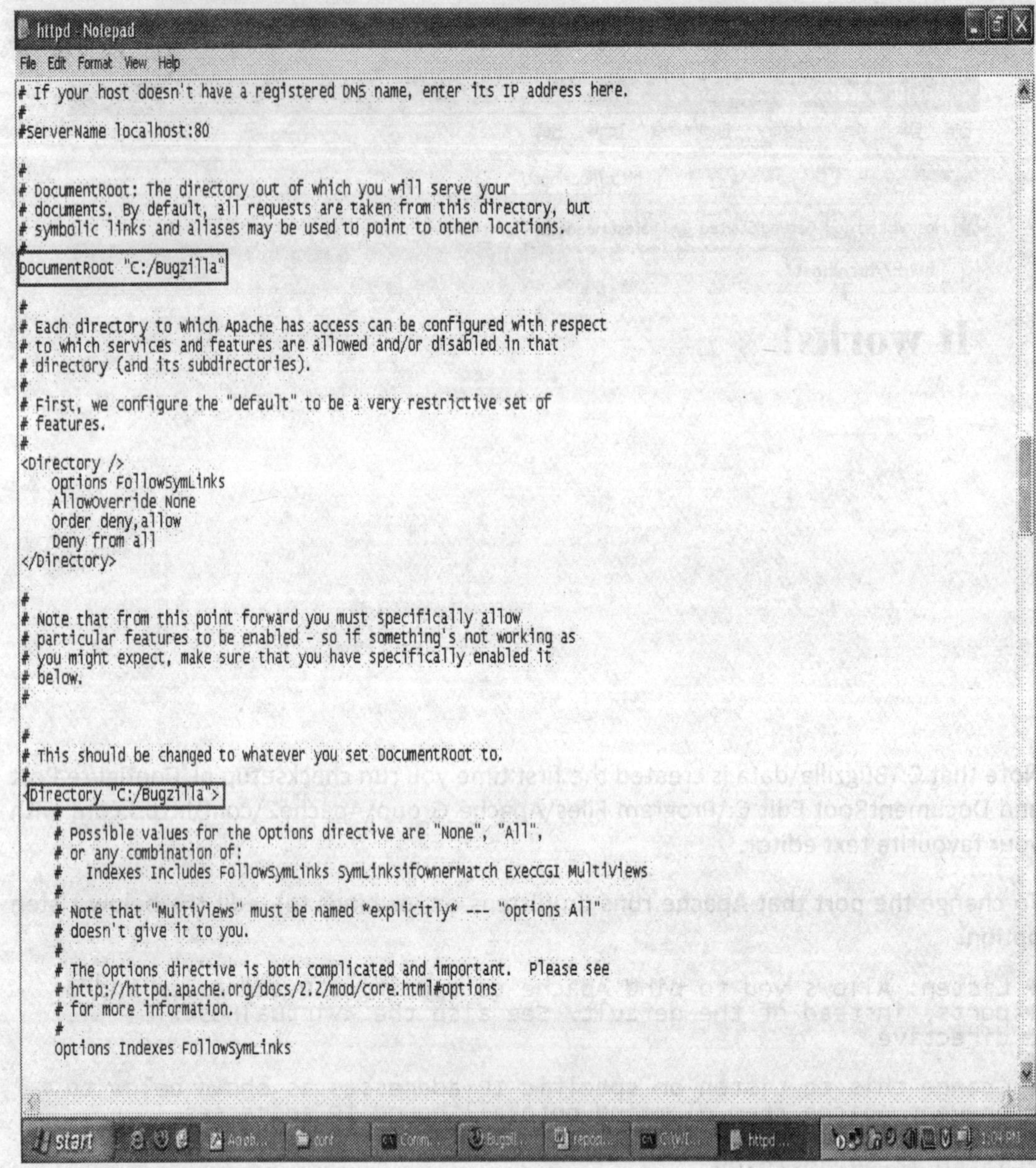

```
# If your host doesn't have a registered DNS name, enter its IP address here.
#
#ServerName localhost:80

#
# DocumentRoot: The directory out of which you will serve your
# documents. By default, all requests are taken from this directory, but
# symbolic links and aliases may be used to point to other locations.
#
DocumentRoot "C:/Bugzilla"

#
# Each directory to which Apache has access can be configured with respect
# to which services and features are allowed and/or disabled in that
# directory (and its subdirectories).
#
# First, we configure the "default" to be a very restrictive set of
# features.
#
<Directory />
    Options FollowSymLinks
    AllowOverride None
    Order deny,allow
    Deny from all
</Directory>

#
# Note that from this point forward you must specifically allow
# particular features to be enabled - so if something's not working as
# you might expect, make sure that you have specifically enabled it
# below.
#

#
# This should be changed to whatever you set DocumentRoot to.
#
<Directory "C:/Bugzilla">
    #
    # Possible values for the Options directive are "None", "All",
    # or any combination of:
    #   Indexes Includes FollowSymLinks SymLinksifOwnerMatch ExecCGI MultiViews
    #
    # Note that "MultiViews" must be named *explicitly* --- "Options All"
    # doesn't give it to you.
    #
    # The Options directive is both complicated and important.  Please see
    # http://httpd.apache.org/docs/2.2/mod/core.html#options
    # for more information.
    #
    Options Indexes FollowSymLinks
```

Configure CGI

To enable CGI support in Apache, you need to enable the CGI handler, by uncommenting the AddHandler cgi-script .cgi line.

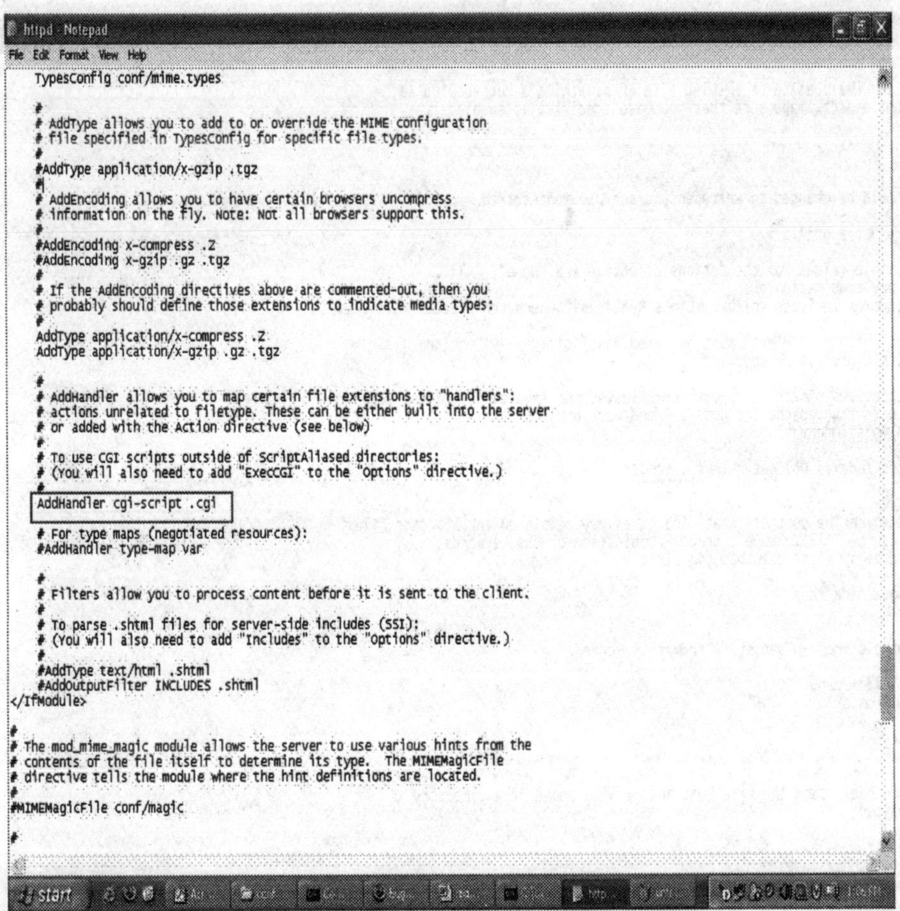

```
    TypesConfig conf/mime.types

    #
    # AddType allows you to add to or override the MIME configuration
    # file specified in TypesConfig for specific file types.
    #
    #AddType application/x-gzip .tgz
    #
    # AddEncoding allows you to have certain browsers uncompress
    # information on the fly. Note: Not all browsers support this.
    #
    #AddEncoding x-compress .Z
    #AddEncoding x-gzip .gz .tgz
    #
    # If the AddEncoding directives above are commented-out, then you
    # probably should define those extensions to indicate media types:
    #
    AddType application/x-compress .Z
    AddType application/x-gzip .gz .tgz

    #
    # AddHandler allows you to map certain file extensions to "handlers":
    # actions unrelated to filetype. These can be either built into the server
    # or added with the Action directive (see below)
    #
    # To use CGI scripts outside of ScriptAliased directories:
    # (You will also need to add "ExecCGI" to the "Options" directive.)
    #
    AddHandler cgi-script .cgi

    # For type maps (negotiated resources):
    #AddHandler type-map var

    #
    # Filters allow you to process content before it is sent to the client.
    #
    # To parse .shtml files for server-side includes (SSI):
    # (You will also need to add "Includes" to the "Options" directive.)
    #
    #AddType text/html .shtml
    #AddOutputFilter INCLUDES .shtml
</IfModule>

#
# The mod_mime_magic module allows the server to use various hints from the
# contents of the file itself to determine its type.  The MIMEMagicFile
# directive tells the module where the hint definitions are located.
#
#MIMEMagicFile conf/magic

#
```

And allow .cgi scripts in the Bugzilla directory by adding the ExecCGI option. We also need to allow Bugzilla's .htaccess file to restrict access to sensitive documents by allowing it to override the defaults. This involves changing AllowOverride None to AllowOverride All. Apache also needs to know to use Perl to execute .cgi files, via the ScriptInterpreterSource directive.

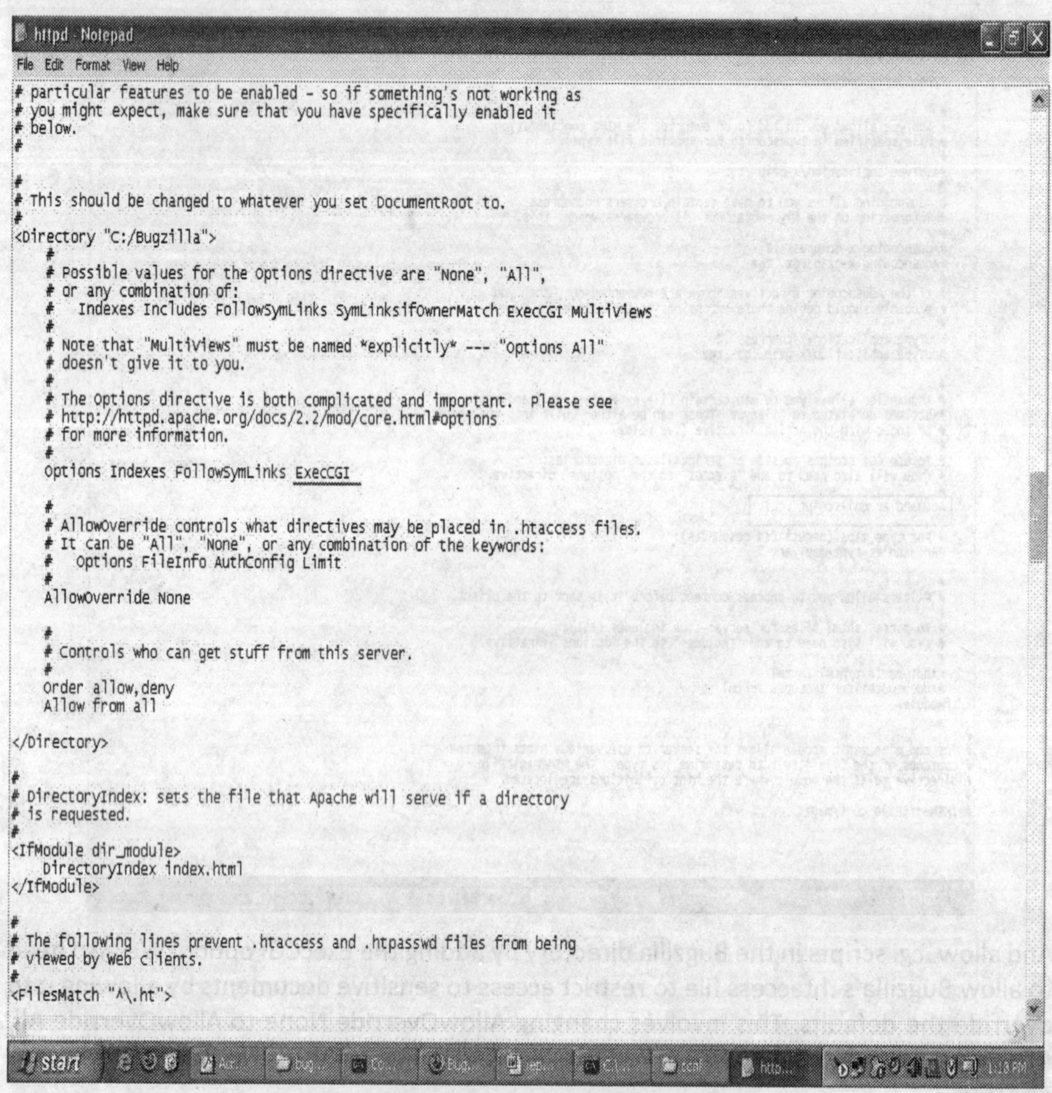

```
# particular features to be enabled - so if something's not working as
# you might expect, make sure that you have specifically enabled it
# below.
#

#
# This should be changed to whatever you set DocumentRoot to.
#
<Directory "C:/Bugzilla">
    #
    # Possible values for the Options directive are "None", "All",
    # or any combination of:
    #   Indexes Includes FollowSymLinks SymLinksifOwnerMatch ExecCGI MultiViews
    #
    # Note that "MultiViews" must be named *explicitly* --- "Options All"
    # doesn't give it to you.
    #
    # The Options directive is both complicated and important.  Please see
    # http://httpd.apache.org/docs/2.2/mod/core.html#options
    # for more information.
    #
    Options Indexes FollowSymLinks ExecCGI

    #
    # AllowOverride controls what directives may be placed in .htaccess files.
    # It can be "All", "None", or any combination of the keywords:
    #   Options FileInfo AuthConfig Limit
    #
    AllowOverride None

    #
    # Controls who can get stuff from this server.
    #
    Order allow,deny
    Allow from all

</Directory>

#
# DirectoryIndex: sets the file that Apache will serve if a directory
# is requested.
#
<IfModule dir_module>
    DirectoryIndex index.html
</IfModule>

#
# The following lines prevent .htaccess and .htpasswd files from being
# viewed by Web clients.
#
<FilesMatch "^\.ht">
```

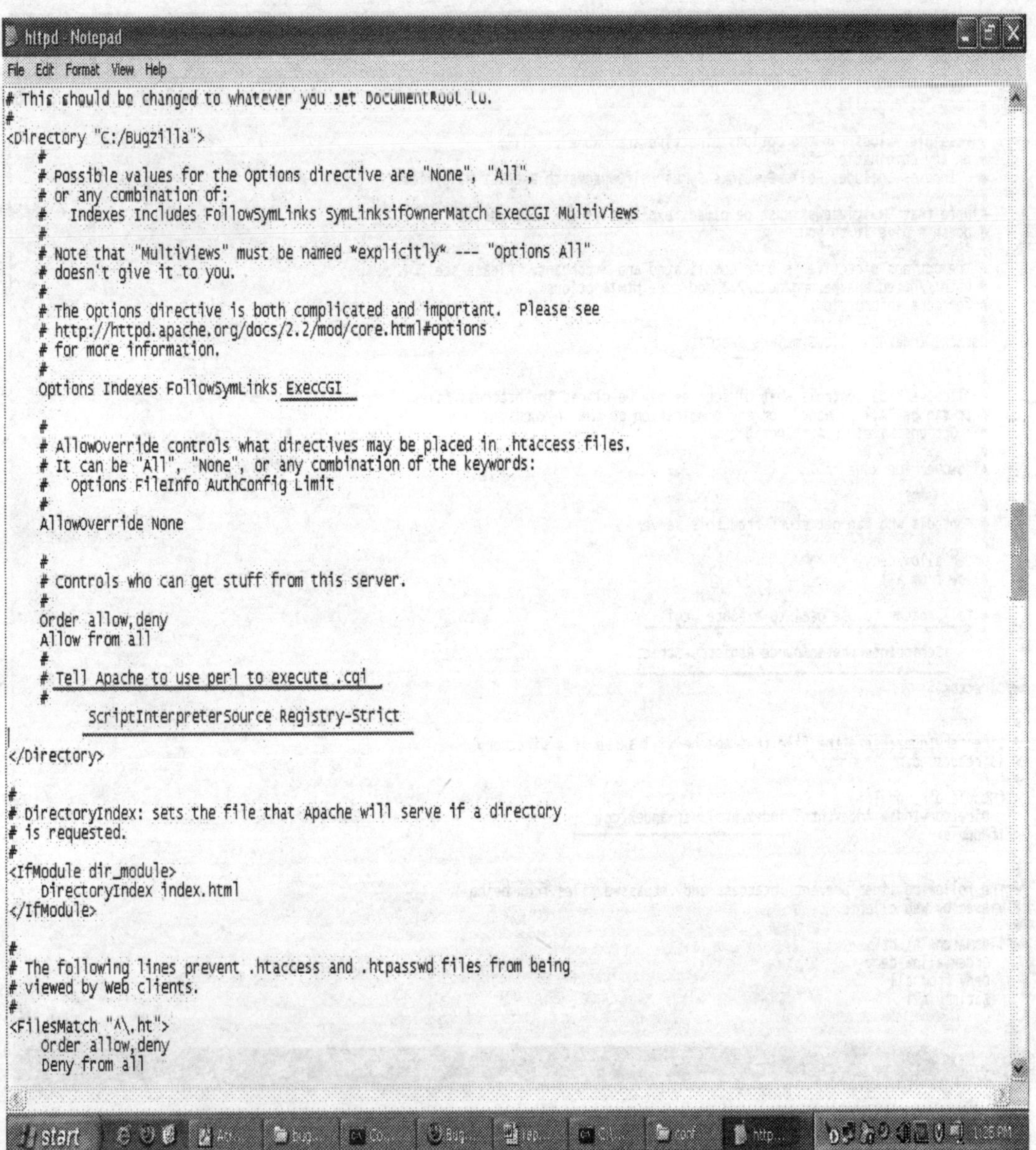

httpd - Notepad

```
# This should be changed to whatever you set DocumentRoot to.
#
<Directory "C:/Bugzilla">
    #
    # Possible values for the Options directive are "None", "All",
    # or any combination of:
    #   Indexes Includes FollowSymLinks SymLinksifOwnerMatch ExecCGI MultiViews
    #
    # Note that "MultiViews" must be named *explicitly* --- "Options All"
    # doesn't give it to you.
    #
    # The Options directive is both complicated and important.  Please see
    # http://httpd.apache.org/docs/2.2/mod/core.html#options
    # for more information.
    #
    Options Indexes FollowSymLinks ExecCGI

    #
    # AllowOverride controls what directives may be placed in .htaccess files.
    # It can be "All", "None", or any combination of the keywords:
    #   Options FileInfo AuthConfig Limit
    #
    AllowOverride None

    #
    # Controls who can get stuff from this server.
    #
    Order allow,deny
    Allow from all
    #
    # Tell Apache to use perl to execute .cgi
    #
        ScriptInterpreterSource Registry-Strict

</Directory>

#
# DirectoryIndex: sets the file that Apache will serve if a directory
# is requested.
#
<IfModule dir_module>
    DirectoryIndex index.html
</IfModule>

#
# The following lines prevent .htaccess and .htpasswd files from being
# viewed by Web clients.
#
<FilesMatch "^\.ht">
    Order allow,deny
    Deny from all
```

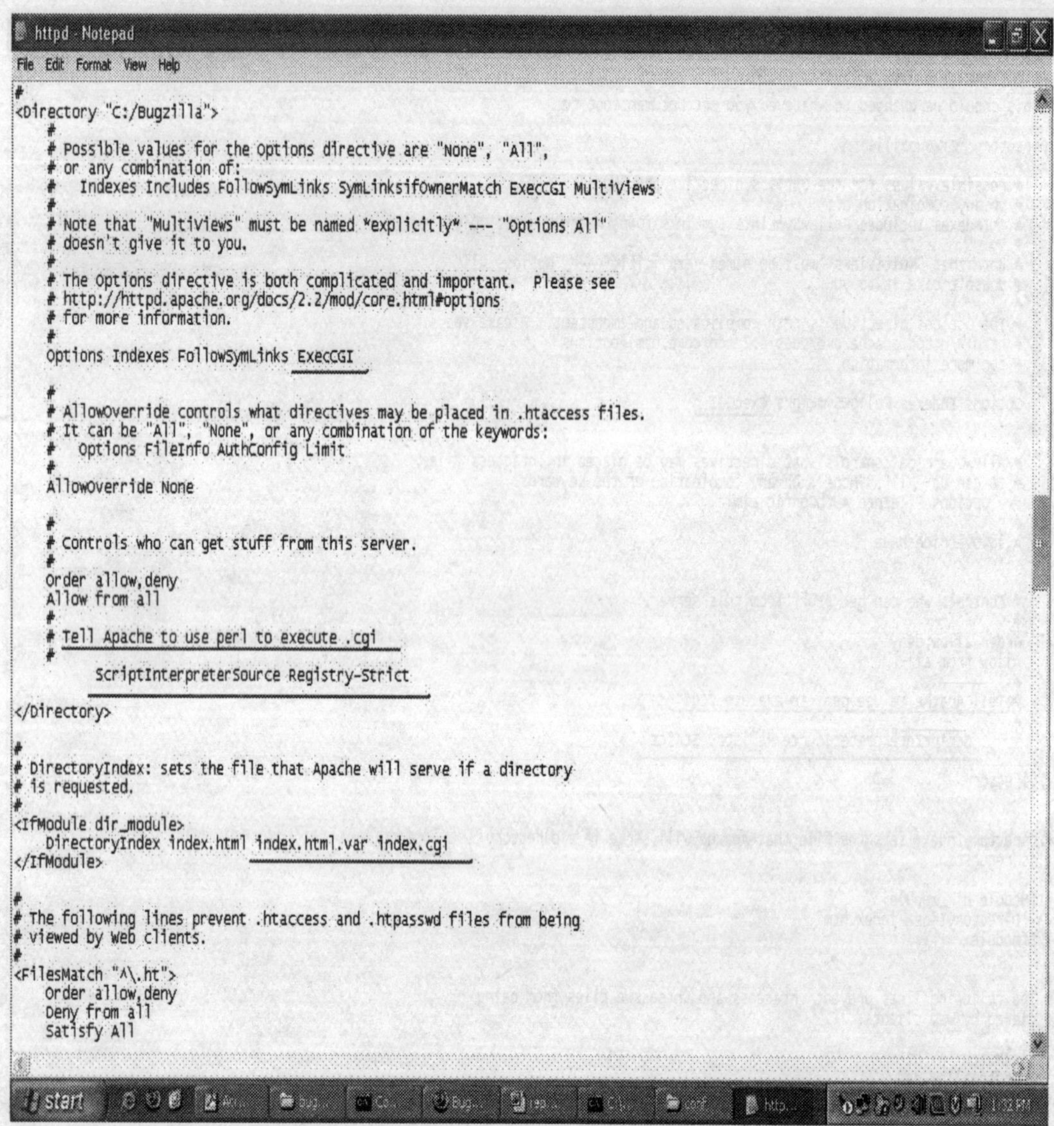


```
#
<Directory "C:/Bugzilla">
    #
    # Possible values for the Options directive are "None", "All",
    # or any combination of:
    #   Indexes Includes FollowSymLinks SymLinksifOwnerMatch ExecCGI MultiViews
    #
    # Note that "MultiViews" must be named *explicitly* --- "Options All"
    # doesn't give it to you.
    #
    # The Options directive is both complicated and important.  Please see
    # http://httpd.apache.org/docs/2.2/mod/core.html#options
    # for more information.
    #
    Options Indexes FollowSymLinks ExecCGI

    #
    # AllowOverride controls what directives may be placed in .htaccess files.
    # It can be "All", "None", or any combination of the keywords:
    #   Options FileInfo AuthConfig Limit
    #
    AllowOverride None

    #
    # Controls who can get stuff from this server.
    #
    Order allow,deny
    Allow from all
    #
    # Tell Apache to use perl to execute .cgi
    #
        ScriptInterpreterSource Registry-Strict
</Directory>

#
# DirectoryIndex: sets the file that Apache will serve if a directory
# is requested.
#
<IfModule dir_module>
    DirectoryIndex index.html index.html.var index.cgi
</IfModule>

#
# The following lines prevent .htaccess and .htpasswd files from being
# viewed by Web clients.
#
<FilesMatch "^\.ht">
    Order allow,deny
    Deny from all
    Satisfy All
```

You also should add index.cgi to the DirectoryIndex list.

```
#
<Directory "C:/Bugzilla">
  #
  # Possible values for the Options directive are "None", "All",
  # or any combination of:
  #   Indexes Includes FollowSymLinks SymLinksifOwnerMatch ExecCGI MultiViews
  #
  # Note that "MultiViews" must be named *explicitly* --- "Options All"
  # doesn't give it to you.
  #
  # The Options directive is both complicated and important.  Please see
  # http://httpd.apache.org/docs/2.2/mod/core.html#options
  # for more information.
  #
  Options Indexes FollowSymLinks ExecCGI

  #
  # AllowOverride controls what directives may be placed in .htaccess files.
  # It can be "All", "None", or any combination of the keywords:
  #   Options FileInfo AuthConfig Limit
  #
  AllowOverride All

  #
  # Controls who can get stuff from this server.
  #
  Order allow,deny
  Allow from all
  #
  # Tell Apache to use perl to execute .cgi
  #
      ScriptInterpreterSource Registry-Strict

</Directory>

#
# DirectoryIndex: sets the file that Apache will serve if a directory
# is requested.
#
<IfModule dir_module>
   DirectoryIndex index.html index.html.var index.cgi
</IfModule>
```

In order for ScriptInterpreterSource Registry-Strict to work, you also need to add an entry to the Registry so Apache will use Perl to execute .cgi files. Create a key HKEY_CLASSES_ROOT\.cgi\Shell\ExecCGI\Command with the default value of the full path of perl.exe with a -T parameter. For exampleC:\Perl\bin\perl.exe –T Type regedit in command prompt, you can see the Registry Editor:

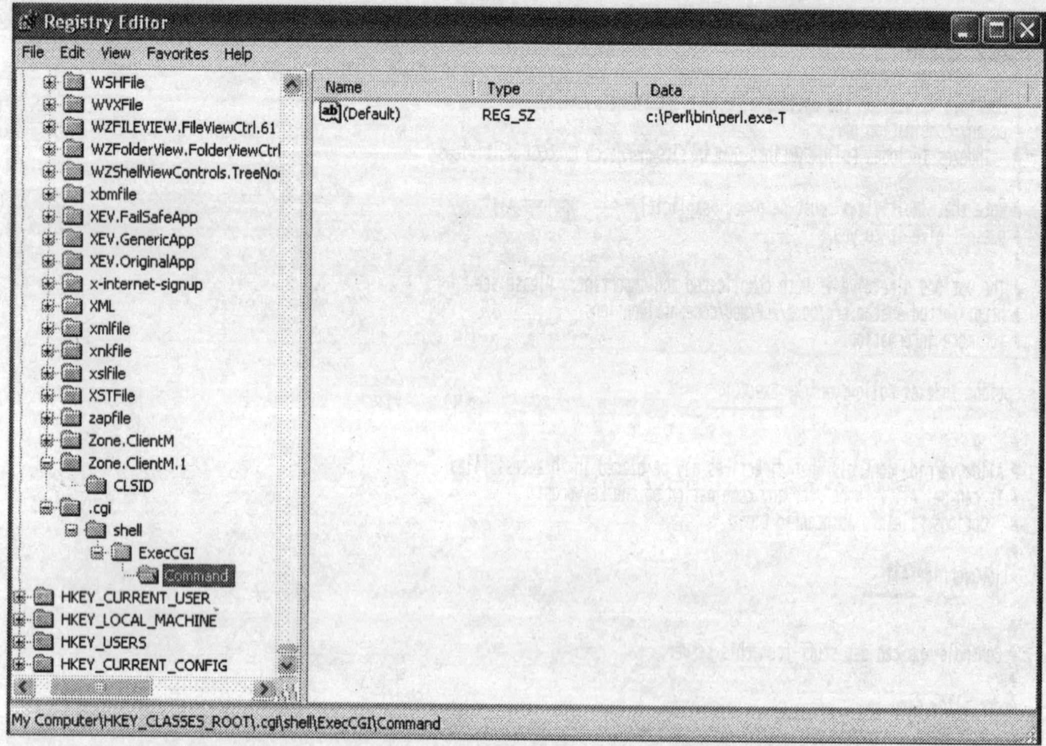

Finally, restart Apache to get it to pick up the changes. While Bugzilla has built in support for SMTP servers, it doesn't (yet) support SMTP authentication or debugging of SMTP errors. If you require SMTP authentiation (including POP before SMTP), you can use Glob's sendmail wrapper. Download and install as per the instructions on that site.If you enable logging inSendmail, you need to ensure that your Apache account has write access to C:\usr\lib.Configure Bugzillachecksetup.pl Runchecksetup.pl. This will check your Perl modules and create localconfig.

```
C:\>cd bugzilla
C:\bugzilla>perl checksetup.pl
Checking perl modules ...
Checking for       AppConfig (v1.52)   ok: found v1.55
Checking for             CGI (v2.93)   ok: found v3.10
Checking for    Data::Dumper (any)     ok: found v2.121_04
Checking for    Date::Format (v2.21)   ok: found v2.22
Checking for             DBI (v1.38)   ok: found v1.48
Checking for      File::Spec (v0.84)   ok: found v3.05
Checking for      File::Temp (any)     ok: found v0.16
Checking for        Template (v2.08)   ok: found v2.13
Checking for      Text::Wrap (v2001.0131) ok: found v2001.09293
Checking for    Mail::Mailer (v1.65)   ok: found v1.67
Checking for        Storable (any)     ok: found v2.13
The following Perl modules are optional:
Checking for              GD (v1.20)   ok: found v2.16
Checking for     Chart::Base (v1.0)    ok: found v2.3
Checking for     XML::Parser (any)     ok: found v2.34
Checking for       GD::Graph (any)     ok: found v1.43
Checking for GD::Text::Align (any)     ok: found v1.18
Checking for     PatchReader (v0.9.4)  ok: found v0.9.5
Most ActivePerl modules are available at Apache's ppm repository.
A list of mirrors is available at
    http://www.apache.org/dyn/closer.cgi/perl/win32-bin/ppms/
You can add the repository with the following command:
    ppm rep add apache http://www.apache.org/dist/perl/win32-bin/ppms/

Checking user setup ...
This version of Bugzilla contains some variables that you may want
to change and adapt to your local settings. Please edit the file
'./localconfig' and rerun checksetup.pl
The following variables are new to localconfig since you last ran
checksetup.pl:   index_html cvsbin interdiffbin diffpath
create_htaccess
webservergroup db_driver db_host db_pass db_sock db_check
C:\bugzilla>
```

Depending upon the Bugzilla version, Bugzilla requires additional Perl modules which we need to be install. For bugzilla 3.0 the following modules are Installed.

1. E-Mail-Send
2. Email-Address.ppd
3. Email-Simple.ppd
4. Module-Pluggable
5. Test-Simple
6. Return-Value
7.Email-MIME-Modifier
8. Email-MIME.ppd
9. Email-MIME-ContentType.ppd
10. /Email-MIME-Encodings

11. MIME-Base64.ppd
12. Email-MessageID.ppd
13. Email-MIME-Creator
14. Email-Reply

The following are the sites where you will be getting the required modules(almost) http://ppm4.activestate.com/PPMPackages/zips/8xx-builds-only/Windows/http://ppm.tcool.org/archives/How to identify required modules for Bugzilla: Click command prompt and Go to Bugzilla Directory (cd Bugzilla) type checksetup.pl. The checksetup.pl script will check the required modules for Bugzilla and mentioning the required perl modules to install. Download the modules from the following sites:

http://ppm4.activestate.com/PPMPackages/zips/8xx-builds-only/Windows/

http://ppm.tcool.org/archives/

```
C:\>cd bugzilla
C:\bugzilla>perl checksetup.pl
Checking perl modules ...
Checking for       AppConfig (v1.52)   ok: found v1.55
Checking for             CGI (v2.93)   ok: found v3.10
Checking for    Data::Dumper (any)     ok: found v2.121_04
Checking for    Date::Format (v2.21)   ok: found v2.22
Checking for             DBI (v1.38)   ok: found v1.48
Checking for      File::Spec (v0.84)   ok: found v3.05
Checking for      File::Temp (any)     ok: found v0.16
Checking for        Template (v2.08)   ok: found v2.13
Checking for      Text::Wrap (v2001.0131) ok: found v2001.09293
Checking for    Mail::Mailer (v1.65)   ok: found v1.67
Checking for        Storable (any)     ok: found v2.13
The following Perl modules are optional:
Checking for              GD (v1.20)   ok: found v2.16
Checking for     Chart::Base (v1.0)    ok: found v2.3
Checking for     XML::Parser (any)     ok: found v2.34
Checking for       GD::Graph (any)     ok: found v1.43
Checking for GD::Text::Align (any)     ok: found v1.18
Checking for     PatchReader (v0.9.4)  ok: found v0.9.5
Most ActivePerl modules are available at Apache's ppm repository.
A list of mirrors is available at
    http://www.apache.org/dyn/closer.cgi/perl/win32-bin/ppms/
You can add the repository with the following command:
    ppm rep add apache http://www.apache.org/dist/perl/win32-bin/ppms/

Checking user setup ...
This version of Bugzilla contains some variables that you may want
to change and adapt to your local settings. Please edit the file
'./localconfig' and rerun checksetup.pl
The following variables are new to localconfig since you last ran
checksetup.pl:   index_html cvsbin interdiffbin diffpath
create_htaccess
webservergroup db_driver db_host db_pass db_sock db_check
C:\bugzilla>
```

Edit localconfig Open C:\Bugzilla\localconfig in your favourite text editor to configure Bugzilla.

You have to tell Bugzilla how to access your database. If you used bugs/bugs, you'll only have to set db_pass.

```
# Enter your database password here. It's normally advisable to specify
# a password for your bugzilla database user.
# If you use apostrophe (') or a backslash (\) in your password, you'll
# need to escape it by preceding it with a '\' character. (\') or (\)
# (Far simpler just not to use those characters.)
';
$db_pass = 'sockmonkey';
```

checksetup.pl Run checksetup.plagain. This time it will build your database tables and initialize Bugzilla.

```
C:\Documents and Settings>cd..

C:\>cd bugzilla

C:\bugzilla>perl checksetup.pl
* This is Bugzilla 3.6 on perl 5.8.9
* Running on WinXP/.Net Build 2600 (Service Pack 2)

Checking perl modules...
Checking for              CGI.pm (v3.21)    ok: found v3.49
Checking for          Digest-SHA (any)      ok: found v5.48
Checking for            TimeDate (v2.21)    ok: found v2.24
Checking for            DateTime (v0.28)    ok: found v0.55
Checking for   DateTime-TimeZone (v0.79)    ok: found v1.19
Checking for                 DBI (v1.41)    ok: found v1.611
Checking for    Template-Toolkit (v2.22)    ok: found v2.22
Checking for          Email-Send (v2.16)    ok: found v2.198
Checking for          Email-MIME (v1.861)   ok: found v1.903
Checking for Email-MIME-Encodings (v1.313)  ok: found v1.313
Checking for Email-MIME-Modifier (v1.442)   ok: found v1.903
Checking for                 URI (any)      ok: found v1.54

Checking available perl DBD modules...
Checking for              DBD-Pg (v1.45)    ok: found v2.17.1
Checking for           DBD-mysql (v4.00)    ok: found v4.005
Checking for          DBD-Oracle (v1.19)    ok: found v1.21

The following Perl modules are optional:
Checking for                  GD (v1.20)    ok: found v2.45
Checking for               Chart (v2.1)     ok: found v2.3
Checking for         Template-GD (any)      ok: found v1.56
Checking for          GDTextUtil (any)      ok: found v0.86
Checking for             GDGraph (any)      ok: found v1.44
Checking for            XML-Twig (any)      ok: found v3.35
Checking for          MIME-tools (v5.406)   ok: found v5.428
Checking for         libwww-perl (any)      ok: found v5.834
Checking for         PatchReader (v0.9.4)   ok: found v0.9.5
Checking for           perl-ldap (any)      ok: found v0.4001
Checking for         Authen-SASL (any)      ok: found v2.1401
Checking for          RadiusPerl (any)      ok: found v0.17
Checking for           SOAP-Lite (v0.710.06) ok: found v0.711
Checking for            JSON-RPC (any)      ok: found v0.96
Checking for          Test-Taint (any)      ok: found v1.04
Checking for         HTML-Parser (v3.40)    ok: found v3.65
Checking for       HTML-Scrubber (any)      ok: found v0.08
Checking for Email-MIME-Attachment-Stripper (any)     ok: found v1.316
Checking for         Email-Reply (any)      ok: found v1.202
Checking for        TheSchwartz (any)       ok: found v1.03
Checking for      Daemon-Generic (any)      ok: found v0.61
Checking for            mod_perl (v1.999022) ok: found v2.000004
```

```
Checking for    MySQL Server (v3.23.41) ok: found v4.0.20a-debug
Creating table user_group_map ...
Creating table series_data ...
Creating table longdescs ...
Creating table dependencies ...
Creating table components ...
Creating table keywords ...
Creating table cc ...
Creating table duplicates ...
Creating table groups ...
Creating table flagtypes ...
Creating table profiles ...
Creating table products ...
Creating table bugs_activity ...
Creating table series_categories ...
Creating table keyworddefs ...
Creating table fielddefs ...
Creating table group_control_map ...
Creating table profiles_activity ...
Creating table group_group_map ...
Creating table user_series_map ...
Creating table bugs ...
Creating table series ...
Creating table versions ...
```

```
Creating table flagexclusions ...
Creating table logincookies ...
Creating table match ...
Creating table bug_group_map ...
Creating table votes ...
Creating table attachments ...
Creating table flags ...
Creating table milestones ...
Creating table tokens ...
Creating table flaginclusions ...
Creating table quips ...
Creating table namedqueries ...
Creating initial dummy product 'TestProduct' ...
Populating duplicates table...
Creating duplicates directory...
Migrating old chart data into database ...
Adding group tweakparams ...
Adding group editusers ...
Adding group creategroups ...
Adding group editcomponents ...
Adding group editkeywords ...
Adding group admin ...
Adding group editbugs ...
Adding group canconfirm ...

Looks like we don't have an administrator set up yet.  Either this is your
first time using Bugzilla, or your administrator's privileges might have
accidently been deleted.
Enter the e-mail address of the administrator: usha.kannappan@symphonysv.com
You entered 'byron@example.com'.  Is this correct? [Y/n] y
Enter the real name of the administrator: usha

Enter a password for the administrator account: sundari0-8

Please retype the password to verify: sundari0-8

'usha.kannappan@symphonysv.com' is now set up as an administrator account.

C:\bugzilla>
```

Parameters

You should now be able to log into to Bugzilla using the account checksetup.pl just created. Point your web browser to http://localhost/,choose Log in to an existing account, and login. Configuring Sendmail for Bugzilla:Download the sendmail from the following site: http://www.glob.com.au/sendmail/ about sendmail.exe is a simple windows console application that emulates sendmail's "-t" option to deliver emails piped via stdin. it is intended to ease running unix code that has /usr/lib/sendmail hardcoded as an email delivery means.

it doesn't support deferred delivery, and requires an smtp server to perform the actual delivery of the messages.

install

- download sendmail.zip
- copysendmail.exe and sendmail.ini to\usr\lib on the drive where the windows (Bugzilla) application is installed

  eg. if your application is installed inc:\bugzilla,sendmail.exe and sendmail.ini need to be copied to c:\usr\lib\sendmail.exe and c:\usr\lib\sendmail.ini.

- configure smtp server and default domain in sendmail.ini

  or

  download the installer (for bugzilla installs)

- C:\usr\lib\sendmail.ini" and Give the appropriate information of your mail Go to the "server smtp_server=" the machine where you installed Bugzilla mail ip address" smtp_port=25 default_domain="The server machine mail IP Address"

  Install IIS on your system. And create default Virtual SMTP

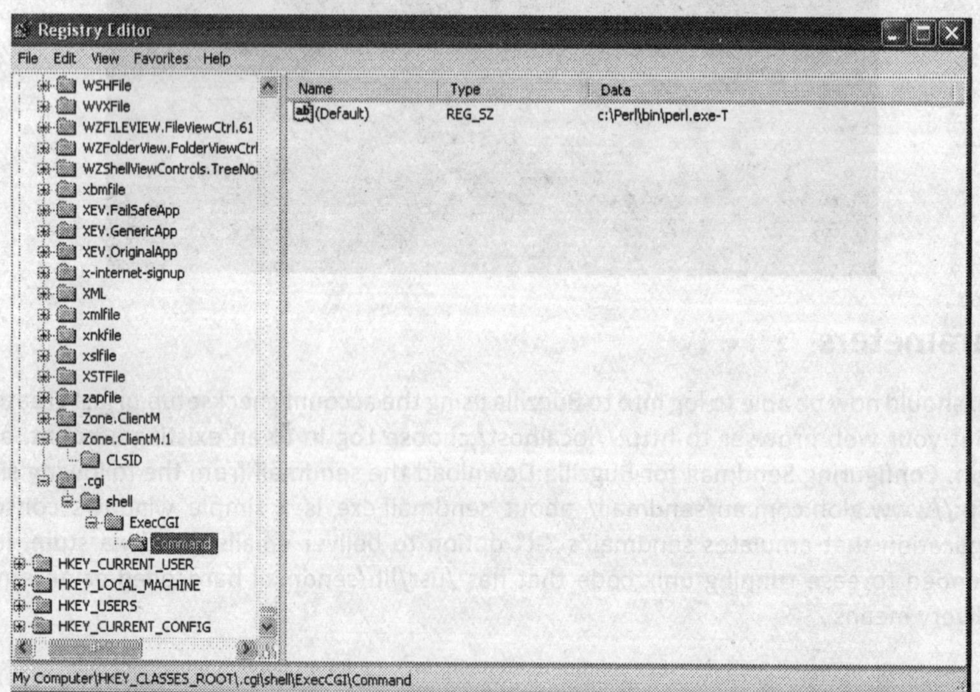

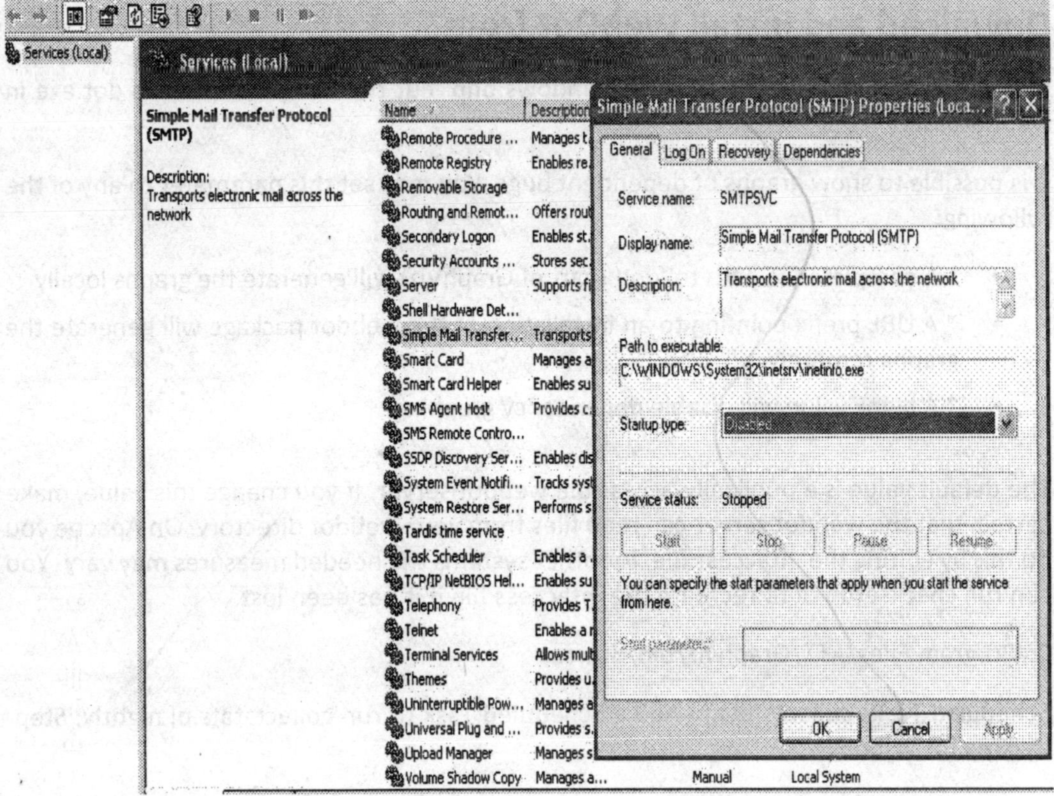

Parameters

You should now be able to log into to Bugzilla using the account checksetup.pl Just created. Point your web browser to http://localhost/, choose Log in to an existing account , and login. In the page footer, choose Parameters. Put in your email address as the maintainer.

Put in the URL to Bugzilla in the urlbase field. This URL will be used in emails, so don't use localhost.

urlbase:

The URL that is the common initial leading part of all Bugzilla URLs.
http://bugzilla.example.com/

Download and install WebDot from

http://www.graphviz.org/Download_windows.php. Put the complete path to dot.exe in webdotbase.

It is possible to show graphs of dependent bugs. You may set this parameter to any of the following:

- * A complete file path to 'dot' (part of GraphViz) will generate the graphs locally.
- * A URL prefix pointing to an installation of the webdot package will generate the graphs remotely.
- * A blank value will disable dependency graphing.

The default value is a publically-accessible webdot server. If you change this value, make certain that the webdot server can read files from your webdot directory. On Apache you do this by editing the .htaccess file, for other systems the needed measures may vary. You can run checksetup.pl to recreate the .htaccess file if it has been lost.

C:/Program Files/ATT/Graphviz/bin/dot.exe

Scheduled Tasks collectstats.pl Add a Scheduled Task to run collectstats.pl nightly. Step-by-step for Windows XP:

1. Control Panel --> Scheduled Tasks --> Add Scheduled Task
2. Next
3. Browse
4. Find perl.exe(normally C:\Perl\bin\perl.exe)
5. Give it a name, such as "Bugzilla Collect Stats"
6. Perfom the task daily at your desired time
7. If you're running Apache as a user, not as SYSTEM, enter that user here. Otherwise you're best off creating an account that has write access to the Bugzilla directory and using that
8. Tick "Open Advanced Properties.." and click Finish
9. Append the script name to the end of the "Run" field. eg C:\Perl\bin\perl.exe C:\Bugzilla\collectstats.pl
10. Change "start in" to the Bugzilla directory whineatnews.pl

Add a Scheduled Task to run

whineatnews.pl nightly.

The steps for setting up whineatnews.pl are as per collectstats.pl whine.pl

Add a Scheduled Task to run whine.pl nightly. The steps for setting up whine.pl are as per collectstats.pl, except whine.pl needs to run in Perl's Taint mode. The command line needs to include the -T option:

C:\Perl\bin\perl.exe -T C:\Bugzilla\whine.pl

Backing up Bugzilla

You may want to backup the entire Bugzilla directory. It's small and you'll get all your settings and customisations on your backup media. The most important component of Bugzilla to backup is the Bugzilla Database. It contains all your Bugs, Users, Attachments, pretty well everything. Like most databases, backups with MySql are performed by generating a dump of the database and backing up the dump. Schedule the mysqldump utility to create the dump, and add the resulting file to your backup media. You'll find MySql's mysqldump documentation at http://dev.mysql.com/doc/mysql/en/mysqldump.html.

Congratulations, the Bugzilla installation process is complete!

Features

1. Custom Fields
2. mod_perl Support
3. Attachments and Flags on New Bugs
4. Custom Resolutions
5. Per-Product Permissions
6. User Interface Improvements
7. XML-RPC Interface
8. Skins
9. Unchangeable Fields Appear Unchangeable
10. All Emails in Templates
11. No More Double-Filed Bugs
12. Default CC List for Components
13. File/Modify Bugs By Email
14. Users Who Get All Bug Notifications
15. Improved UTF-8 Support
16. mproved UTF-8 Suppor
17. Automatic Update Notification
18. Welcome Page for New Installs
19. QuickSearch Plugin for IE7 and Firefox 2

Bugzilla Lifecycle

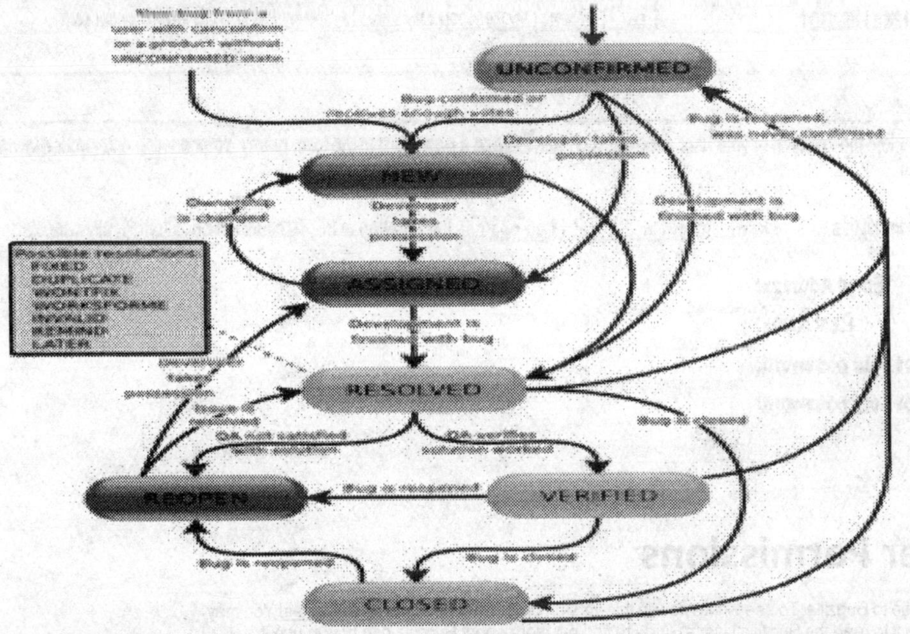

Bugzilla – Main Page

Home | New | Search | [ ] Find | Reports | Requests | New Account | Log In

This is Bugzilla (beta) at XAVIENT INFORMATION SYSTESMS

Welcome to Bugzilla. To see what's new in this version of Bugzilla, see the release notes! You may also want to read the Bugzilla User's Guide to find out more about Bugzilla and how to use it.

Most common actions:

Search existing bug reports
Enter a new bug report
Summary reports and charts

Login:
Password:
☑ Restrict this session to this IP address (using this option improves security)

Login [Forgot my Password]

Open a new Bugzilla account

Add to Sidebar (requires a Mozilla browser like Mozilla Firefox)
Install the Quick Search plugin (requires Firefox 2 or Internet Explorer 7)

Create user

- For creation of new account, first user has to submit his email address to administrator.
- Administrator provides him the link to create a password with email address as a user name.

Bugzilla – Create a new user account

Home | New | Search | [ ] Find | Reports | My Requests | My Votes | Preferences | Log out aroy@xavient.com

This is Bugzilla (beta)

To complete the creation of your user account, you must choose a password in the form below. You can also enter your real name, which optional.

If you don't fill this form before October 8th, 2007 at 11:56 +33000, the creation of this account will be automatically canceled.

Email Address:
Real Name:
Type your password:
Re-type your password:
Send

User Permissions

Welcome to Bugzilla. To see what's new in this version of Bugzilla, see the release notes! You may also want to read the Bugzilla User's Guide to find out more about Bugzilla and how to use it.

Most common actions:

Search existing bug reports
Enter a new bug report
Summary reports and charts

Change password or user preferences
Log out aroy@xavient.com

Add to Sidebar (requires a Mozilla browser like Mozilla Firefox)
Install the Quick Search plugin (requires Firefox 2 or Internet Explorer 7)

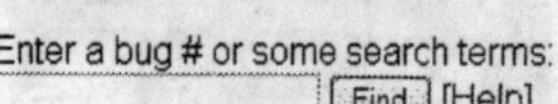

Enter a bug # or some search terms:
Find [Help]

Actions: Home | New | Search | [ ] Find | Reports | My Requests | My Votes | Preferences | Log out aroy@xavient.com
Edit: Parameters | User Preferences | Sanity Check | Users | Classifications | Products | Flags | Custom Fields | Field Valu | Groups | Keywords | Whining
Saved Searches: My Bugs

Group access: **Can turn these bits on for other users**
| **User is a member of these groups**
[☑] ☑ **admin:** Administrators
[☐] ☑ **bz_canusewhineatothers:** Can configure whine reports for other users
[☐] ☑ **bz_canusewhines:** User can configure whine reports for self
[☐] ☑ **bz_sudoers:** Can perform actions as other users
[☐] ☑ **bz_sudo_protect:** Can not be impersonated by other users
[☐] ☑ **canconfirm:** Can confirm a bug or mark it a duplicate
[☐] ☑ **creategroups:** Can create and destroy groups
[☐]* ☐* **editbugs:** Can edit all bug fields
[☐] ☑ **editclassifications:** Can create, destroy, and edit classifications
[☐] ☑ **editcomponents:** Can create, destroy, and edit components
[☐] ☑ **editkeywords:** Can create, destroy, and edit keywords
[☐] ☑ **editusers:** Can edit or disable users
[☐] [☐] **first one:** Access to bugs in the first one product
[☐] [☐] **Industrial Automation System:** Access to bugs in the Industrial Automation System product

Search Bug

Welcome to Bugzilla. To see what's new in this version of Bugzilla, see the release notes! You may also want to read the Bugzilla User's Guide to find out more about Bugzilla and how to use it.

Most common actions:

Search existing bug reports
Enter a new bug report
Summary reports and charts

Change password or user preferences
Log out aroy@xavient.com

Add to Sidebar (requires a Mozilla browser like Mozilla Firefox)
Install the Quick Search plugin (requires Firefox 2 or Internet Explorer 7)

Find a Specific Bug | Advanced Search

Give me some help (reloads page).

Summary: contains all of the words/strings [ ] Search

Classification:	**Product:**	**Component:**	**Version:**	**Target:**
test2 Beta Proj1 Gaming	mobile gaming pc gaming	functional language UI	unspecified	—

A Comment: contains the string
The URL: contains all of the words/strings
Deadline: from [ ] to [ ] (YYYY-MM-DD)

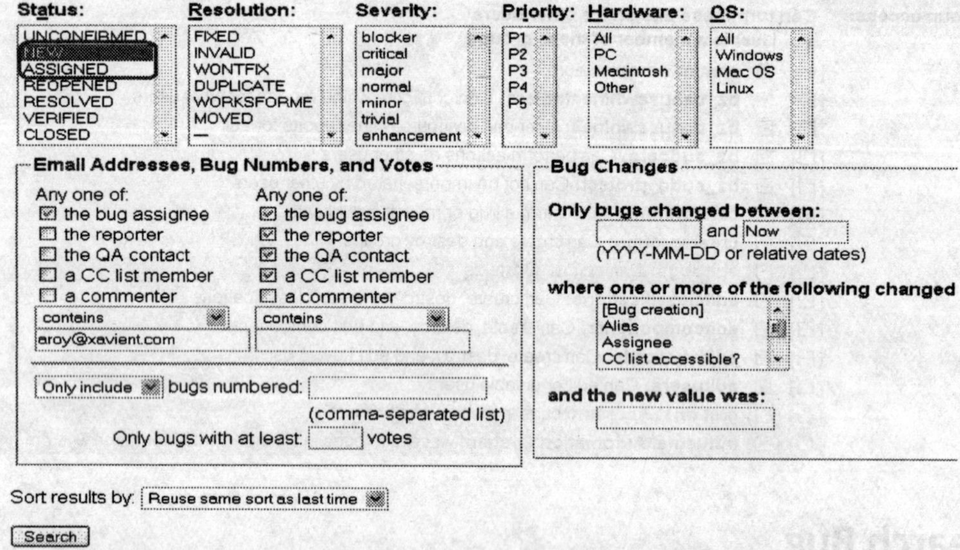
Status:
UNCONFIRMED
NEW
ASSIGNED
REOPENED
RESOLVED
VERIFIED
CLOSED
Resolution:
FIXED
INVALID
WONTFIX
DUPLICATE
WORKSFORME
MOVED
Severity:
blocker
critical
major
normal
minor
trivial
enhancement
Priority:
P1
P2
P3
P4
P5
Hardware:
All
PC
Macintosh
Other
OS:
All
Windows
Mac OS
Linux
Email Addresses, Bug Numbers, and Votes
Any one of:
the bug assignee
the reporter
the QA contact
a CC list member
a commenter
contains
aroy@xavient.com
Only include
bugs numbered:
(comma-separated list)
Only bugs with at least:
votes
Bug Changes
Only bugs changed between:
and Now
(YYYY-MM-DD or relative dates)
where one or more of the following changed
[Bug creation]
Alias
Assignee
CC list accessible?
and the new value was:
Sort results by:
Reuse same sort as last time
Search

New Bug

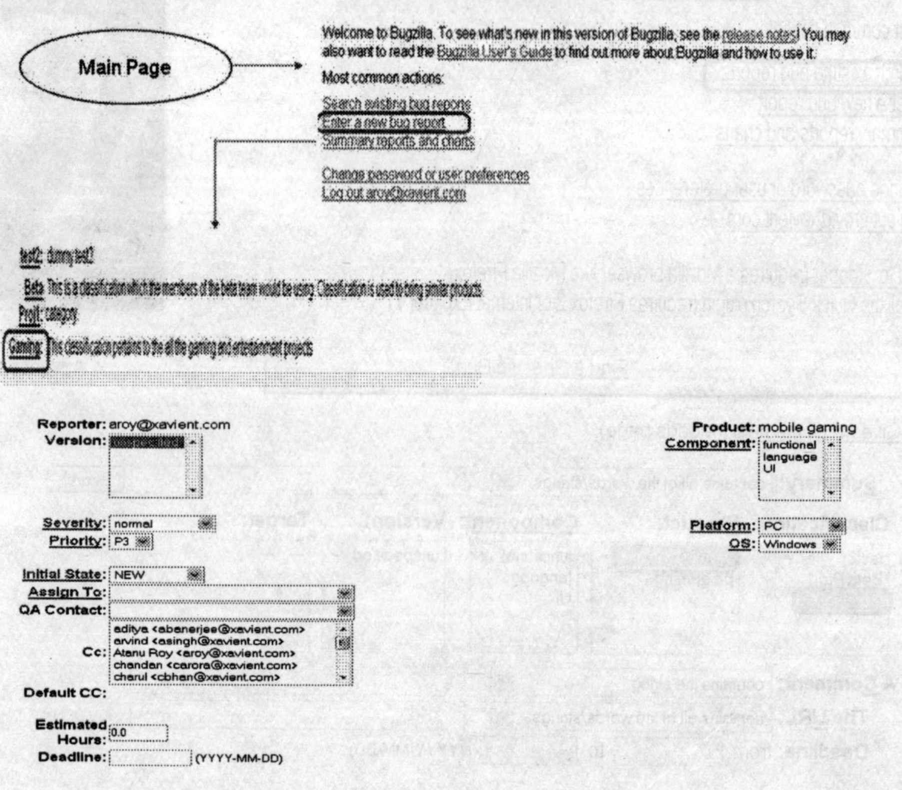
Main Page
Welcome to Bugzilla. To see what's new in this version of Bugzilla, see the release notes! You may also want to read the Bugzilla User's Guide to find out more about Bugzilla and how to use it.
Most common actions:
Search existing bug reports
Enter a new bug report
Summary reports and charts
Change password or user preferences
Log out aroy@xavient.com
Beta: This is a classification which the members of the beta team would be using. Classification is used to bring similar products.
Projt: category
Gaming: This classification pertains to the all the gaming and entertainment projects
Reporter: aroy@xavient.com
Version:
Product: mobile gaming
Component:
functional
language
UI
Severity: normal
Priority: P3
Platform: PC
OS: Windows
Initial State: NEW
Assign To:
QA Contact:
Cc:
aditya <abanerjee@xavient.com>
arvind <asingh@xavient.com>
Atanu Roy <aroy@xavient.com>
chandan <carora@xavient.com>
charul <cbhan@xavient.com>
Default CC:
Estimated Hours: 0.0
Deadline:
(YYYY-MM-DD)

- QA Contact: User responsible for quality assurance of this bug
- Deadline: This field shows the deadline for this bug.
- Estimated Hours: This field shows the original estimated time.

URL: http://
Iteration: —
Summary:
Description:

Initial Description is Private

Attachment: Add an attachment
Depends on:
Blocks:

Only users in all of the selected groups can view this bug:
(Leave all boxes unchecked to make this a public bug.)

Access to bugs in the mobile gaming product

Commit | Remember values as bookmarkable template

- Depends on: This field gives dependency of this bug on the bug specified.
- Blocks: This field specifies the bug which is prevented from being fixed until this bug is fixed
- Selecting the Commit button results into submission of bug and simultaneously an mail is send to the QA contacts of the bug.

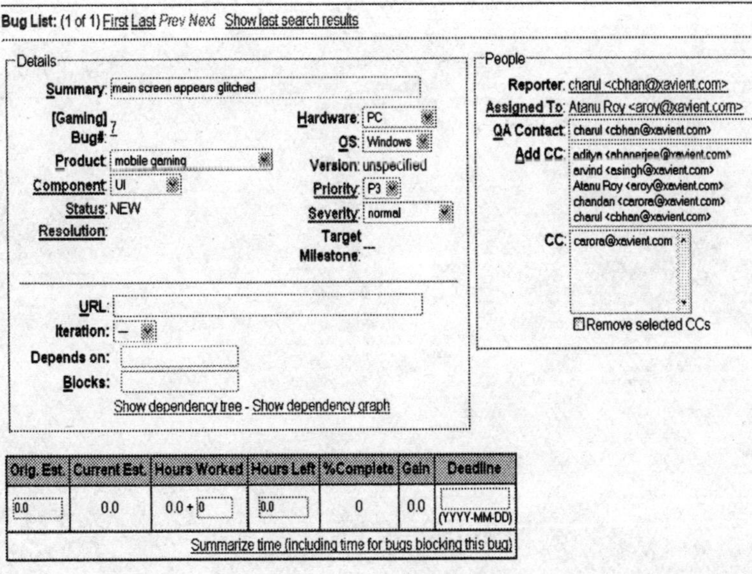

Orig. Est.	Current Est.	Hours Worked	Hours Left	%Complete	Gain	Deadline
0.0	0.0	0.0 + 0	0.0	0	0.0	(YYYY-MM-DD)

Summarize time (including time for bugs blocking this bug)

References

1. http://www.gzip.org/
2. http://www.7-zip.org/ (Extract tar file)
3. **http://www.perl.org**
4. **http://www.mysql.com.**
5. **http://www.postgresql.org/**
6. **http://www.oracle.com/**
7. **http://httpd.apache.org/.**
8. **http://www.bugzilla.org/download/**
9. **http://dev.mysql.com/downloads/mysql/**
10. **http://landfill.bugzilla.org/ppm/**
11. **http://httpd.apache.org/**
12. **http://ppm.tcool.org/archives/**
13. **http://bugzilla.example.com/**
14. **http://www.graphviz.org/Download_windows.php**
15. **https://lists.mozilla.org/listinfo/support-bugzilla (bugzilla mailing list)**
16. **http://www.soberit.hut.fi/T-76.5613/2006/material/T-76.5613_Bugzilla%20 Tutorial_2006.pdf**

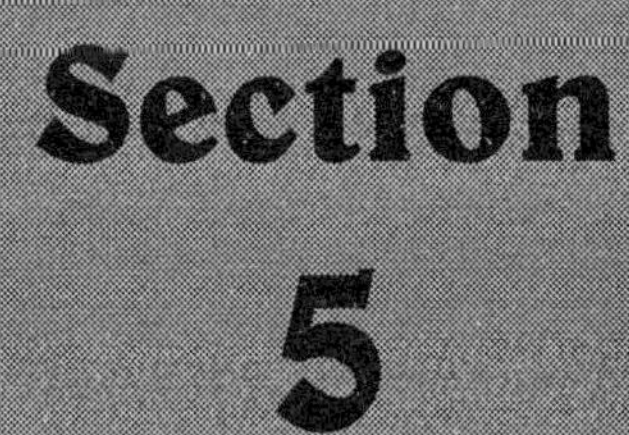

Agile Testing

Agile Methodology

Introduction:

Dictionary Meaning:

Synonyms for Agile

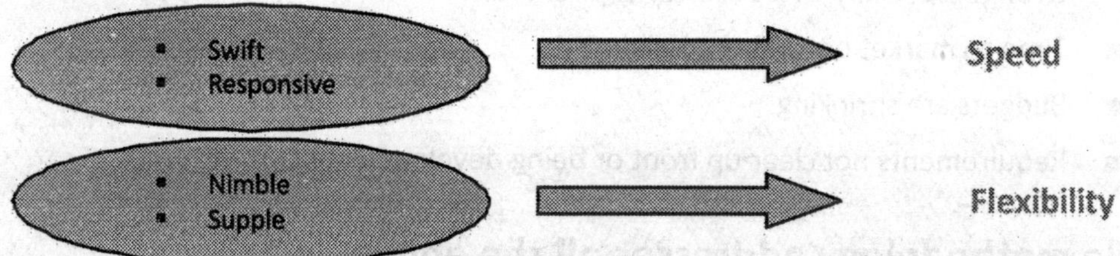

- Traditional methodologies seek to reduce costs according to Boehm's cost of change curve

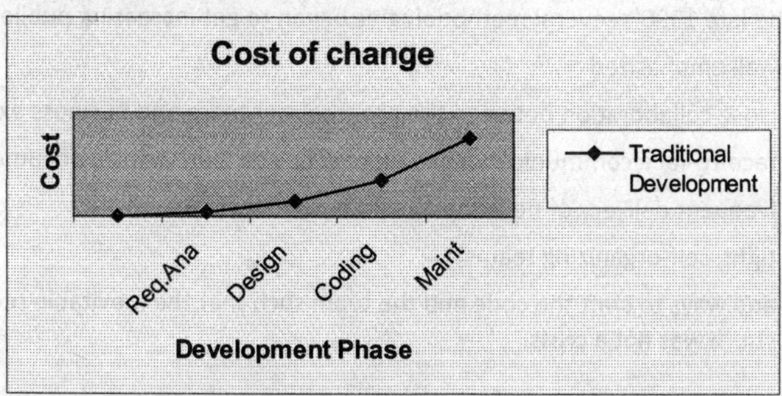

Boehm's Curve

To accomplish this:

- We need lots of up front planning, resulting in "heavy" methodologies
- Every bug caught early saves money, since models are easier to modify than code
- Large investments are made in up front analysis and design models, because of the cost of late error discovery
- This leads to a waterfall mentality with BDUF (Big Design Up Front)
- But that logic is based on development in the 1970's and 1980's

Things have changed a little

- Computing power has increased astronomically
- New tools have dramatically reduced the compile/test cycle
- Used properly, OO languages make software much easier to change
- The cost curve is significantly flattened, i.e. costs don't increase dramatically with time
- Up front modeling becomes a liability – some speculative work will certainly be wrong, especially in a business environment
- Time to market becoming crucial
- Budgets are shrinking
- Requirements not clear up front or being developed concurrently

Agile methodology addresses all the above

Sunrise of Agile

- In the late 1990's several methodologies began to get increasing public attention.
- They all emphasized
  - close collaboration between the programmer team and business experts;
  - face-to-face communication (as more efficient than written documentation);
  - frequent delivery of new deployable business value;
  - tight, self-organizing teams;
  - and ways to craft the code and the team such that the inevitable requirements churn was not a crisis.

- Early 2001 saw a workshop in Snowbird, Utah, USA, where various originators and practitioners of these methodologies met to figure out just what it was they had in common.
- They picked the word "agile" for an umbrella term and crafted the Manifesto

Agile Manifesto

->Individuals and Interactions	->Over processes and tools
->Working Software	->Over comprehensive documentation
->Customer Collaboration	->Over contract negotiation
->Responding to change	->Over following a plan

That is while there is value in the items on the right we value the items on the left more

Principles behind the Agile Manifesto:

- Our highest priority is to satisfy the customer through early and continuous delivery
- Welcome changing requirements, even late in development
- Deliver working software frequently, from a couple of weeks to a couple of months
- Business people and developers must work together daily throughout the project
- Build projects around motivated individuals. Give them the environment and support they need, and trust them to get the job done.
- The most efficient and effective method of conveying information to and within a development team is face-to-face communication
- Working software is the primary measure of progress
- Agile processes promote sustainable development. The sponsors, developers, and users should be able to maintain a constant pace always
- Continuous attention to technical excellence and good design enhances agility
- At regular intervals, the team reflects on how to become more effective, then tunes and adjusts its behavior accordingly

Concluding...

- Agile is a way of approaching a very human endeavour
- With greater acceptance of our own humanity.
- Agile is much more than a "new process".
- It is social change, a culture.
- It is accepting the inevitable (change, humanity, etc) and embracing it.

Agile vs. Waterfall

Waterfall	Agile
Plan driven	Learning driven
Infrequent client communication	Continuous client communication
Deliver once in "Big Bang" fashion, Typically 9 - 12 months	Deliver in short, business-focused releases, Typically in 2 - 3 months
Requirements defined up front	Just-in-time requirements
Develop in distinct phases with interim paper deliverables	Develop and deliver working code in 2-week long iterations
Develop in layers: Presentation, Persistence, Business, etc.	Develop in end-to-end functional slices
View programming as construction	View programming as design
Integration of different layers occurs at end of build phase	Continuously integrate code througout (hourly builds)
Testing as seperate phase at end of project, typically emphasizing functional level	Fully-automated, continuous testing at both functional and unit level
High cost of change	Low cost of change

Agile software development methods

Method Name	Key Points	Special Features
Scrum	Independent, small, self organizing development teams, 30-day release cycles.	Enforce a paradigm shift from the "defined and repeatable" to the "new product development view of Scrum".
XP	Customer driven development, small teams, daily builds	Refactoring – the ongoing redesign of the system to improve its performance and responsiveness to change
DSDM	Application of controls to RAD, use of timeboxing, empowered DSDM teams, active consortium to steer the method development	First truly agile software development method, use of prototyping, several user roles: "ambassador", "visionary" and "advisor"
RUP	Complete software development model including tool support. Activity driven role assignment	Business modeling, tool family support

What is Agile ?

- Agile – A continuous stream of business values
- Agile methods in contrast to traditional ones produce completely developed and tested features at frequent intervals of 2-4 weeks.
- Iterative approaches mean we can trade features for time instead of sacrificing quality

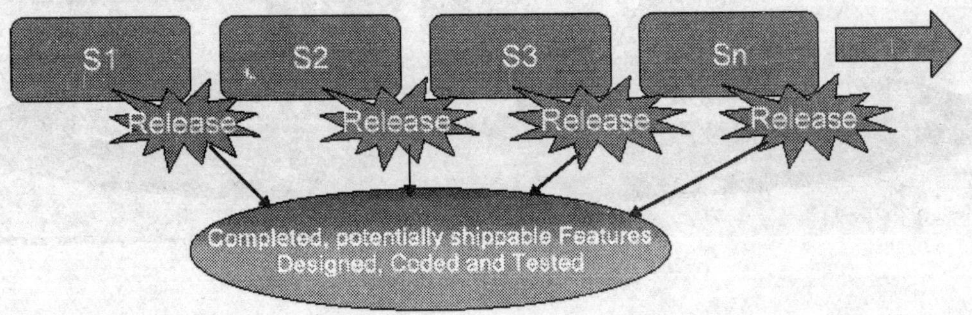

SCRUM

What is SCRUM ?

- **"Scrum" name derived from activity that occurs during rugby match. (A group of players forms around the ball and the team-mates work together, sometimes violently, to move the ball downfield.)**

In IT context it is Project Management Methodology for Agile development

SCRUM Process Flow

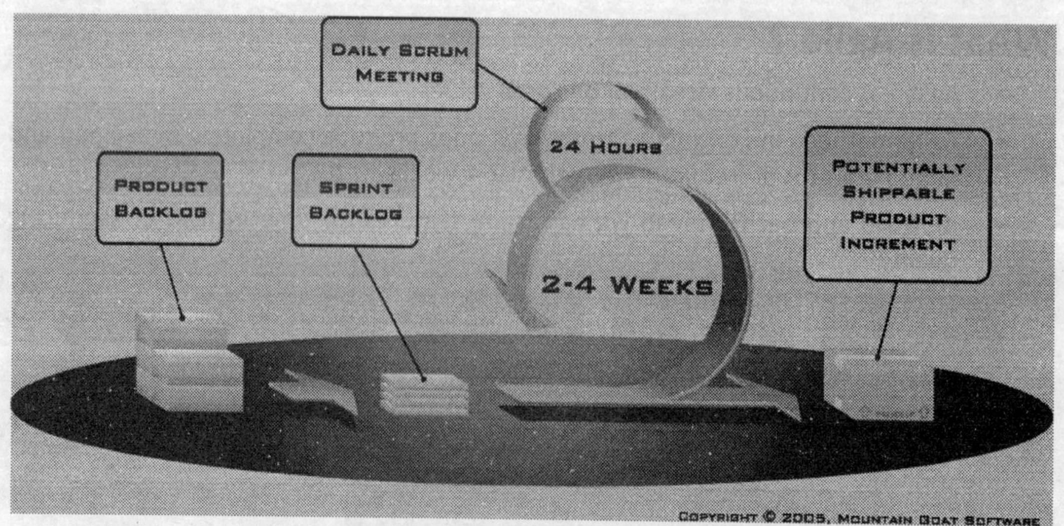

Characteristics of a SCRUM project

- It's a project management methodology
- Wrapper for existing engineering practices
- Scrum works with XP, RUP and any other engineering practice you have adopted
- Believes in empowering the development team
- Advocates working in small team (7-9)
- Consists of only three roles
- Expects to track the progress regularly

Scrum Roles

Role	Responsibilities
Product Owner	• Owns product log and prioritizes • Directs the project, Sprint by Sprint, • Manages ROI through prioritization and release plans
Scrum Master	• Helps the team turn that backlog into functionality • Responsible for enacting Scrum values and practices • Main job is to remove impediments • Fosters team communications • Improves engineering practices and tools • Improving productivity of development team • Organizes and facilitates 'scrum meetings'
Team	• Responsible for managing itself • Has the full authority to do anything to meet the sprint goal • Estimate deliveries • Commit and deliver user stories • Produce quality code

Scrum's Practices

- The Sprint Planning Meeting
- The Sprint
- The Daily Scrum
- The Sprint Review Meeting
- The Sprint Retrospective

Sprint Planning Meeting

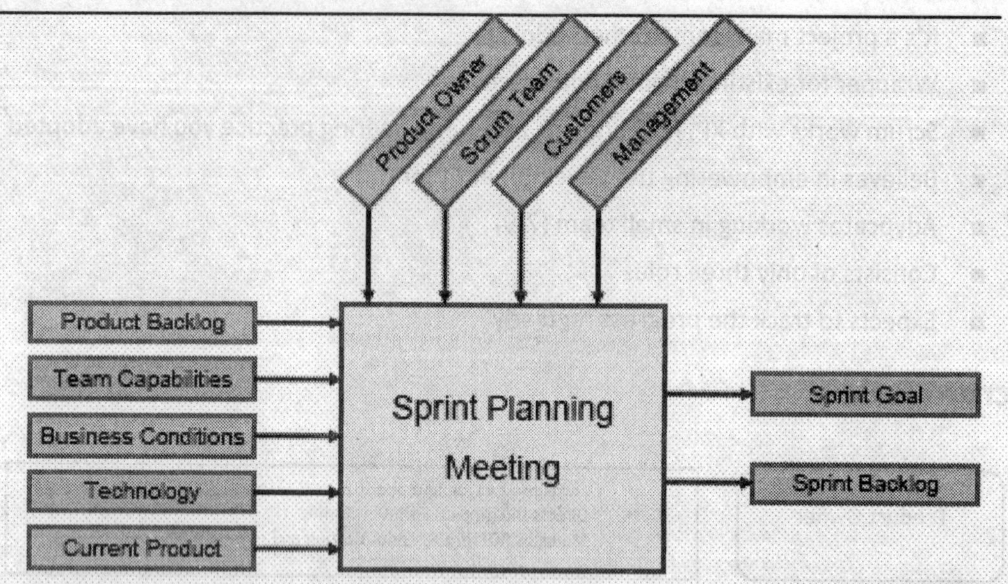

The Sprint Planning Meeting

1. Product Owner describes highest priority features to the Team.
2. Team decides what they can commit to delivering in the Sprint.

Sprint planning: Segment One: Four Hours

- The Product Owner selects the ideal backlog for the coming Sprint and communicates its meaning and importance to the team.
- Team may ask questions.

Sprint Planning : Segment Two: Four Hours

- The Team decides
  - on the sprint goal (a short theme for the sprint)
  - how much it can commit to delivering in the coming Sprint.
- The Product Owner answers questions but does not direct the team's choices.
- The outcome is the Sprint goal and the Sprint Backlog.

Life Sciences

"Support features necessary for population genetics studies."

Database Application

"Make the application run on SQL Server in addition to Oracle."

Financial Services

"Support more technical indicators than company ABC with real-time, streaming data."

Example of Sprint Goal

The Sprint Planning Meeting

- "The Team decides how to turn the selected requirements into an increment of potentially shippable product functionality. The Team devises its own tasks and figures out who will do them."

The Sprint

- Strictly time boxed to 30 consecutive calendar days: it's more important to fall short than to slip the date
- Activities are visible through the Sprint Backlog and Sprint Burndown Charts
- The Product Owner refrains from tinkering with priorities
- Within the sprint, there are many possible engineering practices!
- Changes
    - Team adds new tasks whenever they need to in order to meet the sprint goal
    - Team can move unnecessary tasks
    - But : sprint backlog can only be updated by the team
- Estimates are updated whenever there is new information

Scrum meetings

- Parameters
    - Daily
    - 15-minutes
    - Stand up
    - Not for problem solving

  - Three questions
  - What did you do yesterday ?
  - What will you do today ?
  - What obstacles are in your way ?
  - Scrum master leads the meeting and assesses the responses from each person
- Scrum meetings
  - Help the team to uncover potential problems as early as possible.
  - Daily meetings lead to knowledge socialization and promotes self organizing team structure

Scrum of Scrum

- Carried out when large teams are broken down into smaller teams
- Can be held daily
- Purpose is to coordinate activities and address integration issues
- Team leaders participate
- Following is discussed
  - What did my team do yesterday to advance the objectives of the Sprint
  - What will my team do today
  - What are the barriers that could keep my team from meeting its commitment to the Sprint
- This meeting takes place after daily SCRUMs

The Sprint Review Meeting

- Team presents what is accomplished during the sprint
- Team demonstrates product increment to product owner's satisfaction.
- Time boxed to one hour of prep and four hours of meeting.
- Informality is encouraged.

The Sprint Retrospective

- A retrospective is a ritual gathering of a community at the end of a project to review the events and learn from the experience
- Time boxed to three hours.

- Team, Scrum Master, and (optionally) Product Owner review the last Sprint
- Teams get together to discuss the following
  - What did we do well
  - What did we learn
  - What should we do differently the next time
  - What still puzzles us
- Actionable items are presented to the Product Owner for prioritization as non-functional requirements.

What a Retrospective is NOT

- Retrospectives are NOT about blame
  - Problems (opportunities) arise. The focus is on what we can learn from what happened
- Retrospectives are NOT a witch hunt
- Retrospectives are NOT about gathering specific information
  - They are a free-flowing brainstorm on opportunities and ways to resolve them

Scrum's Artefacts

- The Product Backlog
- The Sprint Backlog

The Sprint Burndown Chart

- The Product Increment

Product Backlog

	Item #	Description	Est	By
Very High				
	1	**Finish database versioning**	16	KH
	2	**Get rid of unneeded shared Java in database**	8	KH
	-	**Add licensing**	-	-
	3	Concurrent user licensing	16	TG
	4	Demo / Eval licensing	16	TG
		Analysis Manager		
	5	File formats we support are out of date	160	TG
	6	Round-trip Analyses	250	MC
High				
	-	**Enforce unique names**	-	-
	7	In main application	24	KH
	8	In import	24	AM
	-	**Admin Program**	-	-
	9	Delete users	4	JM
	-	**Analysis Manager**	-	-
	10	When items are removed from an analysis, they should show up again in the pick list in lower 1/2 of the analysis tab	8	TG
	-	**Query**	-	-
	11	Support for wildcards when searching	16	T&A
	12	Sorting of number attributes to handle negative numbers	16	T&A
	13	Horizontal scrolling	12	T&A
	-	**Population Genetics**	-	-
	14	Frequency Manager	400	T&M
	15	Query Tool	400	T&M
	16	Additional Editors (which ones)	240	T&M
	17	Study Variable Manager	240	T&M
	18	Haplotypes	320	T&M
	19	**Add icons for v1.1 or 2.0**	-	-
	-	**Pedigree Manager**	-	-
	20	Validate Derived kindred	4	KH
Medium				
	-	**Explorer**	-	-
	21	Launch tab synchronization (only show queries/analyses for logged in users)	8	T&A
	22	Delete settings (?)	4	T&A

- A list of all desired work on the project
  - A prioritized list of project requirements or features that provide business value for the customer
- Usually a combination of
  - Story based work
  - Task based work
- List is prioritized by the Product owner
- Items can be added to the backlog at any time (this is how changes are i ntroduced)
- This activity is not intended to analyze the system, merely to scope and list its requirements and not to how it would be done
- The product backlog consists of three types of items:
  - Product functionality - what functions could the system perform to deliver the value anticipated in the product vision.

- Non-functional requirements - for the product to deliver the necessary value, what operational aspects must it demonstrate, such as performance, security, reliability, and cost requirements
- Environmental requirements - what capabilities and environments must be in place for the product to be developed and delivered

The Sprint Backlog

Who	Description	7/22/2007	7/24/2007	7/26/2007	7/31/2007	
	Days left in sprint	15	13	10	8	
	Total Estimated Hours :	90	75	52	14	0
-	**User's guide**	-	-	-	-	-
SM	Start on study variable chapter first draft	20	12	8	0	
SM	Import chapter first draft	10	10	4	4	
SM	Export chapter first draft	10	5	4	2	
-	**Miscelleaneous Small bugs**					
JM	Fix connection leak	8	4	4	0	
JM	Delete queries	8	4	4	0	
JM	Delete analysis	4	4	4	0	
TG	Fix tear-off messaging bug	15	15	10	8	
JM	View pedigree for kindred column in a result set	10	5	5	0	
AM	Derived kindred validation	5	5	0	0	

Scrum master maintains the sprint Backlog by updating it to reflect which tasks are completed and how long the team thinks it will take to complete those that are not yet done

- Scrum team takes the sprint goal and decides what tasks are necessary
- The Sprint Backlog is the list of tasks that the Scrum Team is committing that they will complete in the current Sprint.
- Selected by team at outset of Sprint
- Changes during Sprint as information is discovered
- Okay to use other engineering practices (stories, micro-iterations), but progress must be reported in the backlog
- Managers don't make decisions for the team
- Sprint Backlog is created
- Time estimates must be updated daily

The Sprint Burndown Chart

The estimated work remaining in the Sprint is calculated daily and graphed resulting in a Sprint Burndown chart

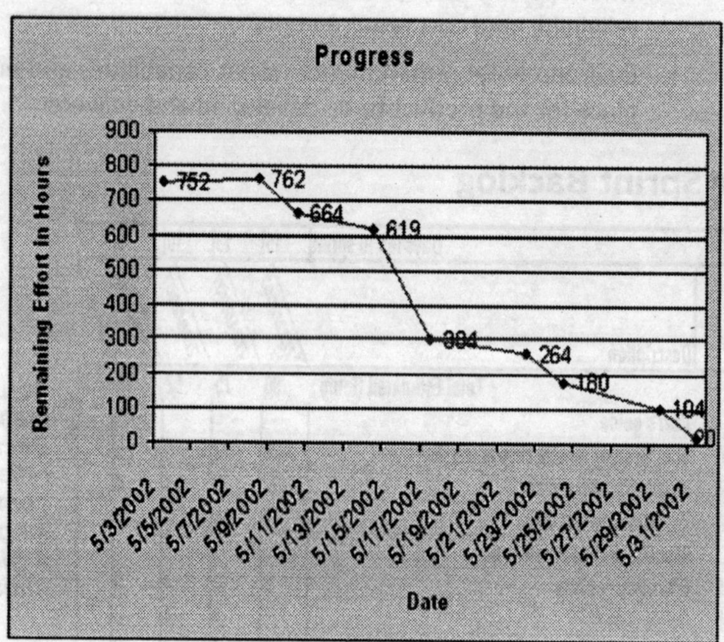

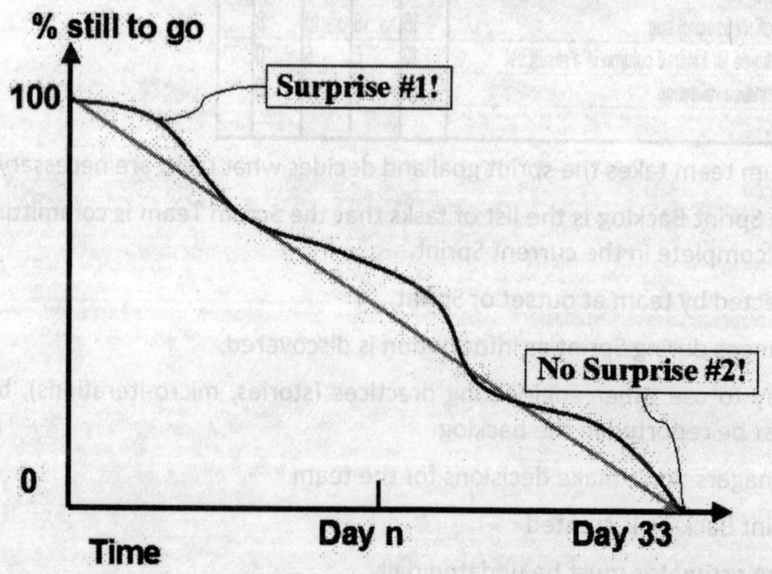

The burn-down chart is emotionally powerful because there is a special feeling about hitting the number zero that helps people get excited about completing their work and pressing forward

The Product Increment

- Delivers measurable value
- "Potentially Shippable": the process can be halted after every Sprint and there will be some value, some ROI
- Must be a product, no matter how incomplete

Who Is Using Scrum?

- Microsoft
- Sun
- Siemens
- Nokia
- Philips
- BBC
- IBM
- US Federal Reserve Bank
- HP
- Motorola
- Trans Union
- Xerox
- Yahoo!

Sample Results After One Year at Yahoo!

- Average productivity change: +36%
- Impact on morale: 52% report better or much better / 9% worse or much worse
- Overall approval rating among teams using it: 85%
- First new product developed: took 1/3 less time than comparable products (and team was split between US and India)

What is Extreme Programming(XP)?

- XP uses an object-oriented approach as its preferred development paradigm
- XP encompasses a set of rules and practices that occur within the context of four framework activities
    - Planning
    - Design
    - Coding
    - Testing

Economics of XP

- Promotes incremental development with minimal up-front design
- Results in a "pay as you go" process, rather than a high up-front investment
- Delivers highest business value first
- XP tends to use small teams, thus reducing communication costs.
- XP puts Customers and Programmers in one place.
- XP prefers index cards to expensive round-trip UML diagramming environments
- XP's practices work together in synergy, to get a team moving as quickly as possible to deliver value the customer wants

XP Values

- XP is based on 4 core values:
  - Communication
  - Simplicity
  - Feedback
  - Courage

XP Roles

- **Customer**
  - Writes User Stories and specifies Functional Tests
  - Sets priorities, explains stories
  - May or may not be an end-user
  - Has authority to decide questions about the stories
- **Programmer**
  - Estimates stories
  - Defines Tasks from stories, and estimates
  - Implements Stories and Unit Tests
- **Coach**
  - Watches everything, sends obscure signals, makes sure the project stays on course
  - Helps with anything

- **Tracker**
  - Monitors Programmers' progress, takes action if things seem to be going off track.
  - Actions include setting up a meeting with Customer, asking Coach or another Programmer to help
- **Tester**
  - Implements and runs Functional Tests (not Unit Tests!)
  - Graphs results, and makes sure people know when test results decline.
- **Doomsayer**
  - Ensures that everybody knows the risks involved
  - Ensures that bad news isn't hidden, glossed over, or blown out of proportion
- **Manager**
  - Schedules meetings (e.g. Iteration Plan, Release Plan), makes sure the meeting process is followed, records results of meeting for future reporting, and passes to the Tracker
  - Possibly responsible to the Gold Owner.
  - Goes to meetings, brings back useful information
  - Pays for pizza
- **Gold Owner**
  - The person funding the project, which may or may not be the same as the Customer

Why 'Extreme'

- Reflects the intensity and fearlessness of athletes in extreme sports
- The XP practices get "turned up" to a much higher "volume" than on traditional projects.

XP : 12 Practices

- The Planning Game
- Small Releases
- Metaphor

- Simple Design
- Testing
- Refactoring
- Pair Programming
- Collective ownership
- Continuous integration
- 40-hour week
- On-site customer
- Coding standards

Stages of an XP project

- Initiation
  - User Stories
  - Release Planning
- Release (each Release is typically 1 - 6 months)
  - Iteration 1 (typically 1 - 3 weeks)
    - Development
    - Deployment
    - Acceptance Testing
  - Iteration 2
    - Development
    - Deployment
    - Acceptance Testing
  - Iteration- n

XP Process flow

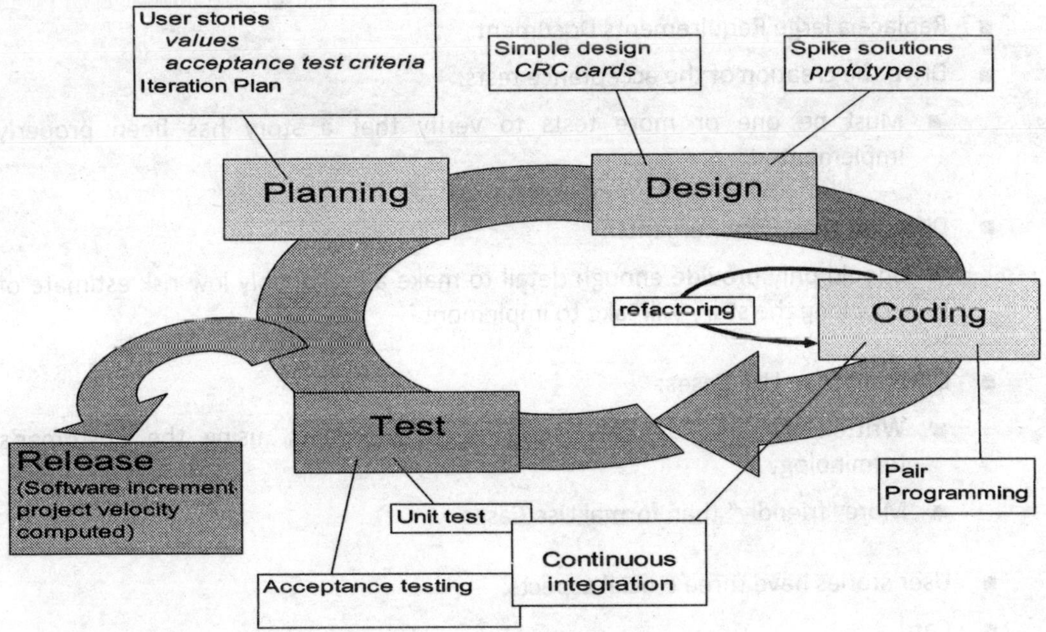

Gathering Requirements

- Responsibilities
  - Key Point: The Customer is responsible for the requirements.
  - Programmers help to gather and clarify requirements. Customers especially need help with non-functional requirements and with working out the details of acceptance tests.
- Documentation
  - User Stories
  - Acceptance Test Cases

User Stories

- A short description of the behavior of the system from the point of view of the Customer
- Use the Customer's terminology without technical jargon
- One for each major feature in the system

- Must be written by the users
- Are used to create time estimates for release planning
- Replace a large Requirements Document
- Drive the creation of the acceptance tests:
  - Must be one or more tests to verify that a story has been properly implemented
- Different than Requirements:
  - Should only provide enough detail to make a reasonably low risk estimate of how long the story will take to implement.
- Different than Use Cases:
  - Written by the Customer, not the Programmers, using the Customer's terminology
  - More "friendly" than formal Use Cases
- User stories have three crucial aspects:
- Card
  - Enough information to identify the story
- Conversation
  - Customer and Programmers discuss the story to elaborate on the details
  - Verbal when possible, but documented when required
- Confirmation
  - Acceptance tests to confirm that the story has been properly implemented

User story – Story card composition

- As (a user)
- I Want to
- So that

- A Customer (for a library)
- Search for a book by category and display the results as a list
- It helps me in selecting the appropriate book

Acceptance tests

- Formal test to determine if a system satisfies its acceptance criteria, i.e. the User Stories!
- Should be automated
- At least one Acceptance Test for each Story

Release Planning

- Stories for a Release are arranged into 1-3 week Iterations
- Higher risk, and higher priority stories in earlier Iterations
- For new system, the 0th Iteration defines the basic skeleton of the application and infrastructure required
- The Release and Iterations have fixed dates for completion – dates are fixed, scope is variable
- This is the Release Plan

Iteration Planning

- Stories for Iteration are broken down into Tasks by Programmers
- Tasks are estimated by all Programmers as a group
- Programmers "sign up" for Tasks, and estimate the time to complete
- Can only sign up for as many points as were completed in the last Iteration
- Once development begins, Project Velocity measures progress

User Stories

- Each story is written by the customer and is **placed on an index card**
- Customer **assigns a value (priority)** to the story based on overall business value of the feature or function
- XP team members assess each story and assign a cost (measured in development weeks) to it.
- If the story requires more than 3 development weeks,
  - customer splits the story into smaller ones
  - assignment of values and cost happens again

- Customer and XP team together decide how to group stories in next release (the next software increment).

Programmer Tests

- Programmer Tests must run at 100% before code is integrated
- Assist with Refactoring (promote Courage)
- Testing frameworks exist for many languages:
  - JUnit for Java
  - CPPUnit for C++
  - NUnit for all .Net languages

Sample Junit test

- First, write the test:

```
import junit.framework.TestCase;
public class TestMovieList extends
    TestCase {
public void testEmptyList() {
MovieList emptyList = new MovieList();
assertEquals( "Empty list should have
    size of 0",
0, emptyList.size() );
}
}
```

- Now write the code to make the test pass.
- First, there is no MovieList class:

```
public class MovieList {
}
```

- Now we need a 'size' method that returns an 'int':

```
public class MovieList {
public int size() {
return 0;
}
}
```

Refactoring

Meaning of word Factoring

$x^2 - 1$ can be factored as $(x - 1)(x + 1)$

What have we done ? We have simplified further

In software refactoring its means

- Rejuvenating old designs
- Removing redundancy
- Eliminating unused functionality

Refactoring is a disciplined technique for restructuring an existing body of code, altering its internal structure without changing its external behavior

Pair programming

- 2 people work together at one PC to create a code for a story
- One person types and thinks tactically about the method being created
- Other thinks strategically about how that method fits into the class

Pair programming – Concerns

- Productivity will be halved
  - With collective code ownership, it will be difficult for programmers to be recognized and compensated
  - It is annoying having someone looking over your shoulder while you program
  - Pair programming will interfere with "flow", which requires solitude and silence

Pair programming – Success trends

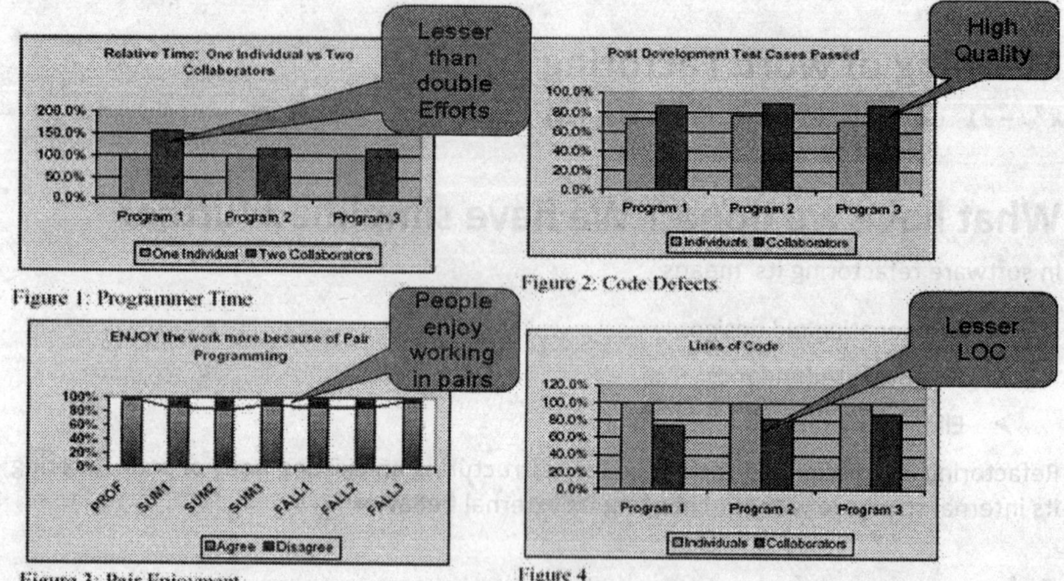

Figure 1: Programmer Time

Figure 2: Code Defects

Figure 3: Pair Enjoyment

Figure 4

Pair programming-Take Care...

Big Visible Charts

- Display important project information not in some formal way, not on the web, not in PowerPoint, but in charts on the wall that no one can miss.

Continuous Integration

- Developers should be integrating and releasing code into the code repository periodically
- Code is released for integration only when 100 % unit test cases have passed
- Benefits
    - Ensure changes are not made to obsolete code causing integration headaches
    - Ensures latest versions of code are being worked on
    - Fixing small problems every few hours takes less time than fixing huge problems just before the deadline

Conclusion

- Open, honest communication
- Rapid feedback at all levels
- Quality Work
- Assume Simplicity
- Incremental Change
- Small initial investment
- Embrace Change
- Travel light
- Local adaptation

Proposed Agile Methodology

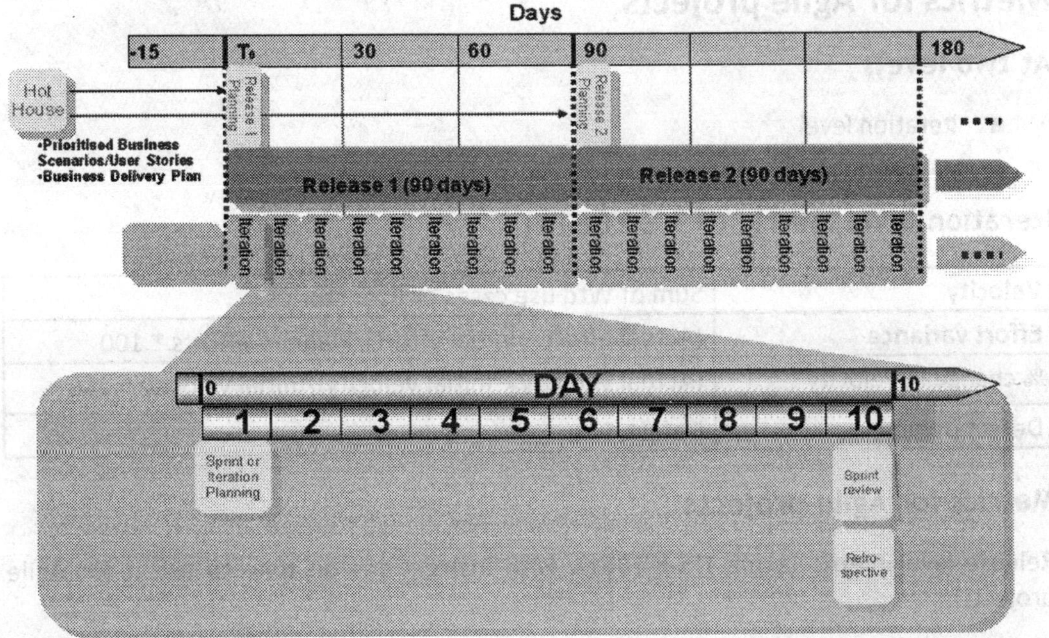

Proposed Agile Methodology

- Scrum as project management methodology
- Some of the XP practices will be adopted

Highlights

- 90 day release cycle
- 2 week sprint (iteration) (can be tailored)

Pre-90 days

- Hot housing

Release

- Iteration 0
- Iteration 1 to (n-1)
- Iteration n

Metrics for Agile projects

At two levels

- Iteration level
- Release level

Iteration level metric (ITS-E-T061A)

Velocity	Sum of Wtd use cases or user stories
Effort variance	(Actual effort – Initial effort)/Planned efforts * 100
% change in velocity	(Actual velocity – Initial velocity)/Initial velocity * 100
Defect Density	Defect/Size

Metrics for Agile projects

Release level metric (same ITS-E-T061A with instructions on how to use it for Agile projects)

% change in velocity	(Actual velocity – planned velocity)/Planned velocity * 100
Effort variance	(Actual efforts – planned effort)/Planned effort * 100

Productivity	Size/Efforts
Defect Density	Total Wtd defects / Size
DRE – coding	
DRE- Component/ integration testing	
Defect seepage – system testing	
% Schedule variance	(Planned days – Actual days)/Planned days * 100

Migrating to Agile

Criteria for selection of projects

- Project Type – Full Life Cycle, Enhancement
- Management – Joint Development of User stories/ Release Plan in Hothouses
- Human Factor - Experienced Skill set, Empowered team
- Infrastructure – CASE tools for Upper Phases, Testing Tools, Configuration Management Tools
- Development Methodology – Iterative, Incremental, Exploratory

Starting Agile

- Find suitable projects to try agile methods out with.
- Start with a team that wants to try and work in an agile way.
- Find customers who want to work in this kind of collaborative way.
- Better to start learning on a project of a more manageable size.
- Take a project that's a little bit more critical than you are comfortable with.
- Find someone more experienced in agile methods to help you learn. (Agile mentor)
- Once you've found a good mentor, follow their advice.

When and Where to use Agile

- Agile approach is recommended when:
    - Domain & Technology are evolving
    - Requirements change
    - Short timelines for delivery

When not to use Agile

- If the people involved aren't interested in the kind of intense collaboration
- Never try to impose agile working on a team that doesn't want to try it.
- Use an agile approach if clients are willing

Some suggestions on implementing Agile

- Continuous integration, making builds as often as needed daily
- Automated testing
- Test driven development
- Simplicity in design using story card task break up
- Refactoring of code for ease of maintenance/ enhancement and to prevent code aging

- Introduce the following people practices:
  - Feedback: daily/weekly/monthly and end of projects
  - Stand up meetings

Agile Challenges

- Documentation – Retain critical information over time
- Design and coding standards for every technology
- Refactoring – frequent refactoring would enable local changes
- Competent manpower (past experience in technology domain) and willing to live with developers' decisions
- Fast feedback from the customer/users
- Physically co-located teams
- Larger programs and distributed teams
- Availability of tools
- Co-ordinating team of teams

Agility versus CMM

- Agility
  - Faster Interactions,

- Lesser Rework (?)
- Tested Code for integration

- CMM
    - Disciplined, auditable Process
    - Predictable process artifacts, project performance
    - Formal Estimation, Scheduling, Planning, Tracking
- CMM Level 5 Practices will not be abandoned; they will co-exist

Tool for agile

SCM	Continuus
Unit Testing	JUnit, Cactus, JavaScope (Code coverage tool)
Build	Ant,Jalopy
Integration	CruiseControl
TestAutomation	Ant,DBUnit
DefectTracking	Continuus

References:

www.agilealliance.com

www.mountaingoatsoftware.com

www.controlchaos.com

IceScrum for Agile

Icescrum2

IceScrum is a web application for using Scrum while keeping the spirit of a collaborative workspace. It also offers virtual boards with post-its for sprint backlog, product backlog and others. The tool offers everything that is in Scrum:

- Roles: Product Owner, ScrumMaster, Team member and StakeHolder .
- The product backlog management with advanced features for prioritizing stories.
- Scrum lifecycle including a roadmap view.
- Release planning.
- Sprint backlog, as a task board facilitating the Scrum ceremonial.
- Management of impediments.
- Chart production such as burndown charts, velocity charts, cumulative flow diagram.

IceScrum offers others agile practices like :

- Roadmap
- Vision
- Features
- User stories
- Acceptance tests associated to stories
- User roles
- Planning poker

Scrum's Roles

- The Product Owner

  -- Owns definition of success

  -- Manages ROI through prioritization and release plans

- The Scrum Master

  -- Owns the process

  -- Teaches the Product Owner and the Team

- The Team

  -- Owns the production and engineering process

"The **Product Owner's** focus is ROI. The Product Owner directs the project, Sprint by Sprint, to provide the greatest ROI and value to the organization."

"The **Scrum Master** is responsible for the success of the project, and he or she helps increase the probability of success by helping the Product Owner select the most valuable product backlog and by helping the Team turn that backlog into functionality." The Scrum Master is not part of the Team.

"The **Team** is responsible for managing itself and has the full authority to do anything to meet the Sprint goal within the guidelines, standards, and conventions of the organization and of Scrum." The Team is responsible for/to:

- Software quality
- Technical implementation of User Stories
- Delivery of functional software increment
- Organize themselves

Scrum Artifacts

Scrum knows 3 main Artifacts:

- Product Backlog
- Burndown Chart
- Sprint Backlog

Product Backlog

The **Product Owner** creates Requirements and User Stories to define his **vision** of the future functionality. These requirements and user stories are not yet planned for a specific release or sprint so they appear in the Product Backlog.

The requirements for the product are listed in the Product Backlog.

- All features and functions for final product
- May be subdivided into releases
- Prioritized by Product Owner
- Initial backlog is established and releases are defined prior to start of Sprints
- Product backlog is reviewed and updated throughout the project
- Time must be allotted during Sprints to allow for this activity

Burndown Chart

The Burndown chart shows the amount of work remaining per Sprint. It is a very useful way of visualizing the correlation between work remaining at any point in time and the progress of the Team(s). It inspects their progress in relation to the Planning by using the Burndown Chart, and makes adjustments as necessary.

Sprint Backlog

According to the priorities of the PO the Team chooses the User Stories which they think they can implement in this Sprint, and the PO assigns these User Stories to the Sprint by setting the Sprint field of each User Story.

After the Sprint is set, the User Stories will appear in the Sprint Backlog automatically. They will not be visible in the Product Backlog anymore because the Product Owner is not allowed to change User Stories once the team has committed to them.

- Features and functions targeted for a single Sprint
    - Frequently broken down into User Stories; especially if function is complex
- May include technical requirements or objectives
    - e.g.; database design, UI standards, architecture documentation

Scrum's Practices

- The Sprint Planning Meeting
- The Sprint
- The Sprint Review Meeting
- The Sprint Retrospective
- The Daily Scrum

The Sprint Planning Meeting

1. Product Owner describes highest priority features to the Team.
2. Team decides what can commit to delivering in the Sprint.

The Sprint

- Strictly time boxed to 30 consecutive calendar days: it's more important to fall short than to slip the date
- Activities are visible through the Sprint Backlog and Sprint Burndown Charts
- The Product Owner refrains from tinkering with priorities
- Within the sprint, there are many possible engineering practices!

The Sprint Review Meeting

- Time boxed to one hour of preparation and four hours of meeting.
- Team demonstrates product increment to product owner's satisfaction.
- Informality is encouraged. PowerPoint is discouraged.
- Chickens are welcome. Comments from chickens are discouraged.

The Sprint Retrospective

- Time boxed to three hours.
- Team, Scrum Master, and (optionally) Product Owner review the last Sprint
- What went well?
- What can be improved?
- Actionable items are presented to the Product Owner for prioritization as non-functional requirements.

The Daily Scrum

- Time boxed to fifteen minutes!
- The Team and the Scrum Master only.
- What have you accomplished since yesterday?
- Are your Sprint Backlog estimates accurate?
- What are you working on today?

Requirements:

* Java Development Kit 1.5 or later,

* A compatible internet browser: Internet Explorer 7+, Firefox 3+, Safari 3+

Download

1. Download the latest Bundle file

   http://www.icescrum.org/en/download-en/

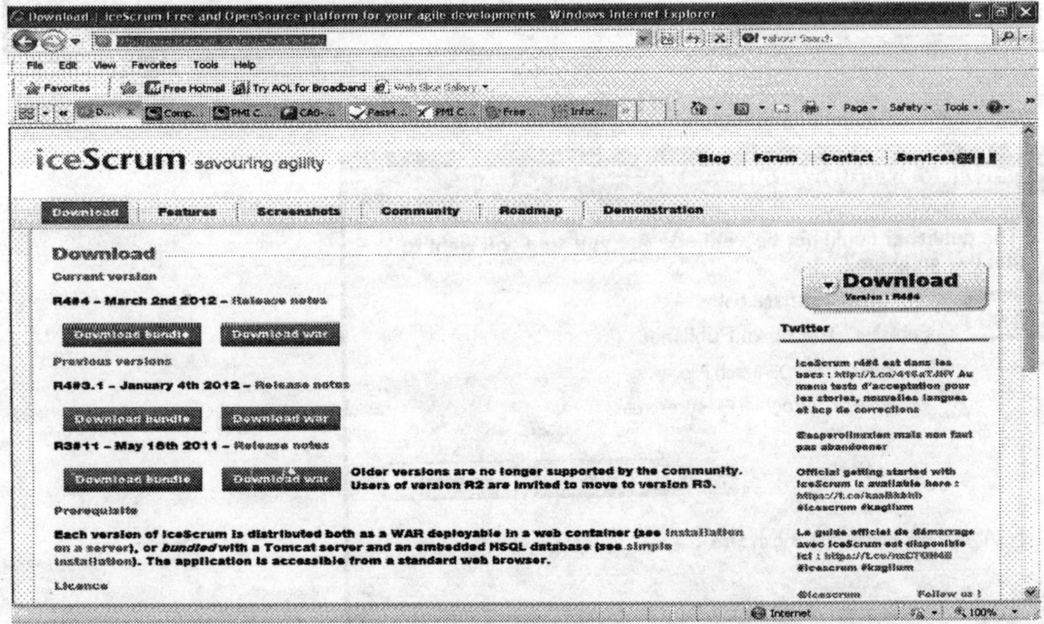

2. Extract the file in a chosen folder

Installation

1. Launch the *icescrum2.bat* file for Windows or *icescrum2.sh* for Unix/Linux systems i.e. click on the icescrum2 Batch File

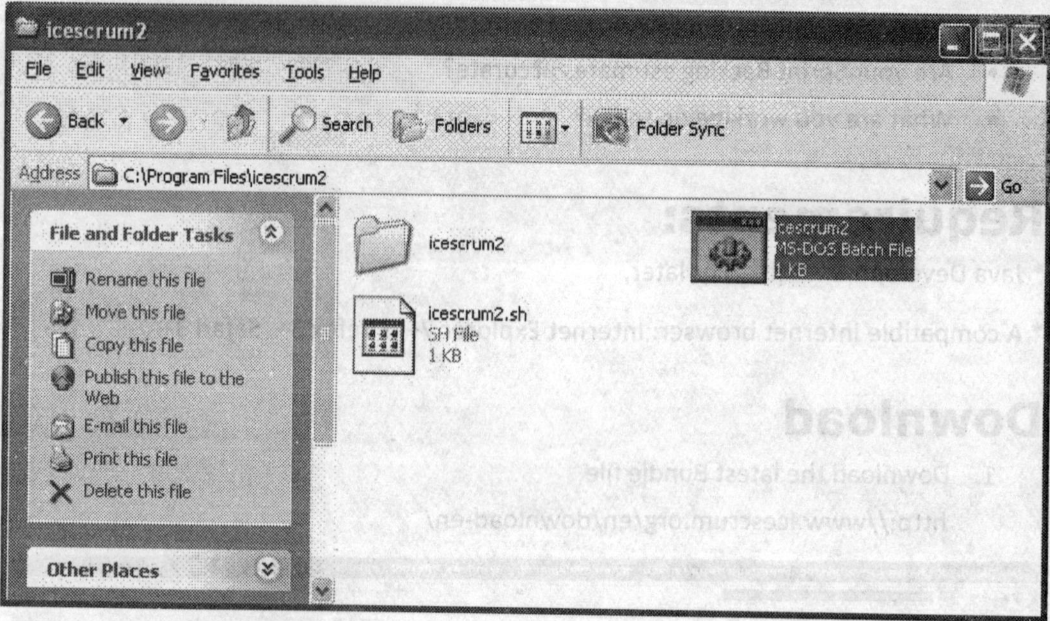

Following window will appear, Click on Run button

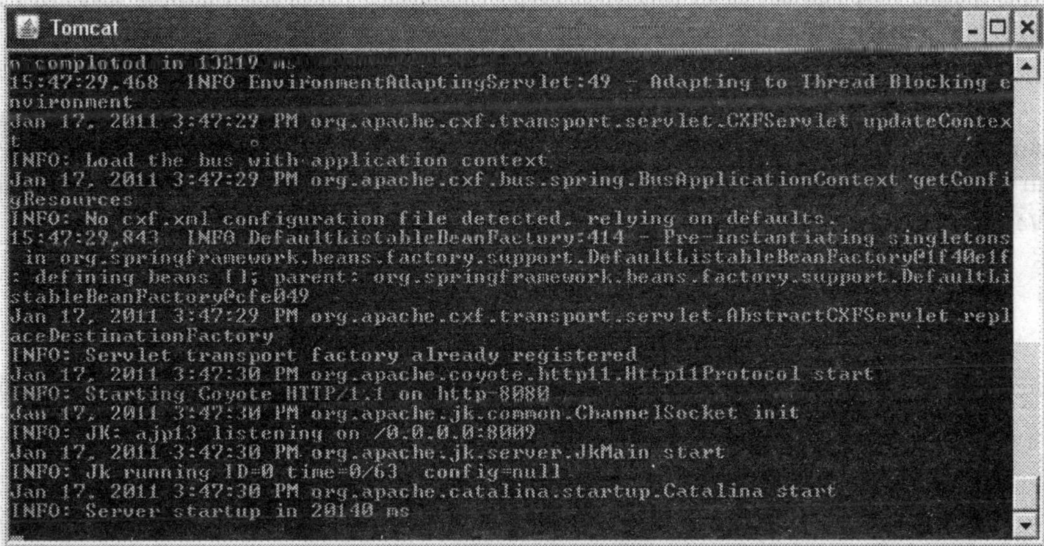

Note : While running Tomcat, following error may occur :

Error : C:\Program Files\Tomcat\apache-tomcat-5.5.23\bin>startup.bat. Neither the JAVA_HOME nor the JRE_HOME environment variable is defined. At least one of these environment variable is needed to run this program

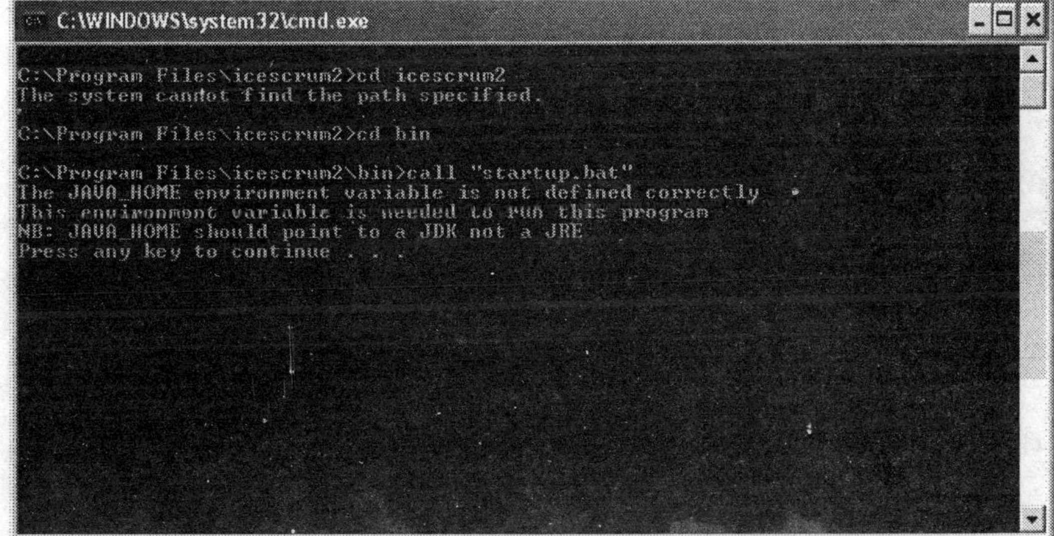

This means that Tomcat can't find your Java installation. There are multiple ways to fix this, but an easy one is to edit the startup.bat file, and put this at the top:

set JAVA_HOME=C:\Program Files\Java\jdk1.6.0

Another way to address this is to add a JAVA_HOME environmental variable to your system. In Windows XP, go to Start --> Control Panel --> System --> Advanced --> Environmental Variables, and add the variable to either user or system variables.

2. Type the URL: http://[host_adress]/[web-app_name] (for example, http://localhost:8080/icescrum2). Following window will appear.

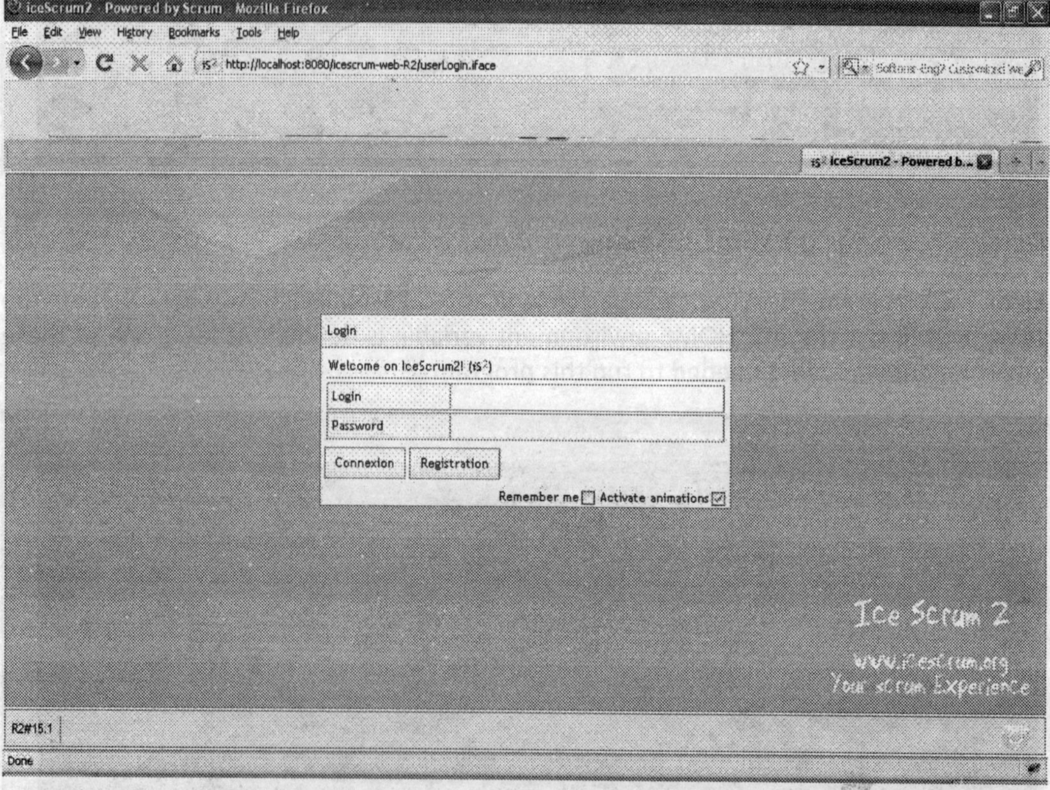

3. You can now start using IceScrum2! You must begin by register yourself. Click on the button "Registration", fill the form and validate. Log in your freshly created account, and give it a try.

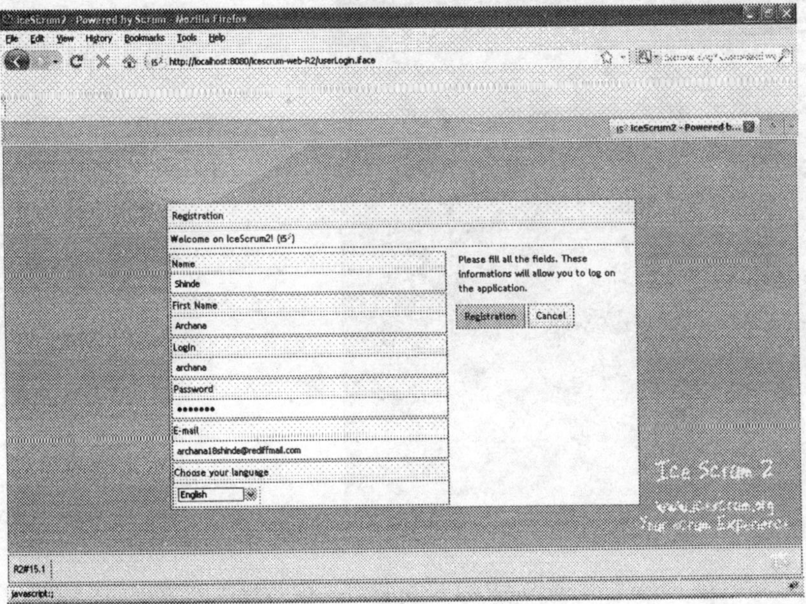

Create Project:

1. Click on project, Select **Create A New Project.**
2. Input the required information.

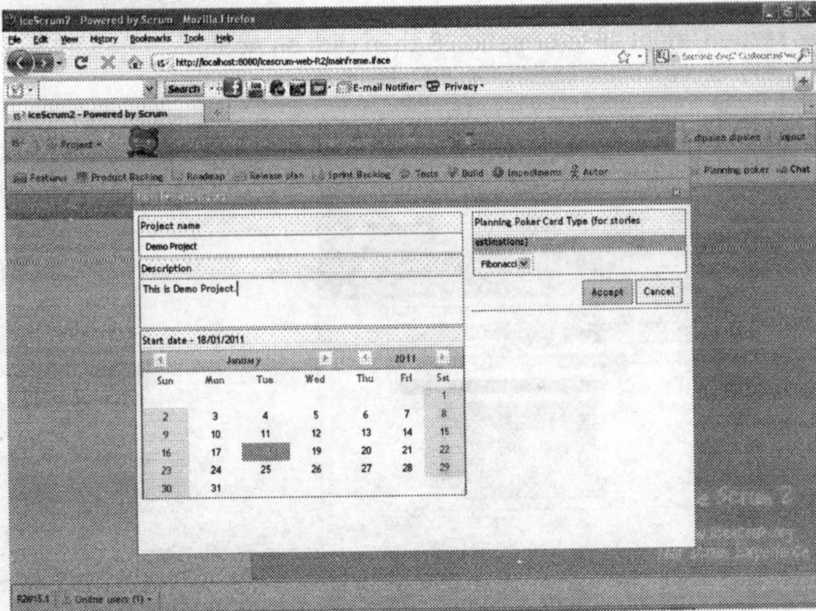

3. By clicking on Accept button, following window will be displayed.

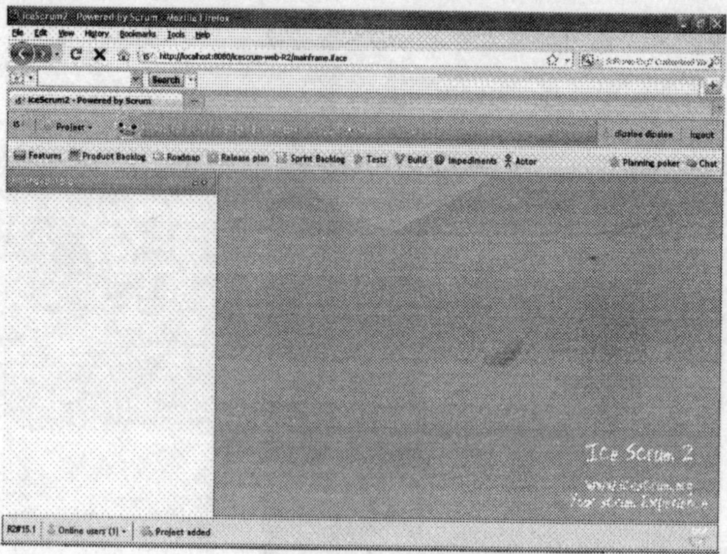

Features

A feature is a high level externally observable service provided by the software that directly fulfills the stakeholders need.

Create Features:

1. In the **Features** section, input all information & then click on Accept.

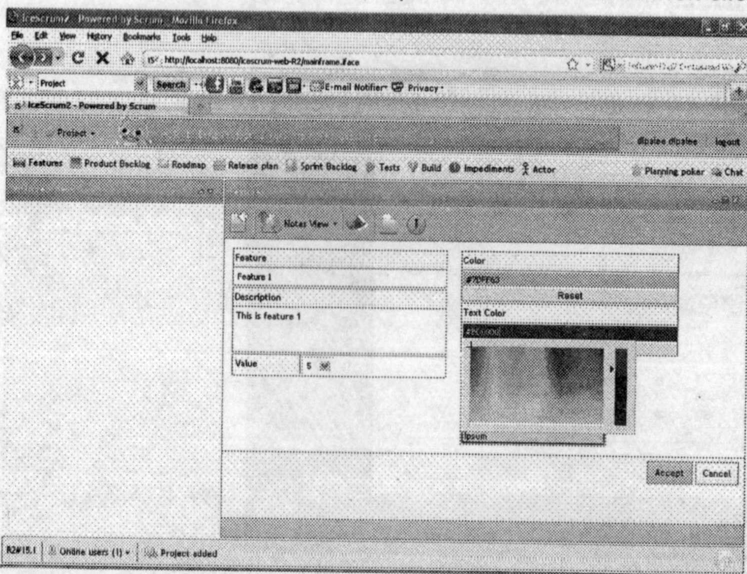

Feature will be created like:

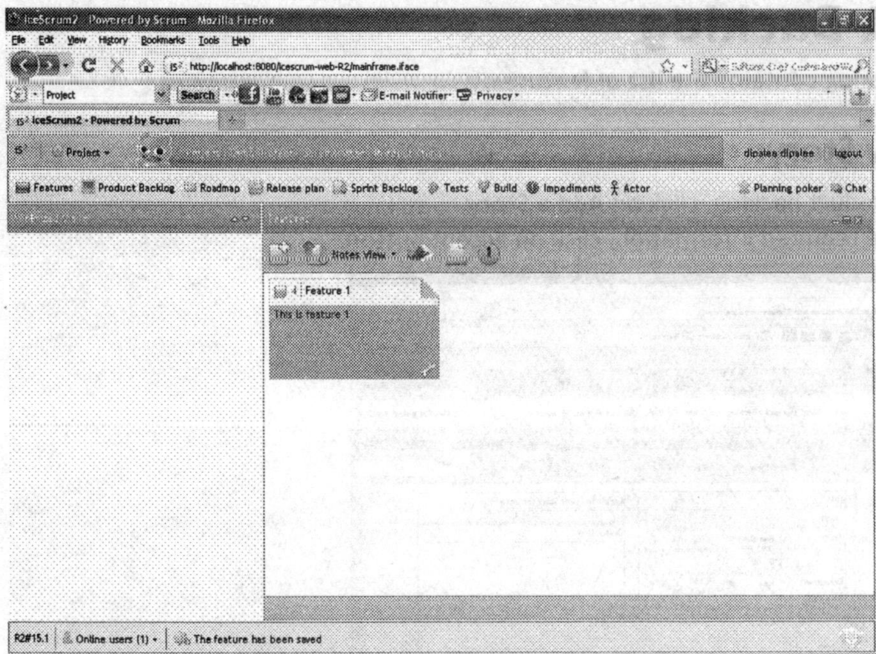

We can create the features as per requirement.

The newly created features are:

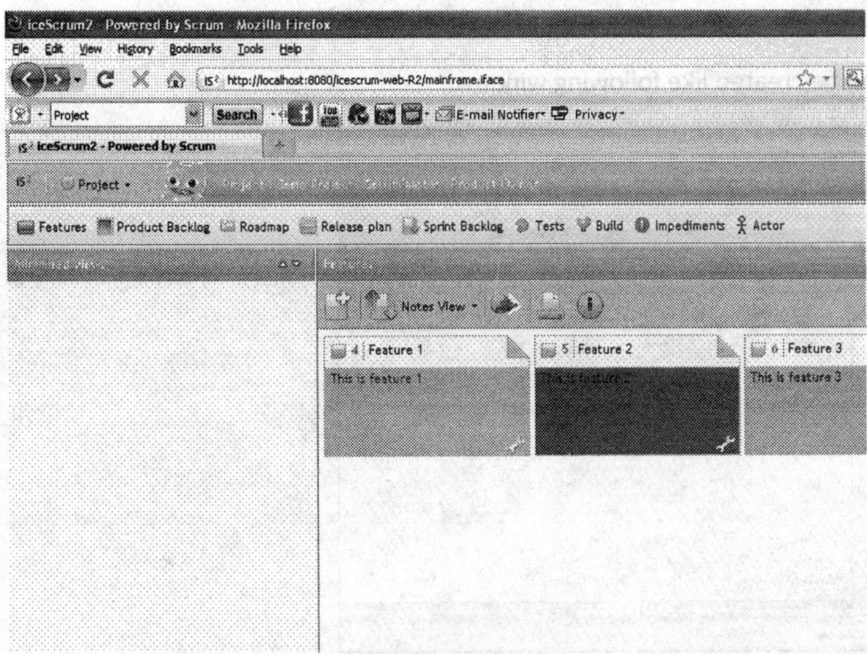

Product Backlog

The product backlog contains the list of features.

Create New Story:

1. In the Product backlog, click on **Add a Story.**
2. Input the required information, click on accept button.

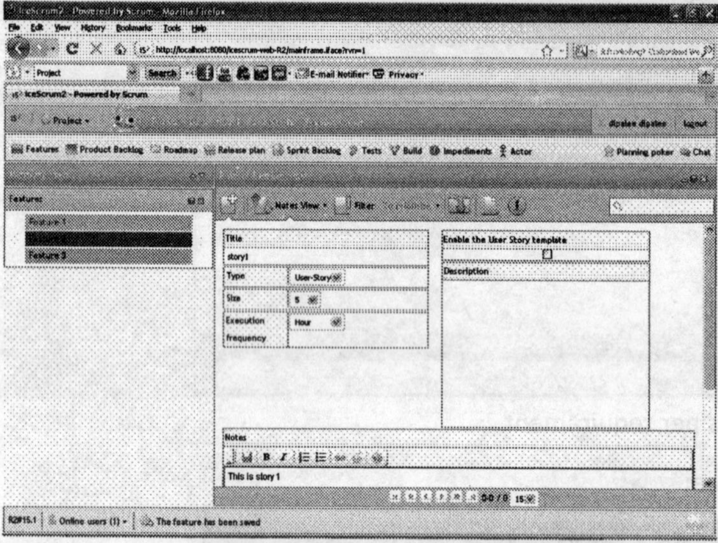

3. Story 1 will be created like following window:

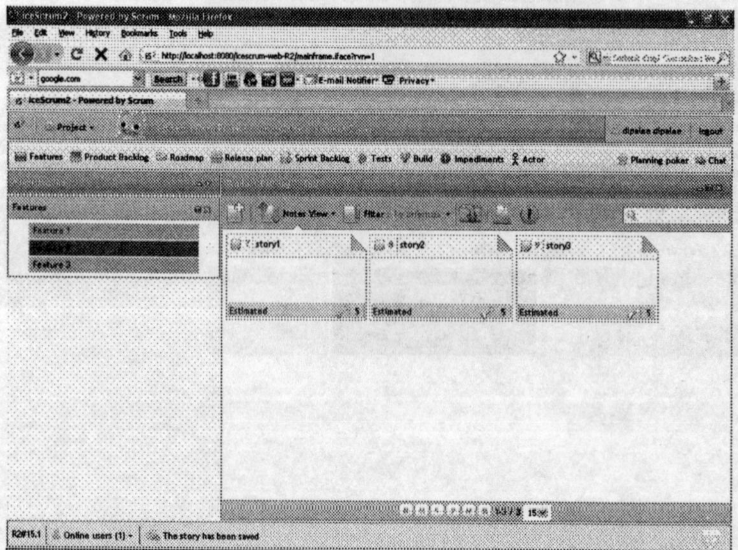

Roadmap

The roadmap shows releases & sprints on a timeline. Created sprints are displayed inside the releases. You can access to the sprints & releases content by clicking the selected object. For the first time, start by creating a releases(+) then go to the releases plan for creating sprints.

Create release:

1. Click on **Add release.**
2. Input the required information(like release name, release goal, sprint duration, start date, end date)
3. Click on accept button.
4. The newly created releases are:

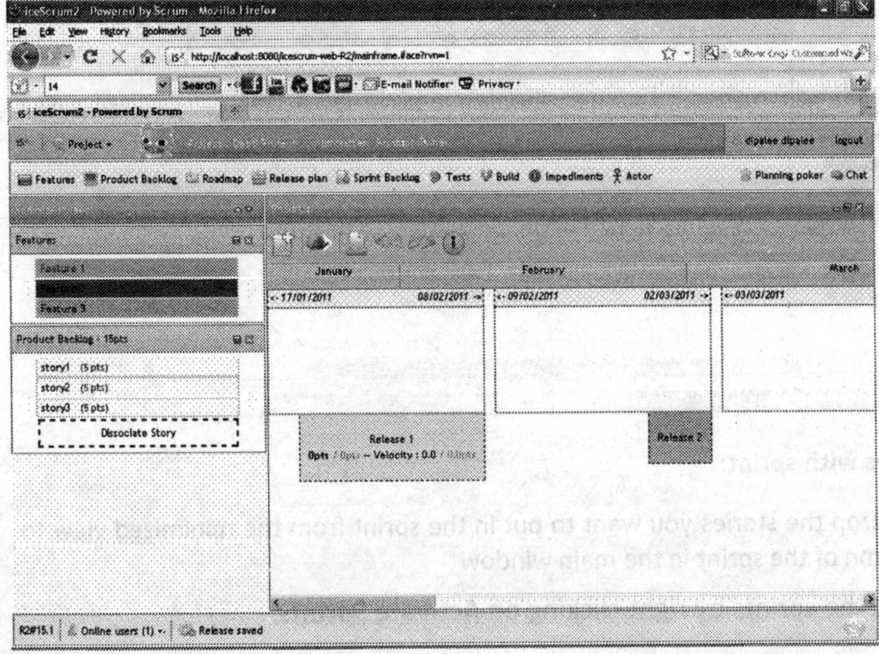

Release Plan

A release plan is the delivery of a version. By extension, in icescrum a release is the period from the beginning of work on this version until it is delivered and through a series of successive sprints. Release plan allows to associate estimated stories from product backlog(visible in the minimized view) by drag & drop on a sprint.

Create sprint:

1. Click on **Create a new Sprint.**
2. Input the required information.
3. Click on accept button.
4. The newly created sprints are:

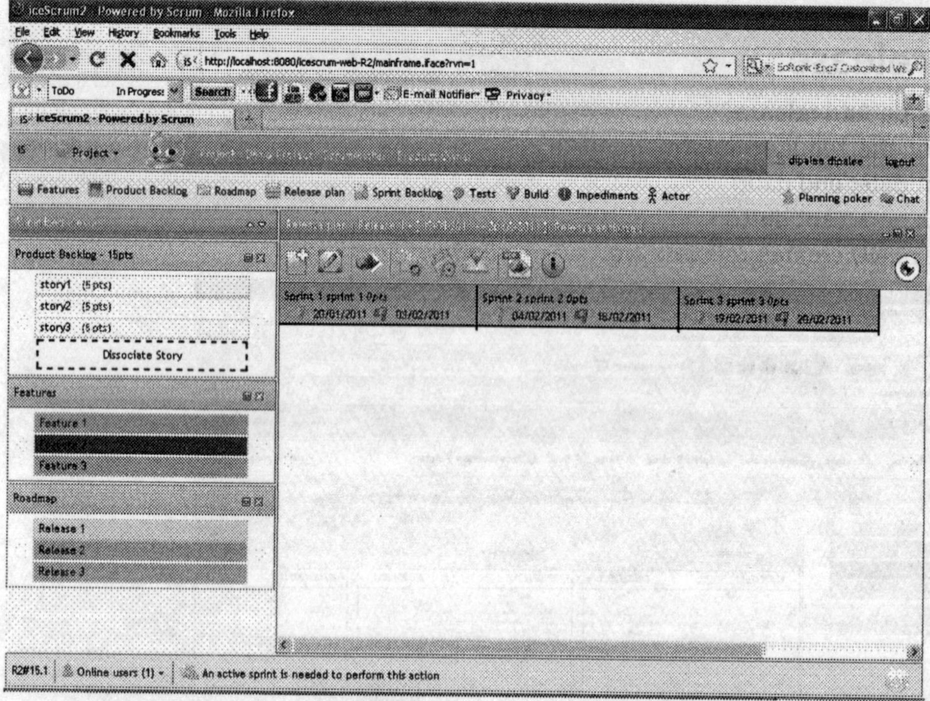

Associate stories with sprint:

1. Drag & drop the stories you want to put in the sprint from the minimized view to the column of the sprint in the main window
2. Activate the sprints by right clicking on **Activate Sprints.**

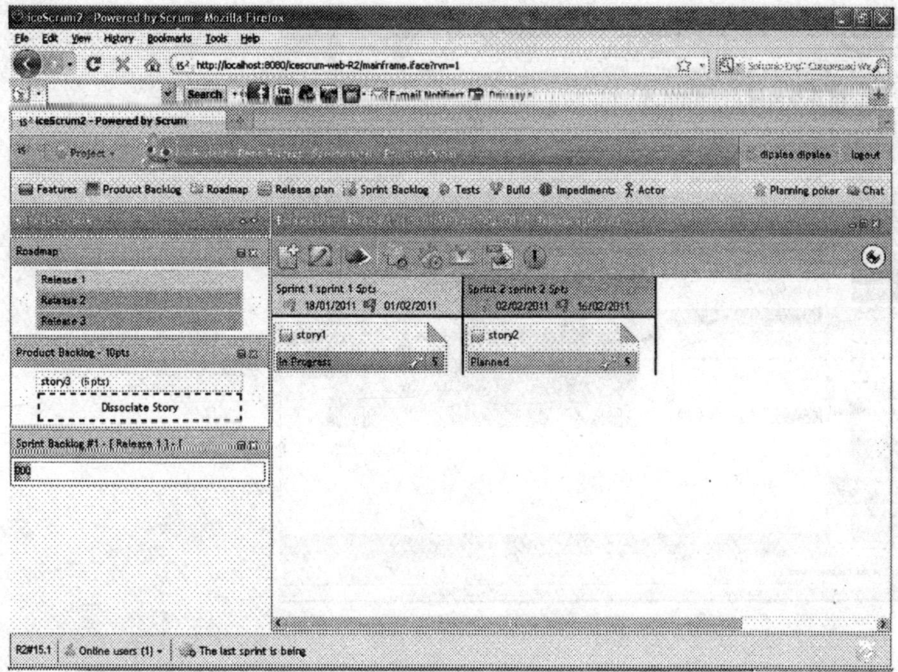

Sprint Backlog

The **sprint backlog** lists all the **tasks** that are to be done in a specific sprint.

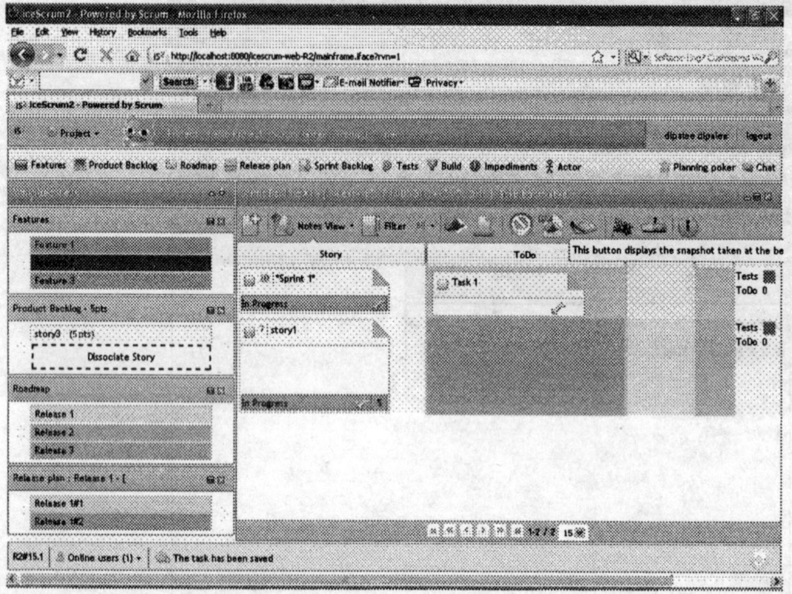

Charts:

1. Release Burndown chart

In the release plan section, click on & then select **Burndown of release.**

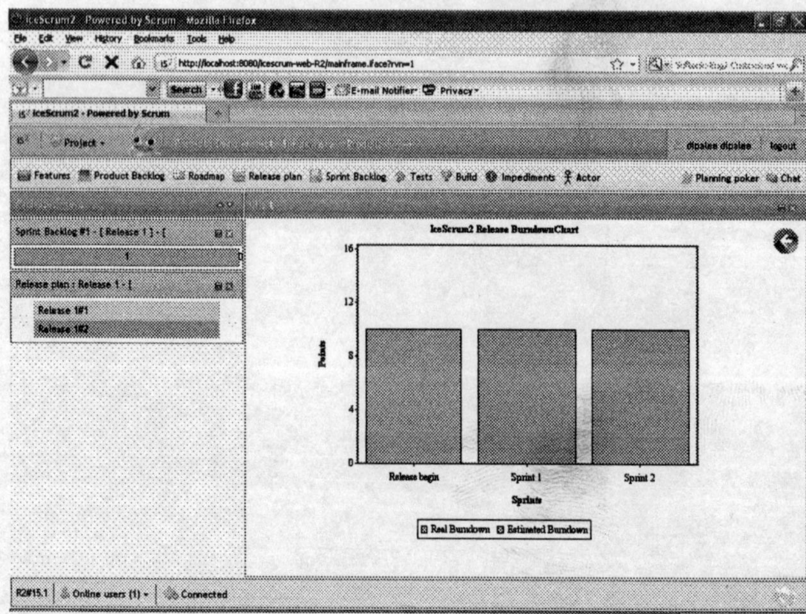

2. Parking lot chart

In the release plan section, click on 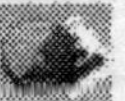 & then select **Parking Lot Chart (Features)**

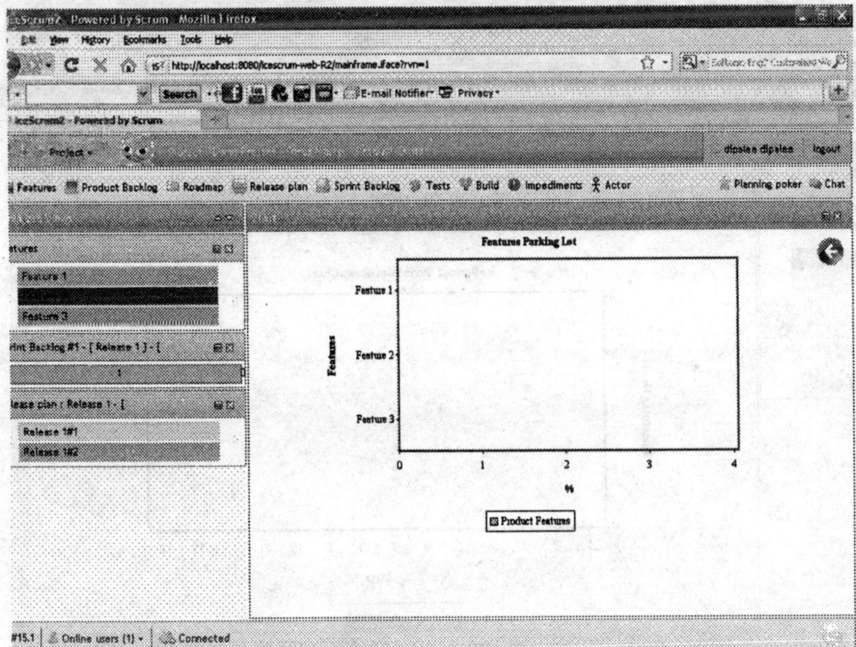

3. Sprint burndown chart

Burndown chart trace the remaining time to do in the sprints every day.

In the sprint backlog section, click & then select **Burndown Chart (Hours)**

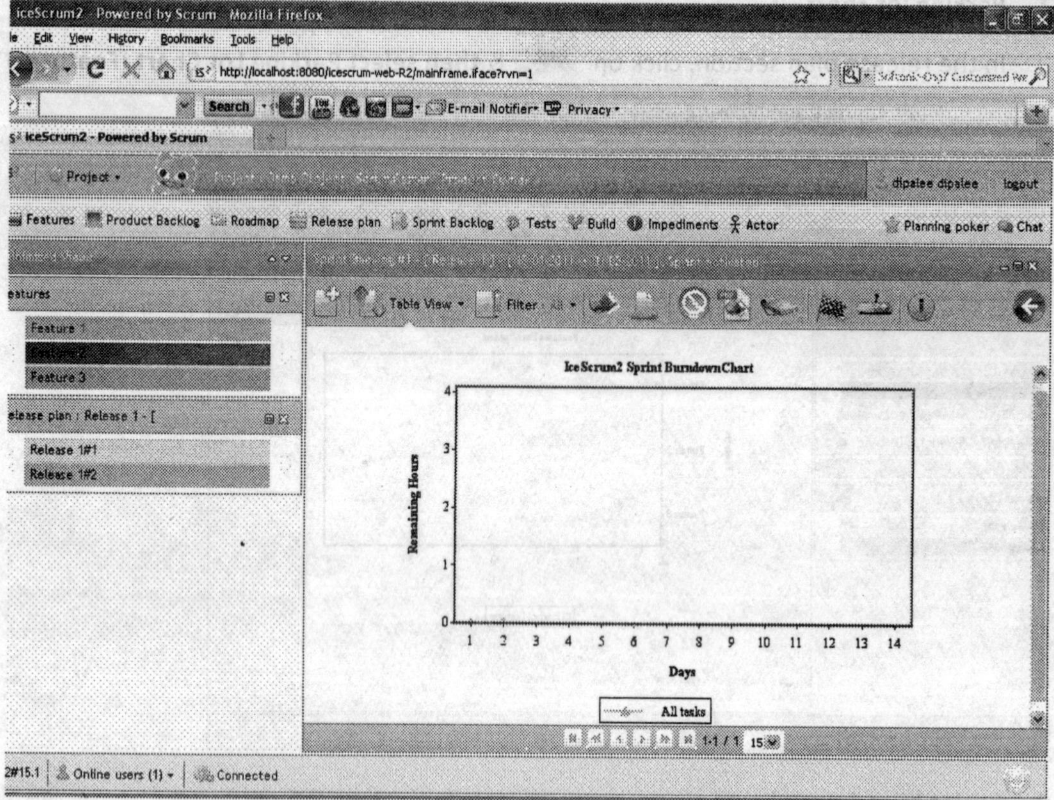

4. Sprint Burnup

3. Sprint burnup compares the number of tasks done to the total number of tasks in the sprint.

4. In the sprint backlog section, click & then select Burnup Chart (Tasks)

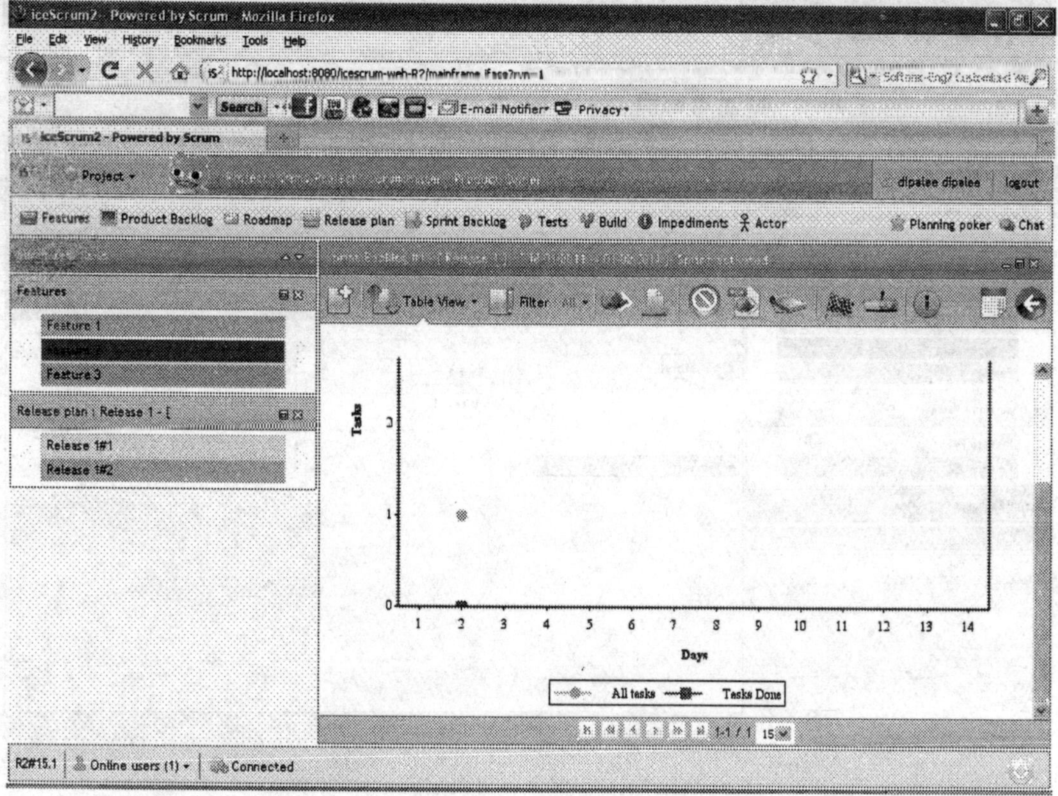

Test

1. Open the **Test** section in the menu where you can see once again the user stories of your sprint.
2. Create new test by entering required information.

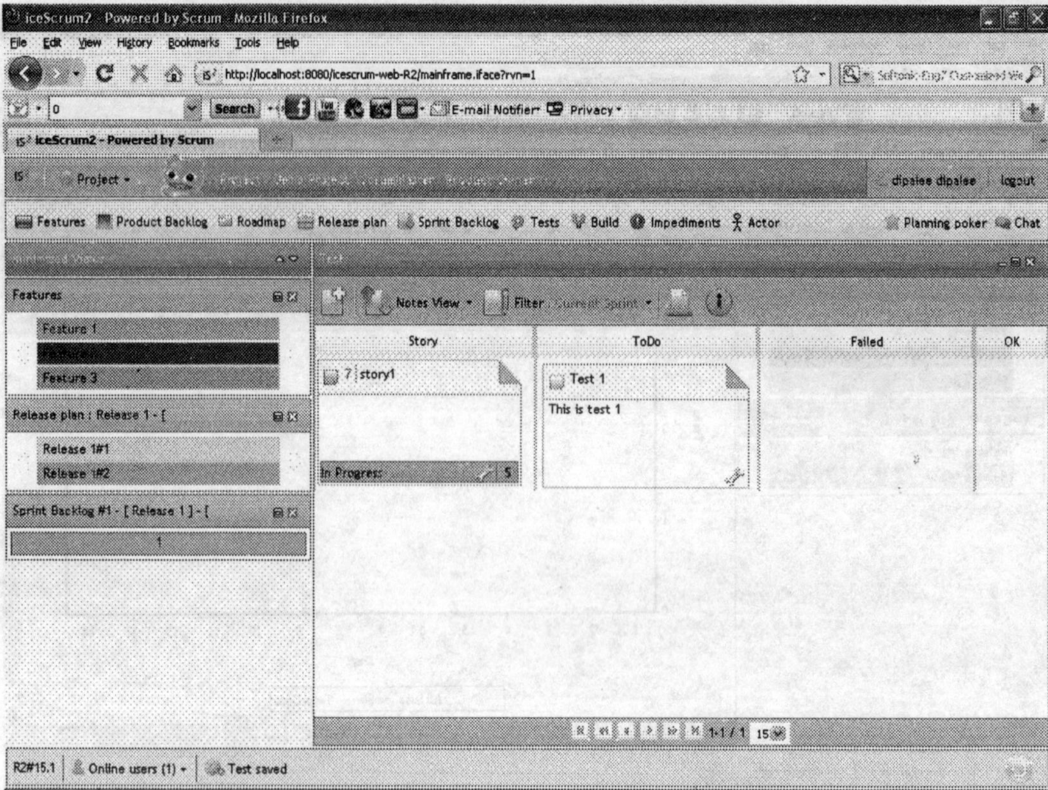

3. Product owner or yourself can change the state of the test.
4. Click on product owner following window will be displayed.

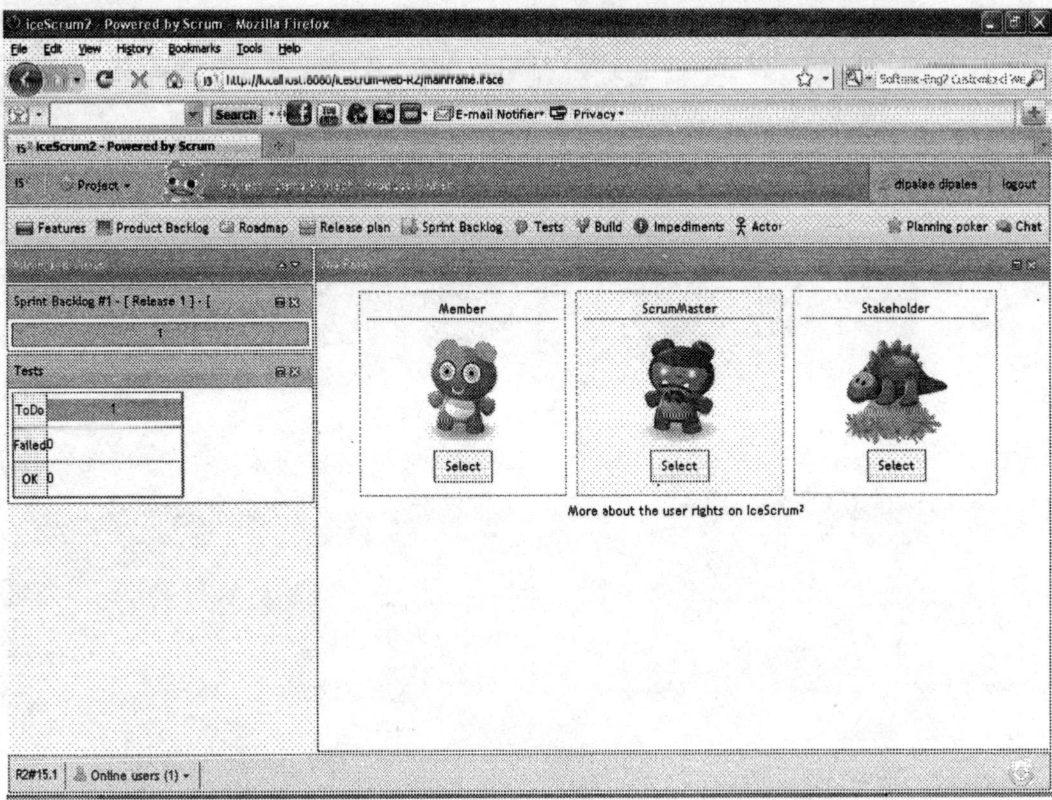

5. There are two possible resulting tests for a test: “Failed” or “Ok”.
6. Change the state as ok:

- In case of ok, the square in the last column of sprint backlog has become green.
- While in case of failure, the square would have become red.

Test Driven Development

Introduction:

What is TDD?

- "Before you write code, think about what it will do.Write a test that will use the methods you haven't even written yet."
- Extreme Programming Applied: Playing To Win
- In principle, it is just about writing the test before the program.
- But in consequence, it leads the developer to
  - First think about "how to use" the component (why do we need the component, what's it for?) and only then about "how to implement".
- So, it's a testing technique as well as a design technique
  - It results into components that are easy to test.
  - It results into components that are easy to enhance and adapt.
- In the end, there is no code without a test.
- The developer can tell at any time
  - whether everything still works as it should, or
  - what exactly does no longer work as it once did.

A test is not something you "do", it is something you "write" and run once, twice, three times, etc.

- It is a piece of code

- Testing is therefore “automated”
- Repeatedly executed, even after small changes

Motivation

- TDD is a technique whereby you write your test cases before you write any implementation code
- Tests drive or dictate the code that is developed
- An indication of “intent”
  - Tests provide a specification of “what” a piece of code actually does
  - Some might argue that “tests are part of the documentation

TDD Stages

- In Extreme Programming Explored (The Green Book), Bill Wake describes the test / code cycle:

1. Write a single test
2. Compile it. It shouldn’t compile because you’ve not written the implementation code
3. Implement just enough code to get the test to compile
4. Run the test and see it **fail**
5. Implement just enough code to get the test to pass
6. Run the test and see it **pass**
7. **Refactor** for clarity and “once and only once”
8. Repeat

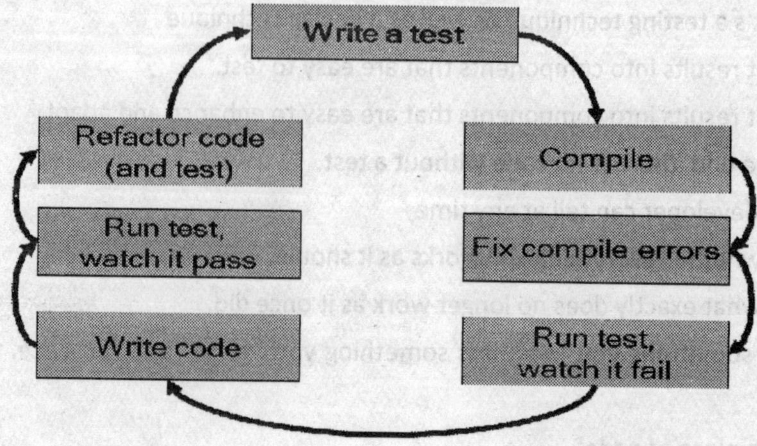

TDD in Delphi

DUnit

- An xUnit implementation for Delphi

xUnit is a colloquial umbrella term

- Platform-specific implementations
  - e.g. sUnit, JUnit, XMLUnit
- Provides classes with methods to help us write test cases
  - TTestCase
  - "Check" functions...

TDD in Delphi using DUnit

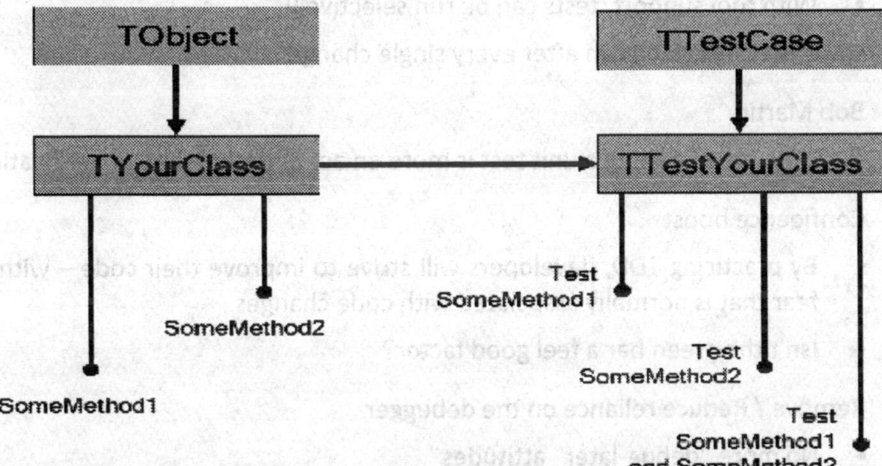

Test Complexity

- Do the simplest thing
  - Dave Astels: "Strive for simplicity"
  - Write a test that fails (red)
  - Make the test pass (green)
  - **Refactor** implementation code (change the internal design)
- Use the compiler – let it tell you about errors and omissions

- One assertion (Check/Assert) per test
    - Subject of furious debate on Yahoo's TDD group

Why TDD?

- Programmers dislike testing
    - They will test reasonably thoroughly the first time
    - The second time however, testing is usually less thorough
    - The third time, well..
- Testing is considered a "boring" task
- Testing might be the job of another department / person
- TDD encourages programmers to maintain an exhaustive set of repeatable tests
    - Tests live alongside the Class/Code Under Test (CUT)
    - With tool support, tests can be run selectively
    - The tests can be run after every single change
- Bob Martin:
    - "The act of writing a unit test is more an act of design than of verification"
- Confidence boost
    - By practicing TDD, developers will strive to improve their code – without the fear that is normally associated with code changes
    - Isn't the green bar a feel good factor?
- Remove / Reduce reliance on the debugger
    - No more "debug-later" attitudes

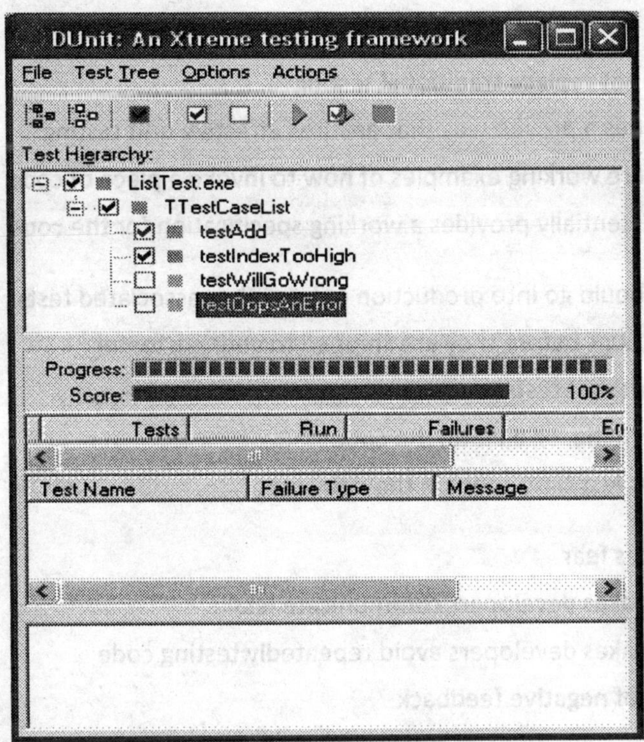

Who should write the tests?

- The programmers should write the tests
  - The programmers can't wait for somebody else to write tests
- TDD promotes "small steps", and lots of them
  - Small steps: the shortest distance between two points
  - Your destination is closer...

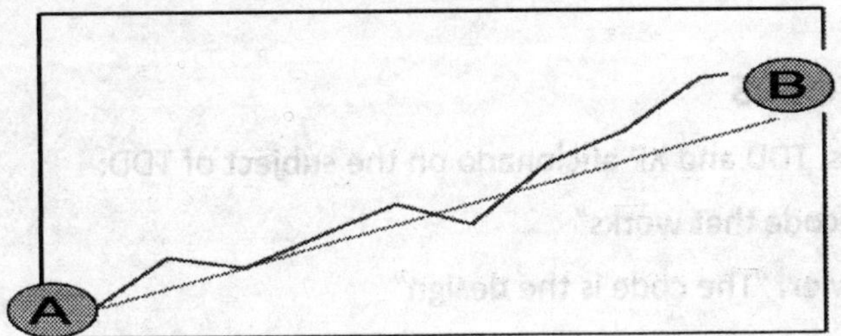

Summary

- TDD does not replace traditional testing
  - It defines a proven way that ensures effective unit testing
  - Tests are working examples of how to invoke a piece of code
    - Essentially provides a working specification for the code
- No code should go into production unless it has associated tests
  - Catch bugs before they are shipped to your customer
- No code without tests
- Tests determine, or dictate, the code
- TDD means less time spent in the debugger
- TDD negates fear
  - Fear makes developers communicate less
  - Fear makes developers avoid repeatedly testing code
  - Afraid of negative feedback
- TDD promotes the creation of a set of "programmer tests"
  - Automated tests that are written by the programmer
  - Exhaustive
  - Can be run over and over again
- TDD allows us to **refactor**, or change the implementation of a class, without the fear of breaking it
  - TDD and refactoring go hand-in-hand

Notable Quotes

- Ron Jeffries, TDD and XP aficionado on the subject of TDD:
  - "clean code that works"
- Martin Fowler: "The code is the design"

References:

- http://www.CraigMurphy.com
- NUnit:http://www.nunit.org
- CSUnit: http://www.csunit.org
- http://groups.yahoo.com/group/csunit
- Mock Objects: http://www.mockobjects.com
- testdrivendevelopment group (Yahoo):
    - http://groups.yahoo.com/group/testdrivendevelopment
- The DUnit group at SourceForge
    - http://dunit.sourceforge.net
- Lutz Roeder's .NET Reflector:
    - http://www.aisto.com/roeder/dotnet
- xUnit implementations:
    - http://www.xprogramming.com/software.htm
    - http://www.junit.org

Use Tools

- Framework for automating the unit tests
    - E.g. Junit
- Integrated development environment
    - For writing tests, using auto-completion and generation of missing code.
    - For running the tests
    - For refactoring
    - E.g. Eclipse
- Build environment
    - For executing tests automatically and during the build process
    - For computing code coverage
    - For generating test reports
    - E.g. Maven

Iterative Software Development

At the start of the iteration, the customer explains the expected functionality to the team. The customer prioritizes for business value and urgency, the team estimates the effort and cost.

Then the team brainstorms the necessary tasks to implement the functionality, details the estimation and team members select their tasks.

During the iteration, the team holds short status meetings in order to discuss the current tasks, the achievements and the problems.

At the end of the iteration, the team demonstrates to the customer the increment of potentially shippable functionality.

Acceptance Testing

- Don'wait until the software has been written in order to start with acceptance testing.
- Write the acceptance tests as soon as possible.
- Build the unit tests upon the acceptance tests.
- Execute the acceptance tests during the iteration to understand the progress.
- Execute the acceptance tests at the end of the iteration in order to verify that the requested functionality has been built.

Why?

Better collaboration between customer and developer, faster feedback

Validates the requirements

- Is that really what we need? ("Do we build the right system?", not just ""Do we build the system in the right way?")
- Typically, validation only occurs at the end of the project (where it's too late).

Targets errors not found by unit testing

- Requirements are mis-interpreted by developer
- Interface of software is not as intended
- Modules don't integrate with each other

Agile Approach to Acceptance Testing

Framework for automating the functional tests
e.g Fit,Fitnesse

Advantages:

- Easy for the user to describe the requirements themselves (no programming, just text)
- Easy for the developer to glue the requirements to the business logic
- Tests are written before the code, so this approach supports TDD
- Inexpensive because the frameworks are open source, execution of the tests can be automated.
- The developer has a clear goal to achieve!

Pairwise Testing

Introduction:

- Increasing dependency on software, networks and distributed applications
- Increasing expectation and need for quality
- Facts of life:
    - More features and complexity
    - Shorter development cycles
    - More reuse of components

Why Pairwise Testing?

- Statistical coverage to find faults

— Improved quality

- Small number of test cases

— Reduced cost

Pairwise Testing Example

- Test 3 new applications on a networked computer
- 4 test configuration factors with 3 values

Operating System	Connection	Browser	Application
XP	Dial-up	IE	App1
Linux	DSL	NetScape	App2
OS X	LAN	Firefox	App3

- 3^4=81 configurations in total – too many
- 3 configurations cover all values individually – but only a few interactions

Pairwise Testing:

- Includes all pairs of interactions between test factors
- Provides a small set of test cases – a practical alternative to testing all combinations
- Started almost 20 years ago

Increasingly popular way to improve quality and reduce cost

Galois Field Example:

- Modulo 3 arithmetic – GF(3)
- Usual + or x, divide by 3 & take remainder

+	0	1	2
0	0	1	2
1	1	2	0
2	2	0	1

x	0	1	2
0	0	0	0
1	0	1	2
2	0	2	1

- Use GF(3) tables to make orthogonal array

Orthogonal Array OA(9;3^3)

- Replace each element in the x table with the corresponding column from the + table

+	0	1	2
0	0	1	2
1	1	2	0
2	2	0	1

x	0	1	2
	0	0	0
0	1	1	1
	2	2	2

	0	1	2
	1	2	0
1	2	0	1
	0	2	1
	1	0	2
2	2	1	0

Orthogonal Array OA(9;3^4)

- Add one column which pairs a different value with every 3 rows

0	0	0	0
0	1	1	1
0	2	2	2
1	0	1	2
1	2	2	0
1	2	0	1
2	0	2	1
2	1	0	2
2	2	1	0

Networked Computer Example

- 4 test configuration factors with 3 values
- Replace numbers in OA(9;3^4) template with test factor values

Operating System	Connection	Browser	Application
0 XP	0 Dial-up	0 IE	0 App1
1 Linux	1 DSL	1 NetScape	1 App2
2 OS X	2 LAN	2 Firefox	2 App3

Networked Computer Example

- Only 9 configurations are needed to cover all 54 pairs of values using OA(9;3^4)

Operating System	Connection	Browser	Application
XP	Dial-up	IE	App1
XP	DSL	NetScape	App2
XP	LAN	Firefox	App3
Linux	Dial-up	NetScape	App3
Linux	DSL	Firefox	App1
Linux	LAN	IE	App2
OS X	Dial-up	Firefox	App2
OS X	DSL	NetScape	App3
OS X	LAN	IE	App1

Design of Experiments

- Ronald A. Fisher analyzed data from crop yield experiments
- Developed new statistical methods to study experimental data
- Pioneered the mathematical principles of experimental design

Orthogonal Arrays

- Calyampudi Radhakrishna Rao introduced Orthogonal Arrays
- Orthogonal Array designs are used in agricultural & manufacturing experiments, clinical trials, market research...
- Results can show effects of factors and how they interact

OAs for Manufacturing

- Genichi Taguchi adapted Fisher's experimental design to improve quality of manufactured goods
- Used OAs to select test parameters in creative ways
- Worldwide influence in improving manufactured quality

OAs for Software Test

- Keizo Tatsumi, Robert Mandl & others applied these ideas to software testing
- Taguchi visited Bell Labs and collaborated with Madhav Phadke
- Orthogonal Array Test System (OATS) offered statistical coverage where exhaustive testing was not possible

StarLAN and StarGROUP

- Client installation test
  - 101 combinations of PCs and OS versions
  - 15 network cards
- Tried to use OATS to reduce number of test configurations
- OATS could not handle our complex configuration constraints correctly
- Generated impossible tests, as in previous example

Networked Computer Example

- Two of the 9 configurations from OA(9;3^4) are invalid

Operating System	Connection	Browser	Application
XP	Dial-up	IE	App1
XP	DSL	NetScape	App2
XP	LAN	Firefox	App3
Linux	Dial-up	NetScape	App3
Linux	DSL	Firefox	App1
Linux	LAN	IE	App2
OS X	Dial-up	Firefox	App2
OS X	DSL	NetScape	App3
OS X	LAN	IE	App1

What to do?

- Skip the bad cases? Then for each case there is no coverage for 5 good pairs, along with the invalid one

- Replace values 'Linux', 'OS X' or 'Int Explorer' to avoid bad pairs? Still miss good pairs
- Solution: Computer search for small number of cases to cover all allowed pairs.

Networked Computer Example

- 11 configurations cover 52 allowed pairs

Operating System	Connection	Browser	Application
XP	Dial-up	NetScape	App1
XP	DSL	Firefox	App2
OS X	DSL	NetScape	App3
OS X	LAN	Firefox	App1
Linux	Dial-up	Firefox	App3
Linux	LAN	NetScape	App2
XP	LAN	IE	App3
OS X	Dial-up	Firefox	App2
Linux	DSL	NetScape	App1
XP	Dial-up	IE	App2
XP	DSL	IE	App1

Constrained Array Test System

- Search among allowed test cases to handle constraints
- Find next "best" test case to minimize uncovered pairs
- Secondary result: fewer test cases than OATS

Types of Arrays

	Orthogonal Arrays	Covering Arrays
All Pairs Test Cases	in equal numbers a few	at least once fewer typically
Fixed Values	OA($18;3^7$)	CA($14;3^7$)
Mixed Values	OA($12;3^1 2^4$)	CA($6;3^1 2^4$)

Pairwise Selection of Input Data

- Identify equivalence classes
  - Analyze functional requirements, use cases
  - Partition factor value combinations for equivalent processing and expected results
- Generate test cases for different classes separately
  - All pairs from each class go to same resulting state
  - Example: Don't mix error combinations with normal combinations

References:

www.testcover.com

Pairwise Testing using Jenny/ JWrap tool

Introduction:

Jenny:

`jenny` is tool for generating regression tests. Any time exhaustive testing looks painful due to the combinatorial explosion of features interactions to be tested, consider using `jenny`. It will cover most of the interactions with far fewer testcases. It can guarantee pairwise testing of all features that can be used together, and it can avoid those feature combinations that cannot.

Features:

- Coded in C language
- Guarantees pair wise testing for all the features paired together

Download:

http://burtleburtle.net/bob/math/jenny.html

JWrap:

JWRAP is the Ms-excel wrapper for Jenny. jenny is a time tested tool for generating test cases. the tool is based on Orthogonal array and paring concept.The tool also has exclude filters to generate robust test cases. works only in Windows.

Jwrap has 2 components:

JWrap Engine: Converts all the jenny format to Human understandable form.
TWrap template: Populates all the values in the spread sheet.

Download:

http://sourceforge.net/projects/jwrap/

<u>Click on Download now button.</u>

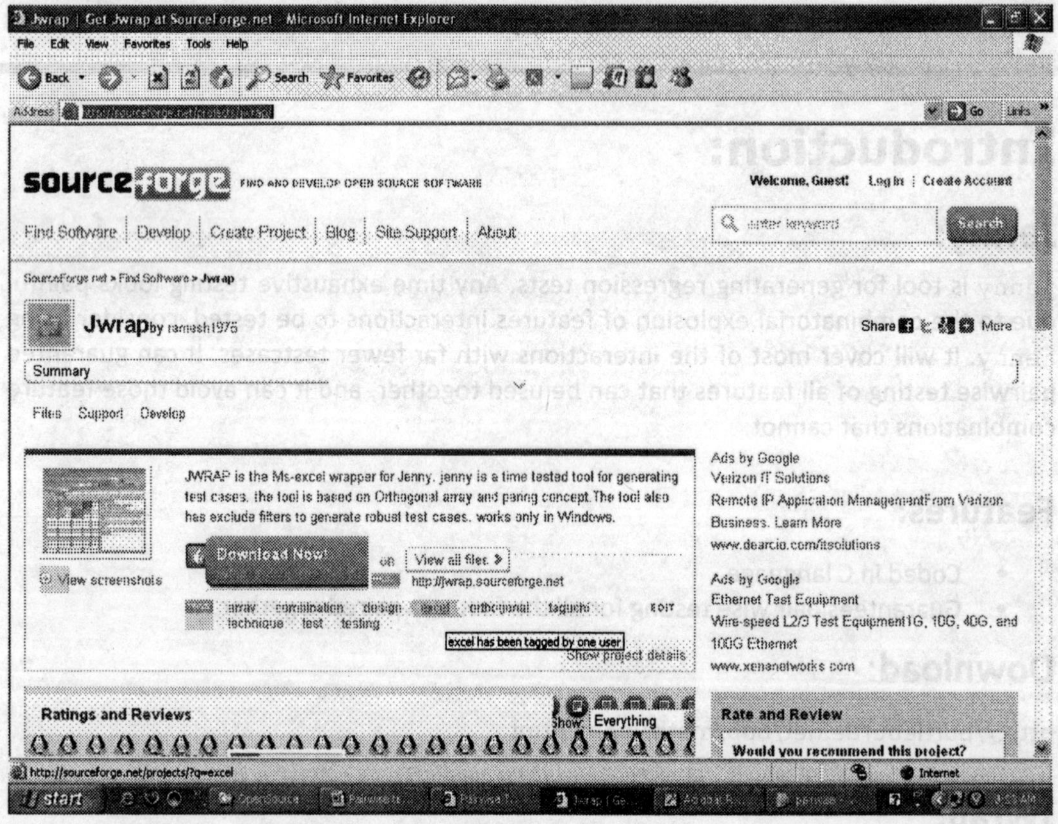

download 'jwrap_2.2.Zip' file and extract to folder.

After extracting 'JWrap2.2.zip' folder will look like this:

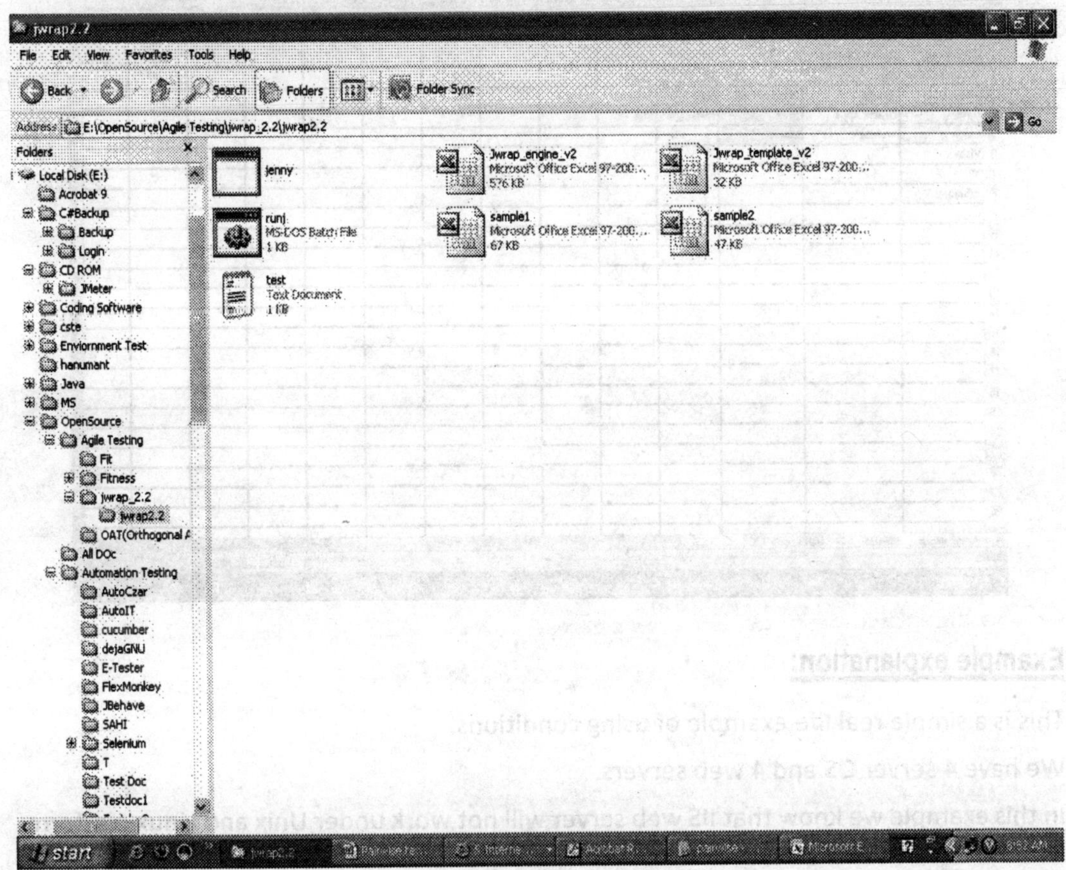

Click on 'Sample1.xls'

OS Server	App/Web server	OS Client	Browser	Database
Windows 2000	IIS	Windows 2000	IE6	Oracle
Windows NT	Apache	Windows XP	IE5	Sybase
Unix	Oracle Apps	Unix	Netscape6	SQL
Linux	Weblogic	Linux		
Vista				
XP				
Windows 7				

Example explanation:

This is a simple real life example of using conditions.

We have 4 server OS and 4 web servers.

In this example we know that IIS web server will not work under Unix and Linux platform. In order to exclude this combination, we should fill color the cells. In this example we fill colored Unix,Linux and IIS in yellow.

In the same way we have client OS and browsers. Again IE5 and IE6 will now work under Linux and UNIX combination so we mark these cells in purple.

When you click on Run button and check with results sheet. You can find that the tool has generated paring combinations and implemented the exclude condition.

So this is the scenario we will going to test:

Click on 'Jwrap_engine_v2.xls'

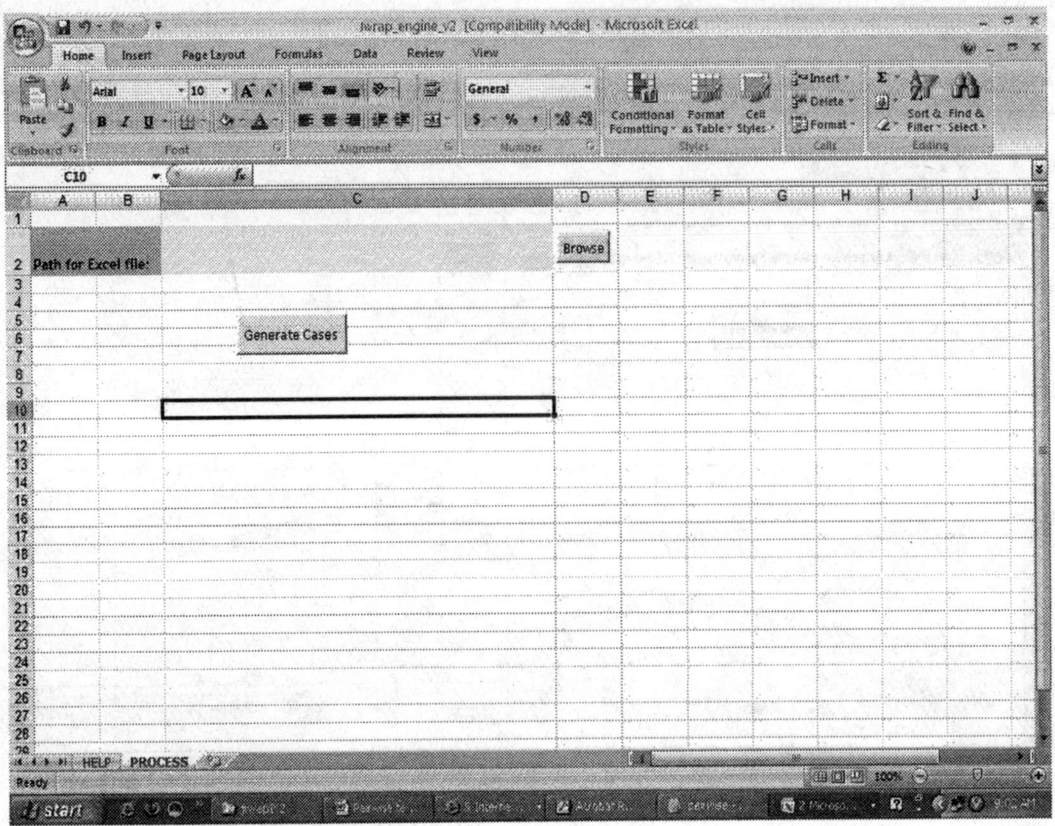

Click on Browser button and select 'Sample1.xls' file

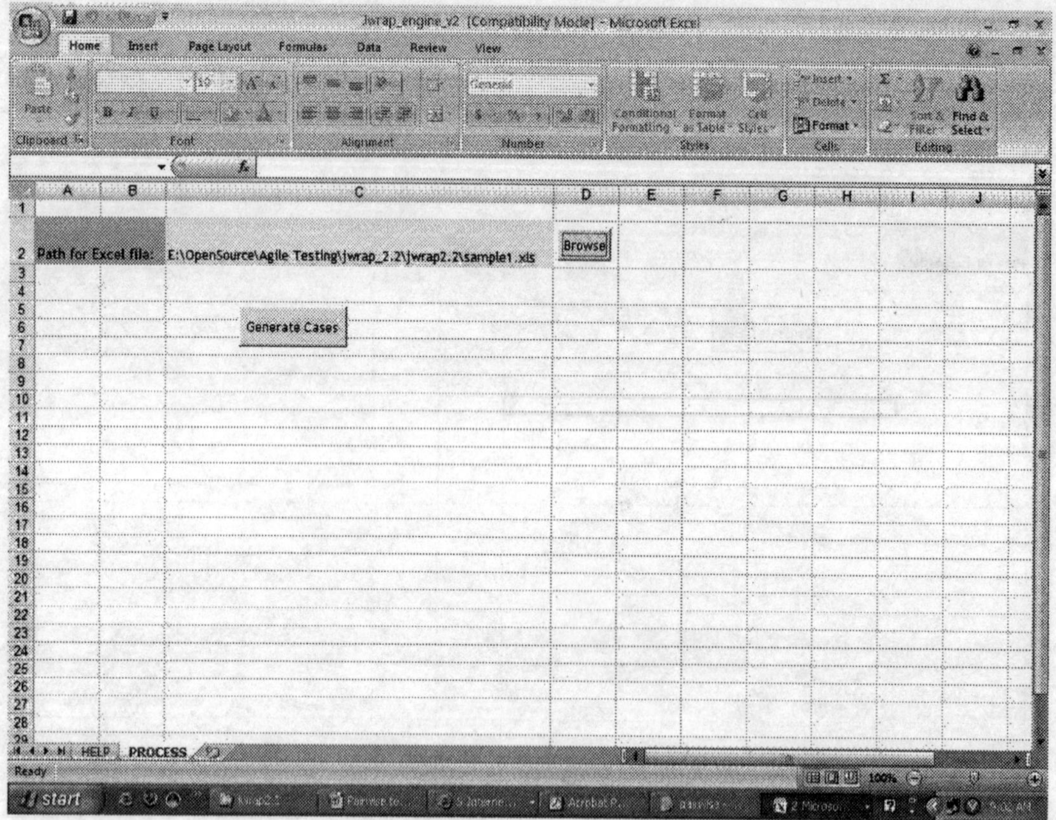

Click on 'Generate Cases'

It will open Sample1.xls and in 'Result tab it will show the Pairwise test result.

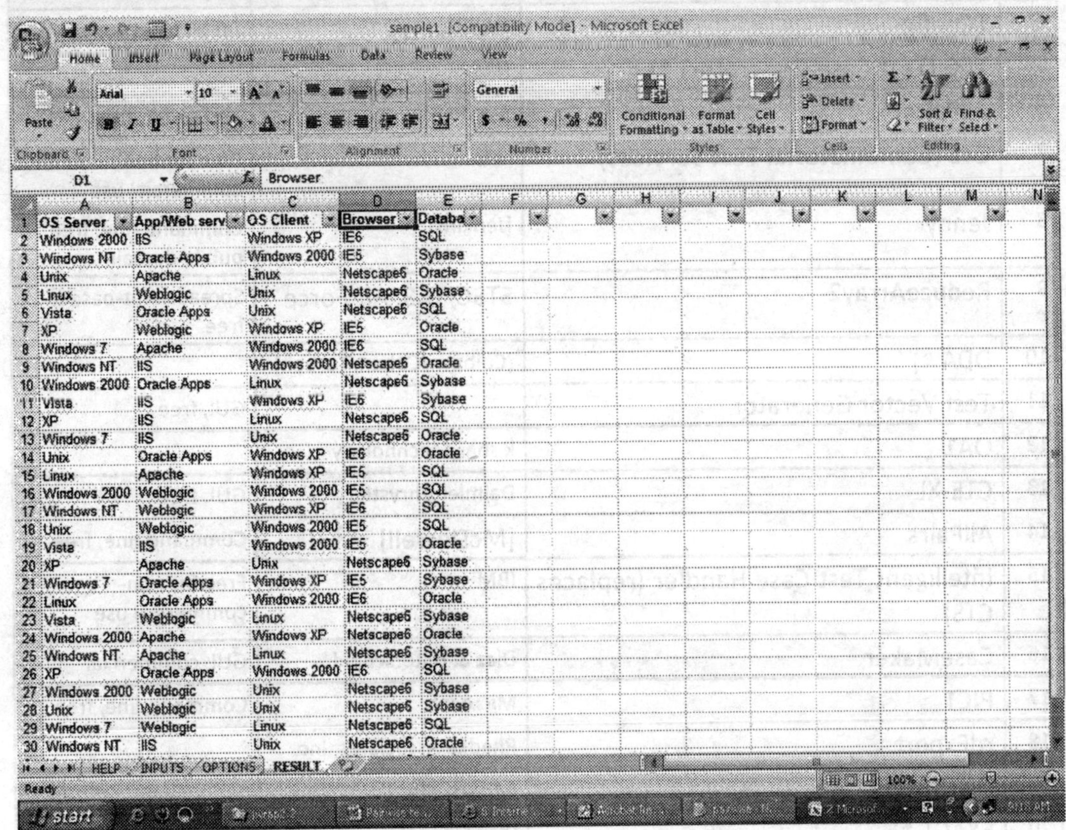

	OS Server	App/Web serv	OS Client	Browser	Databa
2	Windows 2000	IIS	Windows XP	IE6	SQL
3	Windows NT	Oracle Apps	Windows 2000	IE5	Sybase
4	Unix	Apache	Linux	Netscape6	Oracle
5	Linux	Weblogic	Unix	Netscape6	Sybase
6	Vista	Oracle Apps	Unix	Netscape6	SQL
7	XP	Weblogic	Windows XP	IE5	Oracle
8	Windows 7	Apache	Windows 2000	IE6	SQL
9	Windows NT	IIS	Windows 2000	Netscape6	Oracle
10	Windows 2000	Oracle Apps	Linux	Netscape6	Sybase
11	Vista	IIS	Windows XP	IE5	Sybase
12	XP	IIS	Linux	Netscape6	SQL
13	Windows 7	IIS	Unix	Netscape6	Oracle
14	Unix	Oracle Apps	Windows XP	IE6	Oracle
15	Linux	Apache	Windows XP	IE5	SQL
16	Windows 2000	Weblogic	Windows 2000	IE5	SQL
17	Windows NT	Weblogic	Windows XP	IE6	SQL
18	Unix	Weblogic	Windows 2000	IE5	SQL
19	Vista	IIS	Windows 2000	IE5	Oracle
20	XP	Apache	Unix	Netscape6	Sybase
21	Windows 7	Oracle Apps	Windows XP	IE5	Sybase
22	Linux	Oracle Apps	Windows 2000	IE6	Oracle
23	Vista	Weblogic	Linux	Netscape6	Sybase
24	Windows 2000	Apache	Windows XP	Netscape6	Oracle
25	Windows NT	Apache	Linux	Netscape6	Sybase
26	XP	Oracle Apps	Windows 2000	IE6	SQL
27	Windows 2000	Weblogic	Unix	Netscape6	Sybase
28	Unix	Weblogic	Unix	Netscape6	Sybase
29	Windows 7	Weblogic	Linux	Netscape6	SQL
30	Windows NT	IIS	Unix	Netscape6	Oracle

References:

http://www.pairwise.org/tools.asp

Other Pairwise Open Source Tool

Sr. No	Tool Name		
1	CATS (Constrained Array Test System) *)	[Sherwood] Bell Labs.	
2	OATS (Orthogonal Array Test System) *)	[Phadke] AT&T	

3	IPO (PairTest) *)	[Tai/Lei]	
4	TConfig	[Williams]	Java-applet
5	TCG (Test Case Generator) *)	NASA	
6	AllPairs	Satisfice	Perl script, free, GPL
7	CTS (Combinatorial Test Services)	IBM	Free for non-commercial use
8	Jenny	[Jenkins]	Command-line, free, public-domain
9	ReduceArray2	STSC, U.S. Air Force	Spreadsheet-based, free
10	DDA *)	[Colburn/Cohen/Turban]	
11	Test Vector Generator		GUI, free
12	OA1	k sharp technology	
13	CTE-XL	Daimler Chrystler	GUI, free
14	AllPairs	[McDowell]	Command-line, free
15	Intelligent Test Case Handler (replaces CTS)	IBM	Free for non-commercial use
16	CaseMaker	Díaz & Hilterscheid	GUI, commercial
17	PICT	Microsoft	Command-line, free
18	rdExpert	Phadke Associates, Inc.	
19	OATSGen *)	Motorola	
20	EXACT *)	[Yan/Zhang]	
21	AllPairs	MetaCommunications	Free
22	FireEye	NIST	GUI
23	Pairwise Test Case Generator	TestersDesk	Web-based
24	Combo-Test	The Australian eHealth Research Centre	Command-line, free
25	IPO-s *)	[Calvagna/ Gargantini]	

Pairwise Testing using www.testersdesk.com tool

Introduction:

Open URL 'http://www.testersdesk.com/TestersDesk/TestersDesk.jsp'

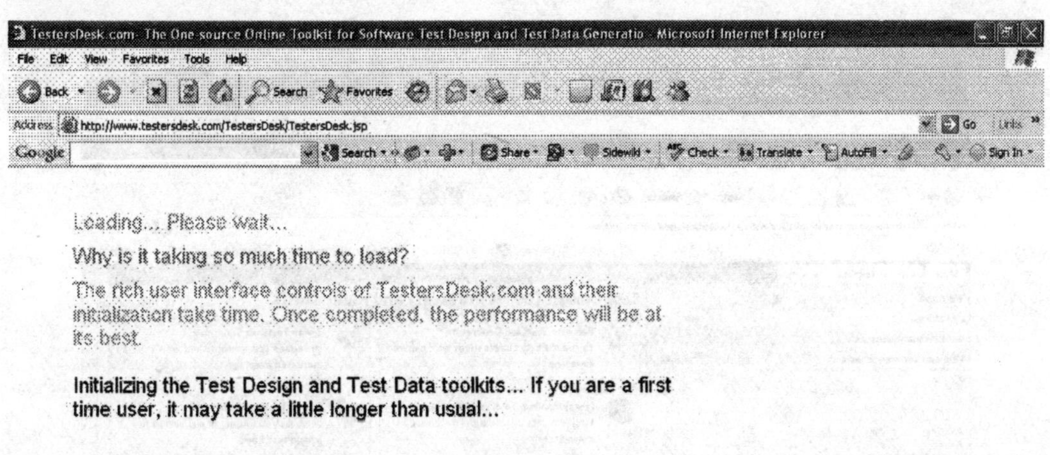

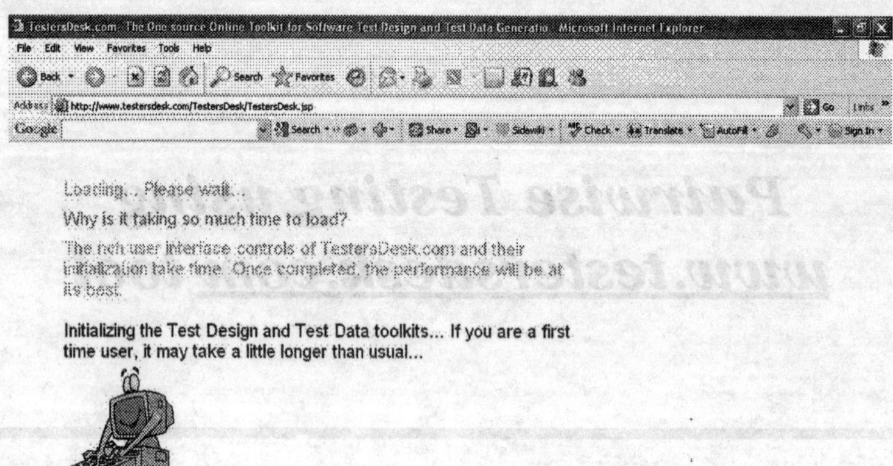
TestersDesk.com The One source Online Toolkit for Software Test Design and Test Data Generatio - Microsoft Internet Explorer
File Edit View Favorites Tools Help
Back Search Favorites
Address http://www.testersdesk.com/TestersDesk/TestersDesk.jsp
Go Links
Loading... Please wait...
Why is it taking so much time to load?
The rich user interface controls of TestersDesk.com and their initialization take time. Once completed, the performance will be at its best.
Initializing the Test Design and Test Data toolkits... If you are a first time user, it may take a little longer than usual...
Opening page http://www.testersdesk.com/TestersDesk/TestersDesk.jsp...
Internet
start

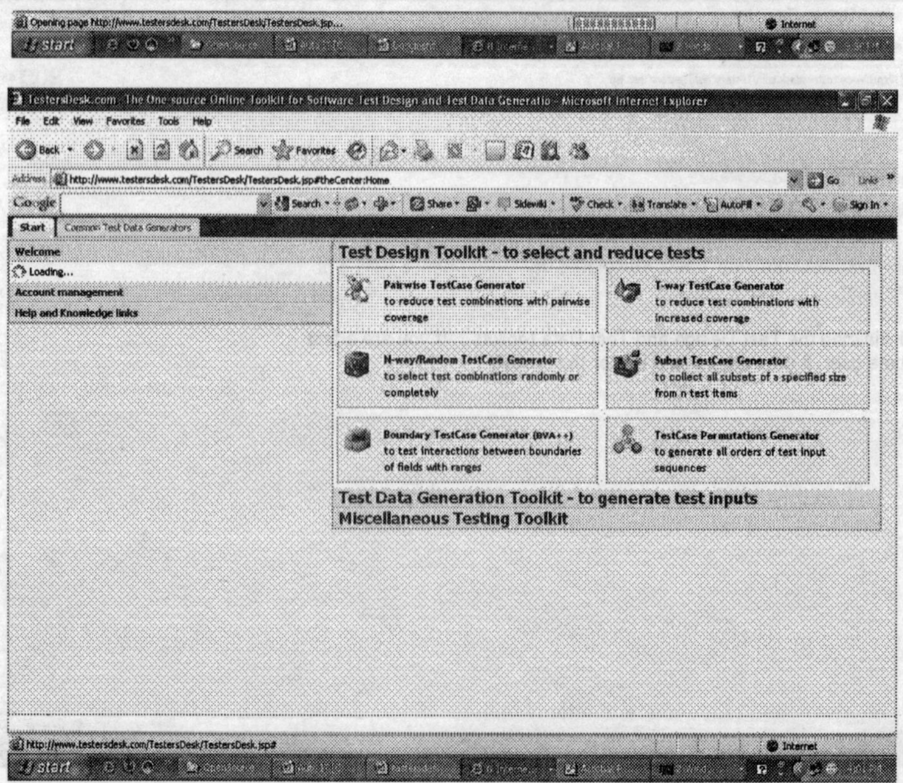
TestersDesk.com The One source Online Toolkit for Software Test Design and Test Data Generatio - Microsoft Internet Explorer
File Edit View Favorites Tools Help
Address http://www.testersdesk.com/TestersDesk/TestersDesk.jsp#theCenter:Home
Start
Common Test Data Generators
Welcome
Loading...
Account management
Help and Knowledge links
Test Design Toolkit - to select and reduce tests
Pairwise TestCase Generator
to reduce test combinations with pairwise coverage
T-way TestCase Generator
to reduce test combinations with increased coverage
N-way/Random TestCase Generator
to select test combinations randomly or completely
Subset TestCase Generator
to collect all subsets of a specified size from n test items
Boundary TestCase Generator (BVA++)
to test interactions between boundaries of fields with ranges
TestCase Permutations Generator
to generate all orders of test input sequences
Test Data Generation Toolkit - to generate test inputs
Miscellaneous Testing Toolkit
http://www.testersdesk.com/TestersDesk/TestersDesk.jsp#
Internet
start

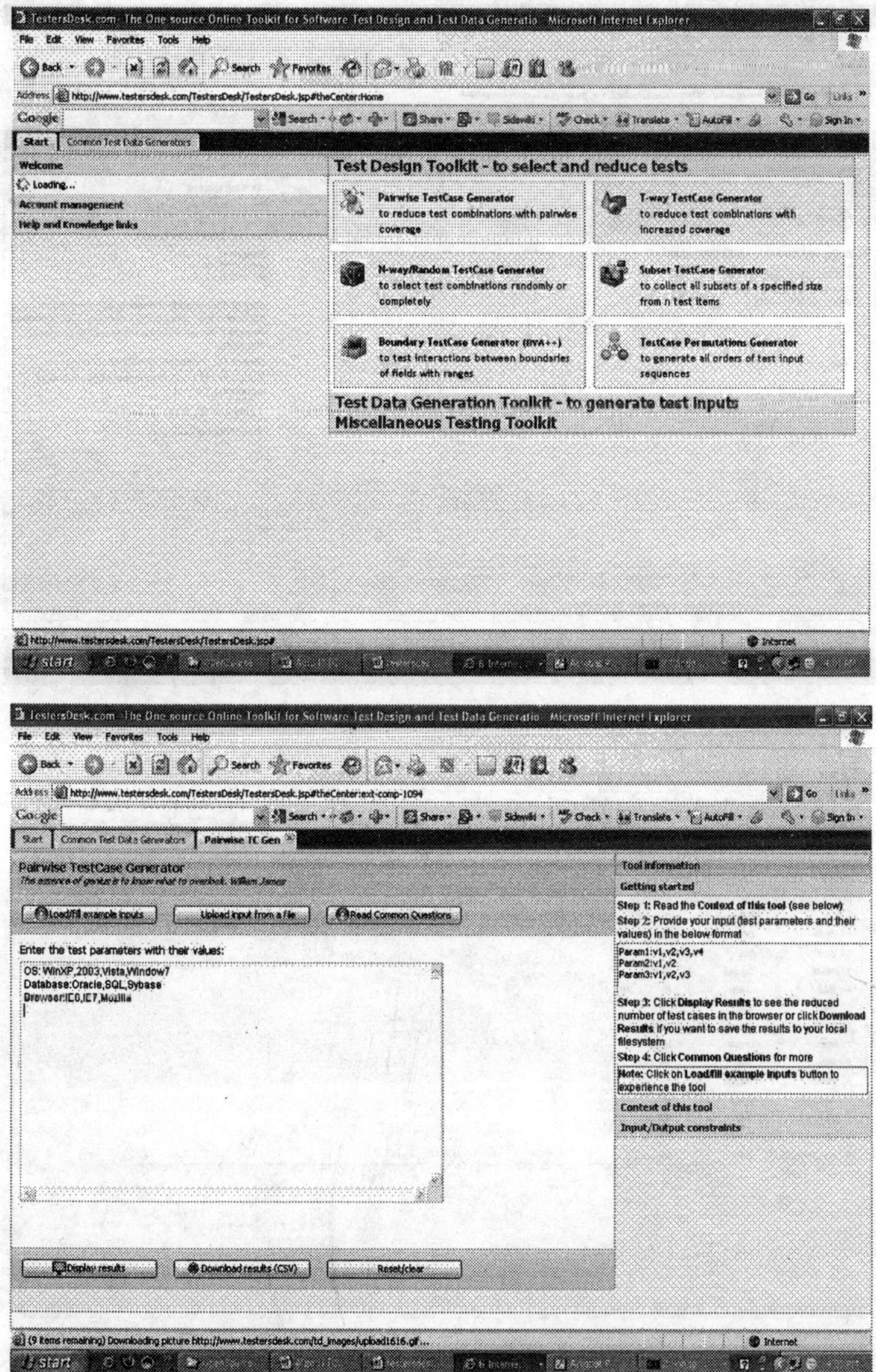

TestersDesk.com: The One source Online Toolkit for Software Test Design and Test Data Generatio - Microsoft Internet Explorer
http://www.testersdesk.com/TestersDesk/TestersDesk.jsp#theCenter:Home
Start
Common Test Data Generators
Welcome
Loading...
Account management
Help and Knowledge links
Test Design Toolkit - to select and reduce tests
Pairwise TestCase Generator
to reduce test combinations with pairwise coverage
T-way TestCase Generator
to reduce test combinations with increased coverage
N-way/Random TestCase Generator
to select test combinations randomly or completely
Subset TestCase Generator
to collect all subsets of a specified size from n test items
Boundary TestCase Generator (BVA++)
to test interactions between boundaries of fields with ranges
TestCase Permutations Generator
to generate all orders of test input sequences
Test Data Generation Toolkit - to generate test inputs
Miscellaneous Testing Toolkit
http://www.testersdesk.com/TestersDesk/TestersDesk.jsp#
TestersDesk.com - The One source Online Toolkit for Software Test Design and Test Data Generatio - Microsoft Internet Explorer
http://www.testersdesk.com/TestersDesk/TestersDesk.jsp#theCenter:ext-comp-1094
Pairwise TC Gen
Pairwise TestCase Generator
Load/fill example inputs
Upload input from a file
Read Common Questions
Enter the test parameters with their values:
OS: WinXP,2003,Vista,Window7
Database:Oracle,SQL,Sybase
Browser:IE6,IE7,Mozilla
Tool information
Getting started
Step 1: Read the Context of this tool (see below)
Step 2: Provide your input (test parameters and their values) in the below format
Param1:v1,v2,v3,v4
Param2:v1,v2
Param3:v1,v2,v3
Step 3: Click Display Results to see the reduced number of test cases in the browser or click Download Results if you want to save the results to your local filesystem
Step 4: Click Common Questions for more
Note: Click on Load/fill example inputs button to experience the tool
Context of this tool
Input/Output constraints
Display results
Download results (CSV)
Reset/clear
(9 items remaining) Downloading picture http://www.testersdesk.com/td_images/upload1616.gif...

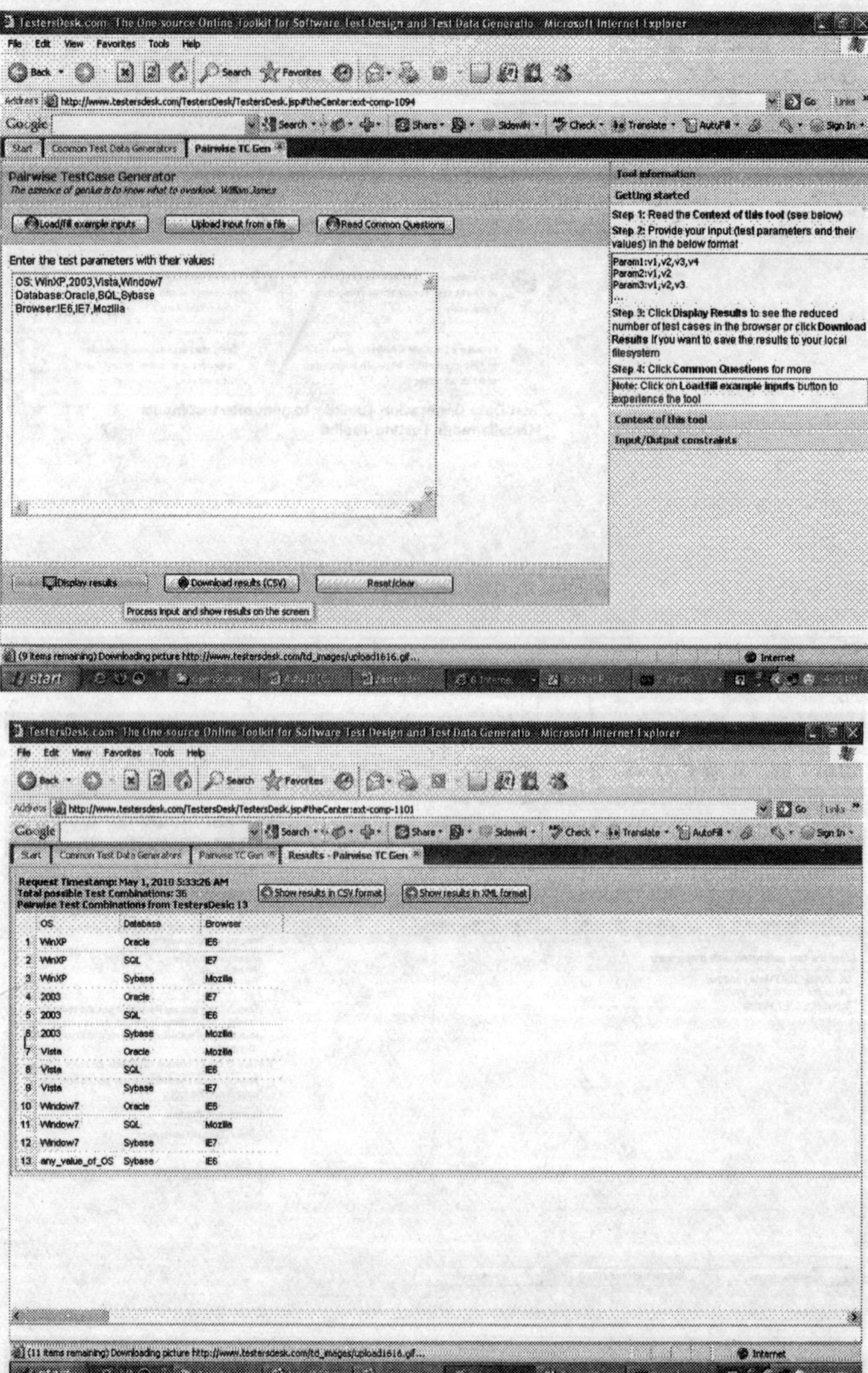
TestersDesk.com: The One-source Online Toolkit for Software Test Design and Test Data Generatio - Microsoft Internet Explorer
File Edit View Favorites Tools Help
http://www.testersdesk.com/TestersDesk/TestersDesk.jsp#theCenter:ext-comp-1094
Start
Common Test Data Generators
Pairwise TC Gen
Pairwise TestCase Generator
The essence of genius is to know what to overlook. William James
Load/fill example inputs
Upload input from a file
Read Common Questions
Enter the test parameters with their values:
OS: WinXP,2003,Vista,Window7
Database:Oracle,SQL,Sybase
Browser:IE6,IE7,Mozilla
Display results
Download results (CSV)
Reset/clear
Process input and show results on the screen
Tool information
Getting started
Step 1: Read the Context of this tool (see below)
Step 2: Provide your input (test parameters and their values) in the below format
Param1:v1,v2,v3,v4
Param2:v1,v2
Param3:v1,v2,v3
...
Step 3: Click Display Results to see the reduced number of test cases in the browser or click Download Results if you want to save the results to your local filesystem
Step 4: Click Common Questions for more
Note: Click on Load/fill example inputs button to experience the tool
Context of this tool
Input/Output constraints
(9 items remaining) Downloading picture http://www.testersdesk.com/td_images/upload1616.gif...
Internet
TestersDesk.com: The One-source Online Toolkit for Software Test Design and Test Data Generatio - Microsoft Internet Explorer
http://www.testersdesk.com/TestersDesk/TestersDesk.jsp#theCenter:ext-comp-1101
Results - Pairwise TC Gen
Request Timestamp: May 1, 2010 5:33:26 AM
Total possible Test Combinations: 36
Pairwise Test Combinations from TestersDesk: 13
Show results in CSV format
Show results in XML format
OS Database Browser
1 WinXP Oracle IE6
2 WinXP SQL IE7
3 WinXP Sybase Mozilla
4 2003 Oracle IE7
5 2003 SQL IE6
6 2003 Sybase Mozilla
7 Vista Oracle Mozilla
8 Vista SQL IE6
9 Vista Sybase IE7
10 Window7 Oracle IE6
11 Window7 SQL Mozilla
12 Window7 Sybase IE7
13 any_value_of_OS Sybase IE6
(11 items remaining) Downloading picture http://www.testersdesk.com/td_images/upload1616.gif...
Internet

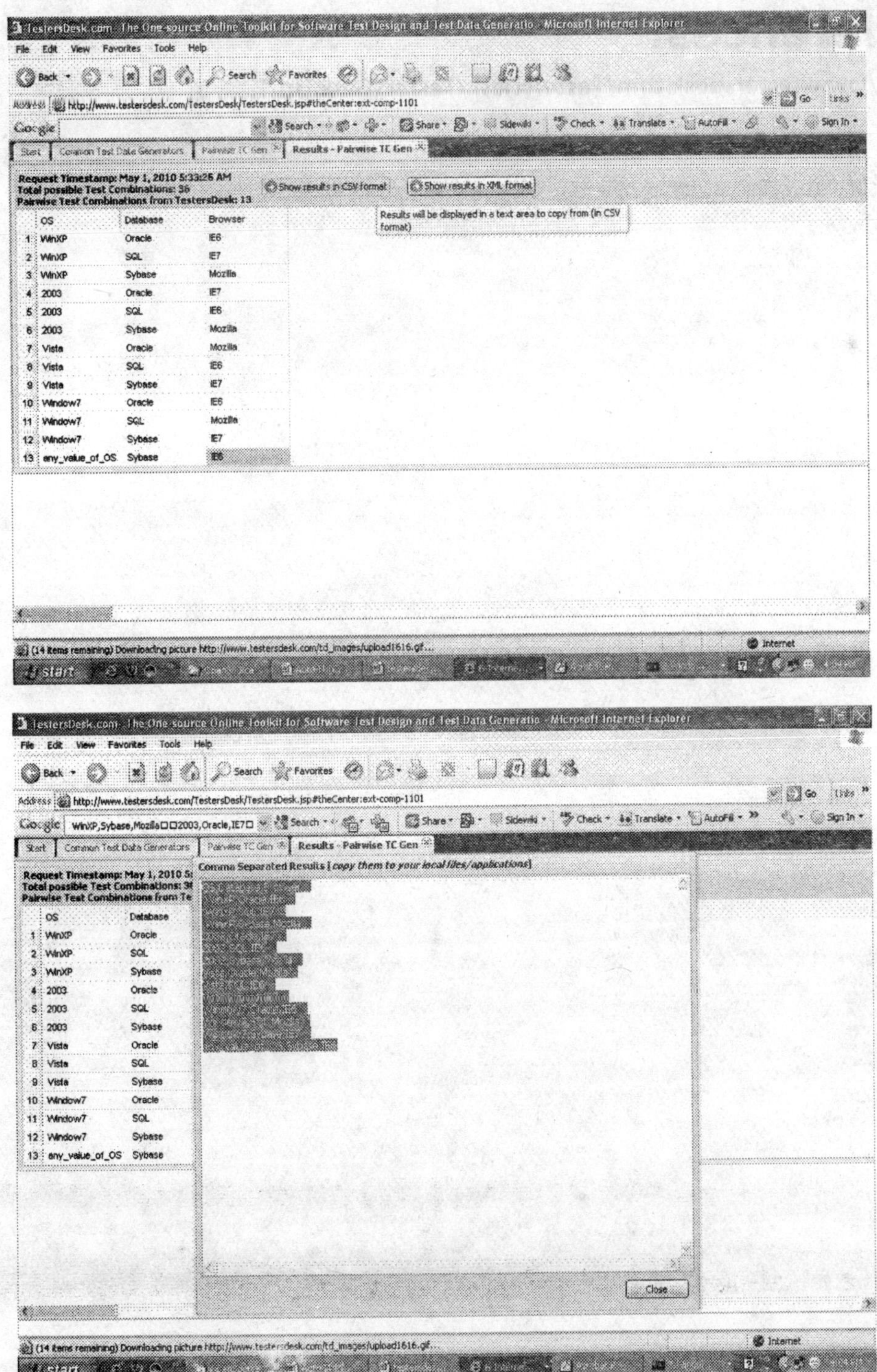
TestersDesk.com - The One-source Online Toolkit for Software Test Design and Test Data Generatio - Microsoft Internet Explorer
File Edit View Favorites Tools Help
http://www.testersdesk.com/TestersDesk/TestersDesk.jsp#theCenter:ext-comp-1101
Start
Common Test Data Generators
Pairwise TC Gen
Results - Pairwise TC Gen
Request Timestamp: May 1, 2010 5:33:26 AM
Total possible Test Combinations: 36
Pairwise Test Combinations from TestersDesk: 13
Show results in CSV format
Show results in XML format
Results will be displayed in a text area to copy from (in CSV format)
OS | Database | Browser
1 WinXP Oracle IE6
2 WinXP SQL IE7
3 WinXP Sybase Mozilla
4 2003 Oracle IE7
5 2003 SQL IE6
6 2003 Sybase Mozilla
7 Vista Oracle Mozilla
8 Vista SQL IE6
9 Vista Sybase IE7
10 Window7 Oracle IE6
11 Window7 SQL Mozilla
12 Window7 Sybase IE7
13 any_value_of_OS Sybase IE6
(14 items remaining) Downloading picture http://www.testersdesk.com/td_images/upload1616.gif...
Internet
start
Comma Separated Results [copy them to your local files/applications]
Close

References:

http://www.testersdesk.com/TestersDesk/TestersDesk.jsp

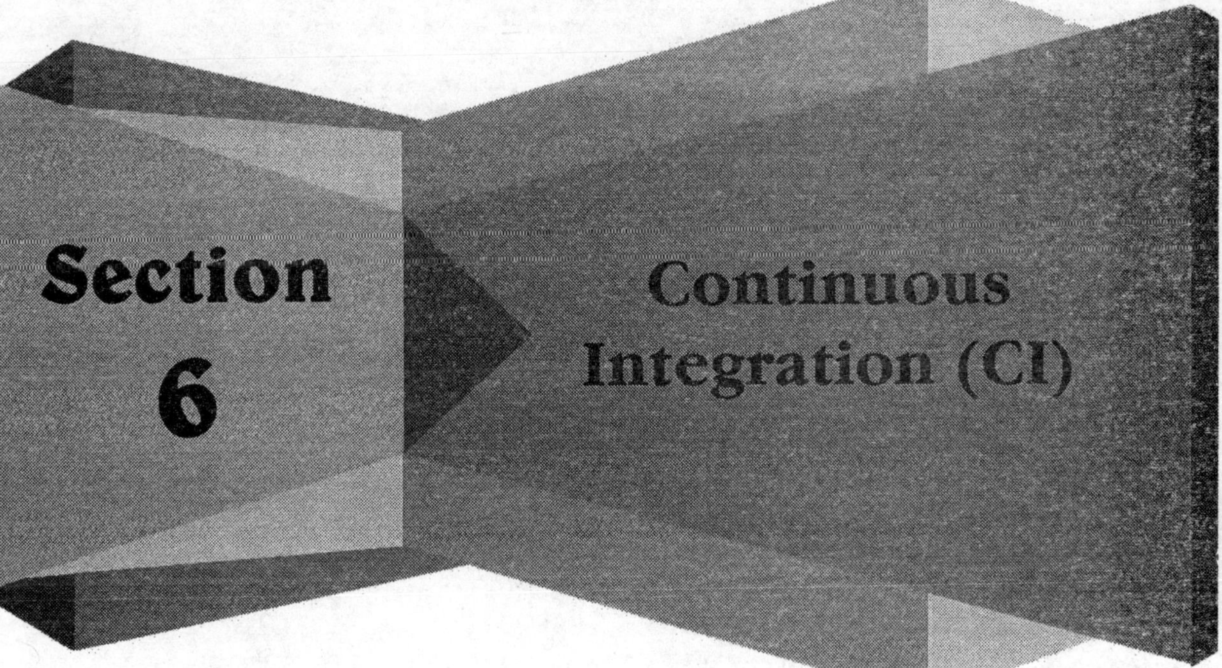
Section
6
Continuous
Integration (CI)

What is continuous integration (CI)?

Continuous integration (CI) is a software engineering practice in which isolated changes are immediately tested and reported on when they are added to a larger code base. The goal of CI is to provide rapid feedback so that if a defect is introduced into the code base, it can be identified and corrected as soon as possible. Continuous integration software tools can be used to automate the testing and build a document trail.

Continuous integration has evolved since its conception. Originally, a daily build

was the standard. Now, the usual rule is for each team member to submit work on a daily (or more frequent) basis and for a build to be conducted with each significant change. When used properly, continuous integration provides various benefits, such as constant feedback on the status of the software. Because CI detects deficiencies early on in development, defects are typically smaller, less complex and easier to resolve.

Best practices of CI include:

- Committing code frequently.
- Categorizing developer tests.
- Using a dedicated integration build machine.
- Using continuous feedback mechanisms.
- Staging builds.

CI originated from within the extreme programming paradigm but the principles can be applied to any iterative programming model, such as agile programming. Traditional development approaches, such as the waterfall model can benefit from using CI methods for the construction stage.

Principles of continuous integration

Continuous integration – the practice of frequently integrating one's new or changed code with the existing code repository – should occur frequently enough that no intervening window remains between commit and build, and such that no errors can arise without developers noticing them and correcting them immediately.[4] Normal practice is to trigger these builds by every commit to a repository, rather than a periodically scheduled build. The practicalities of doing this in a multi-developer environment of rapid commits are such that it's usual to trigger a short timer after each commit, then to start a build when either this timer expires, or after a rather longer interval since the last build. Automated tools such as CruiseControl, Jenkins, Hudson, Bamboo, BuildMaster, AnthillPro or Teamcity offer this scheduling automatically.

Another factor is the need for a version control system that supports atomic commits, i.e. all of a developer's changes may be seen as a single commit operation. There is no point in trying to build from only half of the changed files.

To achieve these objectives, continuous integration relies on the following principles.

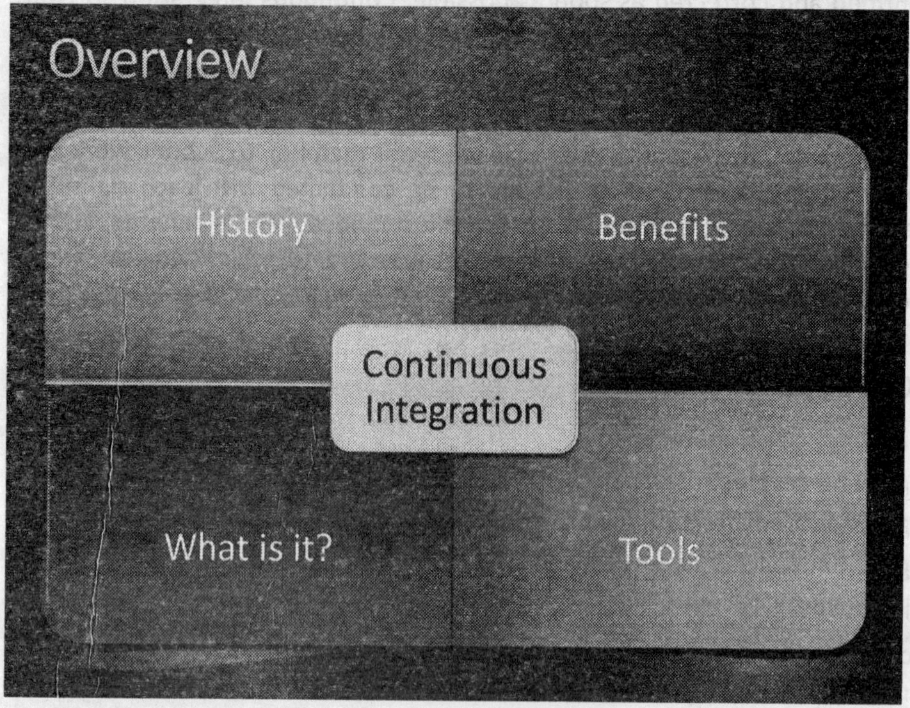

Today many organizations are trying to incorporate Continuous Integration into software development process because years of experience has taught everyone leaving integration to the end of a project is a risk.

-History of Continuous Integration –We will look at how Continuous Integration came to life.

-Benefits of Continuous Integration –We will look at how Continuous Integration can benefit the development, managers and customer relations.

-Theory of Continuous Integration –We will look at high level overview of what pieces are involved in creating Continuous Integration before we go into more detailed discussion.

-Tools of Continuous Integration –Tools are important part of Continuous Integration because tools help manage many of the overheads caused by achieving Continuous Integration.

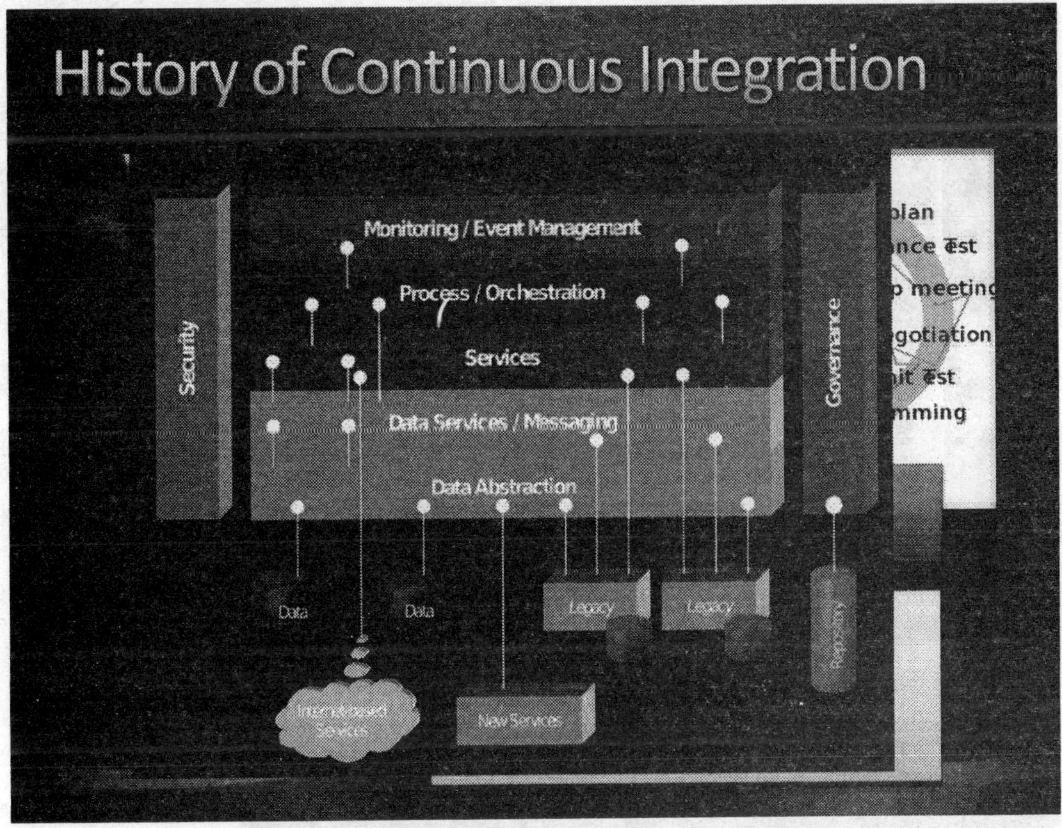

-Many of the practices of Continuous Integration came from XP (Extreme) programming development processas necessity

-Continuous Integration takes into account many of the Best Practices practiced in XP programming

-Martin Fowler promoted Continuous Integration process and along cameopen source product calledCruiseControl from Thoughtworks

-SOAtriggers the need for integration platform.

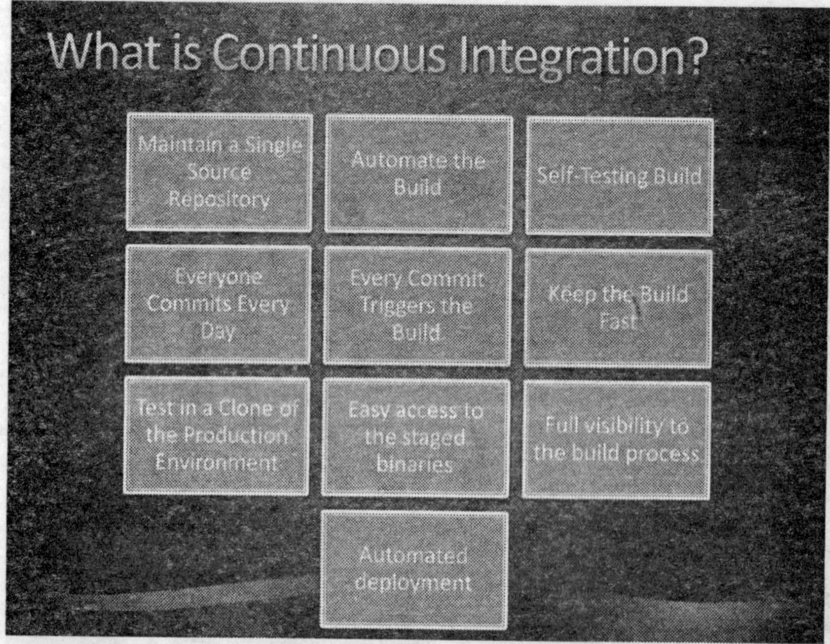

Here is the overview of the practices of Continuous Integration

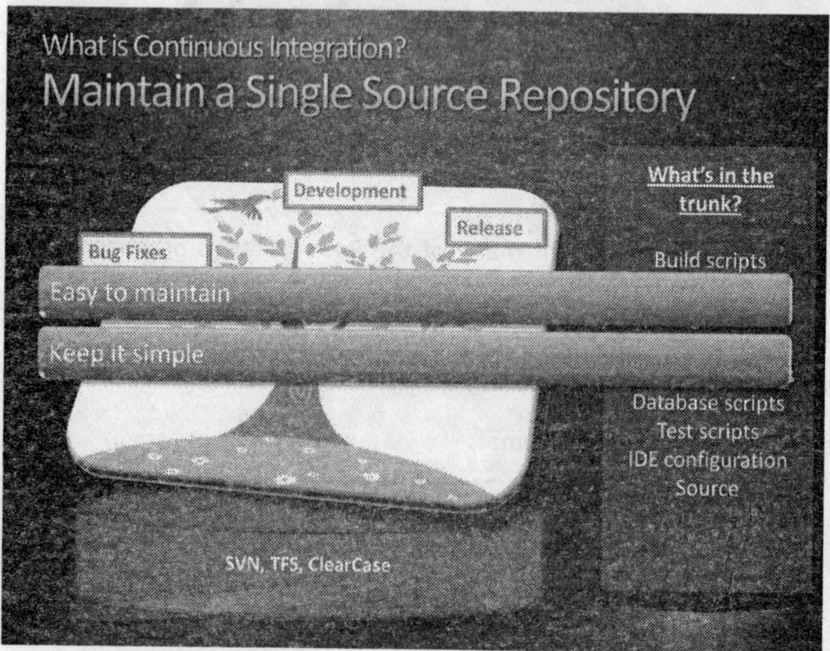

-Need to pick one of Source Code Management tools like: Subversion, ANT

-Include test scripts, configuration files, database schema and scripts, build scripts, install scripts, third party libraries, and IDE configuration.

-Keep the branches to minimum (bug fixes and maintenance, release, and experiments)

Pros:

1)Sources are centralized and thus easy to maintain

2)Everything is in repository and everyone knows where everything is

Cons:

1)Choosing right source control can be difficult because choosing source control depends on the needs of the organization

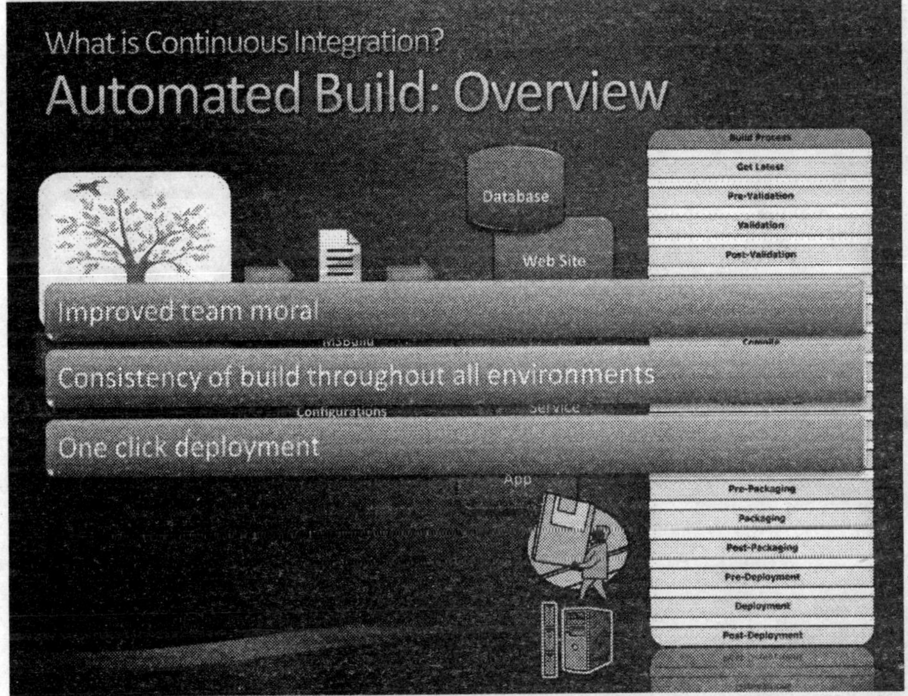

-Sources into running system using build script such as Ant, NAnt,

-Including EVRYTHING in the build things like database schema, database scripts, web site and web service deployment.

-Any one should be able to get the latest source from the repository and execute build on the new machine and have system running.

Pros:

1)Single command converts sources into system.

2)New developers are ready to learn and develop right away because build is automated.

3)Every developers' environments are consistent.

Cons:

1)Introduces scripting language

2)Need to understand and learn new tool sets.

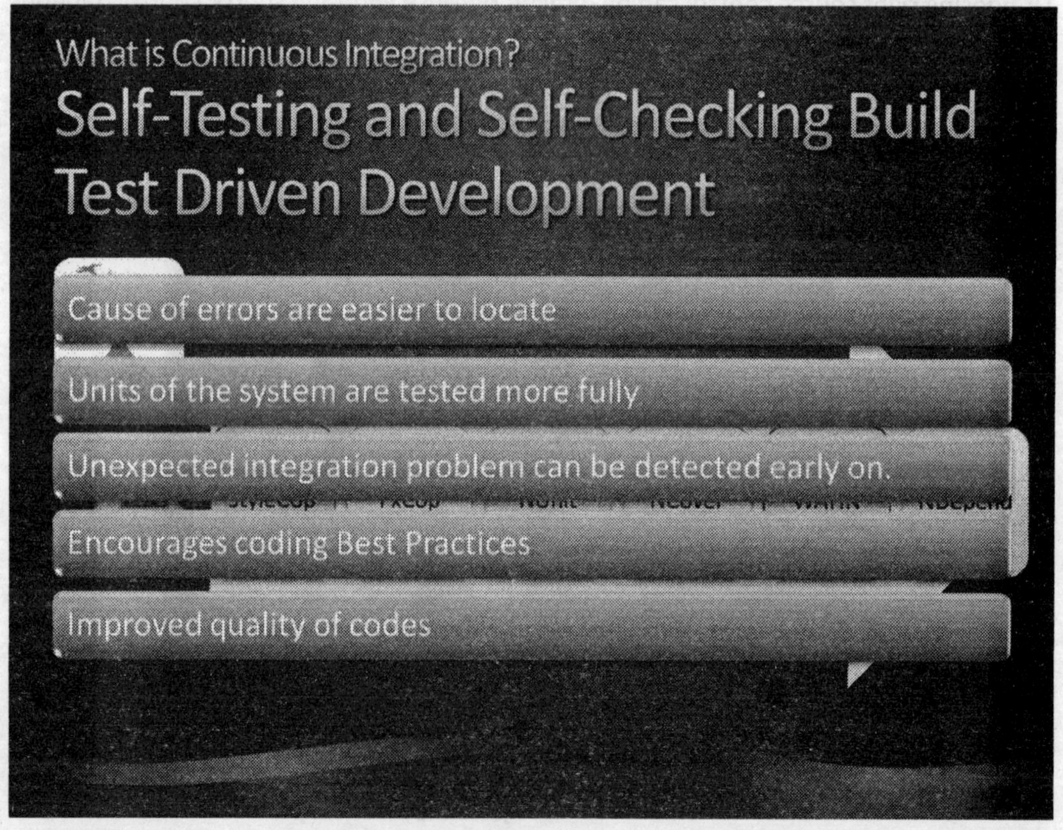

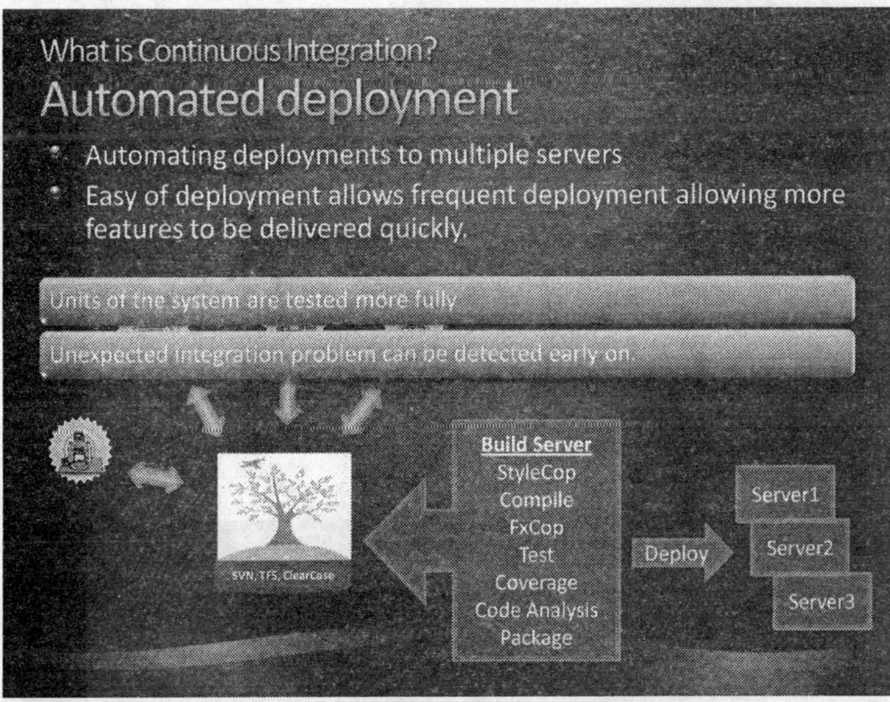
What is Continuous Integration?
Automated deployment
Automating deployments to multiple servers
Easy of deployment allows frequent deployment allowing more features to be delivered quickly.
Units of the system are tested more fully
Unexpected integration problem can be detected early on.
SVN, TFS, ClearCase
Build Server
StyleCop
Compile
FxCop
Test
Coverage
Code Analysis
Package
Deploy
Server1
Server2
Server3

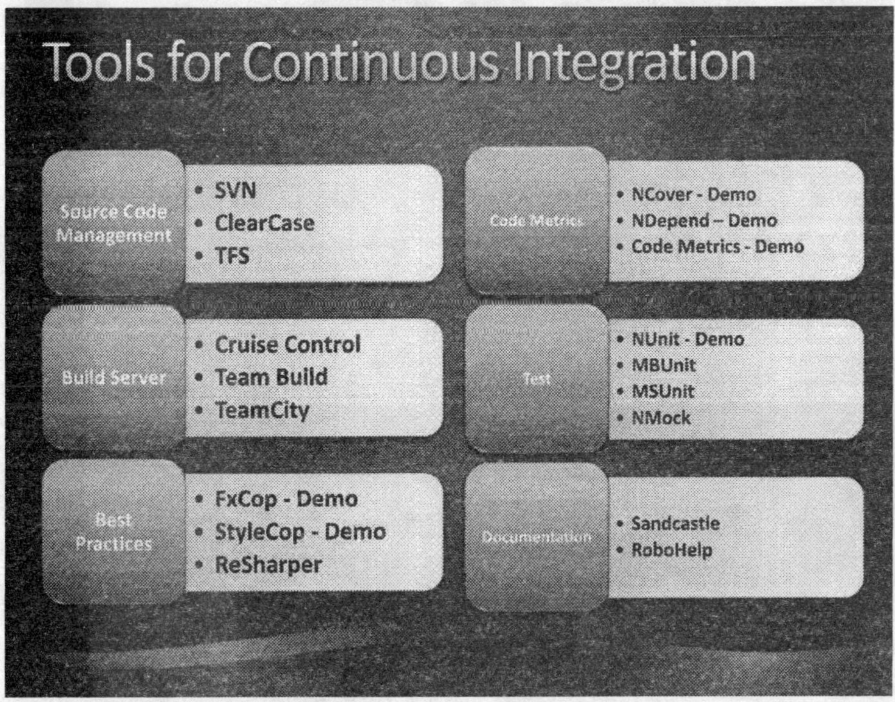
Tools for Continuous Integration
Source Code Management
SVN
ClearCase
TFS
Code Metrics
NCover - Demo
NDepend – Demo
Code Metrics - Demo
Build Server
Cruise Control
Team Build
TeamCity
Test
NUnit - Demo
MBUnit
MSUnit
NMock
Best Practices
FxCop - Demo
StyleCop - Demo
ReSharper
Documentation
Sandcastle
RoboHelp

Choice of tools to use in Continuous Integration has improved drastically in lastfew years; tools are becoming easy to use and powerful, and nicely integrated into GUI based development tools like Visual Studio or Eclipse and usability of tools are becoming seamless. The key considerations for choosing right tools to use are as follow:

1)Command line based to be used in scripting language for automation purpose?

2)Built into Visual Studio?

3)Does it need to be pre installed before the execution?

4)Can it be reused?

5)How easy is it to learn and use?

6)Product is maintained and supported?

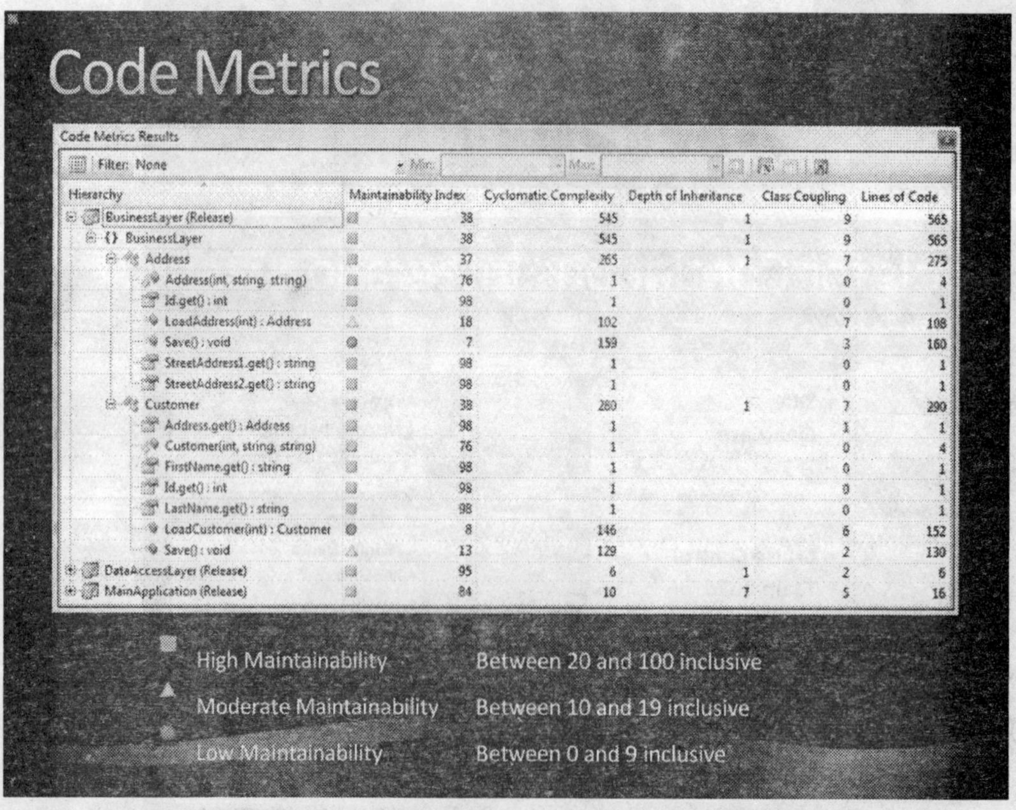

Hierarchy	Maintainability Index	Cyclomatic Complexity	Depth of Inheritance	Class Coupling	Lines of Code
BusinessLayer (Release)	38	545	1	9	565
{} BusinessLayer	38	545	1	9	565
Address	37	265	1	7	275
Address(int, string, string)	76	1		0	4
Id.get() : int	98	1		0	1
LoadAddress(int) : Address	18	102		7	108
Save() : void	7	159		3	160
StreetAddress1.get() : string	98	1		0	1
StreetAddress2.get() : string	98	1		0	1
Customer	38	280	1	7	290
Address.get() : Address	98	1		1	1
Customer(int, string, string)	76	1		0	4
FirstName.get() : string	98	1		0	1
Id.get() : int	98	1		0	1
LastName.get() : string	98	1		0	1
LoadCustomer(int) : Customer	8	146		6	152
Save() : void	13	129		2	130
DataAccessLayer (Release)	95	6	1	2	6
MainApplication (Release)	84	10	7	5	16

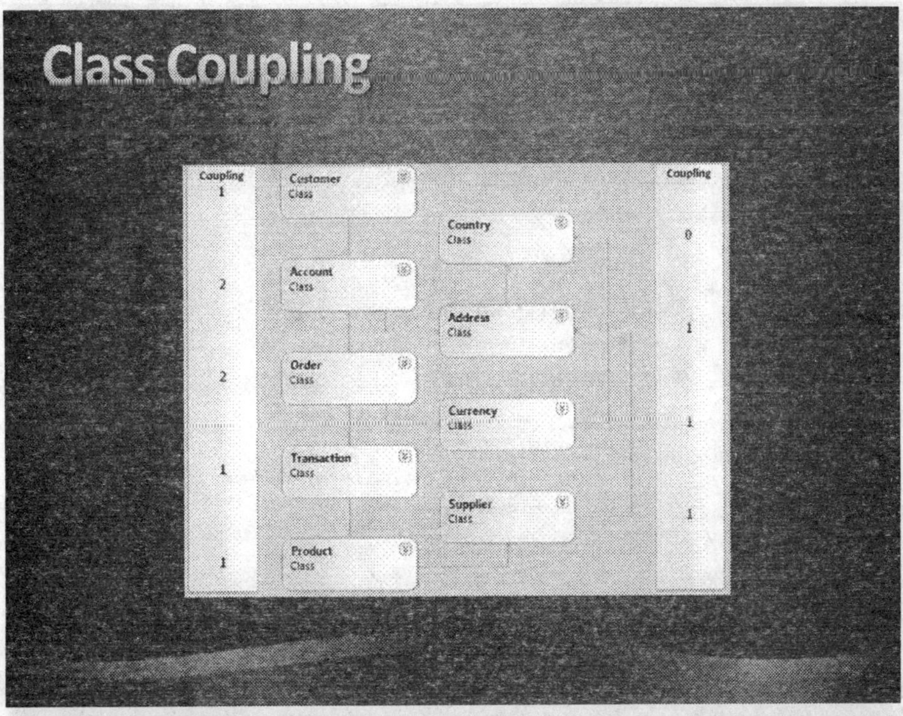
Class Coupling
Coupling
1
2
2
1
1
Customer
Class
Account
Class
Order
Class
Transaction
Class
Product
Class
Country
Class
Address
Class
Currency
Class
Supplier
Class
Coupling
0
1
1
1

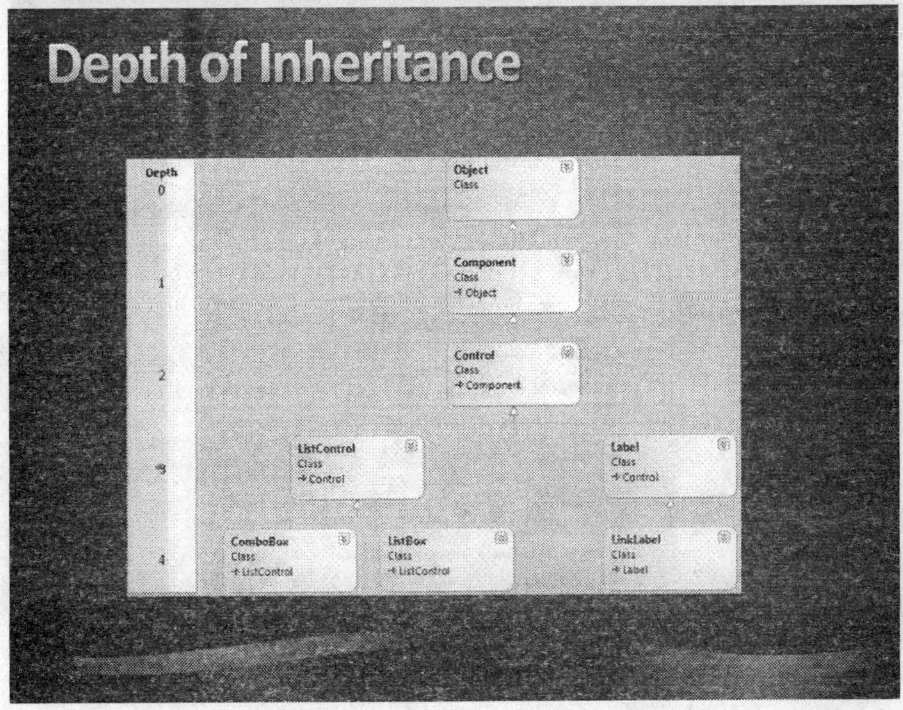
Depth of Inheritance
Depth
0
1
2
3
4
Object
Class
Component
Class
→ Object
Control
Class
→ Component
ListControl
Class
→ Control
Label
Class
→ Control
ComboBox
Class
→ ListControl
ListBox
Class
→ ListControl
LinkLabel
Class
→ Label

Cyclomatic Complexity

```
Complexity
1     bool ParseCommandLine(string[] arguments)
      {
2         if (arguments.Length == 0)
          {
              ShowHelp();
              return false;
          }

3         for (int i = 0; i < arguments.Length; i++)
          {
4             if (arguments[i] == "/?")
              {
                  ShowHelp();
                  return false;
              }

5             if (arguments[i] == "/input")
              {
6, 7              if (arguments.Length > 1 && File.Exists(arguments[i + 1]))
                  {
                      InputFileName = arguments[i++];
                  }
              }
          }

          return true;
      }
```

Lines of Code

```
Lines
      /// <summary>
      ///     Parses the specified command-line arguments.
      /// </summary>
      bool ParseCommandLine(string[] arguments)
      {
          // By default we show help if no
          // command-line arguments are specified
1         if (arguments.Length == 0)
          {
2             ShowHelp();
3             return false;
          }

4         for (int i = 0; i < arguments.Length; i++)
          {
5             if (arguments[i] == "/?")
              {
6                 ShowHelp();
7                 return false;
              }

8             if (arguments[i] == "/input")
              {
                  // We only recognize the /input
                  // switch, if the file name exists
9                 if (arguments.Length > 1 && File.Exists(arguments[i + 1]))
                  {
10                    InputFileName = arguments[i++];
                  }
              }
          }

11        return true;
      }
```

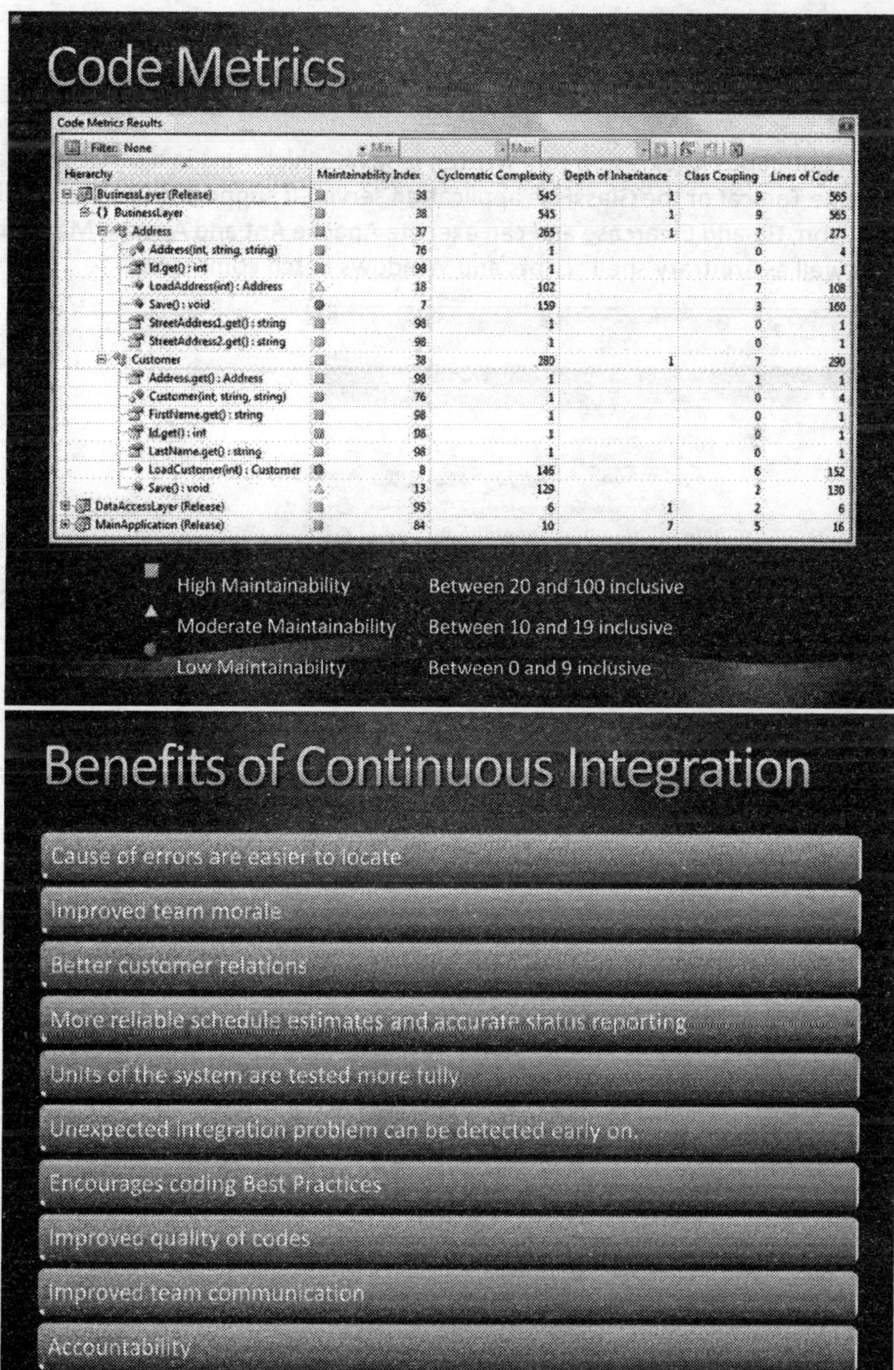

Hierarchy	Maintainability Index	Cyclomatic Complexity	Depth of Inheritance	Class Coupling	Lines of Code
BusinessLayer (Release)	38	545	1	9	565
{} BusinessLayer	38	545	1	9	565
Address	37	265	1	7	275
Address(int, string, string)	76	1		0	4
Id.get() : int	98	1		0	1
LoadAddress(int) : Address	18	102		7	108
Save() : void	7	159		3	160
StreetAddress1.get() : string	98	1		0	1
StreetAddress2.get() : string	98	1		0	1
Customer	38	280	1	7	290
Address.get() : Address	98	1		1	1
Customer(int, string, string)	76	1		0	4
FirstName.get() : string	98	1		0	1
Id.get() : int	98	1		0	1
LastName.get() : string	98	1		0	1
LoadCustomer(int) : Customer	8	146		6	152
Save() : void	13	129		2	130
DataAccessLayer (Release)	95	6	1	2	6
MainApplication (Release)	84	10	7	5	16

Tools Available in Market:

1. Hudson

Hudson is a continuous integration tool written in Java, which runs in a servlet container, such as Apache Tomcat or the GlassFish application server. It supports SCM tools including CVS, Subversion, Git and Clearcase and can execute Apache Ant and Apache Maven based projects, as well as arbitrary shell scripts and Windows batch commands.

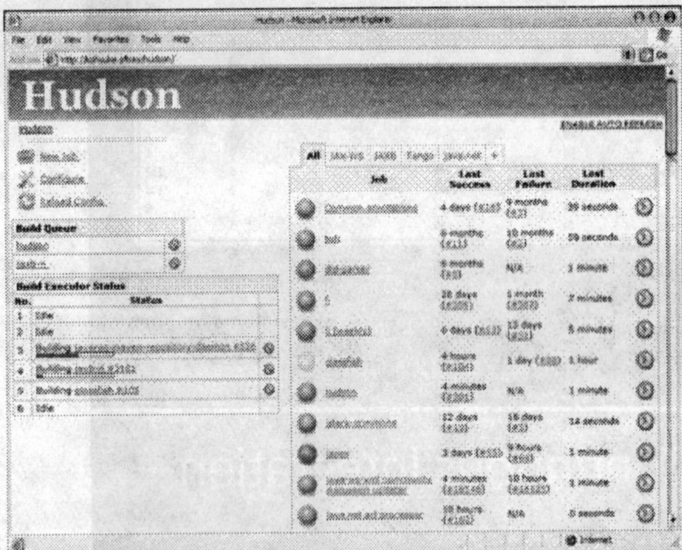

2. CruiseControl NET

CruiseControl.NET is an Automated Continuous Integration server, implemented using the Microsoft .NET Framework.

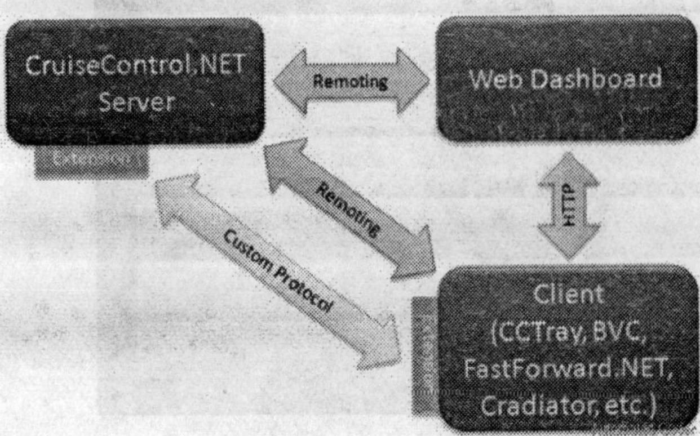

3. Apache Continuum

Apache Continuum is an enterprise-ready continuous integration server with features such as automated builds, release management, role-based security, and integration with popular build tools and source control management systems. Whether you have a centralized build team or want to put control of releases in the hands of developers, Continuum can help you improve quality and maintain a consistent build environment.

4. CABIE

Continuous Automated Build and Integration Environment. Cabie is a multi-platform, multi-cm client/server based application providing both command line and web-based access to real time build monitoring and execution information. Cabie builds jobs based upon configuration information stored in MySQL and will support virtually any build that can be called from the command line. Cabie provides a centralized collection point for all builds providing web based dynamic access, the collector is SQL ba

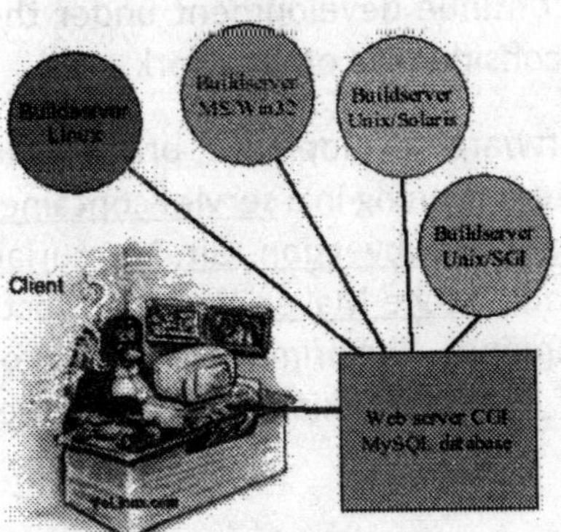

Cabie Architecture

5. CruiseControl

CruiseControl is both a continuous integration tool and an extensible framework for creating a custom continuous build process. It includes dozens of plugins for a variety of source controls, build technologies, and notifications schemes including email and instant messaging. A web interface provides details of the current and previous builds. And the standard CruiseControl distribution is augmented through a rich selection of 3rd Party Tools.

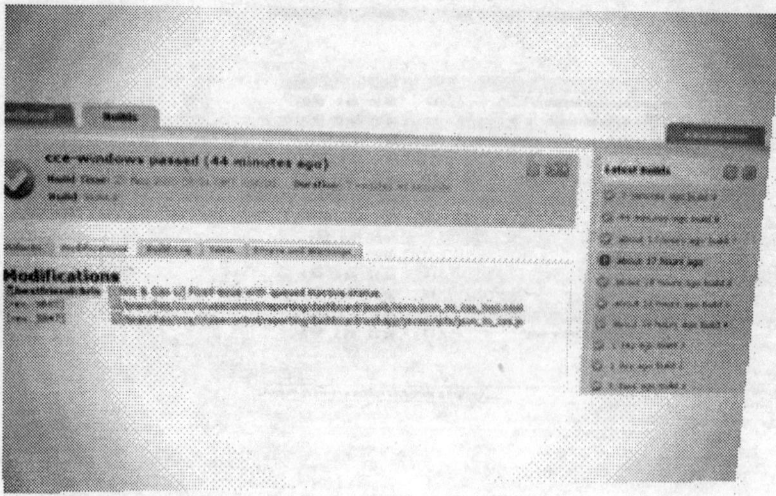

6. Jenkins:

Jenkins, previously known as Hudson, is an open source continuous integration tool written in Java. The project renamed itself after a dispute with Oracle, which claims the right to trademark the Hudson name and has applied for such a trademark as of December 2010.[2] Complicating matters, Oracle has decided to continue development under the Hudson name, creating two parallel versions that each consider the other a fork.

Jenkins provides continuous integration services for software development, primarily in the Java programming language. It is a server-based system running in a servlet container such as Apache Tomcat. It supports SCM tools including CVS, Subversion, Git, Mercurial, Perforce and Clearcase, and can execute Apache Ant and Apache Maven based projects as well as arbitrary shell scripts and Windows batch commands. The primary developer of Jenkins is Kohsuke Kawaguchi.[3] Released under the MIT License, Jenkins is free software.[4]

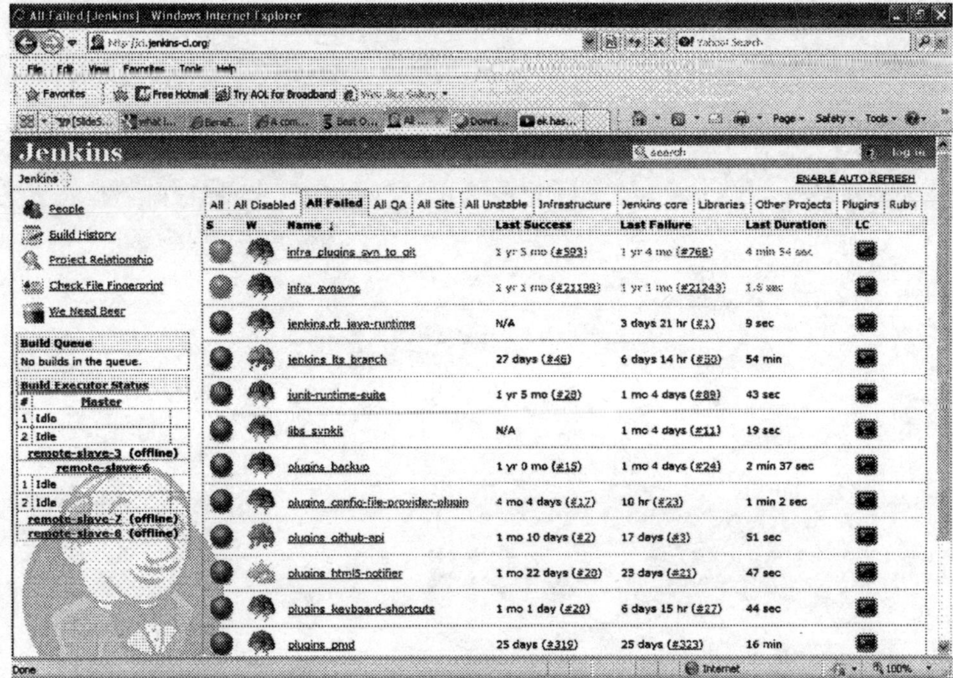
All Failed [Jenkins] - Windows Internet Explorer
Jenkins
search
ENABLE AUTO REFRESH
People
Build History
Project Relationship
Check File Fingerprint
We Need Beer
Build Queue
No builds in the queue.
Build Executor Status
Master
1 Idle
2 Idle
remote-slave-3 (offline)
remote-slave-6
1 Idle
2 Idle
remote-slave-7 (offline)
remote-slave-8 (offline)
All | All Disabled | All Failed | All QA | All Site | All Unstable | Infrastructure | Jenkins core | Libraries | Other Projects | Plugins | Ruby
S W Name ↓ Last Success Last Failure Last Duration LC
infra_plugins_svn_to_git 1 yr 5 mo (#593) 1 yr 4 mo (#768) 4 min 54 sec
infra_svnsync 1 yr 1 mo (#21199) 1 yr 1 mo (#21243) 1.6 sec
jenkins.rb_java-runtime N/A 3 days 21 hr (#1) 9 sec
jenkins_lts_branch 27 days (#46) 6 days 14 hr (#50) 54 min
junit-runtime-suite 1 yr 5 mo (#28) 1 mo 4 days (#89) 43 sec
libs_svnkit N/A 1 mo 4 days (#11) 19 sec
plugins_backup 1 yr 0 mo (#15) 1 mo 4 days (#24) 2 min 37 sec
plugins_config-file-provider-plugin 4 mo 4 days (#17) 10 hr (#23) 1 min 2 sec
plugins_github-api 1 mo 10 days (#2) 17 days (#3) 51 sec
plugins_html5-notifier 1 mo 22 days (#20) 23 days (#21) 47 sec
plugins_keyboard-shortcuts 1 mo 1 day (#20) 6 days 15 hr (#27) 44 sec
plugins_pmd 25 days (#319) 25 days (#323) 16 min
Done
Internet
100%

Selenium – Hudson Integration

Step 1: Create 'SeleniumTest' folder on any drive, I have created on 'C: \SeleniumTest'

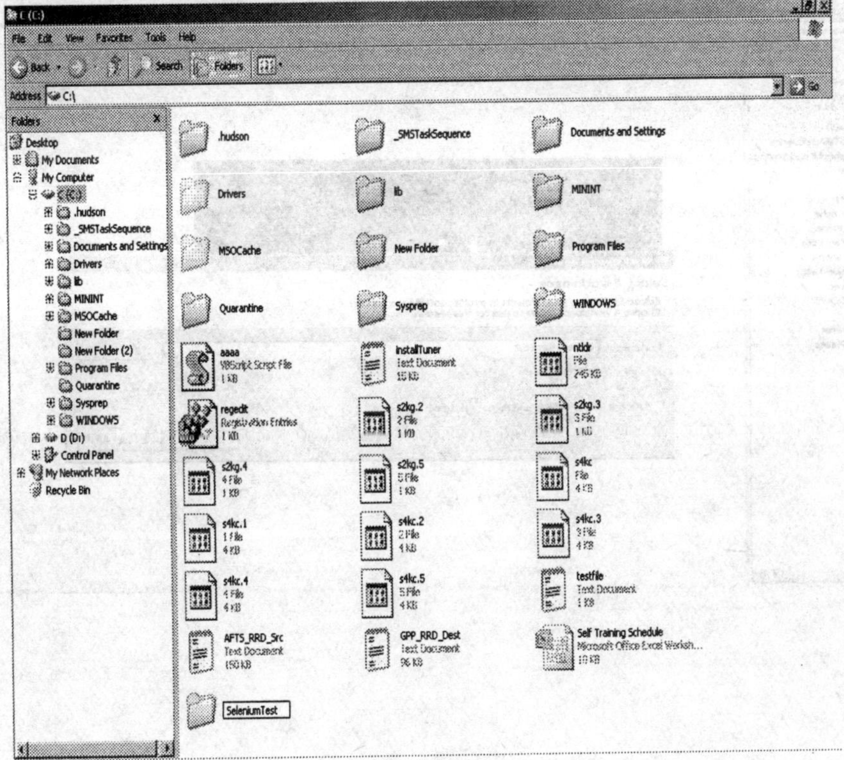

Step 2: Double click on the eclipse setup

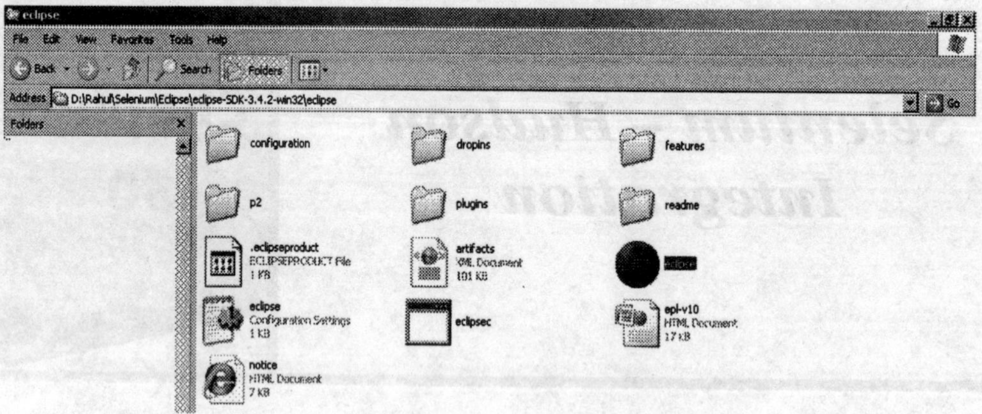

Step 3: select the workspace 'C:\SeleniumTest' and then click 'OK'

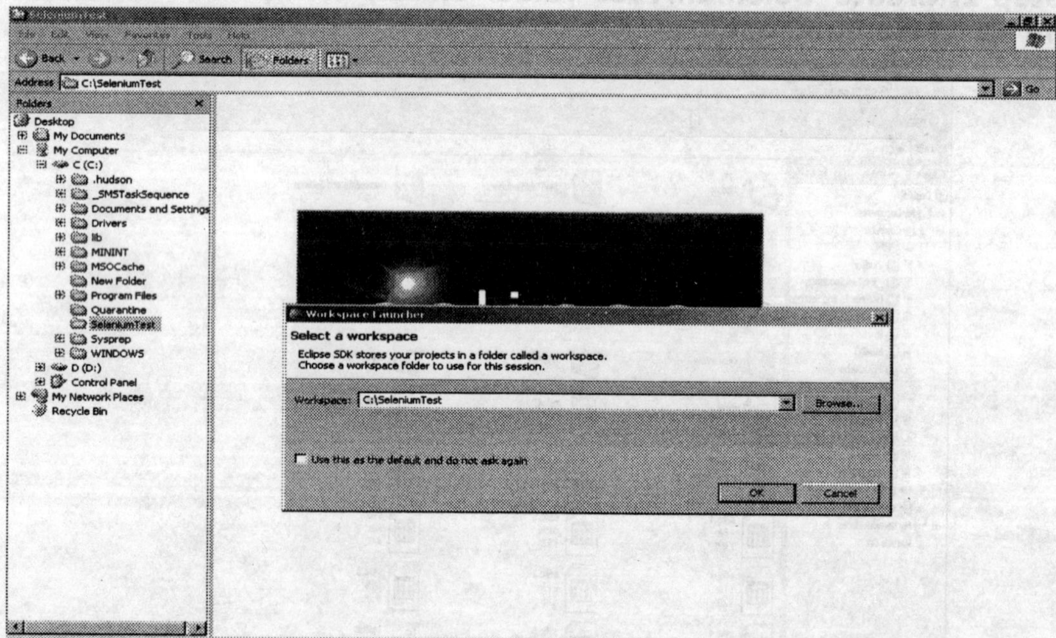

Step 4: click on the button highlighted in red

Step 5: you will see below eclipse window

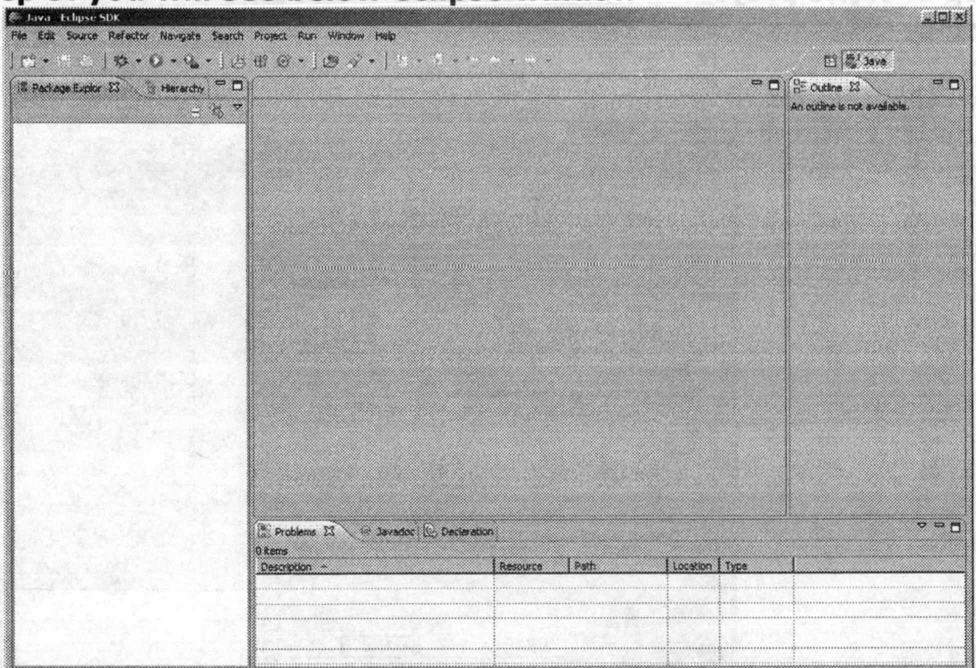

Step 6: Right Click 'New→ Java Project'

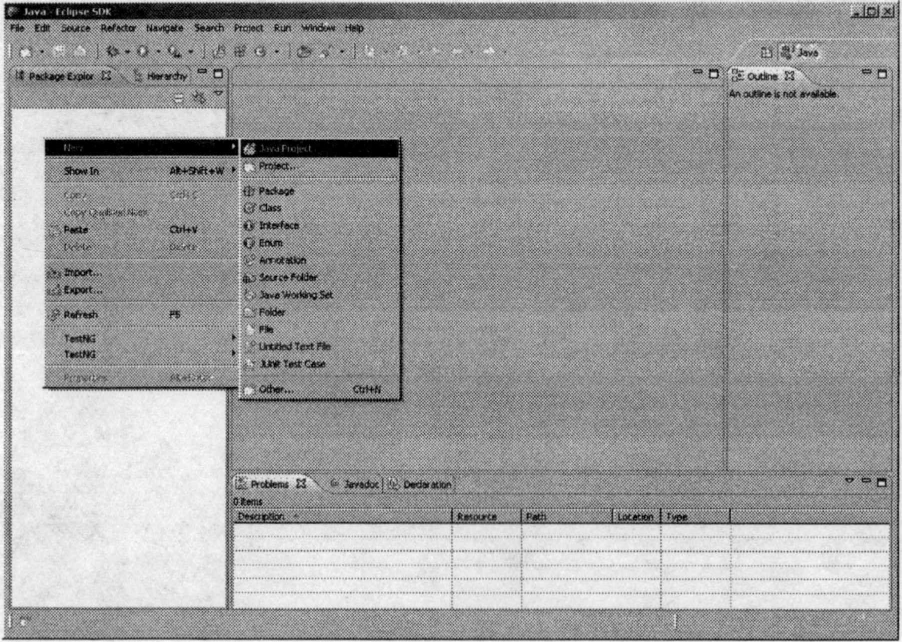

Step 8: Write project name as 'SeleniumHudson'

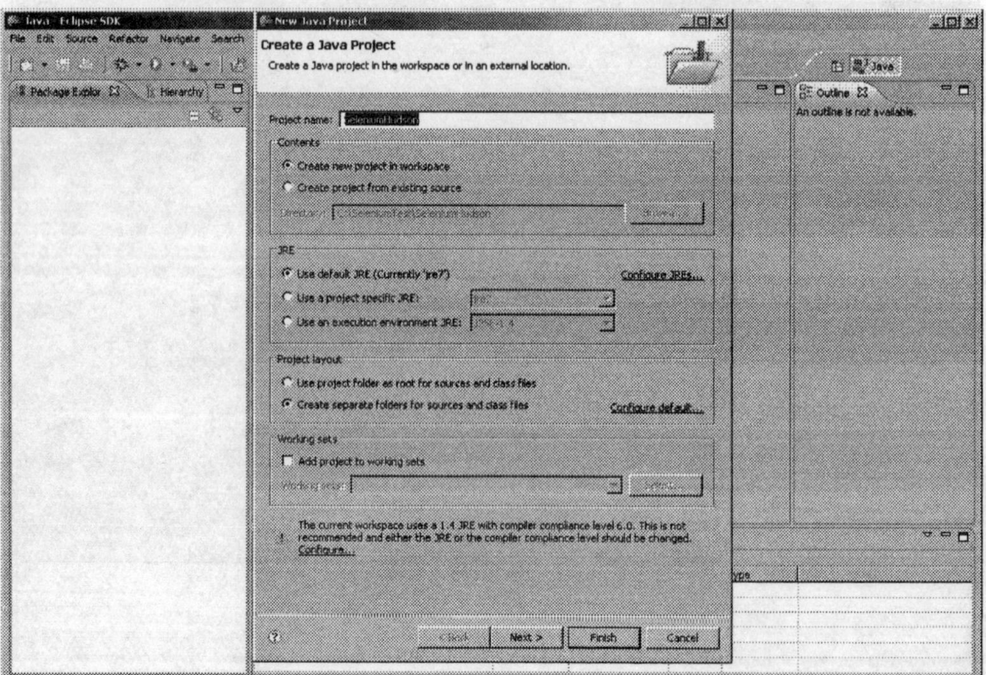

Step 9: you will see that project got created as 'SeleniumHudson'

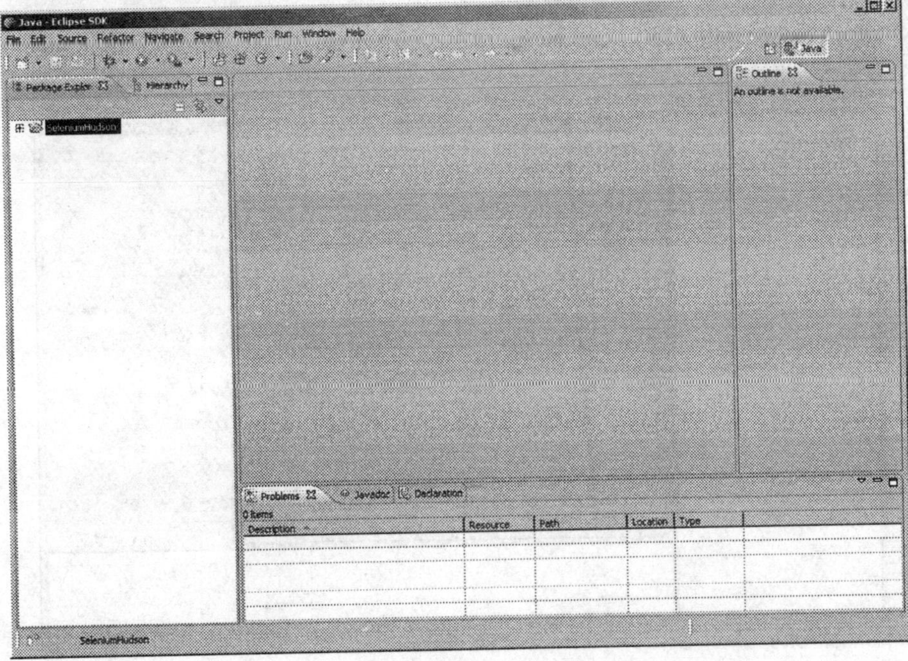

Step 10: Right click on 'SeleniumHudson' project and 'New→ Package'

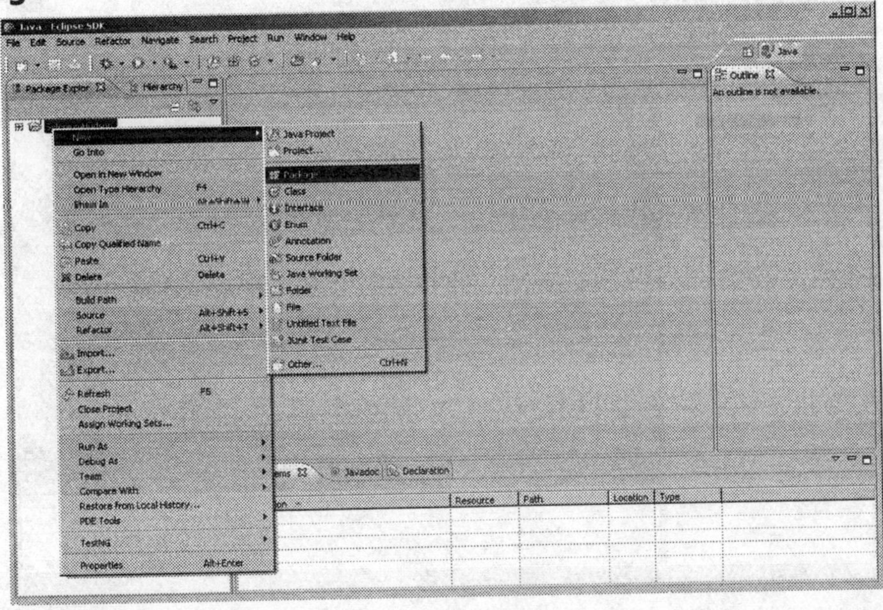

Step 11: Enter Name as 'com.SeleniumIntegration' and then click on 'Finish'

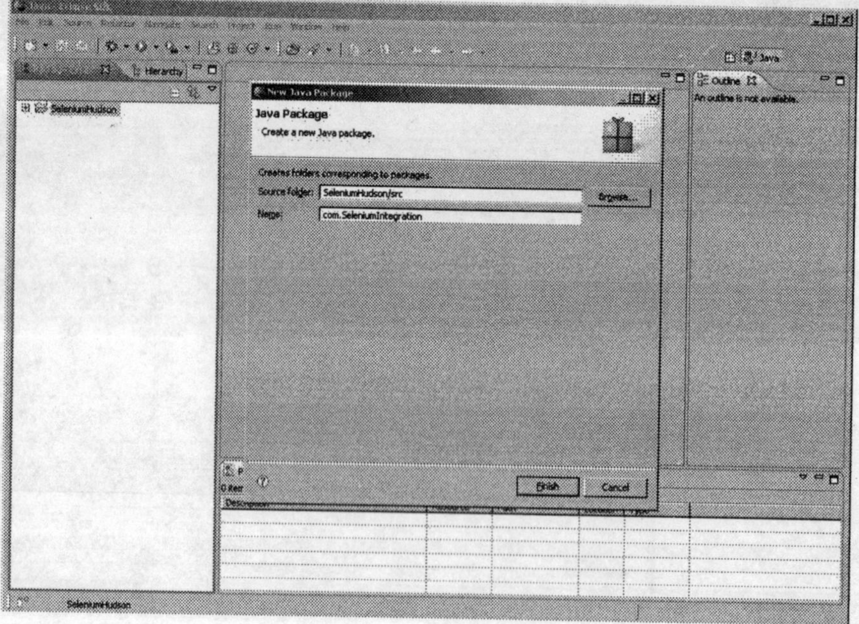

Step 12: you will see ''com.SeleniumIntegration' package has been created.

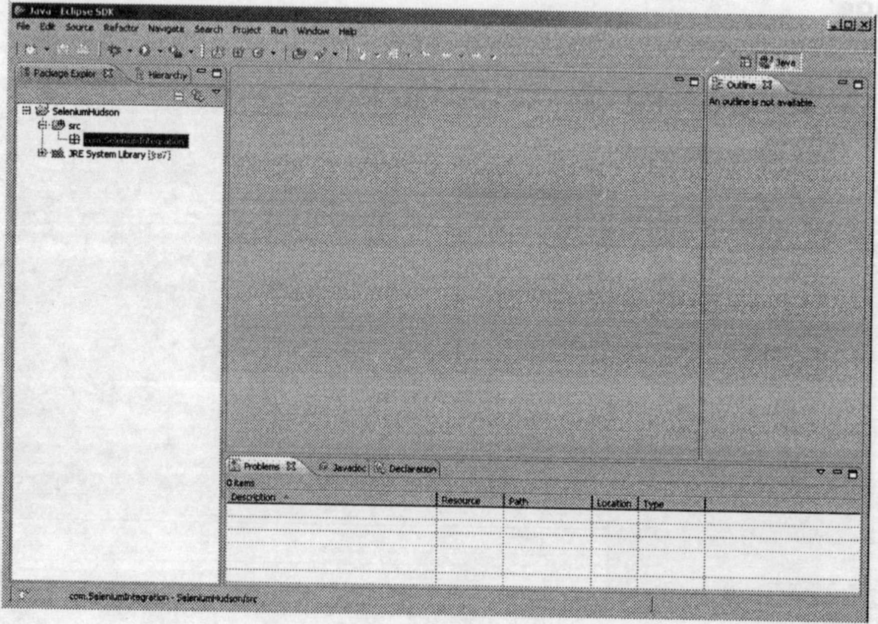

Step 13: Right click on 'com.SeleniumIntegration' package and click on 'New→ Class'

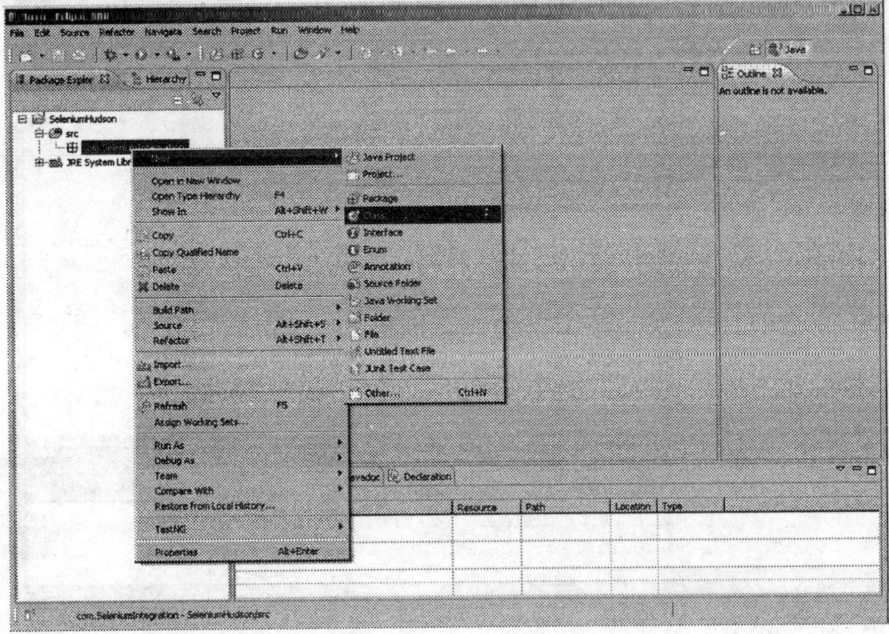

Step 14: Enter Name as 'Seleniumhudsonintegration' and click on 'Finish'

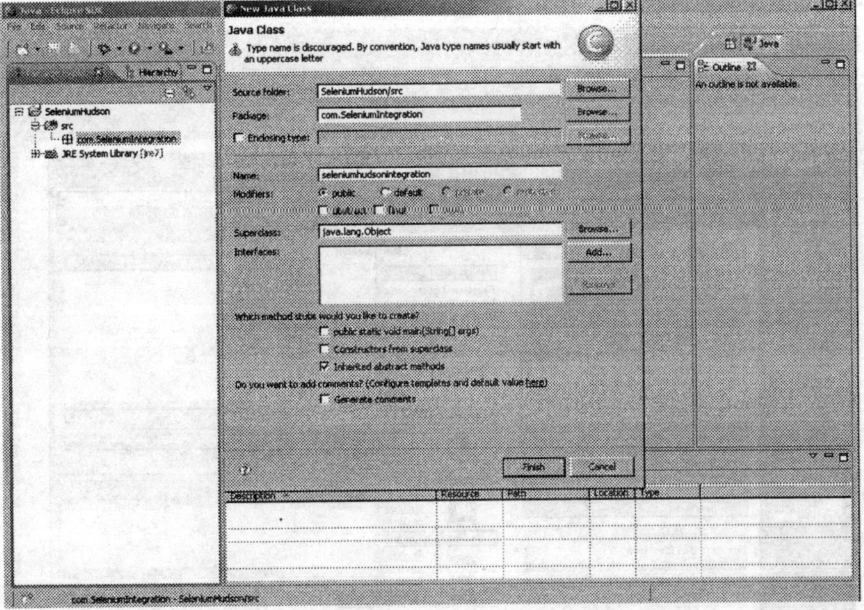

Step 15: you will see below code in the eclipse 'Project Explore' window

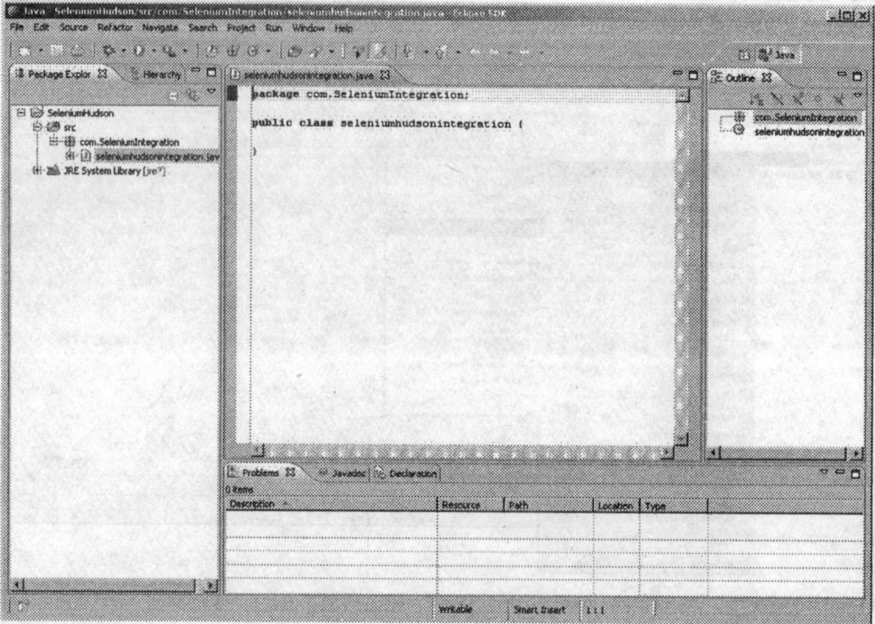

Step 16: open Firefox browser and enter URL "http://newtours.demoaut.com/"

Then click on 'Tools→ Selenium IDE'

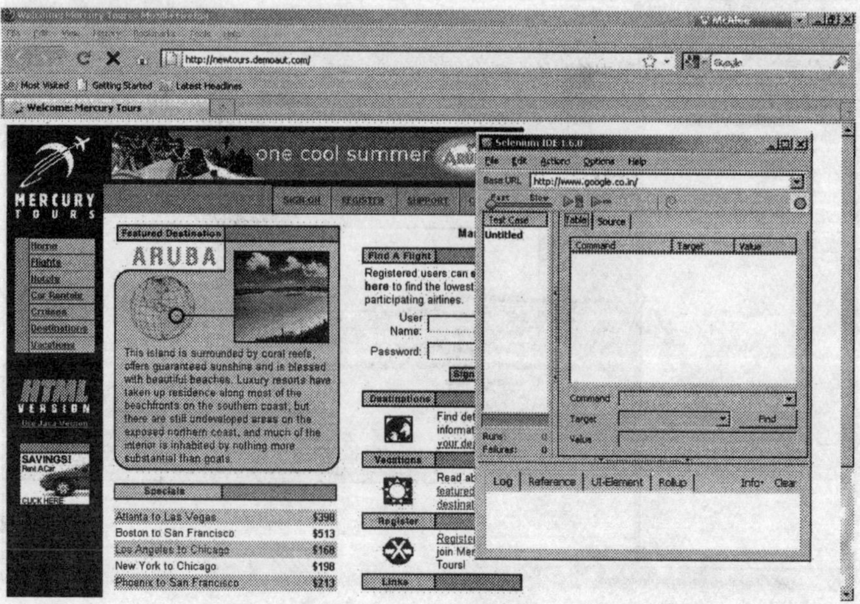

Step 17: record some steps using selenium IDE like

a) Login –Enter user name and password as 'mercury'
b) VerifyTestPresent

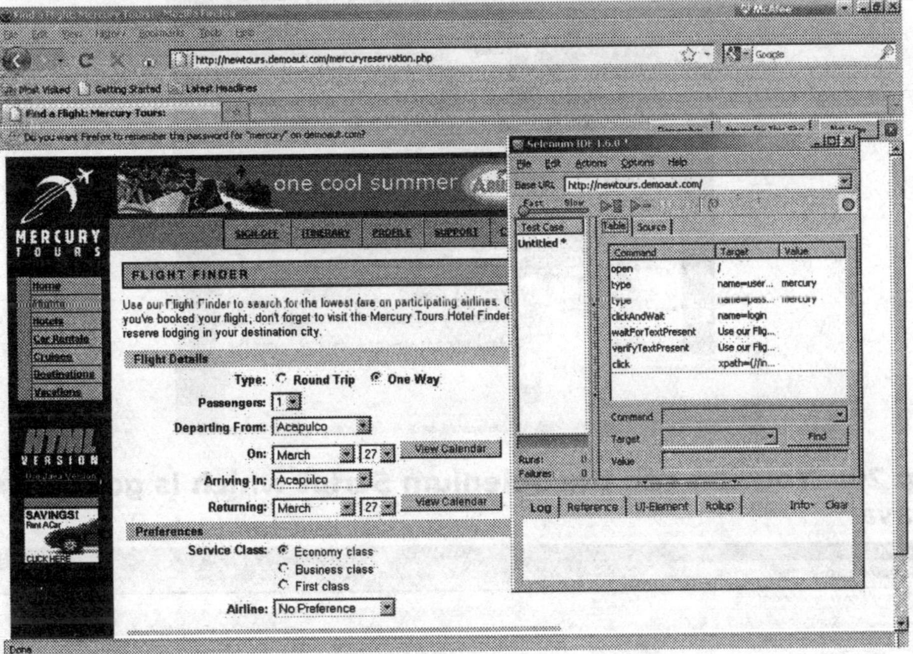

Step 18: in Selenium IDE select 'Options→ Options→ Format→ Junit 4(Remote Control)

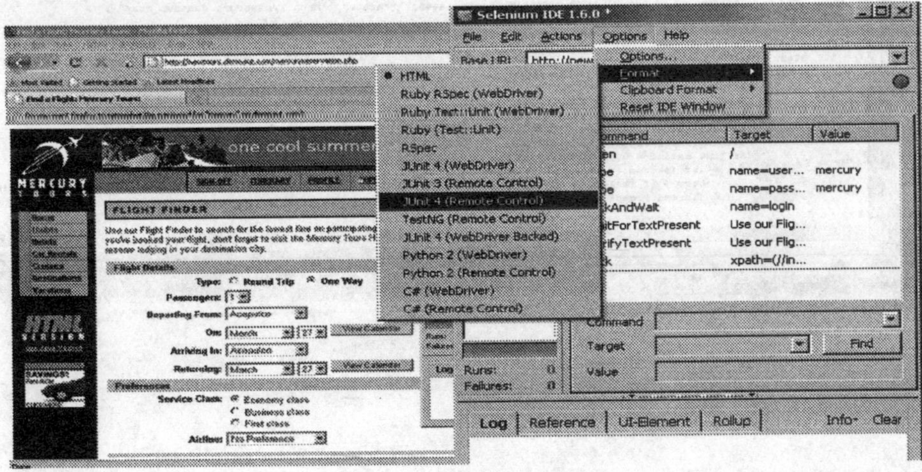

Step 19: click on 'OK'

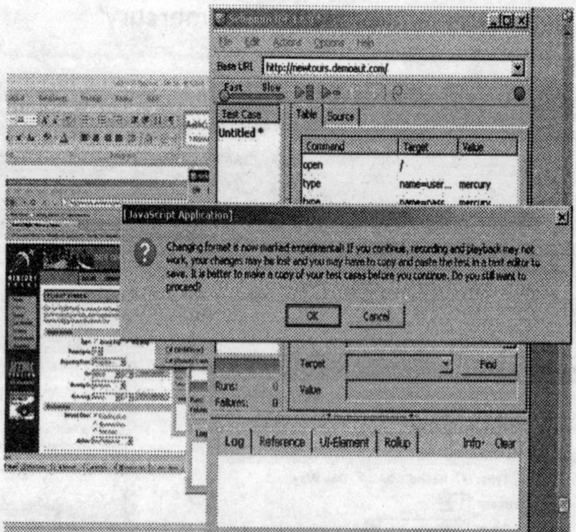

Step 20: You can see the Selenium Script which is got converted in Java

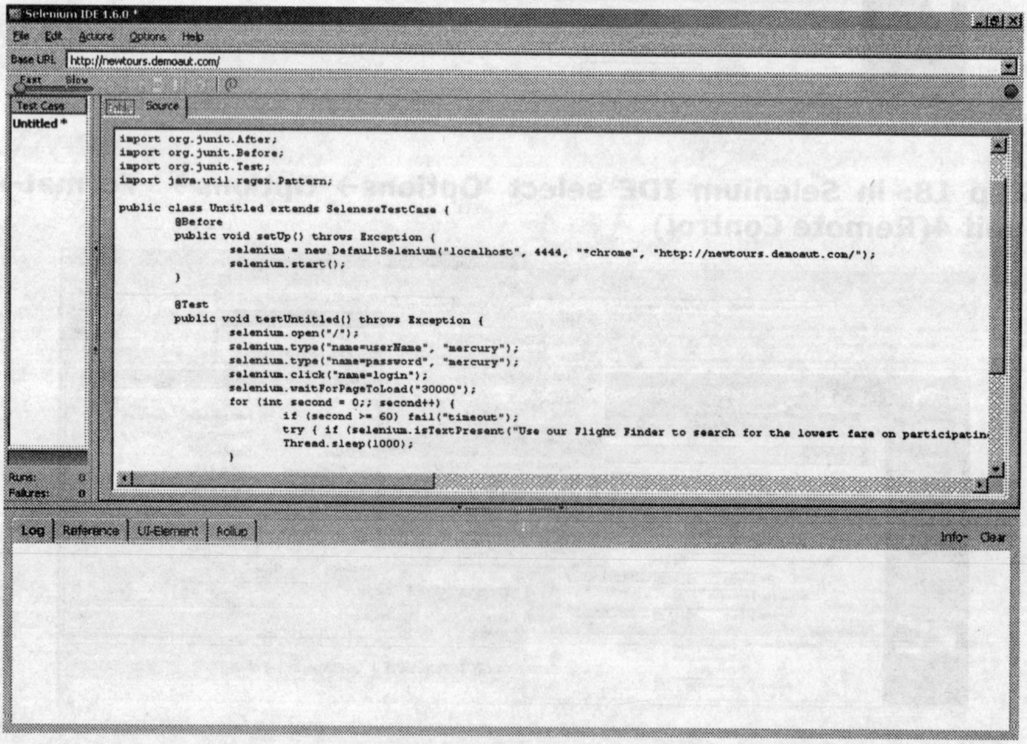

Selenium IDE 1.6.0 *

File Edit Actions Options Help

Base URL http://newtours.demoaut.com/

Test Case | Table | Source

Untitled *

```
import org.junit.After;
import org.junit.Before;
import org.junit.Test;
import java.util.regex.Pattern;

public class Untitled extends SeleneseTestCase {
        @Before
        public void setUp() throws Exception {
                selenium = new DefaultSelenium("localhost", 4444, "*chrome", "http://newtours.demoaut.com/");
                selenium.start();
        }

        @Test
        public void testUntitled() throws Exception {
                selenium.open("/");
                selenium.type("name=userName", "mercury");
                selenium.type("name=password", "mercury");
                selenium.click("name=login");
                selenium.waitForPageToLoad("30000");
                for (int second = 0;; second++) {
                        if (second >= 60) fail("timeout");
                        try { if (selenium.isTextPresent("Use our Flight Finder to search for the lowest fare on participatin
                        Thread.sleep(1000);
                }
```

Runs: 0
Failures: 0

Log | Reference | UI-Element | Rollup   Info · Clear

Step 21: Select the complete code and copy the code

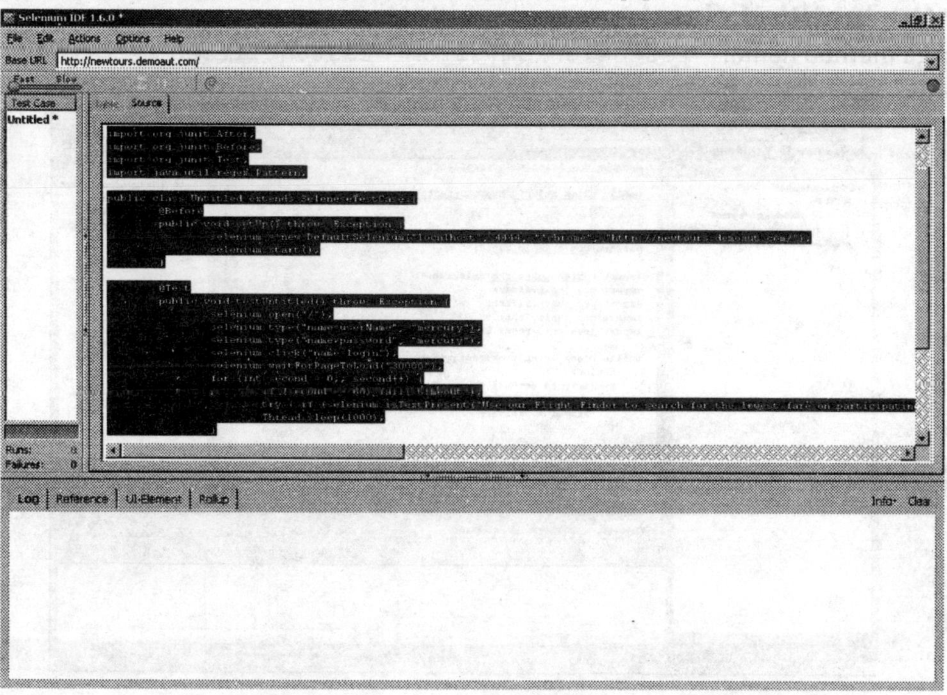

Step 22: Paste the copied code in Eclipse, so your code will look like below screen shot

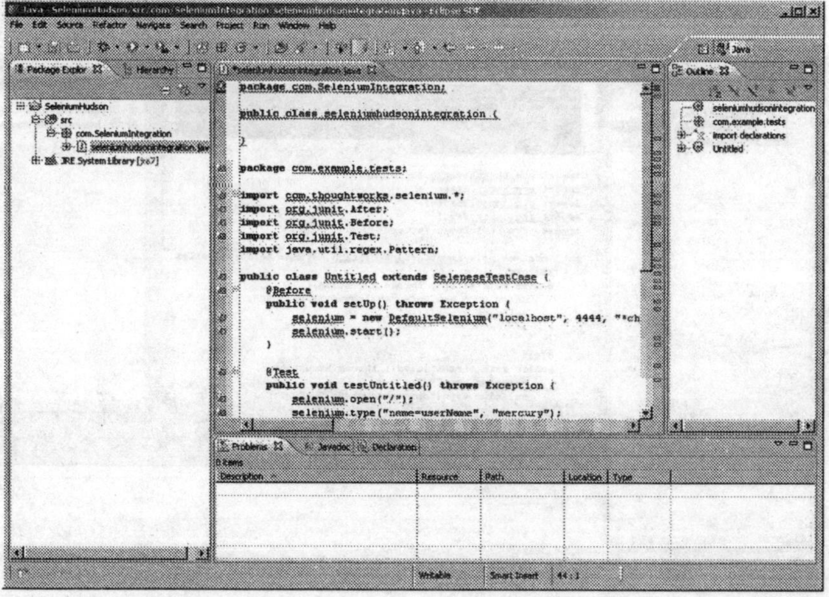

Step 23: change the class name as 'Seleniumhudsonintegration' for the 'untitled class'

Change method name: `'testSelenium'` from `'testUntiltled'`

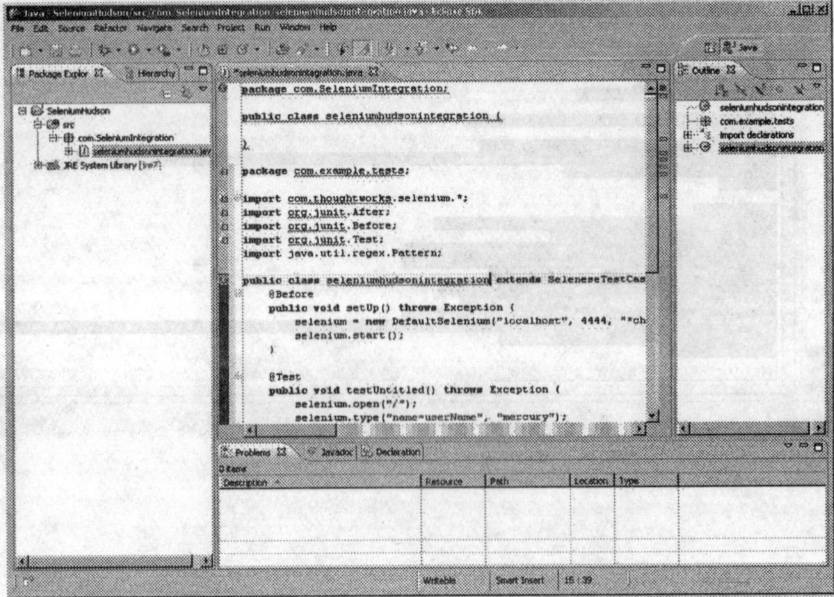

Step 25: Delete the highlighted code in eclipse

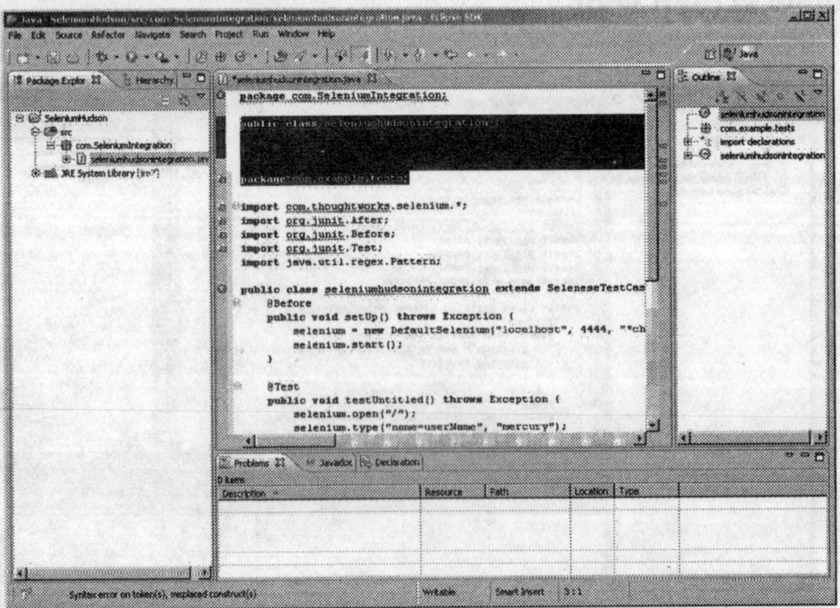

Step 26: So your code will look like below screen shot with some errors

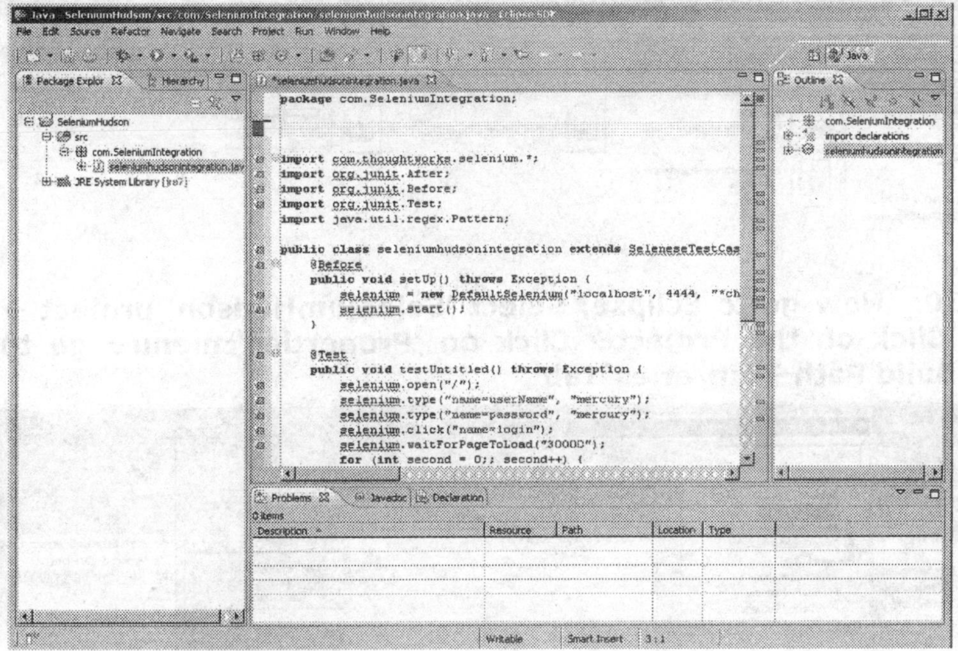

Step 27: Create another folder 'Selenium_Liabraries' in local drive, I have created on

'c:\ Selenium_Liabraries'

Step 28: Download below jar files and put them in 'Selenium_ Liabraries' folder

1. selenium-server-standalone-2.19.0.jar
2. selenium-java-2.19.0.jar
3. junit-4.8.1.jar
4. jxl.jar

Step 29: Download below jar files and put them in 'Selenium_Liabraries' folder

Step 30: Now go to Eclipse; Select 'SeleniumHudson' project → Right Click on the Project→ Click on 'Properties' menu→ go to 'Java Build Path→ Libraries' tab

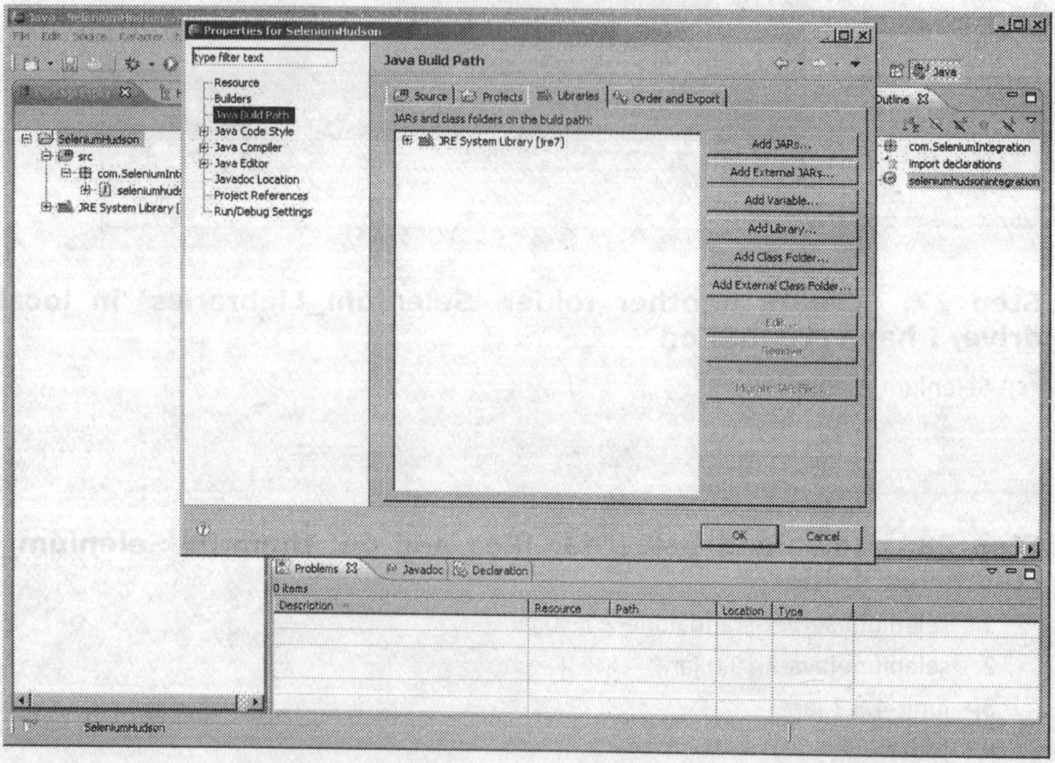

Step 31: Click on 'Add External Jar' Add all the jar files from 'Selenium_Liabraries' folder

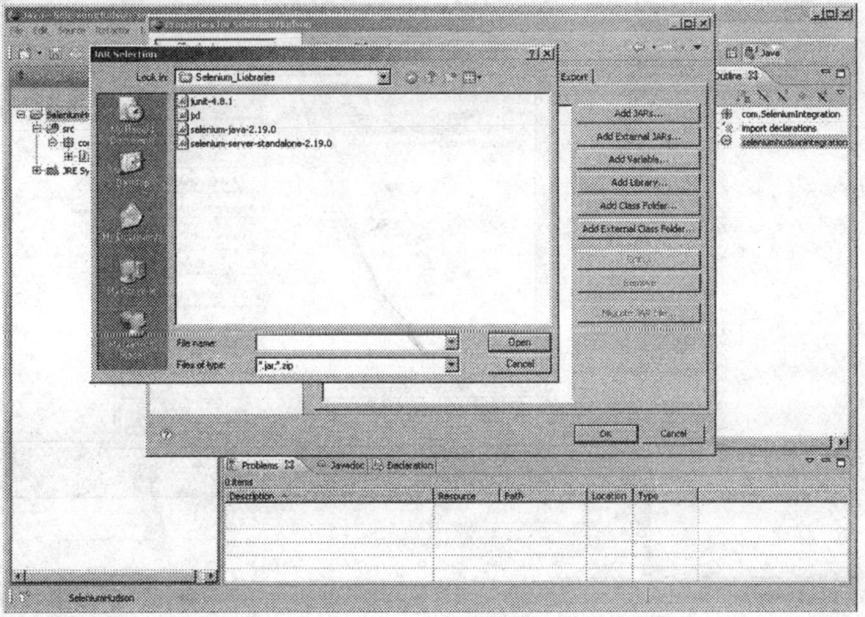

Step 32: Click on 'Add External Jar' Add the entire jar files from 'Selenium_Liabraries' folder and click on 'Open'

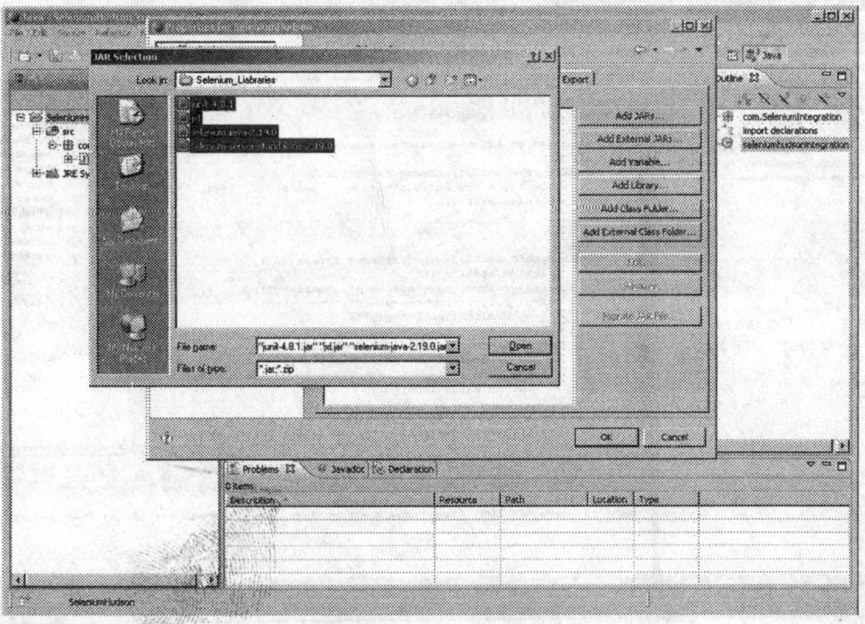

Step 33: Click on 'OK' button

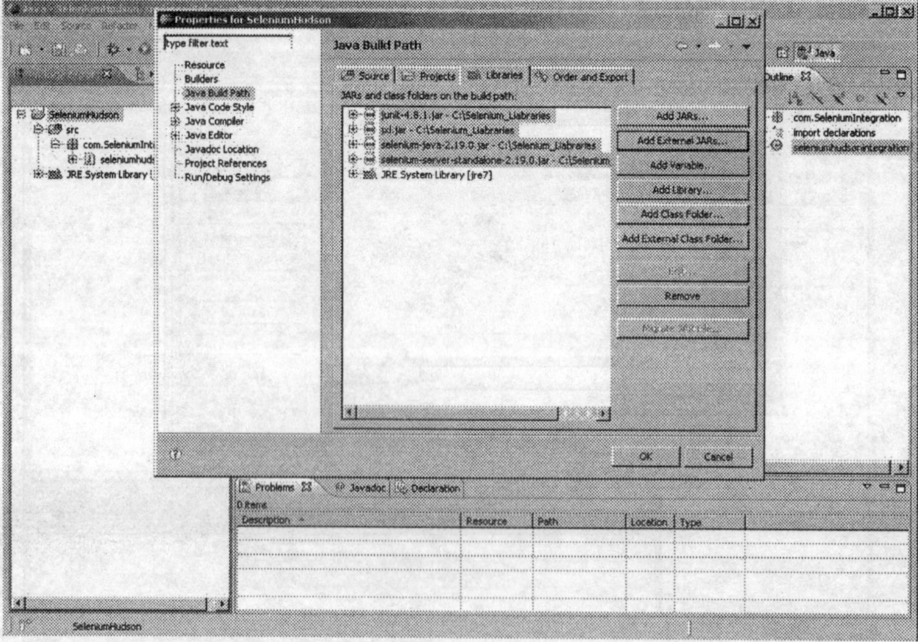

Step 34: After adding all the jar's you will see that all the errors are gone with some warnings, so ignored the warnings

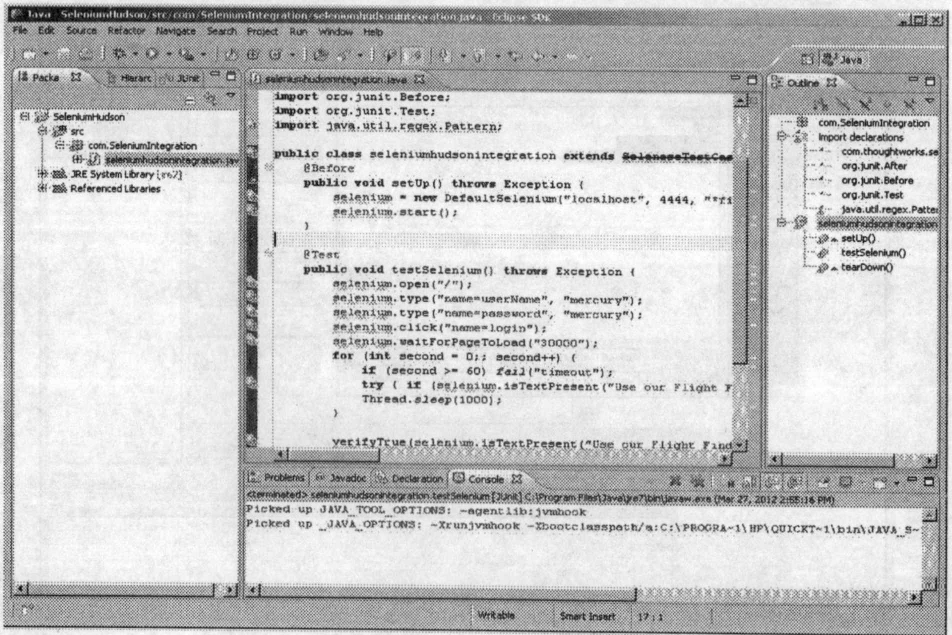

Step 35: Select the 'SeleniumHudson' project → Right Click → Click on 'Export'

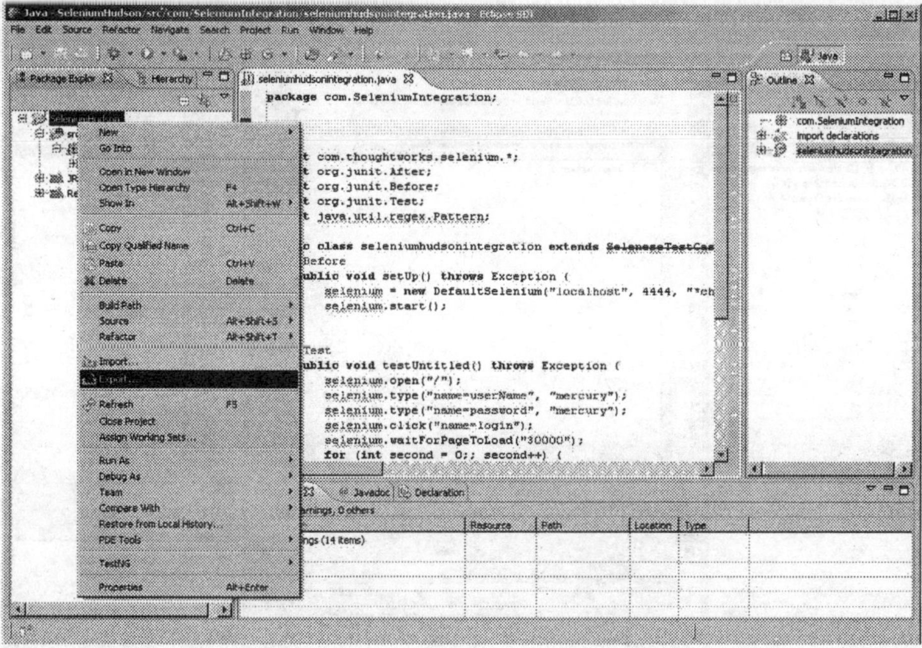

Step 36: Select the 'General→ Ant Buildfiles'

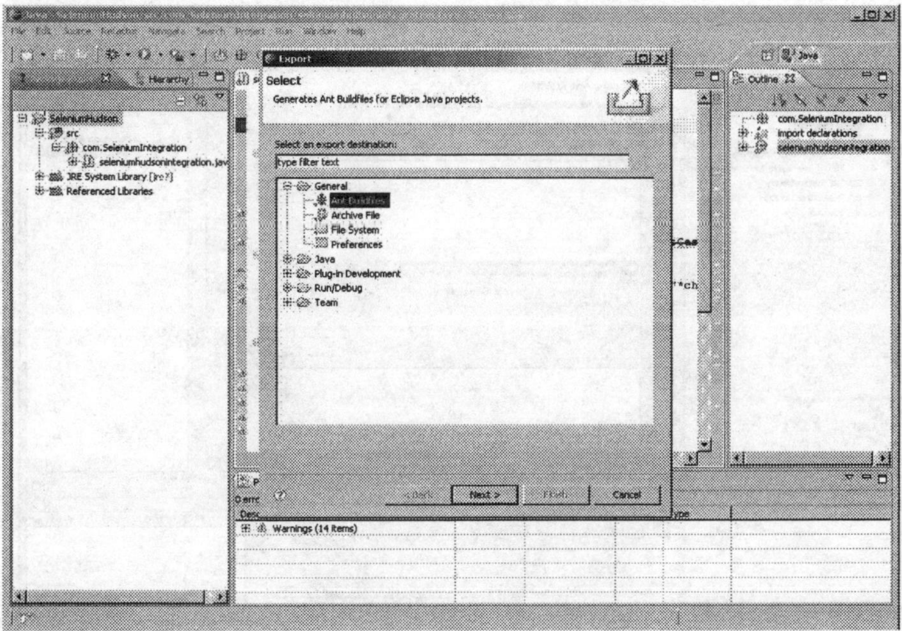

Step 37: Click on 'Finish' by default it takes 'build.xml' name as a Ant buildfile

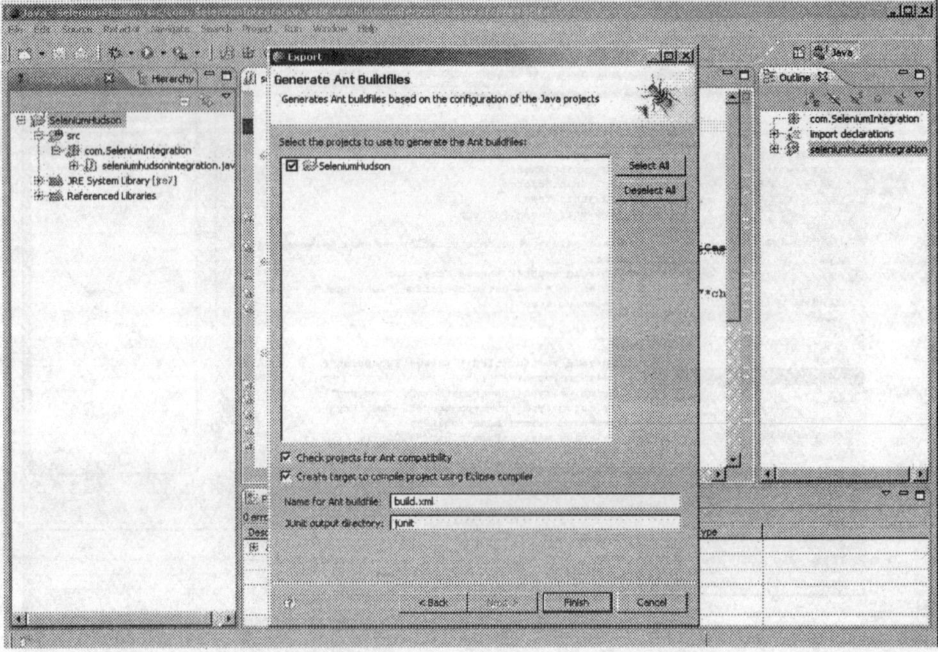

Step 38: Click on ''OK' button

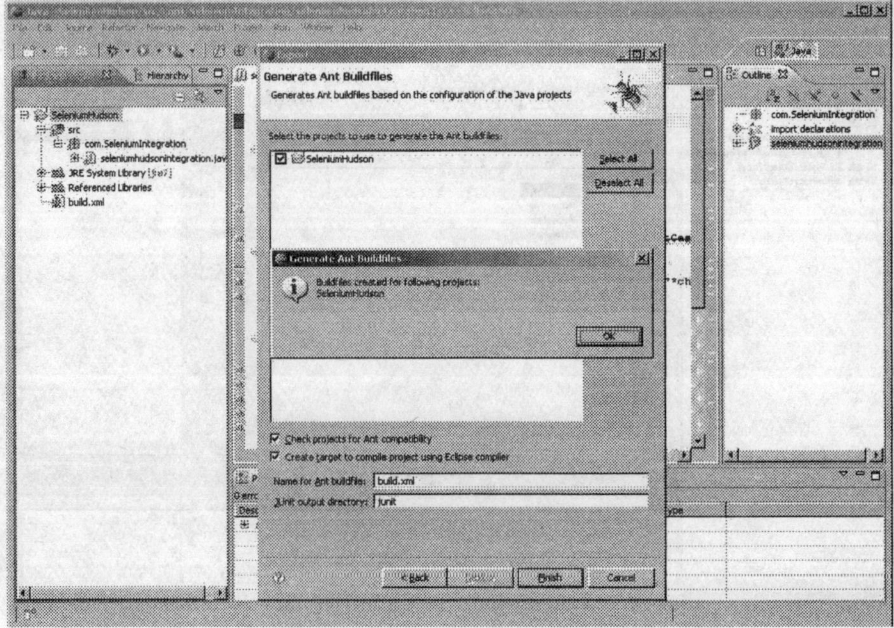

Step 39: You will see the build.xml has been created also change the '*Firefox' instead of '*chrome'

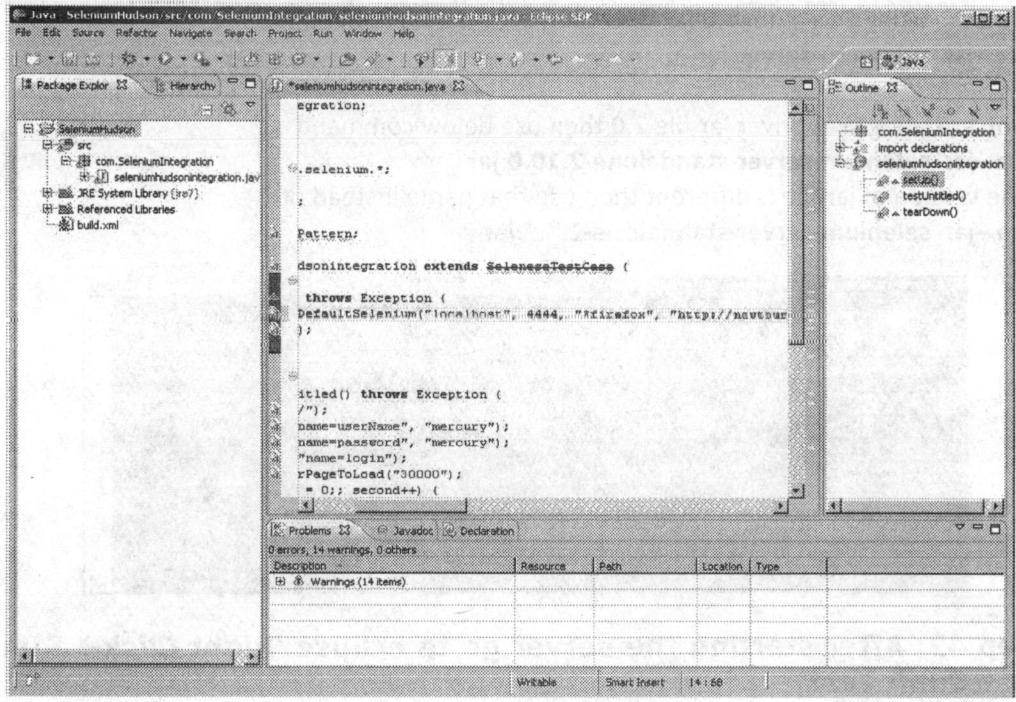

Step 40: go to command prompt and then go to the specified folder where you have created the workspace

e.g. 'C:\Selenium_Liabraries'

```
C:\WINDOWS\system32\cmd.exe
Microsoft Windows XP [Version 5.1.2600]
(C) Copyright 1985-2001 Microsoft Corp.

C:\Documents and Settings\276070>cd C:\Selenium_Liabraries

C:\Selenium_Liabraries>_
```

Step 41: Type below command which will start the selenium RC server

If you are using Selenium 1.0 jar files then type below command

Java –jar selenium-server.jar

Or

If you are using Webdriver jar file 2.0 then use below command

Java –jar selenium-server-standalone-2.19.0.jar

If the version of jar file is different then use that name instead of *

Java –jar selenium-server-standalone-2.*.*.jar

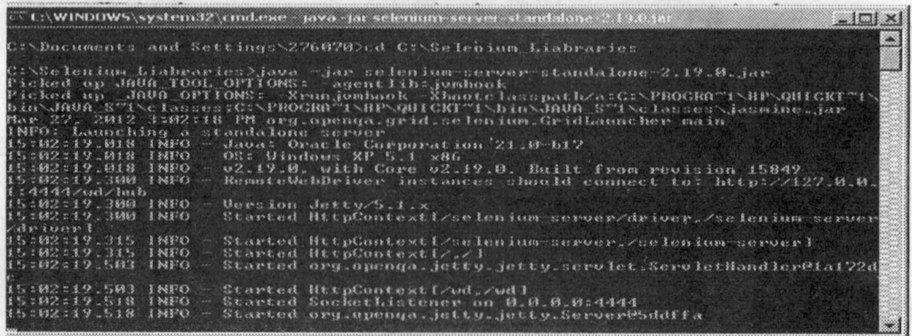

Step 42: After starting the server go to eclipse 'Right Click→ Run As → Junit Test'

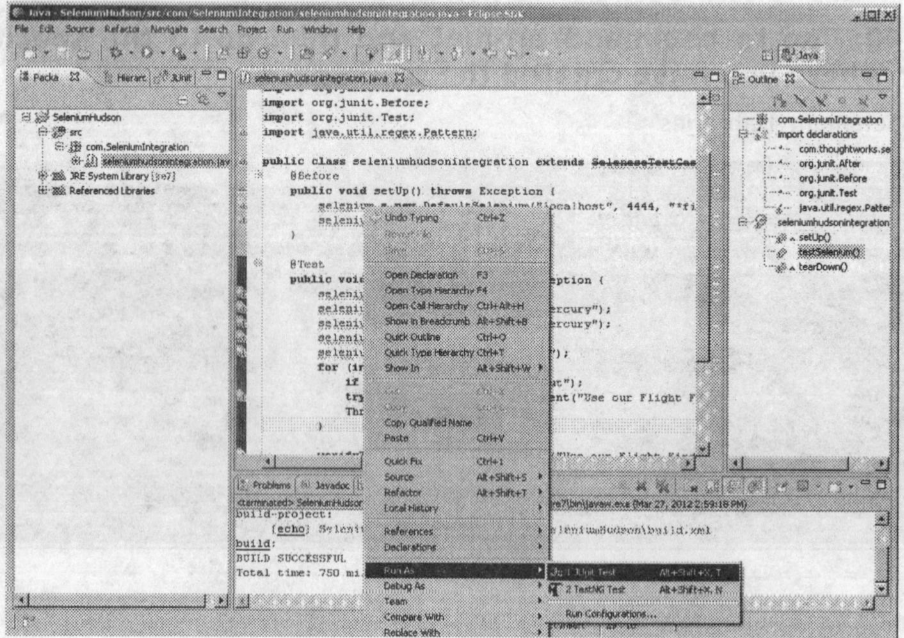

Step 43: It will start the execution

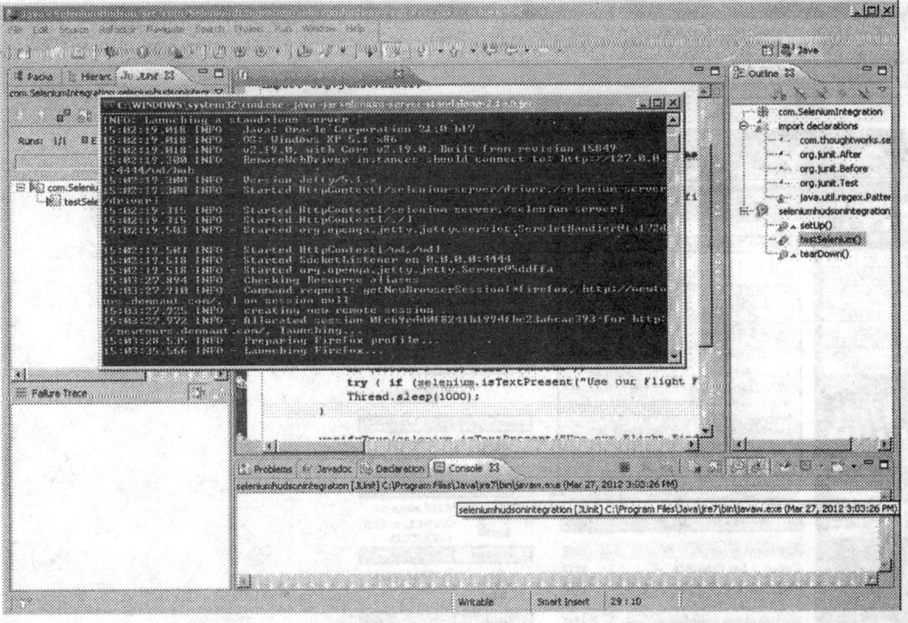

Step 44: It will open Selenium RC server and execute the command on Firefox

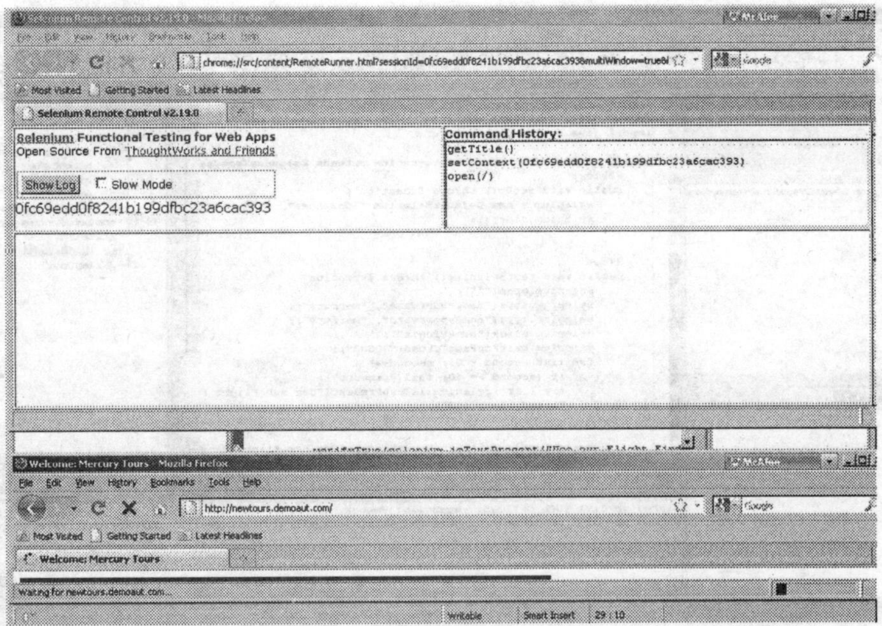

Step 45: It will execute the script as per recorded steps

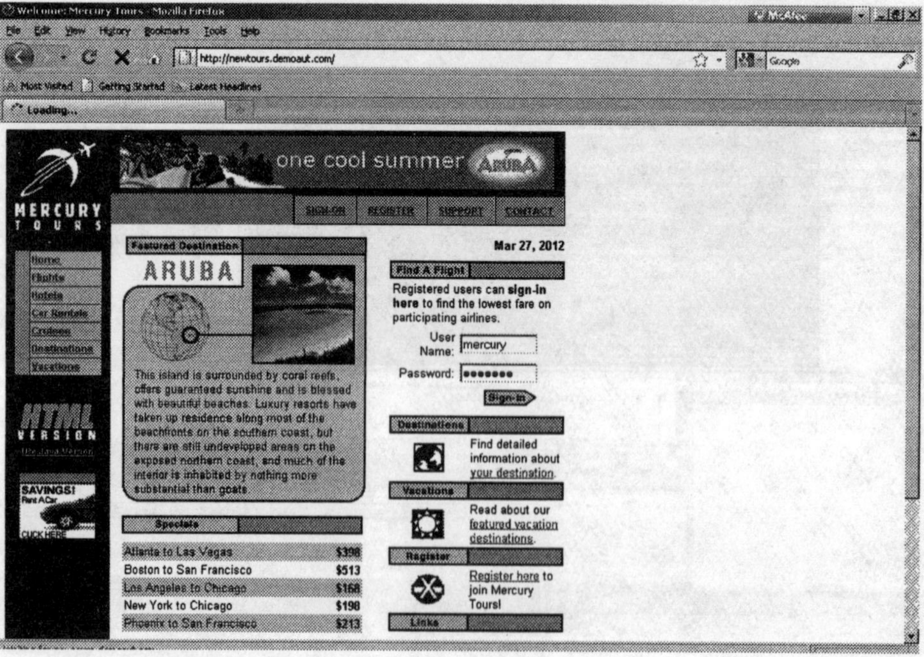

Step 46: Script executed successfully

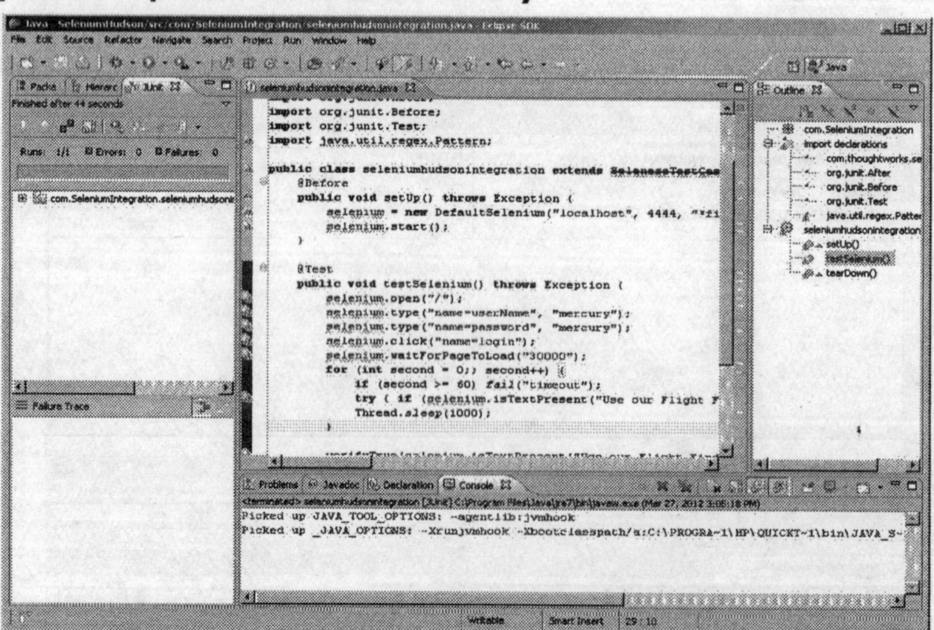

Step 48: build.xml will look like below screen shot

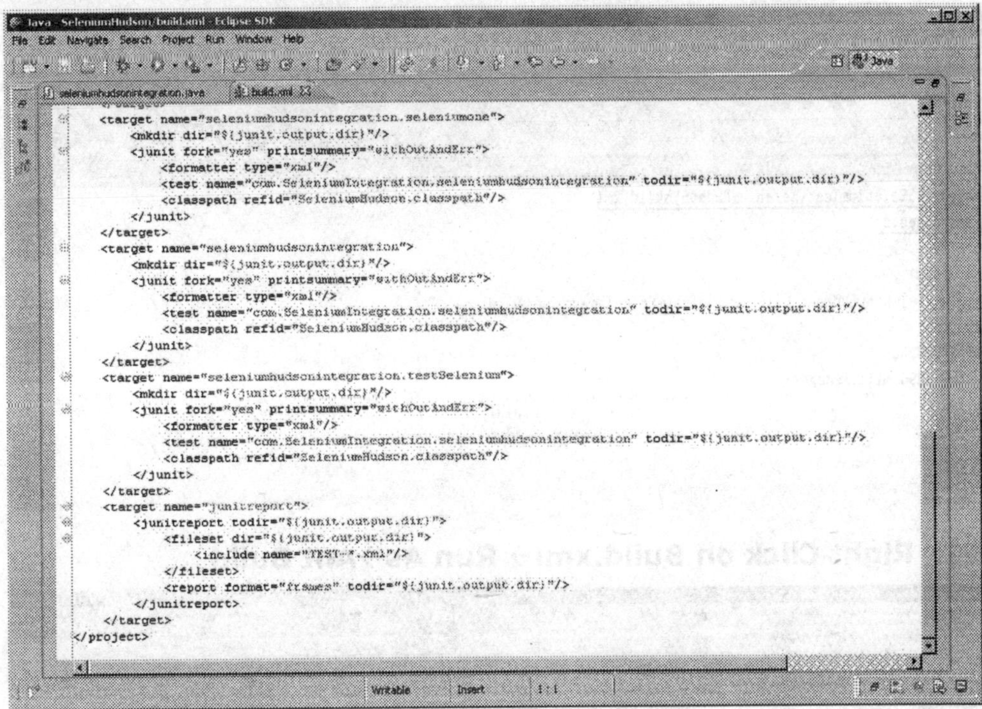

Step 49: Right Click on 'Build.xml' → Run As → Ant Build

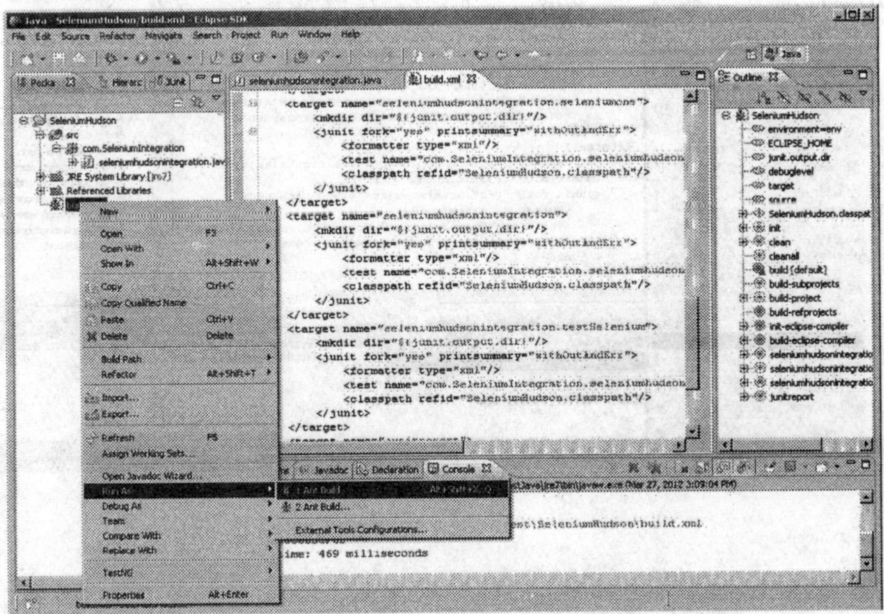

Step 50: you will get message as 'Build Successful'

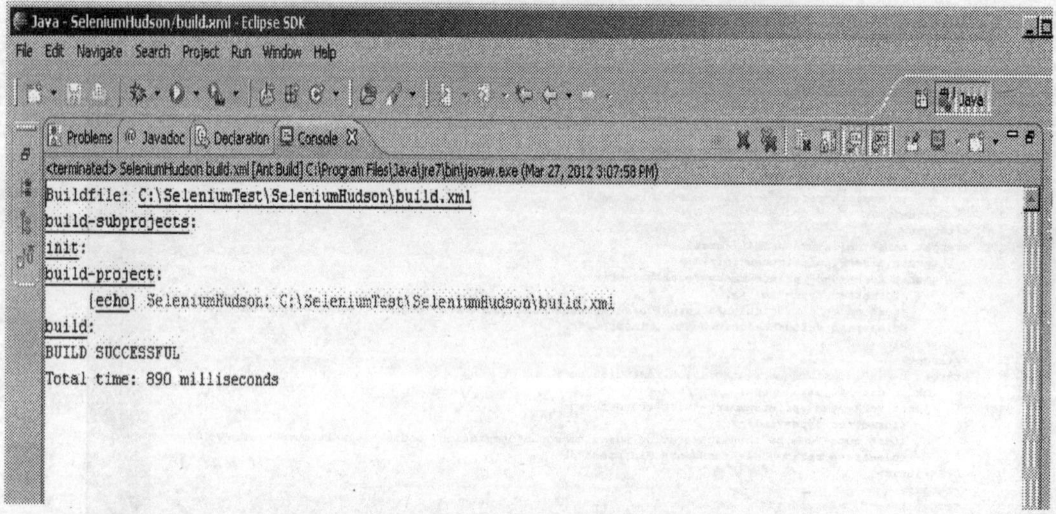

Step 51: Right Click on Build.xml→ Run As→Ant Build

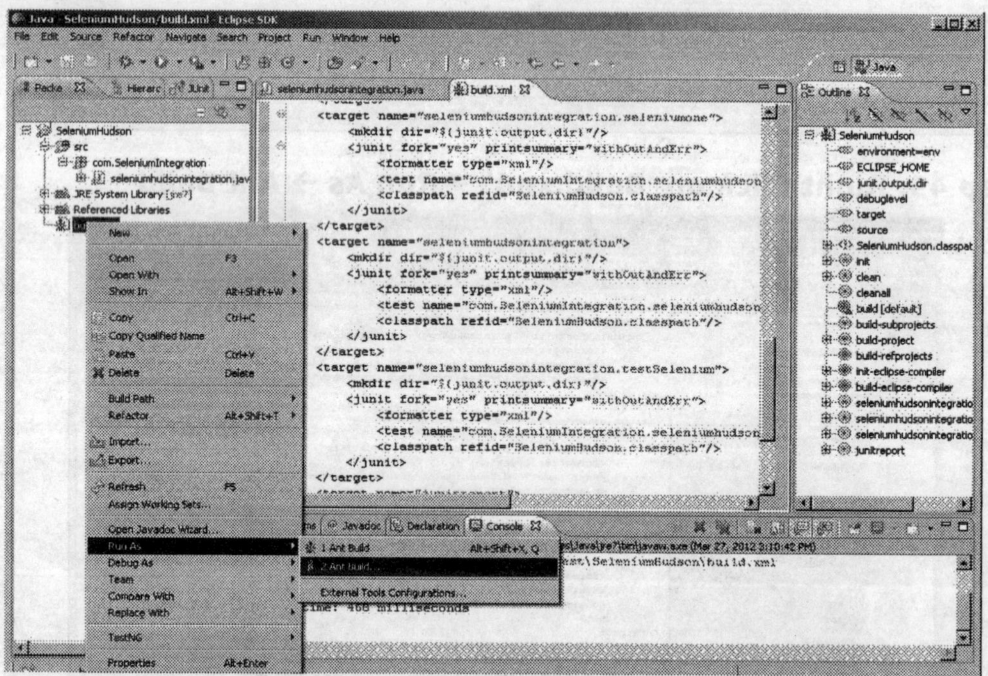

Step 52: Select 'seleniumhudsonintegration.testSelenium' check box

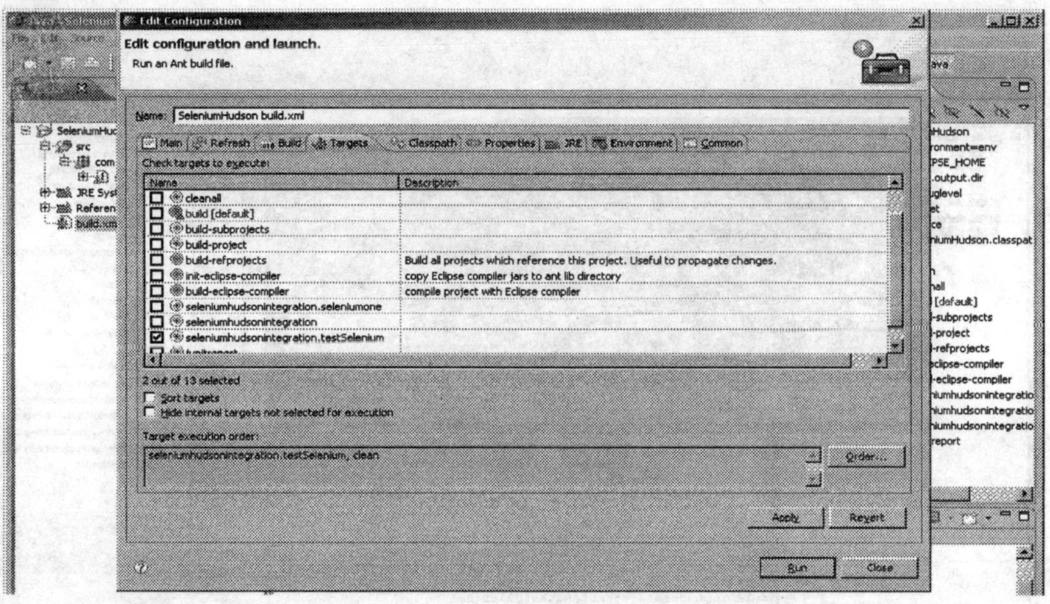

Step 53: It will start the execution

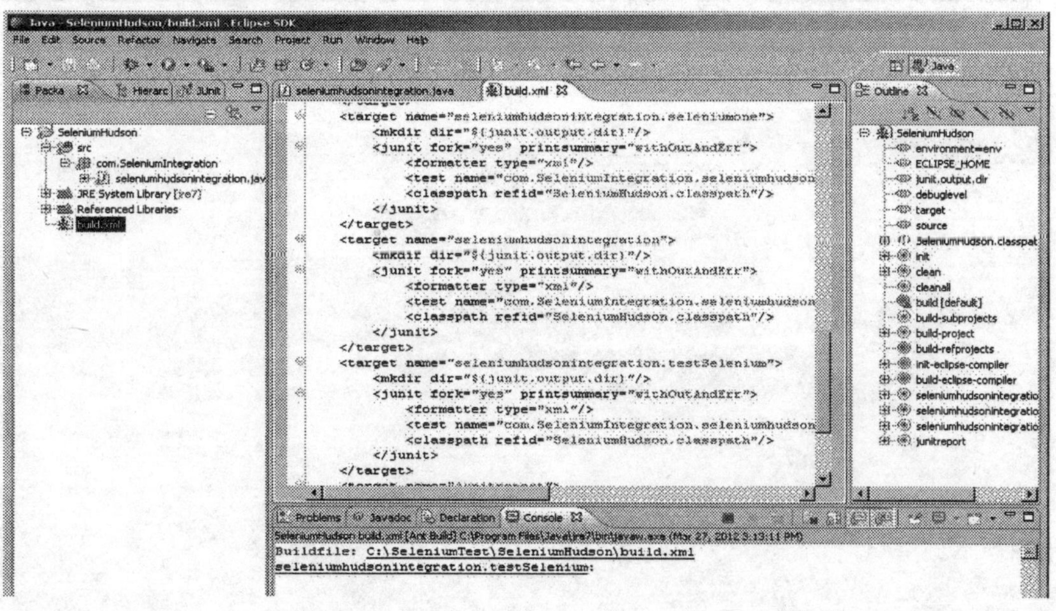

Step 54: It will start the execution and open the Firefox browser and perform the actions

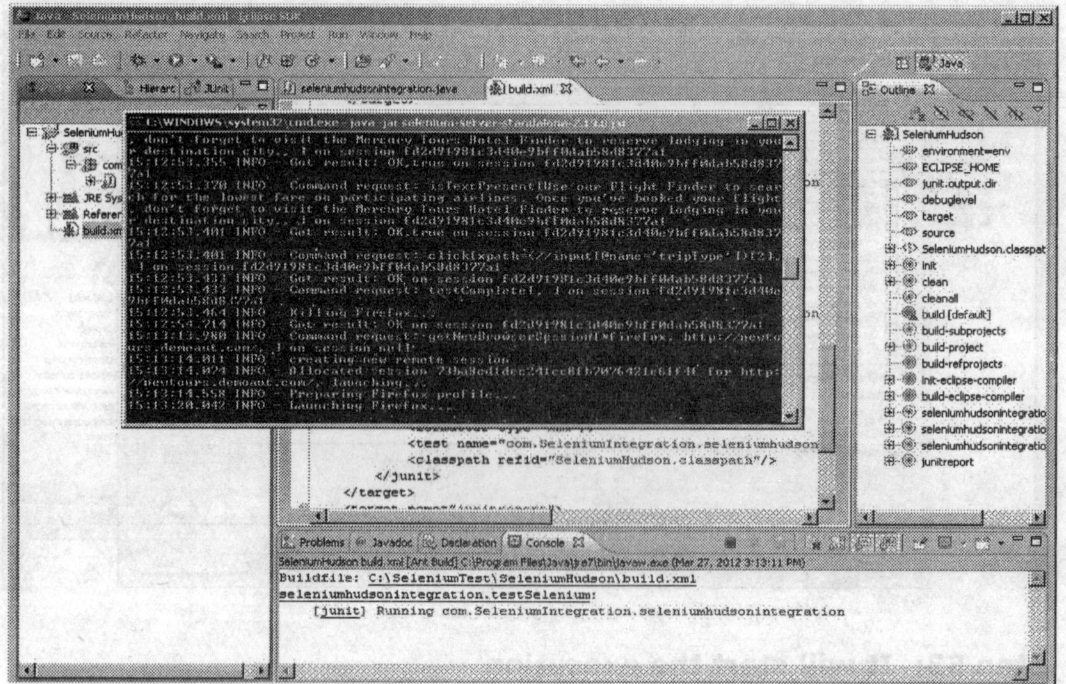

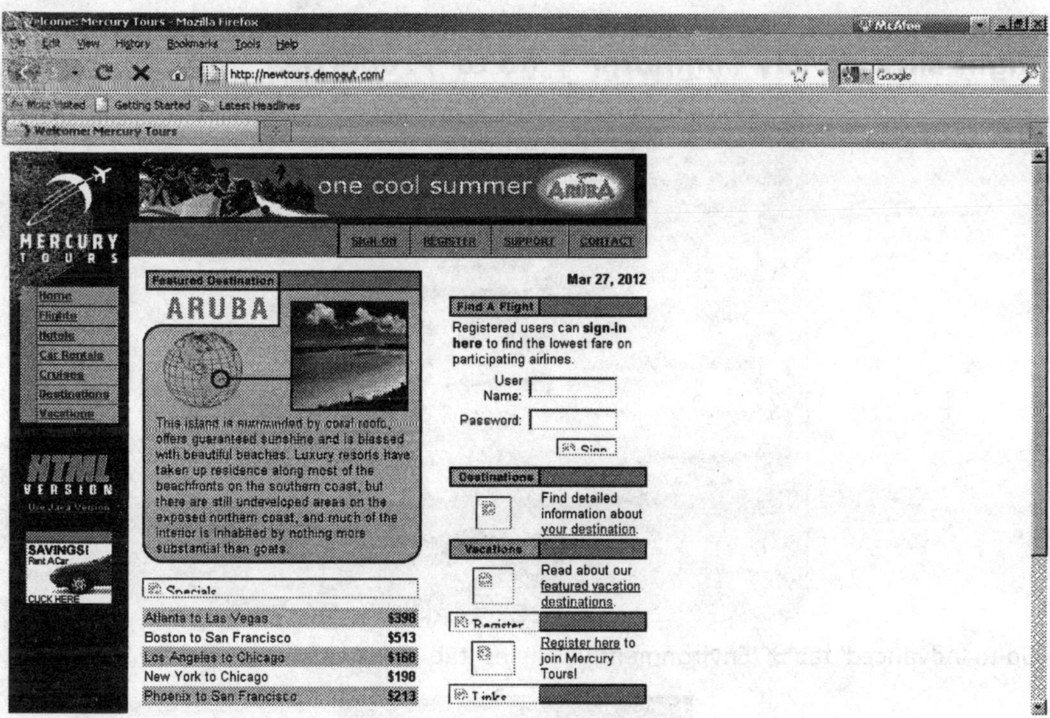

Step 55: After execution we will setup the Hudson

Pre-requisite:

Download ANT from below link:

http://mirror.atlanticmetro.net/apache//ant/binaries/apache-ant-1.8.2-bin.zip

or http://ant.apache.org/bindownload.cgi

download : `.zip` archive: apache-ant-1.8.2-bin.zip

Step 56: after that extract the file and then go to environment variables Right click on 'My Computer'→ go to 'Properties'

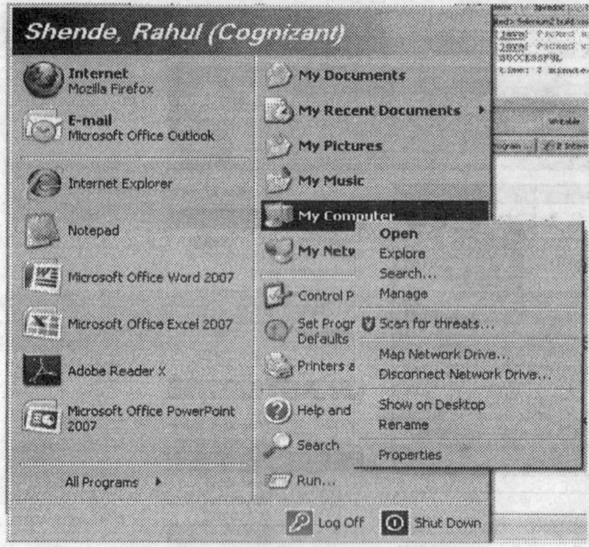

Go to 'Advanced' tab→ 'Environment Variables' tab

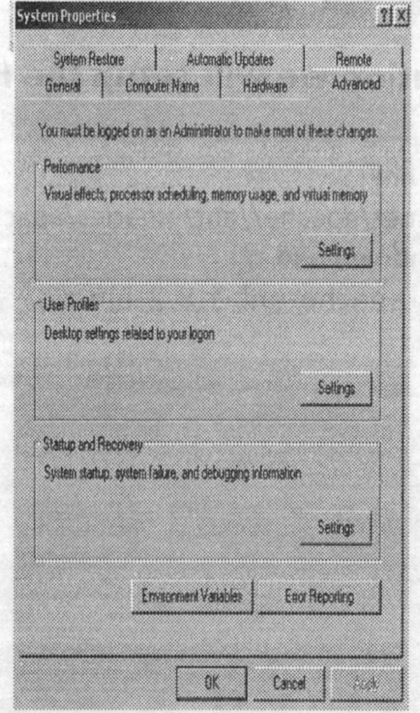

go to 'Path' and 'variable value'→
D:\ANT\bin;

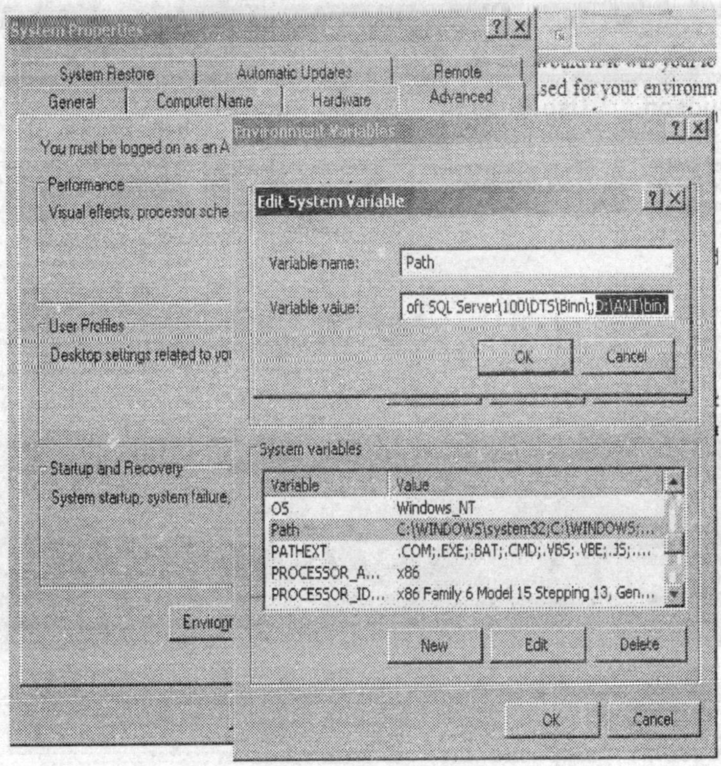

1. then go to command prompt: ant -version

```
C:\WINDOWS\system32\cmd.exe
Microsoft Windows XP [Version 5.1.2600]
(C) Copyright 1985-2001 Microsoft Corp.

C:\Documents and Settings\276070>echo %path%
C:\WINDOWS\system32;C:\WINDOWS;C:\WINDOWS\System32\Wbem;C:\Program F
 Imaging\;C:\Program Files\HP\QuickTest Professional\bin;C:\Program
oft SQL Server\100\Tools\Binn\;C:\Program Files\Microsoft SQL Server
n\;D:\ANT\bin;

C:\Documents and Settings\276070>ant -version
Picked up JAVA_TOOL_OPTIONS: -agentlib:jvmhook
Picked up _JAVA_OPTIONS: -Xrunjvmhook -Xbootclasspath/a:C:\PROGRA~1\
bin\JAVA_S~1\classes;C:\PROGRA~1\HP\QUICKT~1\bin\JAVA_S~1\classes\ja
Unable to locate tools.jar. Expected to find it in C:\Program Files\
b\tools.jar
Apache Ant version 1.6.5 compiled on June 2 2005
```

Step 57: Download Hudson

http://hudson-ci.org/

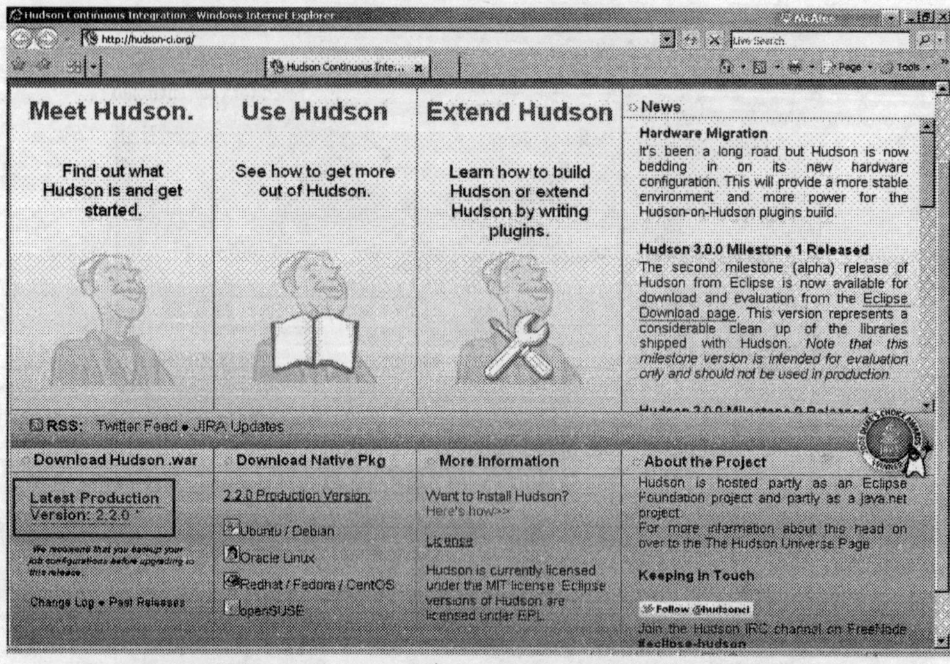

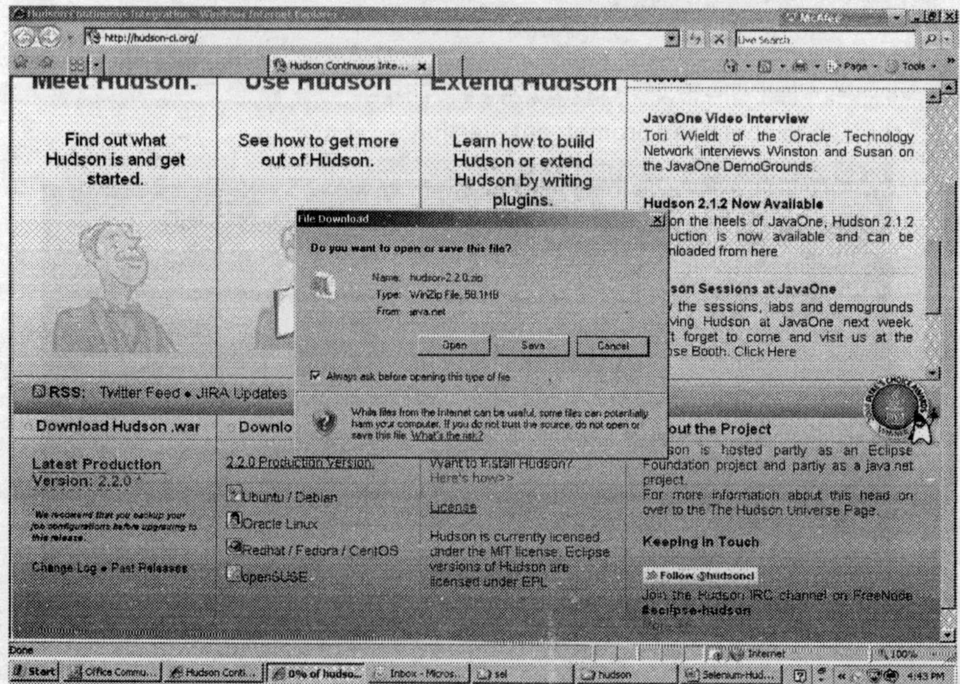

Step 58: Save the file on 'C:\Hudson folder'

Step 59: Download Tomcat:

http://tomcat.apache.org/download-60.cgi

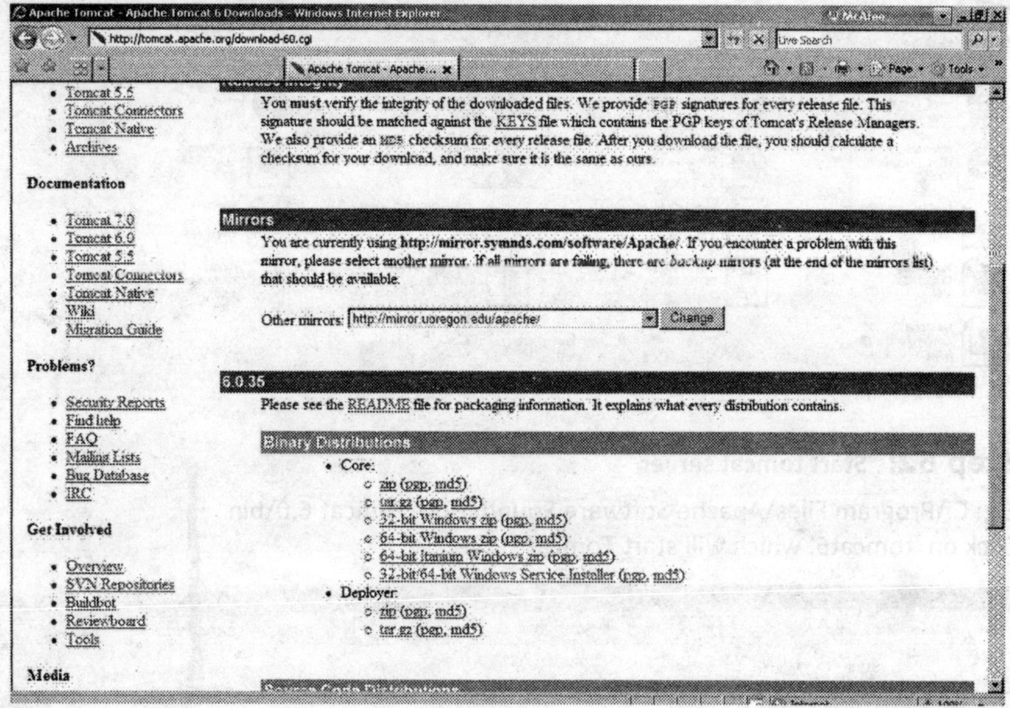

Step 60: Install Tomcat

Step 61: Extract the Hudson folder which you have downloaded and then Deploy or paste Hudson folder where you have installed tomcat server,

*Make sure you change folder name as ' hudson' or if you are using **hudson-2.2.0 setup just copy the setup in webapps**

Here I have installed tomcat in: **C:\Program Files\Apache Software Foundation\Tomcat 6.0\webapps**

So paste the Hudson folder in tomcat webapps folder so your Hudson folder will get deploy

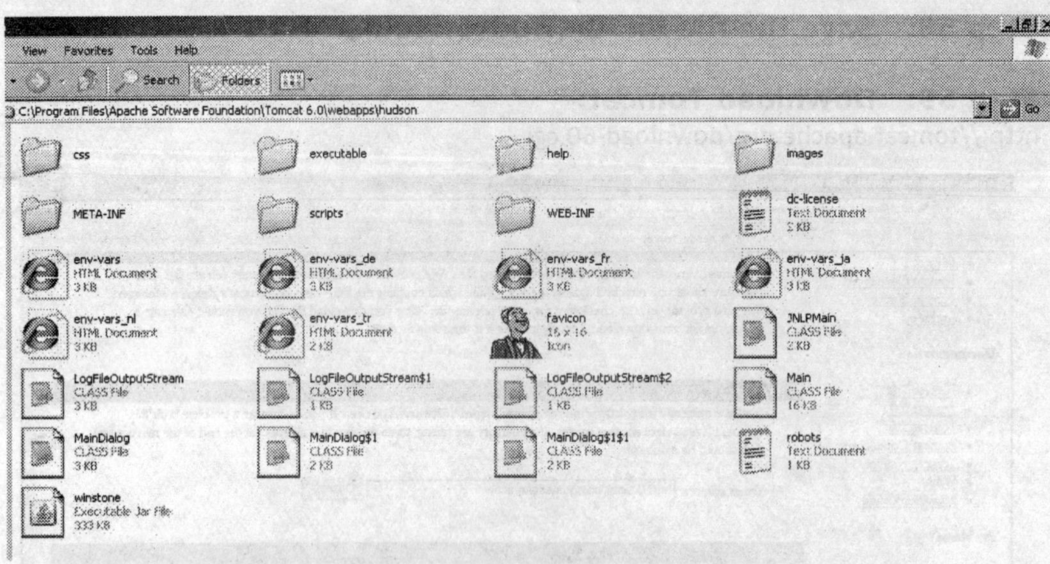

Step 62: Start tomcat server

E.g: C:\Program Files\Apache Software Foundation\Tomcat 6.0\bin
Click on 'tomcat6' which will start Tomcat server

Step 63: tomcat server started

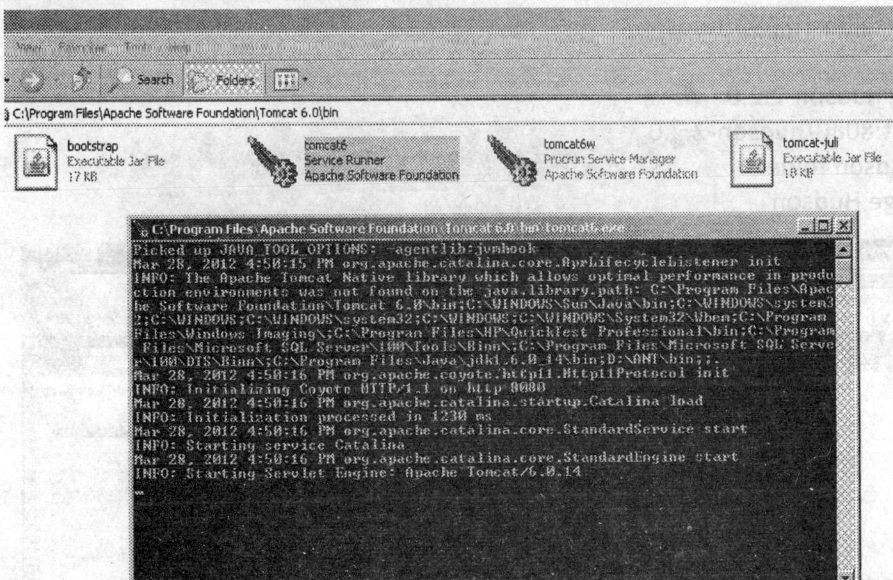

Step 64:

Go to: http://localhost:8080/hudson/
Or
If you are using hudson-2.2.0
http://localhost:8080/hudson-2.2.0
You will see Hudson folder
Click on 'Manage Hudson'

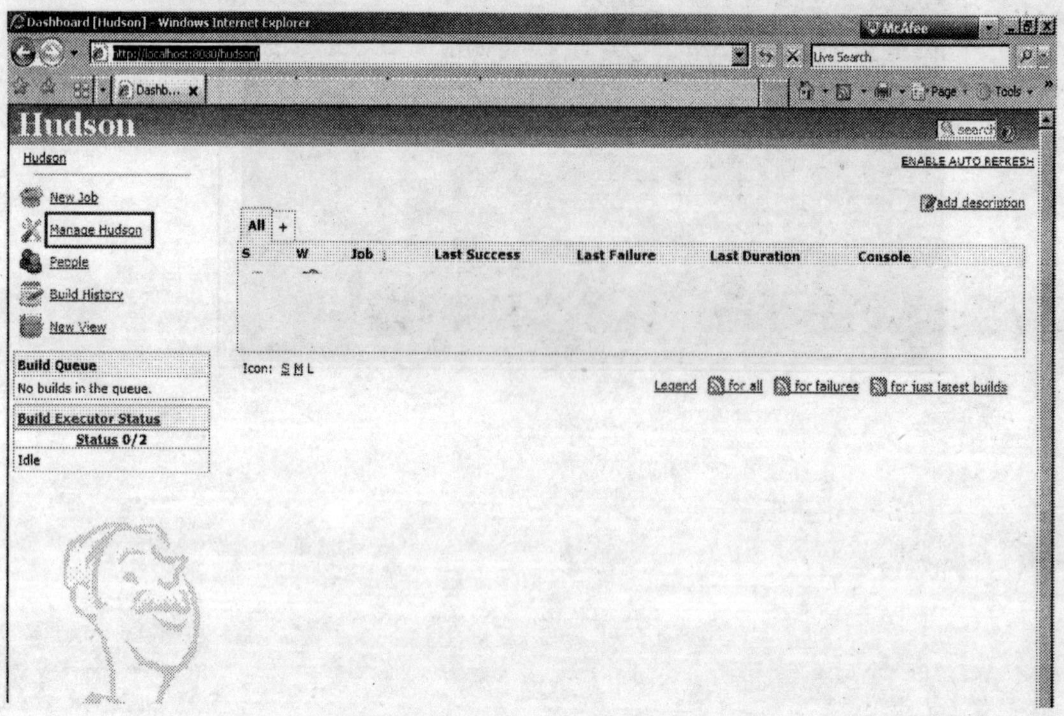

Step 65:

Click on 'configure system'

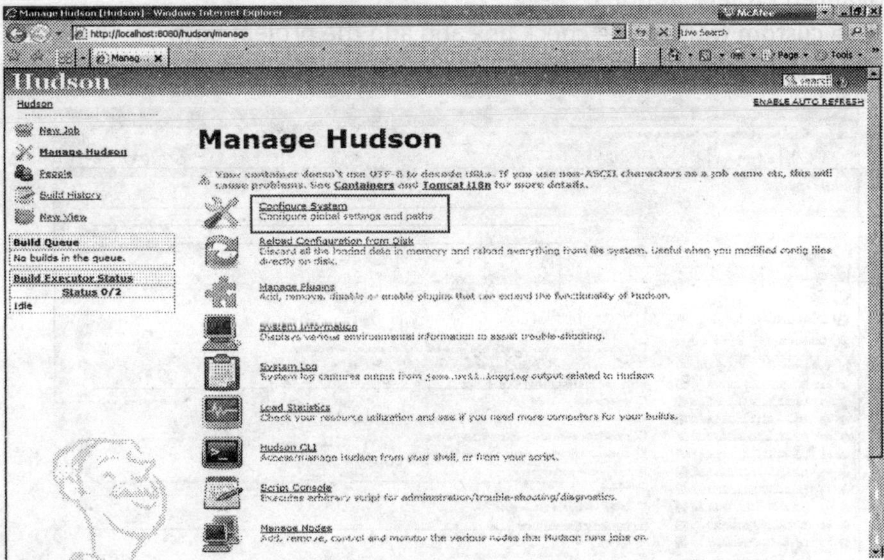

Step 66:

Go to 'ANT' and click on 'Save'
Name: put the name (e.g. SelleniumExample or SeleniumANT)
ANT_HOME: D:\ANT (Put the path where you have downloaded the ANT)

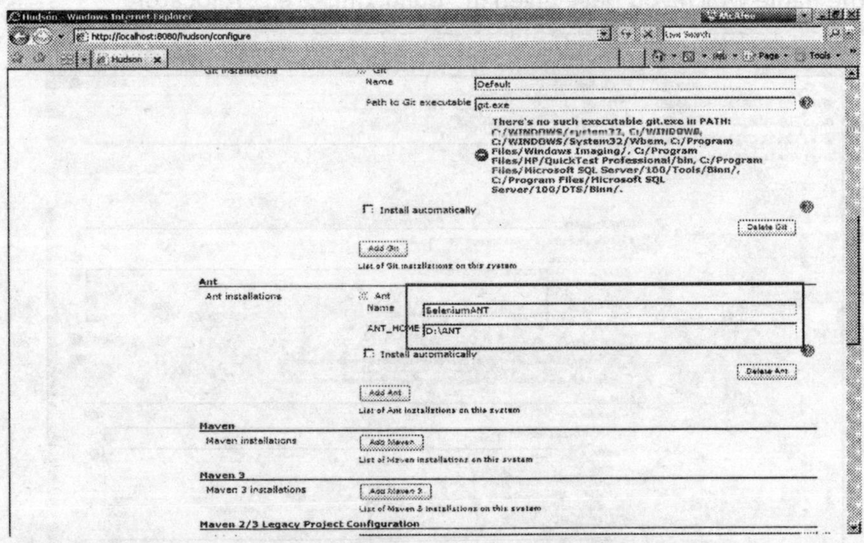

Step 67:

Click on 'configure' link and then add the below configuration:

Go to: Advanced Project Options:

Click on 'Use custom workspace' check box and add the project path 'C:\ Selenium_Liabraries'

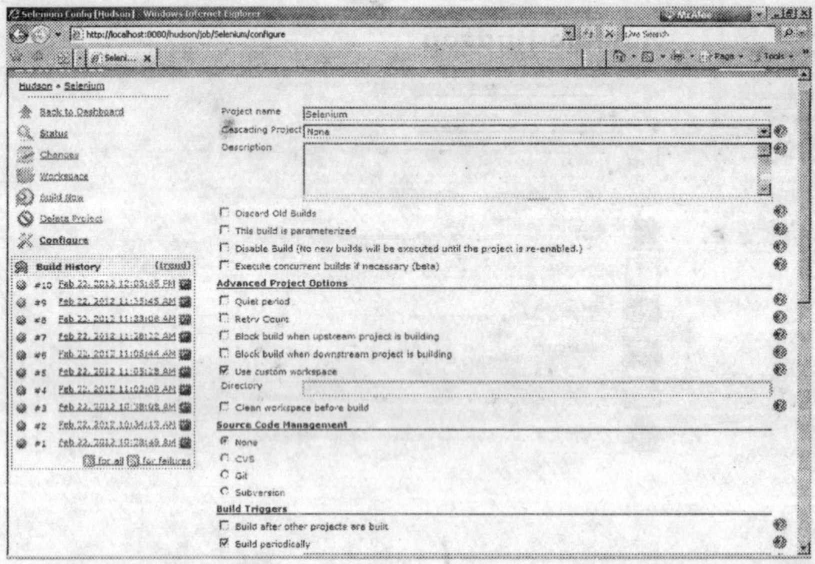

Step 68:

Select 'ANT version' :- the name which you configured in Hudson.

Targets: the name which you have given in ' build.xml'→ e.g. Allocator.

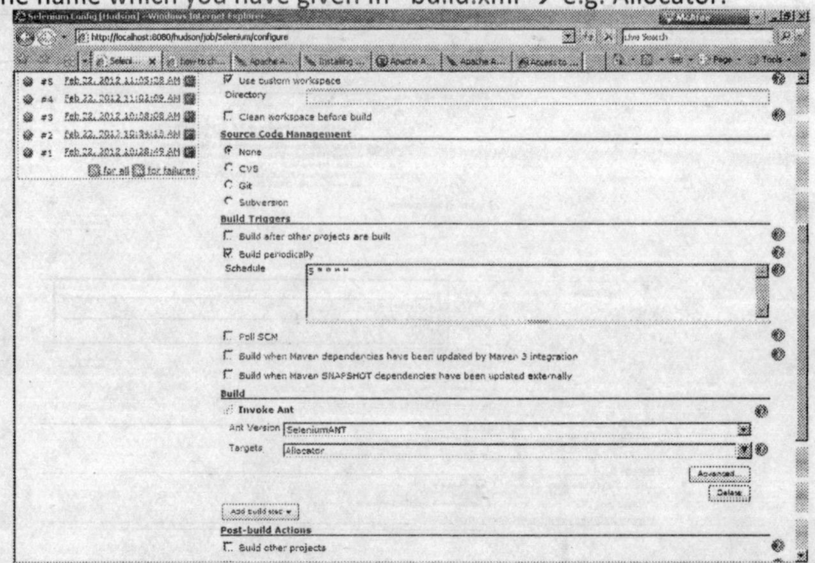

Step 69: Now click on 'Build Now' → it will start the execution and show the result., only start the selenium server. Then you can see the output you can go to 'Console Output'.

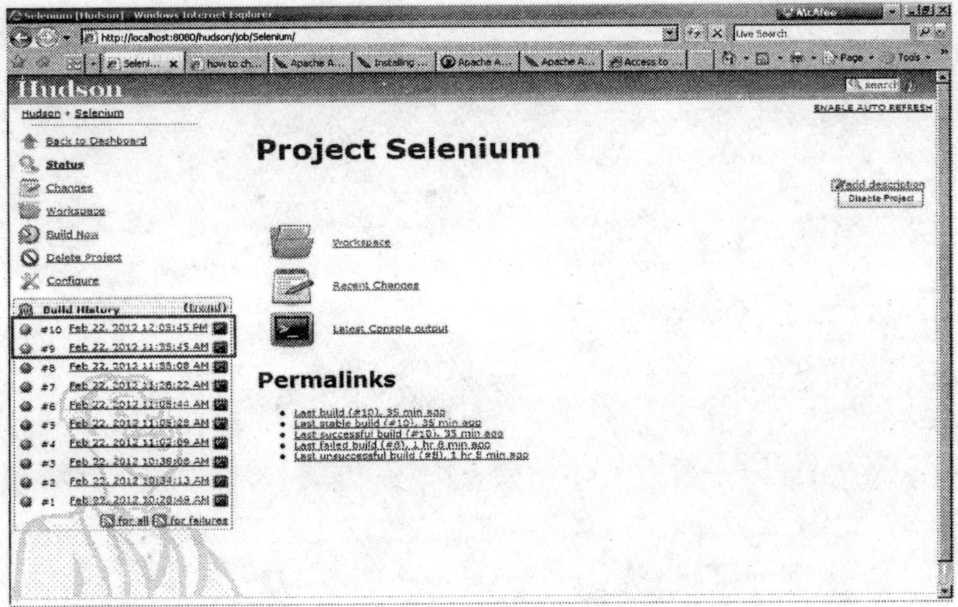

Step 70: So after setup Hudson will refer build.xml and start the execution on the server.

If you go to Build History and click on the links you will get the build output

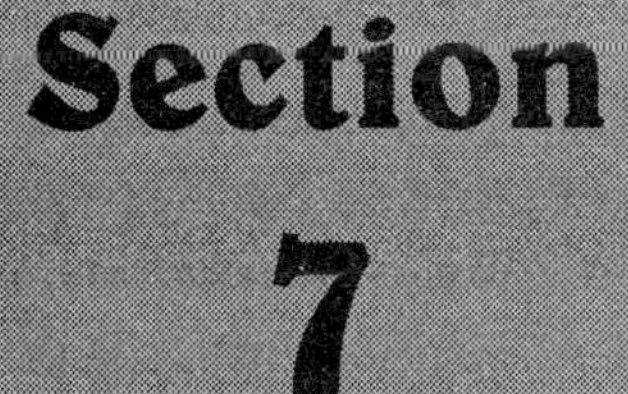

Performance Testing Approach

Introduction:

Performance Testing

- **Performance Tests are tests that determine end to end timing of various time critical business processes and transactions under a particular workload.**
  - It can demonstrate that the system meets performance criteria
  - It can compare two systems to find which performs better
  - It can measure what parts of the system or workload cause the system to perform badly
- **"It is much easier to make measurements than to know exactly what you are measuring." —J. W. N. Sullivan (1928)**

Performance Testing – Definition

- **To evaluate the response time, throughput and utilization of the system, to perform it's required functions in comparison with different versions of the same product(s) or with different competitive product(s).**

Why Performance Testing Is Needed ?

- Ensuring Optimal end-user experience
- Will my application meet the defined response-time requirements of my customers?
- Will my users experience acceptable response times, even during peak hours?
- What system capacity is required to handle expected load?
- Where are the bottlenecks in my multi-user environment?
- How can we detect errors that only occur under real-load conditions?
- How can we optimize the multi-user application before it goes live?

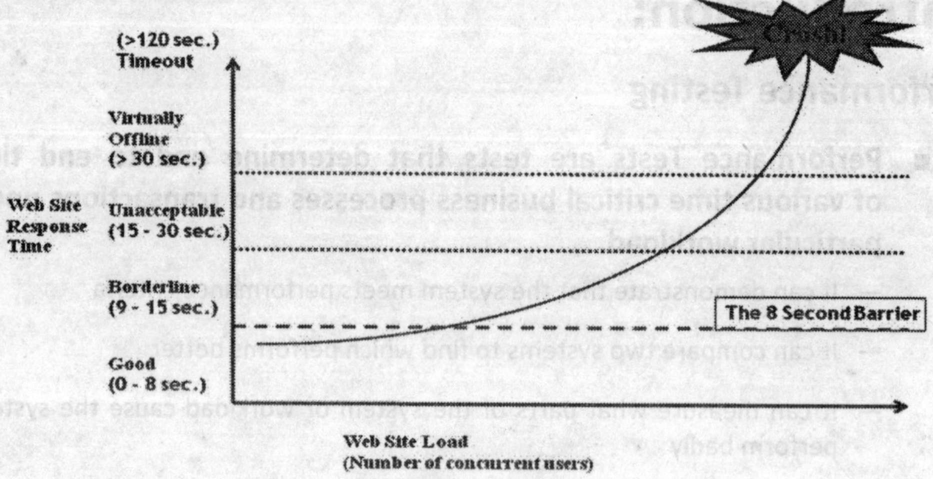

When PT needs to be done – example

- Application is performing well for single user
- Application is ready for production
- Doesn't support more than 10 users
- Response times are not acceptable
- Resource utilization is very high
- Customers are not happy
- Business Impact

How do you know the problem?

- Needs to test the application with more load.
- Monitor the system and identify the issue
- Fix the problem

Avoid performance issues before rolling out to production

Factors governing performance testing

- Throughput
- Response time
- Latency

— Tuning
— Benchmarking
— Capacity planning

- **Throughput**

1. Refers to the number of client requests processed within a certain amount of time.
2. Requests received per hour or operations performed per hour

*Key factor in determining hardware and system requirements

— Transactions per Second
— Web Interactions per Second
— Pages per Second
— Bytes per Second

- **Response time**

1. The delay between point of request and server's response

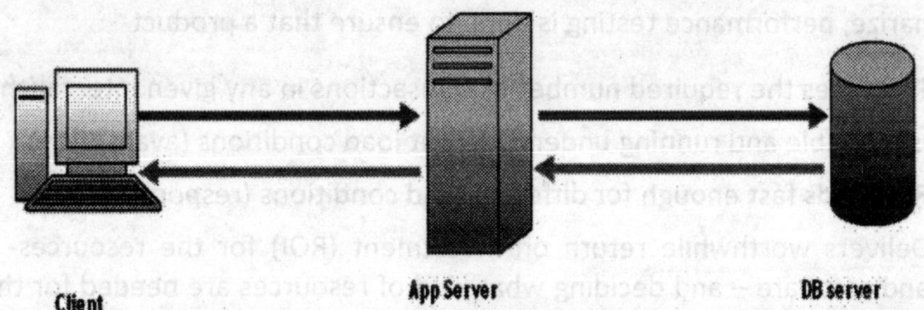

Time in which the system responds for a particular request.
e.g., Time required for Processing a search request.

- **Latency**

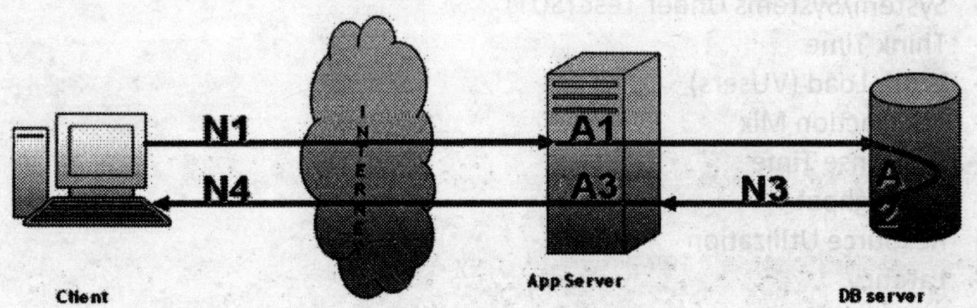

- Network Latency – data to travel from machine to machine (N=N1+N2+N3+N4)

- Application Latency - data to be processed within the server (A=A1+A2+A3)
- Total Latency L = A+N

Tuning

— Tuning is a procedure by which product performance is enhanced.

— Tuning doesn't involve touching the code

— Tuning is done at two levels

- Operating system / infrastructure level tuning
- Application level tuning

Benchmarking and Capacity planning

— Comparison of two products with performance factors is called benchmarking

— The exercise to find out the hardware and software requirements for a particular usage/load is called capacity planning

To Summarize, performance testing is done to ensure that a product

— Processes the required number of transactions in any given interval(throughput)

— Is available and running under different load conditions (availability)

— Responds fast enough for different load conditions (response time)

— Delivers worthwhile return on investment (ROI) for the resources- hardware and software – and deciding what kind of resources are needed for the product for different load conditions (capacity planning)

— Is comparable to and better than that of the competitors (benchmarking.)

Important Terminology

— System/Systems Under Test (SUT)
— Think Time
— Work Load (VUsers)
— Transaction Mix
— Response Time
— Throughput
— Resource Utilization
— Latency

System Under Test

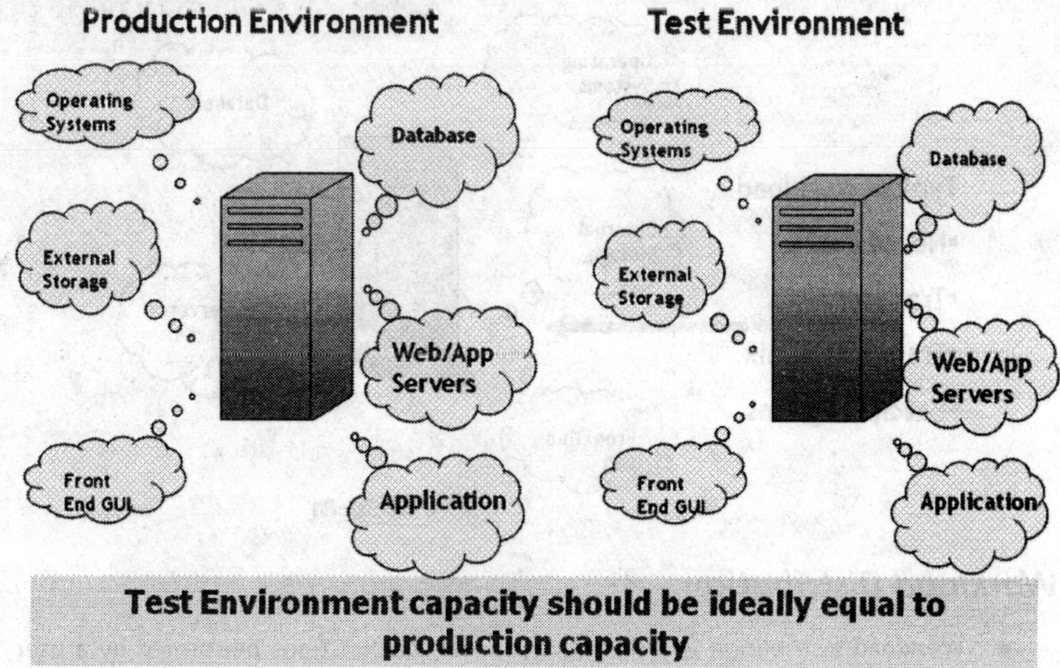

Think Time

- Time taken by the user for performing a new action(transaction) after the previous action (transaction) has been completed.
  - Wait.
  - Read contents of web page.

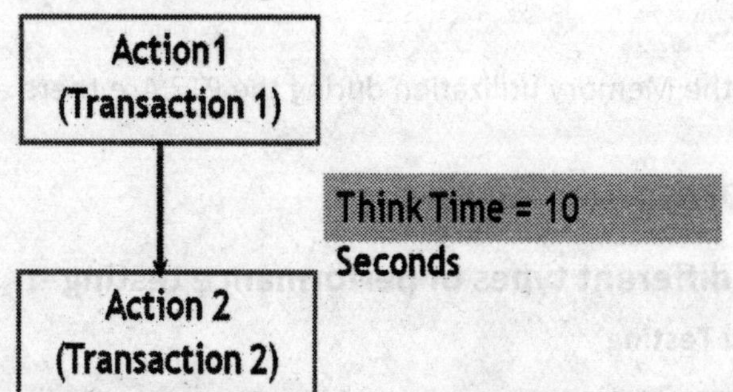

Workload

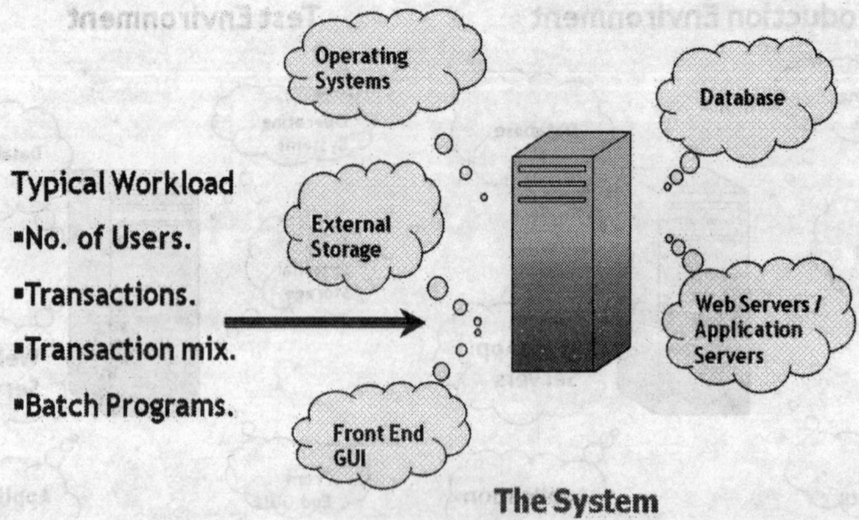

Workload Distribution

- Workload distribution is a representation of the functions performed by a user community on a system. It is based on a percentage of users performing a specific function over a given period of time.

Resource Utilization

- CPU
  — What is the CPU utilization during the PT? Is it crossing the thresholds.

- Memory
  — What is the Memory utilization during the PT? Are there any memory leaks?

Types Of Performance Testing

- **There are different types of performance testing -:**
  - **Load Testing**
  - **Volume Testing**
  - **Stress Testing**
  - **Scalability Testing**

Load Testing

- **Varying the number of users**
- **Varying think times i.e., transaction fire rates**
- **System behavior at various LOADS**
- **Purpose:-**
  - How response times are varying with load ?
  - What is System resource utilization with increase in load?
  - Estimate the hardware capacity for future workloads

Volume Testing

- Vary database entities like policies, accounts

  ex: 100000, 200000, 500000 policies etc

  100GB, 200GB, 500GB etc

  Vary number of users

  100, 200, 500 etc

- **Purpose:-**
  - Response times with increase in database entities?
  - Are query plans changing?
  - What are the system resources consumption with increase in database size?

Stress Testing

- **Find the breaking point of the system.**
  - Max out in Users
  - Increase the transaction rates
  - Run for a long duration
- **Purpose:-**
  - When the system breaks?
  - What is the maximum load the system can support?
  - To find out memory leaks

Scalability Testing

- Checking the system for hardware and user Scalability.

Why do we need a tool?

- **A well-constructed PT answers questions like:**
  - Does the application response quickly enough for the intended users?
  - Will the application handle the expected user load and beyond?
  - Will the application handle the number of transactions required by the business?
  - Is the application stable under expected load and unexpected user loads?
  - Are you sure that users will have a positive experience (i.e., response time) on go-live day?
- **Production environment simulation** -:

  Recreating production environment means that there have to be 1000 online terminals and 1000 testers for these terminals
- **Virtual user technology** -:

  Virtual user is a process, which executes the work flow of an application as if it would have been executed by user from physical machine
- **Problem With Manual Testing** –:
  - Do you have the testing resources
  - Testing Personnel
  - Client machines
  - How do you synchronize users ?
  - How do you collect and analyze results ?
  - How do you achieve test repeatability ?
  - Benefits of Virtual user technology -:
  - It is possible to simulate many users on the same machine, depending upon the RAM of the system
  - Number of testers and terminals required are minimal
  - Repeatable

- **We need a tool to:**
  - Emulate hundreds or thousands of users interacting with the system using minimal hardware.
  - Measure end-user response times.
  - Repeat load in a consistent way.
  - Monitor system components under user load.
  - Provide robust analysis and reporting engine.

Virtual users replaces Manual users

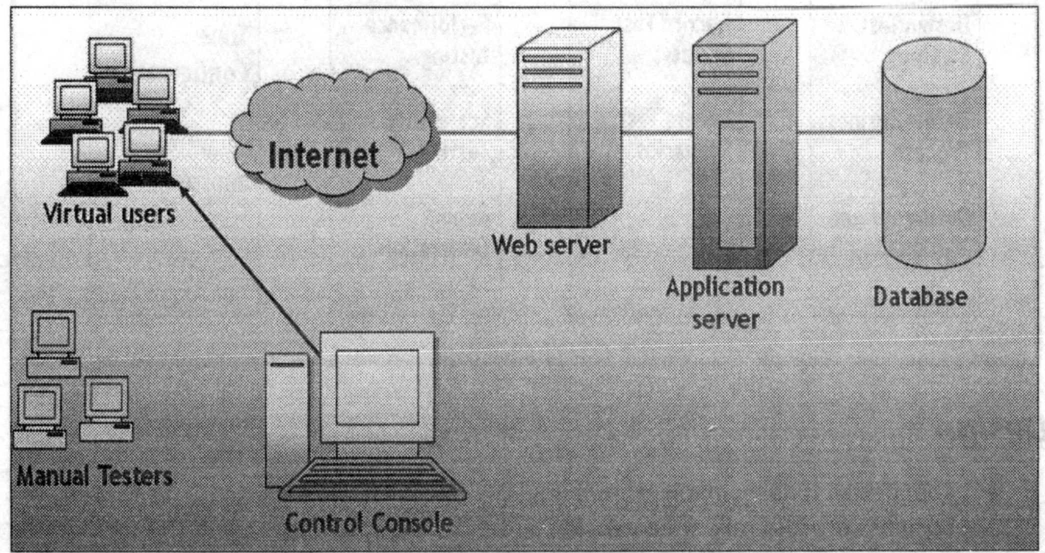

A single console controlling several thousand virtual users replaces manual testers

- Today, automated load testing is the preferred choice for load testing a web application. The testing tools typically use three major components to execute a test. These include:
  - A **control console**, which organizes, drives, and manages the load.
  - **Virtual users**, which are processes used to imitate the real users performing a business process on a client application
  - **Load servers**, used to run the Virtual users.

The Automated Performance testing Process

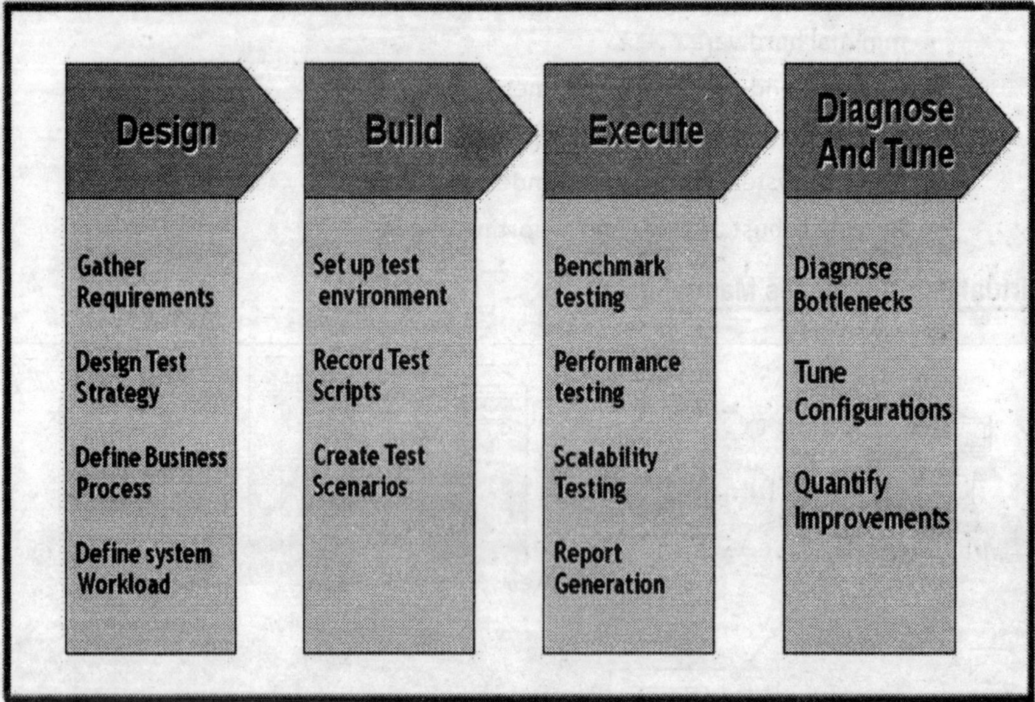

Design

- The design phase involves defining the business processes to be tested, the business process mix of an average or peak production hour, and the overall user and response time goals for the system.
    - Application Overview
    - Business process List
    - Business process Flows
    - A Transaction List
    - Business process diagrams
    - Environment Walkthrough
    - Systems Scope Meeting
    - Production Diagram

Execute

- Among those new to PT, there is misconception that execution is a single event. In fact it is a multi-step process consisting of several types of performance tests.
  - **Baseline** tests verifies that the system and its surrounding environments function within reasonable technical parameters. PT's are run with only 5 to 10 users. Tests should be executed at the start and end of the performance testing process to measure absolute response-time improvement.
  - **Performance** tests simulate a load on a environment to determine the optimal and maximum number of users the system can handle. They should apply real-world user behaviors such as think time, modem emulation, and multi browser types for maximum accuracy.
  - ***Benchmark*** *tests are designed to measure and compare the performance of each machine type, environment, or build of the application in an ideal situation. These are run after the system has been scalability tested to understand the performance impact of different architectures.*
  - ***Soak*** *tests are designed to run the system for a long period of time under load and examine how well the system performs.*
  - ***Peak*** *tests are designed to simulate peak load on the system for a period of time to ensure that the application and the underlying H/W can handle load for reasonable periods of time.*

Diagnose and Tune

- **Monitoring** during a performance test shows what is happening at each tier of the infrastructure, offering more clarity about how the DB server, Web server, App server, or individual apps or processes are performing during the a PT.
- **Analysis:** After a load test is completed , the user can correlate metrics – such as virtual users against CPU or App server CPU to Web server – to determine further information about app behavior.
- **Tuning:** systematically identifying, isolate, and resolve infrastructure performance bottlenecks by modifying the system configuration settings.
- **Diagnostics:** To View how individual tiers, components, and SQL statements impact the overall performance of a business process under Load conditions. Can know how long each component takes and how many times it is called.

Performance Testing using JMeter tool

Introduction:

Apache JMeter is a 100% pure Java desktop application designed to load test client/ server software (such as a web application). It may be used to test performance both on static and dynamic resources such as static files, Java Servlets, CGI scripts, Java objects, databases, FTP servers, and more. JMeter can be used to simulate a heavy load on a server, network or object to test its strength or to analyze overall performance under different load types.

Additionally, JMeter can help you regression test your application by letting you create test scripts with assertions to validate that your application is returning the results you expect. For maximum flexibility, JMeter lets you create these assertions using regular expressions.

History

Stefano Mazzocchi of the Apache Software Foundation was the original developer of JMeter. He wrote it primarily to test the performance of Apache JServ (a project that has since been replaced by the Apache Tomcat project). We redesigned JMeter to enhance the GUI and to add functional-testing capabilities.

JMeter can be used as a unit test tool for JDBC database connection, FTP, LDAP, WebServices,J MS, HTTP and generic TCP connections. JMeter can also be configured as a monitor, although this is typically considered an ad-hoc solution in lieu of advanced monitoring solutions.

But please note that JMeter is not a browser.

Installing JMeter:

- ✓ Download and Install JDK 6 Update 16 from http://java.sun.com/javase/downloads/index.jsp
- ✓ Set Environment variable:
  - ➢ Right click on My Computer → Properties → Advanced → Environment Variables → New
  - ➢ Variable Name = PATH
  - ➢ Variable Value = C:\Program Files\Java\jdk1.6.0_16\bin

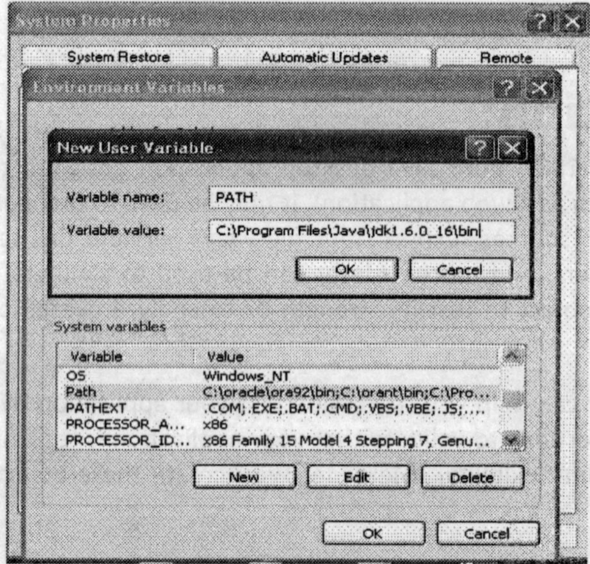

- ✓ Just place the JMeter setup file in C or D drive as this software requires no installation. You can download JMeter from:

http://jakarta.apache.org/site/downloads/downloads_jmeter.cgi

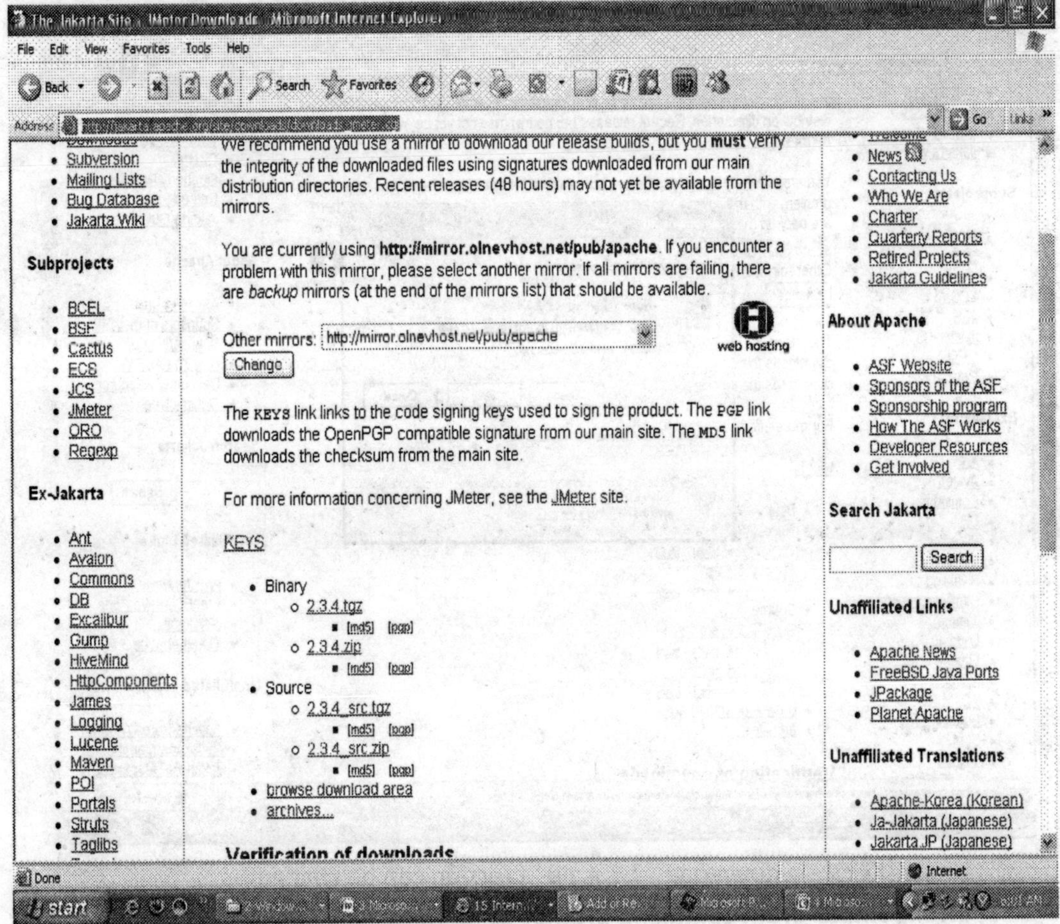

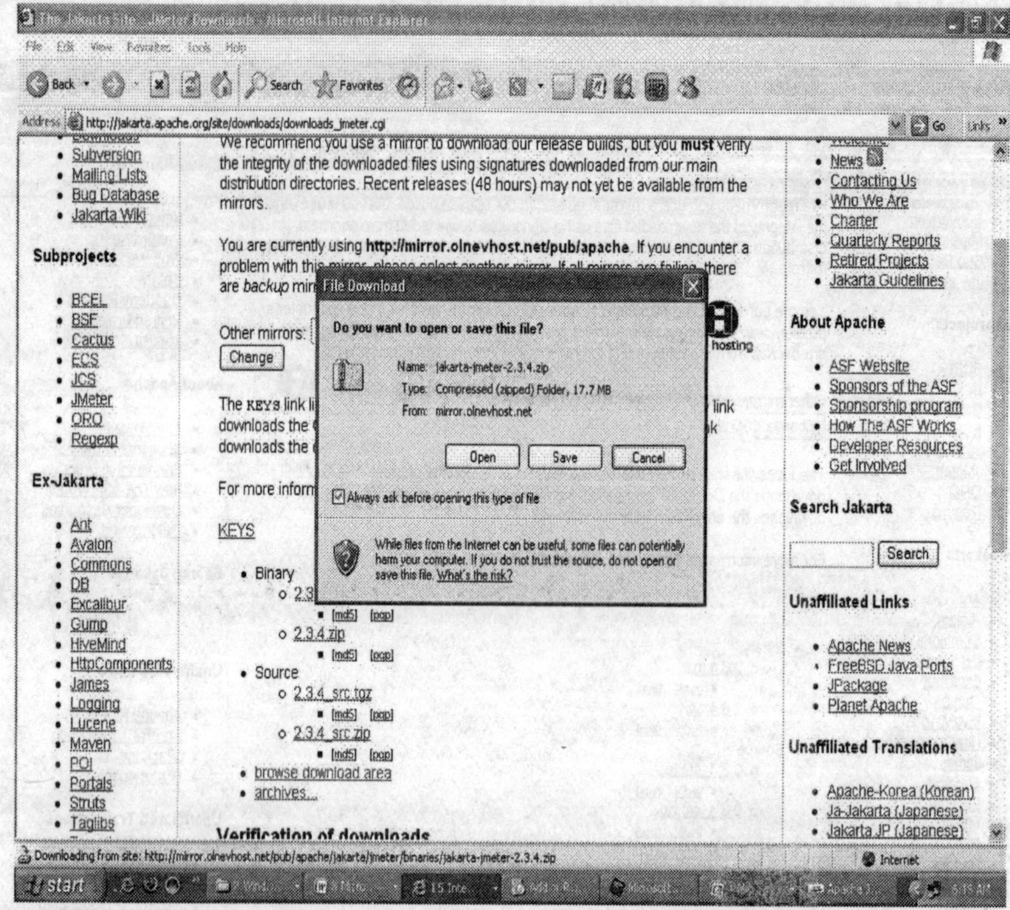

- ✓ Under 'KEYS' --> download '2.3.4.zip ' (Version can be change)
- ✓ Invoke Jmeter from command prompt using the below command and make sure that you are in Jmeter bin folder before executing it:
  - ➤ <cmd>jmeter.bat -H 172.28.0.12 -P 8002

Installation

Note: avoid installing JMeter in a path with spaces in the name. This causes problems for remote testing.

To install a release build, simply unzip the zip/tar file into the directory where you want JMeter to be installed. Provided that you have a JRE/JDK correctly installed and the JAVA_HOME environment variable set, there is nothing more for you to do.

Running JMeter

To run JMeter, run the JMeter.bat (for Windows) or JMeter (for Unix) file.

JMeter's ClassPath

JMeter automatically finds classes from jars in the following directories:

- JMETER_HOME/lib - used for utility jars
- JMETER_HOME/lib/ext - used for JMeter components and add-ons

Folder Structure after download & extract of JMeter

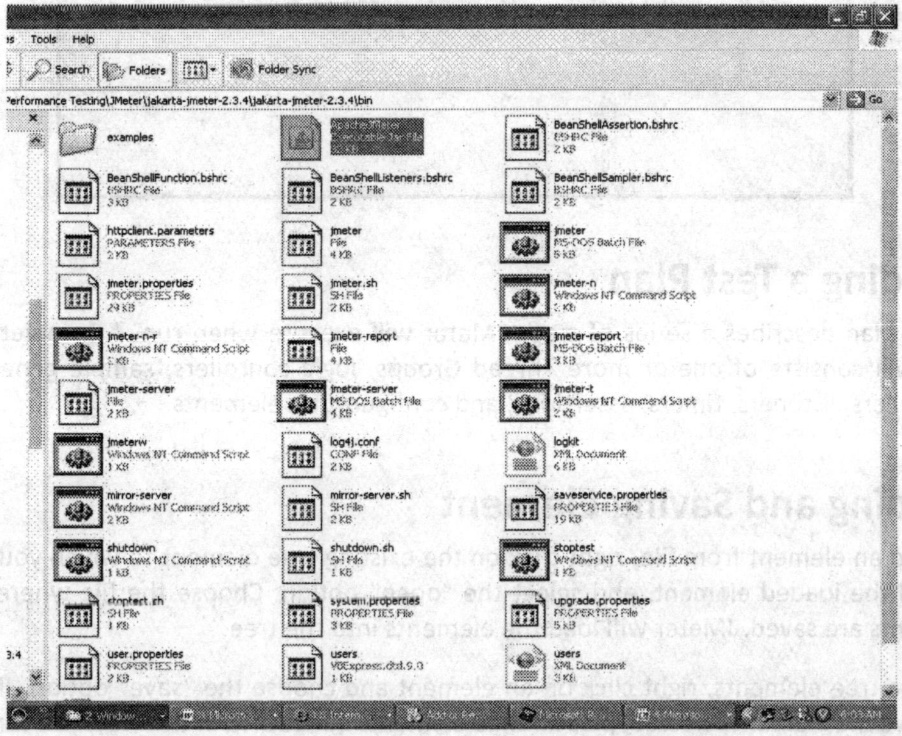

To Start JMeter go to 'Bin' Folder and click on 'ApacheJMeter' jar file it will open JMeter Page.

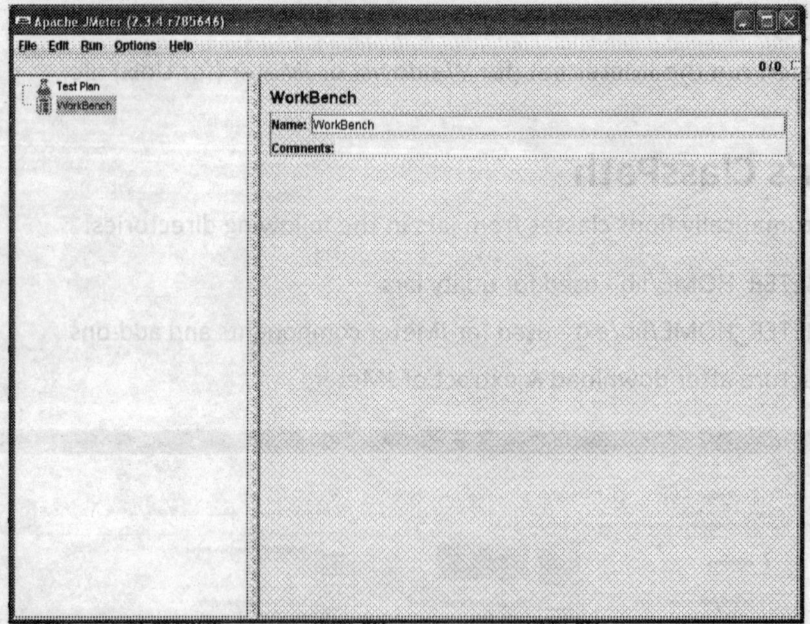

Building a Test Plan

A test plan describes a series of steps JMeter will execute when run. A complete test plan will consiste of one or more Thread Groups, logic conrollers, sample generating controllers, listeners, timers, assertions, and configuration elements.

Loading and Saving Element

To load an element from file, right click on the existing tree element to which you want to add the loaded element, and select the "open" option. Choose the file where your elements are saved. JMeter will load the elements into the tree.

To save tree elements, right click on an element and choose the "save" option. JMeter will save the element selected, plus all child elements beneath it. In this way, you can save test tree fragments, individual elements, or the entire test plan.

Configuring Test Elements

Any element in the test tree will present controls in JMeter's right-hand frame. These controls allow you to configure the behavior of that particular test element. What can be configured for an element depends on what type of element it is.

Saving the Test Plan

Although it is not required, we recommend that you save the Test Plan to a file before running it. To save the Test Plan, select Save Test Plan from the File menu (with the latest release, it is no longer necessary to select the Test Plan element first).

Running a Test Plan

To run your test plan, choose "start" from the "run" menu item. To stop your test plan, choose "stop" from the same menu. When JMeter is running, it shows a small green box at the right hand end of the section just under the menu bar. You can also check the "run" menu. If "start" is disabled, and "stop" is enabled, then JMeter is running your test plan (or, at least, it thinks it is).

There are two types of stop command:

- Stop (Control + '.') - stops the threads immediately
- Shutdown (Control + ',')- requests the threads to stop at the end of any current work

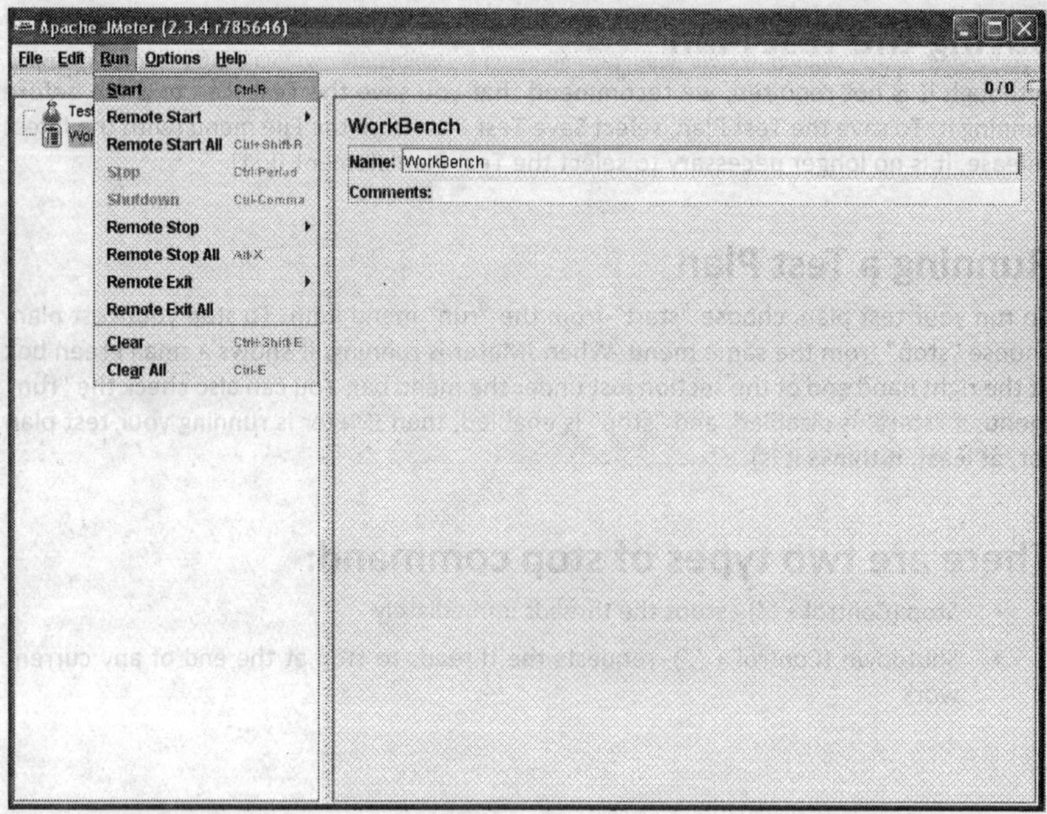

Scoping Rules

The JMeter test tree contains elements that are both hierarchical and ordered. Some elements in the test trees are strictly hierarchical (Listeners, Config Elements, Post-Procesors, Pre-Processors, Assertions, Timers), and some are primarily ordered (controllers, samplers). When you create your test plan, you will create an ordered list of sample request (via Samplers) that represent a set of steps to be executed. These requests are often organized within controllers that are also ordered. Given the following test tree:

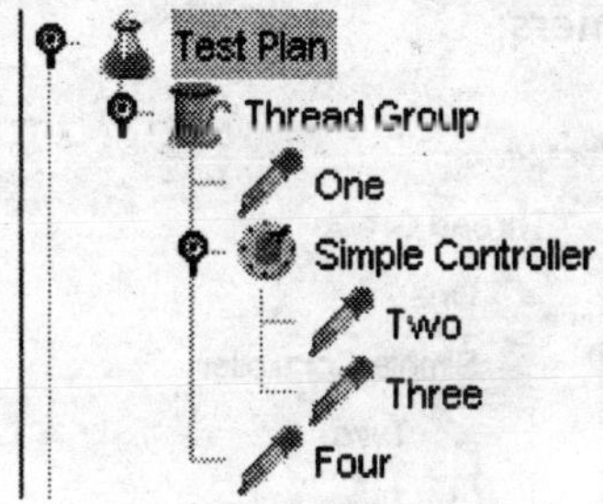

Example test tree

The order of requests will be, One, Two, Three, Four.

Some controllers affect the order of their subelements, and you can read about these specific controllers in the component reference.

Other elements are hierarchical. An Assertion, for instance, is hierarchical in the test tree. If its parent is a request, then it is applied to that request. If its parent is a Controller, then it affects all requests that are descendants of that Controller. In the following test tree:

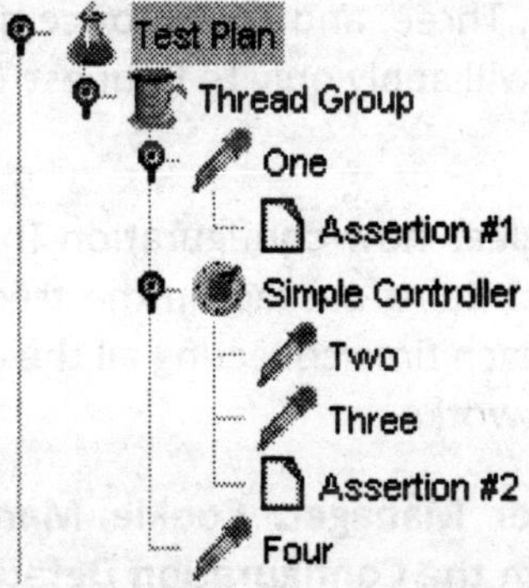

Hierarchy example

Assertion #1 is applied only to Request One, while Assertion #2 is applied to Requests Two and Three.

Another example, this time using Timers:

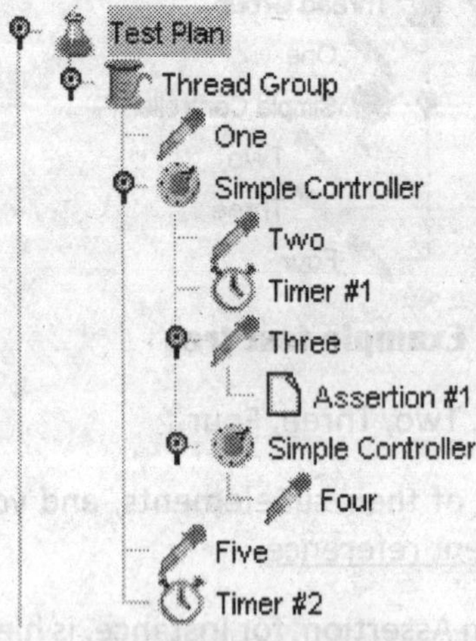

complex example

In this example, the requests are named to reflect the order in which they will be executed. Timer #1 will apply to Requests Two, Three, and Four (notice how order is irrelevant for hierarchical elements). Assertion #1 will apply only to Request Three. Timer #2 will affect all the requests.

Hopefully these examples make it clear how configuration (hierarchical) elements are applied. If you imagine each Request being passed up the tree branches, to its parent, then to its parent's parent, etc, and each time collecting all the configuration elements of that parent, then you will see how it works.

The Configuration elements Header Manager, Cookie Manager and Authorization manager are treated differently from the Configuration Default elements. The settings from the Configuration Default elements are merged into a set of values that the Sampler has access to. However, the settings from the Managers are not merged. If more than one Manager is in the scope of a Sampler, only one Manager is used, but there is currently no way to specify which is used.

Elements of Test Plan

The Test Plan object has a checkbox called "Functional Testing". If selected, it will cause JMeter to record the data returned from the server for each sample. If you have selected a file in your test listeners, this data will be written to file. This can be useful if you are doing a small run to ensure that JMeter is configured correctly, and that your server is returning the expected results. The consequence is that the file will grow huge quickly, and JMeter's performance will suffer. This option should be off if you are doing stress-testing (it is off by default).

If you are not recording the data to file, this option makes no difference.
You can also use the Configuration button on a listener to decide what fields to save.

ThreadGroup

Thread group elements are the beginning points of any test plan. All elements of a test plan must be under a thread group. As the name implies, the thread group element controls the number of threads JMeter will use to execute your test. The controls for a thread group allow you to:

- Set the number of threads
- Set the ramp-up period
- Set the number of times to execute the test

Each thread will execute the test plan in its entirety and completely independently of other test threads. Multiple threads are used to simulate concurrent connections to your server application.

The ramp-up period tells JMeter how long to take to "ramp-up" to the full number of threads chosen. If 10 threads are used, and the ramp-up period is 100 seconds, then JMeter will take 100 seconds to get all 10 threads up and running. Each thread will start 10 (100/10) seconds after the previous thread was begun. If there are 30 threads and a ramp-up period of 120 seconds, then each successive thread will be delayed by 4 seconds.

Ramp-up needs to be long enough to avoid too large a work-load at the start of a test, and short enough that the last threads start running before the first ones finish (unless one wants that to happen).

Start with Ramp-up = number of threads and adjust as needed.
By default, the thread group is configured to loop once through its elements.

Controllers

JMeter has two types of Controllers: Samplers and Logical Controllers.
Samplers tell JMeter to send requests to a server. For example, add an HTTP Request Sampler if you want JMeter to send an HTTP request. You can also customize a request by adding one or more Configuration Elements to a Sampler.

Logical Controllers let you customize the logic that JMeter uses to decide when to send requests. For example, you can add an Interleave Logic Controller to alternate between two HTTP Request Samplers.

Samplers

Samplers tell JMeter to send requests to a server. JMeter samplers include:

- FTP Request
- HTTP Request
- JDBC Request
- Java object request
- LDAP Request
- SOAP/XML-RPC Request
- WebService (SOAP) Request

Each sampler has several properties you can set. You can further customize a sampler by adding one or more Configuration Elements to it. Note that JMeter sends requests in the order that the samplers appear in the tree.

If you are going to send multiple requests of the same type (for example, HTTP Request) to the same server, consider using a Defaults Configuration Element. Each controller has one or more Defaults elements (see below).

Remember to add a Listener to your Thread Group to view and/or store the results of your requests to disk.

If you are interested in having JMeter perform basic validation on the response of your request, add an Assertion to the Request controller. For example, in stress testing a web application, the server may return a successful "HTTP Response" code, but the page may have errors on it or may be missing sections. You could add assertions to check for certain HTML tags, common error strings, and so on. JMeter lets you create these assertions using regular expressions.

Logic Controllers

Logic Controllers let you customize the logic that JMeter uses to decide when to send requests. Logic Controllers may have as child elements any of the following: Samplers (requests), Configuration Elements, and other Logic Controllers. Logic Controllers can change the order of requests coming from their child elements. They can modify the requests themselves, cause JMeter to repeat requests, etc.

To understand the effect of Logic Controllers on a test plan, consider the following test tree:

- Test Plan
  - Thread Group
    - Once Only Controller
      - Login Request (an HTTP Request)
    - Load Search Page (HTTP Sampler)
    - Interleave Controller
      - Search "A" (HTTP Sampler)
      - Search "B" (HTTP Sampler)
      - HTTP default request (Configuration Element)
    - HTTP default request (Configuration Element)
    - Cookie Manager (Configuration Element)

The first thing about this test is that the login request will be executed only the first time through. Subsequent iterations will skip it. This is due to the effects of the Once Only Controller.

After the login, the next Sampler loads the search page (imagine a web application where the user logs in, and then goes to a search page to do a search). This is just a simple request, not filtered through any Logic Controller.

Listeners

Listeners provide access to the information JMeter gathers about the test cases while JMeter runs. The Graph Results listener plots the response times on a graph. The "View Results Tree" Listener shows details of sampler requests and responses, and can display basic HTML and XML representations of the response. Other listeners provide summary or aggregation information.

Additionally, listeners can direct the data to a file for later use. Every listener in JMeter provides a field to indicate the file to store data to. There is also a Configuration button which can be used to choose which fields to save, and whether to use CSV or XML format. **Note that all Listeners save the same data; the only difference is in the way the data is presented on the screen.**

Listeners can be added anywhere in the test. They will collect data only from elements at or below their level.

There are several interesting listeners that come with JMeter.

Timers

By default, a JMeter thread sends requests without pausing between each request. We recommend that you specify a delay by adding one of the available timers to your Thread Group. If you do not add a delay, JMeter could overwhelm your server by making too many requests in a very short amount of time.

The timer will cause JMeter to delay a certain amount of time before each request that a thread makes.

If you choose to add more than one timer to a Thread Group, JMeter takes the sum of the timers and pauses for that amount of time before executing the samplers to which they apply.

Assertions

Assertions allow you to assert facts about responses received from the server being tested. Using an assertion, you can essentially "test" that your application is returning the results you expect it to.

For instance, you can assert that the response to a query will contain some particular text. The text you specify can be a Perl-style regular expression, and you can indicate that the response is to contain the text, or that it should match the whole response.

You can add an assertion to any Sampler. For example, you can add an assertion to a HTTP Request that checks for the text, "</HTML>". JMeter will then check that the text is present in the HTTP response. If JMeter cannot find the text, then it will mark this as a failed request.

To view the assertion results, add an Assertion Listener to the Thread Group. Failed Assertions will also show up in the Tree View and Table Listeners, and will count towards the error %age for example in the Aggregate and Summary reports.

Configuration elements

A configuration element works closely with a Sampler. Although it does not send requests (except for HTTP Proxy Server), it can add to or modify requests.

A configuration element is accessible from only inside the tree branch where you place the element. For example, if you place an HTTP Cookie Manager inside a Simple Logic Controller, the Cookie Manager will only be accessible to HTTP Request Controllers you place inside the Simple Logic Controller (see figure 1). The Cookie Manager is accessible to the HTTP requests "Web Page 1" and "Web Page 2", but not "Web Page 3".

Also, a configuration element inside a tree branch has higher precedence than the same element in a "parent" branch. For example, we defined two HTTP Request Defaults elements, "Web Defaults 1" and "Web Defaults 2". Since we placed "Web Defaults 1" inside a Loop Controller, only "Web Page 2" can access it. The other HTTP requests will use "Web Defaults 2", since we placed it in the Thread Group (the "parent" of all other branches).

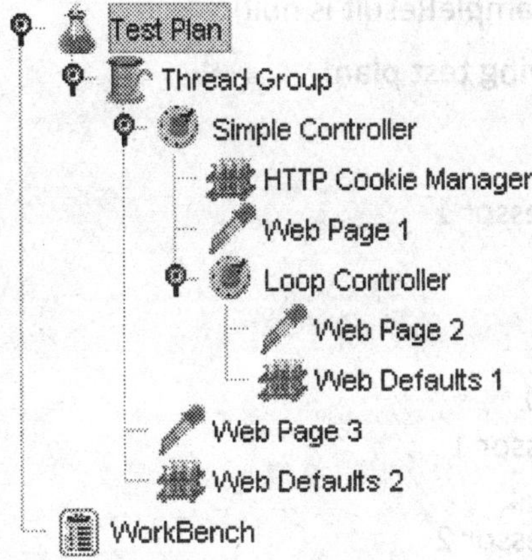

Figure 1 - Test Plan Showing Accessability of Configuration Elements

Pre-Processor elements

A Pre-Processor executes some action prior to a Sampler Request being made. If a Pre-Processor is attached to a Sampler element, then it will execute just prior to that sampler element running. A Pre-Processor is most often used to modify the settings of a Sample Request just before it runs, or to update variables that aren't extracted from response text. See the scoping rules for more details on when Pre-Processors are executed.

Post-Processor Element

A Post-Processor executes some action after a Sampler Request has been made. If a Post-Processor is attached to a Sampler element, then it will execute just after that sampler element runs. A Post-Processor is most often used to process the response data, often to extract values from it. See the scoping rules for more details on when Post-Processors are executed.

Execution Order

1. Pre-Processors
2. Timers
3. Sampler
4. Post-Processors (unless SampleResult is null)
5. Assertions (unless SampleResult is null)
6. Listeners (unless SampleResult is null)

For example, in the following test plan:

- Controller
    - Post-Processor 1
    - Sampler 1
    - Sampler 2
    - Timer 1
    - Assertion 1
    - Pre-Processor 1
    - Timer 2
    - Post-Processor 2

The order of execution would be:

- Pre-Processor 1
- Timer 1
- Timer 2
- Sampler 1
- Post-Processor 1
- Post-Processor 2
- Assertion 1
- Pre-Processor 1
- Timer 1
- Timer 2
- Sampler 2
- Post-Processor 1
- Post-Processor 2
- Assertion 1

Properties & Variables

JMeter properties are defined in jmeter.properties (see Gettting Started - Configuring JMeter for more details).

Properties are global to jmeter, and are used to define some of the defaults JMeter uses. For example the property remote_hosts defines the servers that JMeter will try to run remotely. Properties can be referenced in test plans - see Functions - read a property- but cannot be used for thread-specific values.

JMeter **variables** are local to each thread. The values may be the same for each thread, or they may be different.

If a variable is updated by a thread, only the thread copy of the variable is changed. For example the Regular Expression Extractor Post-Processor will set its variables according to the sample that its thread has read, and these can be used later by the same thread. For details of how to reference variables and functions, see Functions and Variables

Building a web Test Plan

In this section, you will learn how to create a basic Test Plan to test a Web site. You will create five users that send requests to two pages on the Jakarta Web site. Also, you will tell the users to run their tests twice. So, the total number of requests is (5 users) x (2 requests) x (repeat 2 times) = 20 HTTP requests. To construct the Test Plan, you will use the following elements: Thread Group, HTTP Request, HTTP Request Defaults, and Graph Results.

Adding Users

The first step you want to do with every JMeter Test Plan is to add a Thread Group element. The Thread Group tells JMeter the number of users you want to simulate, how often the users should send requests, and the how many requests they should send.

Go ahead and add the ThreadGroup element by first selecting the Test Plan, clicking your right mouse button to get the Add menu, and then select Add --> ThreadGroup.

You should now see the Thread Group element under Test Plan. If you do not see the element, then "expand" the Test Plan tree by clicking on the Test Plan element.

Next, you need to modify the default properties. Select the Thread Group element in the tree, if you have not already selected it. You should now see the Thread Group Control

Panel in the right section of the JMeter window (see Figure 5.1 below)

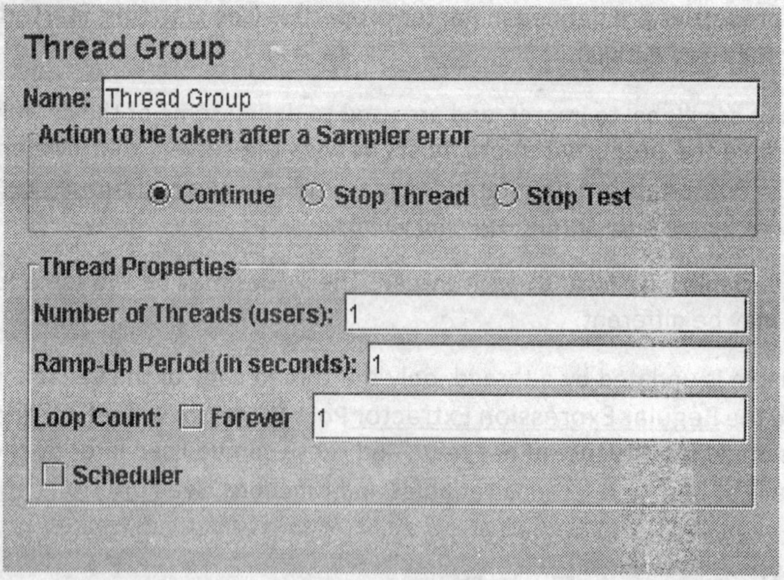

Figure 5.1. Thread Group with Default Values

Start by providing a more descriptive name for our Thread Group. In the name field, enter Jakarta Users.

Next, increase the number of users (called threads) to 5.

In the next field, the Ramp-Up Period, leave the the default value of 0 seconds. This property tells JMeter how long to delay between starting each user. For example, if you enter a Ramp-Up Period of 5 seconds, JMeter will finish starting all of your users by the end of the 5 seconds. So, if we have 5 users and a 5 second Ramp-Up Period, then the delay between starting users would be 1 second (5 users / 5 seconds = 1 user per second). If you set the value to 0, then JMeter will immediately start all of your users.

Finally enter a value of 2 in the Loop Count field. This property tells JMeter how many times to repeat your test. If you enter a loop count value of 1, then JMeter will run your test only once. To have JMeter repeatedly run your Test Plan, select the Forever checkbox.

See Figure 5.2 for the completed Jakarta Users Thread Group.

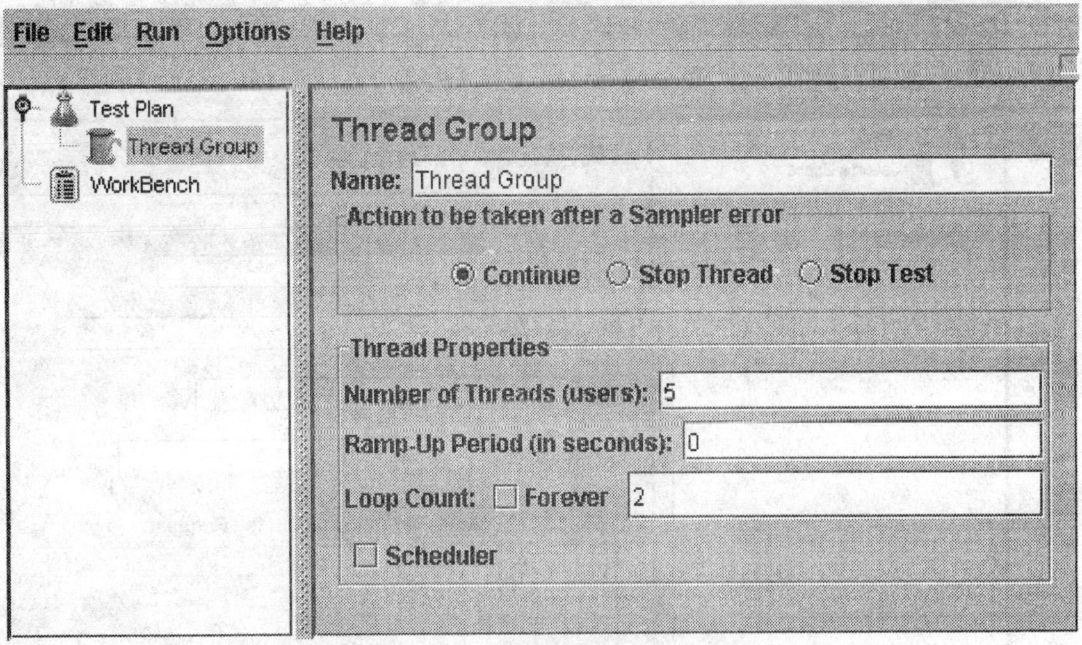

Figure 5.2. Jakarta Users Thread Group

Adding Default HTTP Request properties

Now that we have defined our users, it is time to define the tasks that they will be performing. In this section, you will specify the default settings for your HTTP requests. And then, in section 5.3, you will add HTTP Request elements which use some of the default settings you specified here.

Begin by selecting the Jakarta Users (Thread Group) element. Click your right mouse button to get the Add menu, and then select Add --> Config Element --> HTTP Request Defaults. Then, select this new element to view its Control Panel (see Figure 5.3).

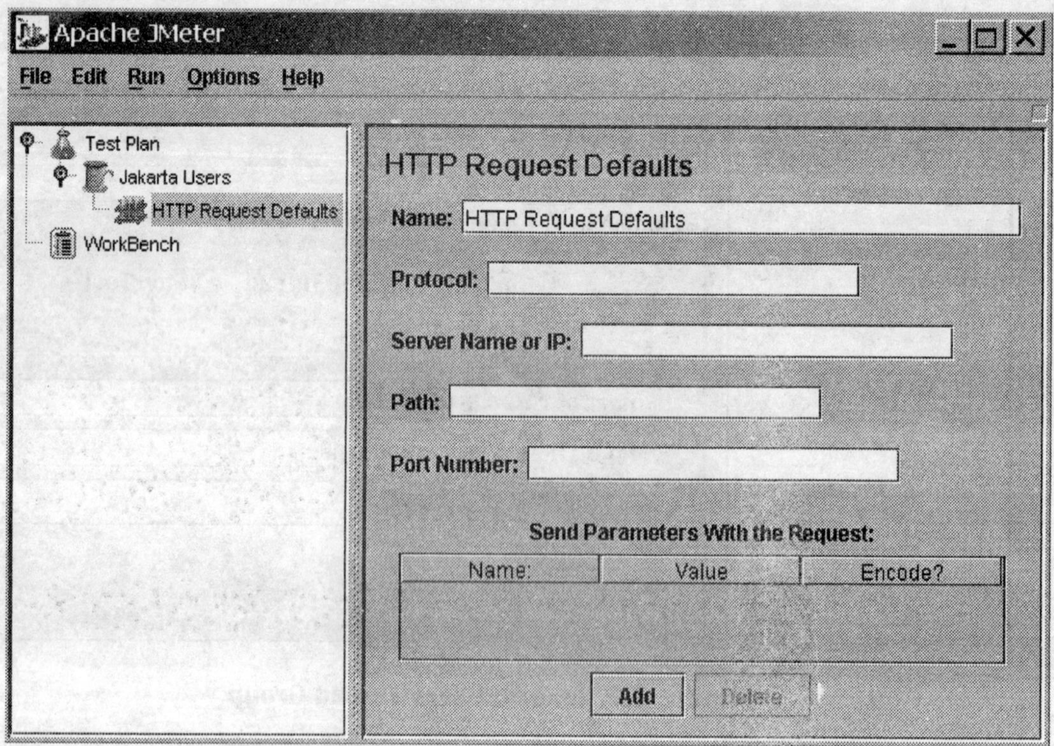

Figure 5.3. HTTP Request Defaults

Like most JMeter elements, the HTTP Request Defaults Control Panel has a name field that you can modify. In this example, leave this field with the default value.

Skip to the next field, which is the Web Server's Server Name/IP. For the Test Plan that you are building, all HTTP requests will be sent to the same Web server, jakarta.apache.org. Enter this domain name into the field. This is the only field that we will specify a default, so leave the remaining fields with their default values.

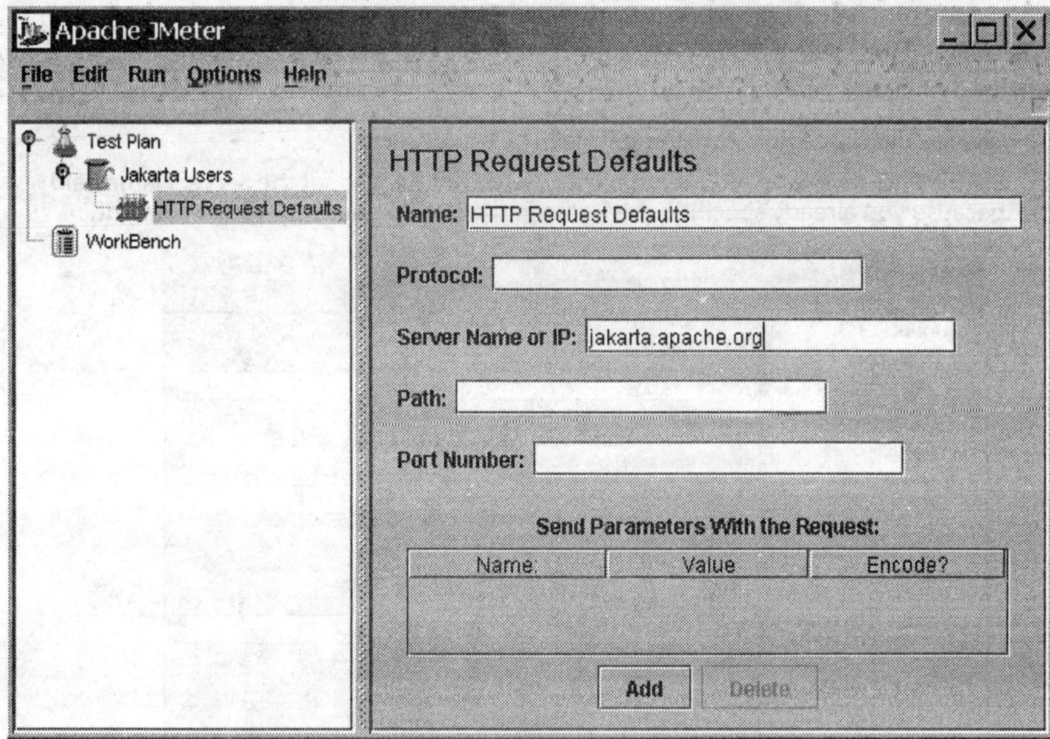

Figure 5.4. HTTP Defaults for our Test Plan

Adding Cookie Support

Nearly all web testing should use cookie support, unless your application specifically doesn't use cookies. To add cookie support, simply add an HTTP Cookie Manager to each Thread Group in your test plan. This will ensure that each thread gets its own cookies, but shared across all HTTP Request objects.

To add the HTTP Cookie Manager, simply select the Thread Group, and choose Add --> Config Element --> HTTP Cookie Manager, either from the Edit Menu, or from the right-click pop-up menu.

Adding HTTP Request

In our Test Plan, we need to make two HTTP requests. The first one is for the Jakarta home page (http://jakarta.apache.org/), and the second one is for the Project Guidelines page (http://jakarta.apache.org/site/guidelines.html).

Start by adding the first HTTP Request to the Jakarta Users element (Add --> Sampler --> HTTP Request). Then, select the HTTP Request element in the tree and edit the following properties (see Figure 5.5):

1. Change the Name field to "Home Page".
2. Set the Path field to "/". Remember that you do not have to set the Server Name field because you already specified this value in the HTTP Request Defaults element.

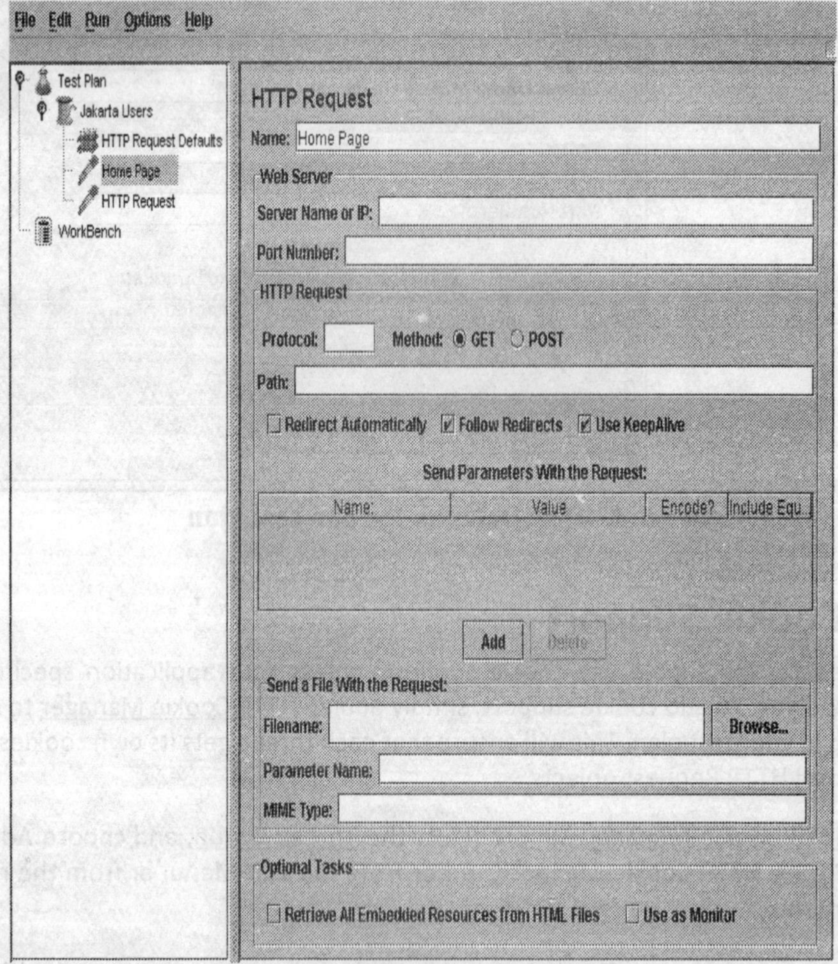

Figure 5.5. HTTP Request for Jakarta Home Page

Next, add the second HTTP Request and edit the following properties (see Figure 5.6:

1. Change the Name field to "Project Guidelines".
2. Set the Path field to "/site/guidelines.html".

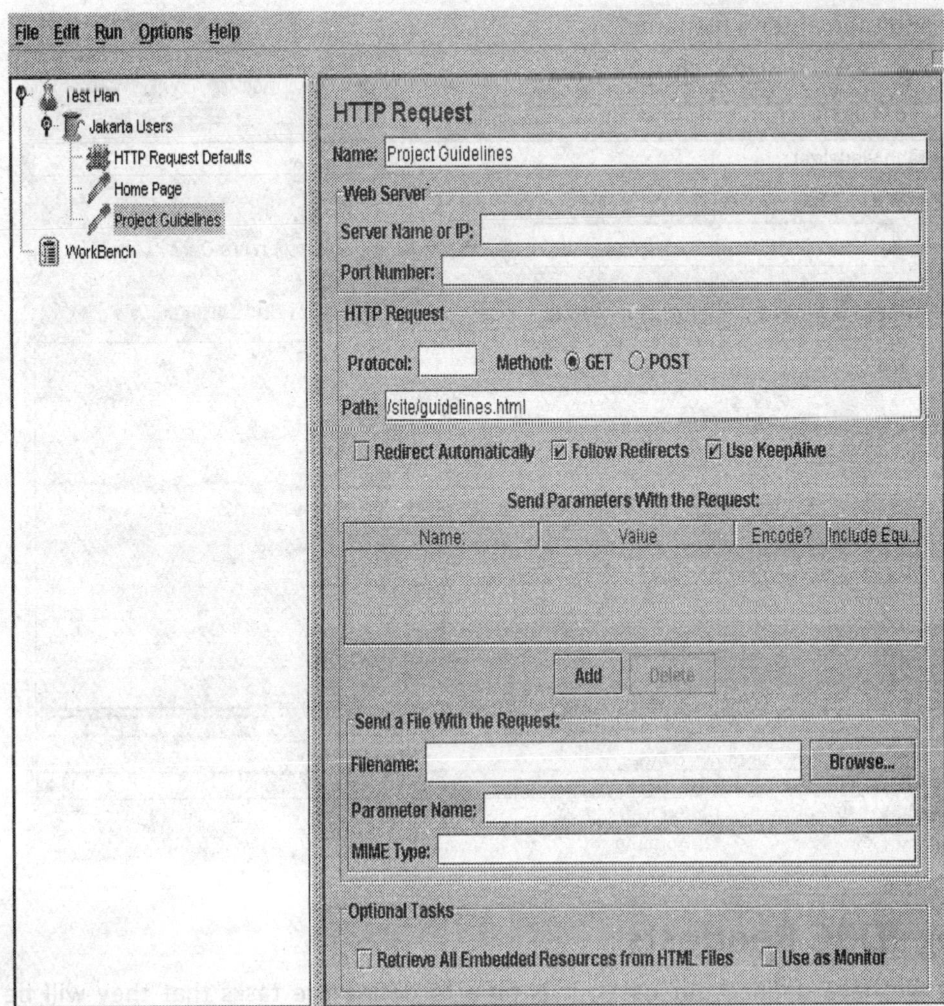

Figure 5.6. HTTP Request for Jakarta Project Guidelines Page

Adding a Listener to View Store the Test Results

The final element you need to add to your Test Plan is a Listener. This element is responsible for storing all of the results of your HTTP requests in a file and presenting a visual model of the data.

Select the Jakarta Users element and add a Graph Results listener (Add --> Listener --> Graph Results). Next, you need to specify a directory and filename of the output file. You can either type it into the filename field, or select the Browse button and browse to a directory and then enter a filename.

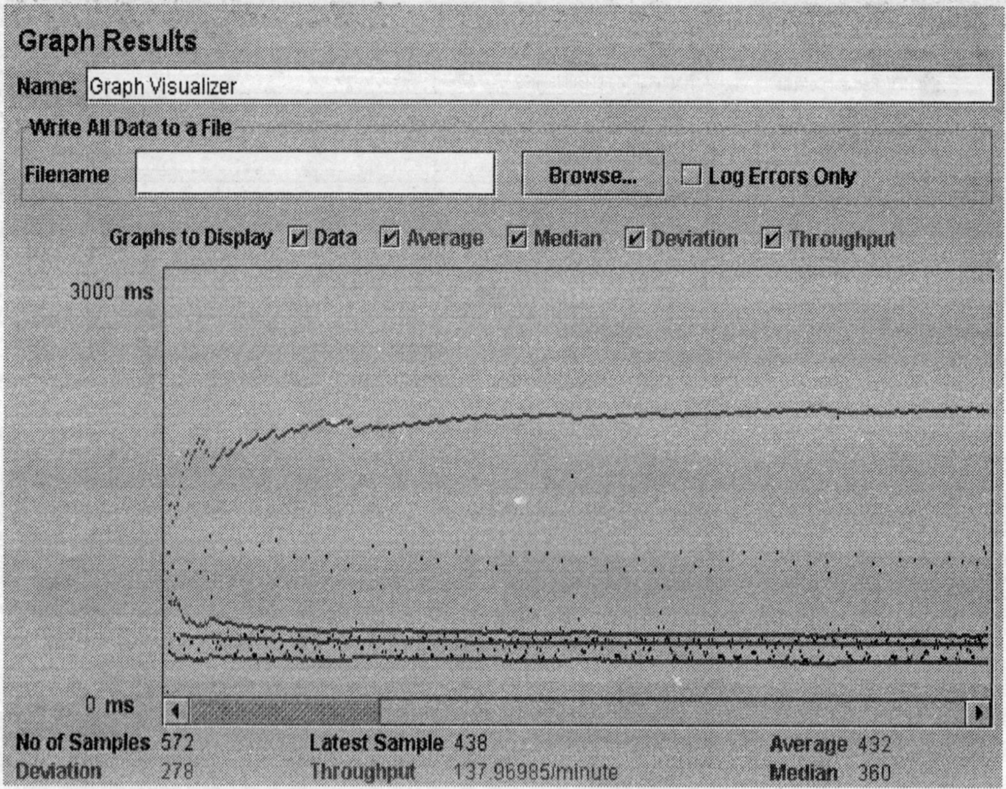

Adding JDBC Requests

Now that we have defined our users, it is time to define the tasks that they will be performing. In this section, you will specify the JDBC requests to perform.

Begin by selecting the JDBC Users element. Click your right mouse button to get the Add menu, and then select Add --> Config Element --> JDBC Connection Configuration. Then, select this new element to view its Control Panel (see Figure 7.3).

Set up the following fields (these assume we will be using a local MySQL database called test):

- Variable name bound to pool. This needs to uniquely identify the configuration. It is used by the JDBC Sampler to identify the configuration to be used.
- Database URL: jdbc:mysql://localhost:3306/test

- JDBC Driver class: com.mysql.jdbc.Driver
- Username: guest
- Password: password for guest

The other fields on the screen can be left as the defaults.

JMeter creates a database connection pool with the configuration settings as specified in the Control Panel. The pool is referred to in JDBC Requests in the 'Variable Name' field. Several different JDBC Configuration elements can be used, but they must have unique names. Every JDBC Request must refer to a JDBC Configuration pool. More than one JDBC Request can refer to the same pool.

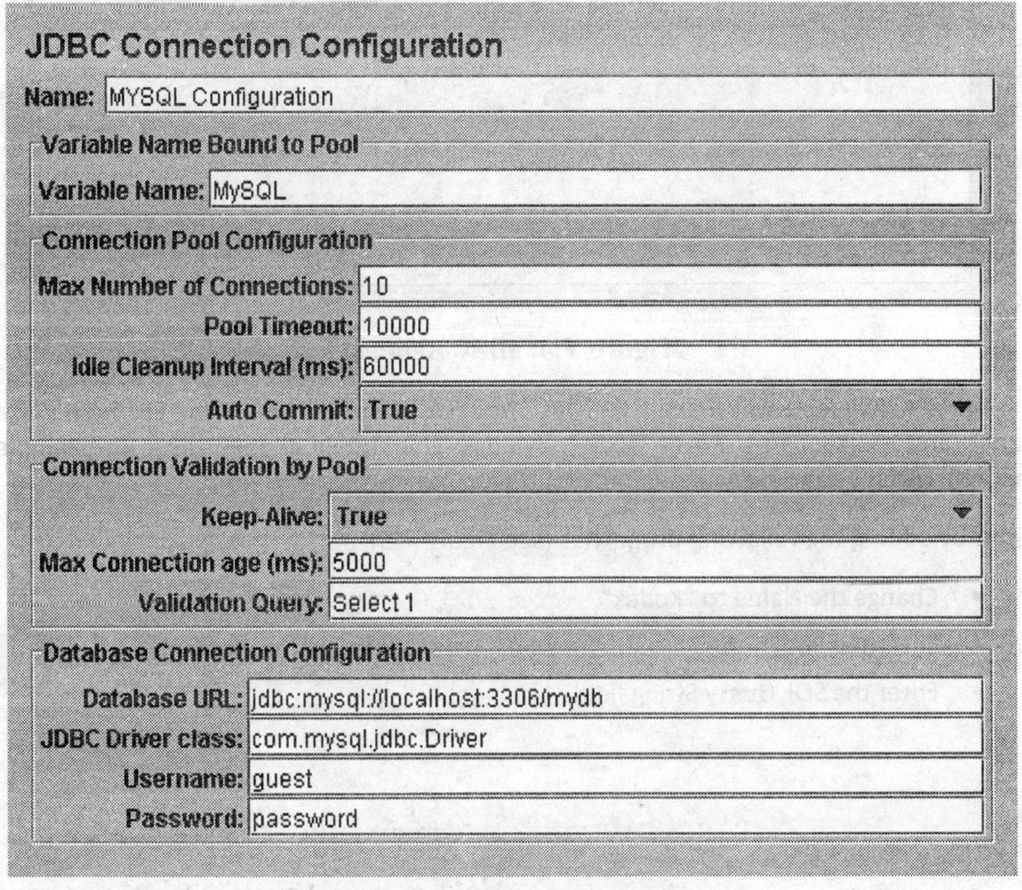

Figure 7.3. JDBC Configuration

Selecting the JDBC Users element again. Click your right mouse button to get the Add menu, and then select Add --> Sampler --> JDBC Request. Then, select this new element to view its Control Panel (see Figure 7.4).

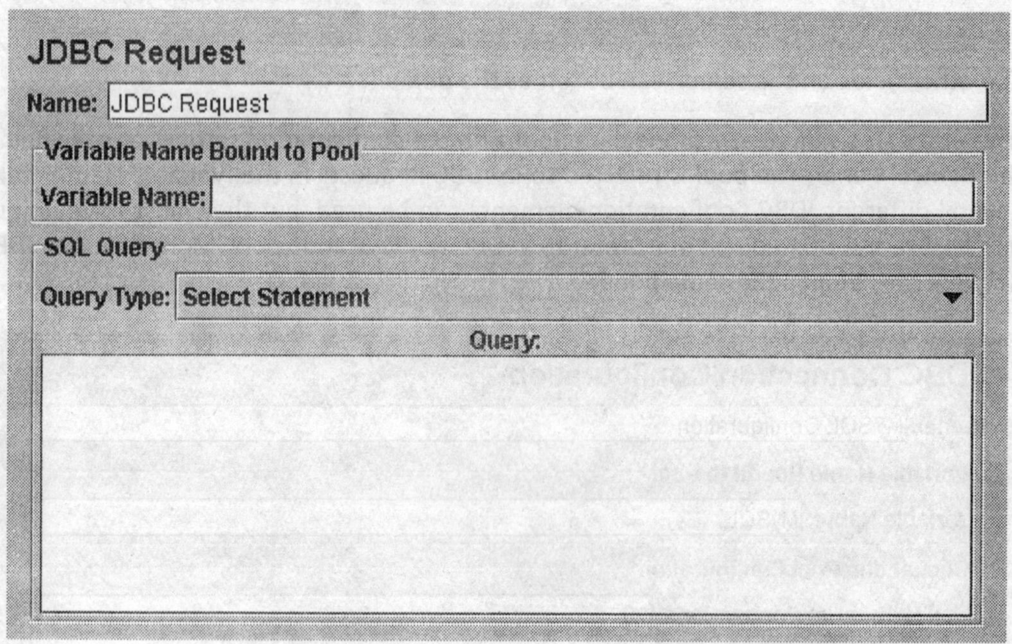

Figure 7.4. JDBC Request

In our Test Plan, we will make two JDBC requests. The first one is for Eastman Kodak stock, and the second is Pfizer stock (obviously you should change these to examples appropriate for your particular database). These are illustrated below.

Start by editing the following properties (see Figure 7.5):

- Change the Name to "Kodak".
- Enter the Pool Name: MySQL (same as in the configuration element)
- Enter the SQL Query String field.

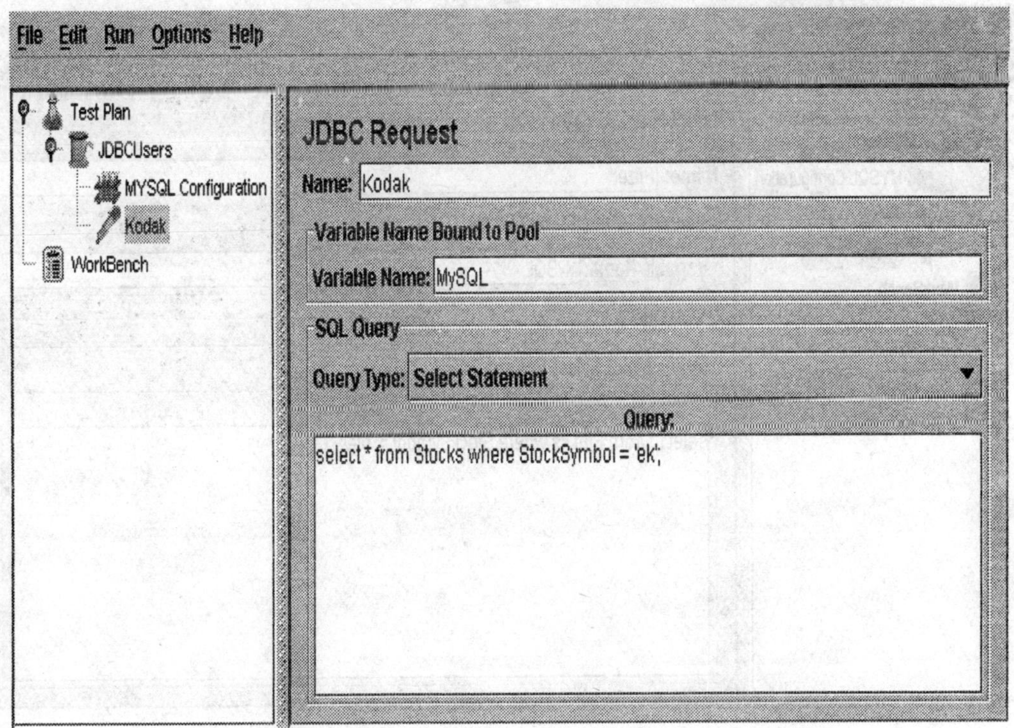

Figure 7.5. JDBC Request for Eastman Kodak stock

Next, add the second JDBC Request and edit the following properties (see Figure 7.6):

- Change the Name to "Pfizer".
- Enter the SQL Query String field.

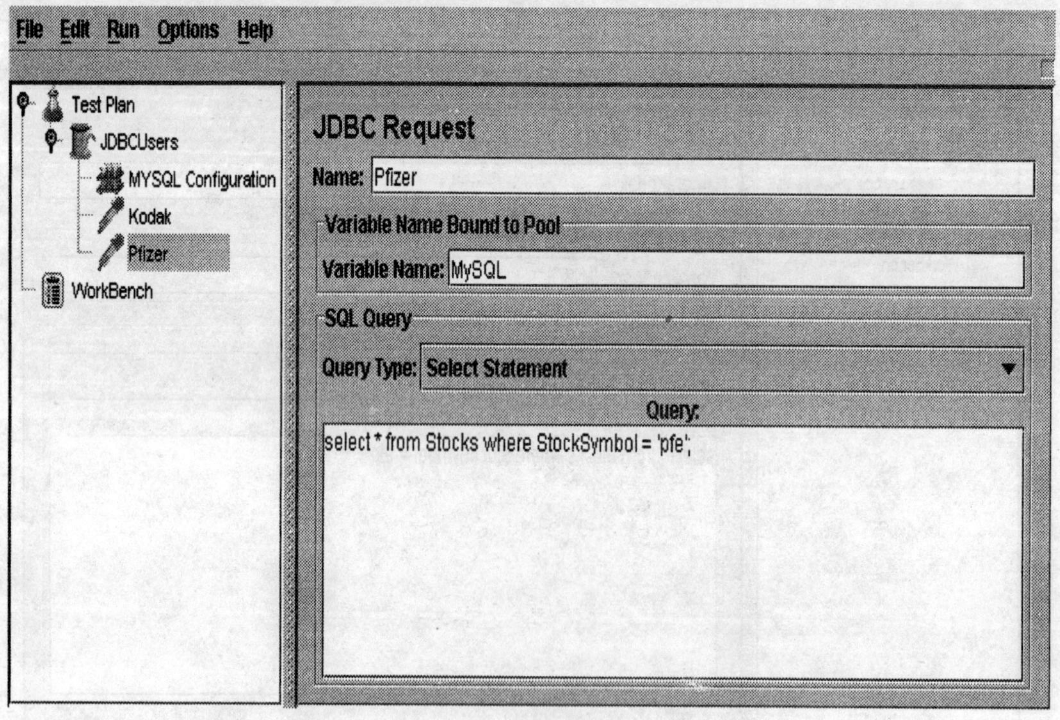

Adding a Listener to View/store the Test Results

The final element you need to add to your Test Plan is a Listener. This element is responsible for storing all of the results of your JDBC requests in a file and presenting a visual model of the data.

Select the JDBC Users element and add a Graph Results listener (Add --> Listener --> Graph Results).

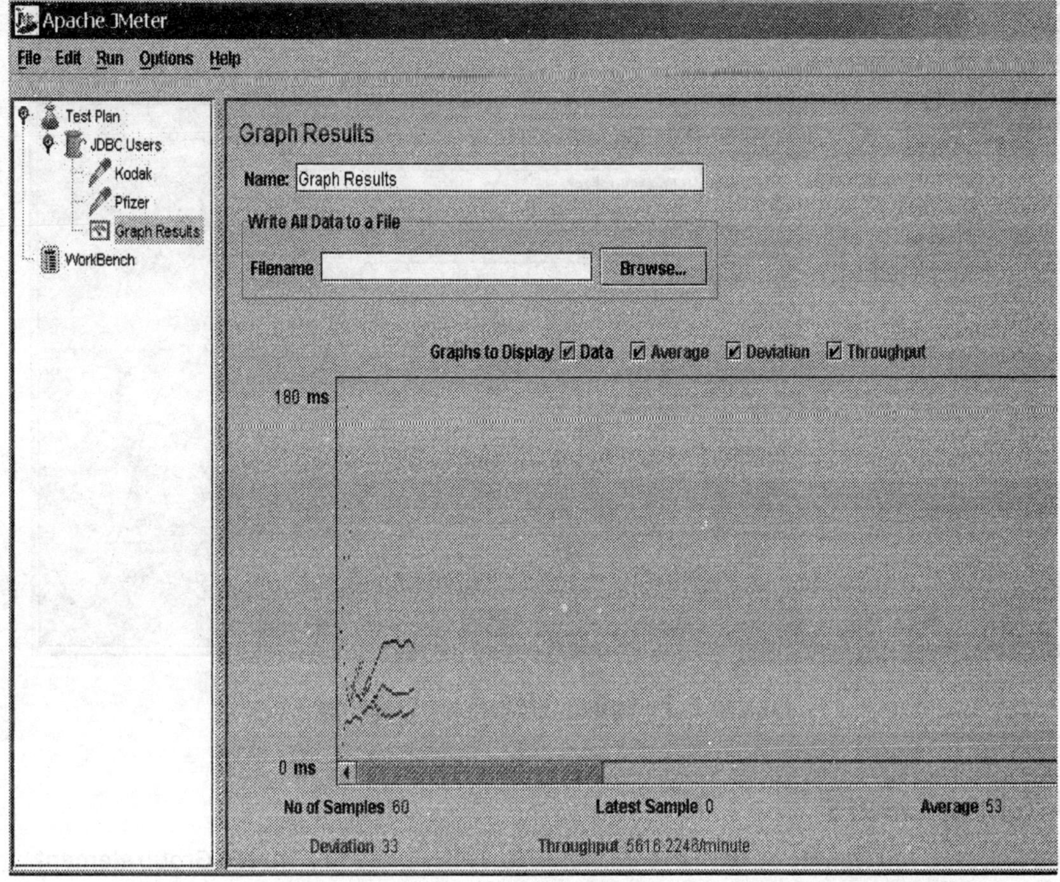

Figure 7.7. Graph results Listener

Adding a Listener to View/ Store the Test Results

The final element you need to add to your Test Plan is a Listener. This element is responsible for storing all of the results of your FTP requests in a file and presenting a visual model of the data.

Select the O'Reilly Users element and add a Spline Visualizer listener (Add --> Listener --> Spline Visualizer).

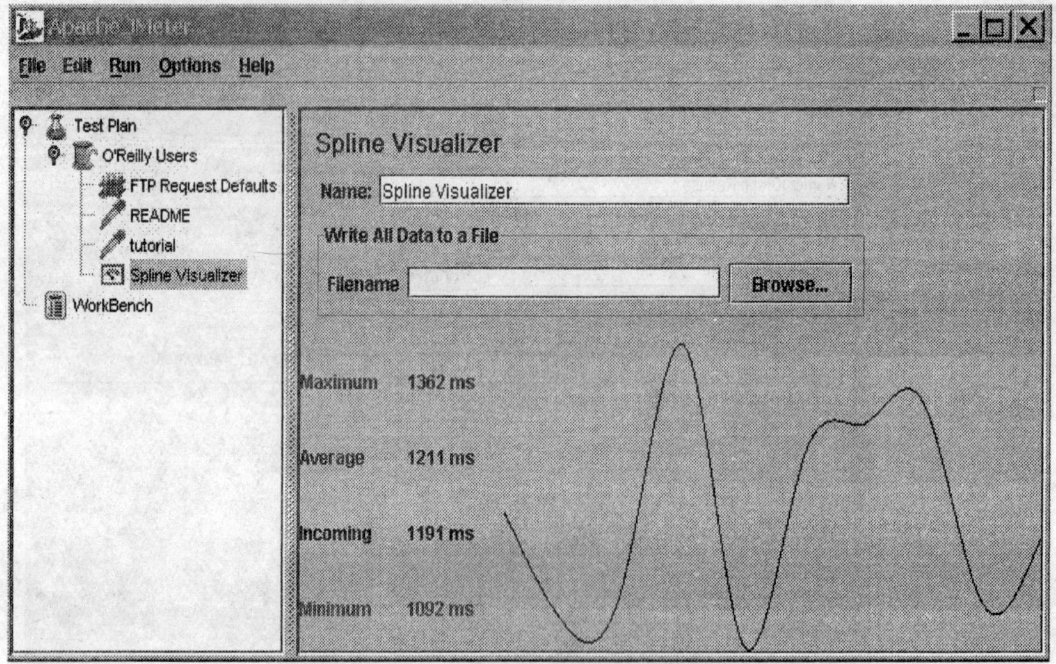

Figure 8.7. Spline Visualizer Listener

Adding Users

The first step you want to do with every JMeter Test Plan is to add a Thread Group element. The Thread Group tells JMeter the number of users you want to simulate, how often the users should send requests, and the how many requests they should send.

Go ahead and add the Thread Group element by first selecting the Test Plan, clicking your right mouse button to get the Add menu, and then select Add --> Thread Group.

You should now see the Thread Group element under Test Plan. If you do not see the element, then "expand" the Test Plan tree by clicking on the Test Plan element.

Next, you need to modify the default properties. Select the Thread Group element in the tree, if you have not already selected it. You should now see the Thread Group Control Panel in the right section of the JMeter window (see Figure 10.1 below)

Figure 10.1. Thread Group with Default Values

Start by providing a more descriptive name for our Thread Group. In the name field, enter Jakarta Users.

Next, increase the number of users (called threads) to 10.

In the next field, the Ramp-Up Period, leave the the default value of 0 seconds. This property tells JMeter how long to delay between starting each user. For example, if you enter a Ramp-Up Period of 5 seconds, JMeter will finish starting all of your users by the end of the 5 seconds. So, if we have 5 users and a 5 second Ramp-Up Period, then the delay between starting users would be 1 second (5 users / 5 seconds = 1 user per second). If you set the value to 0, then JMeter will immediately start all of your users.

Finally, clear the checkbox labeled "Forever", and enter a value of 2 in the Loop Count field. This property tells JMeter how many times to repeat your test. If you enter a loop count value of 0, then JMeter will run your test only once. To have JMeter repeatedly run your Test Plan, select the Forever checkbox.

See Figure 10.2 for the completed Jakarta Users Thread Group.

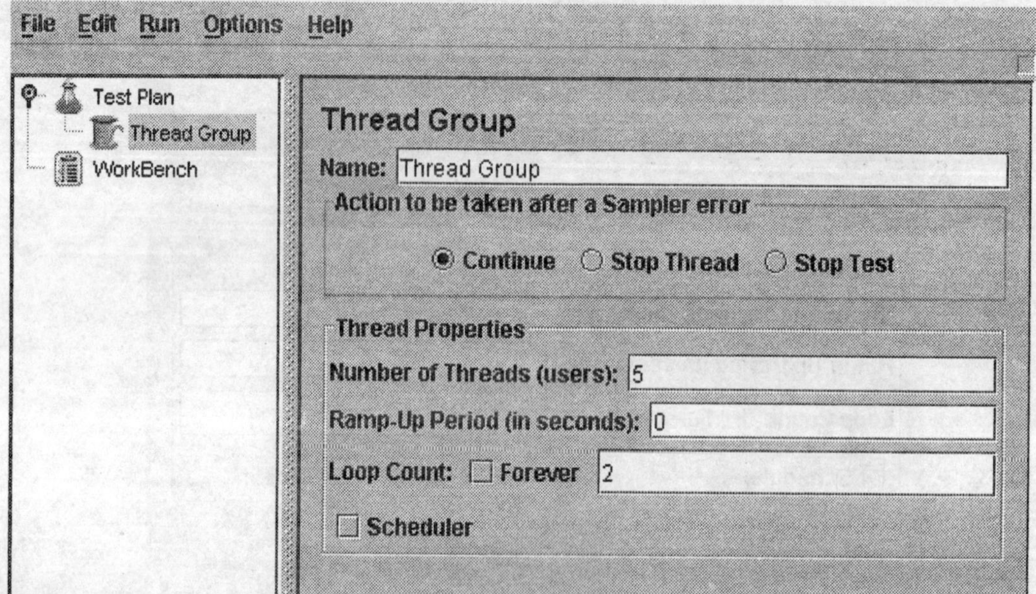

References:

http://jakarta.apache.org/site/downloads/downloads_jmeter.cgi

Performance Testing using OpenSTA tool

Chapter 32

Introduction:

- History
  - Develop by Cyrano, a French software company
  - Released into public domain in 2001
- Collector: System resource monitor script
- Commander: Main UI and test launcher
- Modeling: Script development
- SCL: Script Control Language
- Task Group: Load scenario script or Collector script
- Test: Set of scripts comprising load scenario and related results
- Timers: Start-Stop transaction timing markers for actions to be timed
- Variables: Script Parameters

Features:

Capabilities

- **Applications it will test**
  - Protocols: Standard http/https only (not Oracle 11i, SAP, RMI, web services...)
  - Development technologies: D/HTML, javascript, XML payloads, jvm servers (not java applets, "latest technologies")
- **Functionality**
  - Script development: 7/10 (Handles sessionid cookies; UI intuitivess "ok"; SCL language support "good")
  - Test/Debug: 6/10 (Need error-handling and content checks to ensure script functioning properly)
  - Test execution: 7/10 (slow refresh on summary stats Results analysis: 3/10 (built-in graphs limited; need to do much in Excel)
- **Robustness**
  - Excellent thread model; spawns a new thread only when it needs it to drive more load
  - Sometimes hangs, crashes (must manually clean up processes and sometimes reboot)
  - Conflicts with other load testing tools' listener processes (run only one at a time)
- **Limitations**
  - Does not record with IE7 or Firefox – needs IE6
  - Max of 1664 users per Commander session
  - Watch out for
    - Trip-ups with https
    - Too many parameter files can create file open bottleneck, throttling load
    - Code your own error handling of http 400 and 500 errors

Open STA 1.4.4

The OpenSTA toolset supplies performance testing software for evaluating Web Application Environments (WAEs). It is built on the OpenSTA Architecture which is a distributed testing architecture that enables you to create and run versatile production monitoring and HTTP/S load Tests. It can be employed at all stages of WAE development as well as being used to continuously monitor system performance once an WAE goes live.

Use the OpenSTA toolset to develop Tests which monitor and collect performance data from live WAEs within a production environment and to create load Tests which include HTTP/S load element, known as Scripts, to help assess the performance of WAEs during development. The OpenSTA toolset enables you to run Tests against the same target system within both load testing and production monitoring scenarios. This means that you can directly compare the performance of the target system within these two environments.

Within the OpenSTA toolset, use Commander to create Collectors and Scripts, then create and run the Tests which incorporate them in order to generate the performance data you need.

Download & Install

- V.1.4.3 12/04 is current release
- 5.7 MB download
- Windows installer
- Runs on XP, W2K, NT SP5
- Installer (usually) runs flawlessly
    - http://www.opensta.org/download.html
    - http://sourceforge.net/projects/opensta/files/ostaw32/1.4.4/ostaw32-x86-1404.msi/download

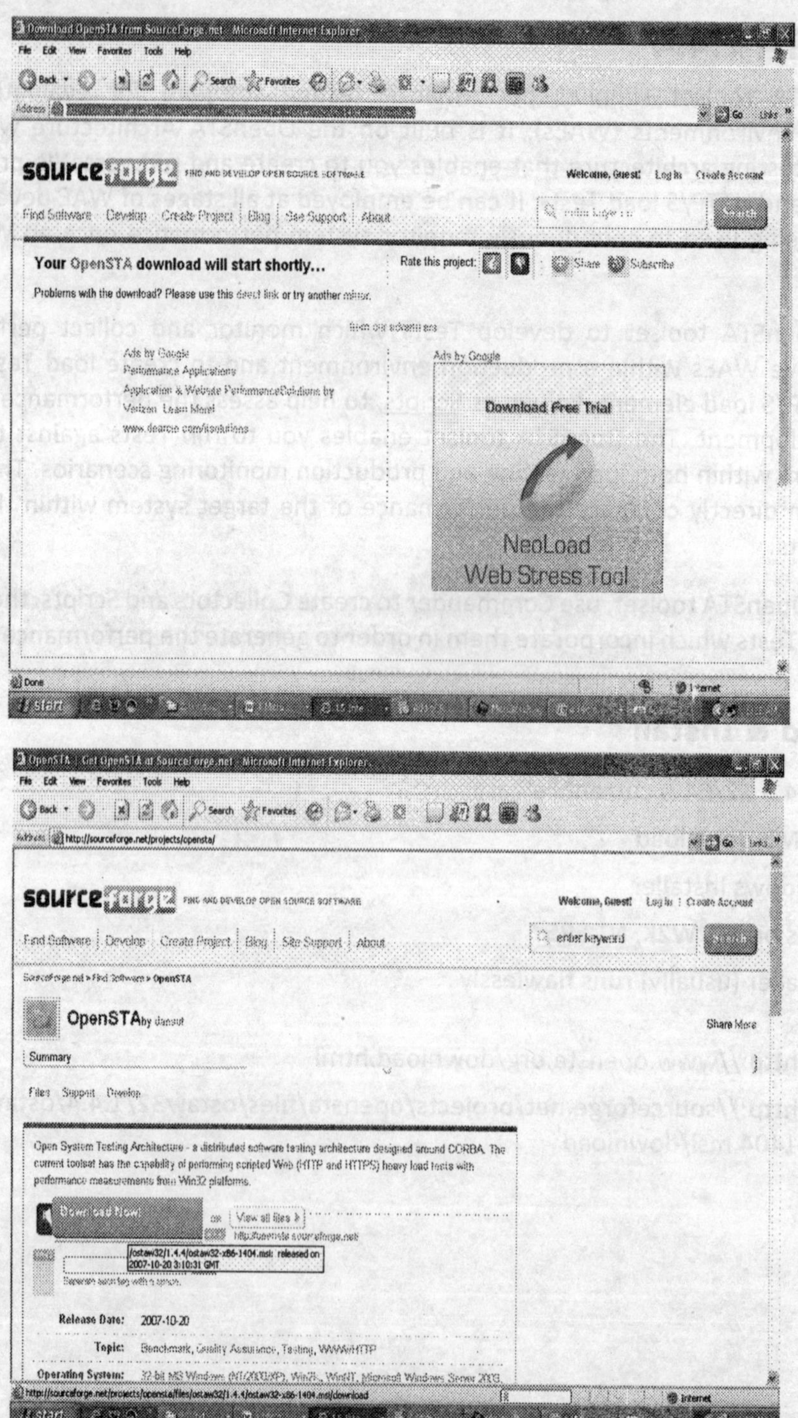
Download OpenSTA from SourceForge.net - Microsoft Internet Explorer
File Edit View Favorites Tools Help
sourceforge FIND AND DEVELOP OPEN SOURCE SOFTWARE
Welcome, Guest! Log In Create Account
Find Software Develop Create Project Blog Site Support About
Your OpenSTA download will start shortly...
Rate this project:
Share Subscribe
Problems with the download? Please use this direct link or try another mirror.
Ads by Google
Performance Applications
Application & Website PerformanceSolutions by Verizon. Learn More!
www.dearcio.com/itsolutions
Ads by Google
Download Free Trial
NeoLoad
Web Stress Tool
Done
Internet
OpenSTA | Get OpenSTA at SourceForge.net - Microsoft Internet Explorer
http://sourceforge.net/projects/opensta/
sourceforge FIND AND DEVELOP OPEN SOURCE SOFTWARE
Welcome, Guest! Log In Create Account
Find Software Develop Create Project Blog Site Support About
enter keyword
SourceForge.net > Find Software > OpenSTA
OpenSTA by dansut
Share More
Summary
Files Support Develop
Open System Testing Architecture - a distributed software testing architecture designed around CORBA. The current toolset has the capability of performing scripted Web (HTTP and HTTPS) heavy load tests with performance measurements from Win32 platforms.
Download Now!
or View all files
http://opensta.sourceforge.net
/ostaw32/1.4.4/ostaw32-x86-1404.msi: released on 2007-10-20 3:10:31 GMT
Release Date: 2007-10-20
Topic: Benchmark, Quality Assurance, Testing, WWW/HTTP
Operating System:
http://sourceforge.net/projects/opensta/files/ostaw32/1.4.4/ostaw32-x86-1404.msi/download
Internet

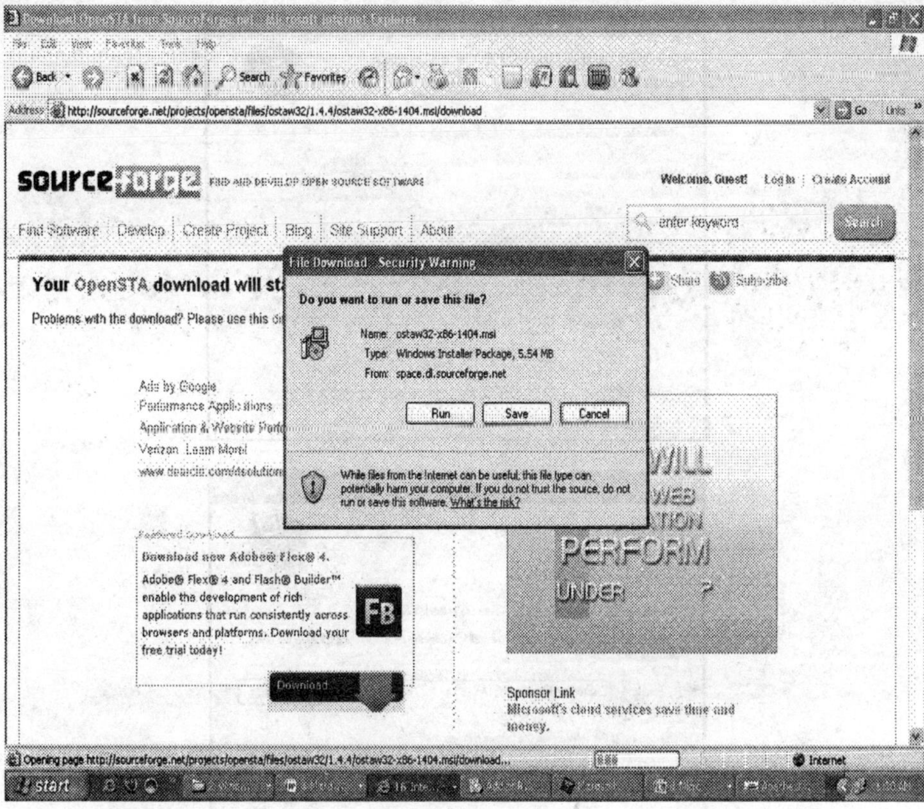

Click on 'Run'

Internet Explorer - Security Warning
The publisher could not be verified. Are you sure you want to run this software?
Name: ostaw32-x86-1404.msi
Publisher: Unknown Publisher
Run
Don't Run
This file does not have a valid digital signature that verifies its publisher. You should only run software from publishers you trust. How can I decide what software to run?

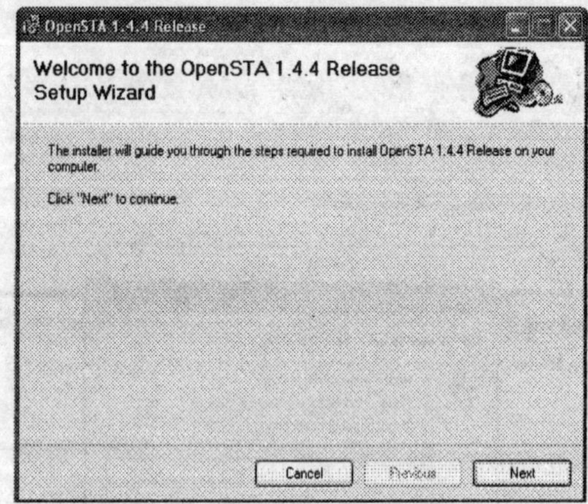
OpenSTA 1.4.4 Release
Welcome to the OpenSTA 1.4.4 Release Setup Wizard
The installer will guide you through the steps required to install OpenSTA 1.4.4 Release on your computer.
Click "Next" to continue.
Cancel
Previous
Next

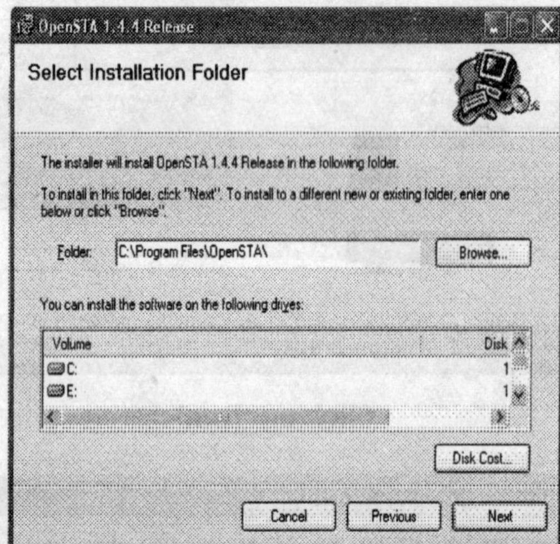
OpenSTA 1.4.4 Release
Select Installation Folder
The installer will install OpenSTA 1.4.4 Release in the following folder.
To install in this folder, click "Next". To install to a different new or existing folder, enter one below or click "Browse".
Folder:
C:\Program Files\OpenSTA\
Browse...
You can install the software on the following drives:
Volume
Disk
C:
E:
Disk Cost...
Cancel
Previous
Next

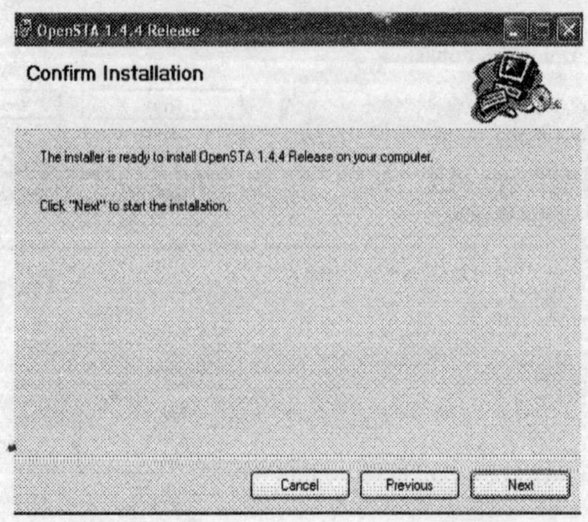
OpenSTA 1.4.4 Release
Confirm Installation
The installer is ready to install OpenSTA 1.4.4 Release on your computer.
Click "Next" to start the installation.
Cancel
Previous
Next

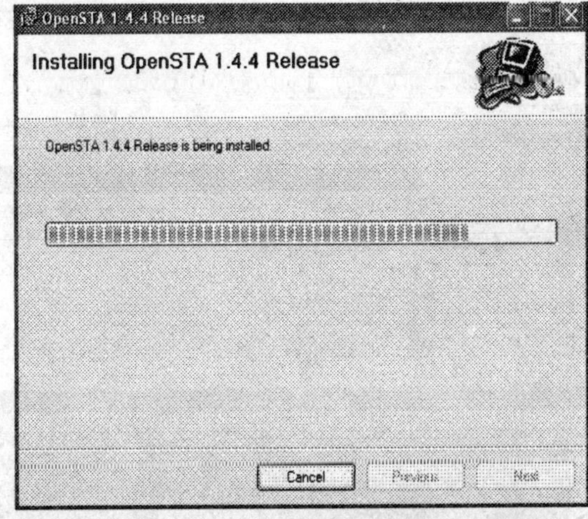
OpenSTA 1.4.4 Release
Installing OpenSTA 1.4.4 Release
OpenSTA 1.4.4 Release is being installed.
Cancel
Previous
Next

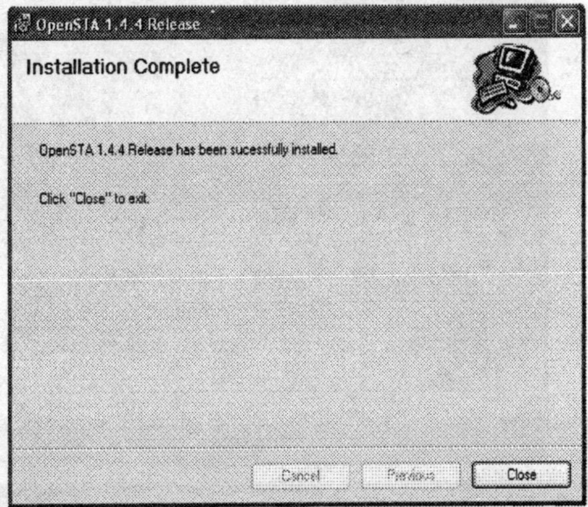
OpenSTA 1.4.4 Release
Installation Complete
OpenSTA 1.4.4 Release has been sucessfully installed.
Click "Close" to exit.
Cancel
Previous
Close

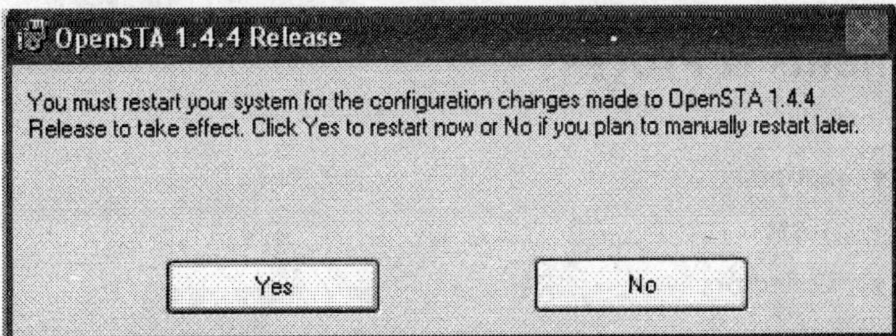
OpenSTA 1.4.4 Release
You must restart your system for the configuration changes made to OpenSTA 1.4.4 Release to take effect. Click Yes to restart now or No if you plan to manually restart later.
Yes
No

Select 'OpenSTA' from Start-> Program Files -> OpenSTA -> OpenSTA Commander

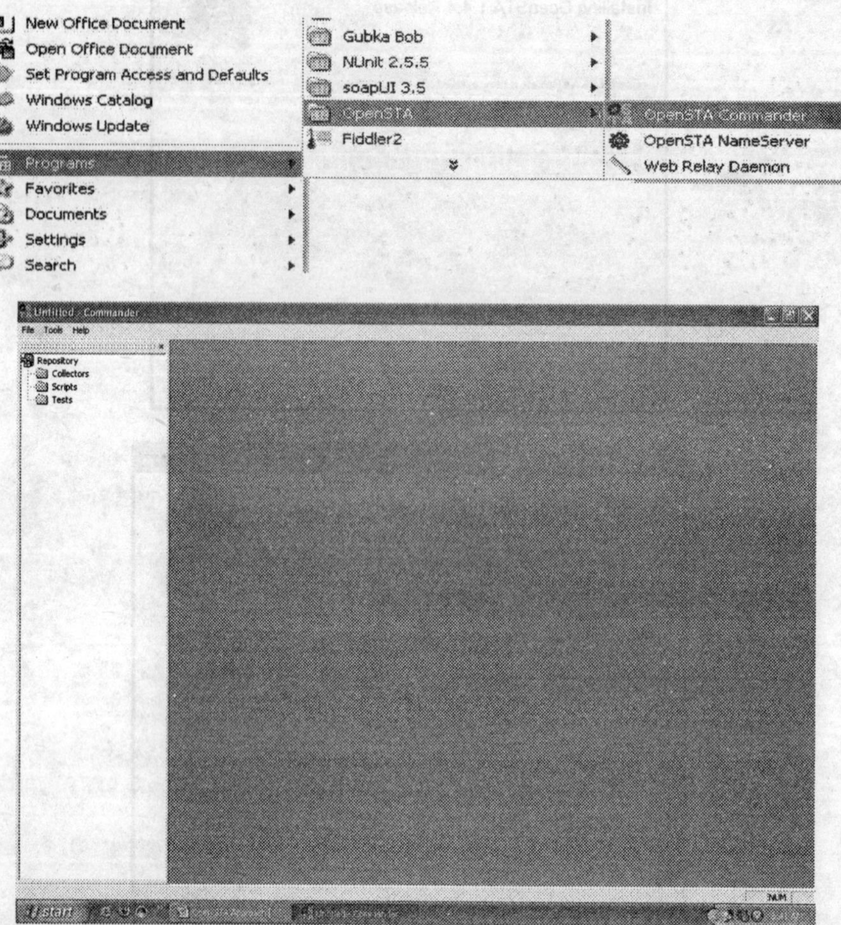

Components & Process

- Commander
  - Scripts
  - Tests
  - Collectors
- OpenSTA Name Server

  Step 1: Develop test scripts

  Record, parameterize user-entered data, parameterize dynamic system data, adjust think-times & timers, test/debug

Step 2: Define & Launch Test
Define load scenario; configure Collectors; launch test; monitor interactively

Step 3: Export, Graph, & Analyze Results
Select & filter results; export; generate graphs; analyze & interpret.

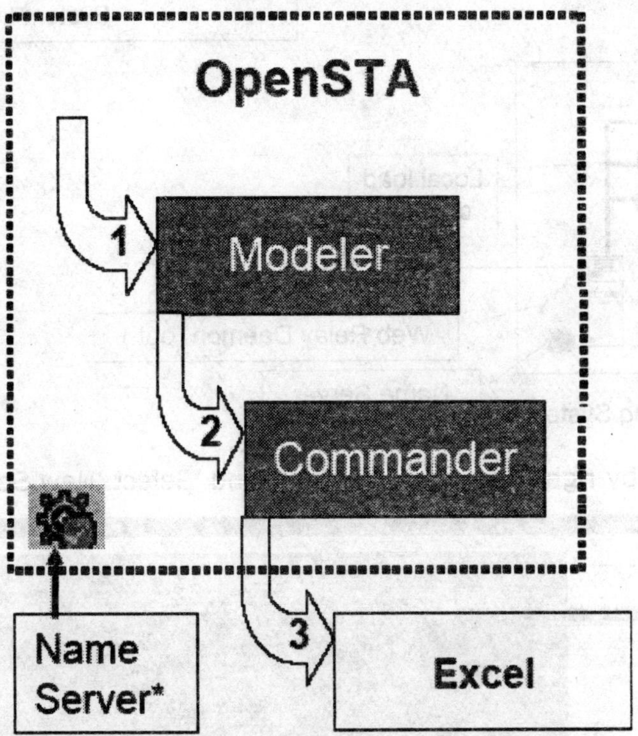

Architecture

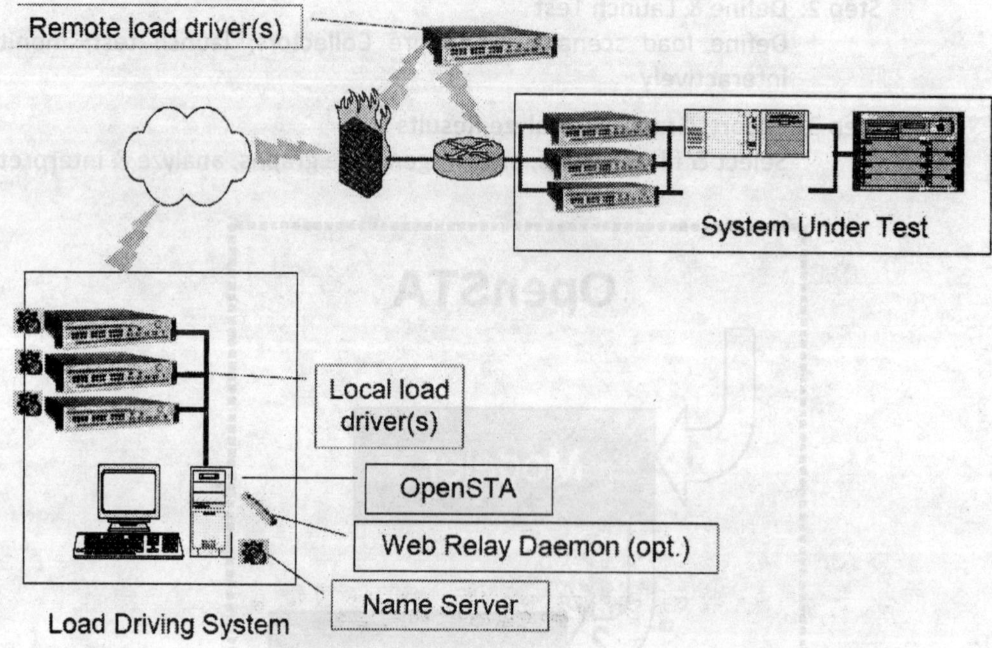

Add new script by right clicking on 'Scripts' and 'Select 'New Script-> HTTP'

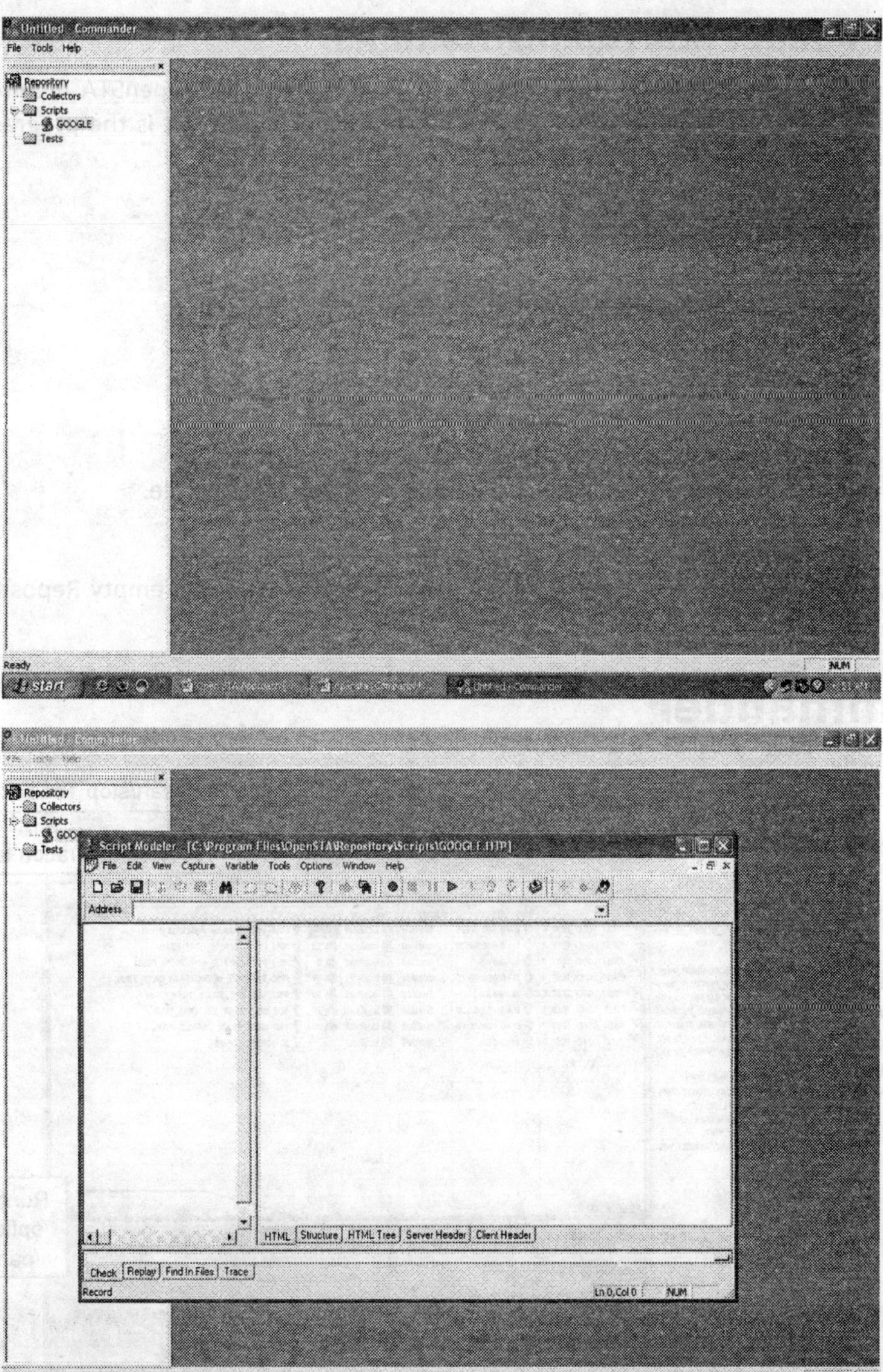
Untitled - Commander
File Tools Help
Repository
Collectors
Scripts
GOOGLE
Tests
Ready
NUM
Script Modeler - [C:\Program Files\OpenSTA\Repository\Scripts\GOOGLE.HTP]
File Edit View Capture Variable Tools Options Window Help
Address
HTML
Structure
HTML Tree
Server Header
Client Header
Check
Replay
Find In Files
Trace
Record
Ln 0, Col 0
NUM

Commander Startup Instructions

Commander is the Graphical User Interface that runs within the OpenSTA Architecture and functions as the front end for all Test development activity. It is the program you need to run in order to use HTTP/S Load.

Launch Commander

- Click **Start > Programs > OpenSTA > OpenSTA Commander.**
  Or,

1. Click **Start > Run.**
2. Enter the application path and program file:
   \Program Files\OpenSTA\BaseUI\OSCommander.exe
   or click **Browse**, then locate and double-click the program file.
3. Click **OK** to launch Commander.

   Note: When you startup Commander for the first time an empty Repository is automatically created in the program directory structure.

Commander

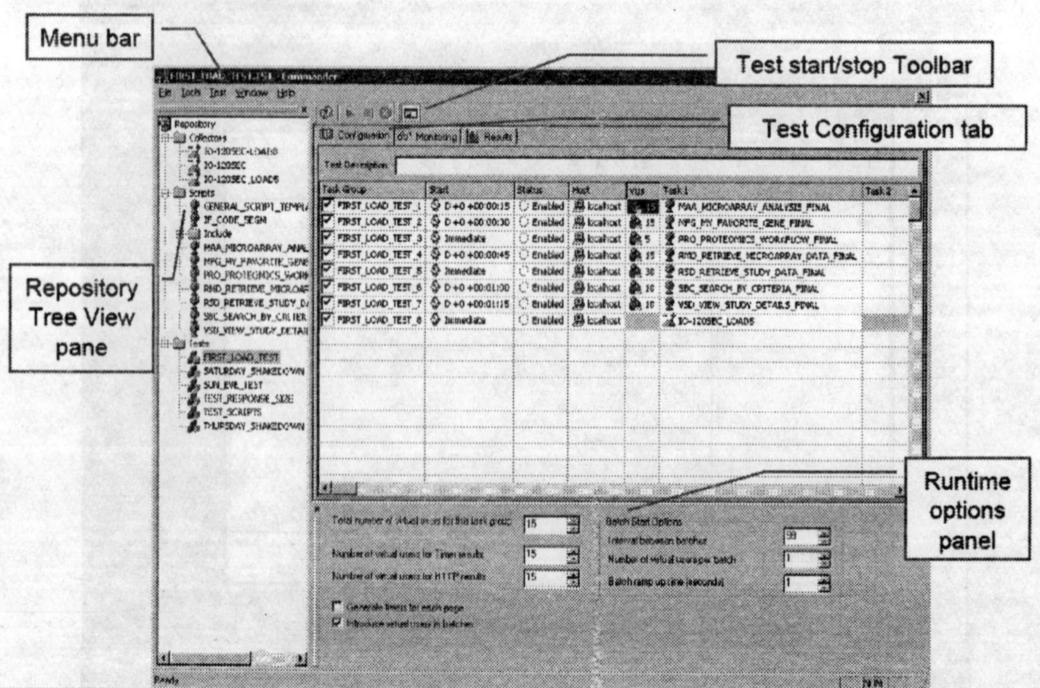

Commander: Monitoring a Test

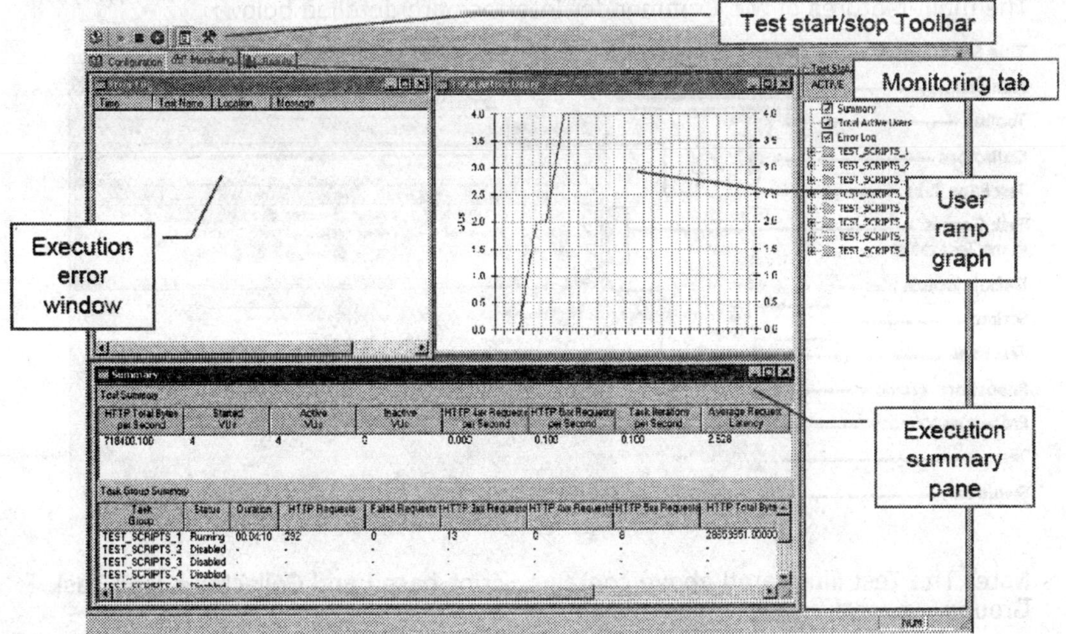

Commander: Exporting Results

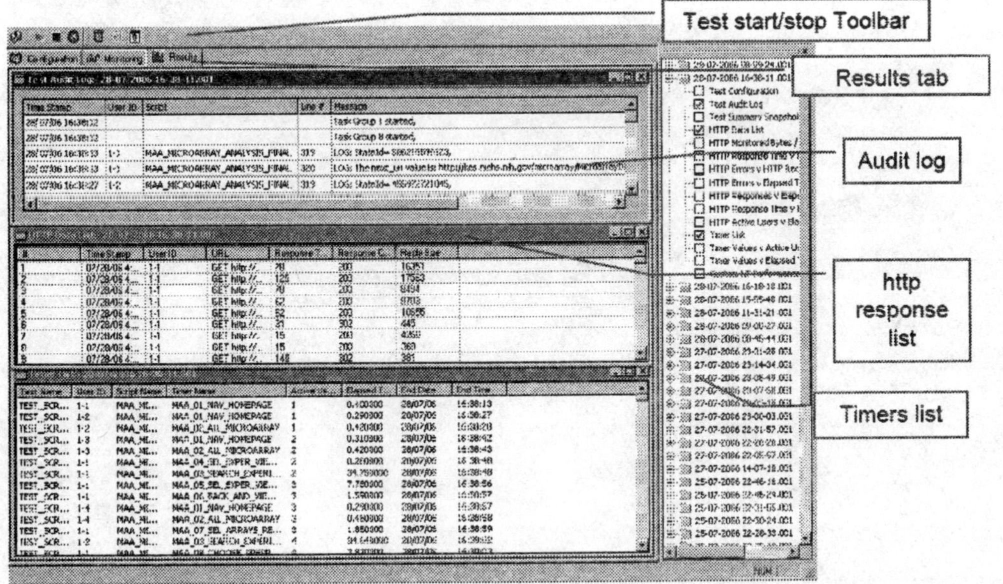

The Commander Interface

The main features of the Commander interface are detailed below:

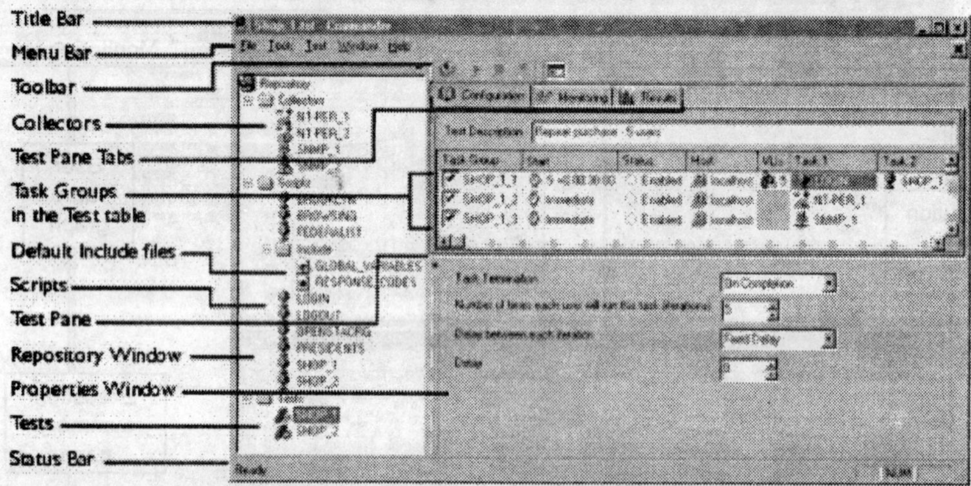

Note: The Test illustrated above contains Script-based and Collector-based Task Groups.

Create a New Script

1. In Commander select **File > New Script > HTTP**.

   Or: In the Repository Window, right-click **Scripts**, and select **New Script > HTTP**.

   The Script appears in the Repository Window with a small crossed red circle over the Script icon, indicating that the file has no content. As soon as you open the Script and record a Web session, the icon changes to reflect this and appears.
2. Give the new Script a name within the Repository Window, which must be an OpenSTA Dataname, with the exception that the name can be up to 60 characters long, then press **Return**.
3. Double-click the new Script icon, to launch Script Modeler.
4. Click the Record button, in the Capture/Replay Toolbar, or select **Capture > Record**, to begin the HTTP/S capture process.

   This action launches the Gateway and the Web browser you have selected.

   Your browser's Home page Internet option is overridden by Script Modeler when you start recording. The setting is replaced with **about:blank**, which specifies that your home page will be a blank HTML page. This ensures that your normal Home page is not launched and recorded in the Script.

   Note: The Gateway is launched in Local recording mode by default unless you have chosen Remote recording mode.
5. Type in a URL and hit **Return** or select a URL from the browser's URL Address bar. Then use the browser as normal to perform the actions you want to record in your Script.

   Tip: Use the Add Comment button in the Capture/Replay Toolbar to add comments while you are recording a Web session, or select **Capture > Insert Comments**. They are used to assist you when monitoring a single stepping session. The time taken to add a comment is not recorded in the Script.
6. After you have completed the browser actions you need, switch back to Script Modeler from the browser and click the Stop button, in the Capture/Replay Toolbar to end the recording. Or, close the browser.

   Tip: If you have more than one Script to record use to end a recording, to save repeatedly closing and opening the browser.

   When you have finished recording the Script the SCL formatted data is displayed in the Script Pane as illustrated below:

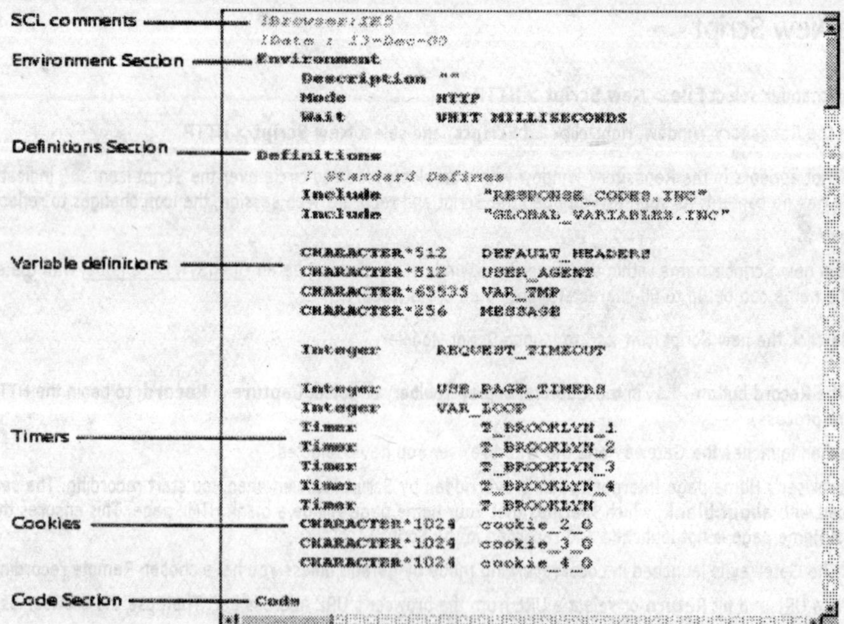

7. Before you save your new Script you need to compile it using the Syntax Check option to ensure the validity of the recording.

   Select **Capture > Syntax Check** or click [icon], in the Capture/Replay Toolbar. Compilation results are reported in the Output Pane. If compilation is unsuccessful, you may need to re-record the Script or model the contents to resolve the problem.

   Note: You can record over the top of an existing Script until you achieve the content you need.

8. After compilation replay the Script to check the activity you have recorded.

   Select **Capture > Replay** or click [icon], in the Capture/Replay Toolbar

9. When you have finished recording, click [icon], in the Standard Toolbar to save your Script in the Repository, or click **File > Save**.

10. Select **File > Close** to close the current Script or **File > Exit** to exit Script Modeler.

    Note: If you have unsaved Scripts open in Script Modeler, you are automatically prompted to save them before the program closes. Closing down Script Modeler also closes the browser which restores your original browser settings.

The Script Recording Process

Script Modeler creates a Script exactly as the browser requested the Web pages and their contents. They are created by the Gateway and consist of SCL code, including GET, POST and HEAD commands, which represent corresponding HTTP/S instructions.

Scripts represent HTTP/S browser requests in SCL code and are saved in a .HTP file. During the same recording session the corresponding WAE responses are recorded by the Gateway in a .ALL file. This includes DOM, HTML and Web page structure data. The full detail of a Web session is stored in these two files.

After you have clicked the Record button in the Capture/Replay Toolbar and entered the first URL in your browser's Address text box, the WAE responds by sending the HTTP/S data that forms the content of the Web page displayed by your browser.

Loading a Web page involves parsing or compiling the Web page structure from the raw HTTP/S data returned by the WAE in response to the URL or PRIMARY GET. The content is then rendered on screen by the browser whilst concurrently making additional, asynchronous requests on other TCP connections via secondary GETs for the remaining contents of the Web page. The browser continues to issue requests and render any remaining content until the Web page is fully loaded. The Gateway records and formats this information.

The Script Modeler HTTP/S capture process is illustrated below:

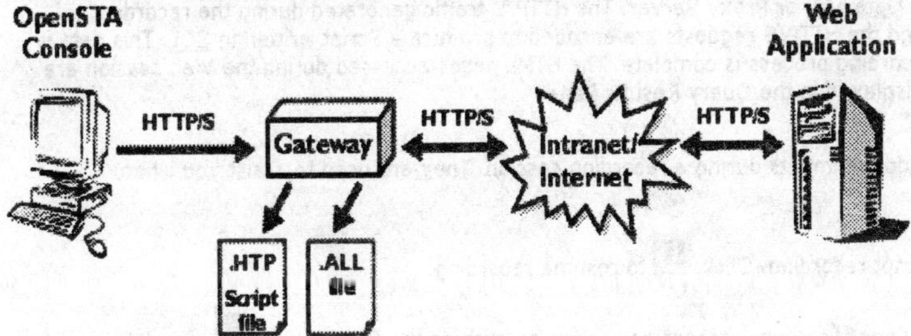

Browser requests hit the target WAE via the Gateway, across the Internet or other network. Browser requests are recorded by the Gateway as a Script (.HTP file). WAE responses are recorded by the Gateway in a .ALL file.

Note: OpenSTA Console refers to a computer which has an installation of OpenSTA. This includes the OpenSTA Architecture and Commander and it may also include the Repository, where all Test related files and results are stored. The PC will also have a Web browser installed and is typically the home for the Gateway. In this diagram the Gateway is shown as separated from the OpenSTA Console to clarify the Script recording process.

Capture/Replay Toolbar

The Capture/Replay Toolbar is used to control the Script recording process. It is located below the Menu Bar in the Script Modeler window. You can use it to record multiple Scripts during the same Web browser session

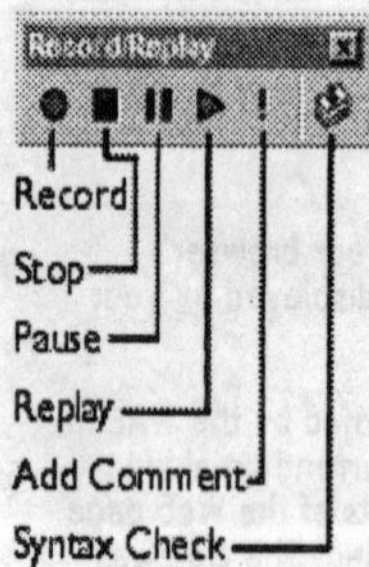

Click the Record button, in the Capture/Replay Toolbar to begin the HTTP/S capture process. This action launches your Web browser which in turn activates the Gateway, or Proxy Server. The HTTP/S traffic generated during the recording session is intercepted by the Gateway and the HTTP/S requests are encoded to produce a Script written in SCL. This data is displayed in the Script Pane after the recording process is complete. The HTML pages accessed during the Web session are recorded in a separate file and can be displayed in the Query Results Pane.

Use the Add Comment button, to add comments during a recording session. They are used to assist you when monitoring a single stepping session.

Use the Pause button to suspend Script recording. Click to resume recording.

When you have recorded everything you need, end your recording session by clicking the Stop button, or close down the browser.

Use the Syntax Check button to compile the current Script. The SCL compiler is launched and generates an object file called a .TOF file. This is the file that is executed by a Task Group Executer when a Test is run.

Use the Replay button to compile the current Script and replay it within Script Modeler to ensure that it is valid. Replay activity can be monitored using the Output Pane.

Create Additional Scripts

Once you have launched Script Modeler you can record additional Scripts.

1. In Script Modeler, select **File > New.**

   Shortcut: Click , in the Standard Toolbar, or press **Ctrl** + N.

2. Click the Record button , in the Capture/Replay Toolbar, or select **Capture > Record**, to begin the HTTP/S capture process.
3. In the Script Name dialog box, give the new Script a name, which must be an OpenSTA Dataname, with the exception that the name can be up to 60 characters long.

Script Modeler

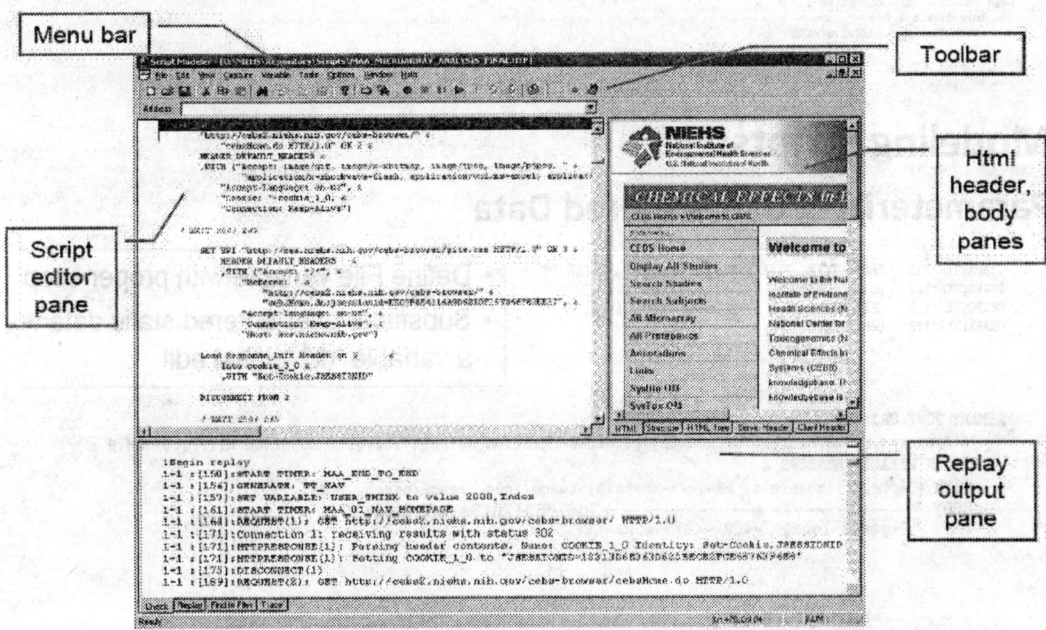

Modeling Scripts: Cookies

```
Definitions
    ! Standard Defines
    Include         "RESPONSE_CODES.INC"
    Include         "GLOBAL_VARIABLES.INC"

    CHARACTER*512   USER_AGENT
    Integer         USE_PAGE_TIMERS
    CHARACTER*256   MESSAGE

    Timer           MFG_END_TO_END
    Timer           mfg_02_disp_annotations
    Timer           mfg_01_nav_homepage
    Timer           mfg_04_sort_by_probe
    Timer           mfg_03_submit_request
    Timer           mfg_mutex
    CHARACTER*1024  cookie_1_0
    CHARACTER*1024  cookie_3_0
    CHARACTER*1024  cookie_8_0

PRIMARY GET URI "http://cebs2.niehs.nih.gov/cebs-browser/ HTTP/1.0" ON 1 &
    HEADER DEFAULT_HEADERS &
    ,WITH {"Accept: image/gif, image/x-xbitmap, image/jpeg, image/pjpeg, " &
          "application/vnd.ms-powerpoint, application/vnd.ms-excel, application/msword, " &
          "application/x-shockwave-flash, */*", &
      "Accept-Language: en-us", &
      "Connection: Keep-Alive"}

Load Response_Info Header on 1      &
    Into cookie_1_0 &
    ,WITH "Set-Cookie,JSESSIONID"
```

- Defined automatically during Record
- Handled automatically during replay

Modeling Scripts:

Parameterizing User-Entered Data

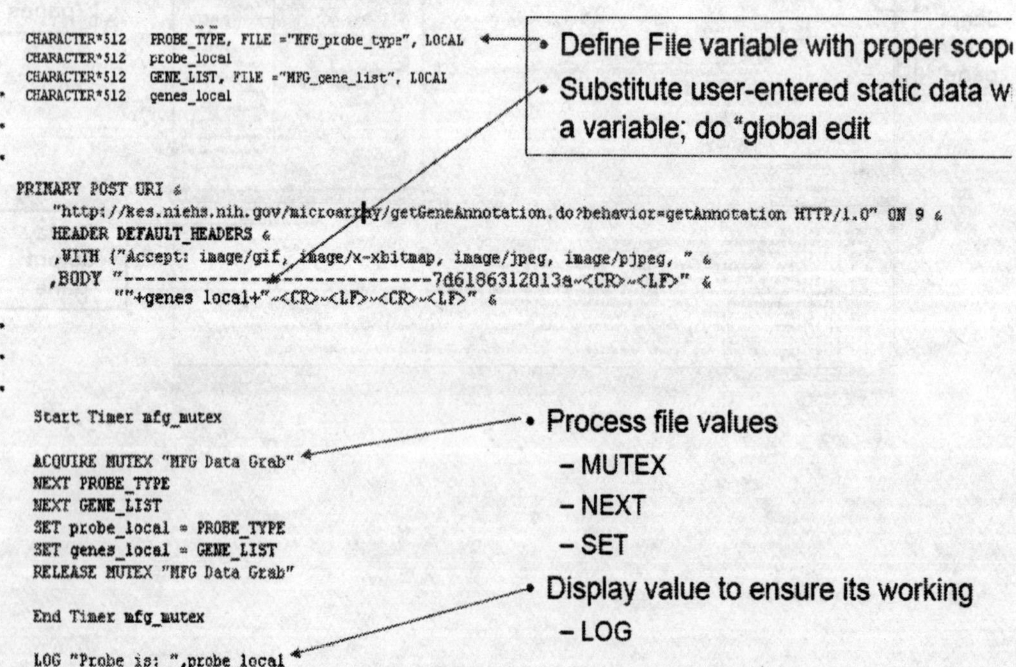

Modeling Scripts:

Capturing System Response Values

```
PRIMARY GET URI "http://kes.niehs.nih.gov/cebs-browser/microarray.do?behavior=gene HTTP/1.0"
    ON 7 &
    HEADER DEFAULT_HEADERS &
    ,WITH {"Accept: image/gif, image/x-xbitmap, image/jpeg, image/pjpeg, " &
          "application/vnd.ms-powerpoint, application/vnd.ms-excel, application/msword, " &
          "application/x-shockwave-flash, */*", &
        "Referer: " &
          "http://cebs2.niehs.nih.gov/cebs-browser/" &
          "cebsHome.do;jsessionid=AD212AA43880FFD0EBD4061F8F16496B", &
        "Accept-Language: en-us", &
        "Connection: Keep-Alive", &
        "Host: kes.niehs.nih.gov", &
        "Cookie: "+cookie_3_0}

LOAD RESPONSE_INFO HEADER ON 7 &
INTO next_url &
,WITH   "Location"
SET StateID_capture = ~EXTRACT (82, 15, next_url)

LOG "StateId= ", StateID_capture
```

- Load Response Header/Body into a buffer (character array)
- Parse desired value and load into a variable
- Do global replace so it gets "fed back" on later urls

```
PRIMARY GET URI &
    "http://kes.niehs.nih.gov/microarray/" &
        "MicroarrayDispatcher.do?behavior=gene&StateId="+StateID_capture+" HTTP/1.0" ON 8 &
    HEADER DEFAULT_HEADERS &
    ,WITH {"Accept: image/gif, image/x-xbitmap, image/jpeg, image/pjpeg, " &
          "application/vnd.ms-powerpoint, application/vnd.ms-excel, application/msword, " &
          "application/x-shockwave-flash, */*", &
        "Referer: " &
          "http://cebs2.niehs.nih.gov/cebs-browser/" &
          "cebsHome.do;jsessionid=AD212AA43880FFD0EBD4061F8F16496B", &
        "Accept-Language: en-us", &
        "Connection: Keep-Alive", &
        "Host: kes.niehs.nih.gov", &
        "Cookie: "+cookie_3_0}
```

Directory Structure

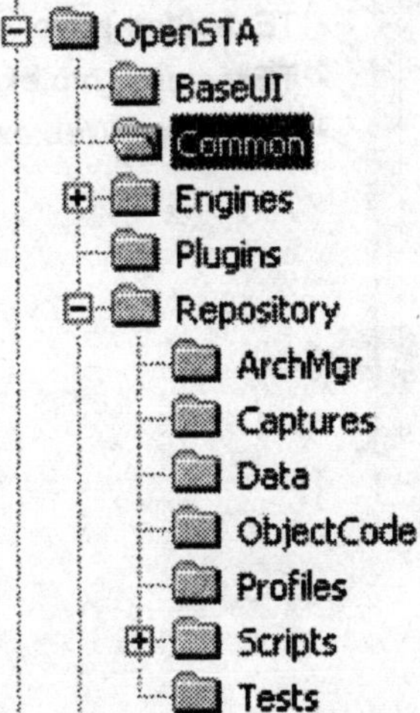

- Base directory; location pointed to by Tools/Repository Path
  - – Main applications
  - – DLLs
  - – More DLLs, exes, ini files
  - – More DLLs

– **Test assets (by project)**

- <EMPTY>
- Screen shots <.ALL>
- Data files <.FVR>
- Compiled scripts <.tof, .scd>
- Collector scripts <.NTP>
- Scripts (source SCL code) <.HTP>
- Tests
  - – Load scenarios <Full_Load_1>
    - » Test results folders <09-06-2006-10.000>

Architecture: Processes

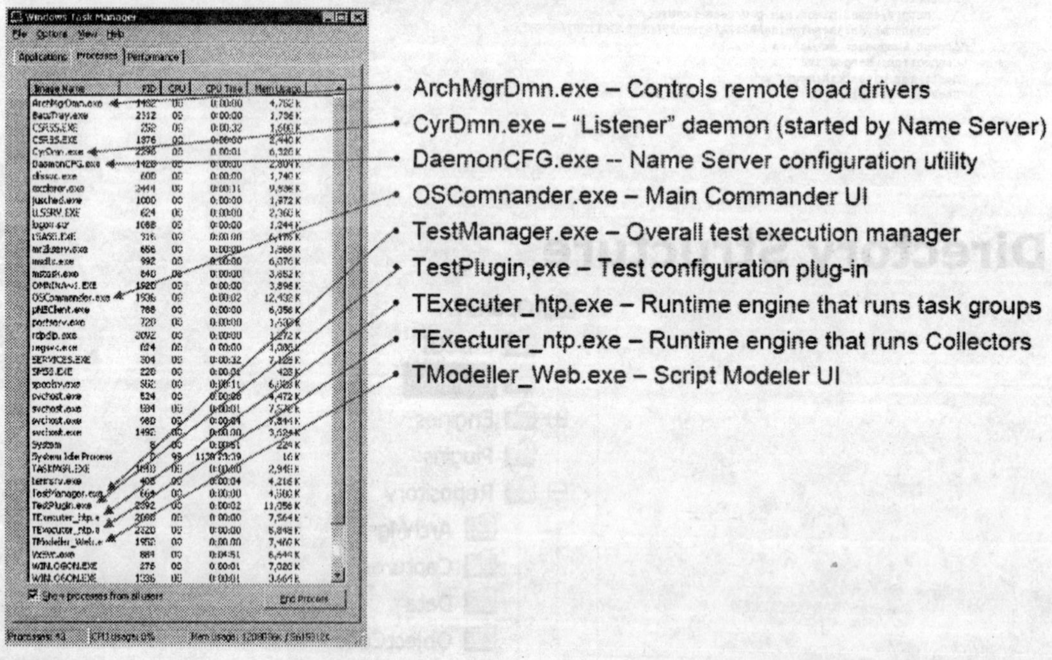

Parameterization in open STA

Consider the Scenario, parameter zing the Username and Password In Login screen,

1. Record the script
2. Create a dataset for username and password in different notepads and save it with extension **.fvr**
3. Copy the created files and place it in the **Data** Folder of OpenSTA installation directory,

Ex: C:\Program Files\OpenSTA\Repository\Data

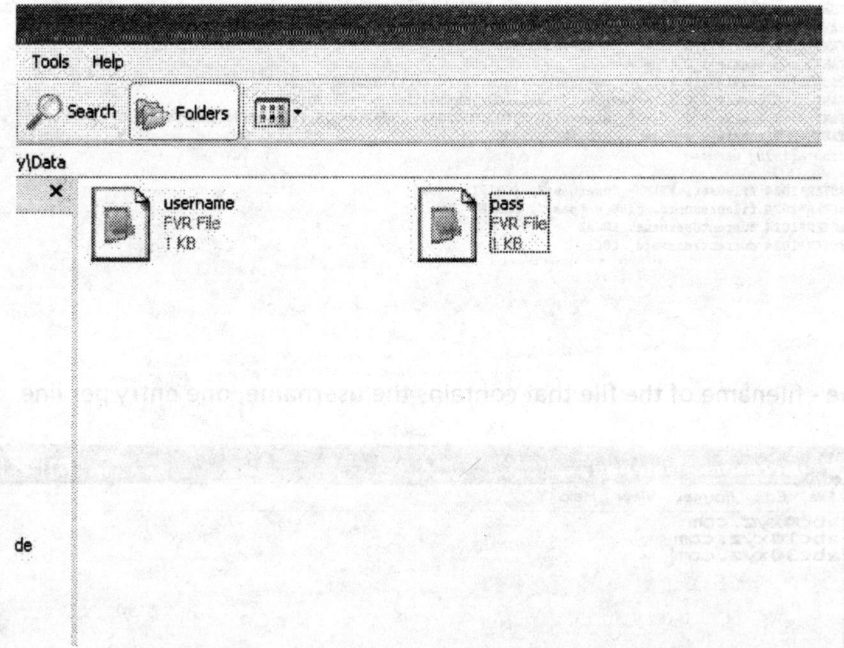

4. Under the **Definition** section of the recorded script place the following lines,

```
CHARACTER*512 fileuser, FILE = "username", SCRIPT
CHARACTER*512 filepassword, FILE = "pass", SCRIPT
CHARACTER*100 currentUsername, LOCAL
CHARACTER*100 currentPassword, LOCAL
```

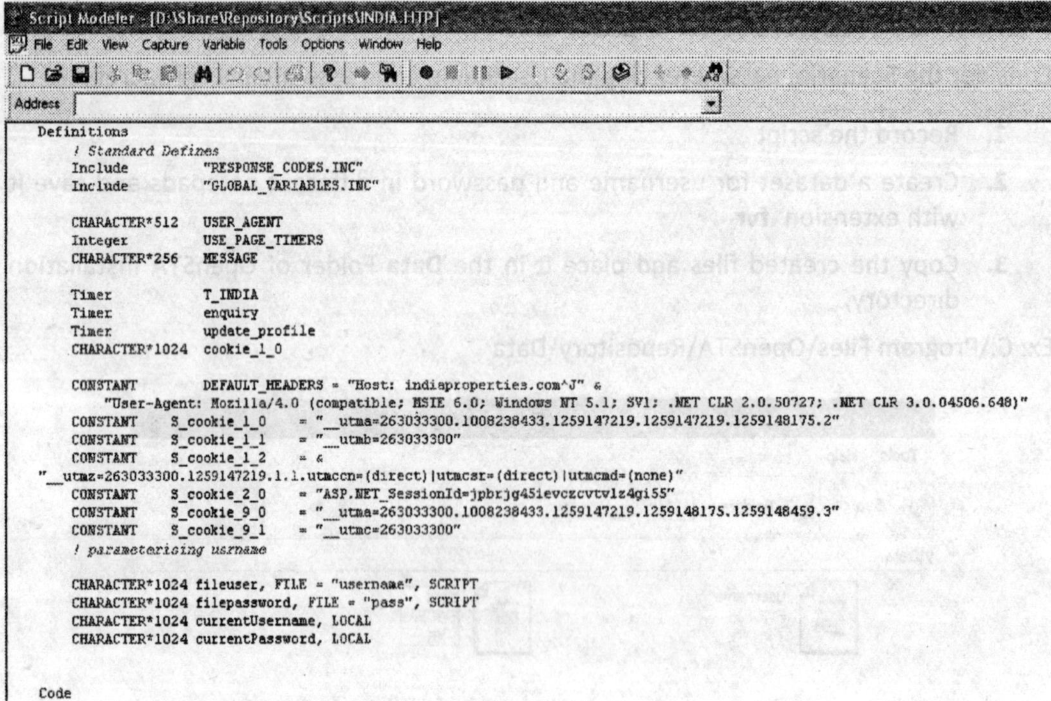

Note:

username - filename of the file that contains the username, one entry per line

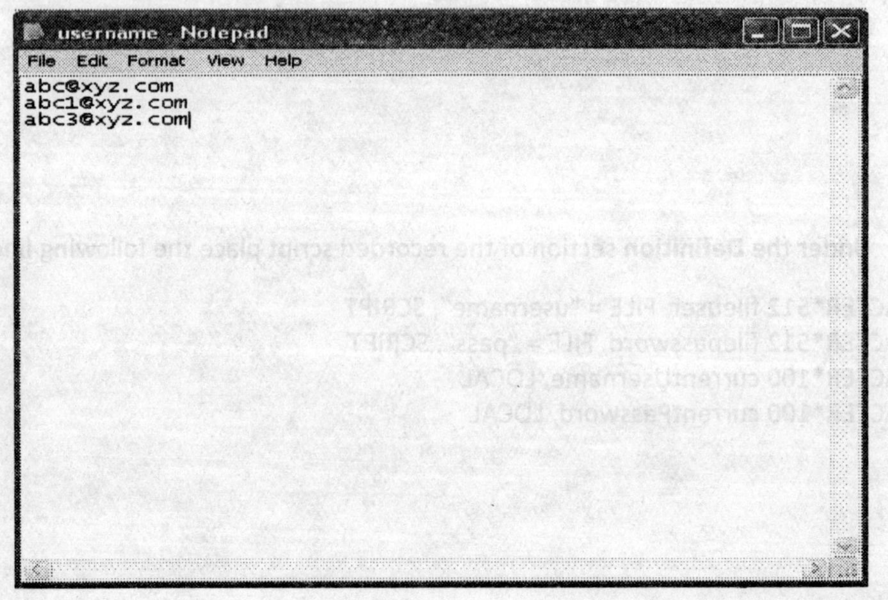

pass - filename of the file that contains the password, one entry per line

5. In the script recorded, just above the url where the login data will be passed, place the following code,

ACQUIRE MUTEX “Logn”
NEXT fileuser
NEXT filepassword
SET currentusername = fileuser
SET currentpassword = filepassword

LOG “User: “, fileuser, “ - Password: “, filepassword
LOG “User: “, currentUsername, “ - Password: “, currentPassword

RELEASE MUTEX “Logn”

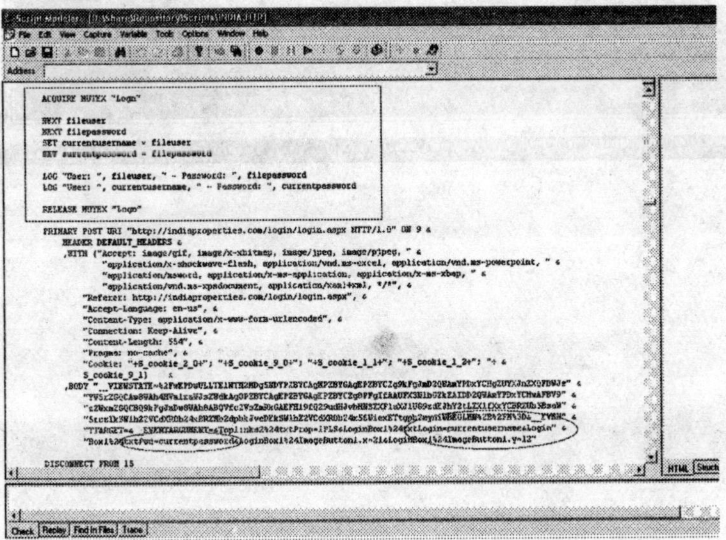

Make sure you use the mutex, or each thread may not use a distinct value from the list/ file.

6. In the Url section replace the values passed in login with the variables we have created i.e **currentusername** for Username and **currentpassword** for Password.

7. Run the Script, different values will be passed for different iterations from the file created.

8. In Result section check the **Test Audit Log** check box, you can see the log with variables you passed during test.

Constrain

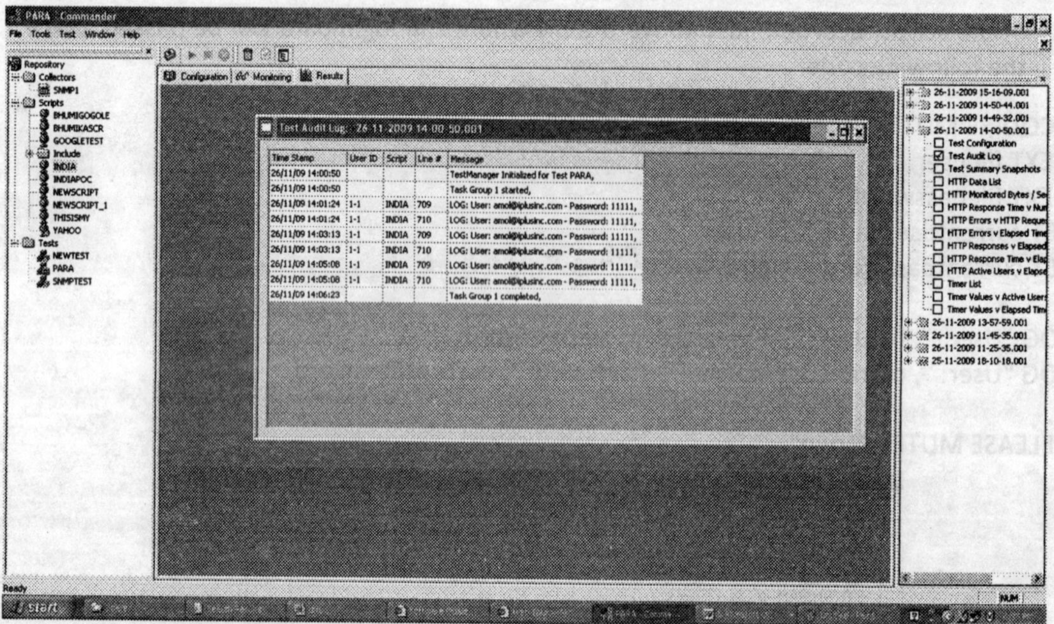

Open STA Distributed Tests

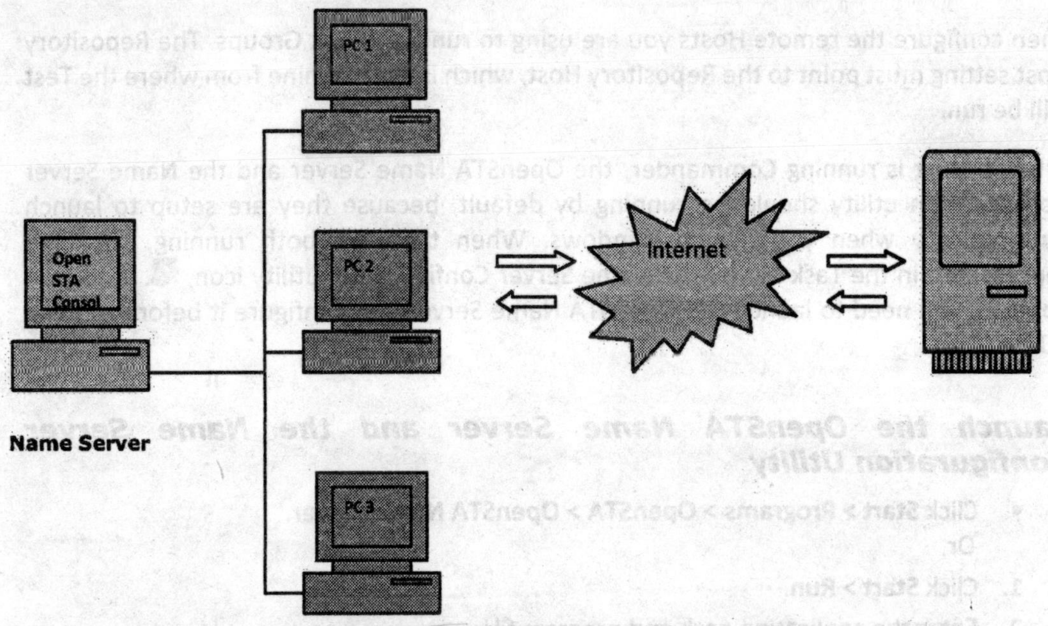

HTTP/S Load supplies a distributed software testing architecture based on COBRA which enables you to utilize remote Host computers to run the Task Groups that comprise a Test. A Task Group can be run by a Task Group Executer process on a remote Host or the Rep^sitory Host during a Test-run.

Define the Host you want to run a Task Group when you add a Script or Collector to a Test. Open the Configuration tab of the Test Pane then click on the Host column table cell in the selected Task Group and using the Properties Window to select a Host

Open STA Name Server

Before you can start a distributed Test the Hosts you have chosen to run the Task Groups must have the **Open STA Name Server** installed, running and correctly configured. Use the Name Server Configuration utility to configure the OpenSTA Name Server settings on all the Hosts running Windows in your Test network.

Before starting a Test-run, make sure that the OpenSTA Name Server is running on the Repository Host and that the Repository Host setting points to itself. You can configure this by right-clicking, in the Task Bar and selecting the **Configure** option. Then specify the Repository Host setting by typing **localhost**, the computer name or the IP address of the Repository Host in the Repository Host text box. You will need to restart the OpenSTA Name Server to implement the configuration changes you make.

Then configure the remote Hosts you are using to run your Task Groups. The Repository Host setting must point to the Repository Host, which is the machine from where the Test will be run.

When a Host is running Commander, the OpenSTA Name Server and the Name Server Configuration utility should be running by default, because they are setup to launch automatically when you launch Windows. When they are both running, they are represented in the Task bar by the Name Server Configuration utility icon, . If no icon appears, you need to launch the OpenSTA Name Server and configure it before running a Test.

Launch the OpenSTA Name Server and the Name Server Configuration Utility

- Click **Start > Programs > OpenSTA > OpenSTA Name Server.**
  Or,

1. Click **Start > Run.**
2. Enter the application path and program file:
3. **\Program Files\OpenSTA\Server\DaemonCFG.exe**
4. or click **Browse**, then locate and double-click the program file.
5. Click **OK.**

Change the Repository Host Setting of the OpenSTA Name Server

1. In the Task Bar, right-click .
2. Select **Configure** from the menu, to display the OpenSTA Name Server dialog box.
3. Remote Hosts must point to the Repository Host:
   In the Repository Host text box enter the computer name or IP address of the Repository Host which will be used to run the Test.

   The Repository Host must point to itself:
   In the Repository Host text box type **localhost**, or enter the computer name or IP address of the Repository Host.

4. Click **OK.**
   Note: You will need to restart the OpenSTA Name Server to implement the configuration changes you make.
   Always start the OpenSTA Name Server on the Repository Host before configuring and restarting the OpenSTA Name Server on remote Hosts. If the

OpenSTA Name Server shuts down on the Repository Host, you must restart the OpenSTA Name Server on all remote Hosts.

Start the OpenSTA Name Server

When the OpenSTA Name Server has stopped, the Name Server Configuration utility icon appears in the Task Bar with a small crossed red circle over it, .

1. In the Task Bar, right-click .
2. XSelect **Start Name Server** from the menu.

   The Name Server Configuration utility icon appears in the Task Bar.

Stop the OpenSTA Name Server

When the OpenSTA Name Server is running, the Name Server Configuration utility icon appears in the Task Bar with a small ticked green circle over it, .

In the Task Bar, right-click .

1. Select **Stop Name Server** from the menu.
2. Click **Yes** in the dialog box that appears to confirm your choice.
3. Click **OK** to close the confirmation dialog box.

   The Name Server Configuration utility icon appears in the Task Bar.

Shutdown the OpenSTA Name Server

In the Task Bar, right-click or .

1. Select **Start Name Server** from the menu.
2. Click **Yes** in the dialog box that appears to confirm your choice.

Configuration Steps for the Repository Host Machine Name Server

1) Don't Change the Repository host name if you want to make your machine as server.

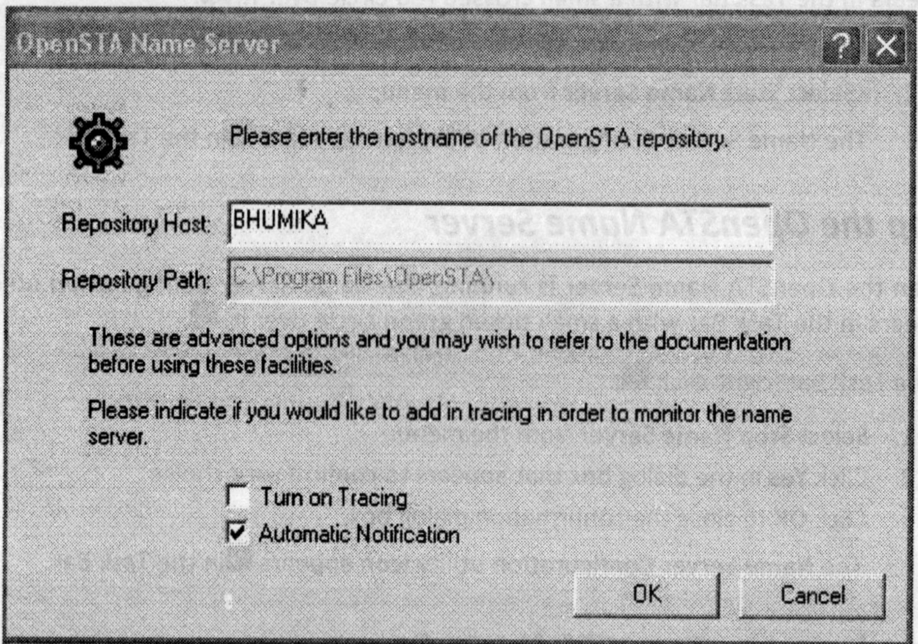

2) Right click on My Computer >> Properties>> Advanced Tab >> Environment variable ->System variable.

OR

Set path variables into Control Panel>>System->Advance->Environment variable ->System variable

3) Select Path variable from system Variables and click on Edit button.

In to variable value write down whole path where you have installed Open STA (Example "C:\Program Files\OpenSTA\Common")

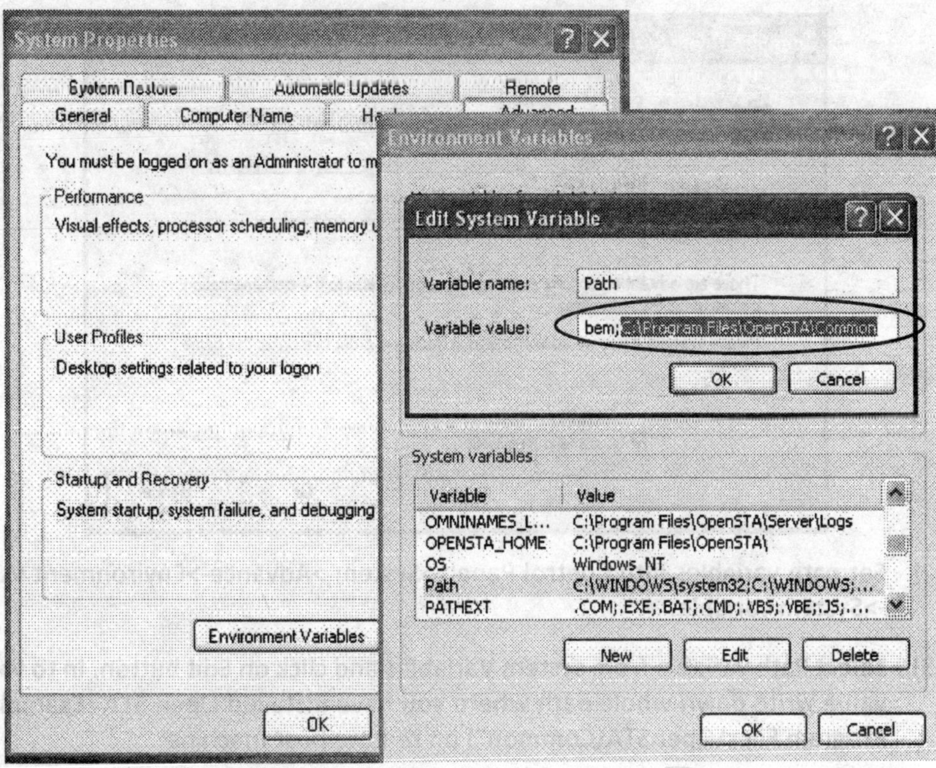

Steps for the Name server configuration on Remote Host Machine

1) Right click on Name Server symbol on task bar and click on "Configure..." menu as shown in the figure below

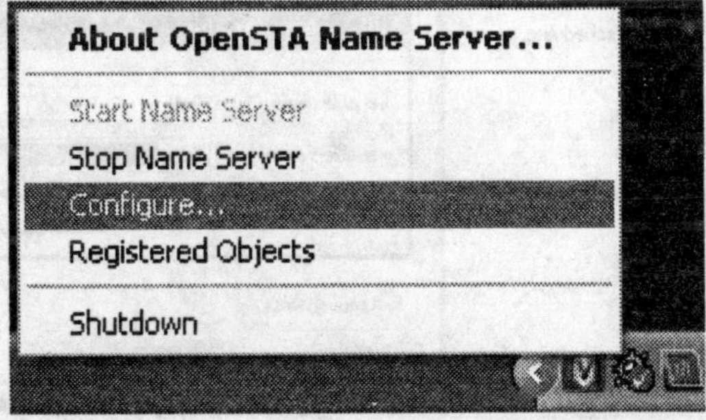

2) Change Repository Host name to your server name or IP address of your server.

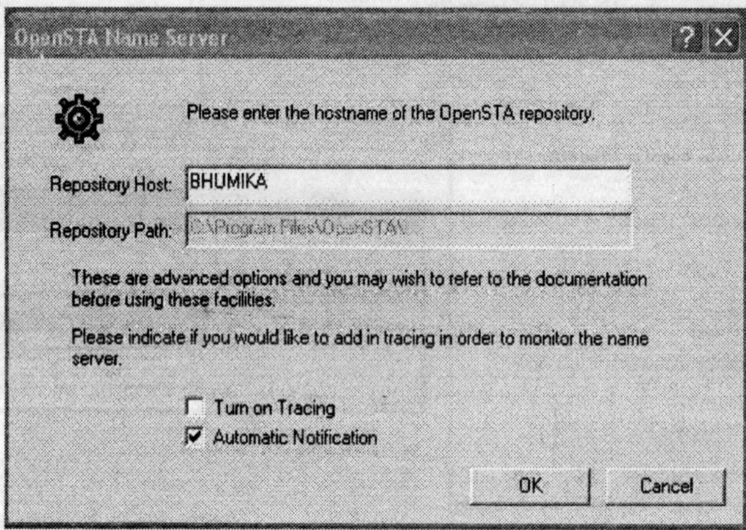

2) Set path variables into Control Panel>>System->Advance->Environment variable ->System variable.

3) Select Path variable from system Variables and click on Edit button. In to variable value write down whole path where you have installed Open STA (Example "C:\Program Files\OpenSTA\Common") on remote host machine

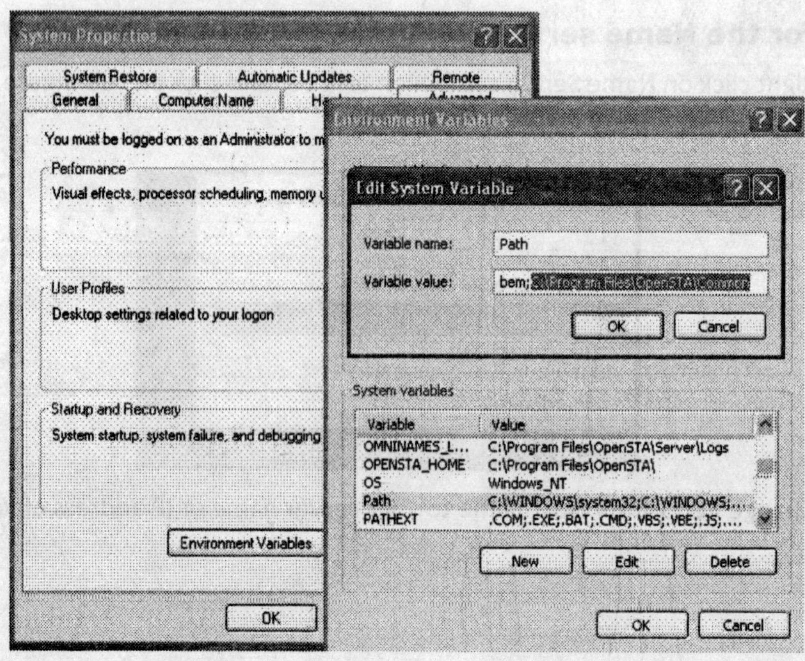

How to check Remote Host machine connected with Repository host server

1. Start Menu->Open STA commander of Repository Host server.
2. Click on Tool ->Architecture Manager

In the Architecture Manager window you will see all your Remote Host machines information as seen in the below figure.

All the remote host machines are displayed under the repository host machine name.

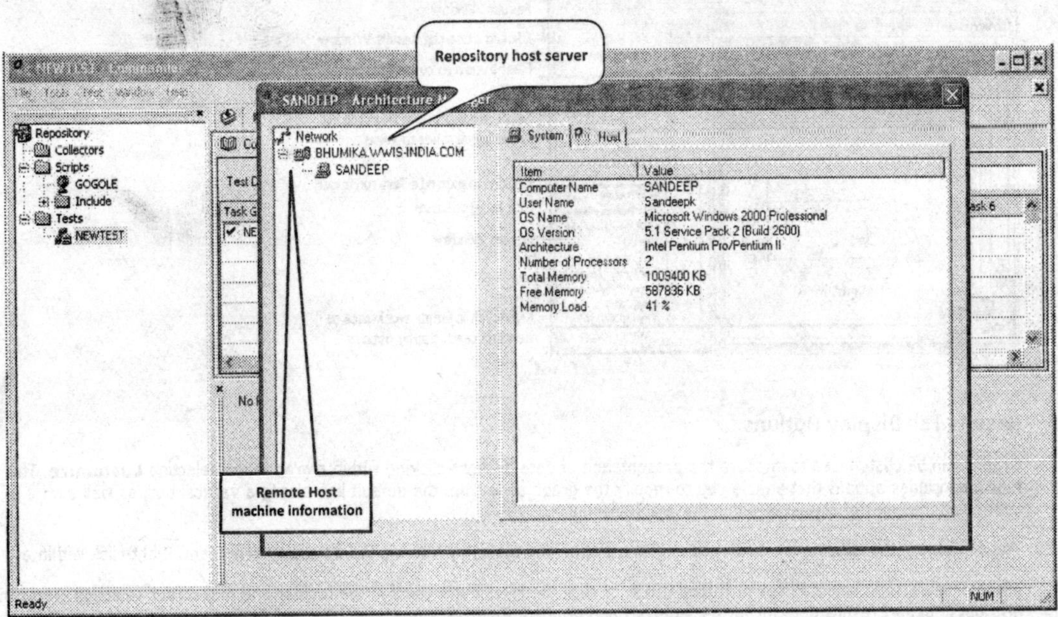

Results Tab

Results are stored in the Repository after a Test-run is complete. You can view them by working from the Repository Window to open the Test you want, then click on the **Results** tab in the Test Pane. Use the Results Window to select the results you want to view in the workspace of the Test Pane. You can reposition the Results Window by floating it over the Main Window to give yourself more room for results display, or close it once you have selected the results options you want to view.

The Results Tab of the Test Pane

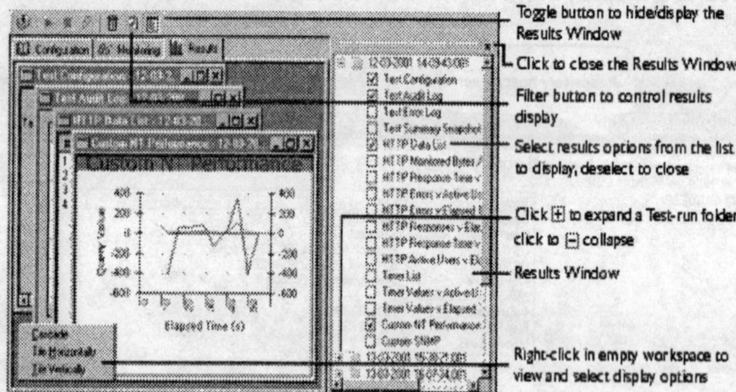

Results Tab Display Options

Graphs can be customized to improve the presentation of data by right-clicking within a graph then selecting **Customize.** This function includes options that enable you to modify the graph style from the default line plot to a vertical bar, as well as controlling the color of elements within the graph display.

You can control the information displayed in some graphs and tables by filtering the data they represent. Right-click within a graph or table, then select **Filter** or **Filter URLs**, or click the Filter button in the toolbar and make your selection. You can also opt to export results data for further analysis and printing. Right-click and select **Export to Excel** or **Export** from the menu.

You can also zoom in on a graph by clicking and dragging over the area of the graph you want to study. Use the **Windows** option to control the presentation of results options in the Test Pane, or right-click within the empty workspace of the Test Pane to access these functions as illustrated in the diagram above.

Display Test Audit Log Data

1. Open a Test and click the Results tab in the Test Pane.

   The Results Window opens automatically listing all Test-runs associated with the current Test. Results are stored in date and time stamped folders.
2. In the Results Window, click ⊞ next to a Test-run folder or double-click on it to open the folder and display the available results.
3. Click the **Test Audit Log** results option in the list.

   Audit information is displayed in the Results tab in table format:

Test Audit Log - 15-03-2001 09-05-06.001

Time Stamp	User ID	Script	Line #	Message
15/03/01 09:05:06				D:\Program Files\OpenSTA\Engines\BD_SYB_
15/03/01 09:05:06				Start Test BD_SYB_TEST,
15/03/01 09:05:06				D:\Program Files\OpenSTA\Engines\BD_SYB_
15/03/01 09:05:06				Start Test BD_SYB_TEST_1,
15/03/01 09:05:37	192_168_1_8-1348-0	BD_SYB_TEST_1		Start Script,
15/03/01 09:05:37	192_168_1_8-1348-0	BD_SYB		Start Script,
15/03/01 09:05:47	192_168_1_8-1348-1	BD_SYB_TEST_1		Start Script,
15/03/01 09:05:47	192_168_1_8-1348-1	BD_SYB		Start Script,
15/03/01 09:07:58	192_168_1_8-1348-0	BD_SYB		End Script,
15/03/01 09:07:58	192_168_1_8-1348-0	BD_SYB_TEST_1		End Script,
15/03/01 09:08:48	192_168_1_8-1348-1	BD_SYB		End Script,
15/03/01 09:08:48	192_168_1_8-1348-1	BD_SYB_TEST_1		End Script,
15/03/01 09:08:59				End Test BD_SYB_TEST_1,
15/03/01 09:09:10				End Test BD_SYB_TEST,

Tip: Display multiple graphs and tables concurrently to compare results using the Results Window.

Note: Click ☒, in the Title Bar of a graph or table to close it or deselect the display option in the Results Window.

Tip: You can export the data displayed in the Test Audit Log by right-clicking within the table and selecting **Export**. The data is exported in CSV format.

HTTP Data List

The HTTP Data List stores details of the HTTP requests issued by the Scripts included in a Test when it is run. This data includes the response times and codes for all the HTTP requests issued. The amount of HTTP data recorded depends on the Logging level specified for a Script-based Task Group when you created the Test and defined the Virtual User settings to be applied. The Logging level setting controls the number of Virtual Users that statistics are gathered for and can be edited from the Configuration tab of the Test Pane.

The data is presented in a table and can be sorted by clicking on the column headings to reverse the display order of the data entries. These results can also be filtered by right-clicking inside the table and selecting the **Filter** option. Use the **Export** right-click menu option to export data in .CSV text file format which allows them to be imported into other data analysis and report generating tools.

Display the HTTP Data List

1. Open a Test and click the **Results** tab in the Test Pane.

   The Results Window opens automatically listing all Test-runs associated with the current Test. Results are stored in date and time stamped folders.

2. In the Results Window, click ⊞ next to a Test-run folder or double-click on it to open the folder and display the available results.

3. Click the **HTTP Data List** display option in the list to open it in the Test Pane.

   HTTP Data List information is displayed in table format:

HTTP Data List - 15-03-2001 09-05-06.001

#	Time Stamp	User ID	URL	Response Time	Response Code	Reply Size
1	15-Mar-01 09:05:37	192_168_1_8-...	GET http://Aky/s...	12	200	1023
2	15-Mar-01 09:05:38	192_168_1_8-...	GET http://Aky/s...	1	200	4106
3	15-Mar-01 09:05:38	192_168_1_8-...	GET http://Aky/s...	1	200	1117
4	15-Mar-01 09:05:39	192_168_1_8-...	GET http://Aky/s...	0	200	1004
5	15-Mar-01 09:05:39	192_168_1_8-...	GET http://Aky/s...	0	200	776
6	15-Mar-01 09:05:39	192_168_1_8-...	GET http://Aky/s...	0	200	884
7	15-Mar-01 09:05:39	192_168_1_8-...	GET http://Aky/s...	1	200	6373
8	15-Mar-01 09:05:40	192_168_1_8-...	GET http://Aky/s...	1	200	3814
9	15-Mar-01 09:05:40	192_168_1_8-...	GET http://Aky/s...	1	200	7745
10	15-Mar-01 09:05:45	192_168_1_8-...	GET http://Aky/s...	1	200	3635
11	15-Mar-01 09:05:46	192_168_1_8-...	GET http://Aky/s...	1	200	2445
12	15-Mar-01 09:05:47	192_168_1_8-...	GET http://Aky/s...	0	200	1023
13	15-Mar-01 09:05:48	192_168_1_8-...	GET http://Aky/s...	0	200	1117
14	15-Mar-01 09:05:48	192_168_1_8-...	GET http://Aky/s...	0	200	4106
15	15-Mar-01 09:05:48	192_168_1_8-...	GET http://Aky/s...	0	200	884
16	15-Mar-01 09:05:49	192_168_1_8-...	GET http://Aky/s...	0	200	776
17	15-Mar-01 09:05:49	192_168_1_8-...	GET http://Aky/s...	0	200	6373
18	15-Mar-01 09:05:49	192_168_1_8-...	GET http://Aky/s...	1	200	7745
19	15-Mar-01 09:05:49	192_168_1_8-...	GET http://Aky/s...	0	200	1004
20	15-Mar-01 09:05:50	192_168_1_8-...	GET http://Aky/s...	0	200	3814
21	15-Mar-01 09:05:51	192_168_1_8-...	GET http://Aky/s...	50942	200	1034
22	15-Mar-01 09:05:55	192_168_1_8-...	GET http://Aky/s...	0	200	3635
23	15-Mar-01 09:05:56	192_168_1_8-...	GET http://Aky/s...	0	200	2445
24	15-Mar-01 09:06:00	192_168_1_8-...	GET http://Aky/s...	91187	200	1034
25	15-Mar-01 09:07:58	192_168_1_8-...	GET http://Aky/s...	1	200	3635
26	15-Mar-01 09:08:48	192_168_1_8-...	GET http://Aky/s...	1	200	3635

Tip: Right-click within the table and use the menu options to **Filter** and **Export** the data.

Note: Click ☒, in the Title Bar of a graph or table to close it or deselect the display option in the Results Window.

Display Custom Collector Graphs

1. Open a Test and click the **Results** tab in the Test Pane.

   The Results Window opens automatically listing all Test-runs associated with the current Test. Results are stored in date and time stamped folders.

2. In the Results Window, double-click on a Test-run folder or click ⊞ , to open it and display the available results.
3. Click the **Custom NT** or **Custom SNMP** from the list results option to open your selection in the Test Pane.

   The Custom NT Performance Graph is displayed below:

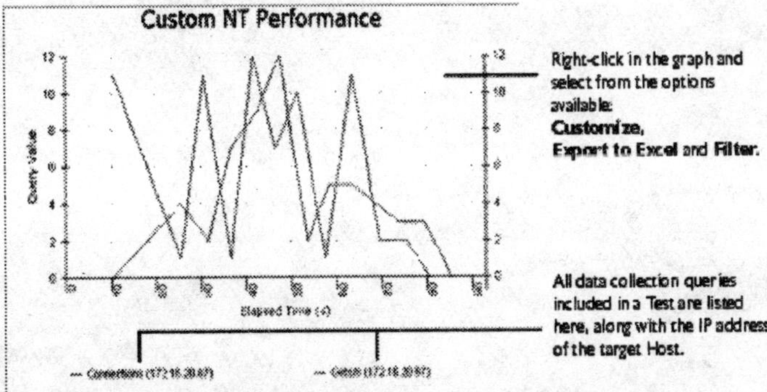

Note: Graphs are displayed in the default line plot style. Right-click within a graph and select **Customize** from the menu to change their appearance.

Tip: Right-click within the graph and use the menu options to **Customize, Export to Excel** and **Filter** the data.

Tip: Display multiple graphs and tables concurrently to compare results using the Results Window.

Note: Click , in the Title Bar of a graph or table to close it or deselect the display option in the Results Window.

Performance Testing using Fiddler tool

What is Fiddler?

Fiddler is a Web Debugging Proxy which logs all HTTP(S) traffic between your computer and the Internet. Fiddler allows you to inspect all HTTP(S) traffic, set breakpoints, and "fiddle" with incoming or outgoing data. Fiddler includes a powerful event-based scripting subsystem, and can be extended using any .NET language.

Fiddler is freeware and can debug traffic from virtually any application, including Internet Explorer, Mozilla Firefox, Opera, and thousands more.

Features:

- Freeware Web Debugging Platform
- Easily installed from www.fiddler2.com
- Runs as a local proxy; registers as system proxy while capturing
- View, analyze and modify web traffic from any application that supports a proxy; including most devices (e.g. Windows Mobile)
- Enables HTTPS interception via self-signed certificate
- Extremely extensible, via JavaScript or .NET assemblies

Intercepting Web Traffic

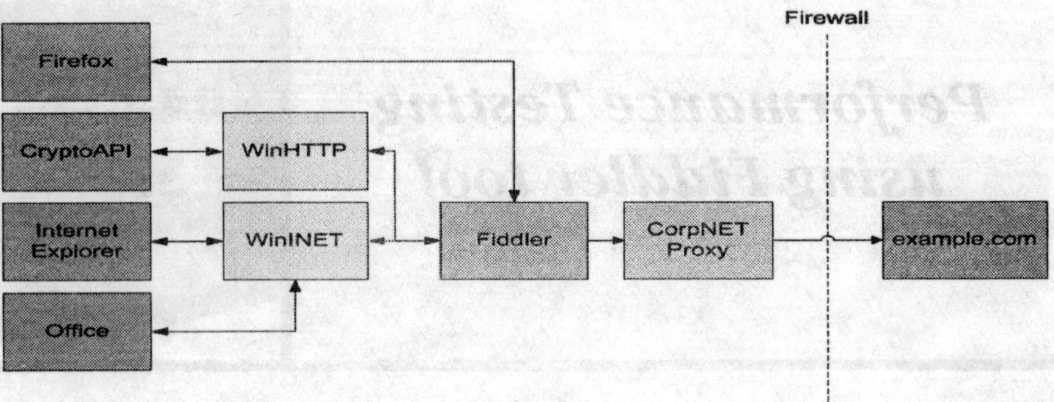

HTTPS support

- Man-in-the-middle – Intercepts HTTPS CONNECT tunnels and shows raw traffic

#	Result	Protocol	Host	URL	Body	Content-Type
4	200	HTTP	CONNECT	www.fidelity.com:443	590	
5	200	HTTPS	www.fidelity.com	/	11,212	text/htm
6	200	HTTP	CONNECT	www.fidelity.com:443	590	
7	200	HTTPS	www.fidelity.com	/nav/homepage_nav.js	1,209	applicati
8	200	HTTP	CONNECT	www.fidelity.com:443	590	

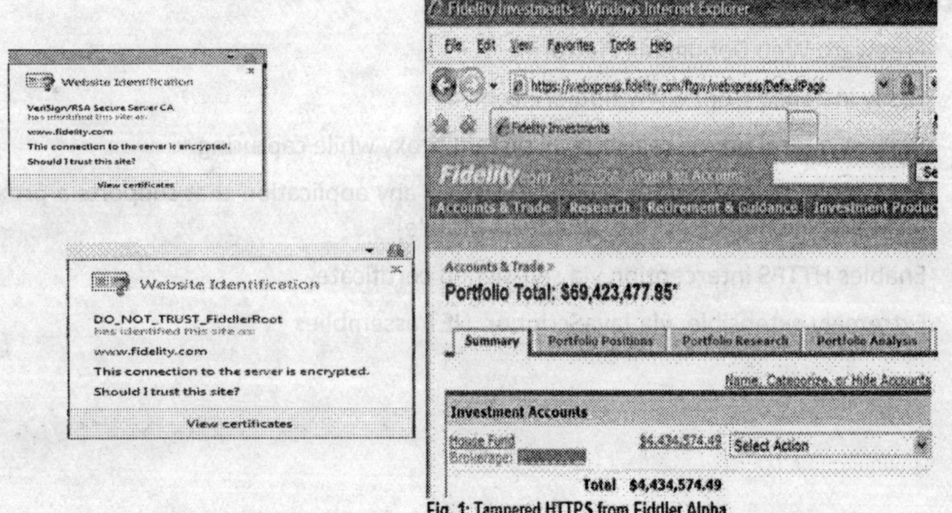

Fig. 1: Tampered HTTPS from Fiddler Alpha

Fiddler for Performance

Measure / analyze / simulate the end-user experience.

- Measure request size, page weight
- Analyze caching, compression, page composition
- Simulate low-speed / high-latency connections

Performance Statistics

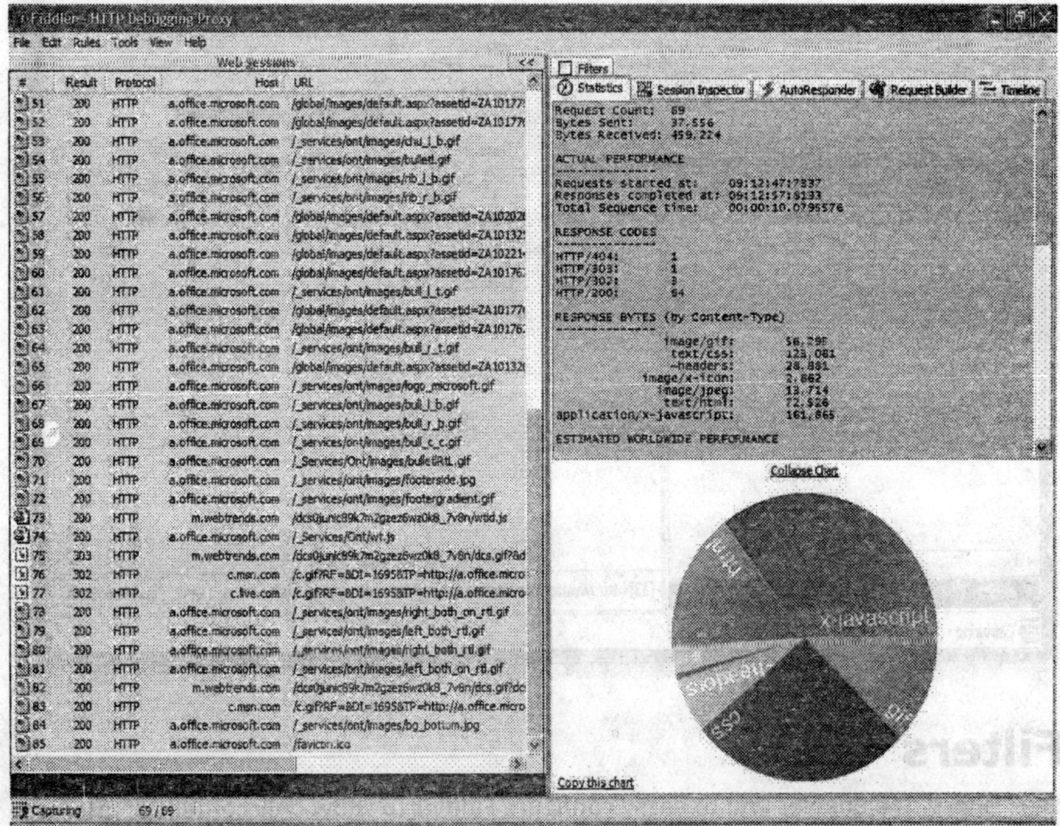

Session Timeline

The "Timeline" tab reveals the timing of request and responses. Right-click the timeline to enable Fiddler's "Streaming" mode.

In the session list, hit the "P" key to select the parent of the current request; hit the "C" key to select the current request and all of its children (sub-downloads).

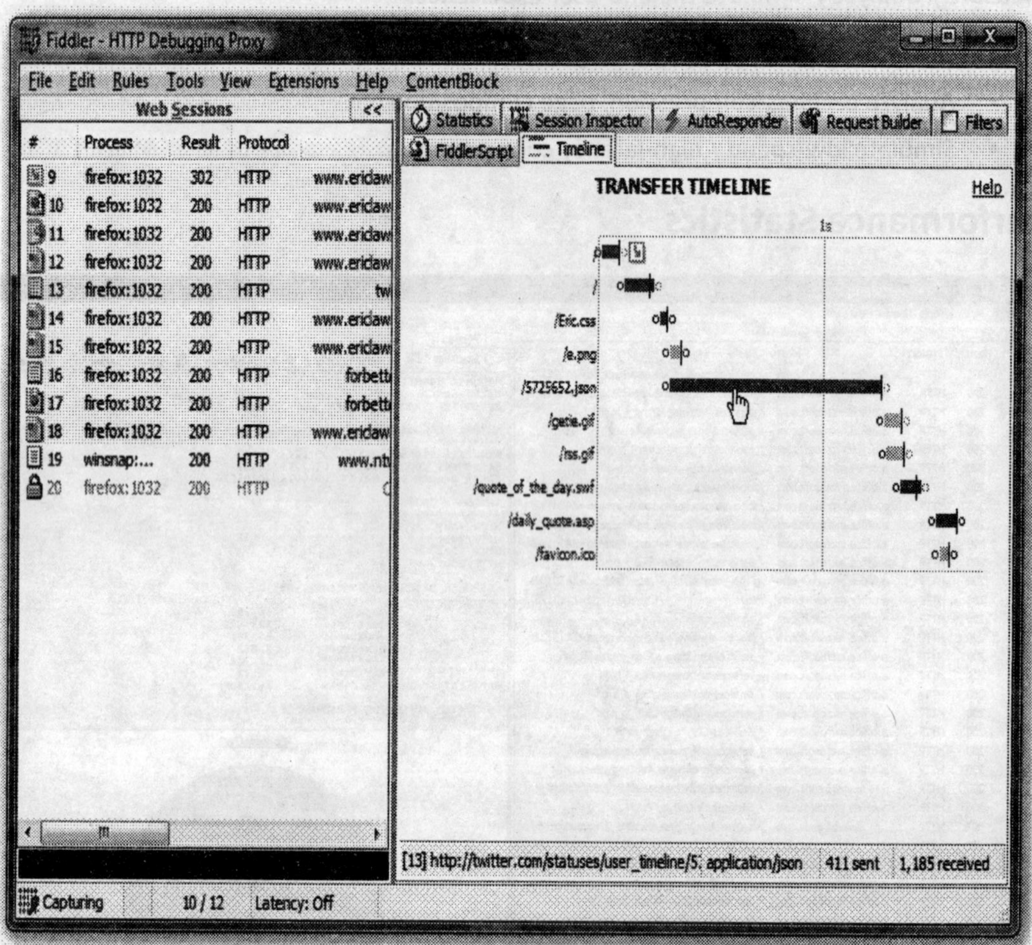

Filters

The "Filters" tab enables you to easily configure Fiddler to show only content of interest. Custom Rules written in JavaScript are more powerful, but the Filters tab is often all you'll need.

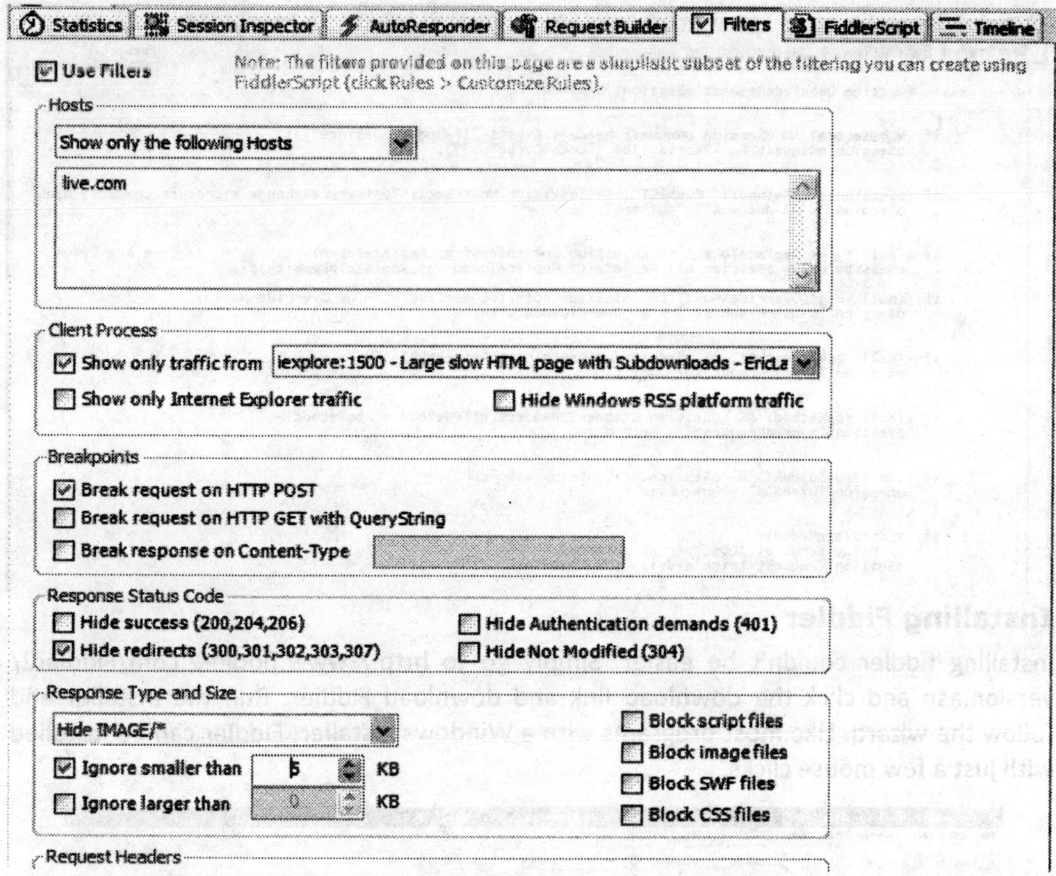

Custom Rules

Custom Rules written in JavaScript enable very powerful traffic filtering and modification. You can extend the Fiddler user-interface using rules. See http://www.fiddler2.com/fiddler/dev/ for more information.

Statistics | Session Inspector | AutoResponder | Request Builder | Filters | FiddlerScript | Timeline | Gallery

Save Script   OnBeforeRequest   OnBeforeResponse   OnExecAction   Find...

```
static function OnBeforeRequest(oSession: Session)
{
    if (m_bUseLocal && oSession.oRequest.headers.Exists("If-Modified-Since")){
        oSession.oRequest.FailSession(304, "LocalCache", "");
    }

    if (oSession.HTTPMethodIs("CONNECT") && (oSession.HostnameIs("primary.exchange.microsoft.com") || oSes
        oSession["x-no-decrypt"]="outlook";
    }

    if ((null != gs_ReplaceToken) && (oSession.url.indexOf(gs_ReplaceToken)>-1)){      // Case sensitive
        oSession.url = oSession.url.Replace(gs_ReplaceToken, gs_ReplaceTokenWith);
    }
    if ((null != gs_OverridenHost) && (oSession.host.toLowerCase() == gs_OverridenHost)){
        oSession["x-overridehost"] = gs_OverrideHostWith;
    }

    if ((null!=bpRequestURI) && oSession.uriContains(bpRequestURI)){
        oSession["x-breakrequest"]="uri";
    }

    if ((null!=bpMethod) && (oSession.oRequest.headers.HTTPMethod == bpMethod)){
        oSession["x-breakrequest"]="method";
    }

    if ((null!=uiBoldURI) && oSession.uriContains(uiBoldURI)){
        oSession["ui-bold"]="QuickExec";
    }

    if (m_SimulateModem){
        // Delay sends by 300ms per KB uploaded.
        oSession["request-trickle-delay"] = "300";
    }
```

Installing Fiddler

Installing fiddler couldn't be easier. Simply go to http://www.fiddler2.com/Fiddler2/version.asp and click the download link and download Fiddler. Run the installer and follow the wizard. Like most programs with a Windows installer, Fiddler can be installed with just a few mouse clicks.

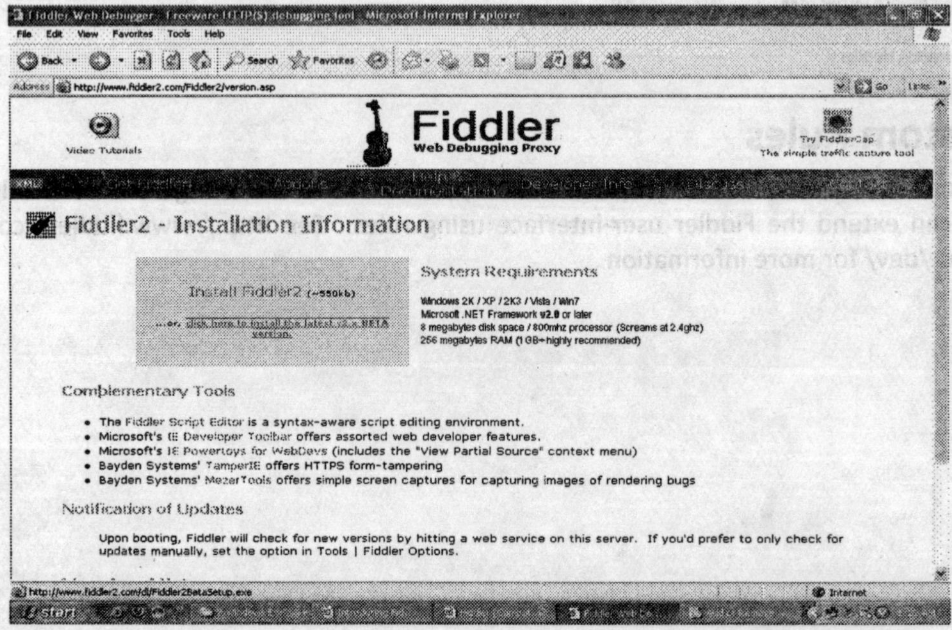

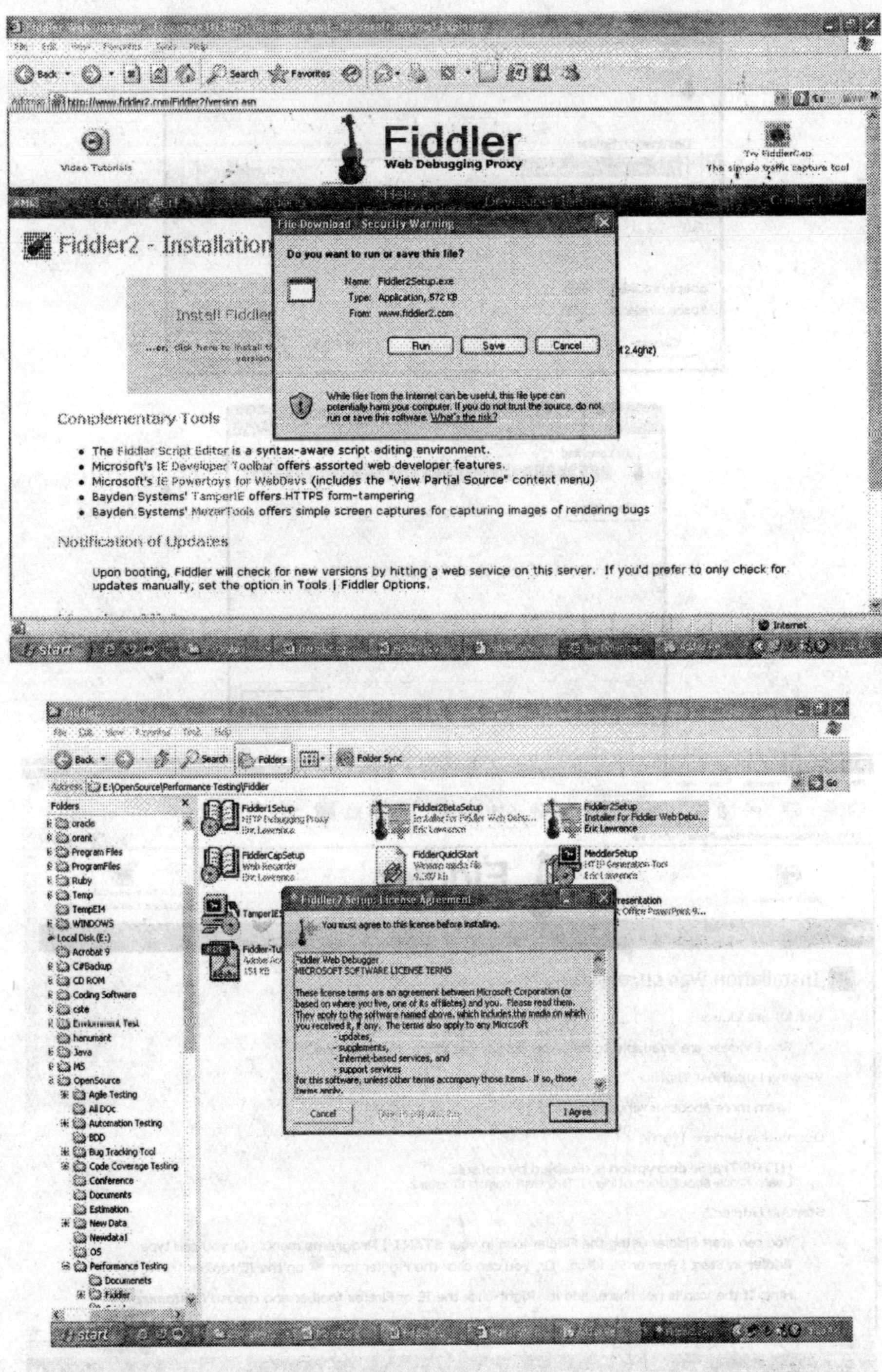
Fiddler
Web Debugging Proxy
Video Tutorials
Fiddler2 - Installation
File Download - Security Warning
Do you want to run or save this file?
Name: Fiddler2Setup.exe
Type: Application, 572 KB
From: www.fiddler2.com
Run
Save
Cancel
While files from the Internet can be useful, this file type can potentially harm your computer. If you do not trust the source, do not run or save this software. What's the risk?
Complementary Tools
The Fiddler Script Editor is a syntax-aware script editing environment.
Microsoft's IE Developer Toolbar offers assorted web developer features.
Microsoft's IE Powertoys for WebDevs (includes the "View Partial Source" context menu)
Bayden Systems' TamperIE offers HTTPS form-tampering
Bayden Systems' MezerTools offers simple screen captures for capturing images of rendering bugs
Notification of Updates
Upon booting, Fiddler will check for new versions by hitting a web service on this server. If you'd prefer to only check for updates manually, set the option in Tools | Fiddler Options.
E:\OpenSource\Performance Testing\Fiddler
Fiddler2 Setup: License Agreement
You must agree to this license before installing.
Fiddler Web Debugger
MICROSOFT SOFTWARE LICENSE TERMS
These license terms are an agreement between Microsoft Corporation (or based on where you live, one of its affiliates) and you. Please read them. They apply to the software named above, which includes the media on which you received it, if any. The terms also apply to any Microsoft
- updates,
- supplements,
- Internet-based services, and
- support services
for this software, unless other terms accompany those items. If so, those terms apply.
Cancel
I Agree

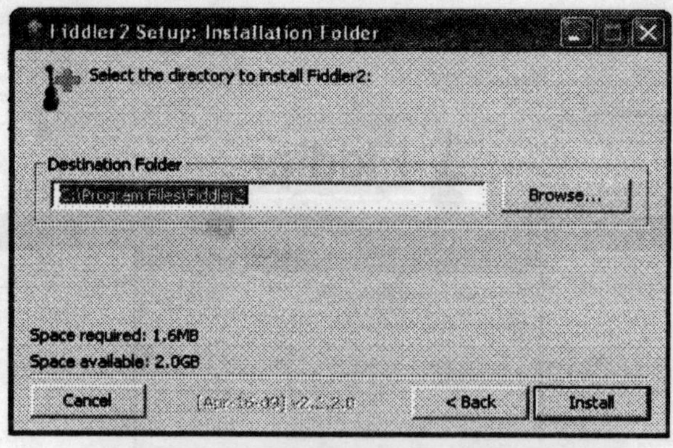
Fiddler2 Setup: Installation Folder
Select the directory to install Fiddler2:
Destination Folder
C:\Program Files\Fiddler2
Browse...
Space required: 1.6MB
Space available: 2.0GB
Cancel
< Back
Install

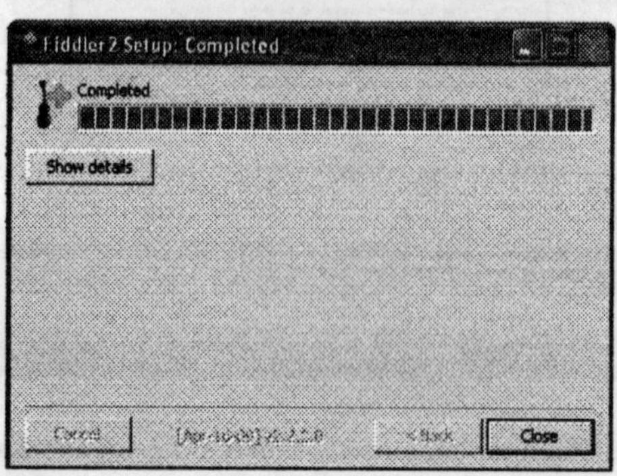
Fiddler2 Setup: Completed
Completed
Show details
Cancel
< Back
Close

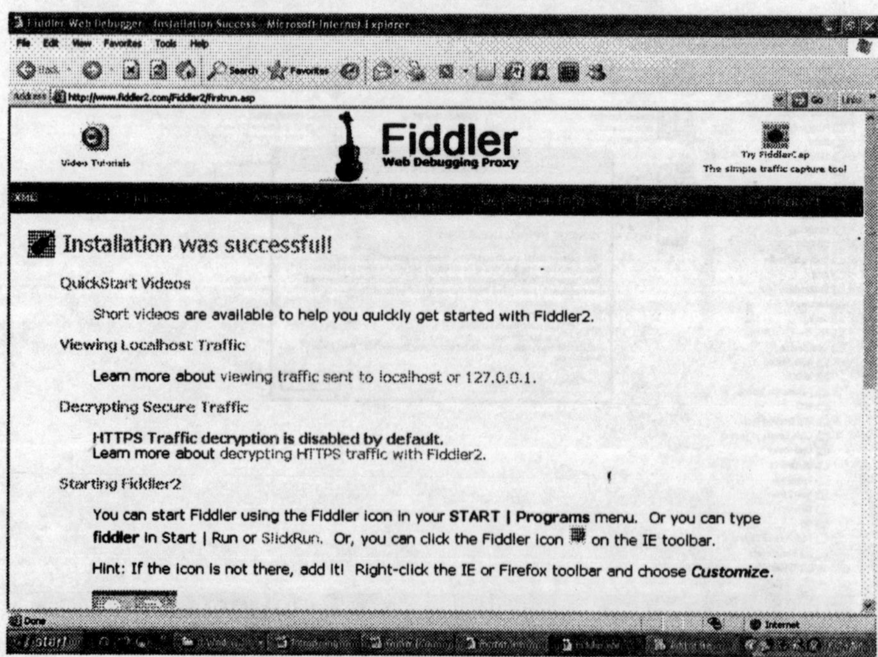
Fiddler
Web Debugging Proxy
Video Tutorials
Try FiddlerCap
The simple traffic capture tool
Installation was successful!
QuickStart Videos
Short videos are available to help you quickly get started with Fiddler2.
Viewing Localhost Traffic
Learn more about viewing traffic sent to localhost or 127.0.0.1.
Decrypting Secure Traffic
HTTPS Traffic decryption is disabled by default.
Learn more about decrypting HTTPS traffic with Fiddler2.
Starting Fiddler2
You can start Fiddler using the Fiddler icon in your START | Programs menu. Or you can type fiddler in Start | Run or SlickRun. Or, you can click the Fiddler icon on the IE toolbar.
Hint: If the icon is not there, add it! Right-click the IE or Firefox toolbar and choose Customize.

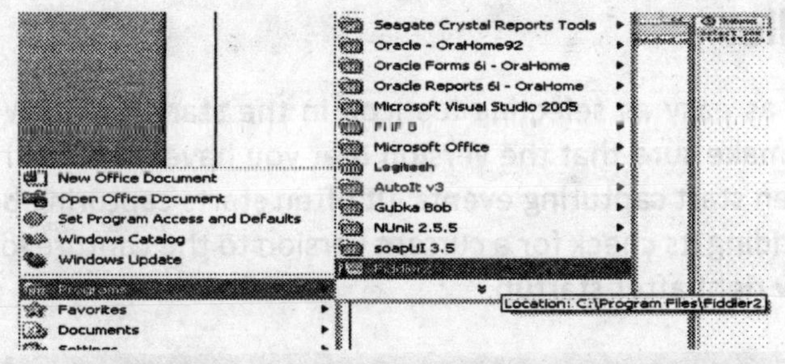
Seagate Crystal Reports Tools
Oracle - OraHome92
Oracle Forms 6i - OraHome
Oracle Reports 6i - OraHome
Microsoft Visual Studio 2005
Microsoft Office
Logitech
AutoIt v3
Gubka Bob
NUnit 2.5.5
soapUI 3.5
New Office Document
Open Office Document
Set Program Access and Defaults
Windows Catalog
Windows Update
Programs
Favorites
Documents
Location: C:\Program Files\Fiddler2

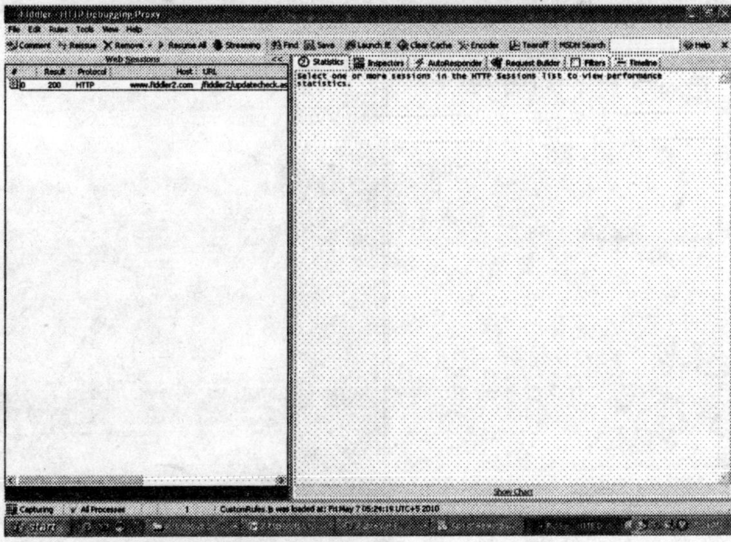

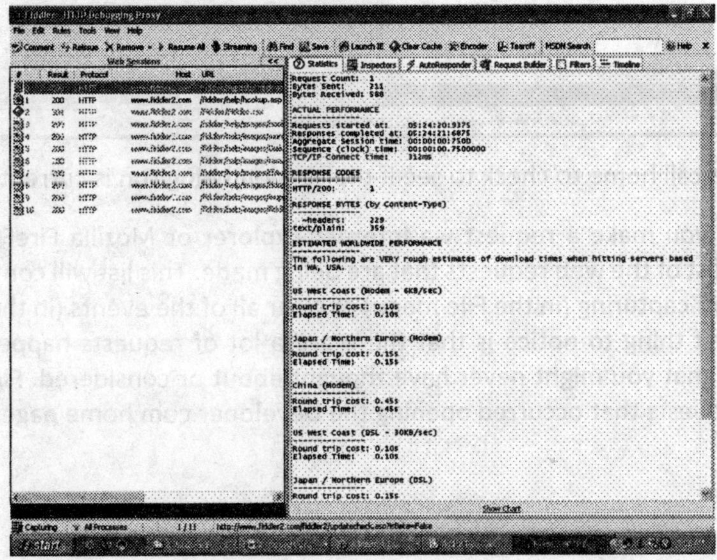

Running Fiddler

Running Fiddler is as easy as selecting it's icon in the start menu. When Fiddler starts up it will check to make sure that the version that you have is the current version of the software. It will then start capturing events. (It often starts capturing before it checks for a new version — adding its check for a current version to the capture log.) Figure 1 shows the Fiddler window right after startup.

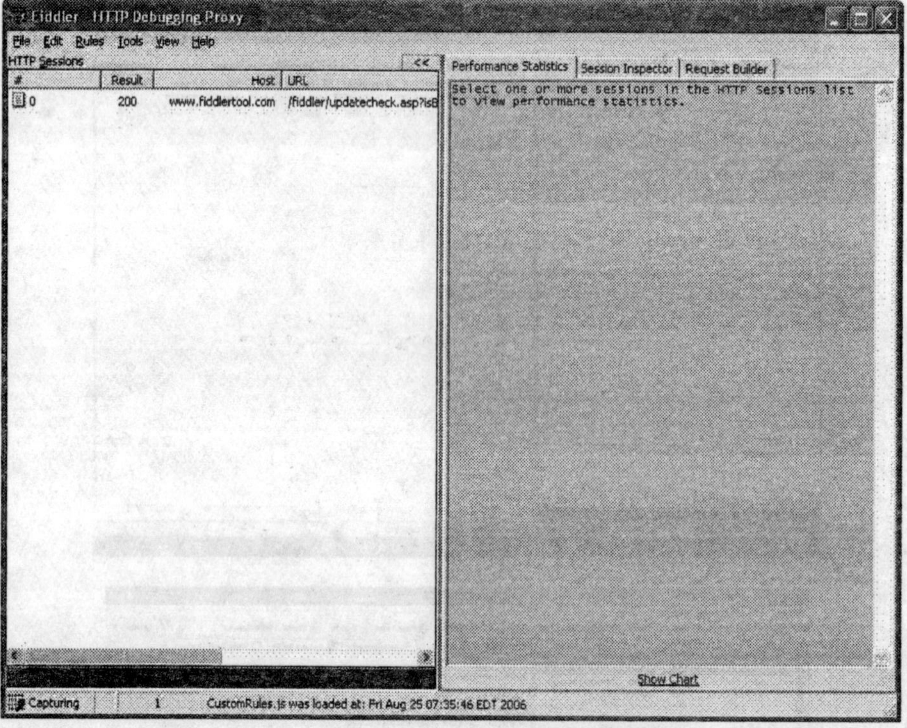

Fiddler makes a call home to check to see if the version being run is current.

If at this point you make a request via Internet Explorer or Mozilla FireFox and you'll instantly see a list of the web requests that are being made. This list will continue to grow until you turn off capturing (in the File menu) or clear all of the events (in the Edit menu). Perhaps the first thing to notice is that there are a lot of requests happening &mash; many of which that you might never have thought about or considered. Figure 2 shows some of the requests that occurred opening the Developer.com home page.

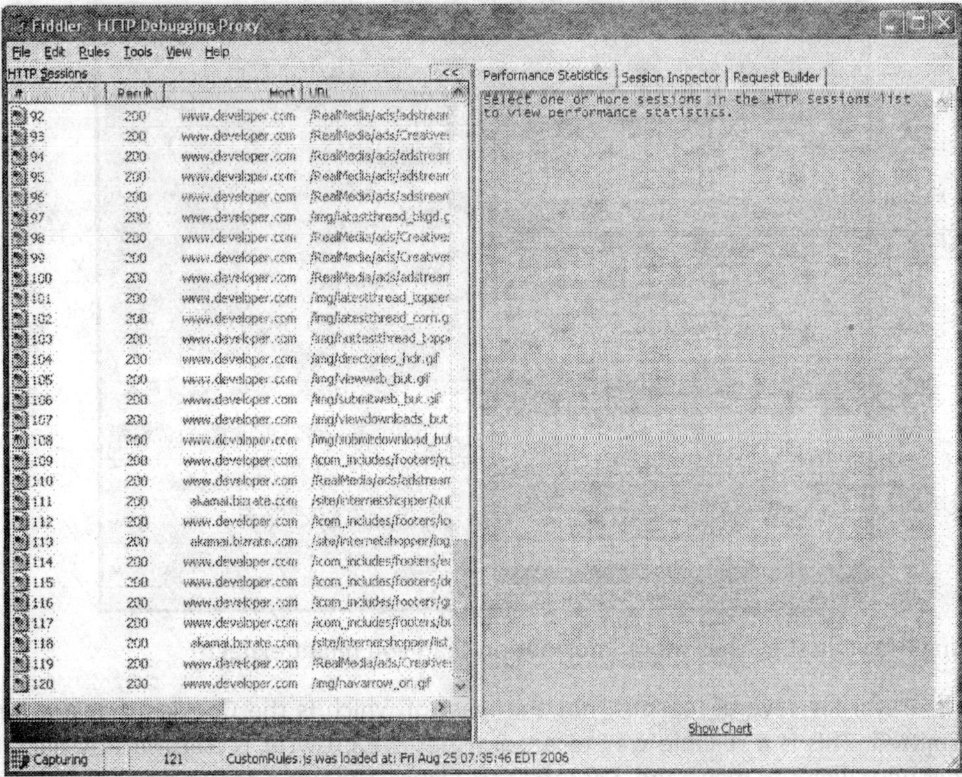

A single web page can be made up of over 100 individual requests.

Fiddler is helpful in two ways, the first way you've already seen. Requests are instantly logged and displayed in summary. However, this just tells you overall what happened it doesn't allow you to dig into the details to understand what is happening with each request. That's why you need to dig into the Session Inspector.

Session Inspector

By simply clicking on one of the sessions in the session list on the left the right hand side of the screen will show you the estimated performance statistics for the session. While this information isn't particularly helpful, the information on the other tabs can be. By clicking the Session Inspector tab you'll see the contents of the request that you sent. The headers button is pressed down by default so you'll see all of the headers in the request. Figure 3 shows the detail of one request made to Developer.com.

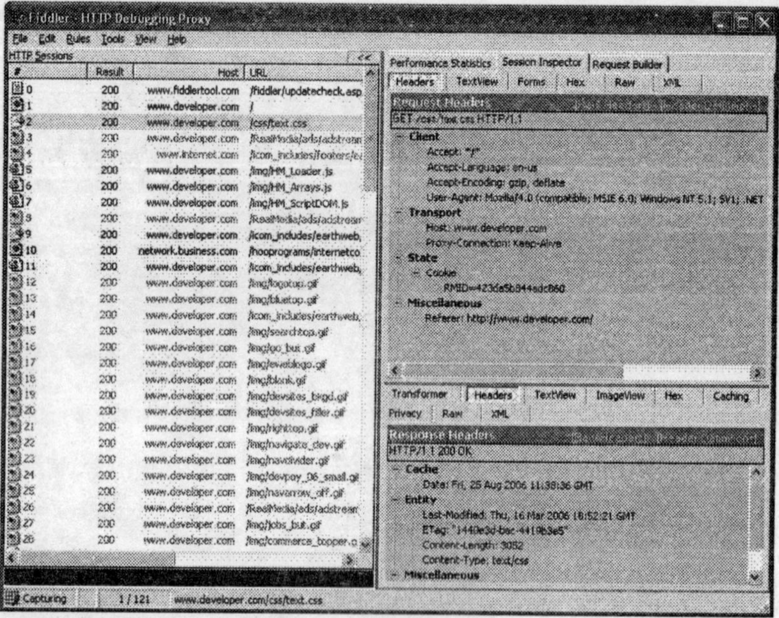

Getting the style sheet has more information than you might expect

This is useful for several reasons, not the least of which is the Cookies that are being transmitted. This is a reliable way to ensure that the browser is transmitting back the cookies your web site may need. For instance, Figure 3 shows a cookie being transmitted to retrieve the Cascading Style Sheet (CSS).

In the bottom half of the right hand side is the response. This is the entire response being sent back to the client browser. By clicking the Headers button you'll see the headers transmitted with the response. This is important because it includes cache directives, cookies, and additional information about the response. This can be used to see whether your web page is transmitting cookies back to the client.

You can also click the text view button to see text type files that are returned or image view for the images that are returned. This allows you to see specifically what was returned to the browser before it was interpreted. This is a much more convenient view than hitting view source on each page you come to — changing the request you're looking at is as simple as clicking on a new request on the left hand side. In addition, since all requests are logged any redirect that you get — that you wouldn't be able to do a show source on in Internet Explorer will also be visible. Figure 4 shows the image view of the request for the EARTHWEB logo.

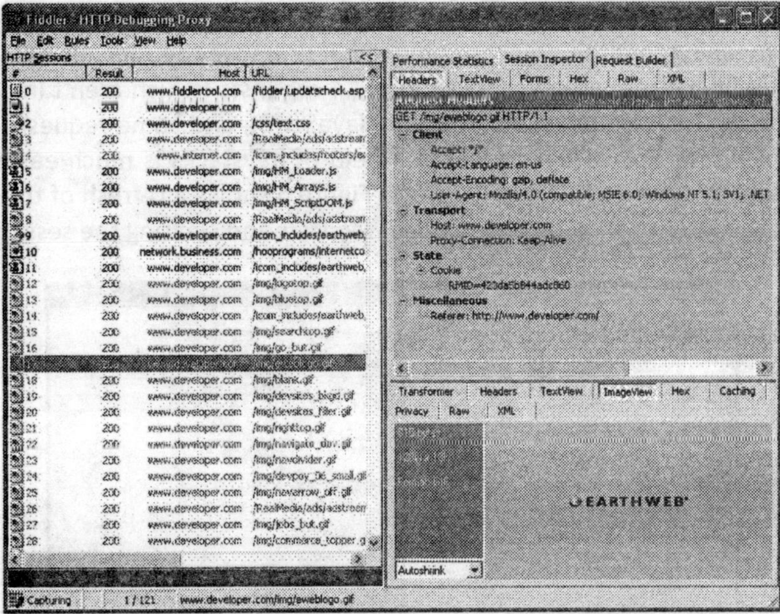

Quickly view what a response contains with the text view or image view.

Of course, with all this information it's easy to become overwhelmed. Just opening the home page of developer.com my browser issued more than 100 requests. Because of this it may make sense to add some filtering so that you can focus on the results that you need.

Filtering the Results

Sifting through hundreds of requests as you navigate your application can be daunting. Minimizing the requests that you don't want to see can become invaluable. There are two key rules that you can add that will filter the results. They are:

- **Hide all 200s** — This rule will remove all of the successful web requests. (An HTTP status code of 200 means success.)This is handy when you're just trying to walk around the application looking for problems and don't want to have to look through all of the successes to find the missing files, content expiration intervals that aren't properly set, etc.

- **Hide Image Requests** — In some ways more valuable than hiding the successful requests. Since there's rarely debugging that you're trying to do on how images come down you can hide the image requests.

If I turn on both Hide all 200s and Hide Image Requests I get one session logged in fiddler. It has a 302 meaning that the object has moved. If I remove the Hide all 200s option and leave the hide image requests, I get a total of 14 requests (which aren't images). These requests include the main page, style sheets, JavaScript, and some requests to fetch ad content. Looking for the virtual needle in a field of haystacks is much easier once you reduce the search down to just one haystack. Figure 5 shows a refresh of the Developer.com home page after turning on *Hide Image Requests* and clearing the sessions.

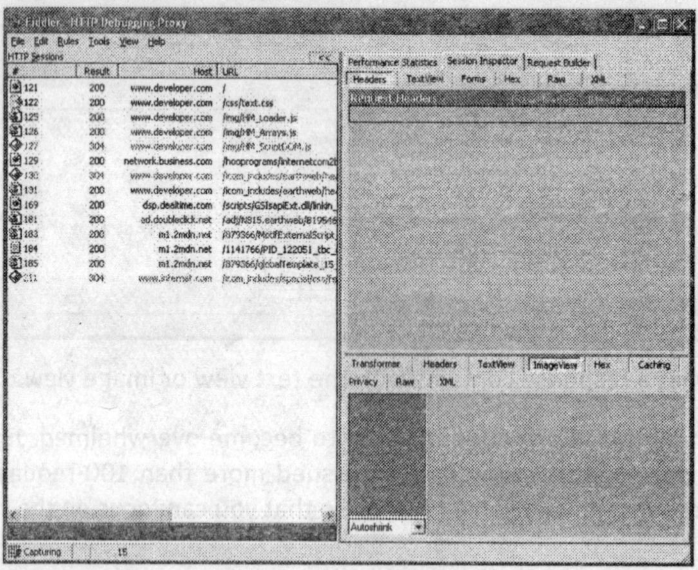

Fewer is better when you're trying to sift through data to find what you want.

Common Observations with Fiddler

Once you've filtered the results you're left with the unenviable task of figuring out what the results mean. If you're tracking down the details of what cookies and form postings are traveling back and forth then it's simply a matter of walking through the details. However, what if you're looking at the general health of the application? What do you do with the results that you find? The following sections quickly discuss each HTTP status that you can get back, what it means, and what to do about it.

301 — Moved Permanently

This HTTP status means that a redirect was used – and that the redirect told the browser that the redirect would remain in effect indefinitely. The URL that the web browser asked for has permanently moved to a new location. This may mean that your application is referring to a directory on the web site without a final slash. So if the reference is http://www.thorprojects.com/blog the reference should be http://www.thorprojects.com/blog/ because blog isn't a file it's a directory.

302 — Object Moved

This type of status is a temporary redirect. This is the kind of redirect that most developers are familiar with. It tells the web browser that the object has temporarily moved to a new location. These are normal for applications that post back to the same page, validate the input, perform the operation, and then redirect the user to another page. These generally don't represent a problem unless there are a lot of them.

304 — Not Modified

This type of status indicates that the web browser asked the server if the image had been modified since the browser had cached it. The browser sent a request for the file but indicated in the request that it had a cached copy and that the web server shouldn't bother sending it back unless it changed. This typically indicates that the cache control headers aren't present in the responses the browser is receiving. As a result it caches the response but has to check with the web server to see if its cache is still valid. This can be a performance problem. Since not a lot of data is transmitted it doesn't have a huge impact on overall bandwidth, however, because there can be many of these requests the latency of each call to check whether an image has changed or not can add up to a significant wait time for the user. By setting caching headers in the response that the browser receives these 304 statuses can all but be eliminated.

400 — Bad Request

This status code means that the web server didn't understand the request from the client. Although this occurs rarely it can be a problem if it's occurring frequently. This typically points to components integrated into the web server, such as ISAPI filters, which are mangling the request but can sometimes point to poorly encoded data in the request.

404 — Not Found

This status message is the most infamous status on the Internet. It means that the web server couldn't find the content that was requested. If this is the main page that the user has requested this will be obvious as they get a 404 page. However, if it's for a JavaScript file, a CSS file, or other supporting files for the page, the user may not know anything is wrong. The best solution here is to track down the references and update them.

500 — Server Error

This status message is a bit more ominous than the others here. It's more ominous because it means that the server wasn't able to complete the processing of the request. This can indicate a greater server problem or at the very least instability that should be addressed. As with other errors it may be hidden in an embedded object and can be easily missed.

502 — Connection Issue

This status message indicates that a connection message couldn't be made to the server. This could mean that the name wasn't translated or that there are problems in the underlying transport of packets to the server. Either case indicates a broader networking issue. You'll need to make sure that you have thoroughly tested the underlying network before continuing to debug the issue.

Conclusion

Fiddler is the electronic equivalent of an X-Ray that can get into the traffic going between your web application and the web server to make sure that everything is OK. Fiddler can tell you what was wrong in a specific interaction and can show you at a glance what problems there are with the overall conversation. It's an invaluable tool for anyone who develops web applications — no matter whether that development is in .NET, Java, Cold Fusion, or some other language.

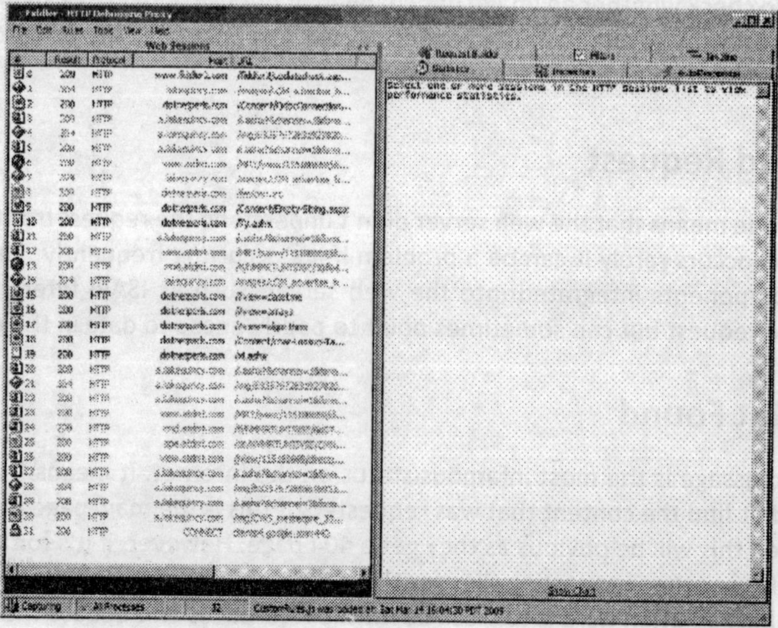

1. HTTP and Fiddler

For the example, I will examine private caching in ASP.NET. I required a private cache in ASP.NET, meaning one that only the **browser** would keep. Then I use Fiddler to see what happens

2. Getting started

You don't need to change any code to use Fiddler, but here I show the ASP.NET code so we can see what it does. We enable ASP.NET caching and use Fiddler to make sure it works right.

3. How can I force client-side caching?

You can't. But you can allow it. You can use HttpCachePolicy in ASP.NET to indicate to the browsers that they don't need to re-download pages every time.

4. Add client caching in ASP.NET

Here we tell browsers to cache pages in their memory. This saves network accesses, and makes everything faster. Use HttpCachePolicy in ASP.NET.

```
//
// Suggest browsers cache the page.
//
Response.Cache.SetCacheability(HttpCacheability.Private);

Response.Cache.SetExpires(DateTime.Now.AddMinutes(5));
```

5. How can I use Fiddler?

Open it alongside Internet Explorer, Google Chrome, or Safari. Fiddler is a **HTTP debugging proxy**, and we use it to see HTTP connections. It is not only for ASP.NET or IIS. Similar tools are available in Firebug and Safari.

- **The left side shows connections.**
  These connections are made. The first column shows the Result, which is 200 for HTTP success. Other codes are the famous 404, and 302.
- **It uses special icons.**
  on the left side, blue indicates requests and green indicates downloads. You see when a page wasn't in the client-side cache.

6. Server-side caching

Servers can also cache HTML on their end, but Fiddler can't distinguish these loads. Server-cached pages will still be sent even if they haven't changed.

7. Use Fidder to check caching

You should make it in such a manner that when the user clicks back, your page loads from the browser cache. Visitors click the site icon multiple times. Test this with Fiddler.

8. Use Fiddler with GZIP compression

You can use Fiddler to see how much GZIP compression would help your website. Click the radio button on the **Transformer** tab to count bytes.

Use HexView. You can read the raw binary in GZIP files using HexView. I used this to see the original file names in my GZIP files. This is useful for low-level server bugs.

9. Use Fiddler's ImageView

On the ImageView tab, you can see the images that are sent through HTTP. This is useful for dynamic images, such as those in ASHX handlers. [ASP.NET ASHX Handler Tutorial-dotnetperls.com]

10. Use Fiddler to examine headers

On the right side of Fiddler (which you can open by double clicking on an item in the left pane), click on Inspectors -> Headers. These are the raw HTTP headers.

11. Statistics and more

On the statistics pane, Fiddler offers some estimates about transfer times. I have not found these to be useful. Use web benchmarks instead. [ASP.NET HTTP Compression Overvie - dotnetperls.com]

12. Summary

Caching is complex, but tools like Fiddler or Firebug make it **much easier to debug**. Using private caching on dynamic pages is important. I explore cache expiration and show code to allow output caching elsewhere on this site.

How do I configure an application to use Fiddler?

Fiddler is an HTTP Proxy running on port 8888 on your local PC. You can configure any application which accepts a HTTP Proxy to run through Fiddler so you can debug its traffic.

WinINET-based applications (E.g. Microsoft Office, Internet Explorer, etc) should automatically use Fiddler while it's running and the "Capture Traffic" box is checked on the Fiddler File menu.

If they do not, they can be configured to use Fiddler by setting the appropriate option in the Internet Explorer **Tools | Internet Options | Connections | LAN Settings** dialog. (You can also get to this dialog in the **Tools | Internet Options** menu inside Fiddler).

Can I monitor RAS, VPN, or dialup connections?

Fiddler 2.2.0.3 and later introduces a new option which enables automatic monitoring of dialup or VPN connections:

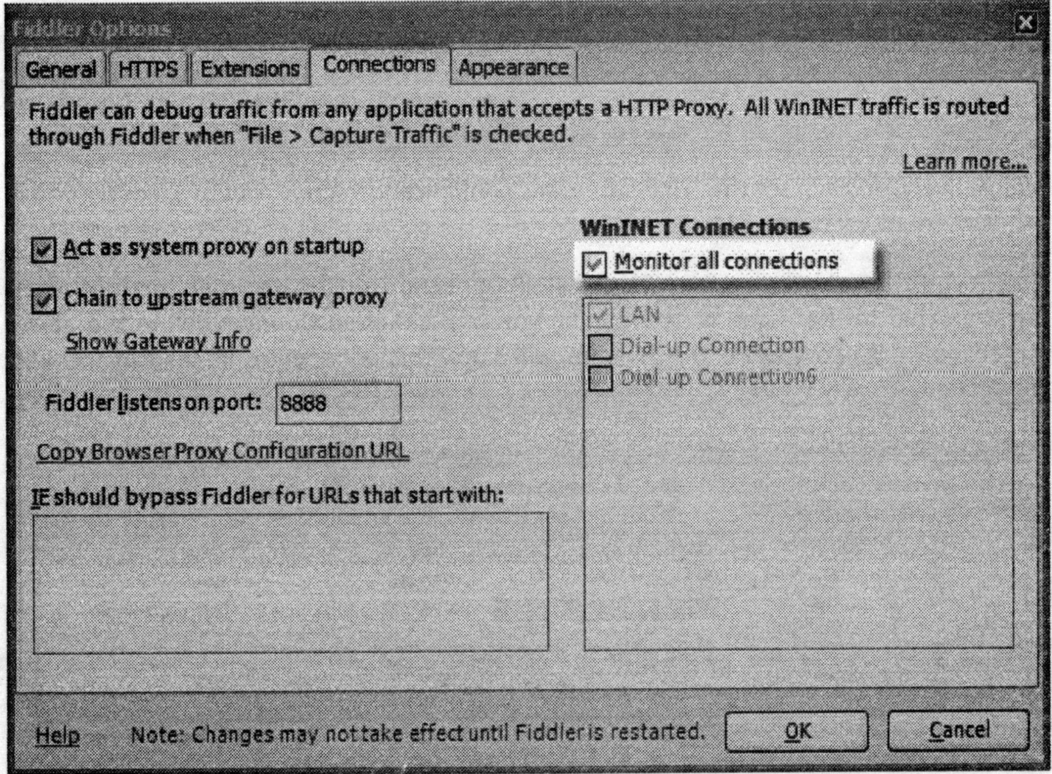

Otherwise, you'll need to set the Proxy Configuration manually. Set the proxy for your VPN/dialup connection as follows:

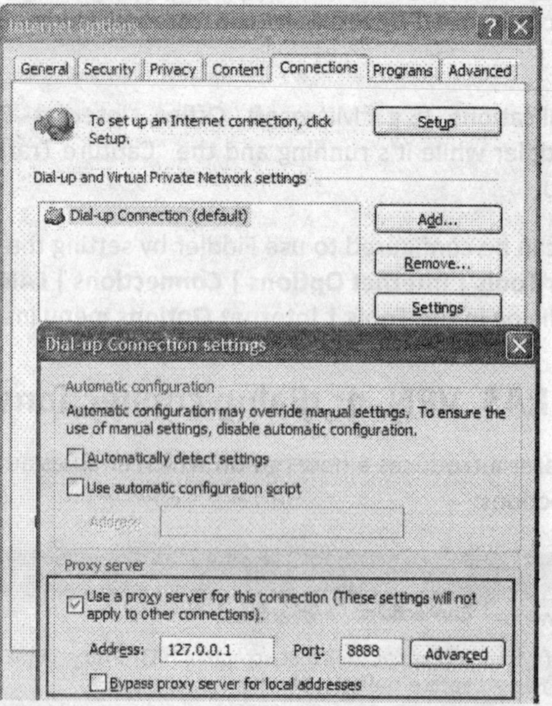

Alternatively, you can set the "Use automatic configuration script" option as described in the "Other browsers" tip below.

Note: If you *always* have an active VPN or dialup connection, set the **HookConnectionNamed** registry value to the name of the Connection (e.g. "Dial-up Connection" in the above screenshot). When you do this, Fiddler will hook this connection instead of the LAN connection.

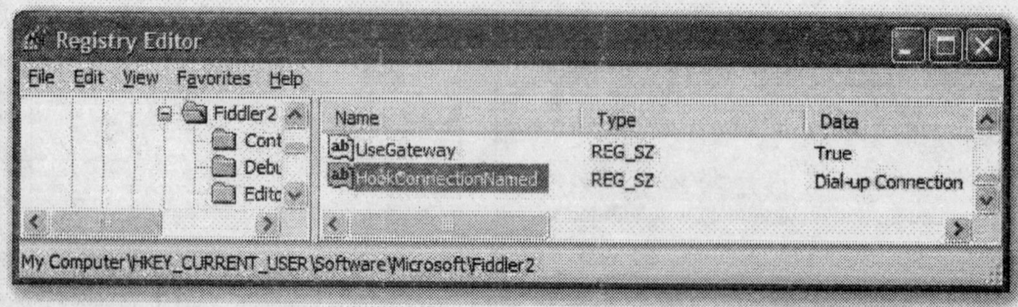

Note: IE will always use the proxy settings from any active VPN connection, without regard to whether or not that VPN connects to the Internet.

How can I configure a .NET v1.1 application to use Fiddler?

If you're coding a .NET application, K Scott Allen's blog shows a simple way to hook Fiddler temporarily for debugging purposes:

```
GlobalProxySelection.Select = new WebProxy("127.0.0.1", 8888);
```

Note that you might not even need to do this-- The Framework should autodetect the WinINET proxy when the .NET application starts. Note that this means that Fiddler must be started BEFORE your application if your application is to autodetect Fiddler.

Another setting to check is in machine.config, ensure the following is present:

```
<proxy usesystemdefault="true" />
```

If all else fails, you can manually specify the proxy on an individual WebRequest object, like so:

```
objRequest = (HttpWebRequest)WebRequest.Create(url);
objRequest.Proxy= new WebProxy("127.0.0.1", 8888);
```

Important: Regardless of other settings, .NET will always bypass the Fiddler proxy for URLs containing *localhost*. So, rather than using localhost, change your code to refer to the machine name. For instance:

Does not show in Fiddler: http://localhost/X509SignCodeService/X509SigningService.asmx
Shows in Fiddler: http://mymachine/X509SignCodeService/X509SigningService.asmx

How can I configure a .NET v2.0 application to use Fiddler?

It's even easier. See: http://msdn.microsoft.com/en-us/magazine/cc300743.aspx for details.

How can I configure a Java application to use Fiddler?

Per http://www.davidreilly.com/java/java_network_programming/#2.4 you should be able to do something like:

```
jre -DproxySet=true -DproxyHost=127.0.0.1 -DproxyPort=8888 MyApp
```

Why don't I see traffic sent to http://localhost or http://127.0.0.1?

IE7 and the .NET Framework are hardcoded not to send requests for Localhost through any proxies, and as a proxy, Fiddler will not receive such traffic.

The workaround is to use your machine name as the hostname instead of Localhost or 127.0.0.1. So, for instance, rather than hitting http://**localhost**:8081/mytestpage.aspx, instead visit http://**machinename**:8081/mytestpage.aspx.

...Or, if you're using Fiddler v2.1.8 or later, just use **http://ipv4.fiddler** to hit localhost on the IPv4 adapter, or use **http://ipv6.fiddler** to hit localhost on the IPv6 adapter. This works especially well with the Visual Studio test webserver (codename: Cassini) because the test server only listens on the IPv4 loopback adapter.

Lastly, you could Customize your Rules file like so:

static function OnBeforeRequest(oSession:Fiddler.Session){
if (oSession.HostnameIs("MYAPP")) **{oSession**.host = "127.0.0.1:8081";}
}

...and then just hit http://myapp, which will act as an alias for 127.0.0.1:8081.

How can I configure a WinHTTP application to use Fiddler?

You can either directly configure the WinHTTP application to point to Fiddler, in code, or you can use the following command at the command prompt to tell WinHTTP to use Fiddler:

On XP or below:

proxycfg -p http=127.0.0.1:8888;https=127.0.0.1:8888

...or this one to force WinHTTP to use WinINET's proxy settings:

proxycfg -u

On Vista or above:

netsh winhttp set proxy 127.0.0.1:8888

Can I configure IEMobile on PocketPC to use Fiddler?

Yes. This works over desktop-passthrough (ActiveSync connection).

On the device, set the HTTP proxy to be "ppp_peer:8888"

On your desktop, open port 8888 in Windows Firewall (Control Panel)

ActiveSync->Connection Settings... This Computer is connected to: "Work Network"

(Automatic will clobber the setting you did from #1)

Start Fiddler as you normally would Tools->Fiddler Options... check "Allow remote clients to connect" (Restart Fiddler) Connect your device to ActiveSync, fire up IEMobile and browse away...

Can I configure Fiddler to debug traffic from another machine (even a Mac or Unix box)?

Yes.

1. Start Fiddler on a Windows machine named (for example) WINBOX1.
2. In Fiddler, click to make sure Tools / Fiddler Options / *Allow remote clients to connect* is checked. (Restart Fiddler if this box wasn't already checked.)
3. On the other machine (Mac/Unix/Windows) set the proxy settings to WINBOX1:8888.

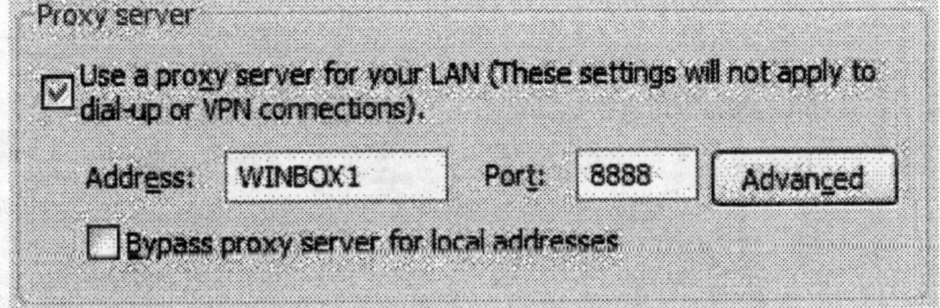

The second machine will now send its traffic through Fiddler running on WINBOX1.

How to configure other browsers to use Fiddler?

Current versions of Internet Explorer, Google Chrome, Apple Safari, and Opera all automatically use Fiddler when Fiddler is configured to Capture Traffic. (Opera requires that you start Fiddler **before** starting Opera).

Every browser allows you to connect a proxy server; usually this is the Options (or

Preferences) menu. You can either point directly at Fiddler (address: 127.0.0.1, port: 8888), or you can use Proxy Auto-configuration.

The advantage of auto-configuration is that Fiddler rewrites the configuration script when it is attached and detached, meaning you shouldn't need to manually enable or disable the proxy in your client depending on whether or not Fiddler is loaded. Simply restart the browser and the new setting is detected.

To configure Firefox to point at Fiddler, click Tools / Options / Advanced / Network / Settings, and adjust the settings like so:

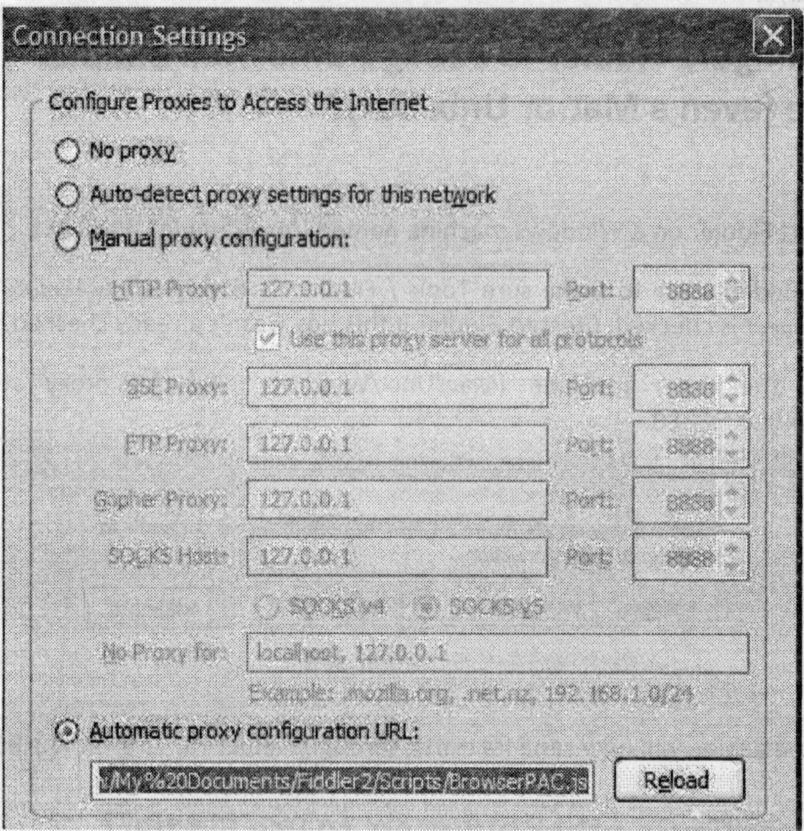

You can get the correct auto-configuration URL from Fiddler by clicking Tools / Fiddler Options / Connections, and clicking the "Copy Browser Proxy Configuration URL" link.

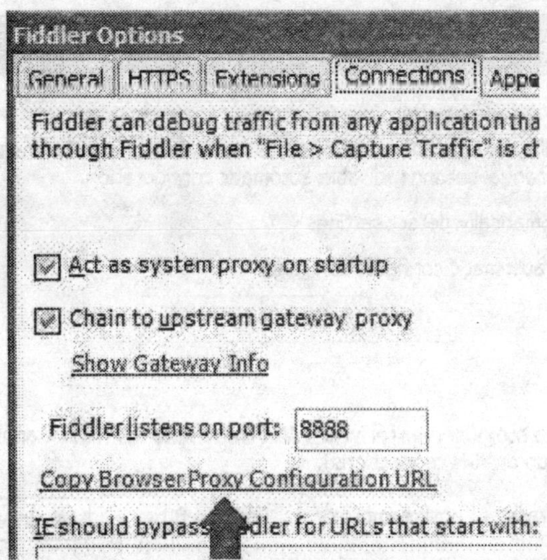

Can Fiddler "chain" to a manually-specified upstream proxy?

Yes, Fiddler supports chaining to another proxy. So, you end up with an architecture like so:

To configure Fiddler to use an upstream proxy:

1. Close Fiddler.
2. Inside IE, choose Tools | Internet Options | Connections.
3. Click the "LAN Settings" button.
4. On the dialog, set the options exactly as follows, replacing the "upstreamproxy" and "80" with the address and port of your proxy.

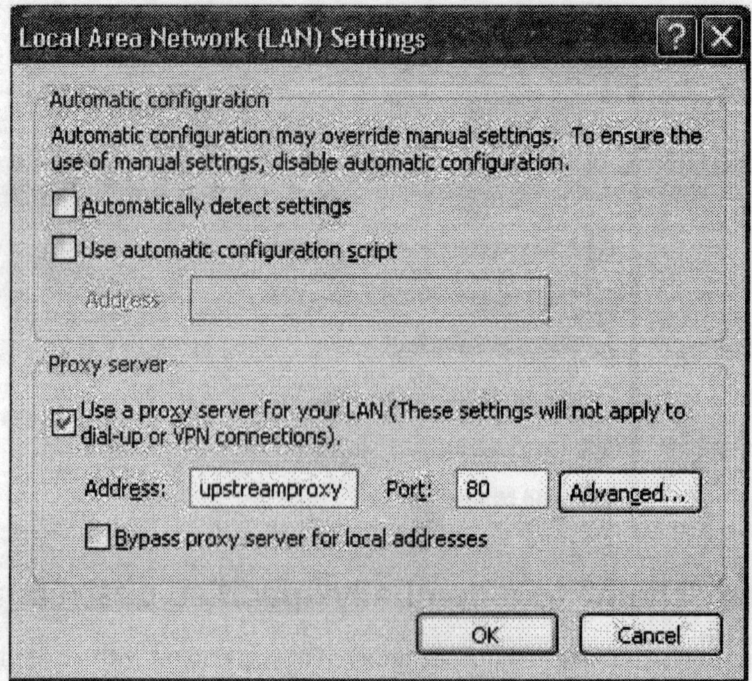

5. Hit Ok.
6. Close IE.
7. Start Fiddler.
8. In Fiddler, choose Help | About Fiddler.
9. You should see the upstream proxy listed in the About box.

Traffic Modification

- Redirect requests to a particular datacenter
- Simulate a downed server
- Prototype the performance cost of site changes
- Etc...

Traffic Archives

•Preserves the traffic and timings in compressed .SAZ (Session Archive ZIP) format•Great for regressing bugs

••Remote user capture using FiddlerCap

Tip: .SAZ files are maintained as ZIP archives. If you rename a .SAZ file to .ZIP, you can open it with Windows Explorer or WinZip and explore the traffic and timings stored within.

FiddlerCap - *www.fiddlercap.com*

FiddlerCap is a lightweight, easy-to-use client that archives traffic in .SAZ format. It's used by the Windows Live product support team and the IE Beta team for repro capture from non-technical users. SAZ files can be submitted by email or bug reporting systems for analysis by the product team.

Several simple configuration options are available. By default, the tool minimizes capture size by dropping binary response bodies (e.g. images/video) but retaining their headers for analysis.

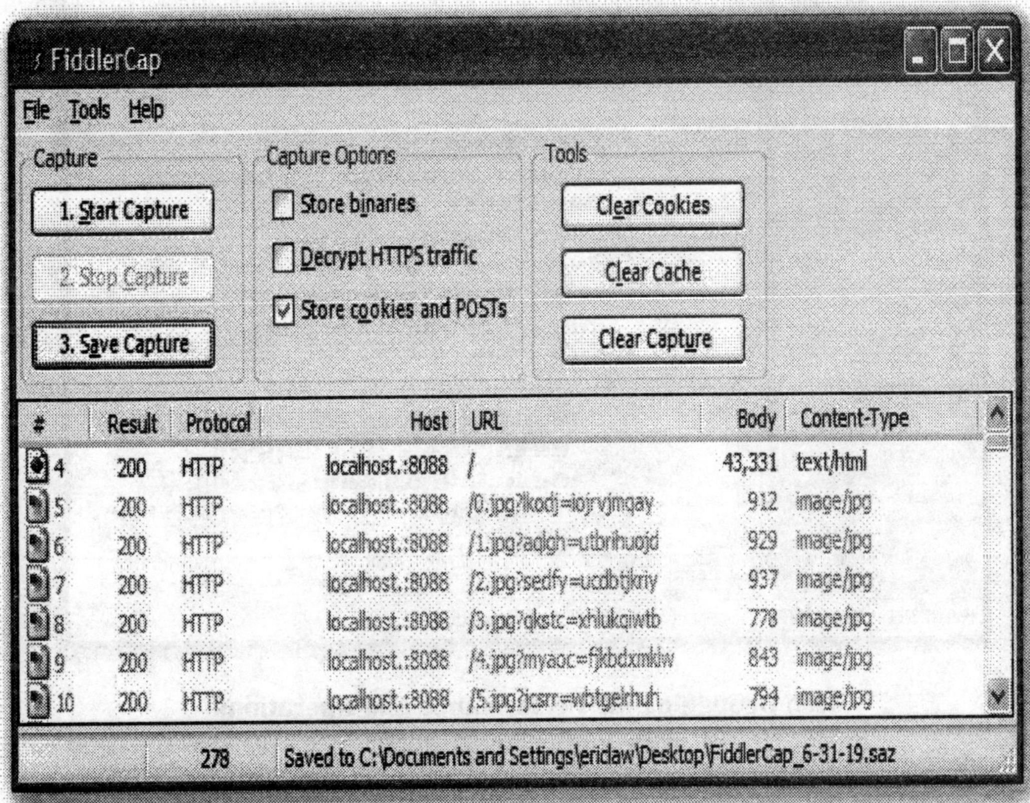

Meddler - www.fiddler2.com/meddler/

Meddler is a complementary tool to Fiddler. It is a simple scriptable HTTP server that allows full control over response headers, content, and connection handling. It can be useful for testing client code or performing offline demos.

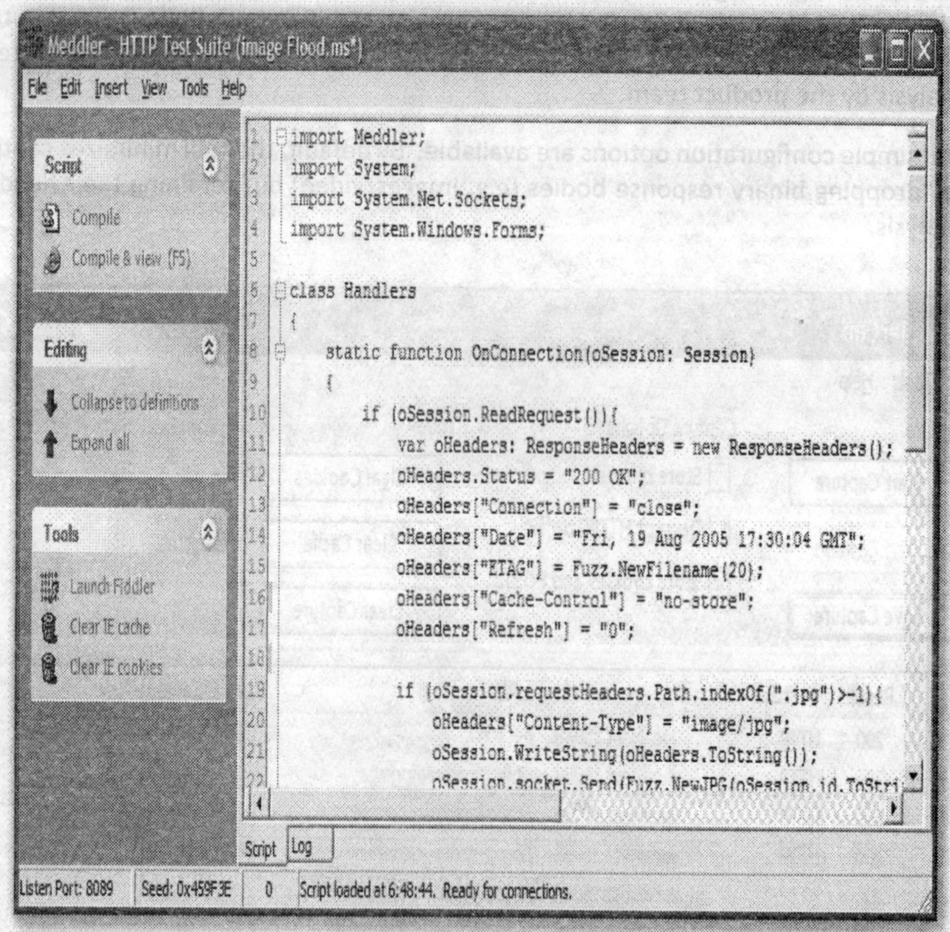

Web Debugging for Performance and Operations
www.fiddler2.com/perf/

Learn More...

www.fiddler2.com/fiddler/help/ for tutorials, demonstration videos, references, RSS, and the Fiddler Discussion Group

www.fiddler2.com/perf/ for performance-related content

Performance Testing Tool List

Sr No	Tool	Description
1	**Grinder**	The Grinder is a Java load-testing framework making it easy to orchestrate the activities of a test script in many processes across many machines, using a graphical console application
2	**Hammerhead 2 - Web Testing Tool**	Hammerhead 2 is a stress testing tool designed to test out your web server and web site. It can initiate multiple connections from IP aliases and simulated numerous (256+) users at any given time. The rate at which Hammerhead 2 attempts to pound your site is fully configurable, there are numerous other options for trying to create problems with a web site (so you can fix them)
3	**httperf**	Httperf is a tool for measuring web server performance. It provides a flexible facility for generating various HTTP workloads and for measuring server performance. The focus is not on implementing one particular benchmark but on providing a robust, high-performance tool that facilitates the construction of both micro and macro level benchmarks. The three distinguishing characteristics of httperf are its robustness, which includes the ability to generate and sustain server overload, support for the HTTP/1.1 and SSL protocols, and its extensibility

4	**http_load**	http_load runs multiple HTTP fetches in parallel, to test the throughput of a Web server. However, unlike most such test clients, it runs in a single process, to avoid bogging the client machine down. It can also be configured to do HTTPS fetches
5	**OpenWebLoad**	OpenWebLoad is a tool for load testing web applications. It aims to be easy to use and providing near real-time performance measurements of the application under test
6	**Siege**	SIEGE is an http regression testing and benchmarking utility. It was designed to let web developers measure the performance of their code under duress, to see how it will stand up to load on the internet. It lets the user hit a webserver with a configurable number of concurrent simulated users. Those users place the webserver "under siege." SCOUT surveys a webserver and prepares the urls. txt file for a siege. In order to perform regression testing, siege loads URLs from a file and runs through them sequentially or randomly. Scout makes the process of populating that file easier. You should send out the scout, before you lay siege
7	**WebLOAD**	WebLOAD Open Source is a fully functional, commercial-grade performance testing product based on WebLOAD, Radview's flagship product that is already deployed at 1,600 sites. Available for free download and use, WebLOAD is a commercial-grade open source project with more than 250 engineering years of product development. Companies that require commercial support, additional productivity features and compatibility with third-party protocols have the option of purchasing WebLOAD Professional directly from RadView

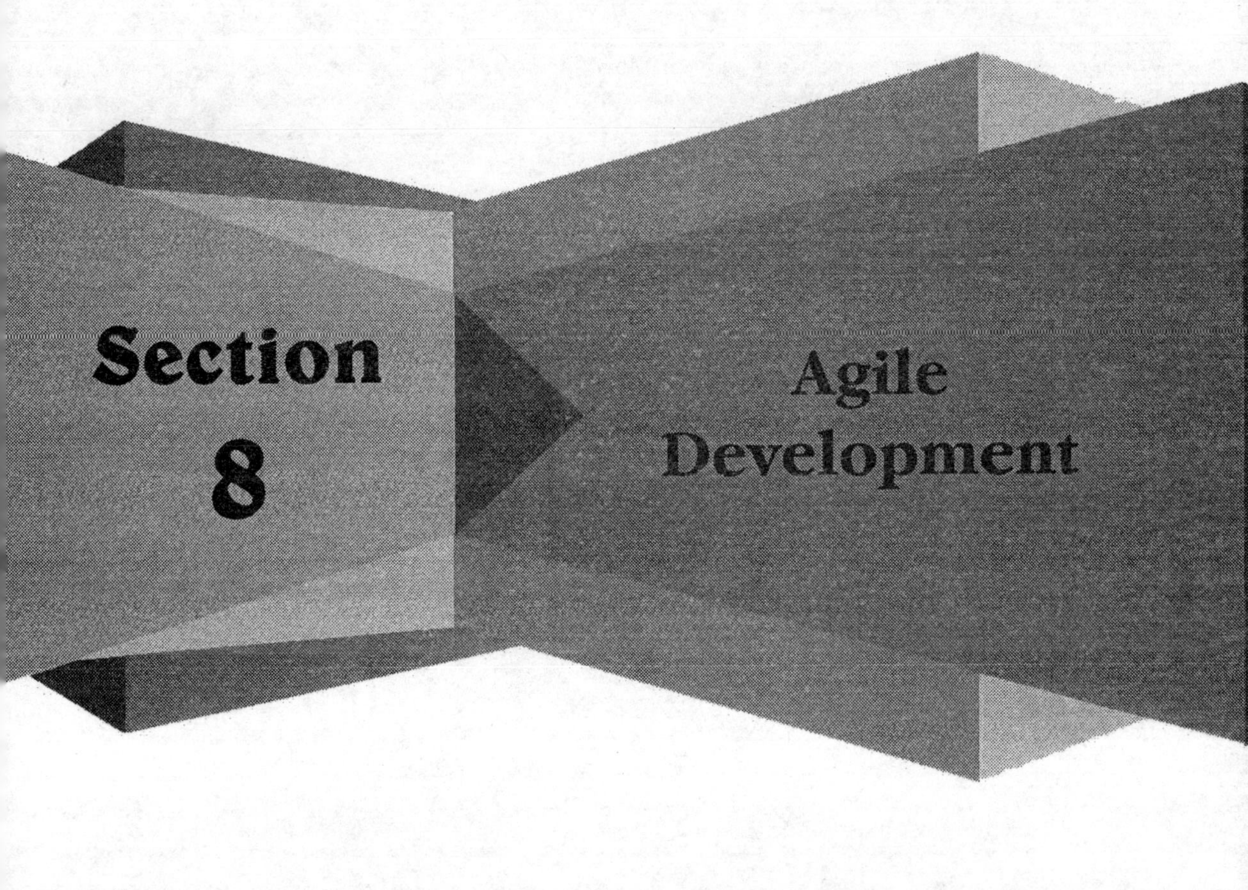
Section
8
Agile
Development

Unit Testing Is About Going Faster

Unit Testing is about delivering working software quickly. That means you need to be able to write the code quickly, get it to work (avoid and fix defects) and to be able to change and maintain the code in future. The fastest way to deliver working software is to write correct code, straight off, in one sitting, to a known set of requirements. Most programmers can't write code that's perfect, and most customers change their minds about the features they want (this is a good thing – we're embracing change). Your response as a programmer to the reality of imperfect code is to write unit tests to help check your work.

Mike Mason

http://mikemason.ca/2004/01/29#032UnitTestingIsAboutGoingFaster

When To Write Tests

Martin Fowler makes this easy for you. He says, "Whenever you are tempted to type something into a print statement or a debugger expression, write it as a test instead."...

Here are a couple of the times that you will receive a reasonable return on your testing investment:

- ***During Development - When you need to add new functionality to the system, write the tests first. Then you will be done developing when the test runs.***
- ***During Debugging - When someone discovers a defect in your code, first write a test that will succeed if the code is working. Then debug until the test succeeds.***

- **JUnit Test Infected: Programmers Love Writing Tests**

http://junit.sourceforge.net/doc/testinfected/testing.htm

What Is A Test?

- At the high-level, a test is a requirement. As every trained project manager knows, a project requirement must be "clear and testable." Automated tests are just automatic requirement checks.
  - There are tools, like FITnesse and Mercury's Quality Center, that handle this from the high level (functional and acceptance tests). This presentation will focus on the lower level unit tests.

- Probably the easiest way to think of what a good unit test is, is that it's something that verifies a piece of functionality's "contract."
  - Pre-conditions: Those things that must be true before you run the code. (Example: The object's buffer has been initialized.)
  - Post-conditions: Those things that must be true after you run the code. (Example: This method will never return null.)
  - Invariants: Those things that must always be true. (Example: The list size will always be greater than or equal to 0.)

What Makes a Good Unit Test? Part 1

- It sufficiently tests the contract. It doesn't need to be complete, just "sufficient."
  - If it's complex code, then have lots of tests.
  - If it's a simple accessor, then you don't need a test.
  - Most things are in between...
- It runs quickly. Part of the point is to make it in such a manner that you're able to run them regularly, so speed plays into that.
  - It's much easier to fix a bug you introduced five minutes ago than one you did five weeks ago...
- Tests are independent.
  - If you have dependencies between tests, or have to do tons of setup, then it's a pain to write tests and to run them.
  - Loosely coupled functionality enables independent tests.
  - <u>Write loosely coupled, highly cohesive code!</u>
- Run the tests regularly. (Ideally, use something like CruiseControl to run the complete test suite run automatically after you check code in.)
  - One of the seriously cool benefits of having the automated tests is that it gives you automatic regression testing.
  - You can be "fearless" when you need to make changes, because you don't have to worry that you might've broken something.

Writing Good Tests

- If you do all the stuff that you know you're supposed to anyway (loose coupling, high cohesion, etc.), writing tests is really easy. :-)
- ***Seriously***: Loosely coupled and highly cohesive software is much easier to test than tightly coupled systems, or ones where it's hard to tell what something is really ***for*** (low cohesion).
- There's a lot of Patterns for making that easier, like Inversion of Control, Strategies, etc.
- Writing the test before you write the code guarantees that your code is "testable."
- With very few exceptions, code that is hard to test is a HUGE flag that the design is bad (ie, tightly coupled, low cohesion).

Example of How To Think of Tests

- The required functionality for a particular service (getVersionsForProductId) is the ability to get a list of all versions for a given product id. If there's no product for that id, then an exception is thrown. If there's no versions for a valid product id, then an empty list is returned.

The Tests That Are Needed

- Starting from the easiest to the hardest:
  - If there's no product for that id, then an exception is thrown (pre-condition)
  - If there's no versions for a valid product id, then an empty list is returned (post-condition)
  - If there are versions for a product id, then a non-empty list of all the versions is returned (post-condition)

Implementing the Tests

```
def testInvalidProduct
 begin
  vers = getVersionsForProductId(-99)
  assert(false, "Should have thrown an exception, but got: "+vers.to_s)
 rescue
```

```
    # an exception should've been thrown
  end
end
def testNoVersionsForProduct
  # 1234 is a legit product id, but we know it doesn't have any versions
  vers = getVersionsForProductId(1234)
  assert(vers.length == 0, "Got versions back: "+vers.to_s)
end
def testListOfVersionsForProduct
  # 2345 is a legit product id, and we know it has versions
  vers = getVersionsForProductId(2345)
  assert(vers.length > 0, "Didn't get any versions back")
end
```

Why Unit Test

- It will make your life easier
- Better code
- Better designs
- Code is easier to maintain later
- Confidence when you code

Test-driven Development using JUnit

History

- Kent Beck developed the first xUnit automated test tool for Smalltalk in mid-90's
- Beck and Gamma (of design patterns Gang of Four) developed JUnit on a flight from Zurich to Washington, D.C.
- Martin Fowler: "Never in the field of software development was so much owed by so many to so few lines of code."
- Junit has become the standard tool for Test-Driven Development in Java (see Junit.org)
- Junit test generators now part of many Java IDEs (Eclipse, BlueJ, Jbuilder, DrJava)
- Xunit tools have since been developed for many other languages (Perl, C++, Python, Visual Basic, C#, ...)

What is JUnit?

- Regression testing framework
- Used for unit testing in Java
- Open Source
- Released under IBM's CPLJUnit is a testing framework used for unit testing.
- Testing is an important activity in the development, and there are different levels of testing. There are unit testing, integration testing, regression testing, load balancing testing, etc.

- JUnit framework is designed to help you with the lowest level of testing, unit testing.
- CPL is Common Public License

Where Does JUnit Come From?

- JUnit's web site: http://junit.org/index.htm
- Eclipse includes JUnit
  - Eclipse provides new GUI to run JUnit test cases and suites
- You can run your unit tests outside of Eclipse
  - If you wish using TestRunner
  - Using JUnit's Window

Why create a test suite?

- Obviously you have to test your code—right?
  - You can do *ad hoc* testing (running whatever tests occur to you at the moment), or
  - You can build a test suite (a thorough set of tests that can be run at any time)
- Disadvantages of a test suite
  - It's a lot of extra programming
    - True, but use of a good test framework can help quite a bit
- You don't have time to do all that extra work
  - *False!* Experiments repeatedly show that test suites reduce debugging time more than the amount spent building the test suite
- Advantages of a test suite
  - Reduces total number of bugs in delivered code
  - Makes code much more maintainable and refactorable

Architectural overview

- JUnit test framework is a package of classes that lets you write tests for each method, then easily run those tests
- **TestRunner** runs tests and reports **TestResults**

- You test your class by extending abstract class ***TestCase***
- To write test cases, you need to know and understand the **Assert** class

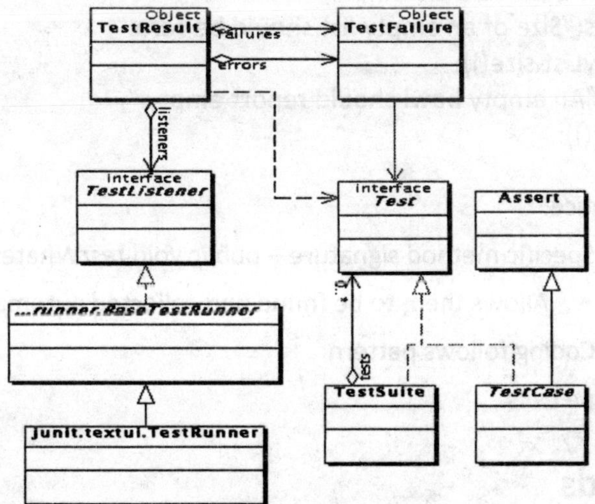

Writing a TestCase

- To start using JUnit, create a subclass of *TestCase*, to which you add test methods
- Here's a skeletal test class:

```
import junit.framework.TestCase;
public class TestBowl extends TestCase {
} //Test my class Bowl
```

- Name of class is important – should be of the form ***Test***MyClass or MyClass***Test***
- This naming convention lets TestRunner automatically find your test classes

Writing methods in TestCase

- Pattern follows *programming by contract* paradigm:
    - Set up preconditions
    - Exercise functionality being tested
    - Check postconditions

- Example:

```
public void testEmptyList() {
    Bowl emptyBowl = new Bowl();
    assertEquals("Size of an empty list should be zero.",
        0, emptyList.size());
    assertTrue("An empty bowl should report empty.",
emptyBowl.isEmpty());
}
```

- Things to notice:
    - Specific method signature – public void *test*Whatever()
        - Allows them to be found and collected automatically by JUnit
    - Coding follows pattern

Notice the assert-type calls...

Assert methods

- Each assert method has parameters like these: *message, expected-value, actual-value*
- Assert methods dealing with floating point numbers get an additional argument, a tolerance
- Each assert method has an equivalent version that does not take a message – however, this use is not recommended because:
    - messages helps documents the tests
    - messages provide additional information when reading failure logs
- assertTrue(String *message*, Boolean *test*)
- assertFalse(String *message*, Boolean *test*)
- assertNull(String *message*, Object *object*)
- assertNotNull(String *message*, Object *object*)
- assertEquals(String *message*, Object *expected*, Object *actual*) (uses equals method)
- assertSame(String *message*, Object *expected*, Object *actual*) (uses == operator)
- assertNotSame(String *message*, Object *expected*, Object *actual*)

More stuff in test classes

- Suppose you want to test a class Counter
- public class CounterTest
  extends junit.framework.TestCase {
  - This is the unit test for the Counter class
- public CounterTest() { } //Default constructor
- protected void setUp()
  - Test *fixture* creates and initializes instance variables, etc.
- protected void tearDown()
  - Releases any system resources used by the test fixture
- public void testIncrement(), public void testDecrement()
  - These methods contain tests for the Counter methods increment(), decrement(), etc.
  - Note capitalization convention

JUnit tests for Counter

```
public class CounterTest extends junit.framework.TestCase {
    Counter counter1;
    public CounterTest() { }  // default constructor

    protected void setUp() {  // creates a (simple) test fixture
       counter1 = new Counter();
    }

    public void testIncrement() {
       assertTrue(counter1.increment() == 1);
       assertTrue(counter1.increment() == 2);
    }

    public void testDecrement() {
       assertTrue(counter1.decrement() == -1);
    }
}
```

Note that each test begins with a *brand new* counter

This means you don't have to worry about the order in which the tests are run

TestSuites

- TestSuites collect a selection of tests to run them as a unit
- Collections automatically use TestSuites, however to specify the order in which tests are run, write your own:

```
public static Test suite() {
        suite.addTest(new TestBowl("testBowl"));
        suite.addTest(new TestBowl("testAdding"));
        return suite;
}
```

- Should seldom have to write your own TestSuites as each method in your TestCase should be independent of all others
- Can create TestSuites that test a whole package:

```
public static Test suite() {
        TestSuite suite = new TestSuite();
        suite.addTestSuite(TestBowl.class);
        suite.addTestSuite(TestFruit.class);
        return suite;
}
```

Installation

http://www.eclipse.org/downloads/

://www.eclipse.org/downloads/download.php?file=/eclipse/downloads/drops/R-3.5.2-201002111343/eclipse-SDK-3.5.2-win32.zip

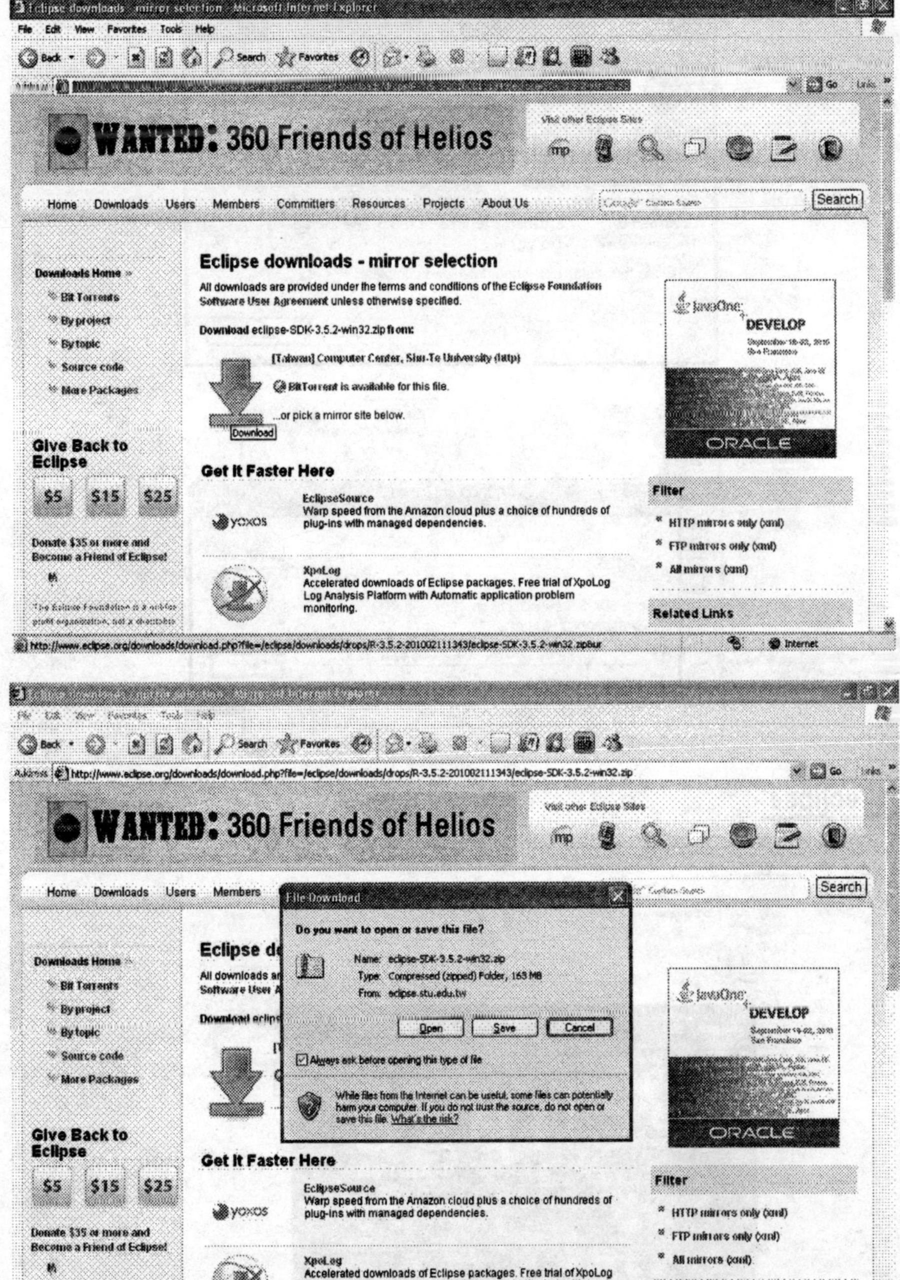
Eclipse downloads - mirror selection - Microsoft Internet Explorer
File Edit View Favorites Tools Help
WANTED: 360 Friends of Helios
Home Downloads Users Members Committers Resources Projects About Us
Search
Eclipse downloads - mirror selection
All downloads are provided under the terms and conditions of the Eclipse Foundation Software User Agreement unless otherwise specified.
Download eclipse-SDK-3.5.2-win32.zip from:
[Taiwan] Computer Center, Shu-Te University (http)
BitTorrent is available for this file.
...or pick a mirror site below.
Download
Downloads Home
Bit Torrents
By project
By topic
Source code
More Packages
Give Back to Eclipse
$5 $15 $25
Donate $35 or more and Become a Friend of Eclipse!
Get It Faster Here
EclipseSource
Warp speed from the Amazon cloud plus a choice of hundreds of plug-ins with managed dependencies.
XpoLog
Accelerated downloads of Eclipse packages. Free trial of XpoLog Log Analysis Platform with Automatic application problem monitoring.
DEVELOP
ORACLE
Filter
HTTP mirrors only (xml)
FTP mirrors only (xml)
All mirrors (xml)
Related Links
http://www.eclipse.org/downloads/download.php?file=/eclipse/downloads/drops/R-3.5.2-201002111343/eclipse-SDK-3.5.2-win32.zip&url
Internet
http://www.eclipse.org/downloads/download.php?file=/eclipse/downloads/drops/R-3.5.2-201002111343/eclipse-SDK-3.5.2-win32.zip
File Download
Do you want to open or save this file?
Name: eclipse-SDK-3.5.2-win32.zip
Type: Compressed (zipped) Folder, 163 MB
From: eclipse.stu.edu.tw
Open Save Cancel
Always ask before opening this type of file
While files from the Internet can be useful, some files can potentially harm your computer. If you do not trust the source, do not open or save this file. What's the risk?
Start downloading from site: http://eclipse.stu.edu.tw/eclipse/downloads/drops/R-3.5.2-201002111343/eclipse-SDK-3.5.2-win32.zip
Findbugs-Plugin for Eclipse - Microsoft Word

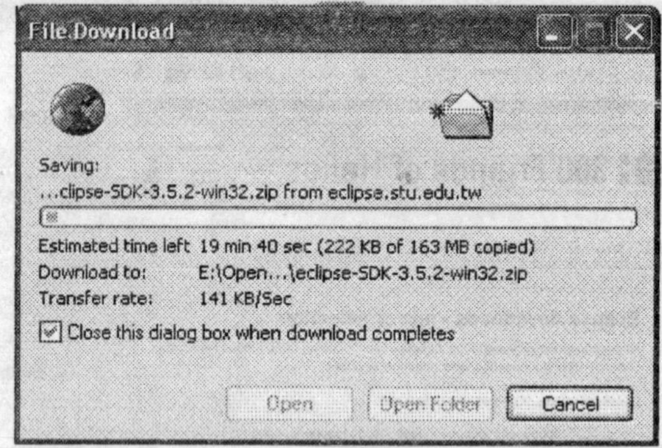

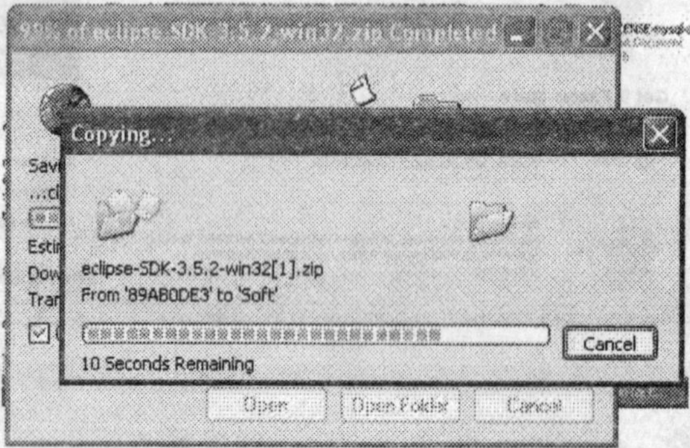

Click on 'eclipse'

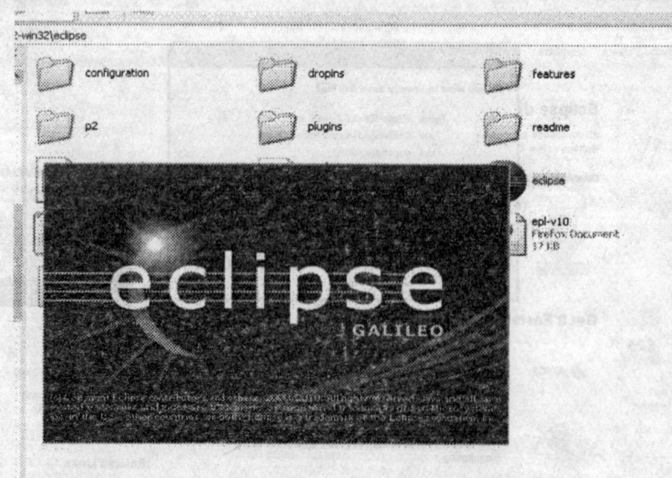

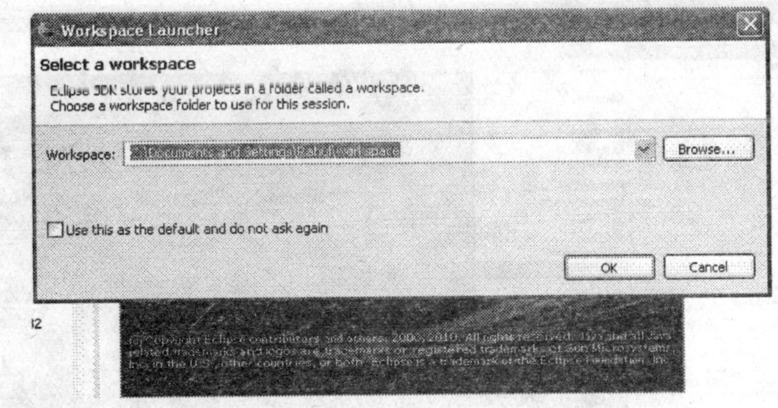

Workspace Launcher
Select a workspace
Eclipse SDK stores your projects in a folder called a workspace.
Choose a workspace folder to use for this session.
Workspace:
Browse...
Use this as the default and do not ask again
OK
Cancel

Java - Eclipse SDK
File Edit Navigate Search Project Run Window Help
Welcome
Welcome to Eclipse
start

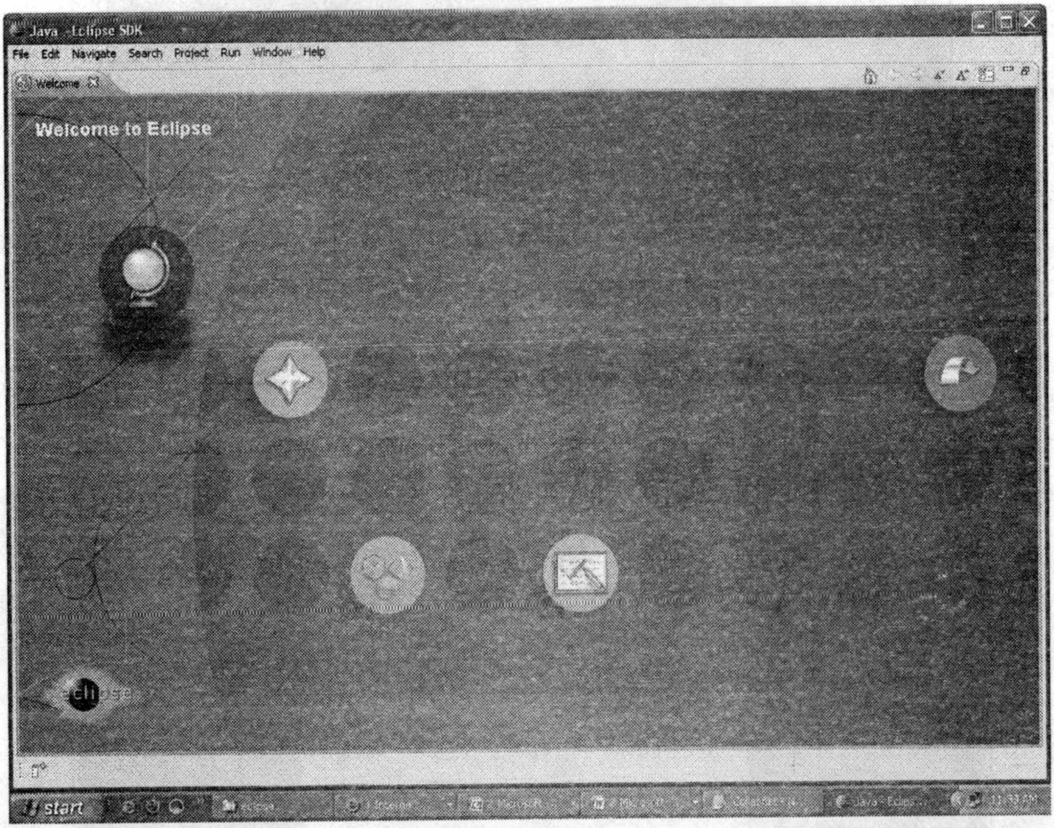

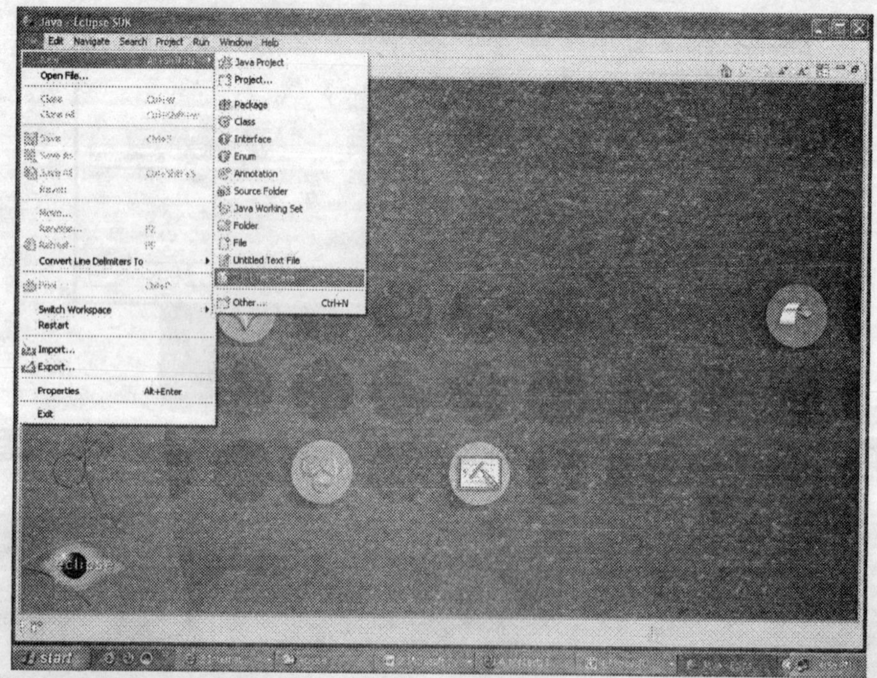
Java - Eclipse SDK
Edit Navigate Search Project Run Window Help
Open File...
Convert Line Delimiters To
Switch Workspace
Restart
Import...
Export...
Properties Alt+Enter
Exit
Java Project
Project...
Package
Class
Interface
Enum
Annotation
Source Folder
Java Working Set
Folder
File
Untitled Text File
Other... Ctrl+N
start

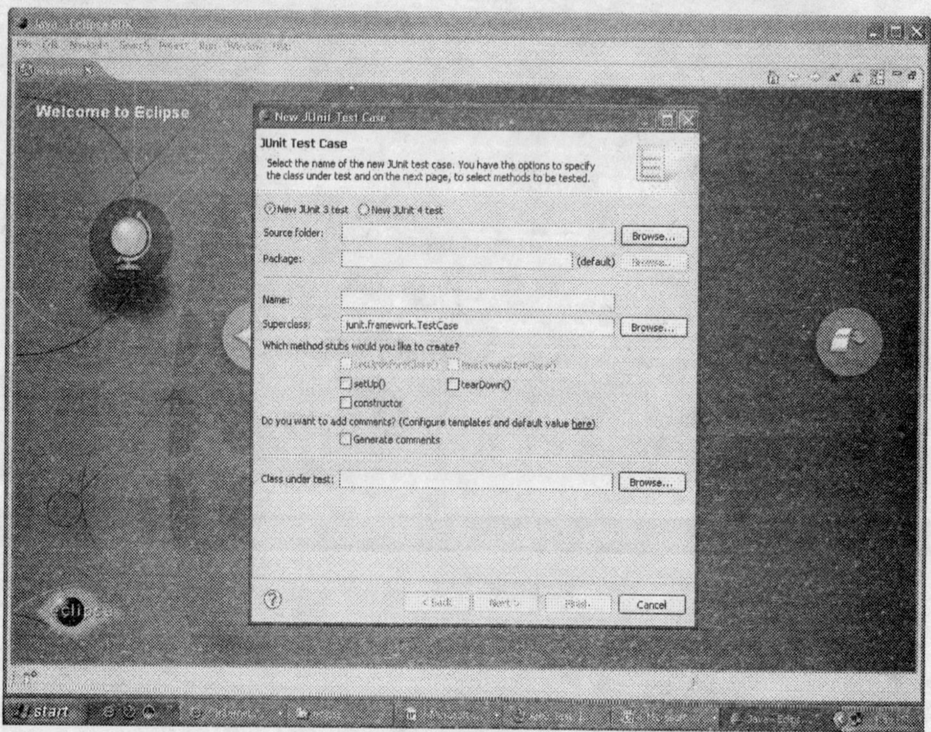
Java - Eclipse SDK
Welcome to Eclipse
New JUnit Test Case
JUnit Test Case
Select the name of the new JUnit test case. You have the options to specify the class under test and on the next page, to select methods to be tested.
New JUnit 3 test
New JUnit 4 test
Source folder:
Browse...
Package:
(default)
Name:
Superclass:
junit.framework.TestCase
Browse...
Which method stubs would you like to create?
setUp()
tearDown()
constructor
Do you want to add comments? (Configure templates and default value here)
Generate comments
Class under test:
Browse...
Cancel
start

- Eclipse preferences can be set in the JUnit Preferences window
- For the most part you can leave these alone
- Filters needed to identify packages, classes, or patterns that should not be shown in the stack trace of a test failure

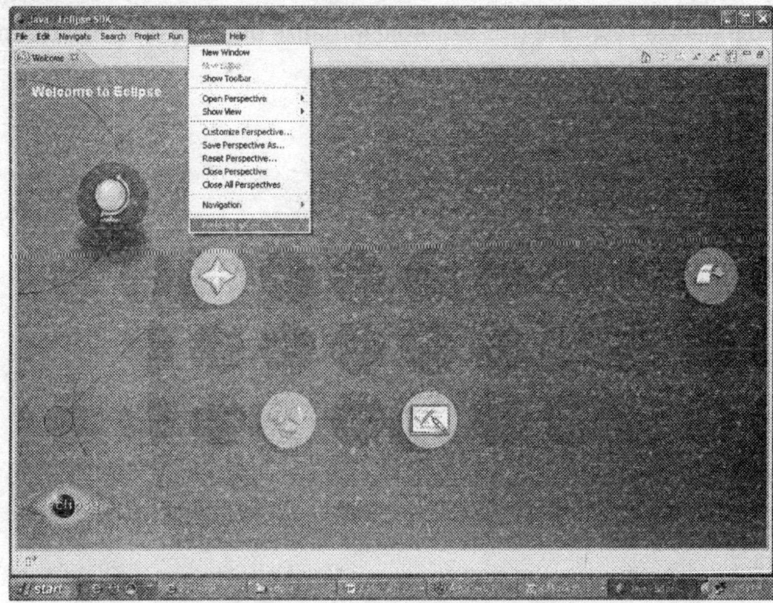

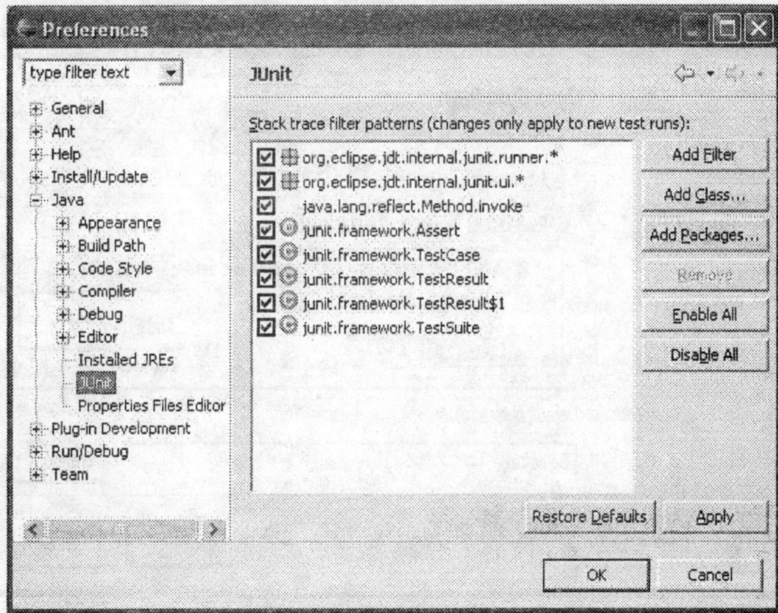

JUnit Test Cases

When you use JUnit for unit testing you write test cases. These test cases are implemented as subclasses of TestCase, which is part of the JUnit framework. The test cases correspond to Java classes, and contain code used for testing of classes' methods.

It is possible to initialize test case (for example initialize objects) and also clean it up after testing is performed.

- Test case
    - Runs multiple tests
- Implemented a subclass of TestCase
- Define instance variables that store the state of the tests in the class
- Initialize TestCase by overriding setUp method

Clean-up after test case is done by overriding tearDown method

Creating TestCases in Eclipse...

- Create a new package to contain your test case classes
- Add the JUnit JAR file to the project's buildpath
- Or, will be done for you the first time you build a test case

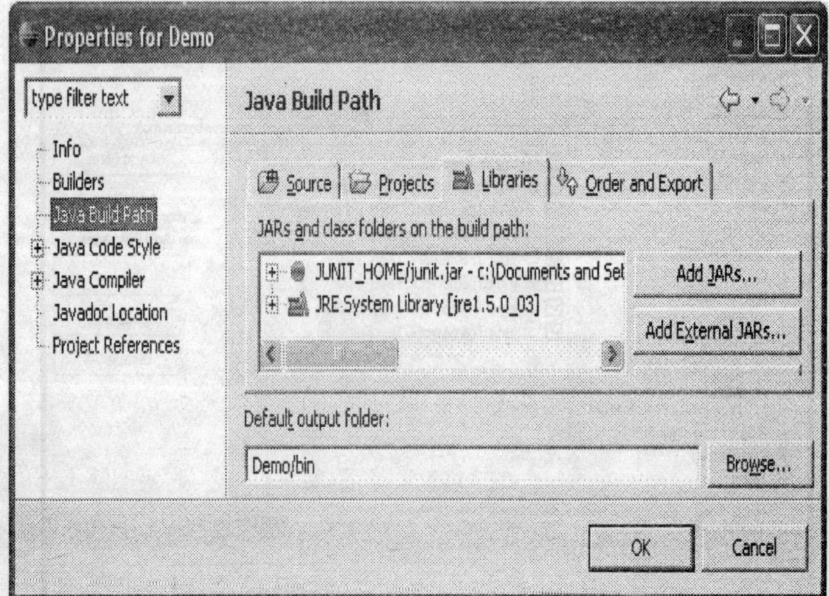

Creating TestCases in Eclipse

- Select your testing package
- From the context menu select New → JUnit Test Case
- In the next Window fill in the name of your test case

This will create the corresponding class in your testing package

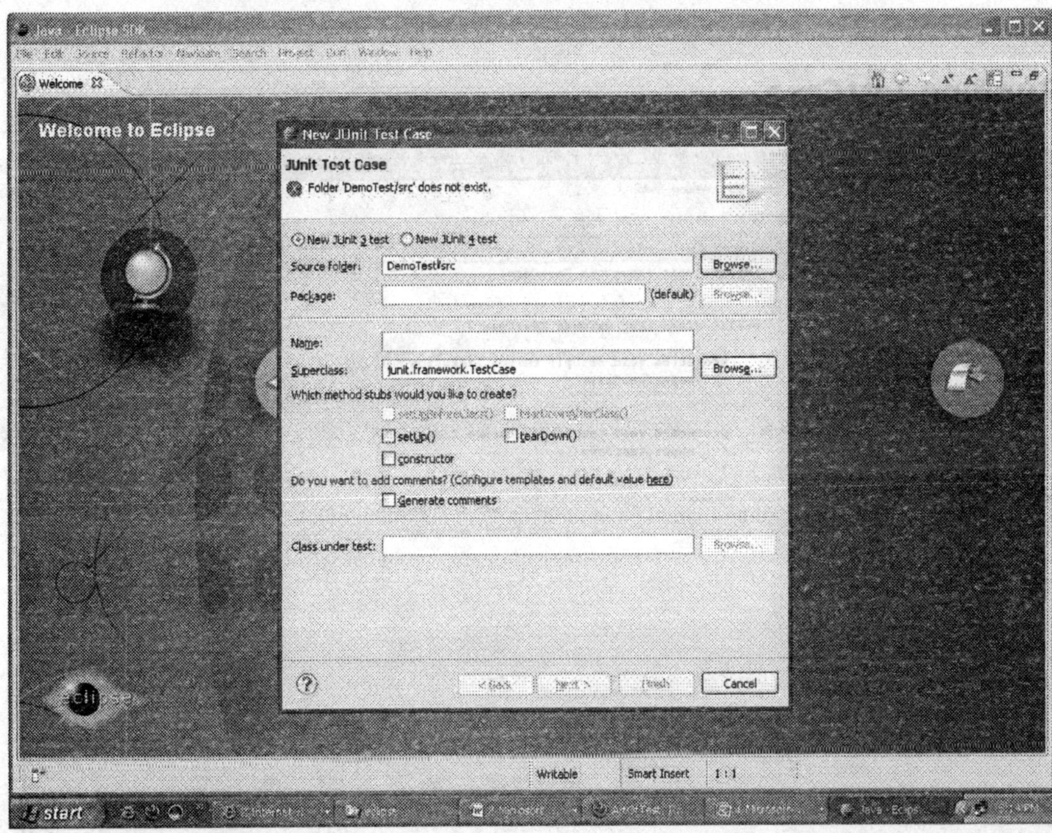

TestCase Template

```
package com.espirity.course.testing;
import junit.framework.TestCase;
public class FirstTestCase extends TestCase {
        public FirstTestCase(String arg0) {
                super(arg0);
        }
        public static void main(String[] args) {
```

```
	}
	protected void setUp() throws Exception {
		super.setUp();
	}
	protected void tearDown() throws Exception {
		super.tearDown();
	}
}
```

Running TestCase

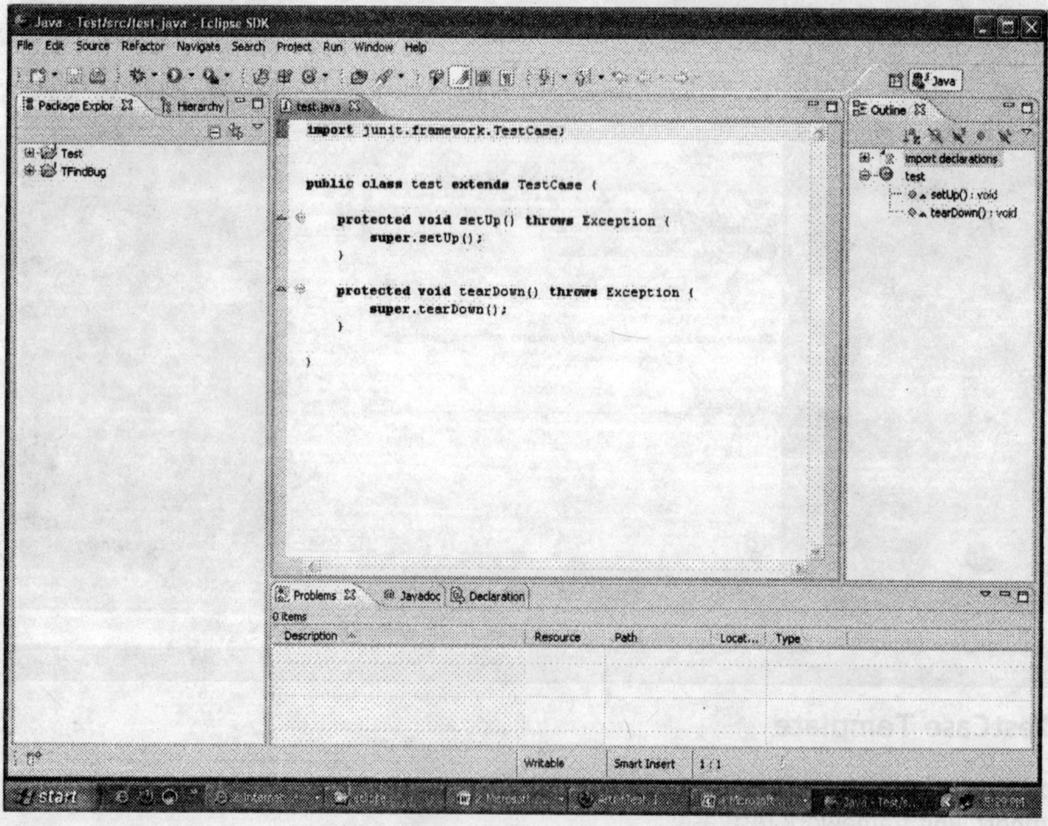

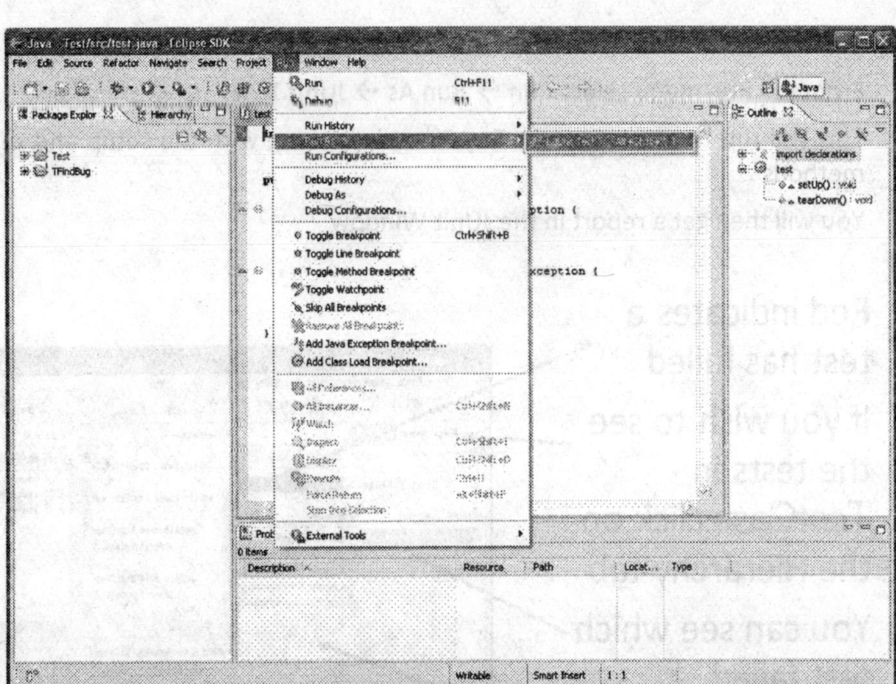

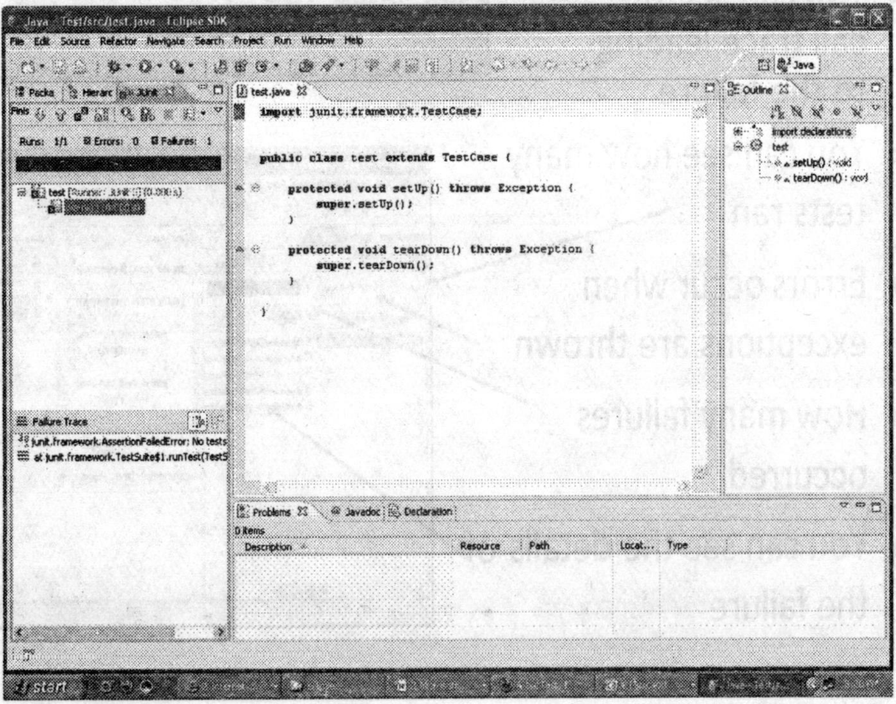

- Select TestCase class
- From the Run menu select Run → Run As → JUnit Test
- This will run the tests in your TestCase class along with the setup and teardown methods
- You will then get a report in the JUnit Window

- Red indicates a test has failed
- If you wish to see the tests in TestCase click on the Hierarchy tab
- You can see which test failed
- You can see the call trace leading to the failure

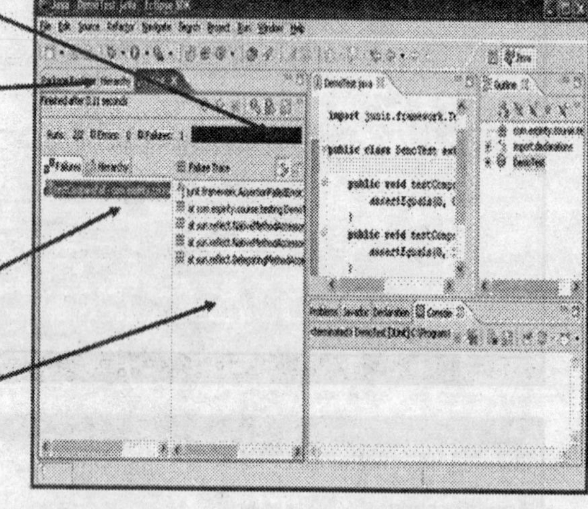

- You can see how many tests ran
- Errors occur when exceptions are thrown
- How many failures occurred
- You can see the details of the failure

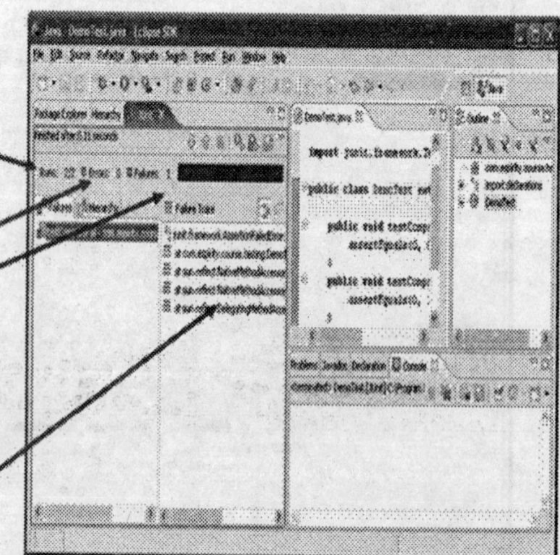

Creating JUnit TestSuite...

- Test Suite
  - Runs multiple test cases or suites
- Implemented as subclass of TestSuite
- To create a TestSuite
  - Select your testing package
  - From the context menu select New → Other... → Java → JUnit

Then from the Wizard select JUnit Test Suite

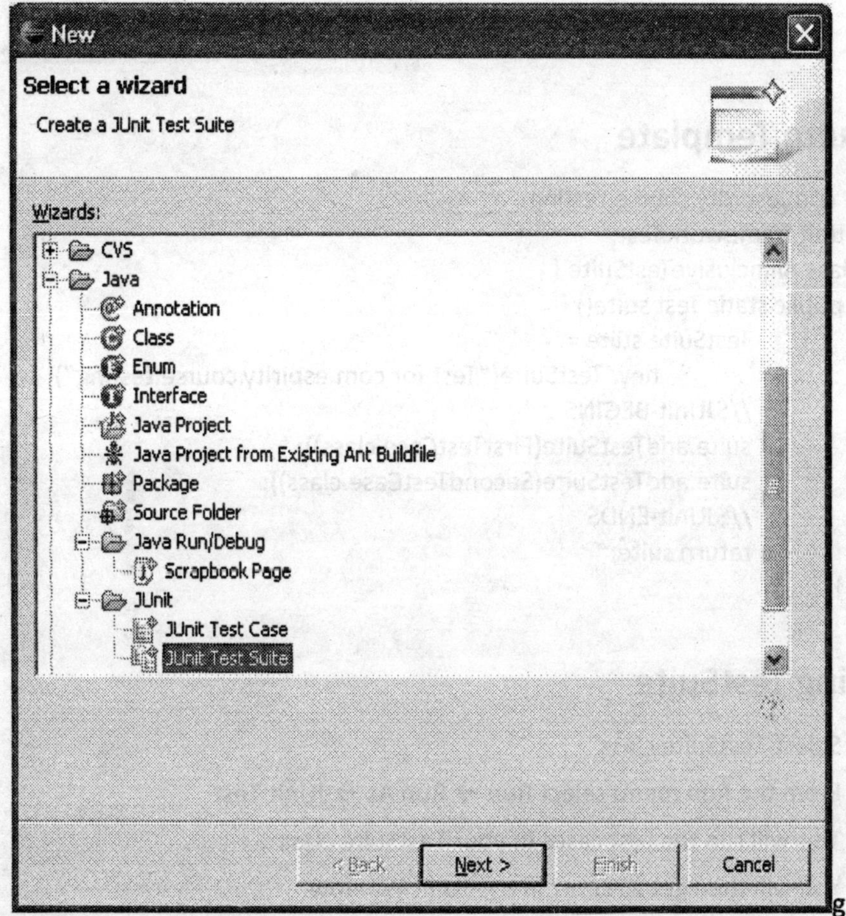

...Creating JUnit TestSuite

- Fill in the name of your TestSuite Class
- Select the TestCases to include in your TestSuite

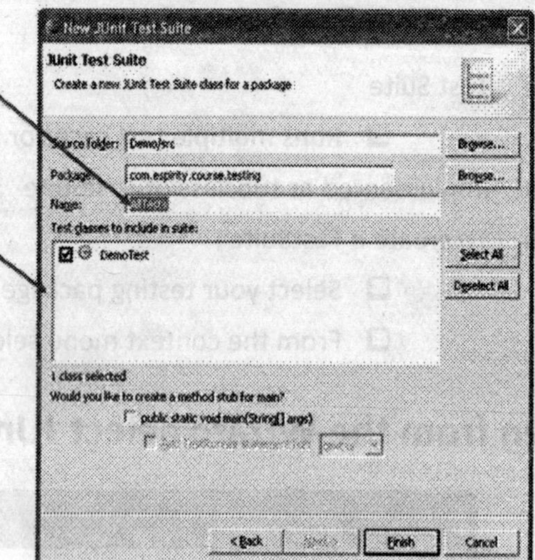

TestSuite Template

```
package com.espirity.course.testing;
import junit.framework.Test;
public class AllInclusiveTestSuite {
        public static Test suite() {
                TestSuite suite =
                        new TestSuite("Test for com.espirity.course.testing");
                //$JUnit-BEGIN$
                suite.addTestSuite(FirstTestCase.class));
                suite.addTestSuite(SecondTestCase.class));
                //$JUnit-END$
                return suite;
        }
}
```

Running TestSuite

- Select TestSuite class
- From the Run menu select Run → Run As → JUnit Test
- This will run the test cases in your TestSuite class
- You will then get a report in the JUnit Window

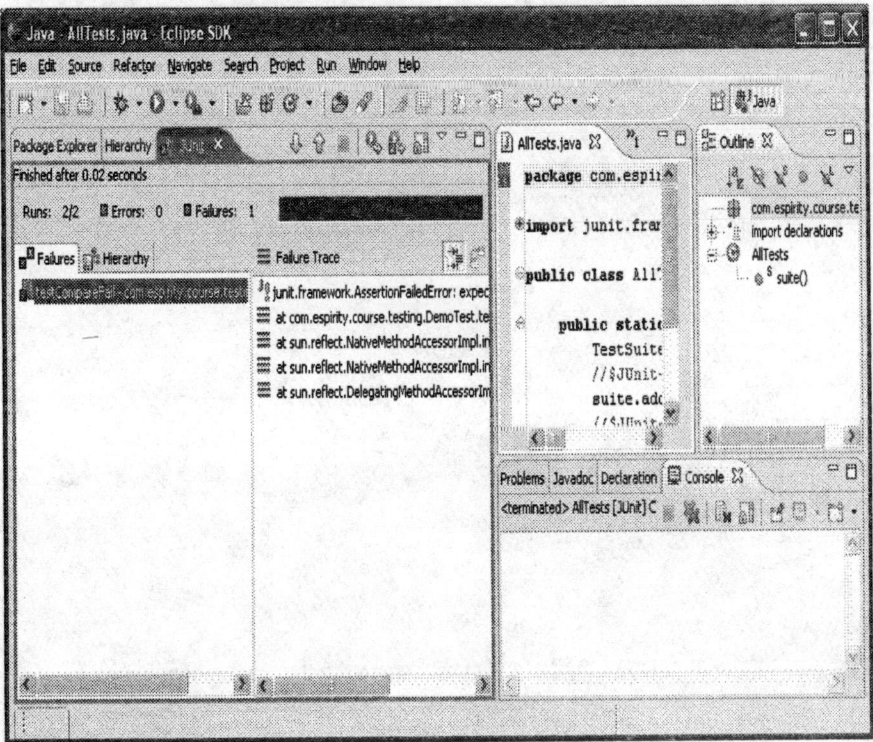

References:

http://www.thecoadletter.com

http://sourceforge.net/projects/cppunit

http://www.junit.org

Test-driven Development using NUnit

- Drive the design and construction of your
- code on one unit test at a time
- Write a test that the system currently fails
- Quickly write the code to pass that test
- Remove any duplication from the code
- Move on to the next test

TDD Benefits

- Focuses your efforts on specific concrete test cases and helps pace development (micro-iterations)
- Provides continuous feedback about whether your code is
- working
- --Boosts confidence when working on complex systems
- Evolves code to do exactly what you need and no more
- Provides a suite of tests you can run often to be sure your code is always working.

  --Code is easier to change without inadvertently breaking dependent code

  --Means better assurance when integrating your code into CVS, VSS

Introducing XUnit

- Original framework developed for Smalltalk by Kent Beck
- Versions for most programming languages (CppUnit for C++, JUnit for Java, Nunit for .NET etc)
- Simple concepts

  -- Test fixture : a class that contains one or more test methods

  -- Test method : a method that executes a specific test

  -- Test runner : an application that finds and executes test methods on test fixtures

  -- Assertion : a Boolean expression that describes what must be true when some action has been executed

  -- Expected Exception : the type of an Exception we expect to be thrown during execution of a test method

  -- Setup : Code that is run before every test method is executed (eg, logging in as a particular user or initializing a singleton)

  -- Teardown : Code that is run after every test method has finished (eg, deleting rows
- from a table that were inserted during the test)

What to Test: BICEP

B Are the boundary conditions correct?

I Can you check inverse relationships?

C Can you cross check using other means?

E Can you force an error condition to happen?

P Are the performance characteristics acceptable?

Stubs and Mocks

Stub Defined

" A portion is a portion of code that is inserted at runtime in place of real code, in order to isolate calling code from the real implementation. The intent is to replace a complex behavior with a simpler one that allows independent testing of some portion of real code."

Mock Objects Defined

"A mock object is an object created to stand in for an object that your code will be collaborating with. Your code can call methods on the mock object, will deliver results as set up by your tests."

When are stubs appropriate?

Objects that are expensive to create to manipulate
At the edges of a system, or around complex clusters of objects
Course-grained testing, integration testing

When are mocks appropriate?

Real object has non-deterministic behavior
Real object is difficult to set up
Real object has behavior that is difficult to cause
Real object is slow
Source: http://c2.com/cgi/wiki?MockObjects

What is NUnit

- NUnit is a unit-testing framework for all .Net languages.
- It has been written entirely in C#.

Important nUnit Links

- http://www.nunit.org
- http://nunit.org/download.html
- http://sourceforge.net/projects/nunit/

How to Install Nunit:

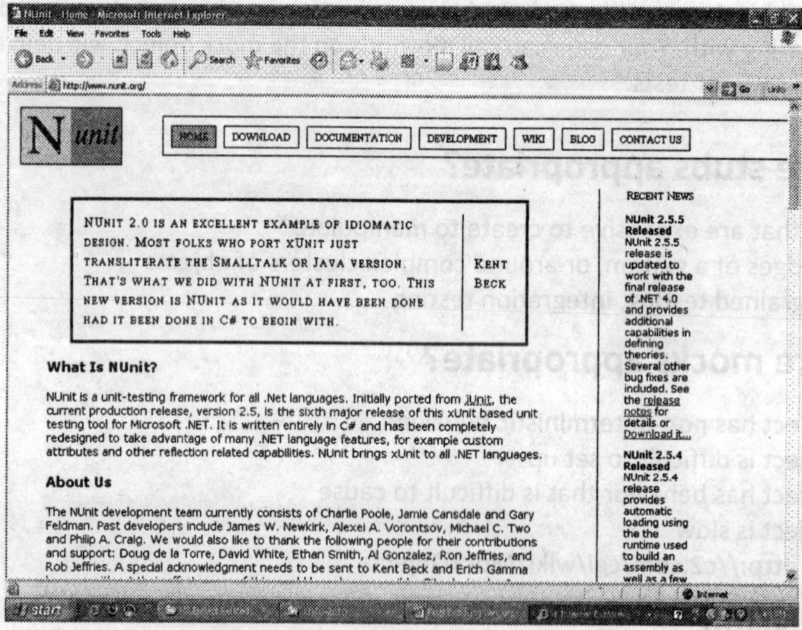

http://www.nunit.org/

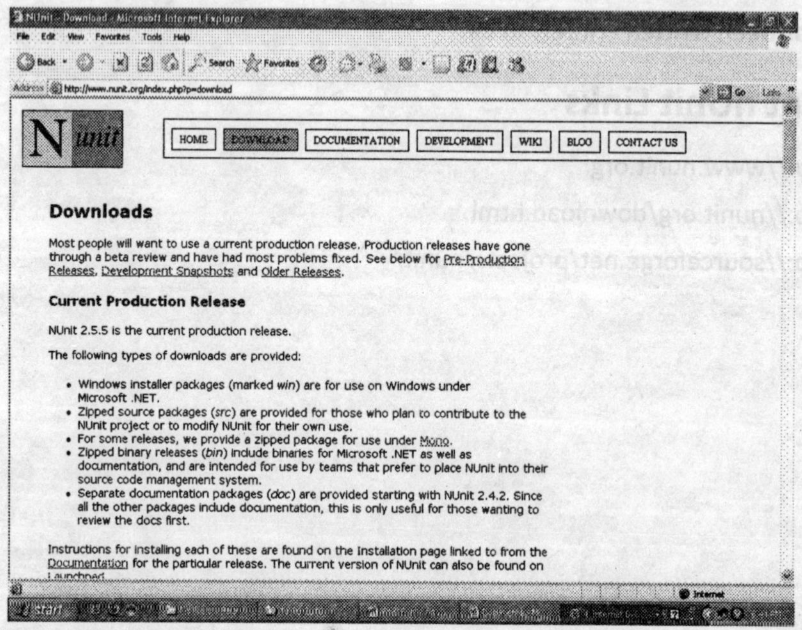

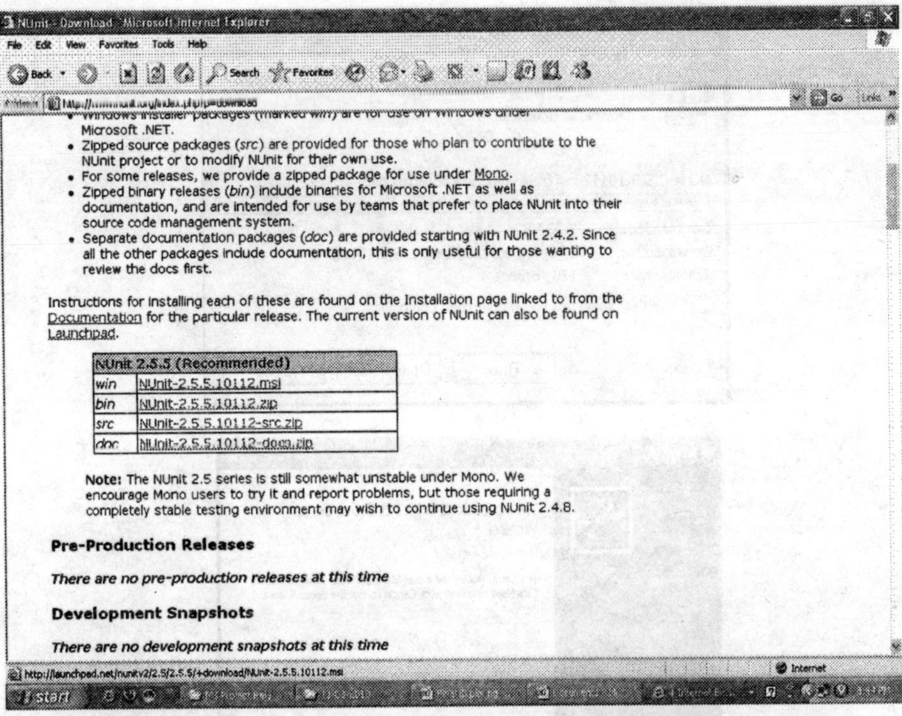
NUnit - Download - Microsoft Internet Explorer
File Edit View Favorites Tools Help
Microsoft .NET.
Zipped source packages (src) are provided for those who plan to contribute to the NUnit project or to modify NUnit for their own use.
For some releases, we provide a zipped package for use under Mono.
Zipped binary releases (bin) include binaries for Microsoft .NET as well as documentation, and are intended for use by teams that prefer to place NUnit into their source code management system.
Separate documentation packages (doc) are provided starting with NUnit 2.4.2. Since all the other packages include documentation, this is only useful for those wanting to review the docs first.
Instructions for installing each of these are found on the Installation page linked to from the Documentation for the particular release. The current version of NUnit can also be found on Launchpad.
NUnit 2.5.5 (Recommended)
win NUnit-2.5.5.10112.msi
bin NUnit-2.5.5.10112.zip
src NUnit-2.5.5.10112-src.zip
doc NUnit-2.5.5.10112-docs.zip
Note: The NUnit 2.5 series is still somewhat unstable under Mono. We encourage Mono users to try it and report problems, but those requiring a completely stable testing environment may wish to continue using NUnit 2.4.8.
Pre-Production Releases
There are no pre-production releases at this time
Development Snapshots
There are no development snapshots at this time
http://launchpad.net/nunitv2/2.5/2.5.5/+download/NUnit-2.5.5.10112.msi
Internet

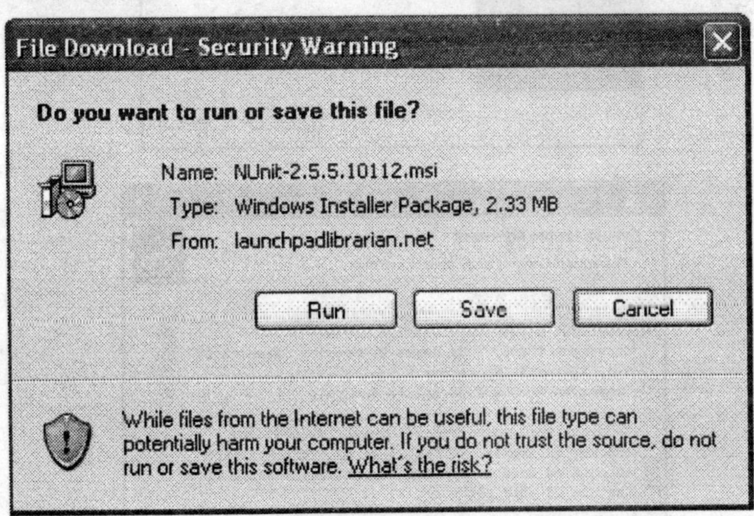
File Download - Security Warning
Do you want to run or save this file?
Name: NUnit-2.5.5.10112.msi
Type: Windows Installer Package, 2.33 MB
From: launchpadlibrarian.net
Run
Save
Cancel
While files from the Internet can be useful, this file type can potentially harm your computer. If you do not trust the source, do not run or save this software. What's the risk?

Click on 'Run'

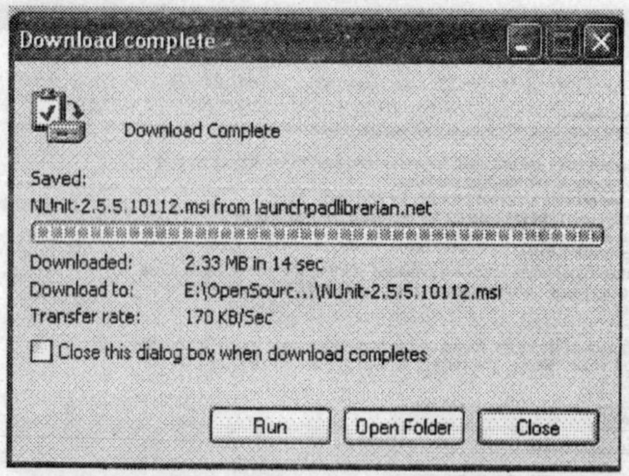
Download complete
Download Complete
Saved:
NUnit-2.5.5.10112.msi from launchpadlibrarian.net
Downloaded: 2.33 MB in 14 sec
Download to: E:\OpenSourc...\NUnit-2.5.5.10112.msi
Transfer rate: 170 KB/Sec
Close this dialog box when download completes
Run
Open Folder
Close

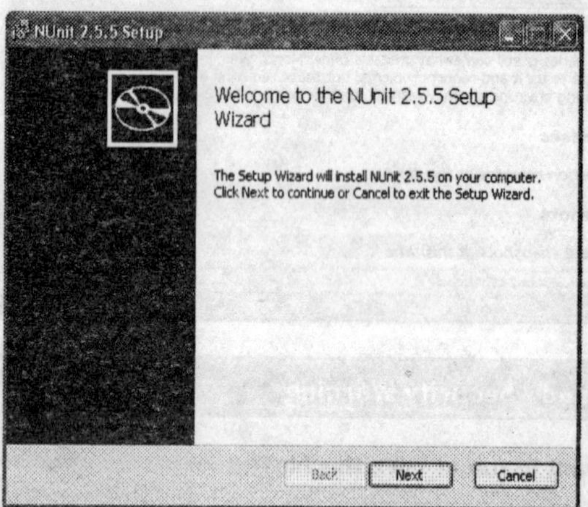
NUnit 2.5.5 Setup
Welcome to the NUnit 2.5.5 Setup Wizard
The Setup Wizard will install NUnit 2.5.5 on your computer. Click Next to continue or Cancel to exit the Setup Wizard.
Back
Next
Cancel

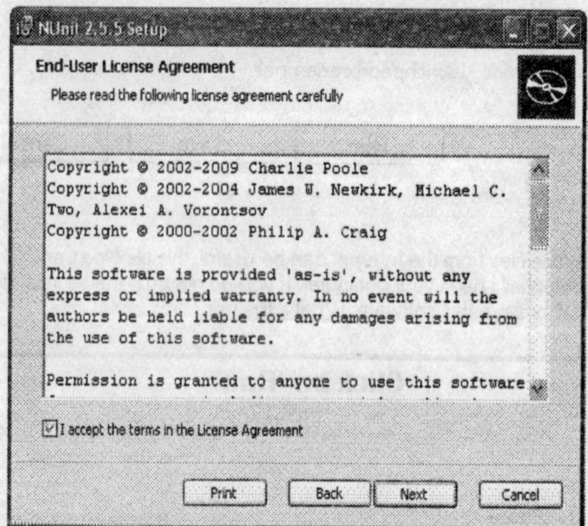
NUnit 2.5.5 Setup
End-User License Agreement
Please read the following license agreement carefully
Copyright © 2002-2009 Charlie Poole
Copyright © 2002-2004 James W. Newkirk, Michael C. Two, Alexei A. Vorontsov
Copyright © 2000-2002 Philip A. Craig
This software is provided 'as-is', without any express or implied warranty. In no event will the authors be held liable for any damages arising from the use of this software.
Permission is granted to anyone to use this software
I accept the terms in the License Agreement
Print
Back
Next
Cancel

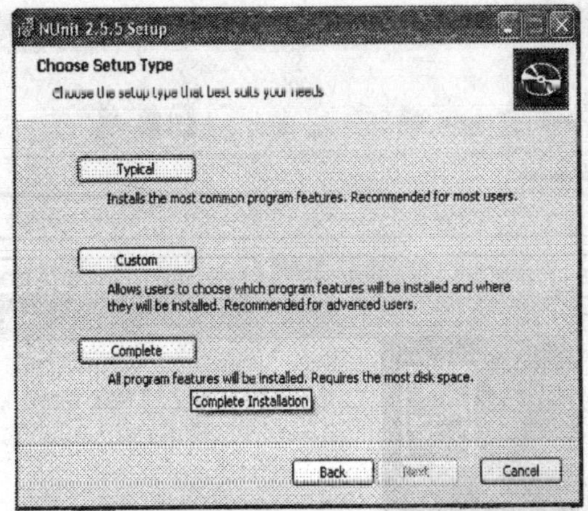
NUnit 2.5.5 Setup
Choose Setup Type
Choose the setup type that best suits your needs
Typical
Installs the most common program features. Recommended for most users.
Custom
Allows users to choose which program features will be installed and where they will be installed. Recommended for advanced users.
Complete
All program features will be installed. Requires the most disk space.
Complete Installation
Back
Next
Cancel

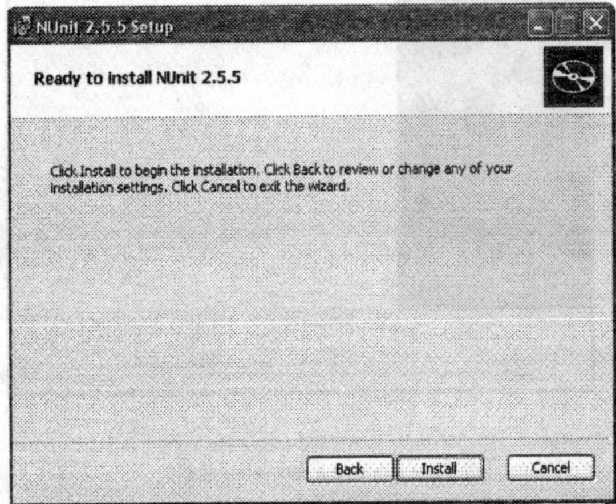
NUnit 2.5.5 Setup
Ready to install NUnit 2.5.5
Click Install to begin the installation. Click Back to review or change any of your installation settings. Click Cancel to exit the wizard.
Back
Install
Cancel

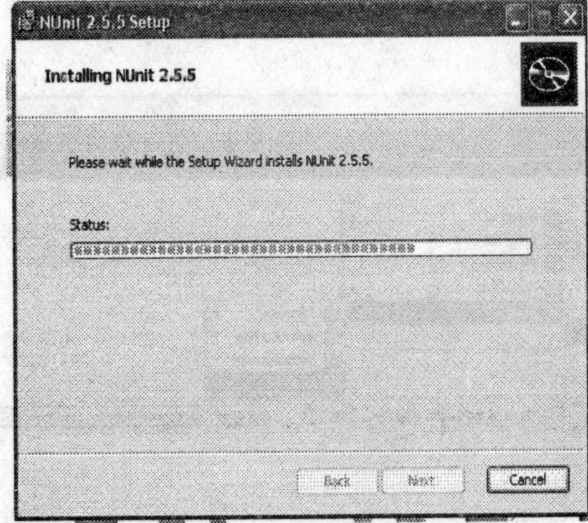
NUnit 2.5.5 Setup
Installing NUnit 2.5.5
Please wait while the Setup Wizard installs NUnit 2.5.5.
Status:
Back
Next
Cancel

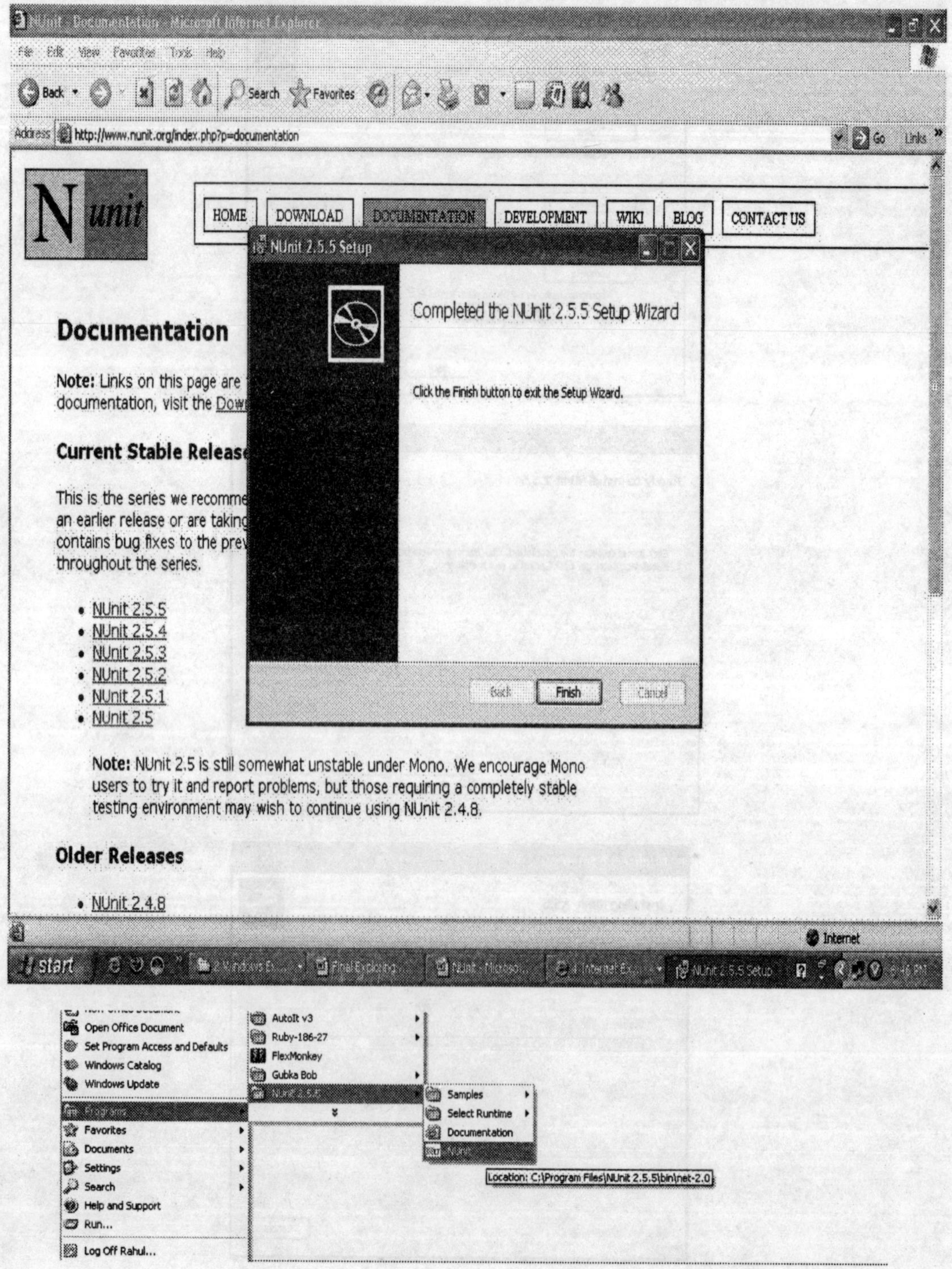
NUnit - Documentation - Microsoft Internet Explorer
http://www.nunit.org/index.php?p=documentation
HOME
DOWNLOAD
DOCUMENTATION
DEVELOPMENT
WIKI
BLOG
CONTACT US
NUnit 2.5.5 Setup
Completed the NUnit 2.5.5 Setup Wizard
Click the Finish button to exit the Setup Wizard.
Back
Finish
Cancel
Documentation
Note: Links on this page are
documentation, visit the Dow
Current Stable Releas
This is the series we recomme
an earlier release or are taking
contains bug fixes to the prev
throughout the series.
NUnit 2.5.5
NUnit 2.5.4
NUnit 2.5.3
NUnit 2.5.2
NUnit 2.5.1
NUnit 2.5
Note: NUnit 2.5 is still somewhat unstable under Mono. We encourage Mono users to try it and report problems, but those requiring a completely stable testing environment may wish to continue using NUnit 2.4.8.
Older Releases
NUnit 2.4.8
Internet
start
Open Office Document
Set Program Access and Defaults
Windows Catalog
Windows Update
Programs
Favorites
Documents
Settings
Search
Help and Support
Run...
Log Off Rahul...
AutoIt v3
Ruby-186-27
FlexMonkey
Gubka Bob
NUnit 2.5.5
Samples
Select Runtime
Documentation
NUnit
Location: C:\Program Files\NUnit 2.5.5\bin\net-2.0

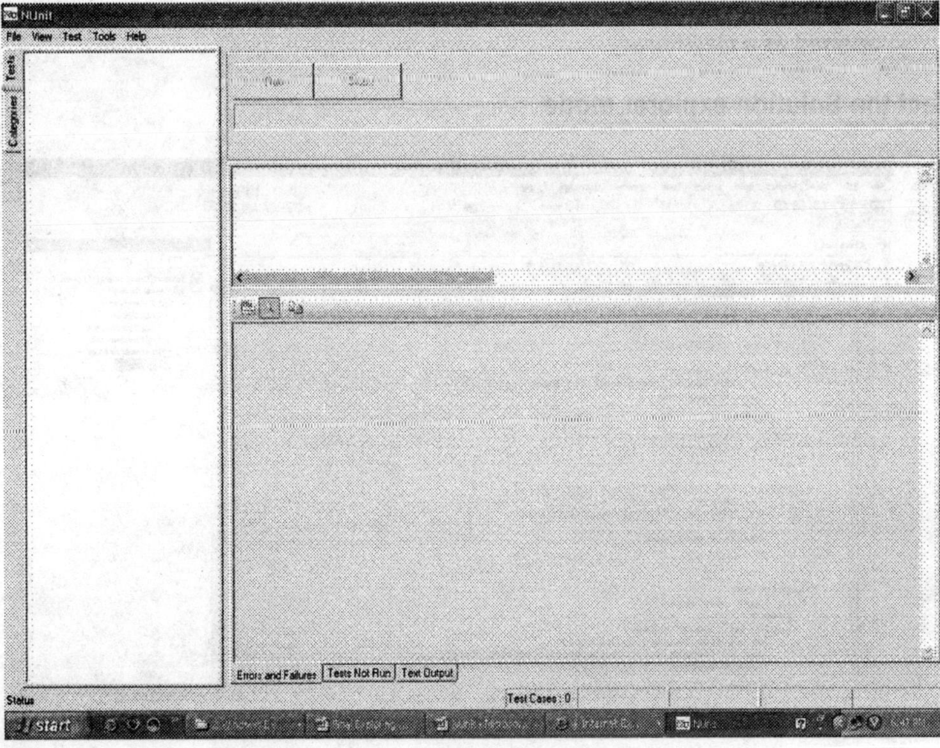

The Input & Output of nUnit

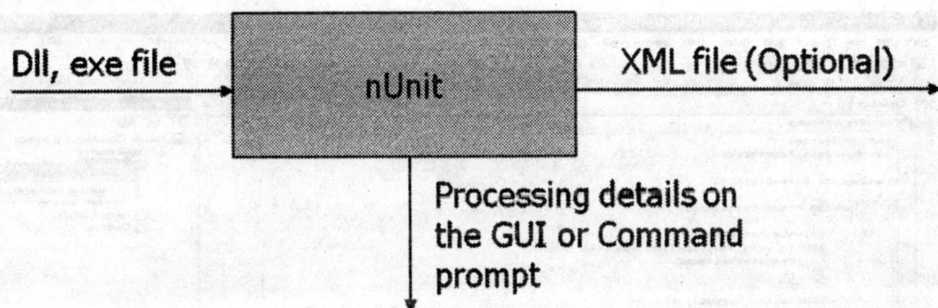

The 2 operational modes

- GUI mode
- Console mode (. net)

Things to do before testing

- Add nunit.frameworks.dll to your project references. This dll resides in nunit\bin folder.

- The next few screen shots show how to add this dll file if your project has been opened as a classlibrary.

Select the Solution explorer mode

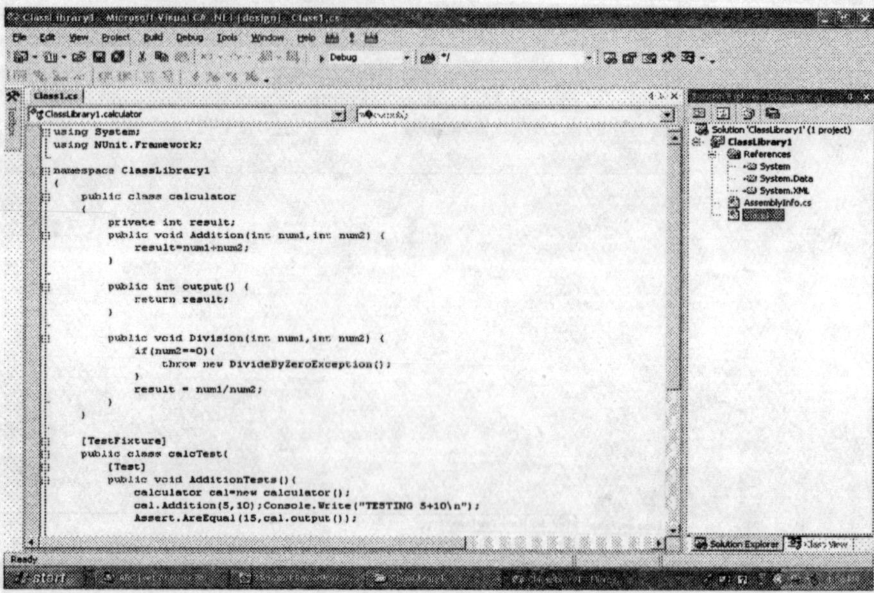

Right click references and select Add reference

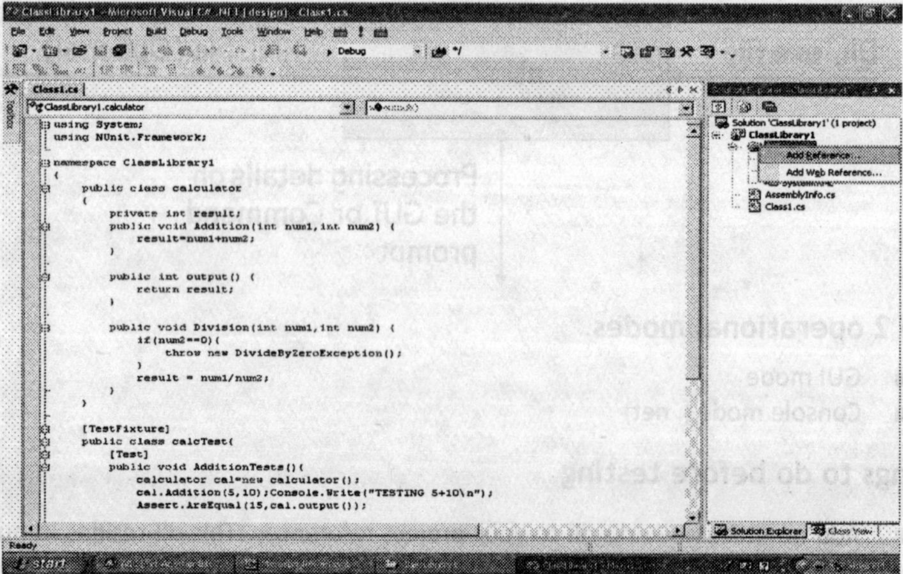

Select Browse

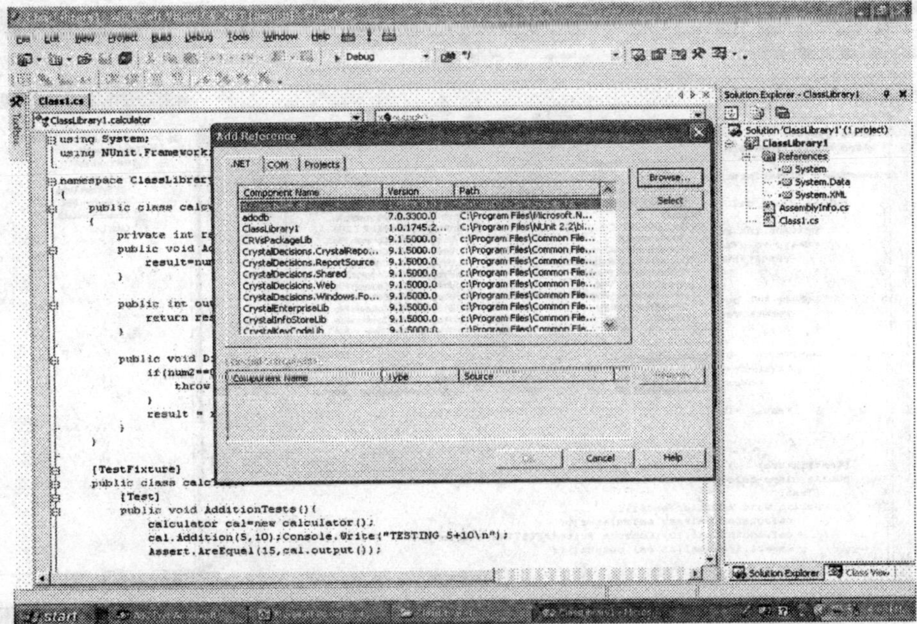

Goto the nunit\bin directory, choose nunit.framework.dll and press open.

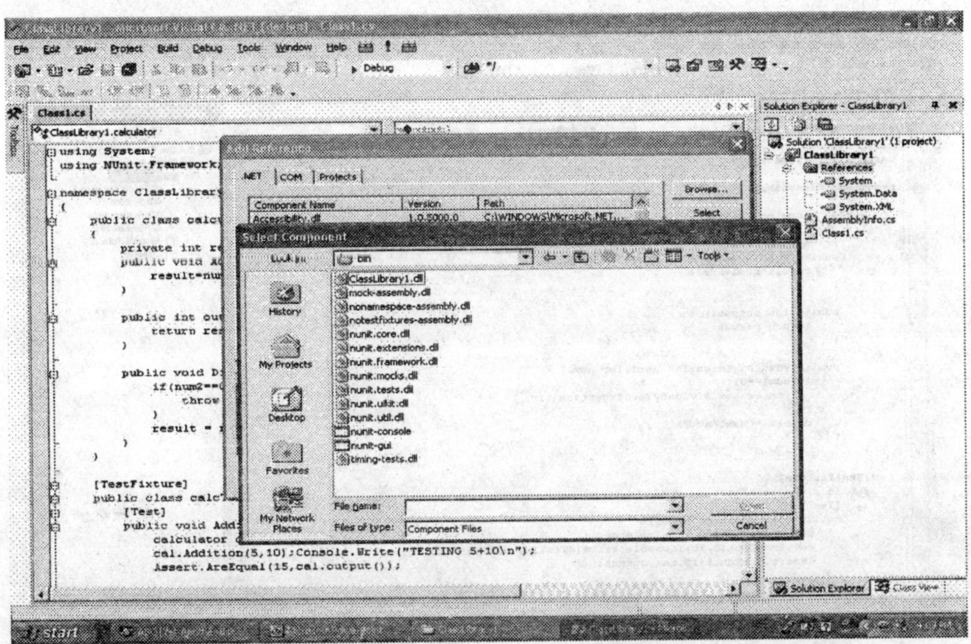

Now press ok in the Add reference page

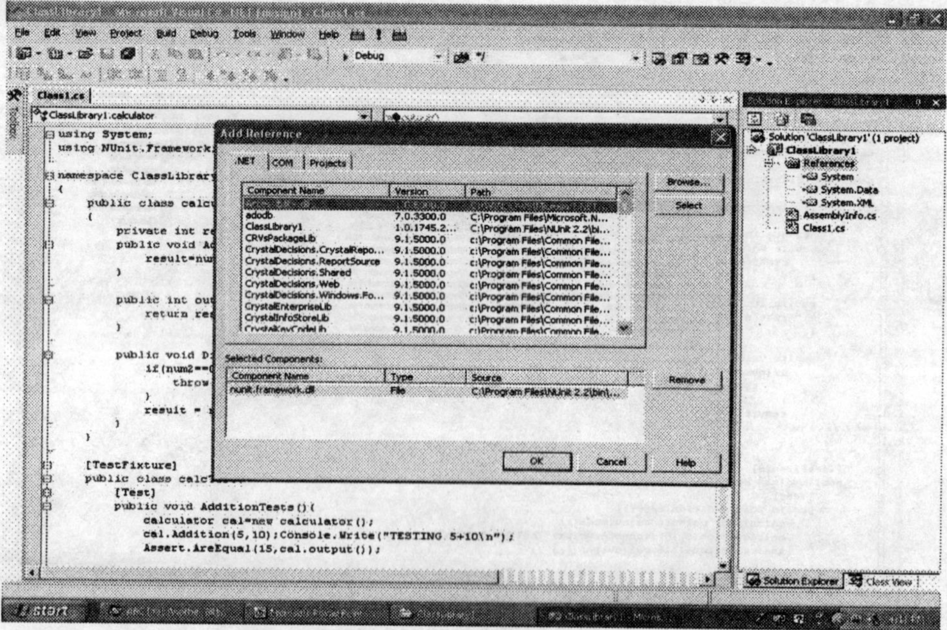

The dll has been added to your reference list.

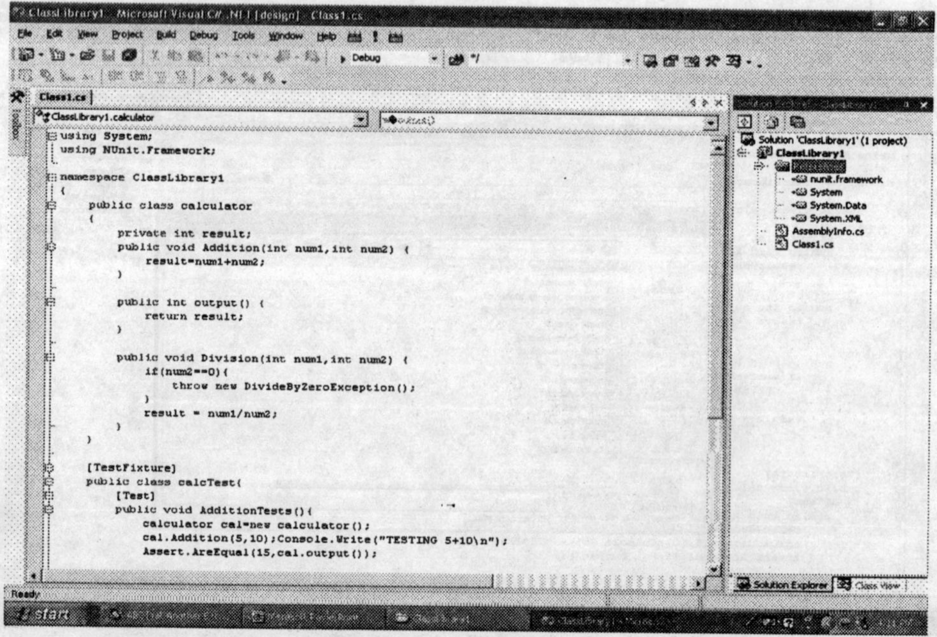

In your code, add using nunit.framework.

```
using System;
using NUnit.Framework;

namespace ClassLibrary1
{
    public class calculator
    {
        private int result;
        public void Addition(int num1,int num2) {
            result=num1+num2;
        }
        public int output() {
            return result;
        }

        public void Division(int num1,int num2) {
            if(num2==0){
                throw new DivideByZeroException();
            }
            result = num1/num2;
        }
    }

    [TestFixture]
    public class calcTest{
        [Test]
        public void AdditionTests(){
            calculator cal=new calculator();
            cal.Addition(5,10);Console.Write("TESTING 5+10\n");
            Assert.AreEqual(15,cal.output());
```

Add testfixture to your program

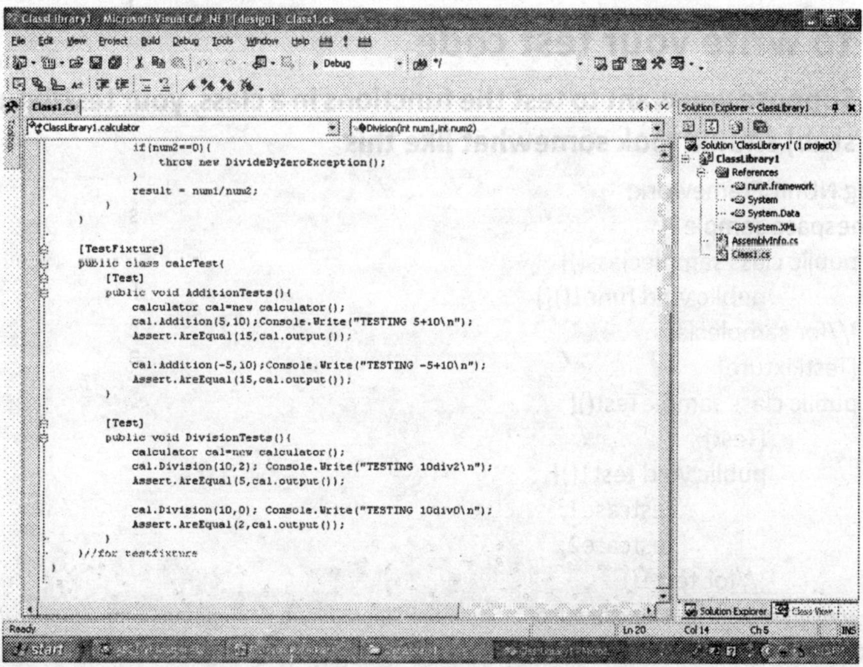

TestFixture Example

```
[TestFixture]
public class calcTest{
	[Test]
	public void AdditionTests(){
		calculator cal=new calculator();
		cal.Addition(5,10); //CASE 1
		Assert.AreEqual(15,cal.output());

		cal.Addition(-5,10); // CASE 2
		Assert.AreEqual(15,cal.output());
	}
	[Test]
	public void DivisionTests(){
		calculator cal=new calculator();
		cal.Division(10,2); // CASE 1
		Assert.AreEqual(5,cal.output());
		cal.Division(10,0);  //CASE 2
		Assert.AreEqual(2,cal.output());
	}
}//for testfixture
```

How to write your test code

- **Suppose you want to test the functions in a class, your testfixture(test stub) should look somewhat like this**

```
using NUnit.Framework;
Namespace sample1{
	public class sampleclass(){
		public void func1(){}
	}//for sampleclass
	[TestFixture]
	public class sampleTest(){
		[Test]
		public void test1(){
			testcase1;
			testcase2;
		}//for test1()
	}//for sampleTest textfixture
}//for namespace
```

Calculator Example

```
using System;
using NUnit.Framework;

namespace ClassLibrary1
{
        public class calculator
        {
                private int result;
                public void Addition(int num1,int num2){
                        result=num1+num2;
                }
                public int output(){
                        return result;
                }
                public void Division(int num1,int num2){
                        if(num2==0){
                                throw new DivideByZeroException();
                        }
                        result = num1/num2;
                }
        }

[TestFixture]
        public class calcTest
        {
                [Test]
                public void AdditionTests(){
                        calculator cal=new calculator();
                        cal.Addition(5,10);Console.Write("TESTING 5+10\n");
                        Assert.AreEqual(15,cal.output());

                        cal.Addition(-5,10);Console.Write("TESTING -5+10\n");
                        Assert.AreEqual(5,cal.output());
                }
                [Test]
                public void DivisionTests(){
                        calculator cal=new calculator();
                        cal.Division(10,2); Console.Write("TESTING 10div2\n");
```

```
                        Assert.AreEqual(5,cal.output());
                        cal.Division(10,0); Console.Write("TESTING 10div0\n");
                        Assert.AreEqual(0,cal.output());
                }
        }//for testfixture
}//for namespace
```

Build the Project

- After the testfixture is complete, build the project. This will create a dll file which will reside in projectname\bin\debug folder.

LOCATION of dll

- In this example I am copying the dll file from projectname\bin\debug folder to nunit\bin folder for my convenience.
- But this is not a requirement when we are testing and the dll can be run from projectname\bin\debug folder.

Location of exe files

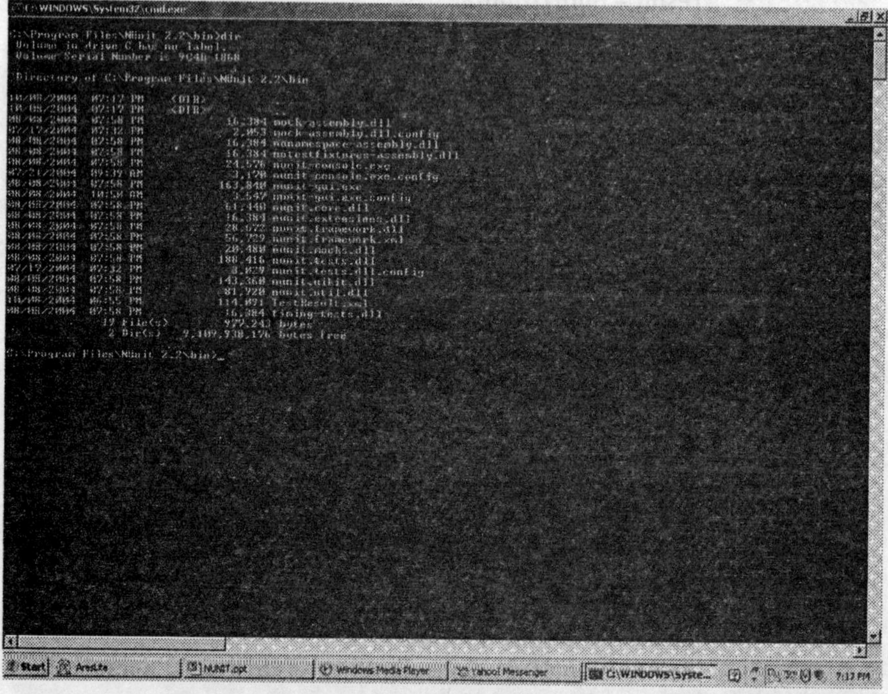

Starting the GUI from console

The GUI can be started from the console by executing

nunit-gui.exe [inputfilename][options]

Ex: nunit-gui.exe nunit.tests.dll –run

This option will load the dll file and run the test.

* Options with their values are separated by an equal, colon or a space.

Starting the GUI from console

- nunit-gui.exe [inputfilename][options]

Options:

/help short format: /?
/config=STR project config to load
/noload suppress loading of last proj
/run Automatically run after load
/fixture=STR Fixture to test

GUI MODE

- The steps to be followed are
  - Load the Dll file.
  - Select Run.
  - View the errors if any on the GUI screen.
  - Save the output XML if necessary.

Select open in the NUNIT GUI

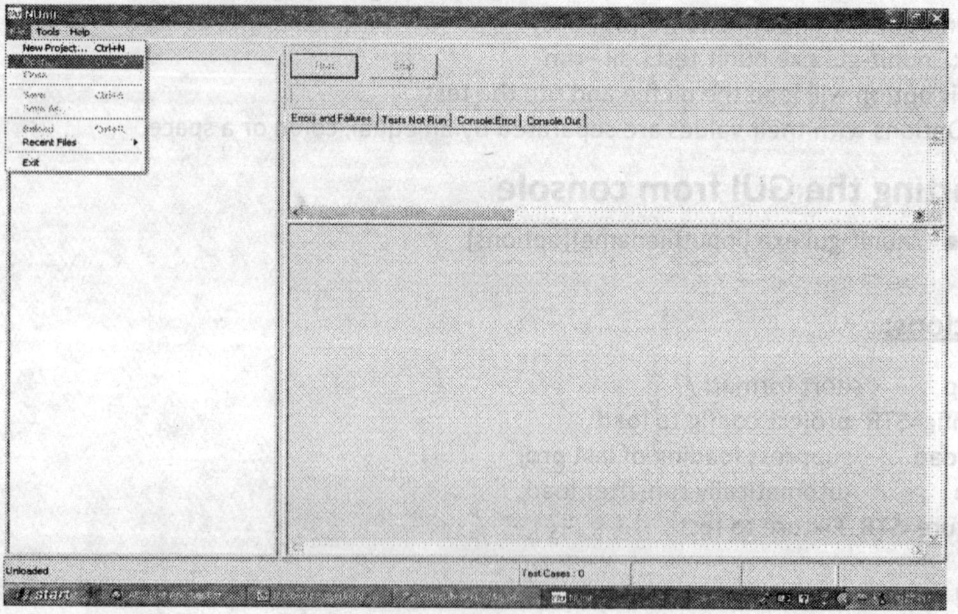

Select the dll which you want to test(In this case, we have moved the dll to the nunit\bin folder)

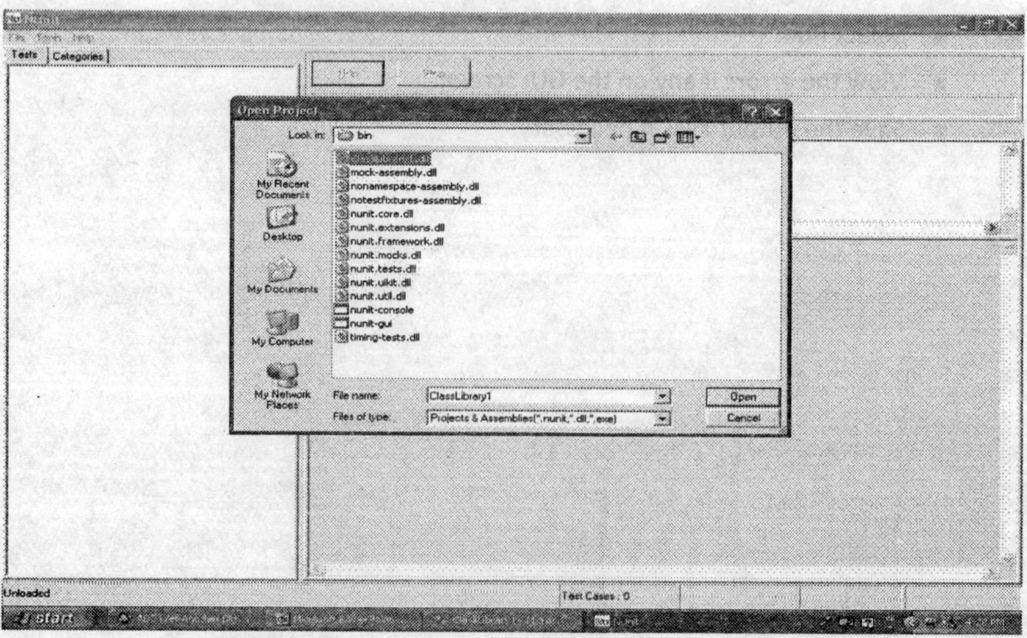

Runs Perfectly

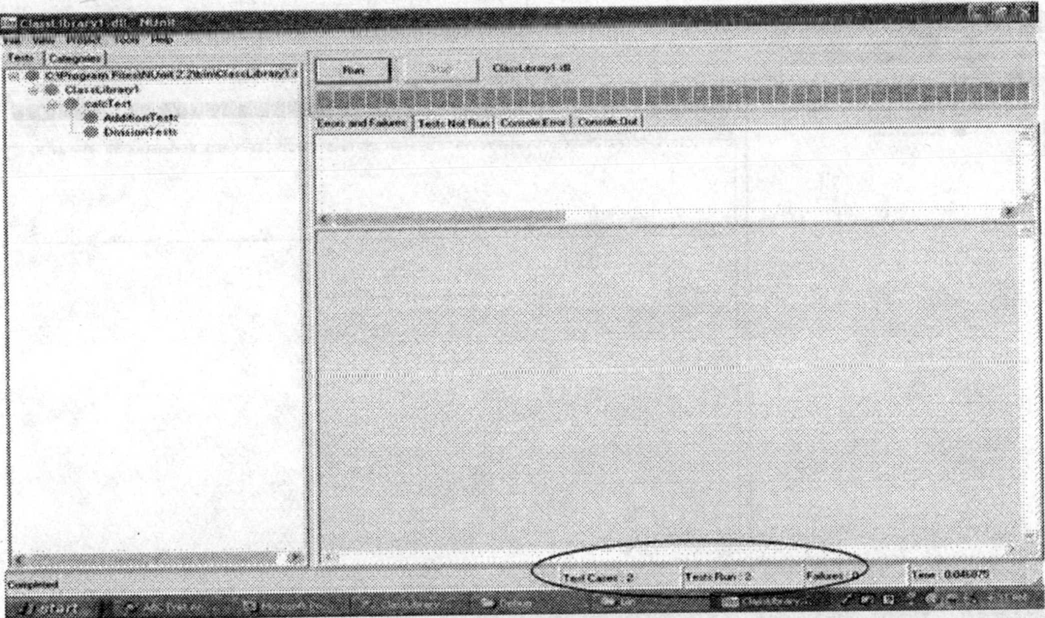

Tests Fail

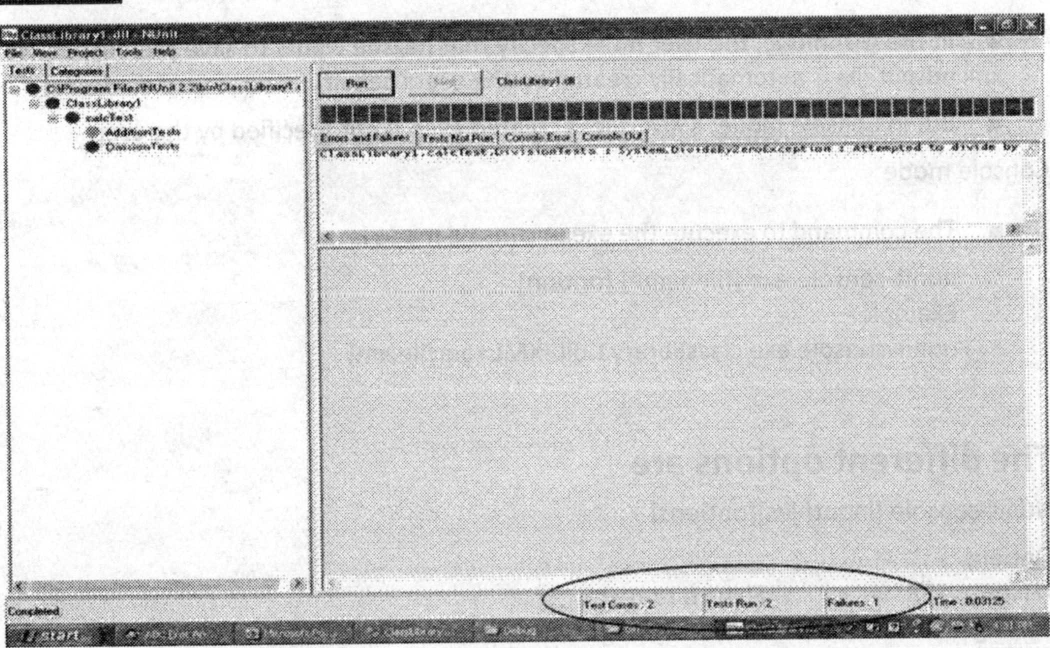

To save the output in an XML file

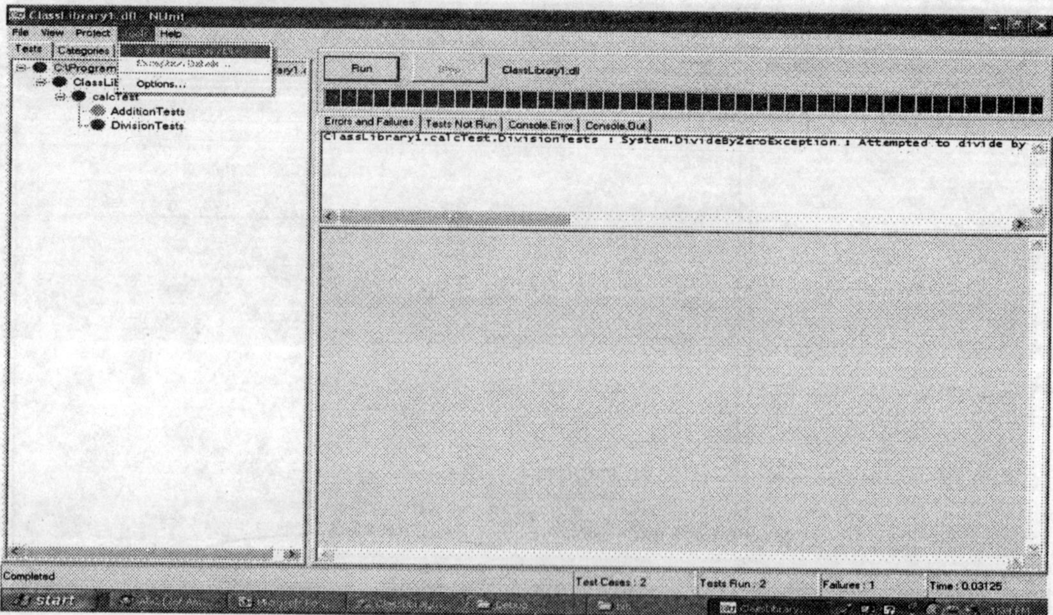

Writing in the output file

- In the GUI mode, the user must specify that he/she wants to save the output. No xml output file is automatically created on the users behalf.
- But in Console mode, a XML file is created even if not specified by the user.

Console mode

- The command to execute the exe in console mode is

  nunit-console.exe [filename] [option]
  Example:
  nunit-console.exe classlibrary1.dll -XML=ourfile.xml

The different options are

Nunit-console [inputfiles][options]

Options

/Fixture=STR Fixture to test
/config=STR project configuration to load
/XML=STR Name of XML output file

/transform=STR	name of transform file
/xmlConsole	display XML to the console
/output=STR	File to receive test output (short :/out=STR)
/err=STR	File to receive test error output
/labels	Label each test in stdout
/include = STR	list of categories to include
/exclude = STR	list of categories to exclude
/noshadow	disable shadow option
/thread	runs thread on a separate thread
/wait	wait for input before closing console window
/nologo	Do not display the logo
/help	Display help (short format: /?)

Runs Perfectly

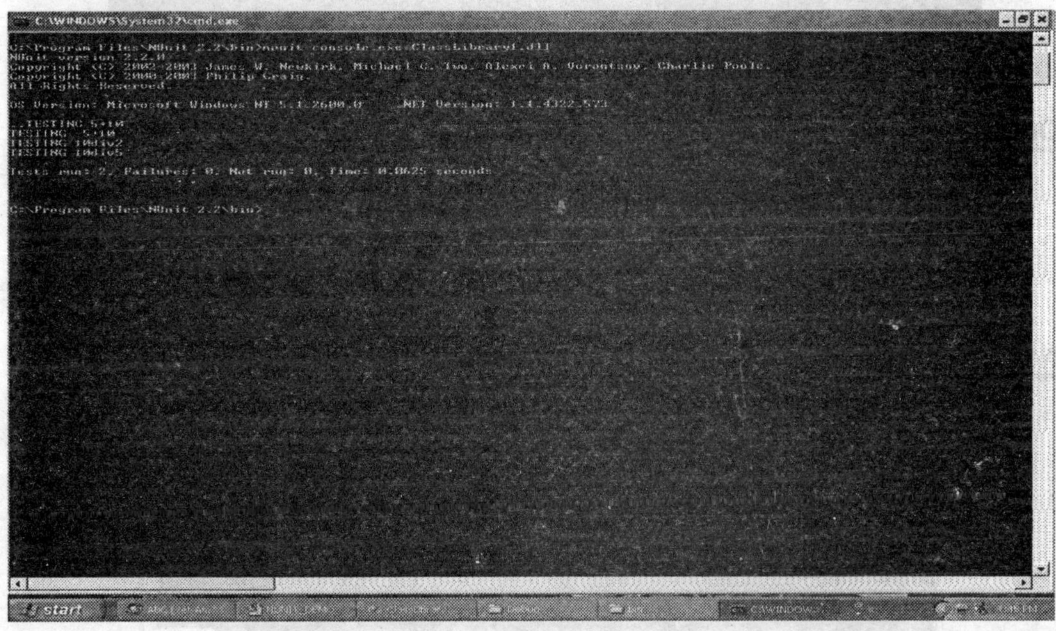

Test Fails

Output file

- As mentioned earlier, in console mode the xml file is automatically created as testresult.xml in the nunit\bin folder.
- The user can change the name of the output file by saying -XML = newfilename.xml as shown in the previous slide.

Now lets Examine the Output file (test passed)

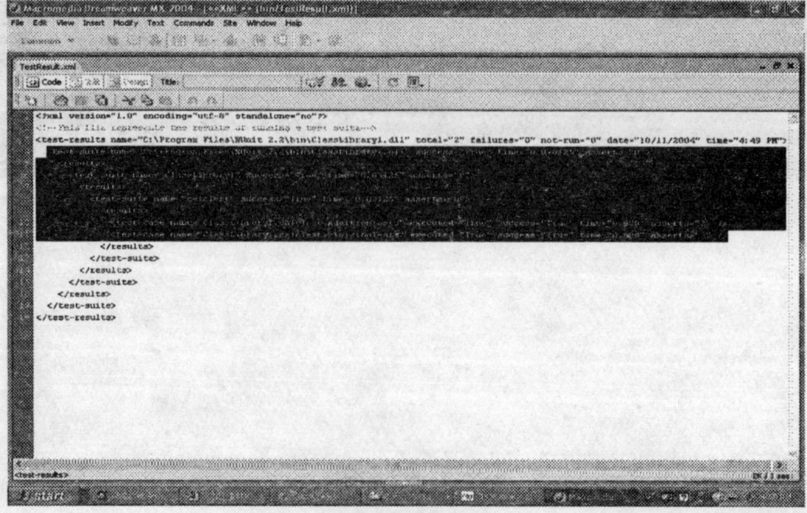

Test Failed

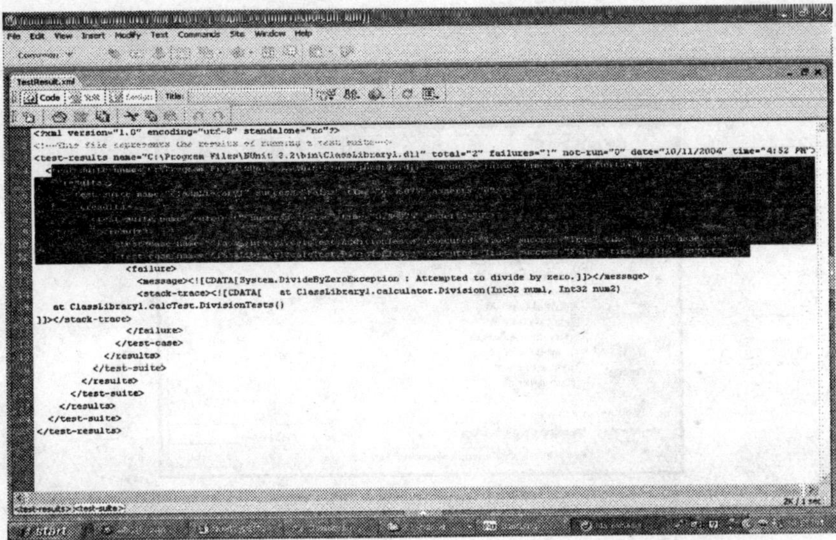

Proposed Architecture

- The architecture which has been proposed by the architect is
  - The user shall run his tests in the console mode of the nUnit tool after the dll has been created by the nAnt tool.
  - The output XML file shall be sent to the User Interface to accommodate information about the user, date, time and other related information.

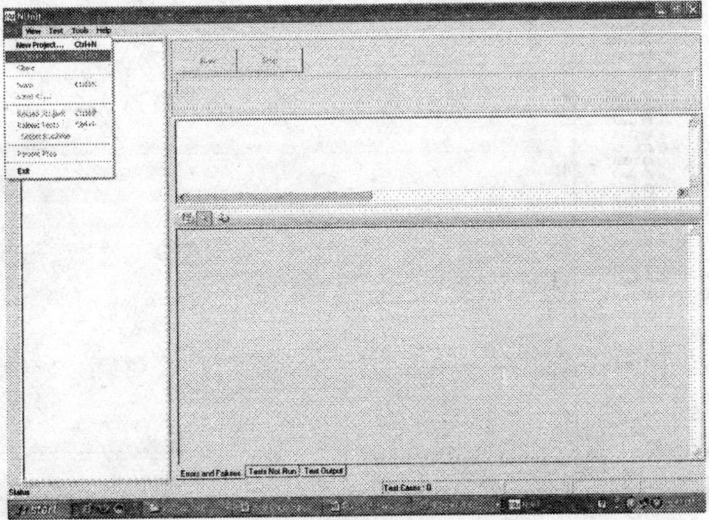

Open dll file

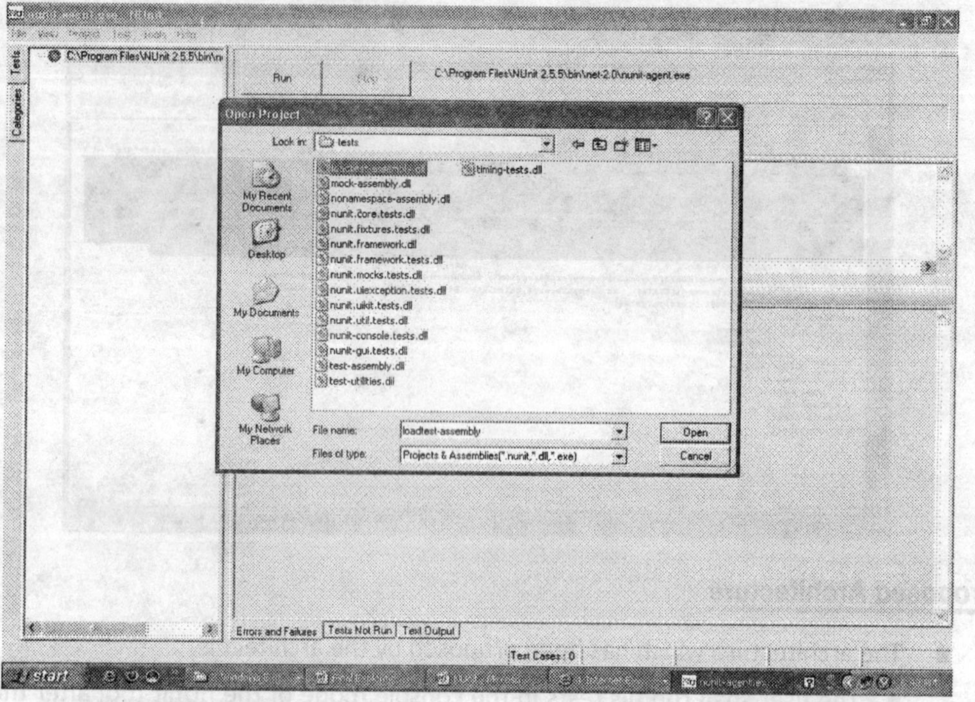

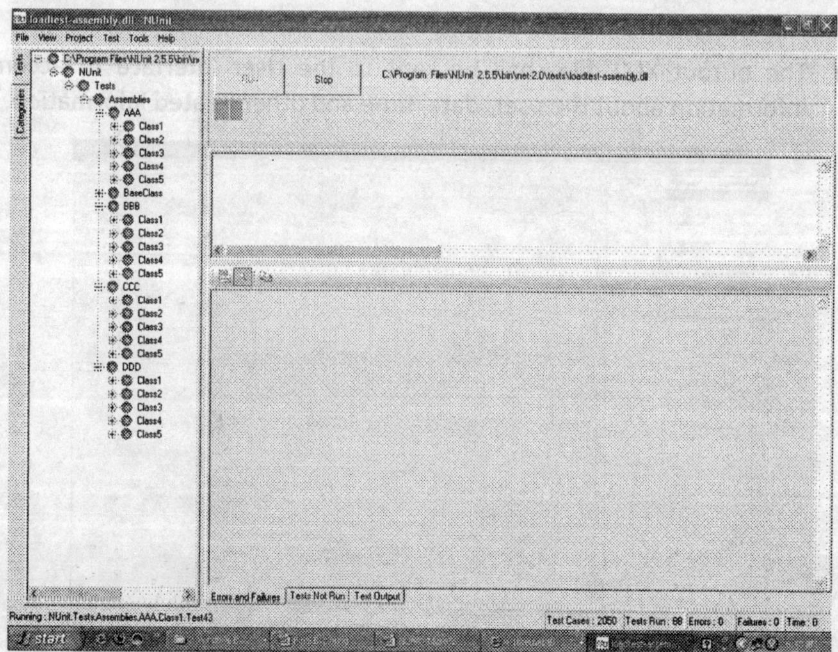

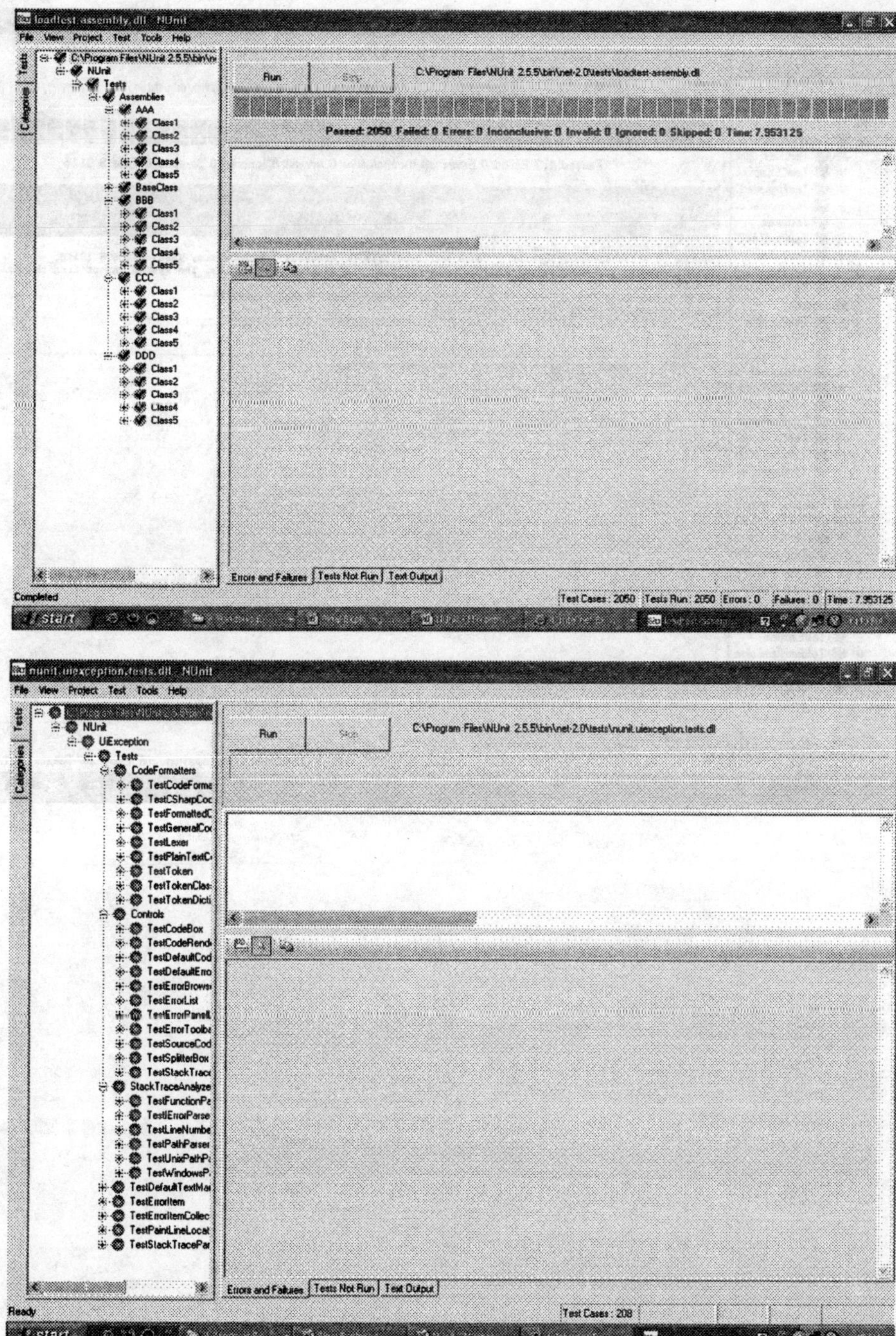

Click on 'Run'

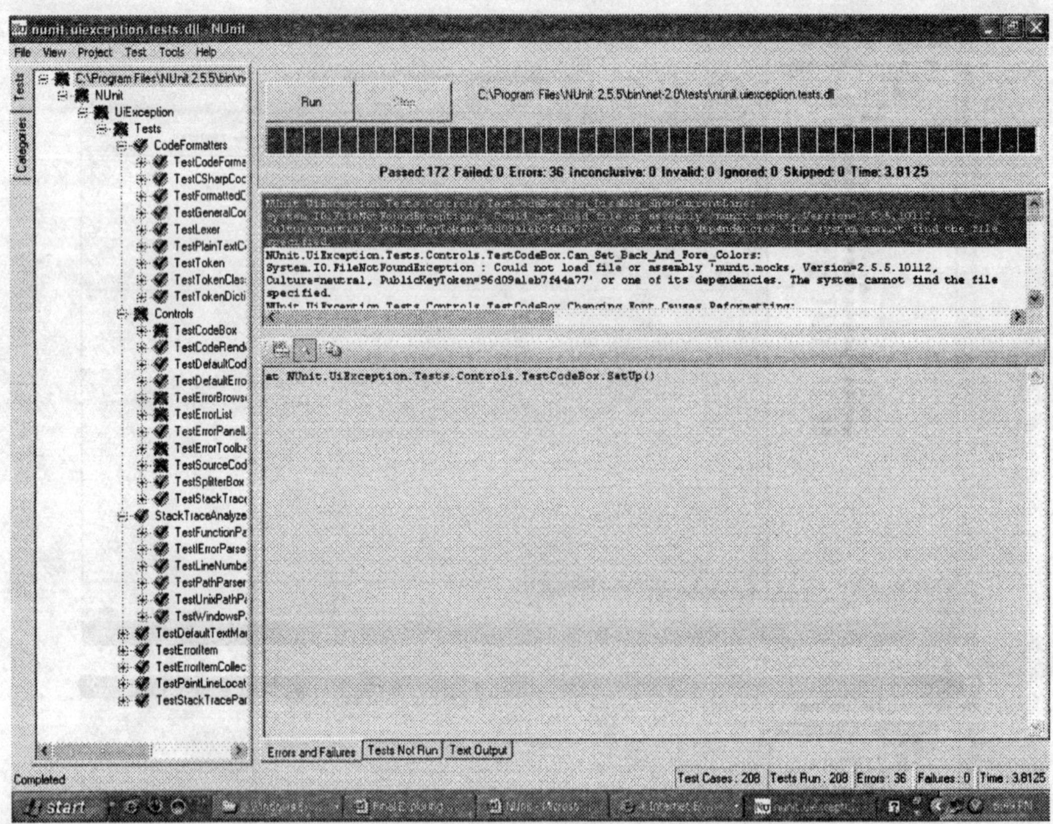
nunit.uiexception.tests.dll - NUnit
File View Project Test Tools Help
Run
C:\Program Files\NUnit 2.5.5\bin\net-2.0\tests\nunit.uiexception.tests.dll
Passed: 172 Failed: 0 Errors: 36 Inconclusive: 0 Invalid: 0 Ignored: 0 Skipped: 0 Time: 3.8125
NUnit.UiException.Tests.Controls.TestCodeBox.Can_Set_Back_And_Fore_Colors:
System.IO.FileNotFoundException : Could not load file or assembly 'nunit.mocks, Version=2.5.5.10112, Culture=neutral, PublicKeyToken=96d09a1eb7f44a77' or one of its dependencies. The system cannot find the file specified.
at NUnit.UiException.Tests.Controls.TestCodeBox.SetUp()
Tests
Categories
NUnit
UiException
Tests
CodeFormatters
TestLexer
TestToken
Controls
TestCodeBox
TestErrorList
TestSplitterBox
TestErrorItem
Errors and Failures
Tests Not Run
Text Output
Completed
Test Cases : 208
Tests Run : 208
Errors : 36
Failures : 0
Time : 3.8125
start

TDD Golder Rule:

Never write model code unless you have a test that requires it

TDD Best Practices

- Only work on one test at a time

  → Don't write a whole bunch of tests and then try to pass them all in one go

- Write test assertions self-explanatory so other developers can readily see what the code is supposed to be doing just by reading the tests
- Make the structure of your test projects follow the structure of the projects they are testing so developers can easily navigate from the tests to the code they are testing and vice-versa
- Keep the tests small

  → More than 15 minutes on the same test is probably too long. You will lose focus.

  → If a test looks complicated, think of ways to break it down. If a test involves several methods or classes that you'll have to write to pass the test then either:

    - Write tests for those first and work your way up to the bigger test (bottom-up TDD)
    - Fake them to pass this test and then work your way down to implement each of them one test at a time (top-down TDD)

- If you're working in a team, integrate your code changes after every few unit tests (say, every hour or two) to make sure there aren't any nasty surprises waiting for you in someone else's changes
- If you're working alone, end every day with one broken test to help you quickly refocus the next morning
- If you're working in a team, never ever leave with broken tests!
- Automate acceptance tests, too (this is a challenge, I must warn you) so that you can be confident when you're done and ready to release it to the customer.

TDD & Continuous Integration

- Before integrating your code changes tell all team members that you are about to. Until you have a successful build on the integration server, nobody else should consider integrating their changes
- Get any changed files that have been checked in to your team's repository (eg VSS, CVS) since you last checked out the code and merge those with your changes
- Run all of the tests
- Do not integrate if any of the tests fail
- If all tests pass then check in your code changes
- Do a build with the latest code in the repository on the integration server and run all of the tests against that build
- If all the tests pass then you have a successful build and other developers can start to integrate
- If any tests fail then you have a broken build, which means nobody else can start integrating – your team's priority is now to find out why the test(s) fail and fix the problem ASAP

References:

http://www.nunit.org/index.php?p=equalityAsserts&r=2.5.5

http://www.ecs.syr.edu/faculty/fawcett/handouts/Seminar_BrownBag/CodingAndUnitTest/NUNIT.ppt.

http://www.testdriven.com

http://www.xprogramming.com

http://workspaces.gotdotnet.com/tdd

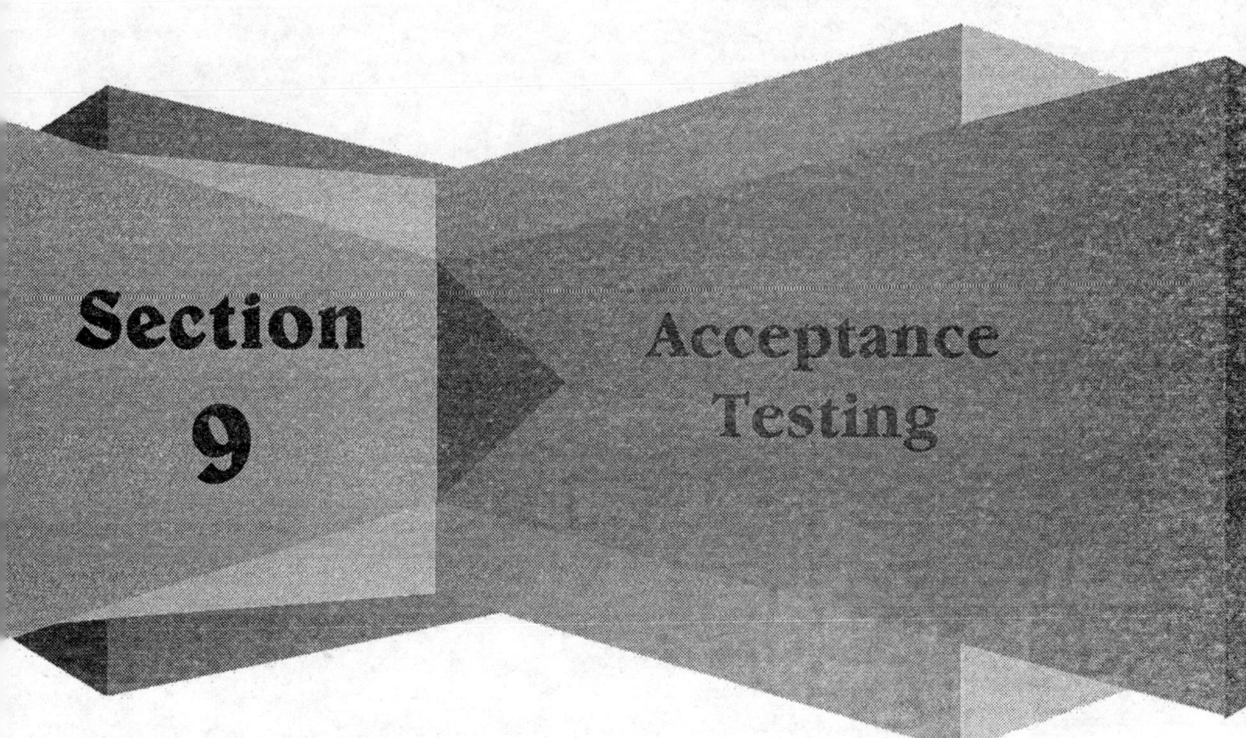
Section
9
Acceptance
Testing

What is UAT (User Acceptance Testing)

- **User Acceptance Testing** is a process where the actual users of the system test the remediated functionality to make sure there are no errors or defects.
- The users will "Accept" the system when all testing has passed.

The objective of software development is to develop the software that meets the true needs of the user, not just the system specifications.

To accomplish this, testers should work with the users early in a project to clearly define the criteria that would make the software acceptable in meeting the user needs.

Acceptance Testing Concepts

- **Software acceptance** is an incremental process of approving or rejecting software systems during development or maintenance, according to how well the software satisfies predefined criteria.
- **Acceptance decisions** occur at pre-specified times when processes, support tools, interim documentation, segments of the software, and finally the total software system must meet predefined criteria for acceptance.
- **The final acceptance decision** occurs with verification that the delivered documentation is adequate and consistent with the executable system and that the complete software system meets all buyer requirements.
- **Formal final software acceptance testing** must occur at the end of the development process. It consists of tests to determine whether the developed system meets predetermined functionality, performance, quality, and interface criteria.
- **Acceptance testing** involves procedures for identifying acceptance criteria for interim life cycle products and for accepting them.

As a life cycle process, software acceptance enables:

- Early detection of software problems (and time for the customer or user to plan for possible late delivery)
- Preparation of appropriate test facilities
- Early consideration of the user's needs during software development

The Customer or User's Responsibilities in Acceptance Testing

- Ensure user involvement in developing system requirements and acceptance criteria.

- Identify interim and final products for acceptance, their acceptance criteria, and schedule.
- Plan how and by whom each acceptance activity will be performed.
- Plan resources for providing information on which to base acceptance decisions.
- Schedule adequate time for buyer staff to receive and examine products and evaluations prior to acceptance review.
- Prepare the Acceptance Plan.
- Respond to the analyses of project entities before accepting or rejecting.
- Approve the various interim software products against quantified criteria at interim points.
- Perform the final acceptance activities, including formal acceptance testing, at delivery.
- Make an acceptance decision for each product

Acceptance Testing Measures the Software's "Fit"

- Is the software "fit" for use?
- Does it "fit" into the customer's business process?

The Four Components of Fit

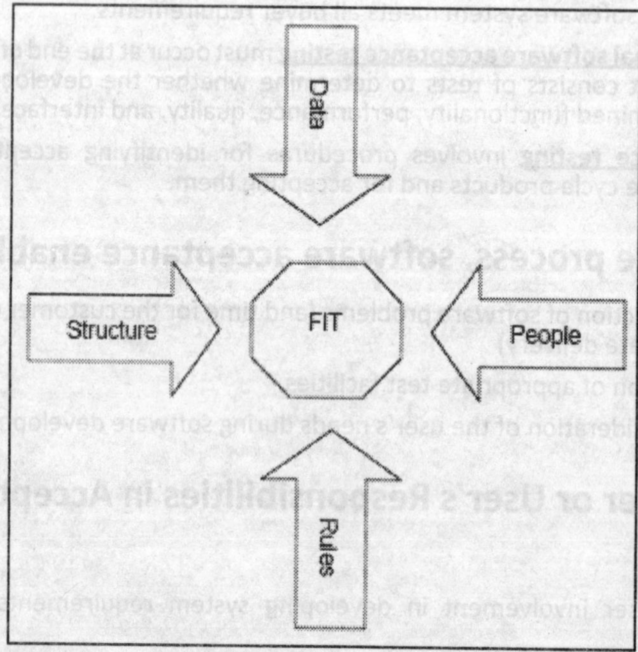

The Four Components of "Fit"

- **Data**

  The reliability, timeliness, consistency, and usefulness of the data included in the automated application.

- **People**

  People should have the skills, training, aptitude, and desire to properly use and interact with the automated application.

- **Structure**

  The structure is the proper development of application systems to optimize technology and satisfy requirements.

- **Rules**

  The rules are the procedures to follow in processing the data.

At a minimum the user will have the following roles in acceptance testing:

- Defining acceptance criteria in a testable format.
- Providing the use cases that will be used in acceptance testing.
- Training user personnel in using the new software system.
- Providing the necessary resources, primarily user staff personnel, for acceptance testing.
- Comparing the actual acceptance testing results with the desired acceptance testing results (NOTE: This may be performed using testing software).
- Making decisions as to whether additional work is needed prior to placing the software in operation, whether the software can be placed in operation with additional work to be done, or whether the software is fully acceptable and can be placed into production as is.

Acceptance Criteria that "Should" be in the Requirements Specifications

Functionality Requirements

These requirements relate to the business rules that the system must execute.

Performance Requirements

These requirements relate to operational aspects, such as time or resource constraints.

Interface Quality Requirements

These requirements relate to connections from one component to another component of processing (e.g., human-machine, machine-module).

Overall Software Quality Requirements

These requirements specify limits for factors or attributes such as reliability, testability, correctness, and usability.

Example of Required Information to Document Acceptance Criteria

Table 21. Example of Required Information to Document Acceptance Criteria

Criteria	Action
Hardware/Software Project	The name of the project being acceptance-tested. This is the name the user or customer calls the project.
Number	A sequential number identifying acceptance criteria.
Acceptance Requirement	A user requirement that will be used to determine whether the corrected hardware/software is acceptable.
Critical / Non -Critical	Indicate whether the acceptance requirement is critical, meaning that it must be met, or non-critical, meaning that it is desirable but not essential.
Test Result	Indicates after acceptance testing whether the requirement is acceptable or not acceptable, meaning that the project is rejected because it does not meet the requirement.
Comments	Clarify the criticality of the requirement; or indicate the meaning of the test result rejection. For example: The software cannot be run; or management will make a judgment after acceptance testing as to whether the project can be run.

Acceptance Criteria Example

Project Description	Type of system; life cycle methodology; user community of delivered system; major tasks system must satisfy; major external interfaces of the system; expected normal usage; potential misuse; risks; constraints; standards and practices.
User Responsibilities	Organization and responsibilities for acceptance activities; resource and schedule requirements; facility requirements; requirements for automated support; special data, and training; standards, practices, and conventions; updates and reviews of acceptance plans and related products.
Administrative Procedures	Anomaly reports; change control; record-keeping; communication between developer and manager organizations.
Acceptance Description	Objectives for entire project; summary of acceptance criteria; major acceptance activities and reviews; information requirements; types of acceptance decisions; responsibility for acceptance decisions.

http://www.agilemodeling.com/artifacts/useCaseDiagram.htm

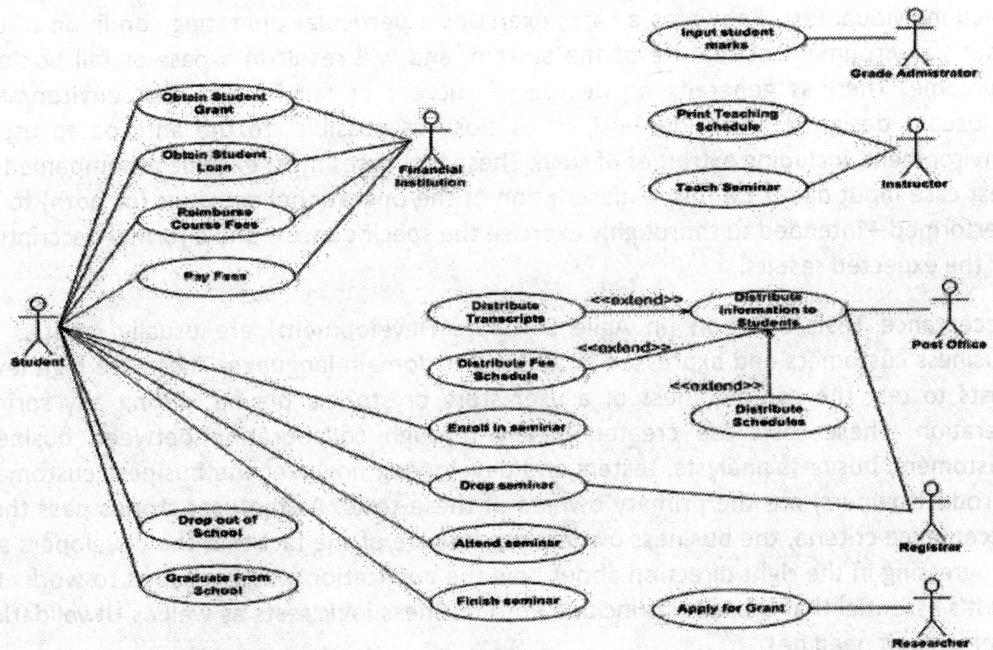

Scott W. Ambler

- **Using System boundary boxes to indicate releases:**

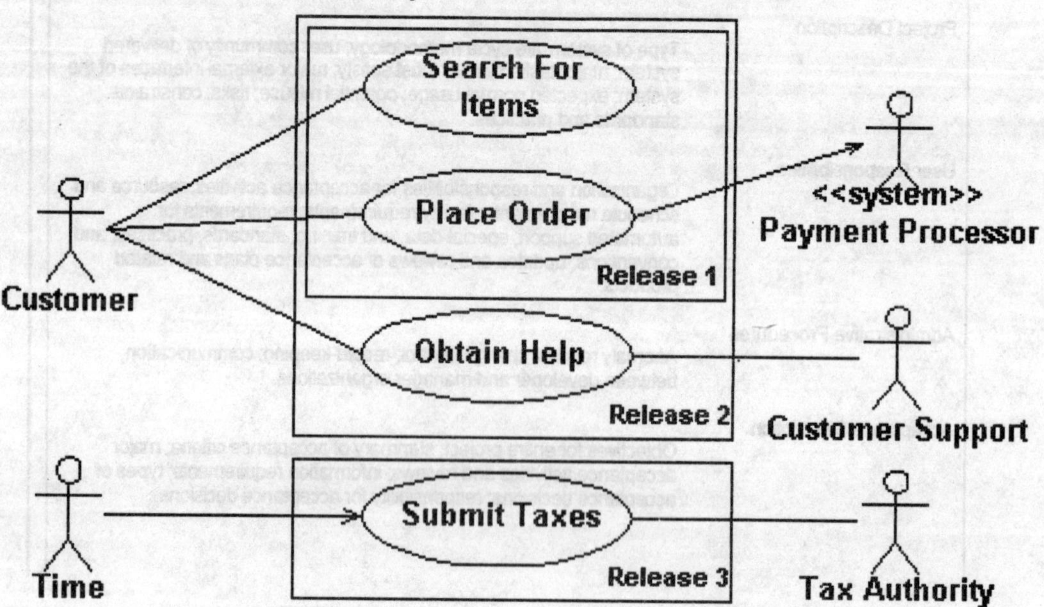

Acceptance testing generally involves running a suite of tests on the completed system. Each individual test, known as a case, exercises a particular operating condition of the user's environment or feature of the system, and will result in a pass or fail boolean outcome. There is generally no degree of success or failure. The test environment is usually designed to be identical, or as close as possible, to the anticipated user's environment, including extremes of such. These test cases must each be accompanied by test case input data or a formal description of the operational activities (or both) to be performed—intended to thoroughly exercise the specific case—and a formal description of the expected results.

Acceptance Tests/Criterion (in Agile Software Development) are usually created by business customers and expressed in a business domain language. These are high level tests to test the completeness of a user story or stories 'played' during any sprint/iteration. These tests are created ideally through collaboration between business customers, business analysts, testers and developers, however the business customers (product owners) are the primary owners of these tests. As the user stories pass their acceptance criteria, the business owners can be sure of the fact that the developers are progressing in the right direction about how the application was envisaged to work and so it's essential that these tests include both business logic tests as well as UI validation elements (if need be).

Acceptance test cards are ideally created during sprint planning or iteration planning meeting, before development begins so that the developers have a clear idea of what to develop. Sometimes (due to bad planning!) acceptance tests may span multiple stories (that are not implemented in the same sprint) and there are different ways to test them out during actual sprints. One popular technique is to mock external interfaces or data to mimick other stories which might not be played out during an iteration (as those stories may have been relatively lower business priority). A user story is not considered complete until the acceptance tests have passed.

Process

The acceptance test suite is run against the supplied input data or using an acceptance test script to direct the testers. Then the results obtained are compared with the expected results. If there is a correct match for every case, the test suite is said to pass. If not, the system may either be rejected or accepted on conditions previously agreed between the sponsor and the manufacturer.

The objective is to provide confidence that the delivered system meets the business requirements of both sponsors and users. The acceptance phase may also act as the final quality gateway, where any quality defects not previously detected may be uncovered.

A principal purpose of acceptance testing is that, once completed successfully, and provided certain additional (contractually agreed) acceptance criteria are met, the sponsors will then sign off on the system as satisfying the contract (previously agreed between sponsor and manufacturer), and deliver final payment.

[edit] User acceptance testing

User Acceptance Testing (UAT) is a process to obtain confirmation by a Subject Matter Expert (SME), preferably the owner or client of the object under test, through trial or review, that a system meets mutually agreed-upon requirements. In software development, UAT is one of the final stages of a project and often occurs before a client or customer accepts the new system.

Users of the system perform these tests, which developers derive from the client's contract or the user requirements specification.

Test designers draw up formal tests and devise a range of severity levels. It is preferable that the designer of the user acceptance tests not be the creator of the formal integration and system test cases for the same system, however there are some situations where this may not be avoided. The UAT acts as a final verification of the required business function and proper functioning of the system, emulating real-world usage conditions on behalf of the paying client or a specific large customer. If the software works as intended and without issues during normal use, one can reasonably infer the same level of stability in production. These tests, which are usually performed by clients or end-users, are not usually focused on identifying simple problems such as spelling errors and cosmetic problems, nor show stopper defects, such as software crashes; testers and developers previously identify and fix these issues during earlier unit testing, integration testing, and system testing phases.

The results of these tests give confidence to the clients as to how the system will perform in production. There may also be legal or contractual requirement for acceptance of the system.

[edit] Q-UAT - Quantified User Acceptance Testing

Quantified User Acceptance Testing (Q-UAT or, more simply, the Quantified Approach) is a revised Business Acceptance Testing process which aims to provide a smarter and faster alternative to the traditional UAT phase.[citation needed] Depth-testing is carried out against Business Requirement only at specific planned points in the application or service under test. A reliance on better quality code delivery from Development/Build phase is assumed and a complete understanding of the appropriate Business Process is a pre-requisite. This methodology if carried out correctly results in a quick turnaround against plan, a decreased number of test scenarios which are more complex and wider in breadth than traditional UAT and ultimately the equivalent confidence level attained via a shorter delivery window, allowing products/changes to be brought to market quicker.

The Approach is based on a ‘gated’ 3-dimensional model the key concepts of which are:

- Linear Testing (LT, the 1st dimension)
- Recursive Testing (RT, the 2nd dimension)
- Adaptive Testing (AT, the 3rd dimension).

The four ‘gates’ which conjoin and support the 3-dimensional model act as quality safeguards and include contemporary testing concepts such as:

- Internal Consistency Checks (ICS)
- Major Systems/Services Checks (MSC)
- Realtime/Reactive Regression (RTR).

The Quantified Approach was shaped by the former “guerilla” method of Acceptance Testing which was itself a response to testing phases which proved too costly to be sustainable for many small/medium-scale projects.

[edit] Acceptance testing in Extreme Programming

Acceptance testing is a term used in agile software development methodologies, particularly Extreme Programming, referring to the functional testing of a user story by the software development team during the implementation phase.

The customer specifies scenarios to test when a user story has been correctly implemented. A story can have one or many acceptance tests, whatever it takes to ensure the functionality works. Acceptance tests are black box system tests. Each acceptance test represents some expected result from the system. Customers are responsible for verifying the correctness of the acceptance tests and reviewing test scores to decide which failed tests are of highest priority. Acceptance tests are also used as regression tests prior to a production release. A user story is not considered complete until it has passed its acceptance tests. This means that new acceptance tests must be created for each iteration or the development team will report zero progress.[2]

Types of acceptance testing

Typical types of acceptance testing include the following

User acceptance testing

This may include factory acceptance testing, i.e. the testing done by factory users before the factory is moved to its own site, after which site acceptance testing may be performed by the users at the site.

Operational acceptance testing

Also known as operational readiness testing, this refers to the checking done to a system to ensure that processes and procedures are in place to allow the system to be used and maintained. This may include checks done to back-up facilities, procedures for disaster recovery, training for end users, maintenance procedures, and security procedures.

Contract and regulation acceptance testing

In contract acceptance testing, a system is tested against acceptance criteria as documented in a contract, before the system is accepted. In regulation acceptance testing, a system is tested to ensure it meets governmental, legal and safety standards.

Alpha and beta testing

Alpha testing takes place at developers' sites, and involves testing of the operational system by internal staff, before it is released to external customers. Beta testing takes place at customers' sites, and involves testing by a group of customers who use the system at their own locations and provide feedback, before the system is released to other customers. The latter is often called "field testing".

Test Case Document Example

Step #	Execution Procedure or Input	Expected Result or Output	Passed/Failed
CLN1	*Add a New Client, Status Incomplete*		
CLN1 1.1	Log in to the CMIS application with a valid User ID and Password.	Logged in to CMIS.	
CLN1 1.2	Click the Add New Client link.	New Client page opens.	
CLN1 1.3	Complete all the required fields (listed in the Required Fields list at the right of the screen) and any non-required fields, click Save.	The data entered or selected is saved.	
CLN1 1.4	Click the Guardian menu tab.	Guardian/Spouse screen opens.	
CLN1 1.5	Complete all the required fields and any non-required fields, click Save.	The data entered or selected is saved.	
CLN1 1.6	Click the Financial menu tab.	Financial page opens.	
CLN1 1.7	Complete all the required fields and any non-required fields, click Save.	The data entered or selected is saved.	
CLN1 1.8	Click the Insurance menu tab.	Insurance page opens.	
CLN1 1.9	Choose 'No' for the following fields: Medicaid Determination and Applied for CHIP. Click Save.	The data entered or selected is saved.	
CLN1 1.10	Click the Medical menu tab.	Medical page opens.	
CLN1 1.11	Complete all the required fields and any non-required fields, click Save.	The data entered or selected is saved.	
CLN1 1.12	Click the Client Info tab at the right of the screen.	The Client Status is listed as Incomplete (I).	

List of Acceptance Testing Frameworks

- Framework for Integrated Test (*Fit*)
- FitNesse, a fork of Fit
- ItsNat Java AJAX web framework with built-in, server based, functional web testing capabilities.
- Selenium (software)
- iMacros
- Ranorex
- Watir
- Test Automation FX
- StoryTestIQ (STIQ) a mash-up of Selenium and the FitNesse wiki

Framework for Integrated Test (FIT)

Framework for Integrated Test, or "Fit", is an open-source tool for automated customer tests. It integrates the work of customers, analysts, testers, and developers.

Customers provide examples of how their software should work. Those examples are then connected to the software with programmer-written test fixtures and automatically checked for correctness. The customers' examples are formatted in tables and saved as HTML using ordinary business tools such as Microsoft Excel. When Fit checks the document, it creates a copy and colors the tables green, red, and yellow according to whether the software behaved as expected.

Fit was invented by Ward Cunningham in 2002. He created the initial Java version of Fit. As of June 2005, it has up-to-date versions for Java, C#, Python, Perl, PHP and Smalltalk.

Although Fit is an acronym, the word "Fit" came first, making it a backronym. Fit is sometimes italicized but should not be capitalized. In other words, "Fit" and "*Fit*" are appropriate usage, but "FIT" is not.

Fit includes a simple command-line tool for checking Fit documents. There are third-party front-ends available. Of these, FitNesse is the most popular. FitNesse is a complete IDE for Fit that uses a Wiki for its front end. As of June 2005, FitNesse had forked Fit, making it incompatible with newer versions of Fit, but plans were underway to re-merge with Fit.

References:

http://en.wikipedia.org/wiki/Framework_for_Integrated_Test

http://en.wikipedia.org/wiki/Acceptance_testing

User Acceptance Testing Using Fitnesse / Fit

Introduction of Fitnesse

— Two pieces of Fitnesse

- FIT (Framework for Acceptance Tests)
- Fitnesse

➢ Allows specifications to be written in HTML, Excel or Wiki format

➢ Can use any language underneath (runners for .NET, Java, Python, Ruby and others)

What is Fitnesse / Fit?

➢ Fitnesse is a web server, wiki and an automation testing tool for testing.

➢ It supports acceptance testing rather than unit testing.

➢ It requires no configuration or set up.

➢ It is a wiki based system easy for creating ,running and organizing FIT test tables.

➢ Fit test tables are easy to read and understand.

➢ Tests are expressed as tables of input data and expected output data

Features

- FitNesse enables customers, testers, and programmers to learn what their software should do, and to automatically compare that to what it actually does do.
- It creates a feedback loop between customers, testers and programmers.
- FitNesse allows users of a developed system to enter specially formatted input (its format is accessible to non-programmers).
- It creates a link between customer expectations and output data

How It Works

- The Framework for Integrated Test (Fit) is the most well-known implementation (*open source framework*) of the table-based acceptance testing approach.
- Fit lets customers and analysts write "executable" acceptance tests using simple HTML tables.
- Developers write "fixtures" to link the test cases with the actual system itself.
- Fit compares these test cases, written using HTML tables, with actual values, returned by the system, and highlights the results with colors and annotations.

- User enters the input, interprets it and tests are created automatically.
- These tests are then executed by the system and output is returned back to the user.
- The advantage of this approach is very fast feedback from users.
- Fit needs hooks to the software under test; these hooks are called fixtures.

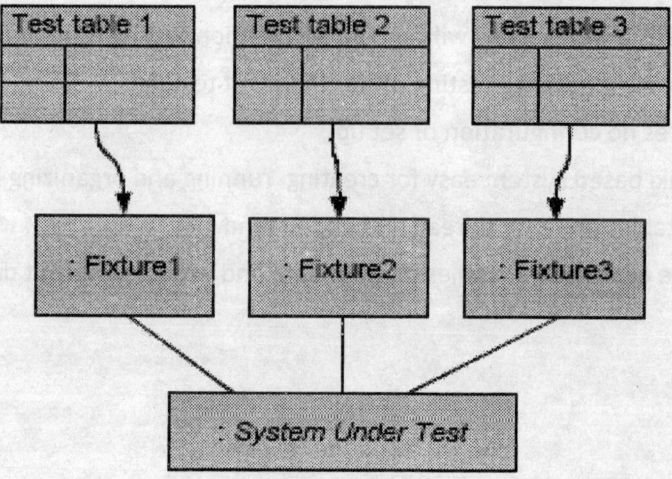

Pre requisite:

All you require in order to start using fitnesse is Java 5 (or higher). Only a JRE (Java Runtime Environment) is required and not the full-blown JDK (Java Development Kit).

There is a good chance that Java is already installed on your system and you can verify whether it is ready to run fitnesse by opening a command prompt and typing the following command:

```
java -version
```

If the system responds with a java version that is 1.5 or greater, you are ready to download and run fitnesse.

You can download Java from here: http://www.java.com/download.

How to Install:

http://fitnesse.org/

It really takes very little time and effort to get FitNesse running on your machine.

1. Go to http://fitnesse.org/FrontPage.FitNesseDevelopment.DownLoad and click on the most recent fitnesse.jar file.
    - If this is a brand new installation, just put it in some convenient empty directory.
    - If this is an update, then copy it on top of the old fitnesse.jar in your current installation.
2. Type java -jar fitnesse.jar
    - It will ask you to be patient as it installs or updates.
    - When it's done, it will ask you to reload fitnesse. Type java -jar fitnesse.jar again.
    - If you have nothing running on port 80 on your machine, you should see a message similar to the following:
        - Fitnesse (*date code*) Started...
        - on port 80
        - using path '.'

- using dir 'FitNesseRoot'
- Not logging.

If you don't see this, you may have something running on port 80 already,

- So try the command java -jar fitnesse.jar -p 8080
- If you are still having trouble then check out FitNesseWontStart.

1. Start up a browser and go to http://localhost
    - *or if you had to edit run.bat in step 3 then go to http://localhost:8080.*
2. The main FitNesse screen should come up. That's it. You're ready to start using FitNesse.

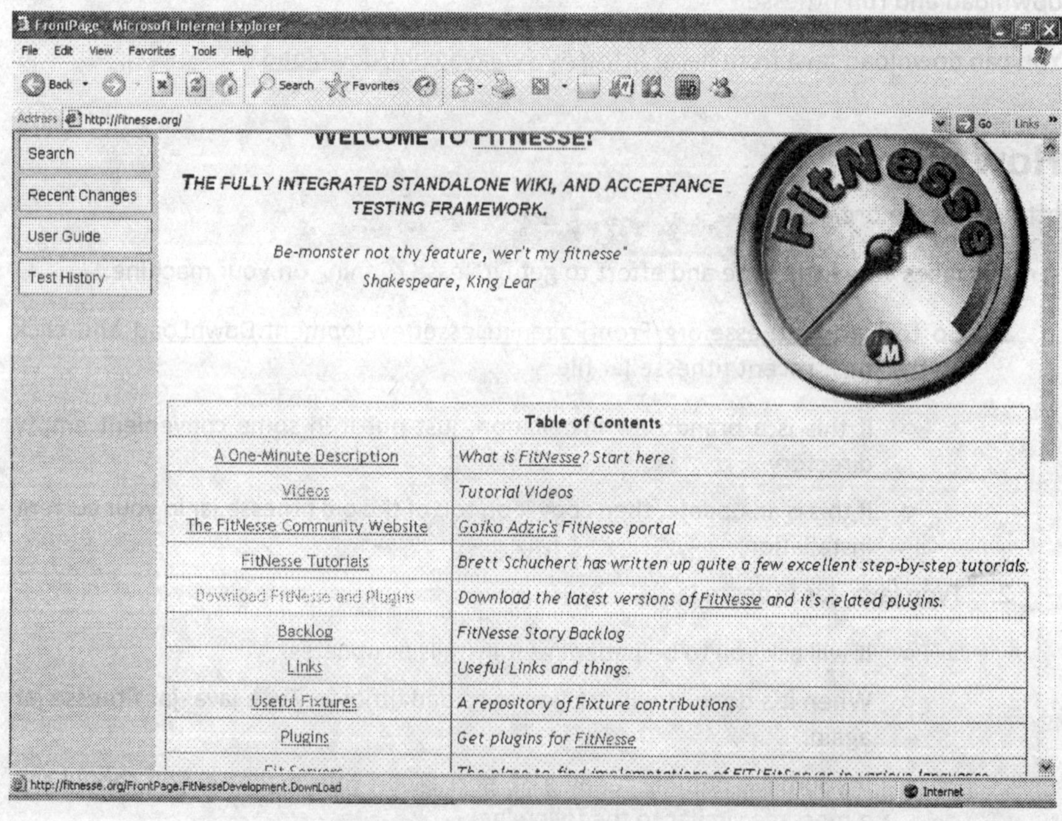

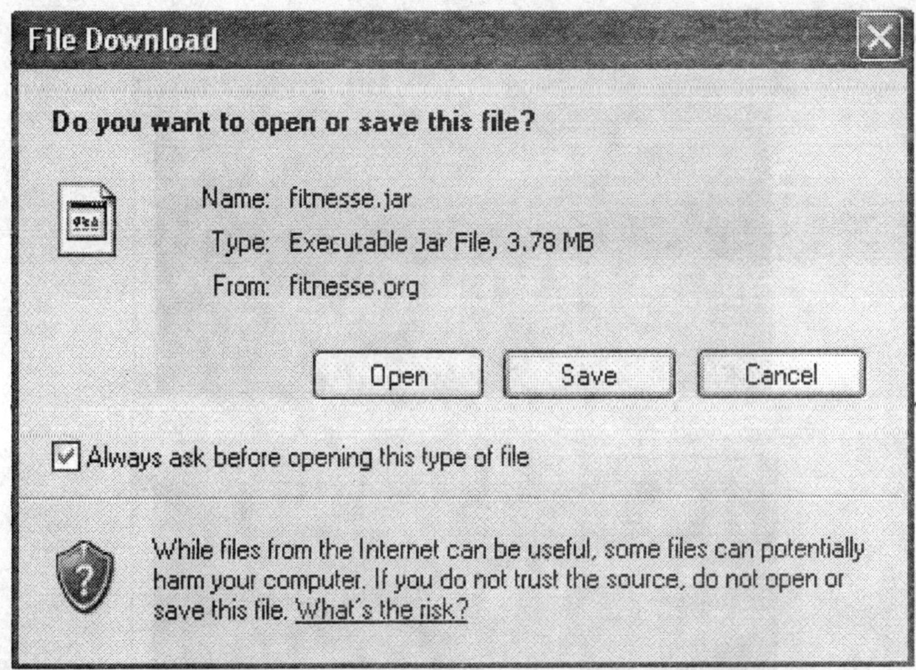
File Download
Do you want to open or save this file?
Name: fitnesse.jar
Type: Executable Jar File, 3.78 MB
From: fitnesse.org
Open
Save
Cancel
Always ask before opening this type of file
While files from the Internet can be useful, some files can potentially harm your computer. If you do not trust the source, do not open or save this file. What's the risk?

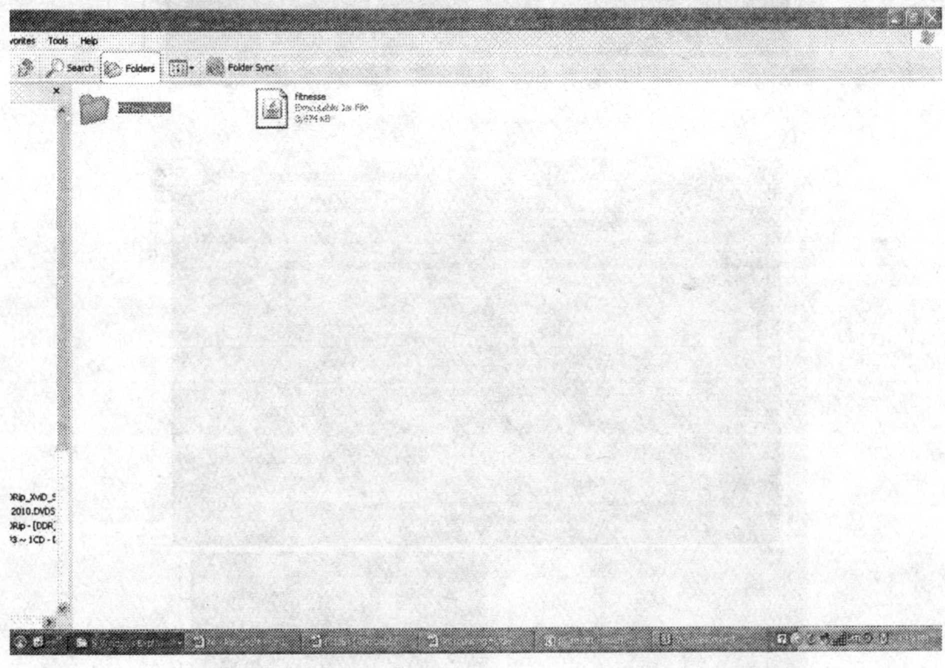
Tools
Help
Search
Folders
Folder Sync
fitnesse

Open Commance Prompt and type: java -jar fitnesse.jar

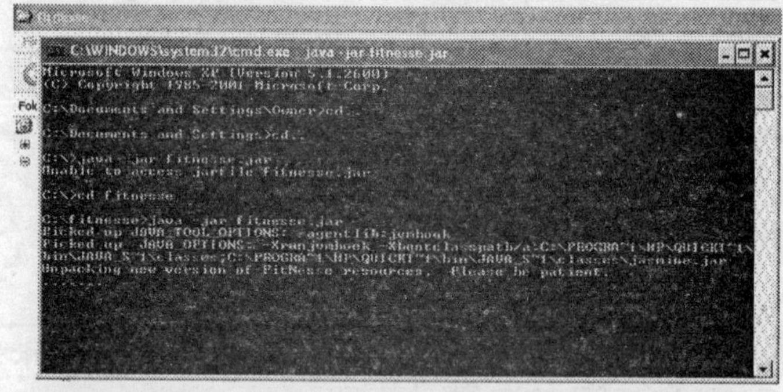

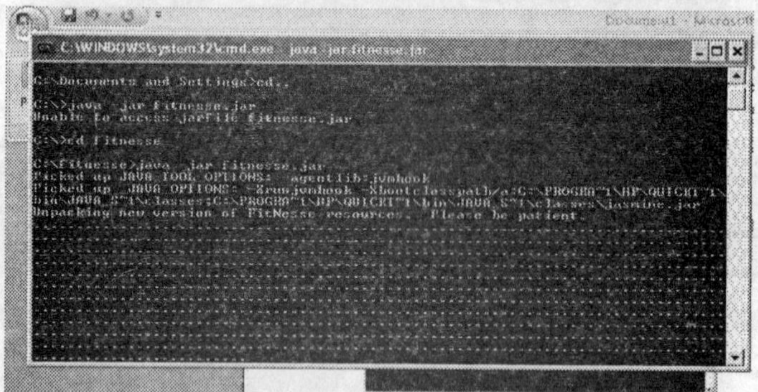

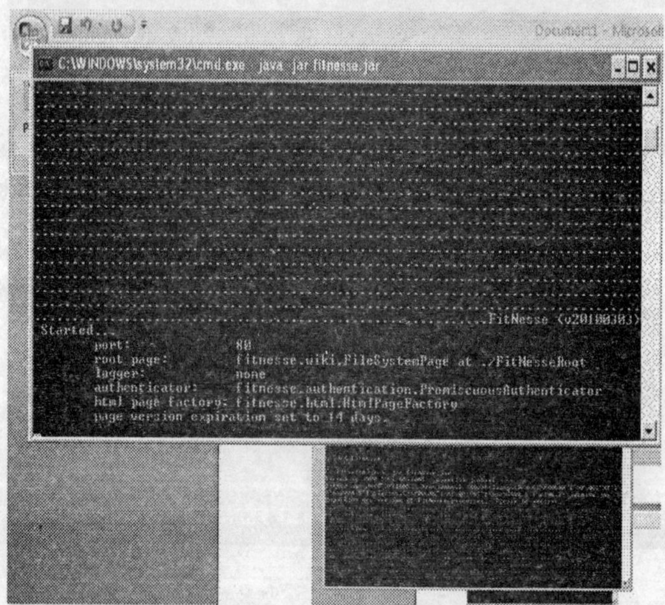

After installation goto IE and type 'http://localhost/FitNesse'

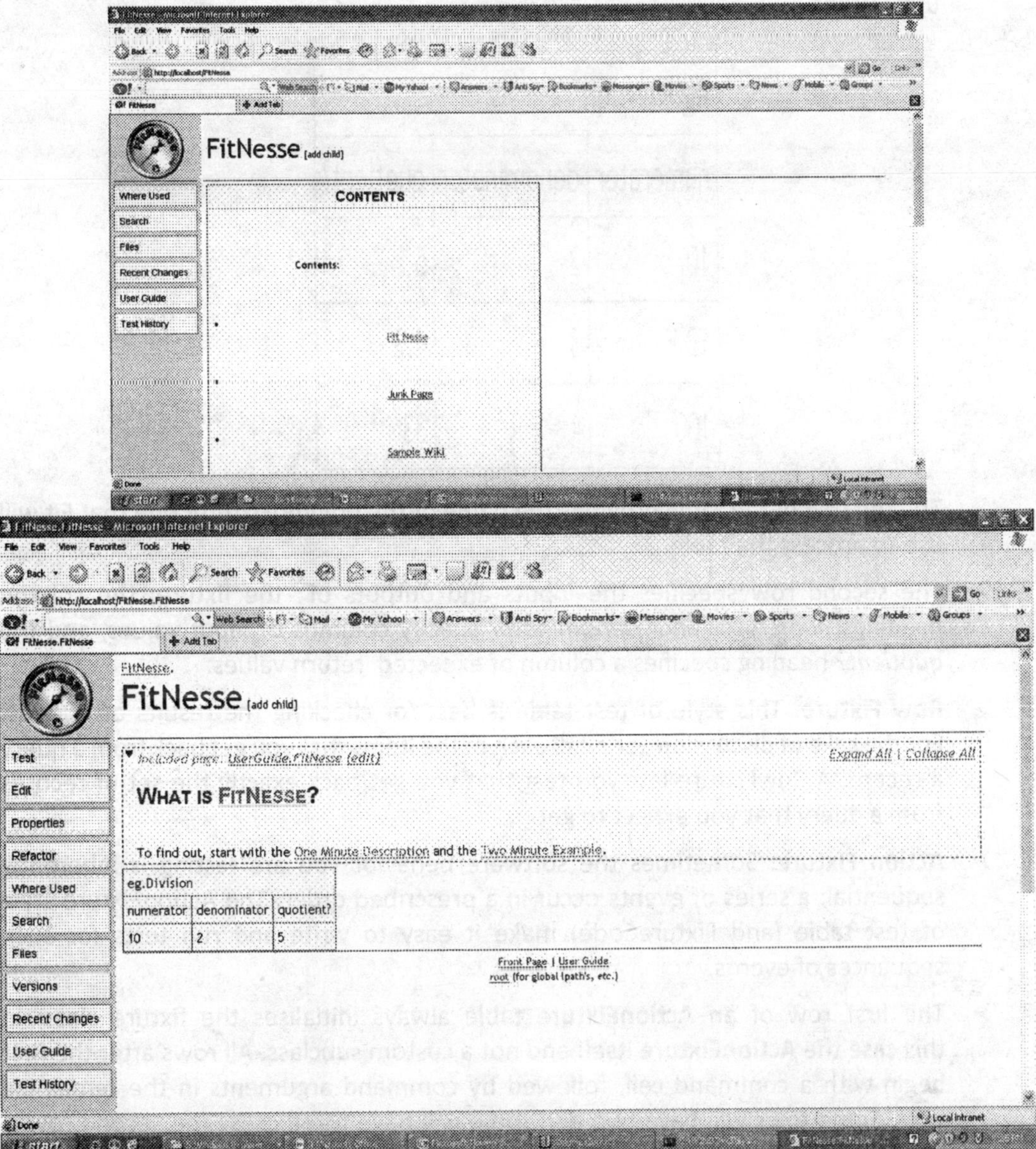

Tables in FITNESSE

➤ **Column Fixture:** This table style is probably the most generally useful in FitNesse. Many kinds of software features can be tested with ColumnFixture: any feature that can be expressed as rows of inputs and outputs.

- **ColumnFixture** has the advantages of being easy to design and easy to understand.

eg.Division		
numerator	denominator	quotient?
10	2	5
12.6	3	4.2
100	4	33

- The top row of the table provides the name of the ColumnFixtureCode that Fit will use to process the table.
- The second row specifies the inputs and outputs of the fixture; the column headings *numerator* and *denominator* specify columns of input values, and the *quotient?* heading specifies a column of expected return values.
- **Row Fixture:** This style of test table is best for checking the results of queries. For the sake of discussion, let's call each of the items that you get back from a query a record. A RowFixture lets you test that you get back exactly the set of records from a query that you expect to get.
- **Action Fixture:** Sometimes the software behavior you are testing is inherently sequential: a series of events occur in a prescribed order. The ActionFixture style of test table (and FixtureCode) make it easy to write and run tests for such sequences of events.
- The first row of an **ActionFixture** table always initialises the fixture class, in this case the **ActionFixture** itself and not a custom subclass. All rows after the first begin with a command cell, followed by command arguments in the remaining cells. Some rows will have two and some will have three cells. The second row is typically used for the **start** command, which expects one argument — the class name for the actual fixture to automate. After that, you can use the following commands to describe the test:

  check — executes a method and verifies its value.
  press — executes a **void** method without testing anything.
  enter — executes a method and passes an argument to it.

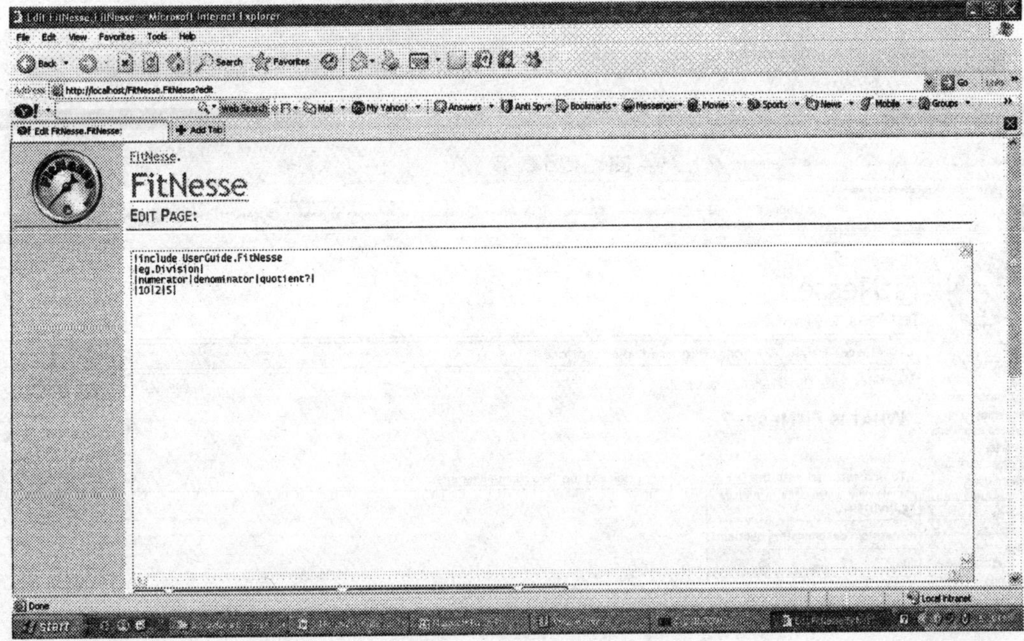


```
!include UserGuide.FitNesse
|eg.Division|
|numerator|denominator|quotient?|
|10|2|5|
```

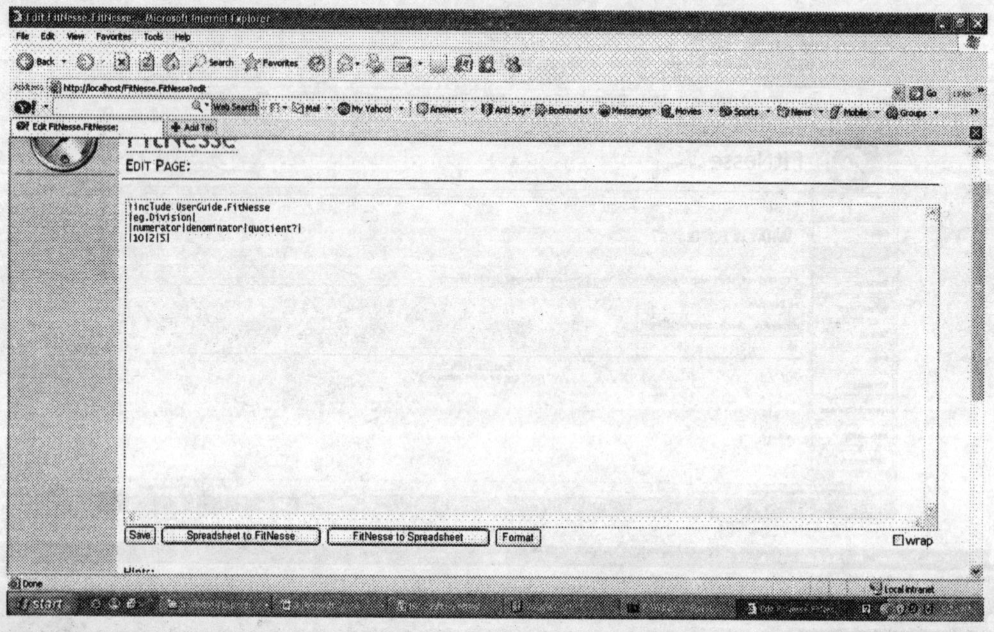
Edit FitNesse.FitNesse: - Microsoft Internet Explorer
http://localhost/FitNesse.FitNesse?edit
EDIT PAGE:
!include UserGuide.FitNesse
|eg.Division|
|numerator|denominator|quotient?|
|10|2|5|
Save
Spreadsheet to FitNesse
FitNesse to Spreadsheet
Format
wrap

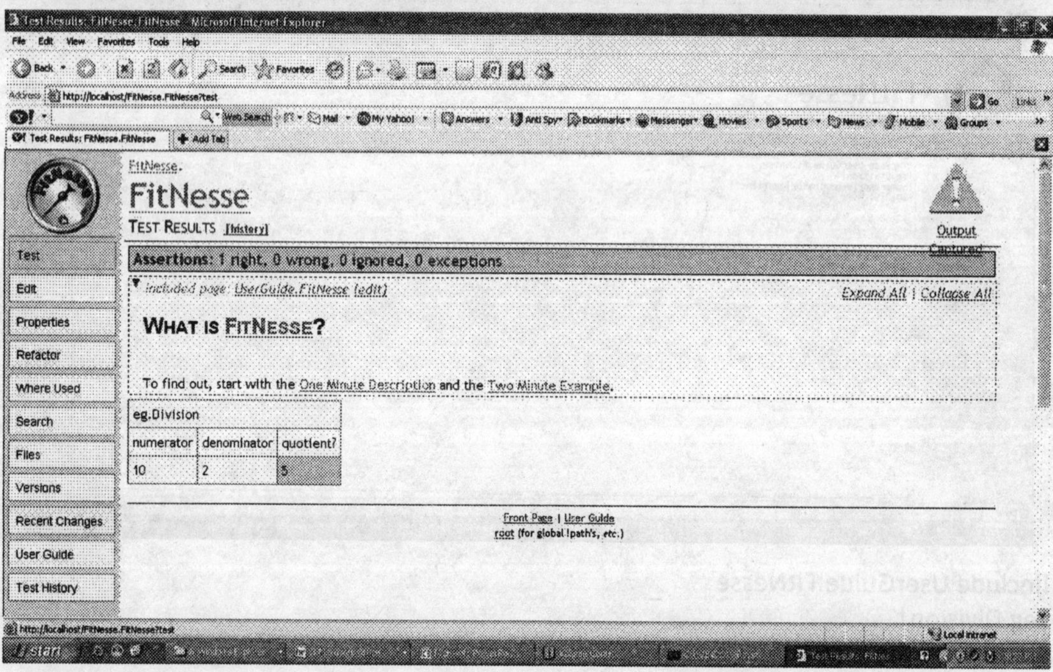
Test Results: FitNesse.FitNesse - Microsoft Internet Explorer
http://localhost/FitNesse.FitNesse?test
FitNesse
TEST RESULTS [history]
Output Captured
Assertions: 1 right, 0 wrong, 0 ignored, 0 exceptions
included page: UserGuide.FitNesse (edit)
Expand All | Collapse All
WHAT IS FITNESSE?
To find out, start with the One Minute Description and the Two Minute Example.
eg.Division
numerator denominator quotient?
10 2 5
Test
Edit
Properties
Refactor
Where Used
Search
Files
Versions
Recent Changes
User Guide
Test History
Front Page | User Guide
root (for global !path's, etc.)

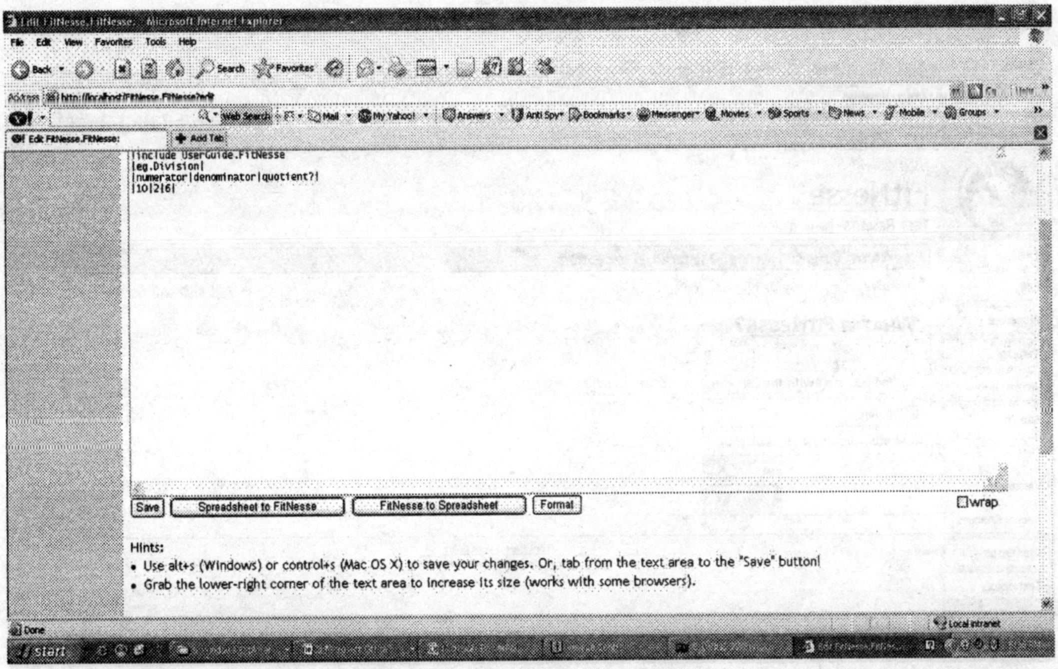

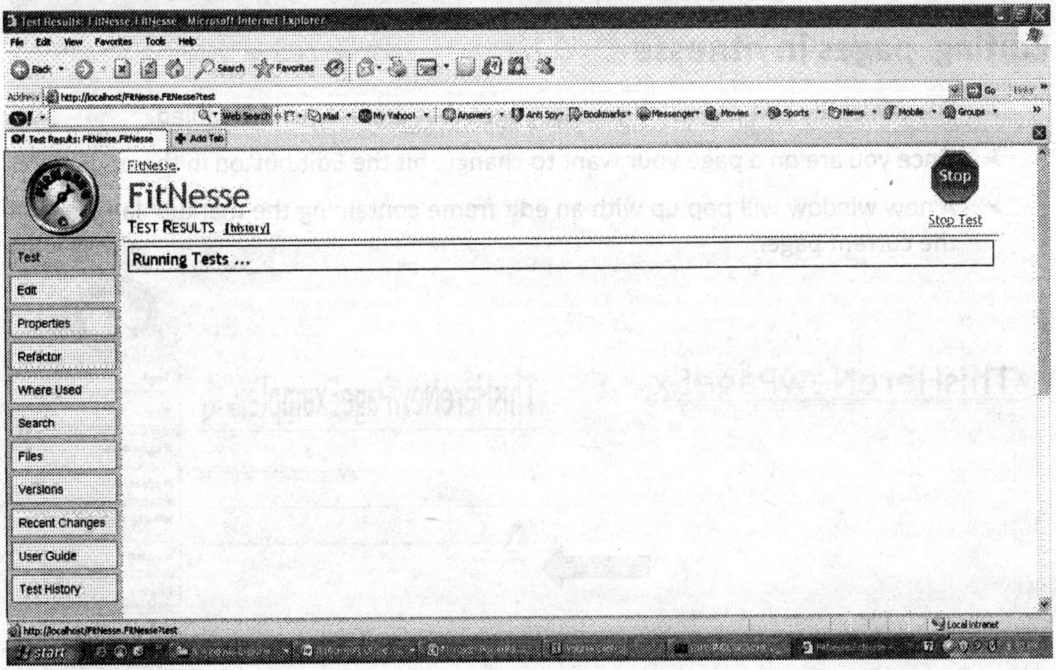

```
!include UserGuide.FitNesse
|eg.Division|
|numerator|denominator|quotient?|
|10|2|6|
```

Save | Spreadsheet to FitNesse | FitNesse to Spreadsheet | Format | wrap

Hints:

- Use alt+s (Windows) or control+s (Mac OS X) to save your changes. Or, tab from the text area to the "Save" button!
- Grab the lower-right corner of the text area to increase its size (works with some browsers).

FitNesse.

FitNesse

TEST RESULTS [history]

Stop

Stop Test

Running Tests ...

Test

Edit

Properties

Refactor

Where Used

Search

Files

Versions

Recent Changes

User Guide

Test History

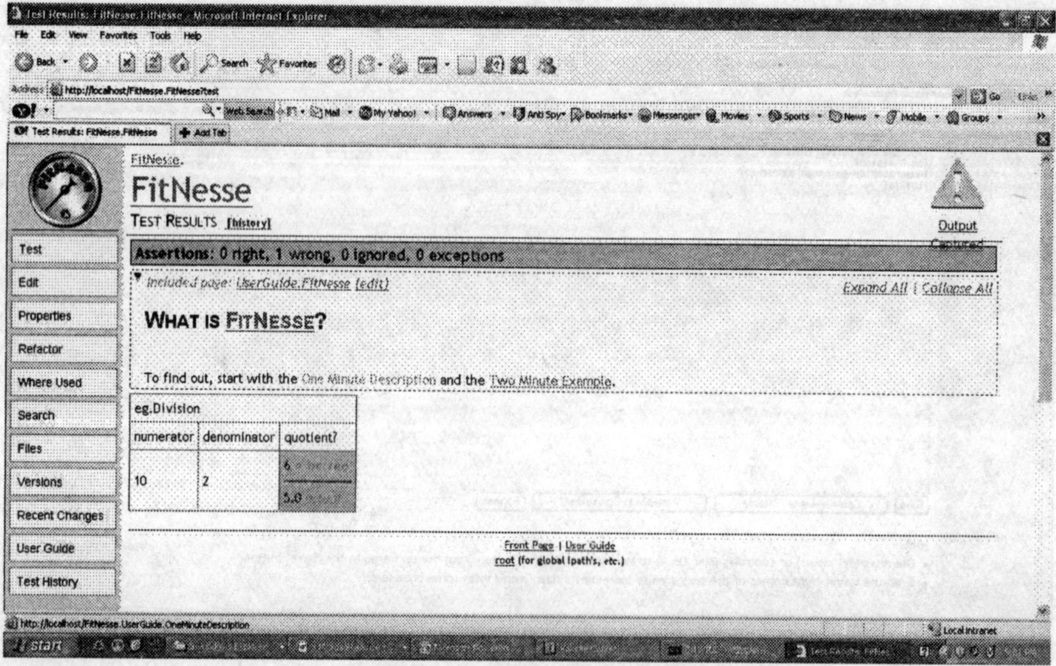

Editing pages in fitnesse

- We can easily edit pages in fitnesse, pages that are only edit–enabled.
- Once you are on a page your want to change, hit the Edit button in the upper left.
- A new window will pop up with an edit frame containing the markup language of the current page.

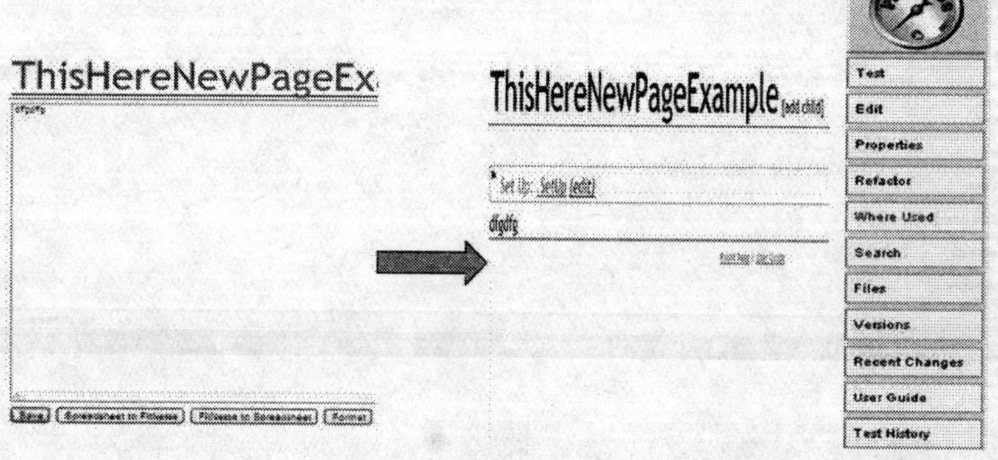

Fixture code and column fixture

- Fixture code is the actual code in any language.
- A simple division example:

Class path:

- The wiki markup widget you use is the !path widget.
- !path D:\Fitnesse\fitnesse\bin

```
import fit.ColumnFixture;

public class Division2 extends ColumnFixture
{

    public double numerator1, denominator1;


    public void setNumerator1(double numerator)
    {
        this.numerator1 = numerator;
    }
    public void setDenominator1(double denominato:
    {
        this.denominator1 = denominator;
        }
    public double quotient1()
    {
        return numerator1/denominator1;
        }


    public static void main (String args[])
    {
        new Division2();
    }
    }
```

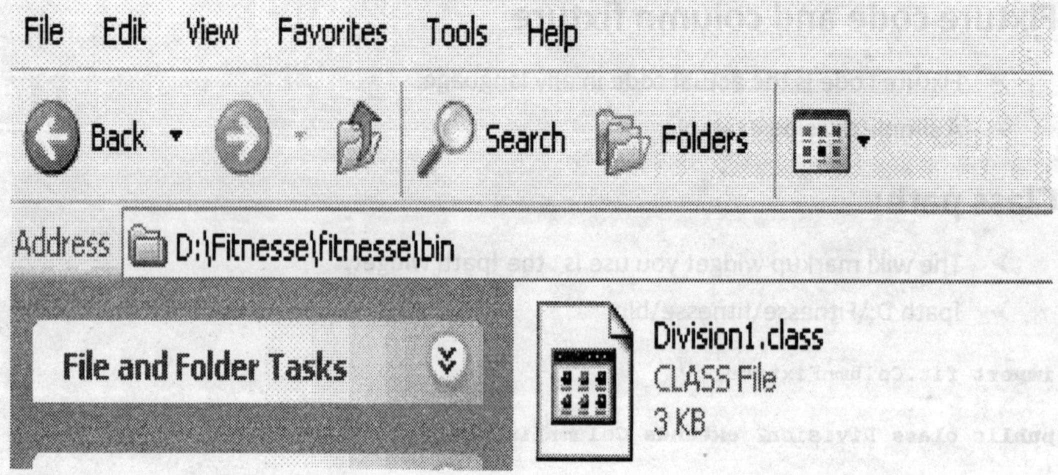

Fixture code

In the edit enabled page of fitnesse ,write the class path

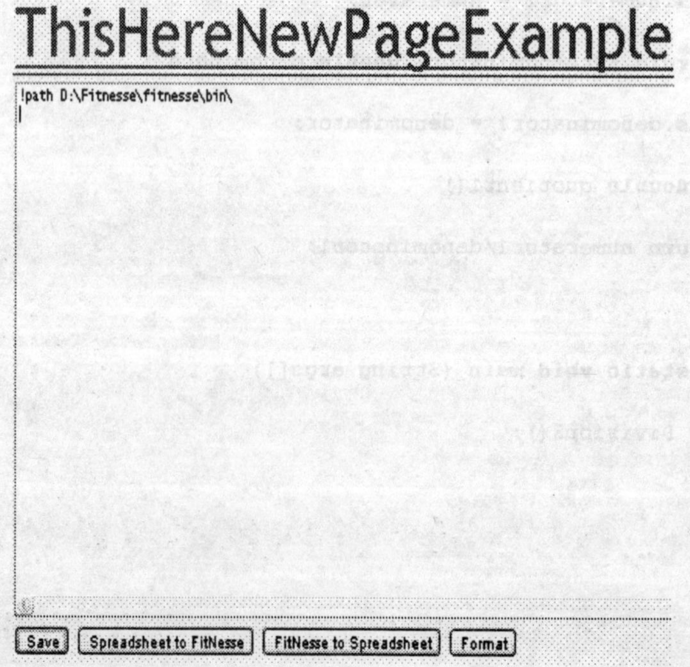

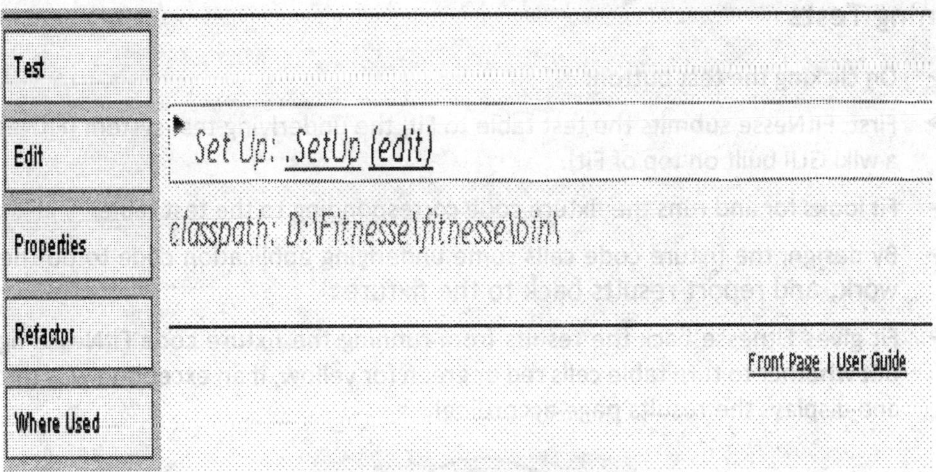

➢ On clicking the save button, class

path definition looks like:

Test Tables

➢ In the edit-enabled page of fitnesse wiki,we can create a test table based on the desired fixture code in eg.Java.

➢ On clicking the save button,table looks like:

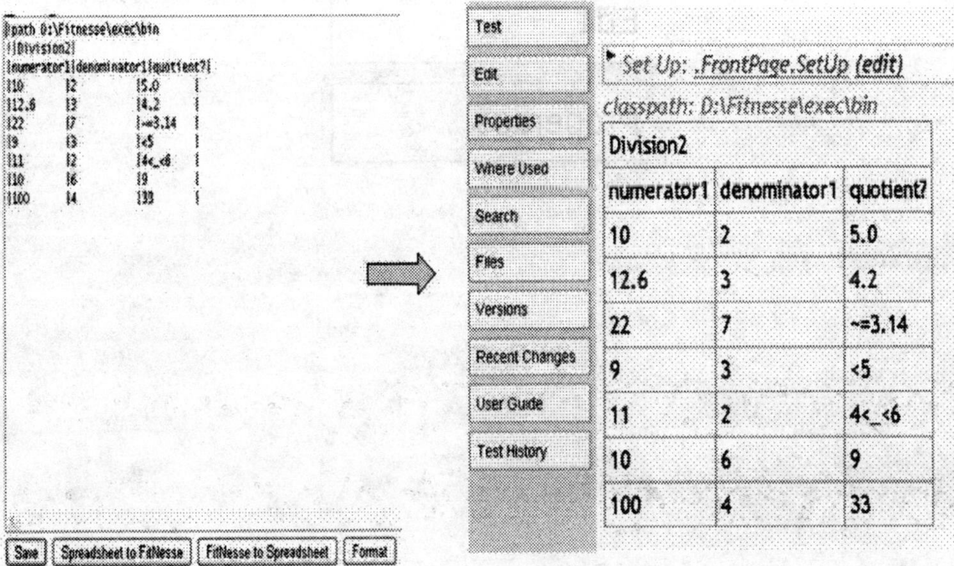

Division2		
numerator1	denominator1	quotient?
10	2	5.0
12.6	3	4.2
22	7	~=3.14
9	3	<5
11	2	4<_<6
10	6	9
100	4	33

Running Tests

- On clicking the test button:
- First, FitNesse submits the test table to Fit, the underlying test system (FitNesse is a wiki GUI built on top of Fit).
- Fit looks for and runs the fixture code corresponding to the test table.
- By design, the fixture code calls some underlying application code to do the real work, and report results back to the fixture
- Fit gives Fitnesse back the results from running the fixture code FitNesse figures out whether to turn table cells red or green (or yellow, if an exception was thrown) and displays the results page accordingly

Test
Edit
Properties
Where Used
Search
Files
Versions
Recent Changes
User Guide
Test History

classpath: D:\Fitnesse\exec\bin

Division2		
numerator1	denominator1	quotient?
10	2	5.0
12.6	3	4.2
22	7	~=3.14 *Could not parse: ~=3.14, expected type: double.*
9	3	**3.0**<5
11	2	4<**5.5**<6
10	6	9 *expected* 1.6666666666666667 *actual*
100	4	33 *expected* 25.0 *actual*

- Green color indicates that our output is correct.
- Red color indicates that our output is different from actual value , i.e. , there is an error.
- Yellow color indicates exceptions in our fixture code.

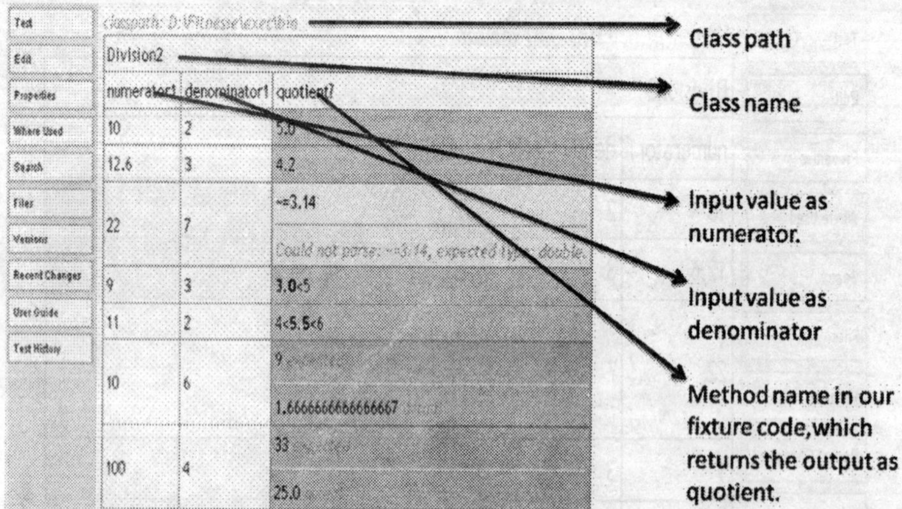

Fixture code and Action Fixture

- **For eg:**
- **Table format:**

```
!path D:\Fitnesse\exec1\bin\
!|ActionFixture|
|start|ss|
|enter|firstPart|Hello|
|enter|secondPart|World|
|press|join|
|check|together|Hello, World|
```

Test screen:

Set Up: .SetUp (edit)

classpath: D:\Fitnesse\exec1\bin

ActionFixture		
start	ss	
enter	firstPart	Hello
enter	secondPart	World
press	join	
check	together	Hello, World

- Fixture code:

```
public class ss extends fit.Fixture
{
private String first, second, both;
public void firstPart(String s){
first=s;
}
public void secondPart(String s){
second=s;
}
public void join(){
both=first+ ", "+second;
}
public String together(){
return both;
}
}
```

- **For eg:**
- **Table format:**

!path D:\Fitnesse\exec1\bin\	→ Class path
!|ActionFixture|	→ Format for action fixture
|start|ss|	→ Class name
|enter|firstPart|Hello|	→ Method name 1
|enter|secondPart|World|	→ Method name 2
|press|join|	→ Method name 3
|check|together|Hello, World|	→ Method name 4,that returns first part and second part

Test screen

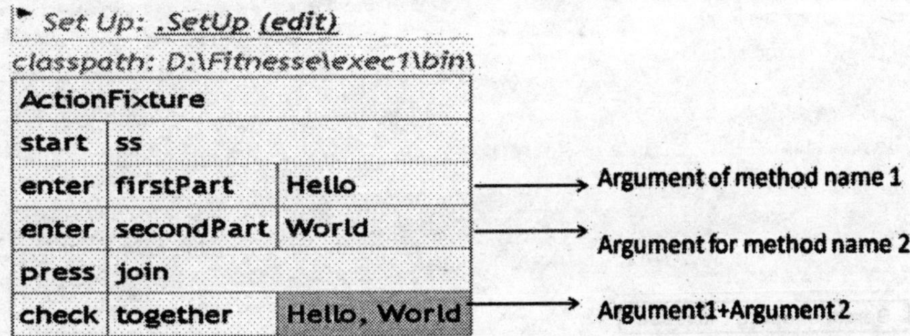

Set Up: .SetUp (edit)

classpath: D:\Fitnesse\exec1\bin

ActionFixture		
start	ss	
enter	firstPart	Hello
enter	secondPart	World
press	join	
check	together	Hello, World

Running multiple outputs

- **Fixture code:**

```
public class table2 extends ActionFixture{
private String first, second, third,fourth,both,both1;
public void input1(String s){
first=s;}
public void  input2(String s){
second=s;}
public void  input3(String s){
third=s;}
public void  input4(String s){
fourth=s;}
public void join(){
both=first+second;}
public String output1(){
   return both;}
public void join1(){
both1=third+fourth;}
public String output2(){
   return both1;}
```

Test table:

```
!define TEST_SYSTEM {fit}
!path D:\Fitnesse\exec1\bin
!|fit.ActionFixture|
|start|table2|
|enter|input1|u1|
|enter|input2|u2|
|enter|input3|u3|
|enter|input4|u4|
|press|join|
|check|output1|u1u2|
|press|join1|
|check|output2|u3u4|
```

Save | Spreadsheet to FitNesse

Running multiple outputs

variable defined: TEST_SYSTEM=fit

classpath: D:\Fitnesse\exec1\bin

fit.ActionFixture			
start	table2		➤ Class name
enter	input1	u1	➤ Function name1 with argument as u1
enter	input2	u2	➤ Function name 2 with argument as u2
enter	input3	u3	➤ Function name 3 with argument as u3
enter	input4	u4	➤ Function name 4 with argument as u4
press	join		➤ Function join
check	output1	u1u2	➤ Function output1 executing u1&u2
press	join1		
check	output2	u3u4	➤ Function output2 executing u3&u4

References:

http://storustiq.sourceforge.net

http://mojo.codehaus.org/selenium-maven-plugin/

http://fitnesse.org/FitNesse.UserGuide.DownloadingAndInstallingFitNesse

http://www.cs.tut.fi/tapahtumat/testaus06/juhain.pdf

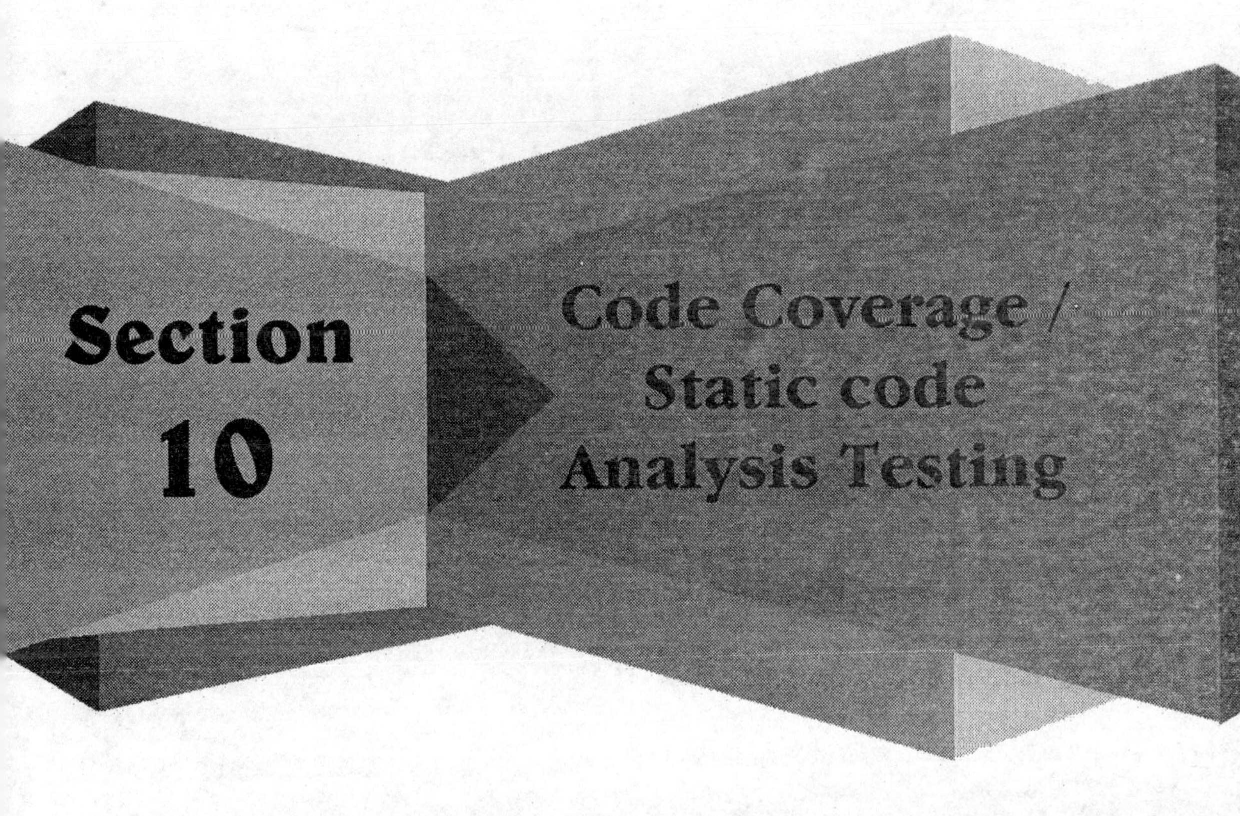

Section
10
Code Coverage /
Static code
Analysis Testing

Code Coverage Testing

Introduction

- Code coverage describes the degree to which the source code of an application has been tested
- Code coverage is a form of testing that looks at the code directly and as such comes under the heading of white box testing
- Code coverage analysis is done during unit testing and system testing, to know the coverage of unit test cases and system test cases respectively
- Code coverage analysis has three phases:

Phases in Code Coverage

- Code Coverage Testing
  - Prepare the coverage environment
  - Enable coverage profiling and run tests
  - Disable coverage profiling and generate a report

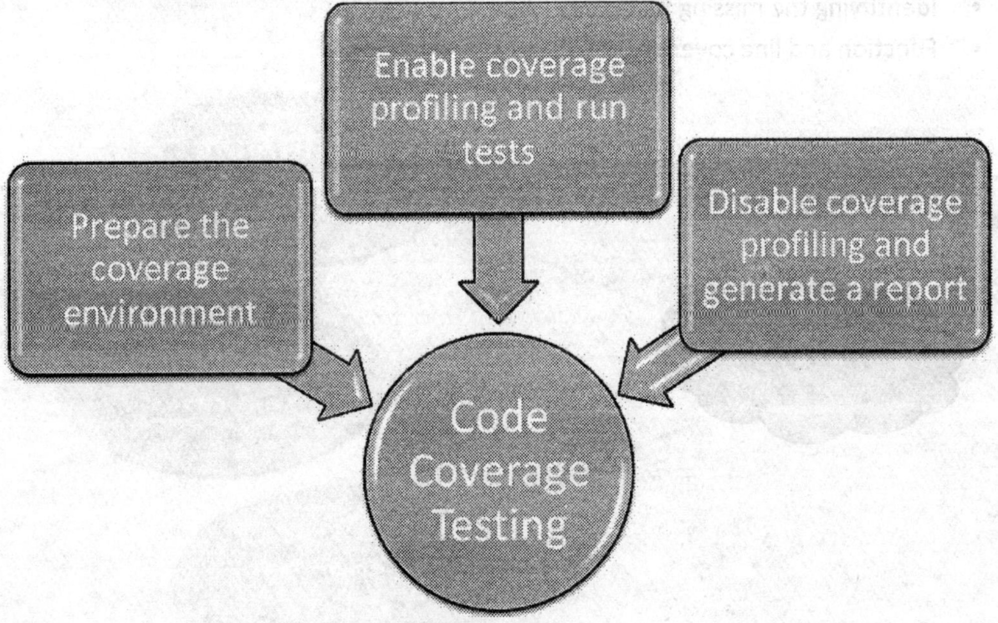

Approach for Code Coverage Testing

- **Prepare the coverage environment**

  In this phase we determine which constructors, methods, and properties are in the assemblies under coverage

- **Enable coverage profiling and run tests**

  Irrespective of tests pass or fail we need to analyze how much of the code base of the product under test is touched by the tests. In other words, even if every test fails, but code coverage is 100 percent

- **Disable coverage profiling and generate a report**

  Once disabling of coverage profiling is done we didn't continue gathering information. Report generator collects the information about all methods that could potentially be touched.

Why to do Code Coverage Testing?

- Identifying the dead code
- Identifying the missing test cases
- Function and line coverage

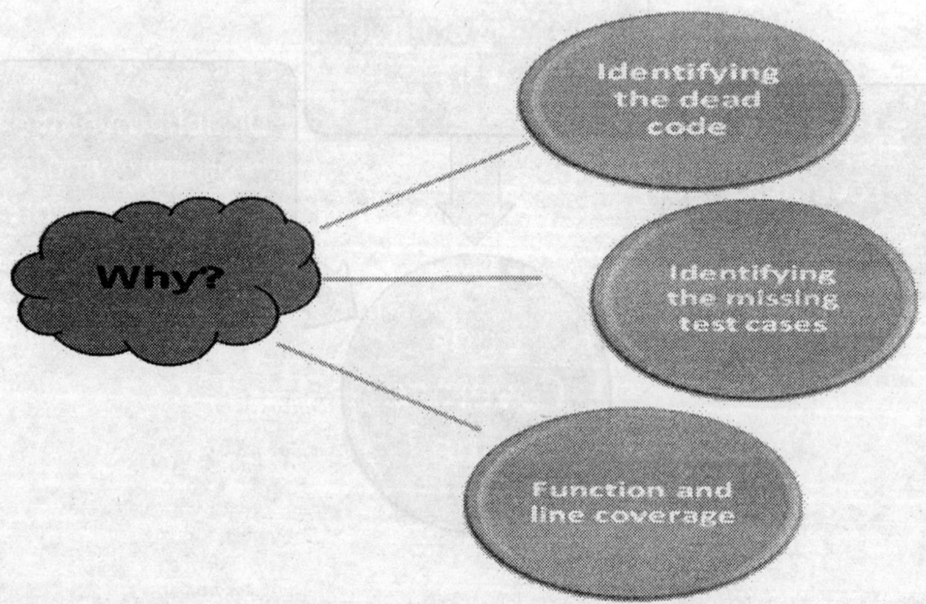

- ### Identifying the dead code :

  Coverage output shows that if some functions are not called, after analyzing we can identify whether the code is un-touched as no required use case exists or code is dead code

- ### Identifying the missing test cases :

  Coverage output reports can also be useful in identifying the extra tests (exceptional cases), which we were missed out earlier

- ### Function and line coverage :

  Coverage output reports can useful to find how many functions,how may lines have been covered in the application code and how many times as a particular method is been called.

Code Coverage Testing using PartCover tool

http://sourceforge.net/projects/partcover/

PartCover | Get PartCover at SourceForge.net - Microsoft Internet Explorer
File Edit View Favorites Tools Help
Address: http://sourceforge.net/projects/partcover/

sourceforge FIND AND DEVELOP OPEN SOURCE SOFTWARE
Welcome, Guest! Log In | Create Account
Find Software | Develop | Create Project | Blog | Site Support | About
SourceForge.net » Find Software » PartCover
PartCover by mr2dark, oregu
Share More
Summary
Files Support Develop
This is analog for NCover application, but have some advantages. See latest news on http://partcover.blogspot.com
Download Now! OR View all files »
http://partcover.blogspot.com/
EDIT
Show project details
Ads by Google
Agile Testing Course
Agile Testing Training ClassesLondon, Oslo and Copenhagen
www.softwaretest.doodlekit.com
Ads by Google
Agile Testing Course
Agile Testing Training ClassesLondon, Oslo and Copenhagen
www.softwaretest.doodlekit.com
Ratings and Reviews
Show: Everything
Thumbs up:
Thumbs down:
Rate and Review
Would you recommend this project?
Done
Unknown Zone
start

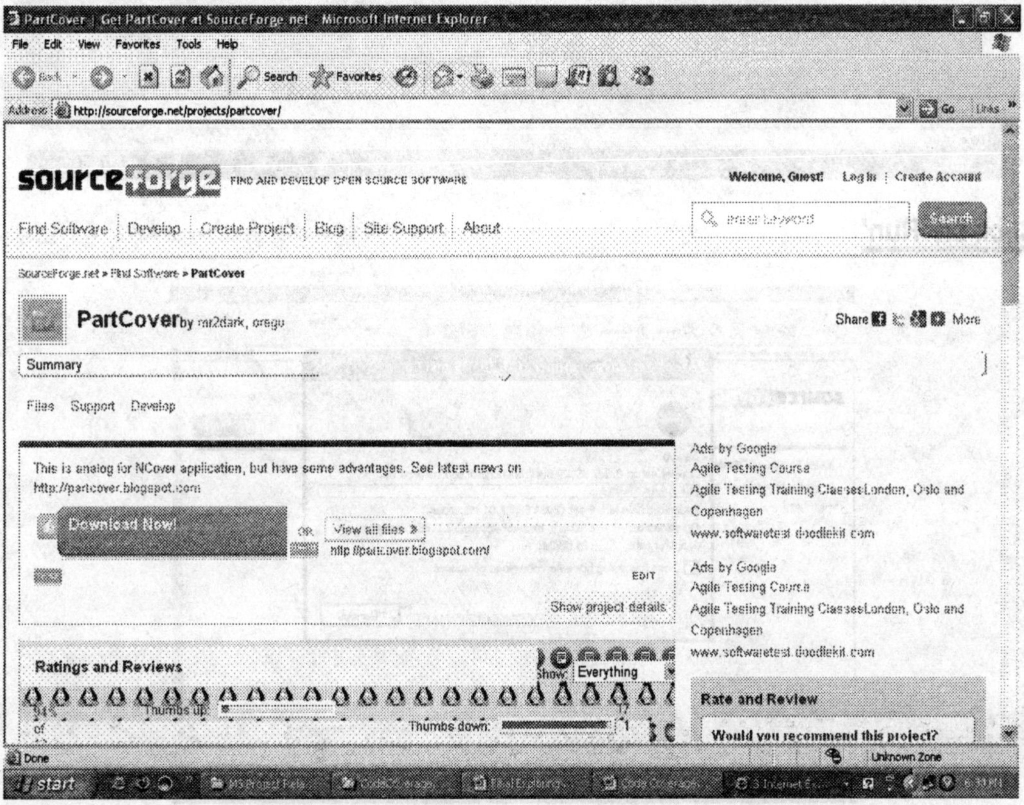

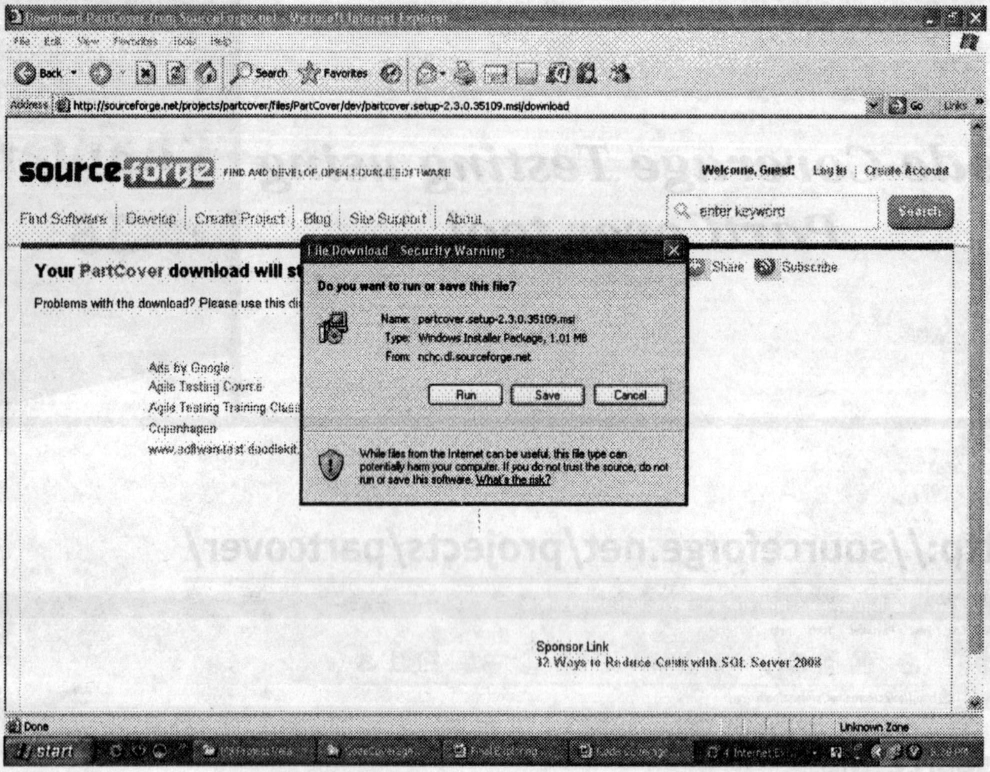

Address http://sourceforge.net/projects/partcover/files/PartCover/dev/partcover.setup-2.3.0.35109.msi/download
sourceforge FIND AND DEVELOP OPEN SOURCE SOFTWARE
Welcome, Guest! Log In | Create Account
Find Software | Develop | Create Project | Blog | Site Support | About
Your PartCover download will st
Problems with the download? Please use this di
File Download - Security Warning
Do you want to run or save this file?
Name: partcover.setup-2.3.0.35109.msi
Type: Windows Installer Package, 1.01 MB
From: nchc.dl.sourceforge.net
Run
Save
Cancel
While files from the Internet can be useful, this file type can potentially harm your computer. If you do not trust the source, do not run or save this software. What's the risk?
Share Subscribe
Ads by Google
Agile Testing Course
Agile Testing Training Class
Copenhagen
Sponsor Link
12 Ways to Reduce Costs with SQL Server 2008
Done
Unknown Zone

Click on 'Run'

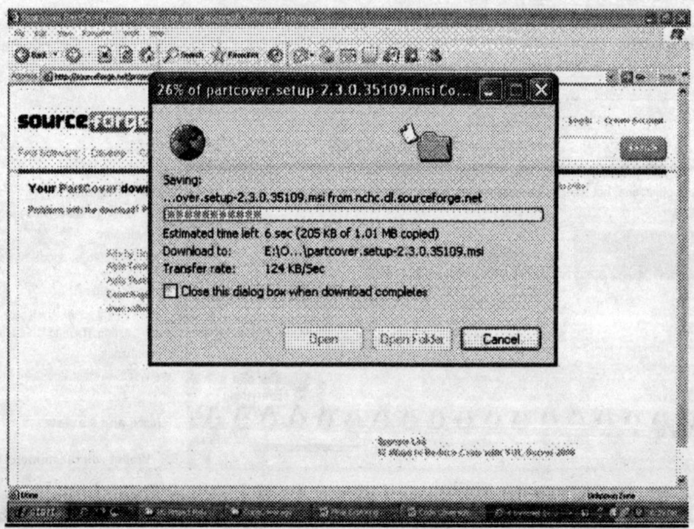
26% of partcover.setup-2.3.0.35109.msi Co...
Saving:
...over.setup-2.3.0.35109.msi from nchc.dl.sourceforge.net
Estimated time left 6 sec (205 KB of 1.01 MB copied)
Download to: E:\O...\partcover.setup-2.3.0.35109.msi
Transfer rate: 124 KB/Sec
Close this dialog box when download completes
Open
Open Folder
Cancel

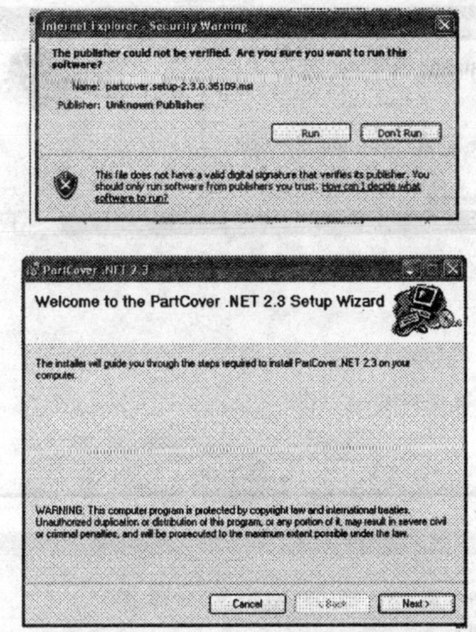
Internet Explorer - Security Warning
The publisher could not be verified. Are you sure you want to run this software?
Name: partcover.setup-2.3.0.35109.msi
Publisher: Unknown Publisher
Run
Don't Run
This file does not have a valid digital signature that verifies its publisher. You should only run software from publishers you trust. How can I decide what software to run?
PartCover .NET 2.3
Welcome to the PartCover .NET 2.3 Setup Wizard
The installer will guide you through the steps required to install PartCover .NET 2.3 on your computer.
WARNING: This computer program is protected by copyright law and international treaties. Unauthorized duplication or distribution of this program, or any portion of it, may result in severe civil or criminal penalties, and will be prosecuted to the maximum extent possible under the law.
Cancel
< Back
Next >

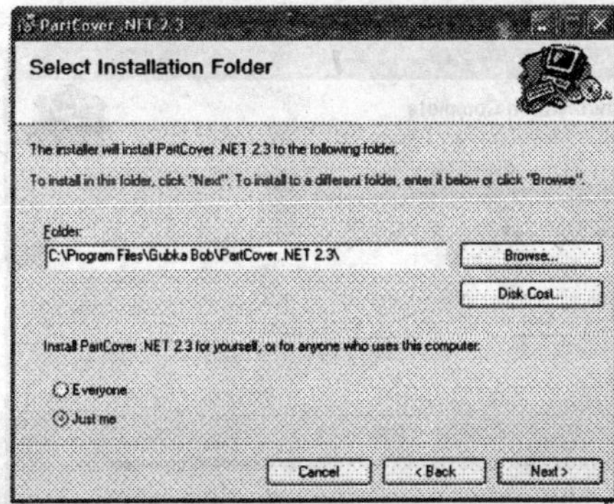
PartCover .NET 2.3
Select Installation Folder
The installer will install PartCover .NET 2.3 to the following folder.
To install in this folder, click "Next". To install to a different folder, enter it below or click "Browse".
Folder:
C:\Program Files\Gubka Bob\PartCover .NET 2.3\
Browse...
Disk Cost...
Install PartCover .NET 2.3 for yourself, or for anyone who uses this computer:
Everyone
Just me
Cancel
< Back
Next >

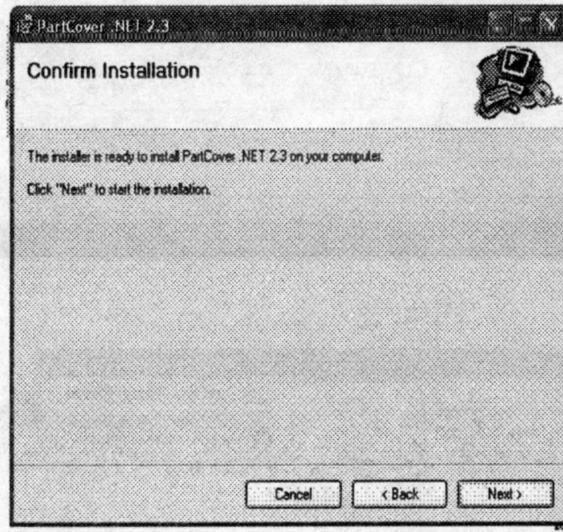
PartCover .NET 2.3
Confirm Installation
The installer is ready to install PartCover .NET 2.3 on your computer.
Click "Next" to start the installation.
Cancel
< Back
Next >

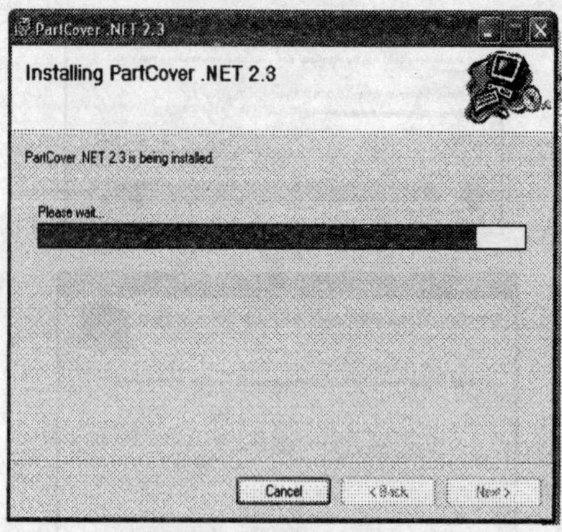

PartCover .NET 2.3
Installing PartCover .NET 2.3
PartCover .NET 2.3 is being installed.
Please wait...
Cancel
< Back
Next >

http://sourceforge.net/projects/partcover/
sourceforge
PartCover .NET 2.3
Installation Complete
PartCover .NET 2.3 has been successfully installed.
Click "Close" to exit.
Please use Windows Update to check for any critical updates to the .NET Framework.
Close
PartCover
Summary
This is analog for NCover application.
http://partcover.blogspot.com
Download Now!
Release Date: 2009-06-17
Topic: Profiling
Operating System: All 32-bit MS Windows (95/98/NT/2000/XP)
Agile Testing Course
Ads by Google
start
Internet

Windows Catalog
Windows Update
Programs
Favorites
Documents
Settings
Ruby-186-27
FlexMonkey
PartCover Browser Manual
PartCover Console Manual

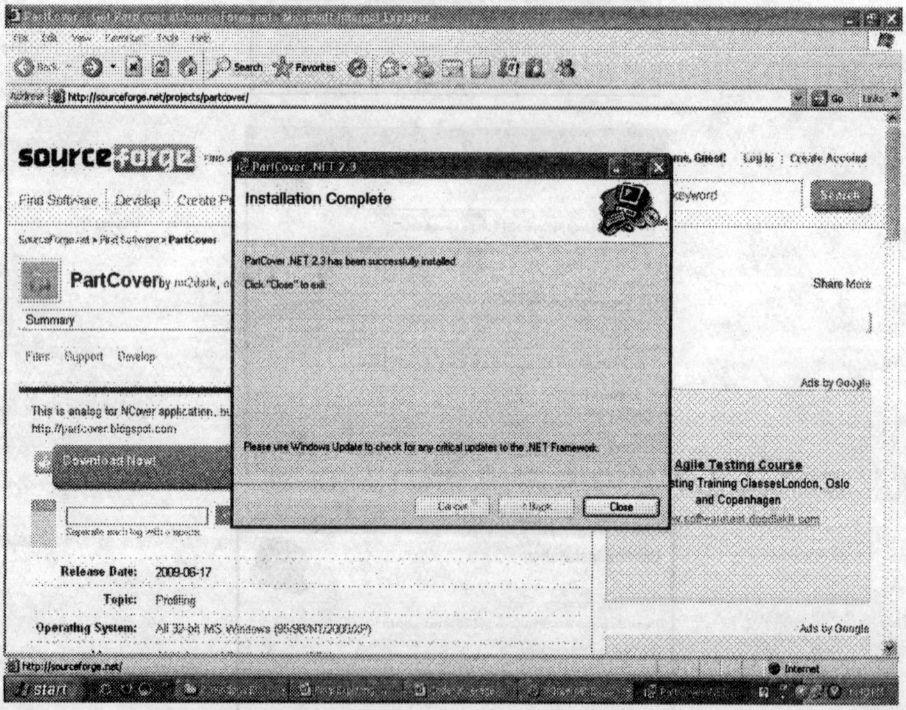

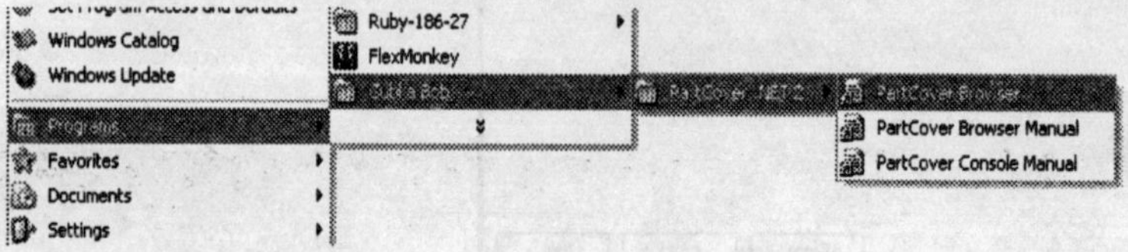

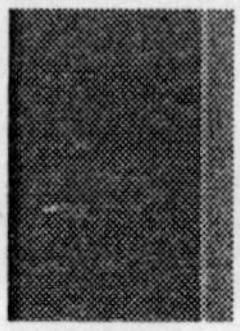

Code Coverage testing using Part Cover for ASP.Net application

Below screen shot showing how to configure the ASP.Net application with Part Cover Tool. In Tool bar Click the 'File' Tab and click the 'Run Target' option.

Once we click the 'Run Target' option on pop up will appear. Below screen shot represents the same. There we need to configure the required paths like

- **Executable File:** Points to your testing exe file. In our case, we use the NUnit console exe file. This is what it runs against the tests.
- **Working Directory:** The directory of your executable file.
- **Working Arguments:** Arguements you pass into your executable file to get the tests to run. In the case of NUnit, it takes in a DLL file that contains all of your annotated test-cases and tests.
- **Rules:** Specifies which classes (not methods, but only classes) that you want to generate coverage for.

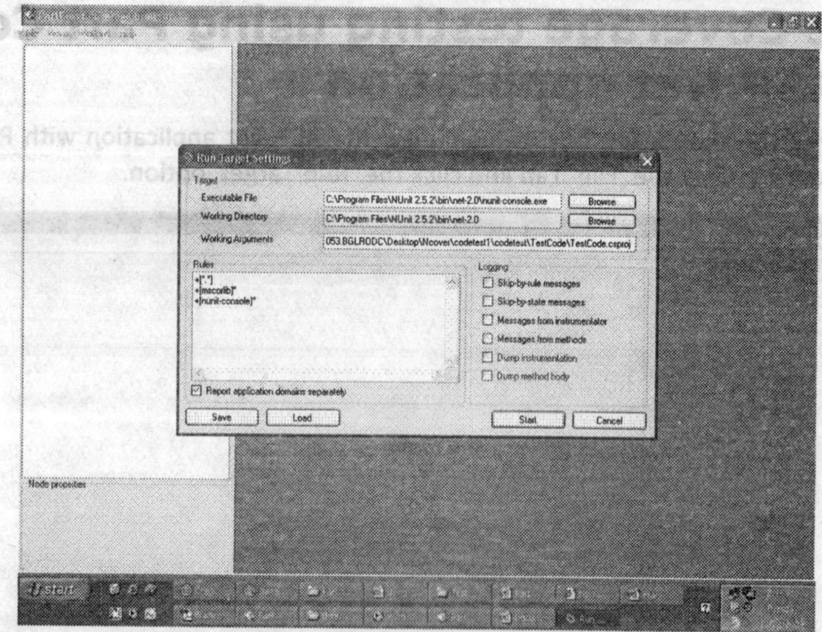

Once we mapping the respective paths click the 'Start' button. The tool will start the N Unit console and respective class files and test cases are imported into tool and did the code coverage for those files.

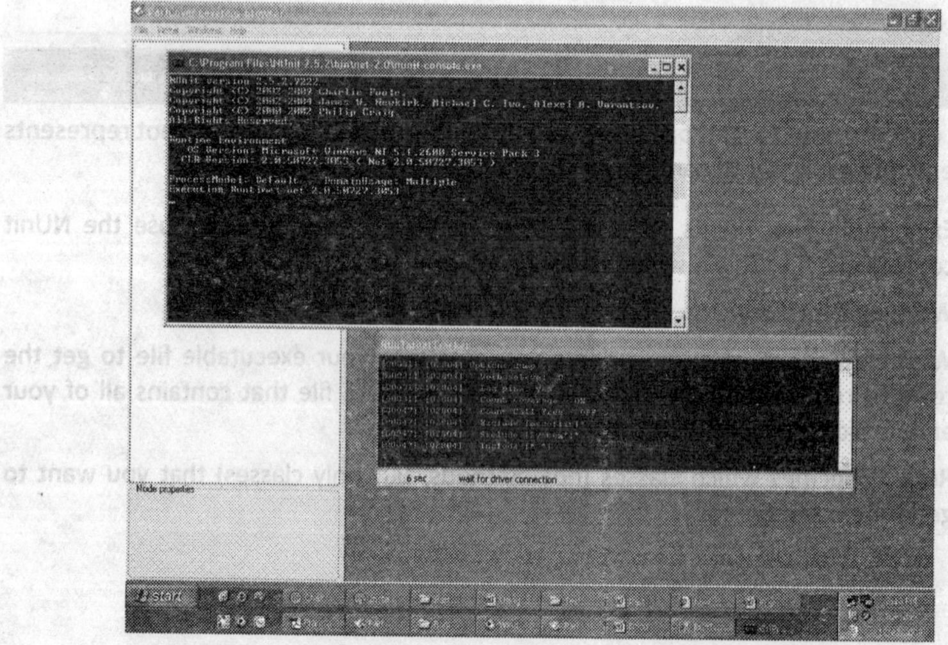

If we want to view the coverage reports go to 'View' tab in tool bar there we find out the 'View coverage Details' option click on that, below screen shot should be getting. There we can find out that which are the lines are executed and which are lines are skipped, and which class files and methods cover under code coverage are testing.

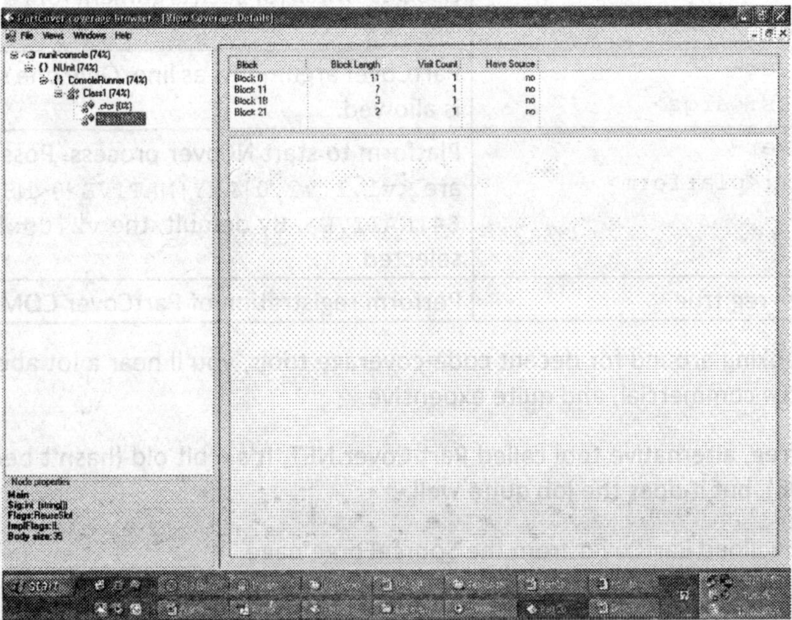

Using PartCover and NUnit for Code-Coverage

Part Cover is analog for NCover application, but has some advantages. It specifies which assemblies and classes you want to report and can work not only assemblies that have debug symbols. Manuals are included and will be placed in program directory. It is an Open Source tool to calculate unit test code coverage. Current Version of this tool is Part Cover 2.2. Part Cover comes along with its GUI PartCover Browser .This application is GUI wrapper over PartCover.exe (console version). Parameters for running PartCover.exe (console version).

The tool has a command prompt option, so running from Nant is no problem, and the report is generated as xml, so integrate it with CC.net should not be an issue, the even provide two XSLT files to display the report based on the assembly or based on the class very neat!!!.

To invoke code coverage with PartCover and define its arguments, use the following switches:

Switch	Description
`/partcover:<exe>`	Use to invoke PartCover. Enter the path to `PartCover.exe`
`/partcover-arg:<arg>`	Use this switch for each argument for `PartCover.exe`
`/partcover-arguments:<args>`	PartCover arguments as line. Only one such switch is allowed.
`/partcover-platform:<platform>`	Platform to start NCover process. Possible values are `<v1.1|v2.0|ANY|NATIVE>@<MSIL|x86|x64|NATIVE>`. By default, the `v2.0@x86` value is selected.
/partcover-reg:true	Perform registration of PartCover COM object

If you're looking around for decent code-coverage tools, you'll hear a lot about NCover, which is now commercial, and quite expensive.

There's a free, alternative tool called Part Cover.NET. It's a bit old (hasn't been updated since ~2008), but it does the job quite well.

You can download PartCover from the SourceForge page.

Once you've done that, setting it up can be a bit tricky for lack of information available. You need, as with any application, to specify where the testing-tool is (in our case, NUnit) and where the test-files binary is (so it can run the tests and calculate code-coverage).

Here's a screenshot of some working configuration from clicking on File > Run Target:

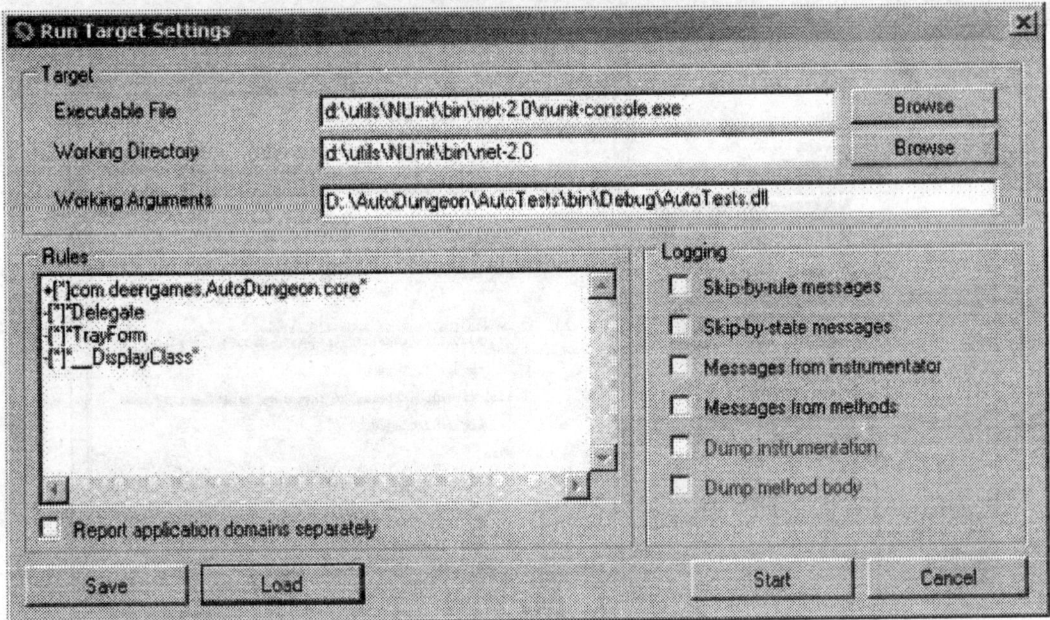

The data in the fields are:

- **Executable File:** Points to your testing exe file. In our case, we use the NUnit console exe file. This is what it runs against the tests.
- **Working Directory:** The directory of your executable file.
- **Working Arguments:** Arguements you pass into your executable file to get the tests to run. In the case of NUnit, it takes in a DLL file that contains all of your annotated test-cases and tests.
- **Rules:** Specifies which classes (not methods, but only classes) that you want to generate coverage for. Let's look at a sample positive and negative rule:
    - +[*]com.deengames.AutoDungeon.core*: Generate coverage for all of the classes in the com.deengames.AutoDungeon.core package, and all sub-packages (eg. com.deengames.AutoDungeon.core.controllers will be included, but core.deengames.AutoDungeon.tests will not). The [*] means, look in any project.

- -[*]*Delegate: Don't generate coverage for any class that ends in the word "Delegate." This is because delegates have all inherited methods, and we don't need to really test those.

Once you're ready, hit Start to start. You will see a pop-up for the NUnit console exe file running the tests, then you should see results, like so:

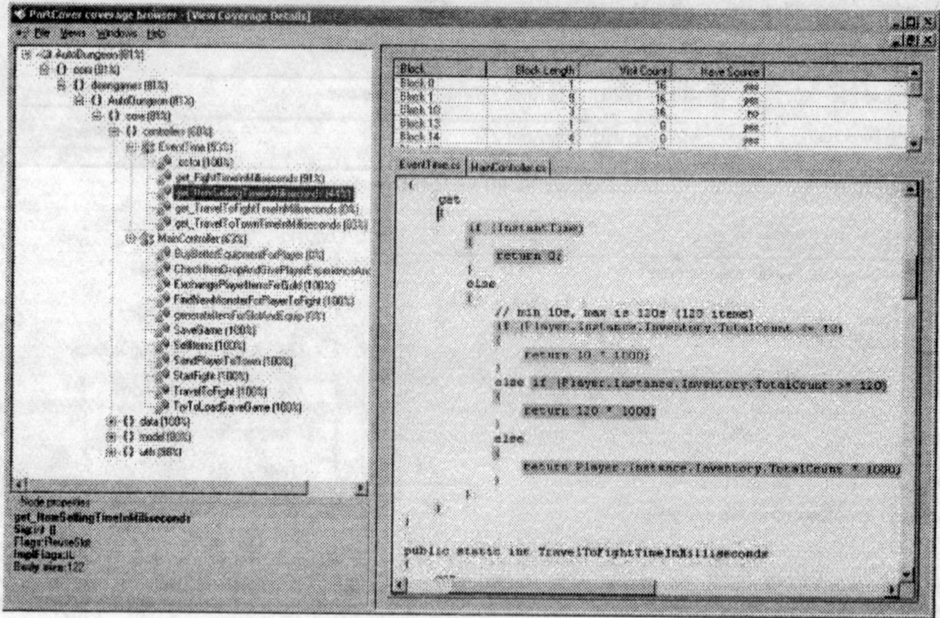

At this point, I recommend you go to Run Target again and save your configuration into an XML file that you check in to your source-control. You will add and remove classes and packages over time. You can click Cancel to return to the coverage report.

The left side shows you a hierarchical tree of namespaces and classes, and code coverage at each namespace, sub-namespace, and class-level. Once you go to Views > View Coverage Detail, you'll see the panel on the right. Red lines of code are not covered by any test, and green lines are executed in at least one test.

You can also see method-level coverages. As a rule of thumb, 80% is pretty decent for code-coverage (since 100% is sometimes very hard and obscure to attain).

Also, as a reminder, code-coverage does not mean your tests are good. Code coverage means, some code, somewhere, in some test, hits that line; it could even just be setup code that doesn't check anything! So use this as a guideline, not a hard-and-fast rule to tell you if you're done testing.

And that's NUnit and PartCover in a nutshell!

References:

http://www.csharpcity.com/using-partcover-and-nunit-for-code-coverage/

Code Analysis using Firebug tool

Chapter 39

What is Firebug?

The most popular and powerful web development tool

- Inspect HTML and modify style and layout in real-time
- Use the most advanced JavaScript debugger available for any browser
- Accurately analyze network usage and performance
- Extend Firebug and add features to make Firebug even more powerful

Firebug integrates with Firefox to put a wealth of web development tools at your fingertips while you browse. You can edit, debug, and monitor CSS, HTML, and JavaScript live in any web page.

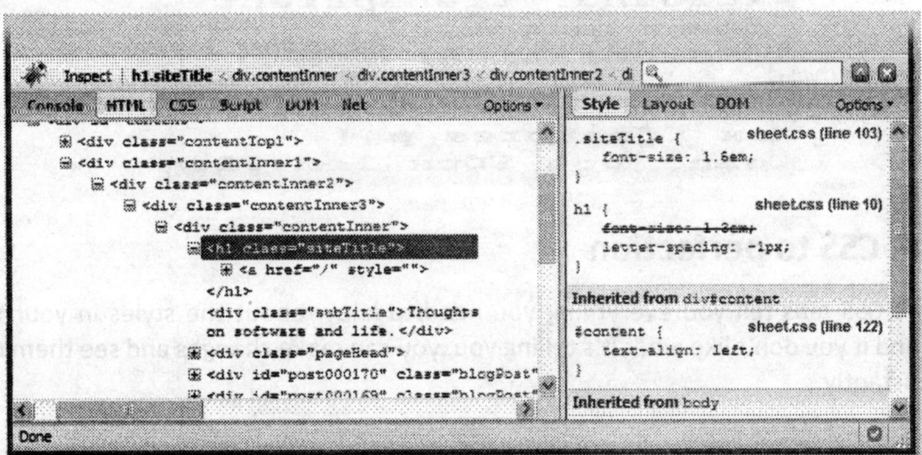

Features

Just the way you like it

Firebug is always just a keystroke away, but it never gets in your way. You can open Firebug in a separate window, or as a bar at the bottom of your browser. Firebug also gives you fine-grained control over which websites you want to enable it for.

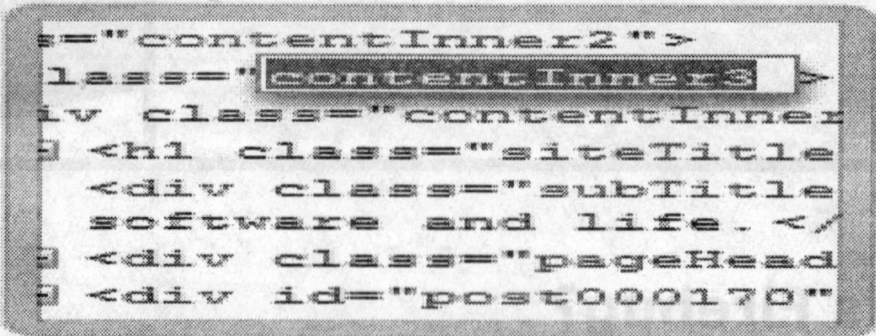

Inspect and edit HTML

Firebug makes it simple to find HTML elements buried deep in the page. Once you've found what you're looking for, Firebug gives you a wealth of information, and lets you edit the HTML live.

Tweak CSS to perfection

Firebug's CSS tabs tell you everything you need to know about the styles in your web pages, and if you don't like what it's telling you, you can make changes and see them take effect instantly.

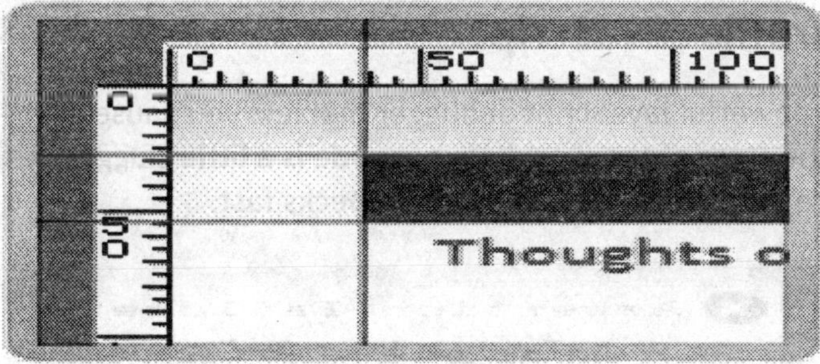

Visualize CSS metrics

When your CSS boxes aren't lining up correctly it can be difficult to understand why. Let Firebug be your eyes and it will measure and illustrate all the offsets, margins, borders, padding, and sizes for you.

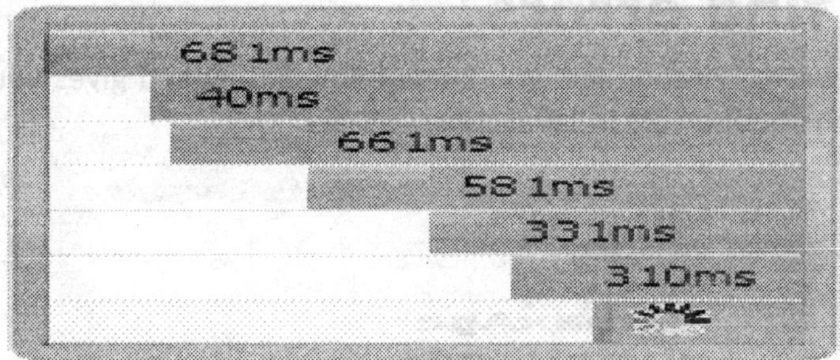

Monitor network activity

Your pages are taking a long time to load, but why? Did you go crazy and write too much JavaScript? Did you forget to compress your images? Are your ad partner's servers taking a siesta? Firebug breaks it all down for you file-by-file.

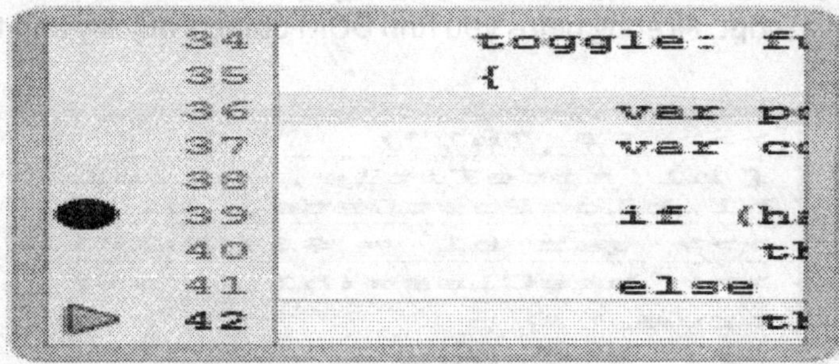

Debug and profile JavaScript

Firebug includes a powerful JavaScript debugger that lets you pause execution at any time and have look at the state of the world. If your code is a little sluggish, use the JavaScript profiler to measure performance and find bottlenecks fast.

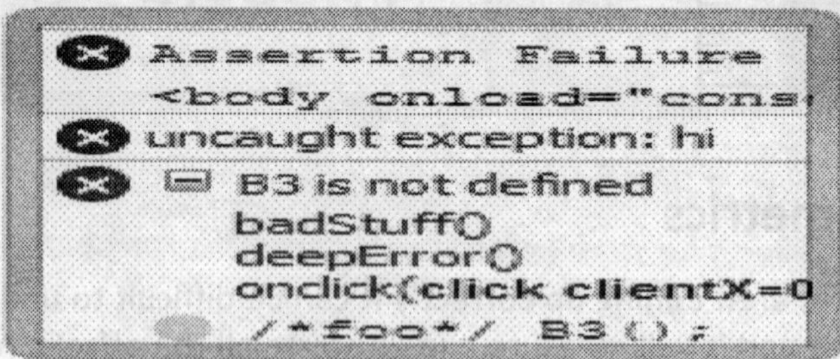

Quickly find errors

When things go wrong, Firebug lets you know immediately and gives you detailed and useful information about errors in JavaScript, CSS, and XML.

Explore the DOM

The Document Object Model is a great big hierarchy of objects and functions just waiting to be tickled by JavaScript. Firebug helps you find DOM objects quickly and then edit them on the fly.

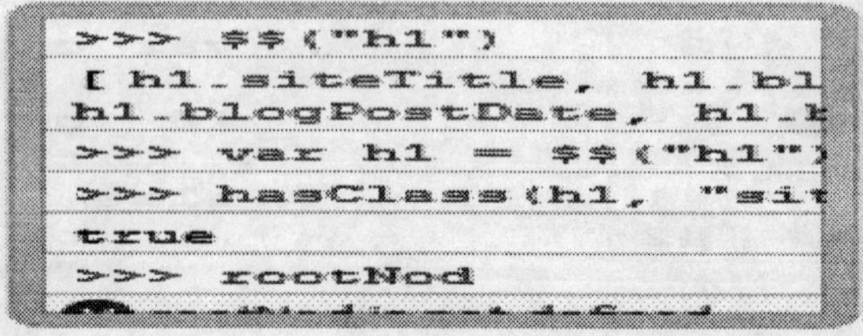

Execute JavaScript on the fly

The command line is one of the oldest tools in the programming toolbox. Firebug gives you a good fashioned command line for JavaScript complete with very modern amenities.

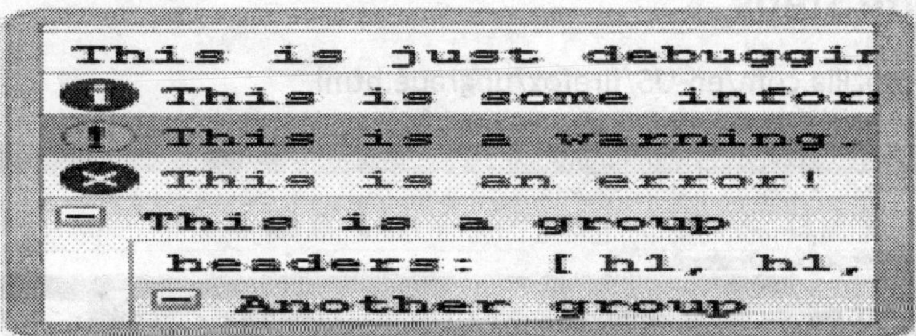

Logging for JavaScript

Having a fancy JavaScript debugger is great, but sometimes the fastest way to find bugs is just to dump as much information to the console as you can. Firebug gives you a set of powerful logging functions that help you get answers fast.

Installing firebug:

http://getfirebug.com

Installation Steps

http://www.mozilla.com/en-US/firefox/upgrade.html

Mozilla Download - Microsoft Internet Explorer
Back
Search
Favorites
Address http://www.mozilla.com/en-US/products/download.html?product=firefox-3.6.3&os=win&lang=en-US
Go
Links
mozilla
Products
Add-ons
Support
Community
About
Firefox!
Your dow
in a few s
7% of Firefox Setup 3.6.3.exe Completed
Saving:
Firefox Setup 3.6.3.exe from ftp-stud.hs-esslingen.de
Estimated time left 1 min 2 sec (450 KB of 7.96 MB copied)
Download to: E:\OpenSour...\Firefox Setup 3.6.3.exe
Transfer rate: 123 KB/Sec
Close this dialog box when download completes
Open
Open Folder
Cancel
Just follow these easy steps to
1.
2.
3.
Done
Mozilla Download - Microsoft Internet Explorer
Internet
start

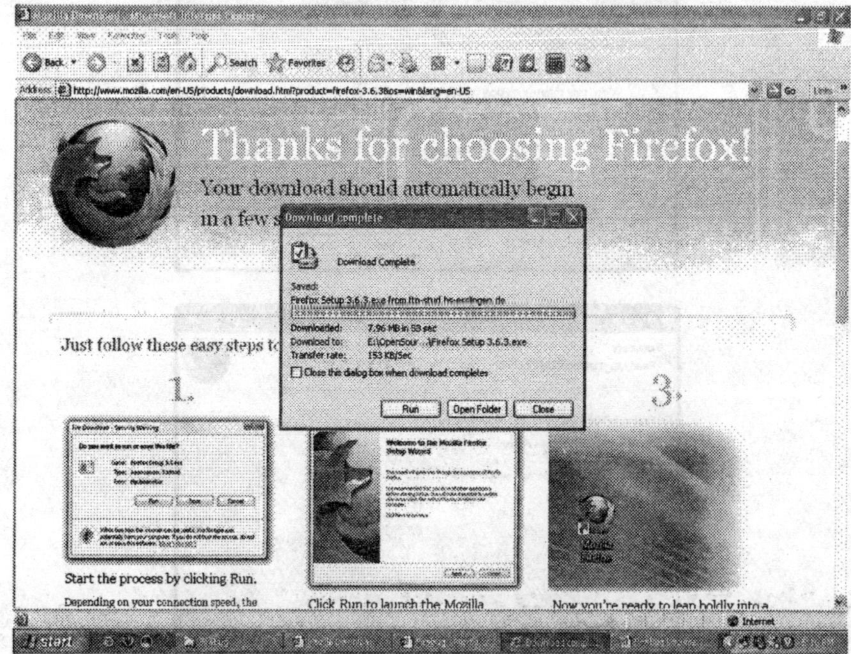
Back
Search
Favorites
Address http://www.mozilla.com/en-US/products/download.html?product=firefox-3.6.3&os=win&lang=en-US
Go
Links
Thanks for choosing Firefox!
Your download should automatically begin
in a few s
Download complete
Download Complete
Saved:
Firefox Setup 3.6.3.exe from ftp-stud.hs-esslingen.de
Downloaded: 7.96 MB in 53 sec
Download to: E:\OpenSour...\Firefox Setup 3.6.3.exe
Transfer rate: 153 KB/Sec
Close this dialog box when download completes
Run
Open Folder
Close
Just follow these easy steps to
1.
3.
Start the process by clicking Run.
Depending on your connection speed, the
Click Run to launch the Mozilla
Now you're ready to leap boldly into a
Internet
start

Click on 'Run'

47% Extracting
Cancel

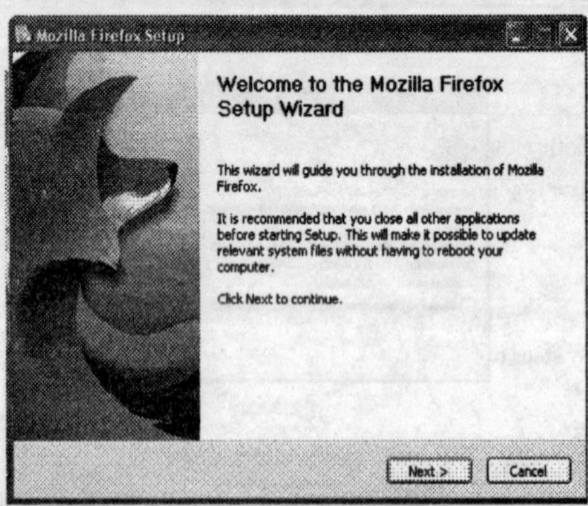
Mozilla Firefox Setup
Welcome to the Mozilla Firefox Setup Wizard
This wizard will guide you through the installation of Mozilla Firefox.
It is recommended that you close all other applications before starting Setup. This will make it possible to update relevant system files without having to reboot your computer.
Click Next to continue.
Next >
Cancel

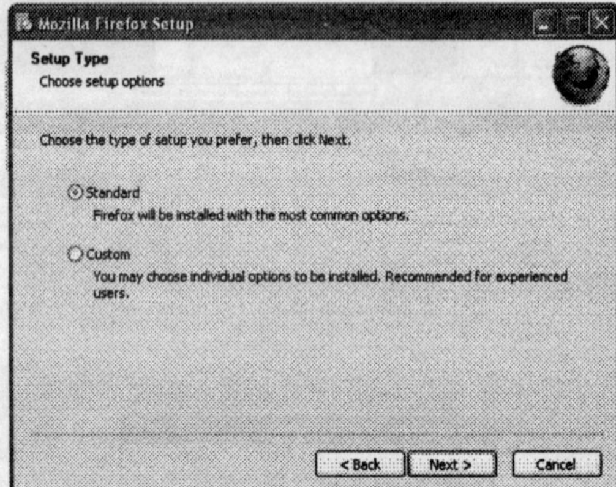
Mozilla Firefox Setup
Setup Type
Choose setup options
Choose the type of setup you prefer, then click Next.
Standard
Firefox will be installed with the most common options.
Custom
You may choose individual options to be installed. Recommended for experienced users.
< Back
Next >
Cancel

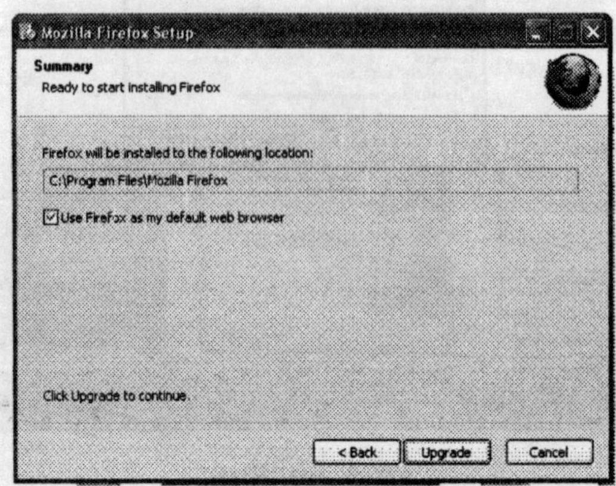
Mozilla Firefox Setup
Summary
Ready to start installing Firefox
Firefox will be installed to the following location:
C:\Program Files\Mozilla Firefox
Use Firefox as my default web browser
Click Upgrade to continue.
< Back
Upgrade
Cancel

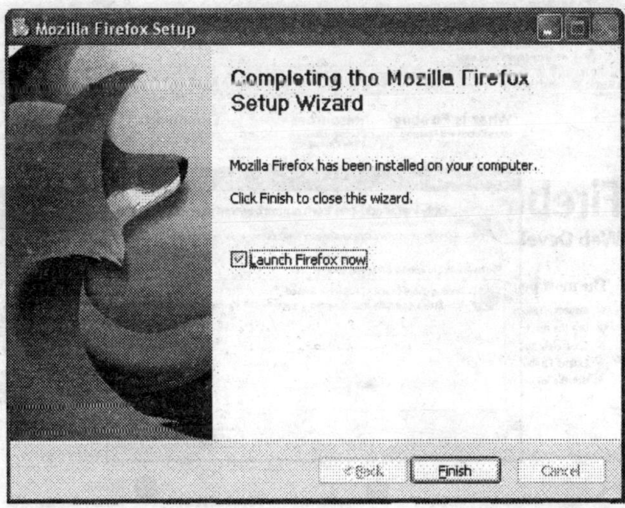

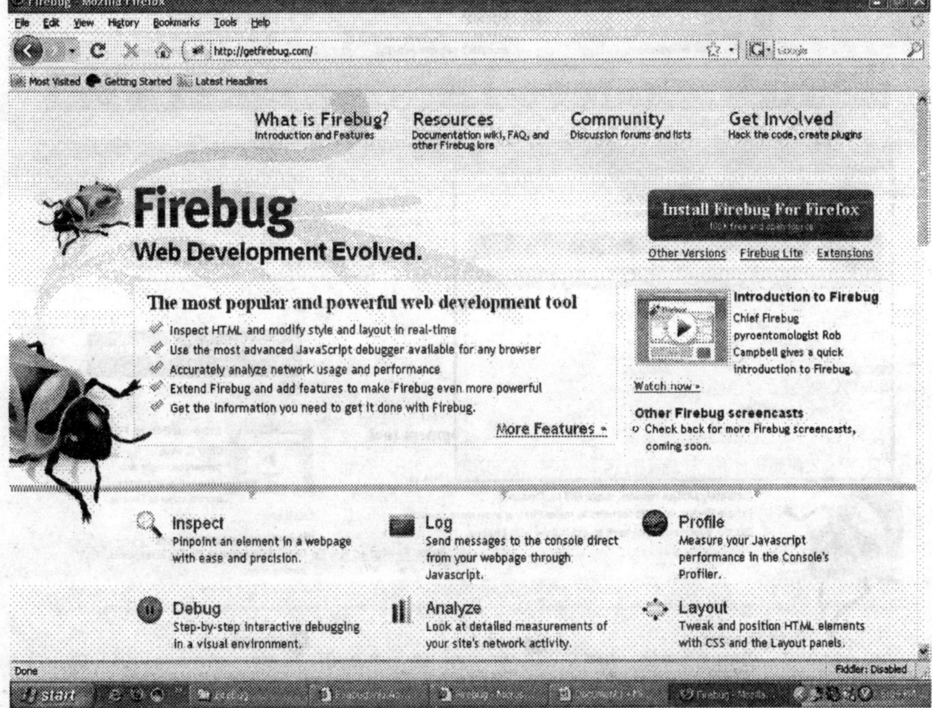

Click on 'Install Firebug for Firefox' button on webpage

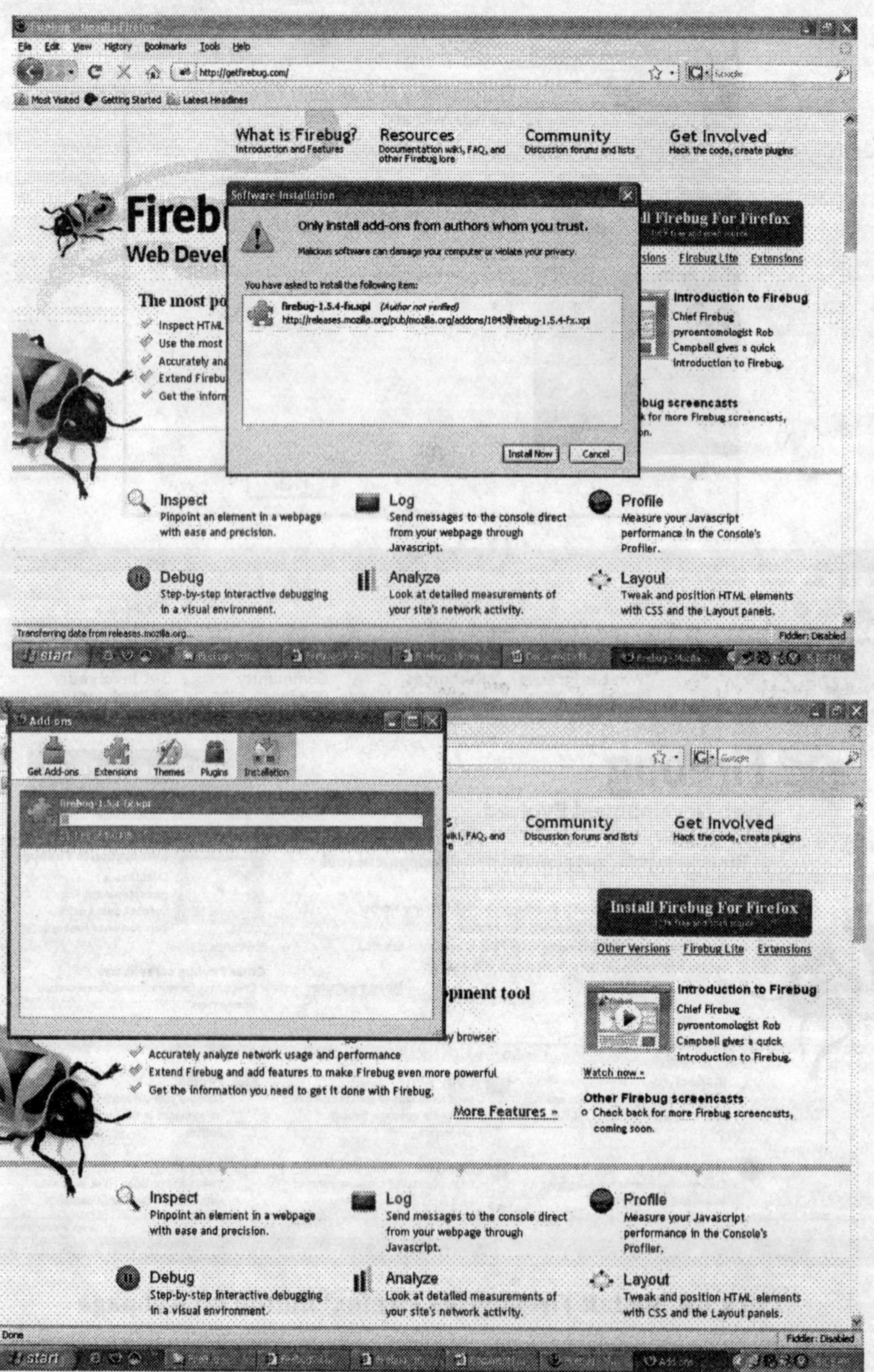
File Edit View History Bookmarks Tools Help
http://getfirebug.com/
Most Visited Getting Started Latest Headlines
What is Firebug?
Introduction and Features
Resources
Documentation wiki, FAQ, and other Firebug lore
Community
Discussion forums and lists
Get Involved
Hack the code, create plugins
Software Installation
Only install add-ons from authors whom you trust.
Malicious software can damage your computer or violate your privacy.
You have asked to install the following item:
firebug-1.5.4-fx.xpi (Author not verified)
Install Now
Cancel
Introduction to Firebug
Chief Firebug pyroentomologist Rob Campbell gives a quick introduction to Firebug.
Inspect
Pinpoint an element in a webpage with ease and precision.
Log
Send messages to the console direct from your webpage through Javascript.
Profile
Measure your Javascript performance in the Console's Profiler.
Debug
Step-by-step interactive debugging in a visual environment.
Analyze
Look at detailed measurements of your site's network activity.
Layout
Tweak and position HTML elements with CSS and the Layout panels.
Transferring data from releases.mozilla.org...
Fiddler: Disabled
Add-ons
Get Add-ons
Extensions
Themes
Plugins
Installation
Community
Discussion forums and lists
Get Involved
Hack the code, create plugins
Install Firebug For Firefox
Other Versions
Firebug Lite
Extensions
Introduction to Firebug
Chief Firebug pyroentomologist Rob Campbell gives a quick introduction to Firebug.
Watch now »
Other Firebug screencasts
Check back for more Firebug screencasts, coming soon.
Accurately analyze network usage and performance
Extend Firebug and add features to make Firebug even more powerful
Get the information you need to get it done with Firebug.
More Features »
Inspect
Pinpoint an element in a webpage with ease and precision.
Log
Send messages to the console direct from your webpage through Javascript.
Profile
Measure your Javascript performance in the Console's Profiler.
Debug
Step-by-step interactive debugging in a visual environment.
Analyze
Look at detailed measurements of your site's network activity.
Layout
Tweak and position HTML elements with CSS and the Layout panels.
Done
Fiddler: Disabled

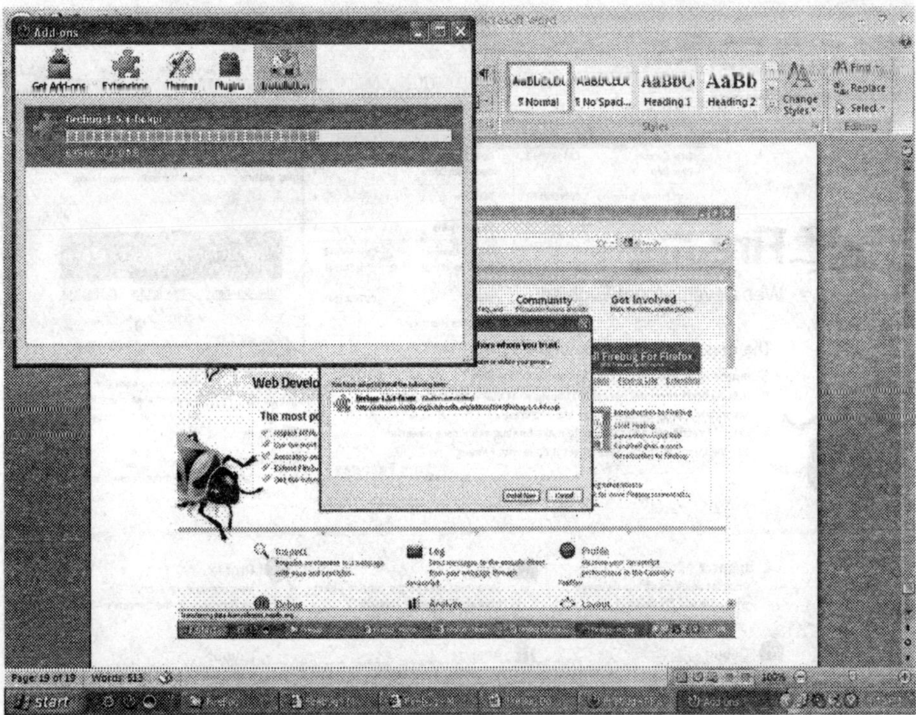
Add-ons
Get Add-ons
Extensions
Themes
Plugins
Installation
Normal
No Spaci...
Heading 1
Heading 2
Change Styles
Find
Replace
Select
Styles
Editing
Community
Get Involved
Web Develo
The most po
Log
Profile
Debug
Analyze
Layout
Page 19 of 19
Words: 513
100%
start

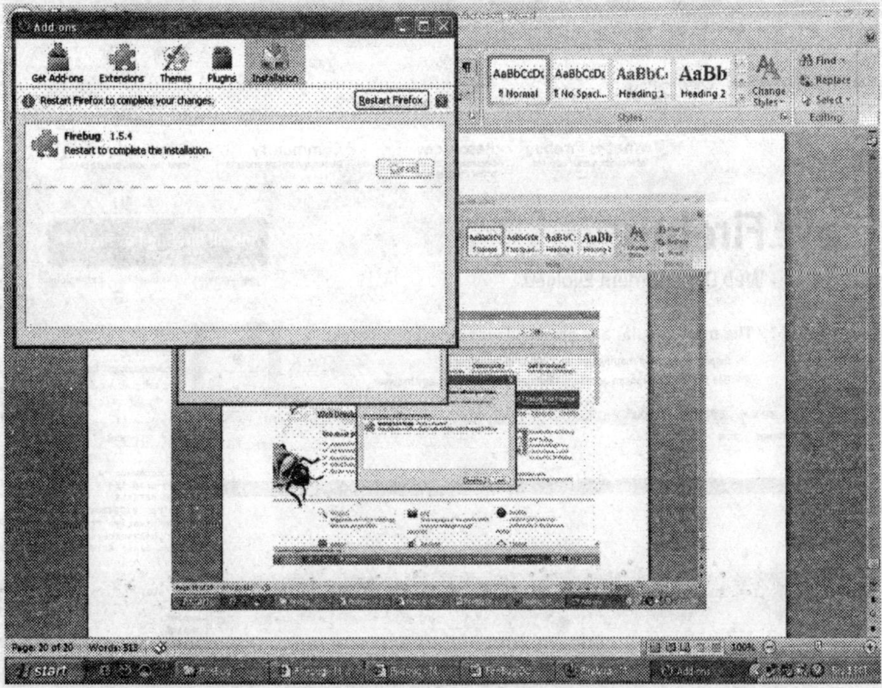
Add-ons
Get Add-ons
Extensions
Themes
Plugins
Installation
Restart Firefox to complete your changes.
Restart Firefox
Firebug 1.5.4
Restart to complete the installation.
Cancel
Normal
No Spaci...
Heading 1
Heading 2
Change Styles
Find
Replace
Select
Styles
Editing
Page: 20 of 20
Words: 513
100%
start

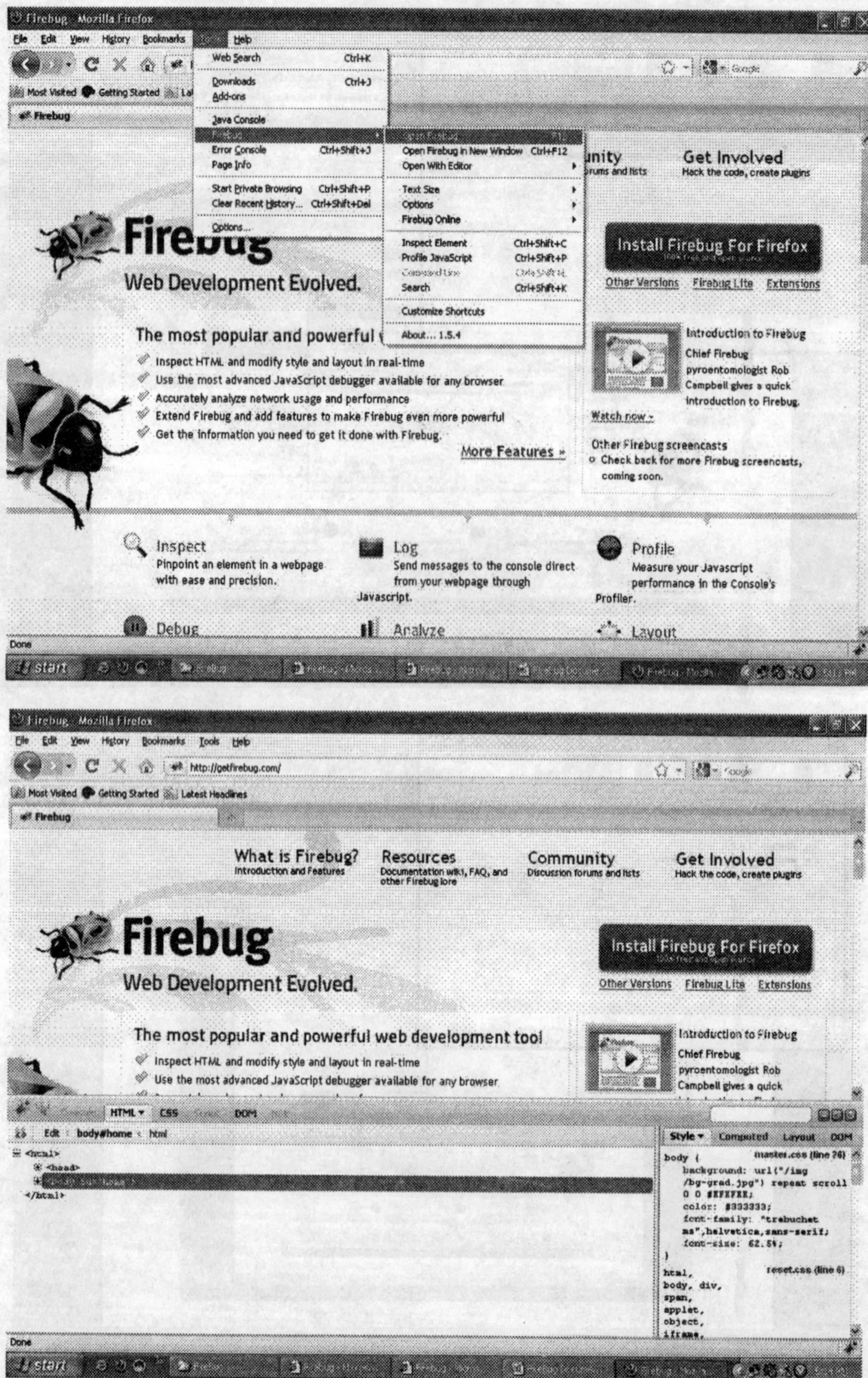

FireBuglite for IE/Safari/Opera

It will automatically install firebuglite in IE

http://getfirebug.com/firebuglite

Firebug is an extension for Firefox, but what happens when you need to test your pages in Internet Explorer, Opera, and Safari?

The solution is Firebug Lite, a JavaScript file you can insert into your pages to simulate some Firebug features in browsers that are not named "Firefox".

Firebug Lite creates the variable "firebug" and doesn't affect or interfere with HTML elements that aren't created by itself.

Screenshots:

IE
Opera
Safari

Latest Version: 1.2.1 (2008-09)

Installing Firebug Lite 1.2

Insert this line of code into any page that you want to contain Firebug lite:

```
<script type='text/javascript'
    src='http://getfirebug.com/releases/lite/1.2/firebug-lite-compressed.js'></script>
```

Firebug Lite as bookmarklet

Drag the following link to your bookmark toolbar and use Firebug Lite on any page:
Firebug Lite

Configuring Firebug Lite

Height of the firebug lite form is resizeable in latest version;

```
<script type="text/javascript">
firebug.env.height = 500;
</script>
```

Also, developers can use their own css file;

```
<script type="text/javascript">

firebug.env.css = "/myown/firebug.css"
</script>
```

Using Firebug Lite Offline

Download the source

Import firebug-lite-compressed.js or firebug-lite.js into your site's directory. Find "firebug-lite.css" URL on the javascript file which you imported and replace this with offline address of firebug-lite.css file.

```
<script language="javascript" type="text/javascript"
   src="/path/to/firebug/firebug-lite.js"></script>
```

Commands

Now FBLite supports all basic commands of Firebug.

firebug.watchXHR: Use this function to watch the status of XmlHttpRequest objects.

```
var req = new XmlHttpRequest;
firebug.watchXHR(req);
```

firebug.inspect: Now elements can be inspected in javascript code:

```
firebug.inspect(document.body.firstChild);
```

On some browsers, the console object is already declared. If you observe errors in Safari, for instance, use the console commands in this fashion:

```
firebug.d.console.cmd.log("test");
firebug.d.console.cmd.dir([ "test" ]);
```

Notes

On some browsers, the console object is already declared. If you observe errors in Safari, for instance, use the console commands in this fashion:

```
firebug.d.console.cmd.log("test");
firebug.d.console.cmd.dir([ "test" ]);
```

Firebug Lite creates the variables "firebug" and doesn't affect or interfere HTML elements that aren't create by itself.

File bug reports and request new features

Firebug is in constant development. If you find an issue, or want a certain feature or improvement, file it on the Firebug Issue Tracker so someone can take a look at it.

If you're looking for help with an issue, there are Firebug users and developers active in the Firebug Google Groups as well as the Firebug IRC channel.

Improve the code

Firebug is open source. Patches (or bug reports) are welcome! John Barton's introduction to the source may be helpful.

Firebug Working Group

The Firebug Working Group seeks to advance the Open Source development of Firebug for the benefit of the worldwide web development community.

The Firebug Working Group newsgroup is our primary communication channel

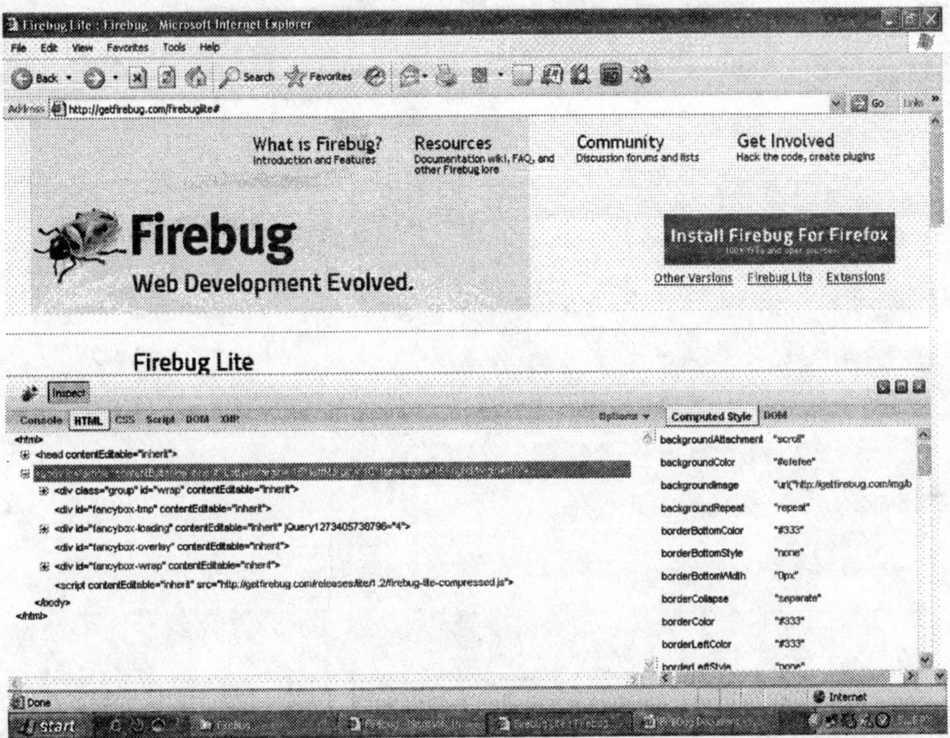

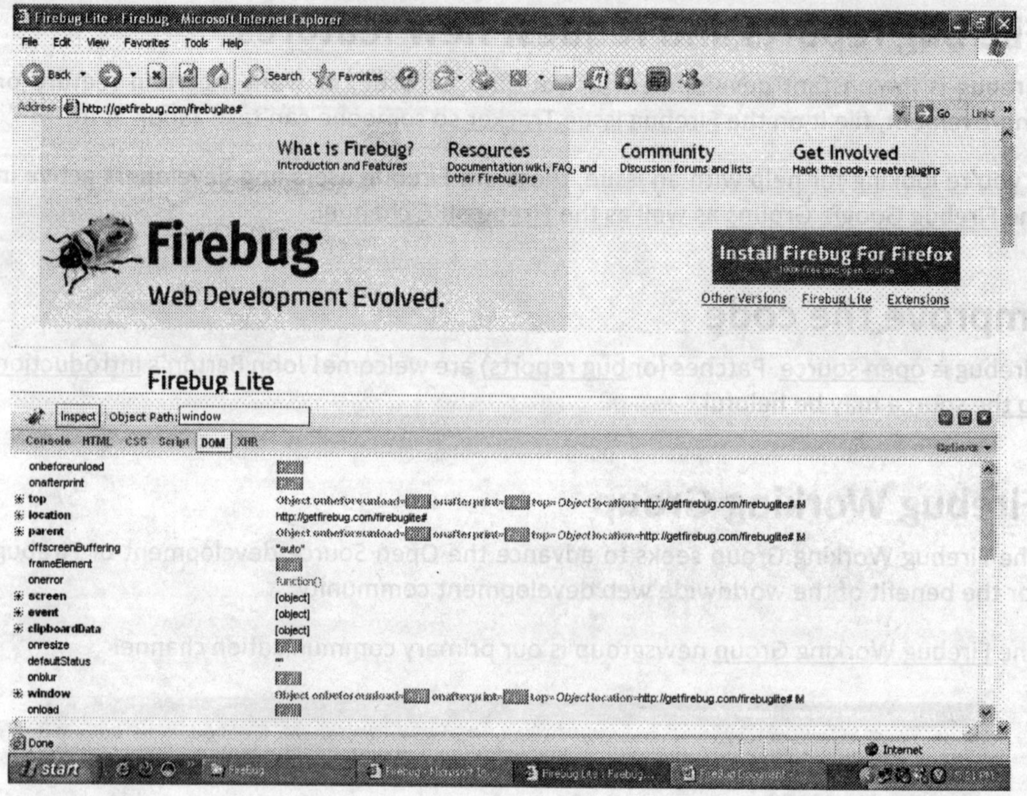
Firebug Lite : Firebug - Microsoft Internet Explorer
http://getfirebug.com/firebuglite#
What is Firebug?
Introduction and Features
Resources
Documentation wiki, FAQ, and other Firebug lore
Community
Discussion forums and lists
Get Involved
Hack the code, create plugins
Firebug
Web Development Evolved.
Install Firebug For Firefox
Other Versions
Firebug Lite
Extensions
Firebug Lite
Inspect
Object Path: window
Console HTML CSS Script DOM XHR
onbeforeunload
onafterprint
top
location
parent
offscreenBuffering
frameElement
onerror
screen
event
clipboardData
onresize
defaultStatus
onblur
window
onload
http://getfirebug.com/firebuglite#
"auto"
function()
[object]
Done
Internet

Chapter 40

Code Coverage Testing using Findbug tool

Static Code Analysis Tools - Find bugs

http://findbugs.sourceforge.net/downloads.html

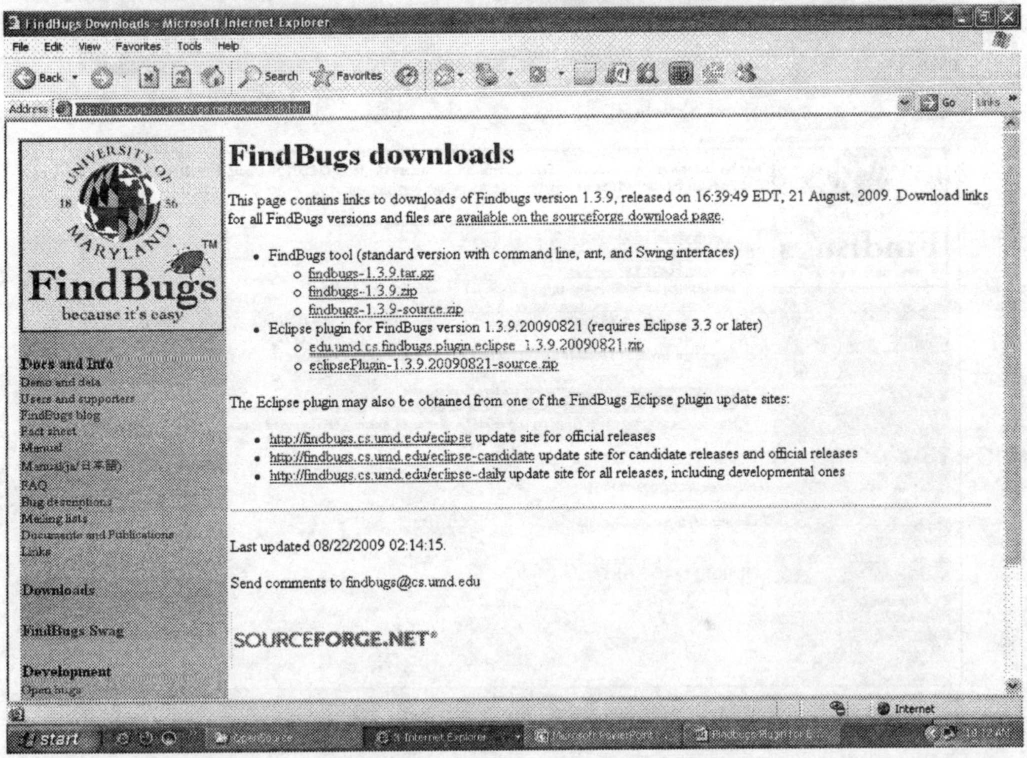

FindBugs Downloads - Microsoft Internet Explorer
File Edit View Favorites Tools Help
Back Search Favorites
Address
Go Links
UNIVERSITY OF MARYLAND
18 56
TM
FindBugs
because it's easy
Docs and Info
Demo and data
Users and supporters
FindBugs blog
Fact sheet
Manual
Manual(ja/日本語)
FAQ
Bug descriptions
Mailing lists
Documents and Publications
Links
Downloads
FindBugs Swag
Development
Open bugs
FindBugs downloads
This page contains links to downloads of Findbugs version 1.3.9, released on 16:39:49 EDT, 21 August, 2009. Download links for all FindBugs versions and files are available on the sourceforge download page.
FindBugs tool (standard version with command line, ant, and Swing interfaces)
findbugs-1.3.9.tar.gz
findbugs-1.3.9.zip
findbugs-1.3.9-source.zip
Eclipse plugin for FindBugs version 1.3.9.20090821 (requires Eclipse 3.3 or later)
edu.umd.cs.findbugs.plugin.eclipse_1.3.9.20090821.zip
eclipsePlugin-1.3.9.20090821-source.zip
The Eclipse plugin may also be obtained from one of the FindBugs Eclipse plugin update sites:
http://findbugs.cs.umd.edu/eclipse update site for official releases
http://findbugs.cs.umd.edu/eclipse-candidate update site for candidate releases and official releases
http://findbugs.cs.umd.edu/eclipse-daily update site for all releases, including developmental ones
Last updated 08/22/2009 02:14:15.
Send comments to findbugs@cs.umd.edu
SOURCEFORGE.NET®
Internet
start

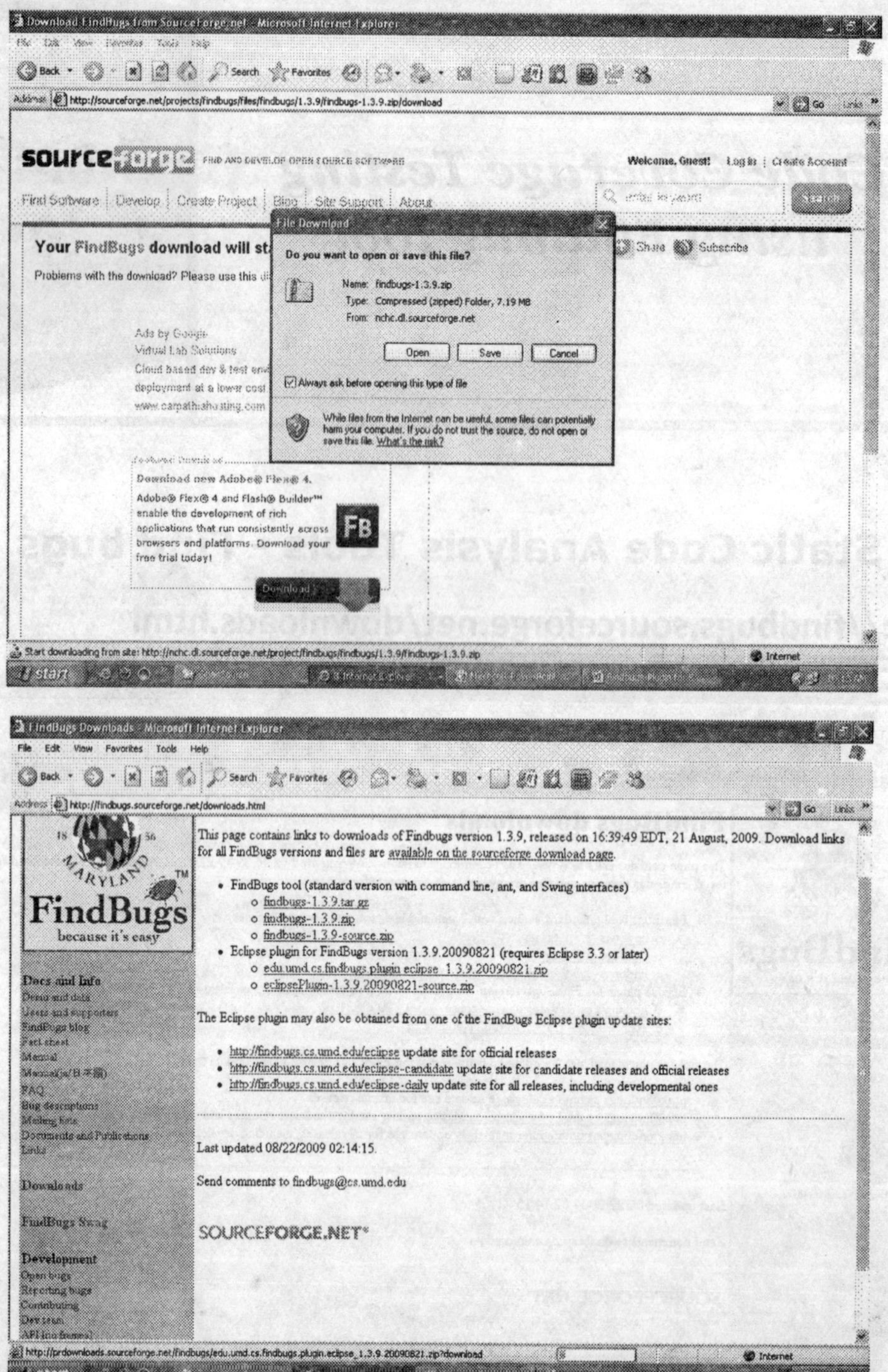
Download FindBugs from SourceForge.net - Microsoft Internet Explorer
http://sourceforge.net/projects/findbugs/files/findbugs/1.3.9/findbugs-1.3.9.zip/download
File Download
Do you want to open or save this file?
Name: findbugs-1.3.9.zip
Type: Compressed (zipped) Folder, 7.19 MB
From: nchc.dl.sourceforge.net
Open
Save
Cancel
Always ask before opening this type of file
While files from the Internet can be useful, some files can potentially harm your computer. If you do not trust the source, do not open or save this file. What's the risk?
Your FindBugs download will st
Problems with the download? Please use this di
Download new Adobe® Flex® 4.
Adobe® Flex® 4 and Flash® Builder™ enable the development of rich applications that run consistently across browsers and platforms. Download your free trial today!
Start downloading from site: http://nchc.dl.sourceforge.net/project/findbugs/findbugs/1.3.9/findbugs-1.3.9.zip
FindBugs Downloads - Microsoft Internet Explorer
http://findbugs.sourceforge.net/downloads.html
This page contains links to downloads of Findbugs version 1.3.9, released on 16:39:49 EDT, 21 August, 2009. Download links for all FindBugs versions and files are available on the sourceforge download page.
FindBugs tool (standard version with command line, ant, and Swing interfaces)
findbugs-1.3.9.tar.gz
findbugs-1.3.9.zip
findbugs-1.3.9-source.zip
Eclipse plugin for FindBugs version 1.3.9.20090821 (requires Eclipse 3.3 or later)
edu.umd.cs.findbugs.plugin.eclipse_1.3.9.20090821.zip
eclipsePlugin-1.3.9.20090821-source.zip
The Eclipse plugin may also be obtained from one of the FindBugs Eclipse plugin update sites:
http://findbugs.cs.umd.edu/eclipse update site for official releases
http://findbugs.cs.umd.edu/eclipse-candidate update site for candidate releases and official releases
http://findbugs.cs.umd.edu/eclipse-daily update site for all releases, including developmental ones
Last updated 08/22/2009 02:14:15.
Send comments to findbugs@cs.umd.edu
SOURCEFORGE.NET
FindBugs
because it's easy
Docs and Info
Downloads
FindBugs Swag
Development
http://prdownloads.sourceforge.net/findbugs/edu.umd.cs.findbugs.plugin.eclipse_1.3.9.20090821.zip?download

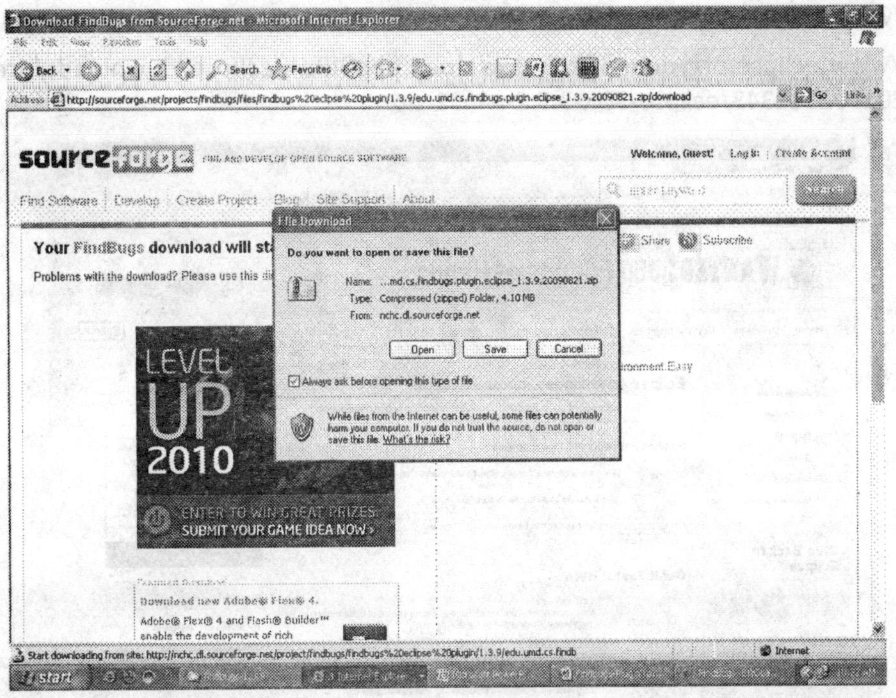
Download FindBugs from SourceForge.net - Microsoft Internet Explorer
http://sourceforge.net/projects/findbugs/files/findbugs%20eclipse%20plugin/1.3.9/edu.umd.cs.findbugs.plugin.eclipse_1.3.9.20090821.zip/download
Welcome, Guest! Log in Create Account
Find Software Develop Create Project Blog Site Support About
Your FindBugs download will st
Problems with the download? Please use this di
File Download
Do you want to open or save this file?
Name: ...md.cs.findbugs.plugin.eclipse_1.3.9.20090821.zip
Type: Compressed (zipped) Folder, 4.10 MB
From: nchc.dl.sourceforge.net
Open Save Cancel
Always ask before opening this type of file
While files from the Internet can be useful, some files can potentially harm your computer. If you do not trust the source, do not open or save this file. What's the risk?
LEVEL UP 2010
ENTER TO WIN GREAT PRIZES
SUBMIT YOUR GAME IDEA NOW
Download new Adobe® Flex® 4.
Adobe® Flex® 4 and Flash® Builder™ enable the development of rich
Start downloading from site: http://nchc.dl.sourceforge.net/project/findbugs/findbugs%20eclipse%20plugin/1.3.9/edu.umd.cs.findb
Internet
start

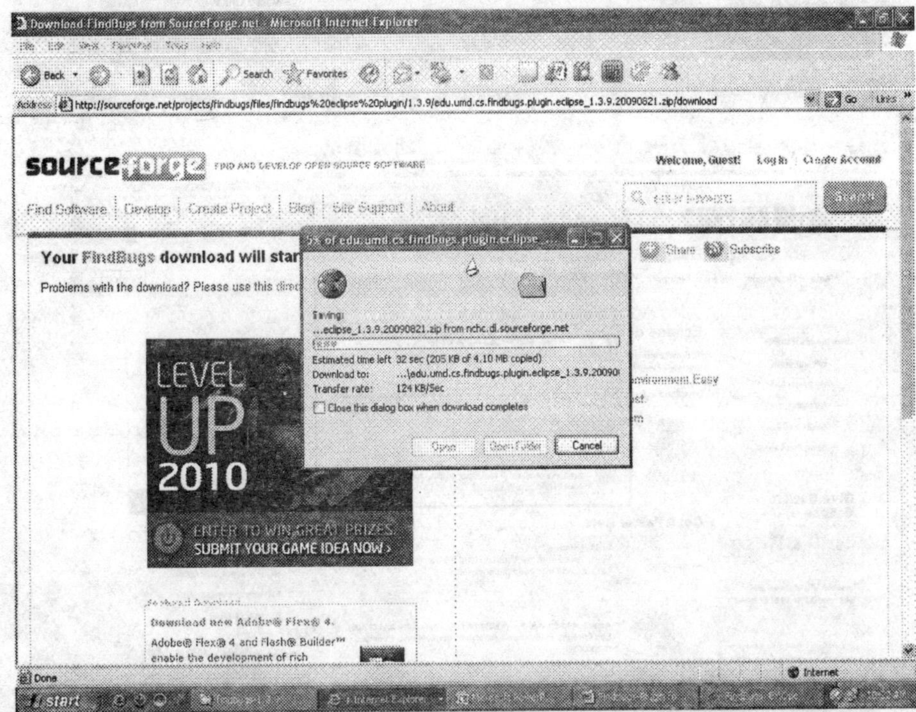
Download FindBugs from SourceForge.net - Microsoft Internet Explorer
http://sourceforge.net/projects/findbugs/files/findbugs%20eclipse%20plugin/1.3.9/edu.umd.cs.findbugs.plugin.eclipse_1.3.9.20090821.zip/download
Welcome, Guest! Log in Create Account
Find Software Develop Create Project Blog Site Support About
Your FindBugs download will star
Problems with the download? Please use this direc
5% of edu.umd.cs.findbugs.plugin.eclipse...
Saving:
...eclipse_1.3.9.20090821.zip from nchc.dl.sourceforge.net
Estimated time left 32 sec (205 KB of 4.10 MB copied)
Download to: ...\edu.umd.cs.findbugs.plugin.eclipse_1.3.9.20090
Transfer rate: 124 KB/Sec
Close this dialog box when download completes
Open Open Folder Cancel
LEVEL UP 2010
ENTER TO WIN GREAT PRIZES
SUBMIT YOUR GAME IDEA NOW
Download new Adobe® Flex® 4.
Adobe® Flex® 4 and Flash® Builder™ enable the development of rich
Done
Internet
start

http://www.eclipse.org/downloads/

http://www.eclipse.org/downloads/download.php?file=/eclipse/downloads/drops/R-3.5.2-201002111343/eclipse-SDK-3.5.2-win32.zip

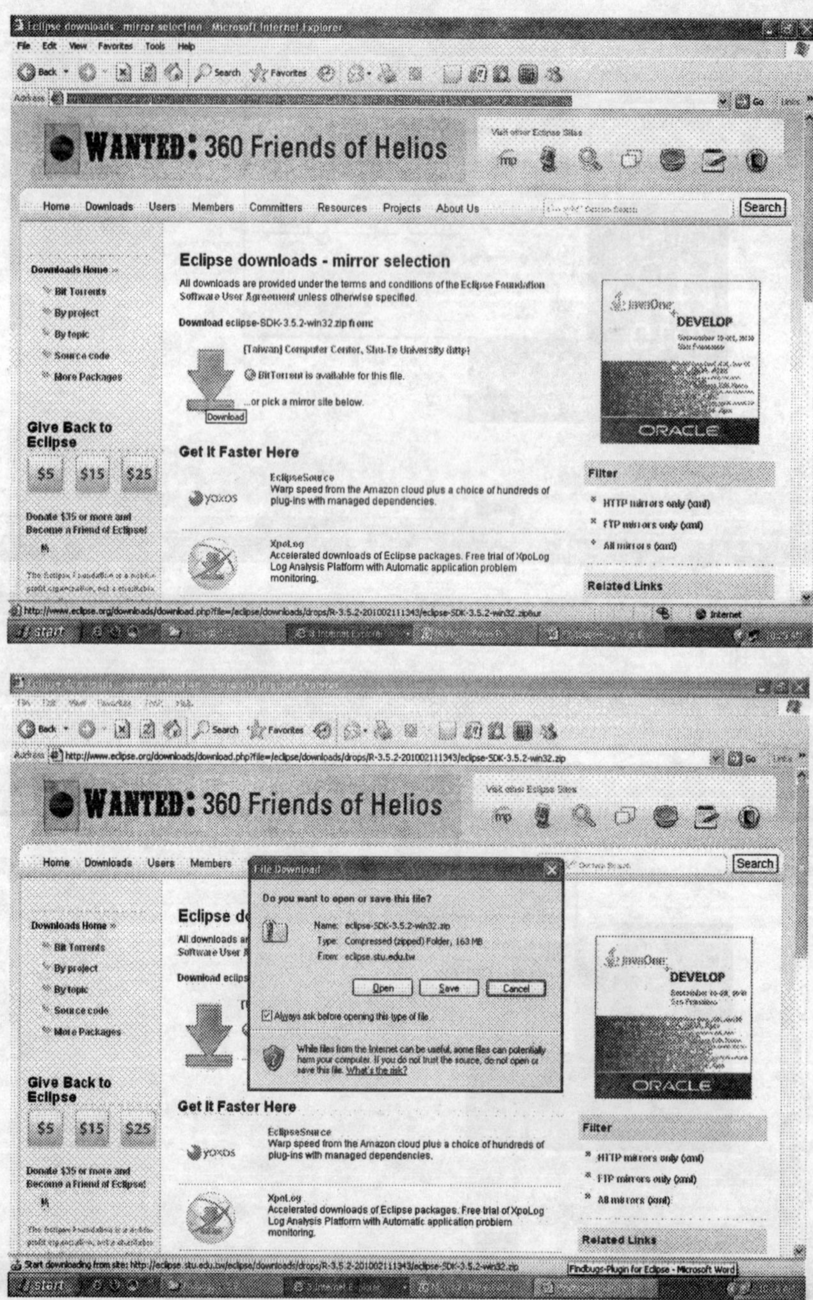

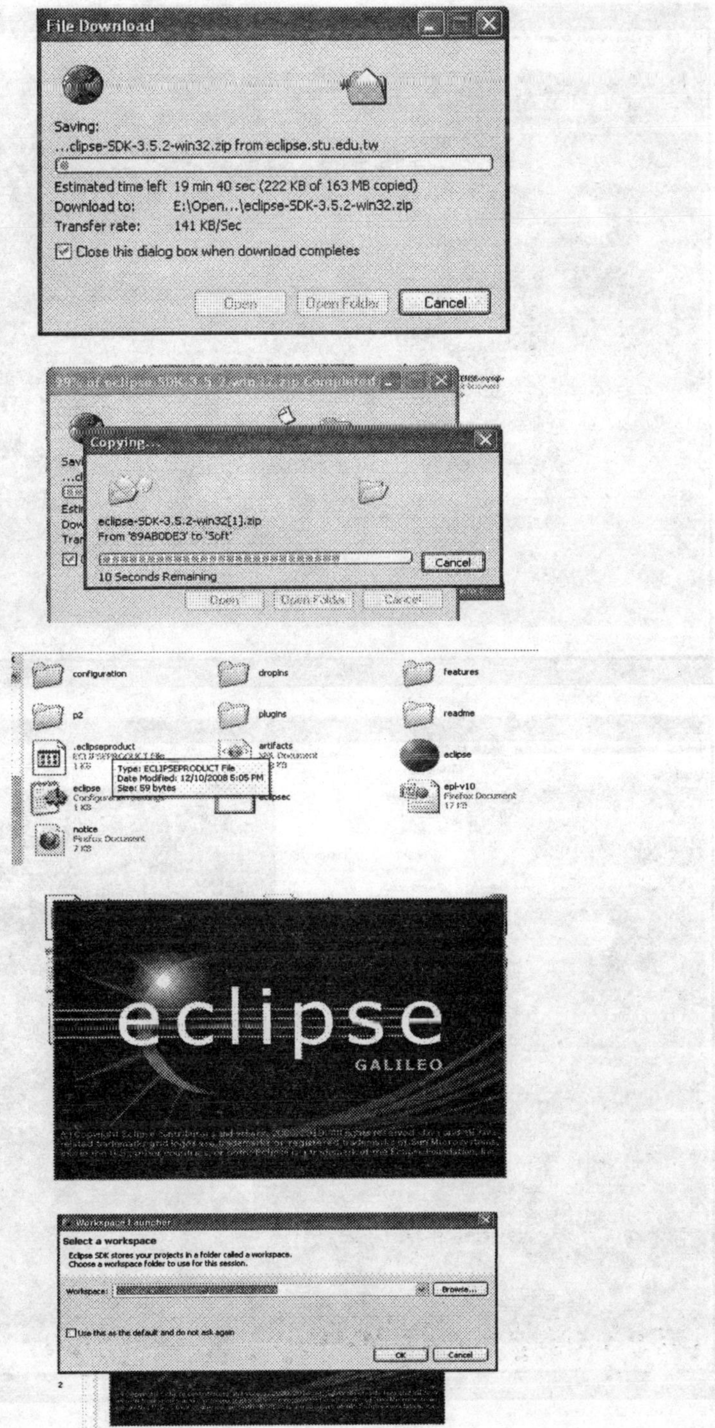
File Download
Saving:
...clipse-SDK-3.5.2-win32.zip from eclipse.stu.edu.tw
Estimated time left 19 min 40 sec (222 KB of 163 MB copied)
Download to: E:\Open...\eclipse-SDK-3.5.2-win32.zip
Transfer rate: 141 KB/Sec
Close this dialog box when download completes
Open
Open Folder
Cancel
Copying...
eclipse-SDK-3.5.2-win32[1].zip
From '69AB0DE3' to 'Soft'
Cancel
10 Seconds Remaining
configuration
dropins
features
p2
plugins
readme
.eclipseproduct
artifacts
eclipse
Type: ECLIPSEPRODUCT File
Date Modified: 12/10/2008 5:05 PM
Size: 59 bytes
eclipse
epl-v10
Firefox Document
notice
Firefox Document
eclipse
GALILEO
Workspace Launcher
Select a workspace
Eclipse SDK stores your projects in a folder called a workspace.
Choose a workspace folder to use for this session.
Workspace:
Browse...
Use this as the default and do not ask again
OK
Cancel

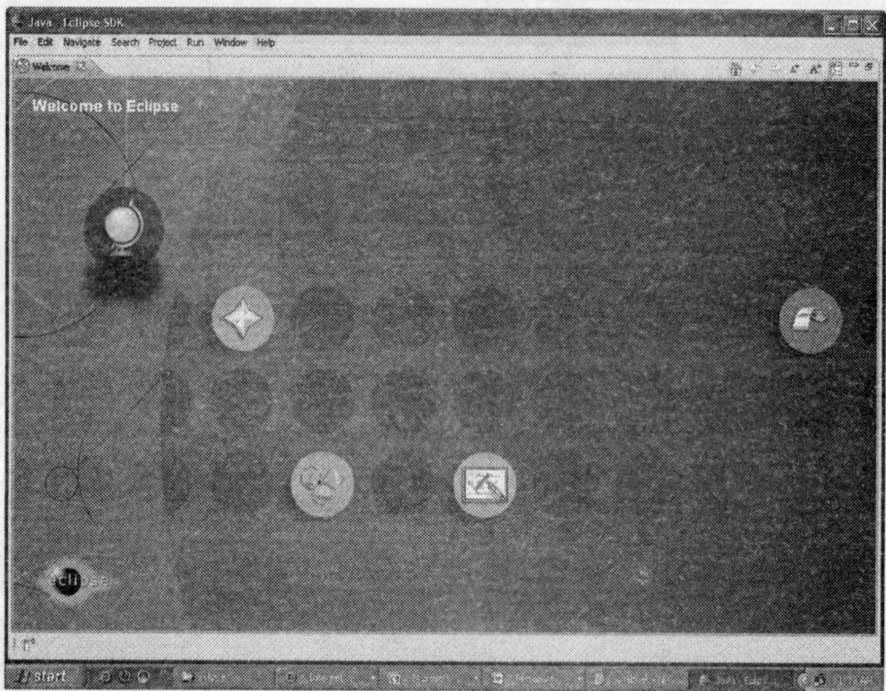
Java - Eclipse SDK
File Edit Navigate Search Project Run Window Help
Welcome
Welcome to Eclipse
start

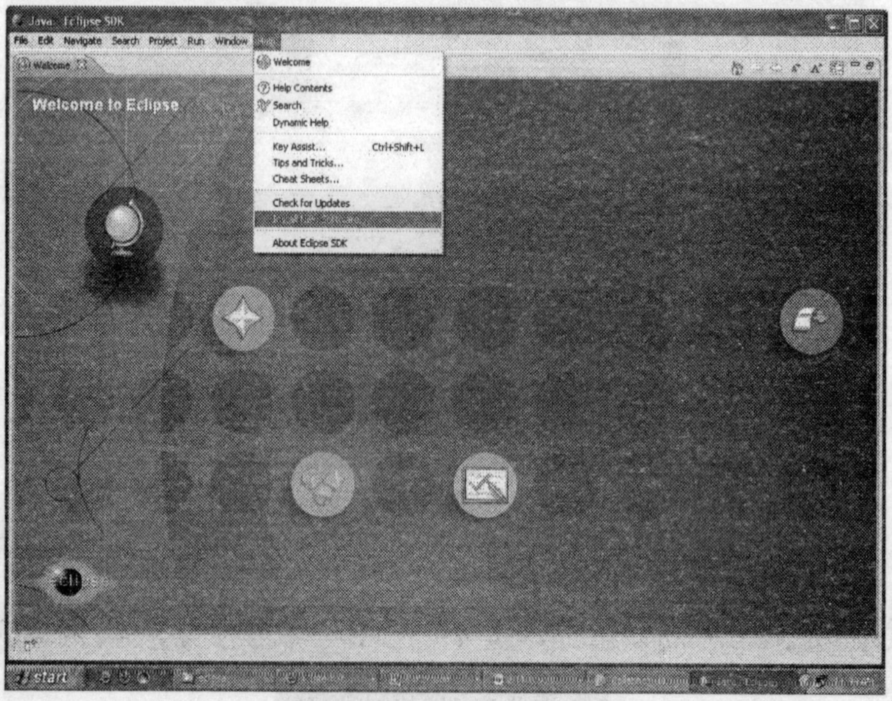
Java - Eclipse SDK
File Edit Navigate Search Project Run Window
Welcome
Welcome to Eclipse
Welcome
Help Contents
Search
Dynamic Help
Key Assist... Ctrl+Shift+L
Tips and Tricks...
Cheat Sheets...
Check for Updates
About Eclipse SDK
start

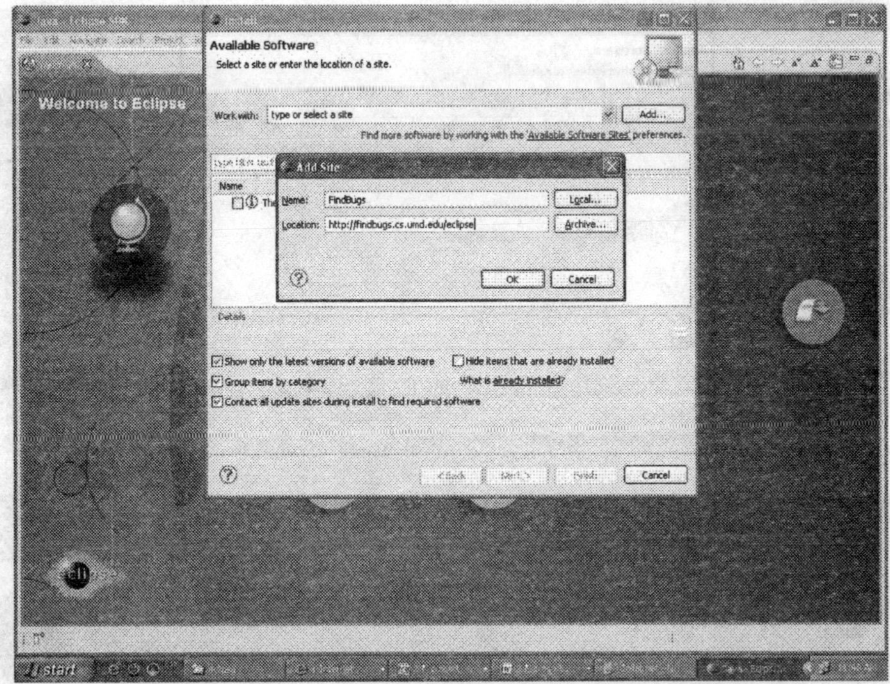
Available Software
Select a site or enter the location of a site.
Welcome to Eclipse
Work with: type or select a site
Add...
Find more software by working with the 'Available Software Sites' preferences.
Add Site
Name:
Name: FindBugs
Local...
Location: http://findbugs.cs.umd.edu/eclipse
Archive...
OK
Cancel
Details
Show only the latest versions of available software
Hide items that are already installed
Group items by category
What is already installed?
Contact all update sites during install to find required software
Cancel

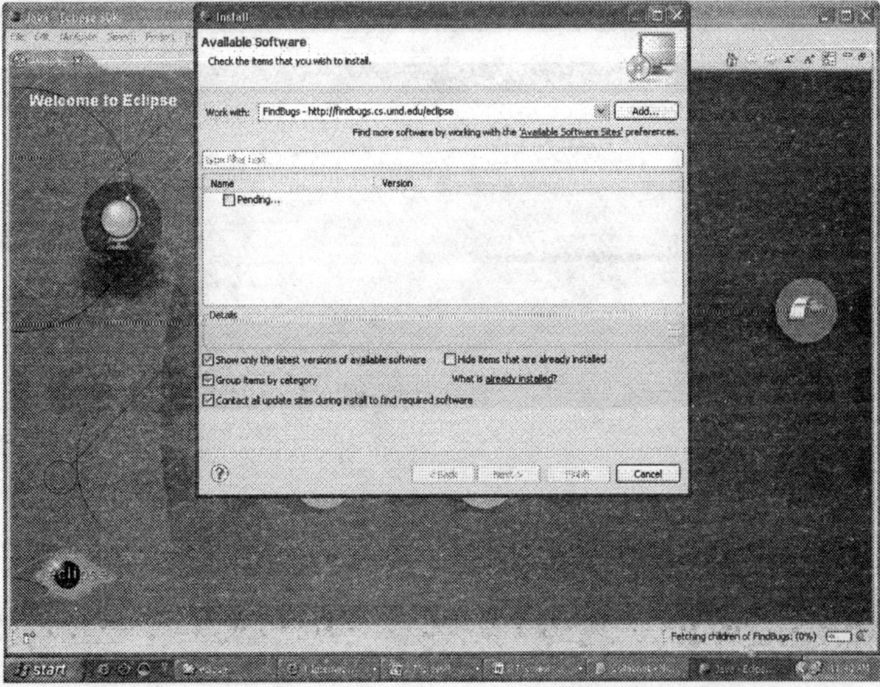
Install
Available Software
Check the items that you wish to install.
Welcome to Eclipse
Work with: FindBugs - http://findbugs.cs.umd.edu/eclipse
Add...
Find more software by working with the 'Available Software Sites' preferences.
Name
Version
Pending...
Details
Show only the latest versions of available software
Hide items that are already installed
Group items by category
What is already installed?
Contact all update sites during install to find required software
Cancel
Fetching children of FindBugs: (0%)

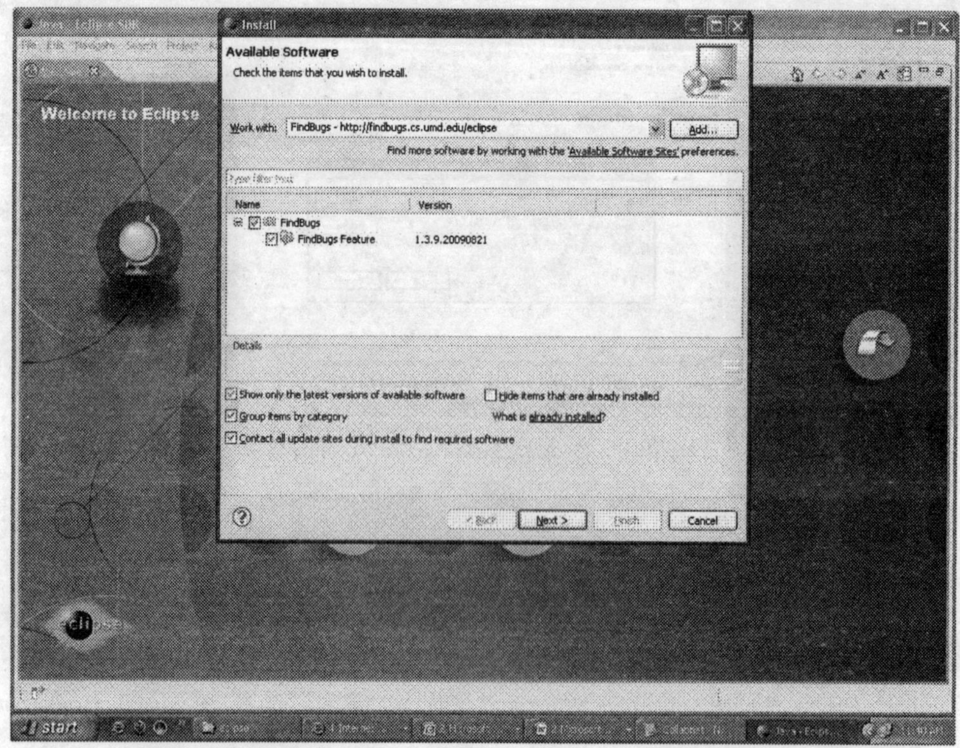
Install
Available Software
Check the items that you wish to install.
Work with: FindBugs - http://findbugs.cs.umd.edu/eclipse
Add...
Find more software by working with the 'Available Software Sites' preferences.
Name
Version
FindBugs
FindBugs Feature
1.3.9.20090821
Details
Show only the latest versions of available software
Hide items that are already installed
Group items by category
What is already installed?
Contact all update sites during install to find required software
< Back
Next >
Finish
Cancel
Welcome to Eclipse

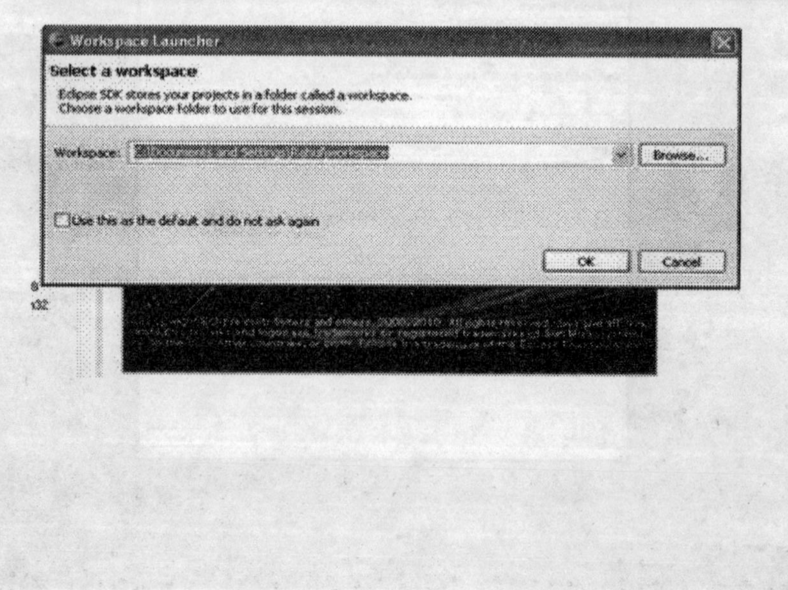
Workspace Launcher
Select a workspace
Eclipse SDK stores your projects in a folder called a workspace.
Choose a workspace folder to use for this session.
Workspace:
Browse...
Use this as the default and do not ask again
OK
Cancel

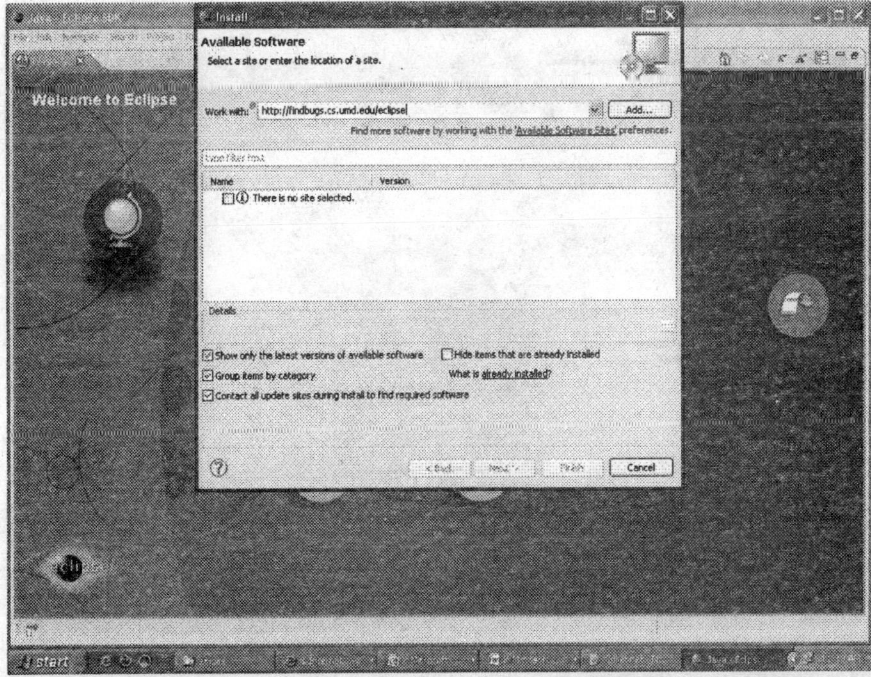
Install
Available Software
Select a site or enter the location of a site.
Work with: http://findbugs.cs.umd.edu/eclipse
Add...
Find more software by working with the 'Available Software Sites' preferences.
Name
Version
There is no site selected.
Details
Show only the latest versions of available software
Hide items that are already installed
Group items by category
What is already installed?
Contact all update sites during install to find required software
Cancel
Welcome to Eclipse

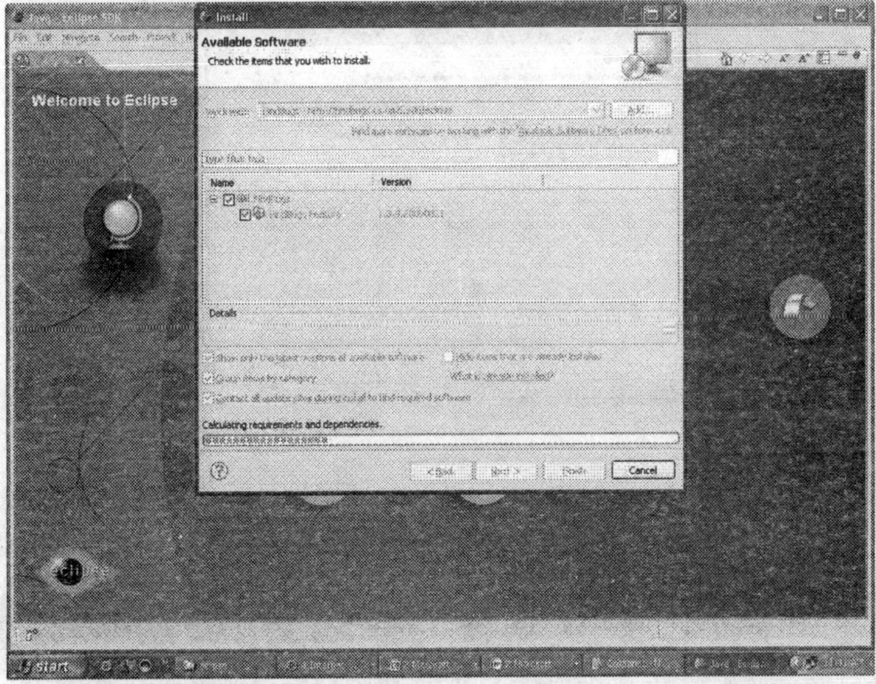
Install
Available Software
Check the items that you wish to install.
Name
Version
Details
Calculating requirements and dependencies.
Cancel
Welcome to Eclipse

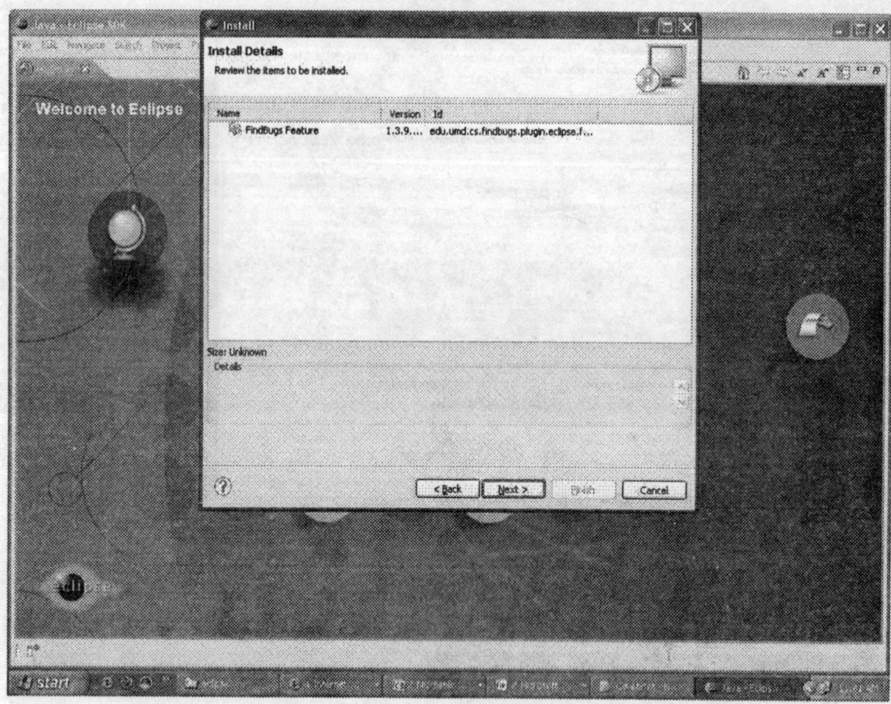
Install
Install Details
Review the items to be installed.
Welcome to Eclipse
Name
Version
Id
FindBugs Feature
1.3.9....
edu.umd.cs.findbugs.plugin.eclipse.f...
Size: Unknown
Details
< Back
Next >
Finish
Cancel

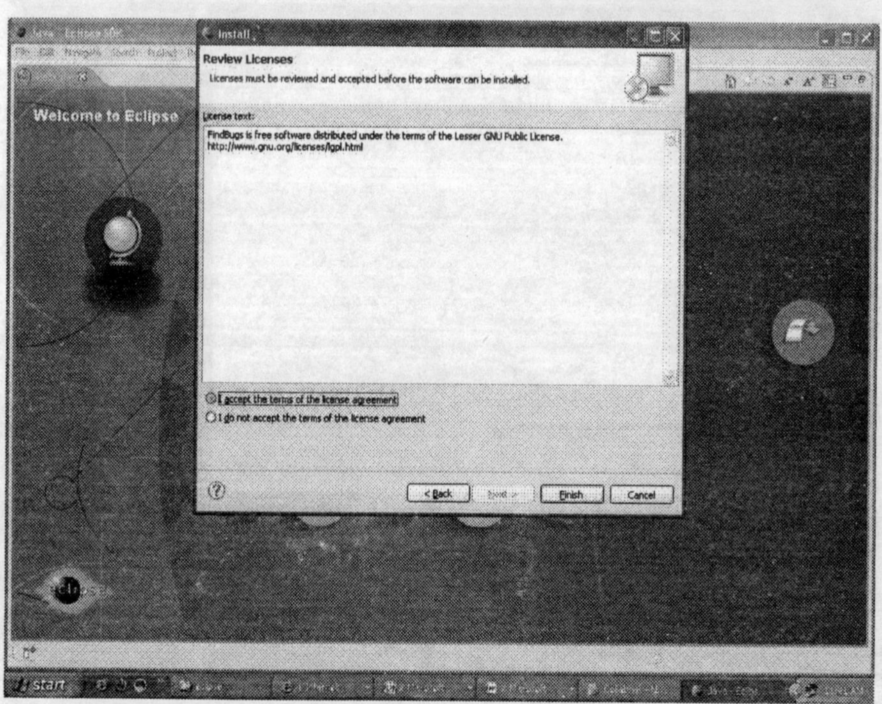
Install
Review Licenses
Licenses must be reviewed and accepted before the software can be installed.
Welcome to Eclipse
License text:
FindBugs is free software distributed under the terms of the Lesser GNU Public License.
http://www.gnu.org/licenses/lgpl.html
I accept the terms of the license agreement
I do not accept the terms of the license agreement
< Back
Next >
Finish
Cancel

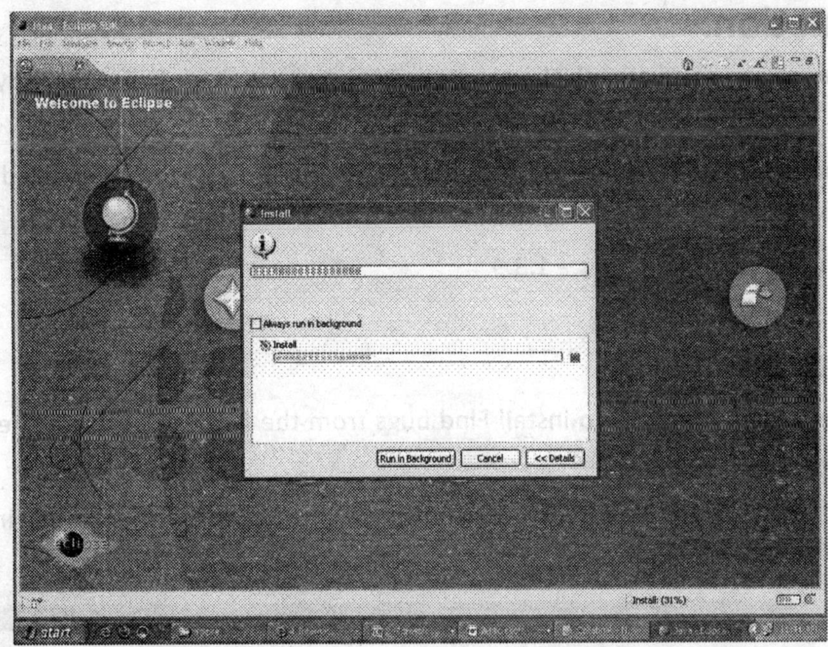

After Installation it will ask to 'Restart Eclipse', so please restart Eclipse to update the changes.

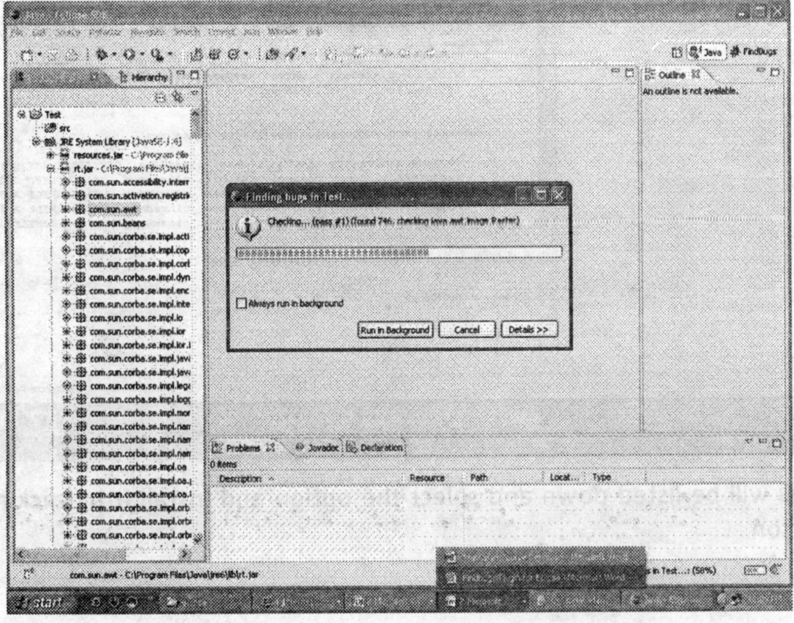

Introduction:-

- An open source software which uses static analysis to look for bugs in java byte-code developed by The University of Maryland.

- It requires JDK 1.5.0 or later to run, but it will analyze programs compiied for any version

- Current version of find bugs – 1.3.9

Installation:-

- Use the update manager to install Find bugs from the find bugs update site http://findbugs.cs.umd.edu/eclipse

- Select *"Help -> Install New Software"* and specify the above mentioned URL in "Work with:" drop down box

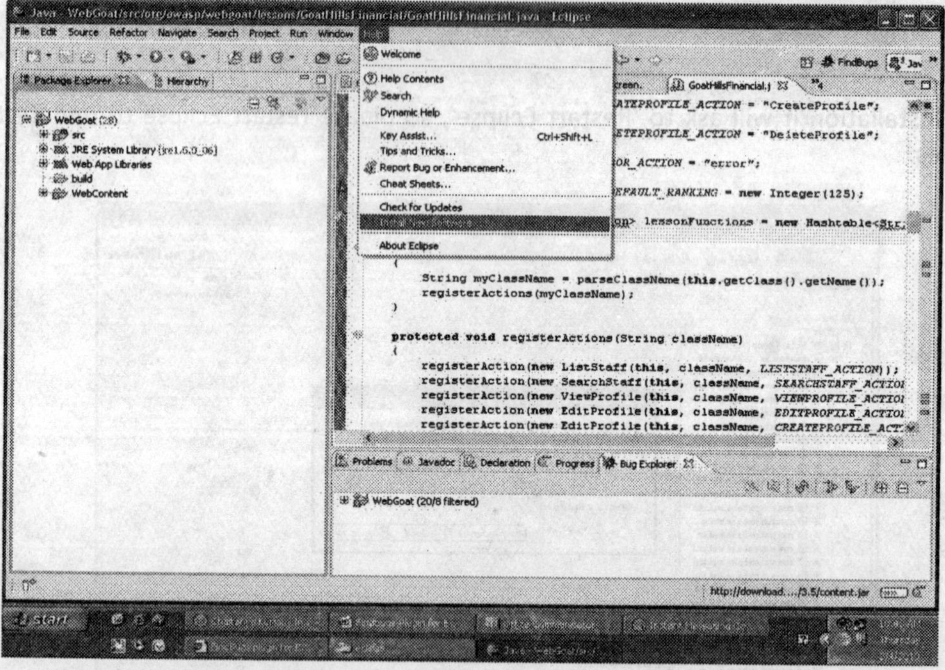

- Find bugs will be listed down and select the option and install it by clicking on the Next button

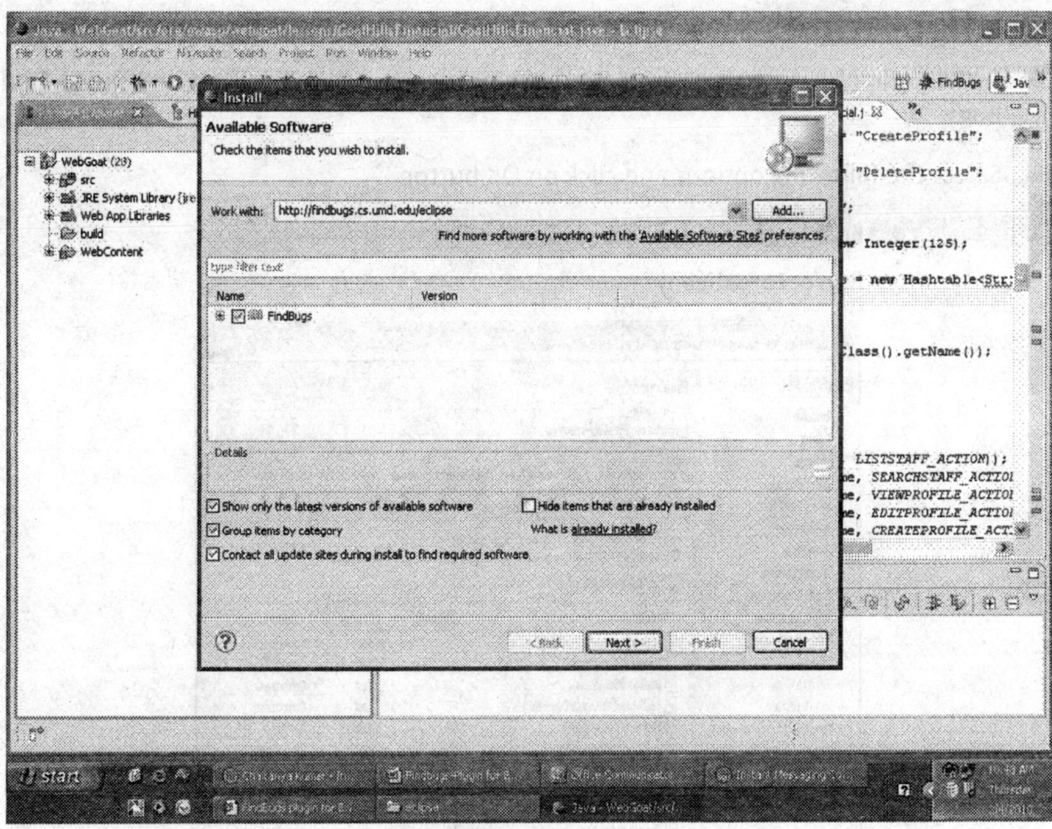

Finally click the 'Finish' button for configuring find bugs with eclipse.

Configuration:-

- Activate find bugs for your project via the properties of your project and select Find Bugs

- Select the following options and click on OK button

    - Enable project specific settings
    - Run automatically

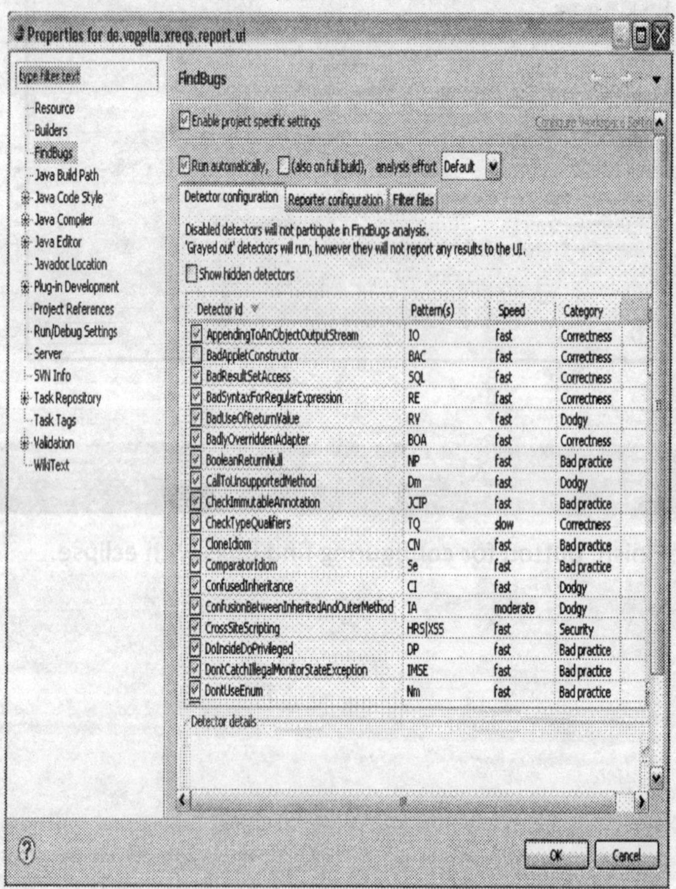

The following points are to be noted from the above picture.

1. All the detector ids can be selected.

2. Analysis effort – Minimal, Default, Maximal
   Minimal – Report all bugs

Default – Report medium and high priority bugs
Maximal – Report only high priority bugs

3. Report configuration – Bug categories that can be displayed in the report will be selected here.

Using Findbugs:-

Run Analysis :

- Run find bugs by right clicking on the project and select *"Findbugs -> Findbugs "*

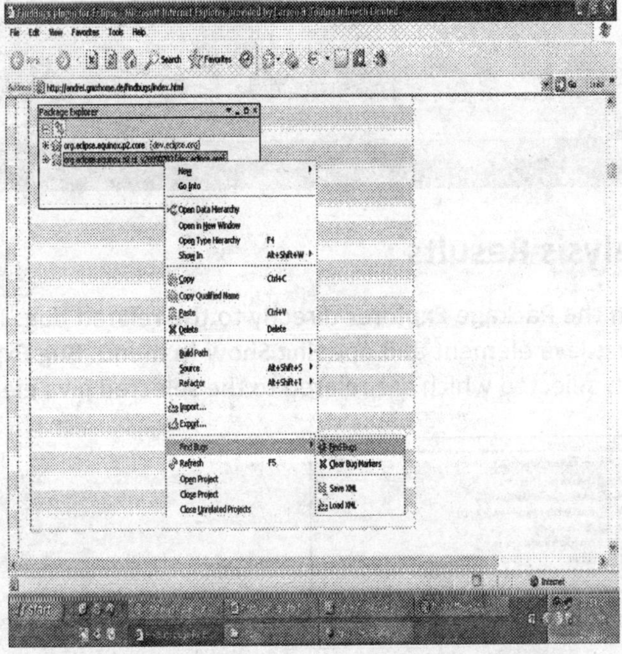

Show Analysis Results :

After FindBugs analysis is done, results are available in **Bug Explorer** view and also shown as **label decorations** for the project/package/file. To enable such decorations go to **Window->Preferences->General-Appearance->Label Decorations**:

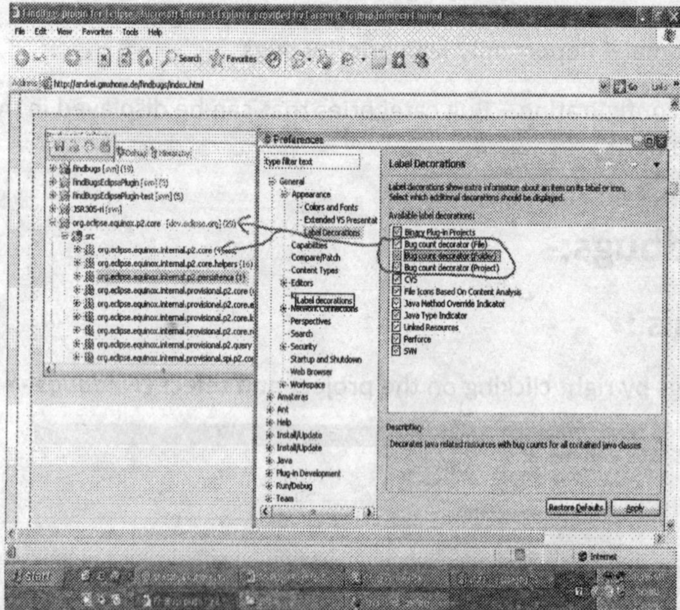

Examine Analysis Results :

You can jump from the **Package Explorer** directly to the related bugs in **Bug Explorer** by selecting interesting Java element and opening **Show In** menu. **Bug Explorer** view shows up with all the bugs selected which are related to the selected java element:

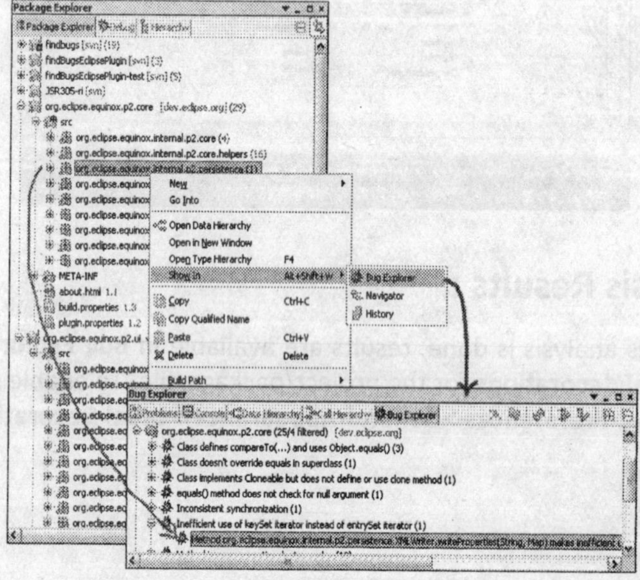

Another possibility is to switch perspective: **Window->Open Perspective->FindBugs** or via "**Ctrl+3 -> FindBugs**":

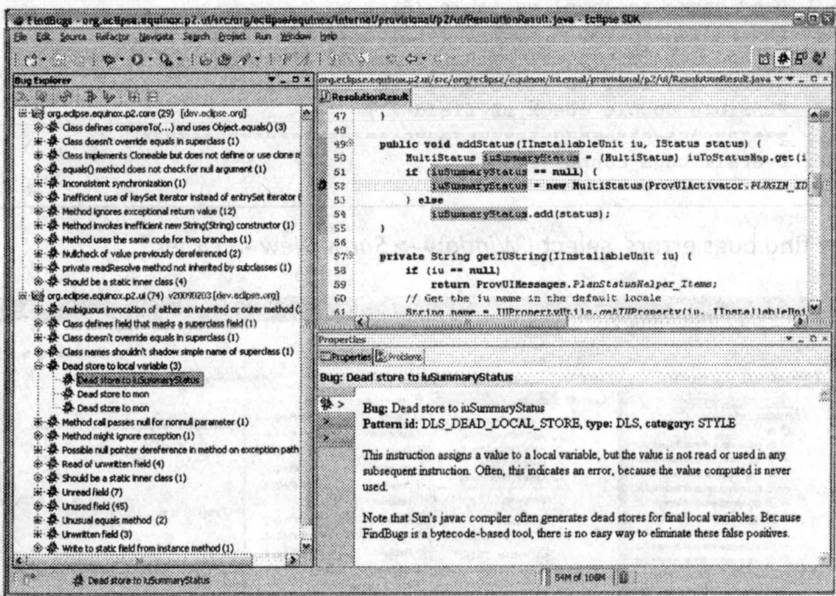

Eclipse **Properties** view follows selection in the **Bug Explorer** view and shows properties for selected element(s).In case there are more information available, it uses additional tabs. For example, each bug instance has it's own **annotations** tab:

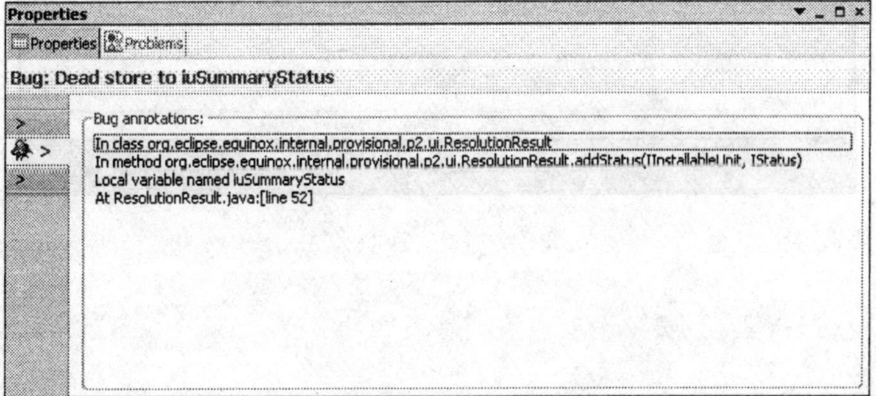

It is also possible to select multiple elements in the **Bug Explorer** view. In this case, **Properties** view will show summary of bugs reported for the current selection:

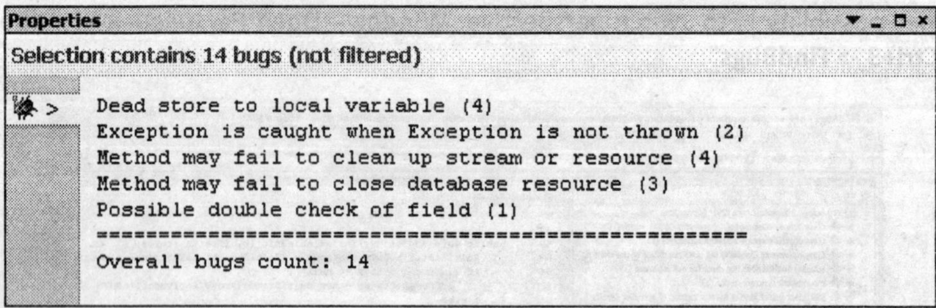

- To see find bugs errors, select *"Window -> Show View -> Other"*

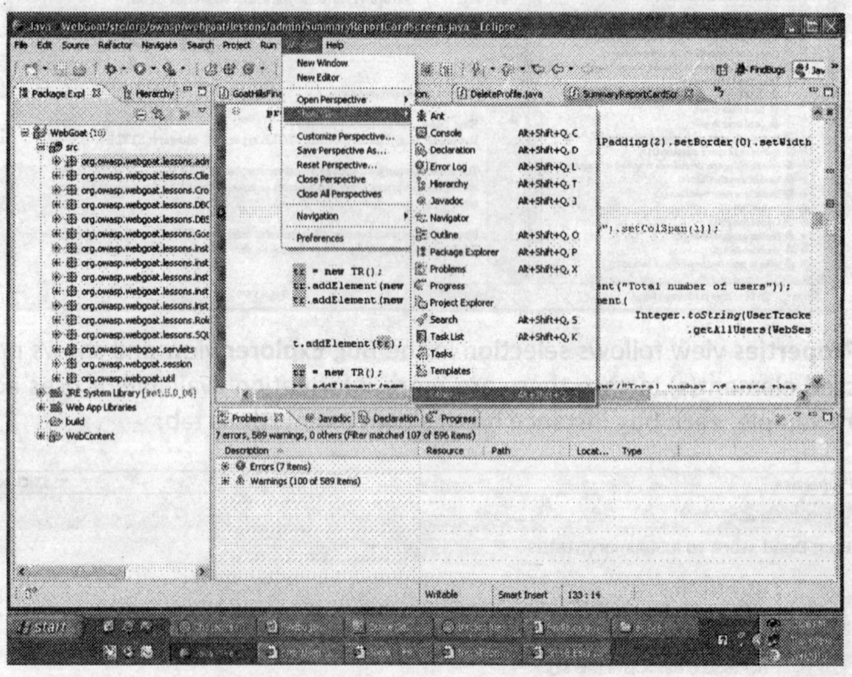

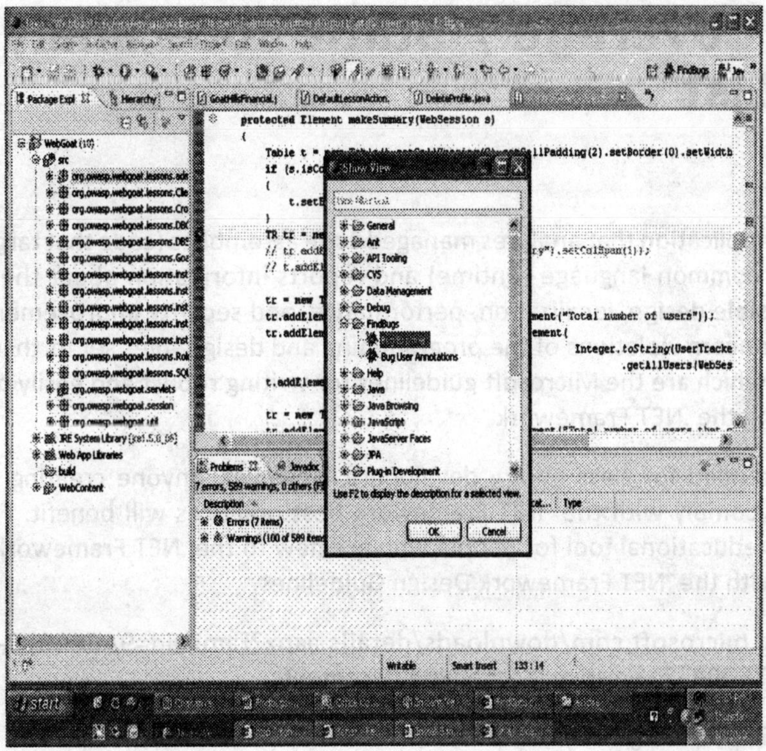

References:

http://findbugs.sourceforge.net/

http://andrei.gmxhome.de/findbugs/index.html

Code Coverage / Static code analysis Tool List

fxcop

FxCop is an application that analyzes managed code assemblies (code that targets the .NET Framework common language runtime) and reports information about the assemblies, such as possible design, localization, performance, and security improvements. Many of the issues concern violations of the programming and design rules set forth in the Design Guidelines, which are the Microsoft guidelines for writing robust and easily maintainable code by using the .NET Framework.

FxCop is intended for class library developers. However, anyone creating applications that should comply with the .NET Framework best practices will benefit. FxCop is also useful as an educational tool for people who are new to the .NET Framework or who are unfamiliar with the .NET Framework Design Guidelines.

http://www.microsoft.com/downloads/details.aspx?familyid=9AEAA970-F281-4FB0-ABA1-D59D7ED09772&displaylang=en#Requirements

http://en.wikipedia.org/wiki/FxCop

EMMA

- EMMA can instrument classes for coverage either offline (before they are loaded) or on the fly (using an instrumenting application classloader).
- Supported coverage types: class, method, line, basic block. EMMA can detect when a single source code line is covered only partially.
- Coverage stats are aggregated at method, class, package, and "all classes" levels.
- Output report types: plain text, HTML, XML. All report types support drill-down, to a user-controlled detail depth. The HTML report supports source code linking.
- Output reports can highlight items with coverage levels below user-provided thresholds.
- Coverage data obtained in different instrumentation or test runs can be merged together.

http://emma.sourceforge.net/downloads.html

PMD:

PMD scans Java source code and looks for potential problems like:

- Possible bugs - empty try/catch/finally/switch statements
- Dead code - unused local variables, parameters and private methods
- Suboptimal code - wasteful String/StringBuffer usage
- Overcomplicated expressions - unnecessary if statements, for loops that could be while loops
- Duplicate code - copied/pasted code means copied/pasted bugs

http://pmd.sourceforge.net/

References:

http://java-source.net/open-source/code-coverage

http://csharp-source.net/open-source/code-coverage

http://www.codecoveragetools.com/

Section
11
Source
Version Control

What Is Source Control?

- "A place to store all the various revisions of the stuff you write while developing an application." – David Thomas and Andrew Hunt, *Pragmatic Version Control Using CVS*
- Also called "Version Control" or "Revision Control"
- "Any practice which tracks and provides control over changes to source code." – http://en.wikipedia.org/wiki/Version_control

Why Use Source Control?

- Single source of record
- File version management
- Release version management
- Single point of backup
- Aggressive refactoring
- Consistent, repeatable builds
- Communication and teamwork
- Change history
- Parallel development

Source Control Concepts

- Repository or Depot
- Development Workspace
- Code line
- Change Task
- Workspace Update
- Commit
- Branch
- Label or Tag
- Locking vs. Non-locking

Repository (Depot)

The single storage location for all your files, directories, versions, branches, et al.

Development Workspace

Your private copies of the files and directories for a project or projects, usually on your hard drive.

Codeline

A set of versions of files, also known as a "branch" (or "stream" in AccuRev).

Change Task

A changeset, or set of changes, that should be tracked as a single unit Workspace Update

The process of bringing modifications from the repository into your development workspace.

Commit

The process of pushing modifications from your development workspace to the repository.

Branch

An isolated set of versions of files, kept separate from and worked in parallel to the main codeline.

Label or Tag

A snapshot of versions of files at a specific point in time.

Locking vs. Non-locking

- Locking
  - Lock, modify, unlock

  - No one else can make changes to file while you have it checked out

- Non-locking
  - Copy, modify, merge
  - Others can continue to develop while you make your changes
- Clear Winner: Non-locking

Locking slows development, setting up roadblocks and breaking people's concentration—people have to wait on each other, sometimes you expend energy chasing people down, sometimes those people have gone on vacation.

Sometimes people edit the file without checking it out, causing even greater problems.

Locking often gives false sense of security.

Locking proponents shrink at the thought of non-locking systems, sure that such chaos can only result in errors. These are people who have never worked in the non-locking model.

As teams get larger, locking gets much harder, while non-locking doesn't.

Source control vs. version control

- Source Code Management
  - More of a "total solution" that includes things like bug tracking, Wiki
- Version Control / Revision Control
  - This is what Subversion does

Version Control Steps

- **Create a repository of project files (code)**
- **CHECKOUT a working copy of the code to working directory**
- **Edit code**

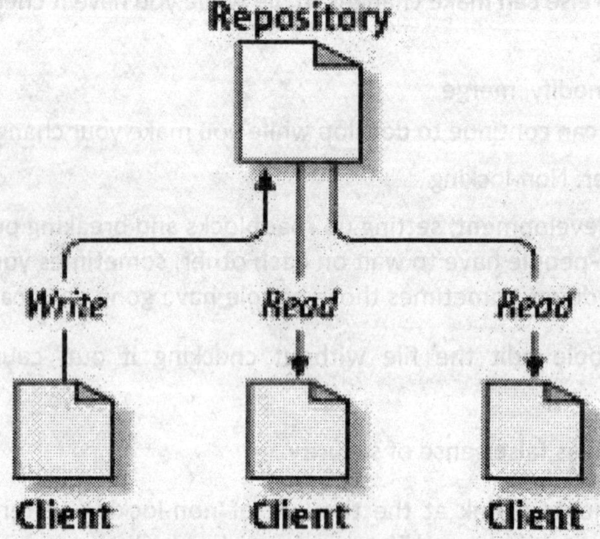

- COMMIT your changes back into the repository
- If someone else changed the same file as you, resolve differences to the changed files as needed (MERGE)
- UPDATE your working copy before continuing work the next time

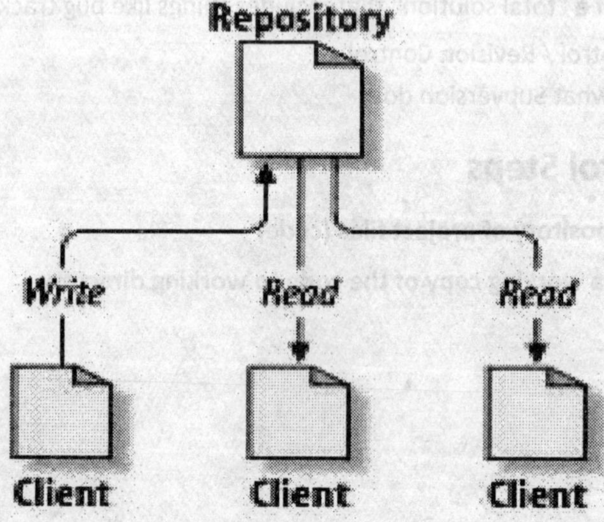

Version control models

File sharing: the problem to avoid

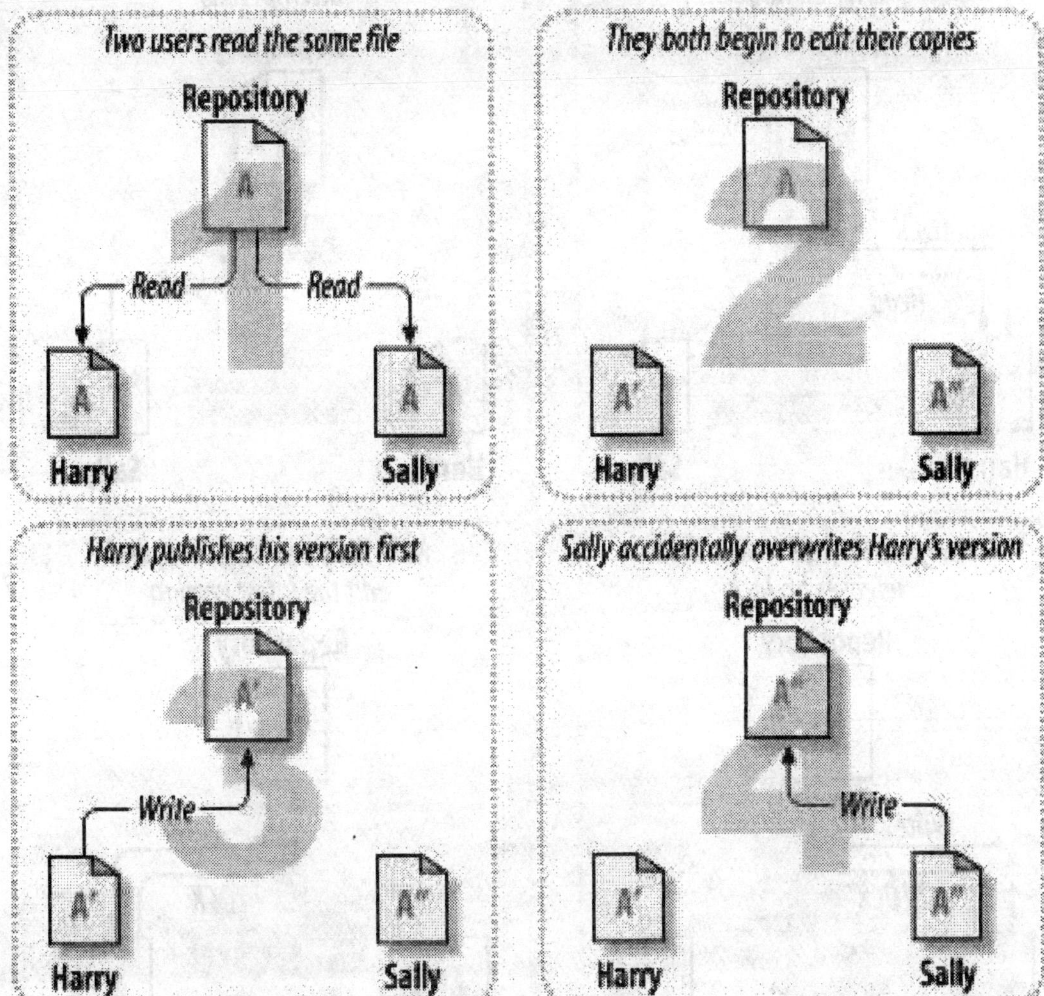

Lock-Modify-Unlock

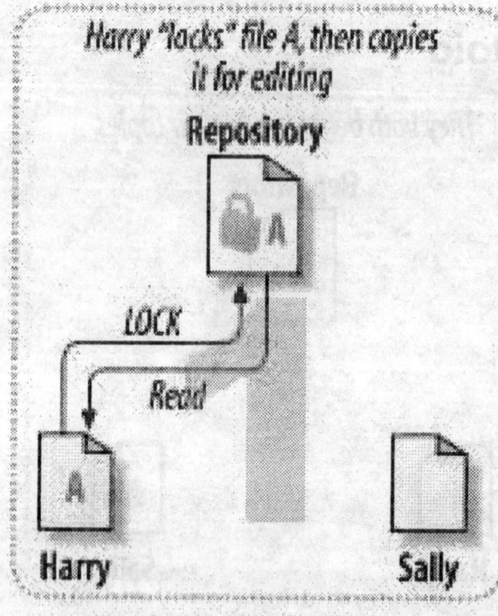

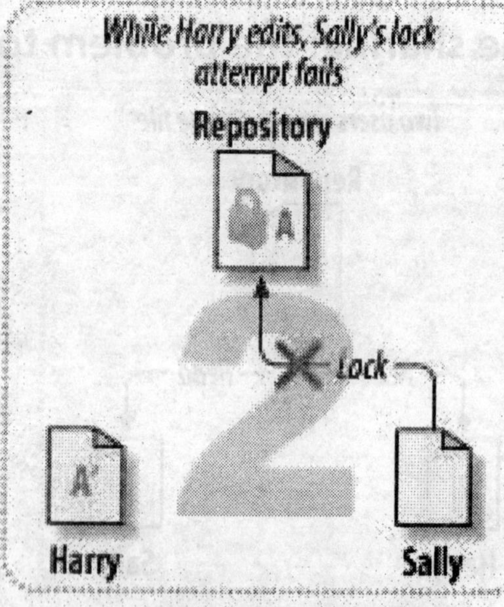

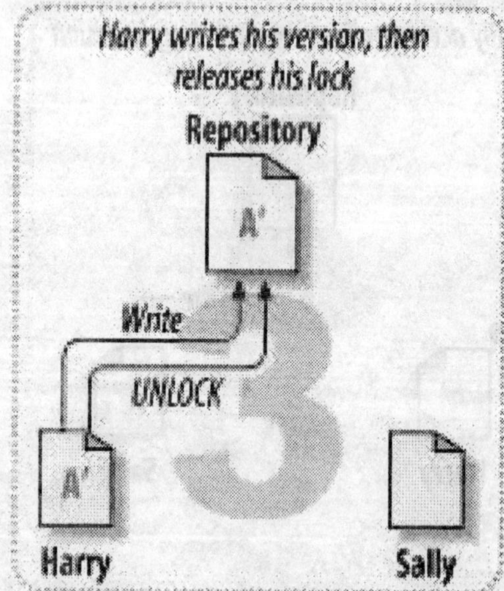

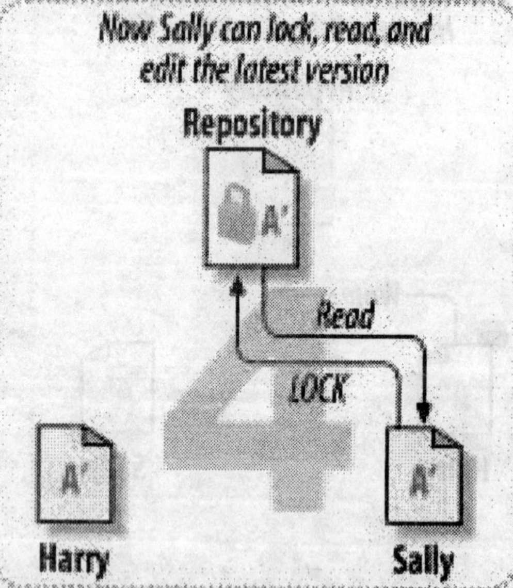

Copy-Modify-Merge

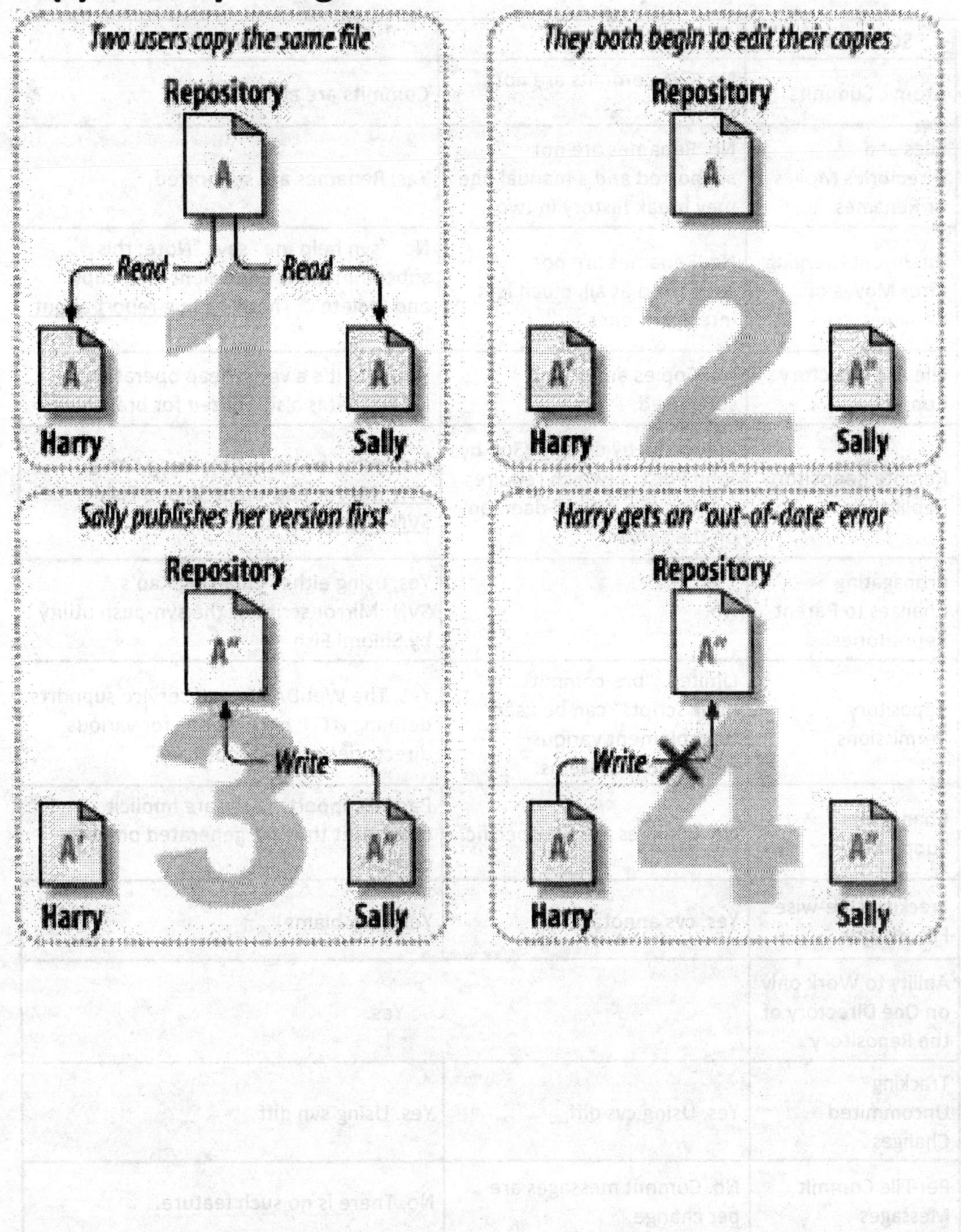

CVS vs Subversion

SCM feature:	CVS	Subversion
Atomic Commits	No. CVS commits are not atomic.	Commits are atomic.
Files and Directories Moves or Renames	No. Renames are not supported and a manual one may break history in two.	Yes. Renames are supported.
Intelligent Merging after Moves or Renames	No. Renames are not supported at all, much less intelligent ones.	No. "svn help me" says "Note: this subcommand is equivalent to a 'copy' and 'delete'." There's a bug report about it.
File and Directory Copies	No. Copies are not supported.	Yes. And it's a very cheap operation (O(1)) that is also utilized for branching.
Remote Repository Replication	Indirectly, by using CVSup by John Polstra (which requires running the cvsupd daemon on the server)	Indirectly, by using Chia-liang Kao's SVN::Mirror add-on or Shlomi Fish' SVN-Pusher utility.
Propagating Changes to Parent Repositories	No.	Yes, using either Chia-Ling Kao's SVN::Mirror script or the svn-push utility by Shlomi Fish.
Repository Permissions	Limited. "pre-commit hook scripts" can be used to implement various permissions systems.	Yes. The WebDAV-based service supports defining HTTP permissions for various directories of the repository.
Changesets' Support	No. Changes are file-specific.	Partial support. There are implicit changeset that are generated on each commit.
Tracking Line-wise File History	Yes. cvs annotate	Yes. (svn blame)
Ability to Work only on One Directory of the Repository	Yes.	
Tracking Uncommited Changes	Yes. Using cvs diff	Yes. Using svn diff
Per-File Commit Messages	No. Commit messages are per change.	No. There is no such feature.

Documentation	Excellent. There are many online tutorials and resources and an online book. The command line client also provides an online comprehensive help system.	Very good. There is a free online book and some online tutorials and resources. The book is written in DocBook/XML and so is convertible to many different formats. The command-line client also provides a good online help system that can be used as a reference.
Ease of Deployment	Good. Out of being the de-facto standard, CVS is available on most systems and is easy to deploy.	A Subversion service requires installing an Apache 2 module (if one wishes to use HTTP as the underlying protocol) or its own proprietary server. The client requires only the Subversion-specific logic and the Neon WebDAV library (for HTTP). Installation of the components is quite straightforward, but will require some work, assuming Subversion does not come prepackaged for one's system.
Command Set	A simple command set that includes three most commonly used commands (cvs commit, cvs update and cvs checkout) and several others.	A CVS-like command set which is easy to get used to for CVS-users.
Networking Support	Good. CVS uses a proprietary protocol with various variations for its client/ server protocol. This protocol can be tunneled over an SSH-connection to support encryption.	Very good. The Subversion service can use either WebDAV+DeltaV (which is HTTP or HTTPS based) as its underlying protocol, or its own proprietary protocol that can be channeled over an SSH connection.
Portability	Good. Client works on UNIX, Windows and Mac OS. Server works on UNIXes and on Windows with a UNIX emulation layer.	Excellent. Clients and Servers work on UNIX, Windows and Mac OS X.
Web Interface	Yes. CVSweb, ViewVC, Chora, and wwCVS.	Yes. ViewVC, SVN::Web, WebSVN, ViewSVN, mod_svn_view, Chora, Trac, SVN::RaWeb::Light, SVN Browser, Insurrection and perl_svn. Aside from that, the Subversion Apache service provides a rudimentary web-interface.

Availability of Graphical User-Interfaces.	Very good. There are many available GUIs: WinCVS, Cervisia (for KDE), TortoiseCVS (Windows Explorer plug-in).	Very good. There are many available GUIs: RapidSVN (cross-platform), TortoiseSVN (Windows Explorer plug-in), Jsvn (Java), etc. Most of them are still under development.

References:

http://versioncontrolblog.com/comparison/CVS/Subversion/index.html

Version Control Using TortoiseSVN

How to download and install

– Visit the download site of tortoiseSVN

http://tortoisesvn.net/downloads

– Click "32-bit installer"

Should look something like:

"TortoiseSVN-1.4.3.8645-win32-svn-1.4.3.msi"
(Version numbers may be different.)

Download:

http://sourceforge.net/projects/tortoisesvn/

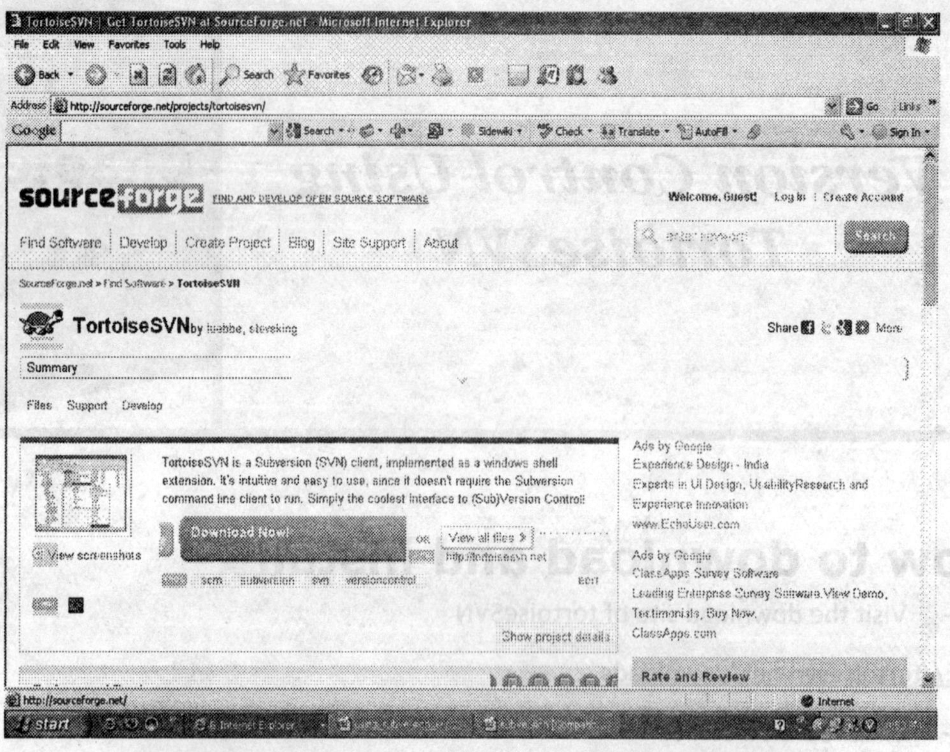
TortoiseSVN - Get TortoiseSVN at SourceForge.net - Microsoft Internet Explorer
File Edit View Favorites Tools Help
Back
Search
Favorites
Address http://sourceforge.net/projects/tortoisesvn/
Go
Links
Google
Search
Sidewiki
Check
Translate
AutoFill
Sign In
sourceforge
FIND AND DEVELOP OPEN SOURCE SOFTWARE
Welcome, Guest! Log In | Create Account
Find Software | Develop | Create Project | Blog | Site Support | About
Search
SourceForge.net > Find Software > TortoiseSVN
TortoiseSVN by luebbe, steveking
Share
More
Summary
Files Support Develop
TortoiseSVN is a Subversion (SVN) client, implemented as a windows shell extension. It's intuitive and easy to use, since it doesn't require the Subversion command line client to run. Simply the coolest Interface to (Sub)Version Control!
Download Now!
or
View all files
View screenshots
scm subversion svn versioncontrol
Show project details
Ads by Google
Experience Design - India
Experts in UI Design, UsabilityResearch and Experience Innovation
www.EchoUser.com
Ads by Google
ClassApps Survey Software
Leading Enterprise Survey Software.View Demo, Testimonials, Buy Now.
ClassApps.com
Rate and Review
http://sourceforge.net/
Internet
start

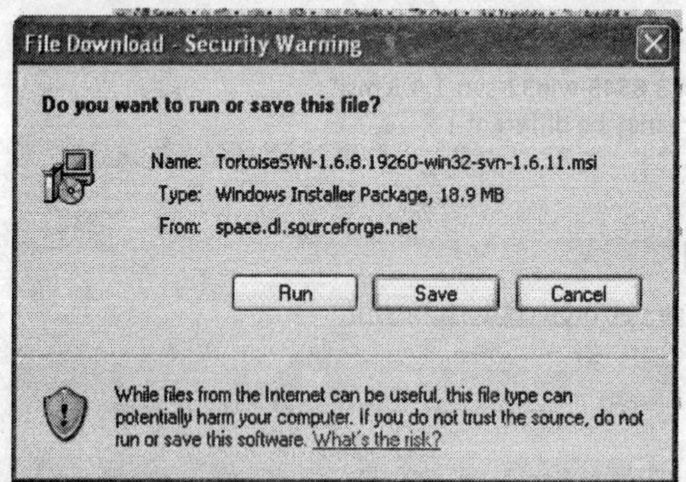
File Download - Security Warning
Do you want to run or save this file?
Name: TortoiseSVN-1.6.8.19260-win32-svn-1.6.11.msi
Type: Windows Installer Package, 18.9 MB
From: space.dl.sourceforge.net
Run
Save
Cancel
While files from the Internet can be useful, this file type can potentially harm your computer. If you do not trust the source, do not run or save this software. What's the risk?

Click on 'Run'

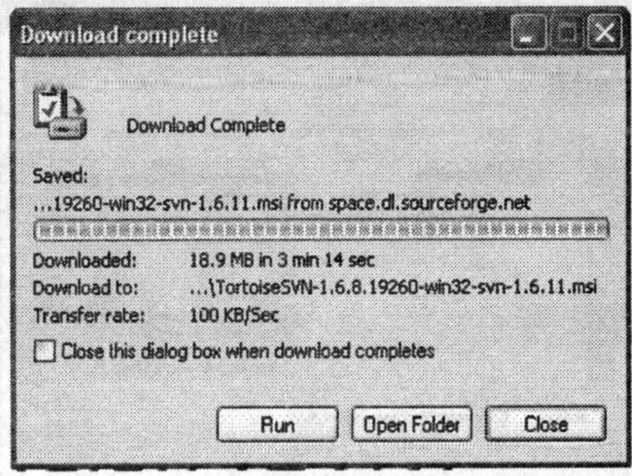
Download complete
Download Complete
Saved:
...19260-win32-svn-1.6.11.msi from space.dl.sourceforge.net
Downloaded: 18.9 MB in 3 min 14 sec
Download to: ...\TortoiseSVN-1.6.8.19260-win32-svn-1.6.11.msi
Transfer rate: 100 KB/Sec
Close this dialog box when download completes
Run
Open Folder
Close

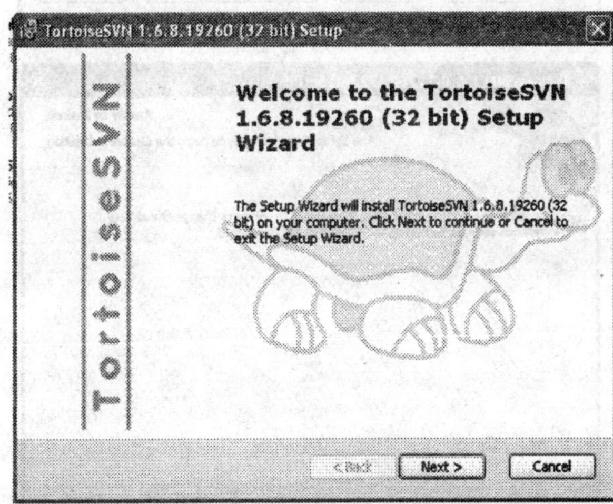
TortoiseSVN 1.6.8.19260 (32 bit) Setup
TortoiseSVN
Welcome to the TortoiseSVN 1.6.8.19260 (32 bit) Setup Wizard
The Setup Wizard will install TortoiseSVN 1.6.8.19260 (32 bit) on your computer. Click Next to continue or Cancel to exit the Setup Wizard.
< Back
Next >
Cancel

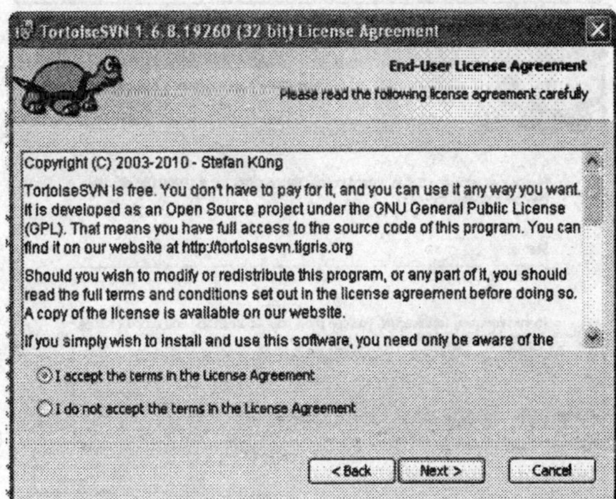
TortoiseSVN 1.6.8.19260 (32 bit) License Agreement
End-User License Agreement
Please read the following license agreement carefully
Copyright (C) 2003-2010 - Stefan Küng
TortoiseSVN is free. You don't have to pay for it, and you can use it any way you want. It is developed as an Open Source project under the GNU General Public License (GPL). That means you have full access to the source code of this program. You can find it on our website at http://tortoisesvn.tigris.org
Should you wish to modify or redistribute this program, or any part of it, you should read the full terms and conditions set out in the license agreement before doing so. A copy of the license is available on our website.
If you simply wish to install and use this software, you need only be aware of the
I accept the terms in the License Agreement
I do not accept the terms in the License Agreement
< Back
Next >
Cancel

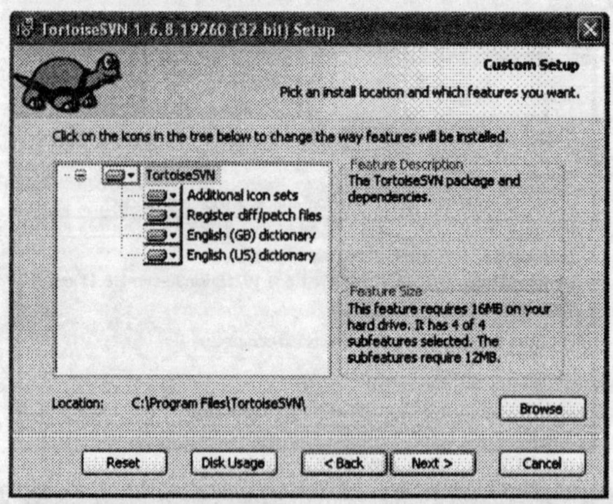
TortoiseSVN 1.6.8.19260 (32 bit) Setup
Custom Setup
Pick an install location and which features you want.
Click on the icons in the tree below to change the way features will be installed.
TortoiseSVN
Additional icon sets
Register diff/patch files
English (GB) dictionary
English (US) dictionary
Feature Description
The TortoiseSVN package and dependencies.
Feature Size
This feature requires 16MB on your hard drive. It has 4 of 4 subfeatures selected. The subfeatures require 12MB.
Location: C:\Program Files\TortoiseSVN\
Browse
Reset
Disk Usage
< Back
Next >
Cancel

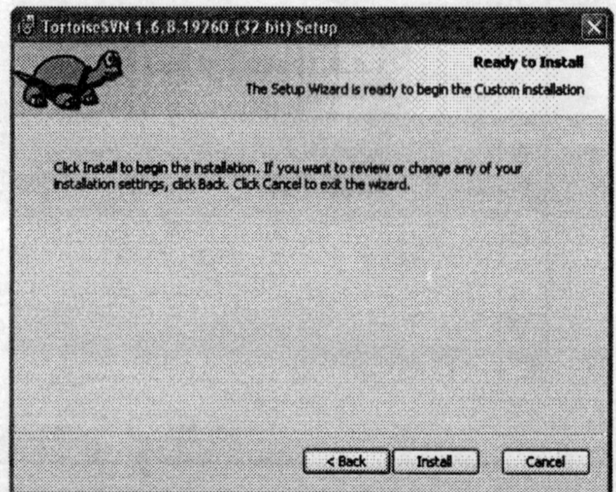
TortoiseSVN 1.6.8.19260 (32 bit) Setup
Ready to Install
The Setup Wizard is ready to begin the Custom installation
Click Install to begin the installation. If you want to review or change any of your installation settings, click Back. Click Cancel to exit the wizard.
< Back
Install
Cancel

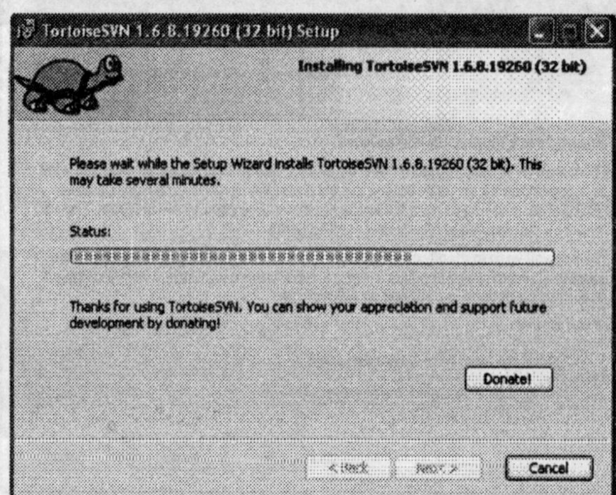
TortoiseSVN 1.6.8.19260 (32 bit) Setup
Installing TortoiseSVN 1.6.8.19260 (32 bit)
Please wait while the Setup Wizard installs TortoiseSVN 1.6.8.19260 (32 bit). This may take several minutes.
Status:
Thanks for using TortoiseSVN. You can show your appreciation and support future development by donating!
Donate!
< Back
Next >
Cancel

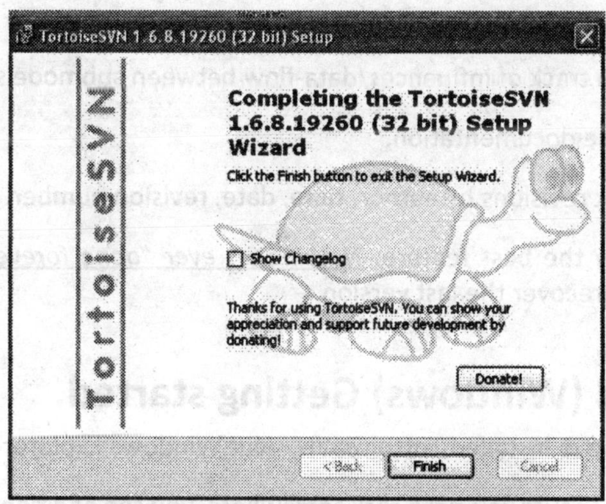

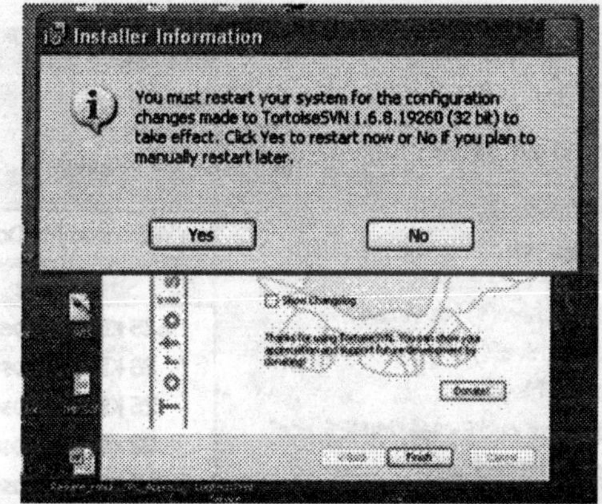

Using Subversion

- When collaborating, it is important to manage changes in the models. For example:
  - — To create or edit a submodel
    - E.g. Habitat suitability is replaced with another method of computing habitat values.
  - — To submit a "rough copy" of a model to the repository for review by collaborators at another institution.
  - — To keep track of data needed from other submodels.

  - Can submit a "data request" to all model developers

— To keep track of influences/data-flow between submodels.

— To revise documentation.

— To track revisions by author, time, date, revision number.

— Possibly the best feature: <u>*Nothing is ever "gone forever*</u>", since you can always recover the last version.

TortoiseSVN (Windows) Getting started

— Once you have installed TortoiseSVN, your Windows Explorer will be modified

  - Whenever you right-click somewhere, you see additional menu- items

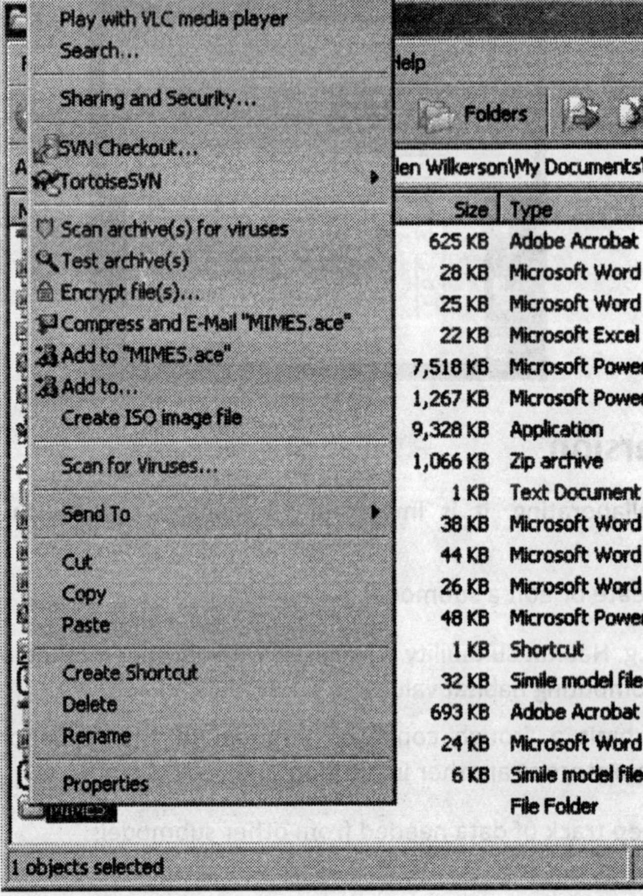

TortoiseSVN:

Common Subversion tasks

- Add a new file to the repository
- Modify an existing file in the repository

Note: For more information on this in the tortoiseSVN help:

- Right click anywhere
- Choose TortoiseSVN->Help

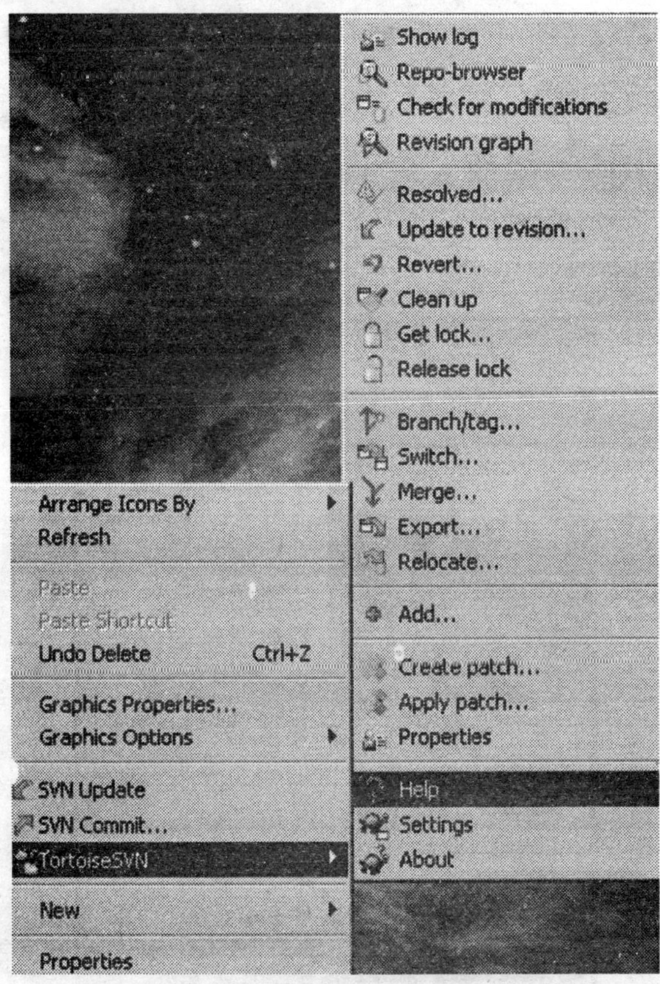

TortoiseSVN:

Add a new file to the repository

Overview:

— heckout appropriate folder from the repository

(The folder where you will put your model.)

— Create file

(model file or other – documentation, etc.)

— "Add"

— "Commit"

— Checkout appropriate folder from the repository

— Start the "Repo-browser"

— (Repository browser)

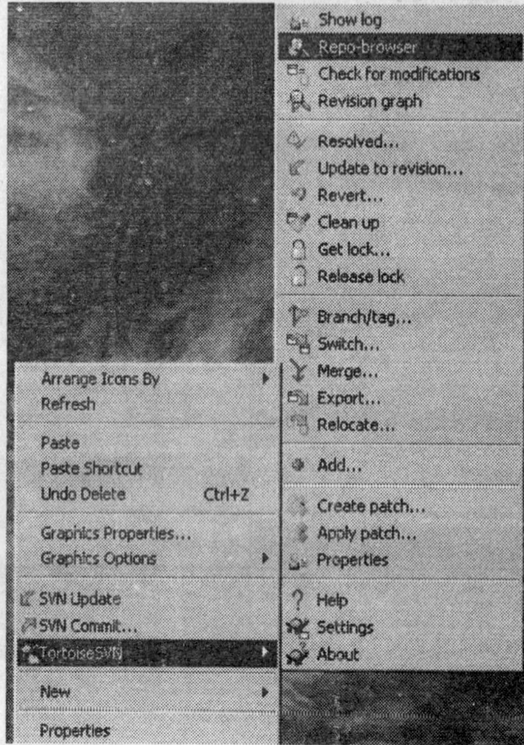

— Choose the folder where your new model belongs (Here, chose Aesthetic/)

— Right-click on the folder and choose "Checkout..."

— A "Checkout" window appears

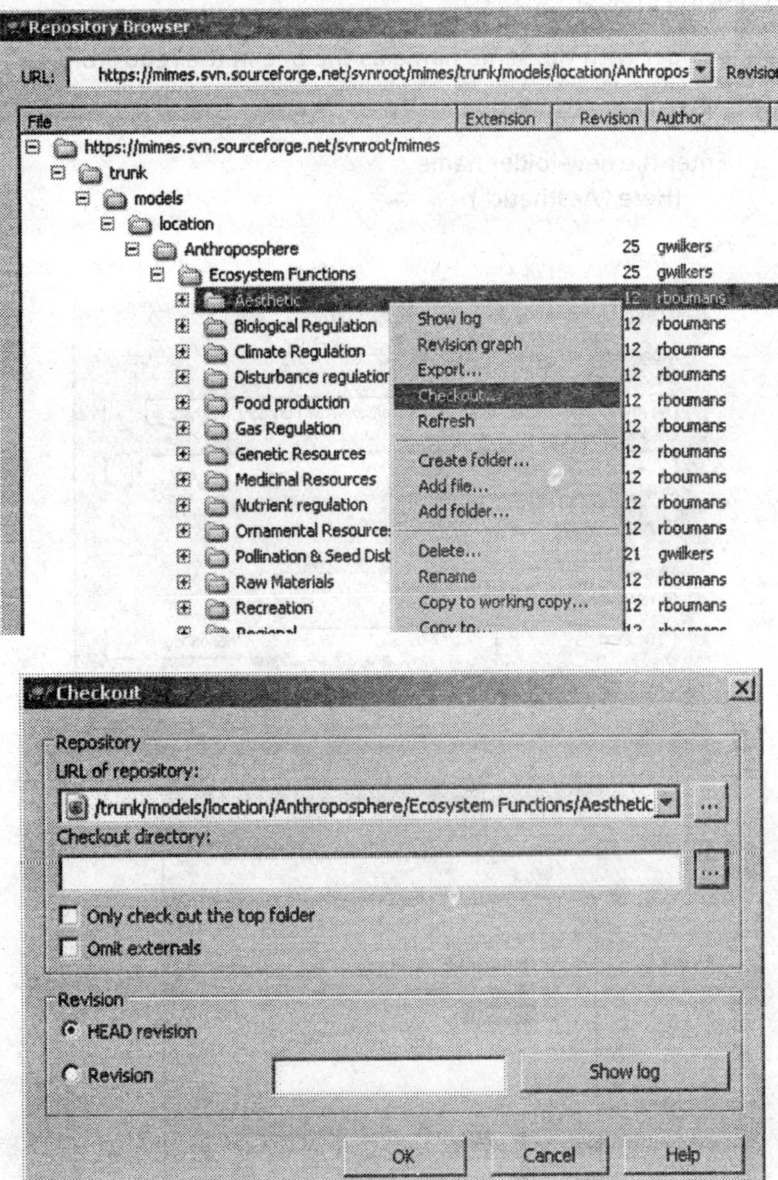

- Click the "..." next to "Checkout Directory"
- A "Browse for Folder" window appears
- Browse to the folder on your computer where you want to create a local copy of the repository folder
- Create a folder with the same name as the one in the repository
  - Click "Make New Folder"
  - Enter the new folder name
    (Here "Aesthetic")
- Click "OK"

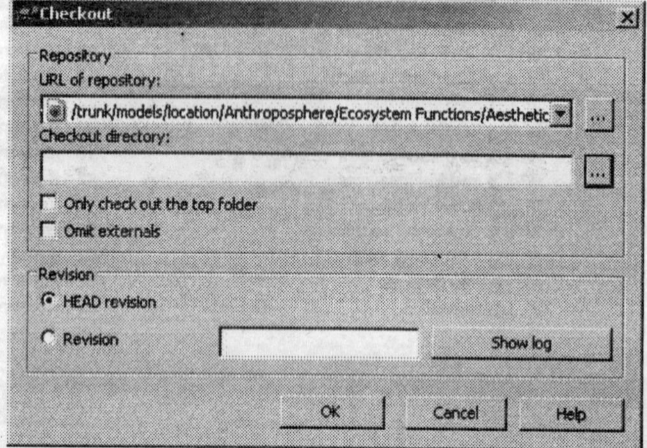

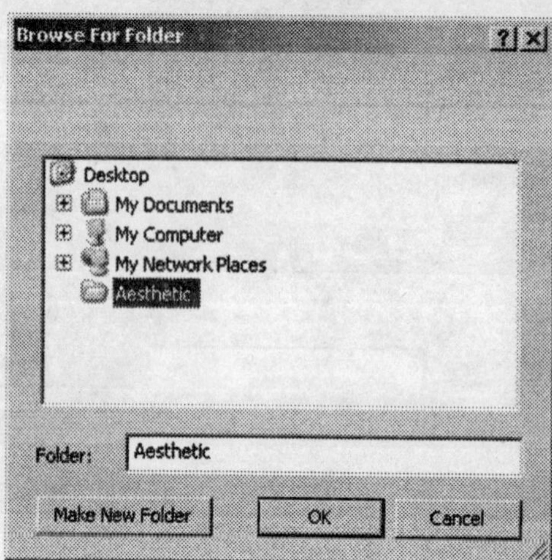

- This window appears telling you what has been downloaded:
- The folder you created now looks like this
- 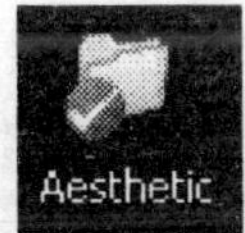

- It contains the files from the repository

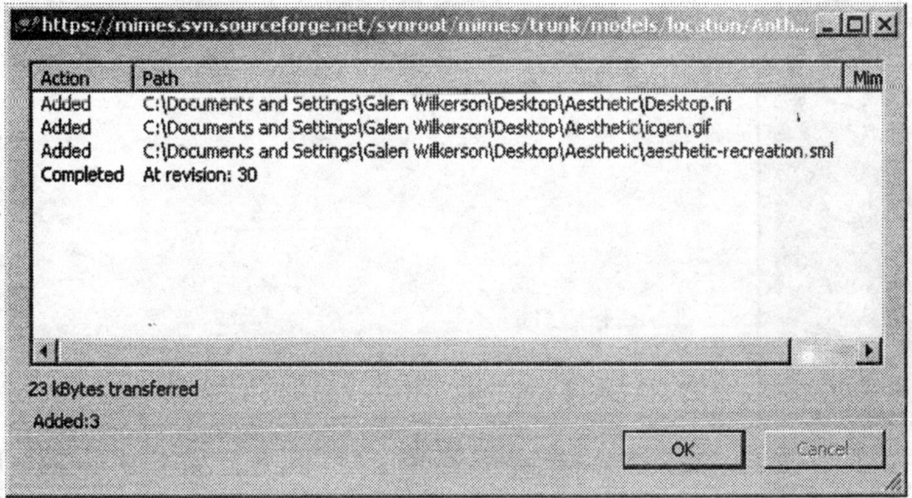

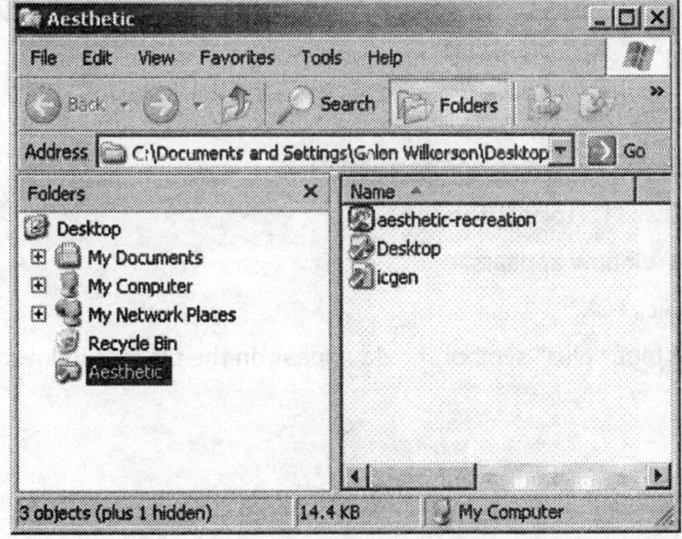

— Move, copy, or create a new file that will be added to the repository

  ○ Give the file a descriptive name to distinguish it from other files (Remember, we are adding a new file.)

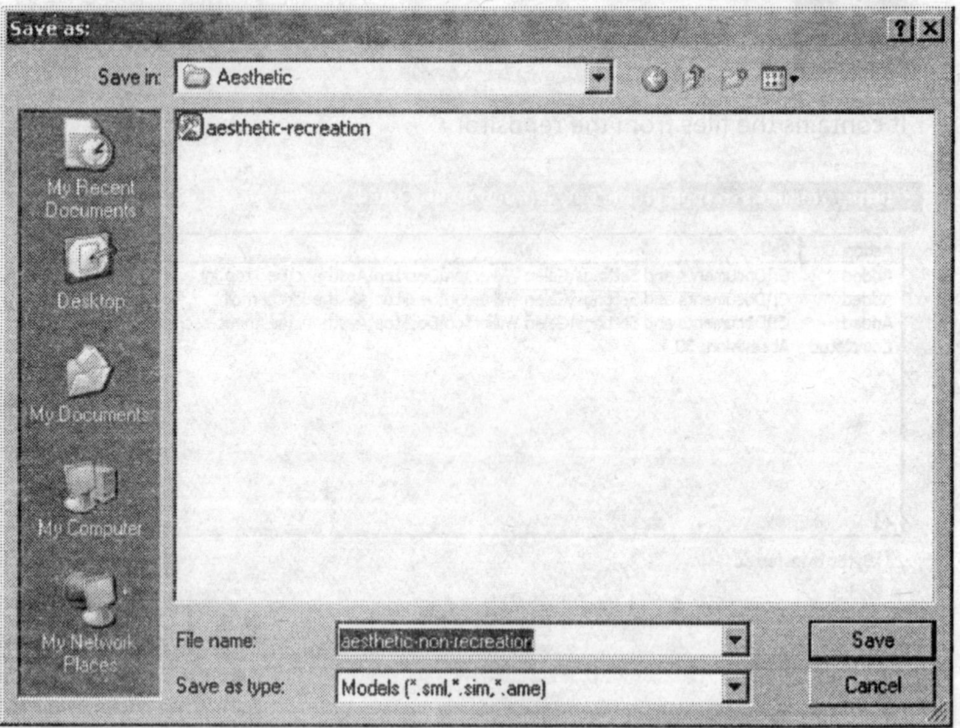

— Use "Add" to add it to the local repository

  ○ Right-click the new file
  ○ (Here, right-click on "Aesthetic")
  ○ Click "TortoiseSVN->Add"
  ○ A window appears
  ○ Click "OK"
  ○ A blue "plus" symbol should appear on the file in Windows Explorer:

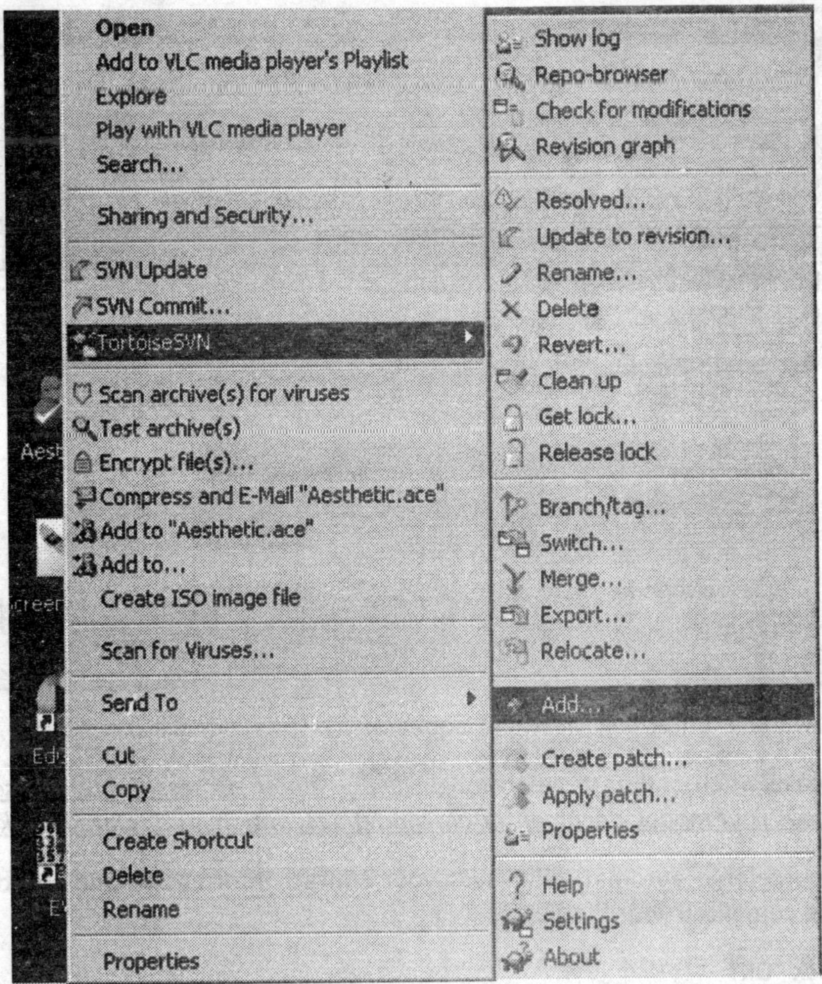

— Right-click on the file you just added

— Choose "SVN Commit..." to commit it to the Sourceforge MIMES repository:

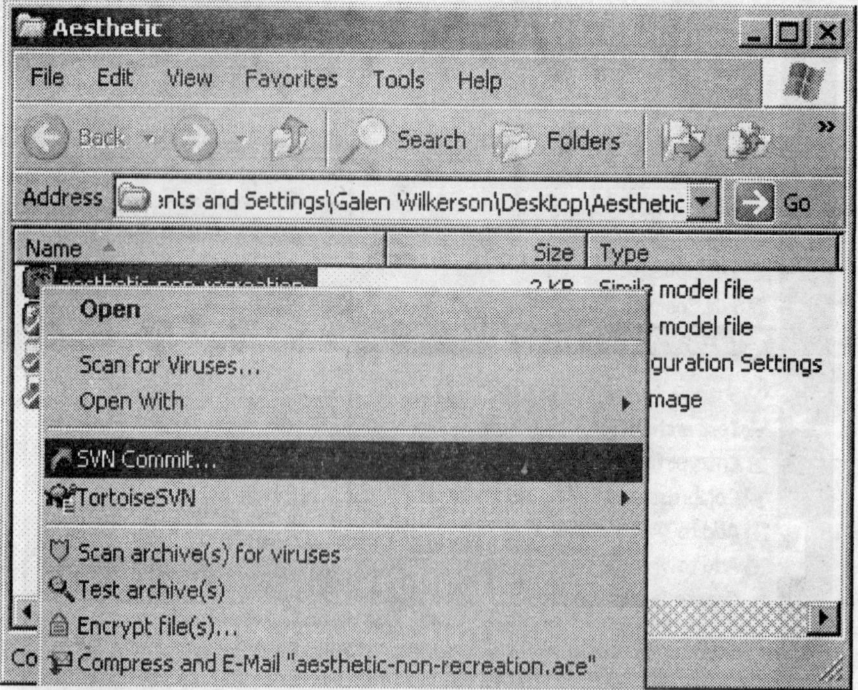

— A window "Enter Log Message" appears:

— Please when adding a new model, _always enter a message telling something about your model, documentation, a brief description, and related work_.

— (Sourceforge automatically saves your contact information and the date/time you commited your file.)

— Click "OK"

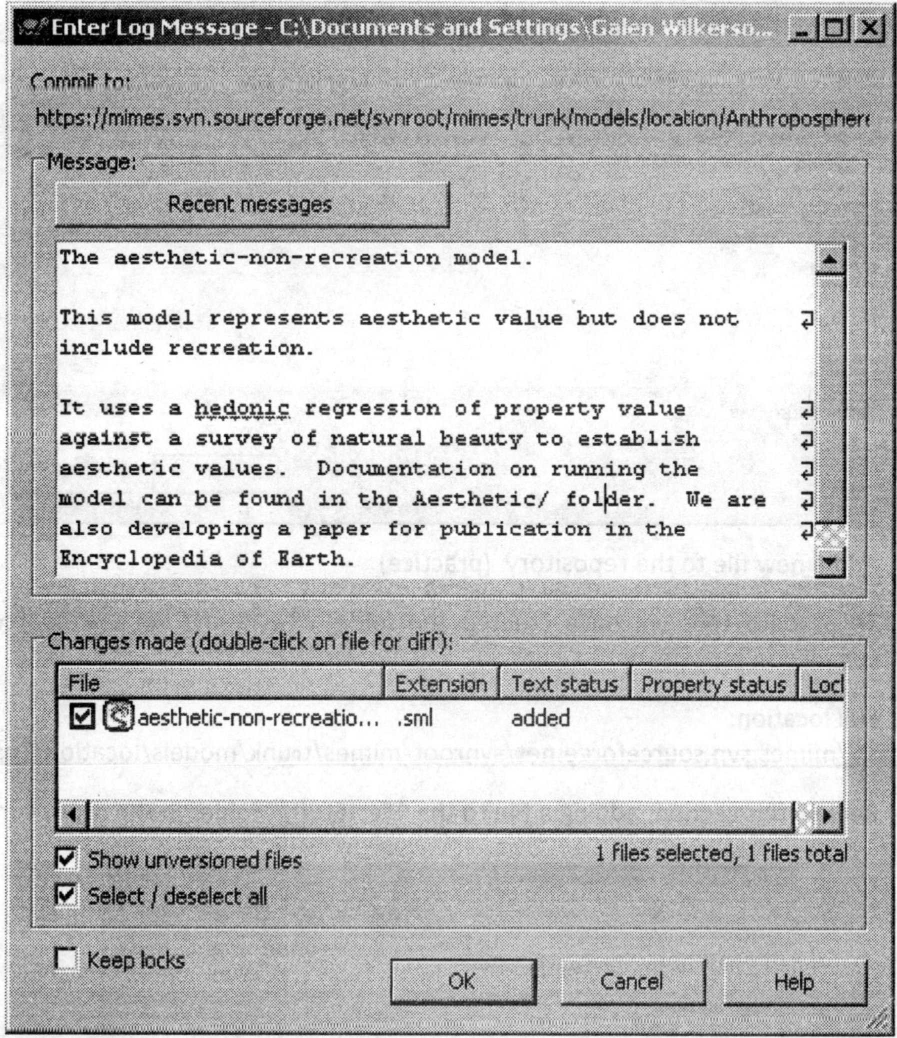

— This window appears:

— Once it says "Completed"

— you have added a file to the repository!

— Congratulations!

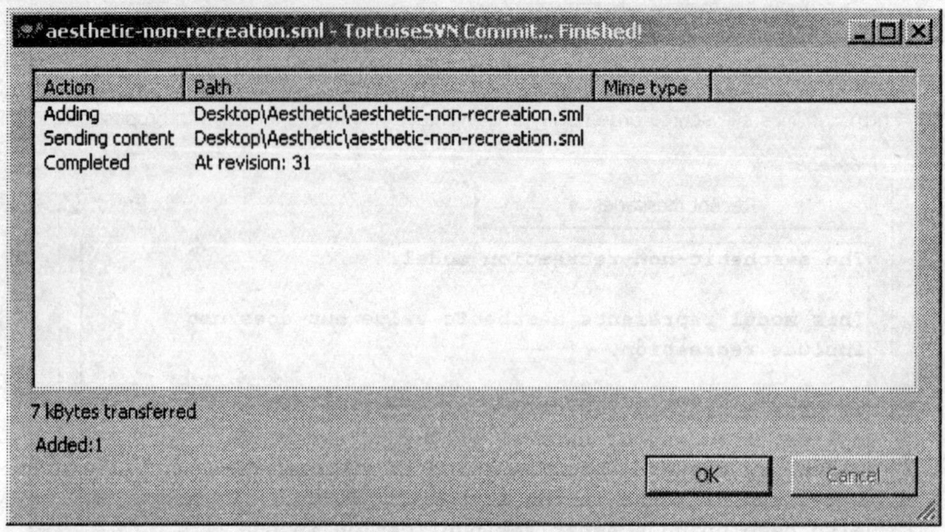

- Add a new file to the repository (practice)
- To practice this, we have created the folder "TestStuff/" in the Sourceforge subversion repository
- Full location:
https://mimes.svn.sourceforge.net/svnroot/mimes/trunk/models/location/TestStuff
- Review this section, adding a file to the "TestStuff/" folder in the repository

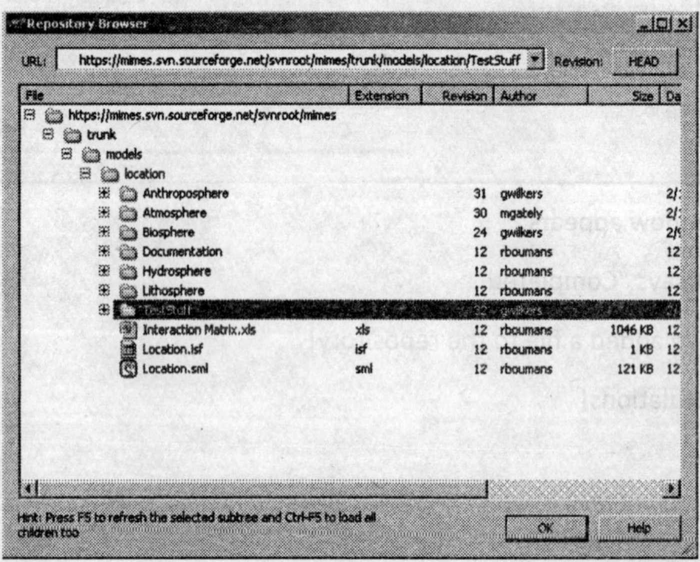

TortoiseSVN:

Modify an existing file in the repository

Overview:

- "Check out" the folder containing the file to be modified
- Edit and save the file on your computer
  - "Commit" the changes you have made
- Checkout appropriate folder from the repository
  - Start the "Repo-browser"

(Repository browser)

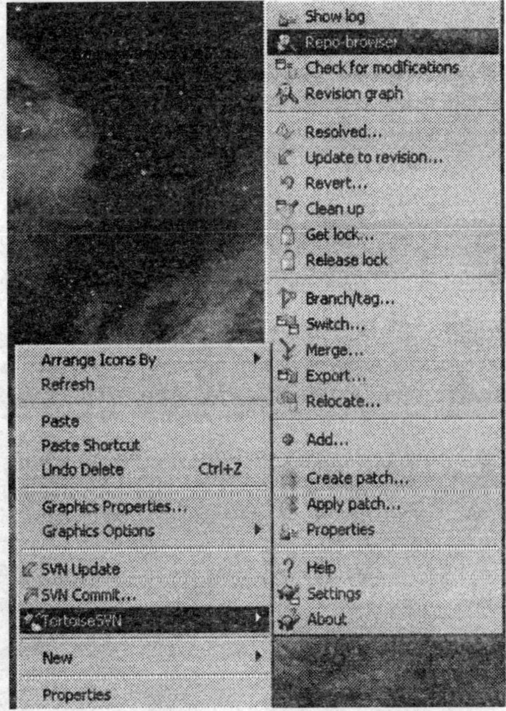

- Choose the folder containing the file you want to edit
  (Here, have chosen Aesthetic/)
- Right-click on the folder and choose "Checkout..."
- A "Checkout" window appears

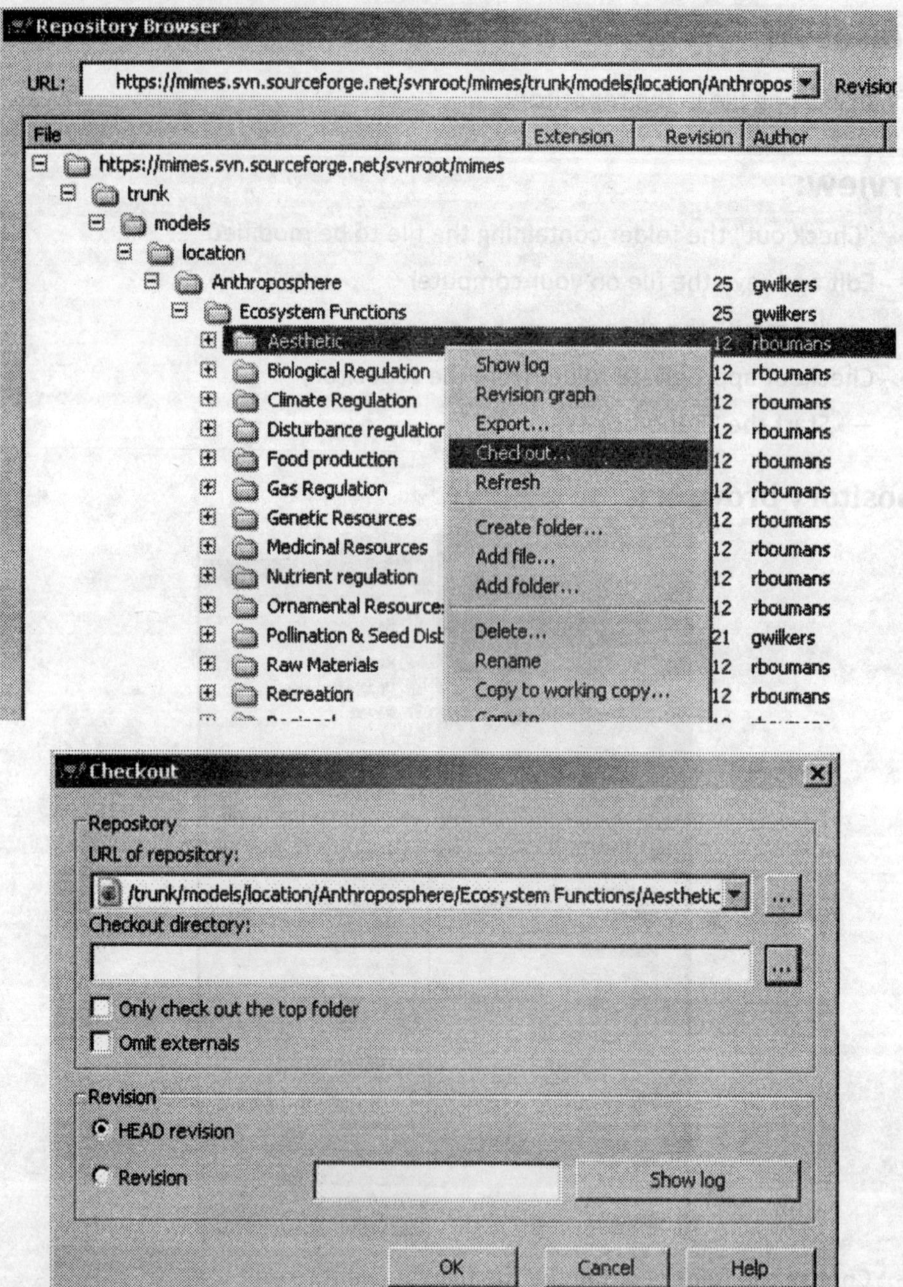

— Click the "..." next to "Checkout Directory"
— A "Browse for Folder" window appears

- Browse to the folder on your computer where you want to create a local copy of the repository folder
- Create a folder with the same name as the one in the repository
  - Click "Make New Folder"
  - Enter the new folder name
- (Here "Aesthetic")
- Click "OK"

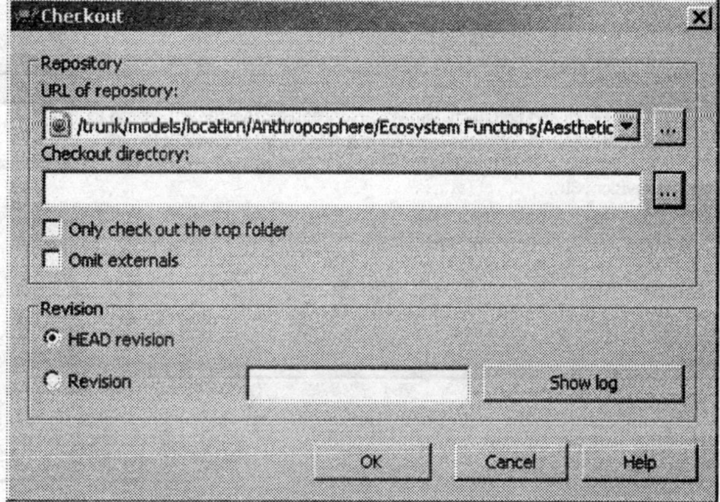

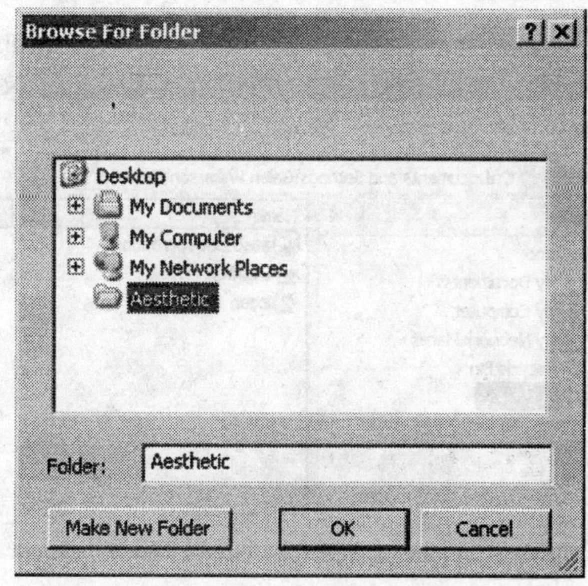

— This window appears telling you what has been downloaded:

— The folder you created now looks like this:

— 

— It contains the files from the repository

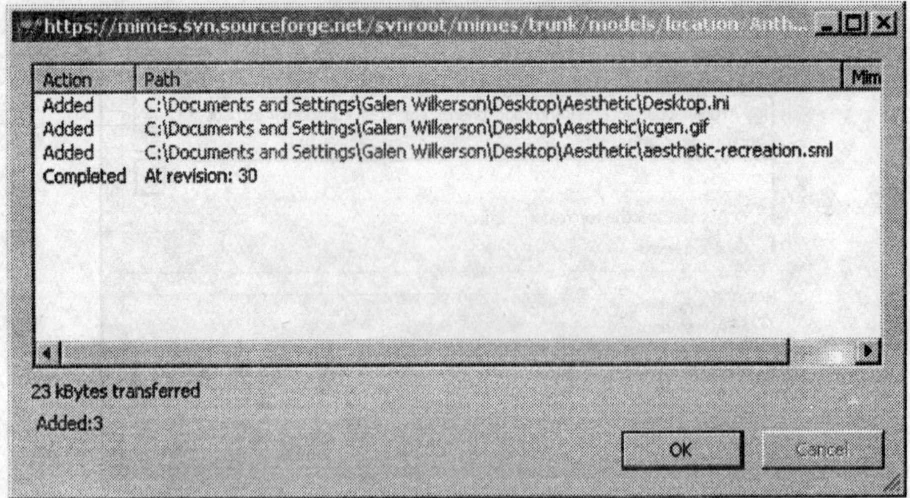

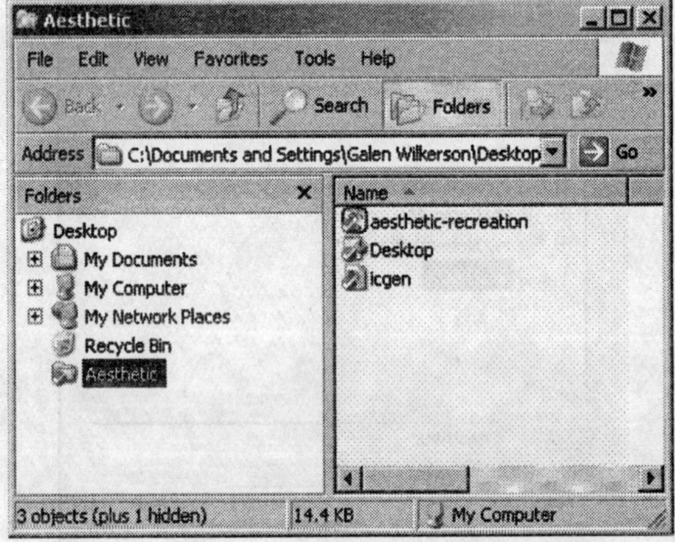

— Double-click the file you want to open

— Edit the file (In Simile, for example)

— Save it

— The file now appears like this:

— (This means it has been modified but changes have not been "committed" to the repository.)

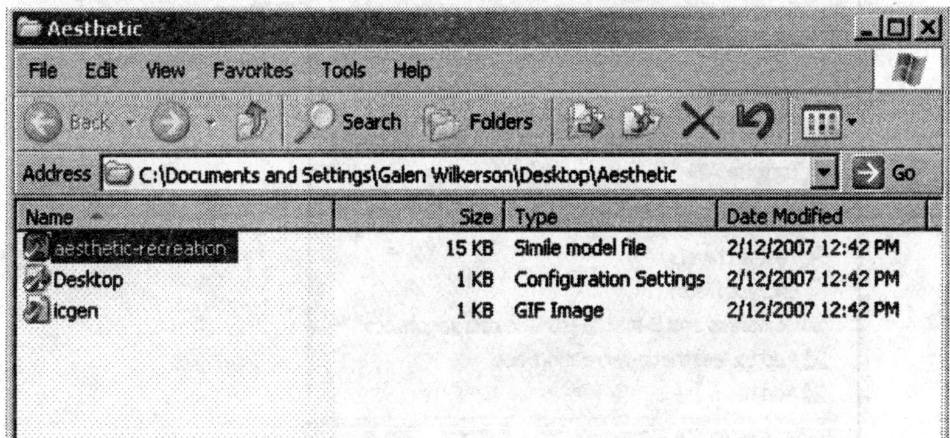

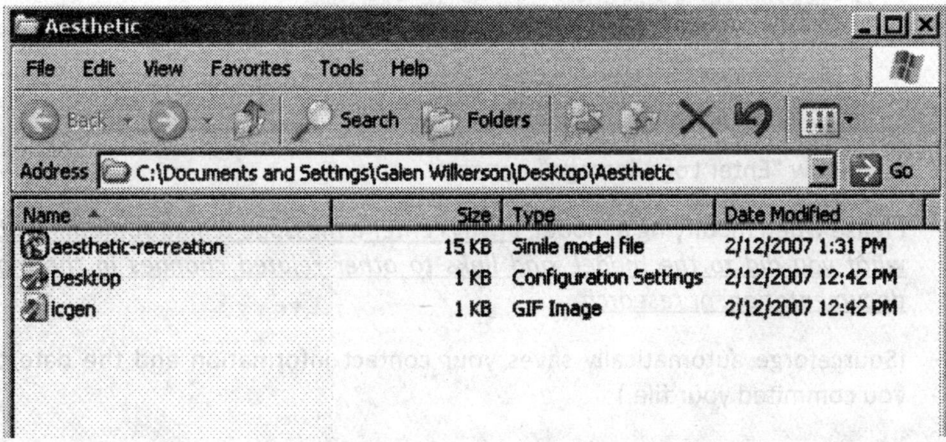

— Right-click the file you want to commit

— Choose "SVN Commit..."

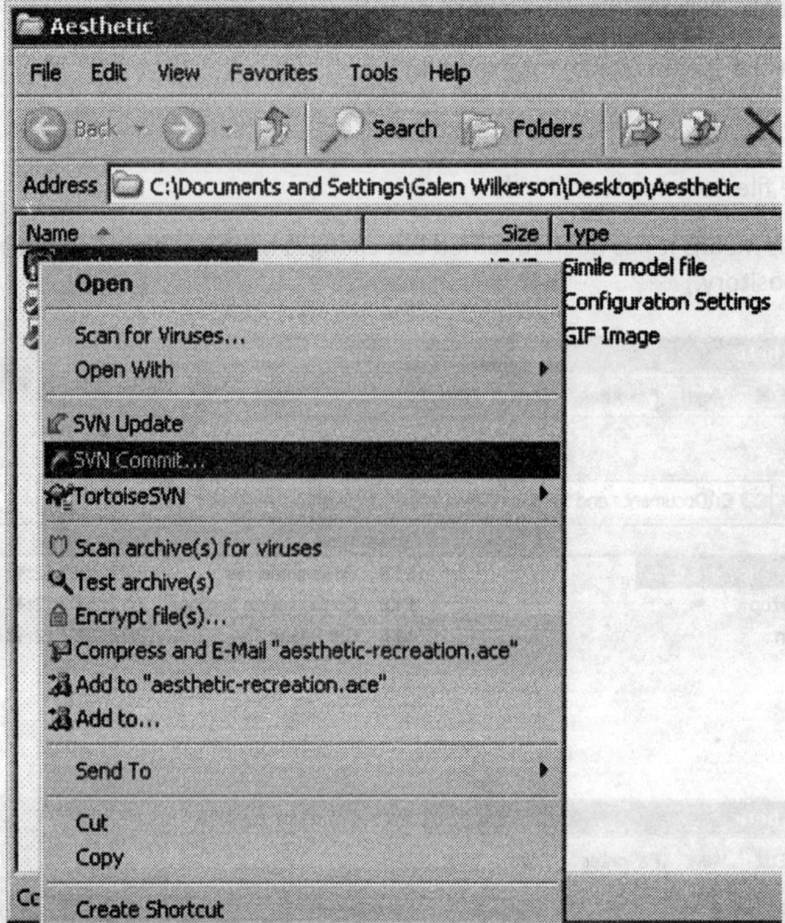

— A window "Enter Log Message" appears:

— Please when modifying a model, *always enter a message telling something about what you did to the model, and links to other related changes in the model, documentation, or research.*

— (Sourceforge automatically saves your contact information and the date/time you commited your file.)

— Click "OK"

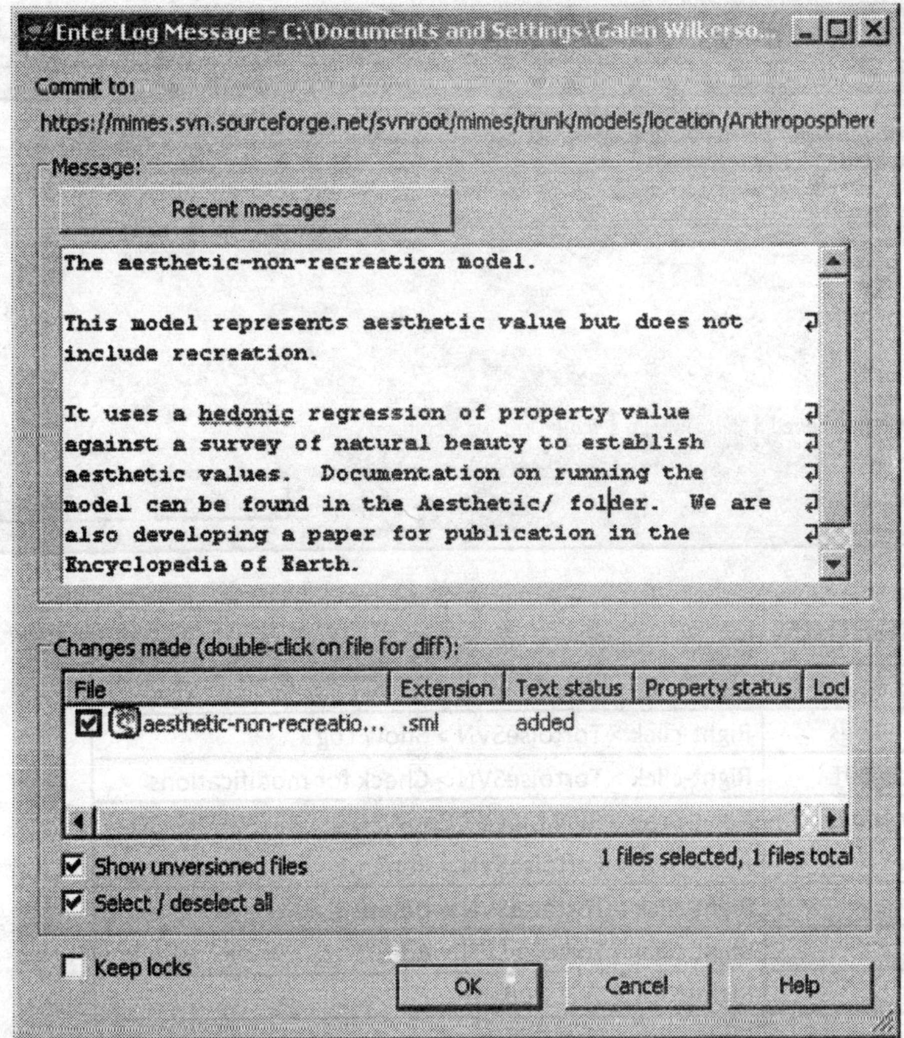

— This window appears:

— Once it says "Completed"

— you have modified the repository!

— Congratulations!

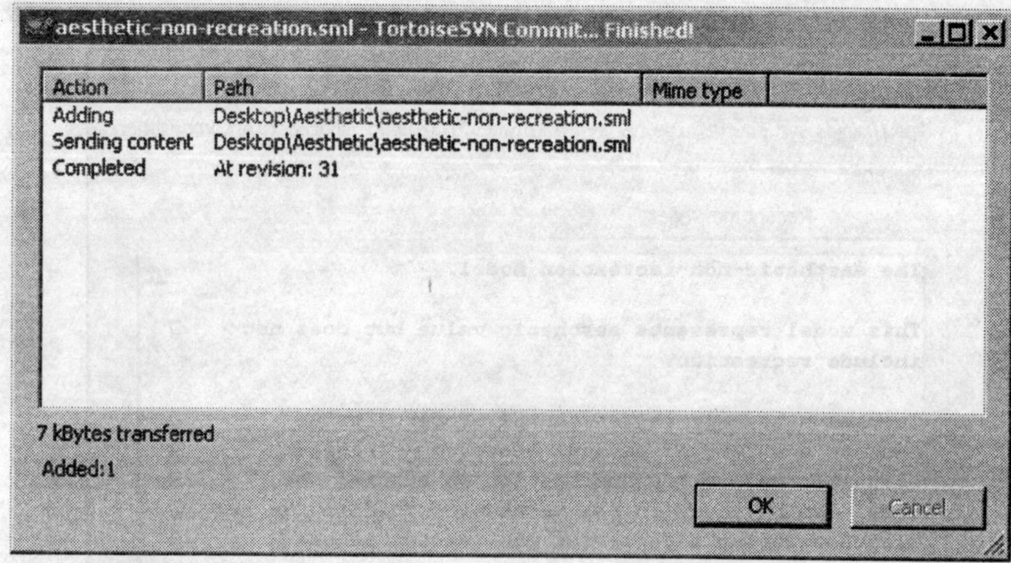

Commands:

Commit changes	Right click > SVN Commit
Examine Logs	Right-click > TortoiseSVN > Show Log
Status or Diff	Right-click > TortoiseSVN > Check for modifications
Copy or Move	Right-drag > SVN Move / Copy
Rename	Right click > TortoiseSVN > Rename
Delete	Right click > TortoiseSVN > Delete
Add	Right click > TortoiseSVN > Add
Update	Right click > SVN Update
Checkout	Right-click > SVN Checkout
Help	Right-click > TortoiseSVN > Help

Ref:

Galen Wilkerson
Gund Institute for Ecological Economics
University of Vermont

Version Control Using Collabnet SVN

What is Subversion?

Subversion is a free/open-source version control system. That is, Subversion manages files and directories, and the changes made to them, over time. This allows you to recover older versions of your data, or examine the history of how your data changed. In this regard, many people think of a version control system as a sort of "time machine".

Subversion can operate across networks, which allows it to be used by people on different computers. At some level, the ability for various people to modify and manage the same set of data from their respective locations fosters collaboration. Progress can occur more quickly without a single conduit through which all modifications must occur. And because the work is versioned, you need not fear that quality is the trade-off for losing that conduit

—if some incorrect change is made to the data, just undo that change.

Some version control systems are also software configuration management (SCM) systems.

These systems are specifically tailored to manage trees of source code, and have many features that are specific to software development—such as natively understanding programming languages, or supplying tools for building software. Subversion, however, is not one of these systems. It is a general system that can be used to manage any collection of files. For you, those files might be source code—for others, anything from grocery shopping lists to digital video mixdowns and beyond.

Subversion's Features

Subversion provides:

Directory versioning

CVS only tracks the history of individual files, but Subversion implements a "virtual" versioned filesystem that tracks changes to whole directory trees over time. Files and directories are versioned.

True version history

Since CVS is limited to file versioning, operations such as copies and renames—which might happen to files, but which are really changes to the contents of some containing directory—aren't supported in CVS. Additionally, in CVS you cannot replace a versioned file with some new thing of the same name without the new item inheriting the history of the old—perhaps completely unrelated—file. With Subversion, you can add, delete, copy, and rename both files and directories. And every newly added file begins with a fresh, clean history all its own.

Atomic commits

A collection of modifications either goes into the repository completely, or not at all. This allows developers to construct and commit changes as logical chunks, and prevents problems that can occur when only a portion of a set of changes is successfully sent to the repository.

Versioned metadata

Each file and directory has a set of properties—keys and their values—associated with it. You can create and store any arbitrary key/value pairs you wish. Properties are versioned over time, just like file contents.

Choice of network layers

Subversion has an abstracted notion of repository access, making it easy for people to implement new network mechanisms. Subversion can plug into the Apache HTTP Server as an extension module. This gives Subversion a big advantage in stability and interoperability, and instant access to existing features provided by that server—

authentication, authorization, wire compression, and so on. A more lightweight, standalone Subversion server process is also available. This server speaks a custom protocol which can be easily tunneled over SSH.

Consistent data handling

Subversion expresses file differences using a binary differencing algorithm, which works identically on both text (human-readable) and binary (human-unreadable) files. Both types of files are stored equally compressed in the repository, and differences are transmitted in both directions across the network.

Efficient branching and tagging

The cost of branching and tagging need not be proportional to the project size. Subversion creates branches and tags by simply copying the project, using a mechanism similar to a hard-link. Thus these operations take only a very small, constant amount of time.

Hackability

Subversion has no historical baggage; it is implemented as a collection of shared C libraries with well-defined APIs. This makes Subversion extremely maintainable and usable by other applications and languages.

- Commits as true atomic operations (interrupted commit operations would otherwise cause repository inconsistency or corruption).
- Renamed/copied/moved/removed files retain full revision history.
- The system maintains versioning for directories, renames, and file metadata (but not for timestamps). Users can move and/or copy entire directory-trees very quickly, while retaining full revision history.
- Versioning of symbolic links.
- Native support for binary files, with space-efficient binary-diff storage.
- Apache HTTP Server as network server, WebDAV/Delta-V for protocol. There is also an independent server process called svnserve that uses a custom protocol over TCP/IP.
- Branching and tagging as cheap operations, independent of file size (though Subversion itself does not distinguish between a tag, a branch, and a directory)
- Natively client–server, layered library design.

- Client/server protocol sends diffs in both directions.
- Costs proportional to change size, not to data size.
- Parsable output, including XML log output.
- Open source licensed — Apache License in the projected 1.7 release; prior versions use a derivative of the Apache Software License, v1.1
- Internationalized program messages.
- File locking for unmergeable files ("reserved checkouts").
- Path-based authorization.
- Language bindings for PHP, Python, Perl, and Java.
- Full MIME support - users can view or change the MIME type of each file, with the software knowing which MIME types can have their differences from previous versions shown.

Introduction

In software development, **Apache Subversion** (formerly called **Subversion**[1], command name **svn**) is a revision control system initiated in 2000 by CollabNet Inc. Developers use Subversion to maintain current and historical versions of files such as source code, web pages, and documentation. Its goal is to be a mostly-compatible successor to the widely used Concurrent Versions System (CVS).

The open source community has used Subversion widely: for example in projects such as Apache Software Foundation, Free Pascal, FreeBSD, GCC, Django, Ruby, Mono, SourceForge, ExtJS, Tigris.org, PHP and MediaWiki. Google Code also provides Subversion hosting for their open source projects. BountySource systems use it exclusively. CodePlex offers access to Subversion as well as to other types of clients.

The corporate world has also started to adopt Subversion. A 2007 report by Forrester Research recognized Subversion as the sole leader in the Standalone Software Configuration Management (SCM) category and as a strong performer in the Software Configuration and Change Management (SCCM) category.[2]

Subversion uses the Apache License, making it open source.

History

The Subversion project started in 2000 as an effort to write an open-source version-control system which operated much like CVS but which fixed the bugs and supplied some features missing in CVS. By 2001, Subversion had advanced sufficiently to host its own source code.[3] In November 2009 Subversion was accepted into Apache Incubator: this marked the beginning of the process to become a standard top-level Apache project. [4] It became a top-level Apache project on February 17 2010[5]

Subversion's Architecture

"Subversion's Architecture" illustrates a "mile-high" view of Subversion's design.

Subversion's Architecture

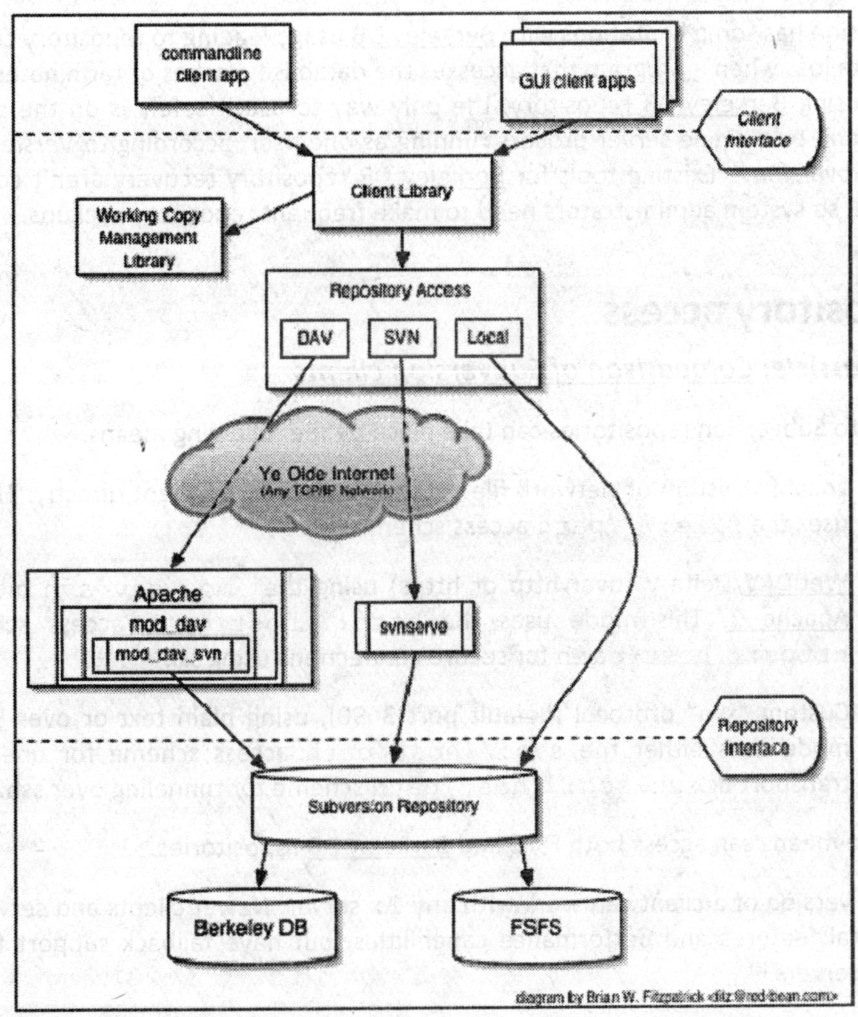

Repository types

Subversion offers two types of repository storage — FSFS and Berkeley DB.

FSFS

FSFS works faster on directories with a large number of files and takes less disk space, due to less logging.[6]

Berkeley DB

Subversion has some limitations with Berkeley DB usage leading to repository corruption and data loss when a program that accesses the database crashes or terminates forcibly. When using Berkeley DB repository, the only way to use it safely is on the dedicated server and by a single server process running as one user, according to *Version Control with Subversion*.[7] Existing tools for Berkeley DB repository recovery aren't completely reliable, so system administrators need to make frequent repository backups.

Repository access

Main article: Comparison of Subversion clients

Access to Subversion repositories can take place by the following means:

1. Local filesystem or network filesystem,[8] accessed by client directly. This mode uses the `file:///path` access scheme.

2. WebDAV/Delta-V (over http or https) using the `mod_dav_svn` module for Apache 2. This mode uses the `http://host/path` access scheme or `https://host/path` for secure connections using ssl.

3. Custom "svn" protocol (default port 3690), using plain text or over SSH. This mode uses either the `svn://host/path` access scheme for unencrypted transport or `svn+ssh://host/path` scheme for tunneling over ssh.

All three means can access both FSFS and Berkeley DB repositories.

Any 1.x version of a client can work with any 1.x server. Newer clients and servers have additional features and performance capabilities, but have fallback support for older clients/servers.[9]

Layers

Internally, a Subversion system comprises several libraries arranged as layers. Each performs a specific task and allows developers to create their own tools at the desired level of complexity and specificity.

Fs

The lowest level; it implements the versioned filesystem which stores the user data.

Repos

Concerned with the repository built up around the filesystem. It has many helper functions and handles the various "hooks" that a repository may have, e.g. scripts that run when an action is performed. Together, Fs and Repos constitute the "filesystem interface".

mod_dav_svn

Provides WebDAV/Delta-V access through Apache 2.

Ra

Handles "repository access", both local and remote. From this point on, repositories are referred to using URLs, e.g.

- `file:///path/` for local access,
- `http://host/path/` or `https://host/path/` for WebDAV access, or
- `svn://host/path/` or `svn+ssh://host/path/` for the SVN protocol.

Client, Wc

The highest level. It abstracts repository access and provides common client tasks, such as authenticating users or comparing versions. Subversion clients use the Wc library to manage the local working copy.

Filesystem

One can view the Subversion filesystem as "two-dimensional"[10]. Two coordinates are used to unambiguously address filesystem items:

- **Path** (regular path of Unix-like OS filesystem)
- **Revision**

Each revision in a Subversion filesystem has its own *root*, which is used to access contents at that revision. Files are stored as links to the most recent change; thus a Subversion repository is quite compact. The system consumes storage space proportional to the number of changes made, not to the number of revisions.

The Subversion filesystem uses transactions to keep changes atomic. A transaction operates on a specified revision of the filesystem, not necessarily the latest. The transaction has its own *root*, on which changes are made. It is then either committed and becomes the latest revision, or is aborted. The transaction is actually a long-lived filesystem object; a client does not need to commit or abort a transaction itself, rather it can also begin a transaction, exit, and then can re-open the transaction and continue using it. Multiple clients can access the same transaction and work together on an atomic change.

Properties

One important feature of the Subversion filesystem is properties: simple *name=value* pairs of text. Properties occur in two different places in the Subversion filesystem. The first is on filesystem entries (i.e., files and directories). These are versioned just like other changes to the filesystem. Users can add any property they wish, and the Subversion client uses a set of properties, which it prefixes with 'svn:'.

`svn:executable`

Makes files on Unix-hosted working copies executable.

`svn:mime-type`

Stores the MIME type of a file. Affects the handling of diffs and merging.

`svn:ignore`

A list of filename patterns to ignore in a directory. Similar to CVS's. `cvsignore` file.

`svn:keywords`

A list of keywords to substitute into a file when changes are made. The file itself must also reference the keywords as `$keyword$` or `$keyword:...$`. This is used to maintain certain information (e.g., author, date of last change, revision number) in a file without human intervention.

The keyword substitution mechanism originates from rcs[11] and from cvs.

`svn:eol-style`

Makes the client convert end-of-line characters in text files. Used when the working copy is needed with a specific EOL style. "native" is commonly used, so that EOL's match the user's OS EOL style. Repositories may require this property on all files to prevent inconsistent line endings, which can cause a problem in itself.

`svn:externals`

Allows parts of other repositories to be automatically checked-out into a sub-directory.

`svn:needs-lock`

Specifies that a file is to be checked out with file permissions set to read-only. This is designed for use with the locking mechanism. The read-only permission reminds one to obtain a lock before modifying the file: obtaining a lock makes the file writable, and releasing the lock makes it read-only again. Locks are only enforced during a commit operation. Locks can be used without setting this property. However, that is not recommended, because it introduces the risk of someone modifying a locked file; they will only discover it has been locked when their commit fails.

`svn:special`

This property isn't meant to be set or modified directly by users. As of 2010 only used for having symbolic links in the repository. When a symbolic link is added to the repository, a file containing the link target is created with this property set. When a Unix-like system checks out this file, the client converts it to a symbolic link.

`svn:mergeinfo`

Used to track merge data (revision numbers) in Subversion 1.5 (or later). This property is automatically maintained by the `merge` command, and it is not recommended to change its value manually.[12]

Subversion also uses properties on revisions themselves. Like the above properties on filesystem entries the names are completely arbitrary, with the Subversion client using certain properties prefixed with 'svn:'. However, these properties are not versioned and can be changed later.

`svn:date`

the date and time stamp of a revision

`svn:author`

the name of the user that submitted the change(s)

`svn:log`

the user-supplied description of the change(s)

Branching and tagging

Subversion uses the inter-file branching model from Perforce[13] to handle branches and tags. A branch is a separate line of development.[14] Tagging involves creating a snapshot of the repository's content, which, unlike a branch, is not expected to change in the future.

The system sets up a new branch or tag by using the 'svn copy' command, which should be used in place of the native operating system mechanism. Subversion does not create an entire new file version in the repository with its copy. Instead, the old and new versions are linked together internally and the history is preserved for both. The copied versions take up only a little extra room in the repository because Subversion saves only the differences from the original versions.

All the versions in each branch maintain the history of the file up to the point of the copy, plus any changes made since. One can "merge" changes back into the trunk or between branches. To Subversion, the only difference between tags and branches is that changes should not be checked into the tagged versions. Due to the differencing algorithm, creating a tag or a branch takes very little additional space in the repository.

Visualization of a very simple Subversion project

Current limitations and problems

Release 1.6.* of Subversion only allows directory access control and lacks more granular file access control. That problem dramatically restricts the use of Subversion in projects where directories are not structured to address the functional separation among various objects. For example, directories like lib, src, bin do not address security and access control in most cases.

A known problem in Subversion affects the implementation of the file and directory **rename** operation. As of 2010, Subversion implements the renaming of files and directories as a "copy" to the new name followed by a "delete" of the old name. Only the names change, all data relating to the edit history remains the same, and Subversion will still use the old name in older revisions of the "tree". However, Subversion may become confused when files are modified and moved in the same commit. This can also cause problems when a move conflicts with edits made elsewhere,[15] for example during merging branches.[16] The Subversion 1.5 release addressed some of these scenarios while others remain problematic.[17]

As of 2010 Subversion lacks some repository-administration and -management features. For instance, someone may wish to edit the repository to permanently remove all historical records of certain data. Subversion does not have built-in support to achieve this simply.[18]

Subversion stores additional copies of data on the local machine, which can become an issue with very large projects or files, or if developers work on multiple branches simultaneously. These .svn directories on the client side can become corrupted by ill-advised user activity,[19] although a repair tool is provided ("svn cleanup").

Subversion does not store the modification times of files. As such, a file checked out of a subversion repository will have the 'current' date (instead of the modification time in the repository), and a file checked into the repository will have the date of the check-in (instead of the modification time of the file being checked in). This might not always be what is wanted.[20]

Subversion does not use a distributed revision control model. Some users of version control systems see this as detrimental; famously, Linus Torvalds has attacked[21] Subversion's centralised model. Ben Collins-Sussman, one of the designers of Subversion, believes a centralised model would help prevent "insecure programmers" from hiding their work from other team members.[22]

While Subversion stores filenames as Unicode, it does not specify if *precomposition* or *decomposition* is used for certain accented characters (such as é). Thus, files added in SVN clients running on some operating systems (such as OS X) use *decomposition* encoding, while clients running on other operating systems (such as Linux) use *precomposition* encoding, with the consequence that those accented characters do not display correctly if the local SVN client is not using the same encoding as the client used to add the files.[23][24]

Subversion tags

This subsection focuses on *tags* but parts of it also apply to *branches*.

Revision numbers are difficult to remember in any version-control system. For this reason most systems offer symbolic *tags* as user-friendly references to them. Subversion does not have such a feature and what its documentation recommends to use instead is very different in nature. Instead of implementing tags as references to points in history, Subversion recommends taking snapshots and storing them in a well-known subdirectory ("`tags/`") in the space of the repository tree.

This history-to-space projection causes at least two problems:

1. Once a snapshot has been taken, the system does not remember which revision it came from. This is the difference between a *copy* and a *reference*. This makes some operations less convenient and others impossible. For instance a naive `svn diff -r tag1:tag2 myfile` does not work; it is slightly more complicated than that to achieve. Other operations like

   `svn log -r tag1:tag2 myfile` are just impossible.

2. When two (ideally independent) object types live in the repository tree, a "fight to the top" can ensue. In other words it is often difficult to decide at which level to create the "tags/" subdirectory:

```
trunk/componentfoo/              componentfoo/trunk/
     /componentbar/      or                  /tags/1.1/
tags/1.1/componentfoo/           componentbar/trunk/
        /componentbar/                       /tags/1.1/
```

To address such problems, posters on the Subversion mailing lists have suggested a new feature called "labels".[25] SVN labels would more closely resemble the "tags" of other systems such as CVS or git. As of 2010 this suggestion has not progressed.

Development and implementation

Main article: Software that uses Subversion

CollabNet has continued its involvement with Subversion, but the project runs as an independent open source community. In November 2009 the project was accepted into the Apache Incubator, aiming to become part of the Apache Software Foundation's efforts.[26] Since March 2010, the project is formally known as Apache Subversion, being a part of the Apache Top-Level Projects.[27]

In October 2009 WANdisco announced the hiring of core Subversion committers as the company moved to become a major corporate sponsor of the project. This included Hyrum Wright, president of the Subversion Corporation and release manager for the Subversion project since early 2008, who joined the company to lead its open source team.[28]

The Subversion open-source community does not provide binaries, but potential users can download such from volunteers, from CollabNet, the initiator of the Subversion project or WANdisco. While the Subversion project does not include an official graphical user interface (GUI) for use with Subversion, third parties have developed a number of different GUIs, along with a wide variety of additional ancillary software.

```
CollabNet Subversion Server and Client v1.6 (for Windows)

Certified platforms: Windows XP SP2, Win 2003(Standard Edition)
R2
    Apache version: 2.2.11

    Prerequisite: You must have administrative privileges to
    install and uninstall CollabNet Subversion.

IMPORTANT: Apache version upgraded from 2.0 to 2.2

    With the CollabNet Subversion 1.5.0 release, we upgraded
    the included Apache server version from 2.0 to 2.2. This
    is consistent with the packages we provide for other
    operating systems, and also upgrades our package to the
    best available version of Apache.

    This is important to existing users because your current
    Apache 2.0 server configuration cannot be automatically
    updated to the format of the Apache 2.2 configuration
    file. If you allow the installer to upgrade your
existing
    installation, it backs up your Apache conf, logs, and htdocs
    folders so that you can refer to your previous configuration
    when configuring your
new
    server.
```

Subversion, once installed, has a number of different pieces. The following is a quick overview of what you get. Don't be alarmed if the brief descriptions leave you scratching your head—there are plenty more pages in this book devoted to alleviating that confusion.

svn
The command-line client program.

svnversion

A program for reporting the state (in terms of revisions of the items present) of a working copy.

svnlook

A tool for directly inspecting a Subversion repository.

svnadmin

A tool for creating, tweaking or repairing a Subversion repository.

svndumpfilter

A program for filtering Subversion repository dump streams.

mod_dav_svn

A plug-in module for the Apache HTTP Server, used to make your repository available to others over a network.

svnserve

A custom standalone server program, runnable as a daemon process or invokable by SSH; another way to make your repository available to others over a network.

svnsync

A program for incrementally mirroring one repository to another over a network.

Installation:

http://www.open.collab.net/downloads/subversion/

Download 'Collabnet SubVersion Server and Client v1.6.11 (For Windows)

This package includes server and client

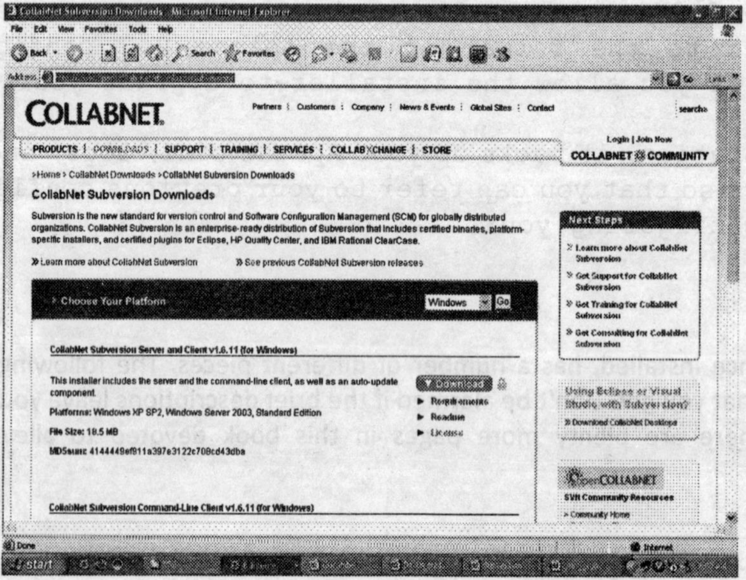

You have to register to the collabnet site then you can download the exe. Registration takes 2 minutes and it's free.

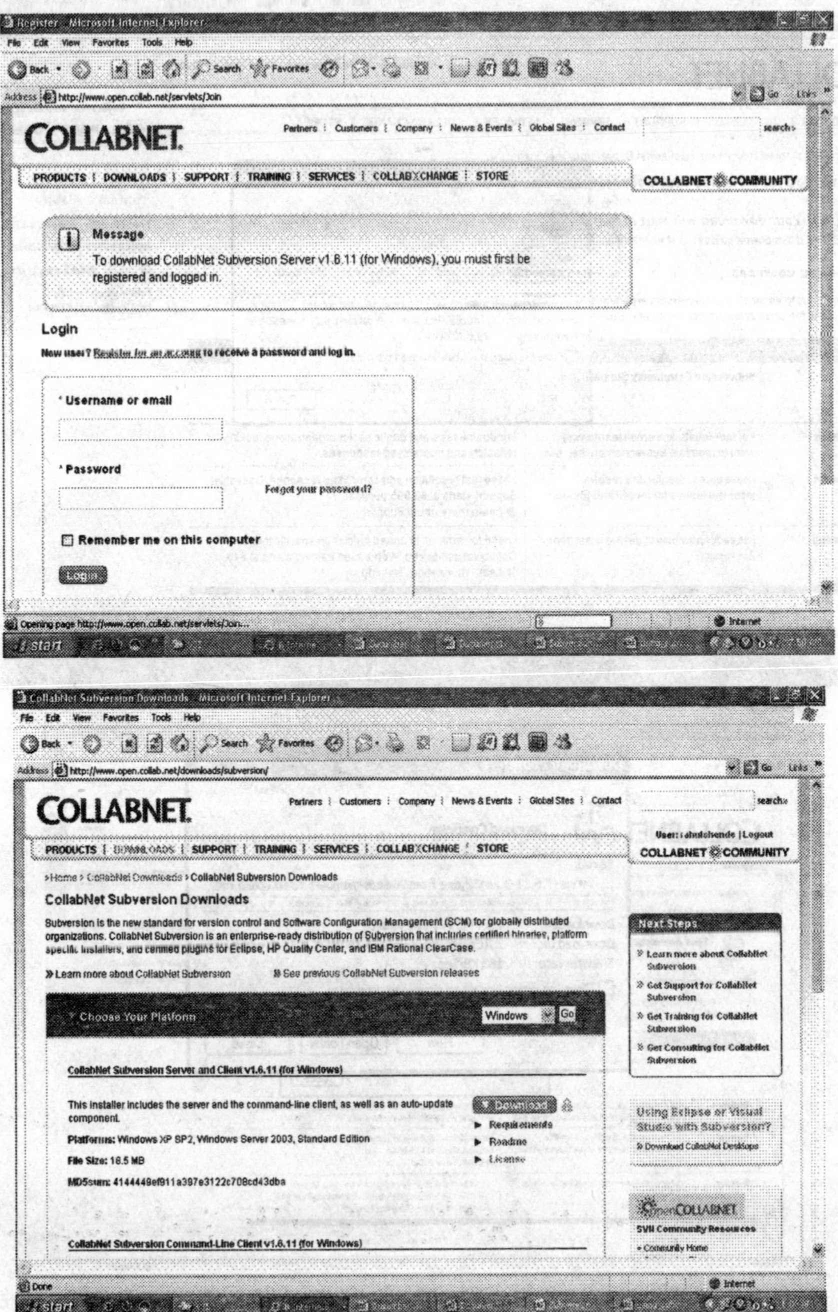

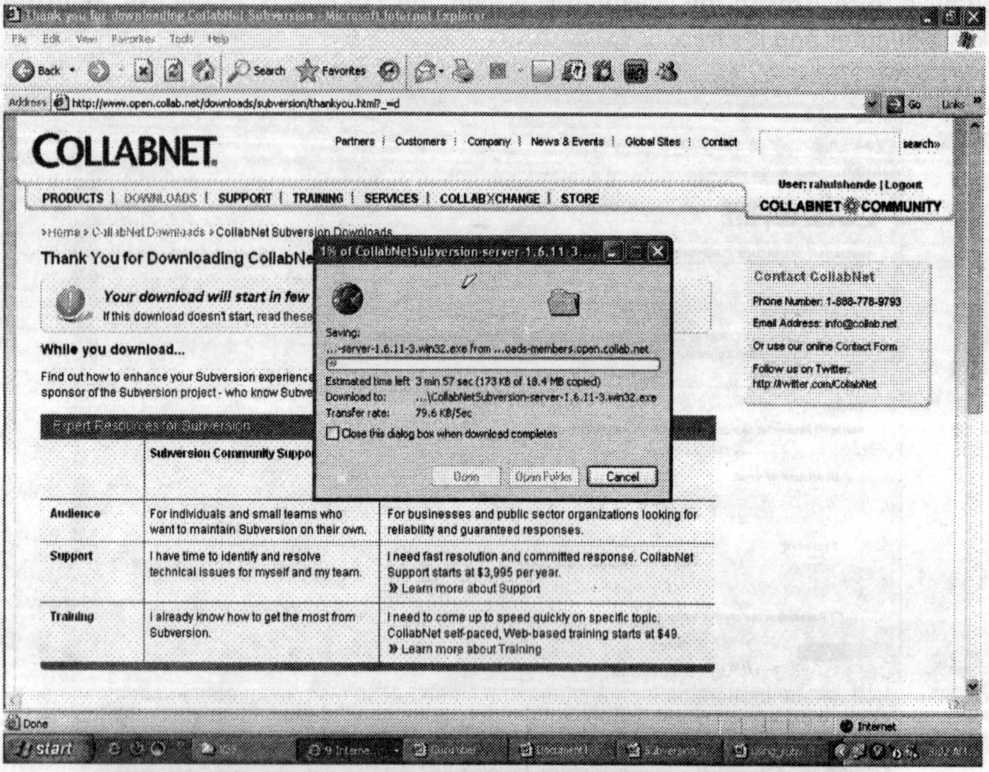

Thank you for downloading CollabNet Subversion - Microsoft Internet Explorer
http://www.open.collab.net/downloads/subversion/thankyou.html?_=d
COLLABNET
Partners | Customers | Company | News & Events | Global Sites | Contact
PRODUCTS | DOWNLOADS | SUPPORT | TRAINING | SERVICES | COLLABXCHANGE | STORE
COLLABNET COMMUNITY
Thank You for Downloading CollabNe
Your download will start in few
While you download...
1% of CollabNetSubversion-server-1.6.11-3...
Saving:
...-server-1.6.11-3.win32.exe from ...oads-members.open.collab.net
Estimated time left 3 min 57 sec (173 KB of 18.4 MB copied)
Download to: ...\CollabNetSubversion-server-1.6.11-3.win32.exe
Transfer rate: 79.6 KB/Sec
Close this dialog box when download completes
Open | Open Folder | Cancel
Contact CollabNet
Phone Number: 1-888-778-9793
Email Address: info@collab.net
Or use our online Contact Form
Follow us on Twitter:
http://twitter.com/CollabNet
Expert Resources for Subversion
Subversion Community Support
Audience | For individuals and small teams who want to maintain Subversion on their own. | For businesses and public sector organizations looking for reliability and guaranteed responses.
Support | I have time to identify and resolve technical issues for myself and my team. | I need fast resolution and committed response. CollabNet Support starts at $3,995 per year. » Learn more about Support
Training | I already know how to get the most from Subversion. | I need to come up to speed quickly on specific topic. CollabNet self-paced, Web-based training starts at $49. » Learn more about Training
Done
Internet

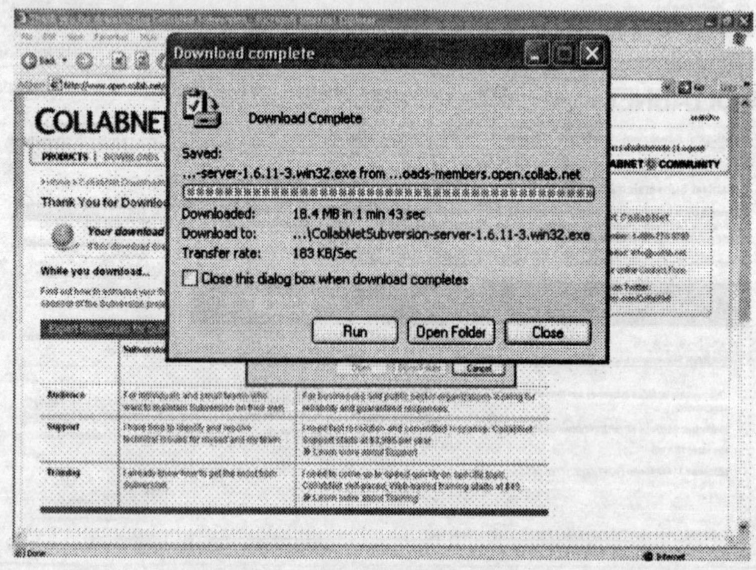
Download complete
Download Complete
Saved:
...-server-1.6.11-3.win32.exe from ...oads-members.open.collab.net
Downloaded: 18.4 MB in 1 min 43 sec
Download to: ...\CollabNetSubversion-server-1.6.11-3.win32.exe
Transfer rate: 183 KB/Sec
Close this dialog box when download completes
Run
Open Folder
Close
COLLABNET

Click on 'Run'

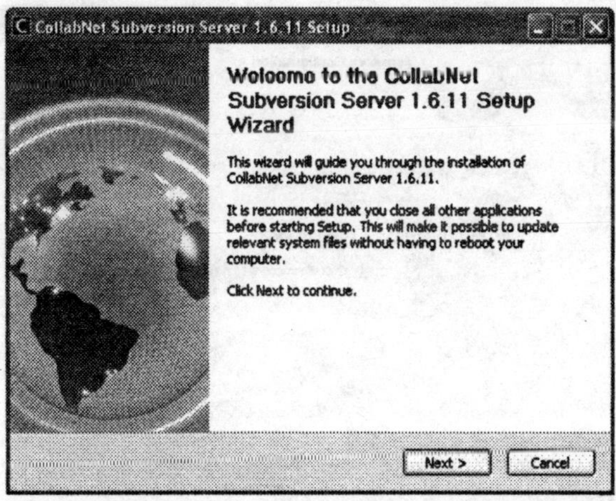
CollabNet Subversion Server 1.6.11 Setup
Welcome to the CollabNet Subversion Server 1.6.11 Setup Wizard
This wizard will guide you through the installation of CollabNet Subversion Server 1.6.11.
It is recommended that you close all other applications before starting Setup. This will make it possible to update relevant system files without having to reboot your computer.
Click Next to continue.
Next >
Cancel

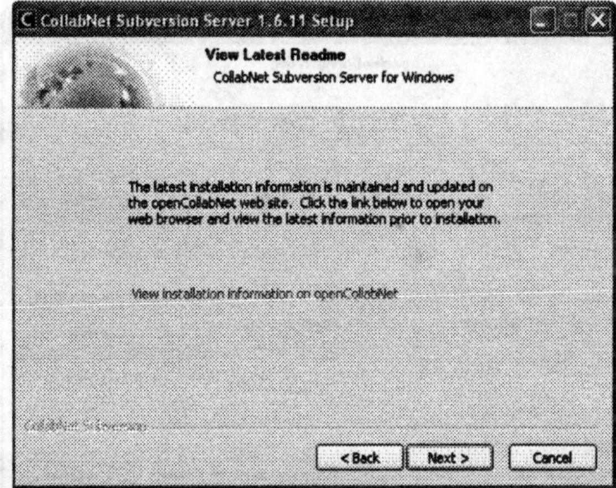
CollabNet Subversion Server 1.6.11 Setup
View Latest Readme
CollabNet Subversion Server for Windows
The latest installation information is maintained and updated on the openCollabNet web site. Click the link below to open your web browser and view the latest information prior to installation.
View installation information on openCollabNet
< Back
Next >
Cancel

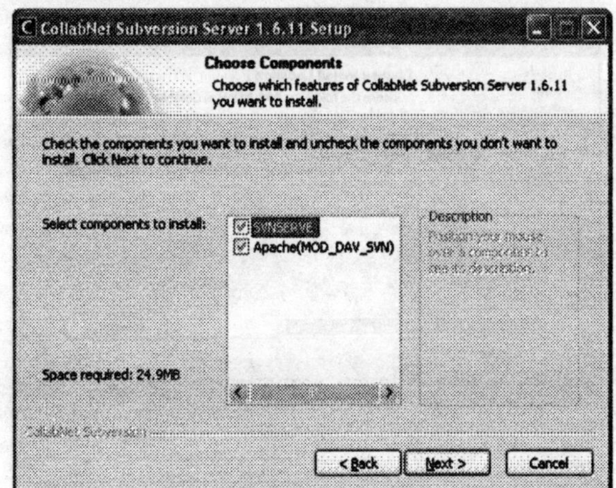
CollabNet Subversion Server 1.6.11 Setup
Choose Components
Choose which features of CollabNet Subversion Server 1.6.11 you want to install.
Check the components you want to install and uncheck the components you don't want to install. Click Next to continue.
Select components to install:
SVNSERVE
Apache(MOD_DAV_SVN)
Description
Space required: 24.9MB
< Back
Next >
Cancel

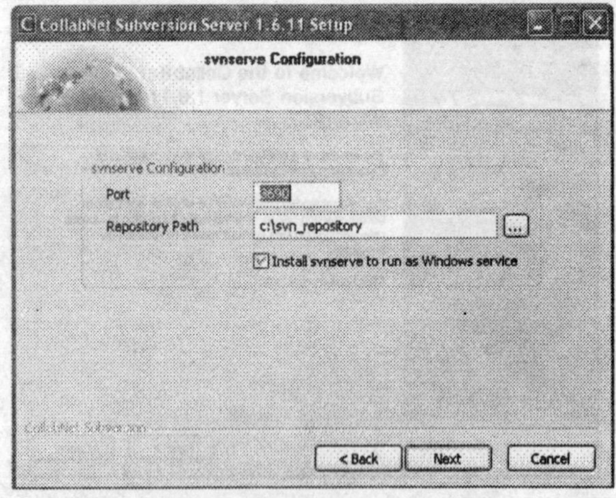
CollabNet Subversion Server 1.6.11 Setup
svnserve Configuration
svnserve Configuration
Port
3690
Repository Path
c:\svn_repository
Install svnserve to run as Windows service
CollabNet Subversion
< Back
Next
Cancel

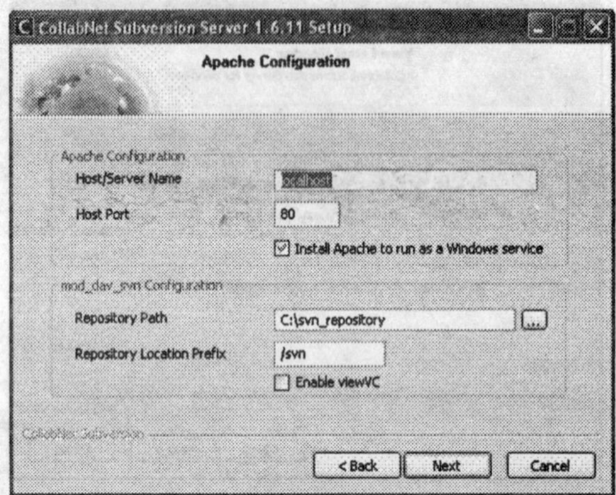
CollabNet Subversion Server 1.6.11 Setup
Apache Configuration
Apache Configuration
Host/Server Name
localhost
Host Port
80
Install Apache to run as a Windows service
mod_dav_svn Configuration
Repository Path
C:\svn_repository
Repository Location Prefix
/svn
Enable viewVC
CollabNet Subversion
< Back
Next
Cancel

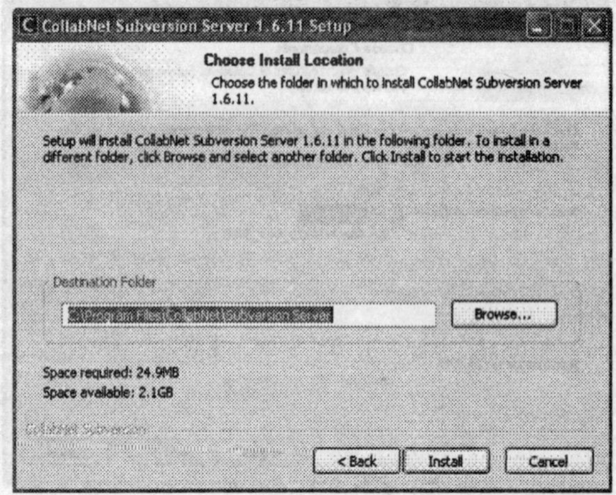
CollabNet Subversion Server 1.6.11 Setup
Choose Install Location
Choose the folder in which to install CollabNet Subversion Server 1.6.11.
Setup will install CollabNet Subversion Server 1.6.11 in the following folder. To install in a different folder, click Browse and select another folder. Click Install to start the installation.
Destination Folder
Browse...
Space required: 24.9MB
Space available: 2.1GB
CollabNet Subversion
< Back
Install
Cancel

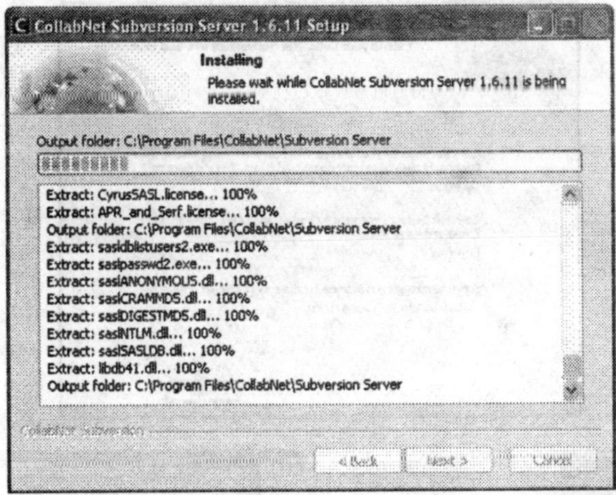
CollabNet Subversion Server 1.6.11 Setup
Installing
Please wait while CollabNet Subversion Server 1.6.11 is being installed.
Output folder: C:\Program Files\CollabNet\Subversion Server
Extract: CyrusSASL.license... 100%
Extract: APR_and_Serf.license... 100%
Output folder: C:\Program Files\CollabNet\Subversion Server
Extract: sasldblistusers2.exe... 100%
Extract: saslpasswd2.exe... 100%
Extract: saslANONYMOUS.dll... 100%
Extract: saslCRAMMD5.dll... 100%
Extract: saslDIGESTMD5.dll... 100%
Extract: saslNTLM.dll... 100%
Extract: saslSASLDB.dll... 100%
Extract: libdb41.dll... 100%
Output folder: C:\Program Files\CollabNet\Subversion Server
CollabNet Subversion
< Back
Next >
Cancel

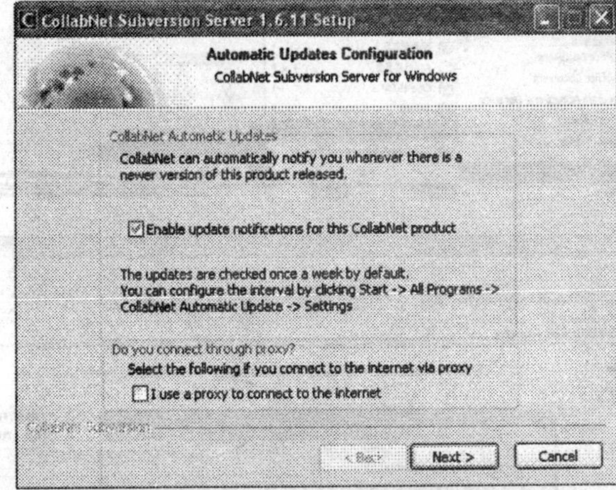
CollabNet Subversion Server 1.6.11 Setup
Automatic Updates Configuration
CollabNet Subversion Server for Windows
CollabNet Automatic Updates
CollabNet can automatically notify you whenever there is a newer version of this product released.
Enable update notifications for this CollabNet product
The updates are checked once a week by default.
You can configure the interval by clicking Start -> All Programs -> CollabNet Automatic Update -> Settings
Do you connect through proxy?
Select the following if you connect to the internet via proxy
I use a proxy to connect to the internet
CollabNet Subversion
< Back
Next >
Cancel

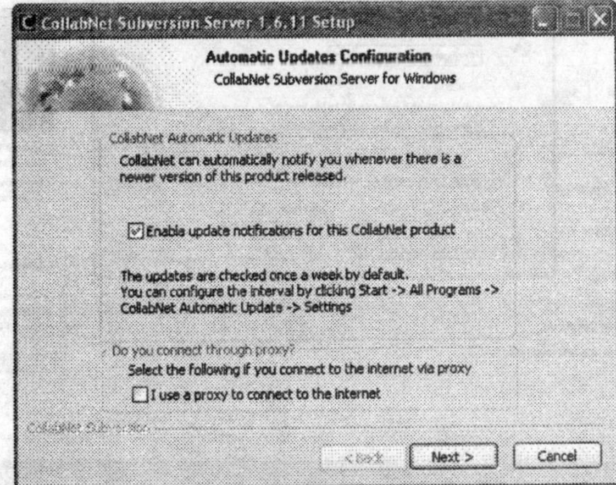
CollabNet Subversion Server 1.6.11 Setup
Automatic Updates Configuration
CollabNet Subversion Server for Windows
CollabNet Automatic Updates
CollabNet can automatically notify you whenever there is a newer version of this product released.
Enable update notifications for this CollabNet product
The updates are checked once a week by default.
You can configure the interval by clicking Start -> All Programs -> CollabNet Automatic Update -> Settings
Do you connect through proxy?
Select the following if you connect to the internet via proxy
I use a proxy to connect to the internet
CollabNet Subversion
< Back
Next >
Cancel

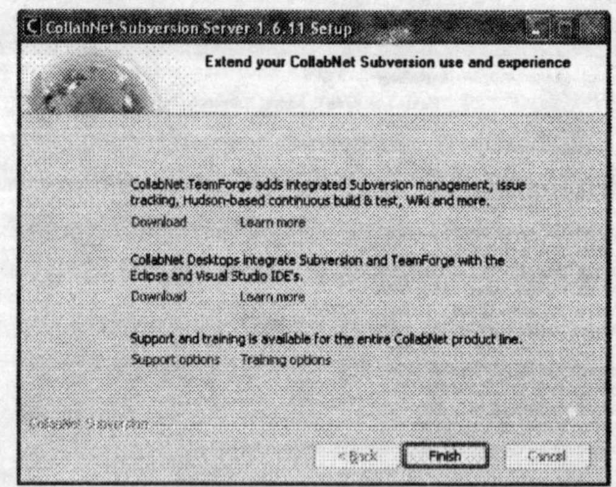
CollabNet Subversion Server 1.6.11 Setup
Extend your CollabNet Subversion use and experience
CollabNet TeamForge adds integrated Subversion management, issue tracking, Hudson-based continuous build & test, Wiki and more.
Download Learn more
CollabNet Desktops integrate Subversion and TeamForge with the Eclipse and Visual Studio IDE's.
Download Learn more
Support and training is available for the entire CollabNet product line.
Support options Training options
Finish
Cancel

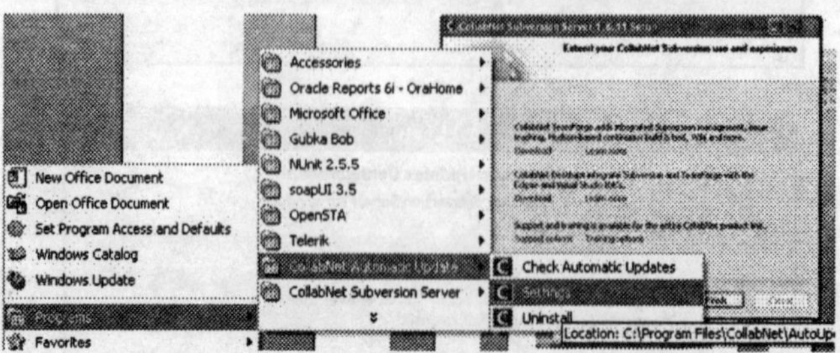
Accessories
Oracle Reports 6i - OraHome
Microsoft Office
Gubka Bob
NUnit 2.5.5
soapUI 3.5
OpenSTA
Telerik
CollabNet Subversion Server
New Office Document
Open Office Document
Set Program Access and Defaults
Windows Catalog
Windows Update
Favorites
Check Automatic Updates
Uninstall
Location: C:\Program Files\CollabNet\AutoUp

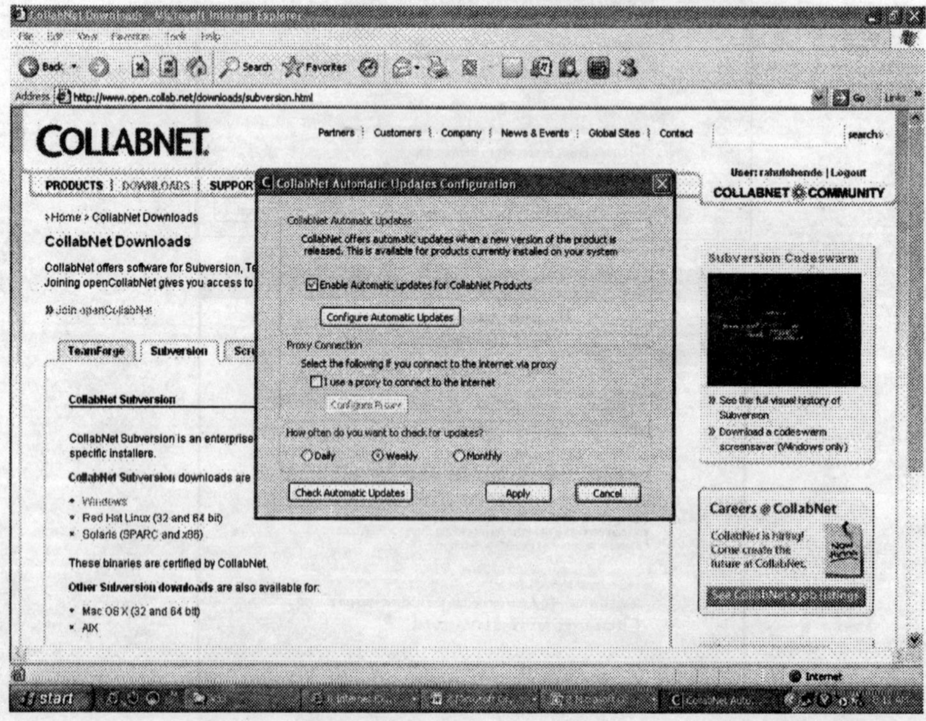
Address http://www.open.collab.net/downloads/subversion.html
COLLABNET
Partners Customers Company News & Events Global Sites Contact
PRODUCTS
CollabNet Automatic Updates Configuration
CollabNet Automatic Updates
CollabNet offers automatic updates when a new version of the product is released. This is available for products currently installed on your system
Enable Automatic updates for CollabNet Products
Configure Automatic Updates
Proxy Connection
Select the following if you connect to the internet via proxy
I use a proxy to connect to the internet
How often do you want to check for updates?
Daily Weekly Monthly
Check Automatic Updates
Apply
Cancel
>Home > CollabNet Downloads
CollabNet Downloads
TeamForge Subversion
CollabNet Subversion
Red Hat Linux (32 and 64 bit)
Solaris (SPARC and x86)
These binaries are certified by CollabNet.
Other Subversion downloads are also available for:
Mac OS X (32 and 64 bit)
AIX
COLLABNET COMMUNITY
Careers @ CollabNet
Internet

This package include only client , so you can install this client on different machine. **CollabNet Subversion Command Line Client v1.6 (for Windows)**

Certified platforms: Windows XP SP2, Windows Server 2003(Standard Edition) R2

If you have an existing version of Subversion installed, examine the PATH environment variable after installation to make sure it points to the version of Subversion you want to use.

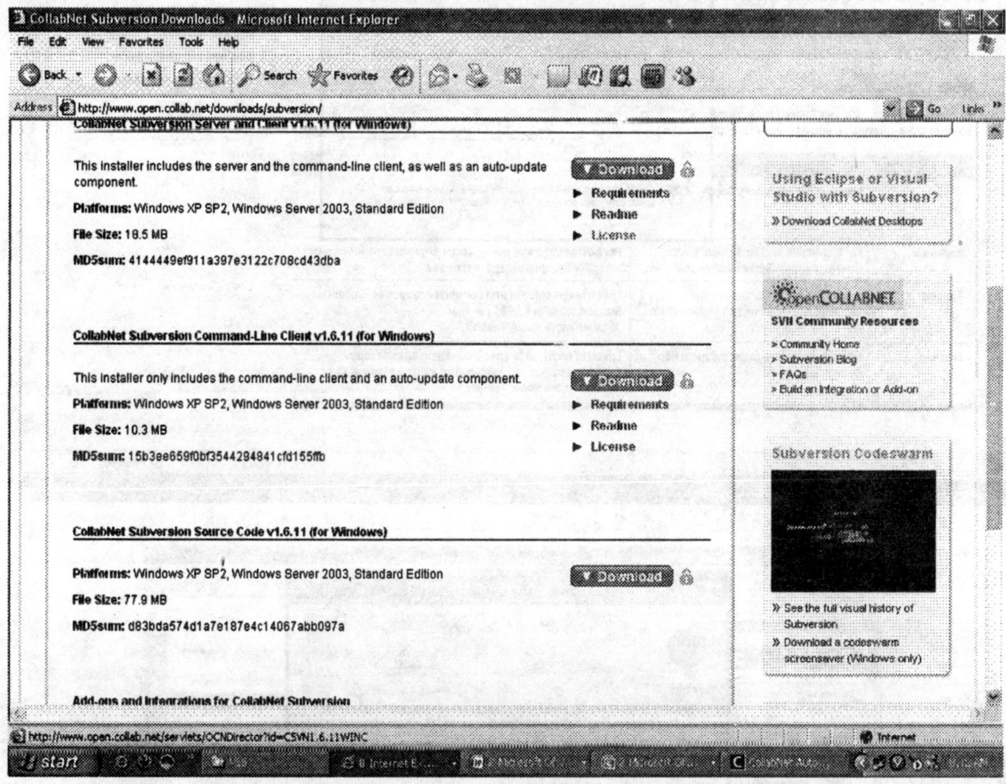

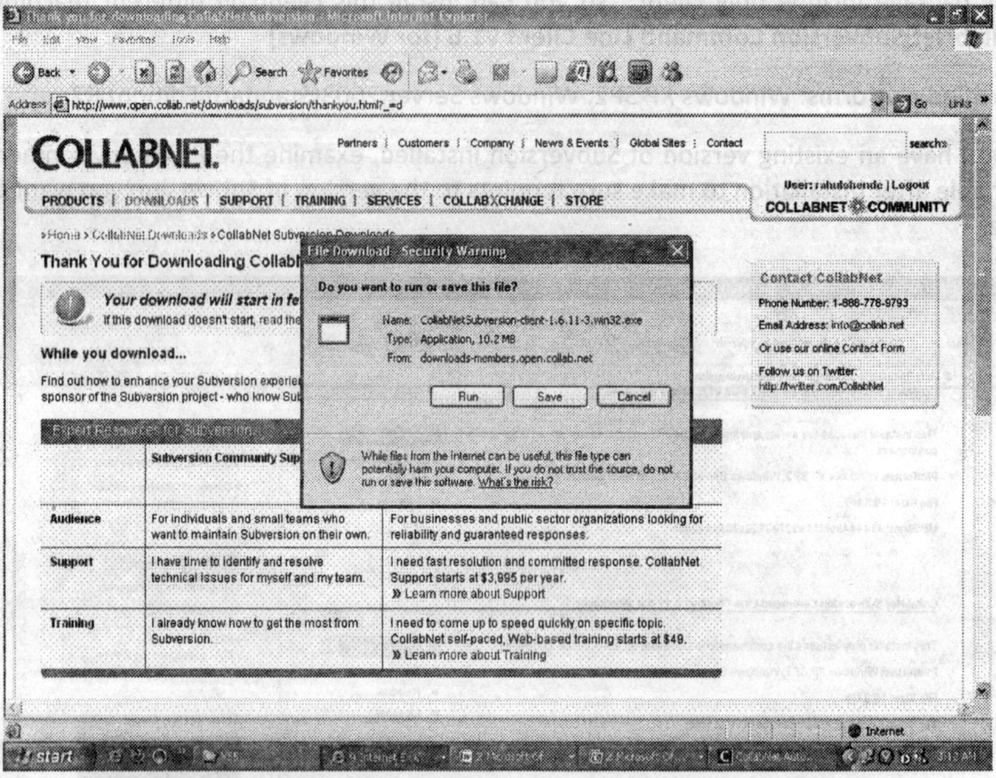

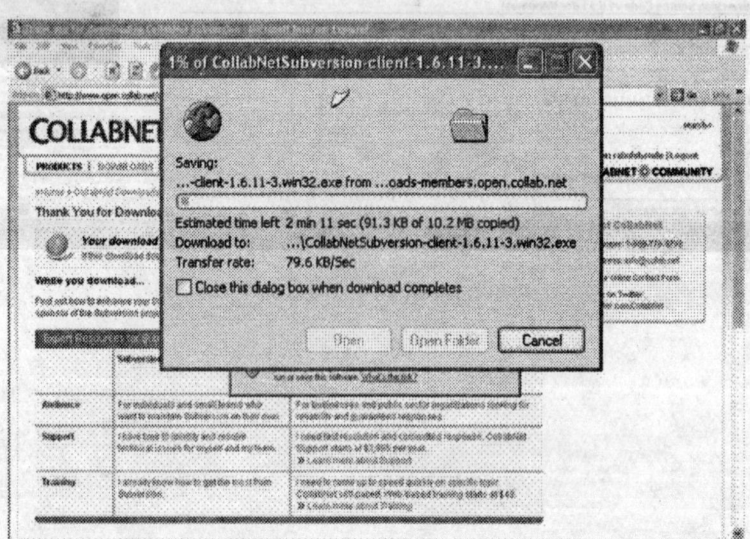
1% of CollabNetSubversion-client-1.6.11-3....
Saving:
...-client-1.6.11-3.win32.exe from ...oads-members.open.collab.net
Estimated time left 2 min 11 sec (91.3 KB of 10.2 MB copied)
Download to: ...\CollabNetSubversion-client-1.6.11-3.win32.exe
Transfer rate: 79.6 KB/Sec
Close this dialog box when download completes
Open
Open Folder
Cancel

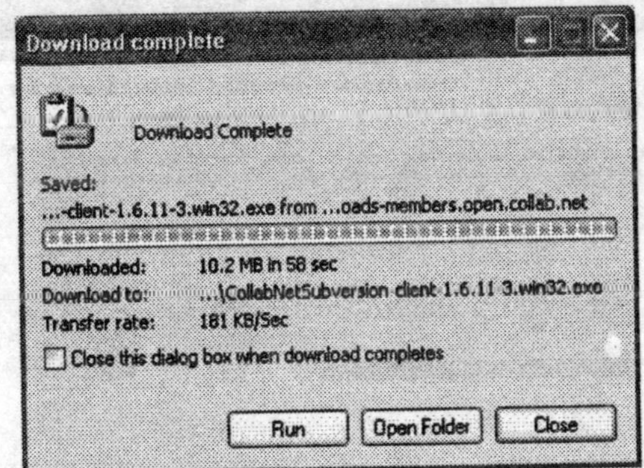
Download complete
Download Complete
Saved:
...-client-1.6.11-3.win32.exe from ...oads-members.open.collab.net
Downloaded: 10.2 MB in 58 sec
Download to: ...\CollabNetSubversion client 1.6.11 3.win32.exe
Transfer rate: 181 KB/Sec
Close this dialog box when download completes
Run
Open Folder
Close

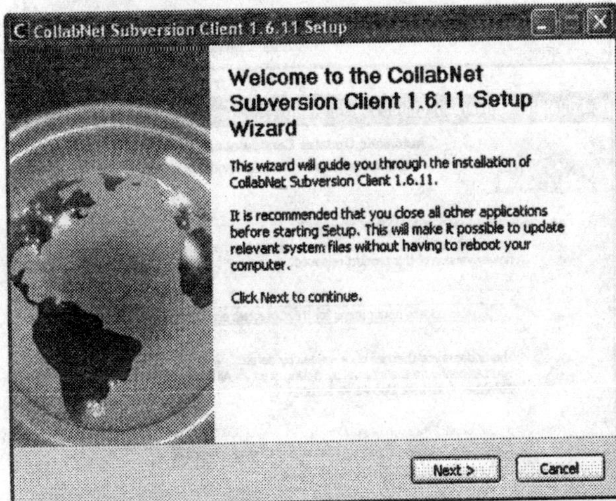
CollabNet Subversion Client 1.6.11 Setup
Welcome to the CollabNet Subversion Client 1.6.11 Setup Wizard
This wizard will guide you through the installation of CollabNet Subversion Client 1.6.11.
It is recommended that you close all other applications before starting Setup. This will make it possible to update relevant system files without having to reboot your computer.
Click Next to continue.
Next >
Cancel

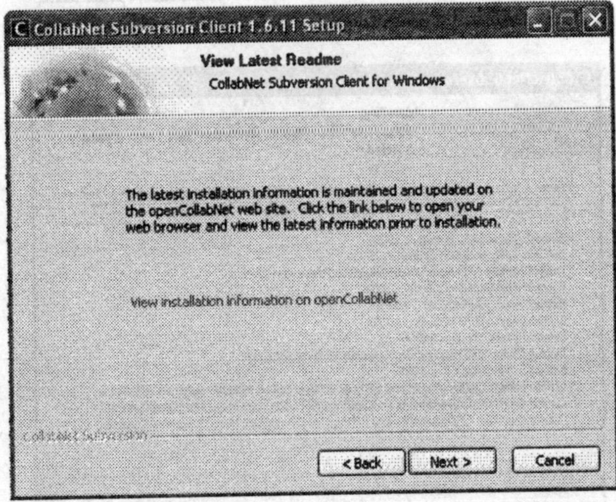
CollabNet Subversion Client 1.6.11 Setup
View Latest Readme
CollabNet Subversion Client for Windows
The latest installation information is maintained and updated on the openCollabNet web site. Click the link below to open your web browser and view the latest information prior to installation.
View installation information on openCollabNet
< Back
Next >
Cancel

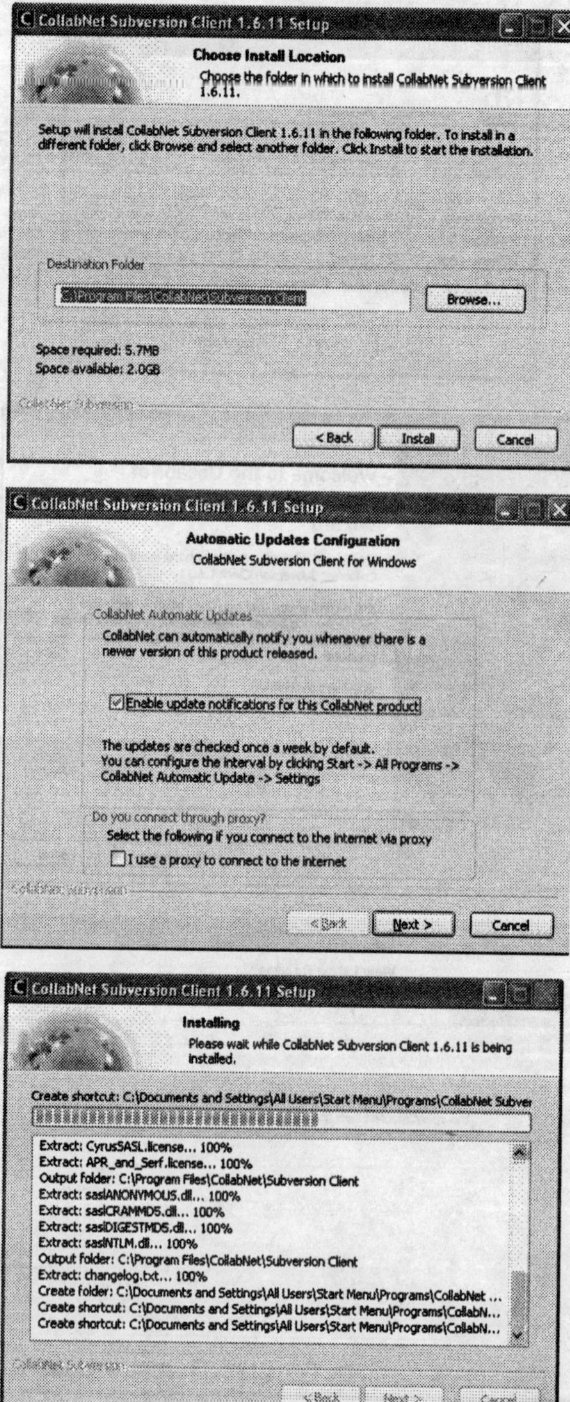
CollabNet Subversion Client 1.6.11 Setup
Choose Install Location
Choose the folder in which to install CollabNet Subversion Client 1.6.11.
Setup will install CollabNet Subversion Client 1.6.11 in the following folder. To install in a different folder, click Browse and select another folder. Click Install to start the installation.
Destination Folder
C:\Program Files\CollabNet\Subversion Client
Browse...
Space required: 5.7MB
Space available: 2.0GB
< Back
Install
Cancel
CollabNet Subversion Client 1.6.11 Setup
Automatic Updates Configuration
CollabNet Subversion Client for Windows
CollabNet Automatic Updates
CollabNet can automatically notify you whenever there is a newer version of this product released.
Enable update notifications for this CollabNet product
The updates are checked once a week by default.
You can configure the interval by clicking Start -> All Programs -> CollabNet Automatic Update -> Settings
Do you connect through proxy?
Select the following if you connect to the internet via proxy
I use a proxy to connect to the internet
< Back
Next >
Cancel
CollabNet Subversion Client 1.6.11 Setup
Installing
Please wait while CollabNet Subversion Client 1.6.11 is being installed.
Create shortcut: C:\Documents and Settings\All Users\Start Menu\Programs\CollabNet Subver
Extract: CyrusSASL.license... 100%
Extract: APR_and_Serf.license... 100%
Output folder: C:\Program Files\CollabNet\Subversion Client
Extract: saslANONYMOUS.dll... 100%
Extract: saslCRAMMD5.dll... 100%
Extract: saslDIGESTMD5.dll... 100%
Extract: saslNTLM.dll... 100%
Output folder: C:\Program Files\CollabNet\Subversion Client
Extract: changelog.txt... 100%
Create folder: C:\Documents and Settings\All Users\Start Menu\Programs\CollabNet ...
Create shortcut: C:\Documents and Settings\All Users\Start Menu\Programs\CollabN...
Create shortcut: C:\Documents and Settings\All Users\Start Menu\Programs\CollabN...
< Back
Next >
Cancel

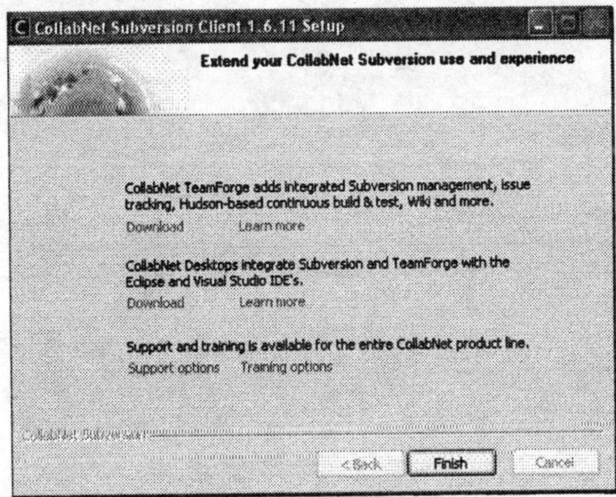

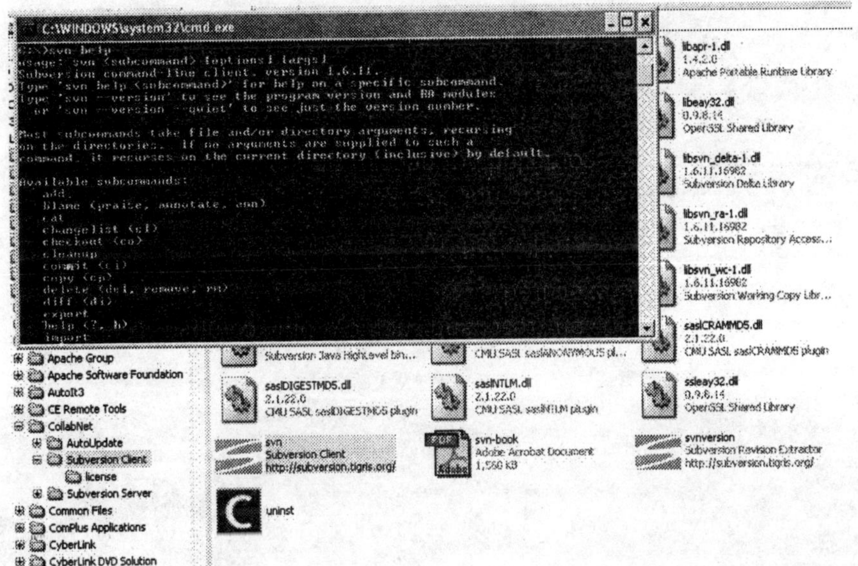

References:

http://www.abbeyworkshop.com/howto/misc/svn01/

After installation of SVN you will get below book:

C:\Program Files\CollabNet\Subversion Client\svn-book

Build Control Using ANT

ANT (Another Nice Tool)

What is Ant?

- Java-based Build tool from Apache
- De facto standard for building, packaging, and installing Java applications
- Accomplishes same objectives that make does on Unix based systems
- Files are written in XML

Why Ant?

- Unlike makefiles, Ant files work cross platform
  - No need for multiple, complex makefiles depending on the operating system.
  - Tasks declared in platform independent way; Ant engine translates to OS specific commands.
- Easy to create own Ant "tasks", in addition to core tasks

How Does Ant Work?

- Ant commands (or tasks) are implemented by Java classes
  - many are built-in
  - others come in optional JAR files
  - custom commands can be created

- Each project using Ant will have a build file
  - typically called build.xml since Ant looks for this by default
- Each build file is composed of targets
  - these correspond to common activities like compiling and running code
- Each target is composed of tasks
  - executed in sequence when the target is executed
  - like make, Ant targets can have dependencies for example, modified source files must be compiled before the application can be run
- Targets to be executed
  - can be specified on the command line when invoking Ant
  - if none are specified then the default target is executed
  - execution stops if an error is encountered so all requested targets may not be executed
- Each target is only executed once
  - regardless of the number of other targets that depend on it
  - for example the "test" and "deploy" targets both depend on "compile" the "all" target depends on "test" and "deploy" but "compile" is only executed once when "all" is executed
- Some tasks are only executed when they need to be
  - for example, files that have not changed since the last time they were compiled are not recompiled not necessarily a good thing

Installing Ant

- Download Ant binary distribution from:
  http://ant.apache.org/bindownload.cgi
- Set ANT_HOME to where you installed Ant
- Include $ANT_HOME/bin in PATH
- Make sure JAVA_HOME is set to point to JDK

Set environment variables

- define ANT_HOME to be the location where Ant was unzipped

- for example, C:\Java\Ant
- define JAVA_HOME to be the location where the JDK is installed
- for example, C:\jdk1.3
- add to CLASSPATH
- a JAXP-compliant XML parser such as Xerces
- download zip file marked "latest binaries" from http://xml.apache.org/dist/xerces-j
- unzip it and add xerces.jar to CLASSPATH
- add to PATH
- %ANT_HOME%\bin

Running Ant

- Type "ant" at the command line
- Automatically looks for build.xml file in current directory to run
- Type "ant –buildfile buildfile.xml" to specify another build file to run.

Ant Output

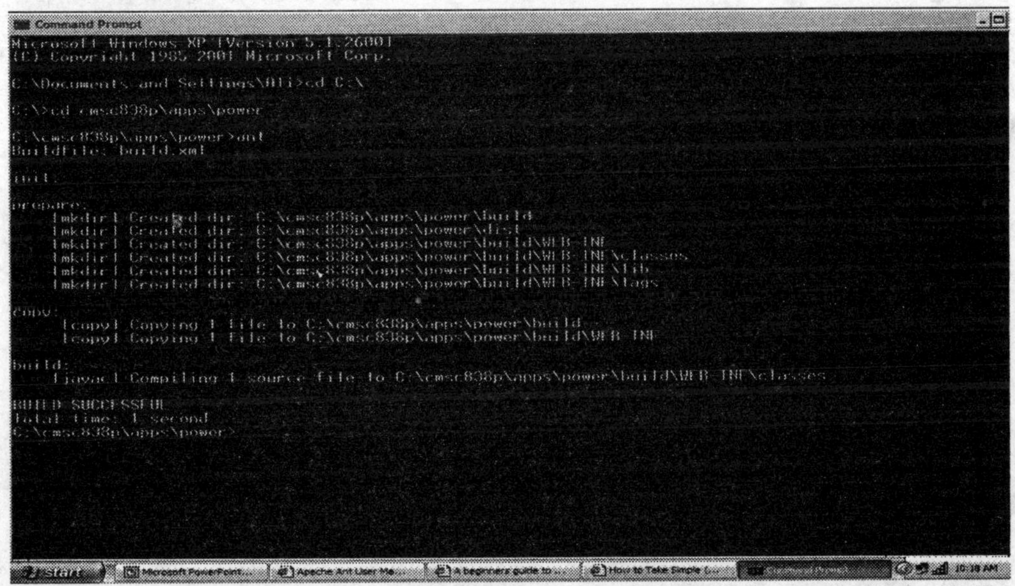

Sample build.xml

```
<project name="MyProject" default="dist" basedir=".">
 <property name="src" location="src"/>
 <property name="build" location="build"/>
 <property name="dist"  location="dist"/>
 <target name="init">
  <tstamp/>
  <mkdir dir="${build}"/>
 </target>
 <target name="compile" depends="init" >
  <javac srcdir="${src}" destdir="${build}"/>
 </target>
 <target name="dist" depends="compile" >
  <mkdir dir="${dist}/lib"/>
  <jar jarfile="${dist}/lib/MyProject-${DSTAMP}.jar" basedir="${build}"/>
 </target>
 <target name="clean" >
  <delete dir="${build}"/>
  <delete dir="${dist}"/>
 </target>
</project>
```

Ant Overview: Project

- Each build file contains exactly one project and at least one target
- Project tags specify the basic project attributes and have 3 properties:
  - name
  - default target
  - basedir
- Example: <project name="MyProject" default="build" basedir=".">

Ant Overview: Targets

- Target is a build module in Ant
- Each target contains task(s) for Ant to do
- One must be a project default

- Overall structure of targets:

<target name="A"/>
<target name="B" depends="A"/>
<target name="C" depends="B"/>
<target name="D" depends="C,B,A"/>

Ant Overview: Tasks

- Each target comprises one or more tasks
- Task is a piece of executable Java code (e.g. javac, jar, etc)
- Tasks do the actual "build" work in Ant
- Ant has core (built in) tasks and the ability to create own tasks
- Example:
- <target name="prepare" depends="init" >
- <mkdir dir="${build}" />
- </target>
- <target name="build" depends="copy" >
- <javac srcdir="src" destdir="${build}">
- <include name="**/*.java" />
- </javac>
- </target>

Ant Overview: Core Tasks

- javac – Runs the Java Compiler
- java – Runs the Java Virtual Machine
- jar (and war) – Create JAR files
- mkdir – Makes a directory
- copy – Copies files to specified location
- delete – Deletes specified files
- cvs – Invokes CVS commands from Ant

Sample Build File

(Contains common targets used for servlet projects)

Sample Build File

(contains common targets used for servlet projects)

```
<?xml version="1.0" encoding="UTF-8"?>
<project name="Web App." default="deploy" basedir=".">

  <!-- Define global properties. -->
  <property name="appName" value="shopping"/>
  <property name="buildDir" value="classes"/>
  <property name="docDir" value="doc"/>
  <property name="docRoot" value="docroot"/>
  <property name="junit" value="/Java/JUnit/junit.jar"/>
  <property name="srcDir" value="src"/>
  <property name="tomcatHome" value="/Tomcat"/>
  <property name="servlet" value="${tomcatHome}/lib/servlet.jar"/>
  <property name="warFile" value="${appName}.war"/>
  <property name="xalan" value="/XML/Xalan/xalan.jar"/>
  <property name="xerces" value="/XML/Xalan/xerces.jar"/>
```

relative directory references are relative to this

target that is run when none are specified

Some of these are used to set **"classpath"** on the next page. Others are used in task parameters.

Where possible, use **UNIX-style paths** even under Windows. This is not possible when Windows directories on drives other than C must be specified.

Sample Build File

Sample Build File (Cont'd)

```
<path id="classpath">
  <pathelement path="${buildDir}"/>
  <pathelement path="${xerces}"/>
  <pathelement path="${xalan}"/>
  <pathelement path="${servlet}"/>
  <pathelement path="${junit}"/>
</path>

<target name="all" depends="test,javadoc,deploy"
 description="runs test, javadoc and deploy"/>
```

used in the compile, javadoc and test targets

means that the test, javadoc and deploy targets must be executed before this target

doesn't have any tasks of its own; just executes other targets

Using ANT

- ant -projecthelp
  - lists targets in build.xml of the current directory
  - example output

```
Searching for build.xml ...
Buildfile: C:\XMLProgLabs\Framework\build.xml
Main targets:

 clean          deletes all generated files
 compile        compiles source files
 deploy         deploys the war file to Tomcat
 dtd            generates a DTD for Ant build files
 javadoc        generates javadoc from all .java files
 prepare        create output directories
 test           runs all JUnit tests
 undeploy       undeploys the war file from Tomcat
 war            builds the war file
```

> Targets with no description attribute are listed as **"Subtargets"** after the main targets. These are typically only invoked by other targets via dependencies or using the Ant and AntCall built-in tasks discussed later.

- ant [*options*] [*target-names*]
  - runs targets with specified names, preceded by targets on which they depend
  - can specify multiple target-names separated by spaces
  - omit target-name to run the default target
  - -D option specifies a property that can be used by targets and tasks
    `-D`*`property-name=property-value`*
    - can specify more than one of these
- ant -help
  - lists other command-line options

ANT OUTPUT

- Indicates the tasks that were executed
  - for example

blank lines were removed so this would fit on the page

```
Searching for build.xml ...
Buildfile: C:\XMLProgLabs\Framework\build.xml
prepare:
    [mkdir] Created dir: C:\XMLProgLabs\Framework\classes
compile:
    [javac] Compiling 26 source files to C:\XMLProgLabs\Framework\classes
war:
      [war] Building war: C:\XMLProgLabs\Framework\shopping.war
undeploy:
   [delete] Deleting directory C:\Tomcat\webapps\shopping
   [delete] Deleting: C:\Tomcat\webapps\shopping.war
deploy:
     [copy] Copying 1 files to C:\Tomcat\webapps
BUILD SUCCESSFUL
Total time: 5 seconds
```

Ant Overview: Writing Own Task

- Create a Java class that extends org.apache.tools.ant.Task
- For each attribute, write a setter method that is public void and takes a single argument
- Write a public void execute() method, with no arguments, that throws a BuildException -- this method implements the task itself

Ant Overview: Properties

- Special task for setting up build file properties:
- Example:

  <property name="src" value="/home/src"/>

- Can use ${src} anywhere in build file to denote /home/src
- Ant provides access to all system properties as if defined by the <property> task

Ant Overview: Path Structures

- Ant provides means to set various environment variables like PATH and CLASSPATH.

- Example of setting CLASSPATH:

```
    <classpath>
  <pathelement path="${classpath}"/>
  <pathelement location="lib/helper.jar"/>
</classpath>
```

Command Line Arguments

- -buildfile buildfile – specify build file to use
- targetname – specify target to run (instead of running default)
- -verbose, -quiet, -debug – Allows control over the logging information Ant outputs
- -logger classname – Allows user to specify their own classes for logging Ant events

IDE Integration

- Eclipse, NetBeans, JBuilder, VisualAge, and almost any other Java IDE has Ant integration built-in to the system
- Refer to each IDE's documentation for how to use Ant with that IDE

Web Development with Ant

- Tomcat comes with special Ant tasks to ease Web application development and deployment
- Copy $TOMCAT_HOME/server/lib/catalina-ant.jar to $ANT_HOME/lib
- Ant tasks for Tomcat:

  - install
  - reload
  - deploy
  - remove

Documentation/References

- Download: http://ant.apache.org/bindownload.cgi
- User Manual: http://ant.apache.org/manual/index.html
- Sun's Web development tutorial (Ant and JSPs): http://java.sun.com/webservices/docs/1.2/tutorial/doc/GettingStarted3.html
- Java Development with Ant, by Erik Hatcher and Steve Loughran

Build Control Using NANT

Ant Vs. NAnt

NAnt is a free .NET build tool. In theory it is kind of like make without make's wrinkles. In practice it's a lot like Ant.

For downloading NAnt:
http://nant.sourceforge.net/ for NAnt
http://ant.apache.org/manual/ For Ant
http://sourceforge.net/projects/nant/files/nant/0.91-alpha1/nant-0.91-alpha1-bin.zip/download

NAnt is different. Instead of a model where it is extended with shell-based commands, NAnt is extended using task classes. Instead of writing shell commands, the configuration files are XML-based, calling out a target tree where various tasks get executed. Each task Is run by an object that implements a particular Task interface.

Granted, this removes some of the expressive power that is inherent in being able to construct a shell command such as 'find . -name foo -exec rm {}', but it gives you the ability to be cross-platform - to work anywhere and everywhere. And hey, if you really need to execute a shell command, NAnt has an <exec> task that allows different commands to be executed based on the OS it is executing on.

Installaing NANt:

Installation

[This is preliminary documentation and subject to change.]

NAnt is available in either a source or binary distribution. The binary distribution is all you need to use NAnt to build your projects, including creating your own custom tasks, types and functions.

If you are upgrading NAnt from a previous version, you must never install over the top of your previous installation. Delete or rename the existing installation directory before installing the new version of NAnt.

Installing from binaries

1. Download the binary distribution archive. Either nant-bin.zip or nant-bin.tar.gz will work, the contents of each archive are the same.

2. Remove any previous versions of NAnt you may have installed.

3. Extract the contents of the archive to the location you wish to install NAnt (eg: C:\Program Files\NAnt in windows, or /usr/local/nant in Linux)

4. Ensure the bin folder in your NAnt installation is in your PATH environment variable.

    - In Windows, a common method to do this is to create an environment variable ANT_HOME that contains the folder you installed NAnt to.
    - Then add %NANT_HOME%\bin to your PATH variable.
    - Both of these should be System variables.

5. Open a new command prompt (shell) and type nant -help. If successful, you should see a usage message displaying available command line options.

6. (optional) Download and install NAnt-contrib or other third party extensions to NAnt.

Installing from source

1. Download the source distribution archive. Either nant-src.zip or nant-src.tar.gz will work, the contents of each archive are the same.

2. Remove any previous versions of NAnt you may have installed.

3. Extract the contents of the archive to a temporary location. This should **not** be the location you wish to install NAnt to.

4. Open a command prompt and change into the folder you extracted the archive to.

5. Depending on your environment, build the NAnt distribution:

Install NAnt using Microsoft .NET

- **GNU Make**

  make install MONO= MCS=csc prefix=*installation-path*
  eg. make install MONO= MCS=csc prefix="C:\Program Files"

- **NMake**

  nmake -f Makefile.nmake install prefix=installation-path
  eg. nmake -f Makefile.nmake install prefix="C:\Program Files"

Install NAnt using Mono

- **GNU Make**

  make install prefix=*installation-path*
  eg. make install prefix="C:\Program Files"

- **NMake**

  nmake -f Makefile.nmake install MONO=mono CSC=mcs prefix=installation-path

  eg. nmake -f Makefile.nmake install MONO=mono CSC=mcs prefix=/usr/local/

This will first build a bootstrap version of NAnt, and then use that to build and install the full version to installation-path/NAnt.

6. Follow the instructions as for a binary release from step 4.

NAnt is a superb tool for building applications. It's fast, extendable, and easy to learn and use. It's also a derivative of a great Java based tool called Ant. Recently I've been having to learn Ant so that I could replace a bunch of hodge-podge batch files in our middle-ware system that is built in Java. Every time I added a new java source file, or had to update an IDL, I had to go modify and run a batch file as well.

Now, I'll admit, I'm the scoundrel who created those batch files to begin with. Honestly, I didn't know any better and they served their purpose well. We haven't done any major development to this system in a couple of years so they haven't had to have more than a mild freshening in that time. Currently I'm doing some extentions to our existing integrations and adding a new integration as well and suddenly realized how much I depend on my NAnt based build system. I quickly drank some of my own kool-aid and went and downloaded Ant.

I had read that Ant and NAnt were related but incompatible for the most part. This is true, but the concepts are basically the same, so once you know how to do something in one it should be easy to accomplish in the other, right? Right??

Well, that really depends on what you are trying to accomplish. There are some fundamental differences between Ant and NAnt:

- Ant doesn't have functions
- Ant has a much more robust and mature set of tasks than does NAnt
- Extending NAnt is easier than extending Ant due to attributes
- NAnt lets you define inline C# to extend on the fly, Ant does not (as far as I can tell)

After a few minutes of head scratching and WTF am I looking at moments with the Ant documentation, I started piecing together the bits where the two products are the same and where they differ. I've put together a little tutorial that will hopefully help any .Net developers needing to play in the Java pool for a while.

Ant for NAnt Users

Introduction

Ant, like NAnt, is an XML-based scripting system that is specialized for performing software builds. Whereas NAnt is primarily designed for building .Net and its related techonologies, Ant is primarily designed for Java and GCC. Note that I said "primarily." This is because both products are completely extensible and one can easily be extended to accomplish the tasks of the other.

This may lead you to a logical question, "Why were these redundant products created?" That's a fair question, and in my opinion it really comes down to the fact that NAnt was borne out of the fact that C# is simply easier to build an extensible API than Java. Ant could have been (and actually has in Ant-Contrib) extended to include functionality for .Net, but the creators of NAnt saw opportunities to make NAnt a superior product to Ant. Whether you feel they succeeded in this goal is based on whether you are primarily a Java developer or a .Net developer.

XML Build Script Concepts

Since Ant and Nant are related products, they share many of the same concepts. They both use XML files that have a root node called a Project. The project node contains child nodes called Tasks that perform the actual work build. There is a wide range of tasks available to both Ant and Nant and in many cases they perform the same job.

The project node is equivalent to a constructor. Any tasks that are included in the project node executed upon the loading of the script. The project node can also contain tasks that indicate a Target. Targets are actions that the caller or script can perform. Most software build systems include commons target task nodes such as Clean, Build, and Install.

Each task contains attributes that pass control data to the code underlying the task. Tasks can also utilize Types, which are XML nodes that denote data instead of actions. Both Ant and NAnt have specialized types to handle collections of files, references, etc.

Here's a sample build script in Ant:

```
<project name="default" default="Hello">
    <target name="Hello">
        <echo message="Hello, Ant User!" />
    </target>
```

```
    <target name="Goodbye">
        <echo message="Goodbye, Ant User!" />
    </target>
</project>
```

This script defines a project named "default" which contains two targets, "Hello" and "Goodbye." The "default" project also has the "Hello" target set as its default. This means that if you were to execute the script without specifying a target on the command line that the "Hello" target will be executed by default. Both the "Hello" and "Goodbye" targets define echo tasks to be executed by the script.

Of course, Ant and Nant being related and all, you should know that this script will run equally well from both Ant and NAnt! Don't take this to mean that this will always be the case, though. Ant and NAnt differ significantly once you move beyond the basic concepts, with NAnt introducing a paradigm of functions that makes scripts a lot easier to build and maintain, but totally breaks any backwards compatibility with Ant at the script level. If you are a seasoned NAnt user, you should know right now that Ant does not have functions and that's that. You will have to learn about the ways that Ant overcomes this with specialized tasks that populate properties.

http://nant.sourceforge.net/
http://nant.sourceforge.net/release/0.85-rc2/help/introduction/installation.html

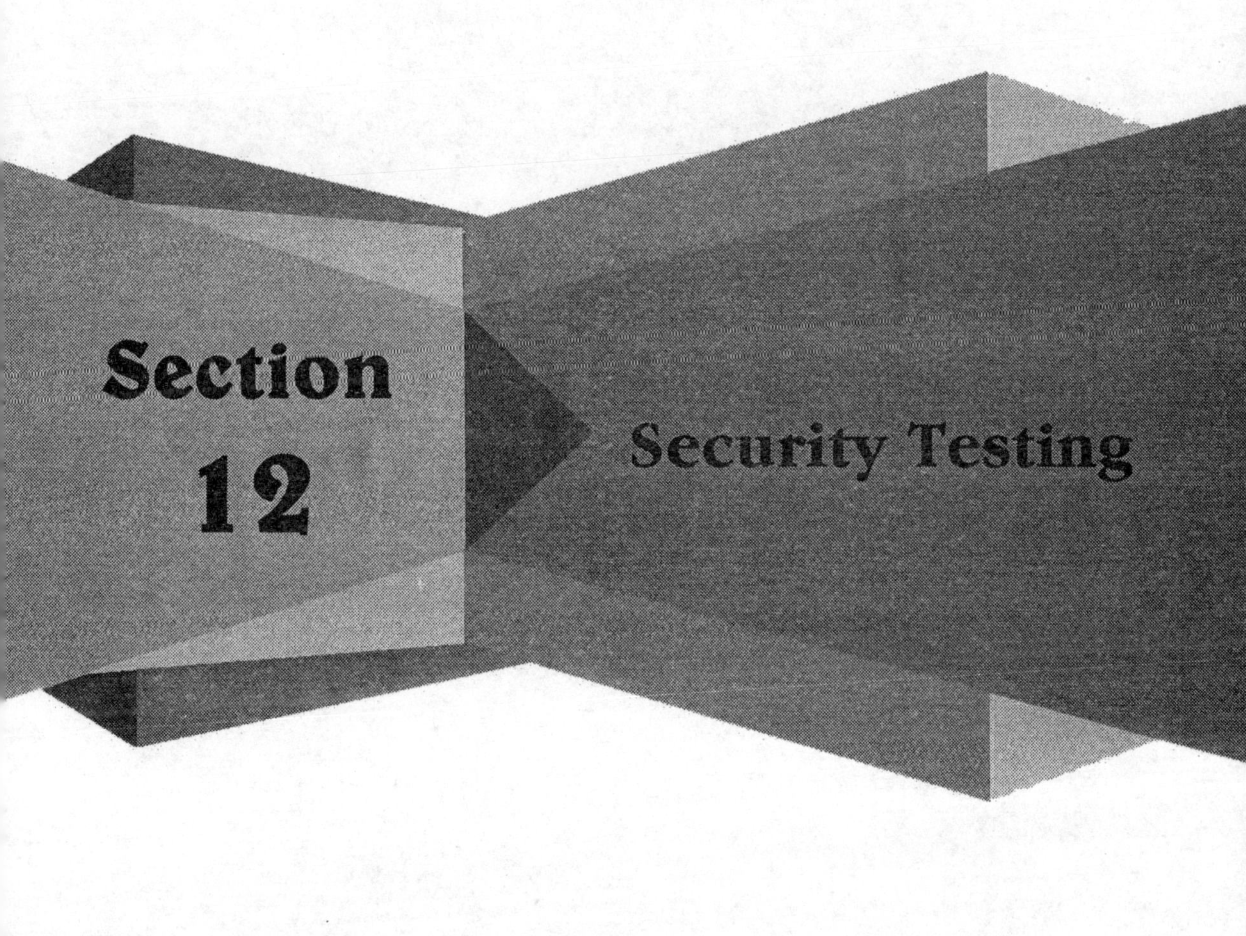
Section
12
Security Testing

Why Security Testing

- Security Capabilities of Vendor to be mandatory criteria for selection of outsourcing partners
- Regulatory Compliance(PCI), user demand(Web2.0) and enterprise Modernization(SOA) are driving awareness and action for security testing
- By 2010, non compliance to PA-DSS (Payment Application Data Security Standard) would have direct business impact on ISV
- By 2011, 50% of organizations will use a Single Vendor who have Security Testing as an inherent component of SLC
- Security Testers are facing the challenge of Testing becoming more specialized
- Constantly Increasing pressure of finding Security Issues early in the cycle
- The cost and lack of coverage of reactive security is driving companies toward proactive measures – building security into the application development process

Business Case

- Company Description:
  - A large business information provider with a user base of 5 M users and daily transactions of 10000 records
  - The application had to conform to security regulations
  - There was an ongoing issue of content data theft in the application which was high in the agenda of CIO
- Strategy adopted for Implementing Security Testing

An engagement model which comprises of 3 sessions of vulnerability Assessment and Penetration testing in one year for 3 Releases of Product Solution of PCI Readiness deployed for the application which included: Pre Assessment and gap analysis Gap mitigation in Application Security issues, IT Policies, Network Security Security Awareness Trainings

- Networks and software are becoming increasingly complex.
- New Vulnerabilities are identified almost each day and Attacks are greatly increased.
- Constant update and Patch management
- One single breach can lead to Financial loss, Loss of reputation, customer Confidence and Brandname.

- 80% of all Security Breaches are due to Web Vulnerabilities – Gartner
- Over 95% of the Web Applications are Vulnerable
- Applications are developed with more focus on the Funtionality than Security.

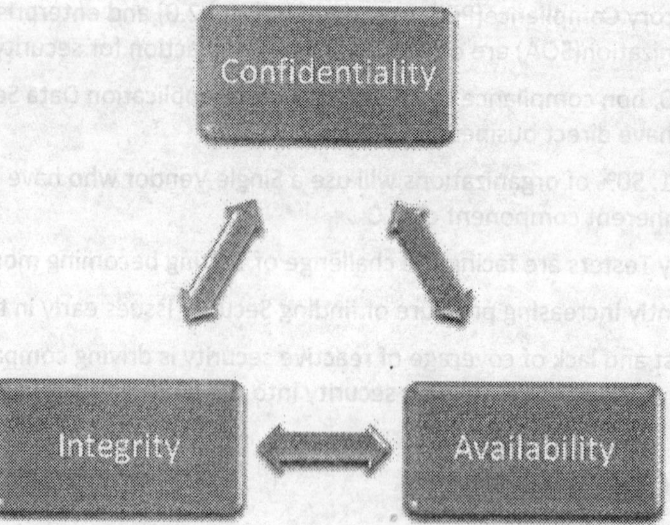

What is Security Testing

Security Testing: (The) Testing process to protect a System from threats Testing whether the system meets its specified security objectives

Attack and its types

Attack is any action to compromise the security of the information of the organization. Attack is the exploit on a system by a human or a program.

Common Attack Types:

- Penetration
- Leakage
- Spoofing (Session Hijack, Man-in-the-middle)
- Password Crackers (Exploitation of Authentication)
- Viruses, Worms, Trojan Horses
- SQL Injection

- Buffer Overflows
- Malicious Use
- Denial of Service

Threats and Vulnerabilities

Vulnerability - Any weakness, administrative process, or act or physical exposure (caused by errors in procedures, code, design or implementation) that makes an information asset susceptible to exploit by a threat.

Threat - A potential cause of an unwanted impact to a system or organization.

Example:

Vulnerability – Open Ports

Threat - Insecure Communication

Vulnerability – Incorrect Error Handling

Threat – Information Leakage

What is Threat Modeling?

Threat Modeling is a technique used to identify threats, attacks, vulnerabilities and countermeasures in a system.

Threat Modeling helps us to:-

- Identify security objectives
- Identify relevant threats
- Identify relevant vulnerabilities and countermeasures

Process In Threat Modeling

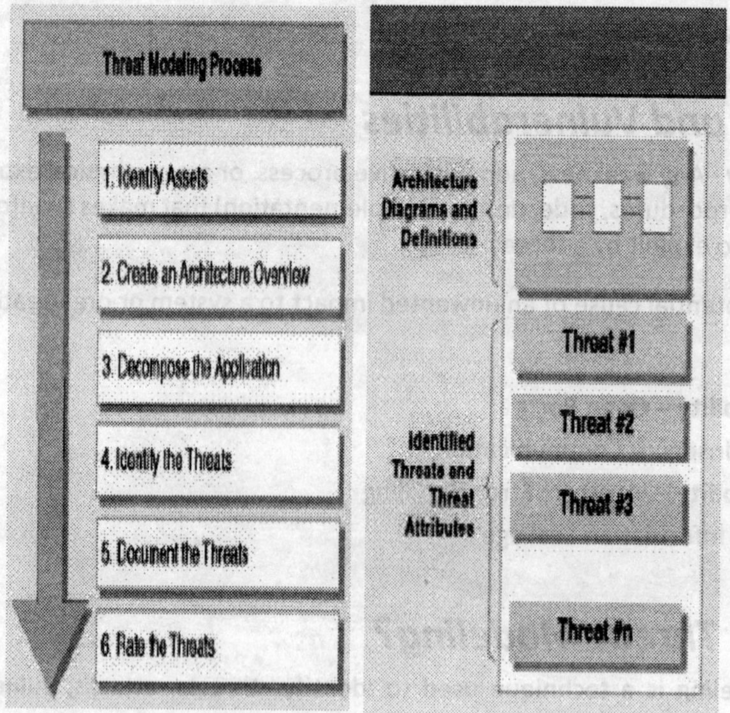

Identify Assets : Identify the assets that needs to be protected. The assets could be entry point in the system, APIs, Web Services, confidential data, etc.

Architecture Overview : Identify all the functions in the application, its architecture & physical configuration, and the technologies that are going to be used. The potential vulnerabilities in the design and the implementation of the application should be analyzed.

Decompose Application : Breakdown the application to identify the following:- Trust Boundaries , Entry Points, Exit Points, Data Flows

Identify Threats : S.T.R.I.D.E threat categorizing technique can be used on threat targets

Document Threats :

- Document the threats identified by entering the data into the Threat Modeling (title, target, type, risk, threat tree, bug number)
- Threat trees allow identify failure modes and better understanding of how a threat might become an attack.

Attack/Threat Tree :

- It is used to determine valid attack paths which are in fact vulnerabilities
- Root node is a high level goal
- Child nodes show paths to that goal

Layers of Security Testing

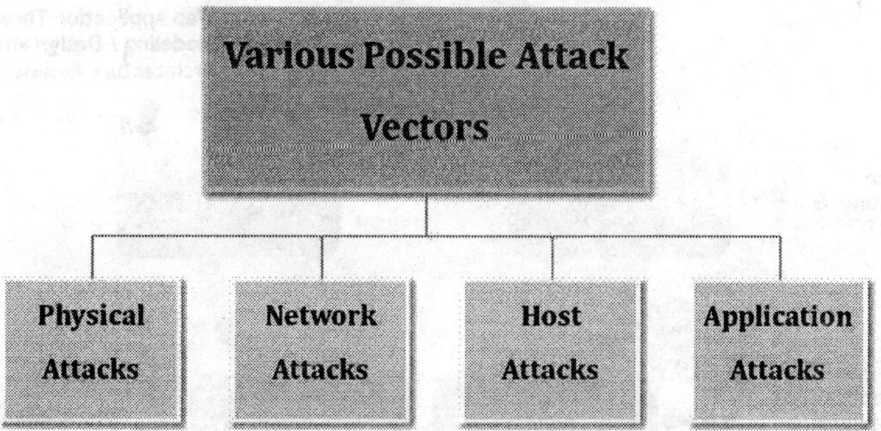

Mapping Security Testing with SDLC

Phase Activity	Standard Software Development Process Artifact	Security-specific artifact
Analysis	Use Case	Misuse Case
	Functional and non-functional requirements	
	Glossary	
Design	Object modelling	Threat Model
	Design Patterns	Data Classification
		Security Integration Design
Coding	Unit Tests	Unit Hacks
	Code Development	Countermeasure and detection development
Deployment	Build and configuration	Security Baseline
	Operational processes	Response processes
		Integration to Overall Security Architecture

Application Security Assessment - Approach

Our Approach

- In line with OWASP
- Implementing Security Throughout the SDLC
- Combination of Manual and Automated Techniques

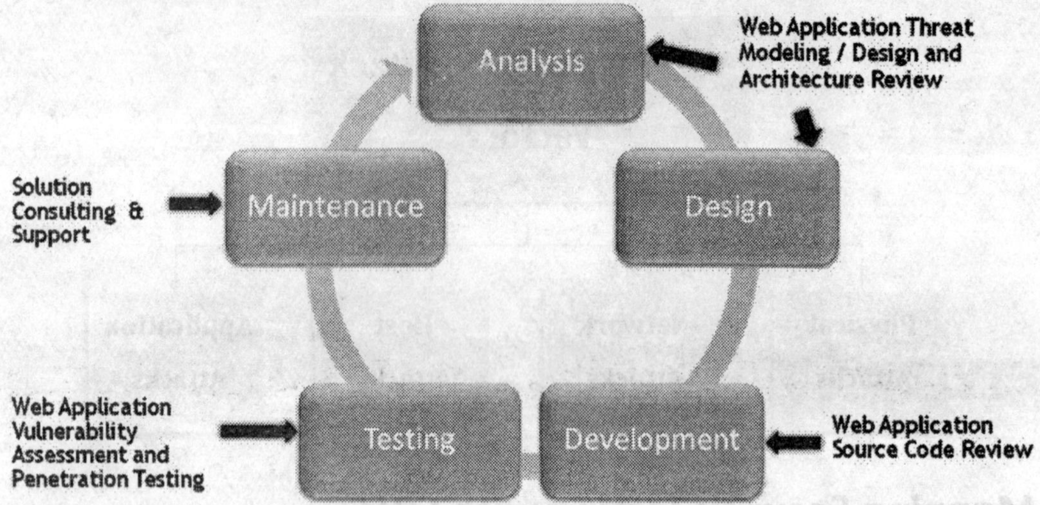

Web Application Threat Modeling / Design and Architecture Review

- Understand Business case and Functionality of the Application
- Review Policies and Standards
- Identifying Information Assests and Security Risks
- Understand Application Security needs
- Review Security Requirements

Network Vulnerability Assessment and Penetration Testing

Methodology

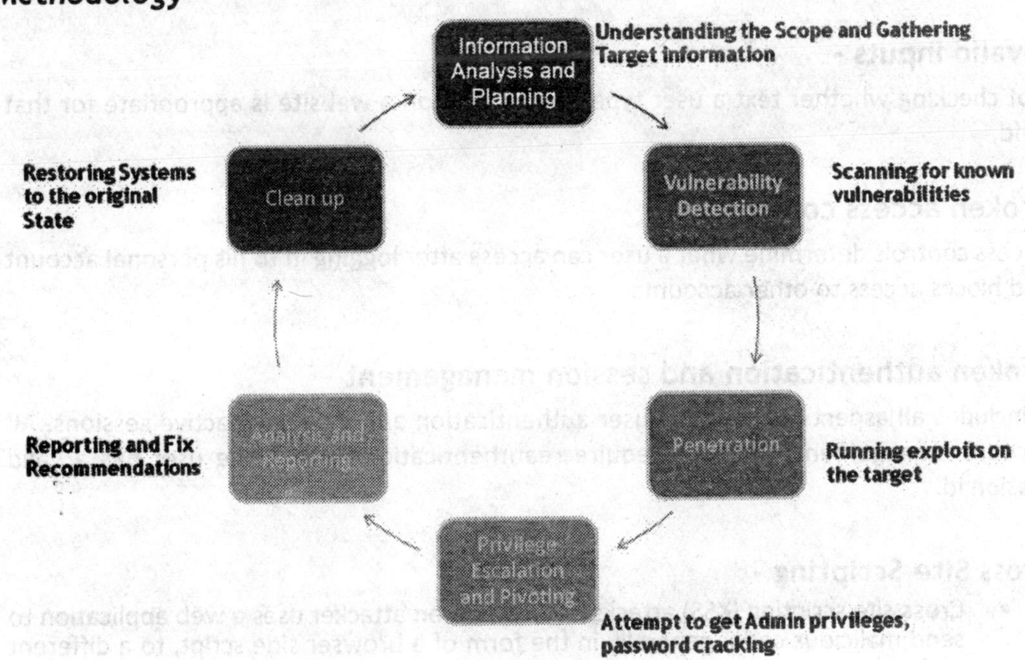

Common Web Vulnerabilities

Penetration Testing -

Identify methods of gaining access to a system by using common tools and techniques used by attackers. The tester acts like an attacker and attempts to find and exploit vulnerabilities.

Spoofing -

Technique used to gain unauthorized access to computer where intruder send message to a computer with an IP address indicating that message coming from trusted host.

Buffer Overflows -

Condition exists when a program attempts to put more data in a buffer than it can hold or when a program attempts to put data in a memory area past a buffer

Denial of Service -

Attempt to make a computer resource unavailable to its intended users.

Invalid inputs -

Not checking whether text a user types into a field on a website is appropriate for that field.

Broken access control -

Access controls determine what a user can access after logging in to his personal account and blocks access to other accounts

Broken authentication and session management -

It includes all aspects of handling user authentication and managing active sessions. All account management functions require reauthentication even if the user has a valid session id.

Cross Site Scripting -

- Cross-site scripting (XSS) attacks occur when an attacker uses a web application to send malicious code, generally in the form of a browser side script, to a different end user.

SQL Injection -

- Allow attackers to relay malicious code through a web application to another system.
- SQL injection attacks are also known as SQL insertion attacks

Cookie Issue -

- Some times users personal information is stored in cookies and if someone hack the cookie then hacker can get access to your personal information. Even corrupted cookies can be read by different domains and lead to security issues.

Session Issue -

- Session hijacking is when a hacker takes over a session between two machines. Most authentications only occur at the start of a session, this allow hacker to gain access to a machine.

Information Leakage -

Information Leakage is when a web site reveals sensitive data, such as developer comments or error messages, which may aid an attacker in exploiting the system. Sensitive information may be present within HTML comments, error messages, source code, or simply left in plain sight.

Main categories of Information Leakage:

- Comments left in code
- Verbose error messages

Comments left in code

```
<TABLE border="0" cellPadding="0" cellSpacing="0" height="59" width="591">
    <TBODY>
        <TR>
    <!--If the image files are missing, restart VADER -->
<TD bgColor="#ffffff" colSpan="5" height="17" width="587"> </TD>
        </TR>
```

Verbose Error Messages

The following was returned when placing an apostrophe into the username filed of a login page:

Verbose error message: An Error Has Occurred. Error Message:

System.Data.OleDb.OleDbException: Syntax error (missing operator) in query expression ‘username = ‘’’ and password = ‘g’’. at

System.Data.OleDb.OleDbCommand.ExecuteCommandTextErrorHandling (Int32 hr) at

System.Data.OleDb.OleDbCommand.ExecuteCommandTextForSingleResult (tagDBPARAMS dbParams, Object& execute Result) at

Cross Site Request Forgery

It is an attack that tricks the victim into loading a page that contains a malicious request. It inherits the identity and privileges of the victim to perform an undesired function on victim’s behalf, like change the victim’s e-mail address, home address, or password, or purchasing something

- The Open Web Application Security Project (OWASP) is dedicated to finding and fighting the causes of insecure software. The OWASP Foundation is a 501c3 not-for-profit charitable organization that ensures the ongoing availability and support for our work.

- Participation in OWASP is free and open to all.
- Everything here is free and open source.
- Main objectives: producing tools, standards and documentations related to Web Application Security.
- Thousands active members, 82 local chapters in the world
- Millions of hits on www.owasp.org

Web Application Penetration Testing

- What is a Web Application Penetration Testing?
  - ▶ The process involves an active analysis of the application for any weaknesses, technical flaws or vulnerabilities
- What is a vulnerability?
  - ▶ A weakness on a asset that makes a threat possible
- Our approach in writing this guide
  - ▶ Open
  - ▶ Collaborative
- Defined testing methodology
  - ▶ Consistent
  - ▶ Repeatable
  - ▶ Under quality

Testing paragraph template

- **Brief Summary**

  Describe in "natural language" what we want to test. The target of this section is non-technical people (e.g.: client executive)
- **Description of the Issue**

  Short Description of the Issue: Topic and Explanation
- **Black Box testing and example**
  - ▶ How to test for vulnerabilities:
  - ▶ Result Expected:

- **Gray Box testing and example**
  - How to test for vulnerabilities;
  - Result Expected:
- References
  - **Whitepapers**
  - **Tools**

Black Box vs. Gray Box

Black Box

✓ The penetration tester does not have any information about the structure of the application, its components and internals

Gray Box

✓ The penetration tester has partial information about the application internals. E.g.: platform vendor, sessionID generation algorithm

White box testing, defined as complete knowledge of the application internals, is beyond the scope of the Testing Guide and is covered by the OWASP Code Review Project

Information Gathering

- The first phase in security assessment is of course focused on collecting all the information about a target application.
- Using public tools it is possible to force the application to leak information by sending messages that reveal the versions and technologies used by the application
- Available techniques include:
  - Raw HTTP Connections (netcat)
  - The good ol' tools: nmap, amap, ...

- Web Spiders
- Search engines ("Google Dorking")
- SSL fingerprinting
- File extensions handling
- Backups and unreferenced files
- **Application Fingerprint**

Knowing the version and type of a running web server allows testers to determine known vulnerabilities and the appropriate exploits to use along the tests. **Netcat** is the tool of choice for this very well known technique

```
$ nc 216.48.3.18 80
HEAD / HTTP/1.0
HTTP/1.1 200 OK
Date: Mon, 16 Jun 2003 02:53:29 GMT
Server: Apache/1.3.3 (Unix)  (Red Hat/Linux)
Last-Modified: Wed, 07 Oct 1998 11:18:14 GMT
ETag: "1813-49b-361b4df6"
Accept-Ranges: bytes
Content-Length: 1179
Connection: close
Content-Type: text/html
```

Other hints can be found by sending the server a malformed request, for instance a "GET / HTTP/3.0"

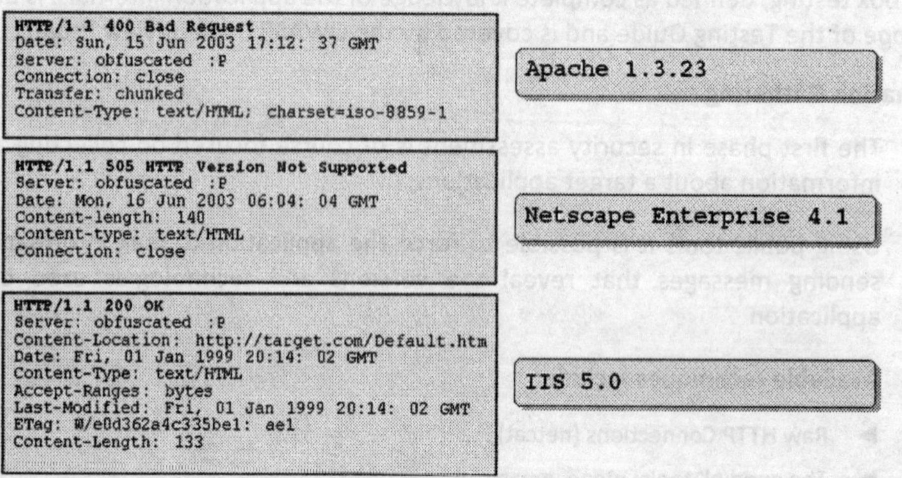

```
HTTP/1.1 400 Bad Request
Date: Sun, 15 Jun 2003 17:12: 37 GMT
Server: obfuscated :P
Connection: close
Transfer: chunked
Content-Type: text/HTML; charset=iso-8859-1
```

Apache 1.3.23

```
HTTP/1.1 505 HTTP Version Not Supported
Server: obfuscated :P
Date: Mon, 16 Jun 2003 06:04: 04 GMT
Content-length: 140
Content-type: text/HTML
Connection: close
```

Netscape Enterprise 4.1

```
HTTP/1.1 200 OK
Server: obfuscated :P
Content-Location: http://target.com/Default.htm
Date: Fri, 01 Jan 1999 20:14: 02 GMT
Content-Type: text/HTML
Accept-Ranges: bytes
Last-Modified: Fri, 01 Jan 1999 20:14: 02 GMT
ETag: W/e0d362a4c335be1: ae1
Content-Length: 133
```

IIS 5.0

The good news is that each server has a favourite way to order headers !

Here are the results for some common web servers when responding to a "HEAD / HTTP/1.0" command:

Apache 1.3.23	IIS 5.0	Netscape Enterprise 4.1	SunONE 6.1
Date	Server	Server	Server
Server	Content-Location	Date	Date
Last-Modified	Date	Content-Type	Content-Length
ETag	Content-Type	Last-Modified	Content-Type
Accept-Ranges	Accept-Ranges	Content-Length	Last-Modified
Content-Length	Last-Modified	Accept-Ranges	
Connection:	ETag	Connection	
Content-Type	Content-Length		

Security Testing Tool Selection Parameters

- Test coverage and completeness
- Accuracy or "false-positive" rate
- Ability to create custom tests
- Ease of use
- Reporting Capabilities
- Cost
- ROI

Security Testing Tools

Open source security testing tools:

- Babel Enterprise
- BFBTester - Brute Force Binary Tester
- CROSS
- Flawfinder
- Gendarme
- Metasploit
- Nessus
- Nikto
- Oedipus
- OSSTMM - Open Source Security Testing Methodology Manual
- WebScarab
- Wireshark

References:

http://www.OWASP.org

http://csrc.nist.gov/

http://en.wikipedia.org/wiki/Security_Testing

http://www.owasp.org/OWASP_Testing_Project

Security Testing Using WebScarab Tools

The interactive HTTP proxy WebScarab – Installation and basic use

This text will explain in detail how to install and use WebScarab. While the explanation will use the Windows operationg system as an example, WebScarab will also run under Linux, MacOS X or any other operating system supporting Java.

One more thing: Please don't let the number of pages of this instruction intimidate you: Everything is explained in all detail and nearly every step is illustrated by screen shots, which of course makes the number of pages grow considerably.

Java Installation

WebScarab needs Java to execute (JRE is sufficient, JDK not necessary) in any version not older than 1.4. Many computers will already have this installed; if this is the case with your computer can be checked in Control Panel / Add or Remove Programs. If you don't have Java already installed, you can download the current JRE here: http://java.sun.com/javase/downloads/index.jsp ; please choose "Java Runtime Environment (JRE) 6.0 Update n"(click "Download"); click the radiobutton "Accept License Agreement" and choose your operating system on the resulting page (e.g. "Windows Platform - J2SE(TM) Runtime Environment 6.0 Update n") and choose "Windows Offline Installation, Multilanguage"

(although the online installation should work as well).

Download WebScarab

http://sourceforge.net/projects/owasp/files/WebScarab/

You should find the WebScarab software for download somewhere on the ACSAC pages (probably close to description of this tutorial); if so, please download it from there, and proceed to the installation section. If for some reason you cannot download from the ACSAC pages, you can download WebScarab from its home page at http://www.owasp.org/index.php/Category:OWASP_WebScarab_Project or you can also go to the download page directly:

http://sourceforge.net/project/showfiles.php?group_id=64424&package_id=61823 . Please download WebScarab from this page by choosing the file webscarab-installer-20070504-1631.jar:

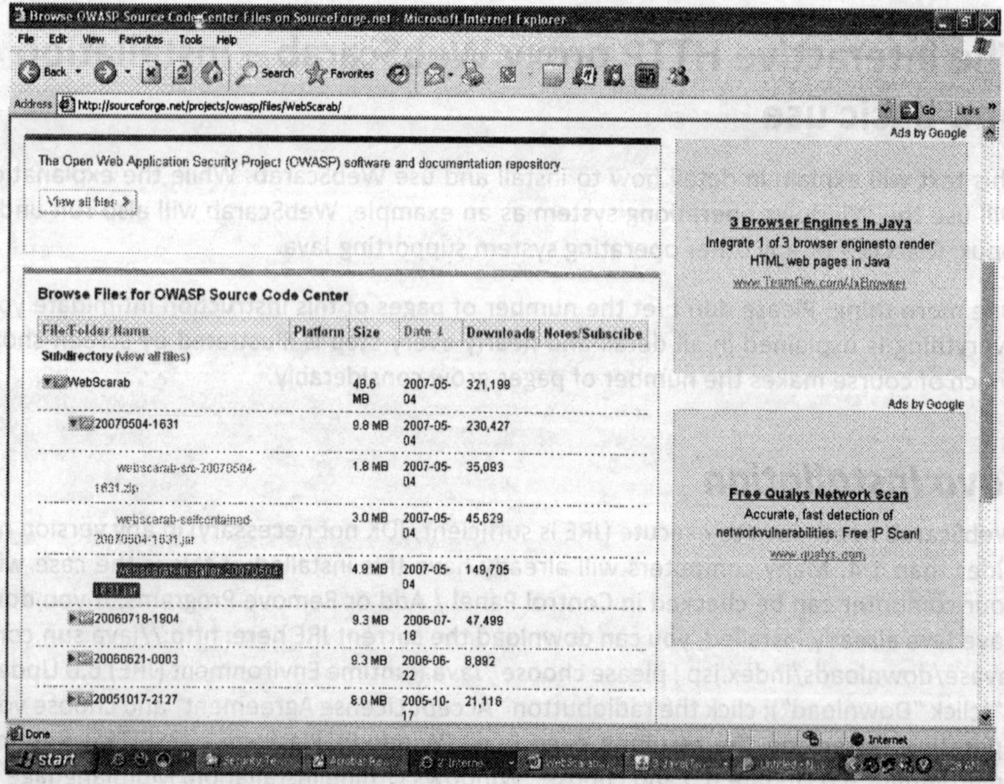

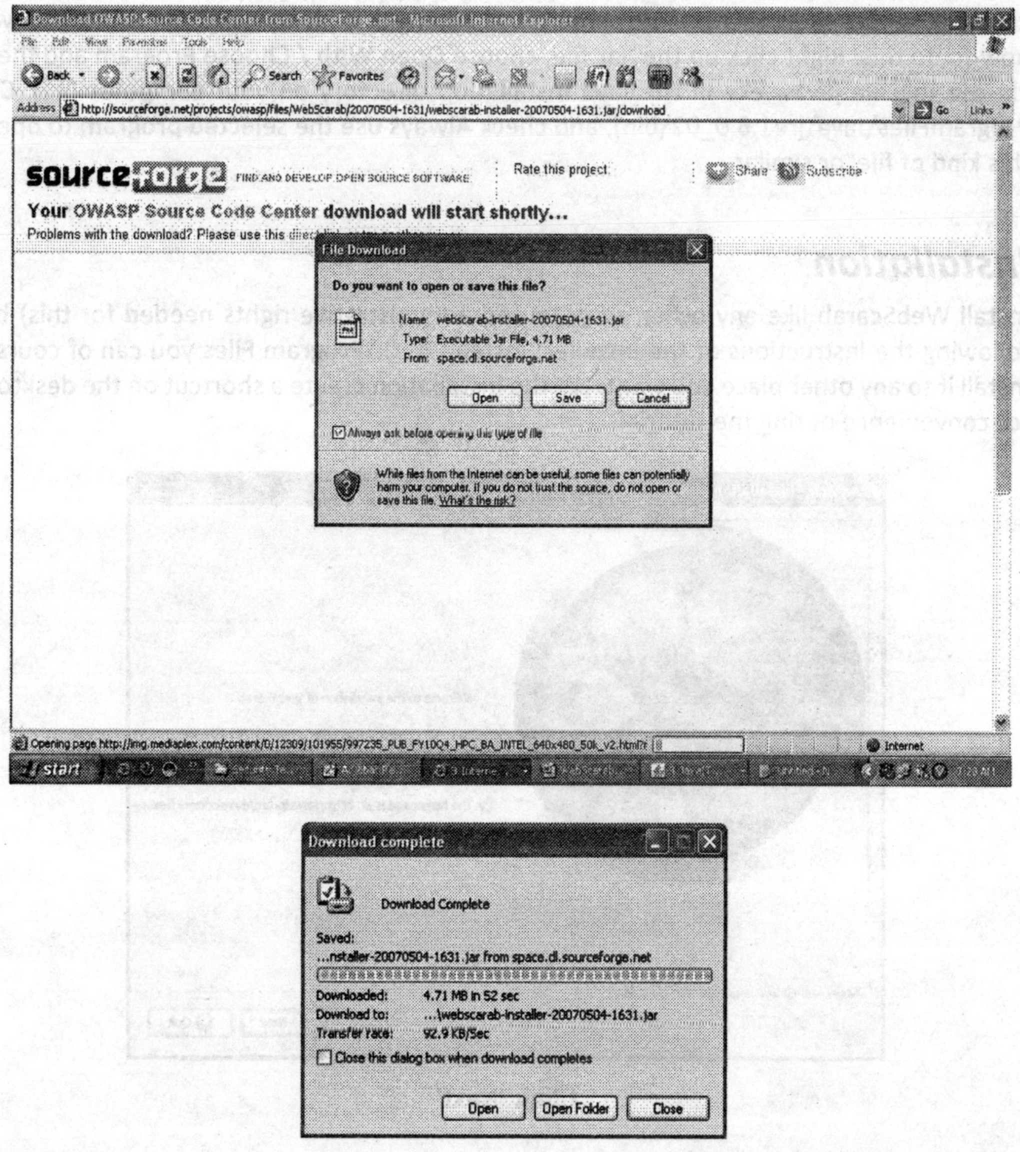

Clicking on that file name may or may not lead you to an intermediate page where you can choose one of a list of file server mirrors (or where one is chosen automatically for you).

Please save the downloaded file in a suitable place (e.g. on your desktop) and install the software by double clicking on the file; installation should start automatically.

If installation does not start automatically, it may be because your Windows does not know yet how to execute a .jar file (namely, by handing that file to Java). If so, tell Windows how to do this: Right click on the .jar file, choose Open With / Choose Program and then choose the file javaw.exe in the Java installation directory on your computer (e.g. C:\ProgramFiles\Java\jre1.6.0_02\bin), and check Always use the selected program to open this kind of file"or similar.

Installation

Install WebScarab like any other program (no administrative rights needed for this) by following the instructions of the installer; instead of C:\Program Files you can of course install it to any other place you want. Let the installation create a shortcut on the desktop for convenience during the tutorial.

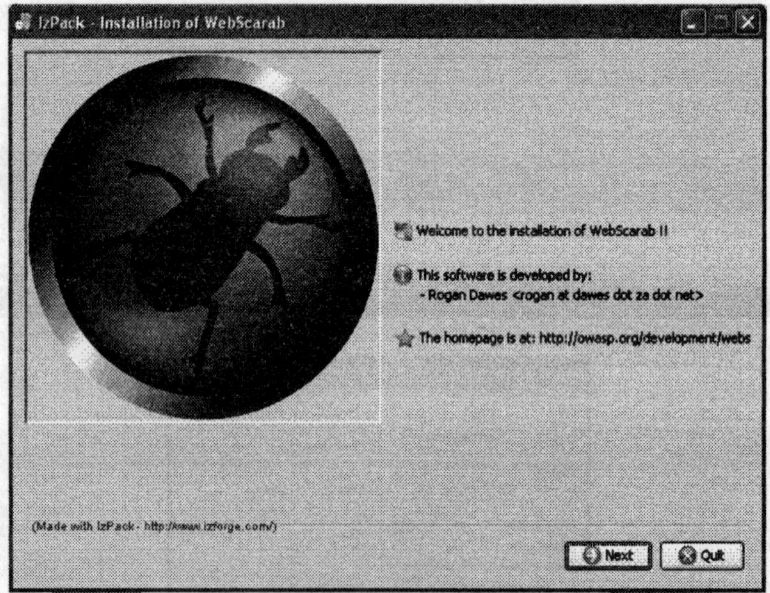

Click 'Next'

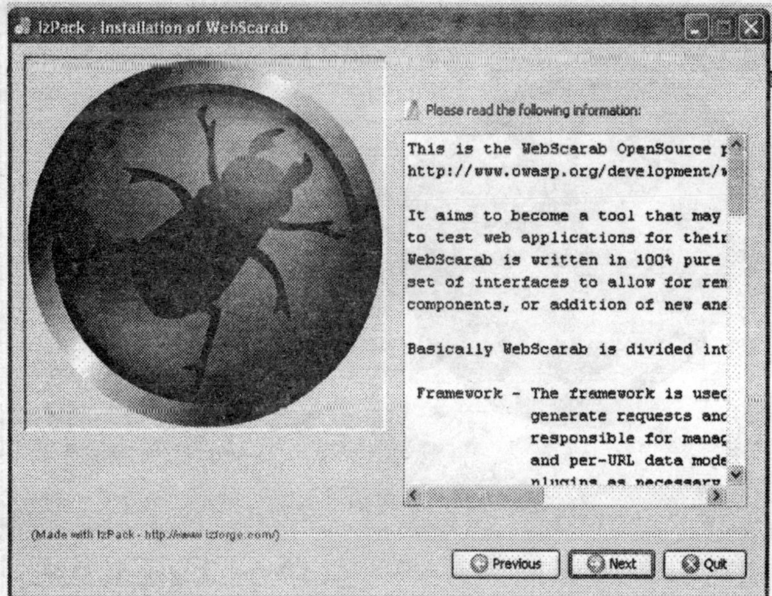
IzPack - Installation of WebScarab
Please read the following information:
This is the WebScarab OpenSource p
http://www.owasp.org/development/w
It aims to become a tool that may
to test web applications for their
WebScarab is written in 100% pure
set of interfaces to allow for rem
components, or addition of new and
Basically WebScarab is divided int
Framework - The framework is used
generate requests and
responsible for manag
and per-URL data mode
(Made with IzPack - http://www.izforge.com/)
Previous
Next
Quit

Click 'Next'

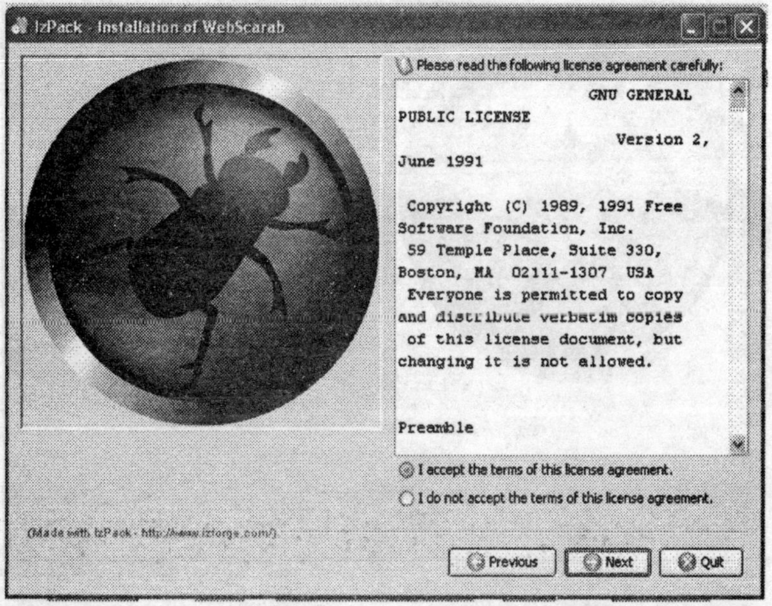
IzPack - Installation of WebScarab
Please read the following license agreement carefully:
GNU GENERAL
PUBLIC LICENSE
Version 2,
June 1991
Copyright (C) 1989, 1991 Free
Software Foundation, Inc.
59 Temple Place, Suite 330,
Boston, MA 02111-1307 USA
Everyone is permitted to copy
and distribute verbatim copies
of this license document, but
changing it is not allowed.
Preamble
I accept the terms of this license agreement.
I do not accept the terms of this license agreement.
(Made with IzPack - http://www.izforge.com/)
Previous
Next
Quit

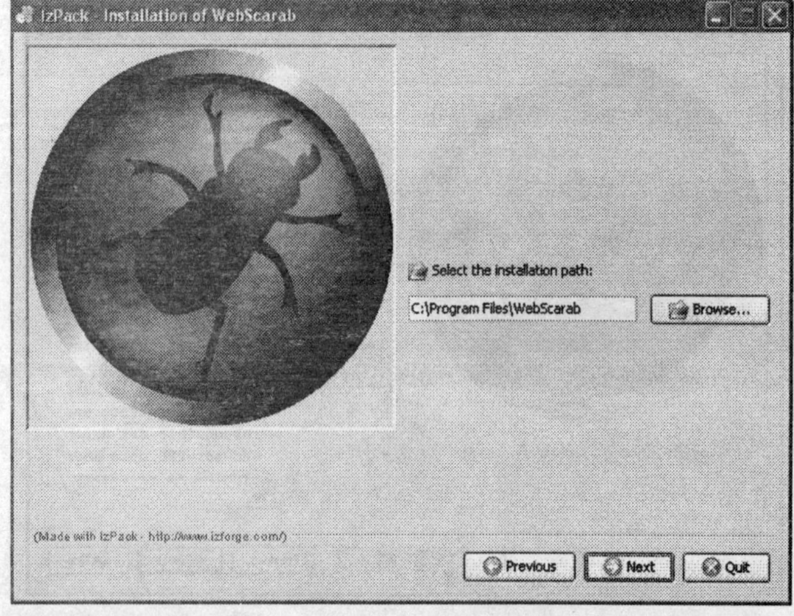
IzPack - Installation of WebScarab
Select the installation path:
C:\Program Files\WebScarab
Browse...
(Made with IzPack - http://www.izforge.com/)
Previous
Next
Quit

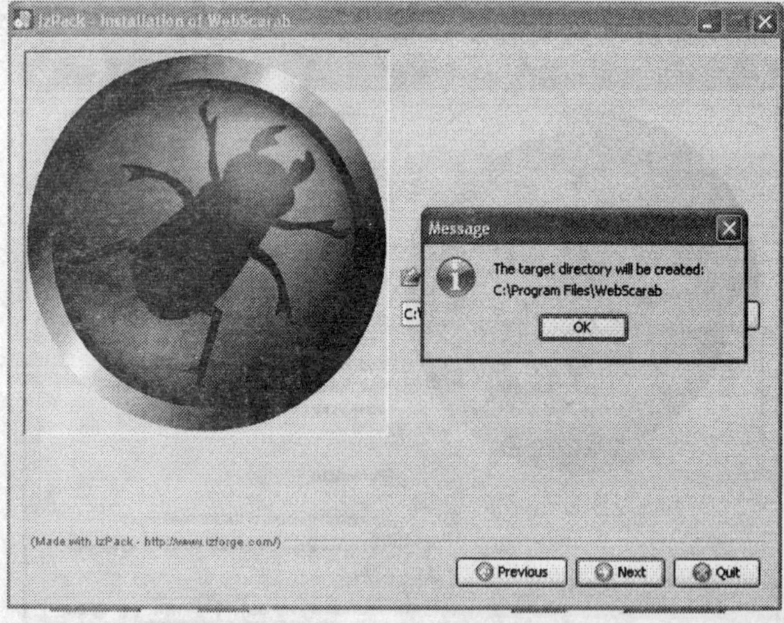
IzPack - Installation of WebScarab
Message
The target directory will be created:
C:\Program Files\WebScarab
OK
(Made with IzPack - http://www.izforge.com/)
Previous
Next
Quit

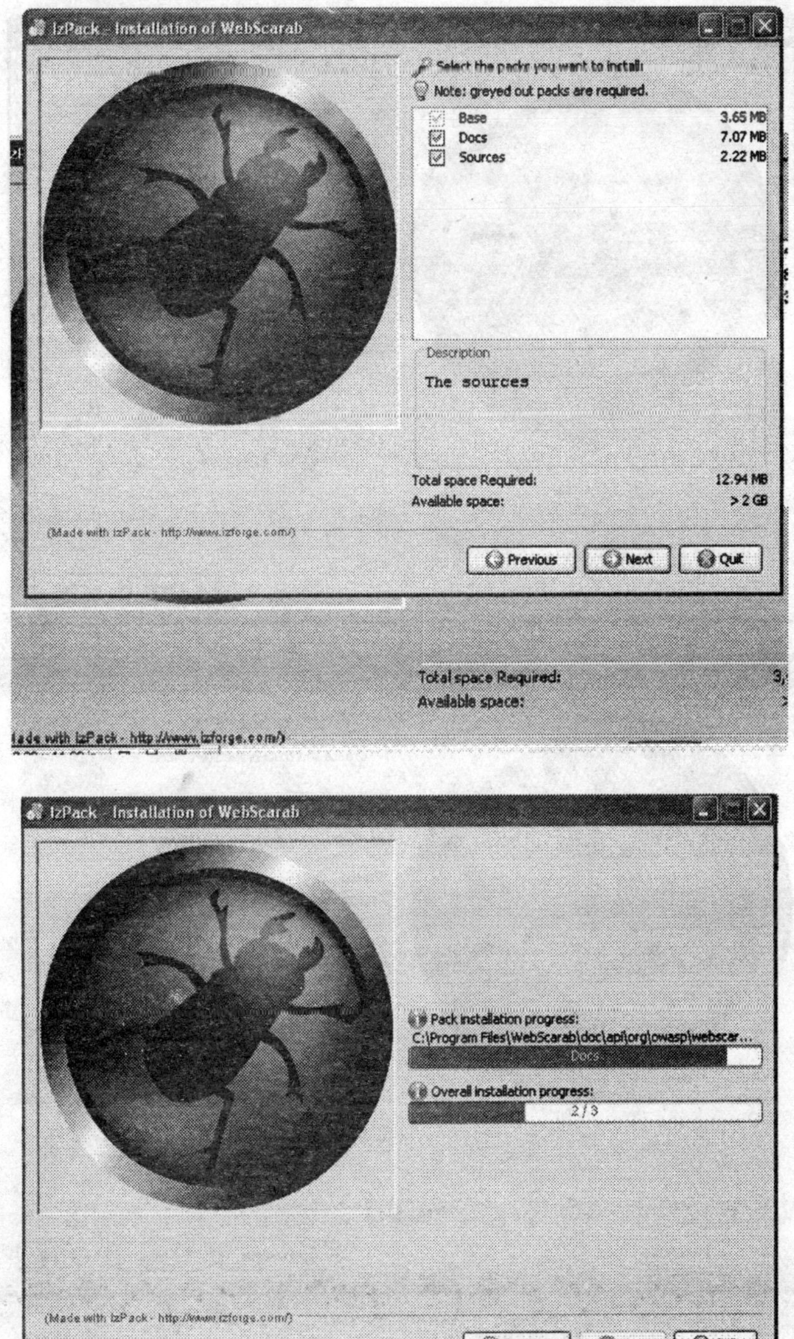
IzPack - Installation of WebScarab
Select the packs you want to install:
Note: greyed out packs are required.
Base 3.65 MB
Docs 7.07 MB
Sources 2.22 MB
Description
The sources
Total space Required: 12.94 MB
Available space: > 2 GB
(Made with IzPack - http://www.izforge.com/)
Previous
Next
Quit
Total space Required:
Available space:
IzPack - Installation of WebScarab
Pack installation progress:
C:\Program Files\WebScarab\doc\api\org\owasp\webscar...
Docs
Overall installation progress:
2 / 3
(Made with IzPack - http://www.izforge.com/)
Previous
Next
Quit

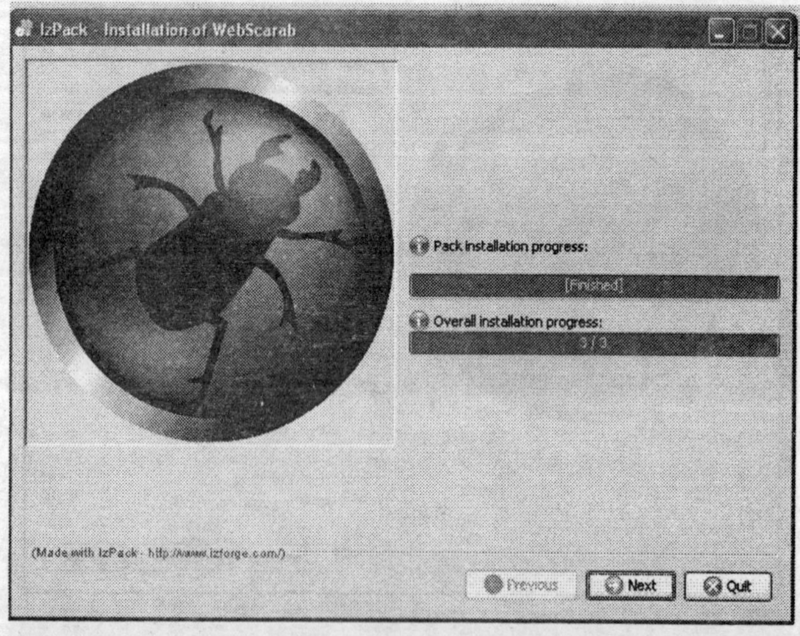
IzPack - Installation of WebScarab
Pack installation progress:
[Finished]
Overall installation progress:
3 / 3
(Made with IzPack - http://www.izforge.com/)
Previous
Next
Quit

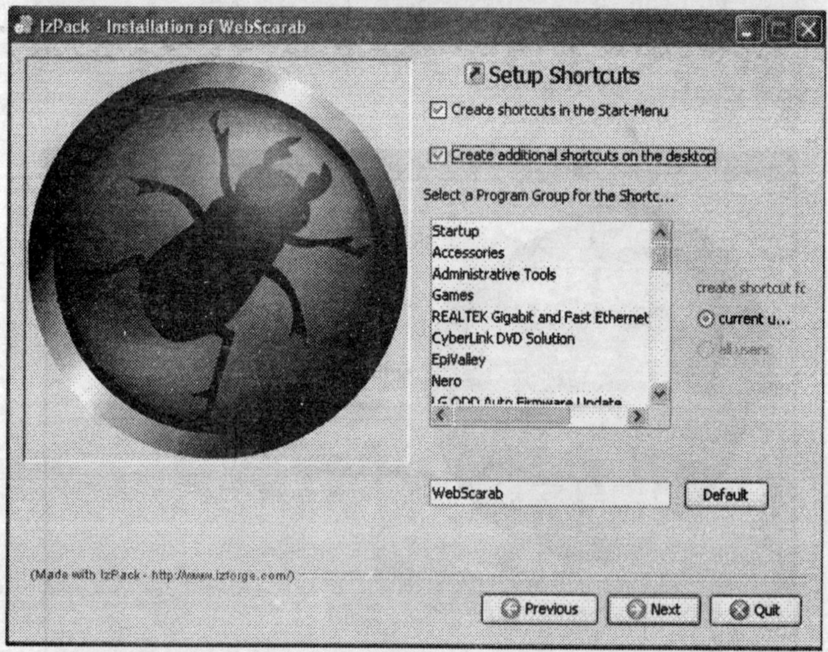
IzPack - Installation of WebScarab
Setup Shortcuts
Create shortcuts in the Start-Menu
Create additional shortcuts on the desktop
Select a Program Group for the Shortc...
Startup
Accessories
Administrative Tools
Games
REALTEK Gigabit and Fast Ethernet
CyberLink DVD Solution
EpiValley
Nero
create shortcut fc
current u...
WebScarab
Default
(Made with IzPack - http://www.izforge.com/)
Previous
Next
Quit

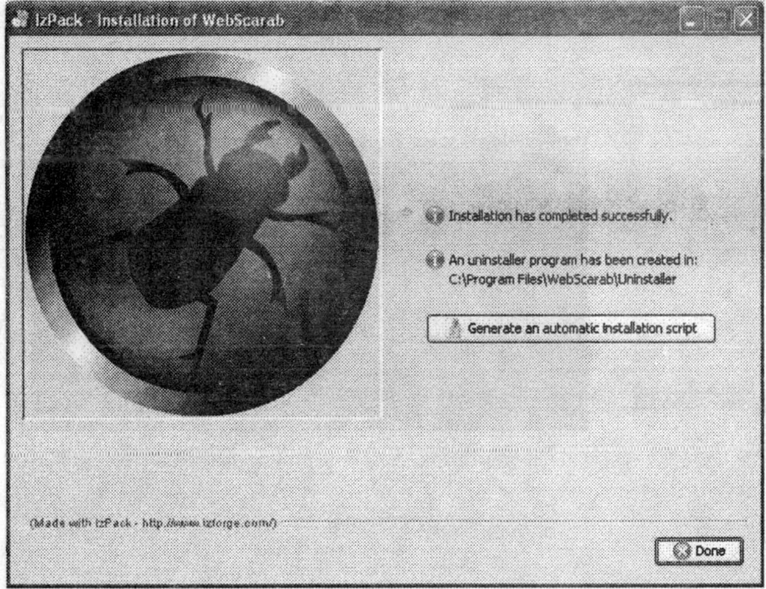

Starting WebScarab

After installation, you can start WebScarab by double clicking on the desktop shortcut just created (or by double clicking on the .jar in the directory where you installed WebScarab). If double clicking does not work, it may be because your Windows does not know yet how to execute a .jar file. The solution to that was described earlier in this text, at the end of the “Download” section. After a successful start, WebScarab should look like this:

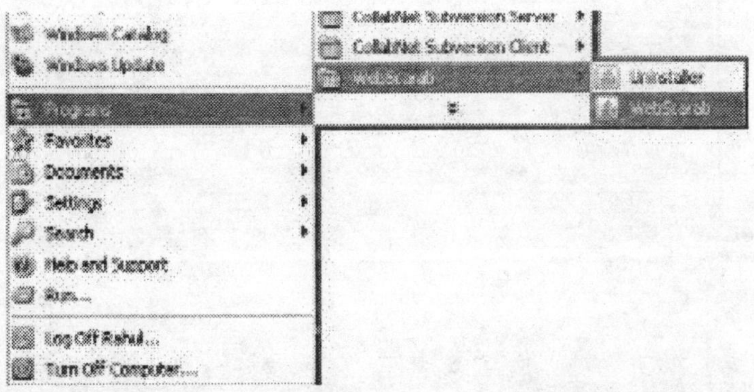

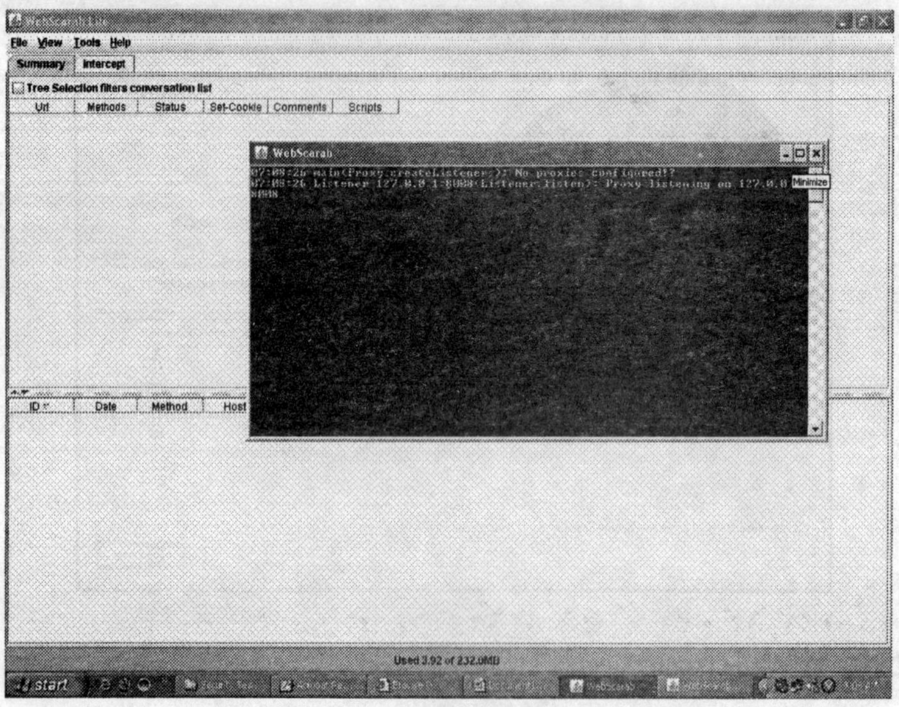

WebScarab Lite
File View Tools Help
Summary Intercept
Intercept requests :
Case Sensitive Regular Expressions ?
Methods
Include Paths matching :
Exclude paths matching :
GET
POST
HEAD
PUT
DELETE
TRACE
PROPFIND
OPTIONS
Intercept responses :
Only MIME-Types matching :
Used 4.15 of 232.0MB
start

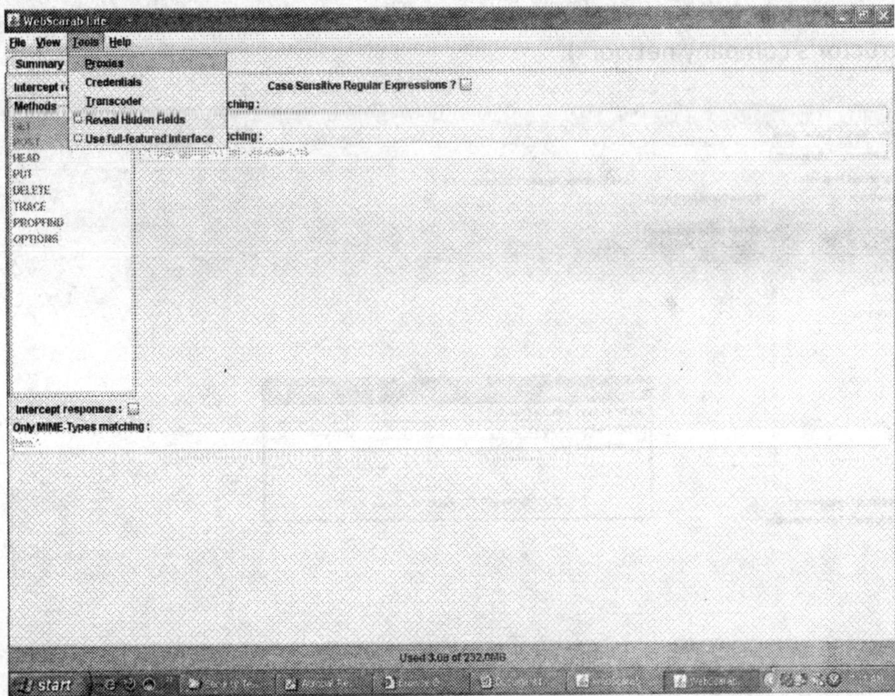

Configuration

1) Set your external proxy in WebScarab

Start WebScarab, choose Tools / Proxies, and enter the name, port, and possibly exceptions of **your site's** HTTP proxy. Which one that is depends on your current network location: It may be the proxy of your company, or your home ISP, or none at all (in the latter case, you can just skip this step). If you don't know these settings, but can see web pages alright with Internet Explorer, you can copy Internet Explorer's settings using the "Get IE settings" button (only available on Windows). If that does not work, you copy the settings manually by reading them from IE's settings, to be found in the Tools menu of Internet Explorer: Tools /Internet Options / Connection / LAN Settings / Proxy Server.

During the actual tutorial at the conference, you will be in a dedicated wireless network where no such HTTP proxy is needed; accordingly, please delete the proxy settings in WebScarab at the start of the tutorial. However, to test WebScarab at your current location, you will need to enter the HTTP proxy settings that apply to you there (the instructor cannot help you to find out these settings; please ask a colleague or your help desk if you don't know these settings).

Here is an example for the HTTP proxy settings (do not copy: these are valid only within the instructor's company network):

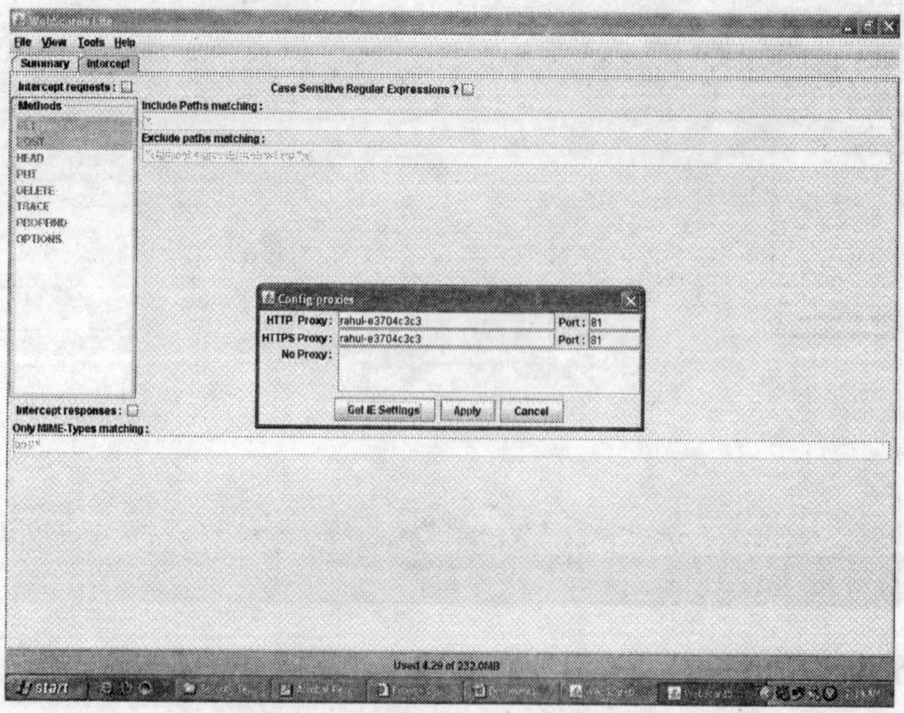

2) Set WebScarab as internal proxy in your browser

Now we need to tell the browser that, for the duration of using WebScarab, it should no longer use its usual external proxy, but instead use WebScarab as its proxy ("internal proxy").

We show how to do this for the Internet Explorer and Firefox browsers (for other browsers, such as Opera or Safari, you should easily find this out yourself):

Firefox

Please go to the following place:Tools / Options / Advanced / Network / Connection / Settings Please enter localhost as the HTTP proxy, and 8008 as the port. Make sure that localhost does not(!) appear in the "No Proxy for" list:

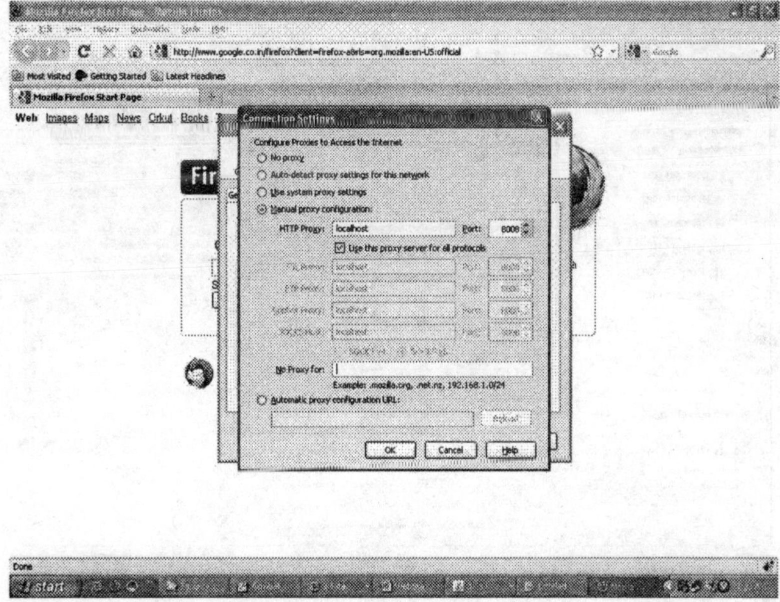

Internet Explorer

Please go to the following place: Tools / Internet Options / Connections / LAN Settings Check "Use a proxy server for your LAN" and uncheck(!) "Bypass proxy server for local Addresses":

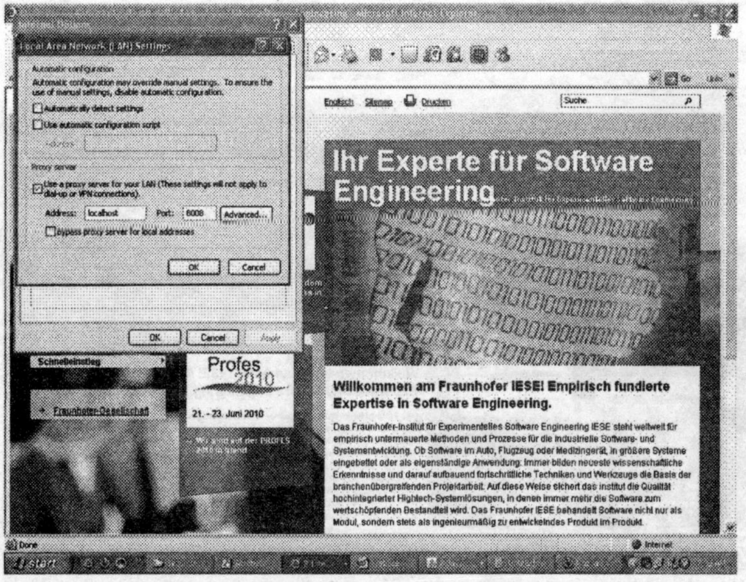

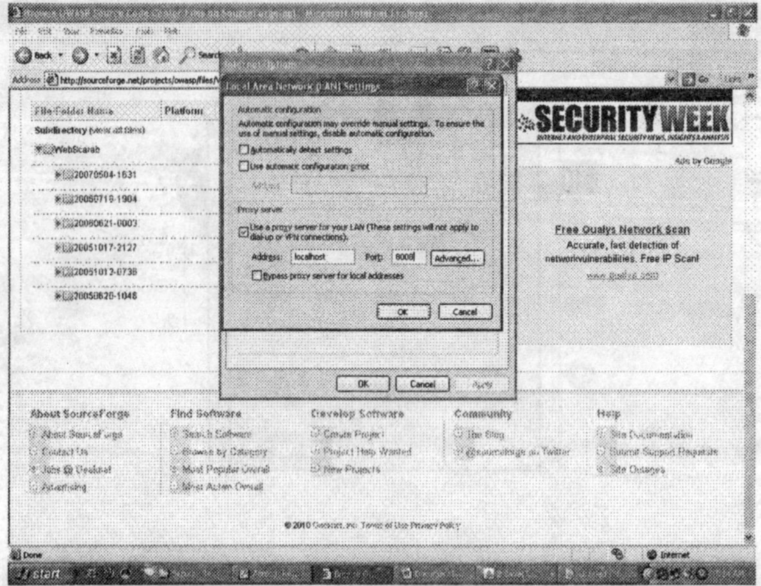

From now on, you need to have WebScarab running when you want to view a web page with your browser. It's best if you test this right now – you should be able to see a page in the browser, and the URL of that page should appear in the list of seen URLs in WebScarab's "Summary"-Tab (I've used the page www.iese.fraunhofer.de as an example in the picture below):

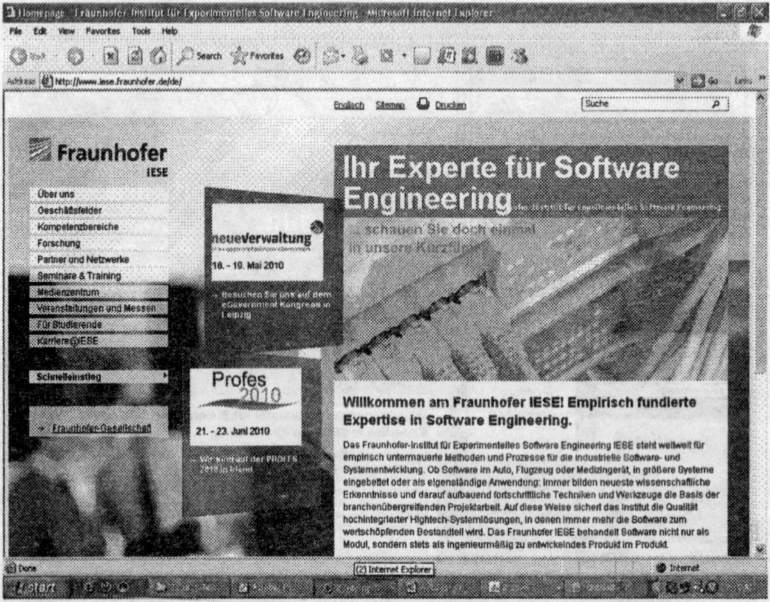

These steps are also described in the „WebScarab Tutorial "http://www.owasp.org/index.php/WebScarab_Tutorial (but note that the screen shots there show the "full" user interface, not the "lite" one we use in this tutorial).

If you use WebScarab more than a few times, it becomes cumbersome to switch the browser's proxy repeatedly between WebScarab and the external proxy of your network. To ease this, if you use the Firefox browser, you can install an add-on named SwitchProxy from https://addons.mozilla.org/firefox/125/; this lets you change the browser's proxy with a single click, once you have entered the proxies to choose from as a list.

Usage

WebScarab offers many flexible and automatable features to record, generate, edit, store and retrieve HTTP requests and responses, well as searching web sites, visualize session ids, and a few auxiliary functions for character encoding. However, most of these functions are not visible in the "lite" user interface (which is the default and which is sufficient for this tutorial); they can be accessed by choosing "Use full-featured interface" from the "Tools" menu).

For the tutorial, we need only two functions of WebScarab:

1) Intercept, change and forward HTTP requests

2) Encode/decode character strings in Base64 and URL encoding

Both are shown in the following. If you want to know what else WebScarab can do (not needed for this tutorial), switch to the full-featured interface and consult the user manual at http://dawes.za.net/rogan/webscarab/docs/ which is more detailed than what WebScarab shows under Help / Contents.

1) Intercept, change and forward HTTP requests

Please check "Intercept Request" on the "Intercept" tab:

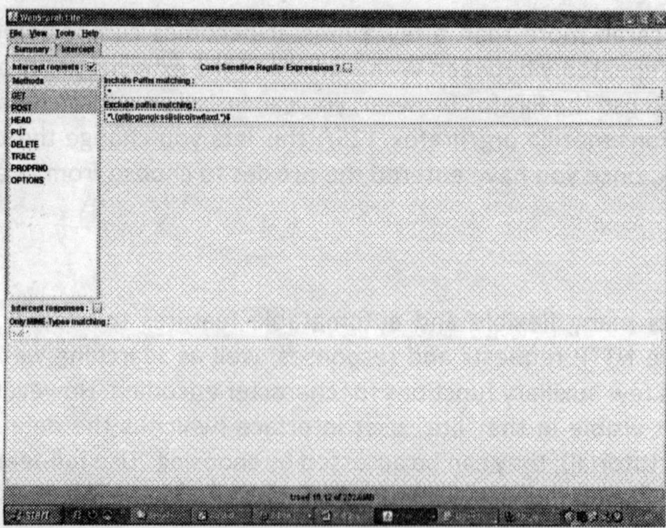

Make sure that both GET and POST are active (i.e. with a blue background) – if not, activate them by control-leftclick.

If you now want to view a web page with your browser, the HTTP request is intercepted by WebScarab and displayed for editing (the WebScarab icon in the desktop task bar is blinking):

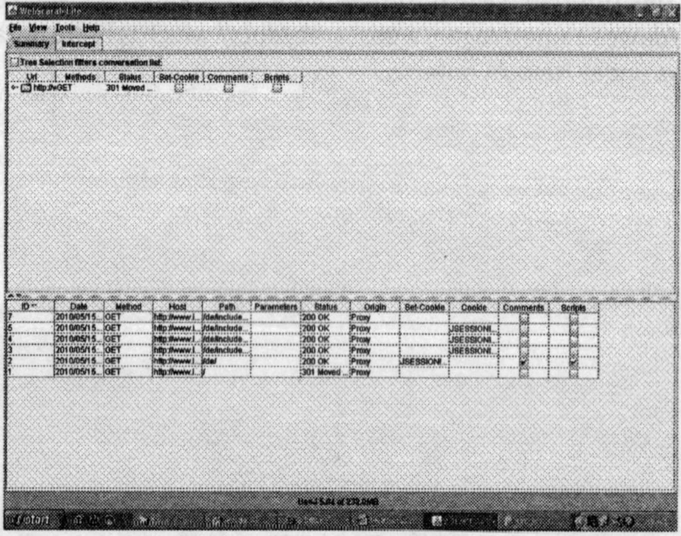

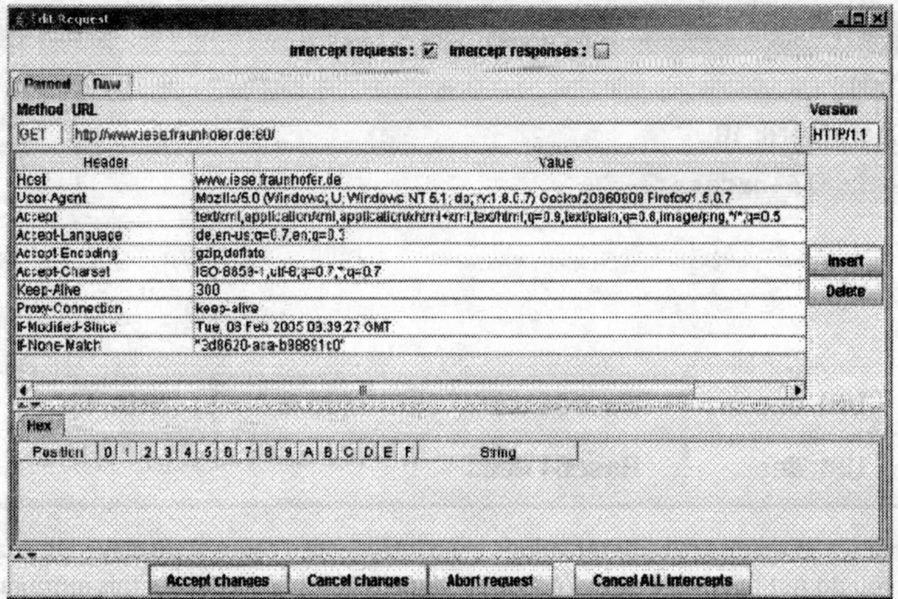

Here you see an HTTP request for http://www.iese.fraunhofer.de. The request may be shown and edited in tabular form ("Parsed", as in the picture above) or in linear textual form ("Raw"). After editing, you should uncheck "Intercept requests" (on the top, in the middle of the window), before you forward the edited request with "Accept changes" to its real destination (here: the web server at www.iese.fraunhofer.de). If you forget to uncheck, all subsequent requests will also be intercepted and offered for editing, and you have to click "Accept Changes" quite a few times until the requested page finally appears in the browser.

2) (De-)Coding of strings in base64 or URL encoding

In HTTP, parameters in request URLs are URL-encoded (the "%" encoding; replaces blanks and special characters). HTTP authorization headers, for example, are base64-encoded. Under "Tools/Transcoder" WebScarab offers a little tool to encode and decode such strings (also MD5 and SHA-1 hashes, but these are not needed for the tutorial). The strings can be pasted into and copied from the transcoder window by the usual ctrl-C / ctrl-V keys. The picture shows a string that was just URL-encoded:

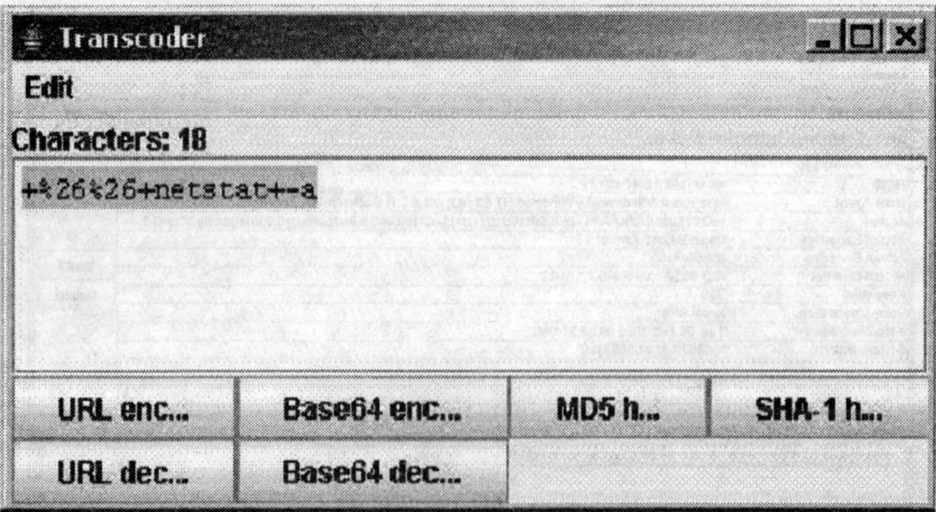

Note that when editing parameter values in an intercepted request displayed in "Parsed" mode, you do not need to encode/decode manually: WebScarab does this automatically in that mode, i.e. you see the parameter values "as they should arrive", and you can also write them in that way. (In "Raw" mode, you see parameter values URL-encoded and need to make sure that any of your changes are also URL-encoded.)

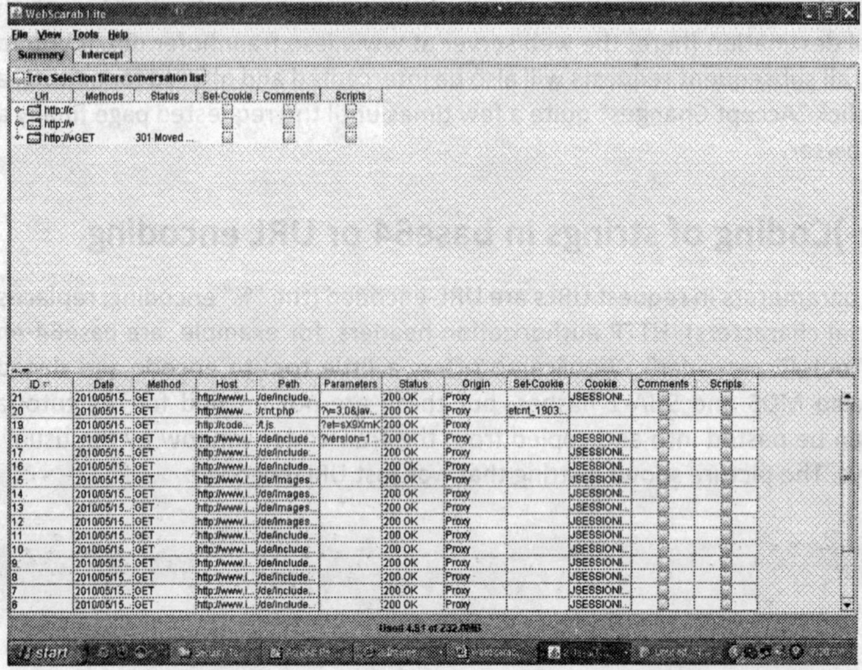

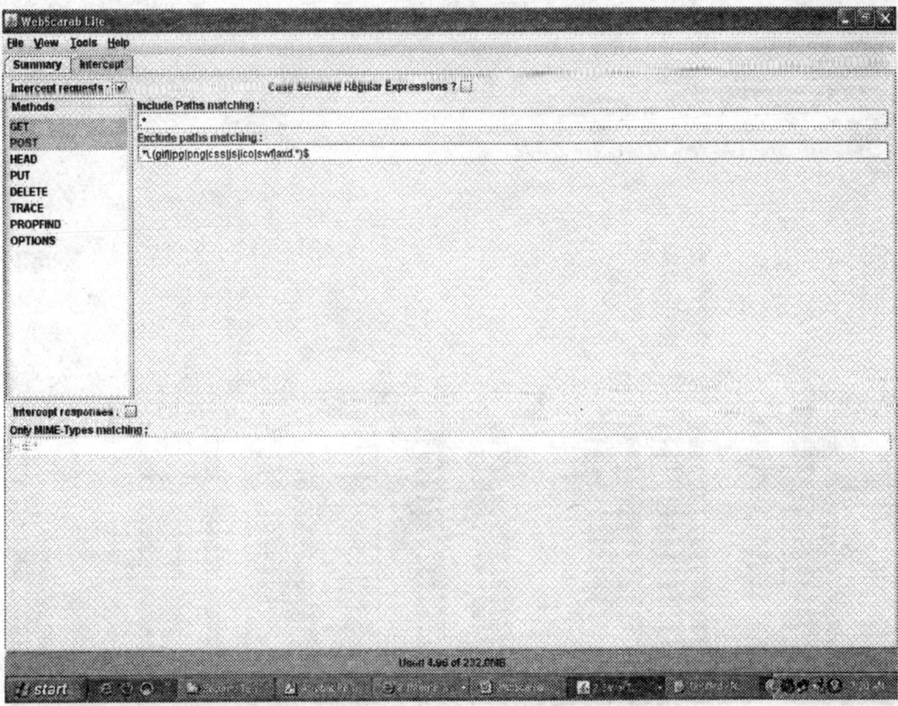

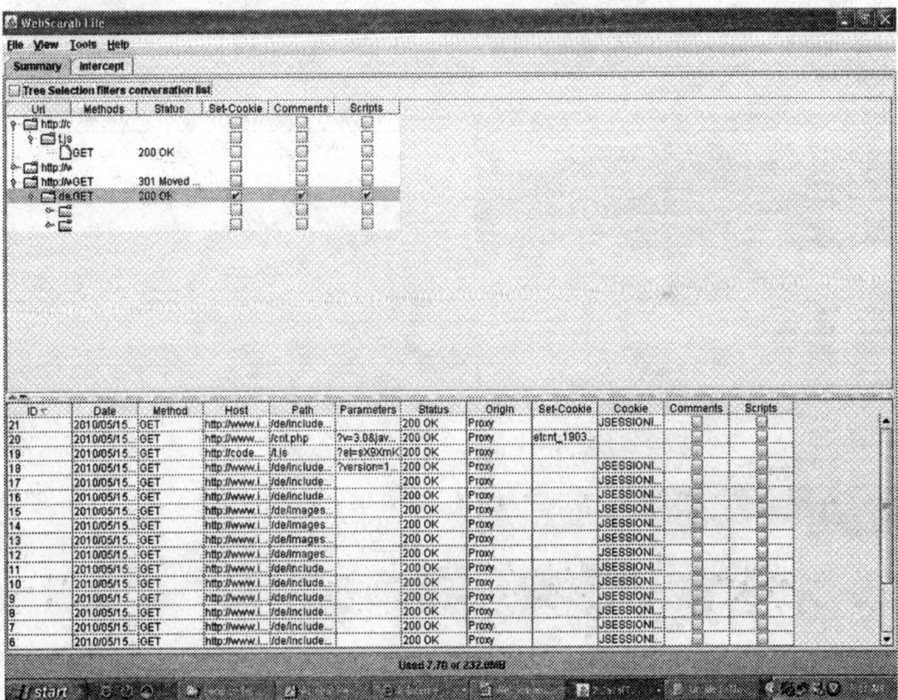

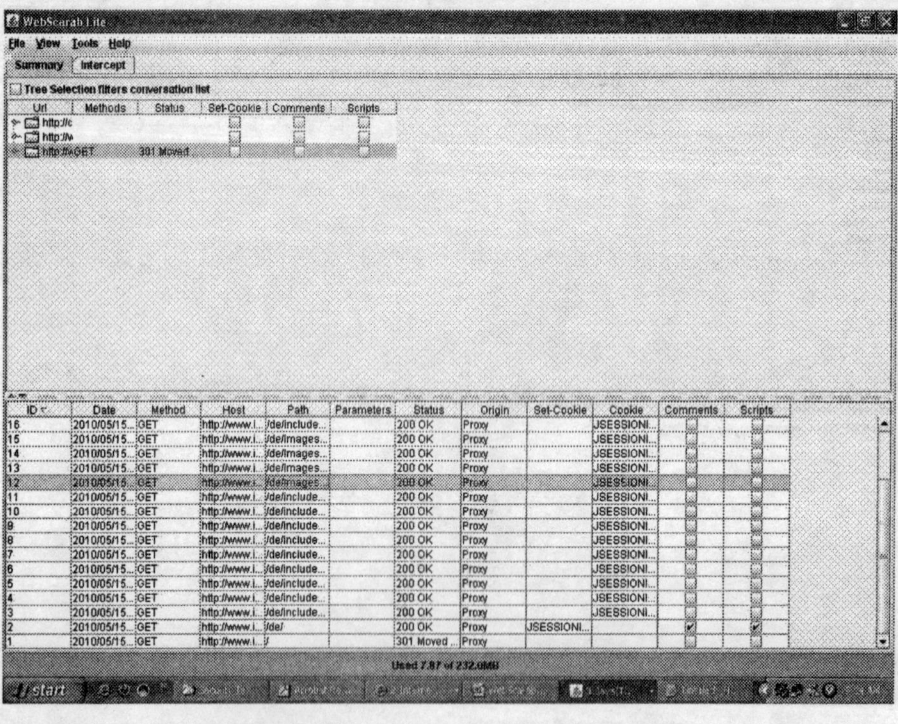
WebScarab Lite
File View Tools Help
Summary Intercept
Tree Selection filters conversation list
Url Methods Status Set-Cookie Comments Scripts
ID Date Method Host Path Parameters Status Origin Set-Cookie Cookie Comments Scripts
Used 7.87 of 232.0MB
start

WebScarab - conversation 55
Previous Next 55 - GET http://l.addthiscdn.com:80/live/t00/250lo.gif 200 OK
Parsed Raw
Method URL Version
GET HTTP/1.1
Header Value
Accept */*
Referer http://s7.addthis.com/static/r07/sh16.html
Accept-Lan... en-us
Accept-Enc... gzip, deflate
User-Agent Mozilla/4.0 (compatible; MSIE 6.0; Windows NT 5.1; SV1; .NET CLR 1.1.4...
Host l.addthiscdn.com
Proxy-Conn... Keep-Alive
Parsed Raw
Version Status Message
HTTP/1.1 200 OK
Header Value
Server Apache
Last-Modifi... Thu, 22 Apr 2010 10:57:48 GMT
ETag "b991b4-2b-484d12e614300"
Accept-Ran... bytes
Content-le... 43
Content-Ty... image/gif
Expires Sat, 15 May 2010 01:58:18 GMT
Cache-Con... max-age=0, no-cache, no-store
Pragma no-cache
Date Sat, 15 May 2010 01:58:18 GMT
Connection close
start

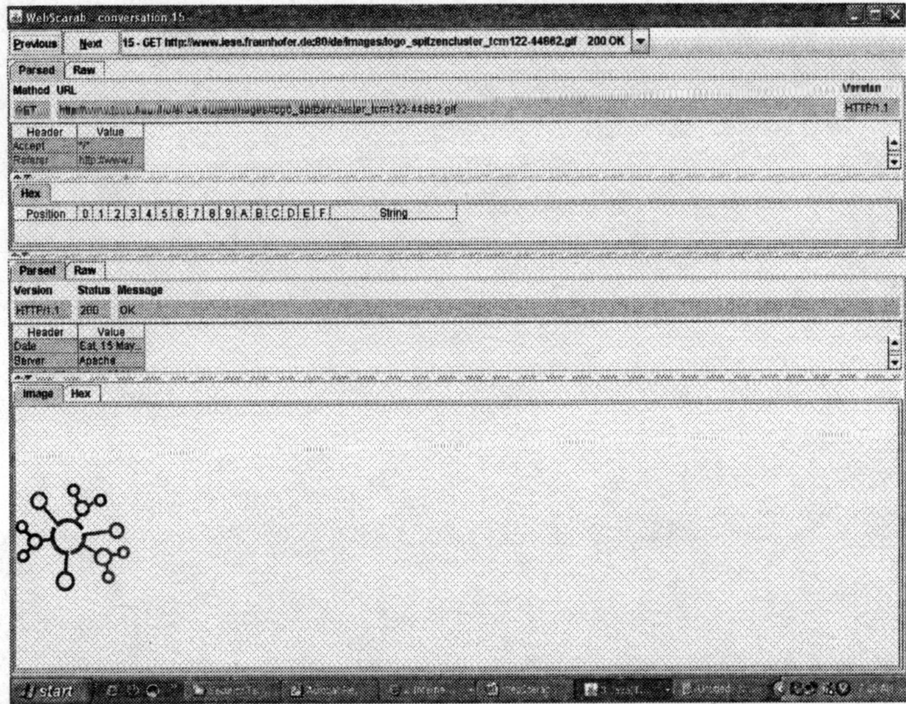

Reference:

Dr. Holger Peine, Fraunhofer IESE

Holger.Peine@iese.fraunhofer.de

Section
13
SOA Testing

Evolution of Software Architecture:

- ♦ Stand-alone
- ♦ Client Server
- ♦ Distributed "n-tier"
- ♦ Web Services
- ♦ Service Oriented

➢ Stand-alone Architecture:

✓ Tightly coupled collections of data and function residing on a single machine.

✓ Reuse, redesign, and replacement of component parts can be very difficult.

➢ Client Server Architecture:

✓ Tightly coupled collections of data and functions reside on a single machine (server).

✓ Reuse, redesign, and replacement of component parts can be very difficult.

✓ Unique in that the multiple users access the application from remote machines (clients).

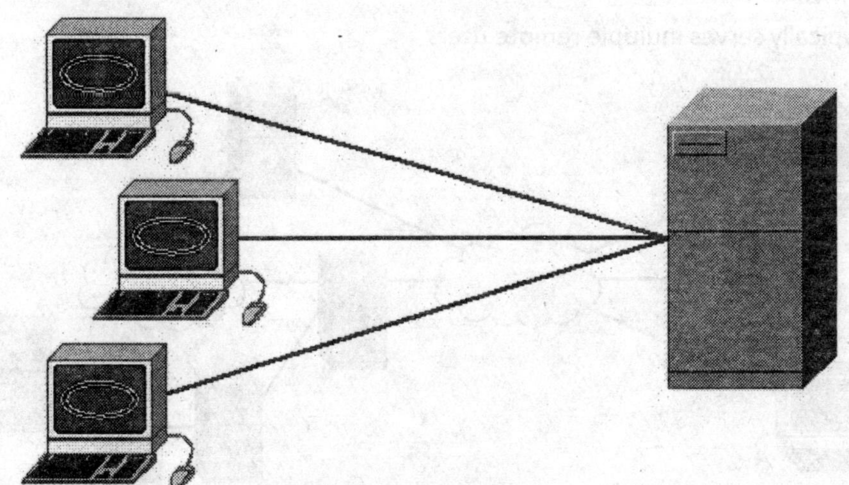

➢ Distributed "n-tier" Architecture:

✓ Loosely or tightly coupled collections of data and function residing on multiple machines.

✓ Reuse, redesign, and replacement of component parts may or may not be very difficult.

✓ Typically serves multiple remote users.

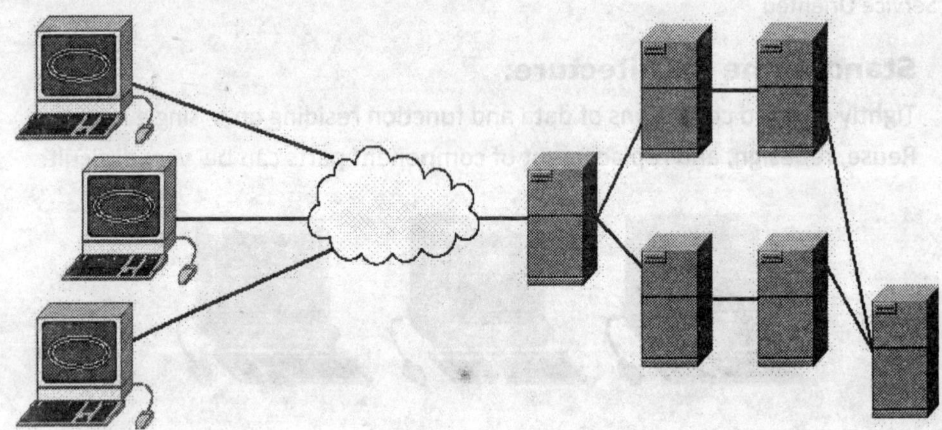

➢ Web Services Architecture:

✓ Loosely or tightly coupled collections of data and function residing on multiple machines.

✓ One or more collection of data and/or function built and hosted externally.

✓ Reuse, redesign, and replacement of component parts may or may not be very difficult.

✓ Typically serves multiple remote users.

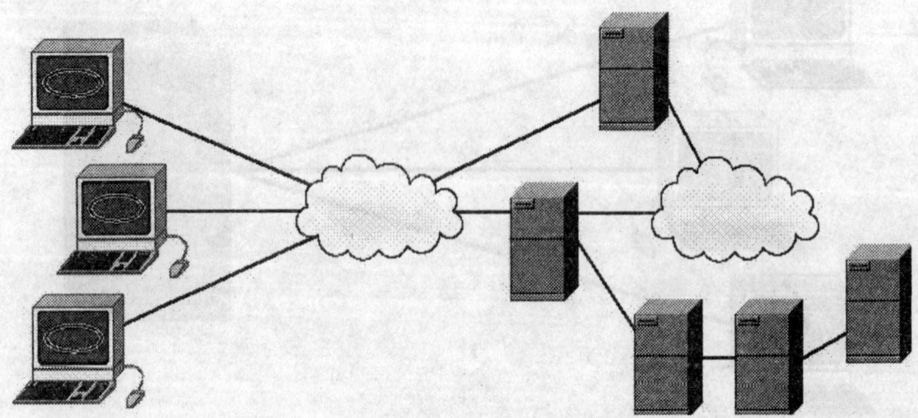

➢ Service Oriented Architecture:

✓ Loosely coupled collections of data and function residing on multiple internal or external machines.

✓ Often, collections communicate through a single interface.

✓ Reuse, redesign, and replacement of component parts should not be very difficult.

✓ Typically serves multiple remote users.

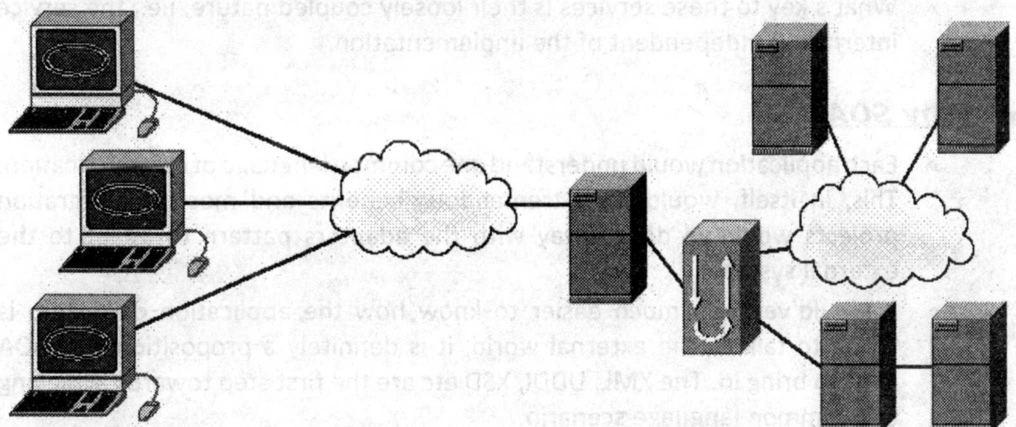

■ What is SOA?

» A service-oriented architecture is essentially a collection of services. These services communicate with each other. The communication can involve either simple data passing or it could involve two or more services coordinating some activity. Some means of connecting services to each other is needed.

» *Service-oriented architecture (SOA) is an evolution of distributed computing based on the request/reply design paradigm for synchronous and asynchronous applications.*

» *Application's business logic or individual functions are modularized and presented as services for consumer/client applications.*

» A ***Service*** is a function that is well-defined, self-contained, and does not depend on the context or state of other services.

» Services are what you connect together using Web Services.

» A ***Service*** is the endpoint of a connection. Also, a service has some type of underlying computer system that supports the connection offered. The combination of services - internal and external to an organization - makes a service-oriented architecture.

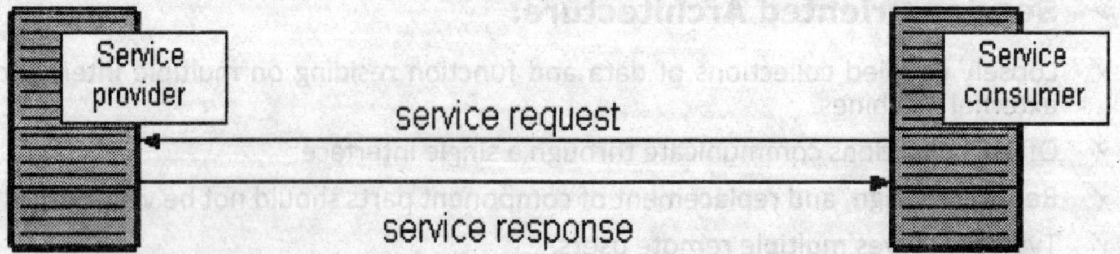

» What's key to these services is their loosely coupled nature; i.e., the service interface is independent of the implementation.

- ***Why SOA?***

» Each application would understand one common language of communication. This, in itself, would have tremendous benefits and most of integration projects would've done away with the adapters pattern to adapt to the external systems.

» It would've been much easier to know how the application or system is trying to talk to the external world, it is definitely a proposition that SOA aims to bring in. The XML, UDDI, XSD etc are the first step towards achieving this common language scenario.

» For any business, SOA translates the business benefits into several ways. It can mean effectively integrating diverse systems for developing highly scalable dynamic collaborative applications by connecting to various systems on the fly.

Conclusion of SOA:

» - Thus if we look at it, SOA is an architecture, It is more than any particular set of technologies, such as web services; it transcends them, and in a perfect world, it is totally independent of them.

» - SOA is an application architecture within which all functions are defined as independent services with well defined invokable interfaces that can be called in defined sequence to form business process.

» - Adapting to the SOA and exposing the systems an processes in an enterprise in a service-oriented way helps develop business agility and adaptability.

Benefits of SOA

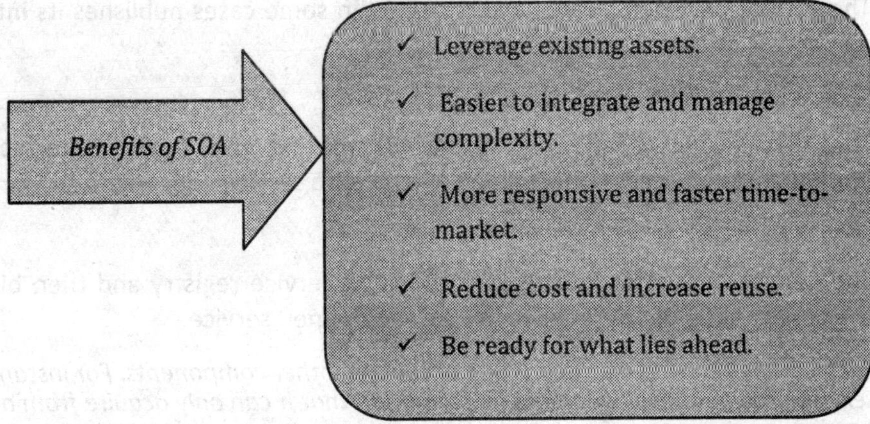

SOA Components – Basic Components Basic Components of SOA:

- ✓ ***Service Provider***
- ✓ ***Service Consumer***
- ✓ ***Service Registry***

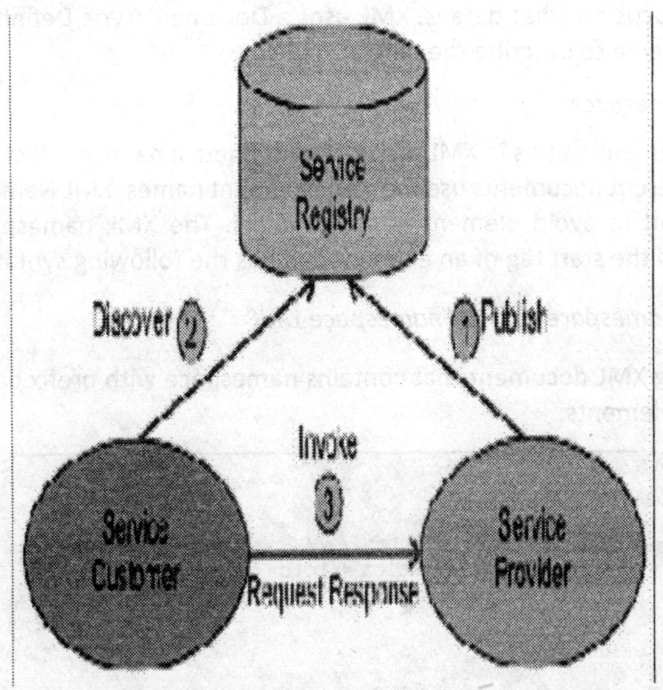

✓ *Service Provider:*

The service provider creates a service and in some cases publishes its interface and access information to a service registry.

✓ *Service Consumer:*

The service registry is responsible for making the service interface and implementation access information available to service consumers.

✓ *Service Registry:*

The service consumer locates entries in the service registry and then binds to the service provider in order to invoke the defined service.

✓ *Each component can also act as one of the two other components. For instance, if a service provider needs additional information that it can only acquire from another service, it acts as a service consumer.*

SOA Components – XML

Following are the key components of SOA described bellow:

XML:

XML stands for Extensible Markup Language. XML is designed to describe data and to focus on what data is. XML uses a Document Type Definition (DTD) or an XML Schema to describe the data.

✓ ***XML Namespace:***

Since element names in XML are not predefined, a name conflict will occur when two different documents use the same element names. XML Namespaces provide a method to avoid element name conflicts. The XML namespace attribute is placed in the start tag of an element and has the following syntax:

Xmlns: *namespace-prefix="namespace URI"*

Example showing XML document that contains namespace with prefix both forparent as well as its child elements:

```
<h: table xmlns:h="http://www.w3.org/TR/html4/">
  <h:tr>      <h:td>tables </h:td>
              <h:td>stationary</h:td>
  </h:tr>
  </h:table>
```

When a namespace is defined in the start tag of an element, all child elements with the same prefix are associated with the same namespace. Defining a default namespace for an element saves us from using prefixes in all the child elements.

It has the following syntax: xmlns="*namespaceURI*"

Example showing XML document that contains only namespace both for parent as well as its child elements:

```
<table xmlns="http://www.w3.org/TR/html4/">
    <tr> <td>tables</td>
        <td>stationary</td>
    </tr>
</table>
```

SOA Testing Life Cycle:

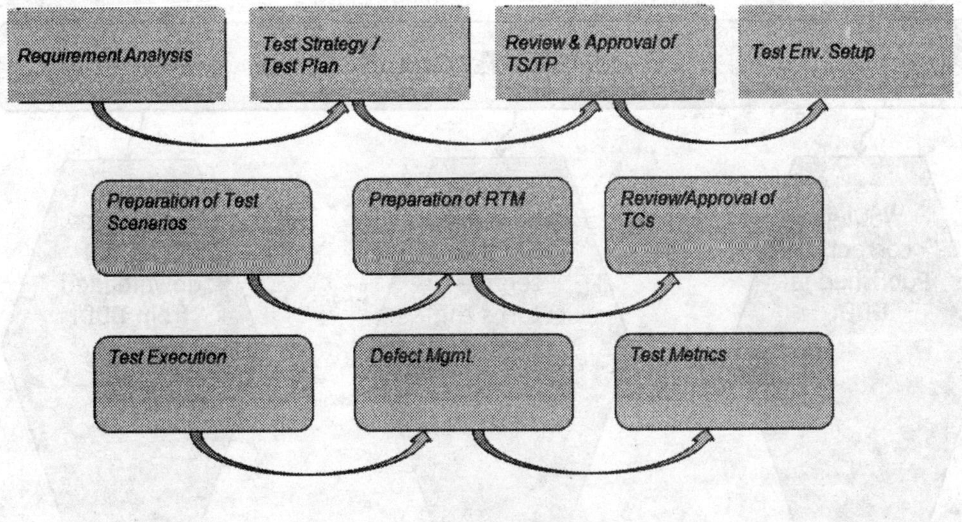

Different Types of SOA Testing

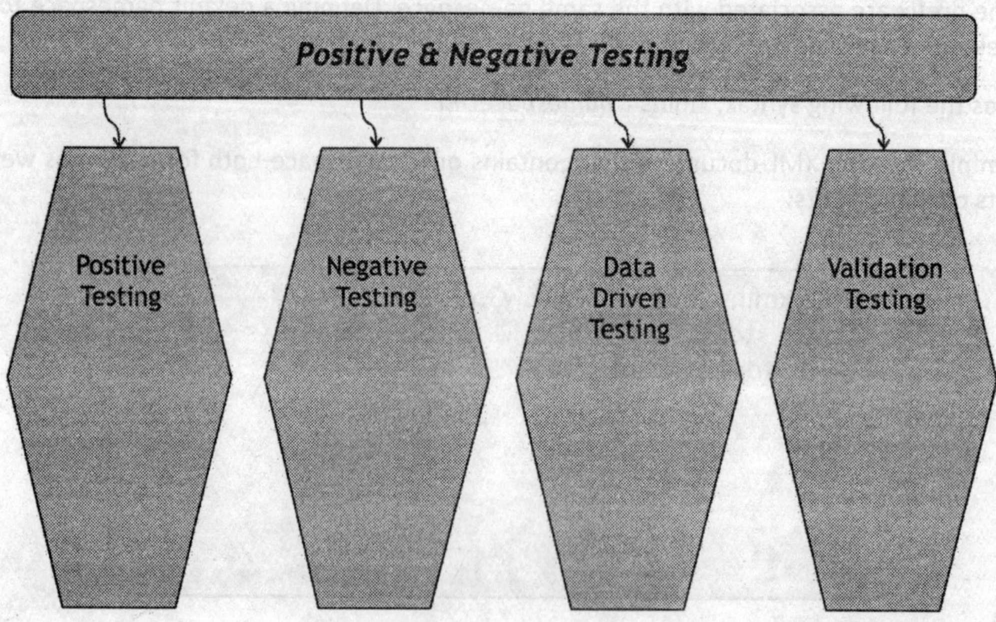

Different Types of SOA Testing

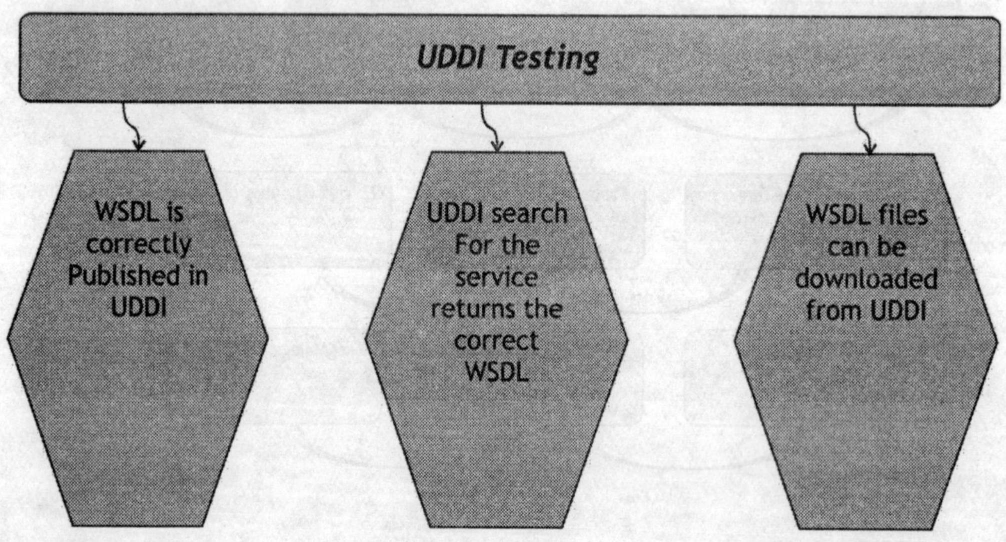

Different Types of SOA Testing

Test at Service Registry:

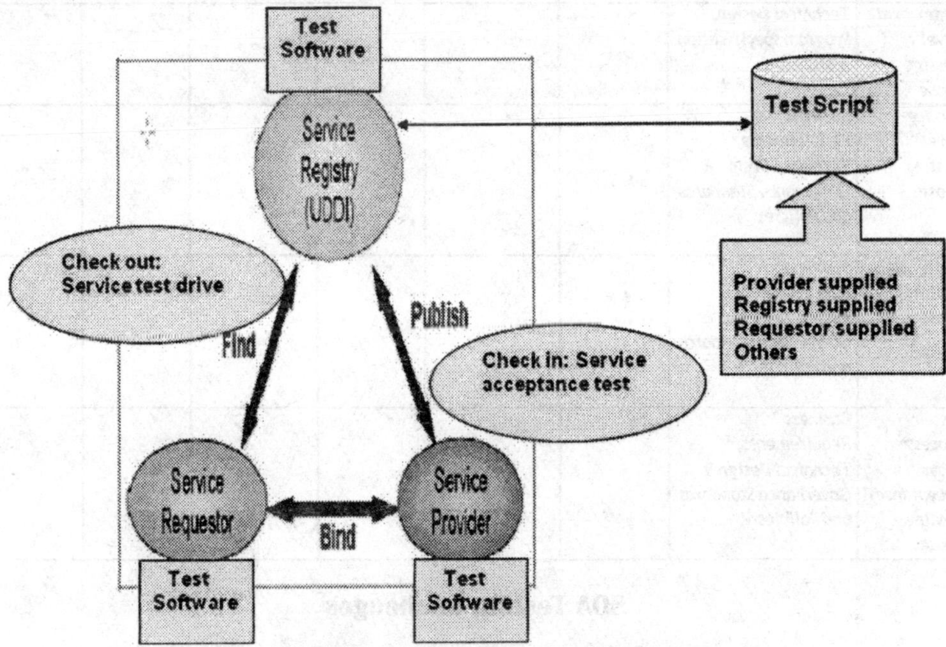

SOA Functional Testing Phases

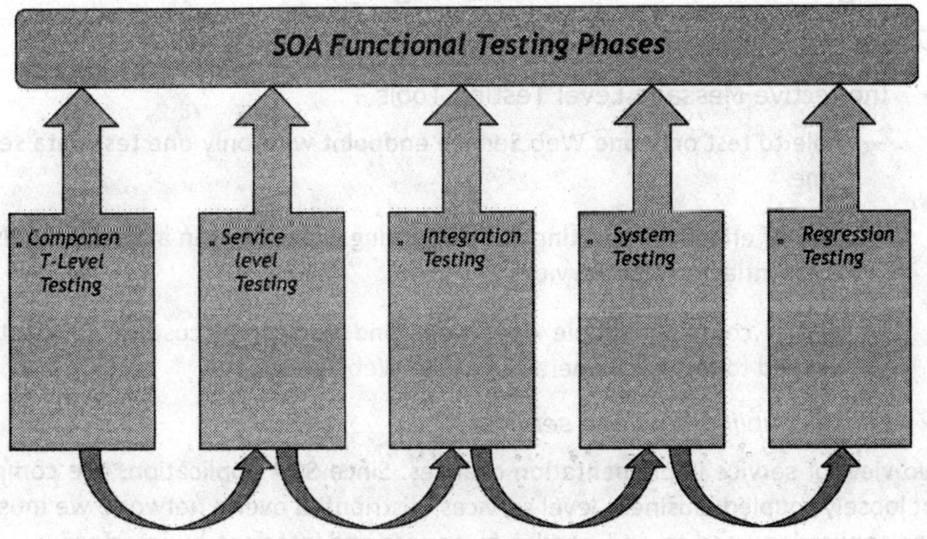

SOA Functional Testing Phases

TEST PHASES	Guiding Documents	Functional	Performance	Interoperability	Backward Compatibility	Compliance	Security
Component-Level Testing Phase	*Technical Design, Program specification & Standards*	✓				✓	✓
Service-Level Testing Phase	*Business Requirements, Technical Design & Governance Standards and Policies*	✓	✓			✓	✓
Integration Testing Phase	*Business Requirements, Technical Design & Governance Standards and Policies*	✓		✓	✓		✓
System/ Process (User Acceptance) Testing Phase	*Business Requirements, Technical Design & Governance Standards and Policies*	✓	✓	✓	✓	✓	✓

SOA Testing Challenges

Challenges involved in SOA Testing:

- *No GUI :* Integration-centric, rather than screen-centric.
- Ineffective Message Level Testing Tools -
  - Able to test only one Web Service endpoint with only one test data set at a time
  - Lack of effective reporting and debugging capabilities in available tools that is essential for Web Services.
  - WSDLs contain multiple operations and so several custom data sets are needed to test each operation of the Web Service
- *Loose coupling between services*

No view of service implementation changes. Since SOA applications are composed of loosely coupled, business-level services, distributed over a network, we must test the application...end-to-end, service-by-service and interface-by-interface.

SOA Testing using SOAPUI tool

Chapter 46

Introduction about SOAP UI:

SOAPUI is a tool which is used for testing web services. This document contains the brief description about SOAPUI and how it works for web services testing. The version of Soap UI describe is- **SoapUI 3 .0.1.**

Installation:

SoapUI can be downloaed from the below url-
http://www.soapui.org/

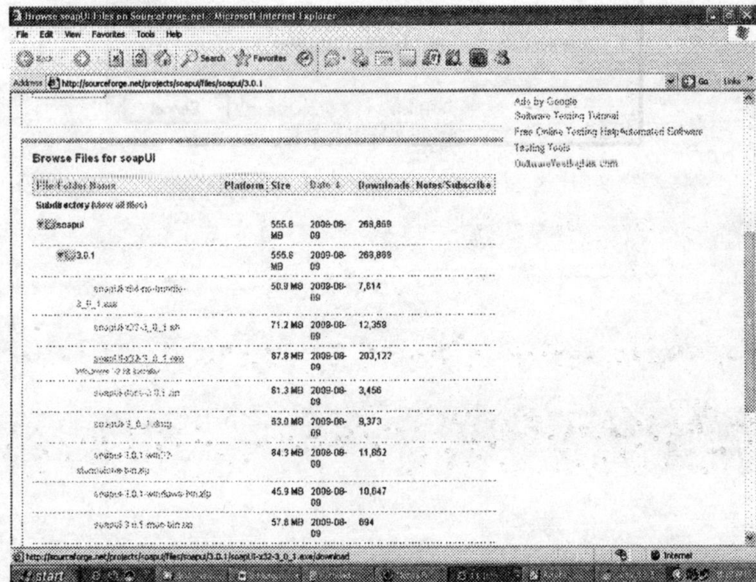

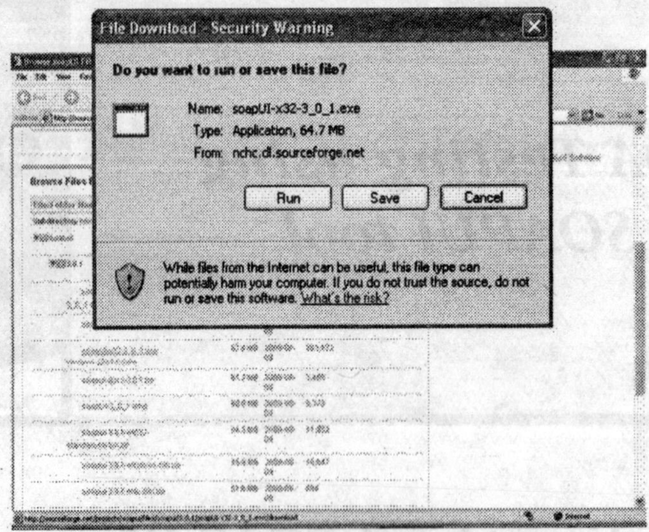
File Download - Security Warning
Do you want to run or save this file?
Name: soapUI-x32-3_0_1.exe
Type: Application, 64.7 MB
From: nchc.dl.sourceforge.net
Run
Save
Cancel
While files from the Internet can be useful, this file type can potentially harm your computer. If you do not trust the source, do not run or save this software. What's the risk?

Click on 'Run'

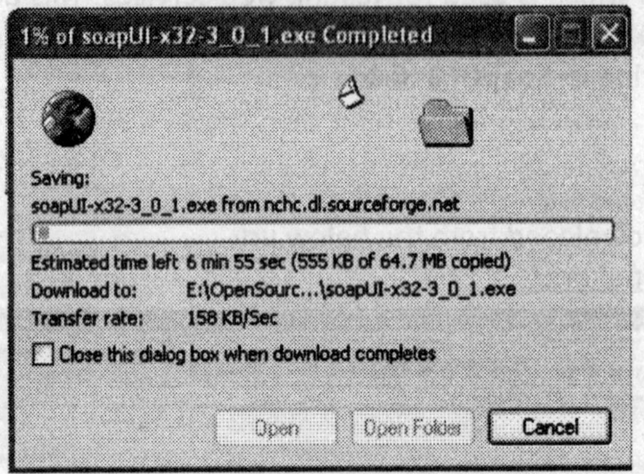
1% of soapUI-x32-3_0_1.exe Completed
Saving:
soapUI-x32-3_0_1.exe from nchc.dl.sourceforge.net
Estimated time left 6 min 55 sec (555 KB of 64.7 MB copied)
Download to: E:\OpenSourc...\soapUI-x32-3_0_1.exe
Transfer rate: 158 KB/Sec
Close this dialog box when download completes
Open
Open Folder
Cancel

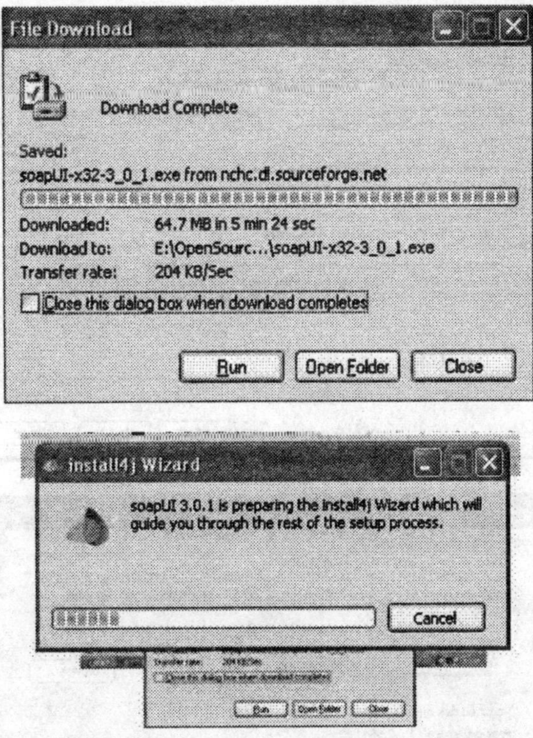
File Download
Download Complete
Saved:
soapUI-x32-3_0_1.exe from nchc.dl.sourceforge.net
Downloaded: 64.7 MB in 5 min 24 sec
Download to: E:\OpenSourc...\soapUI-x32-3_0_1.exe
Transfer rate: 204 KB/Sec
Close this dialog box when download completes
Run
Open Folder
Close
install4j Wizard
soapUI 3.0.1 is preparing the install4j Wizard which will guide you through the rest of the setup process.
Cancel

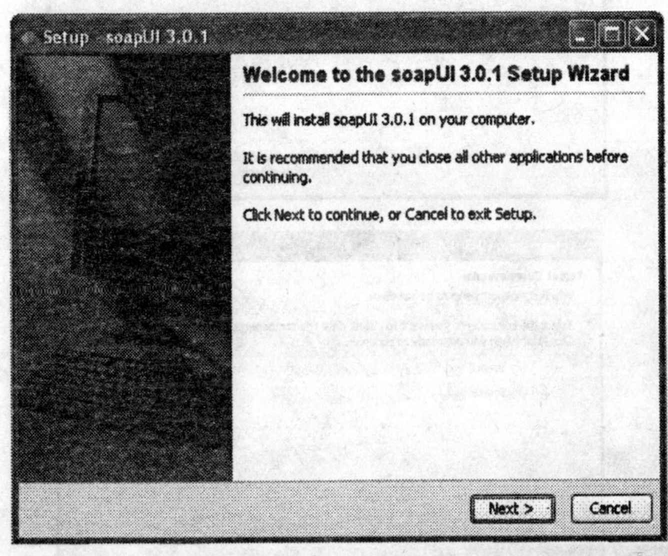
Setup - soapUI 3.0.1
Welcome to the soapUI 3.0.1 Setup Wizard
This will install soapUI 3.0.1 on your computer.
It is recommended that you close all other applications before continuing.
Click Next to continue, or Cancel to exit Setup.
Next >
Cancel

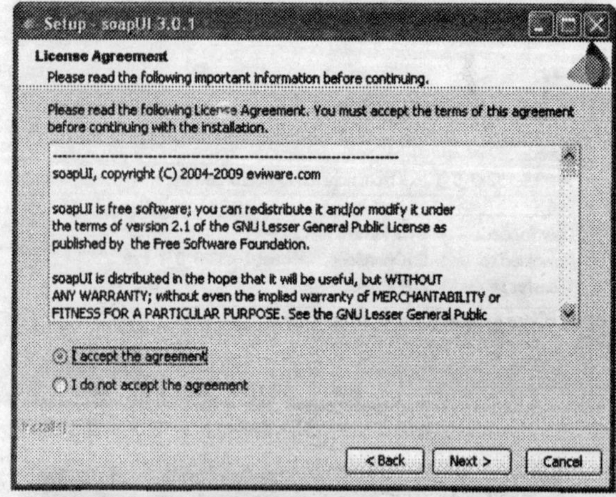
Setup - soapUI 3.0.1
License Agreement
Please read the following important information before continuing.
Please read the following License Agreement. You must accept the terms of this agreement before continuing with the installation.
soapUI, copyright (C) 2004-2009 eviware.com
soapUI is free software; you can redistribute it and/or modify it under the terms of version 2.1 of the GNU Lesser General Public License as published by the Free Software Foundation.
soapUI is distributed in the hope that it will be useful, but WITHOUT ANY WARRANTY; without even the implied warranty of MERCHANTABILITY or FITNESS FOR A PARTICULAR PURPOSE. See the GNU Lesser General Public
I accept the agreement
I do not accept the agreement
< Back
Next >
Cancel

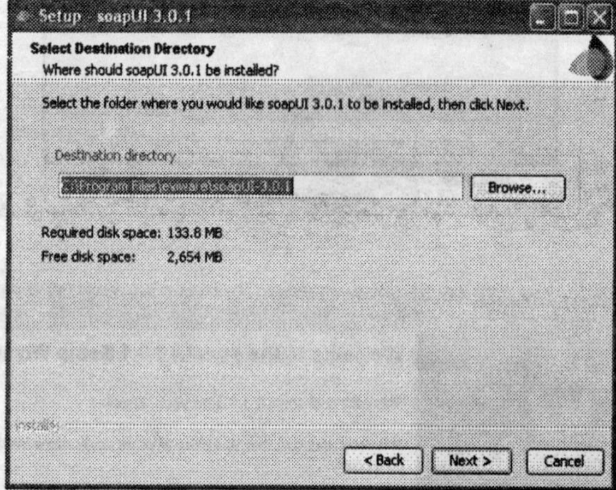
Setup - soapUI 3.0.1
Select Destination Directory
Where should soapUI 3.0.1 be installed?
Select the folder where you would like soapUI 3.0.1 to be installed, then click Next.
Destination directory
Browse...
Required disk space: 133.8 MB
Free disk space: 2,654 MB
< Back
Next >
Cancel

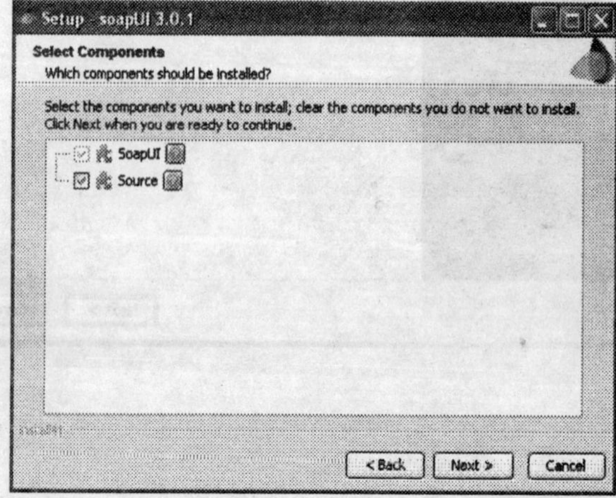
Setup - soapUI 3.0.1
Select Components
Which components should be installed?
Select the components you want to install; clear the components you do not want to install. Click Next when you are ready to continue.
SoapUI
Source
< Back
Next >
Cancel

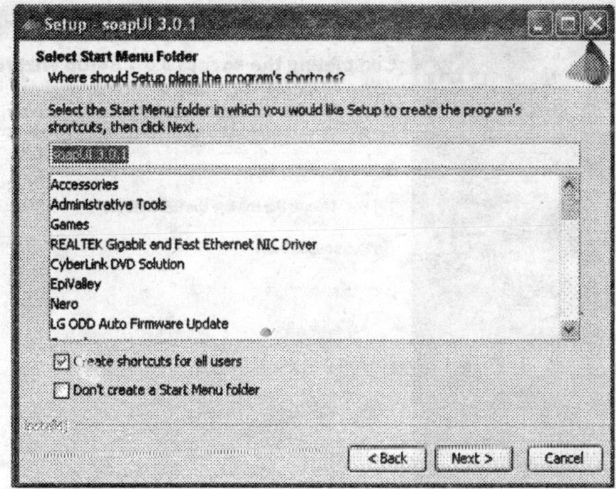
Setup - soapUI 3.0.1
Select Start Menu Folder
Where should Setup place the program's shortcuts?
Select the Start Menu folder in which you would like Setup to create the program's shortcuts, then click Next.
soapUI 3.0.1
Accessories
Administrative Tools
Games
REALTEK Gigabit and Fast Ethernet NIC Driver
CyberLink DVD Solution
EpiValley
Nero
LG ODD Auto Firmware Update
Create shortcuts for all users
Don't create a Start Menu folder
< Back
Next >
Cancel

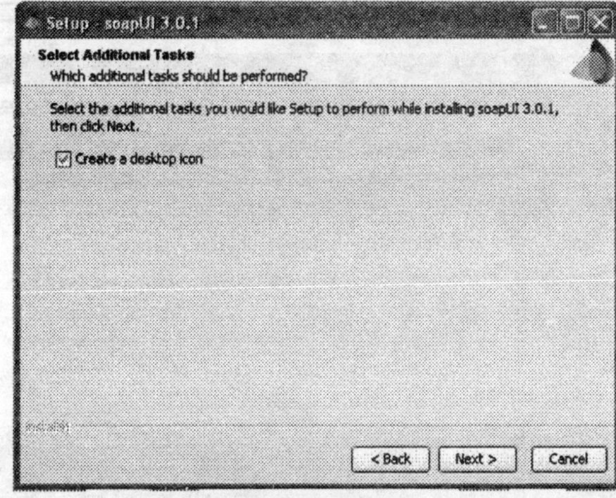
Setup - soapUI 3.0.1
Select Additional Tasks
Which additional tasks should be performed?
Select the additional tasks you would like Setup to perform while installing soapUI 3.0.1, then click Next.
Create a desktop icon
< Back
Next >
Cancel

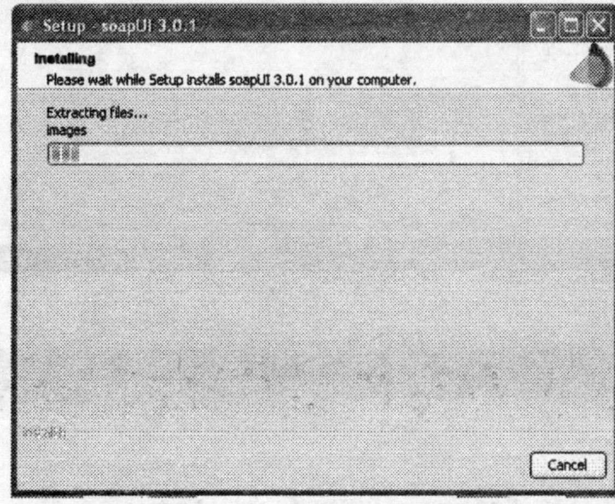
Setup - soapUI 3.0.1
Installing
Please wait while Setup installs soapUI 3.0.1 on your computer.
Extracting files...
images
Cancel

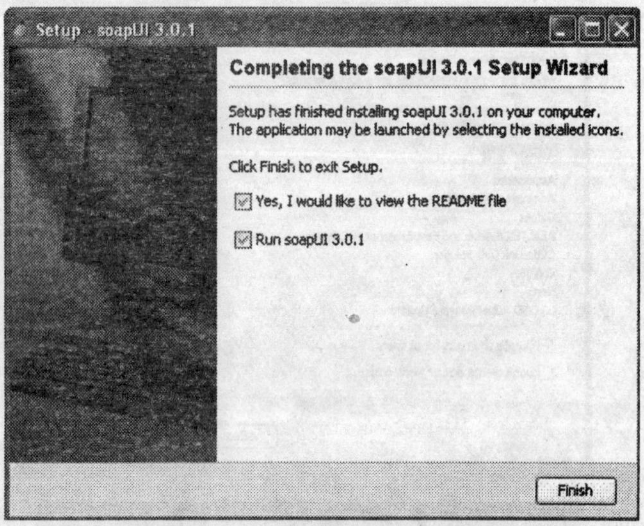

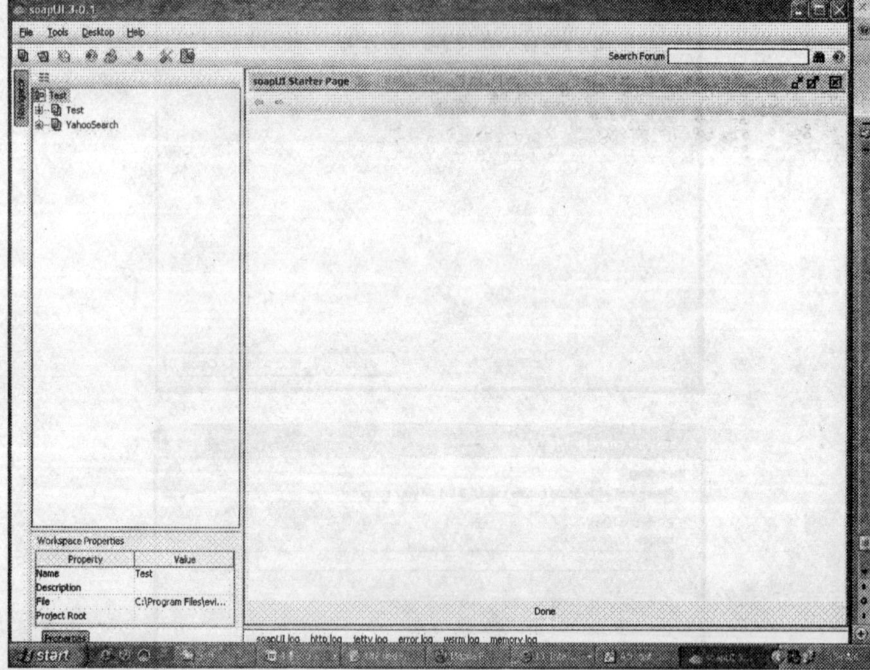

1. Open SoapUI tool.

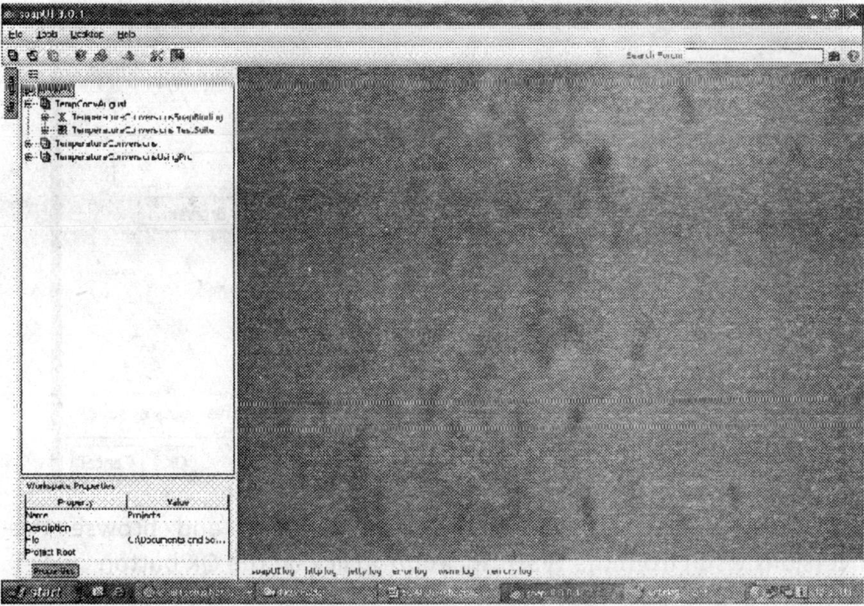

2. Right click on the Projects in the above screen the following are the options that will be displayed:

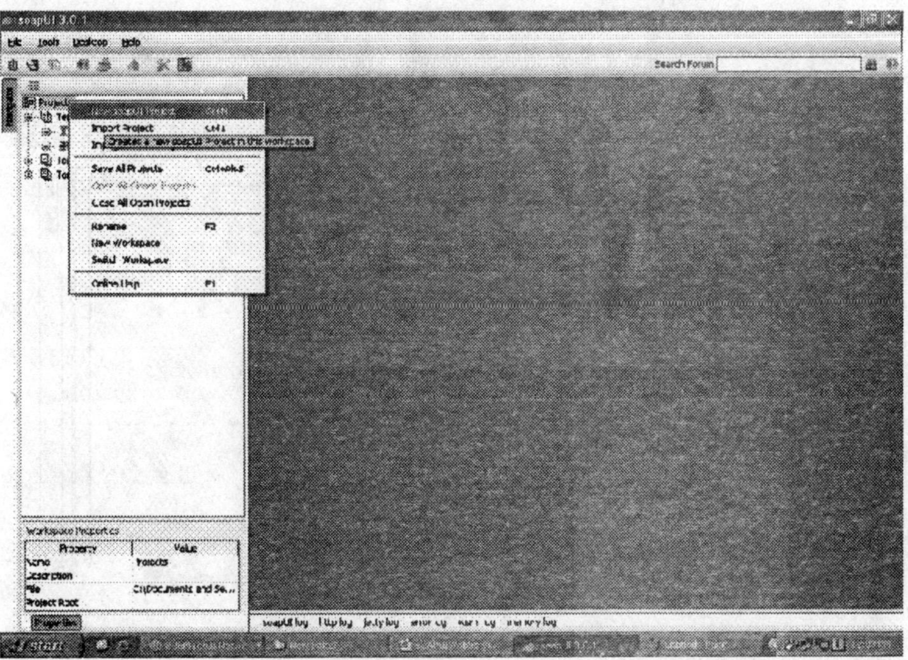

3. Select the New WSDL Project then the following pop up will be displayed:

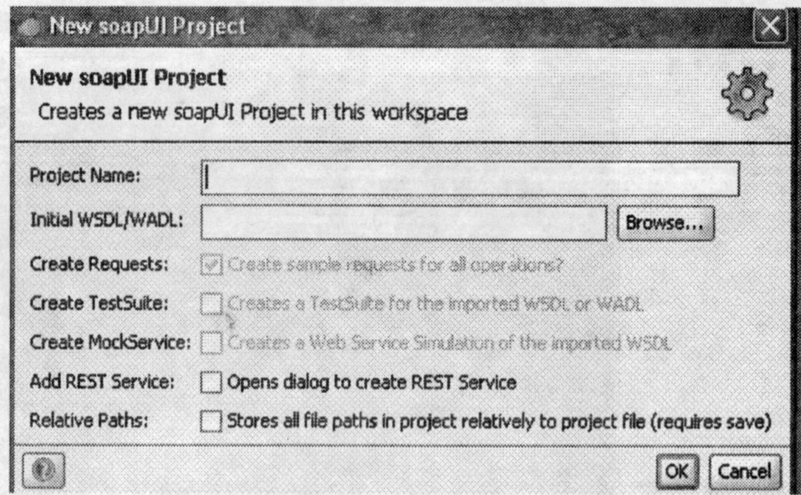

Specify the Name of the Project in the **Project Name** and browse the WSDL (TempConversions.wsdl) from the **WSDL location** > click on the OK button.

➢ Select the check box 'Create TestSuite' if you want to create a Test Suite.

The following picture shows the entire tree structure after the Web service being imported:

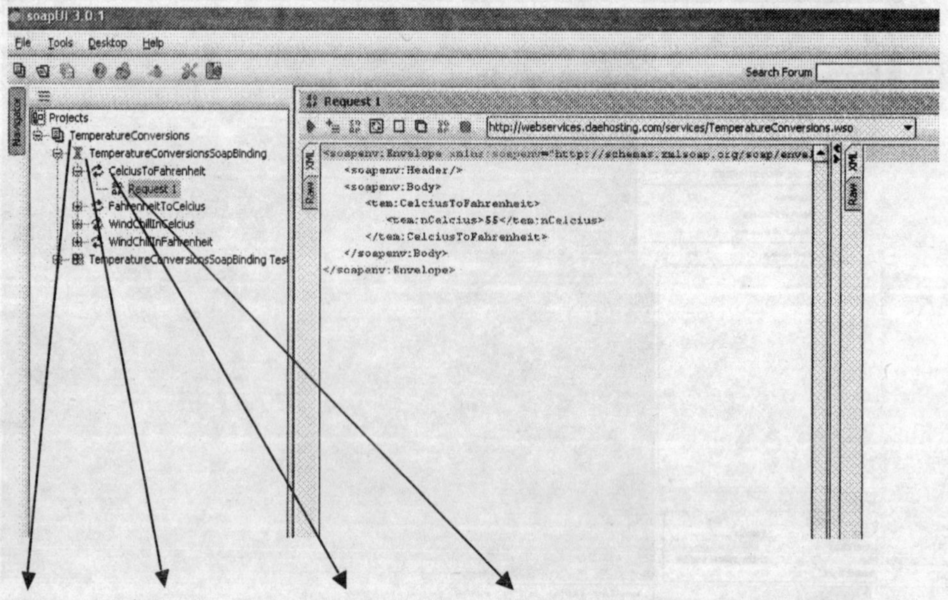

Double Click on the Request then the new window will be displayed which looks like this:

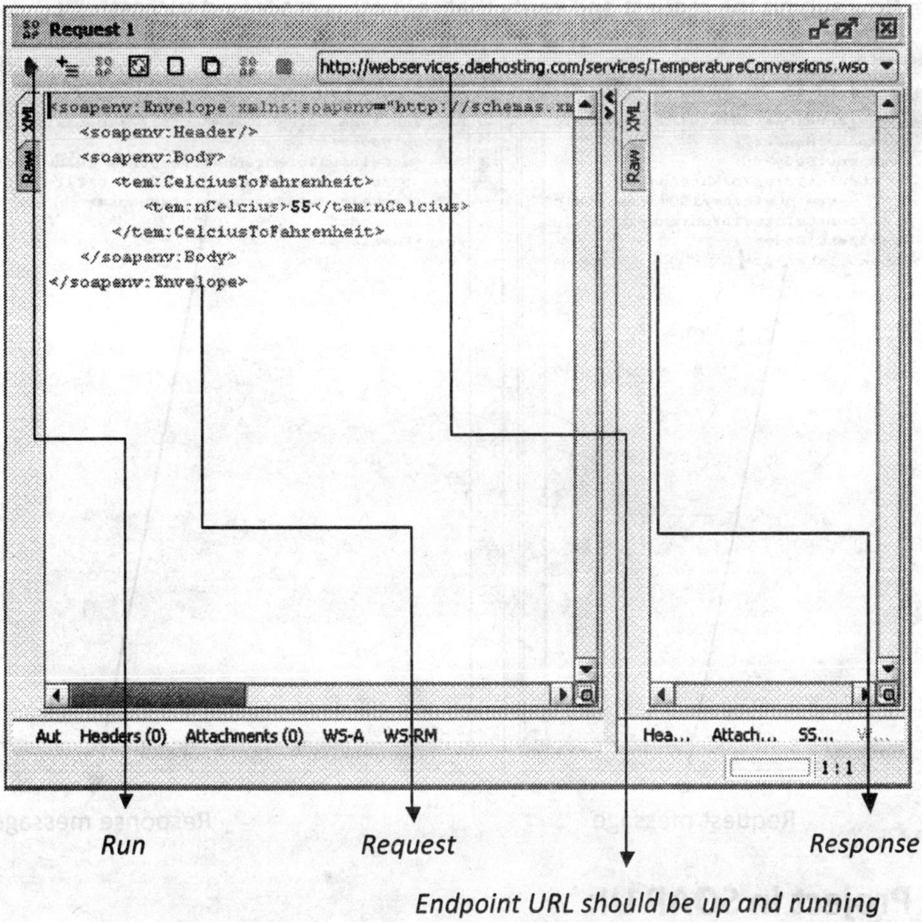

Run Request Response

Endpoint URL should be up and running

- In the above request there are elements with question marks where in we need to provide the values (inputs), validate the request and submit the request.
- To ***validate*** the request right click on the request and click on the validate if the request is correct then it shows Validation Ok Pop-Up window, as shown below-

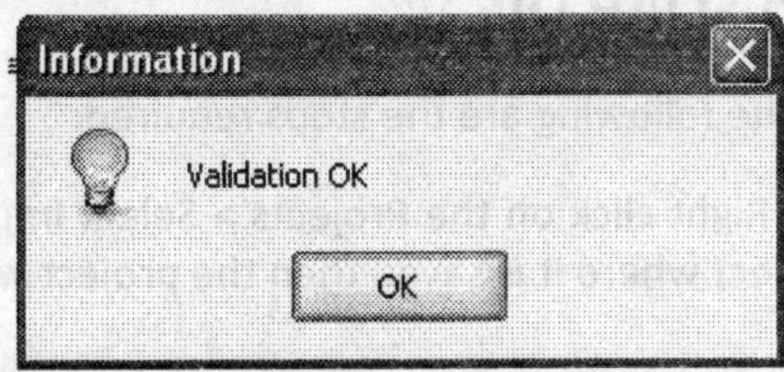

- The green color button specifies the Run or Submit the Request for the specified Endpoint URL.
- Now submit the request and verify that request is processed successfully.

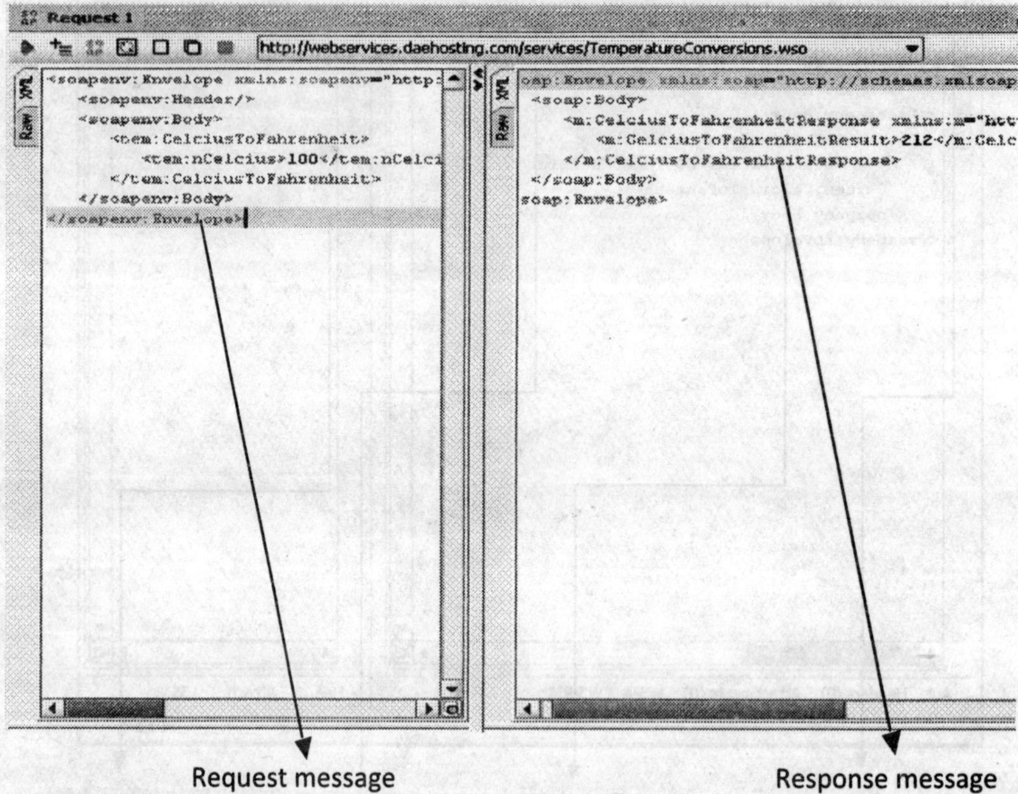

Save Project in SOAP UI:

You can save the project by right click on the project and save project. The project will be saved in .xml format which we call as workspace. This workspace can be sent to others & can work on by importing the project.

Import Project into SOAP UI:

To import the project the following are the steps required:

Navigate to Projects > Right click on the Projects > Select Import Project and select the location of the project where it is saved then the project will be added into SOAP UI automatically.

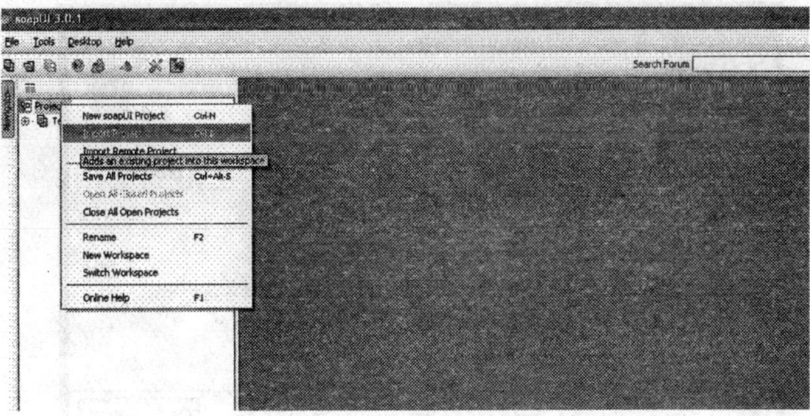

Create Project using URL Location:

Navigate to Projects > Right Click on the Project and Specify the Project name and click on the Ok button.

Now Right Click on the Project Created > Select Add WSDL from URL > provide the URL Location where the WSDL is located > click on the OK button. The Web service should be successfully added in to the project created.

The following Screen shot explains about the same:

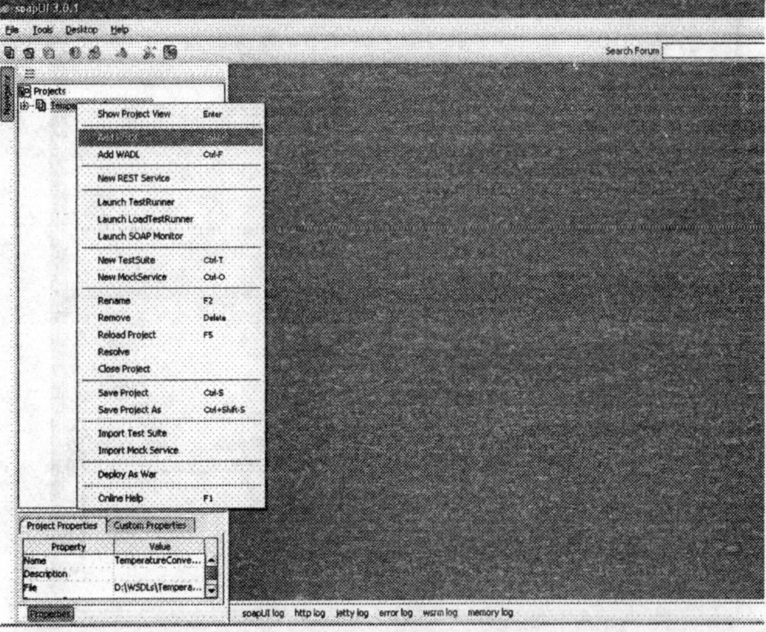

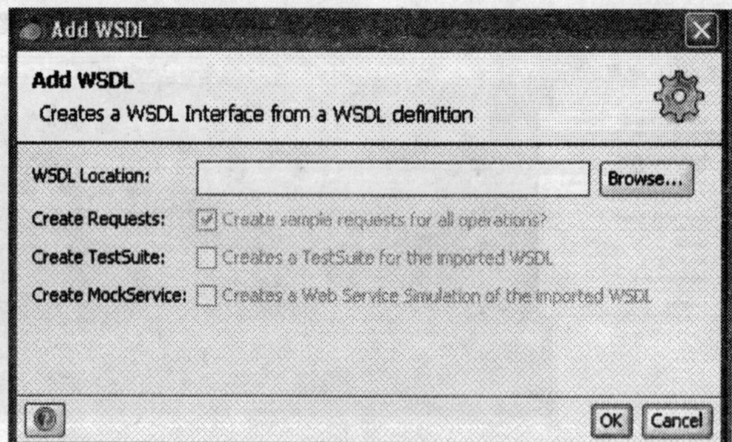

Show Project View in the SOAP UI:

To get the Overview of the project > right click on the project > Click on Show project View then the screen with all the details about the project is displayed.

Following Screen shot explains about it:

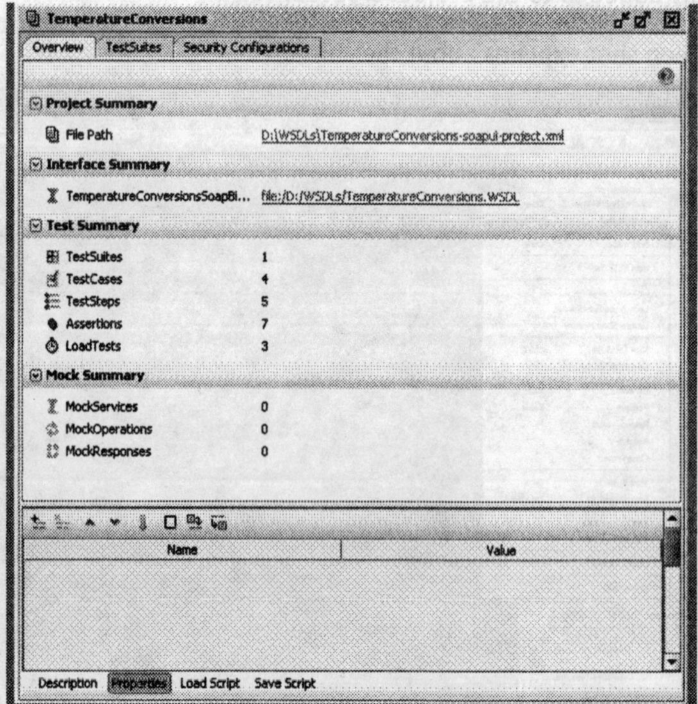

Test Suites and Test cases in SOAP UI:

We can also prepare the Test suite which consists of the set of test cases for each operation in the web service this can be done as follows:

1. Navigate to the project created > Right Click on the project and select New TestSuite > Mention the name of the TestSuite by default we will mention the Operation Name so that it will be easy to recognize.
2. Right Click on the Test Suite Created > Click on the New Test Case > Mention the name of the test case as what the test case does and click on the OK button.
3. Go to Test Case and right click on the Test Case > Navigate to Add Step > Select Test Request and click on the Ok button > Select the Operation that needs to be added in the Test case > Click on the Ok button. Test Step is added to the Test Case Created.

The following Screen shot gives you the brief idea of how to create Test Suite > Test Case > Test Request.

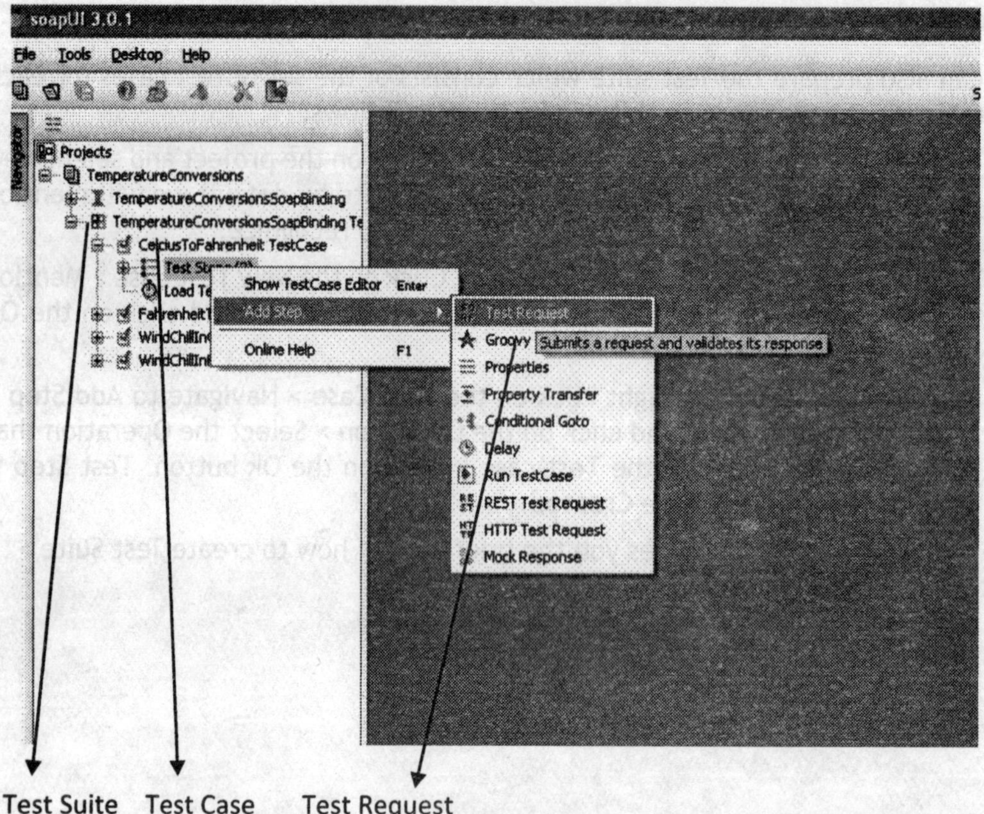

Test suite and test cases helps in executing the test cases which we have written manually and will reduce the time whenever new build is deployed instead of creating and executing each test case just go to the Test suite and run the test cases so that we can identify the health check of the build.

How and Why Assertions are used in SOAP UI:

Assertions are used in SOAP UI to validate the schema, SOAP Response, whether it is (SOAP Fault, Not a SOAP Fault) and Contains (whether the code and message expected in response are valid).

To add the assertions following steps needs to be followed:

1. Navigate to Test Request > Click on the Assertions button and specify the assertion that are needed for the request.

Following Screen shot explains about it:

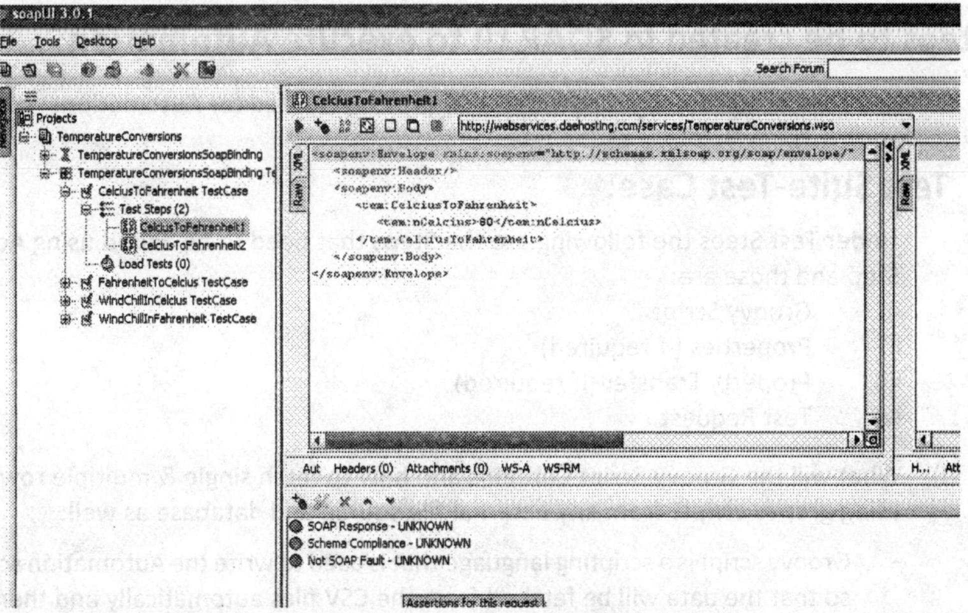

In the above Screen shot there are five assertions added to the test request depending on the test case that we are performing.

i) ***SOAP Response***: Validates whether the Response message received is a valid SOAP response or not.

ii) ***Schema Compliance***: Validates the WSDL Schema from the location where we have added the WSDL.

iii) ***Not SOAP Fault:*** Specifies that the request is not a SOAP Fault.

In the above Screen shot you can find the some of the logs buttons which will capture the information based on the operation that we perform some of them are given below.

A) ***SOAP UI log:*** Captures all the information that we perform in the SOAP UI. For ex: If we save the Project that will be captured in the SOAP UI log, etc.

B) *Error log:* Captures the information if there is any error in the response side.

C) ***Memory log:*** Specifies the Memory Usage of the SOAP by the Web services.

SOAP UI Automation:

Steps to be created in SOAP UI to execute Automation:

The following is the hierarchy that needs to be created for Automation:

Test Suite-Test Case:

Under Test Steps the following are the Steps that need to be added using Add Step and those are:

i) Groovy Script
ii) Properties (If required)
iii) Property Transfer (If required)
iv) Test Request.

i) What will the Groovy Script Contains and how to fetch single & multiple rows using groovy scripts from any external file source and database as well:

- Groovy script is a scripting language that is used to write the Automation scripts so that the data will be fetched from the CSV files automatically and then run the record by submitting them in the request.

1. This groovy Script describes about the location from where the file should be picked up and set the property into context.

   Then it replaces values in the SOAP request as an input and run the request. Also this script saves the corresponding response into your local disk, which would be useful for keeping a track of request executed and its corresponding response. Find the screen shot for Groovy Script:

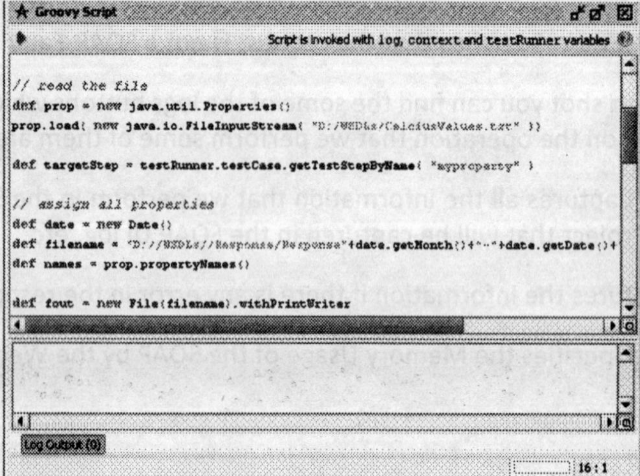

Launch test runner for a project:

Right Click on the project select the Launch test runner then the following screen will be displayed.

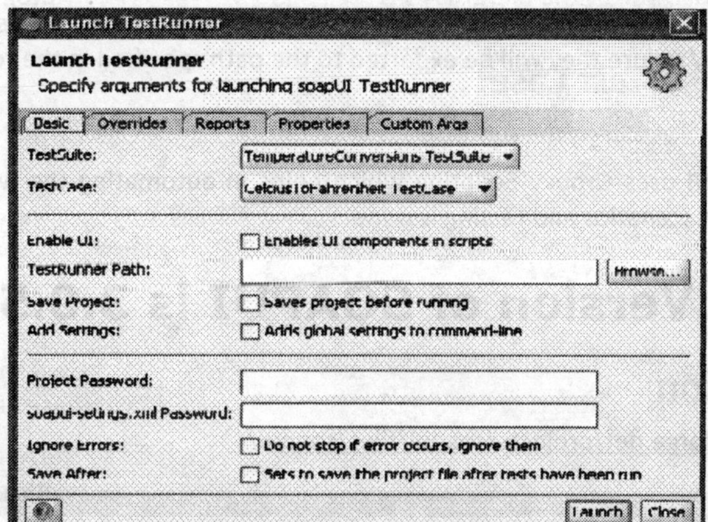

Select the particular Test Suite and Test case that needs to be executed.

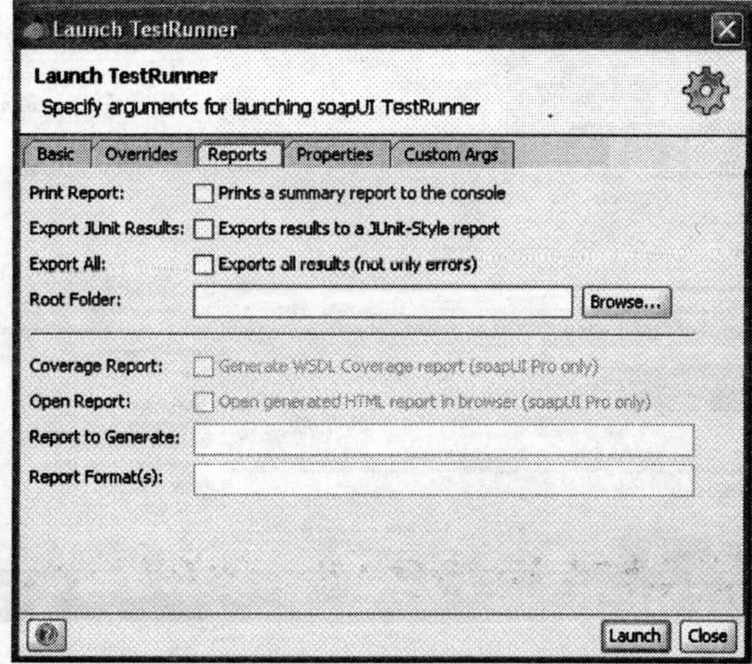

Select the report types you want after the execution and give a specified path where you want to export the result in the Root folder by clicking the Browse button.

Click on "Launch".

Then new window is opened where you can see the status of each test step. If the test step is success/ failure they will be exported to the path specified in the root folder.

Summary:

Hence SOAP UI uses Groovy Scripting which helps in automating the web services by which 100% of scenarios and testing is done.

Latest Version of SOAPUI is 3.0.5

Installation

http://sourceforge.net/projects/soapui/files/soapui/

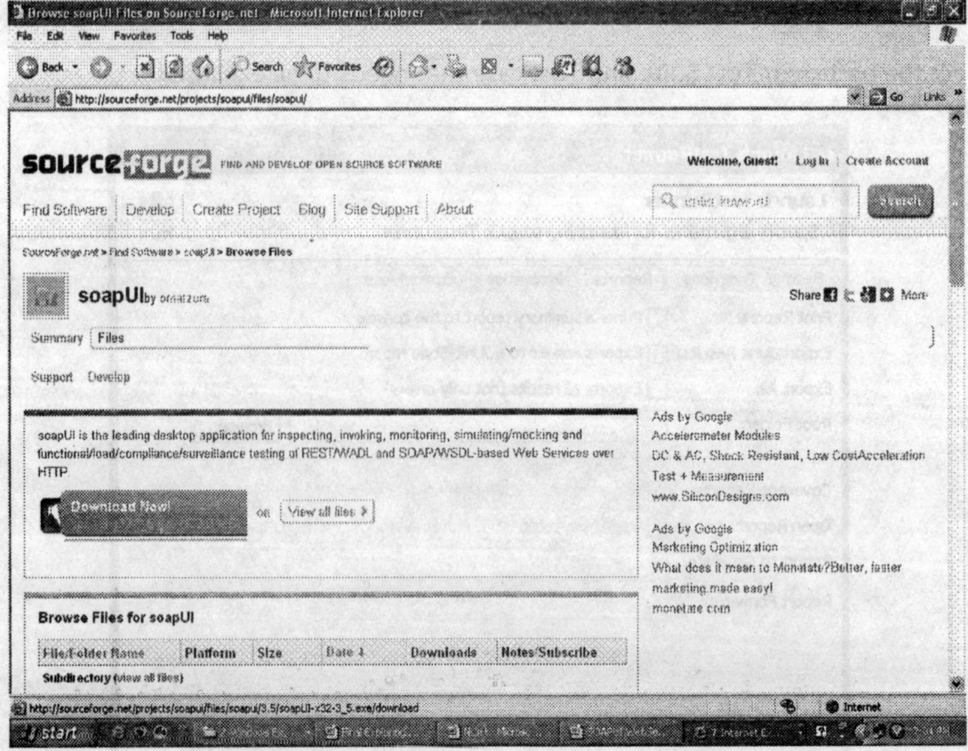

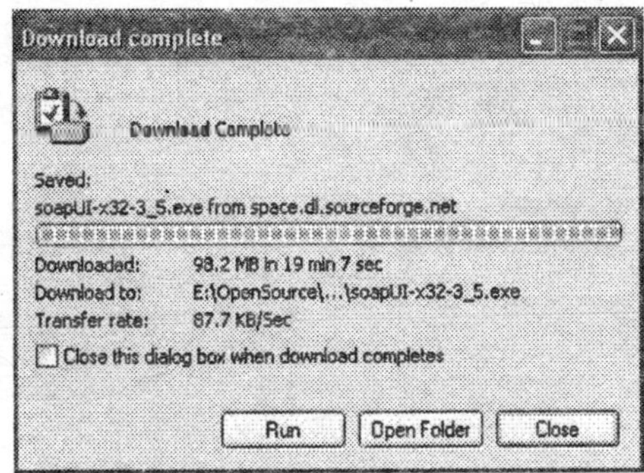
Download complete
Download Complete
Saved:
soapUI-x32-3_5.exe from space.dl.sourceforge.net
Downloaded: 98.2 MB in 19 min 7 sec
Download to: E:\OpenSource\...\soapUI-x32-3_5.exe
Transfer rate: 87.7 KB/Sec
Close this dialog box when download completes
Run
Open Folder
Close

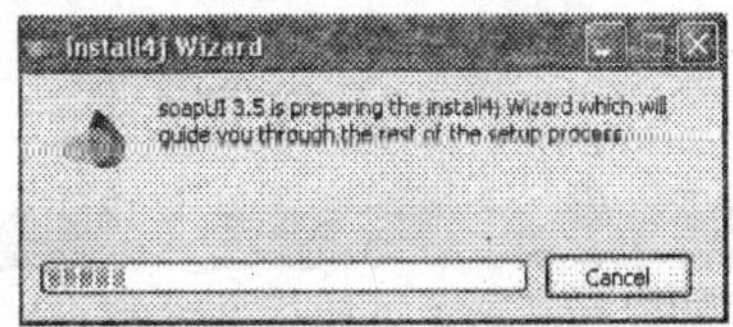
Install4j Wizard
soapUI 3.5 is preparing the install4j Wizard which will guide you through the rest of the setup process.
Cancel

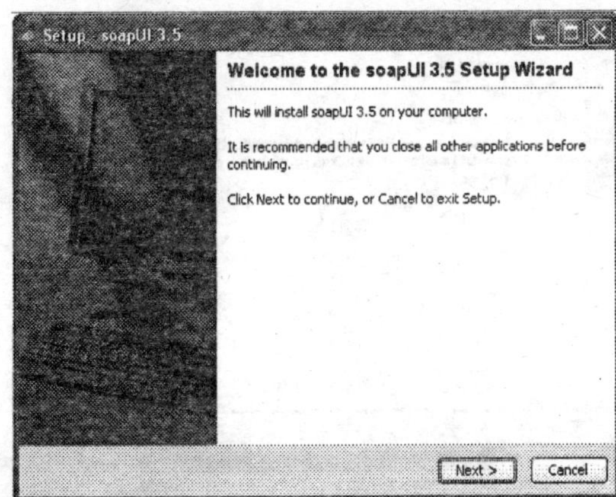
Setup - soapUI 3.5
Welcome to the soapUI 3.5 Setup Wizard
This will install soapUI 3.5 on your computer.
It is recommended that you close all other applications before continuing.
Click Next to continue, or Cancel to exit Setup.
Next >
Cancel

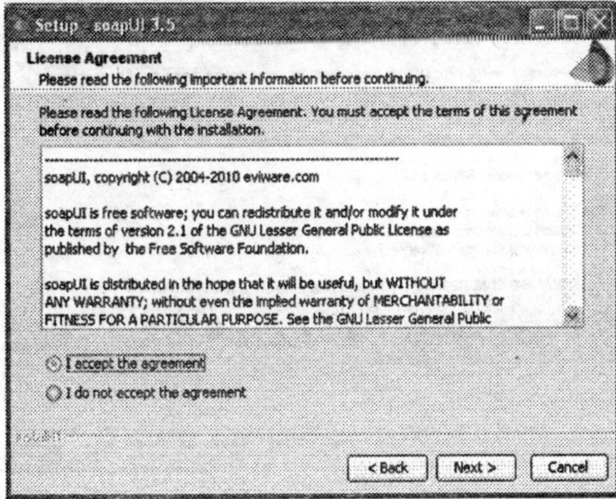
Setup - soapUI 3.5
License Agreement
Please read the following important information before continuing.
Please read the following License Agreement. You must accept the terms of this agreement before continuing with the installation.
soapUI, copyright (C) 2004-2010 eviware.com
soapUI is free software; you can redistribute it and/or modify it under the terms of version 2.1 of the GNU Lesser General Public License as published by the Free Software Foundation.
soapUI is distributed in the hope that it will be useful, but WITHOUT ANY WARRANTY; without even the implied warranty of MERCHANTABILITY or FITNESS FOR A PARTICULAR PURPOSE. See the GNU Lesser General Public
I accept the agreement
I do not accept the agreement
< Back
Next >
Cancel

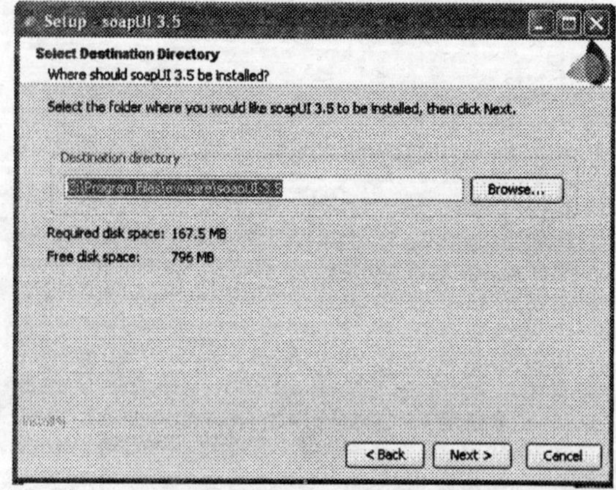
Setup - soapUI 3.5
Select Destination Directory
Where should soapUI 3.5 be installed?
Select the folder where you would like soapUI 3.5 to be installed, then click Next.
Destination directory
Browse...
Required disk space: 167.5 MB
Free disk space: 796 MB
< Back
Next >
Cancel

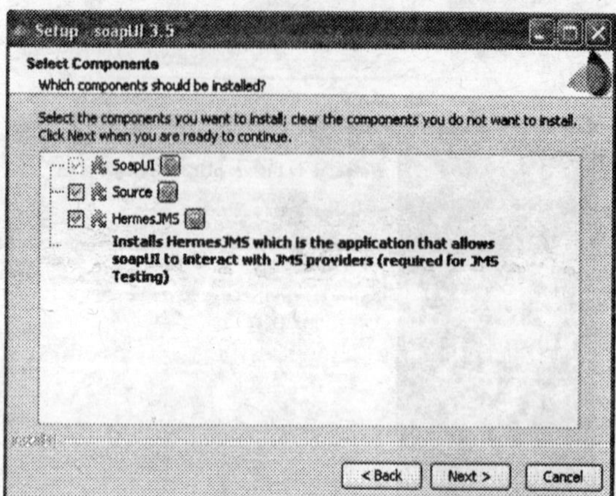
Setup - soapUI 3.5
Select Components
Which components should be installed?
Select the components you want to install; clear the components you do not want to install. Click Next when you are ready to continue.
SoapUI
Source
HermesJMS
Installs HermesJMS which is the application that allows soapUI to interact with JMS providers (required for JMS Testing)
< Back
Next >
Cancel

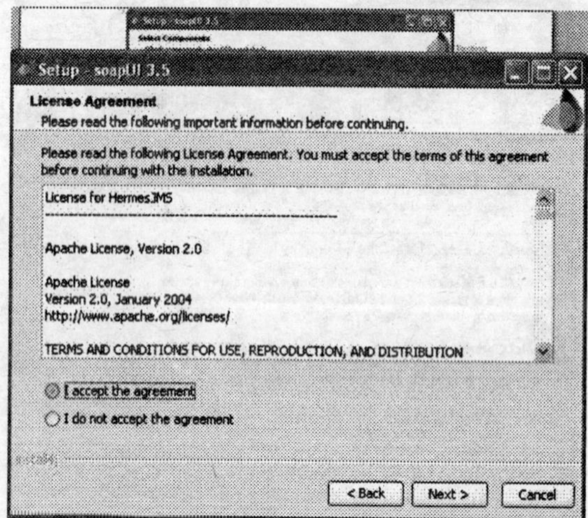
Setup - soapUI 3.5
License Agreement
Please read the following important information before continuing.
Please read the following License Agreement. You must accept the terms of this agreement before continuing with the installation.
License for HermesJMS
Apache License, Version 2.0
Apache License
Version 2.0, January 2004
http://www.apache.org/licenses/
TERMS AND CONDITIONS FOR USE, REPRODUCTION, AND DISTRIBUTION
I accept the agreement
I do not accept the agreement
< Back
Next >
Cancel

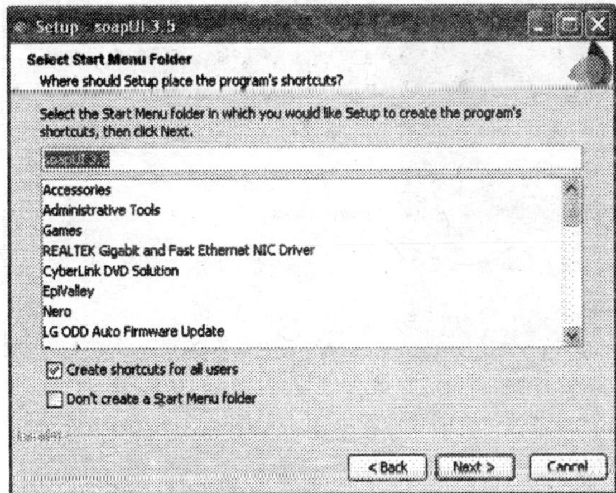
Setup - soapUI 3.5
Select Start Menu Folder
Where should Setup place the program's shortcuts?
Select the Start Menu folder in which you would like Setup to create the program's shortcuts, then click Next.
Accessories
Administrative Tools
Games
REALTEK Gigabit and Fast Ethernet NIC Driver
CyberLink DVD Solution
EpiValley
Nero
LG ODD Auto Firmware Update
Create shortcuts for all users
Don't create a Start Menu folder
< Back
Next >
Cancel

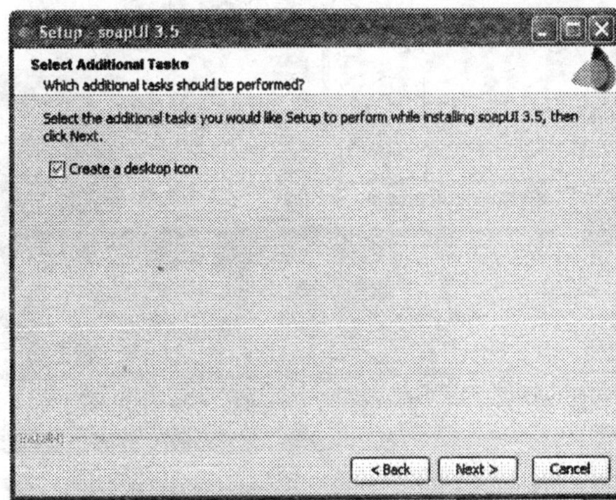
Setup - soapUI 3.5
Select Additional Tasks
Which additional tasks should be performed?
Select the additional tasks you would like Setup to perform while installing soapUI 3.5, then click Next.
Create a desktop icon
< Back
Next >
Cancel

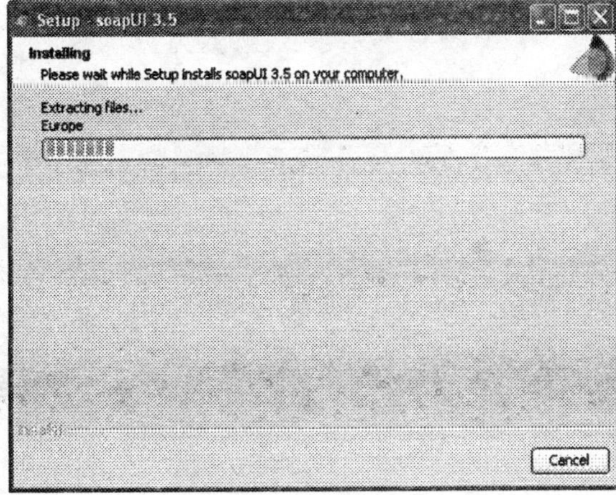
Setup - soapUI 3.5
Installing
Please wait while Setup installs soapUI 3.5 on your computer.
Extracting files...
Europe
Cancel

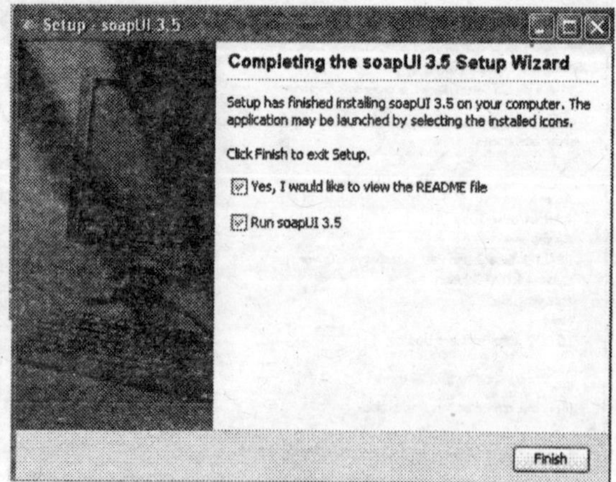
Setup - soapUI 3.5
Completing the soapUI 3.5 Setup Wizard
Setup has finished installing soapUI 3.5 on your computer. The application may be launched by selecting the installed icons.
Click Finish to exit Setup.
Yes, I would like to view the README file
Run soapUI 3.5
Finish

eviware
soapUI
Download professional version at
www.eviware.com
3.5

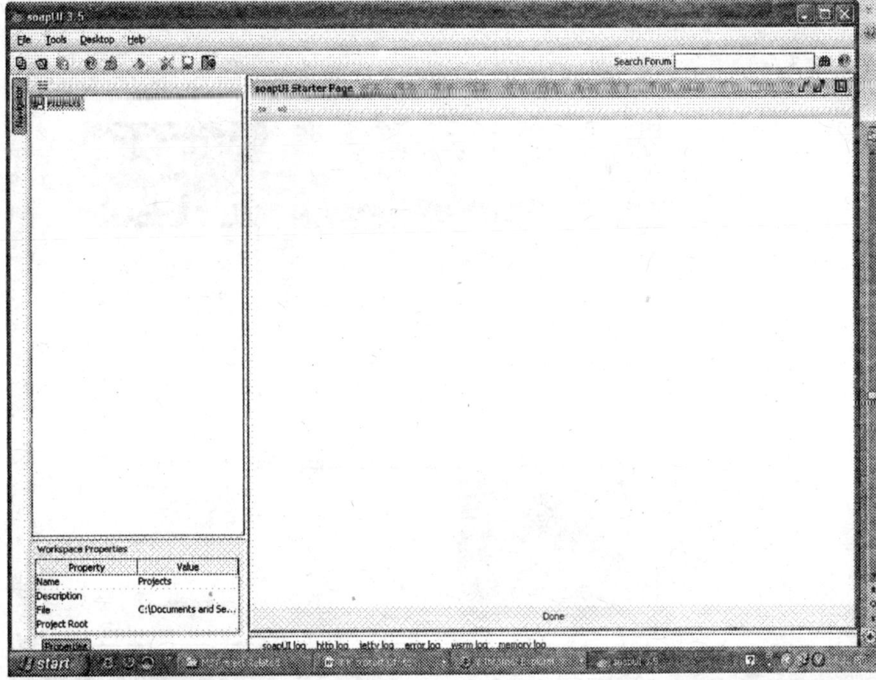
soapUI 3.5
File Tools Desktop Help
Search Forum
soapUI Starter Page
Projects
Workspace Properties
Property
Value
Name
Projects
Description
File
C:\Documents and Se...
Project Root
Done
soapUI log http log jetty log error log wsrm log memory log
start

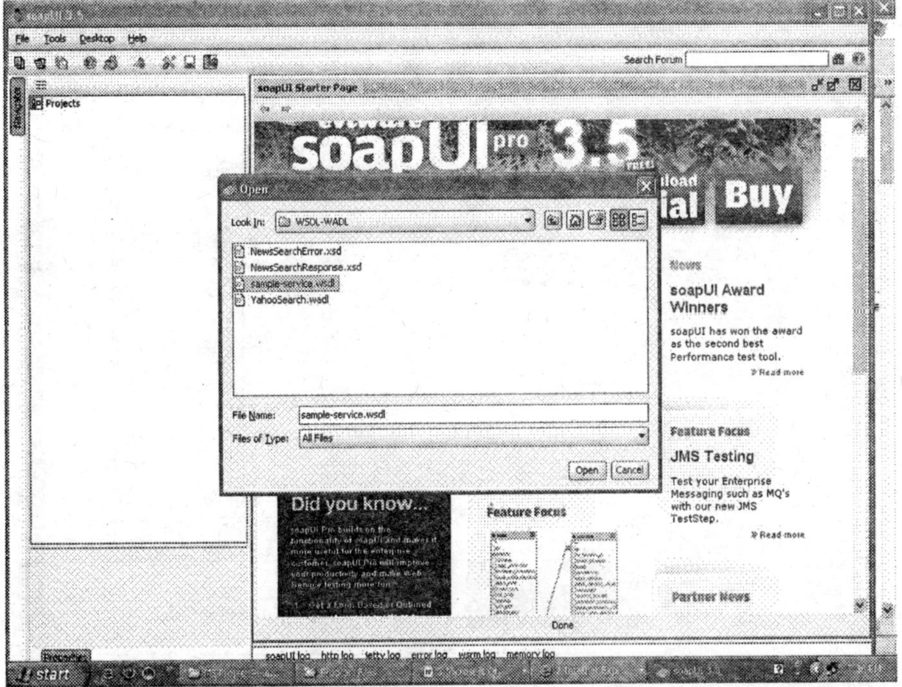
soapUI 3.5
File Tools Desktop Help
Search Forum
soapUI Starter Page
Projects
soapUI pro 3.5
Buy
Open
Look In:
WSDL-WADL
NewsSearchError.xsd
NewsSearchResponse.xsd
sample-service.wsdl
YahooSearch.wsdl
File Name:
sample-service.wsdl
Files of Type:
All Files
Open
Cancel
soapUI Award Winners
soapUI has won the award as the second best Performance test tool.
Feature Focus
JMS Testing
Test your Enterprise Messaging such as MQ's with our new JMS TestStep.
Did you know...
Feature Focus
Partner News
Done
soapUI log http log jetty log error log wsrm log memory log
start

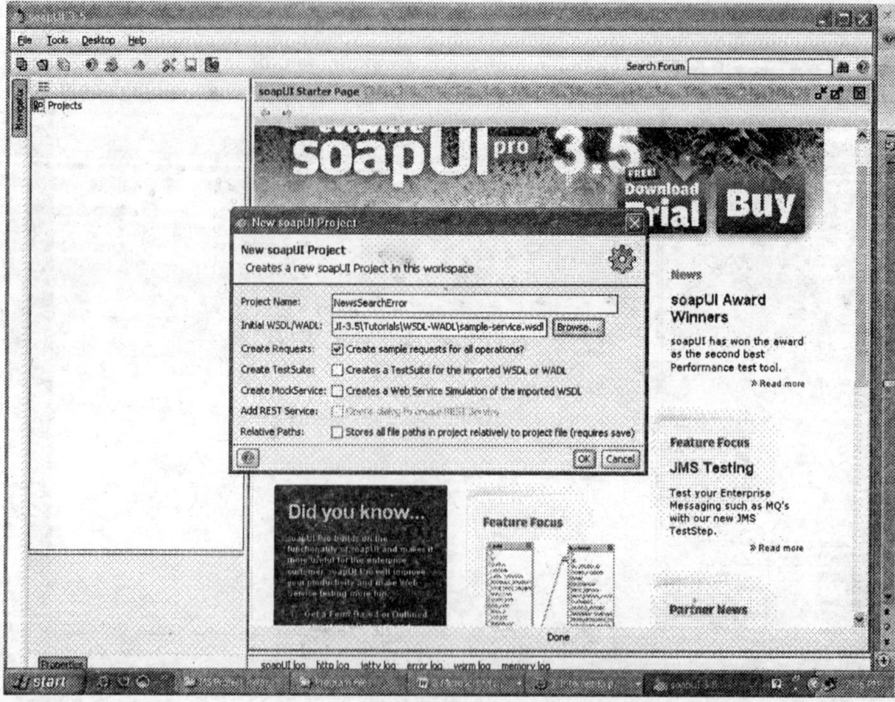
File Tools Desktop Help
Search Forum
Projects
soapUI Starter Page
soapUI pro 3.5
FREE! Download Trial
Buy
New soapUI Project
New soapUI Project
Creates a new soapUI Project in this workspace
Project Name: NewsSearchError
Initial WSDL/WADL: JI-3.5\Tutorials\WSDL-WADL\sample-service.wsdl Browse...
Create Requests: Create sample requests for all operations?
Create TestSuite: Creates a TestSuite for the imported WSDL or WADL
Create MockService: Creates a Web Service Simulation of the imported WSDL
Add REST Service:
Relative Paths: Stores all file paths in project relatively to project file (requires save)
OK Cancel
News
soapUI Award Winners
soapUI has won the award as the second best Performance test tool.
» Read more
Feature Focus
JMS Testing
Test your Enterprise Messaging such as MQ's with our new JMS TestStep.
» Read more
Did you know...
Feature Focus
Partner News
Done
soapUI log http log jetty log error log wsrm log memory log
start

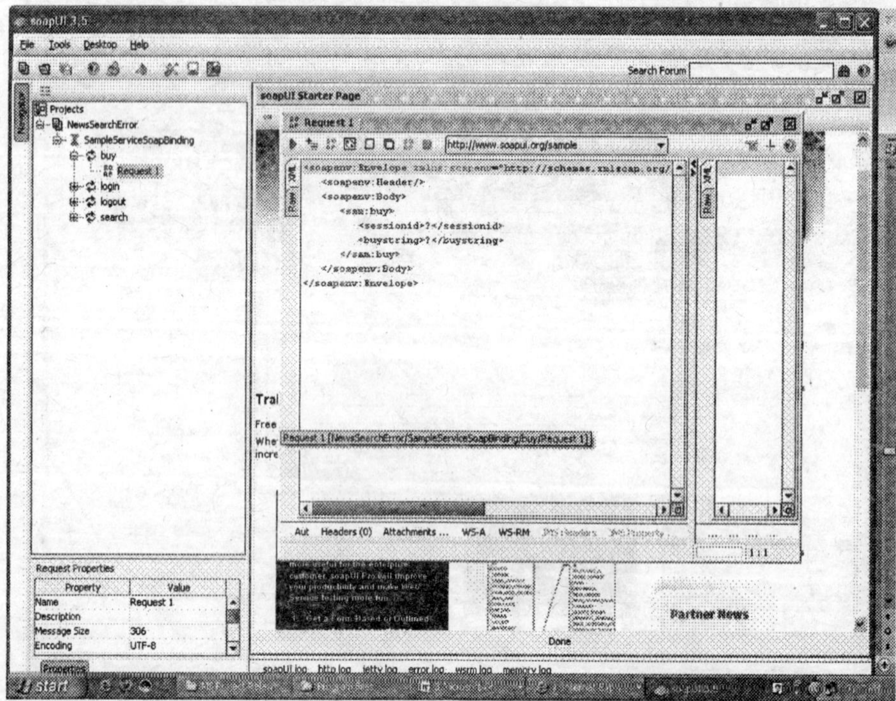
soapUI 3.5
File Tools Desktop Help
Search Forum
Projects
NewsSearchError
SampleServiceSoapBinding
buy
Request 1
login
logout
search
soapUI Starter Page
Request 1
http://www.soapui.org/sample
<soapenv:Envelope xmlns:soapenv="http://schemas.xmlsoap.org/
<soapenv:Header/>
<soapenv:Body>
<sam:buy>
<sessionid>?</sessionid>
<buystring>?</buystring>
</sam:buy>
</soapenv:Body>
</soapenv:Envelope>
Request 1 [NewsSearchError/SampleServiceSoapBinding/buy/Request 1]
Aut Headers (0) Attachments ... WS-A WS-RM
1:1
Request Properties
Property Value
Name Request 1
Description
Message Size 306
Encoding UTF-8
Partner News
Done
soapUI log http log jetty log error log wsrm log memory log
start

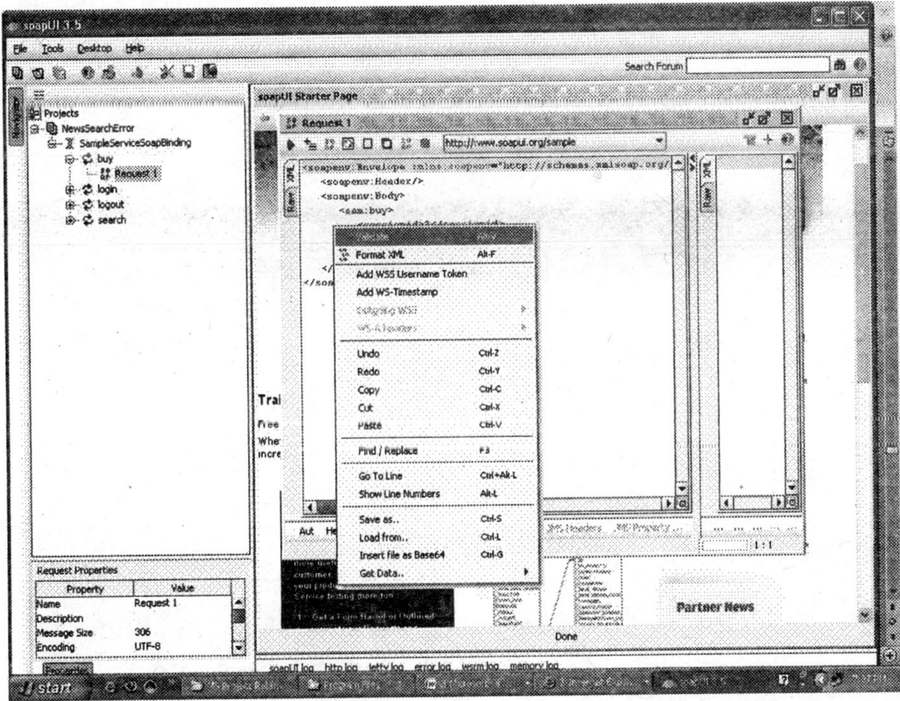
soapUI 3.5
File Tools Desktop Help
Search Forum
Projects
NewsSearchError
SampleServiceSoapBinding
buy
Request 1
login
logout
search
soapUI Starter Page
Request 1
http://www.soapui.org/sample
Format XML Alt-F
Add WSS Username Token
Add WS-Timestamp
Undo Ctrl-Z
Redo Ctrl-Y
Copy Ctrl-C
Cut Ctrl-X
Paste Ctrl-V
Find / Replace F3
Go To Line Ctrl+Alt-L
Show Line Numbers Alt-L
Save as.. Ctrl-S
Load from.. Ctrl-L
Insert file as Base64 Ctrl-G
Get Data..
Request Properties
Property
Value
Name
Request 1
Description
Message Size
306
Encoding
UTF-8
Partner News
Done
soapUI log
http log
jetty log
error log
wsrm log
memory log
start

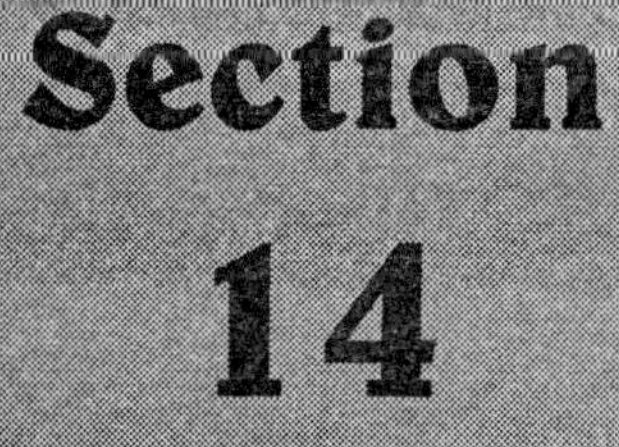

Section 14

Setting up Test Lab

What is a test lab?

Before launching straight into the business of setting up and managing a test lab, let's define what a test lab is. Two definitions taken from Rex Black's book

"Managing the Test Process" [1999] will help us here:
"A test laboratory is a place where testing is conducted."

This may seem to be stating the obvious, but in fact encourages us to consider every setting in which testing takes place as a test lab. So even if you are testing from your normal workplace, planning and organization are needed before you can begin your test execution.

"Testers must perform controlled experiments, dealing with measurements and known quantities."

This second statement appeals to my scientific background. A test lab must provide an environment in which to conduct these controlled experiments. And the environment must stable, ordered and reproducible. Having been responsible for establishing test labs in 2 large projects, I will draw on my experience to provide practical suggestions and some tips and tricks from the real world, which should jump start test managers new to this area and perhaps provide some new ideas to old hands. Apart from the theory, the paper also covers a case study from one of the projects.

Five Ws and an H

Setting up a test lab from scratch can be a large and complex task. It is in fact a small project and as for all projects it helps to have a plan. The five Ws are the five planning questions: Who? What? When? Where? and Why? For this project we need to add an H: How? Answering these questions will help us to state our goals and then define the ways and means to achieve them. It is important to be clear about your objectives. The obvious goal is to set up a test lab.

WHO?

- Who will be doing the testing?
- Who will be using the test lab?
- Is the lab for one project? The whole organization?
- Will more than one test team need to be accommodated?
- How many people at any one time?

WHAT?

- What will they be testing?
- What type of testing will be performed?
- Functional acceptance testing?
- Performance testing?
- User acceptance testing?
- Operations acceptance testing?

WHEN?

- When do you need a fully functional test lab?
- Is a staged implementation possible?
- Are there any other time constraints? e.g. delivery dates for hardware

WHY?

- Why do you need a test lab?
- Be prepared to answer this question! Setting up a dedicated test lab isn't cheap. You will need to justify the expense to your managers.

  To decide whether a virtual or a physical test lab is required there are again questions to help:
- Can all the testing be performed in a normal office environment?
- Are there particular hardware requirements?
- Are there particular software requirements that are not part of the standard workplace or which cannot be installed there?
- Are there special security issues?
- Does access to the test environment need to be restricted?

The test lab inventory

- The test lab inventory covers all the facilities and physical resources you will need in your test lab.
- Space
- **(Computer) hardware**

  Obviously you are going to need PCs or workstations. Are there any other particular hardware requirements? Do you need special printers? Are you testing a Computer Telephone Integration (CTI) application with special telephony requirements? Are other special peripherals required?

Once you have your shopping list for hardware, be sure to check that the room proposed as the test lab has enough electrical power sockets and network connection points and that they are in the right place. Having to run extension cables around the room is an accident waiting to happen

Establishing a controlled environment

Once the hardware is set up, the next step is to define the software requirements.

Baseline installation

For high level testing, the PC or workstation should reflect as closely as possible the production environment, where the application will be used once deployed. Not only should the operating system and middleware be considered, it is also important to have any other applications installed which will be used and exist concurrently with the application under test (AUT) in the final live environment. At the very latest in the User Acceptance Test the application must be tested running in parallel to other applications to rule out any compatibility issues.

Test tools

Decide which test tools will be installed where. Although some tests tools will have to be installed on the test PCs e.g. capture/replay tools, one should be aware that every test tool that is installed takes you one step further away from the live environment. It is worth considering having a separate PC in the lab that provides access to test tools not directly related to test execution, e.g. test management tools, bug tracking tools.

Application under test

It is unlikely that you will be able to get away with only one installation of the AUT, unless you have a well-established system that is in the maintenance phase of its life cycle. So you will need to decide how many installations are required. I would strongly recommend that performance testing be separated from functional testing. It is worth considering having separate installations for different testing groups, i.e. functional acceptance testers, user acceptance testers and operations acceptance testers should all have their own installations. Other constraints to consider are the number of releases it may be necessary to test in parallel and whether the installation can easily be made to access different databases. The latter, if possible, may enable you to reduce the number of installations by assigning separate databases to the different test groups and using time slots for the testing.

Other requirements

Will development be given direct access to the test environment? There is undoubtedly a need to be able to transfer information, such as trace files, log files, protocols, from the test environment to the development environment in electronic form. There are a number of possible ways of achieving this, including e-mail, a LAN connection, CDs, memory sticks.

Finally you are going to need test user accounts. These allow you to assign different roles and responsibilities to the user. Without this flexibility you will be unable to properly test all the functionality of the application.

Keeping chaos at bay

Having defined the requirements for the environment and probably done your first installation, now is the time to start getting your processes defined. In the heat of the testing (who-ever heard of calm, leisurely testing?) if you don't have well defined and practical processes, you will soon find your test environment deteriorating into an uncontrolled chaos.

These are some examples of activities you may want to have processes defined for:

- Installing a new release of the AUT
- Upgrading the baseline installation
- Applying patches to the installation
- Test data load and maintenance
- Taking backups of the testware
- Booking time and resources in the test lab

The processes should be as practical as possible. Try to eliminate all unnecessary bureaucracy. It also helps to have the processes documented in a form, which is easy to refer to and understand at a glance. I have found that RASCI charts are a good way to do this. A RASCI (responsible, approves, supports, is consulted and is informed) chart is a simple tool that can be used to identify roles and responsibilities in a process to make sure ownership, approval, support, consultation and communication responsibilities are assigned.

It is a good idea to collect all this information together into a Test Handbook, which of course then belongs to the reference material that is made available in the test lab. I have found it extremely useful to make checklists (excel sheets), which list the activities, in the order they are to be performed and have tick boxes for each task to record progress (very useful if you get interrupted by something e.g. a phone call). The checklists belong to my philosophy of making important information readily available to everyone. If you run out of time when documenting your processes then just make the checklists. It is a simple truth that anything, which has a practical use and adds value, will be kept up to date. Similarly I make good use of whiteboards in the test lab to display pieces of transient but vital information. Post-its are put to use to mark up the test PCs with information such as which operating system is installed, which installation of the AUT they are hooked up to, etc.

Better data, better testing

I quote James Lyndsay in heading. This was the title he gave to a tutorial he held at EuroSTAR 2002. And I can only agree with him wholeheartedly. If you think you've finished, when you have defined your requirements and processes, then think again. You need to put some serious thought into managing your test data. Controlling test data is part of dealing with known quantities, which in turn leads to reliable test results.

Test data defined

Test data can be divided into 3 types, Lyndsay [2001]:

- Environmental data

That tells the system about its technical environment, e.g. directory paths

- Setup data

That tells the system about the business rules, e.g. tariff structures

- Input data

Is entered into the system by normal functions of the system.

Subdivide input data into 2 categories:

- Primary input data

That is entered into the system during test execution as part of the test case.

- Secondary input data

That exists in the system before a test is executed and that affects or is affected by and is a prerequisite for the test execution.

Environmental data is loaded manually, usually during installation. It often causes lots of problems the first time you try to install the AUT in your test environment and keeps you in constant touch with development, while you try to get a clean, functioning installation. Be sure to keep good notes during this painful birth and document it all. Setup data is also usually loaded manually using a system administration tool associated with the application. Input data is naturally part of test case design.

Environmental data and setup data are normally fairly stable and not subject to frequent change. Input data is transient data and therefore more likely to decay over time and during test execution. Although all types of test data need to be managed, it is the input data that will require most attention.

Managing test data

Even if you have multiple installations you will still have more than one tester using the test data in an installation. To prevent cross-contamination of test results caused by multiple updates to test data, it is sensible to divide the test data into logical data sets and to assign a particular data set to a tester. The data sets must be defined so that data used in one area, will not affect the results of tests in another area. Typically the data sets are defined at the level of a business object. Customer data may be divided into logical sets based on a range of values for the customer number. Product data can be divided based on product groups, e.g. one logical set contains all kitchen appliances, another all bedroom furniture.

Another useful concept is that of test data partitions, Lyndsay [2001]:

- Safe area

No test changes the test data, so the area can be trusted.

- Change area

Tests may change the test data, but must reset or reload the data after testing.

- Scratch area

Existing data cannot be trusted, testers use at their own risk.

The use of data sets and partitions rely on the discipline of the testers in sticking to the rules. They are not in themselves a foolproof way of preventing data corruption.

When defining the processes for test data management it is important to decide where the test data will be stored. Will it be inside or outside the test environment? Having a well-defined directory structure for storing test data, which is intuitive to use, will make the data readily available to everyone and also help prevent data contamination.

Another consideration is the format in which the data is stored. There are a number of possibilities here, e.g.:

- In a neutral format (excel sheets)
- Input format/files for utilities
- Using import/export functions of the database.

A case study

In a project for a service provider to the travel industry I was involved in system testing a client/server application for travel agencies. The system test covered functional acceptance testing, usability testing and performance testing. I was managing the test team performing the functional acceptance test. The test lab that we used for the system test ended up being used by the whole organization, for all client/server applications, for system testing, user acceptance testing and operations acceptance testing.

Test lab established

Clearly there were a number of problems that needed resolution before much more testing was done.

Small Test Lab Setup:

The test lab was configured as follows:

- 6 PCs with interchangeable hard disks, 2 per PC with different versions of the Windows operating system
- 2 gateways (X25 and X31)
- 1 PC as a repository for the testware with a DAT drive for taking back Ups
- 1 PC monitoring the server
- In an isolated section of the LAN.

Medium Test Lab Setup:

The test lab was configured as follows:

- 15-20 PCs with interchangeable hard disks, 4 per PC with different versions of the Windows operating system
- 4 gateways (X25 and X31)
- 2 PC as a repository for the testware with a DAT drive for taking back Ups
- 2 PC monitoring the server

- In an isolated section of the LAN.
- Multi browser setup
- Open Source tools as per there testing type

Large Test Lab Setup:

The test lab was configured as follows:

- 35-40 PCs with interchangeable hard disks, 10 per PC with different versions of the Windows operating system
- 8 gateways (X25 and X31)
- 4 PC as a repository for the testware with a DAT drive for taking back Ups
- 4 PC monitoring the server
- In an isolated section of the LAN.
- Multi browser setup
- Open Source tools as per there testing type

How does lab testing benefit me, and why is it necessary?

Even if you are certain that the software is a good product and that there haven't been too many bugs, you can never take too many precautions. Testing can expose problems such as:

- Flaws in the design.
- Inefficient processes.
- Poor performance.
- Incompatibility issues with hardware and/or software.

Testing is also a good way to practice installing and configuring the product before it is presented to the client, and it allows you to learn about the software more thoroughly. It can show how the product will perform in various situations, particularly if the testing is done in an environment that duplicates the one that will be used by the client after the product is deployed.

But most importantly, testing will help you to be prepared in case something goes wrong with the system (hardware or network failures, data corruption, etc.).

Getting started

There are two very important requirements for all testing projects: documentation and budgeting. You can never have too much documentation.

Documentation

Even if it's not a very large project, you should be keeping a record of all your actions from the very beginning. It might seem that you don't need the notes right now, but if you get stuck on a problem later, the documentation can help you trace the problem back to a previous step.

Start with your ideas of what should be accomplished by testing the software, any problems that you foresee, and a list of other people who might need to participate in the testing.

Budgeting

Next, plan a budget for the project. Even in the early stages, you should have enough resources allocated so that you can add more testing components later, if necessary. Remember that you should avoid taking any equipment that is already in the production environment, such as computers or other components currently in use, even occasionally, by office workers or other personnel.

Ideally, you want the testing lab to simulate the production environment, so identical equipment should be purchased for the lab if feasible. It's also best to avoid using the lab testing equipment in the production environment later. That same equipment can be used again in testing sometime in the future.

Although it can be expensive to acquire the equipment and set up the test lab, it is quite possible that the costs can be justified in several ways. Consider the return on investment (ROI):

- If you can use this equipment for other projects, you can save substantial amounts of money in the future.
- Most likely, you will also be able to streamline the testing process over time by discovering more efficient ways to accomplish various tasks.
- The lab can serve as an environment where you can have training for the demonstration of functionality, deployment processes, or resolving problems in a project.

The equipment that will be necessary for the project should include:

- Servers that are identical (or as similar as possible) to the ones in the production environment.
- Client computers corresponding to the ones end users have (including operating systems, other necessary equipment, and software).
- Peripherals like the ones currently in use (printers, etc.). This will allow you to gain

familiarity with the hardware to be used in the deployment and do performance tests.

If necessary, costs can be kept down by purchasing less-expensive equipment, as long as the major components are present. If you are lacking the resources for certain components, you'll still be able to perform specific implementation scenarios on the less-capable equipment. In that case, the servers and client computers must be able to run the same software.

Building the test network

Keep the lab separate from the production network. This will ensure that the testing activities do not affect the production LAN. You should mirror the network that is used in production as closely as possible:

- If you use both Ethernet and Token Ring there, then the lab should include both.
- Use the same models of hubs, routers, switches, and bridges.
- Use the same types of cables, if possible.

After everything is in place, test all the connections before actually installing the servers. If it all checks out, then go ahead and install and configure the servers.

Performing the testing

Now you're ready to start the actual testing. Make sure you have plenty of backups. This will be very important when you test the impact of version upgrades, service packs, patches, and third-party software or add-ons.

Early in the testing stages, it may not be possible to test absolutely everything, but you can start with the most vital elements:

- Test the busiest server on the network.
- Test the slowest client computer.
- Test the least-reliable network link.
- Check who has control over specific administrative rights and thoroughly plan and test the rights as you would with other security features.
- Test all the known components until you have ensured that it can run with good stability.

If it was necessary to make any changes to the design, as specifically directed by the architects of the project and/or the developers, then continue testing until you have reached stability. Once the systems are stable, verify that the components and applications function properly. This step may require several iterations.

Completing the testing project documentation

Now that you have verified that the system works properly, it's time to work on the most important documentation in this project, which covers the following critical areas:

- What were the exact objectives and results of the project?
- What were the techniques and the tools that were used to perform the tests and evaluate the results?
- What were the resources required for the entire project?
- What hardware and software were used and at what stages? List the types and models of all of the hardware, including networking devices. List all the software, versions, updates, and service packs that were used.
- List the names of all the personnel who participated, the departments they came from, the things they did at various times, and when they did these things.
- Write out a full description of the results.
- Explain the resolution of each of the problems.

Test Lab Hardware

The hardware for the lab is described here. Some of this equipment has been purchased, and some target boards have been delivered already.

Here are some of the individual hardware items that will be used in the lab:

- server - accessible from the outside:
- firewall
- host/target combinations
- control modules

According to business test lab can be set:

1) Small
2) Medium
3) Big

Server Configuration:

Particulars	Hardware
RAM	Minimum 2 GB
Hard Disk	As per project Specific (minimum 80 GB)
Internet	2 mbps

PC Configuration

Particulars	Hardware
RAM	Minimum 1 GB
Hard Disk	As per project Specific (minimum 80 GB)
Browser	Multi Browser setup

Open Source VM software's:

XEN

The Xen® hypervisor, the powerful open source industry standard for virtualization, offers a powerful, efficient, and secure feature set for virtualization of x86, x86_64, IA64, ARM, and other CPU architectures. It supports a wide range of guest operating systems including Windows®, Linux®, Solaris®, and various versions of the BSD operating systems.

http://www.xen.org/

http://www.xen.org/products/cloud_source.html

Kernel Based Virtual Machine

KVM (for Kernel-based Virtual Machine) is a full virtualization solution for Linux on x86 hardware containing virtualization extensions (Intel VT or AMD-V). It consists of a loadable kernel module, kvm.ko, that provides the core virtualization infrastructure and a processor specific module, kvm-intel.ko or kvm-amd.ko. KVM also requires a modified QEMU although work is underway to get the required changes upstream.

Using KVM, one can run multiple virtual machines running unmodified Linux or Windows images. Each virtual machine has private virtualized hardware: a network card, disk, graphics adapter, etc.

The kernel component of KVM is included in mainline Linux, as of 2.6.20.

KVM is open source software.

http://www.linux-kvm.org/page/Main_Page

VirtualBox

VirtualBox is a general-purpose full virtualizer for x86 hardware. Targeted at server, desktop and embedded use, it is now the only professional-quality virtualization solution that is also Open Source Software

http://www.virtualbox.org/wiki/VirtualBox

References and Further Reading

- Black, Rex. 1999. Managing the Test Process, Microsoft Press Dustin, Elfreide, Jeff Rashka, John Paul. 1999. Automated Software Testing, Addison-Wesley
- Fewster, Mark, Dorothy Graham. 1999. Software Test Automation, Addison- Wesley
- Lyndsay, James. 2001. The Importance of Data in Functional Testing. Available at http://www.workroom-productions.com/
- Reid, R Dan. 2003. ISO 9000 and more, Quality Progress, Milwaukee, Apr. 2003 Reizer, Neal and Nancy Wang. 2000. Juggling Concurrent Releases, STQE Volume 2, Issue 6 Nov/Dec

Section 15

Cloud Computing Overview

Cloud Computing - Some terms

- Term cloud is used as a metaphor for internet
- Concept generally incorporates combinations of the following
  - Infrastructure as a service (IaaS)
  - Platform as a service (PaaS)
  - Software as a service(SaaS)
- Not to be confused with
  - Grid Computing – a form of distributed computing
    - Cluster of loosely coupled, networked computers acting in concert to perform very large tasks
  - Utility Computing – packaging of computing resources such as computing power, storage, also a metered services
  - Autonomic computing – self managed

Grid Computing

- Share Computers and data
- Evolved to harness inexpensive computers in Data center to solve variety of problems
- Harness power of loosely coupled computers to solve a technical or mathematical problem
- Used in commercial applications for drug discovery, economic forecasting, sesimic analysis and back-office
- Small to big
  - Can be confined to a corporation
  - Large public collaboration across many companies and networks
- Most grid solutions are built on
  - Computer Agents
  - Resource Manager
  - Scheduler
- Compute grids
  - Batch up jobs

- ◻ Submit the job to the scheduler, specifiying requirements and SLA(specs) required for running the job
- ◻ Scheduler matches specs with available resources and schedules the job to be run
- ◻ Farms could be as large as 10K cpus

- Most financial firms has grids like this
- Grids lack automation, agility, simplicity and SLA guarantees

Utility Computing

- More related to cloud computing
  - ◻ Applications, storage, computing power and network
- Requires cloud like infrastructure
- Pay by the drink model
  - ◻ Similar to electric service at home
- Pay for extra resources when needed
  - ◻ To handle expected surge in demand
  - ◻ Unanticipated surges in demand
- Better economics

Cloud computing – History

- Evolved over a period of time
- Roots traced back to Application Service Providers in the 1990's
- Parallels to SaaS
- Evolved from Utility computing and is a broader concept

So although they are often lumped together, the differences between utility computing and cloud computing are crucial. Utility computing relates to the business model in which application infrastructure resources — hardware and/or software — are delivered. While cloud computing relates to the way we design, build, deploy and run applications that operate in an a virtualized environment, sharing resources and boasting the ability to dynamically grow, shrink and self-heal.

Cloud computing

- Much more broader concept
- Encompasses
  - IIAS, PAAS, SAAS
- Dynamic provision of services/resource pools in a co-ordinated fashion
  - On demand computing – No waiting period
  - Location of resource is irrelevant
    - May be relevant from performance(network latency) perspective, data locality
- Applications run somewhere on the cloud
  - Web applications fulfill these for end user
  - However, for application developers and IT
    - Allows develop, deploy and run applications that can easily grow capacity(scalability), work fast(performance), and offer good reliability
    - Without concern for the nature and location of underlying infrastructure
  - Activate, retire resources

Dynamically update infrastructure elements without affecting the business

Clouds Versus Grids

- Clouds and Grids are distinct
- Cloud
  - Full private cluster is provisioned
  - Individual user can only get a tiny fraction of the total resource pool
  - No support for cloud federation except through the client interface
  - Opaque with respect to resources
- Grid
  - Built so that individual users can get most, if not all of the resources in a single request
  - Middleware approach takes federation as a first principle
  - Resources are exposed, often as bare metal
- These differences mandate different architectures for each

Cloud Mythologies

- Cloud computing infrastructure is just a web service interface to operating system virtualization.
  - "I'm running Xen in my data center – I'm running a private cloud."
- Cloud computing imposes a significant performance penalty over "bare metal" provisioning.
  - "I won't be able to run a private cloud because my users will not tolerate the performance hit."
- Clouds and Grids are equivalent
  - "In the mid 1990s, the term grid was coined to describe technologies that would allow consumers to obtain computing power on demand."

Cloud Anatomy

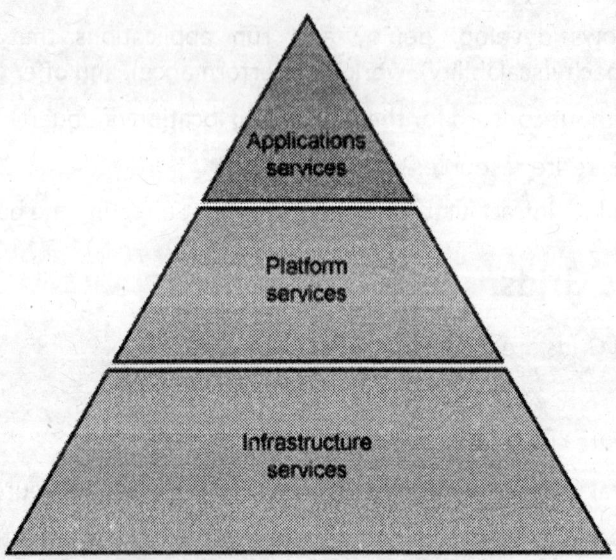

- Application Services(services on demand)
  - Gmail, GoogleCalender
  - Payroll, HR, CRM etc
  - Sugarm CRM, IBM Lotus Live
- Platform Services (resources on demand)
  - Middleware, Intergation, Messaging, Information, connectivity etc

- AWS, IBM Virtual images, Boomi, CastIron, Google Appengine
- Infrastructure as services(physical assets as services)
  - IBM Blue house, VMWare, Amazon EC2, Microsoft Azure Platform, Sun Parascale and more

Cloud Computing – layers

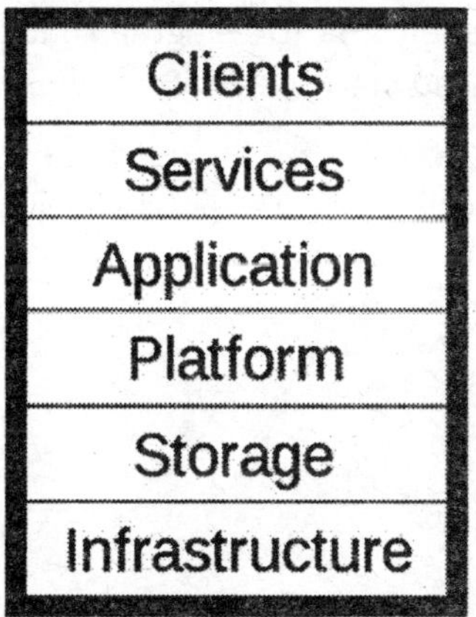

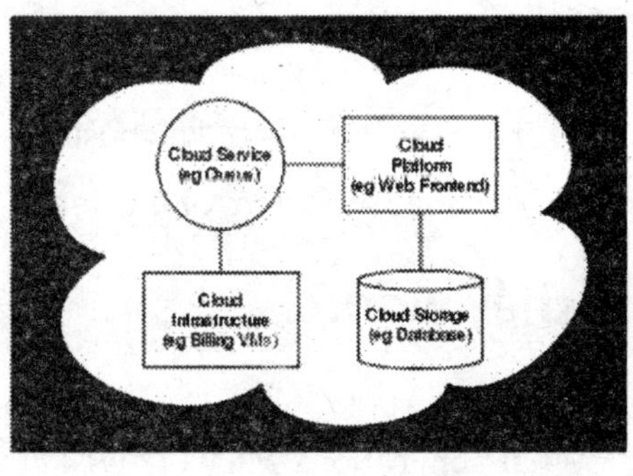

Layers

Architecture

What is a Cloud?

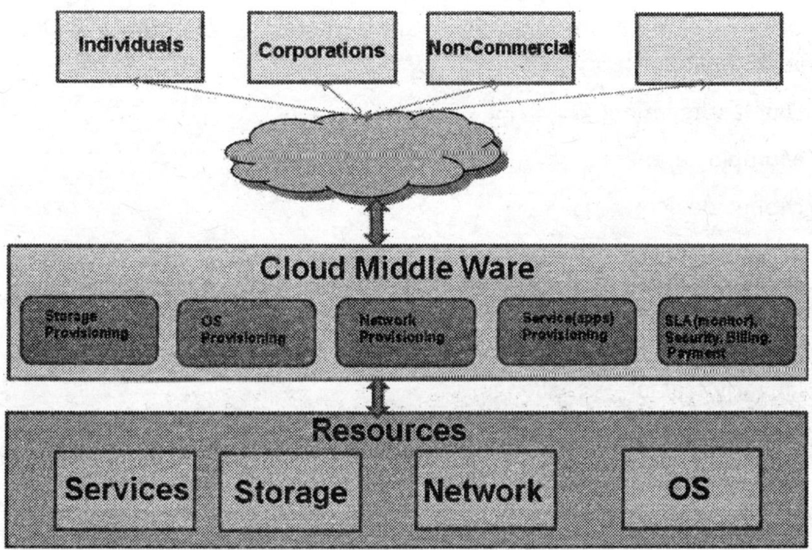

Why cloud computing

- Data centers are notoriously underutilized, often idle 85% of the time
  - Over provisioning
  - Insufficient capacity planning and sizing
  - Improper understanding of scalability requirements etc
- including thought leaders from Gartner, Forrester, and IDC—agree that this new model offers significant advantages for fast-paced startups, SMBs and enterprises alike.
- Cost effective solutions to key business demands
- Move workloads to improve efficiency

How do they work?

- Public clouds are opaque
  - What applications will work well in a cloud?
- Many of the advantages offered by Public Clouds appear useful for "on premise" IT
  - Self-service provisioning
  - Legacy support
  - Flexible resource allocation
- What extensions or modifications are required to support a wider variety of services and applications?
  - Data assimilation
  - Multiplayer gaming
  - Mobile devices

Cloud computing – Characteristics

- Agility – On demand computing infrastructure
  - Linearly scalable – challenge
- Reliability and fault tolerance
  - Self healing – Hot backups, etc
  - SLA driven – Policies on how quickly requests are processed

- Multi-tenancy – Several customers share infrastructure, without compromising privacy and security of each of the customer's data
- Service-oriented – compose applications out of loosely coupled services. One service failure will not disrupt other services. Expose these services as API's
- Virtualized – decoupled from underlying hardware. Multiple applications can run in one computer
- Data, Data, Data
  - Distributing, partitioning, security, and synchronization

Public, Private and Hybrid clouds

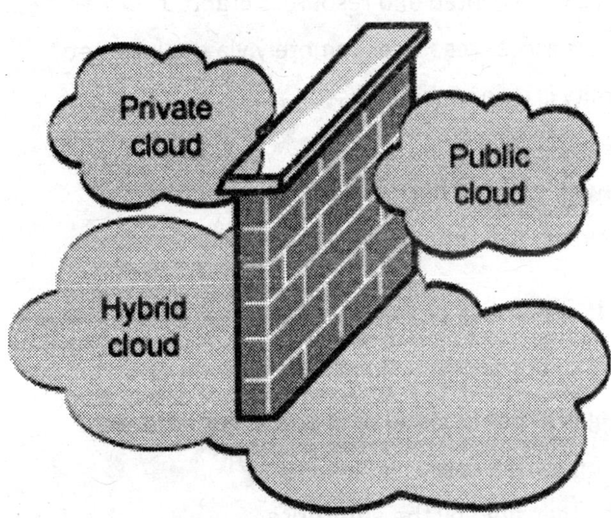

Public clouds

- Open for use by general public
  - Exist beyond firewall, fully hosted and managed by the vendor
  - Individuals, corporations and others
  - Amazon's Web Services and Google appEngine are examples
- Offers startups and SMB's quick setup, scalability, flexibility and automated management. Pay as you go model helps startups to start small and go big
- Security and compliance?

- Reliability concerns hinder the adoption of cloud
    - Amazon S3 services were down for 6 hours

Public Clouds (Now)

- Large scale infrastructure available on a rental basis
    - Operating System virtualization (e.g. Xen, kvm) provides CPU isolation
    - "Roll-your-own" network provisioning provides network isolation
    - Locally specific storage abstractions
- Fully customer self-service
    - Service Level Agreements (SLAs) are advertized
    - Requests are accepted and resources granted via web services
    - Customers access resources remotely via the Internet
- Accountability is e-commerce based
    - Web-based transaction
    - "Pay-as-you-go" and flat-rate subscription
    - Customer service, refunds, etc.

Private Clouds

- Within the boundaries(firewall) of the organization
- All advantages of public cloud with one major difference
    - Reduce operation costs
    - Has to be managed by the enterprise
- Fine grained control over resources
- More secure as they are internal to org
- Schedule and reshuffle resources based on business demands
- Ideal for apps related to tight security and regulatory concerns
- Development requires hardware investments and in-house expertise
- Cost could be prohibitive and cost might exceed public clouds

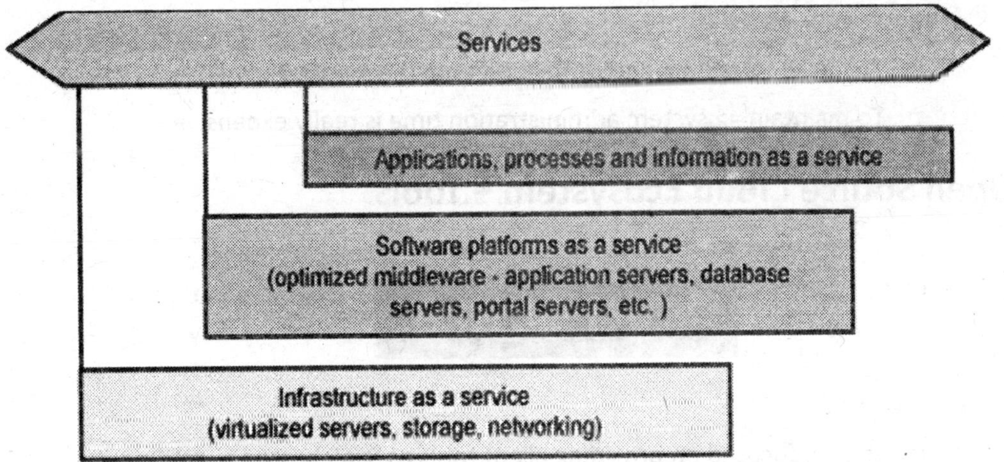

- SOA Enabled cloud computing to what is today
- Physical infrastructure like SOA must be discoverable, manageable and governable
- REST Protocol widely used(Representational State Transfer)

Clouds for Developers

- Ability to acquire, deploy, configure and host environments
- Perform development unit testing, prototyping and full product testing

Open Source Cloud Infrastructure

- Simple
  - Transparent => need to "see" into the cloud
  - Scalable => complexity often limits scalability
  - Secure => limits adoptability
- Extensible
  - New application classes and service classes may require new features
  - Clouds are new => need to extend while retaining useful features
- Commodity-based
  - Must leverage extensive catalog of open source software offerings
  - New, unstable, and unsupported infrastructure design is a barrier to uptake, experimentation, and adoption

- Easy
  - To install => system administration time is expensive
  - To maintain => system administration time is really expensive

Open Source Cloud Ecosystem – Tools

- RightScale
  - Startup focused on providing client tools as SaaS hosted in AWS
  - Uses the REST interface
- Canonical
  - Ubuntu 9.10 (Karmic Koala)
  - Includes KVM and Xen Hypervisors

Open Source Cloud Anatomy

- Extensibility
  - Simple architecture and open internal APIs
- Client-side interface
  - Amazon's AWS interface and functionality (familiar and testable)
- Networking
  - Virtual private network per cloud
  - Must function as an overlay => cannot supplant local networking
- Security
  - Must be compatible with local security policies
- Packaging, installation, maintenance
  - system administration staff is an important constituency for uptake
- Private clouds are really hybrid clouds
  - Users want private clouds to export the same APIs as the public clouds
- In the Enterprise, the storage model is key

- Scalable "blob" storage doesn't quite fit the notion of "data file."
- Cloud Federation is a policy mediation problem
  - No good way to translate SLAs in a cloud allocation chain
  - "Cloud Bursting" will only work if SLAs are congruent
- Customer SLAs allow applications to consider cost as first-class principle
  - Buy the computational, network, and storage capabilities that are required

Open Source Clouds contd.

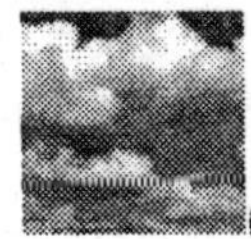

Cloud Computing at UCSB

Open-source implementations of popular cloud systems

Eucalyptus

- Infrastructure-as-a-service (IAAS) framework
- Web services based implementation of elastic/utility/cloud computing infrastructure
- Linux image hosting via virtualization
- Emulates the **Amazon AWS interface** – applications and tools can't tell the difference
- Real use, real users, real impact
  - Distributed with Ubuntu
  - Large international user community

  http://eucalyptus.cs.ucsb.edu

  Lead: Rich Wolski

- Platform-as-a-service (PAAS) framework
- Web services based implementation of **Google AppEngine APIs**
- Runs over Eucalyptus, Amazon EC2, and virtualization layers (Xen/KVM)
- Implements multiple database backends (Hbase, Hypertable, Cassandra, MySQL,...)
- Real use, real users, real impact
  - International user community

  http://appscale.cs.ucsb.edu

  Lead: Chandra Krintz

- Open, extensible, easy to install/use/maintain, transparent, scalable
- Enables investigation of and experimentation with
  - Real applications in real settings
  - IAAS + PAAS interoperation and integration
- Frameworks for investigation the next generation of ***energy efficient*** distributed systems *technologies, languages, applications, and services*

UCSB

Eucalyptus(Elastic Utility Computing Architecture Linking Your Programs To Useful Systems)

Eucalyptus Architecture: WS-Cloud

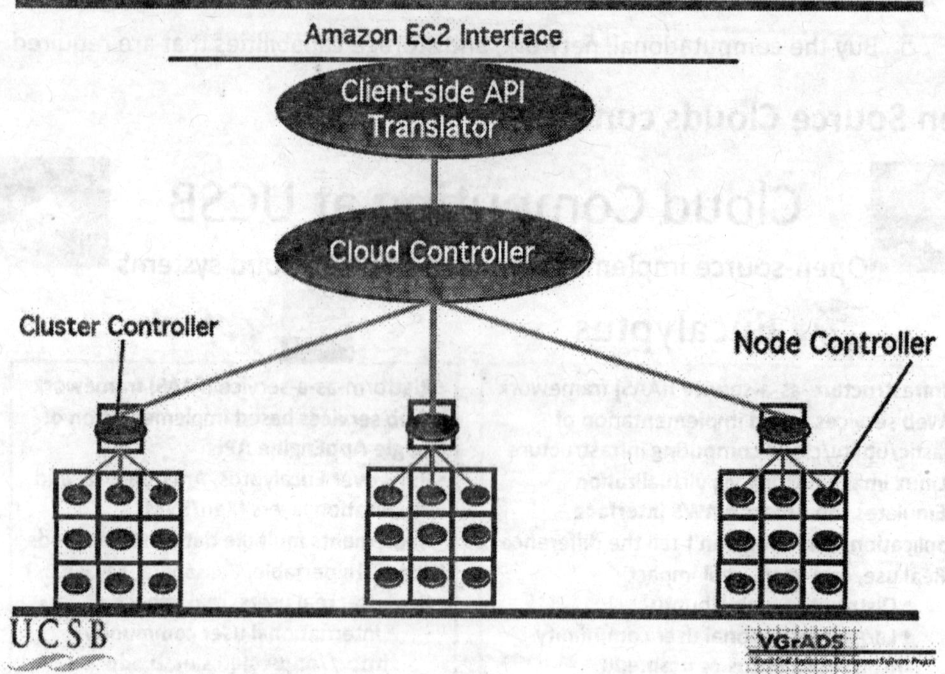

Clouds and Virtualization

- Operating System virtualization (Xen, KVM, VMWare, HyperV) is only apparent for IaaS
  - AppEngine = BigTable
- Hypervisors virtualize CPU, Memory, and local device access as a <u>single</u> virtual machine (VM)
- IaaS Cloud allocation is
  - Set of VMs
  - Set of storage resources
  - Private network

- Allocation is atomic
- SLA
- Monitoring

Cloud Performance

- Extensive performance study using HPC applications and benchmarks
- Two questions:
  - *Performance impact of virtualization*
  - *Performance impact of cloud infrastructure*
- Observations:
  - Random access disk is slower with Xen
  - CPU bound can be faster with Xen -> depends on configuration
  - Kernel version is far more important
  - No statistically detectable overhead

AWS small appears to throttle network bandwidth and (maybe) disk bandwidth

Cloud Infrastructure

- **Network operations center**
- **Physical Infrastructure**
- **Physical Security**
- **Cooling**
- **Power infrastructure, Network Cabling, Fire safety**

Clouds – open for innovation

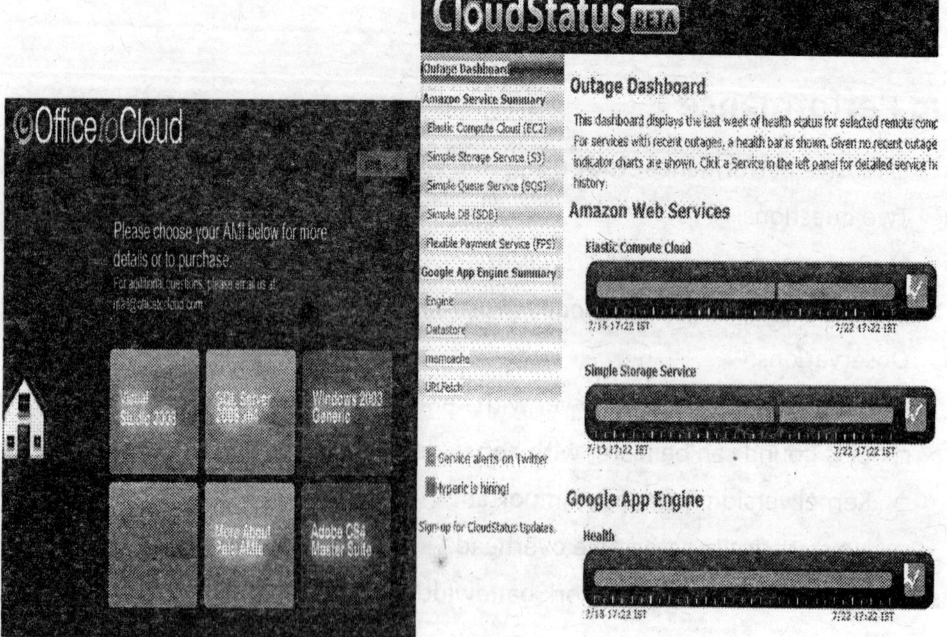

Cloud computing open issues

- Governance
  - Security, Privacy and control
  - SLA guarantees
  - Ownership and control
  - Compliance and auditing
    - Sarbanes and Oxley Act
- Reliability
  - Good servive provider with 99.999% availability
- Cloud independence – Vendor lockin?
  - Cloud provider goes out of business
- Data Security
- Cloud lockin and Loss of control

- Plan for moving data along with Cloud provider

- Cost?
- Simplicity?
- Tools
- Controls on sensitive data?
    - Out of business
- Big and small
    - Scalability and cost outweigh reliability for small businesses
    - Big businesses may have a problem

References: / Cloud articles

ReddyRaja
Research Consultant, IIIT Hyderabad
Vasudev Verma
Associated Professor, IIIT Hyderabad

- http://fif.kr/fisc2009/doc/eom.pdf

- http://blogs.zdnet.com/Hinchcliffe/?p=488&tag=btxcsim
- http://blogs.zdnet.com/Howlett/?p=558&tag=btxcsim
- http://blogs.zdnet.com/BTL/?p=9560&tag=btxcsim
- http://www.businessweek.com/technology/content/aug2008/tc2008082_445669_page_3.htm
- http://www.ibm.com/developerworks/websphere/techjournal/0904_amrhein/0904_amrhein.html
- **http://cloudcomputing.sys-con.com/**

Battle in Cloud:

- Amazon Web Services
- Google App Engine
  - Free upto 500 MB,
    - Free for small scale applications?
    - Universities?
  - Pay when you scale
- GoGrid
- .. Some more Hosting companies
- Where is HP, IBM, Oracle(+sun) and Dell?

ISBN	Title	Author	Year	Price

Shroff Reprints & Original Titles

The X Team Series
(An Imprint of Shroff Publishers)

Computers

ISBN	Title	Author	Year	Price
9789350236321	**.NET Interview Q&A, 164 Pages**	**Harwani**	**2012**	**225.00**
9788184041569	Ajax for Beginners (B/CD), 452 Pages	Bayross	2006	375.00
9788184041972	Application Development with Oracle & PHP on Linux for Beginners, 2/ed (B/CD), 940 Pages	Bayross	2007	650.00
9789350233733	Blogging for Beginners, 268 Pages	Harwani	2011	350.00
9788184046397	C for Beginners, 532 Pages	Mothe	2009	375.00
9789350233900	C Interviews Q&A, 119 Pages [Forthcoming]	Thorat	2011	150.00
9788184046564	C++ for Beginners, 403 Pages	Harwani	2009	375.00
9789350231012	Core Java for Beginners, (B/CD), 892 Pages	Shah	2010	500.00
9788184046694	Database Concepts and Systems for Students, 3/ed, 428 Pgs	Bayross	2009	325.00
9788184048780	HTML for Beginners, 2/ed, 416 Pages	Aibara	2010	500.00
9789350236475	**HTML5 for Beginners, 564 Pages**	**Aibara**	**2012**	**450.00**
9788184047059	Hibernate 3 for Beginners - Covers Java Persistence API (B/CD), 680 Pages	Shah	2009	500.00
9788184045697	Java EE 5 for Beginners, 2/ed **(B/CD)**, 1,192 Pages	Bayross	2008	575.00
9788184049398	Java EE 6 for Beginners, (B/CD), 1092 Pages	Shah	2009	825.00
9788184049411	Java EE 6 Server Programming for Professionals (B/DVD), 1,328 Pages (H/B)	Shah	2010	750.00
9788184048063	Java EE Project using EJB 3, JPA and Struts 2 for Beginners, (B/CD), 1,258 Pages	Shah	2009	1,025.00
9788184043174	Java for Beginners **(B/CD)**, Covers Java SE 6 JDK, 600 Pages	Chavan	2007	450.00
9788184045932	Java for Professionals: A Practical Approach to Java Programming (Covers Java SE 6), 790 Pages	Harwani	2008	525.00
9788184046670	Java for Students, 690 Pages	Pherwani	2009	475.00
9789350233719	Java for Students, 2/ed, 850 Pages	Pherwani	2011	600.00
9788184047097	Java Persistence API in EJB 3 for Professionals, (B/CD) 756 Pgs	Shah	2009	550.00
9788184045925	JavaServer Pages Project for Beginners, **(B/CD)**, 746 Pages	Shah	2008	550.00
9788184045598	Java Server Programming for Professionals, Revised & Enlarged 2/ed (Covers Java EE 5) (B/CD), 1,612 Pages	Bayross	2008	700.00
9788184043594	Java Server Pages for Beginners **(B/CD)**, 872 Pages	Bayross	2007	500.00
9788184048438	Lamp Programming for Professionals, (B/CD), 1,284	Shah	2009	1,275.00
9789350233986	**Mobile Computing for Beginners, 782 Pages**	**Shende**	**2012**	**750.00**
9789350235188	MySQL 5.1 for Professionals (B/CD), 772 Pages	Bayross	2011	650.00

ISBN	Title	Author	Year	Price
9788184045260	Oracle for Professionals **(B/CD)**, 1,420 Pgs	Shah	2008	750.00
9788184043228	PC Hardware for Beginners, 308 Pages	Sangia	2007	225.00
9788184040753	PHP 5.1 for Beginners **(B/CD)**, 1,284 Pages	Bayross	2006	650.00
9788184048445	PHP Project for Beginners, (B/CD), 1,200 Pages	Shah	2010	600.00
9788184047073	Practical ASP.NET 3.5 Projects for Beginners, (B/CD), 550 Pgs	Harwani	2009	450.00
9788184048070	Practical EJB Project for Beginners, 312 Pages	Harwani	2009	325.00
9788184043426	Practical Java Project for Beginners **(B/CD)**, 164 Pages	Harwani	2007	150.00
9788184043419	Practical Web Services for Beginners, 168 Pages	Harwani	2007	150.00
9789350234907	Programming with Pl/SQL for Beginners, 236 Pages	Patil	2011	300.00
9788184049725	QuickTest Professional (QTP) Version 10, 116 Pages	Mallepally	2010	125.00
9789350231241	QTP for Professionals, 480 Pages	Reddy	2010	450.00
9789350236499	**SAP MM for Beginners, 384 Pages**	**Rakshit**	**2012**	**600.00**
9788184048100	SAP SD for Beginners, 324 Pages	Samad	2009	450.00
9789350233894	SAP SD for Beginners 2/ed, 260 Pages	Samad	2011	350.00
9789350236482	**Software Automation Testing Tools for Beginners, 1110 Pages**	**Shende**	**2012**	**1000.00**
9789350236901	**Spring 3 for Beginners, Pages 612**	**Shah**	**2012**	**575.00**
9788184047448	Struts 2 for Beginners, 2/ed, (B/CD), 566 Pages	Shah	2009	450.00
9788184046960	Struts 2 with Hibernate 3 Project for Beginners, (B/CD), 1,042 Pages	Shah	2009	675.00
9788184041071	Visual Basic 2005 for Beginners **(B/CD)**, 1,172 Pages	Bayross	2006	150.00

Other Computer Titles

ISBN	Title	Author	Year	Price
9789350230237	A Primer on Software Quality Models & Project Management, 640 Pages	Mehta	2010	600.00
9788184048827	Art of Creative Destruction: Illustarted Software Testing, Test Automation & Agile Testing, 2/ed, 348 Pages	Puranik	2010	425.00
9788173660030	AS/400 Architecture & Applications, 332 Pages	Lawrence	1993	250.00
9788173660047	AS/400: A Practical Guide to Programming & Operations, 284 Pgs	Zeilenga	1993	225.00
9789350232859	Beginning Web Development for Smartphones Developing Web Applications with PHP, MySQL and jQTouch, 252 Pages	Harwani	2011	300.00
9789350231029	C# 4.0 Programming Made Easy, 624 Pages	Kadam	2011	425.00
9789350230244	Computer Architecture and Maintenance, 320 Pages	Kadam	2010	250.00
9788173660016	CICS: A How-To for Cobol Programmers, 428 Pages	Kirk	1993	300.00
9789350235553	**Data Structure and Algorithm, 492 Pages**	**Rukadikar**	**2012**	**400.00**
9788184048957	FAQ's in MFC and MFC Solutions, Vol I (B/CD) 510 Pages	P. G. Naik	2010	425.00
9788173666810	First Encounter with Java Including BlueJ, 386 Pages	Bhutta	2006	225.00
9789350230275	Instant Oracle, 100 Pages	Shah	2010	75.00
9788173664632	Introducing MySQL, 96 Pages	Oak	2005	50.00
9789350230251	Management Information System (MIS), 176 Pages	Kadam	2010	200.00
9789350231258	Maximum Oracle with Oracle Best Practices, 772 Pages	Puranik	2011	675.00
9788173660023	MVS / VSAM for the Application Programmer, 504 Pages	Brown	1993	325.00
9788184047899	Operating Systems, 2/ed, 408 Pages	Sumitradevi	2009	500.00
9789350236918	**Oracle Financials 11i: A Practical Guide for the Beginners, 2nd Edition, 436 Pgs**	**Peri**	**2012**	**725.00**
9788173668012	Software Defect Prevention Concepts and Implementation, 180 Pages **(H/B)**	Kane & Bajaj	2003	300.00
9789350236307	**Software Testing: Interview Questions, 176 Pages**	**Reddy**	**2012**	**175.00**

ISBN	Title	Author	Year	Price
9788173668814	Strategic Bidding: A Successful Approach, 192 Pgs	Garg	2004	250.00
9788173660078	TCP/IP Companion: A Guide For The Common User, 284 Pages	Arick	1993	225.00
9789350231005	Testing in 30^{+} Open Source Tools (B/CD), 1,080 Pages	Shende	2010	000.00
9788173660429	Vijay Mukhi's ERP Odyssey: Implementing PeopleSoft Financials 7.0/7.5, 528 Pages	Mukhi	1999	350.00

Business, Management & Finance

ISBN	Title	Author	Year	Price
9788184046977	An Introduction to Foreign Exchange & Financial Risk Management, **(B/CD)**, 348 Pages	Lakshman	2009	400.00
9789350230268	Bootstrapping A Software Company, 348 Pages	Yadav	2010	425.00
9788184044287	Breaking the Black Box, **(B/CD)**, 276 Pages	Pring	2008	500.00
9788184044249	Break Your Negative Attitude, 114 Pages	Dr. Mishra	2007	125.00
9789350230220	Complete Guide to Technical Analysis: An Indian Perspective, 612 Pages	Pring	2010	650.00
9788184040425	Developing Analytical Skills: Case Studies in Management, 636 Pages	Dr. Natarajan	2008	500.00
9788173660993	Doing Business with the French, 150 Pages	Jhangiani	1999	150.00
9788184044959	Enabling Event-ful Experiences, 250 Pages	Balachandran	2008	200.00
9788184044744	Ethics, Indian Ethos and Management, 252 Pages	Balachandran	2008	175.00
9789350231227	Financial Decision Modeling Operations Research & Business Statistics (Group II, Paper 5 C.A. Final), 696 Pages	Sridhar	2010	350.00
9789350230794	Financial Management: Problems & Solutions, 4/ed, 1,228 Pgs	Sridhar	2010	750.00
9789350232965	Futures & Options: Equities & Commodities, 4/ed, 392 Pgs	Sridhar	2011	475.00
9789350233917	Globally Distributed Work, 280 Pages	Mehta	2011	425.00
9789350233887	Hospitality Management, 304 pages	Shirke	2011	525.00
9788184040432	How to Eat The Elephant? The CEO's Guide To An Enterprise System Implementation, 104 Pages	Tulsyan	2007	325.00
9789350230459	How to Learn Management from your wife (PB), 96 Pages	Rangnekar	2010	125.00
9789350233108	How to Learn Management from your wife (HB), 96 Pages	Rangnekar	2010	275.00
9788184044447	How to Select Stocks Using Technical Analysis, (B/CD), 338 Pages	Pring	2008	500.00
9788184044164	Logistics in International Business, 2/ed, 428 Pages	Aserkar	2007	450.00
9788184047547	Magic and Logic of Elliott Waves, The, 204 Pages	Kale	2009	500.00
9788184048568	Management Accounting & Financial Analysis for C.A.Final (June 2009), 9/ed, 540 Pages	Sridhar	2009	400.00
9789350235126	Management of Services, 348 Pages	Jain	2011	450.00
9788184044454	Momentum Explained, Volume I (B/CD), 366 Pages	Pring	2008	600.00
9788184044461	Momentum Explained, Volume II (B/CD), 338 Pages	Pring	2008	550.00
9788184047066	Purchasing and Inventory Management, 338 Pages	Menon	2009	475.00
9789350233870	Quantitative Techniques for Project Management, 256 Pages	Velayoudam	2011	600.00
9788173666797	Rules of Origin in International Trade, 238 Pages	Dr. Sathpathy	2005	300.00
9789350233580	Services Marketing, 448 Pages	Balachandran	2011	450.00
9789350233115	Soft Skills In Management, 148 Pages	Rangnekar	2011	125.00
9789350237847	**Strategic Financial Management For C. A. Final, 9/Ed, 904 Pgs.**	**Sridhar**	**2012**	**650.00**
9788173668814	Strategic Bidding: A Successful Approach, 192 Pages	Garg	2004	250.00
9788184043211	Time Your Trades With Technical Analysis **(B/CD)**, 348 Pages	Pradhan	2007	600.00

ISBN	Title	Author	Year	Price
Catering & Hotel Management				
9788173668739	Careers in Hospitality - Hotel Management Entrance Exam Guide, 332 Pages	Rego	2004	200.00
9789350233887	Hospitality Management, 303 Pages [Forthcoming]	Shirke	2011	525.00
9789350230817	Marvels of Indian Snacks, 264 Pages	Shankaran	2011	350.00
9788184044751	Marvels of South Indian Cuisine, 220 Pages	Shankaran	2008	250.00
9788184046687	Marvels of North Indian Cuisine, 196 Pages	Shankaran	2009	325.00
Civil Engineering				
9789350233252	Concrete for High Performance Sustainable Infrastructure, 312 Pages	Newlands	2011	750.00
9789350233245	New Developments in Concrete Construction, 296 Pages	Dhir	2011	750.00
9788173663772	Principles of Environmental Science Engineering and Maintenance, 288 Pages	Dr. Thirumurthy	2004	175.00
9788184048056	Raina's Concrete Bridge Practice: Construction, Maintenance and Rehabiliation 2/ed, 452 Pages (H/B) [14 Full Color Inserts]	Dr. Raina	2010	625.00
9788184048049	Raina's Concrete Bridge: Inspection, Repair, Strengthening, Testing, Load Capacity Evaluation 2/ed, 800 Pages (H/B) [32 Full Color Inserts]	Dr. Raina	2010	1,200.00
9788184047530	Raina's Concrete for Construction: Facts & Practice, 400 Pgs **(H/B)**	Dr. Raina	2009	650.00
9788184047875	Raina's Construction & Contract Management, 2/ed Inside Story, 585 Pages **(H/B)**	Dr. Raina	2009	750.00
9788184043785	Raina's Concrete Bridge Practice, 3/ed : Analysis, Design & Economics, 856 Pages	Dr. Raina	2007	1,000.00
9788184046618	Raina's Field Manual for Highway and Bridge Engineers, 3/ed,1,404 Pages	Dr. Raina	2009	1,800.00
9789350231418	Raina's Handbook for Concrete Bridges, 1500 Pages (H/B) [Forthcoming]	Dr. Raina	2011	TBA
9788184040135	The World of Bridges, 300 Pages **(H/B)** [4 color]	Dr. Raina	2006	500.00
9789350231180	Using Primavera 6: Planning, Executing, Monitoring and Controlling Projects, 228 Pages	Al-Saridi	2010	275.00
Communication				
9789350231265	Knowing Your Word's Worth: A Practical Guide to Communicating Effectively in English, 180 Pages	Shirodkar	2011	175.00
Dental / Health / Medical				
9788173669798	The Balancing Act "A Win Over Obesity", 296 Pages	Dr. Gadkari	2005	225.00
9788184049480	The Balancing Act "Know Your Heart", 368 Pages	Dr. Gadkari	2010	250.00
9788173668975	Splinting Management of MOBILE & Migrating Teeth, 104 Pgs	Dr. Kakar	2004	150.00

ISBN	Title	Author	Year	Price

Economics

9788184043266	Analysing Macroeconomics: A Toolkit for Managers, Executives & Students **(H/B)**, 150 Pages	Rakesh Singh	2007	500.00
9788184044171	Analysing Macroeconomics: A Toolkit for Managers, Executives & Students **(P/B)**, 156 Pages	Rakesh Singh	2007	250.00

Electrical Engineering

9788184043235	Basic Electrical Circuits, 2/ed, 368 Pages	Dr. Salam	2007	250.00

Electronics & Communication

9788173669002	Electronic Components and Materials, 3/ed, 404 Pages	Joshi	2004	175.00

Environmental Engineering

9788173663772	Principles of Environmental Science Engineering and Maintenance, 288 Pgs	Dr. Thirumurthy	2004	175.00

Event Management

9788184044959	Enabling Event-ful Experiences, 250 Pages	Balachandran	2008	250.00

General Titles

9788184045642	Hello Police Station (Marathi), 118 Pages	Shinde	2008	100.00
9789350231760	Mom Don't Spoil Me, 140 Pages	Dr. Mishra	2010	150.00

HRD

9788184047080	Departmental Enquiries: Concept, Procedure & Practice, 534 Pages	Goel	2009	475.00
9788184046229	How To Improve Trainer Effectiveness, 170 Pages	Balachandran	2008	200.00

Law

9789350230800	A Handbook on the Maintenance & Welfare of Parents and Senior Citizens Act, 2007.	Gracias	2010	150.00
9788173664151	Customs Valuation in India 3/ed, 262 Pages	Satapathy	2002	375.00
9788184042481	Laws Of Carriage Of Goods By Sea & Multimodal Transport In India, 92 Pages	Hariharan	2007	60.00
9788173661426	Law of Sale of Goods & Partnership, 228 Pages	Chandiramani	2000	150.00
9789350231289	Social Security, Insurance & The Law, 460 Pgs	Gopalakrishna	2011	600.00

Learning Disability

9789350233924	On the wave of Brain: A Broad Perspective of Learning Disability 300 Pages	Jain	2011	450.00

ISBN	Title	Author	Year	Price

Marine

ISBN	Title	Author	Year	Price
9788184043242	Containerisation, Multimodal Transport and Infrastructure Development in India, 5/ed, 852 Pages	Hariharan	2007	650.00
9788173660375	M.S. (STCW) Rules, 1998 incl. Training & Assessment Programme - 1,216 Pages	DG Shipping	1998	225.00
9788173661419	Maritime Education, Training & Assessment Manual (TAP) - Vol II, 474 Pages	DG Shipping	1999	400.00
9788184043136	Marine Control Technology, 336 Pages	Majumder	2007	400.00
9788173669279	Marine Diesel Engines, 428 Pages	Aranha	2004	250.00
9788184048544	Marine Electrical Technology, 5/ed, 1,250 Pages	Fernandes	2010	750.00
9788173660801	Marine Internal Combustion Engines, 272 Pages	Kane	2003	150.00
9788173660146	Safety Management Systems - An Underconstruction Activity, 98 Pages	Capt. Singhal	1998	95.00
9788173665516	A Textbook on Container & Multimodal Transport Management, 522 Pages	Dr. Hariharan	2002	500.00

Mechanical Engineering

ISBN	Title	Author	Year	Price
9789350236192	**A Glance On Transformer Oil, 96 Pages**	**Pandey**	**2012**	**125.00**

Motivation

ISBN	Title	Author	Year	Price
9788184044249	Break Your Negative Attitude, 114 Pages	Dr. Mishra	2007	125.00
9788173665271	Heads You Win, Tails You Win, 2/ed, 200 Pages	Dr.Mishra	2005	200.00
9789350236208	**Life is Fundamentally Management!, 200 Pages**	**Senthival**	**2012**	**250.00**
9789350230206	Nothing Is Absolute, 274 Pages	Balachandran	2010	300.00

Parenting

ISBN	Title	Author	Year	Price
9789350231760	Mom Don't Spoil Me, 140 Pages	Dr. Mishra	2010	150.00

Patent

ISBN	Title	Author	Year	Price
9788184047882	Breeding Innovation and Intellectual Capital, 2/ed 196 Pgs	Dr.Batra	2009	600.00

Physics

ISBN	Title	Author	Year	Price
9788184043259	Gravitation Demythicised: An Introduction to Einstein's General Relativity and Cosmology for Common Man, 258 Pages	Shenoy	2007	250.00
9788184047929	Study Aid Theoretical Physics - Volume I: Relativistic Theory and Electrodynamics, 418 Pgs	Prof Fai	2010	300.00
9788184047912	Theoretical Physics - Volume I: Relativistic Theory and Electrodynamics, 490 Pages	Prof Fai	2010	400.00

Project Management

ISBN	Title	Author	Year	Price
9789350230237	A Primer on Software Quality Models & Project Management, 640 Pages	Mehta	2010	600.00
9788184048568	Management Accounting & Financial Analysis for C.A.Final 9/ed, 540 Pages	Sridhar	2009	400.00

ISBN	Title	Author	Year	Price

Self-Help

ISBN	Title	Author	Year	Price
9788184047905	Enhancing Soft Skills, 346 Pages	Biswas	2009	375.00
9789350237113	**Secrets of Your Leadership Success, 212 Pages**	**Rao**	**2012**	**350.00**

- **All Prices are in Indian Rupees**
- **Titles Released after January 2012 are marked in Bold.**